Marketing for Hospitality and Tourism

Philip Kotler • John T. Bowen • Seyhmus Baloglu
Contributions by Cristian Morosan

EIGHTH EDITION

Vice President, Portfolio Management: Andrew Gilfillann
Portfolio Manager: Pamela Chirls
Editorial Assistant: Lara Dimmick
Product Marketing Manager: Heather Taylor
Director, Digital Studio and Content Production: Brian Hylands
Managing Producer: Cynthia Zonneveld
Content Producer: Rinki Kaur
Manager, Rights Management: Johanna Burke
Manufacturing Buyer: Deidra Headlee
Full-Service Management and Composition: Integra Software Services, Ltd.
Full-Service Project Manager: Rammohan Krishnamurthy
Cover Design: Studio Montage
Cover Photo: www.tonnaja.com/Moment/GettyImages
Printer/Binder: LSC Communications, Inc.
Cover Printer: Phoenix Color/Hagerstown
Text Font: Melior Com 9/11

Copyright 2021, 2017, 2014 by Pearson Education, Inc. 221 River Street, Hoboken, NJ 07030. All rights reserved. Manufactured in the United States of America. This publication is protected by Copyright, and permission should be obtained from the publisher prior to any prohibited reproduction, storage in a retrieval system, or transmission in any form or by any means, electronic, mechanical, photocopying, recording, or likewise. For information regarding permissions, request forms, and the appropriate contacts within the Pearson Education Global Rights and Permissions department, please visit www.pearsoned.com/permissions/.

Acknowledgments of third-party content appear on the appropriate page within the text.

PEARSON and ALWAYS LEARNING are exclusive trademarks owned by Pearson Education, Inc. or its affiliates in the U.S. and/or other countries.

Unless otherwise indicated herein, any third-party trademarks, logos, or icons that may appear in this work are the property of their respective owners, and any references to third party trademarks, logos, icons, or other trade dress are for demonstrative or descriptive purposes only. Such references are not intended to imply any sponsorship, endorsement, authorization, or promotion of Pearson's products by the owners of such marks, or any relationship between the owner and Pearson Education, Inc., authors, licensees, or distributors.

Library of Congress Cataloging-in-Publication Data
Names: Kotler, Philip, author.
Title: Marketing for hospitality and tourism / Philip Kotler, John T. Bowen, Seyhmus Baloglu.
Description: Eighth edition. | Hoboken : Pearson, [2019] | Includes bibliographical references and index.
Identifiers: LCCN 2019014463| ISBN 9780135209844 | ISBN 0135209846
Subjects: LCSH: Hospitality industry—Marketing. | Tourism—Marketing.
Classification: LCC TX911.3.M3 K68 2019 | DDC 338.4/791068—dc23 LC record available at https://lccn.loc.gov/2019014463

1 2019

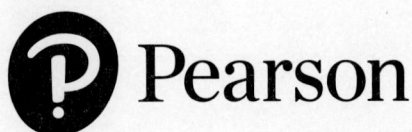

ISBN 10:   0-13-520984-6
ISBN 13: 978-0-13-520984-4
SVE ISBN 10:   0-13-520987-0
SVE ISBN 13: 978-01-3520987-5

This book is dedicated to Nancy, my wife and best friend, with love.
P. K.

With love to my wife, Toni, and children, Casey and Kelly. A special recognition and thank you to my friend and colleague, Jim Makens, who coauthored the previous seven editions of the book. We appreciate his contributions to the past editions, many of which live on in this edition.
J. T. B.

To my wife, Zerrin, and our two sons, Derin and Deniz, with love.
S. B.

BRIEF CONTENTS

PART I Defining Hospitality and Tourism Marketing and the Marketing Process 1

1. Creating Customer Value and Engagement Through Marketing for Hospitality and Tourism 3
2. Services Marketing Concepts Applied to Marketing for Hospitality and Tourism 34
3. Marketing Strategy: Partnering to Build Customer Engagement, Value, and Relationships 57

PART II Understanding the Marketplace and Customer Value 85

4. Analyzing the Marketing Environment 87
5. Managing Customer Information to Gain Customer Insights 116
6. Consumer Markets and Consumer Buying Behavior 156
7. Organizational Buyer Behavior 182
8. Customer-Driven Marketing Strategy: Creating Value for Target Customers 204

PART III Designing Customer Value-Driven Strategy and Mix 233

9. Designing and Managing Products and Brands: Building Customer Value 235
10. Internal Marketing 272
11. Pricing: Understanding and Capturing Customer Value 296
12. Distribution Channels Delivering Customer Value 331

13. Engaging Customers and Communicating Customer Value and Advertising 358

14. Promoting Products: Public Relations and Sales Promotions 395

15. Professional Sales 422

16. Direct, Online, Social Media, and Mobile Marketing 459

PART IV Managing Hospitality and Tourism Marketing 491

17. Destination Marketing 493

18. Next Year's Marketing Plan 536

CONTENTS

To the Student xiii
Preface xvii
About the Authors xx

PART I Defining Hospitality and Tourism Marketing and the Marketing Process 1

1 Creating Customer Value and Engagement Through Marketing for Hospitality and Tourism 3

YOUR PASSPORT TO SUCCESS 5
CUSTOMER ORIENTATION 6
WHAT IS HOSPITALITY AND TOURISM MARKETING? 7
MARKETING IN THE HOSPITALITY AND TRAVEL INDUSTRIES 8
  Importance of Marketing 8
  Tourism Marketing 8
  Definition of Marketing 9
MARKETING HIGHLIGHT 1.1 HOW FOUR SEASONS HOTELS AND RESORTS DELIGHTS ITS CUSTOMERS 9
  The Marketing Process 10
UNDERSTANDING THE MARKETPLACE AND CUSTOMER NEEDS 10
  Customer Needs, Wants, and Demands 10
  Market Offerings: Tangible Products, Services, and Experiences 12
  Customer Value and Satisfaction 12
  Exchanges and Relationships 13
  Markets 13
DESIGNING CUSTOMER VALUE-DRIVEN MARKETING STRATEGY 13
  Selecting Customers to Serve 14
  Marketing Management Orientations 14
PREPARING AN INTEGRATED MARKETING PLAN AND PROGRAM 16
MANAGING CUSTOMER RELATIONSHIPS AND CAPTURING VALUE 16
  Customer Relationship Management 17
  Customer Engagement and Today's Digital and Social Media 19
  Partner Relationship Management 20

CAPTURING VALUE FROM CUSTOMERS 20
  Customer Loyalty and Retention 21
  Growing Share of Customer 21
  Building Customer Equity 21
THE CHANGING MARKETING LANDSCAPE 23
  The Digital Age: Online, Social Media, and Mobile Marketing 23
  Sustainable Marketing—the Call for More Environmental and Social Responsibility 24
  Rapid Globalization 25
  Co-Creation 25
  The Sharing Economy 26
WELCOME TO MARKETING: YOUR PASSPORT TO BECOMING A SUCCESSFUL MANAGER 27
CHAPTER REVIEW 28
IN-CLASS GROUP EXERCISES 30
EXPERIENTIAL EXERCISES 31
REFERENCES 31

2 Services Marketing Concepts Applied to Marketing for Hospitality and Tourism 34

THE SERVICE CULTURE 36
CHARACTERISTICS OF SERVICE MARKETING 36
  Intangibility 36
  Tangible Evidence 37
  Inseparability 38
  Variability 38
  Perishability 40
THE SERVICE PROFIT CHAIN 40
MANAGEMENT STRATEGIES FOR SERVICE BUSINESSES 41
  Managing Service Differentiation 41
  Managing Service Quality 42
MARKETING HIGHLIGHT 2.1 JETBLUE, SOUTHWEST, AND CIRQUE DU SOLEIL PROVIDE THREE EXAMPLES OF SERVICE DIFFERENTIATION 43
  Managing Service Productivity 44
  Resolving Customer Complaints 44
MARKETING HIGHLIGHT 2.2 RECOMMENDATIONS FOR IMPROVING SERVICE QUALITY 45
  Managing Employees as Part of the Product 46
  Managing Perceived Risk 47
  Managing Capacity and Demand 48
CHAPTER REVIEW 53
IN-CLASS GROUP EXERCISES 54
EXPERIENTIAL EXERCISES 54
REFERENCES 54

3 Marketing Strategy: Partnering to Build Customer Engagement, Value, and Relationships 57

NATURE OF HIGH-PERFORMANCE BUSINESS 59
  Stakeholders 59
  Processes 60
  Resources 60
  Organization 60
CORPORATE STRATEGIC PLANNING: DEFINING MARKETING'S ROLE 61
  Defining the Corporate Mission 62
  Setting Company Objectives and Goals 64
  Designing the Business Portfolio 64
MARKETING HIGHLIGHT 3.1 ACCORHOTELS GROUP: MARRIAGE WITH ONEFINESTAY, A LUXURY VACATION RENTAL PLATFORM 66
PLANNING MARKETING: PARTNERING TO BUILD CUSTOMER RELATIONSHIPS 68
  Partnering with Other Company Departments 68
  Partnering with Others in the Marketing System 69
MARKETING STRATEGY AND THE MARKETING MIX 69
  Customer Value-Driven Marketing Strategy 70
  Developing an Integrated Marketing Mix 71
MANAGING THE MARKETING EFFORT 72
  Marketing Analysis 72
  Goal Formulation 75
  Marketing Planning 76
  Implementation 77
  Feedback and Control 77
MEASURING AND MANAGING RETURN ON MARKETING INVESTMENT 77
CHAPTER REVIEW 78
IN-CLASS GROUP ACTIVITIES 80
EXPERIENTIAL EXERCISES 80
REFERENCES 81

PART II Understanding the Marketplace and Customer Value 85

4 Analyzing the Marketing Environment 87

THE COMPANY'S ENVIRONMENT 89
THE MICROENVIRONMENT 89
  The Company 89
  Existing Competitors 90
  Suppliers 91
  Marketing Intermediaries 92
  Customers 94
  Publics 94

THE COMPANY'S MACROENVIRONMENT 95
  Competitors 95
MARKETING HIGHLIGHT 4.1 VISIT INDY—DESTINATION DIGITAL MARKETING 96
  Demographic Environment 97
  The Changing American Family 102
  Economic Environment 103
  Natural Environment 104
  Technological Environment 105
  Political Environment 106
  Cultural Environment 107
RESPONDING TO THE MARKETING ENVIRONMENT 109
  Environmental Scanning 109
CHAPTER REVIEW 110
IN-CLASS GROUP ACTIVITIES 112
EXPERIENTIAL EXERCISES 112
REFERENCES 112

5 Managing Customer Information to Gain Customer Insights 116

MARKETING INFORMATION AND CUSTOMER INSIGHTS 118
  Marketing Information and Today's "Big Data" 119
  Managing Marketing Information 120
THE MARKETING INFORMATION SYSTEM 120
  Assessing Information Needs 120
  Developing Marketing Information 121
MARKETING RESEARCH 129
  Defining the Problem and Research Objectives 130
  Developing the Research Plan 131
MARKETING HIGHLIGHT 5.1 ETHNOGRAPHIC RESEARCH: WATCHING WHAT CONSUMERS REALLY DO 134
MARKETING HIGHLIGHT 5.2 ZMET: GETTING INTO THE HEADS OF CONSUMER 138
MARKETING HIGHLIGHT 5.3 PROS AND CONS OF ONLINE RESEARCH 140
MARKETING HIGHLIGHT 5.4 A "QUESTIONABLE" QUESTIONNAIRE 142
  Implementing the Research Plan 146
  Interpreting and Reporting the Findings 146
MARKETING HIGHLIGHT 5.5 RESEARCH PROBLEM AREAS 147
MARKETING HIGHLIGHT 5.6 HSMAI'S KNOWLEDGE CENTER: A GREAT SOURCE OF MARKETING INFORMATION 148
INTERNATIONAL MARKETING RESEARCH 149
MARKETING RESEARCH IN SMALLER ORGANIZATIONS 150
CHAPTER REVIEW 150
IN-CLASS GROUP ACTIVITIES 152
EXPERIENTIAL EXERCISES 152
REFERENCES 153

6 Consumer Markets and Consumer Buying Behavior 156

A MODEL OF CONSUMER BEHAVIOR 157
PERSONAL CHARACTERISTICS AFFECTING CONSUMER BEHAVIOR 158

viii   Contents

  Cultural Factors 158
  Social Factors 161
MARKETING HIGHLIGHT 6.1 TAPPING SOCIAL MEDIA MOMS AS BRAND AMBASSADORS 164
  Personal Factors 166
  Psychological Factors 169
MARKETING HIGHLIGHT 6.2 SENSORY MARKETING—A POWERFUL TOOL FOR HOSPITALITY BUSINESSES 170
THE BUYER DECISION PROCESS 173
  Need Recognition 173
  Information Search 174
  Evaluation of Alternatives 174
  Purchase Decision 175
  Postpurchase Behavior 175
MARKETING HIGHLIGHT 6.3 UNIQUE ASPECTS OF HOSPITALITY AND TRAVEL CONSUMERS 176
CHAPTER REVIEW 177
IN-CLASS GROUP EXERCISES 178
EXPERIENTIAL EXERCISE 179
REFERENCES 179

7 Organizational Buyer Behavior 182

THE ORGANIZATIONAL BUYING PROCESS 184
  Business Markets 184
  Market Structure and Demand 184
  Nature of the Buying Unit 185
  Types of Decisions and the Decision Process 185
PARTICIPANTS IN THE ORGANIZATIONAL BUYING PROCESS 185
MAJOR INFLUENCES ON ORGANIZATIONAL BUYERS 187
ORGANIZATIONAL BUYING DECISIONS 188
  1. Problem Recognition 188
  2. General Need Description 188
  3. Product Specification 188
  4. Supplier Search 189
  5. Proposal Solicitations 189
  6. Supplier Selection 189
  7. Order-Routine Specification 189
MARKETING HIGHLIGHT 7.1 CORPORATE PROCUREMENT'S INVOLVEMENT IN PURCHASING MEETINGS 190
  8. Performance Review 190
  E-Procurement and Online Purchasing 190
  Business-to-Business Digital and Social Media Marketing 191
HOSPITALITY GROUP MARKETS 192
  Conventions 192
  Convention Bureaus 193
ASSOCIATION MEETINGS 194
  Corporate Meetings 194
  Small Groups 195
  Incentive Travel 195
  SMERFs 196
MARKETING HIGHLIGHT 7.2 GREEN MEETINGS—THE RIGHT THING TO DO FOR THE ENVIRONMENT AND BUSINESS 197

  Segmentation of Group Markets by Purpose of the Meeting 198
  Restaurants as a Meeting Venue 199
DEALING WITH MEETING PLANNERS 199
CHAPTER REVIEW 200
IN-CLASS GROUP EXERCISES 201
EXPERIENTIAL EXERCISE 202
REFERENCES 202

8 Customer-Driven Marketing Strategy: Creating Value for Target Customers 204

MARKETS 206
MARKET SEGMENTATION 206
  Geographic Segmentation 207
  Demographic Segmentation 208
MARKETING HIGHLIGHT 8.1 TARGETING FAMILIES BY TARGETING KIDS 209
  Psychographic Segmentation 211
MARKETING HIGHLIGHT 8.2 W HOTELS: A LIFESTYLE HOTEL 212
  Behavioral Segmentation 213
MARKETING HIGHLIGHT 8.3 DUNKIN' DONUTS: TARGETING THE AVERAGE JOE 214
  Using Multiple Segmentation Bases 215
  Requirements for Effective Segmentation 216
MARKET TARGETING 217
  Evaluating Market Segments 217
  Selecting Market Segments 218
  Choosing a Market-Coverage Strategy 220
MARKET POSITIONING 221
  Positioning Strategies 221
  Choosing and Implementing a Positioning Strategy 222
  Differentiating Competitive Advantages 222
  Choosing the Right Competitive Advantages 225
  Selecting an Overall Positioning Strategy 226
  Communicating and Delivering the Chosen Position 226
  Positioning Measurement: Perceptual Mapping 227
CHAPTER REVIEW 228
IN-CLASS GROUP ACTIVITIES 230
EXPERIENTIAL EXERCISE 230
REFERENCES 230

PART III Designing Customer Value-Driven Strategy and Mix 233

9 Designing and Managing Products and Brands: Building Customer Value 235

WHAT IS A PRODUCT? 237
PRODUCT LEVELS 238
  Core Products 238

Facilitating Products 238
Supporting Products 239
Augmented Product 240
BRANDING STRATEGY 245
Building Strong Brands 245
Brand Equity and Brand Value 246
Brand Positioning 247
Brand Name Selection 248
Leveraging Brands 249
Brand Portfolios 250
MARKETING HIGHLIGHT 9.1 EXTENDING YOUR BRAND TO CHINA: WHAT NAME DO YOU USE? 251
THE NEW-PRODUCT DEVELOPMENT 252
Idea Generation 253
IDEA SCREENING 255
Concept Development and Testing 256
Marketing Strategy 257
Business Analysis 257
Product Development 258
Test Marketing 258
Commercialization 259
PRODUCT LIFE-CYCLE STRATEGIES 259
Introduction Stage 261
Growth Stage 261
Maturity Stage 261
Decline Stage 263
Product Deletion 264
INTERNATIONAL PRODUCT AND SERVICE MARKETING 265
CHAPTER REVIEW 266
IN-CLASS GROUP EXERCISES 267
EXPERIENTIAL EXERCISES 267
REFERENCES 268

10 Internal Marketing 272

INTERNAL MARKETING 273
Post Face-to-Face Guest Relations 274
MARKETING HIGHLIGHT 10.1 PINEHURST RESORT & COUNTRY CLUB "DO WHAT'S RIGHT" 275
THE INTERNAL MARKETING PROCESS 275
Establishment of a Service Culture 276
Development of a Marketing Approach to Human Resources Management 280
Dissemination of Marketing Information to Employees 288
MARKETING HIGHLIGHT 10.2 INTERNAL MARKETING IN ACTION: LEWIS HOTELS 289
CHAPTER REVIEW 292
IN-CLASS GROUP EXERCISES 293
EXPERIENTIAL EXERCISE 293
REFERENCES 293

11 Pricing: Understanding and Capturing Customer Value 296

FACTORS TO CONSIDER WHEN SETTING PRICES 298
Internal Factors Affecting Pricing Decisions 299
External Factors Affecting Pricing Decisions 302
Competitors' Prices and Offers 308
GENERAL PRICING APPROACHES 309
Cost-Based Pricing 309
Break-Even Analysis and Target Profit Pricing 310
Value-Based Pricing 311
Competition-Based Pricing 312
PRICING STRATEGIES 312
New-Product Pricing Strategies 312
Existing-Product Pricing Strategies 313
REVENUE MANAGEMENT 316
MARKETING HIGHLIGHT 11.1 SEGMENTED PRICING: THE RIGHT PRODUCT TO THE RIGHT CUSTOMER AT THE RIGHT TIME FOR THE RIGHT PRICE 316
Dynamic Pricing 319
BAR Pricing 320
Rate Parity 320
Nonuse of Revenue Management 320
Overbooking 321
PSYCHOLOGICAL PRICING 321
Price Endings 321
Promotional Pricing 322
Value Pricing—Low Price Approach 322
MARKETING HIGHLIGHT 11.2 RYANAIR USES VALUE PRICING TO ATTRACT CUSTOMERS AND GAINS REVENUE FROM EXTRA SALES 323
PRICE CHANGES 324
Initiating Price Changes 324
Responding to Price Changes 325
CHAPTER REVIEW 326
IN-CLASS GROUP EXERCISES 328
EXPERIENTIAL EXERCISE 328
REFERENCES 328

12 Distribution Channels Delivering Customer Value 331

PARTNERING TO ADD VALUE 332
Supply Chains and the Value Delivery Network 332
Nature and Importance of Distribution Systems 333
Nature of Distribution Channels 333
HOSPITALITY DISTRIBUTION CHANNELS 336
Direct Channels 337
Online Travel Agencies 338
Global Distribution Systems 339
Travel Agents 340
MARKETING HIGHLIGHT 12.1 CHANGING MARKET DYNAMICS 340
Travel Wholesalers and Tour Operators 341
Specialists: Tour Brokers, Motivational Houses, and Junket Reps 342
Hotel Representatives 343
National, State, and Local Tourist Agencies 343

Consortia and Reservation Systems 343
Restaurant Distribution Channels 344
CHANNEL BEHAVIOR AND THE ORGANIZATION 345
Channel Behavior 345
Channel Organization 346
MARKETING HIGHLIGHT 12.2 RESTAURANT FRANCHISING 348
CHANNEL MANAGEMENT 350
Selecting Channel Members 350
Determining Responsibilities of Channel Members 352
Selecting Business Location 352
CHAPTER REVIEW 354
IN-CLASS GROUP EXERCISES 356
EXPERIENTIAL EXERCISES 356
REFERENCES 357

13 Engaging Customers and Communicating Customer Value and Advertising 358

THE PROMOTION MIX 360
INTEGRATED MARKETING COMMUNICATIONS 360
The New Marketing Communications Model 361
MARKETING HIGHLIGHT 13.1 THANKS, JUST DON'T CALL IT ADVERTISING: IT'S CONTENT MARKETING 363
The Need for Integrated Marketing Communications 365
DEVELOPING EFFECTIVE MARKETING COMMUNICATION 365
A View of the Communication Process 365
STEPS IN DEVELOPING EFFECTIVE COMMUNICATIONS 367
Identifying the Target Audience 367
Determining the Communication Objective 367
Designing the Message 369
Selecting Communication Channels 370
MARKETING HIGHLIGHT 13.2 THANK YOU—A GREAT PERSONAL COMMUNICATION 371
Selecting the Message Source 372
Collecting Feedback 373
SETTING THE TOTAL PROMOTION BUDGET AND MIX 374
Setting the Total Promotional Budget 374
Shaping the Overall Promotion Mix 375
ADVERTISING 379
Major Decisions in Advertising 379
International Advertising Decisions 389
CHAPTER REVIEW 390
IN-CLASS GROUP EXERCISES 392
EXPERIENTIAL EXERCISES 392
REFERENCES 392

14 Promoting Products: Public Relations and Sales Promotions 395

PUBLIC RELATIONS 397
Major Activities of PR Departments 397
MARKETING HIGHLIGHT 14.1 EXTREME SPORTS BRING PUBLICITY AND TOURISTS 399
Publicity 399
THE PUBLIC RELATIONS PROCESS 400
Conducting Research 400
Establishing Marketing Objectives 401
Defining the Target Audience 402
Choosing the PR Message and Vehicles 402
Implementing the Marketing PR Plan 404
Evaluating PR Results 404
PR OPPORTUNITIES FOR THE HOSPITALITY INDUSTRY 405
Promoting Individual Properties 405
Promoting via Storytelling 405
Crisis Management 406
MARKETING HIGHLIGHT 14.2 CHESHIRE'S BEST KEPT STATIONS, CHESHIRE, UNITED KINGDOM 407
Sales Promotion 409
Local Area Marketing (Neighborhood Marketing) 416
CHAPTER REVIEW 417
IN-CLASS GROUP EXERCISES 419
EXPERIENTIAL EXERCISE 419
REFERENCES 419

15 Professional Sales 422

RESULTS 423
MANAGEMENT OF PROFESSIONAL SALES 424
NATURE OF HOSPITALITY SALES 424
Competitive Analysis and Competitive Sets 426
SALES FORCE OBJECTIVES 426
Sales Volume 427
Upselling and Second-Chance Selling 427
Market Share or Market Penetration 427
Product-Specific Objectives 428
SALES FORCE STRUCTURE AND SIZE 428
Territorial-Structured Sales Force 428
Market-Segment-Structured Sales Force 429
Market-Channel-Structured Sales Force 429
Customer-Structured Sales Force 430
Combination-Structured Sales Force 430
Sales Force Size 431

Contents xi

ORGANIZING THE SALES DEPARTMENT   433
   Inside Sales Force   433
   Field Sales Force   434
   Team Sales   435
RELATIONSHIP MARKETING AND STRATEGIC ALLIANCES   436
RECRUITING AND TRAINING A PROFESSIONAL SALES FORCE   437
   Importance of Careful Selection   437
   Establishing a Profile of Desired Characteristics Matching the Corporate Culture   438
   Matching Career Acquisitions with Corporate Objectives   438
   Sales Force Training   439
MANAGING THE SALES FORCE   441
   Selecting Sales Strategies   441
   Sales Force Tactics: Principles of Personal Selling   443
   Motivating a Professional Sales Force   447
   Evaluation and Control of a Professional Sales Force   449
   Peer-to-Peer Sales   452
   Networking   452
SOCIAL SELLING: ONLINE, MOBILE, AND SOCIAL MEDIA TOOLS   453
   Social Selling: Online, Mobile, and Social Media Tools   453
CHAPTER REVIEW   454
IN-CLASS GROUP EXERCISES   456
EXPERIENTIAL EXERCISE   456
REFERENCES   456

16 Direct, Online, Social Media, and Mobile Marketing   459

DIRECT AND DIGITAL MARKETING   461
   The New Direct-Marketing Model   461
   Benefits of Direct and Digital Marketing to Buyers and Sellers   462
   Forms of Direct and Digital Marketing   463
DIGITAL AND SOCIAL MEDIA MARKETING   463
   Marketing, the Internet, and the Digital Age   463
   Online Marketing   465
   Social Media Marketing   469
   Mobile Marketing   474
CUSTOMER DATABASES AND TRADITIONAL DIRECT MARKETING   476
   Database Uses   476
   Personalization, Disclosure of Information, and Value for the Customers   478
RELATIONSHIP MARKETING AND LOYALTY PROGRAMS   479
   Benefits of Customer Relationship Management   480
   Loyalty Programs   481

TRADITIONAL FORMS OF DIRECT MARKETING   483
   Direct-Mail Marketing   483
   Telephone Marketing   483
   Kiosk Marketing   484
   Interactive TV   484
ONLINE PRIVACY AND SECURITY   485
CHAPTER REVIEW   486
IN-CLASS GROUP EXERCISES   487
EXPERIENTIAL EXERCISE   488
REFERENCES   488

PART IV Managing Hospitality and Tourism Marketing   491

17 Destination Marketing   493

MARKETING TOURISM DESTINATIONS   495
   The Globalization of the Tourist Industry   495
   The Tourism Destination   496
   Destination Marketing System   497
   Destination Competitiveness   499
   Sustainable Tourism   502
TOURISM DEVELOPMENT AND INVESTMENTS   505
MARKETING HIGHLIGHT 17.1 CUBA TOURISM DEVELOPMENT: A TIME TRAVEL   506
   Tourism Events and Attractions   507
   Destination Life Cycle: Rejuvenating a Destination   513
SEGMENTING AND MONITORING THE TOURIST MARKET   514
   Agritourism   516
   Space Tourism   517
   Multiday Hiking and Religious Pilgrimages   517
   Medical Tourism   518
   Genealogical Tourism   519
   Identifying Target Markets   519
   Classification of Visitor Segments   520
   Monitoring the Tourist Markets   521
COMMUNICATING WITH THE TOURIST MARKET   522
   Competition for Visitors Involves Image Making   522
   Branding Destinations   523
   Effectiveness of Advertising/Promotion   524
   Developing Packages of Attractions and Amenities   524
   Creating and Managing Visitor Experiences   525
ORGANIZING AND MANAGING TOURISM MARKETING   527
   National Tourism Organizations   527

Regional Tourist Organizations: State Associations and Convention and Tourist Bureaus   528
CHAPTER REVIEW   529
DISCUSSION QUESTIONS   531
EXPERIENTIAL EXERCISE   531
IN-CLASS GROUP ACTIVITIES   531
APPENDIX A: 2018 TRAVEL AND TOURISM COMPETITIVENESS INDEX   531
REFERENCES   532

18 Next Year's Marketing Plan   536

PURPOSE OF A MARKETING PLAN   538
PREPARING A MARKETING PLAN   539
   Section I: Executive Summary   539
   Section II: Corporate Connection   540
   Section III: Environmental Analysis and Forecasting   541
MARKETING HIGHLIGHT 18.1 THE INDIGO PEARL RESORT: FACEBOOK STRATEGY AND PLANNING THE INDIGO PEARL   546
   Section IV: Segmentation and Targeting   546
   Section V: Next Year's Objectives and Quotas   549
   Section VI: Action Plans: Strategies and Tactics   553
   Section VII: Resources Needed to Support Strategies and Meet Objectives   558
   Section VIII: Marketing Control   559
PRESENTING THE PLAN AND PREPARING FOR THE FUTURE   561
   Section IX: Presenting and Selling the Plan   561
   Section X: Preparing for the Future   562
CHAPTER REVIEW   563
IN-CLASS GROUP EXERCISES   564
EXPERIENTIAL EXERCISE   565
REFERENCES   565

Appendix A The Five-Gap Model of Service Quality   567

Appendix B Forecasting Market Demand   571

Case Studies   578

Glossary   635

Index   644

TO THE STUDENT

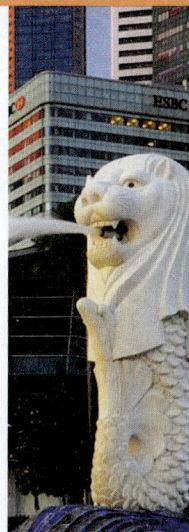

Welcome to the eighth edition!

Marketing for Hospitality and Tourism guides you down the intriguing, discovery-laden road to learning marketing. These are exciting times in hospitality marketing. There is an ever-increasing number of tourists, both domestic and international. This coupled with advances in digital technologies have created a new, more engaging and connected world.

Some of the applications you learn today you will use immediately, while others you may not use until later in your career. Thus, it is important that you have an understanding of the marketing theories and concepts. This will allow you to analyze future situations and make proper decisions. Practices and applications are provided to give you examples of how we currently apply the concepts to industry situations. Finally, we have included marketing highlights, opening cases, written cases, color illustrations, and other features to make learning about marketing interesting and enjoyable. Throughout the text, we provide examples to illustrate how companies are using the marketing principles covered in the book.

Marketing is both an art and science. The art adds some ambiguity to marketing, which makes it difficult for some students. We recommend reading each chapter quickly and then going back and reading it more slowly the second time. This will give you a good understanding of the material in the chapter.

The development of each edition has involved students who tell us which illustrations to use, which examples they find interesting, and which ones we should replace when we are writing the newest edition. We strive to develop a book that is student friendly and clearly explains and illustrates the application of marketing concepts. This has resulted in the book being used around the globe in nine different languages.

We hope you enjoy *Marketing for Hospitality and Tourism* and we wish you success.

Philip Kotler, John T. Bowen, Seyhmus Baloglu

An Indispensable Guide to Successful Marketing in the Hospitality Industry

This book has been written with you in mind—explaining the how and why of everyone's role in marketing. Because customer contact employees are part of our product in hospitality and tourism marketing, marketing is everyone's job. *Marketing for Hospitality and Tourism* gives you an innovative and practical introduction to marketing. Its style and extensive use of examples and illustrations make the book straightforward, easy to read.

Text Organization

PART I: Defining Hospitality and Tourism Marketing and the Marketing Process—Introduces you to the concept of hospitality marketing and its importance.

PART II: Understanding the Marketplace and Customer Value—Helps you understand the role of consumer behavior and how it affects the marketing environment.

PART III: Designing Customer Value-Driven Strategy and Mix—Identifies and explains strategies for promoting products, the various distribution channels and the latest developments in digital marketing.

PART IV: Managing Hospitality and Tourism Marketing—Highlights the latest trends in destination marketing, and planning for the future through development of a marketing plan.

Special Features: Connecting to the Real World

Chapter Opening Cases

Each chapter opens with a mini case showing you how actual hospitality and travel companies have successfully applied marketing. The cases help you understand and remember the concepts presented in the chapter. For example, Chapter 1 illustrates how catering to the customer experience has paid big dividends for Buffalo Wild Wings. B-Dubs is now the United States' number-one seller of chicken wings and largest pourer of draft beer.

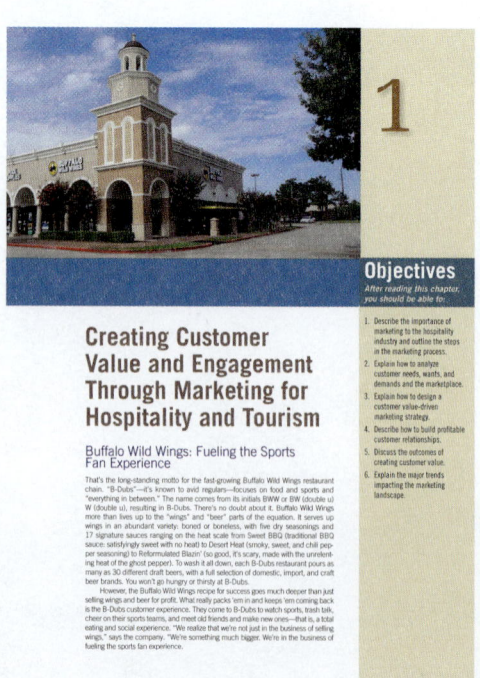

Boxed Marketing Highlights

The boxed segments introduce you to real people and real industry examples, connecting the chapter material to real life.

Marketing HIGHLIGHT 11.1 — Segmented pricing: The right product to the right customer at the right time for the right price

In most hospitality, travel and entertainment products capacity is fixed, but demand varies. In these situations, a common price may result in many people not being able to access the product during prime times and empty seats during off-peak periods. In some products such as airline transportation and events, all seats may not be the same.

Live performances, including sporting events, theater, and concerts, will charge more for seats with great views and less for seats father away from the event. Some airlines charge more for aisle and window seats. Customers wanting better seats with the capacity to pay for these seats will have the opportunity to purchase the seats they want. Those who want to see the event or want to get to a certain destination but want to spend less can purchase less expensive seats. Susan Greco gives an example of an opera company, which went from a single price for all seats to pricing based on the location of the seat, increasing the price for better seats and lowering the price for seats in the back. Seat prices on the weekends were increased and those during the week were reduced. The variety of prices allowed the customers to choose what they would pay and the opera company increased its overall revenue by 9 percent. Some customers who previously could not afford to attend now had the opportunity to attend by selecting tickets further from the stage on weekday nights.

The opera company had introduced a simple form of revenue management. Airlines, hotels, and restaurants call it revenue management and practice it religiously. This allows companies to attract customers by having the right product at the right price for the right customer.

Segmented pricing and yield management aren't really new ideas. For instance, Marriott Corporation used seat-of-the-pants yield-management approaches long before it installed its current sophisticated system. Back when J. W. "Bill" Marriott was a young man working at the family's first hotel, the Twin Bridges in Washington, DC, he sold rooms

Theaters, like the one in the Bellagio Hotel, Las Vegas, where the Cirque du Soleil show "O" is performed, often apply revenue management by charging more for seats with better views and during times when demand is higher.

Full-Color Visuals

Color format with lively photographs, drawings, and tables will maintain your interest and provide visual aids to learning.

■■■ Important Memory Tools

Chapter Objectives

At the start of each chapter, the list will help you focus and organize your thoughts as you are reading. The learning objectives summarize what you need to know after studying the chapter and doing the exercises.

Key Terms

Key marketing and hospitality terms, highlighted and defined in each chapter, provide you with a convenient source for learning and reviewing the professional vocabulary needed for effective communication on the job. These terms are found in each chapter, and a glossary of all the terms can be found at the end of the book.

Chapter Review

At the end of each chapter, a summary of chapter content in outline form helps you review, retain key information, and ties the content of the chapter back to chapter objectives. The format for the chapter review was the suggestion of a student.

■■■ Applying Your Knowledge

Experiential Exercises

These exercises are designed to provide experiences that will illustrate the concepts presented in the chapter and provide experiences that you can draw on in the future.

■■■ Applying Your Critical Thinking Skills

Case Studies

The case studies at the end of the book represent real situations that can be used to analyze actual business situations and come up with solutions to your organization's problem. Sometimes, your instructor will use these cases as the basis of class discussions.

In-Class Group Exercises

These end-of-chapter questions will challenge your students to address real-world applications of the concepts presented in the chapter. They can be done in class to supplement the lectures.

PREFACE

We would like to thank the students and instructors who have used this text in the past. Their support has enabled us to publish the eighth edition of *Marketing for Hospitality and Tourism*, now available in nine languages.

This book is written with the hospitality and travel students in mind. The solicited and unsolicited comments we received from students and instructors have been incorporated into the sixth edition. Students have told us *Marketing for Hospitality and Tourism* is readable and interesting. One student wrote, "I enjoyed reading this book—it didn't seem like I was reading a textbook." In this newest edition, we strive to maintain the same tone. For instructors, we have listened to your comments and made the text flow more smoothly from a teaching perspective.

The authors have extensive experience working with hospitality and travel businesses around the globe. Our understanding of the hospitality and travel business ensures that the end result is a book that clearly explains marketing concepts and shows how they apply to real-life situations.

The book has an international focus, which is especially important in this era of increasing globalization. Business markets have become internationalized—domestic companies are expanding overseas as foreign companies seek to enter domestic markets—therefore, it is crucial that today's students be exposed to business and cultural examples from other parts of the world. Rather than have one chapter devoted to international marketing, we have incorporated examples throughout the text.

This text has truly evolved as a team project. Without the support of our students and faculty at other universities and colleges, this book would not have developed into the leading book in its category. We thank you for your support and acknowledge below some of the people who have been involved in the development of the book.

Instructor Supplements

Instructor's Manual. Includes content outlines for classroom discussion, teaching suggestions, and answers to selected end-of-chapter questions from the text.

TestGen. This computerized test generation system gives you the maximum flexibility in creating and administering tests on paper, electronically, or online. It provides state-of-the-art features for viewing and editing test bank questions, dragging a selected question into a test you are creating, and printing sleek, formatted tests in a variety of layouts. Select test items from test banks included with TestGen for quick test creation, or write your own questions from scratch. TestGen's random generator provides the option to display different text or calculated number values each time questions are used.

PowerPoint Presentations. Our presentations offer clear, straightforward outlines and notes to use for class lectures or study materials. Photos, illustrations, charts, and tables from the book are included in the presentations when applicable.

To access supplementary materials online, instructors need to request an instructor access code. Go to www.pearsonhighered.com/irc, where you can register for an instructor access code. Within 48 hours after registering, you will receive a confirming email, including an instructor access code. Once you have received your code, go to the site and log on for full instructions on downloading the materials you wish to use.

Alternate Versions

eBooks. This text is also available in multiple eBook formats. These are an exciting new choice for students looking to save money. As an alternative to purchasing the printed textbook, students can purchase an electronic version of the same content. With an eTextbook, students can search the text, make notes online, print out reading assignments that incorporate lecture notes, and bookmark important passages for later review. For more information, visit your favorite online eBook reseller or visit www.mypearsonstore.com.

xvii

We Welcome Your Comments, Suggestions, and Questions

We would like to hear your comments on this edition and your suggestions for future editions. Please address comments to Seyhmus Baloglu, seyhmus.baloglu@unlv.edu.

Acknowledgments

We would like to thank the students and the instructors who have used earlier editions of this book and provided feedback that added value to the users of this edition. Thanks go to the following group who provided comments and feedback for this eighth edition: Jamie Cooperstein, Delaware County Community College; Gretchen Friend, Columbus State Community College; Debbie Howarth, Johnson & Wales University; Rick Lagiewski, Rochester Institute of Technology; Mary-Pat Maciolek, Middlesex County College; Melih Madanoglu, Florida Atlantic University; Quantella Noto, Southeast Missouri State University; George Ojie-Ahamiojie Wor-Wic, Community College; Kunsoon Park, South Dakota State University; Joel Reynolds, Niagara University; Gregory Turner, Claflin University; Yasong (Alex) Wang, Indiana University of Pennsylvania; Alvin Yu, St. Cloud State University.

The following people provided reviews of past editions: Tazeem Gulamhusein, University of Houston; Deepak Chhabra, Arizona State University, Tempe; Dan Creed, Metropolitan State University, St. Paul; Jamal Feerasta, College of Applied Science and Technology, University of Akron; Juline Mills, University of New Haven; David Schoenberg, LaGuardia Community College, CUNY; and Nancy Warren, Highline Community College; Jennifer A. Aldrich, Kimberly M. Anderson, James A. Bardi, Jonathan Barsky, David C. Bojanic, Mark Bonn, Jane Boyland, Bonnie Canziani, Harsha E. Chacko, Deepak Chhabra, Dan Creed, Tim H. Dodd, Geralyn Farley, Jamal Feerasta, Andy Feinstein, Michael Gallo, Richard M. Howey, Jeffrey Ivory, Dianne Jolovich, Ed Knudson, Robert J. Kwortnik, Ingrid Lin, Ken McCleary, Juline Mills, H. G. Parsa, Edward B. Pomianoski, Hailin Qu, Allen Z. Reich, Howard F. Reichbart, Joan Remington, Emily C. Richardson, Kisang Ryu, John Salazar, David Schoenberg, Ralph Tellone, Muzzo Uysal, Nancy Warren, Anna Graf Williams, and Gregory R. Wood.

The following people helped with past editions when they were students to make sure the text was student friendly: Shiang-Lih Chen McCain, Jason Finehout, Michael Gallo, Tazeem Gulamhusein, Walter Huertas, Ming (Michael) Liang, Marvel L. Maunder, Tracee Nowlak, Michelle North, Sarah Robinson, and Carrie Tyler.

We appreciate the support and enthusiasm of the companies that provided advertisements and illustrations for this book. These organizations put forth a great deal of effort in finding and providing the materials we requested; working with them was one of the most rewarding parts of producing this book. We would also like to thank our Pearson Team: Daryl Fox, Susan Watkins, and Lara Dimmick. Finally, we would like to thank our families for their support and encouragement.

What's New in the Eighth Edition

The 8th edition of *Marketing for Hospitality and Tourism* is a landmark entry in the long successful history of the market leader. We've thoroughly revised the eighth edition of *Marketing for Hospitality and Tourism* to reflect the major trends and forces impacting marketing in this digital age of customer value, engagement, and relationships. We are very excited that the eighth edition will offer the option of using Pearson's Revel.

- We are very excited that the eighth edition will offer the option of using Pearson's Revel. Revel was designed to help every student come to class ready to learn. To keep students engaged as they read through each chapter, Revel integrates interactives, and assessments directly into the author-created narrative. Thanks to this media-rich presentation of content, students are more likely to complete their assigned reading and retain what they've read. So they'll show up to class better prepared to participate and learn.

- At the end of each chapter we have added a group of In-Class exercises. These are exercises students can perform that reinforce the information being thought in the chapter. They are meant to bring the marketing class to life for the students. They provide an excellent way for instructors to break up their lectures with engaging hands-on exercises to keep the students engaged.

- Cristian Morosan, an expert in digital marketing was brought in to write the chapters on digital and direct marketing and the distribution. There have been sweeping developments in online distribution of hotel rooms, online delivery services for restaurants, and online access to peer-to-peer accommodations. User-generated content on social media can make or break a restaurant, while at the same time providing a useful source of customer information. Listening and gathering data over the Internet has produced large amounts of data, processed by artificial intelligence to give us information that helps us better serve our customers. Dr. Morosan has rewritten Chapters 12 and 16 to include the latest advances in technology and social media.

- One point of differentiation of the text is it has an international focus. The eighth edition provides new discussions and examples of the growth in global marketing. As the world becomes a smaller, more competitive place, marketers face new global marketing challenges and opportunities, especially in fast-growing emerging markets such as China, India, the Middle East, Eastern Europe, and Southeast Asia. In the first chapter, we discuss the growing internationalization of the tourism business. To help your students understand the importance of the global aspect of tourism, we include international examples and illustrations throughout the text. Chapter 9 now includes expanded coverage of branding practices in hospitality on global level and gives examples of generational and lifestyle brands. In Chapter 17, new sections on branding tourist destinations and tourism competitiveness have been added to help students understand how to compete in a global market. The cases include multinational companies and businesses outside of North America. This international approach makes the text relevant to students outside of North American, while showing North American students they can find a truly rewarding career in the area of international business.

- The eighth edition continues to track fast-changing developments in marketing communications and the creation of marketing content. Marketers are no longer simply creating integrated marketing communications programs; they are joining with customers and media to curate customer-driven marketing content in paid, owned, earned, and shared media. You won't find fresher coverage of these important topics in any other hospitality marketing text.

The eighth edition continues to improve on its innovative learning design that has made it the market leader. One design feature of the text is the opening vignette that provides an example of how hospitality companies implement principles that will be discussed in the chapter. New chapter vignettes have been added through the text. The chapter-opening objectives have been revised, reflecting what is covered in the chapter. The end of the chapter summaries have been rewritten to mirror and reinforce the opening objectives. The marketing highlights that provide industry examples of the marketing concepts discussed in the chapter have been updated and will continue to be a valued benefit of the text. New cases have been added to the collection of case studies.

ABOUT THE AUTHORS

Philip Kotler is S. C. Johnson & Son Distinguished Professor of International Marketing at the Kellogg School of Management, Northwestern University. He earned his master's degree at the University of Chicago and his PhD at MIT, both in economics. He is the author of *Marketing Management* (Pearson), now in its fifteenth edition and the most widely used marketing textbook in graduate schools of business worldwide. He has authored dozens of other successful books and has written more than 100 articles in leading journals. He is the only three-time winner of the coveted Alpha Kappa Psi award for the best annual article in the *Journal of Marketing*.

Professor Kotler was named the first recipient of four major awards: the Distinguished Marketing Educator of the Year Award and the William L. Wilkie "Marketing for a Better World" Award, both given by the American Marketing Association; the Philip Kotler Award for Excellence in Health Care Marketing presented by the Academy for Health Care Services Marketing; and the Sheth Foundation Medal for Exceptional Contribution to Marketing Scholarship and Practice. His numerous other major honors include the Sales and Marketing Executives International Marketing Educator of the Year Award; the European Association of Marketing Consultants and Trainers Marketing Excellence Award; the Charles Coolidge Parlin Marketing Research Award; and the Paul D. Converse Award, given by the American Marketing Association to honor "outstanding contributions to science in marketing." A recent Forbes survey ranks Professor Kotler in the top 10 of the world's most influential business thinkers. And in a recent *Financial Times* poll of 1,000 senior executives across the world, Professor Kotler was ranked as the fourth "most influential business writer/guru" of the twenty-first century.

Dr. Kotler has served as chairman of the College on Marketing of the Institute of Management Sciences, a director of the American Marketing Association, and a trustee of the Marketing Science Institute. He has consulted with many major U.S. and international companies in the areas of marketing strategy and planning, marketing organization, and international marketing. He has traveled and lectured extensively throughout Europe, Asia, and South America, advising companies and governments about global marketing practices and opportunities.

John T. Bowen is Professor and former dean of the Conrad N. Hilton College of Hotel and Restaurant Management at the University of Houston and the Barron Hilton Distinguished Chair. He has presented marketing courses and seminars in Asia, Australia, Central America, Europe, and South America. He is a consultant to both large and small hospitality corporations. Before becoming an academic, Professor Bowen held positions in restaurant management at both the unit and corporate level. He is on the editorial boards of the *Cornell Hotel and Restaurant Administration Quarterly*, *Journal of Services Marketing*, *International Journal of Contemporary Hospitality Marketing*, and *Worldwide Hospitality and Tourism Themes*. He is coauthor of *Restaurant Marketing for Owners and Managers*. He has received numerous awards for his teaching and research, including the UNLV Foundation Teaching Award, the Sam and Mary Boyd Distinguished Professor Award for Teaching, Founder's Award for Lifetime Support of Hospitality Graduate Education, and the Board of Regents Outstanding Faculty Member. The Graduate Education & Graduate Student Research Conference presented him with the Founder's Award, to recognize his contribution to graduate education. The Hotel and Lodging Association of Greater Houston recognized him with their lifetime achievement award. He has been a three-time recipient of the annual award from the International Council on Hotel, Restaurant and Institutional Education (CHRIE) for superior published research in the hospitality industry, and he received the John Wiley Award for Lifetime Research Achievement from CHRIE. He was recently cited as one of the five most influential hospitality management faculty in an article published in the *Journal of Hospitality and Tourism Education*. The Mayor of Houston proclaimed November 21, 2014, as John Bowen Day, in recognition of Dr. Bowen's contribution to the hospitality industry and hospitality education.

Dr. Bowen's formal education includes a BS in hotel administration from Cornell University, an MBA and MS from Corpus Christi State University, and a PhD in marketing from Texas A&M University.

Seyhmus Baloglu is Professor and Barrick Distinguished Scholar at the Harrah College of Hospitality, University of Nevada Las Vegas (UNLV), where he has also assumed leadership roles as associate dean of research and director of Harrah Research Center for 10 years. He earned a BS in hotel administration from Cukurova University, an MBA from Hawaii Pacific University, and a PhD in hospitality marketing from Virginia Tech. He has presented marketing courses and seminars in Asia, Australia, Europe, and the

Caribbean. Before joining academia, he held management positions and had diverse background in the industry, including restaurants, hotels, resort clubs, and travel agencies. He has published extensively in leading journals, including *Journal of Business Research*, *Cornell Hospitality Quarterly*, *Journal of Hospitality & Tourism Research*, *International Journal of Hospitality Management*, *Annals of Tourism Research*, *Journal of Travel Research*, *Tourism Management*, *Journal of Travel & Tourism Marketing*, and *Tourism Analysis*. He received grants, contracts, and consulting projects from tourism destinations, gaming resorts, hotels, airports, nightclubs, and supply-chain organizations. He has been named as one of the significant contributors to the hospitality and tourism literature. His work has been cited extensively across multiple disciplines and fields. His research credentials have earned him both an international reputation and placement on the editorial boards of numerous leading journals. He has presented his work at many national and international conferences, seminars, and symposia and served as keynote speaker and panel participant for numerous international conferences. Other books he has coauthored are *Managing and Marketing Tourist Destinations: Strategies to Gain a Competitive Edge* and *Handbook of Scales in Tourism and Hospitality Research*. He is the recipient of numerous and prestigious teaching, research, and service awards. He has been named as the recipient of UNLV Alumni Association's Outstanding Faculty Member of the Year and the John Wiley & Sons Lifetime Research Achievement Award from the International Council on Hotel, Restaurant and Institutional Education (ICHRIE). His other major honors include annual research awards from ICHRIE, the Sam and Mary Boyd Distinguished Professor Awards, the Ace Denken Research Award, the Claudine Williams Distinguished Chair, and Harrah Distinguished Chair.

Contributor

Dr. Cristian Morosan is an associate professor at the Conrad N. Hilton College of Hotel and Restaurant Management at the University of Houston. Prior to joining Hilton College in 2012, he taught marketing at Temple University, Kansas State University, and University of St. Thomas Houston. His work has been funded by regional organizations such as the Hospitality Financial and Technology Professionals, state and local destination organizations, and universities such as University of Houston and Kansas State University. His research has resulted in over 110 peer-reviewed publications that include book chapters, journal articles, invited articles, and conference proceedings, in journals such as *Tourism Management*, *International Journal of Hospitality Management*, *International Journal of Contemporary Hospitality Management*, *Journal of Travel & Tourism Marketing*, *Journal of Travel Research*, *Journal of Hospitality & Tourism Research*, and *Journal of Hospitality Information Technology*. He is the recipient of several prestigious academic awards, including the Teaching Excellence Award for Innovation in Instructional Technology, Stephen Rushmore/HVS Research Excellence Award, The Provost's Certificate of Excellence in Recognition of Extraordinary Achievements, the Barbara S. Stowe Endowed Faculty Development Award and Big 12 Faculty Fellowship Award. He is a member of the Editorial Board of *International Journal of Contemporary Hospitality Management*, *International Journal of Hospitality Information Technology*, and *Tourism Review International*, and has been recognized by the International Council on Hotel, Restaurant and Institutional Education (I-CHRIE) as an outstanding reviewer in the information technology area. He presented his work at I-CHRIE, the International Federation for Information Technologies in Travel and Tourism, the International Hospitality Information Technology Association (where he received the iHITA Best Research Paper awards in 2015 and 2018), Hospitality Financial and Technology Professionals, and Travel and Tourism Research Association. He has numerous media appearances and invited presentations at conferences, colloquia, and workshops throughout North America, Europe and Asia.

Dr. Cristian Morosan earned a Bachelor's of Science from University Ștefan cel Mare Suceava Romania, and Master of Science and PhD from Iowa State University.

Defining Hospitality and Tourism Marketing and the Marketing Process

I

1. Creating Customer Value and Engagement Through Marketing for Hospitality and Tourism
2. Services Marketing Concepts Applied to Marketing for Hospitality and Tourism
3. Marketing Strategy: Building Customer Engagement, Value, and Relationships

1

Courtsey of John Bowen

Objectives
After reading this chapter, you should be able to:

1. Describe the importance of marketing to the hospitality industry and outline the steps in the marketing process.
2. Explain how to analyze customer needs, wants, and demands and the marketplace.
3. Explain how to design a customer value-driven marketing strategy.
4. Describe how to build profitable customer relationships.
5. Discuss the outcomes of creating customer value.
6. Explain the major trends impacting the marketing landscape.

Creating Customer Value and Engagement Through Marketing for Hospitality and Tourism

Buffalo Wild Wings: Fueling the Sports Fan Experience

That's the long-standing motto for the fast-growing Buffalo Wild Wings restaurant chain. "B-Dubs"—it's known to avid regulars—focuses on food and sports and "everything in between." The name comes from its initials BWW or BW (double u) W (double u), resulting in B-Dubs. There's no doubt about it. Buffalo Wild Wings more than lives up to the "wings" and "beer" parts of the equation. It serves up wings in an abundant variety: boned or boneless, with five dry seasonings and 17 signature sauces ranging on the heat scale from Sweet BBQ (traditional BBQ sauce: satisfyingly sweet with no heat) to Desert Heat (smoky, sweet, and chili pepper seasoning) to Reformulated Blazin' (so good, it's scary, made with the unrelenting heat of the ghost pepper). To wash it all down, each B-Dubs restaurant pours as many as 30 different draft beers, with a full selection of domestic, import, and craft beer brands. You won't go hungry or thirsty at B-Dubs.

However, the Buffalo Wild Wings recipe for success goes much deeper than just selling wings and beer for profit. What really packs 'em in and keeps 'em coming back is the B-Dubs customer experience. They come to B-Dubs to watch sports, trash talk, cheer on their sports teams, and meet old friends and make new ones—that is, a total eating and social experience. "We realize that we're not just in the business of selling wings," says the company. "We're something much bigger. We're in the business of fueling the sports fan experience.

Everything about B-Dubs is designed to deliver the ultimate sports experience, for any fan of any sport. The WOW begins the minute you step into any of Buffalo Wild Wings' 1,100 restaurants. This is not your average dark-and-dank sports bar. Instead, a B-Dubs is like a miniature stadium, with high ceilings, ample natural light, and brightly colored furnishings and wall coverings. Every B-Dubs has 60–70 really big flat-screen TVs lining the walls, over the bar, and about everywhere else, ensuring that every table has the best seat in the house no matter what your team or sport is, including live streaming of local college and even high school events. B-Dubs creates an exciting environment that makes it the next best thing to being at the game—or something even better. "We consider ourselves to have 1,100 stadiums," says the chain's vice president for guest experience and innovation.

There's an experience for everyone at Buffalo Wild Wings. The chain appeals to a wide range of customers, from pub-loving sports nuts to families looking for an affordable evening out. Singles and couples gravitate to the bar area; families stick to the carpeted areas with booths. In addition to streaming sports events of all kinds on the big screens, B-Dubs supplies tableside tablets upon which customers can play poker or trivia games. A social jukebox feature lets guests control the music that plays on the restaurant's sound system.

It seems like there's always something happening in a B-Dubs to engage customers and enhance the experience. Take the chain's infamous Blazin' Wing Challenge, which promises a trophy-style T-shirt and a place on the Wall of Fame to any customer who can down a dozen wings with the chain's hottest signature sauce in no more than six minutes. That's no easy feat considering that the Blazin' sauce is 60 times hotter than typical jalapeno sauce. During the six-minute binge, challengers are not allowed to use napkins or utensils, touch their faces, or eat or drink anything other than the wings (no dipping sauces, please). The menu boasts plenty of warnings, and servers advise most people not to even attempt the challenge. And before taking the plunge, each challenger signs a waiver agreeing that she "voluntarily assumes all risk of loss, damage, injury, illness, or death that may be sustained by him or her as a result." As you can imagine, when a challenge is announced over the PA, it usually draws a crowd.

Buffalo Wild Wings never rushes its guests. Whereas many other casual-dining restaurants have a "turn-and-bum" philosophy—cycling as many paying guests as possible through each table—at B-Dubs it's just the opposite. Buffalo Wild Wings encourages people to linger longer, enjoy the food, and soak up the ambiance.

To help make that happen, the chain has created a new staff position at each restaurant. In addition to the usual waitstaff, each table has a Guest Experience Captain. According to B-Dubs chief marketer, the captain is "like a host at any party," moving from table to table, chatting with guests, personalizing their experiences, and making sure their needs are met. Want a special game on one screen with another game on the screen next to it? Your Guest Experience Captain sees to it. Need help with a tablet? Your captain lends a hand. Want to try some new sauces? Your captain will make suggestions and even bring out samples of different sauces with complimentary fries for dipping.

Adding Guest Experience Captains is a major expense, especially when multiplied across shifts in an 1,100 stores. But Buffalo Wild Wings reasons that the captains will more than pay for themselves by enhancing the all-important guest experience, keeping customers around longer, and bringing them back more often. Buffalo Wild Wings restaurants with captains are achieving record levels of customer satisfaction and loyalty compared with those that have not yet brought captains on board.

True to its "ultimate sports experience" mission, Buffalo Wild Wings actively engages its customers digitally and socially outside its restaurants as well as inside. In fact, the company brags that it's the number-one for digital brand in its industry for digital fan engagement. B-Dubs's very active Web site draws three million visitors per month. The brand has more than 12 million Facebook fans, 660,000 Twitter followers, and very active YouTube and Instagram pages. In all, Buffalo Wild Wings creates a host of both in-store and online promotions that inspire camaraderie. "It's about giving customers tools to not just be spectators but advocates of the brand," says the chain.

Catering to the customer experience has paid big dividends for Buffalo Wild Wings. B-Dubs is now the nation's number-one seller of chicken wings and largest pourer of draft beer. Over the past five years, as other casualdining restaurants have struggled with fierce competition and slow growth, B-Dubs's sales have more than tripled and profits are up 250 percent. The chain's hottest wing coating available comes with a warning to B-Dubs's customers: "keep away from eyes, pets, and children." Buffalo Wild Wings performance caught the attention of an investment group and was recently purchased by an investment group. Roark Capital Group, the owner of Wendy's Restaurants, bought Buffalo Wild Wings and created a new company, Inspire Brands, to manage their restaurants. Buffalo Wild Wings provides an example of a company that creates value for its customers, enabling it to capture value from its customers. This is the heart of the marketing process.[1]

▪▪▪ Your Passport to Success

As a manager in a global economy, marketing will greatly assist your personal career and the success of the enterprise you manage. In today's hospitality/travel industry, the customer is global and is king or queen. This title is bestowed not because of hereditary rights but because customers have the ability and power to enhance or damage your career through the purchase choices they make and the positive or negative comments they make to others.

The travel industry is the world's largest industry and the most international in nature. International travel has receipts of over $US1.5 trillion and over 1.33 billion travelers.[2] China's 1.4 billion people take over 5 billion domestic trips each year, spending $US700 billion. The rapid growth of domestic tourism in China, combined with over 150 million inbound tourists, has led to a tremendous growth of hotels, resorts, airport facilities, and other facilities to support tourism.[3] China's outbound tourists number 135 million and are a target market for many tourist destinations. The title "The World's Best Airport" is not held by an American or European airport but by Singapore. The world's best hotel is Hotel Il Pellicano in Tuscany, Italy. There were 15 countries that were home to the top 20 hotels in the world. The best international airline is Air New Zealand.[4]

The world's travel industry is alive, exciting, competitive, and challenging. Hospitality companies and tourism planning/promotion departments are filled with college graduates from across the globe. Competition is strong and getting tougher each day. Yet opportunities are greater than ever before.

Welcome to marketing! Your passport to success!

Today marketing isn't simply a business function: It's a philosophy, a way of thinking, and a way of structuring your business and your mind. Marketing is much more than a new ad campaign. The task of marketing is never to fool the customer or endanger the company's image. Marketing's task is to provide real value to targeted customers, motivate purchase, and fulfil consumer needs.

Marketing, more than any other business function, deals with customers. Creating customer value and satisfaction is at the heart of hospitality and travel industry marketing. Many factors contribute to making a business successful. However, today's successful companies at all levels have one thing in common: They are strongly customer focused and heavily committed to marketing. Accor has become one of the world's largest hotel chains by delivering L'esprit Accor, the ability to anticipate and meet the needs of its guests, with genuine attention to detail.[5] Ritz-Carlton promises and delivers truly "memorable experiences" for its hotels' guests. McDonald's grew into the world's largest restaurant chain by providing its guests with QSC&V (quality, service, cleanliness, and value). These and other successful hospitality companies know that if they take care of their customers, market share and profits will follow.

Singapore's Changi Airport is known for the fantastic interior design, which includes gardens like the one above throughout the airport. Pablo Hidalgo/123RF.

Purpose of a business To create and maintain satisfied, profitable customers. Naruedom Yaempongsa/123RF.

As a manager, you will be motivating your employees to create superior value for your customers. You will want to make sure that you deliver customer satisfaction at a profit. This is the simplest definition of marketing. This book will start you on a journey that will cause your customers to embrace you and make marketing your management philosophy.

Customer Orientation

The **purpose of a business** is to create and maintain satisfied, profitable customers.[6] Customers are attracted and retained when their needs are met. Not only do they return to the same cruise line, hotel, rental car firm, and restaurant, but they also talk favorably to others about their satisfaction.

"What about profits?" Some hospitality managers act as if today's profits are primary and customer satisfaction is secondary. This attitude eventually sinks a firm as it finds fewer repeat customers and faces increasingly negative word of mouth. Successful managers understand that profits are best seen as the result of running a business well rather than as its sole purpose. When a business satisfies its customers, the customers will pay a fair price for the product. A fair price includes a profit for the firm. Managers who forever try to maximize short-run profits are short-selling both the customer and the company. Consider the following episode:

A customer arrived at a restaurant before closing time and was greeted with "What do you want?" Somewhat surprised, the customer replied that he would like to get a bite to eat. A surly voice informed the customer that the restaurant was closed. At this point, the customer pointed to a sign on the door stating that the restaurant was open until 9 P.M. "Yeah, but by the time I clean up and put the food away, it'll be nine, so we're closed." The customer left and went to another restaurant a block away and never returned to the first restaurant.

Let's speculate for a moment. Why was the customer treated in such a shabby manner? Perhaps

- the employee wanted to leave early.
- the employee was suffering from a headache.
- the employee had personal or family problems.

What really happened in the restaurant episode is that this employee once served a customer immediately before closing time, resulting in the employee working until 10:30 P.M. Instead of the corporate office thanking her for serving the customer and staying late, it reprimanded her for putting in extra time. The corporate office wanted to keep down overtime expenses. The employee's response was to close the business by 9 P.M. at any cost. Now the corporate office is happy—they just don't realize they are losing customers and future business. Much of the behavior of employees toward their customers is the result of management philosophy.

The alternative management approach is to put the customer first and reward employees for serving the customer well. Marriott's vice president of sales and marketing services said, "We used to reward restaurant managers for things that were important to us, such as food costs. When have you heard a customer ask for the restaurant's food costs? You have to reward for what customers want from your business."[7]

Chapter 1 Creating Customer Value and Engagement Through Marketing for Hospitality and Tourism

The restaurant creates value for the customer through good customer service and excellent food. Managers and employees need be rewarded for things that are important to the customer. Ammentorp/123RF.

It is wise to assess the customer's long-term value and take appropriate actions to ensure a customer's long-term support. Two studies document this. The Forum Company found that the cost of retaining a loyal customer is just 20 percent of the cost of attracting a new one.[8] Another study found that an increase of five percentage points in customer retention rates yielded a profit increase of 25–125 percent.[9] Accordingly, a hotel that can increase its repeat customers from 35 to 40 percent should gain at least an additional 25 percent in profits.[10] The former president of Scandinavian Airlines summed up the importance of a satisfied customer:

Look at our balance sheet. On the asset side, you can still see so-and-so many aircraft worth so-and-so many billions. But it's wrong; we are fooling ourselves. What we should put on the asset side is the last year SAS carried so-and-so many happy passengers. Because that's the only asset we've got—people who are happy with our service and willing to come back and pay for it once again.[11]

Without customers, assets have little value. Without customers, a new multimillion-dollar restaurant will close, and without customers, a $300 million hotel will go into receivership, with the hotel being sold at a fraction of its book value.

What Is Hospitality and Tourism Marketing?

In the hotel industry, marketing and sales are often thought to be the same, and no wonder: The sales department is one of the most visible in the hotel. Sales managers provide prospective clients with tours and entertain them in the hotel's food and beverage outlets. Thus, the sales function is highly visible, whereas most of the nonpromotional areas of the marketing function take place behind closed doors. In the restaurant industry, many people confuse marketing with advertising and sales promotion. It is not uncommon to hear restaurant managers say that they "do not believe in marketing" when they actually mean that they are disappointed with the impact of their advertising. In reality, selling and advertising are only two marketing functions and often not the most important. Advertising and sales are components of the promotional element of the **marketing mix**. Other marketing mix elements in addition to **promotion** are **product, price**, and **distribution**. Distribution is sometimes called place, allowing the marketing mix to be referred to as the **four P**s. Marketing also includes planning, research, information systems, and understanding buyer behavior.

Marketing mix Elements include product, price, promotion, and distribution (place). Sometimes distribution is called place, resulting in the mix called the four Ps.

The four-P framework calls on marketing professionals to decide on the product and its characteristics, set the price, decide how to distribute their product, and choose methods for promoting their product. For example, McDonald's has a fast-food product. It uses quality ingredients and has developed products that it can sell at prices people expect to pay for fast food. Most people living in an urban area will not spend more than 15 minutes to travel to a McDonald's restaurant. As part of its distribution plan, McDonald's must have restaurants that are conveniently located to its target market. This is why McDonald's has over 15,000 restaurants in North America. This allows McDonald's to make effective use of mass media, such as television, as they can spread the cost out over many restaurants. The marketing mix must be just that—a mix of ingredients to create an effective product/service package for the target market.

If marketers do a good job of identifying consumer needs, developing a good product, and pricing, distributing, and promoting it effectively, the result will be attractive products and satisfied customers. Marriott developed its Moxy concept; Daniel Meyer designed the Shake Shack burger restaurant. They designed differentiated products, offering new consumer benefits. Marketing means "hitting the mark." Peter Drucker, a leading management thinker, put it this way: "The aim of marketing is to make selling superfluous. The aim is to know and understand customers so well that the product or service fits them and sells itself."[12]

This does not mean that selling and promotion are unimportant, but rather that they are part of a larger marketing mix, a set of marketing tools that work together to produce satisfied customers. The only way selling and promoting will be effective is if we first define customer targets and needs and then prepare an easily accessible and available value package.

Marketing in the Hospitality and Travel Industries

Importance of Marketing

Hospitality industry Made up of those businesses that offer one or more of the following: accommodation, prepared food and beverage service, and/or entertainment.

As we have seen, the **hospitality industry** is one of the world's major industries. In the United States, it is the second largest employer. In more than half of the 50 states, it is the largest industry. In this book we focus on the hospitality and travel industries.

Marketing has assumed an increasingly important role in the restaurant sector of the hospitality industry. The entrance of corporate giants into the hospitality market transformed it from a mom-and-pop industry, where individually owned restaurants and hotels were the norm, to an industry dominated by chains. These chains operate in a highly competitive environment where aggressive marketing skills are used to win customers. Almost one-half of the 650,000 restaurants in the United States are part of multiunit operations.[13]

The hotel industry is undergoing a consolidation, with companies such as Accor, Hilton, and Marriott buying hotel chains and operating different brands under one organization. The marketing expertise of these large firms has created a competitive marketing environment. In response to growing competitive pressures, hotel chains are relying more on the expertise of the marketing director. While the marketing director is a full-time marketer, everyone else must be a part-time marketer. All managers must understand marketing. By applying the principles of marketing to your job search, you will be able to enhance your career opportunities and hopefully end up in a job that you will love.

Tourism Marketing

Travel industry The travel industry includes travel agencies, providers of land transportation for tourists, tour operators, resort retailing, entertainment activities for tourists, and convention centers.

The two main industries that comprise the activities we call tourism are the hospitality and travel industries. The **travel industry**, as we define it, includes those organizations outside of the hospitality industry that provide travel services. These organizations include travel agencies, providers of land transportation for tourists, tour operators, resort retailing, entertainment activities for tourists, and convention centers. Hospitality and travel industries are linked, and thus, making a clear demarcation between the two is difficult. The distinction between the two industries is not as important as realizing both industries are highly dependent on each other. Meeting planners choose destinations based on the cost of getting to the destination, the value of the hotels, the quality of restaurants, and evening activities for their attendees.

The success of cruise lines is really the result of coordinated marketing by many travel industry members. For example, the Port of Boston wanted to attract more cruise line business. Massport (the port authority) aggressively marketed Boston to cruise lines. Having convinced the cruise lines to come, they then promoted Boston to key travel agents. This was critical because travel agents account

Cruise ships, such as this one docked in Cozumel, Mexico, can be a good source of tourists. Tonobalaguer/123RF.

for 95 percent of all cruise line business. Boston realized that if the cruise lines ships were leaving Boston with high occupancy levels, the cruise lines would be happy and add more cruises from Boston. The result was that Boston doubled the number of port calls by cruise lines and added $17.3 million to the local economy through this combined marketing effort.

That's only the beginning of travel industry marketing cooperation to promote cruise lines. Airlines, auto rental firms, hotels tour operators, restaurants, and passenger railways cooperatively develop packages with cruise lines. This requires coordination in pricing, promotion, and delivery of those packages. Like Massport, government or quasi-government agencies play an important role through legislation aimed at enhancing the industry and through promotion of regions, states, and nations.[14]

Few industries are as interdependent as travel–hospitality. This interdependence will increase in complexity. The travel industry will require marketing professionals who understand the big picture and can respond to changing consumer needs through creative strategies based on solid marketing knowledge.

Definition of Marketing

Marketing Marketing is the process by which companies create value for customers and society, resulting in strong customer relationships that capture value from the customers in return, while creating value for society.

Marketing must be understood in the sense of satisfying customer needs. If the marketer understands customer needs; develops products that provide superior customer value; and prices, distributes, and promotes them effectively, these products will sell easily. Here is our definition of **marketing**: Marketing is the process by which companies create value for customers and society, resulting in strong customer relationships that capture value from the customers in return, while creating

---

Marketing HIGHLIGHT 1.1 — How four seasons hotels and resorts delights its customers

As the guest's taxi pulled away, Roy Dyment, a doorman at Toronto's Four Seasons, noticed the guest's briefcase still sitting near the entrance to the hotel. Dyment phoned the guest in Washington, D.C., to let him know that he had found the briefcase. He learned that the briefcase contained key documents for an important meeting in the morning. Dyment knew one sure way of getting the briefcase to Washington before the morning meeting—take it himself. He caught a plane and delivered the briefcase. His first concern was taking care of the guest. He didn't worry about getting his boss's approval. Upon his return, instead of getting reprimanded or terminated, he was made employee of the year. Four Seasons is one of the world's great hotel chains that practice the marketing concept. Isadore Sharp, founder and chairman of Four Seasons Hotels and Resorts, states that the company's top priority is a satisfied guest. Concern for the customer starts with top management and flows through the operation. Four Season's corporate culture encourages employees to go that extra mile and respond with concern and dedication to customer needs. Employees are never penalized for trying to serve the customer.

According to a study by Peat Marwick McClintock, Four Seasons is an oddity because many hotel firms place profitability or growth as their number one goal. This, in part, explains why this hotel company has won an international reputation for customer service. Four Seasons has also shown that putting the customer first leads to profits with above-average financial performance and profit percentages that many hotel chains only dream about.[15]

Figure 1–1
A simple model of the marketing process.

value for society. One addition to marketing that has emerged in recent years is the creation of value for society. Today, with increased pressure on the environment and a growing percentage of people living in poverty, it is important that companies engage sustainable methods and support the communities in which they operate.

The Marketing Process

Figure 1–1 presents a simple five-step model of the marketing process. In the first four steps, companies work to understand consumers, develop a value-driven strategy, create a marketing program that delivers superior customer value, build strong customer relationships, and capture value from customers. In the final step, companies reap the rewards of creating superior customer value through sales, profits, and long-term customer equity.

Understanding the Marketplace and Customer Needs

As a first step, marketers need to understand customer needs and wants and the marketplace within which they operate. We now examine five core customer and marketplace concepts: (1) needs, wants, and demands; (2) marketing offerings (tangible products, services, and experiences); (3) value and satisfaction; (4) exchanges and relationships; and (5) markets.

Customer Needs, Wants, and Demands

Needs

Human need A state of felt deprivation in a person.

The most basic concept underlying marketing is that of **human needs**. A human need is a state of felt deprivation. Included are the basic physical needs for food, clothing, warmth, and safety, as well as social needs for belonging, affection, fun, and relaxation. There are esteem needs for prestige, recognition, and fame, and individual needs for knowledge and self-expression. These needs were not invented by marketers, but they are part of the human makeup.

Wants

Human want The form that a human need takes when shaped by culture and individual personality.

The second basic concept to marketing is that of **human wants**, the form human needs take as they are shaped by culture and individual personality. Wants are how people communicate their needs. A hungry person in Papua New Guinea needs food but wants taro, rice, yams, and pork. A hungry person in the United States needs food but wants a hamburger, fries, and a Coke. Wants are described in terms of objectives that will satisfy needs. As a society evolves, the wants of its members expand. As people are

A person who needs food in Malaysia may want Asam Laksa, shown below. While a person in England may want fish and chips. The need is the same, but the want is different. Lim_atos/123RF.

exposed to more objectives that arouse their interest and desire, producers try to provide more want-satisfying products and services. Restaurants were once able to serve generic white wine by the glass. Today, customers are more sophisticated; restaurants now serve chardonnay, sauvignon blanc, viognier, and pinot grigio by the glass. Today's restaurant customers want and expect a good selection of wine.

Many sellers often confuse wants with needs. A manufacturer of drill bits may think that a customer needs a drill bit, but what the customer really needs is a hole. These sellers suffer from "marketing myopia."[16] They are so taken with their products that they focus only on existing wants and lose sight of underlying customer needs. They forget that a physical product is only a tool to solve a consumer problem. These sellers get into trouble if a new product comes along that serves the need better or cheaper. The customer will then have the same need but want a new product.

The restaurant industry is facing a dramatic shift in the way customers purchase meals. Many customers want the restaurant to prepare the meal, but they want to eat it in their own home. Well over half the meals purchased at the nation's restaurants are "takeouts" or delivery to be eaten at home, the office, in the car, or other locations.[17] This dramatic change in eating habits has caused some restaurants to change their delivery and even food preparation area. It has also created new businesses—Uber Eats, Grubhub, and other food delivery services connect the customer with the restaurant, eliminating the need for the customer to drive to the restaurant or for the restaurant to manage its own delivery service. Newer restaurants and renovated restaurants have developed a separate entrance for pick-up orders, so they do not interfere with service to customers in the restaurant. Grocery stores seized the opportunity to have counters with prepared foods to take home as well as freshly prepared meals in convenient microwave containers. Still other entrepreneurs saw an opportunity to create an experience out of cooking your own meal, by removing the hassle of buying multiple ingredients. They simplified the cooking process and created a fun experience by providing everything you need for a meal, including instructions, delivered to your door. These services include Blue Apron, Freshley, and Plated. As wants change, those who understand the new wants have the opportunity to create value for customers.

Demands

People have almost unlimited wants, but limited resources. They choose products that produce the most satisfaction for their money. When backed by buying power, wants become **demands**.

Demands Human wants that are backed by buying power.

Outstanding marketing organizations go to great lengths to learn about and understand their customer's needs, wants, and demands. They conduct customer research. Smart companies also have employees at all levels—including top management—stay close to customers. For example, at Southwest Airlines, all senior executives handle bags, check in passengers, and serve as flight attendants once a quarter. All Disney World managers spend one week per year on the front line—taking tickets, selling popcorn, or loading and unloading rides. Understanding customer needs, wants, and demands in detail provides important input for designing marketing strategies. The city of Santa Fe, New Mexico, has a beautiful and historic opera house, but only a small percentage of the population participated in operas. As Catherine Zacher, president of Santa Fe Economic Development, Inc., said, "Most Americans don't enjoy being yelled at in Italian." However, they did want other forms of entertainment. When the opera house was made available for a variety of musical concerts, the demand created for this contemporary entertainment sold all available seats.[18]

Market Offerings: Tangible Products, Services, and Experiences

Consumer needs and wants are fulfilled through a market offering: a product that is some combination of tangible, services, information, or experiential product components. We often associate the word *product* with a tangible product or one that has physical properties (e.g., the hotel room or the steak we receive in a restaurant). In the hospitality industry, intangible products, such as customer service and experiences, are more important than tangible products. Managers of resorts realize that their guests will be leaving with memories of their stay. They try to create experiences that will generate pleasant memories. At a Ritz-Carlton resort, every evening at sunset, managers set up chairs on the beach, hire a cellist to play relaxing music, and serve champagne to guests. They realize that this event not only creates value for the guests, but it is also an experience that will create a lasting memory of their stay. Marriott provides Dolphin safaris at its Newport Beach property and a water rafting trip at its Utah property. Marriott uses the resources of the destination to create guest experiences that the guest remembers for a lifetime. More broadly, market offerings also include other entities, such as persons, places, organizations, information, and ideas. For example, San Diego runs a "Happiness Is Calling" advertising campaign that invites visitors to come and enjoy the city's great weather and good times—everything from its bays and beaches to its downtown nightlife and urban scenes.[19] Consumers decide which events to experience, which tourist destinations to visit, which hotels to stay in, and which restaurants to patronize. To the consumer these are all products.

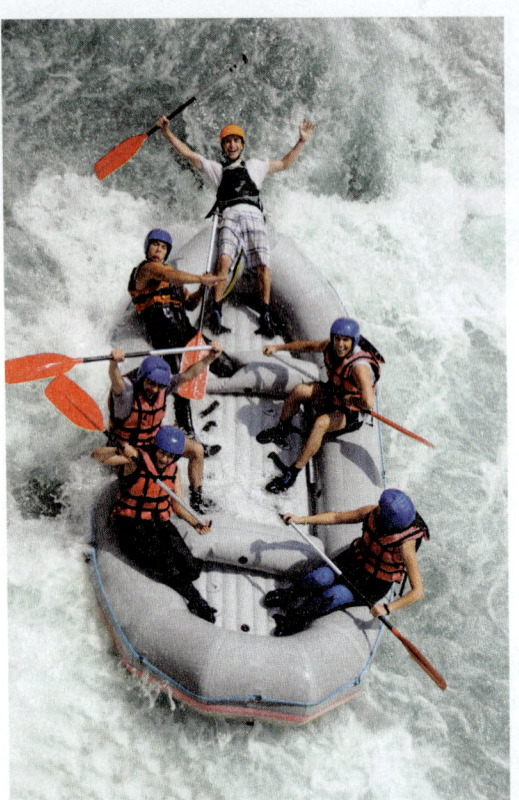

White rafting can create an experience that will be remembered of a lifetime, positive word of mouth about the destination, and a desire to return to the destination. Strahil Dimitrov/123RF.

Customer value The difference between the benefits that the customer gains from owning and/or using a product and the costs of obtaining the product.

Customer expectations Expectations based on past buying experiences, the opinions of friends, and market information.

Customer Value and Satisfaction

Customer value is the difference between the benefits that the customer gains from owning and/or using a product and the costs of obtaining the product. Costs can be both monetary and nonmonetary. One of the biggest nonmonetary costs for hospitality customers is time. Companies are constantly trying to save the guest's time and create value for the guest. For example, digital check using a smartphone allows the guest to bypass the front desk, and at Starbucks, guests can order ahead on their smartphone and have their favorite drink waiting for them when they arrive. Managers must know their customers and understand what creates value for them. This is an ongoing process, as customers and competition change over time.

Customer expectations are based on past buying experiences, the opinions of friends, and market information. If we meet customer expectations, they are satisfied. Marketers must be careful to set the right level of expectations. In the hospitality industry, it is easy to set high expectations because guests will not be able to judge the product until after they have consumed it. For example, an owner can advertise that his or her restaurant serves the best seafood in the city. If this is not true, many customers will leave dissatisfied; the experience did not meet their expectations. The result will be negative reviews on social media. We must understand how we create value for our market and communicate that to our customers and potential customers. For example, we might specialize in fresh, locally caught seafood. Customer satisfaction depends on a product's perceived performance in delivering value relative to a buyer's expectations. If the product's performance falls short of the customer's expectations, the buyer is dissatisfied. If performance matches expectations, the buyer is satisfied. If performance exceeds expectations, the buyer is delighted. Smart companies aim to delight customers by promising only what they can deliver and then delivering more than they promise.

Managers must realize the importance of creating highly satisfied customers, rather than just satisfied customers. On a 7-point scale, with 1 very satisfied

Figure 1–2
Relationship between satisfaction and loyalty behaviors.
Customers were asked to rate on a scale of 1–7 denoting how satisfied they were with their experience after dining in a restaurant. A score of 1 meant they were very satisfied and a score of 7 meant they were very dissatisfied. Scores of 1, 2, and 3 are all on the satisfaction side of the scale; that is, they are all better than a score of 4 (neither satisfied nor dissatisfied), which is the midpoint of the scale. You can see that satisfying the guest is not enough. Only when guests leave very satisfied they are likely to come back. Your goal is to have all guests leave very satisfied.

Even though 3 is still a "positive" score on the above 7-point scale, few customers giving that rating will return.

and 7 very dissatisfied, most managers are happy to receive a 2. However, from Figure 1–2, which shows the results of a guest survey at a Boston hotel,[20] you can see the huge gap between a guest who rates a hotel a 1 and one who rates it a 2. Think of the last time you went to a restaurant and were just satisfied. Would you go back? Probably not. But when you walk out of a restaurant and say, "Wow, that was great!" you will probably return and tell others about your discovery. On social media hundreds or even thousands could see your positive comments.

Exchanges and Relationships

Marketing occurs when people decide to satisfy needs and wants through exchange. **Exchange** is the act of obtaining a desired object from someone by offering something in return. Marketing consists of actions taken to build and maintain desirable exchange relationships with target markets. Beyond simply attracting new customers and creating **transactions**, the goal is to retain customers and grow their business with the company. Marketers want to build strong relationships by consistently delivering superior customer value.

Exchange The act of obtaining a desired object from someone by offering something in return.

Transaction Consists of a trade of values between two parties; marketing's unit of measurement.

Markets

The concept of transactions leads to the concept of a market. A **market** is a set of actual and potential buyers of a product. These buyers share a particular need or want that can be satisfied through exchange relationships.

Marketing involves managing markets to bring about profitable customer relationships. However, creating these relationships takes work. Sellers must search for buyers, identify their needs, design good market offerings, set prices for them, promote them, and deliver them. Activities such as product development, research, communication, distribution, pricing, and service are core marketing activities.

Market A set of actual and potential buyers of a product.

▰▰▰ Designing Customer Value-Driven Marketing Strategy

Once marketing management fully understands consumers and the marketplace, it can design a customer-driven marketing strategy. We define **marketing management** as the art and science of choosing target markets and building profitable relationships with them, while creating value for society. The **marketing manager**'s aim is to find, attract, keep, and grow target customers by creating, delivering, and communicating superior customer value. To design a winning marketing strategy, the marketing manager must

Marketing management The art and science of choosing target markets and building profitable relationships with them, while creating value for society.

Marketing manager A person who is involved in marketing analysis, planning, implementation, and control activities.

answer two important questions: (1) What customers will we serve (what's our target market)? (2) How can we serve these customers best (what's our value proposition)?

Selecting Customers to Serve

The company must first decide who it will serve. It does this by dividing the market into segments of customers (market segmentation) and selecting which segments it will go after (target marketing). Some people think of marketing management as finding as many customers as possible and increasing demand. But marketing managers know that they cannot serve all customers in every way. By trying to serve all customers, they may not serve any customers well. Instead, the company wants to select only customers that it can serve well and profitably. For example, Ritz-Carlton Hotels profitably target affluent travelers; McDonald's restaurants profitably target families.

Choosing a Value Proposition

The company must also decide how it will serve targeted customers—how it will differentiate and position itself in the marketplace. A company's **value proposition** is the set of benefits or values it promises to deliver to consumers to satisfy their needs.

Such value propositions differentiate one brand from another. They answer the customer's question, "Why should I buy your brand rather than a competitor's?" Companies must design strong value propositions that give them the greatest advantage in their target markets.

> **Value proposition** The full positioning of a brand—the full mix of benefits upon which it is positioned.

Marketing Management Orientations

Marketing management wants to design strategies that will build profitable relationships with target consumers. But what philosophy should guide these marketing strategies? What weight should be given to the interests of customers, the organization, and society? Often, these interests conflict with each other. We discuss three alternative concepts under which organizations design and carry out their marketing strategies: selling, marketing, and societal marketing.

The Selling Concept

The **selling concept** holds that consumers will not buy enough of the organization's products unless the organization undertakes a large selling and promotion effort. The aim of a selling focus is to get every possible sale, not to worry about satisfaction after the sale or the revenue contribution of the sale.

The selling concept does not establish a long-term relationship with the customer because the focus is on getting rid of what one has rather than creating a product to meet the needs of the market. Restaurants often advertise when sales start to drop, without first analyzing why sales are dropping. They do not try to change their product to fit the changing market. They sell harder, pushing their products on the customer through increased advertising and couponing. Eventually, they go out of business because their product no longer satisfies the needs of the marketplace.

> **Selling concept** The idea that consumers will not buy enough of an organization's products unless the organization undertakes a large selling and promotion effort.

The selling concept exists within the hospitality industry. A major contributing factor is overcapacity. Virtually every major sector of this industry has suffered from overcapacity. When owners and top management face overcapacity, the tendency is to sell, sell, sell. Why do major sectors such as hotels, resorts, airlines, cruise lines, and even restaurants continuously face overcapacity? A few of the reasons are listed below:

- Pride in being the biggest, having the most capacity.
- A belief that economies of scale will occur as size increases.
- Tax laws that encourage real estate developers to overbuild properties because of the generous tax write-offs.
- Failure to merge revenue management with sales/marketing management.
- Poor or nonexistent forecasting and planning by owners, consultants, financial organizations, and governments.

Figure 1–3
The selling and marketing concepts contrasted.

Starting point	Focus	Means	Ends
Factory	Existing products	Selling and promoting	Profits through sales volume

The selling concept

Market	Customer needs	Integrated marketing	Profits through customer satisfaction

The marketing concept

Marketing concept The marketing management philosophy that holds that achieving organizational goals depends on determining the needs and wants of target markets and delivering desired satisfactions more effectively and efficiently than competitors.

Societal marketing concept The idea that an organization should determine the needs, wants, and interests of target markets and deliver the desired satisfactions more effectively and efficiently than competitors in a way that maintains or improves the consumer's and society's well-being.

Figure 1–4
Three considerations underlying the societal marketing concept.
Source: Kotler, Philip; Armstrong, Gary, *Principles of Marketing*, 16th ed., ©2016, pp. 12, 24, 50. Reprinted and Electronically reproduced by permission of Pearson Education, Inc., New York, NY.

Society
(Human welfare)

Societal marketing concept

Consumers
(Want satisfaction)

Company
(Profits)

The Marketing Concept

The **marketing concept** is a more recent business. The marketing concept holds that achieving organizational goals depends on determining the needs and wants of target markets and delivering the desired satisfaction more effectively and efficiently than competitors.

Amazingly, niche opportunities sometimes remain available long after suppliers recognize the need. This is probably due to difficulties in changing the behavior of those who supply the products, such as the wait staff in a restaurant. The American Association of Retired Persons (AARP) conducted a survey of readers of its magazine, *Modern Maturity*. Fifty-nine percent replied that they frequently ate in a restaurant alone; another 18 percent replied that they sometimes did. Eighty-four percent replied that the service they receive is worse than if they had other people at the table. Some restaurants have established special seating areas for singles with round tables that encourage single diners to sit together. This provides an opportunity for the diners to engage in conversation with other diners and allows the restaurant to conserve seating space. Other restaurants have deuces that face each other, encouraging conversation if it is desired. These restaurants value the single diner and have built up a profitable segment.[21] The marketing concept starts with a well-defined market, focuses on customer needs, and integrates all the marketing activities that affect customers. It meets the organizational goals by creating long-term customer relationships based on customer value and satisfaction. As Herb Kelleher, former CEO of Southwest Airlines, stated, "We don't have a Marketing department: we have a Customer department" (Figure 1–3).

The Societal Marketing Concept

The **societal marketing concept** questions whether the pure marketing concept overlooks possible conflicts between consumer short-run wants and consumer long-run welfare. Is a firm that satisfies the immediate needs and wants of target markets always doing what's best for its consumers in the long run? The societal marketing concept holds that marketing strategy should deliver value to customers in a way that maintains or improves both the consumer's and society's well-being. It calls for sustainable marketing, socially and environmentally responsible marketing that meets the present needs of consumers and businesses while also preserving or enhancing the ability of future generations to meet their needs. Figure 1–4 illustrates the principles of the societal marketing concept.

Even more broadly, many leading business and marketing thinkers are now preaching the concept of shared value, which recognizes that societal needs, not just economic needs, define markets.[22] The concept of shared value focuses on creating economic value in a way

Programs sponsored by a company to such as these employees cleaning up a local park create a team spirit amongst the employees and support the company's and employee's value of being socially responsible. Dolgachov/123RF.

that also creates value for society. A growing number of companies are concerned not just with short-term economic gains but with the well-being of their customers, the depletion of natural resources vital to their businesses, the viability of key suppliers, and the economic well-being of the communities in which they operate.

Two of the sustainability efforts of restaurants include reduction of food waste and locally sourced food, eliminating the carbon fuels used to transport foods. The Sustainable Restaurant Association (SRA) has helped create campaigns that reduce food waste and encourage locally sourced food products. The results of their research found most customers do not ask to take uneaten food home because that 34 percent of the respondents never thought about taking uneaten food home, 25 percent felt embarrassed to ask to take food home, and 24 percent thought restaurants were not allowed to let uneaten food leave the restaurant. Eighteen percent said they would not eat the food at home or thought it was not hygienic. The SRA has been working with restaurants to reduce food waste. Wahaca, a London-based restaurant group, encouraged customers to take home uneaten food through its "Too Good to Waste" campaign. They noticed a 20 percent reduction in plate waste over a six-month period. Pret a Manger, through its "Made Today Gone Today" program, gives over 500,000 meals a year of unsold food to charities.[23]

Preparing an Integrated Marketing Plan and Program

The company's marketing strategy outlines which customers the company will serve and how it will create value for these customers. Next, the marketer develops an integrated marketing program that will actually deliver the intended value to target customers. The marketing program builds customer relationships by transforming the marketing strategy into action. It consists of the firm's marketing mix, the set of marketing tools the firm uses to implement its marketing strategy.

The major marketing mix tools are classified into four broad groups, called the four Ps of marketing: product, price, place, and promotion. To deliver on its value proposition, the firm must first create a need-satisfying market offering (product). It must decide how much it will charge for the offer (price) and how it will make the offer available to target consumers (place). Finally, it must communicate with target customers about the offer and persuade them of its merits (promotion). The firm must blend all of these marketing mix tools into a comprehensive, integrated marketing program that communicates and delivers the intended value to chosen customers. We explore marketing programs and the marketing mix in much more detail in later chapters.

Managing Customer Relationships and Capturing Value

The first three steps in the marketing process—understanding the marketplace and customer needs, designing a customer-driven marketing strategy, and preparing an integrated marketing plan—all lead up to the fourth and most important step: building profitable customer relationships.

Customer Relationship Management

Customer relationship management (CRM) is perhaps the most important concept of modern marketing. CRM involves managing detailed information about individual customers and carefully managing customer "touch points" in order to maximize customer loyalty. A **customer touch point** is any occasion on which a customer encounters the brand and product—from actual experience to personal or mass communications to casual observation. For a hotel, the touch points include reservations, check-in and checkout, frequent-stay programs, room service, business services, exercise facilities, laundry service, restaurants, and bars. For instance, the Four Seasons relies on personal touches, such as a staff that always addresses guests by name, high-powered employees who understand the needs of sophisticated business travelers, and at least one best-in-region facility, such as a premier restaurant or spa.

Sometimes touch points are where you least expect, such as in customer billing. Meeting planners expect to have prompt and accurate billing. Reviewing the bill with the meeting planner during a multiday meeting can help build trust and a strong relationship.

CRM enables companies to provide excellent real-time customer service through the effective use of individualized information. Based on what they know about each valued customer, companies can customize market offerings, services, programs, messages, and amenities. CRM is important because a major driver of a company's profitability is the aggregate value of its customer base. More recently, CRM has taken on a broader meaning. In this broader sense, CRM is the overall process of building and maintaining profitable customer relationships by delivering superior customer value and satisfaction. It deals with all aspects of acquiring, keeping, and growing customers.

Relationship Building Blocks: Customer Value and Satisfaction

The key to building lasting customer relationships is to create superior customer value and satisfaction.

CUSTOMER VALUE. Attracting and retaining customers can be a difficult task. Customers often face a bewildering array of products and services from which to choose. A customer buys from the firm that offers the highest **customer-perceived value**—the customer's evaluation of the difference between all the benefits and all the costs of a market offering relative to those of competing offers. Importantly, customers often do not judge values and costs "accurately" or "objectively." They act on perceived value.

To some consumers, value might mean sensible products at affordable prices. To other consumers, however, value might mean paying more to get more. For example, limited-service restaurants serving food selections usually found in more expensive table-serve restaurants have become popular with customers who are willing to stand in line and place their order at a counter. They then have their food delivered to them at the table rather than having a server come to the table to take their order. They save 10–20 percent on an equivalent meal at a full-service restaurant and often will tip less than they would at a full-service restaurant, creating a perceived value for some customers. Other restaurant customers like to relax with their guests, enjoy conversation, and do not want to stand in line to place an order. To these customers, the perceived value of a full-service restaurant is higher than a limited-service restaurant, and they are willing to pay the extra costs of a full-service restaurant.

CUSTOMER SATISFACTION. **Customer satisfaction** depends on the product's perceived performance relative to a buyer's expectations. If the product's performance falls short of expectations, the customer is dissatisfied. If performance matches expectations, the customer is satisfied. If performance exceeds expectations, the customer is highly satisfied or delighted.

Outstanding marketing companies go out of their way to keep important customers satisfied. Most studies show that higher levels of customer satisfaction lead

---

Customer touch point Any occasion on which a customer encounters the brand and product—from actual experience to personal or mass communications to casual observation.

Customer relationship management (CRM) CRM involves managing detailed information about individual customers and carefully managing customer "touch points" in order to maximize customer loyalty.

Customer-perceived value The customer's evaluation of the difference between all the benefits and all the costs of a market offering relative to those of competing offers.

Customer satisfaction The extent to which a product's perceived performance matches a buyer's expectations.

to greater customer loyalty, which in turn results in better company performance. Companies aim to delight customers by promising only what they can deliver and then delivering more than they promise. Delighted customers not only make repeat purchases but also become willing marketing partners and "customer evangelists" who spread the word about their good experiences to others.

For companies interested in delighting customers, exceptional value and service become part of the overall company culture. A company doesn't need to have over-the-top service to create customer delight. Chick-fil-A, a fast food restaurant chain, is known for its customer service. Thus, customer satisfaction comes not just from service heroics but from how well a company delivers on its basic value proposition and helps customers solve their buying problems. "Most customers don't want to be 'wowed,'" says one marketing consultant. "They [just] want an effortless experience."[24] One of the authors conducted a focus group with hotel business guests. They stated that they just wanted a hassle-free experience. For example, when they turned on the desk lamp, they wanted it to work; when they went to plug in their smartphone on the night plug, they wanted a convenient plug; when they went to take a shower, they wanted the towels to be stocked.

Although a customer-centered firm seeks to deliver high customer satisfaction relative to its competitors, it does not attempt to maximize customer satisfaction. A company can always increase customer satisfaction by lowering its prices or increasing its services. The purpose of marketing is to generate customer value profitably. This requires a very delicate balance: The marketer must continue to generate more customer value and satisfaction but not "give away the house." As long as a company provides its customer with customer satisfaction that customers value, it will have the opportunity to establish a relationship with those customers.

Customer Relationship Levels and Tools

Companies can build customer relationships at many levels, depending on the nature of the target market. At one extreme, a company with many low-margin customers may seek to develop basic relationships with them. For example, McDonald's does not phone, e-mail, or text all of its customers to get to know them. Instead, McDonald's creates engagement and relationships through product experiences, brand-building advertising, Web sites, and social media. On the other hand, casinos have a close relationship with their best customers. They know what they like to eat, drink, and what type of shows they like.

Beyond offering consistently high value and satisfaction, marketers can use specific marketing tools to develop stronger bonds with customers. For example, many companies offer frequency marketing programs that reward customers who buy frequently or in large amounts. Airlines offer frequent-flier programs, hotels give room upgrades to frequent guests, and supermarkets give patronage discounts to "very important customers." These days almost every brand has a loyalty rewards program. Such programs can enhance and strengthen a customer's brand experience. For example, JetBlue's TrueBlue loyalty program offers the usual frequent-flier points and rewards but adds some nice enhancements such as no blackout dates and family sharing. More importantly, the TrueBlue program personalizes the customer experience. Each TrueBlue member has customized Web and mobile pages, complete with a dashboard that shows available points, JetBlue activity history, connections with JetBlue rewards partners, and trip- and flight-planning links. The personalized pages not only make it easy for TrueBlue members to manage their points and rewards, but they are also a handy one-stop trip-planning tool, all geared to an individual member's profile. As one member describes it: "Once you're an official TrueBlue member, go hog wild filling out your profile. Upload that stunning selfie with the blue filter as your member picture, pick your favorite JetBlue destinations, even create an ultimate dream itinerary to the Blue Ridge Mountains, and add it to your TrueBlue 16 Wishlist." JetBlue's pledge to members: "TrueBlue. For your loyalty, we give you ours."[25]

Significant changes are occurring in the nature of customer-brand relationships. Today's digital technologies—the internet and the surge in online, mobile, and social media—have profoundly changed the ways that people on the planet relate to one another. In turn, these events have had a huge impact on how companies and brands connect with customers and how customers connect with and influence each other's brand behaviors.

Customer Engagement and Today's Digital and Social Media

The digital age has spawned a dazzling set of new customer relationship-building tools, from Web sites, online ads and videos, mobile ads and apps, and blogs to online communities and the major social media, such as Twitter, Facebook, YouTube, Snapchat, and Instagram.

Yesterday's companies focused mostly on mass marketing to broad segments of customers at arm's length. By contrast, today's companies are using online, mobile, and social media to refine their targeting and to engage customers more deeply and interactively. The old marketing involved marketing brands to consumers. The new marketing is **customer-engagement marketing** fostering direct and continuous customer involvement in shaping brand conversations, brand experiences, and brand community. Customer-engagement marketing goes beyond just selling a brand to consumers. Its goal is to make the brand a meaningful part of consumers' conversations and lives.

The burgeoning internet and social media have given a huge boost to customer-engagement marketing. Today's consumers are better informed, more connected, and more empowered than ever before. Newly empowered consumers have more information about brands, and they have a wealth of digital platforms for airing and sharing their brand views with others. Thus, marketers are now embracing not only customer relationship management but also customer-managed relationships, in which customers connect with companies and with each other to help forge and share their own brand experiences.

Most marketers now combine their mass-media marketing efforts with a rich mix of online, mobile, and social media marketing that promotes brandconsumer engagement, brand conversations, and brand advocacy among customers. For example, companies post their latest ads and videos on social media sites, hoping they'll go viral. They maintain an extensive presence on Twitter, YouTube, Facebook, Pinterest, Instagram, Snapchat, Vine, and other social media to create brand buzz. They launch their own blogs, mobile apps, online microsites, and consumer-generated review systems, all with the aim of engaging customers on a more personal, interactive level.

Similarly, almost every company has something going on Facebook these days. Starbucks has more than 37 million Facebook "fans"; Coca-Cola has more than 107 million. And every major marketer has a YouTube channel where the brand and its fans post current ads and other entertaining or informative videos. Instagram, LinkedIn, Pinterest, Snapchat, Twitter, all have exploded onto the marketing scene, giving brands more ways to engage and interact with customers. Skilled use of social media can get consumers involved with a brand, talking about it, and advocating it to others.

The key to engagement marketing is to find ways to enter targeted consumers' conversations with engaging and relevant brand messages. Simply posting a humorous video, creating a social media page, or hosting a blog isn't enough. And not all customers want to engage deeply or regularly with every brand. Successful engagement marketing means making relevant and genuine contributions to targeted consumers' lives and interactions.

Consumer-Generated Marketing

A growing part of the new customer dialogue is consumer-generated marketing, by which consumers themselves are playing a bigger role in shaping their own brand experiences and those of others. This might happen through uninvited consumer-to-consumer exchanges in blogs, video-sharing sites, and other digital forums. But increasingly, companies are inviting consumers to play a more active role in shaping products and brand messages. Chili's had a successful campaign on its 40th birthday.

Customer-engagement marketing Fosters direct and continuous customer involvement in shaping brand conversations, experiences, and community.

Almost every company uses multiple social media. Artseen/Shutterstock.

Customer equity The discounted LTVs of all the company's current and potential customers.

Companies want to not only create profitable customers but also "own" them for life, earn a greater share of their purchases, and capture their LTV.

What Is Customer Equity?

The ultimate aim of CRM is to produce high customer equity.[31] **Customer equity** is the discounted LTVs of all the company's current and potential customers. The best approach to customer retention is to deliver products that create high customer satisfaction and high perceived value, resulting in strong customer loyalty. Clearly, the more loyal the firm's profitable customers, the higher the firm's customer equity. Customer equity may be a better measure of a firm's performance than current sales or market share. Whereas sales and market share reflect the past, customer equity suggests the future.[32]

Building the Right Relationships with the Right Customers

Companies should manage customer equity carefully. They should view customers as assets that need to be managed and maximized. But not all customers, not even all loyal customers, are good investments. Surprisingly, some loyal customers can be unprofitable, and some disloyal customers can be profitable. Which customers should the company acquire and retain?

The company can classify customers according to their potential profitability and manage its relationships with them accordingly. Figure 1–5 classifies customers into one of four relationship groups, according to their profitability and projected loyalty.[33] Each group requires a different relationship management strategy. Strangers show low potential profitability and little projected loyalty. There is little fit between the company's offerings and their needs. The relationship management strategy for these customers is simple: Treat them well as a guest but invest in little or no effort in marketing to them. For example, a couple may go out to a nice restaurant twice a year for a special occasion and rotate among their three or four favorite restaurants. In this case, you might want to send an e-mail before their birthday or anniversary offering a complimentary dessert to keep your restaurant at the top of mind. Butterflies are potentially profitable but not loyal. There is a good fit between the company's offerings and their needs. However, like real butterflies, we can enjoy them for only a short while and then they're gone. An example is someone who is traveling and experiencing different destinations and experiences. They enjoy your restaurant, but then they are off to gain a different experience at another restaurant in a new destination. Efforts to convert butterflies into loyal customers are rarely successful. Instead, the company should enjoy the butterflies for the moment. It should create satisfying and profitable transactions with them, capturing as much of their business as possible in the short time during which they buy from the company. Then it should move on and cease investing in them.

Barnacles are highly loyal but not very profitable. There is a limited fit between their needs and the company's offerings. An example is a customer who comes in and orders a sandwich with no sides and no drink. Like barnacles on the hull of a ship, they create drag by taking up space. Barnacles are perhaps the most problematic customers. They should be treated well, as should all guests who are not abusive to other customers or employees. Like strangers, no marketing investment should be made in Barnacles.

True friends are both profitable and loyal. There is a strong fit between their needs and the company's offerings. The firm wants to make continuous relationship investments to delight these customers and engage, nurture, retain, and grow them. It wants to turn true friends into true believers, who come back regularly and tell others about their good experiences with the company.

The point here is an important one: Different types of customers require different engagement and relationship management strategies. The goal is to build

Figure 1–5
Customer relationship groups.
Source: Kotler, Philip; Armstrong, Gary, *Principles of Marketing*, 16th ed., ©2016, pp. 12, 24, 50. Reprinted and Electronically reproduced by permission of Pearson Education, Inc., New York, NY.

	Short-term	Long-term
High Potential profitability	Butterflies	True friends
Low Potential profitability	Strangers	Barnacles

Projected loyalty

an emotional problem. Lack of communication and heterogeneity of guest expectations also lead to service variability. A restaurant customer ordering a medium steak may expect it to be cooked all the way through, whereas the person working on the broiler may define medium as having a warm pink center. The guest will be disappointed when she cuts into the steak and sees pink meat. Restaurants have solved this by developing common definitions of steak doneness and communicating them to the employees and customers. Sometimes the communication to the customer is verbal, and sometimes it is printed on the menu. Customers usually return to a restaurant because they enjoyed their last experience. When the product they receive is different and does not meet their expectations on the next visit, they often do not return. Variability or lack of consistency in the product is a major cause of customer disappointment in the hospitality industry.

When variability is absent, we have consistency, which is one of the key factors in the success of a service business.[5] Consistency means that customers receive the expected product without unwanted surprises. In the hotel industry, this means that a wake-up call requested for 7 A.M. always occurs as planned and that a meeting planner can count on the hotel to deliver coffee ordered for a 3 P.M. meeting break, which will be ready and waiting when the group breaks at that time. In the restaurant business, consistency means that the shrimp scampi will taste the same way it tasted two weeks ago, towels will always be available in the bathrooms, and the brand of vodka specified last week will be in stock next month. Consistency is one of the major reasons for the worldwide success of McDonald's.

Here are three steps hospitality firms can take to reduce variability and create consistency:

1. **Invest in good hiring and training procedures.** Recruiting the right employees and providing them with excellent training is crucial, regardless of whether employees are highly skilled professionals or low-skilled workers. Better-trained personnel exhibit six characteristics: *Competence*—they possess the required skill and knowledge. *Courtesy*—they are friendly, respectful, and considerate. *Credibility*—they are trustworthy. *Reliability*—they perform the service consistently and accurately. *Responsiveness*—they respond quickly to customers' requests and problems. *Communication*—they make an effort to understand the customer and communicate clearly. Excellent hospitality and travel companies such as Marriott and Southwest Airlines spend a great deal of time and effort making sure they hire the right employees. But their attention to employees does not end there. They also invest in their employees by providing ongoing training.

2. **Standardize the service-performance process throughout the organization.** Diagramming the service-delivery system in a service blueprint can simultaneously map out the service process, the points of customer contact, and the evidence of service from the customer's point of view. The guest's experience includes a series of steps he must enact while receiving the service. Behind the scenes, the service provider must skillfully help the guest move from one step to the next. By visually representing the service, a service blueprint can help one understand the process and see potential design flaws. Service blueprints include a line of interaction, line of visibility, and line of internal support. The line of interaction represents the guest's contact with employees. The line of visibility represents those areas that will be visible to the guest and provide tangible evidence of the service. The line of internal interaction represents internal support systems that are required to service the guest.

3. **Monitor customer satisfaction.** Hospitality and travel organizations have many ways they can monitor customer satisfaction. They can use a service to monitor customers' comments on social media. These customer comments, when negative, can allow the business to correct the problem before the guests leave. Analyzing customer comments is a great way to see what customers are saying about your property and your competitors. Use suggestion and complaint systems, customer surveys, and comparison shopping. Hospitality companies have the advantage of knowing their customers. This makes it easy to send a customer satisfaction survey after a guest has stayed in a hotel or used its

If an airplane takes off with 60 empty seats, it forever loses the ability to gain revenue from those seats. This is why airlines use revenue management to help manage their demand. Clement Philippe/Arterra Picture Library/Alamy Stock Photo.

service. Hotel companies often hire a third party to send out satisfaction surveys to recent customers of their franchisees to monitor their performance. Travel intermediaries, such as Travelocity.com, contact guests to see how satisfied they were with a hotel they booked on their site. They realize if a customer had a bad experience they may not use their service again, even though they cannot control the service and quality of the hotels they represent. They try to create a consistent experience and set customer expectations by using a star rating system and publishing customer comments. Firms can also develop customer information databases and systems to permit more personalized, customized service, especially online.

Perishability

Services cannot be stored. A 100-room hotel that sells only 60 rooms on a particular night cannot inventory the 40 unused rooms and then sell 140 rooms the next night. Revenue lost from not selling those 40 rooms is gone forever. Because of service perishability, hotels have tightened their reservation policies. Today many brands require a two-day notice, instead of being able to cancel a reservation the same day by 6 P.M., which used to be the standard. Restaurants are also starting to charge a fee to customers who do not show up for a reservation. They, too, realize that if someone does not show up for a reservation, the opportunity to sell that seat may be lost.

Some hotels will often sell hotel rooms at a very low rate rather let them go unsold. Because of inseparability, this can cause problems. Oftentimes, the discounted rate brings in a different type of customer who is not compatible with the hotel's normal customer. For example, one luxury hotel that normally sold rooms for $300 placed rooms on Priceline's "Name Your Own Price" **opaque channel** for $80. The guest paying $80 a night is not likely to use the food and beverage outlets of that particular hotel, but instead will use less expensive restaurants outside of the hotel or come back into the hotel carrying a bag of food from a nearby fast-food restaurant. Revenue managers must be careful that they maintain a brand's image while at the same time trying to reduce unsold inventory. We will discuss techniques for managing demand at the end of this chapter.

Opaque Channel An opaque channel is one where the customer knows the general location and class of the hotel but does not know the specific name of the hotel she is purchasing.

The Service Profit Chain

In a service business, the customer and the frontline service employee *interact* to create the service. Effective interaction, in turn, depends on the skills of frontline service employees and on the support, processes backing these employees. Thus, successful service companies focus their attention on *both* their customers and their employees. They understand the **service profit chain**, which links service firm profits with employee and customer satisfaction. This chain consists of the following five links:

Service profit chain A model that shows the relationships between employee satisfaction, customer satisfaction, customer retention, value creation, and profitability.[6]

1. **Internal service quality:** Superior employee selection and training, a quality work environment, and strong support for those dealing with customers, which results in satisfied and productive service employees.

2. **Satisfied and productive service employees:** More satisfied, loyal, and hardworking employees, which results in greater service value.

3. **Greater service value:** More effective and efficient customer value creation and service delivery, which results in satisfied and loyal customers.

4. **Satisfied and loyal customers:** Satisfied customers who remain loyal, repeat purchase, and refer other customers, which results in healthy service profits and growth.

5. **Healthy service profits and growth:** Superior service firm performance, which is the end result.

The service profit chains illustrate the importance of employees in creating value for the customer. When properly executed, the service profit chain is self-sustaining. Employees enjoy serving customers who enjoy the product they are delivering, and they become friends with loyal customers who return frequently creating an enjoyable work environment. This example provides an illustration of a well-executed service profit chain. At Four Seasons, satisfying customers is everybody's business. And it all starts with satisfied employees:[7]

Four Seasons has perfected the art of high-touch, carefully crafted service. Whether it's at the tropical island paradise at the Four Seasons Resort Mauritius or the luxurious sub-Saharan "camp" at the Four Seasons Safari Lodge Serengeti, guests paying $1,000 or more a night expect to have their minds read. For these guests, Four Seasons doesn't disappoint. As one Four Seasons Maui guest once told a manager, "If there's a heaven, I hope it's run by Four Seasons." What makes Four Seasons so special? It's really no secret. It's the quality of the Four Seasons staff. Four Seasons knows that happy, satisfied employees make for happy, satisfied customers. So just as it does for customers, Four Seasons respects and pampers its employees.

Four Seasons hires the best people, pays them well, orients them carefully, instills in them a sense of pride, and rewards them for outstanding service deeds. It treats employees as it would its most important guests. For example, all employees—from the maids who make up the rooms to the general manager—dine together (free of charge) in the hotel cafeteria. Perhaps best of all, every employee receives free stays at other Four Seasons resorts, six free nights per year after one year with the company. The room stays make employees feel as important and pampered as the guests they serve and motivate employees to achieve even higher levels of service in their own jobs. Says one Four Seasons staffer, "You come back from those trips on fire. You want to do so much for the guests." As a result of such actions, the annual turnover for full-time employees at Four Seasons is only 18 percent, half the industry average. Four Seasons has been included for 18 straight years on *Fortune* magazine's list of 100 Best Companies to Work For. And that's the biggest secret to Four Seasons' success.

■■■ Management Strategies for Service Businesses

Managing Service Differentiation

Service marketers often complain about the difficulty of differentiating their services from those of competitors. To the extent that customers view the services of different providers as similar, they care less about the provider than the price.

The solution to price competition is to develop a differentiated offering, rather than starting a price war. Competing by reducing price leads to lowering expenses to offset the price reduction. Cuts to employee expenses result in reduced service levels. Cuts in maintenance result in a facility that becomes worn. The offer can include innovative features that set one company's offer apart from that of its competitors. Read the section Marketing Highlight 2–1 to see how three companies were able to compete through creativity and innovation. Still, the service company that innovates regularly usually gains a succession of temporary advantages and an innovative reputation that may help it keep customers who want to go with the best.

Service companies can differentiate their service delivery in three ways: through people, physical environment, and process. The company can distinguish itself by having more able and reliable customer-contact people than its competitors, or it can develop a superior physical environment in which the service product is delivered. It can design a superior delivery process. Finally, service companies can also differentiate their images through symbols and branding. For example, a familiar symbol would be McDonald's golden arches, and familiar brands include Hilton, Shangri-La, and Sofitel.

Managing Service Quality

One of the major ways that a service firm can differentiate itself is by delivering consistently higher quality than its competitors. One can have a number of objective criteria for evaluating a tangible product such as an automobile. For example, how long does it take for an automobile to go from 0 to 60 miles per hour, how many miles to the gallon does it get, and how much leg room does it have. With hospitality products, quality is measured by how well customer expectations are met. The key is to exceed the customers' service-quality expectations. As the chief executive at American Express puts it, "Promise only what you can deliver and deliver more than you promise!" These expectations are based on past experiences, word of mouth, and service firm advertising. If perceived service of a given firm exceeds expected service, customers are apt to use the provider again. Customer retention is perhaps the best measure of quality: A service firm's ability to retain its customers depends on how consistently it delivers value to them. A manufacturer's quality goal might be zero defects, but the service provider's goal is zero customer defections.

The service provider needs to identify the expectations of target customers concerning service quality. In Chapters 4, 5, and 6, we discuss how to obtain information on your customers and how to understand your customers. Knowing your customer is a requisite for delivering quality. Once customer expectations are determined, managers need to develop a service-delivery system that meets the guest's expectations. It is important that the service provider clearly defines and communicates that level to its employees and customers what needs to be delivered to meet customer expectations. Investments in service usually pay off through increased customer retention and sales.

For example, Southwest Airlines has a proactive customer communications team whose job is to find the situations in which something went wrong—a mechanical delay, bad weather, a medical emergency, or a berserk passenger—and then remedy the bad experience quickly, within 24 hours if possible.[8] The team's communications to passengers, usually e-mails or texts these days, have three basic components: a sincere apology, a brief explanation of what happened, and a gift to make it up, usually a voucher in dollars that can be used on their next Southwest flight. Surveys show that when Southwest handles a delay situation well, customers score it 14 to 16 points higher than on regular on-time flights.

Nowadays, social media such as Facebook and Twitter can help companies root out and remedy customer dissatisfaction with service. As discussed in Chapter 4, companies now monitor the digital space to spot customer issues quickly and respond in real time. For example, Southwest has a dedicated team of 29 people who respond to roughly 80,000 Facebook and Twitter posts monthly. A quick and thoughtful response can turn a dissatisfied customer into a brand advocate.[9]

Studies of well-managed service companies show that they share a number of common virtues regarding service quality. First, top service companies are "customer obsessed." They have a philosophy of satisfying customer needs, which wins enduring customer loyalty. Second, well-managed service companies have a history of top management commitment to quality. Management at companies such as Six Senses Hotels and Resorts, Disney, and Chili's looks not only at financial performance but also at service performance. Third, the best service providers set high service-quality standards. A 98 percent accuracy standard may sound good,

Marketing Highlight 2.1: JetBlue, Southwest, and Cirque du Soleil provide three examples of service differentiation

In an industry often characterized by bankruptcies and unhappy customers, two exceptions are Southwest Airlines and JetBlue. The companies have followed very different paths on their way to financial and marketplace success. Southwest, the older of the two, developed an unusual business model for an airline: short hauls only, no travel agents, no meals, no gates at major airports, and no fees. Although the carrier has changed some of those practices, it remains determined to avoid the bag, ticket change, and other fees adopted by competing airlines, believing it would lose $1 billion in revenue from lost bookings otherwise. A true discount airline, Southwest has been able to offer low fares by virtue of a disciplined cost structure that keeps planes in the air and seats filled, all with an informal, friendly style. The company hires employees with outgoing personalities who like to work with people and empowers them to do so.[10]

JetBlue also started with a very different business model from other airlines, primarily targeting leisure travelers at its John F. Kennedy (JFK) hub in New York City. Another discount carrier with a low-cost structure, the company had the advantage of offering comfy seats, live TV, and choice of snacks. JetBlue built a $32 million next to its training facility, JetBlue University. By having their own lodging facility, JetBlue can foster their culture and camaraderie among employees, who come to JetBlue University for training. JetBlue has a strong commitment to customer training with about half of its 22,000 employees visiting the training center every year.[11]

In its more than 25-year history, Cirque du Soleil (French for "circus of the sun") has repeatedly broken loose from circus convention. The company takes traditional ingredients such as trapeze artists, clowns, muscle men, and contortionists and places them in a nontraditional setting with lavish costumes, new age music, and spectacular stage designs. And it eliminates other common circus elements—there are no animals. Each production is loosely tied together with a theme such as "a tribute to the nomadic soul" (Varekai) or "a phantasmagoria of urban life" (Saltimbanco). The group has grown from its Quebec street-performance roots to become a half-billion-dollar global enterprise, with 3,000 employees on four continents entertaining audiences of millions annually. Part of its success comes from a company culture that encourages artistic creativity and innovation and carefully safeguards the brand. One new production is created each year—always in-house—and is unique: There are no duplicate touring companies. In addition to Cirque's mix of media and local promotion, an extensive interactive e-mail program to its million-plus-member Cirque Club creates an online community of fans—20 to 30 percent of all ticket sales come from club members, generating $800 million in revenue annually.[12]

Cirque du Soleil developed a unique form of entertainment by taking the traditional forms of circus entertainment such as trapeze artists and clowns and placing them in a nontraditional setting. The result is a circus for adults that is popular with international audiences, as one does not have to understand the local language to enjoy the show. This makes an ideal form of entertainment for visitors to Las Vegas, home of a number of Cirque de Soleil. Ritu Jethani/123RF.

---

but using this standard, the MGM Grand Hotel would send 50 guests a day to rooms that are already occupied, the Outback Steak house chain would have hundreds of miscooked steaks, and AccorHotels would make hundreds of errors in its central reservation office every week. This level of errors is unacceptable for customer-directed companies. Top service companies do not settle merely for "good" service; they aim for 100 percent defect-free service.

Fourth, the top service firms watch service performance closely, both their own and that of competitors. They use methods such as comparison shopping, customer surveys, suggestions, and complaint forms. Good service companies also communicate their concerns about service quality to employees and provide performance feedback. Ritz-Carlton has daily meetings with its employees to go over customer feedback and to review the guest history of arriving guests. Many quick-service restaurant chains offer customers a chance to win prizes after answering several service-related questions on an internet-based questionnaire.

Managing Service Productivity

With their costs rising rapidly, service firms are under great pressure to increase service productivity, which can be done in several ways. They can train current employees better or hire new ones who will work harder or more skillfully. The provider can "industrialize the service" by adding equipment and standardizing production, as in McDonald's assembly-line approach to fast-food retailing. Finally, a service provider can harness the power of technology. Although we often think of technology's power to save time and costs in manufacturing companies, it also has great—and often untapped—potential to make service workers more productive.

Services have been successful at getting customers involved in the production of the service by using self-service technology (SST). This includes everything from filling your drink at a fast-food restaurant to choosing your flight, selecting your seat and purchasing your airline ticket online. We will discuss SSTs later in this chapter. As technology advances, we now are seeing the use of robots combined with artificial intelligence in hotels and restaurants. The Henn na Hotel in Japan made history when it staffed its front desk robots. Aloft hotels do not offer room service, but some Alofts have enhanced their grab-and-go foods in the lobby with a robot called Butler, which will bring items to the guest's room.[13] Caliburger, a fast-food restaurant, uses a robot to cook hamburgers and place them on buns when they are done. Robots are being used to make coffee drinks, pizza, take orders while offering suggestions, and explaining menu items and delivering food. Proper use of robots can help create customer value if customer service experiences are enhanced.[14]

Companies must avoid pushing productivity so hard that doing so reduces quality. Attempts to industrialize a service or cut costs can make a service company more efficient in the short run. But in making them more efficient, they can become less effective. For example, a restaurant that reduces kitchen payroll may find that it cannot keep up with the orders, resulting in long wait times for food and dissatisfied customers. Thus, in attempting to improve service productivity, companies must be mindful of how they create and deliver customer value. In short, they should be careful not to take the "service" out of service.

Resolving Customer Complaints

Many service companies have invested heavily to develop streamlined and efficient service-delivery systems. They want to ensure that customers will receive consistently high-quality service in every service encounter. Unlike product manufacturers, who can adjust their machinery and inputs until everything is perfect, service quality always varies, depending on the interactions between employees and customers. Problems inevitably occur. As hard as they try, even the best companies have an occasional late delivery, burned steak, or a grumpy employee. A company cannot always prevent service problems, but it can learn from them. Good service recovery can turn angry customers into loyal ones. In fact, good recovery can win more customer purchasing and loyalty than if things had gone well in the first place. Therefore, companies should take steps not only to provide good service every time but also to recover from service mistakes.

To have effective complaint resolution, managers must empower frontline service employees—to give them the authority, responsibility, and incentives that they need to recognize, care about, and tend to customer needs. For example, Marriott places its employees in empowerment training, which encourages them to go beyond their normal jobs to solve customer problems. Empowered employees can act quickly and effectively to keep service problems from resulting in lost customers. According to the Marriott Desert Springs, the major goal for customer-contact employees is to ensure that "guests experience excellent service and hospitality while staying at our resort." Well-trained employees are given the authority to do whatever it takes, on the spot, to keep guests happy. They are also expected to help management ferret out the cause of guests' problems, and to inform managers of ways to improve overall hotel service and guests' comfort.

Marketing Highlight 2.2: Recommendations for improving service quality

Berry, Parasuraman, and Zeithamil, pioneers in conducting academic service research, offer 10 lessons that they maintain are essential for improving service quality across service industries.

1. **Listening.** Understand what customers really want through continuous learning about the expectations and perceptions of customers and noncustomers (e.g., by means of a service-quality information system).
2. **Reliability.** The single most important dimension of service quality. Reliability must be a service priority.
3. **Basic service.** Service companies must deliver the basics and do what they are supposed to do: keep promises, use common sense, listen to customers, keep customers informed, and be determined to deliver value to customers.
4. **Service design.** Develop a holistic view of the service while managing its many details.
5. **Recovery.** To satisfy customers who encounter a service problem, service companies should encourage customers to complain (and make it easy for them to do so), respond quickly and personally, and develop a problem-resolution system.
6. **Surprising customers.** Although reliability is the most important dimension in meeting customers' service expectations, process dimensions such as assurance, responsiveness, and empathy are most important in exceeding customer expectations (e.g., by surprising them with uncommon swiftness, grace, courtesy, competence, commitment, and understanding).
7. **Fair play.** Service companies must make special efforts to be fair, and to demonstrate fairness to customers and employees.
8. **Teamwork.** Teamwork is what enables large organizations to deliver service with care and attentiveness by improving employee motivation and capabilities.
9. **Employee research.** Marketers should conduct research with employees to reveal why service problems occur and what companies must do to solve problems.
10. **Servant leadership.** Quality service comes from inspired leadership throughout the organization; from excellent service-system design; from the effective use of information and technology; and from a slow-to-change, invisible, all-powerful, internal force called corporate culture.[15]

Resolving customer complaints is a critical component of customer retention. One study by the Technical Research Programs Institute found that if a customer has a major complaint, 91 percent will not buy from you again, but if it was resolved quickly, 82 percent of those customers will return. The complaint resolution drops the customer defection from 91 out of 100 to 18 out of 100. With resolution of minor complaints, the defection rate can be reduced to less than 5 out of 100.[16] In complaint resolution there are two important factors. First, if you resolve a complaint, do it quickly—the longer it takes to resolve, the higher the defection rate. Second, seek out customer complaints. If you are unaware of complaints, it is impossible to resolve them.

For example, a businesswoman had just returned from an overseas trip. After a good night's sleep in a New York hotel, she was ready for an American breakfast. She dialed room service, and her breakfast was delivered promptly. A cheerful waiter wheeled the table into the room and positioned it so that the woman could look out the window. He opened the heating compartment and pulled out the breakfast that the woman had been waiting for: a full hot American breakfast. The waiter handed the woman the bill, and she promptly signed the bill and added a handsome tip. Now she was ready to start her breakfast.

The waiter said, "I'm sorry, you will have to pay cash." She explained that she did not have any money with her and pulled out her credit cards, offering the American Express Card she had used to check in to the hotel. The waiter called on the phone and after five minutes it was resolved that the woman could use her credit card. The woman, now upset, sat down to a cold breakfast.[17] If the waiter had been empowered to resolve complaints, he would have been able to leave the room, go down to the front desk, and resolve the problem at the front desk while the woman was enjoying her breakfast.

Complaints should be responded to quickly by a personal form of communication. This could be through responding to a complaint on social media, e-mail, short message service (SMS), or telephone. When responding on social media, try to move the conversation off-line by asking the customer to contact you by e-mail or phone and resolve the complaint. The worst thing a company can do is send out a form of e-mail that shows no empathy to the guest's problem or not respond at all. *Restaurant Business* had an employee contact 25 customer service representatives of restaurant chains, stating she had received poor service. Of the 25 companies contacted, only 15 responded to her complaint. One customer service representative told her, "I'm busy right now, can you call back in a half an hour?" When she called back, the customer service rep said, "Okay, I have a minute now. What's your problem—slow service, is that all? Okay, I can write up a report if you want." Of those restaurants that did respond, only 10 did a good or excellent job of resolving the complaint. The customer service representatives at these restaurants did a nice job of showing concern on the initial phone call and followed up with a letter and coupons. In one case, a regional vice president called the customer back to find out what went wrong.[18]

Another critical area in complaint resolution is that most customers do not complain. They do not give managers a chance to resolve their problem. They just leave and never come back. When a customer does complain, management should be grateful because it gives them a chance to resolve the complaint and gain the customer's repeat business. Most complaints come from loyal customers who want to return, but they also want management to fix the problem so it will not occur on their next visit. Managers must develop ways to encourage customers to complain. Services that scan social media can pick up customers that have commented on your restaurant, allowing management to respond. Managers can train employees to look out for guests who look dissatisfied and try to determine their problems. As one restaurant manager observes, if guests are looking around the restaurant, there is something wrong. We need to find out what is wrong and correct it. If we shift our perspective to see complaints as gifts, we can more readily use the information the complaints generate to grow our own business. Customer complaints are one of the most available yet underutilized sources of customer and market information.[19]

A club manager told us about a surprise the club had from a truly excellent Christmas party. The staff was proud of the way the evening went because everything went as planned. The manager was truly surprised when a member of many years said he wanted to set up a conference call with the food and beverage manager, chef, and the manager to discuss the shortcomings of the event. The call lasted an hour and a half, with many of the complaints considered frivolous by the management team. Through careful listening, the manager was able to separate the symptoms from the real problem. The manager asked his staff to reflect on the call and set a meeting for the next day. He also asked the food and beverage manager to develop a profile of who came to the event. What they discovered is that most of the people attending the event were older retired members who did not have family in the area and were alone during the holidays. Normally the club's parties attracted 45-year-old members and this party was planned for this group, not the 65 and older group who attended the party. This was the essence of the member's complaint: The menu and theme of the party were developed for a much younger group. By listening to what the member was saying and being open to the member's comments, the club's managers discovered the party was developed for the wrong target market. If the member had not complained or the club's managers were not open to the member's complaint, the holiday party would have continued to be developed for the wrong target audience.

Managing Employees as Part of the Product

In the hospitality industry, employees are a critical part of the product and marketing mix. This means that the human resources and marketing departments must work closely together. In restaurants without a human resources department, the restaurant manager serves as the human resource manager. The manager must hire friendly and capable employees and formulate policies that support positive relations between employees and guests. Even minor details related to personnel policy can have a significant effect on the product's quality.[20]

In a well-run hospitality organization, there are two customers: the paying customers and the employees.[21] The task of training and motivating employees to provide good customer service is called internal marketing. In the hospitality industry, it is not enough to have a marketing department focused on traditional marketing to a targeted external market. The job of the marketing department includes encouraging everyone in the organization to practice customer-oriented thinking[22] (see Chapter 10). The following excerpt from *In Search of Excellence* illustrates the importance of well-trained employees in a hospitality operation:

> We had decided, after dinner, to spend a second night in Washington. Our business day had taken us beyond the last flight out. We had no reservations but were near the new Four Seasons, had stayed there once before, and liked it. As we walked through the lobby wondering how best to plead our case for a room, we brace for the usual chilly shoulder accorded to latecomers. To our astonishment, the concierge looked up, smiled, called us by name, and asked how we were. She remembered our names! We knew in a flash why in the space of a brief year the Four Seasons had become the "place to stay" in the District and was a rare first-year holder of the venerated four-star rating.[23]

Managing Perceived Risk

Customers who buy hospitality products experience some anxiety because they cannot experience the product beforehand.[24] This is one of the reasons customers rely on user-generated content on sites such as Yelp, TripAdvisor, and other social media they use. These sources are deemed to be credible sources.

Consider an administrative assistant whose manager asks him to set up a regional sales meeting. Suppose the administrative assistant had never set up a meeting or worked with hotels. If the meeting goes well, his manager will be favorably impressed; if it goes badly, the administrative assistant may be blamed by his manager for the failure. In arranging for the meeting place, the client has to trust the hotel's salesperson. Good hotel salespeople alleviate client fears by letting them know that they have arranged hundreds of successful meetings. The salesperson's claims to professionalism can be affirmed through letters of praise from former clients and a tour of the hotel's facilities. A salesperson must reduce the client's fear and gain the client's confidence.

One way of combating concern is to encourage the client to try the hotel or restaurant in a low-risk situation. Hotels and resorts offer familiarization (FAM) trips to meeting planners and travel agents. Airlines often offer complimentary flight tickets because they are also interested in creating business. Hotels provide rooms, food, beverage, and entertainment at no cost to the prospective client in the hope that this exposure will encourage him or her to recommend the hotel. FAM trips reduce a product's intangibility by letting the intermediary customer experience the hotel beforehand.

The high risk that people perceive when purchasing hospitality products increases loyalty to hotels, restaurants, and event companies that have provided them with a consistent product in the past. Salespeople must have patience and continue calling on prospective clients. At some point, one of their suppliers will make a mistake and they will be open to trying a new supplier. Hospitality companies must strive to satisfy every group, knowing if they make a mistake another company is waiting to take their business.

User-generated content on sites used by travelers to choose hotels, restaurants, and activities can reduce the risk of purchasing. Georgejmclittle/123RF.

Managing Capacity and Demand

Managers have two major options for matching capacity with demand: change capacity or change demand. For example, airlines use dynamic capacity management to adjust capacity to match demand. The airlines swap small aircraft for larger aircraft on flights that are selling out faster than normal. The smaller aircraft are assigned to flights that are expected to have low load factors.[25] If a larger plane is not available, they can reduce demand by eliminating discounted fares and charging a higher fare. The higher fare means that some passengers, often pleasure travelers visiting friends and relatives, will decide not to make the trip or switch to another flight, thus reducing the overall demand. In this section, we discuss capacity management, and in the next section we focus on demand management.

Capacity Management

Corporate management is responsible for matching capacity with demand on a long-term basis; unit managers are responsible for matching capacity with fluctuations in short-term demand. The techniques presented in this section assist in managing short-term demand.

INVOLVE THE CUSTOMER IN THE SERVICE-DELIVERY SYSTEM. Getting the customer involved in service operations expands the number of people that one employee can serve, thus increasing the capacity of the operation. The concept has wide acceptance in food and beverage operations, but modern technology is responsible for its increasing use in the accommodation sector. Perhaps one of the oldest and most common methods of getting the customer involved in the service is a buffet. Customers choose the items they will eat and serve themselves. Customers do not have to decide what they are going to order, place their order with their server, and then wait for the food to be prepared. They simply give their beverage order and go to the buffet. The kitchen can produce more food because they are producing it in bulk, not by individual order, and the front of the restaurant can accommodate more customers, because they are serving themselves. Buffets are thus common during high demand times, such as breakfast in a large hotel or Mother's day.

SSTs can be used to increase capacity, particularly in restaurants by using customers to provide some of the service allowing customers to serve more people. Hotels have developed a system allowing guests to use their smartphone to make reservations, choose their room a day before they arrive, and then use it to access their room when they arrive. Through surveys and by following comments on social media, Hilton found that guests valued the control they received when they were allowed to choose the location of their room and the bedding configuration in the room. There are no employees or employee interaction involved in the process. Hilton is now working on how they create positive interaction with guests in the future to replace the interaction they received with employees at the front desk.[26]

CROSS-TRAIN EMPLOYEES. In a hotel, the demand for all services does not rise and fall in unison. One outlet may experience sudden strong demand while other areas enjoy normal levels. When managers cross-train their employees, they can shift employees to increase the capacity. A hotel restaurant that does only 30 to 40 covers a night cannot justify more than two service people, even though it may have 80 seats. However, such low staffing levels mean that the restaurant may have a difficult time serving more than 60 guests, especially if they arrive at about the same time. Having front-desk staff and banquet staff trained in à la carte service means that the restaurant manager has a group of employees that can be called on if demand for the restaurant on any particular night exceeds the capacity of two service people.

USE PART-TIME EMPLOYEES. Managers can use part-time employees to expand capacity during an unusually busy day or meal period or during the busy months of the year for seasonal businesses. Summer resorts hire part-time staff to work during the summer period. They reduce their staff during the slower seasons and either reduce staff further or close during the low season. Part-time employees allow a hotel or restaurant to increase or decrease its capacity efficiently. Part-time employees can also be used on an on-call basis. Hotels usually have a list of banquet waiters to call for large events. Part-time employees give an organization the flexibility to adjust the number of employees to the level required to meet demand.

RENT OR SHARE EXTRA FACILITIES AND EQUIPMENT. Businesses do not have to be constrained by space limitations or equipment limitations. A hotel with an opportunity to book a three-day meeting from Tuesday to Thursday may have to turn down the business because all the function space is booked Wednesday evening, and there is no space for the group's Wednesday evening dinner. Rather than lose the group, a creative solution would be to suggest the group go outside the hotel for a unique dinner experience. In Paris, the alternative might be a dinner cruise on the Seine. In Arizona, it might be an outdoor steak fry, and in Hong Kong, it could be a dinner at Jumbo, the famous floating restaurant.

Catering firms often purchase only the amount of equipment they use regularly. When they have a busy period, they rent equipment. Renting, sharing, or moving groups to outside facilities can increase capacity to accommodate short-term demand.

SCHEDULE DOWNTIME DURING PERIODS OF LOW DEMAND. Businesses in seasonal resorts have periods of high and low demand. The actions we have discussed so far enable a business to increase capacity to meet peak demand. One way to decrease capacity to match the lower demand is to schedule repairs and maintenance during the low season.

CHANGE THE SERVICE-DELIVERY SYSTEM. One method of changing the service-delivery system that we have discussed is a buffet. Restaurants and entertainment facilities can increase capacity by extending their hours. A hotel coffee shop that is full by 7:30 A.M. may find it useful to open at 6:30 A.M. instead of 7 A.M. If five tables arrive in the first half hour, these should be free in about a half hour, allowing the restaurant to have more tables available during the peak period. Hotels have established grab-and-go food options, where someone wanting a quick meal or snack can choose from a variety of prepared foods and beverages and be on their way. Leaps and bounds, a children's entertainment center that is normally closed at night, offers all-night parties for groups of 20 or more. When the demand exists, the center supplies the capacity by opening at night. Many businesses can increase their capacity by expanding their hours of operation.

Demand Management

In an ideal situation, managers simply expand capacity to meet demand. However, during a citywide convention, a hotel may receive requests for rooms that exceed its capacity. The Saturday before Christmas, a restaurant could book more banquets if it had space, and during a summer holiday, a resort could sell more rooms if it had them. All successful hospitality businesses become capacity constrained. Capacity management allows a business to increase its capacity, but it does not prevent situations where demand exceeds capacity. Demand can be managed in the following ways.

USE PRICE TO CREATE OR REDUCE DEMAND. Price is inversely related to demand for most products. Managers can create more demand for a product by lowering its price and lower demand by raising its price. To create demand, restaurants offer specials on slow days. For example, some Subway restaurants, a submarine sandwich shop, offer two-for-one specials

Tents can provide a memorable outdoor experience venue for special events and enable a hotel or country club to add capacity when their indoor banquet space is booked. Eric Limon/123RF.

Disney's FastPass helps manage demand by allowing guests to avoid waiting for rides for several rides they select with their FastPass. John Raoux/AP Images.

on Tuesdays. Port of Subs (a competitor) offers special discounts after 5 P.M. because most people do not eat sandwiches for the evening meal. Resorts lower prices during the off-season, and city hotels offer weekend specials. Managers must make sure that the market segments attracted by the lower price belong to their desired target markets.

When demand exceeds capacity, managers raise prices to lower demand. On New Year's Eve, many restaurants and nightclubs offer set menus and packages that exceed the normal average check. They realize that even with higher prices, demand remains sufficient to fill to capacity.

USE RESERVATIONS. Hotels and restaurants often use reservations to monitor demand. When it appears they will have more demand than capacity, managers can save capacity for the more profitable segments. Reservations can also limit demand by allowing managers to refuse any further reservations when capacity meets demand.

Although reservations in restaurants can help manage demand, they can also decrease capacity. This is the reason that high-volume mid-priced restaurants do not usually take reservations. A group may arrive 10 minutes late, or one couple of a two-couple party may arrive on time and wait 20 minutes at the table until the other couple shows up. The estimated times of customer arrival and departure may not fit precisely, resulting in tables remaining empty for 20 minutes or more. In high-priced restaurants, guests expect to reserve a table and have it ready when they arrive. Customers of mid-priced restaurants have different expectations, allowing popular restaurants to increase their capacity by having customers queue and wait for the next available table. Queues allow managers to inventory demand for short periods of time and fill every table immediately when it becomes available, eliminating dead time.

To maximize capacity, some restaurants accept reservations for seating at designated times. For example, they may have seating at 6, 8, and 10 P.M. When customers call to make a reservation, the receptionist makes them aware of the seating times and lets them know that the table is theirs for up to two hours. After two hours, another party will be waiting to use the table. The use of seatings increases capacity by ensuring that the restaurant will have three turns and by shifting demand. As the 8 P.M. seating fills, managers can shift demand to either 6 or 10 P.M., depending on the customer's preference. Vallone's restaurant on Mother's day offered a lower price for those who would come in earlier and a higher price for those waiting a prime time. By doing this, the restaurant created more demand for the earlier time, through a combination of pricing and reservations.

In cases where demand is greater than capacity, guests can be asked to prepay or make a deposit. For example, some New Year's Eve parties at hotels and restaurants require that guests purchase their tickets in advance. Resorts often require a nonrefundable deposit with a reservation. By requiring an advance payment, managers help ensure that revenue matches capacity. If a customer fails to arrive, the resort does not lose revenue.

Disneyland has come up with its own form of reservations, FastPass. Guests may go up to one of the rides offering the FastPass service and obtain a reservation to come at a certain time. When the guests come back, they bypass the waiting line and move to the FastPass line, often saving an hour or more in waiting. Guests are limited to one FastPass every four hours to ensure that the rides are able to accommodate both FastPass and regular guests. The beauty of FastPass is that rather than waiting in line, guests can now spend money in the restaurants and shops. By handling demand with FastPass, Disney has created a more satisfying customer experience and also created the opportunity for more sales.

OVERBOOK. Not everyone who reserves a table or books a room shows up. Plans change and people with reservations become no-shows. Overbooking is another method that hotels, restaurants, trains, and airlines use to match demand with capacity. Hotel managers who limit reservations to the number of available rooms frequently find themselves with empty rooms. For example, at one hotel, 20 percent of guests holding nonguaranteed reservations and 5 percent of those holding guaranteed reservations typically do not honor those reservations. If this hotel has 80 guaranteed reservations and 40 nonguaranteed reservations, it will, on average, be left with 12 empty rooms. For a hotel with an average room rate of $200, this can mean a potential annual loss of more than $750,000 in room, food, and beverage revenue.

Overbooking must be managed carefully. Knowing the hotel's customers, past history of the event, availability of rooms at other hotels, and weather conditions are important factors to consider when overbooking. Software systems are available that develop an accurate forecast. When a hotel fails to honor its reservations, it risks losing the future business of guests whose reservations are not honored and possibly the business of their companies and travel agents. Thus, the hotel must walk a fine line between a perfect sell-out, having a room empty or walking a guest. It is better to leave a room unoccupied than to fail to honor a reservation.

Some hotels do nothing for the traveler whose reservation is not honored. Well-managed hotels find alternative accommodations, pay for one night's stay at the new hotel, and provide transportation to the hotel. Smart managers try to get turned-away guests back by offering a free night's stay at their hotel the next day. Hotels that are careless in handling their reservations can be held liable. In one case a travel agent, Rainbow Travel Service, reserved 45 rooms with the Fontainebleau Hilton for clients going to a Miami–Oklahoma football game. The Fontainebleau walked a number of Rainbow's clients, and Rainbow sued for damage to its reputation. A jury awarded the travel agency $250,000. The jury believed that the Fontainebleau should have altered its policy of overbooking by 15 percent because of the demand created by the football weekend.[27]

Revenue management A pricing method using price as a means of matching demand with capacity.

REVENUE MANAGEMENT. Dynamic pricing and overbooking are used in **revenue management** systems. With the help of computer programs, managers are using price, reservation history, and overbooking practices to develop a sophisticated approach to demand management called revenue management, a methodological approach to allocating a perishable and fixed inventory to the most profitable customers. Well-designed revenue management program can increase revenue by 8 percent or more. A 200-room hotel was able to add $600,000 to its top line after implementing revenue management. Its system was designed to maximize revenue per available room (RevPAR). Revenue management techniques have also been designed for restaurants, where they are designed to maximize revenue per available seat (RevPASH). In restaurants, seat utilization along with off-peak pricing are among the tools used to maximize RevPASH.

Properly designed revenue management systems value the business or repeat customers. Thus a customer who stays at a hotel 11 times a year for two nights per stay is treated differently than a one-time convention guest. The frequent loyal guest's business is valued, and some hotel companies have developed corporate rates for these guests that do not fluctuate with the demand for business. They protect these guests. As one can see, the practice of revenue management for a hotel can be very complex. It takes an understanding of forecasting models and the hotel's customer base.[28] For graduates of hospitality programs that enjoy numbers and marketing strategy, revenue management can be an exciting career. The ability to maximize revenue has become such an important management tool that today the position of corporate revenue manager has become a path to the position of corporate vice president of marketing.

USE QUEUING. When demand exceeds capacity and guests are willing to wait, queues form. Sometimes guests make the decision to wait; in other cases they have no choice. For example, a guest is told a restaurant has a 20-minute wait and she decides to wait. However, on occasion, hotel guests may find themselves waiting to check in to a hotel where they have made a reservation.

Voluntary queues, such as waits at restaurants, are a common and effective way of managing demand. Good management of the queue can make the wait more tolerable for the guest. Always overestimate the wait. When the estimated wait is 30 minutes, it is better to tell guests that it will be a 35-minute wait than to tell them they will have a 20-minute wait. Some managers fear that if the wait is too long they will lose guests, so they "shorten" the wait time. Once customers have accepted the wait time, they may sit down and have a drink, but they tend to keep their eyes on their watches. When their names have not been called after the allotted time, they run up to the host and ask where they are on the list. When guests wait longer than they were told they would, they go to their dining table upset and in a mood that makes them tend to look for other service failures. It can be difficult for the restaurant to recover from this initial failure, and many guests leave with memories of an unsatisfactory experience.

If the host tells guests it will be a 35-minute wait and then seats them in 30 minutes, the guests will be delighted. If a guest decides not to accept the wait, the host can suggest a time when the wait will be shorter.

In general, the higher the level of service, the longer the guest is willing to wait. Twenty minutes for sit-down service might be acceptable, whereas a five-minute wait at a fast-food restaurant will be unacceptable. Fast-food restaurants must raise their capacity to meet demand or lose customers.[29]

David Maister, a service expert, provides the following tips for the management of a waiting line:[30]

1. **Unoccupied time feels longer than occupied time.** Entertainment parks have characters who talk to kids in waiting lines, occupying time and making the wait pass faster. Restaurants send customers waiting for a dinner table into their cocktail lounge, where a cocktail and conversation make the time pass more quickly. The Rio Hotel places television monitors over the line for their buffet. The monitors promote different products that the resort has to offer, such as its entertainment and other food and beverage outlets. These are a few examples of how managers can occupy guests' time and make their wait more enjoyable.

2. **Unfair waits are longer than equitable waits.** Guests can become upset and preoccupied with a wait if they feel they are being treated unfairly. Restaurants with a limited number of large tables try to maximize the capacity of these tables. For example, rather than put a party of four at a table for six, the restaurant seats a party of six at the table, even if there are several parties of four in front of them. This sometimes leads to anger on the part of the guests in the passed-over party of four. Because they were next, they feel the host should seat them next. In such cases, the host should explain what is going on to the next party in line. Another example of an unfair wait is when a guest who has been waiting for 20 minutes to check-in finally reaches the front of the line. Just as he is starting to give the details of his reservation to the front-desk clerk, the phone rings. The phone is answered promptly by the clerk, who gets involved in a 10-minute conversation with the caller. Marriott has started a policy of removing phones from the front desk to avoid this distraction and eliminate unfair waits.

3. **Uncertain waits are longer than known, finite waits.** Most travelers have experienced a flight delay. If the agent states the flight will be delayed an hour, the traveler can get something to eat, shop in the stores, or find other activities to fill her time. However, if the traveler is just told there will be a delay and when she asks how long and the agent replies, "I am not sure; it's a mechanical problem," the person often becomes anxious. The anxiety is caused by the uncertain delay. She does not want to leave the gate fearing the plane will be promptly fixed and depart. She is too anxious to relax. The 30-minute delay will seem like an eternity. When possible, we should tell guests the reason for the delay and the expected amount of time of the delay. The reason airlines sometimes do not give delays is because they do not know how long it will take to fix the plane and they do not want people leaving the area. However, they should keep people updated on the progress to reduce the uncertainty.

Maister states that the customer's sense of equity is not always obvious and needs to be managed. Whatever priority rules apply, the service provider must make vigorous efforts to ensure that these rules match with the customer's sense of equity, either by adjusting the rules or by convincing the client that the rules are appropriate.

SHIFT DEMAND. It is often possible to shift the demand for banquets and meetings. A sales manager may want to set up a sales meeting for the end of October or the beginning of November and knows that when the hotel is called to check availability, a date must be given. Suppose that October 31 is picked, although it could have been October 24 or November 7 just as easily. Twenty rooms will be needed the night before and a meeting room on the day of the event. The hotel is forecast to sell out on October 31 but presently has rooms available. The smart manager asks whether October 31 is a firm date. If the date is flexible, the manager shifts the date to a period when the hotel is not projected to sell out and needs the business. When dates are flexible, a smart meeting planner will give several dates and ask for the date when he can get the best prices.

CREATE PROMOTIONAL EVENTS. An object of promotion is to increase demand or, as we will learn later, to shift the demand curve to the left. During slow periods, creative promotions can be an effective way of building business. We discuss promotions later in the book.

The four characteristics of services, intangibility, inseparability, variability, and perishability, create the need for marketing strategies and tactics that are different from goods-producing companies. In the rest of the book we will discuss those strategies and tactics and the principles that support them.

CHAPTER REVIEW

I. The Service Culture. The service culture focuses on serving and satisfying the customer. The service culture has to start with top management and flow down.

  A. Characteristics of service marketing
  1. **Intangibility.** Unlike physical products, services cannot be seen, tasted, felt, heard, or smelled before they are purchased. To reduce uncertainty caused by intangibility, buyers look for tangible evidence that will provide information and confidence about the service.
  2. **Tangible evidence.** Tangible evidence that is not managed properly can hurt a business.
  3. **Inseparability.** In most hospitality services, both the service provider and the customer must be present for the transaction to occur. Customer-contact employees are part of the product. Inseparability also means that customers are part of the product. The third implication of inseparability is that customers and employees must understand the service-delivery system.
  4. **Variability.** Service quality depends on who provides the services and when and where they are provided. Services are produced and consumed simultaneously. Fluctuating demand makes it difficult to deliver consistent products during periods of peak demand. The high degree of contact between the service provider and the guest means that product consistency depends on the service provider's skills and performance at the time of the exchange.
  5. **Perishability.** Services cannot be stored. If service providers are to maximize revenue, they must manage capacity and demand because they cannot carry forward unsold inventory.

II. The Service Profit Chain. The service profit chain is a model that shows relationships between employee satisfaction, customer satisfaction, customer retention, value creation, and profitability. The chain consists of the following five links: internal service quality, satisfied and productive service employees, greater service value, satisfied and loyal customers, and healthy service profits and growth.

III. Management Strategies for Service Businesses

  A. **Managing service differentiation.** The solution to price competition is to develop a differentiated offering. The offer can include innovative features that set one company's offer apart from that of its competitors.
  B. **Managing service quality.** With hospitality products, quality is measured by how well customer expectations are met.
  C. **Manage service productivity.** Service productivity can be increased by better training current employees, hiring new ones, industrializing the service, and harnessing the power of technology.
  D. **Resolving customer complaints.** Resolving customer complaints is a critical component of customer retention.
  E. **Managing employees as part of the product.** In the hospitality industry, employees are a critical part of the product and marketing mix. The human resource and marketing departments must work closely together. The task of internal marketing to employees involves the effective training and motivation of customer-contact employees and supporting service personnel.
  F. **Managing perceived risk.** The high risk that people perceive when purchasing hospitality products increases loyalty to companies that have provided them with a consistent product in the past.
  G. **Managing capacity and demand.** Because services are perishable, managing capacity and demand is a key function of hospitality marketing. First, services must adjust their operating systems to enable the business to operate at maximum capacity. Second, they must remember that their goal is to create satisfied customers. Research has shown that customer complaints increase when service firms operate above 80 percent of their capacity.

IN-CLASS GROUP EXERCISES

Exercises with an asterisk next to them are suitable for individual homework or online assignments. Always provide an explanation for your answer.

1. * Illustrate how a hotel, restaurant, or theater can deal with the intangibility, inseparability, variability, and perishability of the service it provides. Give specific examples.
2. Do you use consumer-generated content from a site like TripAdvisor or Yelp? If so, explain why you think the information is credible. If not, state how you choose a new restaurant. If other consumers acquire information the same way you do, how should managers attract new customers?
3. * Discuss how the service person in a restaurant is part of the product the customer receives when purchasing a meal.
4. Look up several hotels or restaurants on TripAdvisor and review customer comments. Do you think the managers of the company responded to the comments appropriately? Explain the reasons for your answer.
5. Explain in your own words the difference between demand management and capacity management. Give at least two examples of each one. For group work, students could provide examples of how companies they worked for used capacity and demand management.
6. * Visit the Web site of a hotel chain. What does the Web site do to make the product tangible for the customer? Does anything in the site deal with the characteristic of perishables, for example, specials at some of the properties?
7. * Find an example of a blog on a topic that interests you. Are there advertisements on the blog? Does the blogger appear to be sponsored by any companies? Is there information regarding sponsorship? Write a brief report of your observations.

EXPERIENTIAL EXERCISES

Do one of the following:

1. Perishability is very important in the airline industry; unsold seats are gone forever, and too many unsold seats mean large losses. With computerized ticketing, airlines can easily use pricing to deal with perishability and variations in demand.
   a. Go to the Web site of an airline and get a fare for an eight-day stay between two cities it serves. Get prices on the same route for 60 days in advance, two weeks, one week, and tomorrow. Is there a clear pattern to the fares?
   b. When a store is overstocked on ripe fruit, it may lower the price to sell out quickly. What are airlines doing to their prices as the seats get close to "perishing"? Why are tomorrow's fares often higher?
2. Visit a restaurant or a hotel. Observe and record how they manage their customers. This could include how they get them to move through the hotel, stand in line, or throw their trash away in a hotel. Write what you think the business does well and what it does poorly. Explain your answer.
3. Visit a restaurant or hotel and give an example of how they use tangible evidence to tell the customer what type of business they are and how they are run. Things to look at include the exterior of the business, the inside of the business, signage, and employee uniforms. Write what you think the business does well and what it does poorly. Explain your answer.

REFERENCES

1. See Topgolf.com; Brandi Shaffer, (October 27, 2016) "Bloomberg Businessweek Highlights the Appeal, Growth of Topgolf," Bloomberg Businessweek Highlights the Appeal, Growth of Topgolf, https://clubandresortbusiness.com/2016/10/bloomberg-businessweek-highlights-appeal-growth-topgolf/; Rosemary Ayim (November 7, 2014) "Average age of golfers up a massive 15 years since 2009," The Golf Business, http://www.thegolfbusiness.co.uk/2014/11/average-age-golfers-massive-15-years-since-2009/; Statistic Brain (May 3, 2018), "Golf Player Demographic Statistics," https://www.statisticbrain.com/golf-player-demographic-statistics/; Sergio Chapa and Korri Kezar (August 7, 2015), "TopGolf San Antonio breaks alcohol sales records for chain in Texas," *Dallas Business Journal*, https://www.bizjournals.com/dallas/news/2015/08/07/topgolf-san-antonio-breaks-alcohol-sales-records.html; Eric Vician (April 8, 2015), "Topgolf Tampa setting franchise records after just four months," *Tampa Bay Times*, http://www.tampabay.com/news/business/topgolf-tampa-setting-franchise-records-after-just-four-months/2224575 (accessed June 2018).
2. G. Lynn Shostack, "Breaking Free from Product Marketing," *Journal of Marketing* (April 1977): 73–80.
3. Bernard H. Booms and Mary J. Bitner, "Marketing Services by Managing the Environment," *Cornell Hotel and Restaurant Administration Quarterly*, 23, no. 1 (1982): 35–39.
4. Robert C. Ford and Cherrill P. Heaton, "Managing Your Guest as a Quasi-Employee," *Cornell Hotel and Restaurant Administration Quarterly*, 42, no. 2 (2001): 46–61.

5. Diane Schanlensee, Kenneth L. Bernhardt, and Nancy Gust, "Keys to Successful Services Marketing: Customer Orientation, Creed, Consistency," in *Services Marketing in a Changing Environment*, ed. Thomas Bloch et al. (Chicago, IL: American Marketing Association, 1985), pp. 15–18.

6. See James L. Heskett, W. Earl Sasser, Jr., and Leonard A. Schlesinger, *The Service Profit Chain: How Leading Companies Link Profit and Growth to Loyalty, Satisfaction, and Value* (New York: Free Press, 1997); Heskett, Sasser, and Schlesinger, *The Value Profit Chain: Treat Employees Like Customers and Customers Like Employees* (New York: Free Press, 2003); Christian Homburg, Jan Wieseke, and Wayne D. Hoyer, "Social Identity and the Service-Profit Chain," *Journal of Marketing* (March 2009): 38–54; Rachael W. Y. Yee and others, "The Service-Profit Chain: A Review and Extension," *Total Quality Management & Business Excellence* (2009): 617–632.

7. "Four Seasons Hotels and Resorts Named to Fortune List of the '100 Best Companies to Work for,'" March 2, 2015, http://press.fourseasons.com/news-releases/2015/fortune-100-best-companies-to-work-for/; and http://jobs.fourseasons.com and www.fourseasons.com/about_us/ fourseasons.com/about_us/ (accessed September 2016).

8. See Terry Maxon, "Horrible Flight? Airlines' Apology Experts Will Make It Up to You," *McClatchy-Tribune News Service*, (August 24, 2010); Katie Morell, "Lessons from Southwest Airlines' Stellar Customer Service," ehotelier.com, August 29, 2012, http://ehotelier.com/hospitality-news/item.php?id=23931_0_11_0M_C; and Adam Toporek, "Southwest Airlines: A Service Recovery Surprise," B2C, April 24, 2014, www.business2community.com/customer-experience/southwest-airlines-service-recovery-surprise-0886284#dri7dl4r5qW2ESBH.97.

9. See Martha White, "Lost Bags, at 140 Characters, and Airlines Respond," *The New York Times*, October 20, 2015, p. B6.

10. Brad Tuttle, "One Airline That Stubbornly Refuses to Pile on the Fees (for Now)," *Time*, May 7, 2013; Jennifer Rooney, "Southwest Airlines CMO Kevin Krone Explains What's Behind the New Grown-Up Ads," *Forbes*, April 22, 2013; Brad Tuttle, "Southwest Airlines: We're Not Really about Cheap Flights Anymore," *Time*, March 26, 2013; David Whelan, "All Grown Up," *Forbes*, July 18, 2011.

11. Kris van Cleave, "JetBlue's New, Exclusive Orlando 'hotel'," *CBS News*, April 1, 2015, https://www.cbsnews.com/news/jetblue-hotel-lodge-employees-stay-while-training-orlando-florida/ (accessed June 10, 2018); Justin Bachman, "How JetBlue Aims to Grab Some High-Dollar Traffic," *Bloomberg*, June 13, 2013; Robin Farzad and Justin Bachman, "Once High-Flying, JetBlue Returns to Earth," *Bloomberg Businessweek*, April 5, 2012.

12. Dinah Eng, "The Rise of Cirque du Soleil," *Fortune* (November 7, 2011): 39–42; Matt Krantz, "Tinseltown Gets Glitzy New Star," *USA Today*, August 24, 2009; Linda Tischler, "Join the Circus," *Fast Company* (July 2005): 53–58; "Cirque du Soleil," *America's Greatest Brands 3* (2004); Geoff Keighley, "The Factory," *Business 2.0* (February 2004): 102; Robin D. Rusch, "Cirque du Soleil Phantasmagoria Contorts," Brandchannel.com, December 1, 2003.

13. E. Hertzfield (2016), "Will robots ever replace guestroom mini bars," available at http://www.hotelmanagement.net/tech/will-robots-ever-replace-guestroom-minibars (accessed July 26, 2017).

14. See John Bowen and Elizabeth Whalen, "Trends That Are Changing Travel and Tourism," *Worldwide Hospitality and Tourism Themes*, 9, no. 6 (2017): 592–602; https://caliburger.com/ (accessed June 10, 2018); Hertzfield, E. 2016, "Will robots ever replace guestroom mini bars," available at http://www.hotelmanagement.net/tech/will-robots-ever-replace-guestroom-minibars (accessed July 26, 2017).

15. Adapted from Leonard L. Berry, A. Parasuraman, and Valarie A. Zeithaml, "The Lessons for Improving Service Quality," *MSI Reports Working Paper Series, no. 03-Vol* (Cambridge, MA: Marketing Science Institute, 2003): 61–82. See also Leonard I. Berry's books, *On Great Service: A Framework for Action* (New York: Free Press, 2006), *Discovering the Soul of Service* (New York: Free Press, 1999), as well as his articles; Leonard L. Berry, Venkatesh Shankar, Janet Parish, Susan Cadwallader, and Thomas Dotzel, "Creating New Markets through Service Innovation," *Sloan Management Review* (Winter 2006): 56–63; Leonard L. Berry, Stephen H. Haeckel, and Lewis P. Carbone, "How to Lead the Customer Experience," *Marketing Management* (January–February 2003): 18–23; Leonard L. Berry, Kathleen Seiders, and Dhruv Grewal, "Understanding Service Convenience," *Journal of Marketing* (July 2002): 1–17.

16. *Feelings Consultant Marketing Manual* (Bloomington, MN: Better Than Money Corporation, n.d.). The Technical Research Programs Institute does studies on customer complaints and the success of complaint resolution.

17. Linda M. Lash, *The Complete Guide to Customer Service* (New York: Wiley, 1989), pp. 68–69.

18. Majorie Coeyman, "You Call This Service?" *Restaurant Business* (May 15, 1997): 93–104.

19. Janelle Barlow and Claus Moller, *A Complaint Is a Gift* (San Francisco, CA: Berrett-Koehler, 1996).

20. Richard Norman, *Service Management: Strategy and Leadership in Service Businesses* (New York: Wiley, 1984).

21. See Karl Albrecht, *At America's Service* (Homewood, IL: Dow Jones/Irwin, 1988).

22. See Leonard Berry, "Big Ideas in Services Marketing," in *Creativity in Services Marketing*, ed. M. Venkatesan et al. (Chicago, IL: American Marketing Association, 1986), pp. 6–8.

23. Thomas J. Peters and Robert H. Waterman, *In Search of Excellence* (New York: Warner Books, 1982), p. xv.
24. See Valarie A. Zeithaml, "How Consumer Evaluation Processes Differ Between Goods and Services," in *Marketing of Services*, ed. James H. Donnelly and William George (Chicago, IL: American Marketing Association, 1981), pp. 186–190.
25. Sanne de Boer, "The Impact of Dynamic Capacity Management on Airline Seat Inventory Control," *Journal of Revenue and Pricing Management*, 2, no. 4 (2004): 315–320.
26. "Hilton Revolutionizes Hotel Experience with Digital Check-In, Room Selection and Customization, and Check-Out across 650,000-Plus Rooms at More Than 4,000 Properties Worldwide," *Hilton Worldwide*, July 28, 2014, http://news.hiltonworldwide.com/index.cfm/news/hilton-revolutionizes-hotel-experience-with-digital-checkin-room-selection-and-customization-and-checkout-across-650000plus-rooms-at-more-than-4000-properties-worldwide (accessed June 30, 2015).
27. Mark Pestronk, "Finding Hotels Liable for Walking Guests," *Travel Weekly*, 49, no. 37 (1990): 371.
28. Sunmee Choi and Anna S. Mattila, "Hotel Revenue and Its Impact on Customer's Perceptions of Fairness," *Journal of Revenue and Pricing*, 2, no. 4 (2004): 303–314; Karyn Strauss and Jeff Weinstein, "Lesson in Revenue Management," *Hotels* (July 2003): 22; R. G. Cross, *Revenue Management: Hardcore Tactics for Market Domination* (New York: Broadway Books, 1997).
29. Carolyn U. Lambert and Thomas P. Cullen, "Balancing Service and Costs through Queuing Analysis," *Cornell Hotel and Restaurant Administration Quarterly*, 28, no. 2 (1987): 69–72.
30. David H. Maister, "The Psychology of Waiting Lines," in *Service Encounter*, ed. John A. Czepiel, Michael R. Solomon, and Carol F. Surprenant (Lexington, MA: D.C. Heath, 1985).

Objectives

After reading this chapter, you should be able to:

1. Explain the factors of a high-performance business.
2. Discuss the role of marketing in the corporate strategic planning process.
3. Explain how marketing works with its partners to create and deliver customer value.
4. Summarize marketing's role in developing a customer-driven marketing strategy and the marketing mix.
5. Explain the four marketing management functions.
6. Discuss how to measure and manage return on marketing investment.

Jvphoto/Alamy Stock Photo.

Marketing Strategy: Partnering to Build Customer Engagement, Value, and Relationships

Starbucks's Marketing Strategy: Delivering "The Starbucks Experience"

More than 30 years ago, Howard Schultz transformed the coffee industry by bringing a European-style coffeehouse to America. He believed that people needed to slow down—to "smell the coffee" and to enjoy life a little more. The result was Starbucks, founded with a whole new strategy for engaging customers and creating customer value.

Starbucks didn't sell just coffee, it sold "The Starbucks Experience"—"an uplifting experience that enriches people's lives one moment, one human being, one extraordinary cup of coffee at a time." Starbucks gave customers what it calls a "third place"—a place away from home and away from work. At Starbucks, the smells, the sound of beans grinding, watching baristas blend and brew the brand's specialty coffees—all became as much or more a part of the customer experience as the coffee itself.

Over the next two decades, customers flocked to Starbucks cafés. By 2007, some 15,000 Starbucks stores dotted the nation and globe, and the company's sales and profits rose like steam off a mug of hot java. However, Starbucks's enormous success drew a host of competitors. It seemed that every rival—from independent coffeehouses to fast-food restaurants—was peddling its own brand of premium coffee.

To maintain its phenomenal growth in the increasingly overcaffeinated marketplace, Starbucks brewed up an ambitious growth strategy. It opened new stores at a breakneck pace, seemingly everywhere. For example, one three-block stretch in Chicago contained six of the trendy coffee bars. In New York City, there were two Starbucks in one Macy's store. In fact, cramming so many stores so close together caused one satirical publication to run this headline: "A New Starbucks Opens in the Restroom of Existing Starbucks." The company also blanketed the country with Starbucks kiosks and coffee stands everywhere from Target stores and supermarkets to hotel lobbies, and service businesses from airlines to car dealerships proclaimed, "We proudly serve Starbucks coffee."

The more Starbucks grew, however, the more it drifted away from the core mission and values that had made it so successful. The company's almost obsessive focus on growth for growth's sake began to take a toll on the prized Starbucks Experience. Far from its roots as a warm and intimate coffeehouse, Starbucks began to evolve into more of a caffeine filling station. More and more, the premium brand found itself competing with the likes of—gasp!—McDonald's for many of the same customers.

Founder Howard Schultz, who had stepped down as CEO in 2000, expressed concern. In a 2007 memo to Starbucks management, Schultz lamented that the company's push for growth had "led to the watering down of the Starbucks Experience" and that Starbucks was "losing its soul." Schultz was right that something was wrong. By early 2008, when Schultz reassumed his role as Starbucks president and CEO, the company found itself in hot water. For the first time ever, the average number of transactions per U.S. store fell off and same-store sales growth slowed. Within just the previous two years, Starbucks's stock had tumbled nearly 80 percent. According to one analyst, "The financial vultures circled. Obituaries were drafted."

Instead of presiding over the brand's demise, however, Schultz reacted quickly to restore its luster. He cooled the pace of Starbucks's growth, closed underperforming locations, and replaced most of the company's top executives. Most importantly, Schultz laid plans to reestablish the brand's core mission and values and to refocus the company on giving customers the authentic Starbucks Experience. "As we grew rapidly and had phenomenal success," Shultz announced, "we started to lose sight of our focus on the customer and our commitment to continually and creatively enhance the Starbucks Experience." Starbucks needed to shift its focus back to customers—to "reignite the emotional attachment with customers."

To emphasize the point, at a cost of $30 million, Schultz transported 10,000 Starbucks store managers to New Orleans for a morale-building reorientation. A short time later, Starbucks dramatically closed all of its U.S. locations for three hours to conduct nationwide employee training on the basics of producing satisfying customer experiences.

Those early actions began a process of continual renewal by which Starbucks has reignited the Starbucks customer experience through new products, innovative store formats, and new platforms for engaging customers. Beyond improvements in its signature coffee products, Starbucks has developed new products that take the Starbucks Experience into new areas. For example, a few years ago, Starbucks successfully launched Via, an instant coffee that's as good at home as fresh-brewed is in stores. More recently, Starbucks added Fizzio to its menu—freshly carbonated and handcrafted sodas in classic flavors.

The company is also experimenting with new store formats, such as the new high-end Starbucks Reserve Roastery and Tasting Room in Seattle that's part café, part shrine, and part working roastery. Schultz describes the new interactive store as "Niketown meets Apple meets Starbucks"—think of it as the Starbucks Experience on steroids. In another big move, Starbucks purchased Teavana—a specialty tea retailer with more than 400 locations in North America. Schultz sees the Teavana acquisition as pivotal to Starbucks's renewal and reinvention. Tea is "a $90 billion global category, ripe for innovation," he says. "We're going to do for tea what we've done for coffee."

Starbucks's renewal extends the Starbucks Experience well beyond employee relearning, new products, and innovative stores formats. Over the past decade, as much as any brand, Starbucks has built customer engagement and brand community through digital and mobile platforms. Its highly successful mobile payment app, My Starbucks Rewards loyalty program, and prepaid Starbucks Cards now give Starbucks "a direct, real-time, personalized, two-way digital relationship with its customers," says the company's chief digital officer. The Starbucks Rewards mobile payment app has more than 11 million active users, and mobile payments account for 20 percent of all U.S. in-store transactions.

Today, a rejuvenated Starbucks is once again fully engaged with customers and delivering the one-of-a-kind Starbucks Experience. And once again, sales and profits are really perking. Every week, Starbucks serves more than 70 million customers face-to-face in 23,500 stores in 70 countries. Over the past six years, revenues have almost doubled and profits have shot up fivefold.

The moral of the Starbucks story: Good marketing strategy means keeping your eye squarely on delivering customer value. The objective isn't just growth or sales or profits; it's engaging customers in a meaningful way and creating value for them. If a company takes care of customer engagement and value, good performance will result. "It's not just about ringing a register and performing a task," says Schultz. "It's also about creating an emotional, enduring relationship and connection with our... customers. At our core, we celebrate the interaction between us and our customers through the coffee experience. Life happens over coffee."[1]

Nature of High-Performance Business

The major challenge facing today's hospitality companies is knowing how to build and maintain healthy businesses in the face of a rapidly changing marketplace and environment. The consulting firm of Arthur D. Little proposed a model of the characteristics of a high-performance business.[2] It pointed to four factors: stakeholders, processes, resources, and organization. A review of these factors will help set the foundation for our study of strategic marketing.

Stakeholders

Stakeholders Stakeholders include customers, employees, suppliers, and the communities where their business is located and other people or organizations that have an interest in the success of the business.

The starting point for any business is to define the **stakeholders** and their needs. Traditionally, most businesses focused on their stockholders. Today businesses recognize that there are many stakeholders, people, and organizations that have an interest in their success. Stakeholders include customers, employees, suppliers, and the communities where their businesses are located. A business must at least strive to satisfy the minimum expectations of each stakeholder group mentioned above.

A dynamic relationship connects the stakeholder groups. A progressive company creates a high level of employee satisfaction, which leads employees to work on continuous improvements as well as breakthrough innovations. The result is higher-quality products and services, which create high customer and stakeholder satisfaction.

As a response to economic downturn, Hilton Hotels Corporation implemented a strategic goal of creating value for all its stakeholders—customers, owners and shareholders, employees (known as team members), strategic partners, and the communities—and a systematic business model to ensure consistency across properties. To do this, the company adopted the Hilton balance scorecard that measured Hilton's creation of value by integrating all aspects of the business—guest satisfaction, employee satisfaction, mystery shopper reports, financial and revenue management indexes, and brand standards. Over time, the balanced scorecard has been used widely by the Hilton Worldwide to reward teamwork and achieve customer service excellence. The performance measures have evolved to include total quality scorecard (TQS), loyalty score according to SALT (satisfaction and loyalty tracking), and the quality assurance (QA) score. Currently, best hotels are selected and recognized in an annual award ceremony based on these performance metrics.[3]

A critical and sometimes overlooked stakeholder group is that of owners of hotels managed by a hotel management company. Such a company may be one of the well-known flag companies or one that is unknown to the public. Many hotel owners are actually investors and do not wish to manage a property actively, so they contract with an experienced hotel management company.

Hilton Hotels and Resorts use the balanced scorecard concept to manage its hotels. Shown in the picture is the Hilton Hawaiian Village. Courtesy of Steven Heap/123RF.

Processes

Company work is traditionally carried on by departments. However, departmental organization poses some problems. Departments typically operate to maximize their own objectives, not necessarily the company's. Walls go up between departments creating silos, and there is usually less than ideal cooperation. Work is slowed down and plans often are altered as they pass through departments.

Companies are increasingly refocusing their attention on the need to manage processes even more than departments. They are studying how tasks pass from department to department as well as the impediments to creative output. They are now building cross-functional teams that manage core business processes.

Resources

To carry out processes, a company needs such resources as personnel, materials, machines, and information. Traditionally, companies sought to own and control most of the resources that entered the business. Now that is changing. Companies are finding that some resources under their control are not performing as well as those that they could obtain from outside. More companies today have decided to outsource less critical sources. However, they appreciate the need to own and nurture those core resources and competencies that make up the essence of their business. Smart companies are identifying their core competencies and using them as the basis for their strategic planning.

Table 3–1 provides a quick reference concerning organizational resources for use in strategic planning.

Organization

The organizational side of a company consists of its structure, policies, and culture, all of which tend to become dysfunctional in a rapidly changing company. Although structure and policies can be changed, the company's culture is the hardest to change. Successful hospitality companies work hard to maintain a service culture, which was introduced in Chapter 2. In addition to the service culture, they also have

Table 3–1
Strategic Analysis: Questions That Generate Creative Ideas

1. How can this firm take advantage of changes that are expected to occur in society?
2. How can this firm use its relationships with customers to maximize its position in existing or future businesses?
3. Are there any stakeholders that should be seriously considered for partnerships?
4. Does the firm possess any resources or capabilities that are likely to lead to competitive advantage?
5. Are there any resources or capabilities the firm should consider developing to achieve competitive advantage?
6. Can the firm form joint ventures or other alliances with competitors or other stakeholders to acquire valuable knowledge, skills, or other resources?
7. Are there any resources or capabilities the firm does not possess, the absence of which might put it at a competitive disadvantage?
8. Are there any looming threats in the broad environment that the firm should consider in developing its strategy?

Source: Jeffrey S. Harrison, "Strategic Analysis for the Hospitality Industry," *Cornell Hotel and Restaurant Administration Quarterly*, 44, no. 2, April 2003, 152.

to align their organization's structure, policies, and culture to the changing requirements of business strategy. Sometimes structural change and policy change are created by mergers. Other times they are necessary to meet the changing environment. For example, one of the positions being added to organizational structures is that of social media or digital marketing manager. For marketing managers and general managers, it is important that policies and structure support a service culture.

■■■ Corporate Strategic Planning: Defining Marketing's Role

At the corporate level, the company starts the strategic-planning process by defining its overall purpose and mission (see Figure 3–1). This mission then is turned into detailed supporting objectives that guide the whole company. Next, headquarters decides what portfolio of business and products is best for the company and how much support to give each one. In turn, each business and product develops detailed marketing and other departmental plans that support the company-wide plan. This marketing planning occurs at the business unit, product, and market levels. It supports company strategic planning with more detailed plans for specific marketing opportunities.

Each company must find the game plan for long-run survival and growth that makes the most sense given its specific situation, opportunities, objectives, and resources. This is the focus of **strategic planning**—the process of developing and maintaining a strategic fit between the organization's goals and capabilities and its changing marketing opportunities.

Strategic planning sets the stage for the rest of the planning in the firm. Companies usually prepare annual plans, long-range plans, and strategic plans. The annual and long-range plans deal with the company's current businesses and how to keep them going. In contrast, the strategic plan involves adapting the firm to take advantage of opportunities in its constantly changing environment.

Corporate headquarters has the responsibility for setting into motion the whole planning process. Some corporations give a lot of freedom to their business units and let them develop their own strategies. Others set the goals and get heavily involved in the individual strategies. For example, a key success factor for Outback Steakhouse in Korea was attributed to decentralized structure to adapt to local culture and supply procurement.[4] In the mid-1980s, Walt Disney Company set up a powerful, centralized strategic-planning group to guide its direction and growth. Over the next two decades, the strategic-planning group turned the Walt Disney Company into a huge and diverse collection of media and entertainment businesses. The sprawling company grew to include everything from theme resorts and film studios (Walt Disney Pictures, Touchstone Pictures, Pixar, and others) to media networks (ABC Television plus ESPN, Disney Channel, parts of A&E and the History Channel, and a half dozen others) to consumer products and a cruise line. To improve performance, Disney disbanded the centralized strategic-planning unit, decentralizing its functions to Disney division managers. Disney's sound strategic management of its broad mix of businesses has helped it fare better than rival media companies.[5]

The hospitality and tourism industries are international and multicultural. Attitudes and culture sometimes create sharp differences in management style and in the perceived importance of strategic planning, empowerment, and other concepts discussed in this chapter. A study of hospitality managers in Poland, France, and Austria demonstrated differences in risk taking and international vision. Interestingly, Polish managers were shown to have a greater international vision than those in France. The authors concluded that different attitudes of managers in the nations affected the degree of autonomy of the manager.

Strategic planning The process of developing and maintaining a strategic fit between the organization's goals and capabilities and its changing marketing opportunities.

Figure 3–1
Steps in strategic planning.

Corporate level: Defining the company mission → Setting company objectives and goals → Designing the business portfolio

Business unit, product, and market level: Planning marketing and other functional strategies

Managing the business portfolio: Most people think of Tommy Bahama as a clothing retailer, but they also have full-service restaurants attached to 15 of their stores in the United States, as well as a restaurant in Japan. Seyhmus Baloglu.

The authors also believed that the strategy of a hospitality firm and its level of performance were affected by the differing attitudes of managers within the three nations.[6]

Defining the Corporate Mission

A hospitality organization exists to accomplish things such as: to provide a night's lodging, a day of adventure and entertainment for a family, a great dining experience for a couple. At first, it has a clear mission or purpose, but over time, its mission may become unclear as the organization grows, adds new products and markets, or faces new conditions in the environment. When management senses that the organization is drifting, it must renew its search for purpose. Forging a sound mission begins with the following questions: What is our business? Who is the customer? What do customers value? What should our business be? These simple-sounding questions are among the most difficult the company will ever have to answer. Successful companies raise these questions continuously and answer them carefully and completely.

Many organizations develop formal mission statements that answer these questions. A mission statement is a statement of the organization's purpose—what it wants to accomplish in the larger environment. A clear mission statement acts like an "invisible hand" that guides people in the organization. Studies have shown that firms with well-crafted mission statements have better organizational and financial performance.[7]

Some companies define their missions myopically in product or technology terms ("We provide lodging" or "We are a hotel Internet reservations company"). However, a market-oriented mission statement defines the business in terms of satisfying customer needs. The following examples illustrate the difference between a product orientation and a market orientation. A product orientation for Disney would be "We run theme parks." A market orientation would be "We create fantasies—that enable the family to have a great time together and produce memories that will last a lifetime." A product-oriented mission statement for Ritz-Carlton would be "We rent luxury hotel rooms and have fine restaurants." A market-oriented mission statement would be "We create the Ritz-Carlton experience—one that enlivens the senses, instills well-being, and fulfills even the unexpressed wishes and needs of our guests." And Chipotle's mission isn't to sell burritos. Instead, the restaurant promises "Food with Integrity," highlighting its commitment to the immediate and long-term welfare of customers and the environment. To back its mission, Chipotle's serves only the very best natural, sustainable, local ingredients.[8]

Management should avoid making a mission too narrow or too broad. In many cases hospitality companies have gone into businesses that would not fit a marketing-oriented business statement. For example, a fast-food hamburger chain in Texas went into the cattle ranching business because their restaurants used thousands of pounds of beef. They felt they should cut out the middleman and produce their own beef. They soon found out that raising cattle and serving hamburgers took two different sets of business expertise. Mission statements should be realistic. Thai Airlines would be deluding itself if it adopted the mission to become the world's largest airline. However, it could provide excellent service and hospitality for persons flying from the cities that are Thailand's top source of business and/or tourist travelers.

An organization should base its mission on its distinctive competencies. McDonald's could probably enter the solar energy business, but that would not use its core competence.

A company's mission statement should be motivating. Employees need to feel that their work is significant and contributes to people's lives. Missions are at their best when they are guided by a vision, an almost impossible dream. Thomas Monaghan wanted to deliver hot pizza to any home within 30 minutes, and he created Domino's Pizza. Ruth Fertel wanted to provide customers with the finest steak

Some companies like Marriott and Wendy's have public vision statements, but no mission statements. Vision statements are short forward-looking statements. Seyhmus Baloglu.

Corporate mission statement A guide to provide all the publics of a company with a shared sense of purpose, direction, and opportunity, allowing all to work independently, yet collectively, toward the organization's goals.

Corporate values A set of corporate priorities and institutional standards of behavior.

dinners available, and she created Ruth's Chris Steakhouses. Phil Roberts wanted to bring back the warmth and passion of the immigrant southern Italian family-style neighborhood restaurant, so he created Buca di Beppo.[9] James Thomson wanted to create a truly unique and memorable dining experience and created the Witchery by the Castle in Edinburgh, Scotland—one of the United Kingdom's finest. Following that success, James and his team, who were experienced in renovating old buildings, conducted an extensive renovation of a seventeenth-century estate called Prestonfield. Within a short time Prestonfield had gained a reputation as Edinburgh's most opulent retreat, Scotland's most romantic hotel, and one of the top 100 hotels in the world. The restaurant "Rhubarb" within Prestonfield gained an equal reputation.[10] The **corporate mission statement** should stress major policies that the company wants to honor. Policies define how employees should deal with customers, suppliers, competitors, and other important groups.

The company's mission statement should provide a vision and direction for the company for the next 10 to 20 years. Missions are not revised every few years in response to every new turn in the economy. But a company must redefine its mission if that mission no longer defines an optimal course.[11]

Mandarin Oriental manages over 40 hotels across the globe in 26 countries. It is known for operating some of the finest hotels in the world. It describes its vision as delighting and satisfying its guests, and being committed to making a difference every day and continually improving to stay on top.[12]

Finally, as the chapter-opening Starbucks story demonstrates, a company's mission should not be stated as making more sales or profits; profits are only a reward for creating value for customers. Instead, the mission should focus on customers and the customer experience the company seeks to create. Thus, the fast-growing Buffalo Wild Wings restaurant chain's mission isn't just to sell the most wings at a profit.

Customers do, in fact, come to Buffalo Wild Wings to eat wings and drink beer, but also to watch sports, trash talk, cheer on their sports teams, and meet old friends and make new ones—that is, a total eating and social experience. "We realize that we're not just in the business of selling wings," says the company. "We're something much bigger. We're in the business of fueling the sports fan experience." True to that broader mission, Buffalo Wild Wings creates in-store and online promotions that inspire camaraderie. "It's about giving them tools to not just be spectators but advocates of the brand," says the chain. For example, the brand's very active Web site draws 1.4 million visitors per month and its Facebook page has more than 12 million fans. Pursuing a customer-focused mission has paid big dividends for Buffalo Wild Wings. The wing joint's sales have quadrupled in the past eight years and the company brags that it's the number one brand in its industry for fan engagement.[13]

Mission and vision statements are followed by articulation of **corporate values**, which are a set of corporate priorities and institutional standards of behavior. Increasing number of corporations embed social and environmental responsibility in the mission, vision, and values.[14] Hospitality corporations develop mission, vision, and value statements for social and environmental sustainability to communicate what they're doing toward creating a sustainable world and their seriousness on the sustainability front. The values of Shangri-La Hotels and Resorts are rooted in the triple bottom line—economic, environmental, and social: "We envision a community of responsible and educated citizens who are environmentally conscious, practice social responsibility in their daily lives and inspire others to do the same. We commit to operating in an economically, socially and environmentally responsible manner whilst balancing the interests of diverse stakeholders."[15] Starwood Hotels and Resorts briefly state: "At Starwood, we believe sustainable, responsible behavior is a priority—it benefits our business as well as society. And we act on that belief."[16] Marriott International defines their thoughts on sustainability and environment with "We recognize our responsibility to reduce consumption of water, waste and energy in our hotels and corporate offices and are focused on integrating greater environmental sustainability throughout our business," and provides global values and goals such as developing green hotels and inspiring employees and guests to partner with them on sustainability initiatives. The corporation also lists specific areas of focus such as sustainability in hotel kitchens through purchasing organic and responsibly sourced food, planting herb gardens, and sourcing seafood caught in a sustainable manner.[17]

These statements would appeal to minds, hearts, and spirits of younger generations. For example, millennials are very concerned about environmental issues and corporate responsibility. They are more likely to purchase from companies that engage in and commit to social and environmental sustainability.[18]

Setting Company Objectives and Goals

The company needs to turn its mission into detailed supporting objectives for each level of management. Each manager should have objectives and be responsible for reaching them. "The Ritz-Carlton experience enlivens the senses, instills well-being, and fulfills even the unexpressed wishes and needs of our guests." This broad mission leads to a hierarchy of objectives, including business objectives and marketing objectives. Ritz-Carlton's overall objective is to build profitable customer relationships by providing genuine care and comfort for its guests. It does this by understanding what its guests want. This is done by observing guests, seeing how they use the room, and getting employees to provide feedback on what the guests say about Ritz-Carlton and its competitors. Profits can be improved by increasing sales or reducing costs. Sales can be increased by improving the company's share of leisure, group, and transient business markets. These goals then become the company's current marketing objectives.[19]

Marketing strategies and programs must be developed to support these marketing objectives. To increase its market share, Ritz-Carlton may add salespeople to attract the incentive travel market. It may expand its presence in international markets. Ritz-Carlton also realizes that condominiums as part of a Ritz-Carlton hotel project increases the value by 35 percent over an unbranded condominium. Therefore, this becomes an option to provide the cash flow and thus gain financing for new properties.

Each broad marketing strategy must then be defined in greater detail. For example, increasing the incentive travel business may require more salespeople, advertising, and public relations efforts; if so, both requirements will need to be spelled out. In this way, the firm's mission is translated into a set of objectives for the current period.

Designing the Business Portfolio

Most companies operate several businesses. However, they often fail to define them carefully. Businesses are too often defined in terms of products. Companies are in the "hotel business" or the "cruise line business."[20] However, market definitions of a business are superior to product definitions. A business must be viewed as a customer-satisfying process, not a product-producing process. Companies should define their business in terms of customer needs, not products. Expedia group is a highly diversified travel company owning a global portfolio of online travel brands such as Expedia, HomeAway, trivago, Hotels.com, hotwire, Travelocity, Orbitz, Classic Vacations, carrentals.com, SilverRail, and Expedia CruiseShipCenters. Collectively, its portfolio covers virtually every aspect of researching, planning, and booking travel for both leisure and business travelers with varying tastes and budgets.[21]

Management, of course, should avoid a market definition that is too narrow or too broad. Holiday Inns, Inc., the world's largest hotel chain, fell into this trap. There was a time when Holiday Inns broadened its business definition from the "hotel business" to the "travel industry." It acquired Trailways, Inc., then the nation's second-largest bus company, and Delta Steamship, Inc., but it did not manage

Strategic business units (SBUs) A single business or collection of related businesses that can be planned separately from the rest of the company.

these companies well and later divested the properties.[22] Today Holiday Inns is part of the Intercontinental Hotel Group and has refocused on the lodging industry.

Companies have to identify those of its businesses that they must manage strategically. These businesses are called **strategic business units (SBUs)**. An SBU has the following three characteristics:

1. It is a single business or a collection of related businesses that can be planned for separately from the rest of the company.
2. It has its own set of competitors.
3. It has a manager who is responsible for strategic planning and profit performance and who controls most of the factors affecting profits.

The purpose of identifying the company's SBUs is to assign to these units strategic-planning goals and appropriate funding. These units send their plans to company headquarters, which approves them or sends them back for revision. Headquarters reviews these plans to decide which of its SBUs to build, maintain, harvest, and divest. Management cannot rely just on impressions. Analytical tools are needed for classifying businesses by profit potential.

Choice Hotels International has initiated a multifaceted plan to strengthen and revitalize its Comfort brand family, which includes Comfort Inn and Comfort Suites, about 2,000 domestic hotels. The "Comfort: Redefined and Redesigned" plan focuses on three key strategies: removing underperforming properties, refreshing existing hotels, and adding new construction prototypical hotels.[23]

Developing Strategies for Growth

Companies need growth if they are to compete and attract top talent. At the same time, a firm must be careful not to make growth itself an objective. The company's objective must be "profitable growth." Many would add that growth must be environmentally responsible. This is not unilaterally accepted, however.

Marketing has a responsibility to achieve profitable growth for the company. Marketing must identify, evaluate, and select opportunities and lay down strategies for capturing them. The **Ansoff product–market expansion grid** (Figure 3–2) offers a useful framework for examining growth.[24] Management first considers whether it could gain more market share with its current products in its current markets (market concentration strategy). Dunkin' stores in the United States generate about 40 percent of their sales after 11 A.M. The chain started offering discounted menu items and coffee from 3 P.M. to 6 P.M. to increase afternoon business.[25] Starbucks focuses on its loyalty program and mobile payment applications to increase sales.

Next it considers whether it can find or develop new markets for its current products (**market development strategy**). Southwest Airlines began flying internationally to Mexico City and select Caribbean destinations such as Jamaica and Dominican Republic. Hooters' renovate their restaurants and update their menu as an attempt to draw younger generation and female consumers.[26]

Next, management should consider **product development**: offering modified or new products to current markets. By examining these three intensive growth strategies, management ideally will discover several ways to grow. Still, that may not be enough, in which case management must also examine diversification and integrative growth opportunities. For example, Starbucks developed packaged products that can be sold in supermarkets. McDonald's increases its consumer base through product expansion. For example, the introduction of McCafé directly targeted consumers in the booming coffee industry and stole share from companies like Starbucks and Dunkin' Donuts.[27] McDonald's also offers new products such as fruits, salads, and McWrap sandwiches to draw millennials as well as new breakfast menu items to increase coffee sales at its McCafé.[28] InterContinental Hotels Group (IHG) developed EVEN Hotels to target business and leisure travelers who are looking for wellness experience in a hotel stay.

Ansoff product–market expansion grid A matrix developed by cell, plotting new products and existing products with new products and existing products. The grid provides strategic insights into growth opportunities.

Market development strategy Finding and developing new markets for your current products.

Product development Offering modified or new products to current markets.

Figure 3–2
The product–market expansion grid is useful in helping managers visualize and identify market opportunities.

	Existing products	New products
Existing markets	1. Market penetration	3. Product development
New markets	2. Market development	4. Diversification

Diversification Growth

Diversification growth makes sense when good opportunities can be found outside the present businesses. A good opportunity is one where the industry is highly attractive and the company has the mix of business strengths to be successful. Three types of diversification can be considered. First, the company could seek new products that have technological or marketing synergies with existing product lines, even though the products may appeal to a new class of customers (**concentric diversification strategy**). In the mid-2000s, Wyndham Worldwide entered into timeshare business by launching the brand Wyndham Vacation Ownership, to attract independent timeshare and hotel developers to participate in a franchise and affiliation arrangement under the Wyndham brand. The company now operates timeshare resorts throughout the United States, Canada, Mexico, the Caribbean, and the South Pacific.[29] Restaurant Brands, the owner of Burger King and Tim Hortons, has recently paid $1.8 billion to acquire fried chicken chain Popeyes Louisiana Kitchen.[30] Second, the company might search for new products that could appeal to its current customers, although technologically unrelated to its current product line (**horizontal diversification strategy**). Hotels, restaurants, cruise lines, and airlines all pursue this strategy when they sell gift items such as T-shirts, perfume, and luggage. Many restaurants, such as the Hard Rock Café franchise, have found that the sale of restaurant logo clothing in their restaurants is highly profitable and the clothing serves as an excellent advertising medium. Hilton Hotel and Resorts sell beds and in-room amenities online through Hilton to Home Web site.[31]

Diversification opportunities sometimes arise as a result of new technology. A new class of lightweight aluminum ferries can cruise at 55 miles per hour and carry hundreds of passengers. This new technology allows ferries to serve new routes. Opportunities for onboard food and beverage service as well as the ferry service itself will be available to the hospitality/tourism industries.[32]

Finally, the company might seek new businesses that have no relationship to the company's current technology, products, or markets (**conglomerate diversification strategy**). The restaurant we mentioned earlier in this chapter that went into the cattle ranching business is an example of conglomerate diversification.

The company Sodexo of Marseille, France, was experienced and successful in providing hospitality services on ocean liners and cruise ships.[33] The company's founder, Pierre Bellon, decided to expand into other industries with similar needs, such as health-care facilities and schools, and to seek international expansion. Within five years, the company was successful in Belgium, and then expanded to North and South America and went public on the Paris Bourse. In 2008, Sodexo's global expansion led to a name change to Sodexo from Sodexho because in some countries a "xh" is difficult to pronounce.

Companies that diversify too broadly into unfamiliar products or industries can lose their market focus. Thus we see that a company can systematically identify new business opportunities by using a marketing systems framework. Despite the risk, companies that started in one market often desire to enter others considered complimentary. The hospitality industry is witness to this phenomenon. This is by no means a secure strategy because different businesses often require different management style and practices.

Concentric diversification strategy A growth strategy whereby a company seeks new products that have technological or marketing synergies with existing product lines.

Horizontal diversification strategy A product growth strategy whereby a company looks for new products that could appeal to current customers, which are technologically unrelated to its current line.

Conglomerate diversification strategy A product growth strategy in which a company seeks new businesses that have no relationship to the company's current product line or markets.

Marketing HIGHLIGHT 3.1 — AccorHotels group: Marriage with onefinestay, a luxury vacation rental platform

In 2016, AccorHotels, the Paris-based hotel group that owns and operates thousands of hotels around the world, announced the acquisition of onefinestay, a London-based "sharing economy" startup company specializing in luxury serviced home rental, for $170 million. The company also made a commitment of $70 million investment in onefinestay over the next few years to grow the startup's presence globally. Sébastien Bazin, Chairman & CEO of AccorHotels, indicated that "onefinestay has successfully captured a sweet spot: a combination of needs that neither traditional hotels nor new actors of the sharing economy can meet" and the acquisition allowed for value creation related to the rise of private rentals and strengthening Accor's presence in the luxury market.

AccorHotels, Europe's largest hotel groups, has approximately 3,900 hotels in 92 countries. AccorHotels joined luxury vacation home rentals market with onefinestay to expand into the sharing economy, strengthen its response to the threat posed by Airbnb, and further expand its luxury portfolio after companies like Airbnb. Sébastien Bazin, chief executive of Accor, indicated that the goal is to generate 30 percent of Accor's businesses from revenue streams other than hotel rooms within five years.

Onefinestay, launched in 2010, provides hotel experience in the luxury segment of the Serviced Homes market, combining the short-term vacation rental homes and the finest service. The company targets both leisure and business guests by offering hand-picked distinctive private homes with personal service from a personal welcome on arrival to a team on call 24/7. Onefinestay itself oversees each rental and provides toiletries, bedding, and other amenities to serve the high-end guests.

For homeowners, onefinestay aims to provide peace of mind and convenience and handle promotion, pricing, distribution, insurance, guest screening, professional cleaning, management, and maintenance. The company operates a portfolio of over 2,500 properties under exclusive management.

Following the acquisition, onefinestay remained an independent business and guests would still have to visit Onefinestay's Web site to book a stay. When acquired in 2016, it used to operate in four cities. As of today, it operates in seven cities and destinations (London, Rome, Paris, New York, Los Angeles, Hawaii, and Caribbean) (https://www.onefinestay.com/). With additional investment of $70 million and support by AccorHotels, the aggressive growth plans were to scale the platform to over 40 new cities during the next five years, particularly in Europe and Asia.

In 2017, AccorHotels also acquired Squarebreak, a company offering high-end rentals in France, and Travel Keys, a U.S. group that acts as a broker to hire luxury villas. Unlike onefinestay, which focused on urban areas, Travel Keys and Squarebreak are primarily resort focused. The former has a strong presence in the Caribbean while the latter has a European and North African portfolio. Recently, AccorHotels combined and consolidated Travel Keys and Squarebreak under the onefinestay brand to further counter the challenge of Airbnb and other online booking services, increasing the number of rentals offered to 10,000 from about 2,500. Both companies will retain their names but sit under the umbrella brand of onefinestay.[34]

Integrative Growth

Opportunities in diversification, market development, and product development can be seized through integrating backward, forward, or horizontally within that business's industry. A hotel company could select **backward integration** by acquiring one of its suppliers, such as a food distributor, or it could acquire tour wholesalers or travel agents (**forward integration**). MGM Resorts International set up its own tour wholesaler, MGM Resorts Vacations, to sell complete vacation packages of SBUs in its portfolio. Finally, the hotel company might acquire one or more competitors, provided that the government does not bar the move (**horizontal integration**). In 2013, Pinnacle Entertainment offered a $2.8 billion buyout of regional casino rival Ameristar Casinos. The Federal Trade Commission blocked the buyout because the merger would reduce competition, lead to higher prices, and lower quality for customers in the St. Louis, Missouri, and Lake Charles, Louisiana, areas. Pinnacle Entertainment and Ameristar Casinos have agreed to sell casino properties in St. Louis, Missouri, and Lake Charles, Louisiana, to settle and complete the transaction.[35] In 2015, IHG acquired Kimpton Hotels & Restaurants, a boutique hotel and food and beverage operator whose portfolio consisted of 62 hotels and 71 restaurants and bars.[36]

A company can systematically identify new business opportunities by using a marketing systems framework, looking at ways to intensify its position in current product markets, searching for profitable opportunities outside its current businesses, and considering ways to integrate backward, forward, or horizontally in relation to its current businesses.

Backward integration A growth strategy by which companies acquire businesses supplying them with products or services (e.g., a restaurant chain purchasing a bakery).

Forward integration A growth strategy by which companies acquire businesses that are closer to the ultimate consumer, such as a hotel acquiring a chain of travel agents.

Horizontal integration A growth strategy by which companies acquire competitors.

Downsizing

Growth strategies are not the only strategies for a firm to consider. Sometimes downsizing will lead to the long-term viability of a company. There are many reasons a company may want to abandon products or markets. The firm may have grown too fast. In the United States, restaurant chains with publicly traded stock are under intense pressure to grow their sales and net profits each quarter. Restaurant companies will sometimes expand beyond their capabilities to manage the quality across their

Red Lobster uses backward integration by owning its supply chain. Courtesy of Philip Kotler.

rapidly growing chain. When this happens, sales per store start to decline and stock prices follow. When this happens, they will reduce the number of stores they have and consolidate, hopefully moving back into an effective organization. Sometimes, during economic downturns companies will be faced with pruning unprofitable units to focus their resources on the most profitable units. Sometimes the focus of the company will change and it will enter new markets and exit old ones.

Landry's restaurants sold a casual restaurant chain called Joe's Crab Shack. Landry's decided to focus on casinos and upscale restaurants. The lower end Joe's Crab Shack no longer fit into their plans. The CEO of Landry's stated, "Joe's has been an important part of our growth over the years. We are now going in a different strategic direction … Joe's just does not fit well in our future plans."[37] Since divesting Joe's, Landry's has purchased Morton's, an upscale chain of steakhouses, and opened a major casino in Louisiana. When a firm finds brands or businesses that are unprofitable or that no longer fit its overall strategy, it must carefully prune, harvest, or divest them.

Planning Marketing: Partnering to Build Customer Relationships

The company's strategic plan establishes what kinds of businesses the company will operate and its objectives for each. Then, within each business unit, more detailed planning takes place. The major functional departments in each unit—marketing, finance, accounting, purchasing, operations, information systems, human resources, and others—must work together to accomplish strategic objectives.

Marketing plays a key role in the company's strategic planning in several ways. First, marketing provides a guiding philosophy—the marketing concept—that suggests the company strategy should revolve around creating customer value and building profitable relationships with important consumer groups. Second, marketing provides inputs to strategic planners by helping to identify attractive market opportunities and assessing the firm's potential to take advantage of them. Finally, within individual business units, marketing designs strategies for reaching the unit's objectives. Once the unit's objectives are set, marketing's task is to help carry them out profitably.

Customer engagement and value are the key ingredients in the marketer's formula for success. However, as noted in Chapter 1, although marketing plays a leading role, it alone cannot produce engagement and superior value for customers. It can be only a partner in attracting, engaging, and growing customers. In addition to customer relationship management, managers must also practice partner-relationship management. They must work closely with partners in other company departments to form an effective internal value chain that serves customers. For example, most hotels outsource the cleaning of their laundry. They need a reliable supplier that will provide a clean, finished product and deliver it when it is needed. We now take a closer look at the concepts of a company value chain and a value delivery network.

Partnering with Other Company Departments

Each company department can be thought of as a link in the company's internal **value chain**.[38] That is, each department carries out value-creating activities to design, produce, market, deliver, and support the firm's products. The firm's success

Value chain The series of internal departments that carry out value-creating activities to design, produce, market, deliver, and support a firm's products.

depends not only on how well each department performs but also on how well the various departments coordinate their activities.

Ideally, a company's different functions should work in harmony to produce value for consumers. But, in practice, interdepartmental relations are full of conflicts and misunderstandings. The general manager takes the consumer's point of view. But when managers try to improve customer satisfaction, it can cause conflict if all the departments do not put the customer first. For example, the sales department may want a late checkout for an important group, but housekeeping may not want to keep extra staff on to provide this service. If everyone has the interests of the guest and future business in mind, then the departments will work together to provide great guest service.

Yet, general managers must find ways to get all departments to "think consumer" and develop a smoothly functioning value chain. One marketing expert puts it this way: "True market orientation ... means that the entire company obsesses over creating value for the customer and views itself as a bundle of processes that profitably define, create, communicate, and deliver value to its target customers.... Everyone must do marketing regardless of function or department." Says another, "Engaging customers today requires commitment from the entire company. We're all marketers now."[39] Thus, whether you're an accountant, an operations manager, a financial analyst, an IT specialist, or a human resources manager, you need to understand marketing and your role in creating customer value.

Partnering with Others in the Marketing System

In its quest to create customer value, the firm needs to look beyond its own internal value chain and into the value chains of its suppliers, distributors, and, ultimately, its customers. Consider McDonald's. People do not swarm to McDonald's only because they love the chain's hamburgers. Consumers flock to the McDonald's system, not only to its food products. Throughout the world, McDonald's finely tuned value delivery system delivers a high standard of QSCV—quality, service, cleanliness, and value. McDonald's is effective only to the extent that it successfully partners with its franchisees, suppliers, and others to jointly create "our customers' favorite place and way to eat."

More companies today are partnering with other members of the supply chain—suppliers, distributors, and, ultimately, customers—to improve the performance of the customer value delivery network. Competition no longer takes place only between individual competitors. Rather, it takes place between the entire value delivery networks created by these competitors.

Marketing Strategy and the Marketing Mix

The strategic plan defines the company's overall mission and objectives. Figure 3–3 shows marketing's role and activities and summarizes the major activities involved in managing a customer-driven marketing strategy and the marketing mix.

Consumers stand in the center. The goal is to create value for customers and build profitable customer relationships. Next comes **marketing strategy**, the marketing logic by which the company hopes to create customer value and achieve profitable relationships. The company decides which customers it will serve (segmentation and targeting) and how (differentiation and positioning). It identifies the total market and then divides it into caller segments, selects the most promising segments, and focuses on serving and satisfying customers in these segments.

Guided by marketing strategy, the company designs an integrated *marketing mix* made up of factors under its control—product, price, place, and promotion (the four Ps). To find the best marketing strategy and mix, the company engages in marketing analysis, planning, implementation, and control. Through these activities, the company watches and adapts to the actors and forces in the marketing environment. We now look briefly at each activity. Then, in later chapters, we discuss each one in more depth.

Marketing strategy The marketing logic by which the company hopes to create customer value and achieve profitable relationships.

Figure 3–3
Managing marketing strategy and the marketing mix.
Source: Philip Kotler and Gary Armstrong, *Principles of Marketing*, 17th ed., ©2018, p. 50. Reprinted and electronically reproduced by permission of Pearson Education, Inc., New York, NY.

Customer Value-Driven Marketing Strategy

As we emphasized throughout Chapter 1, to succeed in today's competitive marketplace, companies need to be customer centered. They must *win* customers from competitors and then keep and grow them by delivering greater value. But before it can satisfy consumers, a company must first understand their needs and wants. Thus, sound marketing requires a careful customer analysis.

Companies know that they cannot profitably serve all consumers in a given market—at least not all consumers in the same way. There are too many different kinds of consumers with too many different kinds of needs. And most companies are in a position to serve some segments better than others. Thus, each company must divide up the total market, choose the best segments, and design strategies for profitably serving chosen segments. This process involves *market segmentation*, *market targeting*, *differentiation*, and *positioning*.

Market Segmentation

The market consists of many types of customers, products, and needs. The marketer must determine which segments offer the best opportunities. Consumers can be grouped and served in various ways based on geographic, demographic, psychographic, and behavioral factors. The process of dividing a market into distinct groups of buyers who have different needs, characteristics, or behavior and who might require separate products or marketing programs is called **market segmentation**.

A market segment consists of consumers who respond in a similar way to a given set of marketing efforts. It would be difficult to design a hotel concept that was the first choice of consumers for both luxury and budget-minded traveler segments. Companies are wise to focus their efforts on meeting the distinct needs of individual market segments.

Market Targeting

After a company has defined market segments, it can enter one or many of these segments. **Market targeting** involves evaluating each market segment's attractiveness and selecting one or more segments to enter. A company should target segments

---

Market segmentation The process of dividing a market into distinct groups of buyers who have different needs, characteristics, or behavior and who might require separate products or marketing programs.

Market targeting Evaluating each market segment's attractiveness and selecting one or more segments to enter.

in which it can profitably generate the greatest customer value and sustain it over time. A company with limited resources might decide to serve only one or a few special segments or "market niches."

Alternatively, a company might choose to serve several related segments—perhaps those with different kinds of customers but with the same basic wants. Most companies enter a new market by serving a single segment, and if this proves successful, they add segments. Large companies eventually seek full market coverage.

Market Differentiation and Positioning

After a company has decided which market segments to enter, it must decide how it will differentiate its market offering for each targeted segment and what positions it wants to occupy in those segments. A product's *position* is the place the product occupies, relative to competitors' products, in consumers' minds. Marketers want to develop unique market positions for their products. If a product is perceived to be exactly like others on the market, consumers would have no reason to buy it.

Positioning is arranging for a product to occupy a clear, distinctive, and desirable place relative to competing products in the minds of target consumers. As one positioning expert puts it, positioning is "why a shopper will pay a little more for your brand."[40] Thus, marketers plan positions that distinguish their products from competing brands and give them the greatest advantage in their target markets.

CitizenM hotel chain promises "Affordable Luxury." Subway wants you to "Eat Fresh" while Wendy's says "Quality Is Our Recipe." Southwest Airlines, from its founding, has positioned itself as "The LUV Airline," a positioning recently reinforced by the colorful heart in its new logo and plane graphics design. As recent Southwest advertising affirms, "Without a heart, it is just a machine." The airline has "always put Heart in everything it does."

In positioning its product, the company first identifies possible customer value differences that provide competitive advantages on which to build the position. The company can offer greater customer value either by charging lower prices than competitors do or by offering more benefits to justify higher prices. But if the company *promises* greater value, it must then deliver that greater value. Thus, effective positioning begins with differentiation, actually *differentiating* the company's market offering so that it gives consumers more value. Once the company has chosen a desired position, it must take strong steps to deliver and communicate that position to target consumers. The company's entire marketing program should support the chosen positioning strategy.

Positioning Arranging for a product to occupy a clear, distinctive, and desirable place relative to competing products in the minds of target consumers.

Developing an Integrated Marketing Mix

After deciding on its overall marketing strategy, the company is ready to begin planning the details of the marketing mix, one of the major concepts in modern marketing. The marketing mix is the set of controllable, tactical marketing tools that the firm blends to produce the response it wants in the target market. The marketing mix consists of everything the firm can do to influence the demand for its product. The many possibilities can be collected into four groups of variables known as the four Ps: *product*, *price*, *place*, and *promotion*.

Product means the goods-and-services combination the company offers to the target market. *Price* is the amount of money customers must pay to obtain the product. *Place* includes company activities that make the product available to target customers. *Promotion* means activities that communicate the merits of the product and persuade target customers to buy it.

An effective marketing program blends all of the marketing mix elements into an integrated marketing program designed to achieve the company's marketing objectives by delivering value to consumers. The marketing mix constitutes the company's tactical tool kit for establishing strong positioning in target markets.

Some critics think that the four Ps may omit or underemphasize certain important activities. For example, they ask, "Where are services?" Just because they don't start with a *P* doesn't justify omitting them. The answer is that services, such as banking, airline, and retailing services, are products too. We might call them *service products*.

"Where is packaging?" the critics might ask. Marketers would answer that they include packaging as just one of many product decisions. All said, as Figure 3–3 suggests, many marketing activities that might appear to be left out of the marketing mix are subsumed under one of the four Ps. The issue is not whether there should be 4, 6, or 10 Ps so much as what framework is most helpful in designing integrated marketing programs.

There is another concern, however, that is valid. It holds that the four Ps concept takes the seller's view of the market, not the buyer's view. From the buyer's viewpoint, in this age of customer value and relationships, the four Ps might be better described as the four As:[41]

4Ps	4As
Product	Acceptability
Price	Affordability
Place	Accessibility
Promotion	Awareness

Under this more customer-centered framework, *acceptability* is the extent to which the product exceeds customer expectations; *affordability* the extent to which customers are willing and able to pay the product's price; *accessibility* the extent to which customers can readily acquire the product; *and awareness* the extent to which customers are informed about the product's features, persuaded to try it, and reminded to repurchase. The four As relate closely to the traditional four Ps. Product design influences acceptability, price affects affordability, place affects accessibility, and promotion influences awareness. Marketers would do well to think through the four As first and then build the four Ps on that platform.

Thus, although marketers see themselves as selling products, customers see themselves as buying value or solutions to their problems. And customers are interested in more than just the price; they are interested in the total costs of obtaining, using, and disposing of a product. Customers want the product and service to be as conveniently available as possible. Finally, they want two-way communication.

Managing the Marketing Effort

In addition to being good at the *marketing* in marketing management, companies need to pay attention to the *management*. Managing the marketing process requires the four marketing management functions shown in Figure 3–4: *analysis, planning, implementation*, and *control*. The company first develops company-wide strategic plans and then translates them into marketing and other plans for each division, product, and brand. Through implementation, the company turns the plans into actions. Control consists of measuring and evaluating the results of marketing activities and taking corrective action where needed. Finally, marketing analysis provides information and evaluations needed for all of the other marketing activities.

Marketing Analysis

Managing the marketing function begins with a complete analysis of the company's situation. The marketer should conduct a **SWOT analysis**, by which it evaluates the company's overall strengths (S), weaknesses (W), opportunities (O), and threats (T) (see Figure 3–5). Strengths include internal capabilities, resources, and positive situational factors that may help the company serve its customers and achieve its objectives. Weaknesses include internal limitations and negative situational factors that may interfere with the company's performance. Opportunities are favorable

SWOT analysis Evaluates the company's overall strengths (S), weaknesses (W), opportunities (O), and threats (T).

Figure 3–4
The relationship between analysis, planning, implementation, and control.

factors or trends in the external environment that the company may be able to exploit to its advantage. And threats are unfavorable external factors or trends that may present challenges to performance.

The company should analyze its markets and marketing environment to find attractive opportunities and identify environmental threats. It should analyze company strengths and weaknesses as well as current and possible marketing actions to determine which opportunities it can best pursue. The goal is to match the company's strengths to attractive opportunities in the environment while eliminating or overcoming the weaknesses and minimizing the threats.

Internal Environmental Analysis (Strengths and Weaknesses Analysis)

It is one thing to discern attractive opportunities in the environment and another to have the necessary competencies to succeed with these opportunities. Each business needs to evaluate its strengths and weaknesses periodically. Management or an outside consultant reviews the business's marketing, financial, manufacturing, and organizational competencies. Each factor is rated as to whether it is a major strength, minor strength, neutral factor, minor weakness, or major weakness. A company with strong marketing capability would probably show up with the 10 marketing factors all rated as major strengths.

In examining its pattern of strengths and weaknesses, clearly the business does not have to correct all its weaknesses or gloat about all its strengths. The big question is whether the business should limit itself to those opportunities for which it now possesses the required strengths or should consider better opportunities.

Figure 3–5
SWOT analysis: The goal of SWOT analysis is to match the company's strengths to attractive opportunities in the environment while eliminating or overcoming the weaknesses and minimizing threats.

Many hospitality industry specialists believe that to compete effectively, companies such as hotels, resorts, and cruise lines need seamless connectivity within their computer reservation systems (CRS), including a global distribution system (GDS). If a hotel company wishes to increase its international business and its reservations through travel agents, the existence or development of such a system would surely be viewed as a strength. Sometimes a business does poorly not because its department lacks the required strengths, but because employees do not work together as a team. In some hospitality companies, salespeople are viewed as overpaid playboys and playgirls who produce business by practically giving it away to customers. In turn, salespeople often view those in operations as incompetent dolts who

Atlantis Resort on Paradise Island in the Bahamas gained access to Marriot's reservation system when it became part of Marriott's Autograph Collection. Ezpic/Shutterstock.

Macroenvironmental forces Demographic, economic, technological, political, legal, social, and cultural factors.

Microenvironmental forces Customers, competitors, distribution channels, and suppliers.

Marketing opportunity An area of need in which a company can perform profitably.

consistently foul up their orders and provide poor customer service. It is therefore critically important to assess interdepartmental working relationships as part of the internal environmental audit.

Every company must manage some basic processes, such as new product development, raw materials to finished products, sales leads to orders, customer orders to cash payments, and so on. Each process creates value and each process requires interdepartmental teamwork.

External Environmental Analysis (Opportunity and Threat Analysis)

The business manager now knows the parts of the environment to monitor if the business is to achieve its goals. In general, a business unit has to monitor key **macroenvironmental forces** (demographic-economic, technological, political-legal, and social-cultural) and significant **microenvironmental forces** (customers, competitors, distribution channels, and supplies) that will affect its ability to earn profits in the marketplace. The business unit should set up a marketing intelligence system to track trends and important developments. For each trend or development, management needs to identify the implied opportunities and threats.

The terrorist attacks on September 11, 2001, brought a sudden awareness to the worldwide hospitality/tourism industry of the dramatic impact such events can have on business and pleasure travel. This has caused tourism promotion agencies, convention centers, transportation firms, and lodging companies to seriously consider alternative markets, new product design, increased security, emergency energy sources, and many other factors.

The emergence of China, India, and Eastern Europe as new industrial and political powers is seriously affecting hospitality/tourism in ways that were unforeseen. For example, the high quality of health care combined with the low cost in countries such as India has created a new segment of tourism known as medical tourism. At the same time, the Texas Medical Center, one of the world's largest medical centers, has seen its medical tourism from the Middle East decline. In today's rapidly changing environment, external environmental threats and opportunities have taken on new importance in strategic planning.

OPPORTUNITIES. A major purpose of environmental scanning is to discern new opportunities. We define a **marketing opportunity** as follows: an area of need that a company can perform profitably.

Opportunities can be listed and classified according to their attractiveness and the success probability. Success probability depends on whether its business strengths match the key success requirements for operating in the target market and exceed those of competitors. The best performing company will be the one that can generate the greatest customer value and sustain it over time.

The concept of incorporating health and recreation clubs into resorts has been an opportunity for some resorts. Programs are aimed at local markets, allowing members to enjoy the resort facilities and sometimes even stay in the rooms. Membership programs offer opportunities for increased revenue, but there is a negative side if they are not well managed. The online reservation networks and alliances might offer considerable opportunities for the independent boutique hotels or B&Bs (bed and breakfasts) operations in terms of promotion and distribution of their products.

Many opportunities lie in unmet needs of consumers. Recently, new boutique and lifestyle concepts have emerged to appeal to millennial generation, and environmentally and health conscious customers. The list includes Moxy and Edition by Marriott International; W, Aloft, and Element by Starwood Hotels & Resorts Worldwide; Indigo by IHG; and Andaz by Hyatt Hotels Corporation. For example, Element by Westin Hotels and Resorts, an extended hotel, positions itself as an eco-friendly concept offering a balanced experience where guests can "eat right, sleep well, exercise, and relax."[42] IHG has developed the EVEN Hotels brand in response to results from customer research that found both business and leisure guests were frustrated with hotels that did not meet their lifestyle and wellness needs. Even properties feature amenities focusing on menus using fresh and organic ingredients, natural bath products, color LED mood lighting, exercise equipment such as yoga mats in guestrooms, and flexible work space.[43]

THREATS. Some developments in the external environment represent marketing threats. We define an environmental threat as follows: A challenge posed by unfavorable trends or developments that would lead, in the absence of defensive marketing action, to sales or profit deterioration. Threats should be classified according to their seriousness and probability of occurrence. After assembling a picture of major threats and opportunities, the following four outcomes are possible:

1. An ideal business is high in major opportunities and low in major threats.
2. A speculative business is high in both major opportunities and threats.
3. A major business is low in major opportunities and threats.
4. A troubled business is low in opportunities and high in threats.

Traditional institutional food-service providers to hospitals, schools, government offices, and office buildings face the threat of competition from quick service restaurants (QSRs). Many QSRs such as Pizza Hut, Dunkin' Donuts, and Burger King have entered this market. Traditional institutional food-service firms such as Aramark cannot ignore this threat.[44]

Today, the impact of threats is so critical that all hospitality companies must study possible threats and build risk management systems. We have previously spoken of the effects of 9/11, but risks such as mad cow disease and microbial contamination are of vital concern to hospitality companies. Several years ago, "The Jack-in-the-Box QSR chain was linked to 400 illnesses and deaths of three children due to an outbreak of *Escherichia coli* in their hamburgers. The chain was accused of serious deception, irresponsibility, and poor communications."[45] Jack-in-the-Box suffered heavy financial loss for four years and nearly went out of business as a result of the problem. Because microbial outbreaks are possible in any food establishment, they must be considered as risks with prescribed procedures to follow after an outbreak.

Goal Formulation

After the business unit has defined its mission and conducted a SWOT analysis, it can proceed to develop specific objectives and goals.

Very few businesses pursue only one objective. Most business units pursue a mix of objectives, including profitability, sales growth, market share improvement, and cost containment. The business unit sets these objectives and manages by objectives. The business unit should strive to arrange its objectives from most to least important. Where possible, objectives should be stated quantitatively. The objective "increase the return on investment" is not as satisfactory as "increase ROI [return on investment] to 15 percent" or even better, "increase ROI to 15 percent within two years." Objectives support measurable goals. A business should set realistic goals. The levels should arise from an analysis of the business unit's opportunities and strengths, not from wishful thinking.

Finally, the company's objectives need to be consistent. Objectives are sometimes in a tradeoff relationship. Here are some important tradeoffs:

- High profit margins versus high market share
- Deep penetration of existing markets versus developing new markets
- Profit goals versus nonprofit goals
- High growth versus low risk

The hotel industry is faced with unique challenges concerning goal formulation and performance measurement due to management agreements between

In-N-Out Burger offers freshly made burgers and fries to differentiate its product from the larger burger chains. Seyhmus Baloglu.

hotel owners and hotel operating companies. Most industries such as manufacturing, construction, or retailing hire their own management staff rather than contracting with an independent operations management company. "Of all the issues addressed in the negotiation of a hotel management agreement, among the most difficult to resolve is establishing an appropriate performance test that is acceptable to both parties."[46]

Goals indicate what a business unit wants to achieve; strategy answers how to get there. Every business must tailor a strategy for achieving its goals. Although we can list many types of strategies, Michael Porter has condensed them into three generic types that provide a good starting point for strategic thinking.[47]

1. **Overall cost leadership.** Here the business works hard to achieve the lowest costs. The problem with this strategy is that other firms usually emerge with still lower costs. The real key is for the firm to achieve the lowest costs among those competitors adopting a similar differentiation or focus strategy. Red Lobster has its own seafood supply chain to help achieve its low-cost leadership in the market.

2. **Differentiation.** Here the business concentrates on achieving superior performance in an important customer benefit area valued by a large part of the market. The relative importance of customer benefits shifts as demographic and psychographic characteristics of market populations change. In-N-Out differentiates themselves from the big burger chains by using fresh ingredients. The meat is cooked to order and french fries are hand-cut from whole potatoes.

   Although difficult, some firms have been successful by combining low-cost and differentiation strategy, a hybrid approach. Southwest Airlines designed a low-cost delivery system, but does not charge a change fee and bags fly for free.

3. **Focus.** Here the business focuses on one or more narrow market segments rather than going after a large market. The firm gets to know the needs of these segments and pursues either cost leadership or a form of differentiation within the target segments. Food trucks have become increasingly popular in major U.S. cities. They offer specialized and niche menus for those who seek authentic and regional dishes.

   The online air travel industry has provided a good example of these three strategies: Travelocity has pursued a differentiation strategy by offering the most comprehensive range of services to the traveler, Lowestfare has pursued a lowest-cost strategy for the leisure travel market, and Last Minute has pursued a niche strategy by focusing on travelers who have the flexibility to travel on very short notice.[48]

Marketing Planning

Marketing planning involves deciding on marketing strategies that will help the company attain its overall strategic objectives. A detailed marketing plan is needed for each business, product, or brand. The plan begins with an executive summary, which quickly overviews major assessments, goals, and recommendations. The main section of the plan presents a detailed SWOT analysis of the current marketing situation as well as potential threats and opportunities. The plan next states major objectives for the brand and outlines the specifics of a marketing strategy for achieving them.

A *marketing strategy* consists of specific strategies for target markets, positioning, the marketing mix, and marketing expenditure levels. It outlines how the company intends to create value for target customers in order to capture value in return. In this section, the planner explains how each strategy responds to the threats, opportunities, and critical issues spelled out earlier in the plan. Additional sections of the marketing plan lay out an action program for implementing the marketing strategy along with the details of a supporting *marketing budget*. The last section outlines the controls that will be used to monitor progress, measure return on marketing investment, and take corrective action. As a manager or a director of sales of a hospitality business, you will be required to develop a marketing plan every year. A well-developed marketing plan is critical to the success of a business. This is why we have devoted the last chapter of this book to developing a marketing plan.

Implementation

Even a clear strategy and well-thought-out supporting program may not be enough. The firm may fail at implementation. Employees in a company share a common way of behaving and thinking. They must understand and believe in the company's strategy. The company must communicate its strategy to its employees and make them understand their part in carrying it out. To implement a strategy, the firm must have the required resources, including employees with the necessary skills to carry out that strategy.

Feedback and Control

All companies need to track results and monitor new developments in the environment. The environment will change. When it does, the company will need to review its strategies or objectives. Peter Drucker pointed out that it is more important to do the right thing (being effective) than to do things right (being efficient). Excellent companies excel at both.

Once an organization starts losing its market position through failure to respond to a changed environment, it becomes increasingly harder to retrieve market leadership. Organizations, especially large ones, have much inertia. Yet, organizations can be changed through leadership, ideally in advance of a crisis.

The hotel-resort industry faces unique challenges in strategic planning. Most other members of the hospitality industry, such as airlines, cruise lines, and major restaurant chains, may approach strategic planning in much the same manner as a manufacturing company. These organizations have highly centralized management operations in which strategic decisions are made.

▪▪▪ Measuring and Managing Return on Marketing Investment

Marketing managers must ensure that their marketing dollars are being well spent. In the past, many marketers spent freely on big, expensive marketing programs, often without thinking carefully about the financial returns on their spending. They believed that marketing produces intangible creative outcomes, which do not lend themselves readily to measures of productivity or return. But in today's world, all that is changing.[49]

According to a recent study, as finances have tightened, marketers see return on marketing investment as the second biggest issue after the economy. "Increasingly, it is important for marketers to be able to justify their expenses," says one marketer. For a marketing program, says another, marketers need to ask themselves, "Do I have the right combination of strategy and tactics that will generate the most return in terms of share, revenue, and/or profit objectives from my investment?"[50]

In response, marketers are developing better measures of *marketing ROI*. **Return on marketing investment** or marketing ROI is the net return from a marketing investment divided by the costs of the marketing investment. It measures the profits generated by investments in marketing activities.

Return on marketing investment (or marketing ROI) The net return from a marketing investment divided by the costs of the marketing investment. It measures the profits generated by investments in marketing activities.

Dashboards, such as Revinate Dashboard, organize and present data creating an effective way for managers to access and understand key data. Courtesy of Revinate.

A recent survey found that although two-thirds of companies have implemented return on marketing investment programs in recent years, only 22 percent of companies report making good progress in measuring marketing ROI. Another survey of chief financial officers reported that 93 percent of those surveyed are dissatisfied with their ability to measure marketing ROI. The major problem is figuring out what specific measures to use and obtaining good data on these measures.[51]

A company can assess marketing ROI in terms of standard marketing performance measures, such as brand awareness, sales, or market share. Increasingly, however, beyond standard performance measures, marketers are using customer-centered measures such as customer acquisition, customer engagement, customer experience, customer loyalty and lifetime value, and customer equity.

Many companies are assembling such measures into *marketing dashboards*—meaningful sets of marketing performance measures in a single display used to monitor strategic marketing performance. Just as automobile dashboards present drivers with details on how their cars are performing, the marketing dashboard gives marketers the detailed measures they need to assess and adjust their marketing strategies.

There is commercial software that produces dashboards for both lodging and food-service operations. Searchview by TravelClickHotels is designed to give an instant update of one's online presence, including production by online travel agencies (OTAs), page presence of these agencies, your star ratings on the OTA, performance of pay-per-click (PPC) activities, and the individual customer ratings and comments. A company can also compare its ratings with its competitors on sites such as travel click. Restaurant dashboards can include sales mix reports, reports on promotions, coupon redemption, information on each comp, payroll costs, and costs of goods sold. Up until a few years ago intelligence would have been cost prohibitive for the individual property to collect.

A growing number of companies provide dashboards showing customer ratings of a business across selected social media sites and comparing them with those of competitors. These dashboards enhance a manager's ability to monitor user-generated content (UGC) and manage online branding.

Revinate, a Software as a Service (SaaS) tech company, provides such a platform built exclusively for hotels to track and manage their social media reviews and online reputation and to connect with their guests in real time. The company provides benchmarking dashboards including ratings across multiple social media sites, trend analysis to compare a property's performance to that of a competitive set, customer sentiment analysis summarizing positive and negative online reviews, performance reports (ADR, RevPAR [revenue per available room], and Occupancy), and monthly property report.

▬▬▬ CHAPTER REVIEW

I. The Nature of High-Performance Business
A. Stakeholder. Stakeholders include customers, employees, suppliers, and the communities where their business is located and other people or organizations that have an interest in the success of the business. A business must at least strive to satisfy the minimum expectations of each stakeholder group.

B. Processes. Companies build cross-functional teams that manage core business processes in order to be superior competitors.

C. Resources. Companies decide to outsource less critical resources. They identify their core competencies and use them as the basis for their strategic planning.

D. Organization. Companies align their organization's structure, policies, and culture to the changing requirements of business strategy.

II. Corporate Strategic Planning: Defining Marketing's Role
A. Defining the corporate mission. A mission statement is a statement of the organization's purpose—what it wants to accomplish in the larger environment.

B. **Setting company objectives and goals.** The company needs to turn its mission into detailed supporting objectives for each level of management. Marketing strategies and programs must be developed to support these marketing objectives.

C. **Designing the business portfolio.** Market definitions of a business are superior to product definitions. A business must be viewed as a customer-satisfying process, not a product-producing process. Companies should define their business in terms of customer needs, not products. Companies have to identify their strategic business units (SBUs), those single businesses or collections of related businesses that can be planned separately from the rest of the company. SBUs should be assigned strategic-planning goals and funding.
   1. **Developing strategies for growth.** Companies need growth if they are to compete and attract top talent.
      a. Ansoff product–market expansion grid offers a useful framework for examining growth.
   2. **Diversification growth.** Makes sense when good opportunities can be found outside the present businesses
      a. **Concentric diversification strategy.** The company could seek new products that have technological or marketing synergies with existing product lines, even though the products may appeal to a new class of customers.
      b. **Horizontal diversification strategy.** The company might search for new products that could appeal to its current customers, although technologically unrelated to its current product line.
      c. **Conglomerate diversification strategy.** The company might seek new businesses that have no relationship to the company's current technology, products, or markets.
   3. **Integrative growth.** Opportunities in diversification, market development, and product development can be seized through integrating backward, forward, or horizontally within that business's industry.
      a. **Backward integration.** A growth strategy by which companies acquire businesses supplying them with products or services (e.g., a restaurant chain purchasing a bakery).
      b. **Forward integration.** A growth strategy by which companies acquire businesses that are closer to the ultimate consumer, such as a hotel acquiring a chain of travel agents.
      c. **Horizontal integration.** A growth strategy by which a company acquires one or more competitors.
   4. **Downsizing.** When a firm finds brands or businesses that are unprofitable or that no longer fit its overall strategy. It must carefully prune, harvest, or divest them.

III. **Planning Marketing: Partnering to Build Customer Relationships**
   A. **Partnership with other company departments.** The major functional departments in each unit—marketing, finance, accounting, purchasing, operations, information systems, human resources, and others—must work together to accomplish strategic objectives.
   B. **Partnering with others in the marketing systems.** Competition no longer takes place only between individual competitors. Rather, it takes place between the entire value delivery networks created by these competitors.

IV. **Marketing Strategy and the Marketing Mix**
   A. **Customer value-driven marketing strategy.** Before it can satisfy consumers, a company must first understand their needs and wants. Thus, sound marketing requires a careful customer analysis. Each company must divide up the total market, choose the best segments, and design strategies for profitably serving chosen segments.
      1. **Market segmentation.** The market consists of many types of customers, products, and needs. The marketer must determine which segments offer the best opportunities. Consumers can be grouped and served in various ways based on geographic, demographic, psychographic, and behavioral factors.
      2. **Market targeting.** Market targeting involves evaluating each market segment's attractiveness and selecting one or more segments to enter. A company should target segments in which it can profitably generate the greatest customer value and sustain it over time.
      3. **Market differentiation and positioning.** After a company has decided which market segments to enter, it must decide how it will differentiate its market offering for each targeted segment and what positions it wants to occupy in those segments.
   B. **Developing an integrated marketing mix.**
   The marketing mix is the set of controllable, tactical marketing tools that the firm blends to produce the response it wants in the target market. The many possibilities can be collected into four groups of variables known as the four Ps: *product, price, place,* and *promotion* or the four As: *acceptability, affordability, accessibility,* and *awareness*. An effective marketing program blends all of the marketing mix elements into an integrated marketing program designed to achieve the company's marketing objectives by delivering value to consumers.

V. **Managing the Marketing Effort**
   A. **Marketing analysis.** Managing the marketing function begins with a complete analysis of the company's situation. The marketer should conduct a SWOT analysis, by which it evaluates the company's overall strengths (S), weaknesses (W), opportunities (O), and threats (T).

1. **Internal environmental analysis** (strengths and weaknesses analysis)
   a. **Strengths.** Internal capabilities, resources, and positive situational factors that may help the company to serve its customers and achieve its objectives.
   b. **Weaknesses.** Internal limitations and negative situational factors that may interfere with the company's performance.
2. **External environmental analysis** (opportunity and threat analysis). In general, a business unit has to monitor key **macroenvironmental forces** (demographic-economic, technological, political-legal, and social-cultural) and significant **microenvironmental forces** (customers, competitors, distribution channels, and supplies) that will affect its ability to earn profits in the marketplace.

   Opportunities are favorable factors or trends in the external environment that the company may be able to exploit to its advantage. Threats are external factors or trends that may present challenges to performance.

B. **Goal formulation.** After the business unit has defined its mission and conducted a SWOT analysis, it can proceed to develop specific objectives and goals. Most business units pursue a mix of objectives, including profitability, sales growth, market share improvement, and cost containment. There are three generic types of strategies for achieving goals:

1. **Overall cost leadership.** The real key is for the firm to achieve the lowest costs among those competitors adopting a similar differentiation or focus strategy.
2. **Differentiation.** The business concentrates on achieving superior performance in an important customer benefit area valued by a large part of the market.
3. **Focus.** The business focuses on one or more narrow market segments rather than going after a large market.

C. **Marketing planning.** Marketing planning involves deciding on marketing strategies that will help the company attain its overall strategic objectives. A detailed marketing plan is needed for each business, product, or brand.

D. **Implementation.** To implement a strategy, the firm must have the required resources, including employees with the necessary skills to carry out that strategy.

E. **Feedback and control.** All companies need to track results and monitor new developments in the environment. The environment will change. When it does, the company will need to review its strategies or objectives.

VI. **Measuring and Managing Return on Marketing Investment**

A. Marketing managers must ensure that their marketing dollars are being well spent. Return on marketing investment or marketing ROI is the net return from a marketing investment divided by the costs of the marketing investment. It measures the profits generated by investments in marketing activities.

IN-CLASS GROUP ACTIVITIES

Exercises with an asterisk next to them are suitable for individual homework or online assignments. Always provide an explanation for your answer.

1. *Find the mission statement of a hospitality or travel company on the internet. Critique the mission statement against the guidelines for a mission statement, as stated in the text.
2. *Visit the annual report of a hospitality organization (these can usually be accessed through the company's home page). What does the annual report tell you about the organization's strategy?
3. *From your earlier analysis, suggest a strategy from the product–market expansion grid and an appropriate marketing mix to implement the strategy.

EXPERIENTIAL EXERCISES

Do one of the following:

1. Visit two hotels, restaurants, or other hospitality businesses. From your observations write down what you think are the strengths and weaknesses of the businesses. You will be able to observe elements such as location, physical facilities, employee attitude, quality of products, reputation of the brand (if it is a brand), and other factors.
2. Find a strategic alliance between a hotel company and another company (this can be for another hospitality organization or a company outside the hospitality industry). State what you think the benefits of the alliance are for each partner.
3. Conduct a SWOT analysis for a hospitality company near your college.
4. Think about the shopping area near your campus. Assume that you wish to start a business here and are looking for a promising opportunity for a restaurant. Is there an opportunity to open a distinctive and promising business? Describe your target market and how you would serve it differently than current businesses do.

REFERENCES

1. John Kell, "Starbucks Wants Your Phone as Much as It Wants to Sell You Coffee," *Fortune*, July 24, 2015, http://fortune.com/2015/07/24/starbucks-mobile-investments/; David Kaplan, "Starbucks: The Art of Endless Transformation," *Inc.*, June, 2014, pp. 82–86; Laura Lorenzetti, "Fortune's World's Most Admired Companies: Starbucks, Where Innovation Is Always Brewing," *Fortune*, October 30, 2014, http://fortune.com/2014/10/30/starbucks-innovation-cafe-to-classroom/; "Starbucks Corporation: Fiscal 2007 Annual Report," http://media.corporate-ir.net/media_files/irol/99/99518/2007AR.pdf; Julia Hanna, "Starbucks, Reinvented: A Seven-Year Study on Schultz, Strategy, and Reinventing a Brilliant Brand," *Forbes*, August 25, 2014, www.forbes.com/sites/hbsworkingknowledge/2014/08/25/starbucks-reinvented/; Bryan Pearson, "Starbucks Loyalty Program Change Brews Anger, Filters Out Value of Experience," *Forbes*, February 24, 2016, www.forbes.com/sites/bryanpearson/2016/02/24/starbucks-loyalty-change-brews-anger-filters-out-value-of-experience/print/; http://roastery.starbucks.com (accessed September 2016); and Starbucks annual reports and other information accessed at www.starbucks.com, September 2016.

2. See Tamara J. Erickson and Everett Shorey, "Business Strategy: New Thinking for the 90s," *Prism* (4th Quarter 1992): 19–35.

3. Dieter Huckestein and Robert Duboff, "Hilton Hotels: A Comprehensive Approach to Delivering Value for All Stakeholders," *The Cornell HRA Quarterly* (August 28–38, 1999); http://www.bscdesigner.com/bsc-for-hotel-top-management.htm (accessed February 2015); http://news.hiltonworldwide.com/index.cfm/newsroom/detail/26370 (accessed February 2015).

4. Kyuho Lee, Mahmood A. Khan, and Jae-Youn Ko, "Outback Steakhouse in Korea: A Success Story," *The Cornell Hospitality Quarterly*, 49, no. 1 (2008): 62–72.

5. Lisa Richwine, "Disney Earnings Beat Despite Shaky Economy," Reuters.com, February 8, 2012, www.reuters.com/article/2012/02/08/us-disney-idUSTRE8161TE20120208; http://corporate.disney.go.comlinvestors/annual_reports.html (accessed July 2013).

6. Patrick Legoherel, Philippe Callot, Karine Gallopel, and Mike Peters, "Personality Characteristics, Attitude Toward Risk and Decisional Orientation of the Small Business Entrepreneur: A Study of Hospitality Managers," *Journal of Hospitality and Tourism Research*, 28, no. 1 (2004): 117–118.

7. For more on mission statements, see Frank Buytendijk, "Five Keys to Building a High-Performance Organization," *Business Performance Management* (February 2006): 24–29; Joseph Peyrefitte and Forest R. David, "A Content Analysis of Mission Statements of United States Firms in Four Industries," *International Journal of Management* (June 2006): 296–301; Jeffrey Abrahams, *101 Mission Statements from Top Companies* (Berkeley, CA: Ten Speed Press, 2007).

8. See http://www.ritzcarlton.com/en/about/gold-standards and https://www.chipotle.com/food-with-integrity (accessed May 29, 2018).

9. "Mission Statements for the Next Millennium," *Restaurant Hospitality* (December 1998): 46.

10. www.scotland-edinburgh.co.uh/hotel-home.asp, Prestonfield-Edinburgh's most indulgent retreat, 2008.

11. For more discussion, see Laura Nash, "Mission Statements: Mirrors and Windows," *Harvard Business Review* (March/April 1988): 155–156. See also Tom Feltenstein, "Strategic Planning for the 1990s: Exploiting the Inevitable," *Cornell Hotel and Restaurant Administration Quarterly*, 33, no. 3 (1994): 45.

12. See https://www.mandarinoriental.com/about-us/ (accessed May 19, 2018).

13. Based on information from "Buffalo Wild Wings," a 22SQUARED case study, September 5, 2012, http://22squared.com/work/projec/buffalo-wild-wings-flavor-fanatics-case-study; Lauren Johnson, "Buffalo Wild Wings Mobile Campaign Increased Purchase Intent by 45pc," *Mobile Commerce Daily*, April 15, 2013, www.mobilecommercedaily.com/buffalo-wild-wings-mobile-campaign-increases-purchase-intent-by-45pc; Brandon Southward, "The Crowd Goes Wild," *Fortune* (July 22, 2013): 18; www.buffalowildwings.com/about/ (accessed September 2014). Buffalo Wild Wings® is a registered trademark of Buffalo Wild Wings, Inc.

14. Phillip Kotler, Hermawan Kartajaya, and Iwan Setiawan, *Marketing 3.0* (New Jersey: John Wiley & Sons, Inc., 2010).

15. See http://www.shangri-la.com/corporate/about-us/corporate-social-responsibility/sustainability/mission-statement/ (accessed March 2015).

16. See http://www.starwoodhotels.com/corporate/about/citizenship/index.html (accessed February 2015).

17. See http://www.marriott.com/corporate-social-responsibility/corporate-environmental-responsibility.mi (accessed January 2015).

18. See http://www.chicagobusiness.com/article/20140325/OPINION/140329895/corporate-social-responsibility-is-millennials-new-religion (accessed March 2014).

19. See the BASF Innovations Web page, www.corporate.basi.comJenJinnovationenI7idZj-HA6M0bcp4PX (accessed November 2007).

20. Theodore Levitt, "Marketing Myopia," *Harvard Business Review* (July/August 1960): 45–46.

21. See http://www.expediagroup.com/expedia-brands/ (accessed April 15, 2018).

Understanding the Marketplace and Customer Value

4 Analyzing the Marketing Environment

5 Managing Customer Information to Gain Customer Insights

6 Consumer Markets and Consumer Buying Behavior

7 Organizational Buyer Behavior

8 Customer-Driven Marketing Strategy: Creating Value

Courtesy of Castle Rock Adventist Health Campus.

4

Objectives

After reading this chapter, you should be able to:

1. Summarize the components of a company's marketing environment.
2. Describe the microenvironmental forces that affect the company's ability to serve its customers.
3. Describe the macroenvironmental forces that affect the company's ability to serve its customers.
4. Discuss how companies can be proactive rather than reactive when responding to environmental trends.

Analyzing the Marketing Environment

Manna Restaurant: A Popular Community Restaurant Within the Castle Rock Adventist Hospital

Hospitality marketing is by no means confined to the for-profit sector. Today, many nonprofit organizations have embraced marketing concepts. Alumni returning to universities and colleges are often amazed at changes in recreational and eating facilities on campus. Many of these hospitals replicate designs used in the for-profit sector. Hospitals used to have very poor reputations for the quality and presentation of their food. Castle Rock Adventist Hospital in Castle Rock, Colorado, offers an example of a nonprofit organization that carefully developed a winning hospital and restaurant by paying close attention to environmental and societal concerns and blending them with their own lifestyle choices.

Castle Rock, Colorado, a community of over 50,000 residents, has a young (median age 33) and well-educated (45 percent college degrees) population with household incomes well above those for the state of Colorado in general.[1] Located south of Denver, this city looks west to the foothills and then the towering Rocky Mountain Range. Given their scenic location, residents are highly concerned about environmental issues.

Castle Rock Adventist Hospital opened in August 2013 and reflects the environmental and societal concerns of the community. It also reflects the values of its sponsor, the Adventist Health System (AHS), the largest not-for-profit Protestant health-care system in the United States with 38 hospitals, nursing homes, and in-home care agencies supporting 44,000 employees and serving over 4 million people each year. One of these values centers on supporting the community in living as healthy as possible through a wellness model called Creation Health.

The hospital was designed to provide patients with views of the nearby mountains. Research has shown that views of nature from a patient's window create a positive healing environment. A community service the hospital provided is the Garden of Eatin', a largest community in Colorado. Members of the community have access to the garden to grow fresh nutritious natural foods. Other hospital features include a fitness program based on the Creation Health model for wellness based on choice, rest, environment, activity, trust, interpersonal relationships, outlook, and nutrition.

Within the hospital's environment, a new restaurant concept was planned by Chef Dan Skay, a graduate of the Culinary Institute of America, who felt that the restaurant should serve the community, not just hospital staff and patient visitors. Dan and the hospital's chief executive officer (CEO), Todd Folkenberg, believed that the nutrition department should provide healthy dining alternatives for the community. Manna Restaurant was designed to be a destination, full-service restaurant complete with customer-oriented service. Unlike many restaurants, Manna offers community cooking classes to encourage the preparation of healthy meals.

Local sources of provisions are used when possible by Manna Restaurant. Honey supplies are local as are vegetables from the Garden of Eatin'. To help ensure a year-round supply of fresh herbs, the hospital plans to build a hydroponic garden.

Initial challenges were convincing the leadership that a different model of meal service was possible to meet the needs of the staff, as well as guests and the community. Concerns for quick service and staff meals were met by the addition of a c-store (Manna Market) selling barista coffees, convenience items, salad bar, and carryout hot meals. In addition to the Manna Market, the restaurant incorporated a call-ahead service for to-go meals, called Manna on the Move, and patient food service called Bedside Manna.

Menus were designed to be "veggie centric" but not exclusively veggie. Forty to fifty percent of the menu items are veggie. Meat is used in several dishes with quality as an overriding concern. Thus, grass-fed beef and free-range chickens are used.

Project design was a critical factor to ensure customer satisfaction. It called for a kitchen with a central circulation spine to accommodate traffic moving from receiving and storage into the production areas. This allowed food to be delivered to specific areas without interfering with production. Ware washing facilities were strategically placed to allow for delivery of soiled patient meal carts and restaurant dishes through two separate entrances to avoid cross-contamination.

Green design concepts were incorporated with dining and kitchen areas displaying floor to ceiling windows allowing for natural sunlight, a water-efficient dish machine, utility distribution system for equipment flexibility/modification with energy-efficient equipment, and a computer hood system. Moving from a cafeteria model to a traditional restaurant galley resulted in minimized food waste. Some by-products are composted for use in the onsite community gardens. Since opening, wind turbines and solar panels have been added on the roof. These supply up to 30 percent of the facilities' electricity.

Much of the kitchen's equipment was strategically placed to allow visibility from the dining room, including the double-windowed hearth oven. Aesthetic consideration was given to local influences of wood, stone, and iron structures within the restaurant's interior, from local artwork and handcrafted wood community table to the use of Rhyolite (a stone native to Castle Rock) stonework.

Combining patient room service and restaurant kitchens allowed Manna to minimize the amount of equipment needed as compared to normal cafeterias with separate production areas. As a result, a chef-inspired European-style cook island and high-end equipment were purchased to help drive functionality/efficiency and customer appreciation. The design of the open chef exhibition window allowed patrons to dine and view the kitchen while offering minimal intrusion to the chefs. Having a streamlined production area also improved labor efficiency, team work, shared production, and ease of cross training. Separate expo lines and windows for room service and the restaurant allowed smooth delivery of meals, again with customer needs in mind.

Without the need to duplicate production and service areas, the ability to purchase high-end furnishings and kitchen equipment was possible. These additions resulted in fewer repairs and less replacement cost. This efficient service model changed staff load. Fewer cooks allowed more hospitality serving staff, resulting in significant cost savings and high customer satisfaction. In turn, this permitted Manna Restaurant to pay above-market wages to the wait staff.

Manna Restaurant exceeded expectations for the 50-bed hospital by generating an average of $130,000 a month in restaurant revenue. With Manna's quick grab and go market and eclectic contemporary lunch/dinner menu, Manna does approximately 350–400 covers daily with a check average of $9. Approximately 85 percent of traffic into the restaurant is community driven, helping Manna achieve high ratings on YELP for Castle Rock restaurants. Patrons do not have to tip, but often do. As a result, a Foundation was created from tips to fund many local nonprofit and community-wellness-related projects. Fund-related events and projects are communicated to restaurant guests and the community through various projects like FreeCycle, a free bike-rental program within the city.

The overall objective of this project was to meet the proactive health needs of the community by delivering innovative dishes to fuel health and wellness in a nurturing and restful atmosphere. With the chef-driven design and ease of flow from production to delivery, chances for success were enhanced. Like the game of tennis, if you can't serve well, you will never win. All aspects of this design allowed customers to be the ultimate winners!

The Company's Environment

Marketing environment The actors and forces outside marketing that affect marketing management's ability to develop and maintain successful transactions with its target customers.

A company's **marketing environment** consists of outside actors and forces that affect a company's ability to build and maintain successful relationships with its target customers. The marketing environment offers both opportunities and threats. Successful companies know the vital importance of constantly watching and adapting to the changing environment.

Managers who practice marketing will be the trend trackers and opportunity seekers. Good marketers have two special aptitudes. They have disciplined methods—marketing intelligence—for collecting information about the marketing environment. They also spend more time in the customer and competitor environments. By carefully studying the environment, marketers can adapt marketing strategies to meet new marketplace challenges and opportunities.

Microenvironment The forces close to a company that affect its ability to serve its customers: the company, market channel firms, customer markets, competitors, and the public.

Macroenvironment The larger societal forces that affect the whole microenvironment: competitive, demographic, economic, natural, technological, political, and cultural forces.

The marketing environment is made up of a microenvironment and a macroenvironment. The **microenvironment** consists of factors close to the company that affect its ability to serve its customers, the company itself, marketing channel firms, customer markets, and a broad range of publics. The **macroenvironment** consists of larger societal forces that affect the entire microenvironment, that is, demographic, economic, natural, technological, political, competitor, and cultural forces. We first examine the company's microenvironment and then its macroenvironment.

The Microenvironment

Marketing management's job is to build relationships with customers by creating customer value and satisfaction. This requires working closely with the company's microenvironment. These actors are shown in Figure 4–1. They include supplier, market intermediaries, customers, and publics that combine to make up the company's value delivery system.

Figure 4–1
Major actors in the company's microenvironment.

The Company

Marketing managers must work closely with top management and the various company departments. The finance department is concerned with finding and using funds required to carry out the company's plans. The accounting department has to measure revenues and costs to help marketing know how well it is achieving its objectives. Housekeeping is responsible for delivering clean rooms sold by the sales department. Top management sets the company's mission, objectives, broad strategies, and policies. Marketing decisions must be made within the strategies and plans made by top management.

Under the marketing concept, all managers, supervisors, and employees must "think consumer." They should work in harmony to provide superior customer value and satisfaction. Together, all departments have an impact on the marketing department's plans and actions.

Existing Competitors

We include competitors in both the microenvironment and macroenvironment. Existing customers are part of the microenvironment. Every company faces a broad range of existing competitors. The marketing concept holds that a successful company must satisfy the needs and wants of consumers better than its competitors. It must also adapt to the strategies of other companies serving the same target markets. Companies must gain strategic advantage by strongly positioning their product in the minds of consumers.

No single competitive marketing strategy is best for all companies. Each firm must consider its size and industry position in relation to that of its competitors. Large firms with dominant positions in an industry can use strategies that smaller firms cannot afford. Small firms can also choose strategies that give them certain advantages. For example, a large restaurant chain can use its buying power to purchase national advertising, spreading the cost among hundreds or thousands of operations. But small individually owned restaurants are able to adjust quickly to local trends and can offer more menu variety because they do not have to worry about standardizing menu items across thousands of restaurants. Both large and small firms must find marketing strategies that give them specific advantages over competitors. A company should monitor market share when analyzing competitors. Market share is the portion of the target market held by each player.

Managers often fail to identify their competitors correctly. The manager of a Houston seafood restaurant said that his restaurant had no competition because there were no other seafood restaurants within several miles. Months later the restaurant was out of business. Customers decided to spend their money at competitors, either by driving farther to other seafood restaurants or by dining at non-seafood restaurants. Our research has shown that only about 40 percent of the customers that rate a hotel or restaurant as being good will return. The figure jumps to 90 percent when customers give a rating of excellent. Competitive forces are so strong in our industry that being good is no longer good enough. We must strive for excellence.

One of the authors found that although 78 percent of the customers came to a casino regularly and were considered loyal customers, only 34 percent were considered truly loyal. The other 44 percent he called spurious loyals. In addition to having the behavioral loyalty of coming to the casino regularly, true loyals exhibited attitudinal loyalty, and as a result they were more likely to recommend the casino to a friend. Spurious loyals are not emotionally attached to the casino and are likely to leave if a new casino opens. It is important for managers to understand how many of their customers might be at risk if a new competitor opens in their market area.[2]

Every company faces the following four levels of competitors (see Figure 4–2):

1. A company can view its competitors as companies that offer similar products and services to the same customers at a similar price. At this level, McDonald's views its competition as Burger King and Wendy's.

2. A company can see its competitors as all companies making the same product or class of products. Here McDonald's may see its competition as all fast-food restaurants, including KFC, Taco Bell, Jamba Juice, and Arby's.

3. A company can see its competitors more broadly as all companies supplying the same service. Here McDonald's would see itself competing with all restaurants and other suppliers of prepared food, such as the deli section of a supermarket.

4. A company can see its competitors even more broadly as all competitors that compete for the same consumer dollars. Here McDonald's would see itself competing with the self-provision of the meal by the consumer.[3]

Figure 4–2
Levels of competition.
Source: Based on *Analysis for Market Planning*, Donald R. Lehmann and Russell S. Winer, p. 22, 1994, by Richard D. Irwin.

Suppliers Firms and individuals that provide the resources needed by a company and its competitors to produce goods and services.

Inland seafood restaurants need to have reliable suppliers with whom they have developed a good relationship. Duybox/123RF.

Putting this framework into action, Subway sandwich shops came out with advertising targeting second-level competition. The ads stressed the nutritional value of their sandwiches compared with other types of fast food, such as hamburgers. The McDonald's "You deserve a break today" advertising campaign was aimed at the fourth level of competition, telling people to give themselves a break from cooking. Carnival Cruise Lines viewed its competition at the third level, that is, as other vacation destinations, such as Hawaii and Las Vegas.

Suppliers

Suppliers are firms and individuals that provide the resources needed by the company to produce its goods and services. Trends and developments affecting suppliers can, in turn, seriously affect a company's marketing plan. Suppose that a restaurant manager decides to run a live lobster special for the weekend. The seafood supplier promises to supply 200 lobsters for the weekend promotion. Friday morning the supplier calls and reports that lobsters were shorted on the shipment from Boston, and they will not be delivered until Saturday morning. The manager must now find alternative sources or disappoint guests who have reservations for Friday night.

In another case, a restaurant chain wanted to add a new scallop seafood dish to its menu. The corporate office spent six months perfecting the scallop dish. During the development period, the price of scallops doubled. The restaurant would now have to charge a price higher than customers would pay. The project was scrapped. Management must pay attention to changes in supply availability (as affected by shortages and strikes) and supply costs.

Some hotels have contracted with restaurant companies to supply their food and beverage services. The New York-New York in Las Vegas contracted with ARK restaurants to manage its restaurants.[4] These and other hotels are bringing branded restaurants to their hotels to create value for their guests and expose restaurant guests to the hotel. The outsourcing of food and beverage operations allows the hotel to concentrate on lodging while letting a food and beverage specialist handle this area within the hotel. There are several ways to partner with a celebrity chef or branded restaurant. One is paying a licensing fee or management fee for a celebrity chef to oversee a restaurant and put his or her name on the restaurant. The fees generally run from 4 to 7 percent of the gross revenue. The second is a partnering deal where the chef is an equity partner, usually taking a 30–50 percent share of the equity. Additionally, the chef gets a 3–6 percent management fee. This creates more of a commitment on the chef's part because the chef now shares directly in the profits of the restaurant.[5]

On paper this sounds like a great arrangement, and in real life it often works out well. However, the outsourcing is not as simple as it may seem. Focus groups of business travelers have told us that a coffee shop suitable for a business meeting is sometimes the deciding factor in the choice of a hotel. A problem for some hotels that have leased their operations to upscale operators is that upscale restaurant operators often are not interested in the coffee shop and room service operations, and these operations suffer as a result. Another problem is that the leasing of food-service operations ties up hotel space through lease agreements. This can be a problem if the hotel decides to renovate and change the design of the public spaces. When hotel guests complain about poor food service at the front desk, telling the guest that the hotel does not operate the restaurants is *not* an acceptable answer. Thus, service recovery programs need to be worked out between the restaurant and the hotel. Suppliers of food and beverage for a hotel have to be chosen carefully. The concept works best when the restaurant brought in for its brand name operates just the restaurant on an equity basis. The coffee shop, room service, and banquet operations are best left to the hotel to run.

Some restaurant chains have developed close relationships with selected suppliers. The Chick-fil-A chain teamed with THRIVE Farmers, a Costa Rica producer co-op, to provide specialty grade coffee to its restaurant patrons. Under this relationship, coffee farmers can earn as much as 10 times more income than by sales through traditional channels. David Farmer, vice president of Product Strategy and Development for Chick-fil-A, said, "Now we are able to serve our customers an amazing cup of coffee that will also improve the lives of the farmer who grows it."[6] This relationship also provided Chick-fil-A with many public relations opportunities such as through social media and in-store information on coffee cups and paper mats on serving trays.

Tourist destinations need suppliers. Airline service, hotels, restaurants, ground operations, meeting facilities, and entertainment are some of the components of a tourist destination. One of the roles of a regional convention and visitors' bureau (CVB) is to make sure there is a good selection of suppliers of tourist products in their area. They must recruit organizations to provide visitors with a variety of tourist activities and options. CVBs must also work to represent the interests of these suppliers to make sure they do well after they are recruited.

Marketing Intermediaries

Marketing intermediaries Firms that help the company to promote, sell, and distribute its goods to final buyers; they include middlemen, physical distribution firms, marketing service agencies, and financial intermediaries.

Disintermediation The elimination of intermediaries.

Marketing intermediaries help the company promote, sell, and distribute its goods to the final buyers. Intermediaries are business firms that help hospitality companies find customers or make sales. They include travel agents, wholesale tour operators, hotel representatives, and online travel agencies (OTAs), such as Expedia, Travelocity, and Orbitz. The OTAs bundle airfare with hotel rooms, creating value for the customer.

The internet has created both disintermediation and pricing transparency. **Disintermediation** is the elimination of intermediaries. Hotels have created their own internet reservation systems, referred to as Brand.com (where the name of the company replaces "Brand," e.g., Hyatt.com). The brands are now less dependent on

Beverage companies provide marketing support for chain restaurants that distribute its products. Hisham Ibrahim/PhotoV/Alamy Stock Photo.

intermediaries, but still use them to provide extra demand. The demand cannot be filled through direct channels. Small hotels can now distribute their products worldwide over the internet.

When hotels sell to intermediaries who use the internet, they have to be careful of price transparency. For example, group rates for associations often include free rooms for the association directors, which are factored into the hotel room rate. The association is also required to book a set number of rooms to take advantage of the complimentary services. If the group is given a rate of $229 per night for a hotel room and members of the organization can book directly on the hotel's Web site for $209, then the members may choose to book directly rather than going through the association's block. Hotel sales managers should either set the prices of groups the same as group prices or give the group credit toward meeting their room block with people who have booked directly through the hotel. The internet has created many distribution opportunities, but it has also made interactions with intermediaries and end users more complex.

Thus, today's marketers recognize the importance of working with their intermediaries as partners rather than simply as channels through which they sell their products. For example, restaurants serve as intermediaries for soft drink companies when they sign an agreement to exclusively distribute the soft drink company's products to their customers. When Coca-Cola signs on as the exclusive beverage provider for a fast-food chain, such as McDonald's, Wendy's, or Subway, it provides much more than just soft drinks. It also pledges powerful marketing support.[7]

Coca-Cola assigns cross-functional teams dedicated to understanding the finer points of each retail partner's business. It conducts a staggering amount of research on beverage consumers and shares these insights with its partners. It analyzes the demographics of U.S. zip code areas and helps partners determine which Coke brands are preferred in their areas. Coca-Cola has even studied the design of drive-through menu boards to better understand which layouts, fonts, letter sizes, colors, and visuals induce consumers to order certain items. Based on such insights, the Coca-Cola Food Service group develops marketing programs and merchandising tools that help its retail partners improve their beverage sales and profits. Such intense partnering efforts have made Coca-Cola a leader in the U.S. fountain soft drink market. Coca-Cola and other major suppliers realize that they are your partners. If the restaurant does well, they sell their product.

Marketing services agencies are suppliers that help the firm formulate and implement its marketing strategy and tactics. These suppliers include public relations agencies, advertising agencies, and direct mail houses. They work directly with the company's marketing program and also include marketing research firms, media firms, and marketing consulting firms, which help companies target and promote their products to the right markets. These firms vary in creativity, quality, service, and price. The company should regularly review performance and replace service firms that no longer perform well.

Financial intermediaries include banks, credit companies, insurance companies, and other firms that help hospitality companies finance their transactions or insure the risks associated with the buying and selling of goods and services. Rising insurance costs, in particular liquor liability insurance, have forced some hospitality firms out of business. Because rising credit costs, limited credit, or both can seriously affect a company's marketing performance, the company has to develop strong relationships with important financial institutions. Small multiunit chains often feel the pressure to grow to keep their stock price up and their stockholders happy. This is what happened to Boston Market, Fuddrucker's, and Del Taco. These companies reorganized and recovered, but they went through hard times. Companies must be careful that they do not succumb to unmanageable growth expectations.

Marketing services agencies
Marketing research firms, advertising agencies, media firms, marketing consulting firms, and other service providers that help a company to target and promote its products to the right markets.

Financial intermediaries
Banks, credit companies, insurance companies, and other businesses that help finance transactions or insure against the risks associated with the buying and selling of goods.

Customers

The hospitality company needs to study five types of general customer markets closely. Consumer markets consist of individuals and households that purchase hospitality services for leisure activities, medical needs, and gatherings such as reunions, weddings, or funerals. Business markets buy hospitality services to facilitate their business. This can be individual rooms for travelers representing the company or for group meetings the company or organization may conduct. Companies have sales meetings, and associations have annual conventions. Resellers purchase a product and then resell it. For example, a tour operator may purchase airline seats, hotel rooms, ground transportation, and restaurant meals to package a tour, which will be resold to the consumer market. Government markets are made up of government agencies that purchase hospitality services for individual travelers and meetings. They often have room rates that are limited by government per diem rates. Finally, international markets consist of those buyers in other countries, including consumers, businesses, resellers, and governments. Each market type has special characteristics that call for careful study by the seller. We discuss these characteristics in Chapters 6 and 7.

Publics

Public Any group that has an actual or potential interest in or impact on an organization's ability to achieve its objectives.

The company's marketing environment also includes various publics. A **public** is any group that has an actual or potential interest in or impact on an organization's ability to achieve its objectives. We identify the following seven types of publics:

- Financial publics. These influence the company's ability to obtain funds. Banks, investment houses, and stockholders are the major financial publics.

- Media publics. These carry news, features, and editorial opinions. They include newspapers, magazines, and radio and television stations.

- Government publics. Management must take government developments into account. Marketers often consult the company's lawyers on issues of product safety, truth in advertising, and other matters.

- Citizen-action publics. A company's marketing decisions may be questioned by consumer organizations, environmental groups, minority groups, and others. Its public relations department can help it stay in touch with consumer and citizen groups.

- Local publics. These include neighborhood residents and community organizations. Large companies usually appoint a community relations officer to deal with the community, attend meetings, answer questions, and contribute to worthwhile causes.

- General publics. A company needs to be concerned about the general public's attitude toward its products and activities. The public's image of the company affects its buying.

- Internal publics. These include workers, managers, volunteers, and the board of directors. Large companies use newsletters and other means to inform and motivate their internal publics. When employees feel good about their company, this positive attitude spills over to better customer service.

A company can prepare marketing plans for these major publics as well as for its customer markets. Suppose the company wants a specific response from a particular public, such as goodwill, favorable word of mouth, or donations of time or money. The company would need to design an offer to this public that is attractive enough to produce the desired response. For example, casino resorts in Las Vegas discuss how they are making efforts to conserve water when they announce plans for a new resort. They know that local residents and local government will be concerned about this issue.

The Company's Macroenvironment

The company and all of the other actors operate in a larger macroenvironment of forces. Figure 4–3 shows the seven major forces in the company's macroenvironment. In the remaining sections of this chapter, we examine these forces and show how they affect marketing plans.

Competitors

We consider future competitors as part of the macroenvironment. The entrance of future competitors is often difficult to predict and can have a major effect on existing businesses.

Barriers to Entry, Exit, and Competition

Two forces that affect competition are the ability of companies to enter and exit markets.[8] Entry barriers prevent firms from getting into a business, and barriers to exit prevent them from leaving. Low barriers to entry characterize the restaurant industry. It takes a relatively small amount of capital to get started in the restaurant business. This makes it hard to predict future competition. As a result, some restaurant managers open without direct competition and soon find themselves with four or five competitors in a year's time. This phenomenon demonstrates the importance of anticipating competition. Restaurant managers should manage a business as if there is strong competition even if there is none. By taking this approach, the manager will be prepared when competition does arrive.

Hotels have moderately high barriers of entry due to the costs of building a hotel and the scarcity of good locations. High barriers to exit from the industry present a different set of competitive problems. The large capital investment required to build a hotel becomes a sunk cost. As a result, hotels that cannot meet all of their debt payments, taxes, and other fixed costs, but can produce enough gross profit to partially offset these fixed costs, may operate at a loss rather than close their doors. Thus when hotel demand plummets, room supply remains the same. With fewer customers bidding for the same number of hotel rooms in a marketplace, competition becomes intense.

The hotel's competitive environment is affected by another factor: Most hotels are planned during upswings in the business cycle when there is not enough supply to meet demand. But it can take four years or more from the planning stages to the opening of a hotel. By that time the economic cycle may have turned down. Sadly, new hotels often open their doors during a recessionary period.[9] So at a period when existing hotels are struggling to fill their rooms, it is not uncommon for competitors to enter the market.

It is easy to see after reading this section that the competitive environment in the hospitality industry is unpredictable. This is why we include it as part of the

Figure 4–3
Major forces in the company's macroenvironment.

Marketing Highlight 4.1: Visit Indy—Destination digital marketing

"Visit Indy is making a seismic shift in how we promote the destination to leisure visitors with a move into 100 percent digital and social marketing," said Mary Huggard, vice president of Tourism Development for Visit Indy, the publicly supported Destination Marketing Organization (DMO) for the city of Indianapolis, Indiana.

Like the majority of visitor destinations throughout the United States, and indeed, the world, destination promotion had been confined to traditional media such as television, radio, print, and outdoor. A new and creative agency, The Basement, specializing in digital marketing, was recently awarded the Visit Indy account. Changing markets accompanied by growth in Indianapolis called for a new marketing strategy away from messages carried in traditional media. Major reasons for the shift to digital marketing according to Visit Indy were as follows:

- The millennial generation will soon be #1 travel consumer, and they are the first full adopters of technology.
- Digital/social marketing gives Visit Indy the ability to microtarget consumers (right audience, right message, at the right time).
- Digital marketing offers more flexibility to alter advertising/messages based on testing and immediate feedback from audiences.
- Digital/social marketing (if done correctly) moves the consumer from passivity to interaction and engagement—hopefully leading to a higher level of loyalty and sharing with others.
- Tracking results is easier—Visit Indy can track Web analytics for its own purposes and for its co-op attraction partners.
- To locals, social and digital media will be the primary method used to engage them in Visit Indy's Tourism Master Plan process.

Source: Jeff Robertson, vice president of Tourism Development for Visit Indy. Used with permission.

---

macroenvironment. A wealthy person may decide to open a restaurant in your market area that is completely unfeasible, but he or she does it for ego reasons. A hotel company wants to have a presence in your city. The hotel on its own is not feasible, but by giving the company a presence in your city it is able to justify the investment, even though it adds rooms to an already weak market. A wealthy international businessperson wants to invest in real estate and chooses a hotel as a way to implement his or her investment. Although the project is not economically feasible in the short term, this investor is looking at long-term real estate gains. The projects just mentioned all bring capacity to markets that already have too much supply and not enough demand. If the projects were based on economic feasibility, they would not have been built. Investments in the hospitality industry are not always predictable.

The city of Indianapolis is rapidly changing. Brian Phillips, executive creative director of the agency The Basement, compared dynamic changes in Indianapolis to Austin, Texas. "Ten years ago few people considered visiting Indianapolis for great restaurants, theatre, and night life and even fewer considered living downtown."[10] Today, Indy downtown condo development is hot as well as redevelopment of formerly run-down areas, which now embrace trendy restaurants and lively "meet your friends over a drink" places. Like in Austin, truck eateries, interesting boutiques, and breweries are also flourishing.

Brian continued,

"The management team of Visit Indy agreed that digital marketing offers an opportunity to reach micro-market segments based on traditional demographics as well as by psychographics. Digital also allows our client to develop a real interaction with buyers and to understand their behavior. Measurement of the effectiveness of messages is now more precise which should lead to improved productivity in the dollars spent to promote the city. Imagine our ability to reach and influence all market segments including the visiting friend and relatives (VFR) segment and first time Indy visitors. We will be able to show our city block by block with a voice and digital message telling each buyer what he or she is looking for whether it is a Jewish deli, a salon, spa, a museum perhaps a public monument or a wine bar. The use of drones in the delivery of these messages is also under consideration."

Indianapolis has transited into an attractive tourist destination. Sean Pavone/123RF.

Brian continued by saying, "This will require great creative work combined with relevant and attention holding content to micro-market Indy individually to each person. Content will be king! Visitor marketing has often had a nearly indistinguishable look and message by city destinations. Digital based marketing by Visit Indy is intended to set it apart from competitors as we can now speak directly to each visitor and potential visitor. The intention is to create a voice and personality such as that which happens in an interaction between two people. Good conversations are not static. Digital will permit us to adjust and refine our message voice."

Chris Gahl, vice president of Marketing and Communications for Visit Indy, said, "Success will also depend upon 'buy in' by critical sectors of the city."[11] With this in mind, Visit Indy is preparing a Tourism Master Plan with the direct involvement of individuals from the traditional visitor industry as well as from public, quasi-governmental organizations, affected city departments, and the private sector. All participants have been asked to represent their interests, such as putting heads on the beds by the lodging sector, but also to think strategically with a macro view concerning how the city should grow and change to meet the needs of visitors and residents who may today be grade school students.

Mary Huggard spoke for Visit Indy and their agency, The Basement, when she said, "We know that digital marketing is no longer the future, it is the now. The time has come to move direction."

Demographic Environment

Demography The study of human populations in terms of size, density, location, age, sex, race, occupation, and other statistics.

Demography is the study of human populations in terms of size, density, location, age, gender, race, occupation, and other statistics. The demographic environment is of major interest to marketers because it involves people, and people make up markets. The world population is growing at an explosive rate. It now exceeds 7.4 billion people and will grow to 8.5 billion by 2030.[12] The world's large and highly diverse population poses both opportunities and challenges.

Changes in the world demographic environment have major implications for business. For example, consider China. More than a quarter century ago, to curb its skyrocketing population, the Chinese government passed regulations limiting families to one child each. As a result, Chinese children have been showered with attention and luxuries under what's known as the "six-pocket syndromes." As many as six adults—two parents and four doting grandparents—may be indulging the whims of an only child. These children, now ranging in age from newborns to mid-twenties, are affecting markets for everything including restaurants and travel. Parents with only children at home spend about 40 percent of their income on their cherished child.[13]

Starbucks is targeting China's millennials, positioning itself as a new kind of informal but indulgent meeting place.[14] Instead of believing in traditional Chinese collective goals, these young people embrace individuality. "Their view of this world is very different," says the president of Starbucks Greater China. "They have never gone through the hardships of our generation."[15] Starbucks is in sync with that, he says, given its customized drinks, personalized service, and original music compilations. In the United States, about 80 percent of Starbucks business is takeout. In China, Starbucks is a destination with about 90 percent of the consumption on premise. Young people flock to Starbucks to hang out with friends. Starbucks knows that China will become its largest market and is preparing for that day. In 2011, they established a coffee farm and processing facilities in China's southern Yunnan province.[16] The Chinese coffee market has grown significantly in recent years and Starbucks, targeting Millennials, extended its reach to the east of China with a $1.2 billion deal for more than 1,000 coffee shops.[17]

Marketers keep close track of demographic trends and developments in their markets, both at home and abroad. They track changing age and family structures, geographic population shifts, educational characteristics, and population diversity. Here, we discuss the most important demographic trends in the United States.

Changing Age Structure of the Population

The U.S. population is currently about 323 million and may reach almost 364 million by 2030.[18] The single most important demographic trend in the United States is the changing age structure of the population. The U.S. population contains several generational groups. The baby boomers, Generation X, the millennials, and Generation Z have a strong impact on today's marketing strategies.

The Baby Boomers

Baby boomers The 78 million people born between 1946 and 1964.

The post–World War II baby boom produced 78 million **baby boomers**, born between 1946 and 1964. Over the years, the baby boomers have been one of the most powerful forces shaping the marketing environment. Today's baby boomers account for nearly 26 percent of the population, spend about $2 trillion annually, and hold three-quarters of the nation's financial assets.[19]

The maturing boomers are rethinking the purpose and value of their work, responsibilities, and relationships. As they reach their peak earning and spending years, the boomers constitute a lucrative market for travel and entertainment, eating out, spas, and other leisure activities. For example, adults over 50 now account for 80 percent of luxury travel spending in America. Boomers are also digitally active and social media savvy. They are the fastest-growing shopper demographic online.[20]

It would be a mistake to think of the boomers as aging and staid. Many boomers are rediscovering the excitement of life. For example, according to the Travel Industry Association of America, half of all U.S. adults took adventure vacations within the past five years. Some 56 percent of these travelers were boomers. Baby boomers do not feel old; one study found they feel 12 years younger than they actually are.[21] They will spend billions of dollars on travel, looking for active vacations where they can have adventure or explore. Through their continuing education departments, universities have developed educational tours that target the baby boomers. Butterfield and Robinson, agents for upscale biking tours, market two-week bike tours with overnight stays in luxury accommodations to the boomers. Boomers look for value and research their vacations. One of the reasons cruises are popular with boomers is because of the value of the all-inclusive vacation.

Generation X

Generation X A generation of 45 million people born between 1965 and 1979; named Generation X because they lie in the shadow of the boomers and lack obvious distinguishing characteristics; other names include "baby busters," "shadow generation," or "yiffies"—young, individualistic, freedom-minded few.

The baby boom was followed by a "birth dearth," creating another generation of 49 million people born between 1965 and 1979. Author Douglas Coupland calls them **Generation X** because they lie in the shadow of the boomers and lack obvious distinguishing characteristics. Others call them the "baby busters" or the "generation caught in the middle" (between the larger baby boomers and later millennials).

The Generation Xers are defined as much by their shared experience as by their age. Having grown up during times of recession and corporate downsizing, they developed a more cautious economic outlook. They care about the environment and respond favorably to socially responsible companies. Hotel and restaurant companies that are taking initiatives to be environmentally responsible are attractive to this group. Although they seek success, they are less materialistic; they prize experience, not acquisition. For many of the 30 million Gen Xers who are parents, family comes first, career second.[22]

The Gen Xers are a more skeptical bunch. "Marketing to Gen Xers is difficult," says one marketer, "and it's all about word of mouth. You can't tell them you're good, and they have zero interest in a slick brochure that says so. They have a lot of 'filters' in place."[23] Another marketer agrees: "Sixty-three percent of this group will research products before they consider a purchase. They are also creating extensive communities to exchange information. The information swap is trusted and thus is more powerful than any marketing pitch."[24]

The Gen Xers have brought us the quality movement. Food-service operations such as Starbucks, Chipotle's, and Panera Bread are favorites of Gen Xers. They like to be intrigued by menus more than millennials or boomers. They enjoy menus that combine the familiar with the unique. When it comes to vacations, Gen Xers look for a different experience, which means they spend more than boomers. The Gen Xers have set a higher bar for casual dining, business travel, and mid-priced hotels.[25]

Hyatt is positioning Andaz as an unpretentious upscale hotel catering to customers looking for fresh, uncomplicated luxury that is timeless and gimmick free. Andaz is squarely aimed at the maturing Generation X market. Gen Xers are becoming the major market segment for business travel. Like all great demographic segments, they demand alternative brands to those patronized by their parents, the baby boomers. Xers are notoriously uncomfortable with general global brands and prefer to seek out local specialties and experiences. Although their parents might prefer hotels with identical bathrooms from Amsterdam to Zurich, Xers like to celebrate local differences. Andaz caters to this by allowing each of its hotels to celebrate its local autonomy through different designs and offerings. In fact, the word *Andaz* means personal style. Andaz will also cater to the Xer market by offering organic food and environmentally sound operating principles. Hyatt pitches the new hotel as a "luxury lifestyle brand" that "expresses individual style and personal independence in an environment of casual elegance. It offers local personality, innovative design, and a relaxed atmosphere, plus unpretentious, responsive, personalized service."[26]

The Virginia Tourism Corporation (VTC), the state's tourism DMO, is now targeting Gen X families. Virginia's 40-year romance with the baby boomer generation is waning. The VTC, best known for its enduring "Virginia is for Lovers" campaign, is now wooing a new audience: Generation X. They're younger and more adventuresome, and they spend more money on travel in Virginia. VTC research showed that Generation X households contribute about 45 percent of the billions spent on travel in Virginia each year, whereas most boomers are done or almost done with raising their children and lean toward more exotic travel locations farther from home.[27]

Millennials

Millennials (also called Generation Y) Born between 1980 and 2000, these children of the baby boomers number 83 million, dwarfing the Gen Xers and larger even than the baby boomer segment.

Both the baby boomers and Gen Xers will one day be passing the reins to the **millennials** (also called **Generation Y**). Born between 1980 and 2000, these children of the baby boomers number 83 million, dwarfing the Gen Xers and are even larger than the baby boomer segment. With total purchasing power of more than $733 billion, Gen Y represents a huge and attractive market. One thing all of the millennials have in common is their fluency and comfort with computer, digital, and internet technology.[28]

Hotel chains have designed specific concepts and marketing campaigns aimed at millennial needs and lifestyles. Marriott's Moxy, Tru by Hilton, and citizenM are three hotel brands designed specifically to attract millennials. Moxy makes use of its small room size by hanging folding furniture on pegs along one wall. This allows guests to design their room according to their need whether it is for entertainment or work.

Mix these ingredients for success with the Gen X millennial segment: adventure, meeting new friends, great exercise, tons of fun, great tacos, and even a chance to be on national television. This is the Taco Ride, a 9.6-mile, night bike ride that attracts 700–1,500 millennial bike riders weekly.

The ride begins in Council Bluffs, Iowa, and ends in Mineola at the Mineola Steakhouse. The participants ride on the Wabash Trace Nature Trail, a converted railroad right of way. Not all riders complete the trip as many stop at a picnic area known as Margaritaville. Commercial firms aware of the promotional potential join the ride at the steakhouse. Recognizing the fun atmosphere and public interest in the ride, Jennie-O® provided turkey tacos to participants at the Mineola Steakhouse and filmed responses that were later used in advertisements on national television. Budweiser and Miller beers donated T-shirts to help raise funds for a cyclist injured on the ride.[29]

Generation Z People born after 2000 (although many analysts include people born after 1995) who make up the kids, tweens, and teens markets.

Generation Z

Hard on the heels of the millennials is **Generation Z**, young people born after 2000 (although many analysts include people born after 1995 in this group). They spend an estimated $44 billion annually of their own money and influence up to $600 billion of family spending.[30]

Generation Z takes smartphones, tablets, internet-connected game consoles, wireless internet, and digital and social media for granted—they've always had them—making this group highly mobile, connected, and social. They have "digital in their DNA."[31]

Generation Z consumers make up about 25 percent of the U.S. population and have a tremendous amount of influence on family travel decisions and spending. They like adventure travel experiences such as exploring and trying new things and prefer environmentally friendly hotels. They will spend a lot of money on meals offering diverse and cultural tastes. Gen Z is cost-conscious. They do their online research for hospitality and travel purchases and will know if they are getting the best value. Hotel brands that create specialized content are more likely to resonate with them. A visual content that's meaningful, memorable, and entertaining is critical to reaching them. Several hotel brands such as Marriott and W Hotels have used Snapchat contests and co-creation campaigns to engage Gen Z consumers.[32]

Generational Marketing

One way marketers can segment is by forming age-specific segments within each group. Defining people by their birth date may be less effective than segmenting them by their lifestyle, life stage, or the common values they seek in the products they buy. We discuss many other ways to segment markets in Chapter 8.

An Australian company, Green Getaways Australia, offers luxury ecotourism to a niche market that may cross demographics. Green Getaways further segments its niche market by budget or luxury and by type of experience as follows:

- Luxury Ecolodges
- Romantic Getaways
- Treehouse
- Glamping (luxury camping in glamorous tents)

This experience is designed for adults who wish to experience wilderness but wilderness with luxury. Green Getaways promotes sleeping on a latex bed with 1,000 thread count quality sheets.

Treehouse and Glamping are promoted as "not cheap." Will Green Getaways find that their product line is too broad? Will they find that appealing to both the luxury and budget markets is too difficult to maintain/manage at a profit? Experienced marketers would probably say yes to both questions, but one must admire the entrepreneurship and product uniqueness of entrepreneurs like Green Getaways.[33]

Few industries have been affected more by changing demographics than the golf and ski industries. Of the approximately 34,000 worldwide golf courses, 45 percent are in the United States. However, the number of U.S. courses has been in steady decline. In 2015, the Associated Press reported there were 15,372 U.S. courses, down from a peak of 16,052.[34]

Jim Hinckley of Palmer Golf claims, "New golfers are different. They see the sport as entertainment, not competition. For the future, golf has to be thought of as a fun experience not a serious experience." While the play on golf courses is in decline, Topgolf created a rapidly growing golf business by responding to environmental changes. Using radio frequency identification (RFID) chips in their golf balls, Topgolf is able to track a player's balls. The players try to hit different targets on the driving range, and they receive points for how close they hit to the designated target. The games are designed so that novices as well as experienced golfers can enjoy them. A video screen keeps track of the scores. The golf bays were designed with seating. At a small table, a server will bring drinks and food. Topgolf's success in part is due to its food and beverage sales that are routinely more than the golf sales. People come to Topgolf to have a good time.

During a trade show by Snowsports Industries America (SIA), Bill Jensen, a ski industry executive, said, "The industry is facing huge challenges and predicted that 150 of the current U.S. ski resorts would fail." He said there are only 45 ski resorts with climbing revenues.[35] Reasons for this include the following:

- Warmer winter weather with new cycles.
- Demographics in which couples with infants and toddlers are less likely to take ski vacations.
- Financial pressures on the middle class.

Increasing Diversity

Countries vary in their ethnic and racial makeup. At one extreme is Japan, where almost everyone is Japanese. At the other extreme is the United States, with people from virtually all nations. The United States has often been called a melting pot. Instead, the United States seems to have become more of a "salad bowl" in which various groups have mixed together but have maintained their diversity by retaining and valuing important ethnic and cultural differences.

Marketers are facing increasingly diverse markets, both at home and abroad as their operations become more international. The U.S. population is about 76 percent white, with Hispanics at 18 percent and African Americans at about 14 percent. More than 13 percent of the population was born in another country. The nation's ethnic populations are expected to explode in coming decades. By 2060 Hispanics will comprise an estimated 28 percent of the U.S. population, with Asians at 9 percent.[36]

Diversity goes beyond ethnic heritage. For example, there are more than 60 million disabled people in the United States—a market larger than African Americans or Hispanics—representing almost $200 billion in annual spending power. This spending power is likely to increase in the years ahead as the wealthier, freer-spending baby boomers enter the "age of disabilities." Julie Perez sees the difference when she goes to the Divi Hotels resort at Flamingo Beach on the Caribbean island of Bonaire. "It is famous for being totally accessible," she says. "The hotel brochures show the wheelchair access. The dive staff are trained and aware, really want to take disabled people diving. They're not afraid." Perez, aged 35, of Ventura, California, is an experienced scuba diver, a travel agent, and a quadriplegic.[37] People with disabilities appreciate products that work for them, explains Jim Tobias, president of Inclusive Technologies, a consultancy specializing in accessible products. Those with disabilities tend to be brand evangelists for products they love. They typically tell more friends about a favorite product, than a typical satisfied guest.[38]

According to one estimate, 6–7 percent of the population who identify themselves as lesbian, gay, bisexual, and transgender (LGBT) have buying power of $712 billion.[39] The British Tourist Authority (BTA) teamed up with British Airways and the London Tourist Board to target this market. The group worked with WinMark Concepts, a Washington marketing and advertising firm that specializes in advising mainstream companies, on how to target the gay and lesbian market. The company wanted something fun and tasteful as the LGTB market are educated and savvy consumers. One recent magazine ad shows five young to early-middle-age men—the target age group is ages 35 to 50—posing in and around several of London's distinctive red phone booths. The campaign was successful. The communication strategy focused on magazine ads to position Britain as gay and lesbian-friendly destination and database marketing - about 40,000 names across the country for a targeted direct marketing campaign. Since BTA launched the campaign, both United Airlines and Virgin Airways have signed onto the program, as have the tourist boards of Manchester, Brighton, and Glasgow.[40]

As the population in the United States grows more diverse, successful marketers will continue to diversify their marketing programs to take advantage of opportunities in fast-growing segments. Warning issues of race, religion, and politics can produce negative reactions. In March 2015, Starbucks initiated a campaign having U.S. workers write "Race Together" on beverage cups. Several companies had been tying their brands to social issues but the Starbucks campaign was ridiculed on social media by people who said it was opportunistic and inappropriate. Some went so far as to say that it used racial tensions within the United States to boost Starbucks bottom line. Following criticism, Starbucks reviewed this tactic and dropped it.

The Changing American Family

The "traditional household" consists of a husband, wife, and children (and sometimes grandparents). Yet the once American ideal of the two-child, two-car suburban family has lately been losing some of its luster.

In the United States, married couples with children under 18 make up only 19 percent of the nation's 125 million households, married couples without children make up 23 percent, and single parents comprise another 14 percent. A full 34 percent are nonfamily households—single person or adults living together composed of one or both sexes.[41]

More people are divorcing or separating, choosing not to marry, marrying later, or marrying without intending to have children. Marketers must increasingly consider the special needs of nontraditional households because they are now growing more rapidly than traditional households. For example, people in their thirties who are marrying for the first time are used to going out to eat frequently. When they have children they continue to dine out, taking their children with them.

The number of working women has also increased, growing up to 47 percent. Both husband and wife work in the majority of married couple families.[42] This has spawned the need for takeout food, prepared by someone else but eaten at the home dining table. Grocery stores are also preparing heat-and-serve entrées and side dishes. These grocery stores are now seeking graduates of culinary programs and hospitality programs as this business grows. Royal Caribbean targets time-crunched working mothers with budget-friendly family vacations that are easy to plan and certain to wow. Royal Caribbean estimates that, although vacations are a joint decision, 80 percent of all trips are planned and booked by women—who are pressed for time, whether they work or not. Royal Caribbean communicates to mothers that all their vacation will pay off by providing an excellent vacation for the whole family including themselves.[43]

Two decades ago, terms such as *guppies* and *dinks* were commonly discussed in sociological and marketing circles. As millennials have become adults, the terms PANKS (Professional Aunts, No Kids) was developed by Melanie Notkin, a New York marketing executive.

PANKS should be of interest to the hospitality/tourism industry since this group consists of college-educated women in their thirties who are unmarried and childless but devote love and attention to their nephews and nieces. Some of these women take these children on vacation trips, and this group is growing. In 1971, 35 percent of women this age were childless, but had increased to 49 percent by 2016.[44]

Geographic Shifts in Population

This is a period of great migratory movements between and within countries. Americans, for example, are a mobile people, with about 15 percent of all U.S. residents moving each year. Over the past two decades, the U.S. population has shifted toward the Sunbelt states. The West and South have grown, whereas the Midwest and Northeast have lost population.[45] As companies look for new locations, they need to understand both national and local geographic trends relating to shifting populations.

A Better-Educated, More White-Collar, More Professional Population

The U.S. population is becoming better educated. Moreover, nearly two-thirds of high-school graduates now enroll in college within 12 months of graduating.[46] The rising number of educated people will increase the demand for quality products, including luxury hotels, travel, wine, and dining at restaurants that have interesting menus.

Economic Environment

Economic environment The economic environment consists of factors that affect consumer purchasing power and spending patterns. Markets require both power and people. Purchasing power depends on current income, price, saving, and credit; marketers must be aware of major economic trends in income and changing consumer spending patterns.

Markets require buying power as well as people. The **economic environment** consists of factors that affect consumer purchasing power and spending patterns. Nations vary greatly in their levels and distribution of income. Some countries have subsistence economies: They consume most of their own agricultural and industrial output. These countries offer few market opportunities. At the other extreme are industrial economies, which constitute rich markets for many different kinds of goods. Marketers must pay close attention to major trends and consumer-spending patterns both across and within their world markets. Following are some of the major economic trends in the United States.

Changes in Income

Throughout the 1990s, American consumers fell into a consumption frenzy, fueled by income growth, a boom in the stock market, rapid increases in housing values, and other economic good fortune. They bought and bought, seemingly without caution, amassing record levels of debt. However, the free spending and high expectations of those days were dashed by the recession of the early 2000s. In fact, we are now facing the age of the "squeezed consumer." Along with rising incomes in some segments have come increased financial burdens. The collapse of the housing markets in 2008 eliminated the opportunity for many consumers to borrow home equity. They now face repaying debts acquired during earlier spending splurges, increased household and family expenses, and saving ahead for children's college tuition payments and retirement. This reduction in discretionary income created hard times for the restaurant industry as customers cut back both on the number of times they dined out and on the amount they spent when they did dine out.

Over the past three decades, the rich have grown richer, the middle class has shrunk, and the poor have remained poor. The top 1 percent of American families now controls 33.4 percent of the nation's net worth, up 3.3 points from 1989. By contrast, the bottom 90 percent of families now control only 30.4 percent of the net worth, down 3.5 points.[47]

Tango dancers are a popular tourist attraction in Argentina, where favorable currency exchange has resulted in attracting more business meetings and tourists. Vikiri/Shutterstock.

The Super Rich

This presentation is not intended for political or sociological discussion. Instead it is included to introduce a group that is unfamiliar to most people but is a viable market segment for hospitality and tourism.

The world's Super Rich represents 0.5 percent of the world's population but over 38.5 percent of its wealth. Despite a recession, global wealth reached a high of $231 trillion in 2011.

Individuals with a net worth of $50 million or more are located primarily in North America, Europe, and Asia/Pacific. London has become a magnet for the Super Rich of the world (top 1 percent). There is a greater concentration of Super Rich in London than anywhere else on the planet. London has the distinction of having the largest concentration of Russian millionaires outside of Moscow.

Deluxe ultra-long vacations are in demand. Realizing this, Four Seasons offers four-week around-the-world, all-inclusive itineraries for $130,000 per person. All accommodations are at Four Seasons hotels/resorts, which are reached on the Four Seasons Private Jet, ground transportation, planned excursions, meals, and gratuities. According to Chris Norton, Four Seasons executive vice president, Global Products & Operations, these trips are consistently sold out.[48] In 2015, Cunard Lines offered 120 nights on the ocean liner RMS *Queen Mary 2* for $233,998 per person for accommodations in its 2,249-square-foot duplex suite.

The Global Economy

Today the travel industry operates in a global environment. When the exchange rate between the Euro and the U.S. dollar favors the Euro, fewer travelers from America go to Europe, and Americans divert their vacations to locations in the United States and South America.

One of the positive outcomes of currency devaluations in Argentina is that it is gaining as a destination for conventions and meetings. But when international meeting planners move meetings to Santiago, Sao Paulo, Rio de Janeiro, Buenos Aires, and other cities of South America, cities in Asia, Europe, and North America lose these conventions. Argentina, Chile, and Uruguay are all among tourist destinations, attracting over a million visitors. This is in part due to the economic consequences of currency exchange.

Natural Environment

The natural environment involves the natural resources that are needed as inputs by marketers or that are affected by marketing activities. Environmental concerns have grown steadily during the past three decades. In many cities around the world, air and water pollution have reached dangerous levels.

Marketers should be aware of several trends in the natural environment. The first involves growing *shortages of raw materials* including air and water. Air pollution chokes many of the world's large cities, and water shortages are already a big problem in some parts of the United States and the world. By 2030, more than one in three of the world's human beings will not have enough water to drink.[49] Renewable resources, such as forests and food, also must be used wisely. Nonrenewable resources, such as oil, coal, and various minerals, pose a serious problem. Shortages increase construction costs of new hotels, restaurants, and tourist attractions.

A second environmental trend is *increased pollution*. Consider the disposal of garbage and sewage by resorts. In destinations where this is not managed, the groundwater has been polluted, damaging the water supply. The littering of the environment with nonbiodegradable bottles, plastics, and other packaging materials is also a concern. Garbage can be seen on the beaches and back bays of some destinations. Hospitality companies must be good corporate citizens and embrace corporate responsibility. In 2018, Marriott International, joining Starbucks, Hilton Hotels, Hyatt Hotels Corporation, and American Airlines, announced that the corporation will eliminate plastic straws and drink stirrers, approximately 1 billion straws and 250 million stirrers, from all of its 6,500 hotels and resorts worldwide. Marriott has made other moves to reduce its environmental footprint such as replacing small bottles of shampoo and conditioner with in-shower dispensers at many of its hotels, which will eliminate 35 million plastic toiletry bottles annually.[50]

Healthy coral reefs are good for tourism. Coral reefs support businesses and people in the Florida Keys, Bahamas, Mexico, Thailand, Indonesia, Australia, and Mauritius, to name a few. Rafael Ben-Ari/123RF.

The natural environment consists of many amenities that attract tourists, such as forests, clean beaches, pristine streams, wildlife, and clean air. The Maldives, an island nation south of Sri Lanka, has seen its coral reefs bleached by warm water from El Nino. Coral reefs are an important attraction and component of nature-based tourism. Coral reef tourism represents a $19 billion a year in direct economic value to the world from diving, snorkeling, glass-bottom boating, and wildlife watching on reefs.[51] Anyone involved in tourism has an obligation to protect the environment and develop sustainable tourism. The concern for sustainability is increasing and has led to publications such as greenlodgingnews.com and organizations such as Green Restaurant Association.

A third trend is *increased government intervention* in natural resource management. The governments of different countries vary in their concern and efforts to promote a clean environment. Some, such as the German government, vigorously pursue environmental quality. Others, especially many poorer nations, do little about pollution, largely because they lack the needed funds or political will.

Unfortunately, many of these countries often rely on tourism and suffer from the problems mentioned in the preceding paragraphs. The general hope is that companies around the world will accept more social responsibility, and less expensive devices can be found to control and reduce pollution.

Technological Environment

The most dramatic force shaping our destiny is technology, which has given us wireless access to the internet. This has made it possible for individuals to have interactions with others involving both audio and visual connections using programs such as Skype and FreeConference.com. Many organizations now accept a document that has been signed, scanned, and e-mailed instead of a hard copy of the original document. The end result is that speed at which business is occurring has increased dramatically. Sites like LinkedIn and Facebook allow us to keep track of both our business and personal networks.

Technology has affected the hospitality industry in many ways. For example, Intelity has produced a product called ICE (Interactive Customer Experience) that can be accessed from a number of Web-enabled platforms, including smartphones and tablets. Guest services from the hotel such as room service, valet parking, dining room reservations, and spa services can be accessed from the tablet. External reservations at theaters, restaurants, golf courses, and airlines can also be accessed. To prevent theft, the equipment has tracking devices.[52] There are predictions that the front desk will be no longer necessary as guests check-in using their smartphone. The Hen na Hotel in Japan has developed robots that will man the front desk. By reducing the cost of labor, the hotel intends to be the low-price leader in the area. The hotel is using facial recognition as a way for guests to access their rooms.[53]

The application of technology, robots and artificial intelligence (AI), is changing how we do business in the hospitality industry. Hotels adopt these technologies to enhance hotel reputation, create word of mouth, and enhance guest experience. Robots are utilized for delivering amenities and room service items, carrying luggage, handling express check-in and check-out service, and taking care of payment. Some hotels such as Hilton started to use robot concierges. Robotic arms stir, shake, and serve up cocktails at some cruise ships and hotel bars. The hotel industry also adopted AI for digital assistance and voice-activated services. Guests can customize their room by controlling room temperature and lighting remotely or without leaving their bed. The chatbot is the newest way for guests to communicate with their hotel. For example, Cosmopolitan of Las Vegas' AI concierge, Rose, can advise on entertainment and things to do on and around the resort. AccorHotels' Mercure launched the BOT, an AI instant messaging, to provide local stories for travelers to discover the city and neighborhood they are visiting.[54]

One of the most powerful changes is from social media. We will discuss social media in Chapter 14. The smartphone is a versatile tool for travelers. They can book and check on reservations, use it as a boarding pass for airlines, register at a hotel, and use it as a key access to the hotel room. These self-service technologies save the guest time and labor for the hospitality company. This also means that one's Web presence has to be formatted to work well on smartphones. Technology has also helped eliminate the theft of hotel products.[55]

Technology is also helping operations. Washable radio-frequency identification (RFID) chips are being embedded in towels, bathrobes, banquet linen, and other washable linens. This allows management to determine the inventory of linen in storage closets and on the hotel floors. Since it is becoming more common for full-service hotels to send their linen off premise to be cleaned, the RFID chips help the laundry to keep track of the linen

Robotic butlers carry luggage to the room and deliver amenities. Ekkasit keatsirikul/123RF.

Disney is taking RFID technology to a new level with its new MagicBand RFID wristband. Helen Sessions/Alamy Stock Photo.

Political environment Laws, government agencies, and pressure groups that influence and limit the activities of various organizations and individuals in society.

and to locate missing items.[56] Panera had converted 400 of its cafes to an easy-order and fast-delivery model. Customers could place orders using iPads-equipped kiosks for delivery to their tables. This was in response to customer complaints about long order lines.[57] Disney is using MagicBand RFID wristband for personalizing guest experiences. The MagicBand provides Disney with potential mother lode of digital data on guest activities, and movements in minute detail, helping to improve guest logistics, services, and sales.[58]

Marketers must understand and anticipate changes in the technological environment. Because the guest is involved in the service delivery process, technology changes often mean we need to train the guest in how to use the new technology.

Political Environment

Marketing decisions are strongly affected by developments in the **political environment**. This environment consists of laws, government agencies, and pressure groups that influence and limit the activities of various organizations and individuals in society. We cite some current political trends and their implications for marketing management.

Increased Legislation and Regulation Affecting Business

As products become more complex, public concern about their safety increases. Governmental agencies have become involved in the investigation and regulation of everything from fire codes to food-handling practices. Employment and employee practices fall under government regulation, as do sales of alcohol, which vary from state to state and sometimes from precinct to precinct in the same county. Politicians also see travelers as good sources of revenue because nonresidents pay taxes on hotel rooms, rental cars, and many other purchases but cannot vote against them. Hotel taxes are supposed to be used to support tourism; however, the spending of this money has sometimes been used for questionable purchases, such as statues for suburban parks. The hospitality industry must make sure that taxes designed to promote tourism are used effectively. Managers must also work with hotel and restaurant associations to ensure that taxes do not become oppressive. New York City hiked its hotel tax to over 21.25 percent for rooms costing over $100 in 1990. Many meeting and convention planners avoided New York because of the unfriendly tax. Convention business plunged by 37 percent during the next three years, and tax revenues declined despite the tax increase. The real loser was New York City's hospitality industry. New York has since reduced its hotel tax in line with other cities. Proposals offering increases in hotel tax rates by state or city officials usually face strong opposition and protests from hotel association and industry professionals.[59]

Government regulation aims at protecting consumers from unfair business practices. Various government units define unfair consumer practices and offer remedies. Businesses can minimize government intervention through active self-regulation. Such associations as the American Hotel and Motel Association and the National Restaurant Association (NRA) define and encourage good trade practices.

Government regulation also aims to protect society's interests. Profitable business activity does not always improve the quality of life. Thus, regulations are passed to discourage smoking, littering, polluting, over-congestion of facilities, and others in the name of protecting society's interests. Regulation aims to make firms responsible for the social as well as private costs of their activities.

Government regulation and enforcement are likely to increase. Business executives must know the major laws protecting competition, consumers, and society when planning their products and marketing programs.

Changing Government Agency Enforcement

To enforce laws, Congress established federal regulatory agencies: the Federal Trade Commission, the Food and Drug Administration, the Interstate Commerce Commission, the Federal Communications Commission, the Federal Power Commission, the Civil Aeronautics Board, the Consumer Products Safety Commission, the Environmental Protection Agency, and the Office of Consumer Affairs. These agencies can have a major impact on a company's marketing performance. Government agencies have discretion in enforcing the laws, and from time to time, they appear to be overly eager. Lawyers and economists, who often lack a practical sense of marketing and other business principles, frequently dominate the agencies. In recent years, the Federal Trade Commission has added marketing experts to its staff to gain a better understanding of complex issues.

International Politics

Sometimes hospitality companies and products are boycotted or worse because of political differences between countries or groups within a country. McDonald's has become an icon of the United States worldwide and has been the victim of boycotts, bomb threats, and on rare occasions bombs. Here are some of the actions that targeted companies can take:

- Emphasize the company's connections to the local community. In Indonesia, McDonald's launched television ads showing some of the staff of the local franchise owners wearing traditional clothing. In Argentina, where McDonald's entrances were blocked by protestors, the restaurant chain launched a campaign showing a Big Mac with the words "Made in Argentina" stamped on it.

- Adopt a low profile. Avoid conflicts and even press interviews with reporters known to be against your product or company.

- Counter lies and misinformation with professional public relations and advertising. Select a well-versed and believable spokesperson. Do not allow random staff members to be spokespeople.

- Be patient. These kinds of things usually have a life of their own and fade away as protestors and the public lose interest.[60]

Cultural Environment

The cultural environment includes institutions and other forces that affect society's basic values, perceptions, preferences, and behaviors. As a collective entity, a society shapes the basic beliefs and values of its members. The following cultural characteristics can affect marketing decisions.

Persistence of Cultural Values

People in any society hold certain persisting core beliefs and values. For example, most Americans believe in working, getting married, giving to charity, and being honest. Core beliefs and values are passed from parents to children and are reinforced by schools, churches, business, and government. Secondary beliefs and values, however, are more open to change. Believing in marriage is a core belief; believing that people should get married early is a secondary belief.

The hospitality industry is worldwide. Chances are very good that many of you will find yourselves serving in a foreign setting sometime during your career. Cultural norms and cultural prohibitions may affect your managerial roles in ways quite different from those in your native country. For example, hoteliers in Israel are expected to understand and observe the rules of kashruth, or keeping kosher. These are complicated and require constant supervision. Hotels in Israel must have two kitchens, one for meat and one for dairy products. Because kosher meat is expensive in Israel, hotel food costs are higher.[61]

A practice widely followed in China, Hong Kong, and Singapore (and that has also spread to Japan, Vietnam, and Korea), feng shui, means wind and water.

Practitioners of feng shui, or geomancers, recommend the most favorable conditions for any venture, particularly the placement of office buildings and the arrangement of desks, doors, and other items. To have good feng shui, a building should face the water and be flanked by the mountains. It should not block the view of the mountain spirits. The Hyatt Hotel in Singapore was designed without feng shui in mind and had to be redesigned to boost business. Originally, the front desk was parallel to the doors and road, which was thought to lead to wealth flowing out. Furthermore, the doors were facing northwest, which gave easy access to undesirable spirits in. The geomancer recommended designed alterations so that wealth could be retained and undesirable spirits kept out.[62]

Well-being and healthy living have become a way of life for many and cultural trend. Most Americans are overworked and looking for a vacation to refresh both mind and body. They also want to maintain their healthy lifestyle when they travel. Hotels embraced the new trend and offer health and wellness amenities such as 24-hour access to a gym or pool, gluten-free and organic food/drink options, yoga mats, fitness classes, essential oils, ergonomic bed, and even a complete wellness room.[63]

Increased Emphasis on Socially Responsible Actions and Ethics

Written regulations cannot possibly cover all potential marketing abuses, and existing laws are often difficult to enforce. Beyond written laws and regulations, business is also governed by social codes and rules of professional ethics.

SOCIALLY RESPONSIBLE BEHAVIOR. Enlightened companies encourage their managers to look beyond what the regulatory system allows and simply "do the right thing." These firms actively seek out ways to protect the long-run interests of their consumers and the environment.

Today, almost every aspect of marketing involves ethical and societal issues. These issues usually involve conflicting interests and well-meaning people can honestly disagree about the right course of action in a given situation. Companies are now developing policies, guidelines, and other responses to complex social issues.

The boom in internet marketing has created a new set of social and ethical issues. Critics worry about online privacy issues. There has been an explosion in the amount of personal digital data available. Users, themselves, supply some of it. They voluntarily place highly private information on social-networking sites, such as Facebook or LinkedIn, or on genealogy sites that are easily searched by anyone with a computer or a smartphone.

Information is systematically developed by businesses seeking to learn more about their customers, often without consumers realizing that they are under the microscope. Legitimate businesses plant cookies on consumers' PCs and collect, analyze, and share digital data from every move consumers make at their Web sites. Critics are concerned that companies may now know too much and might use digital data to take unfair advantage of consumers. Although most companies fully disclose their internet privacy policies and use data to benefit their customers, abuses do occur.

The number of public-interest groups has increased. These groups take on issues of social responsibility. Cindi Lamb and her five-month-old daughter, Laura, were on their way home from a grocery store when a drunk driver slammed into their car. The accident left the baby paralyzed from the waist down. Cindi was outraged when she discovered the drunk driver was a chronic offender. She set out to change the way judges, police officers, and politicians handled drunk driving. Joining together with her friends and other victims, she formed what is now known as MADD (Mothers Against Drunk Driving). MADD has had a major impact on the hospitality industry by demanding that restaurants be more responsible in their serving of alcohol. MADD is helping push stronger legislation against drinking and driving.

One expert who follows People for the Ethical Treatment of Animals (PETA) states that the organization would like to see all fast-food outlets that serve meat closed. Nishiki Sushi in Sacramento used to serve "Dancing Shrimp," a popular menu item in Japan. The shrimp are served live. Customers are instructed to squeeze lemon juice on the shrimp to make them "dance." PETA asked the restaurant to remove the shrimp from the menu. The restaurant voluntarily removed the shrimp. Certainly, improved treatment of animals would be good, but the complete elimination of animals from human diets is something that the majority of people would not embrace.

The cultural eating practice in Chinese restaurants using shark fins to flavor soup resulted in the near disappearance of some shark populations including hammerhead, mahu, and tiger. Fortunately, a report by the wildlife protection group Wild Aid indicated that demand is declining for shark fins. In Southern China, sales dropped by 82 percent from 2012 to 2015.

Many nations have banned "finning," the practice of catching a shark, cutting off its fins, and then throwing the dismembered animal into the ocean to die.

CAUSE-RELATED MARKETING. To exercise social responsibility and build positive images, many companies are now linking themselves to worthwhile causes. Cause-related marketing has become a primary form of corporate giving. It lets companies "do well by doing good" by linking purchases of the company's products or services with fund-raising for worthwhile causes or charitable organizations. Companies sponsor dozens of cause-related marketing campaigns each year. For example, BJ's Restaurants, through its "Cookies for Kids" program, donates a portion of the sale of every signature "Pizookie" dessert to the Cystic Fibrosis Foundation.

Cause-related marketing has stirred controversy. Critics worry that cause-related marketing is more a strategy for selling than a strategy for giving—that "cause-related" marketing is really "cause-exploitative" marketing. Thus, companies using cause-related marketing might find themselves walking a fine line between increased sales and facing charges of exploitation. However, if handled well, cause-related marketing can benefit the company and the cause. The company gains an effective marketing tool while building a positive public image. The charitable organization or cause gains visibility and important new sources of funding and support.

Responding to the Marketing Environment

Many companies view the marketing environment as an "uncontrollable" element to which they must adapt. They passively access the marketing environment. They analyze environmental forces and design strategies that will help the company avoid the threats.

Environmental management perspective A management perspective in which a firm takes aggressive actions to affect the publics and forces in its marketing environment rather than simply watching and reacting to it.

Other companies take an **environmental management perspective**.[64] Rather than simply watching and reacting, these firms take aggressive action to affect the publics and forces in their marketing environment. Lobbyists are hired to influence legislation affecting their industries and to stage media events to gain favorable press coverage. They run advertorials to shape public opinion and press lawsuits and file complaints. They form contractual agreements to control their distribution channels.

One of the elements of the macroenvironment that can be influenced is the political environment. Companies join trade organizations such as the American Hotel and Lodging Association (AH & LA), the American Society of Travel Agents (ASTA), the Hotel and Catering International Management Association (HCIMA), and the NRA. Trade associations hire lobbyists and form political action committees (PACs) to represent and communicate their industry's concerns to government officials.

Marketing management cannot always affect environmental forces; in many cases, it must settle for simply watching and reacting to the environment. For example, a company would have little success trying to influence geographic population shifts, the economic environment, or major cultural values. But whenever possible, marketing managers take a proactive rather than a reactive approach to the publics and forces in their marketing environment.

Environmental Scanning

Use of an environmental scanning plan has proved beneficial to many hospitality companies. The following steps are involved: (1) Determine the environmental areas that need to be monitored; (2) Determine how the information will be collected, including information sources, the information frequency, and who will be responsible; (3) Implement the data collection plan; and (4) Analyze the data and use them in the market planning process. Part of the analysis is weighing the importance of the trends so the organization can keep the trends in proper perspective.

It is never sufficient simply to collect data about the environment. Managers must turn the data into useful information that will help them make decisions. The information used to make decisions must be reliable, timely, and used in decision making.

It is also important to consider the fact that the environmental factors are linked. When the millennials became teenagers, the total expenditures on food in restaurants and food-service operations exceeded food expenditures in grocery stores for the first time. In 2013, people in the United States purchased more meals outside the home than they ate home-prepared meals. One of the forces behind this change is that both heads of the household are working in many families. The average time spent preparing meals is currently 15 minutes and dropping. No longer is the woman expected to prepare home-cooked meals for the man. Many people prefer to eat at home; they just do not have time to cook. The "home-meal replacement" restaurant developed as a result of these trends. Robert Del Grande's Café Express restaurants in Texas and Arizona and Foodies Kitchen in Metairie, Louisiana, are examples of restaurant concepts creating quality meals with the convenience of self-service.

Grocery stores provide competition to restaurants. Most grocery stores have a food display near the deli counter of microwaveable freshly prepared meals. These entries include pot roast, teriyaki chicken, and pasta dishes. The Hy-Vee grocery stores offers drive-through windows or delivery and curbside pickup for online orders.

These examples show how the elements of the environment are linked. Economic forces result in families with both heads of the household working. This is a demographic statistic that can be tracked over time. Women are also able to build careers and take management positions once reserved for men. We have seen a cultural change where men now participate in home duties and no one member of the household is expected to prepare all meals. Technology has also made it easier to reconstitute food and to warm prepared meals at home. Finally, the competitive environment between grocery stores and quick-service restaurants is expected to heat up. Grocery stores are building elaborate delicatessens with a variety of prepared meals; they have fresh microwaveable meals to go, and online grocery shopping for delivery or curbside pickup may become commonplace in the future. The change in food consumption patterns relates to economic, demographic, technological, cultural, and competitive trends.

CHAPTER REVIEW

I. The Company's Environment. A company's marketing environment consists of outside actors and forces that affect a company's ability to build and maintain successful relationships with its target customers. The microenvironment consists of factors close to the company that affect its ability to serve its customers, the company itself, marketing channel firms, customer markets, and a broad range of publics. The macroenvironment consists of larger societal forces that affect the entire microenvironment, that is, demographic, economic, natural, technological, political, competitor, and cultural forces.

II. Company's Microenvironment. The microenvironment consists of actors and forces close to the company that can affect its ability to serve its customers. The actors in the microenvironment include supplier, market intermediaries, customers, and publics that combine to make up the company's value delivery system.

  A. The company. Marketing managers work closely with top management and the various company departments.

  B. Existing competitors. They are part of the microenvironment and must be monitored closely.

  C. Suppliers. Firms and individuals that provide the resources needed by the company to produce its goods and services.

  D. Marketing intermediaries. Firms that help the company promote, sell, and distribute its goods to the final buyers.

  E. Disintermediation. The elimination of intermediaries.

  F. Marketing services agencies. Marketing research firms, advertising agencies, media firms, and marketing consulting firms help companies to target and promote their products to the right market.

  G. Financial intermediaries. Include banks, credit companies, insurance companies, and other firms that help hospitality companies to finance their transaction or insure risks associated with the buying and selling of goods and services.

  H. Customers. Managers must understand the different types of customers: consumers, business markets, government markets, resellers, and international markets.

  I. Publics. A public is any group that has an actual or potential interest in or impact on an organization's ability to achieve its objectives.

III. Company's Macroenvironment. The macroenvironment consists of larger societal forces that affect the entire microenvironment.
   A. Competitors. Future competitors are part of the macroenvironment. In the hospitality industry competition can be unpredictable.
      1. **Barriers to entry, exit, and competition.** Entry barriers prevent firms from getting into a business, and barriers to exit prevent them from leaving.
   B. Demographic environment. Demography is the study of human populations in terms of size, density, location, age, sex, race, occupation, and other statistics. The demographic environment is of major interest to marketers because markets are made up of people.
      1. **Changing age structure of the population.** The single most important demographic trend in the United States is the changing age structure of the population.
      2. **The baby boomers.** As they reach their peak earning and spending years, the boomers constitute a lucrative market for travel and entertainment, eating out, spas, and other leisure activities. For example, adults over 50 now account for 80 percent of luxury travel spending in America. Boomers are also digitally active and social media savvy. They are the fastest-growing shopper demographic online.
      3. **Generation X.** The Generation Xers are defined as much by their shared experience as by their age. Having grown up during times of recession and corporate downsizing, they developed a more cautious economic outlook. They care about the environment and respond favorably to socially responsible companies.
      4. **Millennials.** Born between 1980 and 2000, these children of the baby boomers number 83 million, dwarfing the Gen Xers and are even larger than the baby boomer segment. With total purchasing power of more than $733 billion, Gen Y represents a huge and attractive market. One thing all of the millennials have in common is their fluency and comfort with computer, digital, and internet technology.
      5. **Generation Z.** Generation Z consists of young people born after 2000 (although many analysts include people born after 1995 in this group). They spend an estimated $44 billion annually of their own money and influence up to $600 billion of family spending. They are highly mobile, connected, and social.
      6. **Generational marketing.** One way marketers can segment is by forming age-specific segments within each group. However, defining people by their birth date may be less effective than segmenting them by their lifestyle, life stage, or the common values they seek in the products they buy.
      7. **Increasing diversity.** Marketers are facing increasingly diverse markets, both at home and abroad as their operations become more international.
   C. The changing American family. Marketers must increasingly consider the special needs of nontraditional households because they are now growing more rapidly than traditional households.
      1. **Geographic shifts in population.** As companies look for new locations, they need to understand both national and local geographic trends relating to shifting populations.
      2. **A better-educated, more white-collar, more professional population.** The rising number of educated people will increase the demand for quality products, including luxury hotels, travel, wine, and dining at restaurants that have interesting menus.
   D. Economic environment. The economic environment consists of factors that affect consumer purchasing power and spending patterns.
      1. **Changes in income.** Over the past three decades, the rich have grown richer, the middle class has shrunk, and the poor have remained poor.
      2. **The Super Rich.** The world's Super Rich represents 0.5 percent of the world's population but over 38.5 percent of its wealth. Individuals with a net worth of $50 million or more are located primarily in North America, Europe, and Asia/Pacific.
      3. **The global economy.** Today, the travel industry operates in a global environment. When the exchange rate between the Euro and the U.S. dollar favors the Euro, fewer travelers from America go to Europe, and Americans divert their vacations to locations in the United States and South America.
   E. Natural environment. The natural environment consists of natural resources required by marketers or affected by marketing activities.
   F. Technological environment. The most dramatic force shaping our destiny today is technology.
   G. Political environment. The political environment is made up of laws, government agencies, and pressure groups that influence and limit various organizations and individuals in society.
      1. **Increased legislation and regulation affecting business.** Governmental agencies have become involved in the investigation and regulation of everything from fire codes to food-handling practices.
      2. **Changing government agency enforcement.** To enforce laws, Congress established federal regulatory agencies: the Federal Trade Commission, the Food and Drug Administration, the Interstate Commerce Commission, the Federal Communications Commission, the Federal Power Commission, the Civil Aeronautics Board, the Consumer Products Safety Commission, the Environmental Protection Agency, and the Office of Consumer Affairs. These agencies can have a major impact on a company's marketing performance.
      3. **International politics.** Sometimes hospitality companies and products are boycotted or worse

because of political differences between countries or groups within a country. Actions companies can take include: emphasizing connections to the local community, accepting a low profile, combatting lies with believable public relations professionals, and being patient.
- H. **Cultural environment.** The cultural environment includes institutions and other forces that affect society's basic values, perceptions, preferences, and behaviors.
    1. **Persistence of cultural values.** People in any society hold certain persisting core beliefs and values. Core beliefs and values are passed from parents to children and are reinforced by schools, churches, business, and government. Secondary beliefs and values, however, are more open to change. If you work in a foreign setting, cultural norms and prohibitions may affect your managerial roles in ways quite different from those in your native country.
    2. **Increased emphasis on socially responsible actions and ethics.** Business is also governed by social codes and rules of professional ethics.
- IV. **Responding to the Marketing Environment.** Many companies view the marketing environment as an "uncontrollable" element to which they must adapt. Other companies take an environmental management perspective. Rather than simply watching and reacting, these firms take aggressive actions to affect the publics and forces in their marketing environment.
    1. **Environmental scanning.** These companies use environmental scanning to monitor the environment which involves: (1) determining areas that need to be monitored, (2) determining how information will be collected, (3) implementing the data collection plan, and (4) analyzing the data and using them in the market planning process. Part of the analysis is weighing the importance of the trends so the organization can keep the trends in proper perspective.

IN-CLASS GROUP ACTIVITIES

*Exercises with an asterisk next to them are suitable for individual homework or online assignments. Students, always provide an explanation for your answer.

1. *On the internet, find how ecotourism is being used to attract tourists by different organizations.
2. *From information you can find on the internet, when do you think space tourism will be a viable form of tourism? What organizations are working to develop space tourism?
3. *Go to Web sites of travel or hospitality companies and find examples of how they are taking measures to sustain and improve the natural environment. Which companies that you examined do you think have the best programs? Explain your answer.
4. *How has the McDonald's concept changed since the 1960s? What environmental forces were behind these changes? How will the McDonald's concept change in the next decade, given the new forces operating in the environment?
5. What environmental trends will affect the success of a first-class hotel chain, such as Hyatt or Sofitel, over the next 10 years? If you were corporate director of marketing for this type of hotel, what plans would you make to deal with these trends?
6. How have environmental trends affected the design of hotels?
7. What environmental trends will affect the success of the Walt Disney Company in the next five years? If you were in charge of marketing at Disney, what plans would you make to deal with these trends?

EXPERIENTIAL EXERCISES

Do one of the following:

1. View the annual reports of several hospitality companies. How did you find out about how they might be changing their business to fit the environment from their annual report? If you do not have access to an annual report, visit the book's Web site for electronic access to annual reports.
2. Choose and visit a restaurant, club, or hotel you feel is designed for one of the generations discussed in the book (e.g., baby boomers, Generation X, echo boomers). After doing some research on the generation, state what the business you chose has done to cater to its target generation.

REFERENCES

1. Castle Rock (Town) Colorado, U.S. Census Bureau, State and County Quick Facts, February 5, 2015, http://quickfacts.census.gov.
2. Seyhmus Baloglu, "Dimensions of Customer Loyalty, Separating Friends from Well Wishers," *Cornell Hotel and Restaurant Administration Quarterly*, 43, no. 1 (2002): 47–59.
3. Philip Kotler, *Marketing Management* (Upper Saddle River, NJ: Prentice-Hall, 1988); Donald R. Lehmann and Russel S. Winer, *Analysis for Marketing Planning* (Plano, TX: Business Publications, 1988).
4. See www.arkvegas.com (accessed July 19, 2018).
5. Tejal Rao, "The New Hotel Cuisine: Don't Bite the Brand That Feeds You," StarChefs.com, May 2007,

http://www.starchefs.com/features/trends/concept/index.shtml (accessed August 2, 2008).

6. Chick-fil-A Looks to Perk Sales by Offering First-Ever Specialty Grade Coffee in QSR Industry, Chick-fil-A.com, 2014, CFA Properties, Inc.

7. Information from Robert J. Benes, Abbie Jarman, and Ashley Williams, "2007 NRA Sets Records," www.chefmagazine.com (accessed September 2007); "Coca-Cola, Fishbowl Partnering to Offer Digital Strategy Solutions for Restaurants," February 20, 2015, https://www.fastcasual.com/news/coca-cola-fishbowl-partnering-to-offer-digital-strategy-solutions-for-restaurants, www.thecoca-colacompany.com/presscenter/presskit_fs.html, and www.cokesolutions.com (accessed July 2018).

8. Michael Porter, *Competitive Strategy* (New York: Free Press, 1980).

9. Melinda Bush, "The Critical Need to Know," *Cornell Hotel and Restaurant Administration Quarterly*, 26, no. 3 (1985): 1.

10. From Brian Phillips, Executive Creative Director of the agency. Copyright © by Visit Indy. Reprinted by permission.

11. From Chris Gahl, Vice President of Marketing and Communications for Visit Indy. Copyright © by Visit Indy. Reprinted by permission.

12. World POPClock, U.S. Census Bureau, www.census.gov (accessed June 2018). This Web site provides continuously updated projections of the United States and world populations.

13. See Clay Chandler, "Little Emperors," *Fortune* (October 4, 2004): 138–150; "China's Little Emperor's," *Financial Times* (May 5, 2007): 1; "Me Generation Finally Focuses on US," Chinadaily.com.cn (August 27, 2008), www.chinadaily.com.cn/china/2008-08/27/content_6972930.htm; Melinda Varley, "China: Chasing the Dragon," *Brand Strategy* (October 6, 2008): 26; Clifford Coonan, "New Rules to Enforce China's One Child Policy," *Irish Times* (January 14, 2009): 12; David Pilling, "Reflections of Life in China's Fast Lane," *Financial Times* (April 19, 2010): 10.

14. Adapted from information in Janet Adamy, "Different Brew: Eyeing a Billion Tea Drinkers, Starbucks Pours It on in China," *Wall Street Journal* (November 29, 2006). Also see, "Where the Money Is," *Financial Times* (May 12, 2007): 5; Laurie Burkitt, "Starbucks Menu Expands in China," *Wall Street Journal*, March 9, 2011.

15. Janet Adamy, "Different Brew: Eyeing a Billion Tea Drinkers, Starbucks Pours It on in China," *Wall Street Journal*, November 29, 2006.

16. Laurie Burkitt, "Starbucks Menu Expands in China," *Wall Street Journal* (March 9, 2011): B.7.

17. "China Millennials Switch to Coffee as Starbucks Pushes East," August 8, 2017, www.bloomberg.com/news/articles/2017-08-08/china-millennials-swap-tea-for-coffee-as-starbucks-pushes-east.

18. U.S. Census Bureau Projections and POPClock Projection, U.S. Census Bureau, www.census.gov (accessed September 2007).

19. Louise Lee, "Love Those Boomers," *Business Week* (October 24, 2005): 94–102; Tom Ramstack, "The New Gray: Boomers Spark Retirement Revolution," *Washington Tones*, December 29, 2005; "Baby Boomers in the United States Have an Estimated Annual Spending Power of over $2 Trillion," *Business Wire*, April 27, 2007.

20. "Generational Marketing: Tips for Reaching Baby Boomers," July 16, 2015, www.mayecreate.com/2015/07/generational-marketingtips-for-reaching-baby-boomers.

21. See Simon Hudson, "Wooing Zoomers: Marketing to the Mature Travelers," *Marketing Intelligence & Planning*, 28, no. 4 (2010): 444–461.

22. Scott Schroder and Warren Zeller, "Get to Know Gen X and Its Segments," *Multichannel News* (March 21, 2005): 55; Jim Shelton, "When Children of Divorce Grow Up," *Knight Ridder Tribune Business News* (March 4, 2007): 1.

23. "Mixed Success: One Who Targeted Gen X and Succeeded—Sort of," *Journal of Financial Planning*, 17, no. 2 (February 2004): 15.

24. Paul Greenberg, "Move Over, Baby Boomers; Gen Xers Want Far More Collaboration with Companies, Both as Consumers and Employees," *CIO* 70 (March 1, 2006): 1.

25. "Generation X: The Forgotten Ones," http://fivestar-food.com/generationx_the_forgotten_ones/ (accessed July 19, 2018); "Marketing Strategies for Boomers and Gen X," January 1, 2017, https://www.nestleprofessional.us/trends/marketing-strategies-boomers-and-gen-x; Betsy Goldberg, "How These 9 Qualities Shape Generation X Travel Choices," June 20, 2016, http://blog.virtuoso.com/tips-and-trends/9-qualities-shape-generation-x-travel-choices/.

26. Adapted from information found in Mark Ritson, "Have You Got the Gen X Factor?" *Marketing* (April 25, 2007): 25; "75 Wall Street to Be a Hyatt Andaz Property" (April 25, 2007), www.hotelchatter.con0taghkndax%20Hotels.

27. Based on information found in Donna C. Gregory, "Virginia Tourism Corp. Marketing to Generation X" (December 29, 2009), www.virginiabusiness.com/index.php/news/article/romancing-generation-x. Also see www.virginia.org/home.asp (accessed November 2010).

28. Deirde van Dyk, "The Generation Y Hotel," *Time* online (www.time.com), June 12, 2008 (accessed August 3, 2008); R. K. Miller and Kelli Washington, *Consumer Behavior* 2009; Piet Levy, "The Quest for Cool," *Marketing News* (February 28, 2009): 6.

29. "Taco Ride Sets New Record," August 18, 2008, http://www.bikeiowa.com/news/334/taco-ridesetsnewrecord; Wabash Trace Nature Trail, http://www.traillink.com/trail/Wabash-trace-nature-trail.aspx; Taco Ride—Wabash Trace Weekly Ride Hosted by Taco Ride, Wabash Trace Nature Trail, Council Bluffs, Iowa, https://www.bikeiowa.com/eventpop/7165/taco-ride-wabash-trace-weekly-ride?lightbox%.

30. See Giselle Abramovich, "15 Mind-Blowing Stats About Generation Z," *CMO*, June 12, 2015, www.cmo.com/articles/2015/6/11/15-mind-blowing-stats-about-generation-z.html; and Jessica Geller, "Move Over,

31. See "GenZ: Digital-In Their DNA"; Shannon Bryant, "'Generation Z' Children More Tech-Savvy; Prefer Gadgets, Not Toys," *Marketing Forecast*, April 3, 2013, www.ad-ology.com/tag/tech-savvychildren/#.U5d9avldV8E; and Brett Relander, "How to Market to Gen Z," *Entrepreneur*, November 4, 2014, www.entrepreneur.com/article/238,998.

32. Abi Mandelbaum, "What Should Your Hotel Know About Generation Z?" March 1, 2016, www.lodgingmagazine.com/what-should-your-hotel-know-about-generation-z/; "Move over Millennials, Hotels Are Shifting Focus to Generation Z," March 13, 2017, www.travelupdate.boardingarea.com/move-millennials-hotels-shifting-focus-generation-z/; Deanna Ting, "Smart Hotel Brands Are Already Thinking About Generation Z," March 14, 2016, www.skift.com/2016/03/14/why-hotel-brands-are-already-thinking-about-generation-z/; Jamie Biesiada, "Expedia Study of Age Groups Includes Nascent Generation Z," January 4, 2018, www.travelweekly.com/Travel-News/Travel-Agent-Issues/Expedia-study-of-age-groups-includes-nascent-Generation-Z.

33. Green Getaways Australia, http://www.greengetawaysaustralia.com.au (accessed July 15, 2018).

34. U.S. Golf Courses in Steady Decline, Associated Press, www.espn.go.com/golfstory.id12461331/, March 11, 2015.

35. Megan Barber, "Ski Industry Expert Says 31% of Today's Ski Areas Are Dying," http://ski.curbed.com/archives/2015. See also Tom Ross, "Era of the Super Pass: Ski Resorts Forced to Adapt and Change with Demographic Cycles," SteamboatToday.com, December 7, 2014.

36. See U.S. Census Bureau, "U.S. Population Projections," https://www.census.gov/newsroom/press-kits/2018/pop-projections.html (accessed June 2019); "2016 American Community Survey—Social Characteristics in the United States," https://www.census.gov/acs/www/data/data-tables-and-tools/data-profiles/2016/ and https://factfinder.census.gov/faces/tableservices/jsf/pages/productview.xhtml?src=bkmkwww.census.gov/population/www/socdemo/foreign/cps2008.html.

37. Dan Fost, "The Fun Factor: Marketing Recreation to the Disabled," *American Demographics*, 20, no. 2 (February 1998): 54–58.

38. Joan Voight, "Accessibility of Disability," *Adweek*, March 27, 2006, 20.

39. For these and other statistics, see Witeck-Combs Communications, "Buying Power of Gay Men and Lesbians in 2008," www.rivendellmedia.com/ngng/executive_summary/NGNGPPT and www.gaymarket.com/ngng/ngng_reader.html (accessed April 2009); Paul Morrissette, "Market to LGBT C," *American Agent and Broker* (July 2010): 50.

40. For these and other examples, see Laura Koss-Feder, "Out and About," *Marketing News* (May 25, 1998): 1, 20; Jennifer Gilber, "Ad Spending Booming for Gay-Oriented Sites," *Advertising Age* (December 6, 1999): 58; John Fetto, "In Broad Daylight," *American Demographics* (February 2001): 16, 20; Robert Sharoff, "Diversity in the Mainstream," *Marketing News* (May 21, 2001): 1, 13; David Goetzl, "Showtime, MTV Gamble on Gay Net," *Advertising Age* (January 14, 2002): 4; Kristi Nelson, "Canada's Gay TV Network Gets Ready for U.S.," *Electronic Media* (Chicago, May 6, 2002).

41. For statistics on family composition, see U.S. Census Bureau, "Family Households," Table Fl, www.census.gov/hhes/families/data/cps2015F.html; and U.S. Census Bureau, "Households by Type, Age of Members, Region of Residence, and Age of Householder: 2015," Table H2, www.census.gov/hhes/families/data/cps2015H.html (accessed September 2016).

42. See Department of Labor, "Facts Over Time: Women in the Labor Force," www.dol.gov/wb/stats/facts_over_time.htm; Pew Research Center, "Breadwinner Moms," May 29, 2013, www.pewsocialtrends.org/2013/05/29/breadwinner-moms/; U.S. Census Bureau, "America's Families and Living Arrangements: 2015," Table FG1, www.census.gov/hhes/families/data/cps2015FG.html (accessed March 2016); and U.S. Census Bureau, "Parents and Children in Stay at Home Parent Family Groups: 1994 to Present," Table SHP-1, www.census.gov/hhes/families/data/families.html (accessed September 2016).

43. See Marissa Miley and Ann Mack, "The New Female Consumer: The Rise of the Real Mom," *Advertising Age* (November 16, 2009): A1.

44. Kelly Spors, "The Two Hottest Niche Markets You've Probably Never Heard Of," April 2014, Open Forum, https://www.americanexpress.com; "Percentage of Childless Women in the United States in 2016, by Age," https://www.statista.com/statistics/241535/percentage-of-childless-women-in-the-us-by-age/ (accessed April 2018).

45. U.S. Census Bureau, "U.S. Mover Rate Remains Stable at About 12 Percent Since 2008, Census Bureau Reports," March 18, 2015, www.census.gov/newsroom/press-releases/2015/cb15-47.html; and U.S. Census Bureau, "Geographical Mobility/Migration," www.census.gov/population/www/socdemo/migrate.html (accessed September 2016).

46. U.S. Census Bureau, "Educational Attainment," https://www.census.gov/data/tables/2017/demo/education-attainment/cps-detailed-tables.html (accessed July 2018).

47. Bradley Johnson, "Recession's Long Gone, but America's Average Income Isn't Budging," *Advertising Age* (April 17, 2006): 22. See also Jeremy Siegel, "Why the Rich Got Richer," *Kiplinger's Personal Finance* (July 2007): 532; Frederic L. Pryor, "The Anatomy of Increasing Inequity of U.S. Family Incomes," *Journal of Socio-Economics* (August 2007): 595.

48. Carrie Coolidge, "Trend Spotting: Grand Tours for High-fliers Between Jobs," *Barron's Penta*, March 2, 2015, 8.

49. Sarah Begley, "UN Report Warns of Serious Water Shortages Within 15 Years," *Time*, March 20, 2015,

http://time.com/3,752,643/un-water-shortage-2030/; The 2030 Water Resources Group, www.2030wrg.org (accessed September 2016); and "The World's Water," Pacific Institute, www.worldwater.org/data.html (accessed September 2016).

50. Dee-Ann Durbin, "Marriott Will Stop Using Plastic Straws in All of Its Hotels by 2019," *Time*, July 18, 2018, http://time.com/5341608/marriott-hotels-plastic-straws-2019/.

51. "How Tourism Can Be Good for Coral Reefs," www.global.nature.org/content/coral-reef-tourism (accessed May 2018).

52. See www.intelitycorp.com (accessed August 18, 2010).

53. Robert Loos, "Robots to Staff Hotel in Japan," *Robotics Today*, February 3, 2015, http://www.roboticstoday.com/news/hotel-androids-robots-to-staff-hotel-in-japan-3106 (accessed July 10, 2015).

54. Tobey Grumet Segal, "How Hotels Are Using Artificial Intelligence to Improve Your Stay," April 4, 2018, www.cntraveler.com/story/how-hotels-are-using-artificial-intelligence-to-improve-your-stay; Corris Little, "Robotic Bartenders Shake up F&B," March 21, 2018, *Hotel Business*, https://www.hotelbusiness.com/web-excl-robotic-bartenders-shake-up-fb/?eid=378696098&bid=2043328; Mariella Moon, "IBM Watson Powers Hilton's Robotic Concierge 'Connie,'" March 9, 2016, https://www.engadget.com/2016/03/09/hilton-robot-concierge-connie/; David Eisen, "AccorHotels Just Predicted 7 Hospitality Trends for 2018," *Hotel Management*, January 9, 2018, www.hotelmanagement.net/operate/accorhotels-just-predicted-7-hospitality-trends-for-2018.

55. "Mobile Phones Replace Room Keys in Stockholm Hotel, Check In and Check Out Without Ever Stopping by the Front Desk," November 2, 2010, http://news.discovery.com/tech/mobile-phones-replace-hotel-keys.html (accessed August 18, 2011).

56. Roger Yu, "Hotels Use RFID Chips to Keep Linens from Checking Out," (July 31, 2011), http://abcnews.go.com/travel/hotels-rfid-chips-linens-checking-story?id=14179579 (accessed August 18, 2011).

57. Machan Dyron, "Flour on His Shoes," CEO Spotlight, Ron Shaich, Panera Bread, Barron's: *The Dow Jones Business and Financial Weekly*, XCV, no. 8 (February 23, 2015): 38–39.

58. See "A $1 Billion Project to Remake the Disney World Experience, Using RFID," www.fastcompany.com/1671616/a-1-billion-project-to-remake-the-disney-world-experience-using-rfid; Brooks Barnes, "At Disney Parks, a Bracelet Meant to Build Loyalty (and Sales)," *New York Times*, January 7, 2013, p. Bl; Claire Swedberg, "MagicBands Bring Convenience, New Services to Walt Disney World," *RFID Journal*, June 16, 2014, www.rfidjournal.com/articles/view?11877; and Christopher Palmeri, "Why Disney Won't Be Taking Magic Wristbands to Its Chinese Park," *Bloomberg*, January 10, 2016, www.bloomberg.com/news/articles/2016-01-10/why-disney-won-t-be-taking-magic-wristbands-to-its-chinese-park.

59. Gene Sloan, "Restaurant Taxes Gain Weight in Cash-Strapped Cities," *USA Today*, International Edition (Asia) (September 28, 1994): B7; see Steve Lackmeyer and David Dishman, "Hotel Tax Hike Opposed by Industry Professionals in Oklahoma," March 28, 2018, *NewsOK*, www.newsok.com/article/5,588,661/hotel-tax-hike-opposed-by-industry-professionals-in-oklahoma.

60. Salah Al Shebil, Adbul A. Rasheed, and Hussam Al-Shammari, "Battling Bigots," *Wall Street Journal* (April, 28, 2007): R6, R11.

61. Kenneth J. Gruber, "The Hotels of Israel: Pressure and Promise," *Cornell Hotel and Restaurant Administration Quarterly*, 28, no. 4 (1988): 42.

62. J. S. Perry Jobson, "Feng Shui: Its Impacts on the Asian Hospitality Industry," *International Journal of Contemporary Hospitality Management*, 6, no. 6 (1994): 21–26; Bernd H. Schmitt and Yigang Pan, "In Asia, the Supernatural Means Sales," *New York Times* (February 19, 1995): sec. 3, 11.

63. Adam Glickman, "6 Hotel Wellness Upgrades That Won't Break the Bank," February 6, 2018, www.hotelmanagement.net/operate/6-wellness-solutions-won-t-break-bank; John Power, "As Fitness and Wellness Become Top Priority for Travelers, Hotels Embracing New Trends," February 7, 2017, www.traveltripper.com/blog/as-fitness-and-wellness-become-top-priority-for-travelers-hotels-embracing-new-trends/.

64. Carl P. Zeithaml and Valarie Zeithaml, "Environmental Management: Revisiting the Marketing Perspective," *Journal of Marketing* (Spring 1984): 46–53.

Aerial view of Caesar's Palace, Las Vegas. Courtesy of Charles Zachritz/Shutterstock.

5

Managing Customer Information to Gain Customer Insights

Joseph, a 30-something New Yorker, recently went on a weekend trip to Atlantic City, New Jersey, where he hoped to stay at one of his favorite Caesars Entertainment resorts and enjoy some gaming and entertainment. Unfortunately for Joseph, he picked a weekend when all hotels were booked solid. But after swiping his Caesars Entertainment Total Rewards card to play the tables, the pit boss came by and directed him to the front desk. He was told that a room had become available, and he could stay in it for a reduced rate of $100 a night. When he checked out two nights later, Joseph was told that all the room charges were on the house.

Was this sudden vacancy a case of lady luck smiling down on an Atlantic City visitor? Or was it a case of a company that knows what managing customer relationships truly means? If you ask any of Caesars Entertainment Total Rewards program members, they will tell you without hesitation that it's the latter. "They are very good at upgrading or in some cases finding a room in a full hotel," Joseph reported later. "And I always liked the fact that no matter where I gambled, Atlantic City, Vegas, Kansas City, or New Orleans, or which of their hotels I gambled in, I was always able to use my [Total Rewards card]."

Caesars Entertainment customers like Joseph aren't the only ones praising its customer relationship management (CRM) capabilities. In fact, Caesars Entertainment's program is considered by CRM experts to set the gold standard. With the Total Rewards program at the center of its business and marketing strategies, Caesars Entertainment has the ability to gather data, convert that data into customer insights, and use those insights to serve up a customer experience like no other.

Objectives

After reading this chapter, you should be able to:

1. Explain the importance of information in gaining insights about the marketplace and customers.
2. Define the marketing information system and discuss how marketing information is developed.
3. Outline the steps in the marketing research process and explain how companies analyze and use marketing information.

Gathering Data

The Total Rewards program has worked well since its beginning in 1998. But through smart investments and a continued focus, Caesars Entertainment has hit the CRM jackpot.

The mechanics of the program go something like this: Total Rewards members receive points based on the amount they spend at Caesars Entertainment facilities. They can then redeem the points for a variety of perks, such as cash, food, merchandise, rooms, and hotel show tickets. The simplicity of Total Rewards gains power in volume and flexibility. Through numerous acquisitions over the past decade, Caesars Entertainment has grown to more than 50 properties under several brands across the United States, including Harrah's, Caesars Palace, Bally's, Planet Hollywood, the Flamingo, and Showboat. Total Rewards members swipe their card every time they spend a dime at one of these properties: checking into 1 of 40,000 hotel rooms, playing 1 of 60,000 slot machines, eating at 1 of 390 restaurants, picking up a gift at 1 of 240 retail shops, or playing golf at 1 of its 7 golf courses. Over 80 percent of Caesars Entertainment customers—55 million in all—use a Total Rewards card. That's roughly one out of six adults in the United States. That's a big pile of data points. Added to this, Caesars Entertainment regularly surveys samples of its customers to gain even more details.

In 2012, the corporation rolled out new features allowing members to earn points and credits outside the company's casinos. Caesars also created a portal through the Total Rewards Web site where customers can earn benefits and points while shopping online at more than 500 retailers.

In 2017, Caesars Entertainment Corporation partnered with Survey Sampling International (SSI) for a new loyalty rewards program called "Say and Play." The partnership offers its Total Rewards members an opportunity to earn Reward Credits by participating in surveys and sharing their opinions. These Reward Credits can be redeemed for hotel stays, free casino play, dining, show tickets, shopping, and spa treatments across Caesars Entertainment hotels and resorts. Caesars also partnered with Wyndham Hotels for cross-marketing and reward redemption options for Wyndham Rewards and Total Rewards members.

Customer Insights

Analyzing all this information gives Caesars Entertainment detailed insights into its casino operations. For example, "visualization software" can generate a dynamic "heat map" of a casino floor, with machines glowing red when at peak activity and then turning blue and then white as the action moves elsewhere. More importantly, Caesars Entertainment uses every customer interaction to learn something new about individuals—their characteristics and behaviors, such as who they are, how often they visit, how long they stay, and how much they gamble and entertain.

From its Total Rewards data, Caesars Entertainment has learned that 26 percent of its customers produce 82 percent of revenues. And these best customers aren't the "high-rollers" that have long been the focus of the industry. Rather, they are ordinary folks from all walks of life—middle-aged and retired teachers, assembly line workers, and even bankers and doctors who have discretionary income and time. Caesars Entertainment "low-roller" strategy is based on the discovery that these customers might just visit casinos for an evening rather than staying overnight at the hotel. And they are more likely to play the slots than the tables. Kris Hart, vice president of brand management for Caesars Entertainment, reports on a survey of 14,000 Total Rewards members. "We did a lot of psychographic segmenting—looking at what were the drivers of people's behavior. Were they coming because of the location? Were they coming because they were incented to do so with a piece of direct mail? Were they coming because they have an affinity for a loyalty program? And that allowed us to look at segments that clumped around certain drivers... and it enabled us to construct our brands and messaging."

Customer Experience

Using such insights, Caesars Entertainment focuses its marketing and service development strategies on the needs of its best customers. Caesars Entertainment sends out over 250 million pieces of direct mail and almost 100 million e-mails to its members every year. A good customer can receive as many as 150 pieces of mail in a given year from one or all of its properties. From the customer's perspective, that might sound like a nightmare. But Caesars Entertainment has tested customer sentiment on receiving multiple mailings from multiple locations, and they actually like it because the information is relevant to them.

Caesars Entertainment is certainly concerned about metrics, such as response rates, click-through rates, revenue, and customer profitability. But Caesars Entertainment's program is one of the best because it places emphasis on knowing how all the outcomes are linked. And because Caesars Entertainment CRM culture extends from the IT department to frontline employees, the gaming giant has an uncanny ability to translate all its data into an exceptional customer experience. Based on customer service scores, employees have their own system for accumulating points and redeeming them for a wide variety of rewards, from iPads to pool equipment. Mystery shoppers are also used to verify performance and train employees to service standards.[1]

Caesars Entertainment combines its service culture with the brain center of Total Rewards. After a day's gaming, Caesars Entertainment knows which customers should be rewarded with free show tickets, dinner vouchers, or room upgrades. In fact, Caesars Entertainment processes customer information in real time, from the moment customers swipe their rewards cards, creating the ideal link between data and the customer experience. Caesars Entertainment chief information officer calls this "operational CRM." Based on up-to-the-minute customer information, "the hotel clerk can see your history and determine whether you should get a room upgrade, based on booking levels in the hotel at that time and on your past level of play. A person might walk up to you while you're playing and offer you $5 to play more slots, or a free meal, or perhaps wish you a happy birthday."

Caesars Entertainment is constantly improving its technology so that it can better understand its customers and deliver a more fine-tuned experience. Most recently, Total Rewards gained the ability to track and reward nongaming spending. This is good for people who don't view themselves as big gamblers. "We wanted to make it relevant to them as well because they could spend a couple of hundred dollars on a room, the spa, food, and shows and not be treated any better than a $50-a-day customer," Norton said. This demonstrates the "total" part of Total Rewards. It isn't a program about getting people into casinos. It's a program designed to maximize the customer experience, regardless of what that experience includes.

Caesars Entertainment's CRM efforts have paid off in spades. The company has found that happy customers are much more loyal. Although customer spending decreases by 10 percent based on an unhappy casino experience, it increases by 24 percent with a happy experience. And Caesars Entertainment Total Rewards customers appear to be a happier bunch. Compared with nonmembers, member customers visit the company's casinos more frequently, stay longer, and spend more of their gambling and entertainment dollars in Caesars Entertainment rather than in rival casinos.

Although Caesars Entertainment and the entire gaming industry were hit hard by the Great Recession, things are turning back around; through its acquisitions and the success of its Total Rewards program, Caesars Entertainment is one of the leading in its industry, with about $5 billion revenue in 2017.[2]

Caesars Entertainment shows us how marketers can use information to gain powerful market insights. Caesars Entertainment harnesses marketing information to gain customer insights while customers have been gaming, booking rooms, making travel arrangements, dining, and enjoying other activities at the company's properties. All this information is stored, analyzed, and used for enhancing customer satisfaction, experience, and loyalty.

Marketing Information and Customer Insights

To create value for customers and to build meaningful relationships with them, marketers must first gain fresh, deep insights into what customers need and want. Such customer insights come from good marketing information. Companies use these customer insights to develop competitive advantage and make better decisions.

But although customer and market insights are important for building customer value and relationships, these insights can be very difficult to obtain. Customer needs and buying motives are often anything but obvious—consumers themselves usually can't tell you exactly what they need and why they buy. To gain good customer insights, marketers must effectively manage marketing information from a wide range of sources.

Marketing Information and Today's "Big Data"

Today's marketers have ready access to plenty of marketing information. With the recent explosion of information technologies, companies can now generate information in great quantities.

Consumers themselves are now generating tons of marketing information. Through their smartphones, PCs, and tablets—via online browsing and blogging, apps and social media interactions, texting and video, and geolocation data consumers now volunteer a tidal wave of bottom-up information to companies and to each other.

Far from lacking information, most marketing managers are overloaded with data and often overwhelmed by it. This problem is summed up in the concept of **Big Data**. The term *Big Data* refers to the huge and complex data sets generated by today's sophisticated information generation, collection, storage, and analysis technologies. Every year, the people and systems of the world generate about a trillion gigabytes of information. That's enough data to fill 2.47 trillion good old CD-ROMs, a stack tall enough to go to the moon and back four times. A full 90 percent of all the data in the world has been created in just the past two years.[3]

Big Data is characterized by three Vs: volume (large amounts of information from hundreds of terabytes to petabytes and beyond), velocity (the increasing rate at which data flows into an organization including real-time delivery), and variety (encompassing structured and unstructured formats: text from social networks, data from apps, Web services, images, GPS [global positioning system] signals, and readings from sensors).

Big Data presents marketers with both big opportunities and big challenges. Many restaurants today use unrelated systems to manage different operations of the business such as in-store sales, online orders and delivery, customer loyalty, and purchase history. Restaurants can effectively use and apply those data by combining them all into one Big Data to gain rich, timely customer insights for server performance, menu trends, customer preferences, and order history.[4] However, accessing and sifting through so much data is a daunting task as Big Data is often external and less structured. It is very challenging to store a photo, a sound bite, a video clip, or social media posts in a way that it can be combined with other digital data and mined for useful insights. Besides, the volume of such data is far more information than any manager can digest. In fact, most marketing managers are overloaded with data and often overwhelmed by it. Still, despite this data glut, marketers frequently complain that they lack enough information of the right kind. Thus, they don't need *more* information—they need *better* information. And they need to make better *use* of the information they already have.

Big Data presents companies with big opportunities to gain rich and timely customer insights. Courtesy of Monty Rakusen/Cultura/Getty Images.

Marketers apply marketing analytics to the large and complex data sets they collect from Web, mobile, social media tracking; customer transactions and engagements; and other sources to dig out meaningful patterns to gain customer insights and gauge marketing performance.[5] Marriott recently started to use a customer analytics company that analyzes more than 300 unique sets of data as well as data from

116 million households to reveal patterns about the number of times someone travels—for business or leisure—where they live and work, what they travel for, who they are, and what's their overall value to the brand. Marriott then takes that information to identify where the demand is nationally, by market and region, for future brand growth.[6]

Managing Marketing Information

Thus, a company's marketing research and information system must do more than simply generate lots of information. The real value of marketing research and marketing information lies in how it is used—in the **customer insights** that it provides. "The value of the market research department is not determined by the number of studies that it does," says the marketing expert, "but by the business value of the insights that it produces and the decisions that it influences."[7]

Based on such thinking, many companies are now restructuring and renaming their marketing research and information functions. They are creating "customer insights teams," headed by a vice president of customer insights and made up of representatives from all of the firm's functional areas. For example, the head of marketing research at Kraft Foods is called the "director of consumer insights and strategy."

Customer insight groups collect customer and market information from a wide variety of sources—ranging from traditional marketing research studies to mingling with and observing consumers to monitoring consumer social media conversations about the company and its products. They mine Big Data from variety of sources. Then they use the marketing information to develop important customer insights from which the company can create more value for its customers. For example, one customer insights group states its mission simply as "getting better at understanding our consumers and meeting their needs."

Customer insights Fresh marketing information-based understanding of customers and the marketplace that become the basis for creating customer value, engagement, and relationships.

▪▪▪ The Marketing Information System

A **marketing information system (MIS)** consists of people, equipment, and procedures to gather, sort, analyze, evaluate, and distribute needed, timely, and accurate information to marketing decision makers. Figure 5–1 illustrates the MIS concept. The MIS begins and ends with marketing managers, but managers throughout the organization should be involved in the MIS. First, it interacts with managers to assess their information needs. Next, it develops needed information from internal company records, marketing intelligence activities, and the marketing research process. Information analysts process information to make it more useful. Finally, the MIS distributes information to managers in the right form and at the right time to help in marketing planning, implementation, and control.

We now take a closer look at the functions of a company's MIS.

Marketing information system (MIS) A structure of people, equipment, and procedures to gather, sort, analyze, evaluate, and distribute needed, timely, and accurate information to marketing decision makers.

Assessing Information Needs

A good MIS balances information that managers would like to have against that which they really need and is feasible to obtain. A company begins by interviewing managers to determine their information needs. For example, Mrs. Field's Cookies provides its managers with sales forecasts with updates each hour. When sales are falling behind, the computer suggests merchandising techniques such as sampling in the mall to pick up sales.[8]

Some managers ask for whatever information they can get without thinking carefully about its cost or usefulness. Too much information can be as harmful as too little. Other busy managers may fail to ask for things they need to know, or managers may not ask for some types of information that they should have. For example, managers might need to know about surges in favorable or unfavorable consumer discussions about their brands on blogs or online social media. Because they do not know about these discussions, they do not think to ask about them.

Figure 5–1
Marketing information system.

For example, managers need to anticipate new competitive product offerings. However, competitors withhold information to prevent their competition from knowing about the product. During KFC's development of one of its sandwiches, only a few corporate managers knew of the project. KFC had developed ingredient specifications for the making of the sandwich, and its suppliers had to sign secrecy agreements. KFC did not want competitors to learn about the new product offering before its test marketing. Yet competitors with a good MIS system might have picked up clues in advance about KFC's plans. They may have heard a bread supplier commenting about KFC's orders for small hamburger-style buns. They may have heard an executive stating how KFC would be strengthening its lunch business. Even with secret agreements, news inadvertently leaks out. Managers who keep their eyes and ears open can pick up on competitive moves using legal and ethical sources of information such as speeches by company executives and trade publications.

The company must estimate the value of having an item of information against the costs of obtaining it. The value depends on how it will be used, and this judgment is highly subjective. Similarly, estimating the cost of obtaining a specific item of information may be difficult.

The costs of obtaining, processing, storing, and delivering information can add up quickly. Sometimes additional information contributes little to improving a manager's decision. Its cost may exceed its benefit. Suppose that a restaurant manager estimates that launching a new menu item without further information will yield a lifetime profit of $500,000. The manager believes that additional information will improve the marketing mix and increase the company's profit to $525,000. It would be foolish to pay $30,000 or more to obtain the additional information. A good MIS balances the information users would like to have against what they really need and what is feasible to offer.

Internal data Internal data consist of electronic databases and nonelectronic information and records of consumer and market information obtained from within the company.

Marketing intelligence Everyday information about developments in the marketing environment that helps managers prepare and adjust marketing plans.

Marketing research The systematic design, collection, analysis, and reporting of data and findings relevant to a specific marketing situation facing a company.

Developing Marketing Information

Information needed by marketing managers can be obtained from **internal data**, **marketing intelligence**, and **marketing research** (see Figure 5–2).

Figure 5–2
Three sources of marketing information.

```
                    Developing marketing information
                    ┌──────────┬──────────┐
          Internal records  Marketing intelligence  Marketing research
```

Internal records
1. Guest information system
   a. Guest comment cards
   b. Listening to/speaking with guests
   c. Automated systems
   d. Mystery shoppers
   e. Point-of-sale information (POS)
2. Corporate customer and marketing intermediary

Marketing intelligence
1. Internal
2. External
3. Competitive

Marketing research
1. Define problem and research objectives
   a. Exploratory
   b. Descriptive
   c. Causal
2. Develop the research plan
   a. Secondary data
   b. Primary data
      i. Ethnographic
      ii. Survey
      iii. Experiment
3. Implement the plan
4. Interpret and report findings

Internal Data

Many companies build extensive internal databases, electronic collections of consumer and market information obtained from data sources within the company network. Marketing managers can readily access and work with information in the database to identify marketing opportunities and problems, plan programs, and evaluate performance. The answers to the questions in Table 5–1 will help managers assess their marketing information needs.

Information in the database can come from many sources. The marketing department furnishes information on customer transactions, demographics, psychographics, and buying behavior. The customer service department keeps records of customer satisfaction or service problems. The accounting department prepares financial statements and keeps detailed records of sales, costs, and cash flows. Operations reports on production schedules, shipments, and inventories. The sales force reports on reseller reactions and competitor activities, and marketing channel partners provide data on point-of-sale (POS) transactions. Marketing managers should take advantage of the information that is currently being generated by various departments. Harnessing such information can provide powerful customer insights and competitive advantage.

Table 5–1
Questions for Assessing Marketing Information Needs

1. What types of decisions do you make regularly?
2. What types of information do you need to make these decisions?
3. What types of useful information do you get regularly?
4. What social media sites can provide useful information?
5. What types of information would you like to get that you are not getting now?
6. What types of information do you get now that you don't really need?
7. What information would you want daily? Weekly? Monthly? Yearly?
8. What topics would you like to be kept informed about?
9. What databases would be useful to you?
10. What types of information analysis programs would you like to have?
11. What would be the four most helpful improvements that could be made in the present information system?

Here is an example of how one company uses its internal database to make better marketing decisions:

> Pizza Hut's database contains detailed customer data on 40 million U.S. households, gleaned from phone orders, online orders, and POS transactions at its more than 6,600 restaurants around the nation. Pizza Hut also uses Facebook to get customers to register for deals, collecting their e-mail, phone number, zip code, and other information. The company can slice and dice the data by favorite toppings, what you ordered last, and whether you buy a salad with your cheese and pepperoni pizza. It then uses all this data to enhance customer relationships, sending customers deals that will create another order. Says one blogger, "So who is always on my mind when I feel like pizza? Who is sending me coupons and free things that make me want to get pizza rather than make dinner? You got it, Pizza Hut. They had me buy in and now they'll have my loyalty. They make it so easy that I wouldn't want to bother getting it anywhere else."[9]

Internal databases usually can be accessed more quickly and cheaply than other information sources, but they also present some problems. Because internal information was often collected for other purposes, it may be incomplete or in the wrong form for marketing decisions. For example, sales and cost data used by the accounting department for preparing financial statements must be adapted for use in evaluating the value of specific customer segment, sales force, or channel performance. Data also age quickly; keeping the database current requires a major effort. In addition, a large company produces mountains of information, which must be well integrated and readily accessible so managers can find it easily and use it effectively. Managing that much data requires highly sophisticated equipment and techniques.

Every company contains more information than any manager can possibly know or analyze. The information is scattered in countless databases, plans, and records, and in the heads of many longtime managers. The company must somehow bring order to its information gold mine, so that its managers can more easily find answers to questions and make informed decisions. Increasingly, companies are creating **data warehouses** to house their customer data in a single, more accessible location. Then, using powerful data mining techniques, they search for meaningful patterns in the data and communicate them to managers. For example, a hotel can use data to examine profiles of customers who respond positively to particular types of promotions and events invitations. Then, the hotel marketing department can identify customers with the same profiles and target them for similar promotions and events.

Data warehouses Collect data from a variety of sources and store it in an accessible location.

Useful marketing information is contained in kitchen production schedules and sales reports, front-desk reports, sales call reports, and functions. Managers can use information gathered from these and other sources to evaluate performance and detect problems and opportunities. Here are some examples of how companies use internal records to make marketing decisions:[10]

- Hotel managers use reservations records and registration information to aid in timing their advertising and sales calls. If most vacationers book February reservations in November, advertising in December will be too late.

- Reservation records also provide information concerning the hotel's top-producing travel agents. Hotel representatives can phone, fax, or visit travel agents to inform them of hotel-sponsored promotional activities in an effort to generate a higher volume of room sales.

- Louisiana found through visitors' studies that most families plan for their summer vacations in the spring. They now advertise to the family market January through May, so their message will be in front of prospective visitors while they are making the vacation decision.

GUEST HISTORY INFORMATION. The single most important element in any hospitality MIS is to have a process for capturing and using information concerning guests. Guest information is vital to improving service, creating effective advertising and

Table 5–2
Specific Guest Information That Might Be Collected

Personal guest information	Type of primary product/service purchased
Name	Examples for a hotel:
Address	Regular sleeping room
Postal code	Suite
E-mail address	Deluxe suite
Phone numbers	Other purchases (cross-purchases)
Home	Examples for a hotel:
Work	Long-distance phone
Cell	Laundry
E-mail	Room service
Number in party	Minibar
Reason for trip	Hotel restaurants
Business	Health club
Pleasure	Recreational facilities
Emergency	Retail products charged to bill
Person who made reservation	Length of stay
Self-days stayed	Specific dates as guest
Employer	Method of arrival
Source of reservation	Personal auto
Name of employer	Rental auto
Address of employer	Tour bus
Title/position	Train
Method of payment	Taxi or limo
Credit card	Member of frequent guest programs
Which?	This hotel (number)
Cash	Others presented for credit
Check	Airline (number)
Bill to company	Company (number)

sales promotion programs, developing new products, improving existing products, and developing marketing and sales plans and using an effective revenue management program. Unfortunately, far too many hospitality firms have only a vague idea of who their guests are.

Specific guest information needs may include any or all of the information shown in Table 5–2. At first appearance this list undoubtedly seems overbearing and unduly inquisitive. The fact is that hospitality companies increasingly collect and use this type of information. Obviously, a hotel, resort, cruise line, or other hospitality company must be very careful not to infringe on the privacy rights of guests or to disturb them. An amazing amount of this information is available from internal records. This requires interfacing with other departments, such as reservations and accounting.

GUEST INFORMATION TRENDS. Information concerning guest trends is vital to planning and revenue/yield management. Types of guest trend information used by hotels, airlines, cruise lines, and auto rental companies include the following:

- Booking patterns
- Cancellations
- Conversion percentages (percentage of inquiries to reservations)

- Overbooking patterns
- Historical trends on occupancy for prime, shoulder, and low seasons
- Yield patterns by season

Guest history records enable hotel marketers to identify repeat guests and their individual needs and preferences. If a guest requests a particular newspaper delivered during one stay, a notation entered into the guest's file will ensure that the newspaper is received during all future visits. If a luxury hotel upgrades its guests to a better room on their fifth visit, its managers are increasing guest satisfaction. Frequent guests appreciate the free upgrade, and many request the higher-priced room on the next visit.

GUEST INFORMATION MANAGEMENT. Acquisition of this critical information cannot be left to chance or the whims of department managers. A system for obtaining guest information may include any or all of the techniques discussed next.

Guest Comment Cards Guest comment cards are often found on dining room tables and in guest rooms or are handed to departing customers. They provide useful information and can provide insights into problem areas in departments and service delivery system to take corrective actions. A problem with guest comment cards is that they may not reflect the opinions of the majority of guests. Commonly, only about 1–2 percent of the people who are very angry or very pleased take the time to complete a card.[11] Thus, comment cards can be useful in spotting problem areas, but they are not a good indication of overall guest satisfaction. Also, if the distribution and control of comment cards is not well thought out, employees may selectively distribute comment cards to guests they feel will give a positive response. Employees may also discard negative comment cards if they have the opportunity to do so. Many companies have the card mailed to a corporate office to avoid this problem.

Listening to and Speaking with Guests Many organizations have developed formal ways of interacting with guests. Hotels offer free receptions in the afternoon for their frequent guests. This not only is a way of saying thank you to the guests but also provides an opportunity for managers to speak with guests. Sea World in Australia requires that managers take several customer surveys every week. This is an excellent way to find out what guests think, and it lets management hear it firsthand. Wyndham hotels now call all guests five minutes before their room service order will arrive. This procedure was developed as a result of a guest's comment. The female business traveler said she often orders room service, takes a shower, gets dressed, and then eats breakfast. The call lets her know when the service person will arrive so she does not get caught in the shower. Wyndham found that all business travelers appreciated this thoughtfulness, and they were able to create a better service based on talking with their customers. Gaining information from your guests lets them know you are interested in them and can help create trust and customer loyalty.[12] Trump Hotel Collection has created a guest preferences program across its brands, named Trump Attaché, to treat every guest like a VIP, with a tenet "No stay should feel like the first." A personal "concierge" is assigned to guests to take care of their individual needs. The company collects and stores every request and all the individual preferences their employees observe about each guest during their stay. The Attaché team contacts the guests prior to their arrival and after their departure to know their likes and dislikes and their preferences, which are also recorded in the database for future visits. The company has observed that this program creates significant and enduring guest loyalty.[13]

If employees are trained to listen to guest comments and feed them back to management, this can be a powerful source of information. Your employees can be like microphones recording guest comments. For this listening to work, management has to feed back to the employees how it is using the information, and there must be trust between the employees and management. Ritz-Carlton makes excellent use of the "listening posts" concept. Horst Schulze, former president of Ritz-Carlton, said, "Keep on listening to customers because they change. And if you want to have 100% satisfied customers then you have to make sure that you listen and change—just in case they change their expectations that you change with them."[14]

Automated Systems The decreasing cost and increasing capacity of automated guest history systems will allow hotels to create close relationships with their customers once again.[15]

Obviously, any hotel property or hospitality company, such as a large cruise line, must use automated systems. A variety of systems are available and should be examined carefully and tested before purchasing. Remember that an automated guest information system is part of broader systems such as database marketing and yield/revenue management.

An automated guest history system can be of great benefit to the sales force. Salespeople can pull guest histories by a specific geographic area, such as a city. This information can greatly assist in a sales blitz by identifying frequent guests who can receive top priority in the blitz. The guest history can also identify former frequent guests who are no longer using the hotel. Salespeople will want to call on these former clients to see if they can regain their business.

An automated guest history system offers a real competitive advantage to a chain, particularly a smaller chain. "By means of a centralized system or network, a group of hotels could share guest information. Imagine how impressed a guest would be if he or she requested a suite, champagne, and a hypoallergenic pillow when staying at a hotel in Boston, then received the same services at a chain affiliate in Maui without even having to ask."[16]

Mystery Shoppers Mystery shopping is estimated to be more than a $1.5 billion industry.[17] Hospitality companies often hire disguised or **mystery shoppers** to pose as customers and report back on their experience. Mystery shoppers are used in all types of operations. McDonald's uses a mystery shopping program to make sure their stores are performing to their standards. They post the results on the Web, making them accessible to local managers and corporate managers.[18] Companies hire mystery shoppers to examine their competitors, as well.

A mystery shopper works best if there is a possibility for recognition and reward for good job performance. This is the concept of positive reinforcement. The most effective mystery shopping systems provide the employees with a list of the items the mystery shoppers will be checking. If employees feel that the only purpose of a disguised shopper program is to report poor service and reprimand them, the program will not fulfill its full potential.

Mystery shoppers Hospitality companies often hire disguised or mystery shoppers to pose as customers and report back on their experience.

Point-of-Sale Information For restaurants, the POS register will undoubtedly offer opportunities to compile and distribute, through a computer, information that is currently entered into reports manually. A POS system could collect information about individual restaurant patrons where credit cards are used.

Some observers of the fast-food industry believe that future POS systems will use expert systems that employ computers using artificial intelligence. One possible scenario is the "computaburger." Data concerning customer preference, order size, and volume will be taken from a POS machine and provided to an expert system. The expert system will then predict and possibly even order a volume of hamburger and the accompanying condiments for specific times in each day.[19]

The casino industry has displayed a high interest in POS systems and their increasing sophistication. Some slot machines are now capable of recording the numbers of play and the win–loss record of frequent players who activate the machines through use of a magnetic card. The player receives points based on the amount of play, and the casino is able to track the playing habits of players using the slot club cards, as discussed in the chapter opening case of Caesars Entertainment. Systems are also in place in most casinos to track players who are brought to the casino by junket reps. Tracking of these players is the responsibility of the pit boss in each gaming area, such as blackjack.

CORPORATE CUSTOMER AND MARKETING INTERMEDIARY INFORMATION. A database of customers/prospects is of great value to a professional sales force. The sales force of Benchmark Hospitality Conference Resorts is trained to go beyond demographic studies and to target prospects by geography and industry segment. Benchmark's salespeople monitor the health of specific industries and qualify prospects. Before arranging a sales meeting with any corporate meeting planner, the salesperson obtains marketing information concerning the prospect, such as the following:

- The industry standing and strategic outlook for growth
- Profit and loss statements from annual reports
- Debt-to-equity ratios
- Corporate culture information
- Data concerning how this company uses meetings

This information can be obtained from annual reports, financial analyses of public companies, and articles on the company, and by talking with company employees. In addition to detailed information concerning prospects, Benchmark expects sales force members to be regular readers of the business press, such as *the Wall Street Journal* and *the New York Times*.[20]

Competitive Marketing Intelligence

Competitive marketing intelligence includes everyday publicly available information about developments in the marketing environment that helps managers prepare and adjust marketing plans and short-run tactics. Marketing intelligence techniques range from observing consumers and competitors firsthand to benchmarking competitor' products, online research, and social media buzz.

INTERNAL SOURCES OF MARKETING INTELLIGENCE. Marketing intelligence can be gathered by a company's executives, front-desk staff, service staff, purchasing agents, and sales force. Employees, unfortunately, are often too busy to pass on important information. The company must sell them on their role as intelligence gatherers and train them to spot and report new developments. Managers should debrief contact personnel regularly.

Hotel owners and managers are essential parts of a marketing intelligence system. John F. Power, the general manager of the New York Hilton and Towers, served in this role on a trip to Japan. "I realized how different a Japanese breakfast is from our own," said Power, "and while most people like to sample the cuisine of the country they are visiting, everyone prefers to eat familiar food for breakfast."

As a result of marketing intelligence gathered on Power's trip, the New York Hilton now serves *miso* soup, *nori* (dried seaweed), *yakizanaka* (grilled fish), raw eggs, *natto* (fermented beans), *oshiako* (pickled vegetables), and rice as an authentic Japanese breakfast buffet.[21]

EXTERNAL SOURCES OF MARKETING INTELLIGENCE. A hospitality company must encourage suppliers, convention and tourist bureaus, and travel agencies to pass along important intelligence. It is worthwhile for a hospitality company to encourage the gathering of this information by treating vendors, salespeople, and potential employees in a friendly and receptive manner. Members of management should be encouraged to join community and professional organizations where they are likely to obtain essential marketing information.

Hotel and restaurant managers are in a particularly good position to acquire excellent information by entertaining key information sources in their properties. Sales force members are excellent conduits of information.

Sometimes rival companies offer you the information. For example, Bob Ayling, ex-chief executive of British Airways, accomplished such a mission when he visited the offices of the recently launched EasyJet. Ayling approached the company's founder, Stelios Haji-Ioannou, to ask whether he could visit, claiming to be fascinated as to how the Greek entrepreneur had made the budget airline formula work. Haji-Ioannou not only agreed but allegedly showed Ayling his business plan. A year later, British Airways announced the launch of Go. "It was a carbon copy of EasyJet," says EasyGroup's director of corporate affairs. "Same planes, same direct ticket sales, same use of a secondary airport, and same idea to sell on-board refreshments. They succeeded in stealing our business model—it was a highly effective spying job."[22]

Monthly Performance at a Glance—My Property vs. Competitive Set

Upper Upscale Urban Hotel 555 Central Ave Any City, ST 12,345–1234 Phone: (555) 121–1212 STR # 1234 ChainID: MgtCo: None Owner: None
For the Month of December 2018   Date Created: January 18, 2019   Monthly Competitive Set Data Excludes Subject Property

December 2018

	Occupancy (%)			ADR			RevPAR		
	My Prop	Comp Set	Index (MPI)	My Prop	Comp Set	Index (ARI)	My Prop	Comp Set	Index (RGI)
Current Month	51.3	54.0	95.0	124.26	126.44	98.3	63.73	68.28	93.3
Year to Date	66.8	71.6	93.3	147.67	158.47	93.2	98.64	113.40	87.0
Running 3 Month	59.4	66.8	88.9	149.58	159.19	94.0	88.86	106.40	83.5
Running 12 Month	66.8	71.6	93.3	147.67	158.47	93.2	98.64	113.40	87.0

December 2018 vs. 2017 Percent Change

	Occupancy			ADR			RevPAR		
	My Prop	Comp Set	Index (MPI)	My Prop	Comp Set	Index (ARI)	My Prop	Comp Set	Index (RGI)
Current Month	-22.7	-16.2	-7.8	-0.8	-2.8	2.0	-23.4	-18.6	-5.9
Year to Date	-8.5	1.2	-9.5	4.4	5.8	-1.3	-4.4	7.0	-10.7
Running 3 Month	-16.6	-2.7	-14.2	-0.5	6.5	-6.5	-17.0	3.6	-19.8
Running 12 Month	-8.5	1.2	-9.5	4.4	5.8	-1.3	-4.4	7.0	-10.7

SMITH TRAVEL RESEARCH, Inc.

The Star report allows a hotel to compare how it is doing compared to a competitive set the management selects. The competitive set statistics are always shown as group data so the hotel is never able to determine the actual statistics for the different members of the competitive set. The Star report is a commonly used tool to provide competitive intelligence in the hotel industry. Provided with permission for Smith Travel Research Monthly Performance at a Glance—My Property vs. Competitive Set. Courtesy of Smith Travel Research.

SOURCES OF COMPETITIVE INFORMATION. Competitive intelligence is available from competitors' annual reports, trade magazine articles, speeches, press releases, brochures, and advertisements. Hotel and restaurant managers should also visit their competitors' premises periodically. As mentioned in Chapter 4, a major consideration in any competitive information system is clearly defining the competition. Marketing intelligence techniques range from benchmarking competitors' products to researching on the internet and monitoring social media buzz.

Social media companies such as Revinate provide hotel reputation benchmarking reports based on hotel review scores in social media sites and services to monitor your competition performance in social media on daily basis. Benchmarking allows hotels to track their performance against the competition and take actions.[23]

"In today's information age, companies are leaving a paper trail of information online," says an online intelligence expert. Today's managers "don't have to simply rely on old news or intuition when making investment and business decisions."[24] Using internet search engines, marketers can search specific competitor names, events, or trends and see what turns up. Intelligence seekers can also pore through any of thousands of online databases. Some are free. For example, the U.S. Securities and Exchange Commission's database provides a huge stockpile of financial information on public competitors. And for a fee, companies can subscribe to more than 3,000 online databases and information search services such as Dialog, DataStar, LEXIS-NEXIS, Dow Jones News Retrieval, UMI ProQuest, and Dun & Bradstreet's Online Access. Hospitality managers can also subscribe to newsletters such as HotelMarketing.com, National Restaurant Association Smart Brief, and HotelOnline.net. One news service, HotelOnline.com, has editions by country, including Brazil, Germany, China, Poland, and Romania. To get your country's edition, add your country's internet abbreviation to the URL, for example, www.HotelOnline.com.br for Brazil.

Associations sometimes collect data from member companies, compile it, and make it available to members for a reasonable fee. Information of this nature can often be misleading because member companies frequently provide incorrect data or may refuse to contribute any statistics if they have a dominant market share.

Marketing Research

Managers cannot always wait for information to arrive in bits and pieces from the marketing intelligence system. They often require formal studies of specific marketing situations and decisions. When McDonald's decided to add salads to its menu, its planners needed to research customers' preferences for types of vegetables and dressings.

Ben's Steakhouse in Palm Beach, Florida, would like to know what percentage of its target market has heard of Ben's, how they heard about Ben's, what they know, and how they feel about the steakhouse. This would enable Ben's Steakhouse to know how effective their marketing communications have been. Casual marketing intelligence cannot answer these questions. Managers sometimes need to commission formal marketing research.

Marketing research is a process that identifies and defines marketing opportunities and problems, monitors and evaluates marketing actions and performance, and communicates the findings and implications to management.[25] Marketing researchers engage in a wide variety of activities. Their 10 most common activities are measurement of market potentials, market-share analysis, the determination of market characteristics, sales analysis, studies of business trends, short-range forecasting, competitive product studies, long-range forecasting, MIS studies, and testing of existing products.

A company can conduct marketing research by employing its own researchers or hiring outside researchers. Most large companies—in fact, more than 73 percent—have their own marketing research departments. But even companies with their own departments hire outside firms to do fieldwork and special tasks.

Marriott International's research priorities are as follows:[26]

- Market segmentation and sizing
- Concept development, product testing, and technology

Marketing research The systematic design, collection, analysis, and reporting of data relevant to a specific marketing situation facing an organization.

Figure 5–3
Marketing research process.

Defining the problem and research objectives → Developing the research plan for collecting information → Implementing the research plan—collecting and analyzing the data → Interpreting and reporting the findings

- Price-sensitivity assessment
- Advertising and promotions assessment
- Sustainability and social impact
- Customer satisfaction, loyalty, and experience

Small hotels or restaurants can obtain research help from nearby universities or colleges with business or hospitality programs. College marketing classes can be used to do exploratory research, find information about prospective customers, and conduct customer surveys. Instructors often arrange for their classes to gain marketing research experience in this way.

The marketing research process consists of four steps (see Figure 5–3): defining the problem and research objectives, developing the research plan, implementing the research plan, and interpreting and reporting the findings.

Defining the Problem and Research Objectives

Managers must work closely with marketing researchers to define the problem and the research objectives. The manager best understands the problem or decision for which information is needed, and the researcher best understands marketing research and how to obtain the information.

Managers must know enough about marketing research to interpret the findings carefully. If they know little about marketing research, they may accept the wrong information, draw the wrong conclusions, or request much more information than they need. Marketing researchers can help the manager define the problem and use the findings correctly.

In one case, a restaurant manager hired a researcher to determine the restaurant's level of awareness among the target market. The manager felt that lack of awareness explained low patronage. The researcher found, to the contrary, that many people were aware of the restaurant but thought of it as a special-occasion rather than an everyday restaurant. The manager had misdefined the problem and the research objective.

Assuming the problem is well defined, the manager and researcher must set research objectives. A marketing research project can have one of three types of objectives: **exploratory research**, to gather preliminary information that will help define the problem and suggest hypotheses; **descriptive research**, to describe the size and composition of the market; and **causal research**, to test hypotheses about cause-and-effect relationships. Managers often start with exploratory research and later follow with descriptive and/or causal research.

A sad example of the need for marketing research was a self-help project initiated on U.S. Indian reservations. A total of 52 hotels were built as a result of promoting and anticipating tourism. Only two survived because of poorly conceived plans. In several cases, hotels were built in seldom-visited remote areas. Marketing research could have provided valuable information, such as visitor trends to the areas, identification of possible market segments, plus their size and travel preferences.[27]

Exploratory research Marketing research to gather preliminary information that will help to better define problems and suggest hypotheses.

Descriptive research Marketing research to better describe marketing problems, situations, or markets, such as the market potential for a product or the demographics and attitudes of consumers.

Causal research Marketing research to test hypotheses about cause-and-effect relationships.

A cruise in Victoria Harbor is a popular tourist activity in Hong Kong. Tourist authorities such as the Hong Kong Tourist Association use research to determine who comes to their cities and what tourist attractions create value for them. Courtesy of Norman Chan/Shutterstock.

Developing the Research Plan

The second marketing research step calls for determining the needed information and developing a data-collection plan.

Determining Specific Information Needs

Research objectives must be translated into specific information needs. When Marriott decided to research a new lower-priced hotel system, it had two goals: to pull travelers away from competitors and to minimize cannibalization of its own existing hotels. This research might call for the following specific information:[28]

- What features should the hotel offer?
- How should the new hotels be priced?
- Where should the hotels be located? Can they safely be located near existing Marriott hotels without incurring cannibalization?
- What are the probable sales and profits?

Gathering Secondary Information

To meet a manager's information needs, researchers can gather secondary data, primary data, or both. **Secondary data** consist of information already in existence somewhere, having been collected for another purpose. **Primary data** consist of information collected for the specific purpose at hand.

Researchers usually start by gathering secondary data. Secondary data are usually obtained more quickly and at a lower cost than primary data. For example, Restaurants USA, published by the National Restaurant Association, provides a yearly projection of sales for food-service establishments, presenting the projections by state and by industry segment. A company has the options of paying a research firm to develop this information or of joining the National Restaurant Association and receiving this information through its publication. The latter is more cost effective. Groups on social media sites can also be good sources of secondary information. LinkedIn, for example, has groups that include hotel sales, revenue management, event management, and lodging, food, and beverage trends.

Using *commercial online databases*, marketing researchers can conduct their own searches of secondary data sources. General database services such as ProQuest and LexisNexis put an incredible wealth of information at the fingertips of marketing decision makers. Beyond commercial services offering information for a fee, almost every industry association, government agency, business publication, and news medium offers free information on their Web sites.

Internet search engines can also be a big help in locating relevant secondary information sources. However, they can also be very frustrating and inefficient. For example, a Marriott marketer Googling "hotel cannibalization" would come up with more than 80,000 hits. Still, well-structured, well-designed online searches can be a good starting point to any marketing research.

Basing decisions on secondary data, however, can also present problems. The required information may not exist. Even when it exists, it might not be very relevant, accurate, current, and impartial. For example, a trade magazine wanted to identify the best hotel chains in the minds of corporate travel managers and travel agents. It distributed its survey as inserts in its magazine. The response rate was less than 0.05 percent. Yet the magazine issued a ranking based on this unreliable response rate.[29] Additionally, if research of this type is not properly designed, it can favor the companies with the most hotels or restaurants because they will be more familiar to the respondent.

Secondary data provide a good starting point for marketing research. However, when secondary sources cannot provide all the needed information, the company must collect primary data.

Secondary data Information that already exists somewhere, having been collected for another purpose.

Primary data Information collected for the specific purpose at hand.

Marketing HIGHLIGHT 5.2 — ZMET: Getting into the heads of consumer

What is the meaning of a brand to consumers? How do consumers feel about a brand? Why are consumers loyal to a particular brand? Standard methods such as surveys do not address these issues at a deep level. Former Harvard Business School marketing professor Gerald Zaltman, with colleagues, developed an in-depth methodology to uncover what consumers think and feel about products, services, brands, and other things. The basic assumption behind the Zaltman Metaphor Elicitation Technique (ZMET) is that most thoughts and feelings are unconscious and shaped by a set of universal deep metaphors, basic orientations toward the world that shape everything consumers think, hear, say, or do. In other words, ZMET assumes that much of subconscious content is based on images, not words.

The ZMET technique works by first asking participants in advance to select a minimum of 12 images from their own sources (magazines, catalogs, family photo albums) to represent their thoughts and feelings about a particular issue or brand. In a one-on-one interview, the study administrator uses advanced interview techniques to explore the images with the participant and reveal hidden meanings. Finally, the participants use a computer program to create a collage with these images that communicates their subconscious thoughts and feelings about the topic. The results often significantly influence marketing actions, as the following example illustrates.

After a ZMET study of slot club members of both local and visitor at a mega resort casino, the property made significant changes in its slot club and gave the players control over their comps. Club members have started to use their cash-back points in exchange for cash, promotional credits, or gift cards at different exchange rates. The events were augmented with greater entertainment and higher prizes. To improve the slot club human aspects, the casino also provided training for managing customer interactions.

Sources: Gerald Zaltman and Lindsay Zaltman, "What Deep Metaphors Reveal About the Minds of Consumers," *Marketing Metaphoria* (Boston: Harvard Business School Press, 2008); Glenn L. Christensen and Jerry C. Olson, "Mapping Consumers' Mental Models with ZMET" *Psychology & Marketing*, 19 (June 2002): 477–502; Emily Eakin, "Penetrating the Mind by Metaphor," *New York Times*, February 23, 2002; Flavia Hendler and Kathryn A. LaTour, "A Qualitative Analysis of Slot Clubs as Drivers of Casino Loyalty," *The Cornell Hospitality Quarterly* (May 2008): 105–121; Gerald Zaltman, *How Customers Think* (Cambridge, MA: Harvard Business School Press, 2003).

Internet surveying is growing in popularity. It offers quick and inexpensive access to many samples. The data are also automatically tabulated, eliminating errors and time. Andriy Popov/123RF.

One theme park management company has developed a survey panel of 11,000 guests. It surveys the members of the panel on a regular basis through the internet. The company's research director claims internet surveying saves him at least $30,000 over telephone surveying and provides good information.[43]

A company can also conduct online experiments. It can experiment with different prices, headlines, or product features on different Web or mobile sites or at different times to learn the relative effectiveness of their offers.

As response rates for traditional survey approaches decline and costs increase, the internet is quickly replacing mail and the telephone as the dominant data-collection methodology. Yet, as popular as online research methods are, smart companies are choosing to use them to augment rather than replace more traditional methods. A director of marketing states, "Online is not a solution in and of itself to all of our business challenges but it does expand our toolkit."

Even smaller companies can use online survey services such as Snap Surveys (www.snapsurveys.com) and SurveyMonkey (www.surveymonkey.com) to create, publish, and distribute their own custom online or mobile surveys in minutes. Jacob Brown, a marketing researcher specializing in internet-based surveys, has these suggestions. As with other surveys, always do a pretest. If you have a limited number of names in your database and don't want to waste them on a pretest, buy a list with similar characteristics and use this list for your pretest.

This is a much better alternative to not pretesting. Look at the number of people who drop

SMS Surveys   Offline Surveys   Online Surveys

Qualtrics is a survey platform provider, helping organizations collect, analyze, and act on customer, employee, and market insights. Courtesy of Qualtrics, LLC.

Online focus groups
Gathering a small group of people online with a trained moderator to chat about a product, service, or organization and gain qualitative insights about consumer attitude and behavior.

out after each question. If there is a high dropout rate after one question, this could indicate problems with that question. If the completion rate is low, but no one question has a high dropout rate, this could indicate the survey is too long. Using simple technology for a consumer market is critical. Don't expect respondents to wait for graphics to load or to reset their monitor's resolution. Internet surveys are quick and can be inexpensive. The response rate can be a problem if they are not properly designed and targeted.[44]

Marketing Highlight 5–3, "Pros and Cons of Online Research," outlines some of the advantages and disadvantages of online research. Online researchers have also begun to use instant messaging (IM) in various ways—to conduct a chat with a respondent, to probe more deeply with a member of an online focus group, or to direct respondents to a Web site.[46] IM is also a useful way to get teenagers to open up on topics.

Just as marketing researchers have rushed to use the internet for quantitative surveys and data collection, they are now also adopting qualitative internet-based research approaches, such as online focus groups, blogs, and social networks. The internet can provide a fast, low-cost way to gain qualitative customer insights. A primary qualitative Web-based research approach is **online focus groups**. Such focus groups offer many advantages over traditional focus groups. Participants can log in from anywhere; all they need is a laptop and a Web connection. Thus, the internet works well for bringing together people from different parts of the country or world, especially those in higher-income groups who can't spare the time to travel to a central site. Also, researchers can conduct and monitor online focus groups from just about anywhere, eliminating travel, lodging, and facility costs. Finally, although online focus groups require some advance scheduling, results are almost immediate.

Online focus groups can take any of several formats. Most occur in real time, in the form of online chat room discussions in which participants and a moderator sit around a virtual table exchanging comments. Alternatively, researchers might set up an online message board on which respondents interact over the course of several days or a few weeks. Participants log in daily and comment on focus group topics.

Although low in cost and easy to administer, online focus groups can lack the real-world dynamics of more personal approaches. To overcome these shortcomings, some researchers are now adding real-time audio and video to their online focus groups. For example, online research firm Channel M2 "puts the human touch back into online research" by assembling focus group participants in people-friendly "virtual interview rooms."[47] Participants are recruited using traditional methods and then sent a Web camera so that both their verbal and nonverbal reactions can be recorded. Participants receive instructions via e-mail, including a link to the Channel M2 online interviewing room and a toll-free teleconference number to call. At the appointed time, when they click on the link and phone in, participants sign on and see the Channel M2 interview room, complete with live video of the other participants, text chat, screen or slide sharing, and a whiteboard. Once the focus group is under way, questions and answers occur in "real time" in a remarkably lively setting. Participants comment spontaneously—verbally, via text messaging, or both. Researchers can "sit in" on the focus group from anywhere, seeing and hearing every respondent. Or they can review a recorded version at a later date.

The internet has become an important new tool for conducting research and developing customer insights. But today's marketing researchers are going even further on the Web—well beyond structured online surveys, focus groups, and Web communities. Increasingly, they are listening to and watching consumers by

Marketing Highlight 5.3: Pros and cons of online research

Advantages

- *Online research is inexpensive.* A typical e-mail survey can cost between 20 and 50 percent less than what a conventional survey costs, and return rates can be as high as 50 percent.

- *Online research is fast.* Online surveys are fast because the survey can automatically direct respondents to applicable questions and transmit results immediately. One estimate says that 75–80 percent of a survey's targeted response can be generated in 40 hours using online methods compared to a telephone survey that can take 70 days to obtain 150 interviews.

- *People tend to be honest online.* Britain's online polling company YouGov.com surveyed 250 people via intercom in a booth and the other half online asking questions such as "Should there be more aid to Africa?" Online answers were deemed much more honest. People may be more open about their opinions when they can respond privately and not to another person whom they feel might be judging them, especially on sensitive topics.

- *Online research is versatile.* Increased broadband penetration offers online research even more flexibility and capabilities. For instance, virtual reality software lets visitors inspect 3D models of products such as cameras, cars, and medical equipment and manipulate product characteristics. Even at the basic tactile level, online surveys can make answering a questionnaire easier and more fun than paper-and-pencil versions.

- *Data are more accurate.* Online interviewing programs enable the survey responses to be tabulated as the respondent is entering them. As in any form of computer-aided interviewing, the next question automatically comes up in branching questions or skip sequences. For example, if a business traveler is to answer one set of questions and a pleasure traveler another set, when asked if you were traveling for business or pleasure, the proper set will come up.

Disadvantages

- *Samples can be small and skewed.* Some 33 percent of households are without internet access in the United States; the percentage is even higher among lower-income groups, in rural areas, and in most parts of Asia, Latin America, and Central and Eastern Europe, where socioeconomic and education levels also differ. Although people older than 65 are one of the fastest growing segments of internet users, they have been light users. Thus, one could expect to get a younger sample through an internet survey. Tourism research has found significant differences in responses received from pen-and-paper surveys and internet surveys, including demographic differences.[45] Although it's certain that more and more people will go online, online market researchers must find creative ways to reach population segments on the other side of the "digital divide." One option is to combine offline sources with online findings. Providing temporary internet access at locations such as malls and recreation centers is another strategy.

- *Online market research is prone to technological problems and inconsistencies.* Marketing researchers have rushed to conduct online research by overusing technology, concentrating on the bells and whistles and graphics while ignoring basic survey design guidelines. Problems also arise because browser software varies. The Web designer's final product may look very different on the research subject's screen.

Sources: "Survey: Internet Should Remain Open to All," www.consumeraffairs.com (accessed January 25, 2006); "Highlights from the National Consumers League's Survey on Consumers and Communications Technologies: Current and Future Use," www.nclnet.org/ (accessed July 21, 2005); Catherine Arnold, "Not Done Net; New Opportunities Still Exist in Online Research," *Marketing News* (April 1, 2004): 17; Louella Miles, "Online, on Tap," *Marketing* (June 16, 2004): 39–40; Suzy Bashford, "The Opinion Formers," *Revolution* (May 2004): 42–46; Nima M. Ray and Sharon W. Tabor, "Contributing Factors; Several Issues Affect e-Research Validity," *Marketing News* (September 15, 2003): 50; Bob Lamons, "Eureka! Future of B to B Research Is Online," *Marketing News* (September 24, 2001): 9–10.

---

actively mining the rich veins of unsolicited, unstructured, "bottom-up" customer information already coursing around the Web. This might be as simple as scanning customer reviews and comments on the company's brand site or shopping sites such as zagat.com or tripadvisor.com. Or it might mean using sophisticated Web-analysis tools of data and text mining to deeply analyze Big Data involving consumer comments and messages found in blogs or on social networking sites, such as Facebook or Twitter. Listening to and watching consumers online can provide valuable insights into what consumers are saying or feeling about brands. As one information expert puts it, "The Web knows what you want."[48]

Perhaps the most explosive issue facing online researchers concerns consumer privacy. Some critics fear that unethical researchers will use the e-mail addresses and confidential responses gathered through surveys to sell products after the research is completed. They are concerned about the use of technologies that collect personal information online without the respondents' consent. Failure to address such privacy issues could result in angry, less-cooperative consumers and increased government intervention. For example, Dunkin' Donuts regularly eavesdrops on consumer online conversations as an important input to its customer relationship building efforts. Take the case of customer Jeff Lerner, who recently tweeted about a loose lid that popped off his Dunkin' Donuts drive-through coffee and soaked his white shirt and new car. Within minutes, Dunkin' picked up Lerner's tweet, sent him a direct message asking for his phone number, called him to apologize, and sent him a $10 gift card. Lerner found Dunkin's actions laudable. "This is social media. This is listening. This is engagement," he stated in a later blog post. However, some disconcerted consumers might see Dunkin's Twitter monitoring as an invasion of their privacy.[49]

SAMPLING PLAN. Marketing researchers usually draw conclusions about large consumer groups by taking a sample. A **sample** is a segment of the population selected to represent the population as a whole. Ideally, the sample should be representative and allow the researcher to make accurate estimates of the thoughts and behaviors of the larger population.

Designing the sample calls for the following four decisions:

1. *Who will be surveyed?* This is not always obvious. For example, to study the decision-making process for a family vacation, should the researcher interview the husband, wife, other family members, the travel agent, or all of these? The researcher must determine what type of information is needed and who is most likely to have it.

2. *How many people should be surveyed?* Large samples give more reliable results than small samples. However, it is not necessary to sample the entire target market or even a large portion to obtain reliable results. If well chosen, samples of less than 1 percent of a population can give good reliability.

3. *How should the sample be chosen?* Sample members might be chosen at random from the entire population (a probability sample), or the researcher might select people who are easiest to obtain information from (a convenience sample). The researcher might also choose a specified number of participants from each of several demographic groups (a quota sample). These and other ways of drawing samples have different costs and time limitations and varying accuracy and statistical properties. The needs of the research project will determine which method is most effective. Table 5–4 lists the various kinds of samples.

Sample (1) A segment of a population selected for marketing research to represent the population as a whole; (2) offer of a trial amount of a product to consumers.

Table 5–4
Types of Samples

Probability Samples	
Simple random sample	Every member of the population has a known and equal chance of selection.
Stratified random sample	The population is divided into mutually exclusive groups (e.g., age groups), and random samples are drawn from each group.
Cluster (area) sample	The population is divided into mutually exclusive groups (e.g., blocks), and the researcher draws a sample of the groups to interview.
Nonprobability Samples	
Convenience sample	The researcher selects the easiest population members from which to obtain information.
Judgment sample	The researcher uses his or her judgment to select population members who are good prospects for accurate information.
Quota sample	The researcher finds and interviews a prescribed number of people in each of several categories.

4. *When will the survey be given?* This is particularly important in personal surveys. The days and hours should be representative of the flow of traffic. For example if 70 percent of the customers come after 7 P.M., then the data collection needs to be heavier in the evening. The type of guest may change depending on the day or time. People working in the area may visit a restaurant at lunch, whereas people living in the area visit the restaurant for dinner. Businesspersons stay at a hotel Sunday through Thursday, and pleasure travelers are heavier users on weekends. Thus, if the population of interest is business travelers, there should be heavier sampling during the week. Failure to match the time the data is collected with business patterns can result in invalid survey results.

RESEARCH INSTRUMENTS. In collecting primary data, marketing researchers have a choice of two main research instruments: the questionnaire and mechanical devices.

You can usually spot several errors in a carelessly prepared questionnaire (see Marketing Highlight 5–4).

Questionnaires The questionnaire is by far the most common instrument, whether administered in person, by phone, by e-mail, or online. Questionnaires are very flexible—there are many ways to ask questions. Closed-end questions include all the possible answers, and subjects make choices among them. Examples include multiple-choice questions and scale questions. Open-end questions allow respondents to answer in their own words. In a survey of airline users, Southwest Airlines might simply ask, "What is your opinion of Southwest Airlines?" Or it might ask people to complete a sentence: "When I choose an airline, the most important

Marketing HIGHLIGHT 5.4 A "questionable" questionnaire

Suppose that the following questionnaire has been prepared by a restaurant manager to build a profile of his or her potential market. How do you as a consumer feel about each question?

1. What is your income to the nearest hundred dollars?
People don't necessarily know their income to the nearest hundred dollars, nor do they want to reveal their income that closely. Furthermore, a questionnaire should never open with such a personal question. Personal questions should be placed at the end of the survey.

2. How often do you go out to eat?
The question is ambiguous. To provide useful information one would need to know, at a minimum, the meal period and type of restaurant.

3. During the business week, how often do you eat breakfast?
1 ____ 2 ____ 3 ____ 4 ____ 5 ____
The responses are not collectively exhaustive. That is, they do not provide all responses possible. What if a person never eats breakfast? The addition of a sixth response, 0 ____, would solve the problem.

4. On average, how much do you spend for lunch?
____ 0 to $2 ____ $2 to $4
____ $4 to $6 ____ $6 to $8
The choices are overlapping. If someone spent $2, $4, or $6, he or she could mark his or her response in one of two spots. Also, the response choices are not collectively exhaustive. If someone spends more than $8, there is nowhere to mark this response.

5. Would you like (name of restaurant) to have live bands on Friday and Saturday night?
Yes ( ) No ( )
The word like does not indicate purchase behavior. Many respondents would answer "yes" because it offers them an entertainment option, but they would not come out on a regular basis. Also, many times there is a cost to adding an extra feature. If the respondent is going to pay for the cost through a cover charge or higher drink prices, it should be addressed. Finally, the question does not specify the type of band. Someone who wants a country-and-western band may answer "yes" and then be disappointed when the manager puts in a heavy metal band.

6. Did you receive more restaurant coupons this April or last April?
Who can remember this?

7. What are the most salient and determinant attributes in your evaluation of restaurants?
What are "salient and determinant attributes"? Don't use big words that the respondent may not understand.

consideration is...." These and other kinds of open-end questions often reveal more than closed-end questions because they do not limit respondents' answers.

Open-end questions are especially useful in exploratory research, when the researcher is trying to find out *what* people think but is not measuring *how many* people think in a certain way. Closed-end questions, on the other hand, provide answers that are easier to interpret and tabulate.

Researchers should also use care in the *wording* and *ordering* of questions. They should use simple, direct, and unbiased wording. Questions should be arranged in a logical order. The first question should create interest if possible, and difficult or personal questions should be asked last so that respondents do not become defensive.

In preparing a questionnaire, the marketing researcher must decide what questions to ask, what form the questions should take, and how to word and sequence the questions. Questionnaires too often omit questions that should be answered and include questions that cannot, will not, or need not be answered. Each question should be examined to ensure that it contributes to the research objectives. Questions that are merely interesting should be dropped. You can usually spot several errors in a carelessly prepared questionnaire (see Marketing Highlight 5–4).

Researchers in the hospitality industry must be extremely careful in developing questions and selecting the sample not to offend respondents unwittingly. This problem is less pervasive with many products, such as building tile or brass fittings. A classic example of a marketing research mistake was made by a U.S. airline. This company offered a special companion price for business travelers with the idea that the companion would be the executive's spouse. Following the promotion, questionnaires were sent to the spouse, not the executive. Such questionnaires innocently asked, "How did you like the recent companion trip?" In several cases the answer was, "What trip? I didn't go!" The airline received angry calls and threats of suits for invasion of privacy or contribution to the breakup of a marriage (Table 5–5).

Mechanical Instruments Researchers also use mechanical instruments to monitor consumer behavior. These methods are as simple as recording how much customers consume to measuring how brain activities change when exposed to different marketing stimuli. Restaurant managers use POS systems to track the sales of menu items. Managers can look for increases in sales of promotional items, to measure the success of a promotion. Customer loyalty programs track the purchasing habits of customers and use this information to offer loyalty rewards. If customers never buy an appetizer, they may be offered an appetizer as a loyalty bonus since this free item is not likely to reduce the customer's check average. Keeping track of what customers consume is a very simple yet very effective way of understanding customer behavior.

Researchers are applying "neuromarketing," measuring brain activity to learn how consumers feel and respond. Marketing scientists using magnetic resonance imaging (MRI) scans and electroencephalography (EEG) devices have learned that tracking brain electrical activity and blood flow can provide companies with insights into what turns consumers on and off regarding their brands and marketing. "Companies have always aimed for the customers heart, but the head may make a better target," suggests one neuromarketer. "Neuromarketing is reaching consumers where the action is: the brain."[50] A neuromarketing study in Germany has suggested that Starbucks's coffee prices are too low, underpriced by a third, which leaves profits on the table.[51] Some recent studies, using the neuroscience technique of facial electromyography (fEMG), offer new insights about hotel advertising effectiveness to differentiate the brands emotionally.[52]

PepsiCo's Frito-Lay unit uses neuromarketing to test commercials, product designs, and packaging. Recent EEG tests showed that, compared with shiny packages showing pictures of potato chips, matte beige bags showing potatoes and other healthy ingredients trigger less activity in an area of the brain associated with feelings of guilt. Needless to say, Frito-Lay quickly switched away from the shiny packaging. Although neuromarketing techniques can measure consumer involvement and emotional responses second by second, such brain

144 Part II Understanding the Marketplace and Customer Value

Table 5-5
Types of Questions

A. Closed-End Questions

Name	Description	Example
Dichotomous	A question offering two answer choices.	"In arranging this trip, did you personally phone Delta?" Yes ☐ No ☐
Multiple choice	A question offering three or more answer choices.	"With whom are you traveling on this flight?" No one ☐ Children only ☐ Spouse ☐ Business associates/friends/relatives ☐ Spouse and children ☐ An organized tour group ☐
Likert scale	A statement with which the respondent shows the amount of agreement or disagreement.	"Small airlines generally give better service than large ones." Strongly disagree 1☐ Disagree 2☐ Neither agree nor disagree 3☐ Agree 4☐ Strongly agree 5☐
Semantic differential	A scale is inscribed between two bipolar words, and the respondent selects the point that represents the direction and intensity of his or her feelings.	Delta Airlines Large X:___:___:___:___:___ Small Experienced ___:___:___:___:X:___ Inexperienced Modern ___:___:___:X:___:___ Old-fashioned
Importance scale	A scale that rates the importance of some attribute from "not at all important" to "extremely important."	"Airline food service to me is" Extremely important 1___ Very important 2___ Somewhat important 3___ Not very important 4___ Not at all important 5___
Rating scale	A scale that rates some attribute from "poor" to "excellent."	"Delta's food service is" Excellent 1___ Very good 2___ Good 3___ Fair 4___ Poor 5___
Intention-to-buy scale	A scale that describes the respondent's intentions to buy.	"If in-flight telephone service were available on a long flight, I would" Definitely buy 1___ Probably buy 2___ Not certain 3___ Probably not buy 4___ Definitely not buy 5___

(continued)

Table 5-5 (*continued*)
Types of Questions

B. Open-End Questions		
Completely unstructured	A question that respondents can answer in an almost unlimited number of ways.	"What is your opinion of Delta Airlines?"
Word association	Words are presented, one at a time, and respondents mention the first word that comes to mind.	"What is the first word that comes to your mind when you hear the following?" Airline _____ Delta _____ Travel _____
Sentence completion	Incomplete sentences are presented, one at a time, and respondents complete the sentence.	"When I choose an airline, the most important consideration in my decision is..."
Story completion	An incomplete story is presented, and respondents are asked to complete it.	"I flew Delta a few days ago. I noticed that the exterior and interior of the plane had very bright colors. This aroused in me the following thoughts and feelings." *Now complete the story.*
Picture completion	A picture of two characters is presented, with one making a statement. Respondents are asked to identify with the other and fill in the empty balloon.	*Fill in the empty balloon.*
Thematic apperception tests (TATs)	A picture is presented, and respondents are asked to make up a story about what they think is happening or may happen in the picture.	*Make up a story about what you see.*

responses can be difficult to interpret. Thus, neuromarketing is usually used in combination with other research approaches to gain a more complete picture of what goes on inside consumers' heads.[53]

PRESENTING THE RESEARCH PLAN. The final stage of developing the research plan is to put the plan in writing so the plan can be reviewed by those involved in the implementation of the plan and those involved in using the results of the research can review the plan. The plan should cover the management problems addressed, the research objectives, information to be obtained, sources of secondary information and/or methods for collecting primary data, and how the results will aid in management decision making. The plan should also include research costs and expected benefits. A written research plan helps ensure that management and researchers have considered all the important aspects of the research and they agree on why and how the research will be done. The manager should review the proposal carefully before approving the project.

Implementing the Research Plan

The researcher puts the marketing research plan into action by collecting, processing, and analyzing the information. Data collection can be done by the company's marketing research staff, which affords the company greater control of the collection process and data quality, or by outside firms. Outside firms that specialize in data collection can often do the job more quickly at lower cost.

The data-collection phase of the marketing research process is generally the most expensive and the most subject to error. The researcher should watch the fieldwork closely to ensure that the plan is implemented correctly and to guard against problems with contacting respondents who refuse to cooperate or who give biased or dishonest answers, and interviewers who make mistakes or take shortcuts.

The collected data must be processed and analyzed to pull out important information and findings. Data from questionnaires are checked for accuracy and completeness and coded for computer analysis. The researcher applies standard computer programs to prepare tabulations of results and to compute averages and other measures for the major variables.

Interpreting and Reporting the Findings

The researcher must now interpret the findings, draw conclusions, and report the conclusions to management. The researcher should avoid overwhelming managers with numbers, complex statistical techniques, and focus. Instead, management desires major findings that will be useful in decision making.

Interpretation should not be left entirely to the researcher. Findings can be interpreted in different ways, and discussions between researchers and managers will help point to the best interpretations. The manager should also confirm that the research project was executed properly. After reviewing the findings, the manager may raise additional questions that can be answered with research data. Researchers should make the data available to marketing managers, so that they can perform new analyses and test relationships on their own.

Interpretation is an important phase of the marketing process. The best research is meaningless if a manager blindly accepts wrong interpretations. Similarly, managers may have biased interpretations. They sometimes accept research results that show what they expected and reject those that did not provide expected or hoped-for answers. Thus, managers and researchers must work closely together when interpreting research results. Both share responsibility for the research process and resulting decisions.

Interpreting and reporting findings is the last step of the four-step research process. It is important for managers to remember that research is a process and that the researcher must proceed through all steps of the process. Marketing Highlight 5–5 explains some of the problems that can occur during a research project.

Information gathered by the company's marketing intelligence and marketing research systems can often benefit from additional analysis to help interpret the

Marketing HIGHLIGHT 5.5 Research problem areas

1. **Making assumptions.** A restaurant was considering adding a piano bar. Researchers developed a customer survey. One question asked customers if they would like entertainment in the lounge, without mentioning the type of entertainment. The customers could answer this question positively, thinking of a dance band. The manager, seeing the positive responses, would put in the piano bar and then wonder why so many customers did not respond to the piano bar. Luckily, this question was modified during a pretest of the survey.

    A country club asked its members if they felt the club needed a renovation. Most members said "yes." The club then paid consultants to draw up designs for the renovations. When these, along with the proposed dues increase, were presented, the members expressed outrage at the higher dues. If the original survey had addressed the costs associated with the renovation, it could have saved thousands of dollars in consulting fees.

2. **Lack of qualitative information.** Most surveys reported in trade magazines provide descriptive information. For example, a study done by Procter & Gamble found that the most important attribute in the decision of frequent travelers to return to a hotel was a clean appearance. To use this information, management needs to know how its guests judge clean appearance. Through focus groups, managers can learn what guests look for to determine whether the room is clean, what irritants there are concerning cleanliness, and other more specific information.

3. **Failing to look at segments within a sample.** Survey results should be analyzed to determine difference between customer groups. Often, the arithmetic means (averages) for each question are calculated, and the survey is analyzed based on this information, which can mask important differences between segments. For example, a club surveyed its membership on how satisfied the members were with the lunches purchased in the dining room. The average of all responses was 2, with 1 being very satisfied, 3 being satisfied, and 5 being not satisfied. However, when the total sample was divided into membership classes, it was found that one category of members had a high level of satisfaction 1.5, whereas another class gave an average rating of 2.7. This information is more useful to management than the overall mean of 2. Management now had to decide whether to invest additional money to build satisfaction for the members who gave the dining room a lower rating or promote its food and beverage room to the satisfied segment.

4. **Improper use of sophisticated statistical analysis.** One researcher reported that faculty size explained a remarkable 96 percent of the enrollment in hospitality management programs housed in business schools. He then presented a formula for projecting student enrollment based on the number of faculty, implying that if a school had three faculty members it would have 251 students, but if two more faculty were hired, it would have 426 students. Schools that base decisions on this formula might be disappointed.

    The researcher claimed that adding a professor would increase enrollment. What happens at most universities is professors are added to meet an increase in student enrollment. The number of faculty and students are positively correlated; however, students create faculty positions, not the other way around.

5. **Failure to have the sample representative of the population.** A sample is a segment of the population selected to represent the population as a whole. Ideally, the sample should be representative so that the researcher can make accurate estimates of the thoughts and behaviors of the larger population. It is common for hotel managers to receive a bonus based on a customer satisfaction score. Sometimes segments of the population give ratings that are lower than other segments, even though they seem satisfied with the service. For example, in one customer satisfaction survey, respondents between 26 and 35 years of age rated the service attributes of the company lower than other segments. However, they also rated the competition lower, making the company's relative satisfaction compared with the competition the same as other segments. This segment did not appear to be displeased with the service; they just tended to rate lower on the scale. When segments like this are present in the population, they can skew the results of the survey if they are overrepresented or underrepresented. If they are underrepresented, the overall satisfaction will increase; if they are overrepresented, the overall satisfaction score will decrease.

findings. This might include advanced statistical analysis to learn more about the relationships within a set of data. Such analysis allows managers to go beyond means and standard deviations in the data and answer such questions as the following:

- What are the major variables affecting sales, and how important is each?
- If the price is raised 10 percent and advertising is increased 20 percent, what will happen to sales?

- What are the best predictors of who are likely to come to my hotel versus my competitor's hotel?
- What are the best variables for segmenting my market, and how many segments exist?

Mathematical models might also help marketers to make better decisions. Each model represents a real system, process, or outcome. These models can help answer the questions "what if" and "which is best." In the past 20 years, marketing scientists have developed a great number of models to help marketing managers make better marketing mix decisions, design sales territories and sales call plans, select sites for retail outlets, develop optimal advertising mixes, and forecast new product sales.

Marketing information has no value until managers use it to make better decisions. The information gathered must reach the appropriate marketing managers at the right time. Large companies have centralized MISs that provide managers with regular performance reports, intelligence updates, and reports on the results of studies. Managers need these routine reports for making regular planning, implementation, and control decisions. But marketing managers also need nonroutine information for special situations and on-the-spot decisions. For example, a sales manager having trouble with an important customer needs a summary of the account's sales during the past year. Or a restaurant manager whose restaurant has stocked out of a best-selling menu item needs to know the current inventory levels in the chain's other restaurants. In companies with centralized information systems, these managers must request the information from the MIS staff and wait. Often, the information arrives too late to be useful.

Recent developments in information handling have led to a revolution in information distribution. With recent advances in microcomputers, software, and communications, many companies are decentralizing their MISs and giving managers direct access to information stored in the systems. In some companies, marketing managers can use a desk terminal to tie into the company's information network. Without leaving their desks, they can obtain information from internal records or outside information services, analyze the information, prepare reports on a word processor, and communicate with others in the network through telecommunications. The internet is an excellent source of marketing information (see Marketing Highlight 5–6).

Marketing HIGHLIGHT 5.6 — HSMAI's Knowledge Center: A great source of marketing information

The Hospitality Sales and Marketing Association International (HSMAI) has refined its Knowledge Center Web site over the last 10 years. HSMAI has done a great job of cataloging hospitality marketing information from a variety of sources.

This searchable portal, which delivers global information and resources on a variety of hospitality marketing topics, is a great resource for marketing professionals and students of hospitality marketing. One can also subscribe to news from the HSMAI Knowledge Center.

The portal features major sections and insights on sales, marketing, and revenue management. The sales section includes articles, presentations, and tools for sales professionals. The marketing section contains information on everything from job descriptions to marketing plans. It also offers insights from industry marketing leaders. Revenue section offers resources to optimize revenue, including presentations, expert articles, and revenue management templates. Like the other sections, these sections feature a blog, allowing members to have a dialogue with each other. Hotels are now hiring managers in the areas of revenue management and social media marketing at the individual property level. Students wishing to obtain a position in this area can keep up-to-date by reading the information and postings on knowledge center.

A wealth of marketing information has been gathered into one searchable site. Knowledge Center can be accessed through www.hsmai.org. HSMAI offers special membership rates for students and faculty members. Students interested in hospitality marketing should become familiar with the HSMAI Web site and take advantage of the resources it offers.

Such systems offer exciting prospects. They allow managers to obtain needed information directly and quickly, and tailor it to their needs. As more managers become skilled in using these systems and as improvements in technology make them more economical, hospitality companies will increasingly use decentralized MISs.

■■■ International Marketing Research

International marketing researchers follow the same steps as domestic researchers, from defining the research problem and developing a research plan to interpreting and reporting the results. However, these researchers often face more and different problems. Although domestic researchers deal with fairly homogeneous markets within a single country, international researchers deal with markets in many different countries. These different markets often vary dramatically in their levels of economic development, cultures and customs, and buying patterns.

In many foreign markets, the international researcher has a difficult time finding good secondary data. Although U.S. marketing researchers can obtain reliable secondary data from dozens of domestic research services, many countries have almost no research services at all. Even the largest international research services operate in only a relative handful of countries. For example, A. C. Nielsen, the world's largest marketing research company, has offices in many countries outside the United States.[54] Thus, even when secondary information is available, it usually must be obtained from many different sources on a country-by-country basis, making the information difficult to combine or compare.

Because of the scarcity of good secondary data, international researchers often must collect their own primary data. Here researchers face problems not encountered domestically. For example, they may find it difficult simply to develop appropriate samples. Although U.S. researchers can use current telephone directories, census tract data, and any of several sources of socioeconomic data to construct samples, such information is largely lacking in many countries. Once the sample is drawn, the U.S. researcher usually can reach most respondents easily by telephone or mail or in person. Reaching respondents is often not so easy in other parts of the world. For example, although there are 79 internet users per 100 people in the United States, there are only 36 internet users per 100 people in Mexico. In Madagascar, the number drops to 2 internet users per 100 people. In other countries, the postal system is notoriously unreliable. In Brazil, for instance, an estimated 30 percent of the mail is never delivered; in Russia, mail delivery can take several weeks. In many developing countries, poor roads and transportation systems make certain areas hard to reach, making personal interviews difficult and expensive.[55]

Differences in cultures from country to country cause additional problems for international researchers. Language is the most obvious culprit. For example, questionnaires must be prepared in one language and then translated into the languages of each country researched. Responses then must be translated back into the original language for analysis and interpretation. This adds to research costs and increases the risks for error.

Translating a questionnaire from one language to another is far from easy. Many points are "lost" because idioms, phrases, and statements mean different things in different cultures. A Danish executive observed, "Check this out by having a different translator put back into English what you've translated from the English. You'll get the shock of your life. I remember [an example in which] 'out of sight, out of mind' had become 'invisible things are insane.'"[56]

Buying roles and consumer decision processes vary greatly from country to country, further complicating international marketing research. Consumers in different countries also vary in their attitudes toward marketing research. People in one country may be very willing to respond; in other countries, nonresponse can be a major problem. For example, customs in some Islamic countries prohibit people from talking with strangers—a researcher simply may not be allowed to speak by phone with women about brand attitudes or buying behavior. High functional illiteracy rates in many countries make it impossible to use a written survey for some segments. In addition, middle-class people in developing countries often make false claims in order to appear well off. For example, in a study of tea consumption in India, over 70 percent of middle-income respondents claimed that they used one of several national brands. However, the researchers had good reason to doubt these results; more than 60 percent of the tea sold in India is unbranded generic tea.

Despite these problems, the recent growth of international marketing has resulted in a rapid increase in the use of international marketing research. Global companies have little choice but to conduct such research. Although the costs and problems associated with international research may be high, the costs of not doing it—in terms of missed opportunities and mistakes—might be even higher. Once recognized, many of the problems associated with international marketing research can be overcome or avoided.

Marketing Research in Smaller Organizations

Managers of small businesses often believe that marketing research can be done only by experts in large companies with large research budgets. But many marketing research techniques can be used by smaller organizations and at little or no expense.

Managers of small businesses can obtain good marketing information by observing what occurs around them. Thus, restaurateurs can evaluate their customer mix by recording the number and type of customers in the restaurant at different times during the day. Competitor advertising can be monitored by collecting advertisements from local media.

Managers can conduct informal surveys using small convenience samples. The manager of a travel agency can learn what customers like and dislike about travel agencies by conducting informal focus groups, such as inviting small groups to lunch. Restaurant managers can talk with customers; hospital food-service managers can interview patients. Restaurant managers can make random phone calls during slack hours to interview consumers about where they eat out and what they think of various restaurants in the area. Managers can also conduct simple experiments. By changing the design in regular direct mailings and watching results, a manager can learn which marketing tactics work best. By varying newspaper advertisements, a manager can observe the effects of ad size and position, price coupons, and media used.

Small organizations can obtain secondary data. Many associations, local media, chambers of commerce, and government agencies provide special help to small organizations. The U.S. Small Business Administration offers dozens of free publications giving advice on topics ranging from planning advertising to ordering business signs. Local newspapers often provide information on local shoppers and their buying patterns.

Sometimes volunteers and colleges carry out research. Many colleges are seeking small businesses to serve as cases for projects in marketing research classes. Sales management classes are eager to do sales blitzes for hotels.

Thus, secondary data collection, observation, surveys, and experiments can be used effectively by small organizations with small budgets. Although informal research is less complex and costly, it must still be done carefully. Managers must think through the objectives of the research, formulate questions in advance, and recognize the biases systematically. If planned and implemented meticulously, low-cost research can provide reliable information for improving marketing decision making.

CHAPTER REVIEW

I. Marketing Information and Customer Insights. To create value for customers and to build meaningful relationships with them, marketers must first gain fresh, deep insights into what customers need and want.

A. Marketing information and today's "Big Data." Big data refers to the huge and complex data sets people and systems generate. It is characterized by volume, velocity, and variety. Marketers apply marketing analytics to the large and complex data sets they collect from Web, mobile, social media tracking; customer transactions and engagements; and other sources to dig out meaningful patterns to gain customer insights and gauge marketing performance.

B. **Managing marketing information.** Customer insight groups collect customer and market information from a wide variety of sources—ranging from traditional marketing research studies to mingling with and observing consumers to monitoring consumer social media conversations about the company and its products. Then they use the marketing information to develop important customer insights from which the company can create more value for its customers.

II. **The Marketing Information System (MIS).** An MIS consists of people, equipment, and procedures to gather, sort, analyze, evaluate, and distribute needed, timely, and accurate information to marketing decision makers.

A. **Assessing information needs.** A good MIS balances information that managers would like to have against that which they really need and is feasible to obtain.

B. **Developing marketing information.** Information needed by marketing managers can be obtained from internal company records, marketing intelligence, and marketing research. The information analysis system processes this information and presents it in a form that is useful to managers.

1. **Internal data.** Internal data consist of information gathered from sources within the company to evaluate marketing performance and to detect marketing problems and opportunities.
2. **Competitive marketing intelligence.** Marketing intelligence includes everyday publicly available information about developments in the marketing environment that helps managers prepare and adjust marketing plans and short-run tactics. Marketing intelligence can come from internal sources or external sources.

III. **Marketing Research.** Marketing research is a process that identifies and defines marketing opportunities and problems, monitors and evaluates marketing actions and performance, and communicates the findings and implication to management. Marketing research is project oriented and has a beginning and an ending. It feeds information into the MIS that is ongoing. The marketing research process consists of four steps: defining the problem and research objectives, developing the research plan, implementing the research plan, and interpreting and presenting the findings.

A. **Defining the problem and research objectives.** There are three types of objectives for a marketing research project. Exploratory research seeks to gather preliminary information that will help to better define problems and suggest hypotheses. Descriptive research seeks to better describe marketing problems, situations, or markets. Causal research tests hypotheses about cause-and-effect relationships.

B. **Developing the research plan.**
1. **Determining specific information needs.** Research objectives must be translated into specific information needs. To meet a manager's information needs, researchers can gather secondary data, primary data, or both.
2. **Gathering secondary information.** Secondary data consist of information already in existence somewhere, having been collected for another purpose.
3. **Planning primary data collection.** Primary data consist of information collected for the specific purpose at hand. Three basic research approaches are observations, surveys, and experiments. **Observational research** is the gathering of primary data by observing relevant people, actions, and situations. **Ethnographic research** involves sending trained observers to watch and interact with consumers in their "natural habitat." **Survey research** gathers data by asking people questions about their knowledge, attitudes, preferences, and buying behavior. The most scientifically valid research is **experimental research**, designed to capture cause-and-effect relationships by eliminating competing explanations of the observed findings. Information can be collected by mail, telephone, personal interview, or online. Marketing researchers usually draw conclusions about large consumer groups by taking a sample. A sample is a segment of the population selected to represent the population as a whole. Designing the sample calls for four decisions: (1) Who will be surveyed? (2) How many people should be surveyed? (3) How should the sample be chosen? (4) When will the survey be given? In collecting primary data, marketing researchers have a choice of primary research instruments: the interview (structured and unstructured), mechanical devices, and structured models such as a test market. Structured interviews make the use of a questionnaire. The final stage of developing the research plan is to put the plan in writing so the plan can be reviewed by those involved in the implementation of the plan and those involved in using the results of the research can review the plan. The plan should cover the management problems addressed, the research objectives, information to be obtained, sources of secondary information and/or methods for collecting primary data, and how the results will aid in management decision making. The plan should also include research costs and expected benefits.

C. **Implementing the research plan.** The researcher puts the marketing research plan into action by collecting, processing, and analyzing the information.

D. **Interpreting and reporting the findings.** The researcher must now interpret the findings, draw conclusions, and report them to management. Information gathered by the company's marketing intelligence and marketing research systems can often benefit from additional analysis. This analysis helps to answer the questions related to "what if" and "which is best." Marketing information has no value until managers use it to make better decisions. The information that is gathered must reach the appropriate marketing managers at the right time.

IN-CLASS GROUP ACTIVITIES

*Exercises with an asterisk next to them are suitable for individual homework or online assignments. Students, always provide an explanation for your answer.

1. You are asked to develop a loyalty program for a hotel or restaurant. Go on the internet and find out what information you can find out about loyalty programs, including existing hotel or restaurant loyalty programs. Write up a summary of your findings. The book's Web site has some suggestions on how to set up your search.

2. Perform an internet search on "social media marketing" to find companies that specialize in monitoring social media. Discuss two of these companies. Then find two more sites that allow free monitoring and discuss how marketers can use these to monitor their brands. Write a brief report of your findings.

3. Suppose you are conducting market research for your favorite hotel or restaurant brand. Sales have been lagging for two quarters, and you are determined to find out why. You decide to host an in-person focus group to gain customer insights into your brand's current product offerings. You are also interested in obtaining feedback on a new product that your brand plans to launch in the next six months. Determine the makeup of your focus group. Who should be invited to the focus group, and why? What types of information would you want to obtain? Identify possible questions to present to the focus group.

4. *You own an elegant, high-priced restaurant in your area and want to improve the level of service offered by your 30-person staff. How could observational research help you accomplish this goal?

5. Compare and contrast internal databases, marketing intelligence, and marketing research as a means for developing marketing information. In your discussion provide a definition of each one and then explain the types of useful information you could gain from internal databases, marketing intelligence, and marketing research. Explain why you would need to use all three.

6. *Researchers usually start the data-gathering process by examining secondary data. What secondary data sources would be available to the manager of a full-service restaurant that wanted to research consumer trends?

7. *Which type of research would be most appropriate in the following situations, and why?
   a. A fast-food restaurant wants to investigate the effect that children have on the purchase of its products.
   b. A business hotel wants to gather some preliminary information on how business travelers feel about the menu variety, food, and service in its restaurants.
   c. A casual restaurant is considering locating a new outlet in a fast-growing suburb.
   d. A fast-food restaurant wants to test the effect of two new advertising themes for its roast beef sandwich sales in two cities.
   e. The director of tourism for your state wants to know how to use his or her promotion dollars effectively.

8. *Focus group interviewing is both a widely used and a widely criticized research technique in marketing. What are the advantages and disadvantages of focus groups? What are some kinds of questions that are appropriate for focus groups to investigate?

9. *What is *Big Data* and what opportunities and challenges does it provide for marketers?

EXPERIENTIAL EXERCISES

Do one of the following:

1. You have been asked to find out how the campus community feels about the food service on campus.
   a. Who is the population for this study?
   b. Develop a sampling plan, including times and places that will provide you with a sample that is representative of the population of interest.

2. Get a customer comment card from a local hospitality company. What, if any, design changes would you make to the form? If you were the manager, how would you use the information collected from the comment cards?

REFERENCES

1. Reprinted by permission from Richard Abowitz.
2. Michael Bush, "Why Harrah's Loyalty Effort Is Industry's Gold Standard," *Advertising Age* (October 5, 2009); Neil A. Martin, "A Tempting Wager," *Barron's*, 86, no. 15 (April 10, 2006): 28, 30; H. Scot Krause, "Caesars Offers Total Rewards through Slot Club," May 17, 2016, www.gamingtoday.com/casino_games/video_casino/article/60446-Caesars_offers_total_rewards_through_slot_club; "Leading Selected Casino Companies Worldwide in 2017, by Revenue," www.statista.com/statistics/257531/leading-casino-companies-worldwide-by-revenue/ (accessed July 2018); "Say and Play Total Rewards Program—CAESARS ENTERTAINMENT," November 29, 2017, www.casinojournal.com/articles/91763-say-and-play-total-rewards-program-caesars-entertainment; Howard Stutz, "Caesars Expands Total Rewards Program," *Las Vegas Review-Journal*, March 1, 2012, www.reviewjournal.com/business/casinos-gaming/caesars-expands-total-rewards-program/; "Wyndham Partners with Caesars for Loyalty Program," June 5, 2017, www.hotelnewsnow.com/Articles/143828/Wyndham-partners-with-Caesars-for-loyalty-program.
3. See "Big Data," Wikipedia, http://en.wikipedia.org/wiki/Big_data (accessed June 2016); Michael Lev-Ram, "What's the Next Big Thing in Big Data? Bigger Data," *Fortune*, June 16, 2014, pp. 233–240; Peter Horst and Robert Duboff, "Don't Let Big Data Bury Your Brand," *Harvard Business Review*, November 2015, pp. 79–86.
4. Kristen Hawley, "Chefs+Tech: How Big Data Enhances Good Hospitality," August 29, 2017, https://skift.com/2017/08/29/chefstech-how-big-data-enhances-good-hospitality/.
5. For more discussion, see Matt Ariker and others, "Quantifying the Impact of Marketing Analytics," *Harvard Business Review*, November 5, 2015, https://hbr.org/2015/11/quantifyingthe-impact-of-marketing-analytics; Martin Kihn, "What's Going on with Marketing Analytics?" *Gartner*, September 30, 2015, http://blogs.gartnencom/martin-kihn/whats-going-onwith-marketing-analytics-2/.
6. David Eisen, "Marriott Bets on Predictive Analytics for Brand Growth," *Hotel Management*, January 31, 2018, https://www.hotelmanagement.net/tech/marriott-builds-its-brands-by-knowing-more-about-you.
7. Mohanhir Sawhney, "Insights into Customer Insights," p. 3.
8. Tom Richman, "Mrs. Field's Secret Ingredient" (October 1987), as cited in *Managing Services* by Christopher Lovelock (Upper Saddle River, NJ: Prentice Hall, 1992): 365–372.
9. See "Pizza Hut and Its Local Agency Win Direct Marketing Association Award," *Pegasus Newswire*, November 18, 2006, www.pegasusnews.com; Jennifer Brown, "Pizza Hut Delivers Hot Results Using Data Warehousing," *Computing Canada* (October 17, 2003): 24; http://newspapergrl.wordpress.com/2006103/22lpizza-hut%E2%80%99s-vip-elub/; www.yum.com/investors/fact/asp (accessed March 2007).
10. John Bowen, "Computerized Guest History: A Valuable Marketing Tool," in *The Practice of Hospitality Management II*, ed. Robert C. Lewis et al. (Westport, CT: AVI, 1990).
11. Mark Lynn, "Making Customer Feedback a Priority—A Key to Inducing Demand and Maximizing Value," *Hospitality Net*, June 28, 2004, http://hospitalitynet.org.
12. Rick Hendrie, "Hear Me Out: Talking, Listening to Current Guests May Be the Best Way to Get More Through the Door," *Nation's Restaurant News* (January 20, 2003): 28+; Cary Jehl Broussard, "Inside the Customer-Focused Company," *Harvard Business Review* (May 2000): S20.
13. See Donald Trump Jr. and Suzie Mills, "Valuing Customer Loyalty—The 76% Factor," http://hotelexecutive.com/business_review/2702/valuingcustomer-loyaltythe76factor (accessed February 2015).
14. James L. Heskett, W. Earl Sasser, Jr., and Leonard A. Schlesinger, *The Service Profit Chain* (New York: Free Press, 1997), p. 67.
15. Chekitan S. Dev and Bernard O. Ellis, "Guest Histories: An Untapped Service Resource," *Cornell Hotel and Restaurant Administration Quarterly*, 32, no. 2 (1991): 31.
16. Tammy P. Bieber, "Guest History Systems: Maximizing the Benefits," *Cornell Hotel and Restaurant Administration Quarterly*, 30, no. 3 (1989): 22.
17. See www.mspa-americas.org/news (accessed August 2018).
18. Carolyn Taschner, "Commentary: Mystery Shopping Is Booming Business," *The Daily Record* (Baltimore) (May 15, 2004); Allison Perlik, "If They're Happy, Do You Know It," *Restaurants and Institutions* (October 15, 2002): 65–70.
19. Joseph F. Durocher and Neil B. Neiman, "Technology: Antidote to the Shakeout," *Cornell Hotel and Restaurant Administration Quarterly*, 31, no. 1 (1990): 35.
20. Burt Cabanas, "A Marketing Strategy for Resort Conference Centers," *Cornell Hotel and Restaurant Administration Quarterly*, 33, no. 3 (1992): 47.
21. "Making Them Feel at Home," *Cornell Hotel and Restaurant Administration Quarterly*, 30, no. 3 (1989): 4.
22. James Curtis, "Behind Enemy Lines," *Marketing* (May 24, 2001): 28–29.
23. https://learn.revinate.com/2018-global-benchmark-report/2018-global-hotel-reputation-benchmark-report/ (accessed August 2018).
24. "Company Sleuth Uncovers Business Info for Free," *Link-Up* (January–February 1999): 1, 8.
25. *American Marketing Association*, officially adopted definition (1987).

26. "Marriott Hotels opens Innovation Lab," June 3, 2013, www.hotelnewsresource.com/article71878.html; Jane L. Levere, "A Campaign From Marriott Aims Younger," June 16, 2013, www.nytimes.com/2013/06/17/business/media/a-campaign-from-marriott-aims-younger.html; www.serve360.marriott.com/wp-content/uploads/2018/06/2017_Sustainability_and_Social_Impact_Report.pdf (accessed August 2018); "Business Analysis of Marriott International," www.revenuesandprofits.com/marriott-international/ (accessed July 2018); "Marriott's First-Ever, Pop-Up Innovation Lab Further Evolves Its Cutting Edge Aloft and Element Hotel Brands," www.news.marriott.com/2017/01/marriotts-first-ever-pop-innovation-lab-evolves-cutting-edge-aloft-element-hotel-brands/ (accessed May 2018); "Here's How Marriott International is Offering Innovative Guest Experiences with Its New Smart Shower Screen and Interactive Lobby Kiosk Technology," www.guestexperience.wbresearch.com/marriott-international-innovative-guest-experiences-strategy-smart-shower-interactive-lobby-kiosk-ty-u (accessed July 2018).

27. "The Entrepreneurial Approach to Indian Affairs," *Cornell Hotel and Restaurant Administration Quarterly*, 29, no. 2 (1988): 5.

28. Jerry Wind, Paul E. Green, Douglas Shifflet, and Marsha Scarbrough, "Courtyard by Marriott: Designing a Hotel Facility with Consumer-Based Marketing," *Interfaces*, 19, no. 1 (1989): 25–47.

29. Robert C. Lewis and Richard E. Chambers, *Marketing Leadership in Hospitality: Foundations and Practices* (New York: Van Nostrand Reinhold, 1989), p. 518.

30. See Halah Touryalai, "Hotel Science: How Marriott & Starwood Hotels Choose Your Room Amenities," *Forbes*, August 6, 2014, http://www.forbes.com/sites/halahtouryalai/2014/08/06/hotel-science-how-marriott-starwood-hotels-choose-your-room-amenities/.

31. Linda Tischler, "Every Move You Make," *Fast Company* (April 2004): 73–75.

32. Spencer E. Ante, "The Science of Desire," *Business Week* (June 5, 2006): 99–106.

33. See Pradeep K. Tyagi, "Webnography: A New Tool to Conduct Marketing Research," *Journal of American Academy of Business* (March 2010): 262–268.

34. Spencer E. Ante, "The Science of Desire," *Business Week* (June 5, 2006): 100. Also see Jan Fulton and Suzanne Gibbs Howard, "Going Deeper, Seeing Further: Enhancing Ethnographic Interpretations to Reveal More Meaningful Opportunities to Design," *Journal of Advertising Research* (September 2006): 246–250.

35. Spencer E. Ante, "The Science of Desire," *Business Week* (June 5, 2006): 100; Rhys Blakely, "You Know When It Feels Like Somebody's Watching You...," *Times* (May 14, 2007): 46; Jack Neff, "Marketing Execs: Researchers Could Use a Softer Touch," *Advertising Age* (January 27, 2009), http://adage.com/article7article_id=134144.

36. Robert Reiss, "How Ritz-Carlton Stays at Top," *Forbes*, October 30, 2009, http://www.forbes.com/2009/10/30/simon-cooper-ritz-leadership-ceo-network-hotels.html.

37. Nancy Trejos, "Guests Help Design the Hotel of the Future," *USA Today*, November 15, 2013, http://www.usatoday.com/story/travel/hotels/2013/11/14/hotel-guests-millennials-design-marriott-holiday-inn/3538573/.

38. Joe L. Welch, "Focus Groups for Restaurant Research," *Cornell Hotel and Restaurant Administration Quarterly*, 26, no. 2 (1985): 78–85.

39. Dorothy Dee, "Focus Groups," *Restaurants USA*, 10, no. 7 (1990): 30–34.

40. Nancy Trejos, "Guests Help Design the Hotel of the Future," *USA Today*, November 15, 2013, http://www.usatoday.com/story/travel/hotels/2013/11/14/hotel-guests-millennials-design-marriott-holiday-inn/3538573/.

41. Robert J. Kwortnik, "Clarifying 'Fuzzy' Hospitality-Management Problems with Depth Interviews and Qualitative Analysis: Properly Conducted Depth Interviews Can Dig to the Sometimes-Confusing Heart of Consumers' Motivation for Hospitality Purchases," *Cornell and Hotel Restaurant Administration Quarterly* (April 2003): 117–129.

42. See "Choice Hotels Launches Plan to Redefine and Redesign its Comfort Brand Family," http://www.hospitalitynet.org/news/4,054,592.html (accessed January 25, 2012).

43. Anne Chen, "Customer Feedback Key for Theme Park," *eWeek* (December 15, 2003): 58.

44. Jacob Brown, "Survey Metrics Ward Off Problems," *Marketing News* (November 11, 2003) accessed online via Business Source Premier, October 12, 2004.

45. Stephen W. Litvin and Goh Hwai Kar, "E-Surveying for Tourism Research: Legitimate Tool or a Researcher's Fantasy?" *Journal of Travel Research* (2001): 308–314.

46. Deborah L. Vence, "In an Instant: More Researchers Use IM for Fast, Reliable Results," *Marketing News* (March 1, 2006): 21.

47. Based on information found at www.channelm2.com/HowOnlineQualitativeResearch.html (accessed December 2010).

48. Stephen Baker, "The Web Knows What You Want," *Business Week* (July 27, 2009): 48.

49. Tina Sharkey, "Who Is Your Chief Listening Officer?" *Forbes*, March 13, 2012, www.forbes.com/sites/tinasharkey/2012/03/13/who-is-your-chief-listening-officer/.

50. Jessica Tsai, "Are You Smarter than a Neuromarketer?" *Customer Relationship Management* (January 2010): 19–20.

51. See Roger Dooley, "Is Starbucks Coffee Too Cheap?" *Forbes*, October 14, 2013, http://www.forbes.com/sites/rogerdooley/2013/10/14/is-starbucks-coffee-too-cheap/.

52. "Neuroscience Study Offers New Insights about Hotel Advertising Effectiveness," *Neuromarketing*, October 31, 2016, http://www.gandrllc.com/neuromarketing/hotel-advertising-effectiveness/.

53. This and the other neuromarketing examples are adapted from Laurie Burkitt, "Neuromarketing: Companies Use Neuroscience for Consumer Insights," *Forbes*, November 16, 2009, www.forbes.com/forbes/2009/1116/marketing-hyundai-neurofocus-brain-waves-battle-for-the-brain.html.

54. Jack Honomichl, "Top Marketing/Ad/Opinion Research Firms Profiled," *Marketing News* (June 2, 1992): H2.

55. For these and other examples, see "From Tactical to Personal: Synovate's Tips for Conducting Marketing Research in Emerging Markets," *Marketing News* (April 30, 2011): 20–22. Internet stats are from http://data.worldbank.org/indicator/IT.NET.USER.P2 (accessed February 2014).

56. Subhash C. Jain, *International Marketing Management*, 3rd ed. (Boston: PWS-Kent, 1990), p. 338. For more discussion on international marketing research issues and solutions, see Warren J. Keegan and Mark C. Green, *Global Marketing*, 8th ed. (Upper Saddle River, NJ: Prentice Hall, 2015), pp. 170–201.

6

Objectives

After reading this chapter, you should be able to:

1. Explain the model of buyer behavior.
2. Outline the major characteristics affecting consumer behavior, and list some of the specific cultural, social, personal, and psychological factors that influence consumers.
3. Explain the buyer decision process and discuss need recognition, information search, evaluation of alternatives, the purchase decision, and postpurchase behavior.

Consumer Markets and Consumer Buying Behavior

Years ago, Taco Bell practically invented the fast-food "value menu," with its "59¢-79¢-99¢" pricing structure. With slogans such as "The Cure for the Common Meal," "Make a Run for the Border," and "Think Outside the Bun," Taco Bell firmly established its affordable Mexican-inspired fare as a unique "more-for-your-money" alternative to the most sought-after burgers and fries offered by dominant McDonald's and other fast-food competitors. Taco Bell grew rapidly into a $6-billion-a-year international brand. Today, it is the sixth largest fast-food chain in the United States and ninth largest in the world. It has not been easy to maintain its position as one of the most popular fast-food chains. Taco Bell has to reinvent itself, changing to meet the ever-changing wants of its customers. In fact, *Fast Company* magazine named Taco Bell as one of the most innovative companies.[1]

In the 2000s, many people were no longer looking for cheap fast food. Americans were looking for fresher, better tasting, healthier eating options, and more contemporary fast-casual atmospheres. So, in early 2012, Taco Bell shifted its positioning from "food as fuel" to "food as experience and lifestyle." It launched a new, innovative lifestyle marketing campaign called "Live Mas" ("mas" is Spanish for "more"). Backed by a $280 million annual budget, the "Live Mas" slogan is designed as a lifestyle rallying cry for Taco Bell's target customers, young adults, who consume a disproportionate share of fast and fast-casual food.

Taco Bell's aspirational "Live Mas" message is crafted to inspire millennials to try new things and to live life to the fullest. The first "Live Mas" ad, called "Pockets," showed a hip of a 20-something man coming into a dim apartment as dawn breaks. He empties his pockets onto a table as he thinks back over the night he's had. Along with the standard wallet, keys, and smartphone, he tosses out a concert ticket stub, a matchbook from a 24-hour psychic, a pair of Kanji dice, and a strip of photo-booth images of himself with a young woman. The last item he pulls out is a blister pack of Taco Bell Fire Sauce, adorned with the new "Live Mas" logo and the message, "You have chosen wisely." It's this last item that brings a smile to his face.

To better engage targeted millennials, Taco Bell now reaches them where they hang out—online, digital, and mobile. Befitting the millennial lifestyle, a significant portion of the "Live Mas" promotion budget goes to social media, digital tools, and other nontraditional channels. Beyond the usual Facebook, Twitter, and Pinterest, Taco Bell uses social media such as Vine, Pheed, and Snapchat for buzz-building announcements, limited-time promotions, and sneak peeks at new products. The revitalized chain watches and participates in online brand conversations with its "Fish-bowl"—Taco Bell's own command center for monitoring social media and generating digital dialogue. For example, the brand achieved 2 billion social media impressions for Cool Ranch Doritos Locos Tacos alone before the product even launched.

Taco Bell was right on track with "Live Mas" and the new lifestyle positioning. The year following the introduction of the campaign, sales soared 8 percent, more than twice the gain of industry leader McDonald's. Ad industry magazine *Advertising Age* named Taco Bell its Marketer of the Year, for going "into innovation overdrive, churning out a string of hot new products, game-changing menus, and an aggressive mix of traditional, social, and digital media that's hitting the mark with Millennials." Further, as YouTube grew in popularity, Taco Bell developed Taco Tales, a series of humorous tales of Taco Bell's employees and customers. Some of these tales have been viewed over a million times. Some of the menu changes Taco Bell has made include the addition of Nacho Fries, which has been its most successful product launch in history. It plays on the popularity of food mashups, mixing popular foods into one (e.g., french fries and nachos). Other mashups include hamburgers served on donuts, burgerizza (hamburger between pizza slices), and glazed donut pie. Another mashup Taco Bell introduced was a chicken nacho, that is, chicken coated in cheese and fried.

In addition to the menu changes, Taco Bell has also made other changes based on the changes in consumer behavior. It began a process of replacing additives and artificial preservatives with natural ingredients and added a delivery service. As millennials have moved to cities so has Taco Bell. It plans to open 300–350 cantina-style locations in the next four years. Most of these will be in cities, where people will walk to the location rather than drive. Thus, they will not have drive-through windows. This is a major change as the drive-through window accounts for more than half of Taco Bell's revenue in suburban locations. The elimination of this feature was a bold move, but it shows an understanding of the urban consumer and the growth of this market. Taco Bell also knows that someone walking to the restaurant is likely to dine-in, and thus the addition of beer and wine can make the experience more enjoyable. They have also added a selection of frozen alcoholic drinks called "Twisted Freezes." For those who don't want to leave their apartment, Taco Bell has partnered with DoorDash delivery service. And for those who are hungry on their way home from a night out, Taco Bell partnered with Lyft to provide a free stop at a Taco Bell for those riding between 9 P.M. and 2 A.M.

Taco Bell provides an example of how a company changes to keep up with changes and anticipated changes in consumer behavior. Understanding consumer behavior is an essential component of effective marketing.[2]

A Model of Consumer Behavior

Today's marketplace has become very competitive with thousands of hotels and restaurants. In addition, during recent years the hospitality and travel industries have undergone globalization. Hotel companies headquartered in nations as diverse as Germany, the United States, and Hong Kong compete aggressively in markets such as Singapore and Japan. The result is a fiercely competitive international market with companies fighting for their share of consumers. To win this battle, they invest in research that will reveal what customers want to buy, which locations they prefer, which amenities are important to them, how they buy, and why they buy.

Figure 6–1
Model of buyer behavior.

Marketing stimuli	Other stimuli	Buyer's black box	Buyer's responses
Product Price Place Promotion	Economic Technological Political Cultural	Buyer characteristics / Buyer decision process	Product choice Brand choice Dealer choice Purchase timing Purchase amount

This is the central question: How do consumers respond to the various marketing stimuli that a company might use? The company that really understands how consumers will respond to different product features, prices, and advertising appeals has a great advantage over its competitors. As a result, researchers from companies and universities are constantly studying the relationship between marketing stimuli and consumer response. Their starting point is the model of buyer behavior shown in Figure 6–1. This figure shows that marketing and other stimuli enter the consumer's "black box" and produce certain responses. Marketers must determine what is in the buyer's black box.

On the left side of Figure 6–1, the marketing stimuli consist of the four Ps: product, price, place, and promotion. Other stimuli include major forces and events in the buyer's environment: economic, technological, political, and cultural. All these stimuli enter the buyer's black box, where they are turned into the set of observable buyer responses shown on the right: product choice, brand choice, dealer choice, purchase timing, and purchase amount.

Marketers must understand how the stimuli are changed into responses inside the consumer's black box. The black box has two parts. First, a buyer's characteristics influence how he or she perceives and reacts to the stimuli. Second, the buyer's decision process itself affects outcomes. In this chapter, we look first at buyer characteristics that affect buying behavior and then examine the buyer decision process.

Personal Characteristics Affecting Consumer Behavior

Consumer purchases are strongly influenced by cultural, social, personal, and psychological characteristics. These factors are shown in Figure 6–2. For the most part, they cannot be controlled by the marketer, but they must be taken into account.

Cultural Factors

Culture The set of basic values, perceptions, wants, and behaviors learned by a member of society from family and other important institutions.

Cultural factors exert the broadest and deepest influence on consumer behavior. We examine the role played by the buyer's culture, subculture, and social class.

Culture is the most basic determinant of a person's wants and behavior. It comprises the basic values, perceptions, wants, and behaviors that a person learns continuously in a society. Today, most societies are in a state of flux. Determinants of

Figure 6–2
Factors influencing behavior.

Cultural	Social	Personal	Psychological	Buyer
Culture Subculture Social class	Reference groups Family Roles and status	Age and life-cycle stage Occupation Economic circumstances Lifestyle Personality and self-concept	Motivation Perception Learning Beliefs and attitudes	

culture learned as a child are changing in societies from Chile to California. Culture is expressed through tangible items such as food, architecture, clothing, and art. Culture is an integral part of the hospitality and travel business. It determines what we eat, how we travel, where we travel, and where we stay. Culture is dynamic, adapting to the environment.

Marketers try continuously to identify cultural shifts in order to devise new products and services that might find a receptive market. For example, the cultural shift toward greater concern about health and fitness has resulted in many hotels adding exercise rooms or health clubs or developing an agreement with a local health club so that their guests can have access to it. The shift toward lighter and more natural food has resulted in menu changes in restaurants. The shift toward lighter-colored and simpler home furnishings is reflected in new restaurant designs.

At the same time, a significant number of consumers seem to be rebelling against foods that are good for them, preferring good taste. Restaurants face a consumer who orders broiled flounder and a light salad only to top it off with high-butterfat ice cream for dessert.

Subculture

Subculture A group of people with shared value systems based on common life experiences and situations.

Each culture contains smaller **subcultures**, or groups of people with shared value systems based on common life experiences and situations. Subcultures include nationalities, religions, racial groups, and geographic regions. Many subcultures make up important market segments, and marketers often design products and marketing programs tailored to their needs. Examples of three such important subculture groups are Hispanic, African American, and Asian consumers. As we discuss them, it is important to note that each major subculture is, in turn, made of many smaller subcultures, each with its own preferences and behavior.

HISPANIC AMERICAN CONSUMERS. *Hispanics* represent a large, fast-growing market. The nation's more than 55 million Hispanic consumers (almost one out of every six Americans) have total annual buying power of $1.7 trillion. The U.S. Hispanic population will surge to more than 130 million by 2030, close to one-third of the total U.S. population. Hispanics are a youthful segment—more than 52 percent of U.S. Hispanics are below age 30.[3] Within the Hispanic market, there exist many distinct subsegments based on nationality, age, income, and other factors. A company's product or message may be more relevant to one nationality over another, such as Mexicans, Costa Ricans, Argentineans, or Cubans.

Although Hispanic consumers share many characteristics and behaviors with the mainstream buying public, there are also distinct differences. They tend to be deeply family-oriented and make shopping a family affair—children have a big say in what brands they buy. Older, first-generation Hispanic consumers tend to be very brand loyal and favor brands and sellers who show special interest in them. Younger Hispanics, however, have shown increasing price sensitivity in recent years and a willingness to switch to store brands. Befitting their youthfulness, Hispanics are more active on mobile and social networks than other segments, making digital media ideal for reaching this segment.[4]

To make people aware of their purchasing power, as well as provide continuing education opportunities, the Hispanic meeting planners have formed the International Association of Hispanic Meeting Planners (IAHMP). Its membership includes meeting planners from the United States, Puerto Rico, Mexico, Portugal, Costa Rica, Panama, Guatemala, and Spain. In the United States, IAHMP is establishing chapters in the states and major cities where Hispanics are in the majority.[5] An example of a company increasing their marketing to Hispanics is Denny's. It increased not only its budget for Spanish language television but also its bilingual social media presence.[6]

AFRICAN AMERICAN CONSUMERS. The U.S. African American population is growing in affluence and sophistication. The nation's more than 44 million black consumers wield almost $1.3 trillion in annual buying power. Although more price conscious than other segments, blacks are also strongly motivated by quality and selection. Brands are important. African American consumers are heavy users of digital and social media, providing access through a rich variety of marketing channels.[7] Many companies develop special products, appeals, and marketing programs for African American consumers. For example, the U.S. Forest Service and the Ad Council recently joined forces to create the "Discover the Forest" public service campaign to raise awareness among families of the benefits for children of getting outside and enjoying nature. One round of the campaign specifically targeted the parents of African American tweens. Although more than 245 million Americans live within 100 miles of a national forest or grassland, research shows that a majority of children in some population segments are not spending active time outdoors. For example, only 37 percent of African American children aged 6–12 participate frequently in outdoor activities compared with 67 percent of the broader U.S. population in that age group. To help close that gap, the U.S. Forest Service and the Ad Council created the "Discover the Forest" campaign, a series of public service messages ranging from billboards and radio commercials to interactive social media and Web site content. With headlines such as "Unplug," "Where Curiosity Blooms," and "Where Imagination Sprouts," the ads targeting African American families promote the discovery and imagination wonders of connecting with the great outdoors and the resulting physical, mental health, and emotional well-being benefits. "The forest is one of those amazing places where kids can flex their imagination muscles through exploration and discovery," says a marketer associated with the campaign. With American markets becoming more diverse, companies are seeking managers who are members of a subculture that is a target market of their business.[8]

The U.S. Forest Service has developed ads to target African Americans to encourage them to utilize U.S. Forest Service Parks on vacations and for day use.
Mark Bowden/123RF.

ASIAN AMERICAN CONSUMERS. Asian Americans are the most affluent U.S. demographic segment. A relatively well-educated segment, they now number more than 18.5 million (5 percent of the population), with annual buying power expected to approach $1.33 trillion by 2022. Asian Americans are the second-fastest-growing subsegment after Hispanic Americans. And like Hispanic Americans, they are a diverse group. Chinese Americans constitute the largest group, followed by Filipinos, Asian Indians, Vietnamese, Korean Americans, and Japanese Americans. Yet, unlike Hispanics who all speak various dialects of Spanish, Asians speak many different languages. For example, ads for the U.S. Census ran in languages ranging from Japanese, Cantonese, Khmer, Korean, and Vietnamese to Thai, Cambodian, Hmong, Hinglish, and Taglish.

As a group, Asian American consumers shop frequently and are the most brand conscious of all the ethnic groups. They can be fiercely brand loyal, especially to brands that work to build relationships with them. As a result, many firms now target the Asian American market. For example, among its many other Asian American targeting efforts, McDonald's has built a special Web site for this segment (www.myinspirasian.com), offered in both English and Asian languages. The community-oriented site highlights how McDonald's is working with and serving the Asian American community.[9]

Cross-Cultural Marketing

Beyond targeting segments such as Hispanics, African Americans, and Asian Americans with specially tailored efforts, many marketers now embrace **cross-cultural marketing**. This is the practice of including ethnic themes and cross-cultural perspectives within the mainstream marketing of the organization. Cross-cultural marketing appeals to consumer similarities across subcultural segments rather than differences.

Many marketers are finding that insights gleaned from ethnic consumers can influence their broader markets. For example, today's youth-oriented lifestyle is influenced heavily by Hispanic and African American entertainers. So it follows that consumers expect to see many different cultures and ethnicities represented in the advertising and products they consume. For instance, McDonald's takes cues from African Americans, Hispanics, and Asians to develop menus and advertising in hopes of encouraging mainstream consumers to buy smoothies, mocha drinks, and snack wraps as avidly as they consume hip-hop and rock "n' roll. "The ethnic

Cross-cultural marketing
This is the practice of including ethnic themes and cross-cultural perspectives within the mainstream marketing of the organization.

TABLE 6–1
McDonald's Global Menu Variations

Country	Noteworthy Menu Items
United States	Big Mac, Chicken McNuggets, Filet-o-Fish, Egg McMuffin, Fries
India	McVeggie, Chicken Maharaja-Mac, McSpicy Paneer
France	Le McBaguette, Le Croque McDo, Le Royal Cheese
Egypt	Beef N Pepper, McArabia (grilled kofta), McFalafel
Israel	McKebab, McFalafel, Big New York and Big Texas (hamburgers)
Japan	Ebi Filet-O, MegaTeriyakl Burger, Bacon Egg and Lettuce Wrap, Shaka Shaka Chicken
China	Prosperity Burger, Taro Pie, McWings, McNuggets with Chili Garlic sauce
Brazil	Banana Pie, McNIflco Bacon, Cheddar McMelt, Big Tasty
Mexico	Big Mac, McChicken, Fries, etc.[11]

consumer tends to set trends," says McDonald's chief marketing officer. "So they help set the tone for how we enter the marketplace." Thus, McDonald's might take an ad primarily geared toward African Americans and run it in general-market media. "The reality is that the new mainstream is multicultural," concludes one cross-cultural marketing expert.[10]

Understanding consumer behavior is difficult enough for companies marketing within the borders of a single country. For companies operating in many countries, however, understanding and serving the needs of consumers can be daunting. Although consumers in different countries may have some things in common, their values, attitudes, and behaviors often vary dramatically. International marketers must understand such differences and adjust their products and marketing programs accordingly. Table 6–1 shows how McDonald's adapts its menu to fit the consumer wants of different cultures.

Social Class

Social classes Relatively permanent and order divisions in a society whose members share similar values, interests, and behaviors.

Almost every society has some form of social class structure. **Social classes** are relatively permanent and ordered divisions in a society whose members share similar values, interests, and behaviors. Social scientists have identified the seven American social classes: upper uppers (1 percent), lower uppers (2 percent), upper middles (12 percent), middle (32 percent), working (38 percent), upper lowers (9 percent), and lower lowers (7 percent).[12]

Social class in newer nations such as the United States, Canada, Australia, and New Zealand is not indicated by a single factor such as income but is measured as a combination of occupation, source of income, education, wealth, and other variables. In many older nations, social class is something into which one is born. Bloodlines often mean more than income or education in such societies. Marketers are interested in social class because people within a given class tend to exhibit similar behavior, including buying behavior. Social classes show distinct product and brand preferences in such areas as food, travel, and leisure activity. There are also language differences between social classes, which means advertisers must compose copy and dialogue that will be familiar to the social class being targeted.

Social Factors

Consumer behavior is also influenced by social factors, including the consumers' groups, family, social roles, and status.

Groups and Social Networks

Group Two or more people who interact to accomplish individual or mutual goals.

Many small **groups** influence a person's behavior. Groups that have a direct influence and to which a person belongs are called "membership groups." In contrast,

Reference groups Groups that have a direct (face-to-face) or indirect influence on a person's attitude or behavior.

Membership groups Groups that have a direct influence on a person's behavior and to which a person belongs.

Aspirational group A group to which a person wishes to belong.

Opinion leaders People within a reference group who, because of special skills, knowledge, personality, or other characteristics, exert influence on others.

Buzz marketing Cultivating opinion leaders and getting them to spread information about a product to others in their community.

reference groups serve as direct (face-to-face) or indirect points of comparison or reference in forming a person's attitudes or behavior. People often are influenced by reference groups to which they do not belong. For example, an aspirational group is one to which the individual wishes to belong, as when a young basketball player hopes to someday emulate basketball star Lebron James and play professionally.

Marketers try to identify the reference groups of their target markets. Reference groups influence consumers in at least three ways: (1) They expose the person to new behaviors and lifestyles; (2) they influence the person's attitudes and self-concept; and (3) they create pressures to conform that may affect the person's product, brand, and vendor choices.

Membership groups include primary groups, such as family, friends, neighbors, and coworkers—specifically, those with whom there is regular but informal interaction. Secondary groups are more formal and have less regular interaction; they include religious groups, professional associations, and trade unions. In some societies, secondary groups may be membership groups. Members of the Mormon faith, for example, are greatly influenced by their religious affiliation. Mormons do not drink alcoholic beverages and, therefore, would not be buyers of wine at a fine restaurant.

People can also be influenced by **aspirational groups** to which they do not belong but would like to. For example, a college freshman may aspire to be part of Hyatt's management team and may identify with this group even though not a member.

The importance of group influence varies by product and brand. It tends to be strongest when the product is visible to others whom the buyer respects. Purchases of products that are used privately are not greatly affected by group influence. Certain nightclubs can be associated with reference groups, attracting people who belong or wish to belong to the groups who frequent the nightclubs. Country clubs and city clubs tend to attract members who want to affiliate with their type of members.

Word-of-Mouth Influence and Buzz Marketing

Word-of-mouth influence can have a powerful impact on consumer buying behavior. The personal words and recommendations of trusted friends, associates, and other consumers tend to be more credible than those coming from commercial sources, such as advertisements or salespeople. One recent study found that only 49 percent of consumers reported that they trust or believe advertising, while 72 percent said they trusted family and friends and 72 percent said they trust online reviews.[13] Most word-of-mouth influence happens naturally: Consumers start chatting about a brand they use or feel strongly about one way or the other. Often, rather than leaving it to chance, marketers can help to create positive conversations about their brands.

Marketers of brands subjected to strong group influence must figure out how to reach **opinion leaders**—people within a reference group who, because of special skills, knowledge, personality, or other characteristics, exert social influence on others. Some experts call this group *the influentials* or *leading adopters*. When these influentials talk, consumers listen. Marketers try to identify opinion leaders for their products and direct marketing efforts toward them. For example, the guest list for the grand opening of a restaurant or the first anniversary of a hotel should include opinion leaders.

Buzz marketing involves enlisting or even creating opinion leaders to serve as "brand ambassadors," who spread the word about a company's products. Many companies now create brand ambassador programs in an attempt to turn influential but everyday customers into brand evangelists. A recent study found that such programs can increase the effectiveness of word-of-mouth marketing efforts by as much as 50 percent.[14] Foodie is an organization in Hong Kong that specializes in the online marketing of food and beverage. They create an online buzz by targeting early adopters and using multiple online channels including digital platforms, Foodie Club, social media, and an award-winning Foodie magazine.[15]

JetBlue's CrewBlue program employs real customers to create buzz on college campuses.[16] Over the past few years, the JetBlue CrewBlue program has recruited a small army of college student ambassadors—all loyal JetBlue lovers. CrewBlue representatives advise JetBlue on its campus marketing efforts, talk up the brand to other students, and help organize campus events, such as JetBlue's BlueDay. Held each fall on 21 campuses, the highly successful event urges students to wear outlandish blue costumes (and, on occasion, blue skin and hair). Students with the best costumes are each given a pair of free airline tickets. The CrewBlue ambassadors are crucial to the success of JetBlue's campus marketing efforts.[17]

Online Social Networks

Online social networks Online social communities—blogs, social networking, Web sites, or even virtual worlds—where people socialize or exchange information and opinions.

Over the past several years, a new type of social interaction has exploded onto the scene—online social networking. **Online social networks** are online communities where people socialize or exchange information and opinions. Social networking communities range from blogs (The Social Girl Traveler, The Wandering Eater, Dan Flying Solo) and message boards (Craigslist) to social media sites (Facebook, Twitter, YouTube, Instagram, Snapchat, LinkedIn) and even communal shopping sites (Amazon.com and Etsy). These online forms of consumer-to-consumer and business-to-consumer dialogue have big implications for marketers.

Marketers are working to harness the power of these new social networks and other "word-of-Web" opportunities to promote their products and build closer customer relationships. Instead of throwing more one-way commercial messages at consumers, they hope to use the internet and social networks to *interact* with consumers and become a part of their conversations and lives.

Sometimes, everyday customers become a brand's best evangelists. For instance, Alan Klein loves the McDonald's McRib—a sandwich made of a boneless pork patty molded into a rib-like shape, slathered in BBQ sauce and topped with pickles and onion. The McRib is sold for only short time periods each year at McDonald's restaurants around the nation. Klein loves it so much that he created the McRib Locator app and Web site (mcrib-locator.com), where McRib fans buzz about locations where they've recently sighted the coveted sandwich.[18]

Dunkin' Donuts uses Vine personality Logan Paul to promote its Dunkin' Donuts app and DD Perks loyalty program with posts on Vine and other social media. As it turns out, Paul is a genuine Dunkin' Donuts fan, so the brand lets him figure out what to say to his more than 8.7 million Vine followers, 5.4 million Facebook fans, and 2.4 million followers on Instagram.[19] Other marketers are working to tap the army of self-made influences already plying the internet—independent bloggers. Believe it or not, there are now almost as many people making a living as bloggers as there are lawyers. The key is to find bloggers who have strong networks of relevant readers, a credible voice, and a good fit with the brand. One of the most popular topics of bloggers is food, including restaurant reviews. Bloggers who have large following can have a positive impact on a restaurant. This results in restaurant managers inviting popular bloggers, with a following that matches the target market, to dine at their restaurant. The popular restaurant blogs such as Much Ado About Fooding provide recipes, interviews with chefs, and restaurant reviews as well. They try to understand their followers and write about topics that will keep them as loyal followers of the site. Some sites focus on specific cities, for example, Grub Street focuses on New York City and has 300,000 Facebook fans and 400,000 Twitter followers. Others such as Road Food cover restaurants across the United States and Canada, with past reviews accessible by state on their Web sites.[20]

But marketers must be careful when tapping into online social networks. Results are difficult to measure and control. Ultimately, the users control the content, so social network marketing attempts can easily backfire. We will dig deeper into online social networks as a marketing tool in Chapter 15.

Family

Family members have a strong influence on buyer behavior. The family remains the most important consumer buying organization in American society and has been researched extensively. Marketers are interested in the roles and influence of the husband, wife, and children on the purchase of different products and services. Husband–wife involvement varies widely by product category and by stage in the buying process. Buying roles change with evolving consumer lifestyles. In the United States, the wife traditionally has been the main purchasing agent for the family, especially in the areas of food, household products, and clothing. But with 71 percent of women holding jobs outside the home and the willingness of husbands to do more of the family's purchasing, all this is changing. For example, women now make or influence up to 80 percent of car-buying decisions, and men account for about 40 percent of food-shopping dollars.[21]

Children also have a strong influence on family buying decisions. The nation's kids and tweens influence up to 80 percent of all household purchases, to the tune of $1.2 trillion of spending annually. In one recent survey, parents with teens reported that their children weigh in heavily on everything from where they eat out (95 percent) and take vacations (82 percent) to what mobile devices they use (63 percent) and cars they buy (45 percent).[22] In Asia, children are also becoming more influential. One study found that 66 percent of Asia's teens were influenced by television advertising and 20 percent by the internet. This is significant because research conducted in Taiwan found that 98 percent of the children have a say in what programs they watch on television. Children all over the world are having an influence on where the family dines when they go out to eat. In the United States, the food industry spends $14 billion advertising to children.[23]

One of the most complex and challenging tasks for a professional event planner is the wedding. It often involves multiple family members from not just one family but two families. The wedding planner needs to determine the role of the bride, the bride's mother, and the groom's family in planning the wedding. In some cases, the bride's mother will have the dominant role and plan the wedding she always wanted for her daughter. On other cases, the bride's mother will let her daughter plan her wedding. Paying for the wedding can also get complicated. For example, the bride's family will pay for the wedding reception, except for the liquor which is paid by the groom's family. As a meeting planner, you will need to work through who is covering the different costs of the wedding, as well as create a balance between the family members of both families.

Marketing HIGHLIGHT 6.1 Tapping social media moms as brand ambassadors

Harnessing the power of mom-to-mom influence: Each year, Disney invites 175–200 moms and their families to its Disney Social Media Moms Celebration in Florida, an affair that's a mix of public relations event, educational conference, and family vacation with plenty of Disney Magic for these important mom influencers. Maria Sbytova/123RF.

America's moms constitute a huge market. Women account for 85 percent of all consumer purchases, and the nation's 85 million moms account for $3.2 trillion worth of annual consumer spending. Moms are also heavy social media sharers and shoppers. They are 20 percent more likely than the general population to use social media, and 44 percent of moms have made a purchase on their smartphones within the past week.

Moreover, many moms rely heavily on social media to share experiences with other moms, including brand and buying experiences. For example, there are as many as 14.2 million U.S. mothers who blog, and some mom bloggers influence millions of followers. Some 55 percent of moms on social media regularly base their buying decisions on personal stories, recommendations, and product reviews that they find in blogs and other social media.

Given these pretty amazing figures, it's not surprising that many marketers now harness the power of mom-to-mom influence by creating or tapping into networks of influential social media moms and turning them into brand ambassadors. Here are two examples: McDonald's and Disney.

McDonald's Mom Bloggers

McDonald's systematically reaches out to key "mom bloggers," who influence the nation's homemakers, who in turn influence their families' eating-out choices. For example,

McDonald's recently hosted 15 influential mom bloggers on an all-expenses-paid tour of its Chicago-area headquarters. The bloggers toured the facilities (including the company's test kitchens), met McDonald's USA president, and had their pictures taken with Ronald at a nearby Ronald McDonald House. McDonald's knows that these mom bloggers have loyal followings and talk a lot about McDonald's in their blogs. So it's turning the bloggers into believers by giving them a behind-the-scenes view. McDonald's doesn't try to tell the bloggers what to say in their posts about the visit. It simply asks them to write one honest recap of their trip. However, the resulting posts (each acknowledging the blogger's connection with McDonald's) were mostly very positive. Thanks to this and other such efforts, mom bloggers around the country are now more informed about and connected with McDonald's. "I know they have smoothies and they have yogurt and they have other things that my kids would want," says one prominent blogger. "I really couldn't tell you what Burger King's doing right now," she adds. "I have no idea."

Disney Social Media Moms

Disney has long recognized the power of moms in social media and the importance moms play in planning family vacations. Five years ago, the company assembled a group called "Disney Social Media Moms," roughly 1,300 carefully selected mom bloggers (and some dads), travel bloggers, and active Disney-focused social media posters.

Disney looks for influential moms who fit the brand's family-friendly focus, use social media heavily, and are active in their communities offline as well as online. One example is Rachel Pitzel, a mother of two and CEO of ClubMomMe, a social and educational group that sponsors events for moms, expectant parents, and families and maintains an active blog. Another is Wendy Wright, a home schooling mother of two and a prolific blogger. Wendy describes herself as a "Disney nut" (she named her cats Mickey and Minnie), and she fills her blog with advice for planning Disney park visits, tips for holding Disney-themed parties, and reviews of Disney movies.

Disney Social Media Moms aren't paid; they participate because of their passion and enthusiasm for all things Disney does. However, they do receive special educational attention from Disney, inside information, and occasional perks. For example, every year, Disney invites 175–200 of the moms and their families for a deeply discounted, four-day trip to attend its annual Disney Social Media Moms Celebration in Florida. The celebration is a mix of public relations event, educational conference, and family vacation with plenty of Disney magic for these important mom influencers.

Being invited to the event is a highlight of the year for many of those who are invited and a disappointment to those who did not receive an invitation. Disney does not reveal the criteria it uses for selecting participants. So those who receive invitations give advice to other bloggers on how to get invited to year's event. This provides more exposure to the event and encourages other bloggers to write about Disney in hopes of getting invited to next year's event. One blogger states there is no way to get yourself invited, Disney finds you. Apparently, Disney has a set of criteria that helps it discover moms who are influencers of their target market, even though they may not necessarily write about Disney.

The Disney Social Media Moms are under no obligation to post anything about Disney, and the company doesn't tell them what to say when they do post. However, the most recent celebration generated 28,500 tweets, 4,900 Instagram photos, and 88 blog posts full of ride reviews, videos of families meeting Disney characters, and a host of overwhelmingly positive comments. "For a big chunk of our guests, it's the moms who are making [travel] decisions," says a top Disney executive. The Disney Social Media Moms effort costs the company very little but effectively harnesses the power of mom-to-mom influence to help sprinkle Disney's magical pixie dust on an important group of buyers.[24]

Roles and Status

Role The activities that a person is expected to perform according to the persons around him or her.

A person belongs to many groups: family, clubs, and organizations. An individual's position in each group can be defined in terms of role and status. A **role** consists of the activities that a person is expected to perform according to the persons around him or her. Common roles include son or daughter, wife or husband, and manager or worker.

Each role influences buying behavior. For example, college students dining with their parents may act differently than when they are dining with peers. A person purchasing a banquet for his church's men's club may be more price conscious than usual if he believes church activities call for frugality. However, same person might be less interested in price and more interested in detail and quality when purchasing a banquet for his company. Thus, a person's role affects his purchasing behavior.

Our roles are also influenced by our surroundings. People dining at an elegant restaurant behave differently than when they dine at a fast-food restaurant. They also have expectations about the roles that employees in different establishments should play. Failure to meet these role expectations creates dissatisfaction.[25] For example, diners at an elegant restaurant might expect waiters to hold their chairs

Businesspeople will behave according to the role they are in and act differently during a business meal compared to when they are enjoying a casual dining experience with friends. Courtesy of Ryan McVay/Photodisc/Getty Images.

during seating. The same diners would be surprised and possibly offended if a person cleaning tables at a fast-food hamburger restaurant assisted with seating.

Each role carries a status reflecting the general esteem given to it by society. People often choose products that show their status in society. For example, a business traveler became upset when all first-class seats were sold on a desired flight. The traveler was forced to fly economy class. When questioned about his concern over flying economy class, the traveler's main concern was what people he knew might think if they saw him sitting in the economy section. He did not seem to be concerned over the lower level of service or the smaller seating space provided by the economy section. These illustrations show how role and status can affect consumer behavior. Many marketing and sales professionals have made serious judgmental errors relative to the role and status of prospective customers.

Personal Factors

A buyer's decisions are also influenced by personal characteristics, such as occupation, age and life-cycle stage, economic situation, lifestyle, personality, and self-concept.

Occupation

A person's occupation affects the goods and services bought. For example, construction workers often buy their lunches from industrial catering trucks that come out to the job site. Business executives purchase meals from a full-service restaurant, whereas clerical employees may bring their lunch or purchase lunch from a nearby quick-service restaurant. Employees of some consulting firms are not allowed to eat in fast-food restaurants. The managers of these companies do not think it creates a proper image to have their clients see a consultant they are billed at $300-an-hour for their services eating in a fast-food restaurant. Marketers try to identify occupational groups that have an above-average interest in their products.

Age and Life-Cycle Stage

The types of goods and services people buy change during their lifetimes. Preferences for leisure activities, travel destinations, food, and entertainment are often age-related. Important age-related factors are often overlooked by marketers. This is probably due to wide differences in age between those who determine marketing strategies and those who purchase the product/service. A study of mature travelers showed that this segment places great importance on grab bars in bathrooms, night lights, legible visible signs in hallways, extra blankets, and large printing on menus. Despite the logical importance of the factors, researchers found that this information "is not usually included in advertising and information listings."[26]

Successful marketing to various age segments may require specialized and targeted strategies. This will almost certainly require segmented target publications and database marketing. It may also require a marketing staff and advertising agency with people of varying ages and cultural backgrounds.

Buying behavior is also shaped by the **family life-cycle** stages. Young unmarried persons usually have few financial burdens, and they spend a good portion of their discretionary income on entertainment. Young married people without children have high discretionary incomes and dine out frequently. In fact, they have a higher frequency of dining out than any other group. A study by the National Restaurant Association found couples with no children spent 60 percent more on food away from home as did married couples with children at home. Once they have children,

Family life cycle The stages through which families might pass as they mature.

Many aging baby boomers still have an active lifestyle and choose to stay at resorts offering outdoor activities. Spotmatik Ltd/Shutterstock.

their purchases from restaurants can change to more delivery and carryout. When the children leave home, the discretionary income can jump, and expenses on dining out increases for people aged 55–74. Marketers often define their target markets in life-cycle terms and develop appropriate products and marketing plans.[27]

One of the leading life-stage segmentation systems is the Nielsen PRIZM Lifestage Groups system. PRIZM classifies every American household into one of 66 distinct life-stage segments, which are organized into 11 major life-stage groups, based on affluence, age, and family characteristics. The classifications consider a host of demographic factors, such as age, education, income, occupation, family composition, ethnicity, and housing, and behavioral and lifestyle factors, such as purchases, free-time activities, and media preferences.

The major PRIZM Lifestage Groups carry names such as "Striving Singles," "Midlife Success," "Young Achievers," "Sustaining Families," "Affluent Empty Nests," and "Conservative Classics," which in turn contain subgroups such as "Brite Lites, Li'l City," "Kids & Cul-de-Sacs," "Gray Power," and "Big City Blues." The "Young Achievers" group includes seven subsegments, with names like "Young Digerati," "Bohemian Mix," and "Young Influentials." The "Young Achievers" group consists of hip, single 20-somethings who rent apartments in or close to metropolitan neighborhoods. Their incomes range from working class to well-to-do, but the entire group tends to be politically liberal, listen to alternative music, and enjoy lively nightlife.[28]

Life-stage segmentation provides a powerful marketing tool for marketers in all industries to better find, understand, and engage consumers. Armed with data about the makeup of consumer life stages, marketers can create targeted, actionable, personalized campaigns based on how people consume and interact with brands and the world around them.

Different life-stage groups exhibit different buying behaviors. Life-stage segmentation provides a powerful marketing tool for marketers in all industries to better find, understand, and engage consumers. Armed with data about the makeup of consumer life stages, marketers can create actionable, personalized campaigns based on how people consume and interact with brands and the world around them.

Economic Situation

A person's economic situation greatly affects product choice and the decision to purchase a particular product. Consumers cut back on restaurant meals, entertainment, and vacations during recessions. They trade down in their choice of restaurants and/or menu items and eat out less frequently, looking for a coupon or deal when they do go out. Marketers need to watch trends in personal income, savings, and interest rates. If economic indicators point to a recession, they can redesign, reposition, and reprice their products. Restaurants may need to add lower-priced menu items that will still appeal to their target markets.

Conversely, periods of economic prosperity create opportunities. Consumers are more inclined to buy expensive wines and imported beers, menus can be upgraded, and air travel and leisure expenditures can be increased. Companies must take advantage of opportunities caused by economic upturns and take defensive steps when facing an economic downturn. Managers sometimes react too slowly to changing economic conditions. It pays to remain continuously aware of the macroenvironment facing customers. Regular reading of publications such as *the Wall Street Journal*, the business section of the local press, and regional economic reports by local and regional banks help to keep managers informed.

The Linq resort in Las Vegas is designed to attract millennials and in general a younger active clientele. The outdoor arcade next to the resort contains shops, restaurants, and bars that are consistent with the lifestyle of many millennials. Diego Grandi/Alamy Stock Photo.

Lifestyle A person's pattern of living as expressed in his or her activities, interests, and opinions.

Personality A person's distinguishing psychological characteristics that lead to relatively consistent and lasting responses to his or her environment.

Self-concept Self-image, the complex mental pictures people have of themselves.

Lifestyle

People coming from the same subculture, social class, and occupation may have quite different lifestyles. A **lifestyle** is a person's pattern of living as expressed in his or her activities, interests, and opinions. Lifestyle portrays the "whole person" interacting with his or her environment. Marketers search for relationships between their products and people who are achievement oriented. A chef may then target his or her restaurants more clearly at the achiever lifestyle. A study of tourists who purchase all-inclusive travel packages versus those who make travel arrangements independently revealed that lifestyle characteristics varied. All-inclusive travel purchasers were "more socially interactive, solicitous, and take their vacations mainly to relax." Tourists who preferred independent travel arrangements were more self-confident and often sought solitude.[29]

The San Diego Padres, like many baseball teams in the United States, have difficulty filling the stadium during day games that are held during the work week and when they play weak teams. Through marketing research, the team's management was able to identify a market segment composed of retired couples with a low income that were very loyal to the Padres. These fans enjoyed seeing the Padres play, didn't care who were playing, and preferred day games. By identifying and marketing to this lifestyle segment who wanted to go to day games, the Padres were able to fill seats in games where they had excess capacity.

Personality and Self-Concept

Each person's personality influences his or her buying behavior. By **personality** we mean distinguishing psychological characteristics that lead to relatively consistent and enduring responses to the environment.

Personality can be useful in analyzing consumer behavior for some product or brand choices. For example, a beer company may discover that heavy beer drinkers tend to rank high in sociability and aggressiveness. This information can be used to establish a brand image for the beer and to suggest the type of people to show in an advertisement.

Stanley Paskie, a 72-year-old head bartender at the Drake Hotel in Chicago's Gold Coast, said, "It's imperative that a bartender possess the human touch. Unfortunately, human relations isn't a required course at the nation's bartending schools where most bartenders now learn the craft. I've had conversations with customers in which I never said a word. I remember one customer who, as he was leaving, said 'thanks for listening to me, fella.' "[30] Paskie believed that a good bartender is part father, part philosopher, part confessor, and part devil's advocate. These traits are undoubtedly important in many areas of hospitality and travel marketing.

Many marketers use a concept related to personality: a person's **self-concept** (also called "self-image"). Each of us has a complex mental self-picture, and our behavior tends to be consistent with that self-image.[31] People who perceive themselves as outgoing and active will be unlikely to purchase a cruise vacation if their perception of cruises is one of elderly persons lying on lounge chairs. They would be more likely to select a scuba-diving or skiing vacation. The cruise line industry has been quite successful in changing its "geriatric" image and now attracts outgoing and active consumers.

Cruise lines, led by Carnival, changed cruising to include night clubs and family activities to attract a younger clientele.

The role of self-concept obviously has a strong bearing on the selection of recreational pursuits, including golf, sailing, dirt bike riding, fishing, and hunting. Anyone who enjoys boating will testify to the difference between boaters who use sails and those who use engines. Yachters/sail boaters refer to those who use engines as "stink potters." Stink potters think of the sailing crowd as stuffy, pretentious, and generally not much fun.

Psychological Factors

A person's buying choices are also influenced by four major psychological factors: motivation, perception, learning, and beliefs and attitudes.

Motivation

A person has many needs at any given time. Some are biological, arising from hunger, thirst, and discomfort. Others are psychological, arising from states of tension, such as the need for recognition, esteem, or belonging. Most of these needs are not strong enough to motivate a person to act at a given point in time. A need becomes a **motive** when it is aroused to a sufficient level of intensity. Creating a tension state causes the person to act to release the tension. One of the most well-known theories of motivation was developed by Abraham Maslow.

Motive A need that is sufficiently pressing to direct a person to seek satisfaction of that need.

MASLOW'S THEORY OF MOTIVATION. Abraham Maslow sought to explain why people are driven by particular needs at particular times.[32] Why does one person spend much time and energy on personal safety and another on gaining the esteem of others? Maslow's answer is that human needs are arranged in a hierarchy, from the most pressing to the least pressing. Maslow's hierarchy of needs in order of importance are physiological needs, safety needs, social needs, esteem needs, and self-actualization needs. A person tries to satisfy the most important need first. When that important need is satisfied, it will stop being a motivator, and the person will then try to satisfy the next most important need. For example, a starving man (need 1) will not take an interest in the latest happenings in the art world (need 5), or in how he is seen or esteemed by others (need 3 or 4), or even in whether he is breathing clean air (need 2). But as each important need is satisfied, the next most important need will come into play.

Normally, needs are prioritized. For example, a college student with $500 to pay for incidental and recreational expenses during the term is unlikely to spend $400 on a trip to Florida over spring break. Instead, the money will probably be spent on smaller purchases of entertainment throughout the semester. If the student unexpectedly receives $2,000, there might be a strong temptation to satisfy a higher-order need.

Perception

A motivated person is ready to act. How that person acts is influenced by his or her perception of the situation. In the same situation, two people with the same motivation may act quite differently based on how they perceive conditions. One person may perceive the waiters at T.G.I. Friday's as casual and unsophisticated, whereas another person may view them as spontaneous with cheerful personalities. Friday's is targeting those in the second group.

Why do people have different perceptions of the same situation? All of us experience a stimulus by the flow of information through our five senses: sight, hearing, smell, touch, and taste. However, each of us receives, organizes, and interprets this sensory information in an individual way. A person receives a great deal of information every day. For example, individuals are exposed to an estimated 3,000–5,000 messages every day. The cluttered digital environment adds 5.3 trillion online display ads shown every year, 400 million tweets sent daily, 144,000 hours of video uploaded daily, and 4.75 billion pieces of information shared on Facebook every day.[33] It is impossible for people to pay attention to all the stimuli surrounding them. This means perception is the process by which an individual selects, organizes, and interprets information to create a meaningful picture of the world.[34] From a marketing standpoint, an individual's perception is reality to them. One can have an excellent restaurant, but if the appearance of the restaurant from the street is that of a very ordinary restaurant many people who would have enjoyed the restaurant will never try it because of their perception, based on the street appearance of the restaurant.

The key word in the definition of perception is *individual*. One person might perceive a fast-talking salesperson as aggressive and insincere; another, as intelligent and helpful. People can emerge with different perceptions of the same object because of three perceptual processes: selective attention, selective distortion, and selective retention.

SELECTIVE ATTENTION. Because a person cannot possibly attend to all the messages they receive, most stimuli are screened out—a process called "selective attention." Selective attention means that marketers have to work hard to attract consumers' notice. The real challenge is to explain which stimuli people will notice. Here are some findings:

- People are more likely to notice stimuli that relate to a current need. A billboard advertising a dinner special at a local restaurant will receive more attention if it is placed so people see it on the way home versus on the other side of the street where people are viewing it on their way to work in the morning.

- People are more likely to notice stimuli that they anticipate. You are more likely to notice promotions for restaurants in a hotel than a promotion for a nearby clothes store.

- People are more likely to notice stimuli whose deviations are large in relation to the normal size of the stimuli. You are more likely to notice an ad offering $35 off the admission to a waterpark versus one offering $10 off.

SELECTIVE DISTORTION. Ever noticed stimuli do not always come across in the way the senders intended? Selective distortion is the tendency to twist information into personal meanings and interpret information in a way that will fit our preconceptions. Often fans of competing sports teams will have a different view of a penalty called in the game. Unfortunately, marketers can't do much about selective distortion.

SELECTIVE RETENTION. People forget much of what they learn but tend to retain information that supports their attitudes and beliefs. Because of selective retention, we are likely to remember good points mentioned about competing products. Selective retention explains why marketers use drama and repetition in sending messages to their target market.

Marketing HIGHLIGHT 6.2 Sensory marketing—A powerful tool for hospitality businesses

Researchers found that servers who briefly touched a customer near the shoulder for 2–3 seconds increased their sales. El Nariz/Shutterstock.

Sensory marketing has been defined as "marketing that engages the consumers' senses and affects their perception, judgment, and behavior." In other words, sensory marketing is an application of the understanding of sensation and perception to the field of marketing. All five senses may be engaged with sensory marketing: sight, sound, smell, taste, and feel. In a *Journal of Consumer Psychology* article, Aradhna Krishna offers an excellent review of the rapidly accumulating academic research on this topic.

In doing so, she notes, "Given the gamut of explicit marketing appeals made to consumers every day, subconscious 'triggers' which may appeal to the basic senses may be a more efficient way to engage consumers." In other words, consumers' own inferences about a product's attributes may be more persuasive, at least in some cases, than explicit claims from an advertiser.

Krishna argues that sensory marketing's effects can be manifested in two main ways. One, sensory marketing can be used subconsciously to shape consumer perceptions of more abstract qualities of a product or service (say, different aspects of its brand personality such as its sophistication, ruggedness, warmth, quality, and modernity). Two, sensory marketing can also be used to affect the perceptions of specific product or service attributes such as its color, taste, smell, or shape. Marketers certainly appreciate the importance of sensory marketing; for example, Westin's White Tea scent was so popular it began to sell it for home use. Based on Krishna's review of academic research in psychology and marketing, we next highlight some key considerations for each of the five senses.

Touch

Touch is the first sense to develop and the last sense we lose with age. People vary in their need for touch. One study found that when a server touched a customer with her hand on near the customer's shoulder for 2–3 seconds, sales increased when compared to customers who did not receive the touch.[34]

Smell

Scent-encoded information has been shown to be more durable and last longer in memory than information encoded with other sensory cues. People can recognize scents after very long lapses of time, and using scents as reminders can cue all kinds of autobiographical memories. Most travelers in the United States will recognize the scent of Cinnabon as they pass by the restaurant in the airport. Pleasant scents have also been shown to enhance evaluations of products and stores. Consumers also take more time and engage in more variety seeking in the presence of pleasant scents.

Sound

Marketing communications by their very nature are often auditory in nature. Even the sounds that make up a word can carry meanings. One study showed that Frosh-brand ice cream sounded creamier than Frish-brand ice cream. Language too can have its own associations. In bilingual cultures where English is the second language—such as Japan, Korea, Germany, and India—use of English in ads signals modernity, progress, sophistication, and a cosmopolitan identity. Ambient music in a store has also been shown to influence consumer mood, time spent in a location, perception of time spent in a location, and spending.

Taste

Humans can distinguish only five pure tastes: sweet, salty, sour, bitter, and umami. Umami comes from Japanese food researchers and stands for "delicious" or "savory" as it relates to the taste of pure protein or monosodium glutamate (MSG). Taste perceptions themselves depend on all the other senses—the way a food looks, feels, smells, and sounds to eat. Thus many factors have been shown to affect taste perceptions, including physical attributes, brand name, product information (ingredients, nutritional information), product packaging, and advertising. Foreign-sounding brand names can improve ratings of yogurt, and ingredients that sound unpleasant (balsamic vinegar or soy) can affect consumers' taste perceptions if disclosed before product consumption.

Vision

Visual effects have been studied in detail in an advertising context. Many visual perception biases or illusions exist in day-to-day consumer behavior. For example, people judge tall thin containers to contain more volume than short fat ones, but after drinking from the containers, people actually feel they have consumed more from short fat containers than tall thin containers, over-adjusting their expectations. Even something as simple as the way a mug is depicted in an ad can affect product evaluations. A mug photographed with the handle on the right side was shown to elicit more mental stimulation and product purchase intent from right-handed people than if shown with the handle on the left side.[36]

Learning

Learning Changes in a person's behavior arising from experience.

When people act, they learn. **Learning** describes changes in an individual's behavior arising from experience. Most human behavior is learned. Learning theorists say that learning occurs through the interplay of drives, stimuli, cues, responses, and reinforcement.

When consumers experience a product, they learn about it. Members of the site-selection committee for a convention often sample the services of competing hotels. They eat in the restaurants, note the friendliness and professionalism of the staff, and examine the hotel's features. Based on what they have learned, a hotel is selected to host the convention. During the convention, they experience the hotel once again. Based on their experience and those of the attending conventioneers, they will be either satisfied or dissatisfied.

Hotels should help guests learn about the quality of their facilities and services. Luxury hotels give tours to first-time guests and inform them of the services offered. Repeat guests should be updated on the hotel's services by employees and by letters and literature.

Beliefs and Attitudes

Belief A descriptive thought that a person holds about something.

Through acting and learning, people acquire beliefs and attitudes, which, in turn, influence their buying behavior. A **belief** is a descriptive thought that a person holds about something. A customer may believe that Novotel has the best facilities and most professional staff of any hotel in the price range. These beliefs may be based on real knowledge, opinion, or faith. They may or may not carry an emotional charge.

Marketers are interested in the beliefs that people have about specific products and services. Beliefs reinforce product and brand images. People act on beliefs. If unfounded consumer beliefs deter purchases, marketers will want to launch a campaign to change them.

Unfounded consumer beliefs can severely affect the revenue and even the life of hospitality and travel companies. Among these beliefs might be the following:

- A particular hamburger chain served ground kangaroo meat.
- A particular airline has poor maintenance.
- A particular country has unhealthy food-handling standards.

People have attitudes about almost everything: religion, politics, clothes, music, and food. An **attitude** describes a person's relatively consistent evaluations, feelings, and tendencies toward an object or an idea. Attitudes put people into a frame of mind for liking or disliking things and moving toward or away from them. Companies can benefit by researching attitudes toward their products. Understanding attitudes and beliefs is the first step toward changing or reinforcing them.

Attitude A person's enduring favorable or unfavorable cognitive evaluations, emotional feelings, and action tendencies toward some object or idea.

Attitudes are very difficult to change. A person's attitudes fit into a pattern and changing one attitude may require making many difficult adjustments. It is easier for a company to create products that are compatible with existing attitudes than to change the attitudes toward its products. There are exceptions, of course, where the high cost of trying to change attitudes may pay off.

There is a saying among restaurateurs that a restaurant is only as good as the last meal served. Attitudes explain in part why this is true. A customer who has returned to a restaurant several times and on one visit receives a bad meal may begin to believe it is impossible to count on having a good meal at that restaurant. The customer's attitudes toward the restaurant begin to change. If this customer again receives a bad meal, negative attitudes may be permanently fixed and prevent a future return. Serving a poor meal to first-time customers can be disastrous. Customers develop an immediate negative attitude that prevents them from returning.

Amusement parks view children as lifelong customers. They want them to come back as parents, aunts, uncles, and grandparents. Fei Wong/123RF.

Attitudes developed as children often influence purchases as adults. Children may retain negative attitudes toward certain vegetables, people, and possibly places. Chances are equally good that they may retain very positive images toward McDonald's and Disneyland. Disney and McDonald's both view children as lifelong customers. They want children to return as teenagers, parents, aunts, uncles, and grandparents and treat them in a manner to ensure future business.

Once negative attitudes are developed, they are hard to change. New restaurant owners often want quick cash flow and sometimes start without investing in training their staff. A new restaurateur complained that customers are fickle. When his restaurant first opened, there were lines of people waiting for a seat. A few months later, he had plenty of empty seats every night. Obviously, he had not satisfied his first guests. Even though he may have subsequently corrected his early mistakes, his original customers had been disappointed, were not returning, and reporting negative comments on social media.

We can now appreciate the many individual characteristics and forces influencing consumer behavior. Consumer choice is the result of a complex interplay of cultural, social, personal, and psychological factors. Many of these cannot be influenced by the marketer; however, they help the marketer to better understand customers' reactions and behavior.

The Buyer Decision Process

We are now ready to look at how consumers make buying decisions. Figure 6–3 shows that the buyer decision process consists of five stages: need recognition, information search, evaluation of alternatives, purchase decision, and postpurchase behavior. This model emphasizes that the buying process starts long before and continues long after the actual purchase. It encourages the marketer to focus on the entire buying process rather than just the purchase decision.

The model appears to imply that consumers pass through all five stages with every purchase they make. But in more routine purchases, consumers skip or reverse some of these stages. A customer in a bar always drink a martini made with their favorite brand of vodka. When the bartender asks what kind of vodka she would like, the guest names her favorite brand without asking what kinds of vodka the bar stocks for suggestions from the bartender. She skips information search and evaluation and goes straight to the purchase stage. This is referred to as an *automatic response loop*.[37] The dream of every marketer is to have customers develop an automatic response to purchase its products. However, this does not typically happen. The model in Figure 6–3 shows the considerations that arise when a consumer faces a new and complex purchase situation.

Need Recognition

The buying process starts when the buyer recognizes a problem or need. The buyer senses a difference between his or her actual state and a desired state. The need can be triggered by internal or external stimuli. For example, a person may feel hungry (internal) or they may see an ad for a Valentine's Day Dinner (external) and realize they need to do something for their significant other on Valentine's Day. From previous experience, the person has learned how to cope with these needs and is motivated toward objects that he knows will satisfy it.

At this stage, marketers must determine the factors and situations that trigger consumer problem recognition. They should research consumers to find out what kinds of needs or problems led them to purchase an item, what brought these needs about, and how they led consumers to choose this particular product.

By gathering such information, marketers can identify stimuli that most often trigger interest in the product and develop marketing programs that involve these stimuli. Marketers can also show how their product is a solution to a problem. For example, T.G.I. Friday's advertised its gift certificates as a solution to Christmas shopping. Friday's food and atmosphere attracts a broad range of people; the gift certificates are easy to buy, avoiding the need to go to crowded shopping centers; and they can be bought in denominations that fit with planned expenditures. Friday's promoted gift certificates as a solution to a common need experienced before Christmas, buying gifts for friends and family.

When looking for a hotel, "business travelers want a hotel to give them the tools to get their work done efficiently, which includes having competent staff members on duty, more than they want personalized services and fancy surroundings."[38] Hotels have responded to this by good work spaces in the rooms and by creating lobbies that support a work environment, through computer spaces, free Wi-Fi, and tables in the food and beverage area where one can enjoy a meal or snack while checking e-mails or conducting work.

The Travel Industry Association of America found that families with both heads of the household employed were finding it difficult to find a week when everyone was free. As a result, this segment needed three- and four-day getaways that could be booked at the last minute because 42 percent of this group makes plans within two weeks of the actual vacation.[39] These examples show that businesses must understand the needs of their customers and how these needs are translated into wants.

Figure 6–3
Buyer decision process.

Need recognition → Information search → Evaluation of alternatives → Purchase decision → Postpurchase behavior satisfaction or dissatisfaction with a purchase? The answer lies in the relationship between consumer expectations and perceived product performance.[42] If the product matches expectations, the consumer will be satisfied. If it falls short, the consumer will experience dissatisfaction.

Consumers base expectations on past experiences and on messages they receive from sellers, friends, and other information sources. If a seller exaggerates the product's likely performance, the consumer will be disappointed. The larger the gap between expectations and performance, the greater the consumer's dissatisfaction. This suggests that sellers must faithfully represent the product's performance so that buyers are satisfied. For example, Bermuda enticed tourists to enjoy the island during the off season at a lower price. It called this period "Rendezvous Time" and advertised that all the island's amenities would be available. When tourists arrived, they found that many facilities and attractions were closed. Hotels had shut down many of their food and beverage facilities because of the slower demand, leaving tourists disappointed. Advertising claims initially brought tourists, but the expectations the tourists had of a full service resort were not met and hotel occupancy dropped by almost 50 percent over a period of six years.[43]

Almost all major purchases result in **cognitive dissonance**, or discomfort caused by postpurchase conflict. Every purchase involves compromise. Consumers feel uneasy about acquiring the drawbacks of the chosen brand and losing the benefits of the rejected brands. Thus, consumers feel some postpurchase dissonance with many purchases, and they often take steps after the purchase to reduce dissonance.[44]

Cognitive dissonance Buyer discomfort caused by postpurchase conflict.

Marketing HIGHLIGHT 6.3 Unique aspects of hospitality and travel consumers

Valarie Zeithaml, a marketing consultant, published a classic article describing how the consumer evaluation process differs between goods and services. Persons purchasing hospitality and travel services rely more on information from personal sources. When looking for a good restaurant, people ask friends or people familiar with the town, such as front-desk employees or the concierge. Restaurants should attempt to affect positively those persons whom potential customers may contact. In larger cities there is a concierge association. Smart restaurateurs seek to host this club, letting their members experience the restaurants.

Postpurchase evaluation of services is important. The intangibility of services makes it difficult to judge the service beforehand. Consumers may seek advice from friends but use the information they receive from actually purchasing the service to evaluate it. The first-time customer is on a trial basis. If the hotel or restaurant satisfies the customers, they will come back.

When purchasing hospitality and travel products, customers often use price as an indication of quality. A business executive who has been under a lot of pressure decides to take a three-day vacation now that the project is complete. She wants luxury accommodations and good food service. She is prepared to pay $275 a night for the room. She calls a hotel that offers a special rate of $99. This hotel may be able to satisfy her needs and has simply dropped its rate to encourage business. In this case, the hotel has dropped its rate too low to attract this customer. Because she has never visited the hotel, she will perceive that the hotel is below her standard. Similarly, a person who enjoys fresh seafood and sees grilled red snapper on the menu for $7.99 will assume that it must be a low-quality frozen product because fresh domestic red snapper usually costs two to three as much. When using price to create demand, care must be taken to ensure that one does not create the wrong consumer perceptions about the product's quality.

When customers purchase hospitality and travel products, they often perceive some risk in the purchase. If customers want to impress friends or business associates, they usually take them to a restaurant they have visited previously. Customers tend to be loyal to restaurants and hotels that have met their needs. A meeting planner is reluctant to change hotels if the hotel has been doing a good job.

Customers of hospitality and travel products often blame themselves when dissatisfied. A man who orders scampi may be disappointed with the dish but not complain because he blames himself for the bad choice. He loves the way his favorite restaurant fixes scampi, but he should have known that this restaurant would not be able to prepare it the same way. When the waiter asks how everything is, he replies that it was okay. Employees must be aware that dissatisfied customers may not complain. They should try to seek out sources of guest dissatisfaction and resolve them. A waiter noticing someone not eating his or her food may ask if he or she could replace it with an alternative dish and suggest some items that could be brought out very quickly.[45]

Dissatisfied consumers may take any of several actions. They may return the product or complain to the company and ask for a refund or exchange. They may initiate a lawsuit or complain to an organization or group that can help them get satisfaction. Buyers may also simply stop purchasing the product and discourage purchases by family and friends. In each of these cases, the seller loses.

Marketers can take steps to reduce consumer postpurchase dissatisfaction and help customers to feel good about their purchases. Hotels can send a letter to meeting planners congratulating them on having selected their hotel for their next meeting. They can place ads featuring testimonials of satisfied meeting planners in trade magazines. They can encourage customers to suggest improvements.

Understanding the consumer's needs and buying process is the foundation of successful marketing. By understanding how buyers proceed through problem recognition, information search, evaluation of alternatives, the purchase decision, and postpurchase behavior, marketers can acquire many clues as to how to better meet buyer needs. By understanding the various participants in the buying process and major influences on buying behavior, marketers can develop a more effective marketing program.

CHAPTER REVIEW

I. **Model of Consumer Behavior.** The company that really understands how consumers will respond to different product features, prices, and advertising appeals has a great advantage over its competitors. As a result, researchers from companies and universities have heavily studied the relationship between marketing stimuli and consumer response. The marketing stimuli consist of the four Ps: product, price, place, and promotion. Other stimuli include major forces and events in the buyer's environment: economic, technological, political, and cultural. All these stimuli enter the buyer's black box, where they are turned into a set of observable buyer responses: product choice, brand choice, dealer choice, purchase timing, and purchase amount.

II. **Personal Characteristics Affecting Consumer Behavior**
  A. **Cultural factors**
   1. Culture is the most basic determinant of a person's wants and behavior. It compromises the basic values, perceptions, wants, and behaviors that a person learns continuously in a society.
   2. **Subculture.** Each culture contains smaller subcultures, groups of people with shared value systems based on common experiences and situations.
   3. **Cross-cultural marketing.** This is the practice of including ethnic themes and cross-cultural perspectives within the mainstream marketing of the organization.
   4. **Social class.** These are relatively permanent and ordered divisions in a society whose members share similar values, interests, and behaviors. Social class in newer nations such as the United States, Canada, Australia, and New Zealand is not indicated by a single factor such as income but is measured as a combination of occupation, source of income, education, wealth, and other variables.

  B. **Social factors**
   1. **Groups and social networks.** Groups that have a direct influence and to which a person belongs are called membership groups. In contrast, reference groups serve as direct (face-to-face) or indirect points of comparison or reference in forming a person's attitudes or behavior.
   2. **Word-of-mouth influence and buzz marketing.** The personal words and recommendations of trusted friends, associates, and other consumers tend to be more credible than those coming from commercial sources. Buzz marketing involves enlisting or creating opinion leaders to serve as "brand ambassadors," who spread the word about a company's products.
   3. **Online social networks.** These networks are online communities where people socialize or exchange information and opinions. Social networking media range from blogs to social networking Web sites, such as Facebook.com and YouTube. Marketers are working to harness the power of these new social networks and other "word-of-Web" opportunities to promote their products and build closer customer relationships.
   4. **Family.** Family members have a strong influence on buyer behavior. The family remains the most important consumer buying organization in American society.
   5. **Role and status.** A role consists of the activities that a person is expected to perform according to the persons around him or her. Each role carries a status reflecting the general esteem given to it by society. People often choose products that show their status in society.

  C. **Personal factors**
   1. **Occupation.** A person's occupation affects the goods and services bought.
   2. **Age and life-cycle stage.** The types of goods and services people buy change during their

lifetimes. As people grow older and mature, the products they desire change. The makeup of the family also affects purchasing behavior. For example, families with young children dine out at fast-food restaurants.
3. **Economic situation.** A person's economic situation greatly affects product choice and the decision to purchase a particular product.
4. **Lifestyle.** Lifestyles profile a person's whole pattern of acting and interacting in the world. When used carefully, the lifestyle concept can help the marketer understand changing consumer values and how they affect buying behavior.
5. **Personality and self-concept.** Each person's personality influences his or her buying behavior. By personality we mean distinguishing psychological characteristics that disclose a person's relatively individualized, consistent, and enduring responses to the environment. Many marketers use a concept related to personality: a person's self-concept (also called self-image). Each of us has a complex mental self-picture, and our behavior tends to be consistent with that self-image.

D. **Psychological factors**
1. **Motivation.** A need becomes a motive when it is aroused to a sufficient level of intensity. Creating a tension state causes a person to act to release the tension.
2. **Perception.** Perception is the process by which a person selects, organizes, and interprets information to create a meaningful picture of the world.
3. **Learning.** Learning describes changes in a person's behavior arising from experience.
4. **Beliefs and attitudes.** A belief is a descriptive thought that a person holds about something. An attitude describes a person's relatively consistent evaluations and feelings.

III. **Buyer Decision Process**
A. **Need recognition.** The buying process starts when the buyer recognizes a problem or need. At this stage, marketers must determine the factors and situations that trigger consumer problem recognition. They should research consumers to find out what kinds of needs or problems led them to purchase an item, what brought these needs about, and how they led consumers to choose this particular product. By gathering such information, marketers can identify stimuli that most often trigger interest in the product and develop marketing programs that involve these stimuli. Marketers can also show how their product is a solution to a problem.
B. **Information search.** An aroused consumer may or may not search for more information. How much searching a consumer does will depend on the strength of the drive, the amount of initial information, the ease of obtaining more information, the value placed on additional information, and the satisfaction one gets from searching. With hospitality and travel products, personal and public sources of information are more important than advertisements. This is because customers do not know what they are going to receive until they have received it. People often ask others—friends, relatives, acquaintances, professionals—for recommendations concerning a product or service. Thus, companies have a strong interest in building such *word-of-mouth sources*.
C. **Evaluation of alternatives.** Unfortunately, there is no simple and single evaluation process used by all consumers or even by one consumer in all buying situations. There are several evaluation processes.
D. **Purchase decision.** In the evaluation stage, the consumer ranks brands in the choice set and forms purchase intentions. Generally, the consumer buys the most preferred brand.
E. **Postpurchase behavior.** The marketer's job does not end when the customer buys a product. Following a purchase, the consumer will be satisfied or dissatisfied and will engage in postpurchase actions of significant interest to the marketer.

IN-CLASS GROUP EXERCISES

*Exercises with an asterisk next to them are suitable for individual homework or online assignments. Always provide an explanation for your answer.

1. *Explain why marketers study buyer behavior and discuss characteristics affecting consumer behavior. Which characteristics do you think would have the greatest impact on your decision to select a restaurant to celebrate a special occasion, such as a birthday or anniversary?
2. *Choose a restaurant concept that you would like to take overseas. How will the factors shown in Figure 6–2 work for or against the success of this restaurant?
3. *Define the consumer market and describe the four major sets of factors that influence consumer buyer behavior. Which characteristics influenced your choice when deciding on the school you would attend? Are those the same characteristics that would influence you when deciding what to do on Saturday night?
4. *Discuss when the family can be a strong influence on buying behavior regarding the choice of restaurants.
5. *Apply the buyer five stages in the decision process to your selection of a destination for your next vacation.
6. *An advertising agency president says, "Perception is reality." What does he mean by this? How is perception important to marketers?

EXPERIENTIAL EXERCISE

Do one of the following:

1. Talk to several people about how they would choose a hotel in a city they have never been to before, a restaurant for a special occasion, or a place to vacation. What did you learn about the buyer decision process from these discussions?

REFERENCES

1. Fast Company, 2015, Most innovative Companies Taco Bill, https://www.fastcompany.com/company/taco-bell

2. Aamer Madhani, "Taco Bell Begins Testing Delivery Service at 200 Stores," *USA TODAY*, July 8, 2015, http://www.usatoday.com/story/money/2015/07/08/taco-bell-to-test-delivery-california-texas/29832469/ (accessed July 10, 2015); Chelsey Dulaney, "Taco Bell, Pizza Hut to Remove Artificial Flavors, Coloring," *Wall Street Journal*, May 26, 2015, http://www.wsj.com/articles/taco-bell-to-remove-artificial-flavors-coloring-1432638320 (accessed July 10, 2015); Maureen Morrison, "Sales Are Going Loco at Taco Bell, Ad Age's Marketer of the Year," *Advertising Age* (September 2, 2013): 2; Shirley Brady, "Taco Bell Promotes New 'Live Mas' Tagline in New Campaign," *Brand Channel*, February 24, 2012, www.brandchannel.com/home/post/2012/02/24/Taco-Beii-Uve-Mas-Doritos-Locos-Tacos-Spots-022412.aspx; Maureen Morrison, "Taco Bell to Exchange 'Think Outside the Bun' for 'Live Mas,'" *Advertising Age*, February 21, 2012, adage.com/print/232849/; Mark Brandau, "Yum Plans to Double U.S. Taco Bell Sales," *Restaurant News*, May 22, 2013, nrn.corn/quick-service/analysts-yum-plans-double-us-taco-bell-sales; Mark Brandau, "Taco Bell NBA Sponsorship to Emphasize Digital, Social Media," *Restaurant News*, October 18, 2013, nm.corn/social-media/taco-bell-nba-sponsorship-emphasize-digital-social-media; and various pages at www.tacobell.com (accessed September 2014); Tristano, D. (2018), "Taco Bell Innovates Again with Nacho," *Forbes*, https://www.forbes.com/sites/darrentristano/2018/03/14/innovative-taco-bell-brand-does-it-again-with-new-nacho-fries-for-a-buck/#3a0a07882b76 (accessed July 6, 2018); Morris, C. (2017), "Taco Bell Is Adding Booze to a Lot of Its Locations," *Fortune*, http://fortune.com/2017/09/22/taco-bell-cantina/ (accessed July 7, 2018); *Wired* (N.D.), "Taco Bell, The World's Most Innovative Companies 2017," https://www.fastcompany.com/company/taco-bell (accessed July 6, 2018); Walsh, D. (2017), "Taco Bell Is Ditching Drive-Thrus and Adding Booze," https://www.foodandwine.com/news/taco-bell-ditching-drive-thrus-and-adding-booze (accessed July 6, 2018).

3. "Advertising Age Hispanic Fact Pack," August 3, 2015, pp. 30–31; Claudia "Havi" Goffan, "Hispanic Market Trends Forecast," Target Latino, http://targetlatino.com/hispanic-market-trends-forecast/ (accessed September 2016); Population Projections, www.census.gov/population/projections/ (accessed September 2016).

4. Lee Vann, "5 Predictions for Hispanic Online Marketing in 2015," *MediaPost*, November 13, 2014, www.mediapost.com/publications/article/238136; and Goffan, "Hispanic Market Trends Forecast."

5. http://www.iahmp.org/ (accessed August 29, 2011).

6. Hernan Tagliani, "3 Ways to Keep Success on a Restaurant's Menu," *Orlando Business Journal*, April 20, 2015, http://www.bizjournals.com/orlando/blog/2015/04/3-ways-to-keep-success-on-a-restaurants-menu.html (accessed July 10, 2015).

7. See "Connecting through Culture: African Americans Favor Diverse Advertising," *Nielsen*, October 20, 2014, www.nielsen.com/us/en/insights/news/2014/connecting-through-culture-african-americans-favor-diverse-advertising.html; and U.S. Census Bureau, "U.S. Population Projections," www.census.gov/population/projections (accessed September 2016).

8. "U.S. Forest Service and Ad Council Launch New Multimedia Public Service Advertising Effort to Encourage African American Families to Discover Nature," June 7, 2012, www.multivu.com/mnr/62047-us-forest-service-ad-council-psa-african-american-families-discover-nature; "US Forest Service Discover the Forest," National Environmental Justice Conference and Training Program, April 4, 2013, www.scribd.com/doc/134213528/US-Forest-Service-Discover-The-Forest#scribd; "Discovering Nature (African-American Market)," www.adcouncil.org/Our-Campaigns/Family-Community/Discovering-Nature-African-American-Market (accessed February 2015); and www.discovertheforest.org (accessed September 2016).

9. See Agnes Constante (2018), "Asian-American buying power rising as population grows, Nielsen report finds," https://www.nbcnews.com/news/asian-america/asian-american-buying-power-rising-population-grows-nielsen-report-finds-n872046 (accessed May 6, 2019) and U.S. Census Bureau, "U.S. Population Projections," www.census.gov/population/projections (accessed September 2016).

10. See Eleftheria Parpis, "Goodbye Color Codes," *Adweek* (September 27, 2010): 24–25; "Ethnic Marketing: McDonald's Is Lovin' It," *Bloomberg BusinessWeek* (July 18, 2010): 22–23; Alex Frias, "5 Tips to Refresh Your Multicultural Marketing Strategy in 2013," *Forbes*, February 8, 2013, www.forbes.com/sites/theyec/2013/02/08/5-tips-to-refresh-your-multicultural-marketing-strategy-in-2013/; Stuart

Elliott, "New Ad Organization to Promote Cross-Cultural Marketing," *New York Times*, August 30, 2013, http://www.nytimes.com/2013/08/31/business/media/new-ad-organization-to-promote-cross-cultural-marketing.html; The Cross-Cultural Marketing and Communications Association, "Total Market," www.theccmca.org/?page_id=3631 (accessed September 2014).

11. "Discover McDonald's Around the World," www.aboutmcdonalds.com/mcd/country/map.html (accessed May 20, 2014); David Griner, "McDonald's 60-Second Meals in Japan Aren't Going So Well," *Adweek*, January 7, 2013; Richard Vines and Caroline Connan, "McDonald's Wins Over French Chef with McBaguette Sandwich," www.bloomberg.com, January 15, 2013; Segolene Poirier, "McDonald's Brazil Has Big Plans," *We Rio Times*, April 8, 2012; Susan Postlewaite, "McDonald's McFalafel a Hit with Egyptians, *Advertising Age*, June 19, 2001.

12. See Richard P. Coleman, "The Continuing Significance of Social Class to Marketing," *Journal of Consumer Research* (December 1983): 264–280; Leon G. Shiffman and Leslie Lazar Kanuk, *Consumer Behavior*, 6th ed. (Upper Saddle River, NJ: Prentice Hall, 1997), p. 388.

13. Barry Levine, "New Marketing Survey, It's the Trust, Stupid," *Venture Beat*, September 29, 2015, http://venturebeat.com/2015/09/29/new-marketing-survey-its-the-trust-stupid/.

14. "Research Reveals Word-of-Mouth Campaigns on Customer Networks Double Marketing Results," *Business Wire* (October 27, 2009).

15. See https://www.afoodieworld.com/ (accessed July 6, 2018).

16. See "JetBlue Lovers Unite to Share Brand Perks with Peers," *WOOMA Case*, www.womma.org/case-study/examples/create-an-evangelism-program/jetblue-lovers-unite-to-share/ (accessed March 2010); Joan Voigt, "The New Brand Ambassadors," *Adweek* (December 31, 2007): 18–19, 26; Rebecca Nelson, "A Citizen Marketer Talks," *Adweek* (December 31, 2007): 19; Holly Shaw, "Buzzing Influencers," *National Post* (March 13, 2009): FP 12; information from www.repnation.com (accessed October 2010).

17. Joan Voigt, "The New Brand Ambassadors," *Adweek* (December 31, 2007): 18–19.

18. Kate Taylor, "For McRib Fans, Search for the Sandwich Is Worth the Effort," *Entrepreneur*, November 21, 2013, www.entrepreneur.com//article/230063# and http://mcriblocator.com (accessed September 2016).

19. See "Dunkin' Donuts Taps Vine Star Logan Paul for Loyalty Program Jolt," *Advertising Age*, November 9, 2015, www.adage.com/print/310271.

20. See Hannah (2017). "Top Restaurant Review Blogs for 2017," https://www.gourmetmarketing.net/top-restaurant-review-blogs-2017/ (accessed July 6, 2018); "Top 100 Restaurant Blogs and Websites to Follow in 2018," https://blog.feedspot.com/restaurant_blogs/ (accessed July 6, 2018).

21. See Darla Dernovsek, "Marketing to Women," *Credit Union Magazine* (October 2000): 90–96; Sharon Goldman Edry, "No Longer Just Fun and Games," *American Demographics* (May 2001): 36–38. Chris Slocumb, "Women Outspend Men 3 to 2 on Technology Purchases," *ClarityQuest*, January 3, 2013, www.clarityqst.com/women-outspend-men-3-to-2-on-technology-pur-chases/; "More Men Are Grocery Shopping, but They Do So Grudgingly, Reports NPD," November 12, 2014, www.npd.com/wps/portal/npd/us/news/press-releases/more-men-are-grocery-shopping-but-they-do-so-grudgingly/; Sarwant Singh, "Women in Cars: Overtaking Men on the Fast Lane," *Forbes*, May 23, 2014, www.forbes.com/sites/sarwantsingh/2014/05/23/women-in-cars-overtaking-men-on-the-fast-lane/; and "Women Make Up 85% of All Consumer Purchases," *BloombergBusiness*, June 22, 2015, www.bloomberg.com/news/videos/b/9e28517f-8del-4e59-bcda-ce536aa50bd6.

22. See "Kids Spending and Influencing Power: $1.2 Trillion Says Leading Ad Firm," Center for Digital Democracy, November 1, 2012, www.democraticmedia.org/kids-spending-and-influendng-power-12-trillion-says-leading-ad-firm; and "How Much Influence Do Teens Wield over Their Parents' Purchase Decisions?" Marketing Charts, June 23, 2015, www.marketingcharts.com/traditional/how-much-influence-do-teens-wield-over-their-parents-purchase-dedsions-56068/.

23. Linda Abu-Shalback Zid, "What's for Dinner," *Marketing Management* (September/October 2004): 6; David Evans and Olivia Toth, "Parents Buy, But Kids Rule," *Media Asia* (November 14, 2003): 22+.

24. Sources: See Mindy Rasledvich, "Harnessing the Power of Mom-to-Mom Influence," Dedicated Media, May 19, 2015, www.dedicatedmedia.com/articles/hamessing-the-power-of-mom-to-mom-influence-2; Elizabeth Segran, "On Winning the Hearts—and Dollars—of Mommy Bloggers," Fast Company, August 14, 2015, www.fast-company.com/3049137; Keith O'Brien, "How McDonald's Came Back Bigger than Ever," *New York Times*, May 6, 2012, p. MM44; "Lisa Richwine, Disney's Powerful Marketing Force: Social Media Moms," Reuters, June 15, 2015, www.reuters.com/article/us-disney-moms-insight-idUSKBN0OV0DX20150615; and "Disney Parks Social Media Moms Celebration," http://disneysmmoms.com/ (accessed September 2016); http://land.allears.net/blogs/kristin-ford/walt_disney_world/disney_social_media_moms_celeb/ (accessed July 6, 2018); https://dixiedelightsonline.com/2018/02/disney-social-media-moms-celebration-2018.html (accessed July 6, 2018).

25. John E. G. Bateson, *Managing Services Marketing* (New York: Dryden, 1989), pp. 291–300.

26. Richard M. Howey, Ananth Mangala, Frederick J. De Micco, and Patrick J. Moreo, "Marketplace Needs

of Mature Travelers," *Cornell Hotel and Restaurant Administration Quarterly*, 33, no. 4 (1992): 19–20.

27. *Consumer Spending in Restaurants 2014*, National Restaurant Association, Washington, D.C., 2015.

28. For more on the PRIZM lifestage segmentation, see "MyBestSegments: Nielsen PRIZM Lifestage Groups," www.claritas.com/MyBestSegments/Default.jsp?ID=7010&menuOption=learnmore&pageName=PRIZM2BLifestage2BGroups&segSystem=PRIZM (accessed September 2014).

29. Jihwan Yoon and Elwood L. Shafer, "An Analysis of Sun-Spot Destination Resort Market Segments: All Inclusive Package Versus Independent Travel Arrangements," *Journal of Hospitality and Tourism Research*, 21, no. 1 (1997): 157–158.

30. Edmund O. Lawler, "50 Years Behind the Bar," *F&B Magazine*, 2, no. 1 (1994): 44.

31. James U. McNeal, *Consumer Behavior: An Integrative Approach* (Boston, MA: Little, Brown, 1982), pp. 83–90.

32. Abraham H. Maslow, *Motivation and Personality*, 2nd ed. (New York: Harper & Row, 1970), pp. 80–106.

33. See "Air on the Side of Humanity," September 17, 2013, www.mullen.com/air-on-the-side-of-humanity/; "The Newest Marketing Buzzword? Human," *Advertising Age*, September 20, 2013, www.adage.com/prinV244261; www.jetblue.com/corporate-social-responsibility/ (accessed September 2014).

34. M. Joseph Sirgy, "Self-Concept in Consumer Behavior: A Critical Review," *Journal of Consumer Research* (December 1982): 287–300.

35. Douglas Kaufman and John Mahoney, "The Effect of Waitresses' Touch on Alcohol Consumption in Dyads," *The Journal of Social Psychology*, 139, no. 3 (1999): 261–267.

36. Sources: Aradhna Krishna, *Sensory Marketing: Research on the Sensuality of Products* (New York: Routledge, 2010); Aradhna Krishna, "An Integrative Review of Sensory Marketing: Engaging the Senses to Affect Perception, Judgment and Behavior," *Journal of Consumer Psychology*, 22 (July 2012): 332–351; Joann Peck and Terry L. Childers, "To Have and to Hold: The Influence of Haptic Information on Product Judgments," *Journal of Marketing*, 67 (April 2003): 35–48; Joann Peck and Terry L. Childers, "Individual Differences in Haptic Information Processing: On the Development, Validation, and Use of the 'Need for Touch' Scale," *Journal of Consumer Research*, 30 (December 2003): 43D–42; Joann Peck and Terry L. Childers, "Effects of Sensory Factors on Consumer Behaviors," Frank Kardes, Curtis Haugtvedt, and Paul Herr, eds., *Handbook of Consumer Psychology* (Mahwah, NJ: Erlbaum, 2008), pp. 193–220; Aradhna Krishna, May Lwin, and Maureen Morrin, "Product Scent and Memory," *Journal of Consumer Research*, 37 (June 2010): 57–67; Eric Yorkston and Geeta Menon, "A Sound Idea: Phonetic Effects of Brand Names on Consumer Judgments," *Journal of Consumer Research*, 31 (June 2004): 43–45; Aradhna Krishna and Rohini Ahluwalia, "Language Choice in Advertising to Bilinguals: Asymmetric Effects for Multinationals Versus Local Firms," *Journal of Consumer Research*, 35 (December 2008): 692–705; Richard F. Yalch and Eric R. Spangenberg, "The Effects of Music in a Retail Setting on Real and Perceived Shopping Times," *Journal of Business Research*, 49 (August 2000): 139–147; France Leclerc, Bernd H. Schmitt, and Laurette Dube, "Foreign Branding and Its Effect on Product Perceptions and Attitudes," *Journal of Marketing Research*, 31 (May 1994): 263–270; Priya Raghubir and Aradhna Krishna, "Vital Dimensions: Antecedents and Consequences of Biases in Volume Perceptions," *Journal of Marketing Research*, 36 (August 1994): 313–326; Ryan S. Elder and Aradhna Krishna, "The 'Visual Depiction Effect' in Advertising: Facilitating Embodied Mental Simulation through Product Orientation," *Journal of Consumer Research*, 38 (April 2012): 988–1003.

37. McNeal, *Consumer Behavior*, p. 77.

38. Anna Mattila, "Consumers' Value Judgments," *Cornell Hotel and Restaurant Administration Quarterly*, 40, no. 1 (1999): 40.

39. "TIA Study: Weekend Trips Increasing in Popularity," *Travel Weekly* (July 2, 2001): 4.

40. For more on word-of-mouth sources, see Philip Kotler, *Marketing Management*, 11th ed. (Upper Saddle River, NJ: Prentice Hall, 2003), pp. 574–575.

41. Seth Stevenson, "Like Cardboard," *Slate* (January 1, 2010); Ashley M. Heher, "Domino's Comes Clean Wit! New Pizza Ads," *Associated Press* (January 11, 2010); Bob Garfield, "Domino's Does Itself a Disservice by Coming Clean About Its Pizza," *Advertising Age* (January 11, 2010); Domino's Pizza, www.pizzaturnaround.com.

42. Priscilla A. LaBarbara and David Mazursky, "A Longitudinal Assessment of Consumer Satisfaction/Dissatisfaction: The Dynamic Aspect of the Cognitive Process," *Journal of Marketing Research* (November 1983): 393–404.

43. Thomas Beggs and Robert C. Lewis, "Selling Bermuda in the Off Season," in *The Complete Travel Marketing Handbook* (Lincolnwood, IL: NTC Business Books, 1988).

44. Leon Festinger, *A Theory of Cognitive Dissonance* (Stanford, CA: Stanford University Press, 1957); Leon G. Schiffman and Leslie Lazar Kanuk, *Consumer Behavior* (Upper Saddle River, NJ: Prentice Hall, 1991), pp. 304–305.

45. Valarie Zeithaml, "How Consumer Evaluation Processes Differ Between Goods and Services," in *Marketing of Services*, ed. James Donnelly and William R. George (Chicago: American Marketing Association, 1981), pp. 186–190.

7

Objectives

After reading this chapter, you should be able to:

1. Summarize key aspects of the organizational buying process.
2. Identify and discuss the importance of the participants in the organizational buying process.
3. Describe the major influences on organizational buyers.
4. Explain the eight stages of the organizational buying process.
5. Identify and describe the group markets in the hospitality industry.
6. Explain how to work productively with meeting planners.

Organizational Buyer Behavior

Picture this: A multiunit casual restaurant company in the United States is getting an increasing number of international inquiries from organizations that want to gain franchising rights for the restaurant brand in their respective countries. The company recently promoted a regional manager, Frank Jones, to director of international development. It dispatches Mr. Jones to Europe, Asia, and Africa to follow up on inquiries from these areas. Mr. Jones stops first in London on his way to Paris. He calls his potential franchises on the phone from an airport business lounge. Mr. Jones handles Parisians with confidence after securing a table at the prestigious restaurant, La Tour d'Argent. He greets his luncheon guest, the president of a large French real estate development company, with the words, "Just call me Frank, Jacques." In Germany, Mr. Jones is a powerhouse. Whisking through a flashy multimedia presentation, showing his prospective clients that he knows how to sell the restaurant concept. Mr. Jones next swings through Saudi Arabia, where he coolly presents a potential client with a proposal in a classy pigskin binder. Heading on to Moscow, Frank strikes up a conversation with a Japanese businessman sitting next to him on the plane. Frank compliments the man on his cuff links several times, recognizing him as a man of importance. As the two say good-bye, the man gifts his cuff links to Frank, presents his business card with both hands, and bows at the waist. Frank places his hand firmly on the man's back to express sincere thanks, and then slips his own business card into the man's shirt pocket.

Frank takes Russia by storm as he meets with the chief executive officer (CEO) of an energy company that wants to diversify into real estate development. Feeling very at ease with the Russian executive, Frank sheds his suit coat, leans back, crosses one foot over the other knee, and slips his hands into his pockets. At his next stop in Beijing, China, Frank talks business over lunch with a group of

Chinese executives. After completing the meal, he drops his chopsticks into his bowl of rice and presents each guest with a gift, an elegant Tiffany clock, as a gesture of his desire to do business.

When he arrived back in the United States, Mr. Jones felt he would be very busy following up with his international clients and working on closing deals with them. He was surprised that he heard nothing from them; even after following up with them there was still no response. Frank has nothing to show for the extended trip but a stack of bills. Before he left on his international trip it looked like there was a promising future for international expansions. Frank was not sure why this interest had evaporated.

This hypothetical case has been exaggerated for emphasis. Americans are seldom such dolts. But experts say success in international business has a lot to do with knowing the territory and its people. By learning English and extending themselves in other ways, the world's business leaders, in non-English speaking countries, have met Americans more than halfway. In contrast, Americans too often do little except assume that others will march to their music. Americans are often ego-centric and expect things to be "American" when they travel. Fast, Convenient, and Easy.

Poor Frank tried, all right, but in all the wrong ways. The British do not, as a rule, make deals over the phone as much as Americans do. It's not so much a "cultural" difference as a difference in approach. A proper Frenchman neither likes instant familiarity nor refers to strangers by their first names. "That poor fellow, Jacques, probably wouldn't say anything, but he'd not be pleased," explains an expert on French business practices. Frank's flashy presentation would likely have been a flop with the Germans, who dislike overstatement and showiness. And to the Saudi Arabians, the pigskin binder would have been considered vile. An American salesperson who actually presented such a binder was unceremoniously tossed out of the country, and his company was blacklisted from working with Saudi businesses. Frank also committed numerous faux pas with his new Japanese acquaintance. Because the Japanese strive to please others, especially when someone admires their possessions, the executive likely felt obligated rather than pleased to give up his cuff links. Frank's "hand on the back" probably labeled him as disrespectful and presumptuous. Japan, like many Asian countries, is a "no contact culture" in which even shaking hands is a strange experience. Frank made matters worse with his casual treatment of the business cards. Japanese people revere the business card as an extension of self and as an indicator of rank. They do not hand it to people; they present it—with both hands. Things didn't go well in Russia, either. Russian business people maintain a conservative, professional appearance, with dark suits and dress shoes. Taking one's coat off during negotiations of any kind is taken as a sign of weakness. Placing hands in one's pockets is considered rude, and showing the bottoms of one's shoes is a disgusting gesture. Similarly, in China, Frank casually dropping his chopsticks could have been misinterpreted as an act of aggression. Stabbing chopsticks into a bowl of rice and leaving them signifies death to the Chinese. The clocks Frank offered as gifts might have confirmed such dark intentions. To "give a clock" in Chinese sounds the same as "seeing someone off to his end." Thus, to compete successfully in global markets, or even to deal effectively with international firms in their home markets, companies must help their managers to understand the needs, customs, and cultures of international business buyers. Several companies now offer smartphone apps that provide tips to international travelers and help prevent them from making embarrassing mistakes while abroad. Cultures around the world differ greatly, and marketers must dig deeply to make certain they adapt to these differences. "When doing business in a foreign country and a foreign culture ... take nothing for granted," advises an international business specialist. "Turn every stone. Ask every question. Dig into every detail."[1]

The hospitality business has become a global business. Companies are sending managers around the globe to find locations for their businesses, sell meetings, and source products. The opening vignette discusses some of the cultural differences one has to be aware of when they conduct business with representatives of international business. One does not have to travel internationally to find differences between business and consumer markets. Business markets differ in many ways from consumer markets. The differences are in market structure and demand, the nature of the buying unit, the types of decisions, and the decision process involved. This chapter will help you understand more efficiently your ability to sell to other businesses as well as your ability to make more effective purchases by understanding the process. We will also discuss group markets that generate business for the hospitality and travel industry.

The Organizational Buying Process

In the previous chapter, you studied final consumer buying behavior and factors that influence it. In this chapter, we'll do the same for business customers—those that buy goods and services for use in producing their own products and services or for resale to others. When selling to final buyers, firms marketing to businesses must engage business customers and build profitable relationships with them by creating superior customer value.

Most large companies sell to other organizations. For example, Marriott sells rooms and meeting space to corporations, associations, and nonprofit organizations. Restaurants sell meetings in private dining rooms to businesses, foodservice supply companies sell food products, equipment and supplies to hotels and restaurants and technology companies sell software and hardware to the hospitality industry. Business-to-business (B-to-B) sales positions provide career opportunities for hospitality students.

Business buyer behavior refers to the buying behavior of organizations that buy goods and services for use in the production of other products and services that are sold, rented, or supplied to others. It also includes the behavior of retailing and wholesaling firms that acquire goods to resell or rent to others at a profit. In the business buying process, business buyers determine which products and services their organizations need to purchase and then find, evaluate, and choose among alternative suppliers and brands. B-to-B marketers must do their best to understand business markets and business buyer behavior. Then they must engage business customers and build profitable relationships with them by creating superior customer value.

Business Markets

The business market is huge. In fact, business markets involve far more dollars and items than do consumer markets. In some ways, business markets are similar to consumer markets. Both involve people who assume buying roles and make purchase decisions to satisfy needs. However, business markets differ in many ways from consumer markets. The main differences are in market structure and demand, the nature of the buying unit, and the types of decisions and the decision process involved.

Market Structure and Demand

Derived demand Organizational demand that ultimately comes from (derives from) the demand for consumer goods.

Organizational demand is **derived demand**; it comes ultimately from the demand for consumer goods or services. It is derived or a function of the businesses that supply the hospitality and travel industry with meetings, special events, and other functions. In many cities one sector provides a disproportionate amount of their economic activity. For example, Boston is a major center for the biotechnology industry, while the energy industry accounts for a large portion of Houston's economy. A downturn in an industry that accounts for high percentage of an area's economy can have an adverse effect on the business spending in those markets.

Through good environmental scanning, hotel managers can identify emerging industries, companies, and associations. They screen these organizations to find good business partners. When they see an industry-specific downturn coming, they can look for industries in the region that are healthy to replace the lost business. Destination marketers also need to understand the importance of derived demand and keep up with environmental changes as they seek to fill a city's convention center.

Nature of the Buying Unit

Compared with consumer purchases, a business purchase usually involves more decision makers and a more professional purchasing effort. Corporations that frequently use hotels for meetings may hire their own meeting planners. Professional meeting planners receive training in negotiating skills. They belong to associations such as Meeting Planners International (MPI), which educates its members in the latest negotiating techniques. A corporate travel agent's job is to find the best airfares, rental car rates, and hotel rates. Therefore, hotels must have well-trained salespeople to deal with well-trained buyers, creating thousands of jobs for salespeople. Additionally, once the meeting is sold, the account is turned over to a convention service manager who works with the meeting planner to make sure the event is produced according to the meeting planner's expectations. Outside the hotel, jobs relating to meetings include corporate meeting planners, association meeting planners, independent meeting planners, and convention and visitor bureau salespersons.

Types of Decisions and the Decision Process

Organizational buying process The decision-making process by which formal organizations establish the need for purchased products and services and identify, evaluate, and choose among alternative brands and suppliers.

Organizational buyers usually face more complex buying decisions than consumer buyers. The **organizational buying process** tends to be more formalized than the consumer process and a more professional purchasing effort. The more complex the purchase, the more likely it is that several people will participate in the decision-making process. The total bill for a one-day sales meeting for 75 people can be tens of thousands of dollars. If a company is having a series of sales meetings around the country, it will be worthwhile to get quotes from several hotel chains and spend time analyzing the bids.

Finally, in the organizational buying process, buyer and seller are often very dependent on each other. Sales is a consultative process. The hospitality organization's staff develops interesting and creative menus, theme parties, and coffee breaks. The staff works with meeting planners to solve problems and works. They also have a close working relationship with their corporate and association customers to find customized solutions to satisfy their needs. Hotels and catering firms retain customers by meeting their current needs and thinking ahead to meet their future needs. For example, consider agricultural and food giant Cargill's Cocoa & Chocolate division.[3] Cargill's Cocoa & Chocolate division sells cocoa and chocolate products to business customers around the world, including giants such as Mars and Mondelez. But its success lies in doing much more than just selling its products. Cargill consults with its customers, drawing on its expertise in the use of cocoa including the production of chocolate. It shows its customers how to use its products to better serve their customers and how to reduce their production costs. For example, Cargill's researchers keep customers up to date on the latest global consumer food trends. Its research and development teams give customers personalized product development support. And its technical services specialists provide help in resolving customer ingredient and applications challenges. Cargill provides its chefs and food scientists to help its customers develop new products that will have value for their client's customers. Thus, more than just selling cocoa and chocolate, Cargill sells customer success in using those products. Cargill realizes their business is derived from the success of the client's businesses.[4]

▰▰▰ Participants in the Organizational Buying Process

Buying center All those individuals and groups who participate in the purchasing and decision-making process and who share common goals and the risks arising from the decisions.

The decision-making unit of a buying organization, sometimes called the **buying center**, is defined as "all those individuals and groups who participate in the purchasing decision-making process, who share common goals and the risks arising from the decisions."[2]

The buying center includes all members of the organization who play any of the six roles in the purchase–decision process:[3]

1. **Users.** Users are those who use the product or service. A user could be a chef, a front-desk clerk, or the client's customer. Although the user does not make the purchase decision they can have a great deal of influence on the buying decision. Smart B-to-B marketers will test their products with the end user before taking them to market. They will also make sure they have good support to train the end user on how to use their product.

2. **Influencers.** Influencers directly influence the buying decision but do not make the final decision themselves. They often help define specifications and provide information for evaluating alternatives. Past presidents of trade associations may exert influence in the choice of a meeting location. Executive secretaries, a spouse, regional managers, and many others can and do exert considerable influence in the selection of sites for meetings, seminars, conferences, and other group gatherings. A good salesperson will do some investigation to find out who the influencers are in the decision-making process.

3. **Deciders.** Deciders select product requirements and suppliers. For example, a company's sales manager for the Denver area selects the hotel and negotiates the arrangements when the regional sales meeting is held in Denver.

4. **Approvers.** Approvers authorize the proposed actions of deciders or buyers. Although the Denver sales manager arranges the meeting, the contracts may need to be submitted to the organization's procurement department for formal approval.

5. **Buyers.** Buyers have formal authority for selecting suppliers and arranging the terms of purchase. Buyers may help shape product specifications and play a major role in selecting vendors and negotiating. The event planner may then take over the process and plan the meeting. In some cases the final agreement would then be turned over to the company's procurement department, who would approve the contract.

6. **Gatekeepers.** Gatekeepers have the power to prevent sellers of information from reaching members of the buying center. For example, a hotel salesperson calling on a meeting planner may have to go through an administrative assistant. This administrative assistant can easily block the salesperson from seeing the meeting planner. This can be accomplished by failing to forward messages, telling the salesperson the meeting planner is not available, or simply telling the meeting planner not to deal with the salesperson. Good salespeople treat all people in their client's organization well and seek to gain the trust of gatekeepers.

The buying center is not a fixed and formally identified unit within the buying organization. It is a set of buying roles assumed by different people for different purchases. Within the organization, the size and makeup of the buying center will vary for different products and for different buying situations. For some routine purchases, one person—say, an administrative assistant—may make the arrangements for a small meeting. It is then approved by his boss. For more complex purchases, the buying center may include people from different levels and departments in the organization.[4]

The buying center concept presents a major marketing challenge. The business marketer must learn who participates in the decision, each participant's relative influence, and what evaluation criteria each decision participant uses. This can be difficult especially since the buying center can be dynamic as members are promoted or leave the company. When a buying center includes multiple

It is important to have good relationships with administrative assistants; they can help you gain an appointment and may influence the purchase decision. ESB Professional/Shutterstock.

participants, the seller may not have the time or resources to reach all. Smaller sellers concentrate on reaching the key buying influencers and deciders. It is important not to go over the decider's head. Most deciders like to feel in control of the purchasing decision; going over a decider's head and working with the boss will be resented. In most cases, the boss will leave the decision up to the decider and the ill will created by not dealing with the decider directly will result in the selection of another company. Larger sellers use multilevel, in-depth selling to reach as many buying participants as possible. Their salespeople virtually "live" with their high-volume customers.

■■■ Major Influences on Organizational Buyers

Business buyers are subject to many influences when they make their buying decisions. Some marketers assume that the major influences are economic. They think buyers will favor the supplier who offers the lowest price or the best product or the most service. They concentrate on offering strong economic benefits to buyers. Such economic factors are very important to most buyers, especially in a tough economy. However, business buyers actually respond to both economic and personal factors. Far from being cold, calculating, and impersonal, business buyers are human and social as well. They react to both reason and emotion.

Figure 7–1 lists various groups of influences on business buyers—environmental, organizational, interpersonal, and individual.[5] Business buyers are heavily influenced by factors in the current and expected economic environment, such as the level of primary demand, the economic outlook, and the cost of money. Business buyers also are affected by technological, political, and competitive developments in the environment. Finally, culture and customs can strongly influence business buyer reactions to the marketer's behavior and strategies, especially in the international marketing environment (as we saw in the opening vignette). The business buyer must watch these factors, determine how they will affect the buyer, and try to turn these challenges into opportunities.

Organizational factors are also important. Each buying organization has its own objectives, strategies, structure, systems, and procedures, and the business marketer must understand these factors well. Questions such as these arise: How many people are involved in the buying decision? Who are they? What are their evaluative criteria? What are the company's policies and limits on its buyers?

The buying center usually includes many participants who influence each other, so interpersonal factors also influence the business buying process. However, it is often difficult to assess such interpersonal factors and group dynamics. Buying center participants do not wear tags that label them as "key decision maker" or "not influential." Others believe that buyers respond to personal factors such as favors, attention, or risk avoidance. A study of buyers in 10 large companies concluded that emotions and feelings play a part in the decision process of corporate decision makers. They respond to "image," buy from known companies, and favor suppliers who show them respect and personal consideration. They "overreact" to real or imagined slights, tending to reject companies that fail to respond or delay in submitting bids.[6]

Figure 7–1
Major influences on business buying behavior.

Environmental	Organizational	Interpersonal	Individual	
Level of primary demand	Objectives	Authority	Age	
Economic outlook	Policies	Status	Education	
Cost of money	Procedures	Empathy	Job position	Buyers
Supply conditions	Organizational structure	Persuasiveness	Personality	
Rate of technological change	Systems		Risk attitudes	
Political and regulatory developments				
Competitive developments				

Participants may influence the buying decision because they control rewards and punishments, are well liked, have special expertise, or have a special relationship with other important participants. Interpersonal factors are often very subtle. Whenever possible, business marketers must try to understand these factors and design strategies that take them into account.

Each participant in the business buying decision process brings in personal motives, perceptions, and preferences. These individual factors are affected by personal characteristics such as age, income, education, professional identification, personality, and attitudes toward risk. Also, buyers have different buying styles. Some may be technical types who make in-depth analyses of competitive proposals before choosing a supplier. Other buyers may be intuitive negotiators who are adept at pitting the sellers against one another for the best deal.

Organizational Buying Decisions

Organizational buyers do not buy goods and services for personal consumption. They buy hospitality products to provide training, to reward employees and distributors, and to provide lodging for their employees. Eight stages of the organizational buying process have been identified and are called *buyphases*.[7] This model is called *buygrid framework*. The eight steps for the typical new-task buying situation are as follows.

1. Problem Recognition

Problem recognition The stage of the industrial buying process in which someone in a company recognizes a problem or need that can be met by acquiring a good or a service.

The buying process begins when someone in the company recognizes a problem or need that can be met by acquiring a good or a service. **Problem recognition** can occur because of internal or external stimuli. Internally, a new product may create the need for a series of meetings to explain the product to the sales force. A human resource manager may notice a need for employee training and set up a training meeting. A CEO may feel that the executive team would benefit from a weekend retreat to reformulate the firm's strategy. Externally, the buyer sees an ad or receives a call from a hotel sales representative who offers a favorable corporate program. Marketers can stimulate problem recognition by developing effective ads and calling on prospects.

2. General Need Description

Having recognized a need, the buyer goes on to determine the requirements of the product and to formulate a general need description. For a training meeting, this would include food and beverages, meeting spaces, AV equipment coffee breaks, and sleeping room requirements. The corporate meeting planner works with others—the director of human resources, the training manager, and potential participants—to gain insight into the requirements of the meeting. Together, they determine the importance of the price, meeting space, sleeping rooms, food and beverages, and other factors.

The hotel marketer can render assistance to the buyer in this phase. Often, the buyer is unaware of the benefits of various product features. Alert marketers can help buyers define their companies' needs and show how their hotel can satisfy them.

3. Product Specification

Once the general requirements have been determined, the specific requirements for the meeting can be developed. For example, a meeting might require 20 sleeping rooms, a meeting room for 25 set up classroom style with a whiteboard and overhead projector, and a separate room for lunch. For larger meetings with an exhibit area, the information need becomes more complex. Information often required includes availability of water, ceiling heights, door widths, security, and procedures for receiving and storing materials prior to the event. Salespersons must be prepared to answer their prospective client's questions about their hotel's capabilities to fulfill the **product specification**. Today, these needs are certain to include technology, including portals for computers, the latest AV equipment, and others.

> **Product specification** The stage of an industrial buying process in which the buying organization decides on and specifies the best technical product characteristics for a needed item.

4. Supplier Search

> **Supplier search** The stage of the industrial buying process in which a buyer tries to find the best vendor.

The buyer now conducts a **supplier search** to identify the most appropriate hotels. The buyer can examine trade directories, do a computer search, or phone familiar hotels. Hotels that qualify may receive a site visit from the meeting planner, who eventually develops a short list of qualified suppliers. Personal recommendations from individuals such as members of management, consultants, lawyers, and others often are seriously considered in the search process.

5. Proposal Solicitations

Once the meeting planner has drawn up a short list of suppliers, qualified hotels are invited to submit proposals. Thus hotel marketers must be skilled in researching, writing, and presenting proposals. These should be marketing-oriented, not simply technical, documents. They should position their company's capabilities and resources so that they stand out from the competition. To do this effectively, one must know the strengths and weaknesses of the competition as well as their own strengths and weaknesses. The salesperson must also understand which of the hotel's features will be perceived as benefits to the meeting planner.

6. Supplier Selection

> **Supplier selection** The stage of the industrial buying process in which a buyer receives proposals and selects a supplier or suppliers.

In this stage, members of the buying center review the proposals and move toward **supplier selection**. They conduct an analysis of the hotel, considering physical facilities, the hotel's ability to deliver service, and the professionalism of its employees. Frequently, the buying center specifies desired supplier attributes and suggests their relative importance.

Technology has made it possible for meeting planners to take a visual tour of the meeting space. Companies such as eMarketing 360 specialize in capturing video images of meeting space and making it accessible to buyers on the Web. Meeting Matrix provides a Web site with meeting information, including room diagrams, and videos of meeting space. This helps meeting planners narrow their selection or even make their selection without visiting the site. The later would likely be made up of buyers who have a lot of faith in the brand. Regardless of the sophistication of communication devices, nothing can substitute for on-site visits. These should be an integral part of the selection process.

Buyers may attempt to negotiate with preferred suppliers for better prices and terms before making the final selections. In the end, they may select a single supplier or a few suppliers. Large restaurants may give most of their business to a preferred food supplier to gain the best prices, but they continue to buy products from a second supplier so they have a backup and are not dependent on one supplier. This also allows comparisons of prices and performance of several suppliers.

7. Order-Routine Specification

> **Order-routine specification** The stage of the industry buying process in which a buyer writes the final order with the chosen supplier(s), listing the technical specifications, quantity needed, expected time of delivery, return policies, warranties, and so on.

The buyer now writes the final order with the chosen hotels, listing the technical **order-routine specifications** of the meeting. The hotel responds by offering the buyer a formal contract. The contract specifies cutoff dates for room blocks, the date when the hotel will release the room block for sale to other guests, and minimum guarantees for food and beverage functions. Many hotels and restaurants have turned what should have been a profitable banquet into a loss by not having or enforcing minimum guarantees.

Marketing HIGHLIGHT 7.1 Corporate procurement's involvement in purchasing meetings

As corporations seek to gain control of their travel and meeting costs they have formalized the company's purchasing of meetings and events. Up until about 10 years ago, most corporate event planners where free to book their own meetings, selecting the venue and specifying the food and beverage requirements as long as it was within the company's budget. Today many companies are involving their procurement department in the process. In the past the procurement department worked with tangible products that had set specifications. This meant the bids they received were all for the same identical product. When purchasing meetings, the procurement department has to understand that when prices are cut for a meeting this often involves the cutting of services. A meeting planner for McDonald's invited their procurement team to see what went on behind the scenes at their annual worldwide convention. The procurement team realized the importance of having suppliers that had worked with the company in the past and had proven they could produce meeting and events that met the objectives of the company. Meeting planners on the other hand must realize that the procurement department is responsible for making sure the company does not overpay for goods and services. From the hotel or event venue's side, this means that the salesperson not only has to sell to the meeting planner, but they also have to help them sell their services to the corporate procurement team by explaining the value delivering to the client and how the value of their location exceeds the value of competitors.

An alternative to in-house procurement is the corporate travel agent. Some companies contract with a corporate travel company which will work with the company's event planners or completely manage and produce the event for the company. Corporate travel companies are typically employed to handle the organization's business travel for individual employees but have expanded their product line to also include business travel and event management.[8]

Part of the supplier search can be site inspection. These association executives are getting a tour of meeting facilities in Hong Kong. Shao-Chun Wang/123RF.

8. Performance Review

Performance review The stage of an industrial buying process in which a buyer rates its satisfaction with suppliers, deciding whether to continue, modify, or drop the relationship.

The buyer does a postpurchase **performance review** of the product. During this phase the buyer determines if the product meets the buyer's specifications and if the buyer will purchase from the company again. It is important for hotels to have at least daily meetings with a meeting planner to make sure everything is going well and to correct those things that did not go well. This manages the buyer's perceived service and helps avoid a negative postpurchase evaluation by the buyer.

Engaging Business Buyers with Digital and Social Marketing

As in every other area of marketing, the explosion of information technologies and online, mobile, and social media has changed the face of the B-to-B buying and marketing process. In the following sections, we discuss two important technology advancements: *e-procurement and online purchasing* and *B-to-B digital and social media marketing*.

E-Procurement and Online Purchasing

e-procurement Purchasing through electronic connections between buyers and sellers, usually done online.

Advances in information technology have dramatically affected the face of the B-to-B buying process. Online purchasing, often called **e-procurement**, has grown rapidly in recent years. Virtually unknown two decades ago, online purchasing is standard procedure for most companies today. In turn, business marketers can connect with customers online to share marketing information, sell products and services, provide customer support services, and maintain ongoing customer relationships. Companies can do e-procurement in any of several ways. They can put their purchasing requests online and invite suppliers to bid for the business. This is commonly done when companies need meetings and/or events and place a request for proposal (RFP) online. Large companies also can conduct e-procurement by setting up their own company buying sites.

Sysco, a large supplier of food and other products for the foodservice industry, has recently purchased "Supplies on the Fly," an online distribution system, which allows customers to place orders for more than 170,000 products. The system saves both the customer and Sysco sales representatives time, as well as being fully integrated into their accounting system.[9] B-to-B e-procurement yields many benefits. First, it saves transaction costs and results in more efficient purchasing for both buyers and suppliers. E-procurement reduces the time between order and delivery. And an online-powered purchasing program eliminates the paperwork associated with traditional requisition and ordering procedures and helps an organization keep better track of all purchases. Finally, beyond the cost and time savings, e-procurement frees purchasing people from a lot of drudgery and paperwork. Instead, they can focus on more strategic issues, such as finding better supply sources and working with suppliers to reduce costs and develop new products.

Meetings Maker, a software package, makes it possible for organizations to book their meetings online with a hotel. The benefit to the meeting organizer is they can find the availability and pricing of meeting rooms and sleeping rooms, food and beverage options, and audio visual packages and book directly online. Meeting planning and booking software has allowed hotel brands such as Hilton as well as individual hotels the ability to book meetings on their Web sites. The benefit to the hotel is for smaller meetings the meeting planner can create their meeting to their specifications, allowing the hotel's sales team to work on larger bookings. For larger meetings, companies can submit online requests for proposals to hotels. Hotels then can submit their proposals online, following up with a contact by a salesperson. Online purchasing has created a competitive environment with the expectation of a fast turnaround for proposals. Larger organizations often have a dedicated person to handle online requests.

The rapidly expanding use of e-procurement, however, also presents some problems. For example, at the same time that the internet makes it possible for suppliers and customers to share business data and even collaborate on product design, it can also erode decades-old customer–supplier relationships. Many buyers now use the power of the internet to pit suppliers against one another and search out better deals, products, and turnaround times on a purchase-by-purchase basis. This created a challenge for those who are suppliers to the hospitality industry to create relationships and provide extra services such as hot shots (an extra delivery, often in a salesperson car), when the chef ran out of a product or forgot to order a product needed for a busy night. It is important for the supplier to show the purchaser the benefits of a strong long-term relationship and the buyer to understand and appreciate these benefits.

Business-to-Business Digital and Social Media Marketing

In response to business customers' rapid shift toward online buying, today's B-to-B marketers are now using a wide range of digital and social media marketing approaches—from Web sites, blogs, mobile apps, e-newsletters, and proprietary online networks to mainstream social media such as Facebook, LinkedIn, YouTube, Google+, and Twitter—to engage business customers and manage customer relationships anywhere, anytime.

B-to-B digital and social media marketing isn't just growing, it's exploding. Digital and social media marketing have rapidly become the new space for engaging business customers. Compared with traditional media and sales approaches, digital and social media can create greater customer engagement and interaction. B-to-B marketers know that they aren't really targeting businesses; they are

B-to-B digital and social media marketing Using digital and social media marketing approaches to engage business customers and manage customers relationship anywhere, anytime.

targeting individuals in those businesses who affect buying decisions. And today's business buyers are always connected via their digital devices—whether it's PCs, tablets, or smartphones.

Digital and social media play an important role in engaging these always-connected business buyers in a way that personal selling alone cannot. Instead of the old model of sales reps calling on business customers at work or maybe meeting up with them at trade shows, the new digital approaches facilitate anytime, anywhere connections between a wide range of people in the selling and customer organizations. It gives both sellers and buyers more control of and access to important information. B-to-B marketing has always been social network marketing, but today's digital environment offers an exciting array of new networking tools and applications. Some B-to-B companies mistakenly assume that today's digital and social media are useful primarily to consumer products and services companies. Digital platforms can be powerful tools for engaging customers and other important publics.

Hospitality Group Markets

One of the most important types of organizational business is group business. It is important for marketing managers to understand the differences between a group market and a consumer market. The group business market is often more sophisticated and requires more technical information than the consumer market. Many group markets book more than a year in advance. During this time, cognitive dissonance can develop; thus, marketers must keep in contact with buyers to assure them that they made the right decision in choosing the seller's hotel.

Convention A specialty market requiring extensive meeting facilities. It is usually the annual meeting of an association and includes general sessions, committee meetings, and special-interest sessions.

The Hong Kong Convention Center is a popular site for major international conventions. Attendees enjoy coming to Hong Kong and its easy accessibility makes it a popular spot for association meetings. Estherpoon/Shutterstock.

The four main categories of group markets are conventions, association meetings, corporate meetings, and SMERF (social, military, educational, religious, and fraternal organizations) groups. Conventions attract large numbers, but meetings occur much more frequently than conventions. The attendance at an association's annual convention can number in the tens of thousands, while a training session put on by an association may have only 20 participants. Thus, associations provide convention centers as well as smaller hotels with business. Corporations can put on large events, such as Hilton's Annual General Managers Conference or smaller regional conferences. When choosing a hotel, an important consideration for a meeting planner is whether the hotel can house the participants. Group business is a very important segment for most hotels. Successful hotels know which groups to attract, how to use group business to fill needed dates, and how to sell groups on the hotel's benefits rather than just price.

The Events Industry Council, previously called the Convention Industry Council, is made up of 33 member organizations. The members represent individuals and organizations involved in the meetings, conventions, and exhibitions industry. The Events Industry Council developed the Accepted Practices Exchange (APEX), which brings a set of standards and best practices to all parties involved in the creation and implementation of a meeting. APEX's event specifications provide a template of a checklist for planning an event, and its glossary brings a common meaning to terms used in the meetings industry. APEX is a great tool for those involved in selling or planning meetings.[10]

Conventions

Conventions are a specialty market requiring extensive meeting facilities. These are usually the annual meeting of an association and include general sessions, committee meetings, and special-interest sessions. Hotels with convention facilities, such as the Chicago Hyatt or the

Atlanta Marriott Marquis, can house small and midsized conventions. Conventions that use a major facility, such as the Jacob Javitts Convention Center in New York, often have tens of thousands of delegates. Citywide conventions that attract thousands of attendees and use hotels throughout the city house their delegates. In the United States there are about 2 million meetings held annually with 251 million people attending those meetings, generating $325 billion in direct spending and $845 in business sales, creating 5.9 million jobs.[11] With this size of market, it is no wonder that this industry attracts the interest of developers, city planners, and various levels of government.

There are 252 convention centers in the United States. California, Florida and Nevada have 20 each, followed by Texas with 20. The largest convention center in the United States in McCormick Place in Chicago with 2.6 million square feet but the largest convention center in the world is the Hannover Messegelände with almost 5 million square feet of space.[12]

Associations usually select convention sites two to five years in advance, with some large conventions planned 10 to 15 years before the event. October is the most popular month for conventions, followed by November, September, and April.[13] Some associations prefer to have their conventions in the same city year after year, whereas others prefer to move to a different area of the country each year.

A convention can be a major source of income for the sponsoring organization. Registration fees from attendees and sales of exhibition space in the trade show are major sources of revenue. A trade show gives suppliers a chance to show and sell their products to the association's members. Companies such as Freeman and GES work with the association and conference center to provide electrical hookups, booth setup, and other services to make sure the trade show exhibitors have the resources they need to set up their exhibits. The price that can be charged for exhibition space is related to the number of attendees. When choosing a convention location, an association looks for sites that will be both accessible and attractive to members. The annual convention is one of the main sources of revenue for many associations, thus balancing the annual budget depends on a good turnout.

Many hotels contract with independent AV companies to supply and maintain this equipment. The AV company can pool its equipment and staff within the city. So, when a group has special AV requirements, the company can bring the equipment and staff needed to produce the event. In large hotels, AV companies have an office in the hotel to store equipment and house technicians. For large meetings, AV companies have on-site technicians to remain with the group during the meeting to correct problems as they occur, thus ensuring that speaker presentations proceed as planned. Under this arrangement, the hotel bills the client for the AV and then pays the AV company an agreed-upon percentage of the charges; for example, 60 percent often goes to the AV company, with the hotel keeping 40 percent.

Billing procedures are also important to convention planners. Billing can create problems for hotels that take it for granted and do not have a customer-oriented accounting department. Professional meeting planners want a bill that is understandable, accurate, and delivered in a timely manner. Without these characteristics, the bill can be a nightmare. Important attributes for a convention planner other than facilities and rates are food quality, billing procedures, and professionalism and attention of the hotel's staff.

Convention Bureaus

Convention bureaus are nonprofit marketing organizations that help hotels sign conventions and meetings. These organizations are often supported by a hotel or by sales tax and are run by chamber of commerce, visitor bureaus, or city and county governments. They are often one of the first sources of information for a convention or meeting planner. A hotel relying on meeting business for a significant portion of its occupancy should have a good working relationship with the convention bureau, which includes active membership in the organization.

Association Meetings

The most important attributes of a destination for an association meeting planner are availability of hotel and facilities, ease of transportation, distance from attendees, and transportation costs. Climate, recreation, and cultural activities are not as important as they are to the convention market because the meeting itself is the major draw. In selecting a hotel, the association meeting planner looks for food quality, rates, meeting rooms, billing procedures, and attributes similar to the convention planner except for exhibition space.[14] Notice that for the association meeting planner, food and beverage are the most important attributes in the selection of the hotel.

Convene polled a group of successful and well-respected meeting planners to determine what they looked for when they selected a meeting location. The top 10 criteria were as follows:

1. Location and accessibility
2. Meeting room capacity
3. Flow and layout of space
4. Quality and capability of AV equipment
5. Room flexibility
6. Decor
7. Intelligent staff, from sales to service
8. Price flexibility
9. Quality of food
10. Participant experience[15]

The need for a location that will be desirable and accessible to their attendees was at the top of the list. The next six items relate to having the proper physical facilities—AV and staff to put on a successful meeting. Although quality of food is number 9, a reputation for serving poor food can eliminate a venue from consideration. Surveys like the one mentioned earlier will give overall results, but it is also important to realize that meeting planners are different. A successful salesperson will develop a package that will meet the wants of the meeting planner.

Membership in the American Society of Association Executives (ASAE) is beneficial for hotels actively pursuing association business. It provides an opportunity to network with association executives and is a source of information on national and local associations. Many of the hotel's corporate clients are also members of trade associations. These customers can become ambassadors for the hotel at their trade association meetings.

Members attend association meetings voluntarily. The hotel should work with meeting planners to make the destination seem as attractive as possible. Making sure that the meeting planner is aware of local attractions, offering suggestions for spousal activities, and assisting in the development of after-convention activities can be useful to the hotel and the meeting planner. It is important to market both the destination and the hotel.

Corporate Meetings

Corporate meeting A meeting held by a corporation for its employees.

For employees of a company, a **corporate meeting** is a command performance. They are directed to attend the meeting without choice. One implication of required attendance is a short lead time. Because corporations do not have to develop and implement a marketing plan to gain attendees, they often plan meetings with a few weeks' lead time. Corporate meetings can range in size from a board meeting for 10 to 12 people to a sales meeting for several hundred people. Overall, 35 percent of corporate meetings are for 10 to 24 people, 29 percent have 25 to 49 attendees, 18 percent have 50 to 99 people, and 18 percent are for over a hundred attendees.[16]

Many corporate meetings are set up by mega agencies, such as American Express and Carlson Wagonlit. These agencies provide travel management services for companies. Thus, when seeking business from corporations, a hotel manager must understand who has the responsibility for booking meetings.[17]

The corporation's major concern is that the meeting be productive and accomplish the company's objectives. Types of corporate meetings include training, management, and planning. Another type of corporate meeting is the incentive meeting, which will be discussed later.

To a corporate meeting planner, the most important attributes in the choice of a destination are the availability of hotels, ease of transportation, transportation costs, and distance from the location to the attendees.

Corporate meeting planners want to ensure that meetings are productive and the corporation gets good value for the money it spends. Their success depends on planning smooth-running meetings. Hotels interested in capturing and retaining corporate meeting business must make sure that meeting rooms are adequate and set up properly. Because meeting planners want attendees to be comfortable, sleeping rooms are important to them. They are also concerned about the quality of food. Recreation and modern indoor exercise facilities may also be important. In a multiday technical meeting, the interaction of the participants outside the formal meetings is valuable. Golf or tennis can be used to encourage participants to interact socially and break up the monotony of the classroom sessions. Similarly, an evening outing to an area restaurant, sporting, or cultural event can serve as an enjoyable break for participants.

Full-service hotels have a number of meeting facilities ranging from a large ballrooms to small meeting rooms. August_0802/Shutterstock.

Incentive travel A reward that participants receive for achieving or exceeding a goal.

African photo safaris have become a popular incentive travel destination. There are a number of luxury facilities, such as this one, that attract incentive groups. GTS Productions/Shutterstock.

Small Groups

The small corporate meeting, less than 50 rooms, has gained the attention of hotel chains. Although small in terms of number of participants, thousands of small meetings are held every month. Many hotels have developed a marketing effort toward small groups. A consistent message sales people should give to small groups is their business is important and will not get lost at our hotel. Some hotels, such as Kimpton Hotels, a collection of boutique hotels, have developed a small group desk designed to help someone planning a small group function. Larger hotels also seek small group functions. The large resorts that are 2,000 rooms plus in Las Vegas also value small groups. The Aria Resort and Casino in Las Vegas has a small group page focusing on leisure customers coming to Las Vegas for a family reunion, wedding, and bachelor or bachelorette party.

Many hotels offer a set price per person for a small group. The price includes meals, breaks, meeting room, AV, and sleeping rooms. The set price makes it easy for meeting planners to understand their costs. Simplifying small meeting arrangements is critical because those who plan small meetings are often not meeting planners.

Incentive Travel

Incentive travel, a unique subset of corporate group business, is a reward participants receive for achieving or exceeding a goal. Companies give awards for both individual and team performance. A hotel salesperson selling incentives must be able to help his or her client justify the expenditure. Reminding the meeting planner of the value of the sales to the company created by the attendees is an excellent way to do this.

Participants must perceive the destination and the hotel as something special. Climate, recreational facilities, and sightseeing opportunities are high on an incentive meeting planners' list of desired attributes.[18] The Caribbean, Hawaii, Europe, and resort destinations within the continental United States are common incentive travel destinations. The right location and excellent facilities are important. Brian Jones, senior vice president sales at Morgans Hotel Group, states, "It is also about creating unique experiences that motivate, celebrate, or educate. The more we speak to these issues the more successful we will be."

Incentive trips used to last from three to seven days; however, the current trend is to keep the trips short and get the participants back to their jobs. Scott Walker, director of incentive and promotion certificates for Hyatt Hotels, states, "I am hearing, 'let's change it from five nights to four, but add extras'. These extras include meals, spa treatments, a round on the golf course, or Hyatt Cheque certificates that they can spend any way they want."[19] The average expenditure per room is high. Winners of incentive trips sometimes receive a cash deposit to their account that can be used for charges to their account or services provided through the hotel, such as rental cars. For example, participants in an incentive trip sponsored by Revlon for the best regional sales performance received a $500 credit on their hotel bill that could be spent as they wished. In such cases the participants spend freely in the hotel's restaurants and bars, often supplementing the credit with their own money. Thus, incentive travel can be very profitable for a hotel.

Incentive travel is handled in-house or by incentive houses, travel agencies, consultants, and travel fulfillment firms that handle only the travel arrangements. The trend is moving away from in-house planners to incentive houses, fulfillment houses, and travel agencies. One reason for the shift is that outside organizations specializing in incentive travel often buy blocks of airline seats and hotel rooms. As a result, they can put together packages more efficiently than in-house planners. Incentive houses usually provide a choice of several locations to the company, so the ultimate choice of location is made by the company, even when it uses an incentive house. Travel destinations and their service suppliers such as resorts must work with both the incentive house and the decision makers within the company.

Destination Choice Factors

Maritz Travel, a company with substantial experience in incentive travel, developed an International Certification Index that reflects travel preferences among 1,000 U.S.-based employees who were eligible to earn incentive travel. The results demonstrated the following:

- Visiting new destinations that seem otherwise unattainable is a key motivator.
- Luxurious trips to sun and sand destinations are preferred.
- Long-haul destinations do not mean lower motivational value. Travel time is considered luxurious.
- Negative factors affecting travel incentives are as follows:
  - General lack of interest in the destination.
  - Previous visit to the destination.
  - Safety concerns regarding the destination.

The Maritz study also showed that the motivational level of travel increases for those who earned previous trips. However, 70 percent want to go someplace new and interesting. This means that incentive planners must continuously offer new destinations to this important group as they clearly represent very important employees or clients for a sponsoring company or organization.[20]

SMERFs

SMERF stands for social, military, educational, religious, and fraternal organizations. On a broader scale, this meeting classification includes smaller specialty organizations that are price sensitive. The individual pays for the majority of the

SMERF SMERF stands for social, military, educational, religious, and fraternal organizations. This group of specialty market has a common price-sensitive thread.

functions sponsored by these organizations, and sometimes the expenses are not tax deductible. As a result, participants are usually price conscious. They want a low room rate and often find the food and beverage within the hotel too expensive, preferring to eat elsewhere or purchase food and eat in their rooms. Because attendees are price sensitive, one of the biggest challenges is to get the attendees to book within the room block.[21] Hotels often provide concessions such as free rooms or a free or reduced food and beverage function based on the number of room nights in the groups' block. If the block does not materialize, the meeting planner is responsible for extra charges.

On the positive side, SMERFs are willing to be flexible to ensure a lower room rate. They are willing to meet during the off-season or on weekends. Weekends are often preferred because most participants attend meetings during their free time. Also, the size of these segments should not be overlooked. In the United States, over 50,000 religious organizations have group travel programs.[22] Thus, SMERFs provide good filler business during off-peak times. If you decide to go into hotel sales upon graduation, there is a good chance you will be assigned to the SMERF market, as it is usually assigned to the most junior salesperson.

Marketing HIGHLIGHT 7.2 Green meetings—The right thing to do for the environment and business

The Events Industry Council provides this definition of a green meeting, "a green meeting or event incorporates environmental considerations to minimize its negative impact on the environment." To promote green meetings to the members of their member organizations, the Events Industry Council has created standards for environmentally sustainable meetings and trains its members in how to use these standards to reduce the carbon footprint of their meetings. For example, one of the initiatives they promote is food rescue programs. The caterer of large meetings often has large quantities of leftover food, with much of this food being thrown away. The Events Industry Council has developed a step-by-step plan; meeting planners can follow this plan to have their caterer rescue unused food from their event and give it to a food bank or an organization providing free meals for those in need. At their convention in Orlando, the National Association for Events and Catering (NACE) followed these guidelines to show NACE members how to develop and implement a food rescue program. The Events Industry Council promotes a fully integrated approach to producing sustainable meetings through its sustainable event professional certificate.

An example of some of the things that can be done to create a more sustainable meeting include the elimination of boxed lunches. Boxed lunches have been an industry standard for a low cost lunch. They use a disposable cardboard box for a container and include packaged chips and often a wrapped desert. The chips and/or cookies are thrown away by those on a diet. A green way to do boxed lunches is to set up a sandwich buffet, with chips, salads, and desserts. This eliminates the package material and waste, since people are likely to take what they will eat. It also saves labor, as packing box lunches is labor intensive. Another example of a sustainability initiative by hotels and restaurants is the installation of a water purification system, enabling them to serve bottled water quality from elegant carafes, eliminating the need to use water in throwaway glass bottles and the shipping of water to the hotel from faraway places. Some provide the water free of charge and others charge banquet customers for the water, similar to a charge for imported water. Other ways of reducing meeting costs include recycling name badges, reducing solid waste, and saving the planner 75 cents per recycled badge. Serving bulk sugar and cream for coffee and tea breaks reduces solid waste from sugar wrappers and cream containers, while cutting the food cost by over 50 percent on those items. Even though some of these initiatives can reduce costs, the Travel Industry Association of America found that over 80 percent of the customers surveyed were willing to spend 6.5 percent more on products and services provided

As a sustainability initiative that provides fresh produce, some hotels have developed rooftop gardens. Julief514/123RF.

by environmentally friendly companies. Green meeting practices can enhance reputation, save money, increase revenue, and are the right thing to do for the planet.

In addition to planning sustainability initiatives into meeting, meeting facilities can be built to meet green standards. The Leadership in Energy and Environmental Design (LEED) Green Building Rating System provides design guidelines for environment-friendly buildings. LEED-certified hotels are found in more than 40 U.S. states, 31 countries and on 4 continents (North and South America, Europe and Asia). There are four levels of LEED certification ranging from certified to Platinum. The first LEED platinum hotel in the United States was the Proximity Hotel in Greensboro, North Carolina. In the United States the number of platinum hotels is still less than 10, there are over 400 hotels that have received one of the levels of LEED certification. A good environmental plan begins with the construction of the building. A second area of sustainability is general facility management. Even for buildings that were not built with sustainability in mind, there are still ways to make the building greener. These include changing incandescent light bulbs to light-emitting diodes (LEDs), recycling programs, and the efficient management of room temperatures, which are just a few ways one can minimize the negative effect of the meeting venue on the environment.

A researcher found that 90 percent of the 140 largest companies in the United States believe that adapting environmentally responsible practices is important for their reputation. For more information on green meetings, see the following Web sites:[23]

Coalition for Environmentally Responsible Economies	www.ceres.org
Environmental Protection Agency—Green Meetings Initiative	www.epa.gov/oppt/greenmeetings
The Green Meeting Industry Council (GMIC)	http://www.gmicglobal.org
Council International Association of Conference Centers	http://www.iacconline.org/environmental-initiatives

Segmentation of Group Markets by Purpose of the Meeting

Besides dividing group markets into convention, association, corporate, and SMERF, they also can be broken into the purpose of the meeting. Four major purposes are conventions, conferences, seminars, and meetings. Table 7–1 shows a matrix describing some of the critical sales decision variables for these types of gatherings. This matrix reflects the general nature of sales decision variables within the group market. Exceptions can and do exist.

Table 7–1
Decision Variable Matrix: Group Markets

Sales Decision Variables	Conventions	Conferences	Seminars	Meetings
Decision makers	Many: committees, chapter presidents, high-ranking officers	Conference organizer, meeting planner	Seminar organizer, boss, secretary	Boss, secretary, regional manager, meeting planner
Decision influencers	Many	Limited	Limited	Few
Degree of politicalization	Highly political	Somewhat political	Personal	Highly personal
Decision time	Years	One year or less	Months	Short time; sometimes one day
Customer price sensitivity	Very	Somewhat	Somewhat	Not highly sensitive
Personal service sensitivity	Low	Moderate	High	Extreme
Opportunity for upsell	Low	Moderate	Moderate	High
Team selling opportunity	Definitely	Sometimes	Probably not	No
Special advertising promotion	Definitely	Usually no	No	No
International	Definitely	Possible	Probably not	Usually not, but opportunities exist (board of directors)
Repeat sales opportunity	Long time, poor	Moderate time	Yes	Definitely
Need for personal sales call (travel)	Probably yes	Probably no	Probably no	Depends on the situation

Restaurants as a Meeting Venue

Restaurants are designing their space so they can take advantage of meetings such as using a room off the main room that can be closed for meetings, giving the restaurant the option of using it as part of the public dining space on Saturday night or as a meeting room during a weekday. According to a meeting research firm, meetings held in space of 700 square feet or less (20 feet by 35 feet) increased by over 25 percent in the past two years. Meetings of 50 people or less can be a great source of business for a restaurant. Many times they are held at off-peak times, such as during a weekday. Restaurant Dante in Boston does a great private events business, with 70 percent of its business coming from small corporate meetings, and it has its own marketing and events manager. Many restaurants are adding private rooms and hiring salespeople to gain their share of the meetings market.[24] Civic organizations such as Rotary, Kiwanis, and Lion Clubs International are important sources of business for restaurants.

Restaurants often have private dining rooms, which provide privacy for a group or can be opened up and used as general seating when they are not booked. Liu Anlin/Shutterstock.

Dealing with Meeting Planners

Discussions over price can either drive the meeting planner and the hotel sales executive apart or bring them together. One successful technique for negotiating with a meeting planner is to determine the group's requirements in detail and work out a package based on needs and budget. Some meeting planners try to negotiate every item separately, starting with the room rate. Then they choose a $65 banquet and try to negotiate the price to $45. In this scenario, every line item becomes a point of contention between the meeting planner and the hotel salesperson.

Taking a consultative approach is much more effective. If the hotel knows that the meeting planner wants to spend $50 for dinner, the chef can develop alternatives within this price range, suggesting something the attendees will enjoy, and the hotel can produce the meal at a profit and sell it for $50. The hotel gains a profitable meeting, and the meeting stays within the planner's budget. Debra Kaufman, an association meeting planner, states that if attendees are able to get work done while they are at the conference they will stay longer.[25] If space is available, the hotel can offer a small meeting room set up with business services, including internet access, computers, and printers. Given the space is available, this can be a low-cost item to the hotel, which has a high value to the meeting planner.

Most group rates are noncommissionable. Meeting planners sometimes turn meetings over to travel agents. If the meeting planner does so without understanding that the rate is noncommissionable, problems can arise when the travel agent tries to collect a commission. If the rates are commissionable, it should be determined during the negotiation process. It is also common for hotels to give one complimentary room night for every 50 room nights that the group produces—another point of negotiation. Suites are usually counted as two rooms. Thus, a suite for three nights would be the equivalent of six room nights. When a hotel has a smaller meeting room that it will not be able to sell during a proposed meeting, it can be used in the negotiation process as a space for the meeting manager to work. The hotel salesperson must look for items that will create value for the meeting planner without creating costs or sacrificing revenue for the hotel.

Many associations have a president, elected from the membership, and a professional executive vice president. The executive vice president usually sets up the meeting. In larger associations there may be a paid executive director, a convention manager, and one or more meeting managers who handle the association's meetings. In some associations the elected officers also like to get involved in the selection of sites and hotels for meetings or conventions. To further complicate matters, the previous year's president usually becomes the chairman of the association's board of directors and therefore can hold great power in the association. It is important for the salesperson to find out who is involved in the decision-making process, both officially and unofficially.

When the vice president of sales asks a junior salesperson to organize a sales meeting, the salesperson is usually unsure of how to proceed with newly assigned and unfamiliar tasks. However, meeting administrators often know the business as well as the hotel salesperson. Salespeople should listen to the meeting administrator to understand his or her requirements. Sometimes meeting administrators know exactly what they want and simply desire a quote for the meeting according to their specifications. If this is the case, a salesperson trying to alter their specifications arbitrarily can appear unprofessional and lose the meeting administrator's business. For example, a hotel salesperson altered the meeting administrator's menu and developed a quotation based on the altered menus. The meeting administrator was planning a series of training sessions to be presented at various locations throughout the United States and had developed menus to meet group needs. This uninvited intrusion by the hotel salesperson infuriated the meeting administrator, who then proceeded to a competitive hotel.

Most meeting planners maintain a history of the group for the purpose of planning future meetings. This includes past dates, locations, and attendance figures. They also have evaluations of past meetings. A salesperson can gain valuable information by asking questions about past conferences. These questions can provide insight into room pickups, attendance at banquets, past problems with a hotel, and what their members have enjoyed. The salesperson should also interview hotels that hosted the conference in past years.

Consider the following expectations of meeting planners.[26] Meeting planners want their calls or e-mails returned the same day they are received. When they ask about the availability of meeting space, they expect a response the same day and a complete proposal in five days. They want check-in and checkout to last no more than four minutes. Most meeting planners want their bill within one week of the event, and 25 percent want it within 2 days. Planners feel that hotel management should empower the convention service manager to solve their problems. They do not want to wait while the convention service manager checks with a superior. Ultimately, when dealing with group business, the hotel has to please both the meeting planner and the meeting planner's clients. These clients include those attending the conference, association executives, and the president or senior officer of a corporation. Jonathan Tisch, president and CEO of Loews Hotels, states, "What we're looking to do is to create a win–win situation. If the senior officer is happy, then the planner's happy, and if the planner's happy we've done our job."[27]

One of the most important aspects of creating a successful function is a prefunction meeting between the hotel staff and the meeting planner. The bell captain should know if a gratuity for his or her staff is included in the package. If it is, Renee Goetz, a meeting planner, states that the staff should be instructed to say, "Thank you, that's been taken care of," when a guest offers a tip. The concierge needs to know the meeting has open nights with no banquets because this will allow the concierge to set aside tables at local restaurants. If garage space is limited, arrangements need to take place to make sure there is adequate space for the group. The hotel staff who will be receiving questions about the event should be briefed. Reservation agents should know the names of the group's VIPs and who should get early check-in privileges. Those responsible for receiving packages for the meeting should know how to store them properly. A prefunction meeting can go a long way in creating a successful event.[28]

CHAPTER REVIEW

I. The Organizational Buying Process. Business customers are those that buy goods and services for use in producing their own products and services for resale, rental, or supply to others. Their purchases often involve large sums of money; complex technical, economic considerations; and interactions among many people at all levels of the organization. Buyer and seller are often very dependent on each other.

A. Market structure and demand. Organizational demand is derived demand; it comes ultimately from the demand for consumer goods or services. It is derived or a function of the businesses that supply the hospitality and travel industry with meetings, special events, and other functions.

B. Nature of the buying unit. Compared with consumer purchases, a business purchase usually involves more decision makers and a more professional purchasing effort.

C. Types of decisions and the decision process. Organizational buyers usually face more complex buying decisions than consumer buyers.

II. **Participants in the Organizational Buying Process.** The decision-making unit of a buying organization, sometimes called the "buying center," is defined as "all those individuals and groups who participate in the purchasing decision-making process, who share common goals and the risks arising from the decisions." These include users, influencers, deciders, approvers, buyers, and gatekeepers.

III. **Major Influences on Organizational Buyers.** Business buyers are influenced by environmental, organizational, interpersonal, and individual factors. Organizational buyers are heavily influenced by the current and expected economic environment. Each organization has specific objectives, policies, procedures, organizational structures, and systems related to buying. The buying center usually includes several participants with different levels of interest, authority, and persuasiveness. Each participant in the buying decision process has personal motivations, perceptions, and preferences. The participant's age, income, education, professional identification, personality, and attitudes toward risk all influence the participants in the buying process.

IV. **The Organizational Buying Decisions**
   A. **Problem recognition.** The buying process begins when someone in the company recognizes a problem or need that can be met by acquiring a good or service.
   B. **General need description.** The buyer goes on to determine the requirements of the product.
   C. **Product specifications.** Once the general requirements have been determined, the specific requirements for the product can be developed.
   D. **Supplier search.** The buyer now tries to identify the most appropriate suppliers.
   E. **Proposal solicitations.** Qualified suppliers are invited to submit proposals. Skilled research, writing, and presentations are required.
   F. **Supplier selection.** Once the meeting planner has drawn up a short list of suppliers, qualified hotels are invited to submit proposals.
   G. **Order-routine specification.** The buyer writes the final order, listing the technical specification. The supplier responds by offering the buyer a formal contract.
   H. **Performance review.** The buyer does postpurchase evaluation of the product. During this phase the buyer determines if the product meets the buyer's specifications and if the buyer will purchase from the company again.

   1. **Engaging business byers with digital and social marketing.** Two important technology advancements are e-procurement and online purchasing and B-to-B digital and social media marketing.

V. **Hospitality Group Markets**
   A. **Conventions.** Conventions are usually the annual meeting of an association and include general sessions, committee meetings, and special-interest sessions. A trade show is often an important part of an annual convention.
      1. **Convention bureaus.** Convention bureaus are nonprofit marketing organizations that help hotels sign conventions and meetings. These organizations are often supported by a hotel or by sales tax and are run by chamber of commerce, visitor bureaus, or city and county governments
   B. **Association meetings.** Associations sponsor many types of meetings, including regional, special-interest, educational, and board meetings.
   C. **Corporate meetings.** A corporate meeting is a command performance for employees of a company. The corporation's major concern is that the meeting be productive and accomplishes the company's objectives.
      1. **Small groups.** Meetings of less than 50 rooms are gaining the attention of hotels and hotel chains.
      2. **Incentive travel.** Incentive travel, a unique subset of corporate group business, is a reward participants receive for achieving or exceeding a goal.
   D. **SMERFs.** SMERF stands for social, military, educational, religious, and fraternal organizations. This group of specialty markets are typically price-sensitive and willing to be flexible to ensure a lower room rate.
   E. **Segmentation of group markets by purpose of meeting.** Group markets can also be broken up by the purpose of the meeting. Four major purposes are conventions, conferences, seminars, and meetings.
   F. **Restaurants as a meeting venue.** Restaurants often have private dining rooms, which provide privacy for a group or can be opened up and used as general seating when they are not booked.
   G. **Dealing with meeting planners.** When negotiating with meeting planners, it is important to try to develop a win–win relationship. Meeting planners like to return to the same property.

▰▰▰ IN-CLASS GROUP EXERCISES

*Exercises with an asterisk next to them are suitable for individual homework or online assignments. Always provide an explanation for your answer.

1. *What is derived demand? Give an example(s) of sources of derived demand for a hotel in your town.
2. *The buying center often has six roles. Why is it important for marketers to understand these roles?
3. *Discuss the major environmental influences that affect the purchase meeting space by IBM (or another corporation of your choice) for its sales meetings.
4. How would a catering sales manager handle a mother and daughter making arrangements for the daughter's wedding differently from a meeting planner from a major corporation wishing to get a quote on a regional

sales meeting, which he or she has already done in five other cities?

5. How can a hotel sales representative identify who is responsible for purchasing meeting space, banquets, and rooms for corporate travelers in the corporate headquarters of an insurance company?

6. *Go to the internet site of a travel organization (e.g., a hotel, cruise line, travel agency, large restaurant). Does it have a separate section for group or organizational purchases? If so, how does the information in the section differ from the organization's consumer site? If it does not have a separate site, go to another organization until you find one that has a separate site for group or organizational purchases.

EXPERIENTIAL EXERCISE

Do one of the following:

1. Talk with persons who travel for business. Ask them if they can choose their own hotel and airlines when they travel for their company. If they can choose their own hotels and airlines, ask if they have any restrictions or guidelines. If they are not able to choose their own hotels and airlines, ask if they have any input into where they stay. How would this information help you market travel products to their organization?

REFERENCES

1. Portions adapted from Susan Harte, "When in Rome, You Should Learn to Do What the Romans Do," *The Atlanta Journal-Constitution* (January 22, 1990): 1, 6. Additional information and examples can be found in Susan Adams, "Business Etiquette Tips for International Travel," *Forbes*, June 6, 2012, www.forbes.com/sites/susanadams/2012/06/15/business-etiquette-tips-for-international-travel; Janette S. Martin and Lillian H. Cheney, *Global Business Etiquette* (Santa Barbara, CA: Praeger Publishers, 2013); "Learn Tips to Do Business in China," *The News-Sentinel*, February 9, 2012, www.news-sentinel.com; and www.cyborlink.com (accessed September 2014).

2. Frederick E. Webster, Jr. and Yoram Wind, *Organizational Buying Behavior* (Upper Saddle River, NJ: Prentice-Hall, 1972), pp. 33–37.

3. Ibid, pp. 78–80.

4. See Marco Link and John H. Fleming, "B2B Companies: Do You Know Who Your Customer Is?" *Business Journal*, November 11, 2014, www.gallup.com/businessjournal/179309/b2b-compa- nies-know-customer.aspx; and Karl Schmidt, Brent Adamson, and Anna Bird, "Making the Consensus Sale," *Harvard Business Review*, March 2015, pp. 107–113.

5. Frederick Webster and Yoram Wind, *Organizational Buying Behavior*, Prentice Hall, 1972.

6. See Edward G. Brierty, Robert W. Eckles, and Robert R. Reeder, *Business Marketing*, 3rd ed. (Upper Saddle River, NJ: Prentice-Hall, 1998), Chapter 3; Murray Harding, "Who Really Makes the Purchasing Decision?" *Industrial Marketing* (September 1966): 76; This point of view is further developed in Ernest Dichter, "Industrial Buying Is Based on Same Only Human Emotional Factors That Motivate Consumer Market's Housewife," *Industrial Marketing* (February 1973): 14–16.

7. See Tom Reilly, "All Sales Decisions Are Emotional for the Buyer," *Selling* (July 2003): 13; Patrick J. Robinson, Charles W. Faris, and Yoram Wind, *Industrial Buying Behavior and Creative Marketing* (Needham Heights, MA: Allyn & Bacon, 1967), p. 14.

8. Hirsch, C., "Rethinking How You Work With Procurement," 2018, http://www.pcmaconvene.org/features/rethinking-how-you-work-with-procurement/ (accessed July 19, 2018).

9. "Sysco Acquisition Expands Online Ordering for Its Customers" (July 1, 2016), https://www.chron.com/business/article/Sysco-acquisition-expands-online-ordering-for-its-8337392.php (accessed July 19, 2018).

10. http://www.eventscouncil.org/APEX.aspx (accessed August 30, 2018); Lynn McCullough, "APEX: A Play-Book for the Meetings Industry," *Hotel Business Review* (September 19, 2007).

11. Loren Edelstein, "U.S. Meetings Industry Generated $845 Billion in Business Sales in 2016," http://www.meetings-conventions.com/News/Industry-Associations/U-S-Meetings-Industry-economic-statistics-$845-Billion-in-Business-Sales-in-2016/ (accessed August 30, 2018)

12. Statista, "Exhibition, Convention and Meeting Industry Facts," https://www.statista.com/topics/1413/exhibitions-convention-and-meetings/ (accessed August 30, 2018).

13. Sarah J. F. Braley, "The Big Picture," *Meetings and Conventions* (October 1998): 2–35; Sarah J. F. Braley, "Meetings Market Report 2008-Associations," *Meeting and Convention Magazine*, "2008 Meetings Report" (August 2008), www.ncmag.com (accessed August 17, 2008).

14. Julie Barker, "The State of the Industry Report," *Successful Meetings* (January 1999): 35–47.

15. Top 10 Factors to Consider When Selecting a Meeting Location (Meeting Planner Forum Session One Recap), Convene, February 3, 2014, http://convene.com/top-10-factors-to-consider-when-selecting-a-

meeting-location-meeting-planner-forum-session-one-recap/ (accessed July 20, 2015).

16. Sarah J. F. Bailey, "Corporate Meetings Market Report," *Meetings and Conventions* (December 1, 2010), http://www.meetings-conventions.com/articles/corporate-meeitngs-market-report/a37846/aspx-?page=3 (accessed September 9, 2011).

17. HSMAI econnect, www.hsami.org (accessed October 24, 2001).

18. Sarah J. F. Braley, "The Big Picture," *Meetings and Conventions* (October 1998): 2–35.

19. Andrea Graham, "Companies Add Perks to Individual Travel Awards," *Corporate Meetings and Incentives* (October 1, 2004), www.cmi.meetingsnet.com (accessed October 24, 2004).

20. Travel White Paper, April 2013, Making Destination Choice Go the Distance, Maritz Travel, www.maritztravel.com, 877–4-MARITZ.

21. Regina McGee, "Getting a Fix on SMERF," *Association Meetings* (April 1, 2004), www.meetingsnet.com (accessed June 18, 2004).

22. "Special Report on the Religious Group Travel Market," http://www.premiertourismmarketing.com/fyi/religious.html (accessed October 24, 2004).

23. "Green Meetings" Convention Industry Council, www.convention/industry.org/StandardsPractices/GreenMeetings.aspx (accessed September 8, 2011); Green Meetings, www.mpiweb.com (accessed September 9, 2011); www.greenmeetings.info/goodforbusiness.htm (accessed August 23, 2008); "Green Meetings Policy," *The National Recycling Coalition* (accessed August 23, 2008); www.ceres.org (accessed August 23, 2008); http://www.eventscouncil.org/sustainability; "Green Meetings Policy," *The National Recycling Coalition* (accessed August 23, 2008); www.ceres.org (accessed August 23, 2008). "Where Can You Say in a LEED Hotel," https://readymag.com/usgbc/hospitality/where/ (accessed August 30, 2018); "LEED Certified Hotels Gaining Momentum," https://www.smartmeetings.com/news/98983/leed-certified-hotels-gaining-momentum (accessed August 30, 2018); "USGBC's New Report Reveals Hospitality Industry Poised for Tremendous Growth in Green Building," https://www.usgbc.org/articles/usgbcs-new-report-reveals-hospitality-industry-poised-tremendous-growth-green-building (accessed August 30, 2018).

24. Naomi Kooker, "Small Meetings Driving Big Hotel, Restaurant Business," *Boston Business Journal* (November 9, 2007).

25. Barker, "The State of the Industry Report," pp. 35–47.

26. Howard Feiertag, "New Survey Reveals Meeting Planners' Priorities," *Hotel and Motel Management* (November 23, 1992).

27. James P. Abbey, *Hospitality Sales and Advertising* (East Lansing, MI: Educational Institute of the American Hotel and Motel Association, 1993), p. 569.

28. See Jonathan Vatner, "Inside Track," *Meetings and Conventions*, www.meetings-conventions.co/printarticles.aspx?pageid=4366 (accessed June 7, 2004).

8

Objectives

After reading this chapter, you should be able to:

1. Define the major steps in designing a customer-driven marketing strategy.
2. List and discuss the major bases for segmenting consumer markets.
3. Explain how companies identify attractive market segments and choose a market-targeting strategy.
4. Discuss how companies differentiate and position their products for competitive advantage.

Customer-Driven Marketing Strategy: Creating Value for Target Customers

CitizenM says: hello! Walk into any citizenM hotel and you'll feel like you are in an oversized living room rather than a hotel lobby. The guests, on arrival, do not see a front desk or a bellboy to pick up their luggage. Instead, citizenM offers self-check-in kiosks that dispense keys. Michael Levie, a hotel executive, and Rattan Chadha, a retail entrepreneur, opened their first hotel in 2008 at Amsterdam Schiphol Airport followed by a second one in Amsterdam city in 2009, and named their hotel brand "citizenM" for mobile citizens. Upon their success, more hotels were added to their portfolio in subsequent years, in Glasgow, London, and Rotterdam. With 30 hotels and 7,000 rooms in 2018, citizenM continues to expand its family of hotels in world-class cities such as Paris, Lyon, Taipei, New York, Shanghai, and Kuala Lumpur.

citizenM, a Dutch hotel chain, targets a segment what it calls the "Mobile Citizen" who uses mobile technology, seeks adventure and authenticity, and appreciates value, convenience, and an unpretentious luxurious place to relax. This new generation of traveler is also protective of their time, and doesn't like wasting it. They want things to be easy, efficient, and friendly. citizenM further defines the target market as frequent travelers and "a mix of explorers, professionals, and shoppers" on a business trip or leisure weekend getaway. This is also a brand for millennials who value a concept that offers good settings for selfies and reliable internet connection to share the experience with friends, families, and fellow mobile citizens.

The definition of luxury has changed for mobile travelers and millennials. Luxury used to be limos, crystal chandeliers, and expensive champagne, but nowadays luxury could be anything, from a great shower in the morning, to fast working Wi-Fi, or a perfect cappuccino. It is always critical to know what your customers need and want. Equally important is what they do not need and want in terms of effective product design, pricing, and experience. citizenM decided to focus on what is relevant for their target market. They not only considered what consumers would value and be willing to pay but also what things could be eliminated without much affecting their willingness to pay. Therefore, facilities and amenities that most travelers rarely use such as a hotel restaurant, spa, concierge, and room service were all excluded. There are no minibars in the rooms, but a fridge with free bottled water. The rooms of citizenM are small but luxurious, with wall-to-wall king-size bed, quality linens, rain shower, mood lighting, and free Wi-Fi and on-demand movies. You can also stream Netflix straight from your device to a large flat screen TV. In-room tablets allow guests to control TV, mood lighting, and music, and surf the Web. At citizenM, there is no room upgrade because every room is the same. As a result of these decisions, citizenM's construction costs and staffing are 40 percent lower than other four-star hotels.

The lobby is designed as a communal living room to work, relax, hang out, network, and meet people. Bookshelves, contemporary art, fireplaces, and large plasma TVs are positioned to get guests out of their rooms and into the common areas. citizenM partnered with Vitra, a Swiss design company, to make sure all the furnishings in the common spaces are modern and stylish.

The social lobby in canteenM also included an open kitchen as central area where one can order coffee, cocktails, and foods offered for guests who prefer to spend their time downstairs rather than in their rooms. It has evolved from a quick grab "n" go to a place where guests can enjoy big breakfasts, warm meals, and selection of fresh drinks and snacks 24/7. Foods are locally sourced and freshly made. Rattan Chadha, one of the citizenM founders, said "The hotel industry thinks we're crazy because we don't have a restaurant. My response is, 'We sell a night of sleep.' So instead, come down to the canteen, get your cappuccino the way you like it, and enjoy it there or back in your room." canteenM is a breakfast bar serving barista brewed coffee, fresh pastries, and hot breakfasts. It's a lunch or evening diner for sushi, signature sandwiches, warm dishes, and drinks and beverages. And in the evenings it's a 24-hour bar with beer on tap, champagne on ice, and cocktails on order.

citizenM also appeals to business travelers as many properties feature societyM meeting rooms—co-working spaces for millennials, designed for multiple purpose, from training and workshops to press events, movie nights, and yoga. Unlimited tea and coffee, espresso machines, mini-fridges, smart TV, audio/visual system, and stationery are offered in the meeting rooms.

Location is an important element that determines the success of hotels. citizenM hotels are centrally located in key cities such as New York, Paris, and London to enjoy the city vibrancy and attract locals to the bar to mingle with the guests. Amsterdam and Rotterdam locations provide free bikes for local experience and guests at citizenM. New York Times Square can work out in a gym with a view.

citizenM does not offer special room rates for different segments or corporate clients. Instead, the properties use dynamic pricing and price all their rooms in real time, dependent on supply and demand conditions when reservations are made.

citizenM creates enticing videos that evoke a sense of local vibe and individualistic personality, promoting the local culture as much as the hotel. Humorous messages, starting with "citizenM says:" are consistently being used in traditional, digital, and social media. For instance, they have created outdoor and subway posters with messages like "citizenM says: to the city that never sleeps, we're here to help." Or "citizenM says: cheat on your other hotel, Sleep with us instead." You can even see a message on your pillow once you enter your room, "citizenM says: I will win in a pillow fight."

citizenM's core business philosophy and positioning statement is to offer an affordable luxury brand for the modern travelers that combines a highly personalized and unique experience with sustainability for a reasonable price. The company has also used differentiation to a great extent. It is a hotel where check-in machines are similar to those at airports; its luxurious, but small, bedrooms resemble those at a cruise ship; its booking and pricing system follows that of low-cost airlines. The downstairs space, referred to as the hotel's "living room" with a "kitchen" as its center of activity, is made to mimic the feel of a luxurious and contemporary home where bedrooms are only used for sleeping, showering, and perhaps watching a free movie.

As far as the service and personalization are concerned, citizenM does not believe in segmenting employees into concierge, check-in, food and beverage. Instead they want their staff to be completely multifunctional and call them ambassadors. They are typical mobile citizens themselves. They are trained as baristas to make coffee, as mixologists to shake a cocktail, but they can also check guests in or out, help them in the room, and they know the city well so they can help with local tips and advice. The guests' preferences are stored in a central database to personalize the room no matter where checked-in. Guests can choose from items such as favorite TV content, music, preferred room temperature, mood lighting, and other preferences, all of which are automatically adjusted once they check in at the kiosk. Any changes made during their stay are automatically stored and the next time the guest checks in, the room will be configured precisely as indicated in the previous stay.

The success of citizenM could be attributed to effective use of market segmentation, concentrated target marketing, and positioning. Travelers today are much more value conscious. They care about quality and "luxury," but they don't want to overspend on things they do not need. By focusing on core customers, eliminating unneeded elements, and product and service differentiation, citizenM has developed a new hotel model that is a high end with low cost that creates affordable luxury.[1]

Markets

Companies today recognize that they cannot appeal to all customers in the marketplace, or at least not all customers the same way. Customers are too numerous, too widely scattered, and too varied in their needs and buying processes. Moreover, the companies themselves vary widely in their abilities to serve different segments of the market. Instead, like citizenM, a company must identify the parts of the market that it can serve best and most profitably. It must design customer-driven marketing strategies that build the right relationships with the right customers.

Market segmentation Dividing a market into direct groups of buyers who might require separate products or marketing mixes.

Market targeting Evaluating each market segment's attractiveness and selecting one or more segments to enter.

Market positioning Formulating competitive positioning for a product and a detailed marketing mix.

Most companies have moved away from mass marketing and toward target marketing—identifying market segments, selecting one or more of them, and developing products and market programs tailored to each. Instead of scattering their marketing efforts (the "shotgun" approach), firms are focusing on the buyers who have great interest in the values they create well (the "rifle" approach).

Figure 8–1 shows the three major steps in target marketing. The first is **market segmentation**, dividing a market into distinct groups that might require separate products and/or marketing mixes. The company identifies different ways to segment the market and develops profiles of the resulting market segments. The second step is **market targeting**, evaluating each segment's attractiveness and selecting one or more of the market segments. The third step is **market positioning**, developing competitive positioning for the product and an appropriate marketing mix.

Figure 8–1
Steps in segmentation, targeting, and positioning.

Market segmentation	Market targeting	Market positioning
1. Identify bases for segmenting the market 2. Develop profiles of resulting segments	3. Develop measures of segment attractiveness 4. Select the target segment(s)	5. Develop positioning for each target segment 6. Develop marketing mix for each target segment

Market Segmentation

Buyers in any market differ in their wants, resources, locations, buying attitudes, and buying practices. Because buyers have unique needs and wants, each is potentially a separate market. Ideally, a seller might design a separate marketing program for each buyer. For example, a caterer can customize the menu, entertainment, and the setting to meet the needs of a specific client.

However, most companies are unable to offer complete segmentation because of cost. Companies, therefore, look for broad classes of buyers who differ in their product needs or buying responses. For example, married adults who vacation with small children have different needs than young single adults.

The restaurant industry offers many examples of segmentation by a variety of variables. The type of service varies from quick service to fine dining. One-segment retail host restaurants are restaurants located in retail outlets such as a Walmart or gas station. This segment now accounts for over $41 billion in the United States.[2] The target market for these restaurants are people who are in the store or are traveling, hungry, and want to make one stop for food and gas. The main benefit is convenience. One of the fastest-growing restaurant segments is the fast-casual segment. These restaurants offer excellent food, but require the customer to order the food themselves and then a server brings it to their table, lowering the labor cost for the restaurant and both the cost of the meal and amount of the tip for the customer. Segmenting restaurants by type of service and location are just two of the many ways of segmenting a restaurant.

There is no single way to segment a market. A marketer has to try different segmentation variables. Table 8–1 outlines major variables that might be used in segmenting consumer markets. Here we look at the *geographic, demographic, psychographic,* and *behavioral* variables used in segmenting consumer markets.

Geographic Segmentation

Geographic segmentation Dividing a market into different geographic units such as nations, states, regions, counties, cities, or neighborhoods.

Geographic segmentation calls for dividing the market into different geographic units, such as nations, states, regions, counties, cities, or even neighborhoods. A company decides to operate in one or several geographic areas by paying attention to geographic differences in customer preferences. For example, within the Central American countries, beans are a dietary staple, yet in one nation consumers prefer red beans while in another black beans are preferred.

Restaurants use geographic data about their customers to determine the extent of their market reach, which could be 2 miles for a fast-food restaurant to 50 miles or more for a specialty restaurant. Information on where customers are coming from can be collected by simply asking customers for their zip code or from more sophisticated studies that create customer databases that include other customer data in addition to the geographic information. The customer origin information can be used to show the decay of a customer base over distance, the effect of competition, and the placement of media.[3]

Multiunit restaurant chains will often focus on a geographic region containing customers that they understand. The geographic focus also creates an opportunity for effective management and promotion. For example, Port of Sub, a sandwich restaurant that started in Nevada, has expanded into a chain that has over 140 restaurants. All of their units are in the west, with the majority in Nevada and the states adjacent to Nevada—Arizona, California, and Utah.

Companies that cover a wide geographic area are localizing their products, services, advertising, promotion, and sales efforts to fit the needs of individual regions, cities, and neighborhoods. For example, Domino's Pizza, the nation's

TABLE 8–1
Major Segmentation Variables for Consumer Markets

Segmentation Variable	Examples
Geographic	Nations, regions, states, counties, cities, neighborhoods, population density (urban, suburban, rural), climate
Demographic	Age, life-cycle stage, gender, income, occupation, education, religion, ethnicity, generation
Psychographic	Social class, lifestyle, personality
Behavioral	Occasions, benefits, user status, usage rate, loyalty status

Source: Kotler, Philip; Armstrong, Gary, *Principles of Marketing,* 16th Ed., ©2016, p. 199. Reprinted and Electronically reproduced by permission of Pearson Education, Inc., New York, NY.

largest pizza delivery chain, keeps its marketing and customer focus decidedly local. Hungry customers anywhere in the nation can use the Domino's online platform or tablet and smartphone apps to track down local coupon offers, locate the nearest store with a global positioning system (GPS) store locator, and even use Domino's Pizza Tracker to follow their pies locally from store to door.[4]

Similarly, one of Marriott International lifestyle brands, Renaissance Hotels, has rolled out its Navigator program, which hyper-localizes guest experiences at each of its 155 lifestyle hotels around the world.[5] Renaissance Hotels' Navigator program puts a personal and local face on each location by "micro-localizing" recommendations for guests' food, shopping, entertainment, and cultural experiences at each destination. The program is anchored by on-site "Navigators" of Renaissance Hotels at each location. Whether it's Omar Bennett, a restaurant-loving Brooklynite at the Renaissance New York Times Square Hotel, or James Elliott at the St. Pancras Renaissance London Hotel, a history buff and local pub expert, Navigators are extensively trained locals who are deeply passionate about the destination and often have a personal connection to the locale. Based on their own personal experiences and ongoing research, they work with guests personally to help them experience "the hidden gems throughout the neighborhood of each hotel through the eyes of those who know it best."

In addition, Renaissance Hotels engage locals in each city to participate by inviting them to follow their local Navigator via social media, as well as adding their own favorites to the system, creating each hotel's own version of Yelp. Navigators then cull through submitted tips and feature the best recommendations alongside their own, for sharing within the hotel lobby or on its Web site and social media channels. Since introducing the hyper-localized Navigator program as part of Renaissance Hotels' "Live Life to Discover" campaign two years ago, the hotel's Web site traffic has grown more than 80 percent, Facebook likes have exploded from 40,000 to more than 915,000, and Twitter followers have surged from 5,000 to 61,000.

The St. Pancras Renaissance Hotel in London is located in a building that formerly housed railway offices. Chan Richie/123RF.

Demographic Segmentation

Demographic segmentation divides the market into segments based on variables such as age, life-cycle stage, gender, income, occupation, education, religion, ethnicity, and generation. Demographic variables are the most popular bases for segmenting customer groups. One reason is that consumer needs, wants, and usage rates often vary closely with demographic variables. Another is that demographic variables are easy to measure. Even when market segments are first defined using other bases, such as personality or behavior, demographic characteristics must be known to assess the size of the market and to reach it efficiently. Now we show you how certain demographic factors have been used in market segmentation.

Demographic segmentation Dividing the market into groups based on demographic variables such as age, gender, family size, family life cycle, income, occupation, education, religion, race, and nationality.

Age and Life-Cycle Stage

Consumer preferences change with age. Some companies offer different products or marketing strategies to penetrate various age and life-cycle segments. Other companies focus on the specific age of life-stage groups. For example, although consumers in all age segments love Disney cruises, Disney Cruise Lines focuses primarily on families with children, large and small. Most of its destinations and shipboard activities are designed with parents and their children in mind. On board, Disney provides trained counselors who help younger kids join in hands-on activities, teen-only

The onboard activities of European River cruises are designed for adult travelers. Leoks/Shutterstock.

spaces for older children, and family-time or individual-time options for parents and other adults. It's difficult to find a Disney Cruise Lines ad or Web page that doesn't feature a family full of smiling faces. In contrast, Viking River Cruises, the deluxe smaller-boat cruise line that offers tours along the world's great rivers, primarily targets older-adult couples and singles. It states on its Web site, "Due to the nature of our cruise itineraries, Viking Cruises does not maintain facilities or services for children aboard cruise vessels."[6]

Marketers must be careful to guard against stereotypes when using age and life-cycle segmentation. Although some 80-year-olds fit the doddering stereotype, others ski and play tennis. Similarly, whereas some 40-year-old couples are sending their children off to college, others are just beginning new families. Thus, age is often a poor predictor of a person's life cycle, health, work or family status, needs, and buying power. Companies marketing to mature consumers usually use positive images and appeals. For example, Disney's "The Grand Adventure" promotes Disney's amusement as a great place for active grandparents to take their grandkids.

Gender

Gender marketing is by no means simplistic. A "typical" male or female does not exist, yet droves of companies have erred in trying to develop and market a product or service for such an individual. It is natural for each of us to think of typical as someone in our respective age, income, and lifestyle. This is always wrong.

Marketing HIGHLIGHT 8.1 Targeting families by targeting kids

Friendly's is a casual restaurant originally known for its ice cream. Friendly's was known for sandwiches and ice cream, but not somewhere where a family would go for dinner. Friendly's management wanted to reposition the restaurant as a place where customers would go for lunch and dinner. Research had shown that when determining where a family will eat, kids have a major influence. In fact, children influenced over $125 billion in restaurant spending. Families with children account for 56 percent of all dollars spent on food away from home. Management realized that parents are pressed for time, and they often feel bad about not spending more time with their children. If Friendly's could make a dining experience that the children would enjoy, the family would have fun together and everyone would be a winner.

To find out what would make a good dining experience for children, Friendly's held focus groups with children. One of the things that came out of the focus groups was that children wanted "real" menus, like their parents' menus. They didn't want placemat menus. The kids also told them what kind of food they wanted, and how they wanted it presented. Besides talking to kids, it is also useful to talk to their parents. At the Kids' Marketing Conference, parents told restaurant managers that comfortable seating was important; kids squirm in hard seats. They also said they did not like play areas in sit-down-service restaurants; they want to be with their kids. They also expect more nutritious meals in a sit-down-service restaurant than they do in a fast-food restaurant.

Friendly's put a kids' coordinator on each shift to make sure the wants of the children were being met. Parents mentioned that having servers who can deal with kids is important. According to image research done before and after the program, Friendly's effort to reposition as a family restaurant was successful, and its image as a good place for kids jumped 50 percent. Notice how Friendly's used marketing research to find out about the market it wanted to target. The marketing information it gathered helped it understand the consumer behavior of the family market, namely, that kids play a major role in where the family dines. Knowing this, Friendly's created a program to make Friendly's a place where children would want to come.[8]

Gender marketing is most effective when combined with lifestyle and demographic information.

According to the Lipstick Economy, a Web Site communicating the purchasing power of woman, "The average adventure traveler is not a male but a 47-year-old female." The author cites a growing segment of single women who are traveling. She cites one of the reasons for this growth is the growth of indies, a term for women over 30 years who are not living with a partner and are without children. Jamie Dunham, president of the branding and marketing company Brandwise, states indies account for almost a third of all adult women. She states they have high discretionary income as they do not have the expense of a family household.[7]

Income Segmentation

Income segmentation Dividing a market into different income groups.

Income segmentation has long been used by marketers of products and services. The lodging industry is particularly effective in using income segmentation. Upper-income guests and corporations serve as targets for country clubs, boxes at sports stadiums, and upscale hotels and resorts. The Four Seasons Miami recently offered a Five Diamond package that included a two-carat Graff diamond eternity band (or another diamond piece designed to your specifications) and a stay in the presidential suite with a bottle of 1990 Dom Perignon Oenotheque champagne, caviar for two, and an 80-minute in-suite couples massage using a lotion infused with real ground diamonds. The price tag: "From $50,000."[9]

Seadream Yacht Club, a small-ship luxury cruise line, calls select guests after every cruise and offers to have the chief executive officer (CEO) fly out to their home and host, at Seadream's expense, a brunch or reception for a dozen of the couple's best friends. The brochure rate of Sundream cruises averages over $2,500 per day per couple. The CEO of a cruise line visiting your home is an impressive gesture. The customers have no trouble getting a group of friends together, many of whom are corporate executives like the visiting CEO. The CEO offers a great rate to the guests and sells several cruises that night as well as more sales are generated in the future through the couple telling their friends about the cruise. One of these visits could generate $100,000 or more in short-term sales, as well as the value of repeat cruises from the newly recruited customer. This has been so successful for Seadream that it has abandoned most traditional advertising.[10] Carnival cruises target the much larger middle-income market. Its cruises start at around $150 per day per couple. Both cruise lines have been successful targeting their chosen target markets.

Fractional ownership is a product clearly designed for the upscale income market. Fractional ownership is partial ownership of a property. For instance, hotel companies such as Hyatt, Ritz-Carlton, Four Seasons, and Starwood will sell one-fourth, one-eighth, or one-sixteenth interest in condominiums built adjacent to one of their hotels. This allows an upper-middle-class person to have access to a multimillion dollar condo. The marketing of fractional ownership (also called residence clubs) is essentially a high-end real estate function, with the sales of the condominiums used to support the financial viability of multi-use development, which also includes the hotel. The concept also spread to exotic car, yacht, and jet ownership.[11]

Income does not always predict which customers will buy a given product or service. Some upscale urban restaurateurs opened branches in upper-middle-class suburbs. They were attracted by high suburban household incomes. But many had to close their doors. Why? Urban dwellers tend to be singles and couples without children. A large portion of their income is discretionary and their lifestyle includes dining out frequently. According to the National Restaurant Association, singles spend more than half of their food budget dining out, whereas married couples spend only 37 percent of their food budget eating out. On the other hand, families in the suburbs often have a high household income, but spend a heavy percentage of their money on housing, automobiles, and children. Singles represent a prime market segment for the restaurant industry.[12]

Psychographic Segmentation

Psychographic segmentation Dividing a market into different groups based on social class, lifestyle, or personality characteristics.

Psychographic segmentation divides buyers into different segments based on social class, lifestyle, or personality characteristics. People in the same demographic group can have very different psychographic characteristics. In Chapter 6, we discussed how the products people buy reflect their lifestyles. As a result, marketers often segment their markets by consumer lifestyles and base their marketing strategies on lifestyle appeals. For example, car-sharing nicher Zipcar rents cars by the hour or the day. But it doesn't see itself as a car-rental company. Instead it sees itself as enhancing its customer's urban lifestyles and targets accordingly. "It's not about cars," says Zipcar's CEO, "it's about urban life." In New York, the rental of a parking place for a car can be as expensive as an apartment in other cities. New York also has good public transportation. Many people living in Manhattan do not have a car. Zipcar becomes their car.[13]

Marketers also use personality variables to segment markets. For example, cruise lines target adventure seekers. Royal Caribbean appeals to high-energy couples and families by providing hundreds of activities, such as rock wall climbing and ice skating. Its commercials urge travelers to "declare your independence and become a citizen of nation—Royal Caribbean, The Nation of Why Not." By contrast, the Regent Seven Seas Cruise Line targets more serene and cerebral adventurers, mature couples, seeking a more elegant ambiance and exotic destinations such as the Orient. Regent invites them to come along as "luxury goes exploring."[14]

Fast-casual restaurant Panera caters to a lifestyle segment of people who want more than just good-tasting food—they want food that's good for them, too. To better meet the needs of this healthy-living lifestyle segment, Panera recently announced that it would soon banish more than 150 artificial preservatives, sweeteners, colors, and flavors from its food. It then launched a marketing campaign tagged "Food as it should be," showing happy customers eating better at Panera. "Eat clean," says one ad, "because clean food just tastes better." According to Panera, food should do more than just fill your stomach. "Food should taste good. It should feel good. It should do good things for you and the world around you. That's food as it should be." If that kind of thinking fits your lifestyle, suggests Panera's head of marketing, "then yeah, come on in...that's why we're here."[15]

Panera Bread, the Mother Bread logo, and Panera Bread Food as it should be are the intellectual property of Panera Bread and are used with permission. Photograph by Brian W. Ferry.

Lifestyle segmentation: Panera caters to a healthy-eating lifestyle segment of people who want more than just good-tasting food—they want food that's good for them, too. Brian W. Ferry.

Social Class

In Chapter 6, we described the six social classes and explained that social class has a strong effect on preferences for cars, clothes, home furnishings, leisure activities, reading habits, and retailers. Afternoon tea at the Ritz-Carlton is aimed at the upper-middle and upper classes. A neighborhood pub near a factory targets the working class. The customers of each of these establishments would probably feel uncomfortable in other establishments.

Lifestyle

Chapter 6 also showed the influence of people's lifestyles on the goods and services that they buy. Marketers are increasingly segmenting the markets by consumer lifestyles. For example, many bars/watering holes are designed for young singles wanting to meet the opposite sex, singles wanting to meet the same sex, and couples wanting to avoid the entire singles scene and enjoy each other's company.

Personality

Marketers use personality variables to segment markets, endowing their products and personalities. For example, cruise lines target adventure

Marketing Highlight 8.2

W Hotels: A lifestyle hotel

You approach the glitzy, contemporary building in London, a 10-story structure encased in a translucent glass veil. Cameras mounted on the roof capture the surrounding skyline and project it onto the building's surface, creating a seamless blend of the building with its setting. Inside, you're greeted by thumping hip-hop music, large mirrored glitter balls, open fires, and a huge Chesterfield sofa that snakes around the lounge bar. You're in a nightclub perhaps, or the latest trendy restaurant. No, you're in the W London, a hotel that offers much more than just rooms for the night.

Starwood Hotels and Resorts operate nine different hotel chains—something for everyone, you might say. But its W Hotels brand stands out from all the rest. In fact, W Hotels doesn't really think of itself as just a hotel chain. Instead, it positions itself as "an iconic lifestyle brand." More than just rooms, W Hotels prides itself on "offering guests unprecedented insider access to a world of 'Wow' through contemporary cool design, fashion, music, nightlife, and entertainment." W Hotels exudes a youthful, outgoing, jet-setting lifestyle that fits its ultra-hip, trendsetter clientele—mostly from the media, music, fashion, entertainment, and consulting industries. For these patrons, W provides an unmatched sense of belonging.

W Hotels's lifestyle positioning starts with unique design. Although most hotel chains churn out cookie-cutter locations in search of a consistent brand image, W Hotels's 54 properties worldwide look nothing alike. W's patrons view themselves as unique, so they demand the same from the hotels they choose. Every W Hotel projects a common "energetic, vibrant, forward-thinking attitude," and an appreciation for fashion, art, and music befitting its lifestyle image. But in terms of design, each W Hotel is "uniquely inspired by its destination, mixing cutting-edge design with local influences."

For example, the W Taipei in Taiwan, located in the Xinyi district near Taipei 101, the city's tallest skyscraper, is designed around the theme of "nature electrified," blending soft wooden walls; geometric, box-shaped shelves; and lighting inspired by Chinese lanterns. The W Koh Samui (in Thailand), an all-villa beach resort, treats guests to the concept of "day and night"—relaxing by the pool by day and partying by night with modern interiors accented by bright flashes of red, off-white terrazzo floors, and wooden decks for private guest pools. The W Bali features an "inside and outside" theme, with grass-like green pillows that bring a bit of outdoors into the rooms and bed headboards made from the skin of stingrays.

With each unique design, however, W maintains a consistent ambiance that leaves no question in guests' minds that they are living the W lifestyle. The W Paris, for example, blends the facade of its historic and elegant 1870s building with the theme of Paris as the "City of Light," all wrapped in W's signature contemporary energy. The hotel design revolves around an oversized backlit digital undulating wall that defines the central core of the building and weaves through the public and private spaces. "Our design feeds off the elegance, richness, and radiance of Paris and W's DNA for infusing a sense of energy," says the head of the hotel's design group. In true W fashion, it brings the historic building to life with a glowing vibrancy.

Under the direction of a global music director, W's long-running Symmetry Live concert series offers guests access to exclusive performances by some of the world's hottest entertainers, such as Cee Lo Green, Janelle Monae, Ellie Goulding, and Theophilus London. This year, W is sponsoring an exclusive traveling exhibition of the photography of Madonna, curated by Rock Paper Photo and sponsored by vitaminwater. The exhibit features never seen before photos of pop star Madonna from the 1980s. The exclusive exhibition celebrates music and fashion, two of the W brand's core passions.

Another constant at W Hotels is first-class service—what W calls "Whatever-Whenever" service. "We aim to provide whatever, whenever, as long as it is legal—something that is very much consistent throughout the W brand," explains one W Hotels's manager. W Hotels don't have concierges; instead, they have "W Insiders." The Insiders go a step beyond. Rather than waiting to be asked for advice, they proactively seek out things they can do to enhance the stay of each guest. In keeping with the brand's lifestyle positioning, insiders stay in tune with special need-to-know happenings and advise guests on all the latest places to see and be seen.

Staying at a W Hotel isn't cheap. The basic W room runs about $450 a night, with top suites running up to five figures. But a W Hotel isn't just a place where you rent a room and get a good night's sleep. It's the design of the place, the contemporary ambiance, what's hanging on the walls, the music that's playing, the other guests who stay there—all of these things contribute mightily to the W's lifestyle positioning and allure to its young, hip, upscale W clientele. It's not just a room—it's part of an entire trendsetter lifestyle.[16]

---

seekers. Royal Caribbean appeals to high-energy couples and families with hundreds of activities such as rock climbing walls and ice skating. By contrast, the Regent Seven Seas Cruise Line targets mature couples seeking a more elegant ambiance and exotic destinations, such as Asia. Regent invites them to come along as "luxury goes exploring."[17]

Behavioral Segmentation

Behavioral segmentation Dividing a market into groups based on consumers' knowledge, attitude, use, or response to a product.

In **behavioral segmentation**, buyers are divided into groups based on their knowledge, attitude, and use or response to a product. Many marketers believe that behavioral variables are the best starting point for building market segments.

Occasion Segmentation

Buyers can be grouped according to occasions when they make a purchase or use a product. Occasion segmentation helps firms build product use. For example, air travel is triggered by occasions related to business, vacation, or family. Airline advertisements aimed at the business traveler often incorporate service, convenience, and on-time-departure benefits in the offer. Airline marketing aimed at the vacation traveler uses price, interesting destinations, and prepackaged vacations. Airline marketing aimed at the family market often shows children traveling alone to visit a relative, under the watchful eye of an airline employee. A message of this nature is particularly relevant to the single-parent segment.

Occasion segmentation can help firms build product use. For example, Mother's Day has been promoted as a time to take your mother or wife out to eat. St. Patrick's Day has been promoted as a night of celebration. Monday holidays, such as Labor Day and Memorial Day, have been promoted as times to enjoy a mini vacation. These are examples of occasion marketing.

The honeymoon market represents an occasion with excellent potential for the hospitality industry. In many cultures, the honeymoon trip is paid for by parents or other family members. As a gift, the honeymoon package may contain upscale products and services such as a hotel suite and first-class airfare. The Japanese honeymoon market is particularly important to the hospitality industry of Guam, Hawaii, New Zealand, and Australia. Group honeymoon tours have proved to be successful, in which several Japanese newlyweds participate in a tour of one or more destinations.

Benefits Sought

Buyers can also be grouped according to the product benefits they seek. After studying patrons and nonpatrons of three types of restaurants—family popular, atmosphere, and gourmet—one researcher concluded that there are five major appeal categories for restaurant customers.[19] The relative importance of food quality, menu variety, price, atmosphere, and convenience factors across each group was studied. It was found that patrons of family-service restaurants sought convenience and menu. Variety patrons of atmosphere restaurants ranked food quality and atmosphere as the top attributes. Patrons of gourmet restaurants valued quality.

Dunkin' Donuts targets everyday Joes who just don't get what Starbucks is all about. Its targeting and positioning are pretty well summed up in its long-running ad slogan "America Runs on Dunkin'."
Tupungato/Shutterstock.

Marketing Highlight 8.3

Dunkin' Donuts: Targeting the average Joe

A few years back, Dunkin' Donuts paid dozens of faithful customers in Phoenix, Chicago, and Charlotte, North Carolina, $100 a week to buy coffee at Starbucks instead. At the same time, the no-frills coffee chain paid Starbucks customers to make the opposite switch. When it later debriefed the two groups, Dunkin' says it found them so polarized that company researchers dubbed them "tribes," each of whom loathed the very things that made the other tribe loyal to their coffee shop. Dunkin' fans viewed Starbucks as pretentious and trendy, whereas Starbucks loyalists saw Dunkin' as plain and unoriginal. Most Dunkin' customers were just looking for a good cup of coffee and didn't want an upholstered chair to sit in when they drank their coffee. They did not understand the sense of community Starbucks's was trying to create.

Dunkin' Donuts is rapidly expanding into a national coffee powerhouse, on par with Starbucks, the nation's largest coffee chain. But the research confirmed a simple fact: Dunkin' is not Starbucks. In fact, it doesn't want to be. To succeed, Dunkin' must have its own clear vision of just which customers it wants to serve and how. Dunkin' and Starbucks target very different customers, who want very different things from their favorite coffee shops. Starbucks is strongly positioned as a sort of highbrow "third place," with (the first two being the home and office) couches, eclectic music, and art-splashed walls. Dunkin' has a decidedly more lowbrow, "everyman" kind of appeal.

Dunkin' Donuts built itself on serving simple fare at a reasonable price to working-class customers. It gained a reputation as a morning pit stop where everyday folks could get their daily donut and caffeine fix. But recently, to broaden its appeal and fuel expansion, the chain has been moving upscale a bit, but not too far. It has spiffed up its stores and added new menu items, such as lattes and non-breakfast items such as breaded chicken sandwiches with barbeque sauce. Dunkin' has also made dozens of store and atmosphere redesign changes, big and small, ranging from adding free Wi-Fi, digital menu boards, and more electrical outlets for laptops and smartphones to playing relaxing background music. Dunkin' franchisees can now redecorate in any of four Starbucks-esque color schemes, including "Dark Roast," "Cappuccino Blend," and "Jazz Brew," which features "dark orange and brown cozy booth seating, as well as hanging light fixtures that lend a soft glow to wall murals printed with words such as 'break,' 'fresh,' and 'quality.'"

However, as it inches upscale, Dunkin' Donuts is being careful not to alienate its traditional customer base. There are no couches in the remodeled stores. Dunkin' even renamed a new hot sandwich a "stuffed melt" after customers complained that calling it a "panini" was too fancy; it then dropped it altogether when faithful customers thought it was too messy. "We're walking [a fine] line," says the chain's vice president of consumer insights. "The thing about the Dunkin' tribe is, they see through the hype."

Dunkin' Donuts's research showed that, although loyal customers want nicer stores, they were bewildered and turned off by the atmosphere at Starbucks. They groused that crowds of laptop users made it difficult to find a seat. They didn't like Starbucks's "tall," "grande," and "venti" lingo for small, medium, and large coffees. And they couldn't understand why anyone would pay so much for a cup of coffee. It was clear the Dunkin' customers not only felt uncomfortable going to a Starbucks's, but they did not understood the concept. The Starbucks customers that Dunkin' paid to switch were equally uneasy in Dunkin' shops. "The Starbucks people couldn't bear that they weren't special anymore," says the ad executive.

Such opposing opinions aren't surprising, given the differences in the two stores' customers. Dunkin's customers include more middle-income blue- and white-collar workers across all age, race, and income demographics. By contrast, Starbucks targets a higher income, more professional group. But Dunkin's researchers concluded that it was more the ideal, rather than income, that set the two tribes apart: Dunkin's tribe members want to be part of a crowd, whereas members of the Starbucks's tribe want to stand out as individuals. Over the past several years, both Dunkin' Donuts and Starbucks have grown rapidly, each targeting its own tribe of customers and riding the wave of America's growing thirst for coffee. Now, both are looking for more growth by convincing "grab-and-go" morning customers to visit later in the day and stick around longer. Although still smaller than Starbucks—which captures a 33 percent U.S. market share versus Dunkin's 16 percent share—Dunkin' is currently the nation's fastest-growing snack and coffee chain. It hopes that the recent repositioning and upgrades will help keep that momentum going. Dunkin' plans to double its number of U.S. stores by 2020.

However, in refreshing its stores and positioning, Dunkin' Donuts has stayed true to the needs and preferences of the Dunkin' tribe. So far so good. For seven years running, Dunkin' Donuts has ranked number one in the coffee category in a leading customer loyalty and engagement survey, ahead of number two Starbucks. According to the survey, Dunkin' Donuts was the top brand for consistently meeting or exceeding customer expectations with respect to taste, quality, and customer service.

Dunkin' Donuts's targeting and positioning are pretty well summed up in its popular ad slogan "America Runs on Dunkin'." No longer just a morning pit stop, Dunkin' now bills itself as America's favorite all-day, everyday stop for coffee and baked goods. Nothing too fancy—just meeting the everyday, all-day needs of the Dunkin' tribe.[18]

Knowing the benefits sought by customers is useful in two ways. First, managers can develop products with features that provide the benefits their customers are seeking. Second, managers communicate more effectively with their customers if they know what benefits customers seek.

At their W Hotels, guests who indicate they are traveling with a pet receive a pet toy and treat at check-in. In the room they will find pet food and water bowls and a bed for their pet. The pet even receives a special treat as part of their turndown service.[20] Those traveling with pets will place a high value on this feature, while it will have no value to those who do not travel with pets.

Thus, a benefit is a positive outcome received from a product feature. Those product features that create positive outcomes for guests create value. Features that do not offer positive outcomes for the guest will have no value.

User Status

Many markets can be segmented into nonusers, former users, potential users, first-time users, and regular users of a product. High-market-share companies such as major airlines are particularly interested in keeping regular users and attracting potential users. Potential users and regular users often require different marketing appeals.

Usage Rate

Markets can also be segmented into light, medium, and heavy product users. Heavy users are often a small percentage of the market but account for a high percentage of total consumption. For example, researchers discovered that 4.1 percent of airline travelers account for 70.4 percent of airline trips, and thus airlines were eager to capture this lucrative market.[21] Clearly, marketers are eager to identify heavy users and build a marketing mix to attract them. Many hospitality firms spread their marketing resources evenly across all potential customers. Seasoned marketers identify heavy users and focus marketing strategies toward them.

Loyalty Status

A market can also be segmented on the basis of consumer loyalty. Consumers of hospitality products can be loyal to brands, such as Courtyard by Marriott, or to companies, such as Qantas Airlines. Others are only somewhat loyal. They may be loyal to two or three brands or favor one brand but buy others. Still other buyers show no brand loyalty at all. They want variety or simply buy whichever brand is cheapest or most convenient. These people will stop at a Hilton Garden Inn or Courtyard by Marriott, depending on which they see first when looking for a motel.

A major reason for increasing customer loyalty is that "loyal customers are price insensitive compared to brand-shifting patrons."[22] In the hospitality and travel industries, marketers attempt to build brand loyalty through relationship marketing. Although manufacturing companies often lack direct contact with their customers, most hospitality and travel marketers do have direct contact. They can develop a guest history database and use this information to customize offers and customer communications.

Millennials do not want to stay 20 times before they get significant rewards. They rate "ability to value me" and "ability to understand my needs" as the most important attributes in creating loyalty.[23] A challenge for hotel and airline marketers will be transitioning the tiered loyalty programs, developed for the baby boomers, to programs that will be meaningful for millennials. They want to feel special from the moment they arrive at the hotel for the first time; they desire experiences that are customized for them.[24] The traditional tier-based programs that require the guest to stay a number of nights before they receive their rewards are, therefore, less effective.[25] citizenM, a hotel brand targeted at millennials, has a one-level loyalty program called "citizen," and when you join, you instantly get 15 percent off the room rates and a more liberal cancellation policy.

Using Multiple Segmentation Bases

Marketers rarely limit their segmentation analysis to only one or a few variables. Rather, they often use multiple segmentation bases in an effort to identify smaller, better-defined target groups. Several business information services—such as

Nielsen, Acxiom, and Experian—provide multivariable segmentation systems that merge geographic, demographic, lifestyle, and behavioral data to help companies segment their markets down to zip codes, neighborhoods, and even households.

One of the leading consumer segmentation systems is Experian's Mosaic USA system. It classifies U.S. households into one of 71 lifestyle segments and 19 levels of affluence, based on specific consumer demographics, interests, behaviors, and passions. Mosaic USA segments carry exotic names such as Birkenstocks and Beemers, Bohemian Groove, Sports Utility Families, Colleges and Cafes, Hispanic Harmony, Rolling the Dice, Small Town Shallow Pockets, and True Grit Americans.[26] Such colorful names help bring the segments to life.

For example, the Birkenstocks and Beemers group is located in the Middle Class Melting Pot level of affluence and consists of 40- to 65-year-olds who have achieved financial security and left the urban rat race for rustic and artsy communities located near small cities. They enjoy cruises and warm weather vacations. They enjoy cooking at home and going out to casual restaurants. Promotions to these restaurants will attract this group.[27]

Bohemian Groove consumers, part of the Significant Singles group, are urban singles aged 45 to 65 living in apartments in smaller cities such as Sacramento, California, and Harrisburg, Pennsylvania. They tend to be laid back, maintain a large circle of friends, and stay active in community groups. They enjoy music, hobbies, and the creative arts. When they go out to eat, they choose places such as the Macaroni Grill or Red Robin.

Mosaic USA and other such systems can help marketers to segment people and locations into marketable groups of like-minded consumers. Each segment has its own pattern of likes, dislikes, lifestyles, and purchase behaviors. Using the Mosaic system, marketers can paint a surprisingly precise picture of who you are and what you might buy. Such rich segmentation provides a powerful tool for marketers of all kinds. It can help companies identify and better understand key customer segments, reach them more efficiently, and tailor market offerings and messages to their specific needs.

Requirements for Effective Segmentation

Although there are many ways to segment a market, all are not equally effective. For example, buyers of restaurant meals could be divided into blond and brunette customers. But hair color does not affect the purchase of restaurant meals. Furthermore, if all restaurant customers buy the same number of meals each month and believe all restaurant meals are of equal quality and are willing to pay the same price, the company would not benefit from segmenting this market.

To be useful, market segments must have the following characteristics:

- *Measurability:* The degree to which the segment's size and purchasing power can be measured. Certain segmentation variables are difficult to measure, such as the size of the segment of teenagers who drink beer primarily to rebel against their parents.

- *Accessibility:* The degree to which segments can be assessed and served. One of the authors found that 20 percent of a college restaurant's customers were frequent patrons. However, frequent patrons lacked any common characteristics. They included faculty, staff, and students. There was no usage difference among part-time, full-time, or class year of the students. Although the market segment had been identified, there was no way to access the heavy-user segment.

- *Substantiality:* The degree to which segments are large or profitable enough to serve as markets. A segment should be the largest possible homogeneous group economically feasible to support a tailored marketing program. For example, large metropolitan areas can support many different ethnic restaurants, but in a smaller town, Thai, Vietnamese, and Moroccan food restaurants might not survive.

- *Actionability:* The degree to which effective programs can be designed for attracting and serving segments. A small airline, for example, identified seven market segments, but its staff and budget were too small to develop separate marketing programs for each segment.

■■■ Market Targeting

Marketing segmentation reveals a company's market-segment opportunities. The firm has to evaluate the various segments and decide how many and which ones to target. We now look at how companies evaluate and select target markets.

Evaluating Market Segments

When evaluating different market segments, a firm must look at three factors: segment size and growth, segment-structured attractiveness, and company objectives and resources.

Segment Size and Growth

A company must first collect and analyze data on current segment sales growth rates and expected profitability for various segments. It will be interested in segments that have the right size and growth characteristics, but "right size and growth" is a relative matter. Some companies want to target segments with large current sales, a high growth rate, and a high profit margin. However, the largest, fastest-growing segments are not always the most attractive ones for every company. Smaller companies often find they lack the skills and resources needed to serve the larger segments or that these segments are too competitive. Such companies may select segments that are smaller but are potentially more profitable.

Segment Structural Attractiveness

A segment might have desirable size and growth and still not offer attractive profits. The company must examine several major structural factors that affect long-run segment attractiveness. For example, a segment is less attractive if it already contains many strong and aggressive competitors. The existence of many actual or potential substitute products may limit prices and profits. For example, supermarkets have entered the take-away-meals market that has had an impact on the fast-food restaurant market. The relative power of buyers also affects segment attractiveness. If the buyers in a segment possess strong bargaining power relative to sellers, they will force prices down, demand more quality services, and set competitors against one another. Large buyers, such as an airline with a hub in Dallas that needs 50 rooms a night for flight crews, will be able to negotiate a low price. Finally, a segment may not be attractive if it contains powerful suppliers who control prices or reduce the quality of ordered goods and services. Suppliers tend to be powerful when they are large and concentrated, when few substitutes exist, or when the supplied product is an important input. In certain areas, restaurants specializing in fresh seafood are limited to a few suppliers.

Landry's Inc. decided to sell Joe's Crab Shack, popular casual seafood restaurant chain, to concentrate on higher-end restaurants. Eleven years later a much larger Landry's bought the chain out of bankruptcy.
Courtesy of Philip T. Kotler.

Company Objectives and Resources

All companies must consider their own objectives and resources in relation to available segments. Some attractive segments can be dismissed quickly because they do not mesh with the company's long-run objectives. Although such segments might be tempting in themselves, they might divert a company's attention and energies away from its main goal. Or they might be a poor choice from an environmental, political, or social responsibility viewpoint. In Chapter 3, we mentioned that Landry's decided to sell Joe's Crab Shack restaurants because it wanted to focus on higher-end restaurants gaming. The sale gave Landry's $192 million to invest in higher-end restaurant chains and eliminated 120 restaurants from Landry's management oversight. Landry's bought the much smaller chain back 11 years later, plus a group of 25 Brick House Tavern restaurants for 55 million.

If a segment fits the company's objectives, it must then decide whether it possesses the skills and resources to succeed in that segment. If the company lacks the strengths needed to compete successfully in a segment and cannot readily obtain them, it should exit or not enter the segment. A company should enter segments only where it can gain sustainable advantages over competitors. Landry's sold Joe's Crab Shack to focus on higher-end restaurants. In 2017, Landry's bought the chain out of bankruptcy for $55 million ($137 million less than it sold for) and received the 25 unit Brickhouse Tavern in the deal. Joe's Crab Shack now only had 75 units and Landry's planned on keeping the best performing 60 units and at the same time selling the Brick House Tavern chain, thus reducing their investment even further. Although Joe's Crab Shack did not originally fit in their long-term plans, Landry's saw an opportunity to gain the best units back and operate a much smaller Joe's Crab Shack chain. One that would contribute to cash flow, and the smaller chain in a lower-end segment could now be managed by a Landry's, a much larger company than it was in 2006. The Landry's example shows that selection of target markets can change over time, but they should be carefully planned and fit into the strategic plans of the organization.[28]

Selecting Market Segments

After evaluating different segments, the company must decide which and how many segments to serve. This is a problem of target-market selection. A target market consists of a set of buyers who share common needs or characteristics that the company decides to serve. Figure 8–2 shows that a firm can adopt one of three market-coverage strategies: undifferentiated marketing, differentiated marketing, and concentrated marketing.

Undifferentiated Marketing

Using an undifferentiated marketing strategy, a company ignores market segmentation differences and goes after the entire market with one market offer. It focuses on what is common in the needs of consumers rather than on differences. It designs a marketing plan that will reach the greatest number of buyers. Mass distribution and mass advertising serve as the basic tools to create a superior image in consumers' minds.

Undifferentiated marketing provides cost economies. The narrow product line keeps down production, inventory, and transportation costs. An undifferentiated advertising program holds down advertising costs. The neglect of segmentation holds down marketing research costs and product development costs.

Public cafeterias sometimes believe they fit this model, but in fact, observation of their customer mix usually reveals a disproportionate number of middle-aged and older customers.

Figure 8–2
Three alternative market-coverage strategies.

(a) No market segmentation
(b) Complete segmentation
(c) Market segmentation by income classes 1, 2, and 3
(d) Market segmentation by age classes A and B
(e) Market segmentation by income-age class

Most contemporary marketers have strong doubts about the strategy in today's competitive environment. It is difficult to develop a product and brand that will satisfy all or even most consumers. When several competitors aim at the largest segments, the inevitable result is heavy competition. Small companies generally find it impossible to compete directly against giants and are forced to adopt market-niche strategies. Larger segments may become less profitable because of heavy marketing costs, including the possibility of price cutting and price wars.

Differentiated Marketing

Using a differentiated marketing strategy, a company targets several market segments and designs separate offers for each. AccorHotels, a French company, has 18 brands of hotels. Included in its brands are international luxury hotels (Sofitel), three-star hotels (Novotel), two-star hotels (Ibis), limited-service hotels (Formula One), and extended-stay hotels featuring served apartments (The Sebel). This segmentation has allowed Accor to become one of the world's foremost hotel groups.

Differentiated marketing typically produces more total sales than undifferentiated marketing. Accor gets a higher hotel room market share with three different brands in one city than if it only had one brand in a city. Sofitel attracts the upscale business traveler. Novotel attracts the mid-scale traveler, whereas Formula One attracts families and the budget traveler. Accor offers a different marketing mix to each target market. At the same time, it has to have marketing plans, marketing research, forecasting, sales analysis, promotion planning, and advertising for each brand. Accor also has two differentiated brands for millennials: Mama Shelter offers an urban concept and lively experience in modern design, whereas JOE&JOE provides a communal place for budget-minded travelers.

Concentrated Marketing

Concentrated marketing is especially appealing to companies with limited resources. Instead of going for a small share of a large market, the firm pursues a large share of one or a few small markets.

There are many examples of concentrated marketing. Four Seasons Hotels, Six Senses, and Rosewood Hotels concentrate on the high-priced hotel room market. Through concentrated marketing, hospitality companies achieve a strong market position in the segments that they serve, thanks to their greater knowledge of those segments' needs. The company also enjoys many operative economies. If the segment is well chosen, the company can earn a high rate of return on investment.

Chuck E. Cheese is a restaurant that targets families with young children. It is difficult to take young children to a table service restaurant, as they get bored easily. Many restaurants provide crayons and paper placemats with games to entertain the children. Chili's offers a computer tablet with games to keep adults as well as children occupied. Chuck E. Cheese has developed an entire restaurant concept focused on families with young kids. It has arcade type games and offers basic food that children enjoy including pizza and sandwiches. Some meals come with tokens for the games; the tokens are also sold separately. Children love coming to Chuck E. Cheese. It provides a nice environment for young families to spend time together.[29] For more on Chuck E. Cheese, see Case 21.

At the same time, concentrated marketing involves higher than normal risks. The particular market segment can turn sour. For this reason, many companies prefer to operate in two or more markets.

Micromarketing—Local Marketing and SoLoMo

Differentiated and concentrated marketers tailor their offers and marketing programs to meet the needs of various market segments and niches. At the same time, however, they do not customize their offers to each individual customer. **Micromarketing** is the practice of tailoring products and marketing programs to suit the tastes of specific individuals and locations. Rather than seeing a customer in every individual, micromarketers see the individual in every customer. One form of micromarketing is **local marketing**.

Local marketing involves tailoring brands and promotions to the needs and wants of local customer groups—cities, neighborhoods, and specific restaurant/hotel/store locations. For example, Omni Hotels and Resorts develop its restaurants to reflect the local culinary offering of the community where the hotel is located.

Micromarketing The practice of tailoring products and marketing programs to suit the tastes of specific individuals and locations.

Local marketing Tailoring brands and promotions to the needs and wants of local customer groups—cities, neighborhoods, and specific restaurant/hotel/store locations.

Marriott's Renaissance Hotels' Navigators and "Live Life to Discover" program help guests to experience "the hidden gems around the unique neighborhood of each hotel through the eyes of those who know it best." SeventyFour/Shutterstock.

SoLoMo (social+local+mobile) Marketing that targets on-the-go consumers as they come and go in key local market areas.

Degree of product homogeneity Undifferentiated marketing is more suited for homogeneous products. Products that can vary in design, such as restaurants and hotels, are more suited to differentiation or concentration.

Market homogeneity If buyers have the same tastes, buy a product in the same amounts, and react the same way to marketing efforts, undifferentiated marketing is appropriate.

Competitors' strategies When competitors use segmentation, undifferentiated marketing can be suicidal. Conversely, when competitors use undifferentiated marketing, a firm can gain an advantage by using differentiated or concentrated marketing.

Advances in communications technology have given rise to new high-tech versions location-based marketing. Thanks to the explosion of net-connected smartphones with GPS capabilities and location-based social networks; companies can now track consumers' whereabouts closely and gear their offers accordingly. Using location-based social media check-in services such as Foursquare or/and local-marketing deal-of-the-day services such as Groupon, retailers can engage consumers with local deals and information.

Increasingly, location-based marketing is going mobile, reaching on-the-go consumers as they come and go in key local market areas. It's called **SoLoMo (social+local+mobile)**.[30] For example, a local restaurant can decide to implement SoLoMo marketing, using platforms such as Foursquare, Yelp, and Facebook, to offer deals only to those located in your neighborhood or city. There are also new sites being developed for SoLoMo marketing, including Kapture, SidewalkAd, and LocalBox.[31] Professor Bill Carroll states, "The Mark Hotel in New York City uses Foursquare's list functionality as a virtual extension of its concierge services." Guests looking for local dining and sightseeing suggestions can follow The Mark on Foursquare. The hotel benefits by promoting its own food and beverage options in its recommendations.[32]

Marriott's Renaissance Hotels has launched its Navigator program which hyper-localizes guest experiences by recommendations for food, shopping, entertainment, and cultural experiences at each destination. This helps guests find the best local experiences and live like local at each of its 160 lifestyle hotels around the world.[33]

When using deals of local marketing, one has to be careful that the business generated by the promotion is profitable. The promotion should be priced so the restaurant makes money on the promotion after paying promotional costs. Also, do promotions only when you have excess capacity to handle the promotion. For example, if you are busy on Friday and Saturday night exclude these periods from the promotion.

Choosing a Market-Coverage Strategy

Companies need to consider several factors in choosing a market-coverage strategy. One factor is the company's resources. When the company's resources are limited, concentrated marketing makes the most sense. Another factor is the **degree of product homogeneity**. Undifferentiated marketing is more suited for homogeneous products. Products that can vary in design, such as restaurants and hotels, are more suited to differentiation or concentration. The product's life-cycle stage must also be considered. When a firm introduces a new product, it may be practical to launch only one version, so undifferentiated or concentrated marketing makes the most sense. For example, the early McDonald's had a very limited selection compared with their present menu selection. In the mature stage of the product life cycle, differentiated marketing becomes more feasible. Another factor is **market homogeneity**. If buyers have the same tastes, buy a product in the same amounts, and react the same way to marketing efforts, undifferentiated marketing is appropriate. Finally, **competitors' strategies** are important. When competitors use segmentation, undifferentiated marketing can be suicidal. Conversely, when competitors use undifferentiated marketing, a firm can gain an advantage by using differentiated or concentrated marketing.

Socially Responsible Target Marketing

Smart targeting helps companies become more efficient and effective by focusing on the segments that they can satisfy best and most profitably. Targeting also benefits consumers; companies serve specific groups of consumers with offers carefully tailored to their needs. However, target marketing sometimes generates controversy and concern. The biggest issues usually involve the targeting of vulnerable or disadvantaged consumers with controversial or potentially harmful products.

For example, fast-food chains have generated controversy over the years by their attempts to target inner-city minority consumers. They've been accused of pitching their high-fat, salt-laden fare to low-income, urban residents who are much more likely than suburbanites to be heavy consumers.

Children are seen as an especially vulnerable audience. Marketers have been criticized for their marketing efforts directed toward children. Critics worry that enticing premium offers and high-powered advertising appeals will overwhelm children's defenses. In recent years, for instance, McDonald's has been criticized by various health advocates and parent groups concerned that its popular Happy Meals offers—featuring trinkets and other items tied in with children's movies—create a too powerful connection between children and the often fat- and calorie-laden meals. McDonald's has responded by putting the Happy Meal on a diet, cutting the overall calorie count by 20 percent, adding fruit to every meal, and promoting Happy Meals only with milk, water, and juice.[34]

Today's marketers are also using sophisticated analytical techniques to track consumers' digital movements and to build detailed customer profiles containing highly personal information. Such profiles can then be used to hypertarget individual consumers with personalized brand messages and offers. Hypertargeting can benefit both marketers and consumers, getting the right brand information into the hands of the right customers. However, if taken too far or used wrongly, hypertargeting can harm consumers more than benefit them. Marketers must use these new targeting tools responsibly.

■■■ Market Positioning

Once a company has chosen its target-market segments, it must decide on a value proposition—how it will create differentiated value for targeted markets and what positions to occupy in those segments. A **product's position** is the way the product is defined by consumers on important attributes—the place the product occupies in consumers' minds relative to competing products. Consumers are overloaded with information about products and services. They cannot reevaluate products every time they make a buying decision. To simplify buying decisions, consumers organize products into categories—they "position" products and companies in their minds.

Marketers do not want to leave their products' positions to chance. They plan positions that will give their products the greatest advantage in selected target markets and then design marketing mixes to create the planned positions. In the fast-food hamburger business, Wendy's promotes never-frozen meat, hot off the grill; Burger King is known for its flame-broiled food; and Smashburger smashes its burger on the grill to sear it. Smashburger hopes the customer will perceive it to have a better quality burger, as it charges more than Wendy's or Burger King.

A hotel brand's position can be viewed from two perspectives—that of the brand's management and that of the guests. The brand's management must have a clear concept of the hotel's intended position. Its promotional efforts must articulate not only what the brand offers, but how its offerings are different from those of other brands. In the final analysis, a brand's position is determined by its customers.

Positioning Strategies

Marketers can follow several positioning strategies. They can position their products based on **specific product attributes**. Product attribute positioning can be dangerous. The attribute has to create a benefit for the consumer. Subway has been successful in positioning its sandwiches as a healthy alternative to fried foods and hamburgers. It features eight sandwiches that have six grams of fat or less. Its "Fresh Fit for Kids" program is aimed at parents. Subway has been effective in

---

Product position The way a product is defined by consumers on important attributes—the place it occupies in consumers' minds relative to competing products.

Specific product attributes Price and product features can be used to position a product.

promoting nutrition, without sacrificing flavor, as nutrition is an important food attribute to many people. Not all companies are successful in selecting meaningful product attributes. The Stamford Hotel in Singapore advertised that it is the world's tallest hotel (now the tallest in Southeast Asia). Most people are interested in service, location, and other attributes when choosing a hotel, but height is not a product attribute that is valued by many people. In fact hotel guests often prefer to stay on lower floors as they perceive they will have a better chance of survival in case of emergency. If one promotes a product attribute that is not usually associated as a benefit, the benefits must be communicated. The Marina Bay Sands Singapore has done a good job at promoting the benefit of height for its swimming pool and SkyBar with these messages: "Imagine soaking in the world's largest rooftop infinity pool and gazing down on the glittering expanse of the city from 57 levels above. After your swim, sunbathe on a luxurious poolside lounger, or relax in the shade of a palm tree with a glass of champagne in hand." "Savour the view from the Marina Bay Sands SkyPark observation deck, the perfect spot from which to survey the world below. Take in the vista of the city spread out before you and the panoramic view of the Singapore Strait as you sip on cocktail creations by Spago mixologists."[35] Notice how the messages from the Marina Bay Sands have an emotional appeal, whereas simply stating you are the tallest hotel is an unemotional fact. In the hospitality industry, appealing to emotions is important.

Finally, products can be positioned against another product class. Cruise ships positioned themselves against other vacation alternatives such as destination resorts, and bed and breakfasts (B&Bs) are positioned as a home-like alternative to other forms of lodging. Airbnb provides a marketplace for individuals to rent their house, apartment, or room to a traveler. Airbnb positions itself as providing unique travel experiences through the diversity of its offerings. These offerings include a lighthouse in Croatia, castles, underground homes, and John Steinbeck's writers' studio. It also includes a room in a common home. Airbnb offers some very inexpensive places to stay in most cities; however, it does not want to position itself as an inexpensive place to stay. Instead Airbnb states, "Airbnb connects people to unique travel experiences."[36]

Choosing and Implementing a Positioning Strategy

Some firms find it easy to choose a differentiation and positioning strategy. For example, a firm well known for quality in certain segments will go after this position in a new segment if there are enough buyers seeking quality. But in many cases, two or more firms will go after the same position. Then each will have to find other ways to set itself apart. Each firm must differentiate its offer by building a unique bundle of benefits that appeals to a substantial group within the segment.

Above all else, a brand's positioning must serve the needs and preferences of well-defined target markets. For example, as discussed previously, although both Dunkin' Donuts and Starbucks are coffee and snack shops, they target very different customers, who want very different things from their favorite coffee seller. Starbucks targets more upscale professionals with more highbrow positioning. In contrast, Dunkin' Donuts targets the "average Joe" with a decidedly more lowbrow, "everyman" kind of positioning. Yet each brand succeeds because it creates just the right value proposition for its unique mix of customers.

Competitive advantage An advantage over competitors gained by offering consumers greater value either through lower prices or by providing more benefits that justify higher prices.

The differentiation and positioning task consists of three steps: identifying a set of differentiating **competitive advantages** on which to build a position, choosing the right competitive advantages, and selecting an overall positioning strategy. The company must then effectively communicate and deliver the chosen position to the market.

Differentiating Competitive Advantages

A hospitality company or a visitor destination must differentiate its products/services from those of its competitors. Differentiation can occur by physical attributes, service, personnel, location, or image.

Physical Attribute Differentiation

Classic hotels such as the Waldorf-Astoria in New York, Palmer House in Chicago, Brown Palace in Denver, and Raffles in Singapore.

The five-star Casa Santo Domingo Hotel in Antigua, Guatemala, was built into the ruins of a sixteenth-century monastery partially destroyed in an earthquake. The architects and interior designers masterfully blended new construction with the remains of the old monastery, including a crypt. The roofless remains of the sanctuary, surrounded by thousands of blazing candles, serves as a popular site for evening weddings.

Unfortunately, many hotels, restaurants, and airlines lack physical differentiation. Motels in particular follow a standard architectural look that provides no differentiation. When this happens, price becomes the primary differentiating factor.

Restaurants such as Chez Panisse in Berkeley, Lidia's in Kansas City, and the chain Chipotle Mexican Grill use natural/organic foods to differentiate themselves. These restaurants have developed a network of farmers to provide fresh products produced to each restaurant's standards.[37]

Differentiation that excites the consumer and offers something new can lead to excellent public relations opportunities, customer loyalty, and greater profits.

The Raffles Hotel is one of the most recognized buildings in Singapore. Alex Cimbal/Shutterstock.

Service Differentiation

Hospitality companies differentiate themselves on service. For example, Hilton offers Hilton Huanying, as a point of service differentiation for the growing Chinese market in 110 of its hotels in markets heavily frequented by Chinese travelers. Huanying takes its name from the Chinese word for "welcome." Hilton conducted market research to determine preferences and needs of Chinese travelers. The service includes a welcome note in simplified Chinese upon arrival, at least one television channel in Mandarin, tea kettles in the room, and a Chinese breakfast.[38]

Unwanted differentiation occurs when a company consistently provides a horrible level of guest service. Such a reputation often requires a change in management or ownership to correct. It is strange that so many members of service industries ignore good customer service. The basics of good customer service are comparable to the Golden Rule: "Do unto others as you would have them do unto you."

Mature consumers place special value on friendly staff, guest name recognition by staff, assistance in making a product decision, opportunities to socialize, and no pressure to leave. These simple services can reap large rewards for members of the hospitality industry.[39] Because so many companies overlook the importance of good service, those who truly emphasize service will achieve positive differentiation.

Personnel Differentiation

Companies can gain a strong competitive advantage through hiring and retaining better people than their competitors. Thus, Singapore Airlines enjoys an excellent reputation largely because of the grade of its flight attendants. Southwest Airlines claimed that a competitor could replicate its low-cost system but would find it more difficult to create the spirit of Southwest's employees.

Personnel differentiation requires that a company select its customer-contact people carefully and train them well. These personnel must be competent and must possess the required skills and knowledge. They need to be courteous, friendly, and respectful. They must serve customers with consistency and accuracy, and they must make an effort to understand their customers, communicate clearly with them, and respond quickly to customer requests and problems. We will discuss how to create personnel differentiation in Chapter 10.

The restaurants along the ocean on Samos Island, Greece, have a competitive advantage over those restaurants that are not on the water. Pawel Kazmierczak/123RF.

Location Differentiation

Location can provide a strong competitive advantage. For example, hotels facing Central Park in New York City have a competitive advantage over hotels a block away. Motels located right off a freeway exit can enjoy double-digit advantages in percentage of occupancy over hotels a block away. Hotels along the River Walk in San Antonio, Texas, have a strong advantage over hotels located off the river. International airlines often use their location as a point of differentiation in their home markets. For example, Qantas promotes itself as Australia's airline and has a strong following in its home market. Hospitality and travel firms should look for benefits created by their location, keeping in mind that this advantage is subject to chance. Factors such as a new highway bypass or criminal activity in a neighborhood can quickly turn an advantage into a problem.

Taco John's 425 quick-service restaurants are located in 25 states. However, their strength has been what the company calls "the Heartland of America." The company started in Cheyenne, Wyoming, and then expanded to places like Scottsbluff, Nebraska, and Rapid City, South Dakota. Most of its locations are still in small to midsized Midwestern towns where it has obviously been successful. It is questionable if this success could be duplicated in towns such as San Antonio, Texas, or Los Angeles. Hospitality companies are well advised to seriously consider what geographic factors may have created their success before expanding too widely. Perhaps the sauces or something else in the product are perfect for people in Nebraska or Minnesota but might not be acceptable in other geographic regions.[40]

Image Differentiation

Even when competing offers look the same, buyers may perceive a difference based on company or brand image. Thus, hospitality companies need to work to establish images that differentiate them from competitors. A company or visitor destination image should convey a singular or distinctive message that communicates the product's major benefits and positioning. In the case of visitor destinations such as tropical locations, it is often impossible to distinguish the advertising of one from another. Most seem to employ beaches, clear water, and other features that do not provide any differentiation from other beach resorts. Developing a strong and distinctive image calls for creativity and hard work. A positive image must be earned. Chili's developed an image as a casual and fun neighborhood restaurant. This image must be supported by everything that the company says and does.

A common mistake made by new owners/operators of a property is to implement a new image/positioning strategy before fully understanding the property, the community, and the market. New owners of the Telluride Ski and Golf Resort announced they would not make this mistake. Instead of announcing grand changes, the new owners said, "Our intentions are to honor unique characteristics that define Telluride. We want to preserve Telluride's authenticity, charm, and casual atmosphere." They further said that they would seek input from the community to develop a shared vision of what the resort should look like.[41]

Starwood Hotels and Resorts Worldwide, acquired recently by Marriott International, has differentiated its hotels, creating an image along emotional and experiential lines for some of the brands:

Sheraton. With the tagline "You don't stay here, you belong," Sheraton is about warm, comforting, and casual. Its core value centers on "connections," an image aided by the hotel's alliance with Yahoo!, which cofounded the Yahoo! Link@Sheraton lobby kiosks and cyber cafes.

Four Points by Sheraton. For the self-sufficient traveler, Four Points strives to be honest, uncomplicated, and comfortable. The brand is all about providing a high level of comfort and little indulgences like free high-speed internet access and bottled water. Its ads feature apple pies and talk about providing guests with "the comforts of home."

W. With a brand personality defined as flirty, for the insider, and an escape, W offers guests unique experiences around the warmth of cool.

Westin. Westin's emphasis on "personal, instinctive, and renewal" has led to a new sensory welcome featuring a white tea scent, signature music and lighting, and refreshing towels. Each room features Westin's own "Heavenly Beds," sold exclusively in the retail market through Nordstrom, further enhancing the brand's upscale image.[42]

Choosing the Right Competitive Advantages

Suppose that a company is fortunate enough to discover several potential competitive advantages. It must now choose the ones on which it will build its positioning strategy.

How Many Differences?

Many marketers think that companies should aggressively promote only one benefit to the target market. Adman Rosser Reeves, for example, said a company should develop a unique selling proposition (USP) for each brand and stick to it. Each brand should pick an attribute and tout itself as number one on that attribute. Buyers tend to remember number one better, especially in an overcommunicated society. Thus, Motel 6 consistently promotes itself as the lowest-priced national chain, and Ritz-Carlton promotes itself as a value leader. What are some number-one positions to promote? The major ones are best quality, best service, lowest price, best value, and best location. A company that hammers away at a position that is important to its target market and consistently delivers on it probably will become the best known and remembered.

Other marketers think that companies should position themselves on more than one differentiating factor. A restaurant may claim that it has the best steaks and service. A hotel may claim that it offers the best value and location. Today, in a time when the mass market is fragmenting into many small market segments, companies are trying to broaden their positioning strategies to appeal to more segments. For example, the Boulders in Arizona promotes itself as a top golf resort and as a luxury resort, giving guests a chance to experience the flora and fauna of the Sonoran Desert. By doing this, the Boulders can attract both golfers and nongolfers.

However, as companies increase the number of claims for their brands, they risk disbelief and a loss of clear positioning. In general, a company needs to avoid three major positioning errors. The first is **underpositioning**, or failing ever to position the company at all. Some companies discover that buyers have only a vague idea of the company or that they do not really know anything special about it. Many independent hotels trying to capture an international market are underpositioned. The Seoul Plaza Hotel, a luxury hotel in Seoul, Korea, is not well known in Europe or North America. To establish positions in distant markets, hotels like the Seoul Plaza are affiliating with marketing groups such as "Leading Hotels of the World" and "Preferred Hotels." The second positioning error is **overpositioning**, or giving buyers too narrow a picture of the company. Finally, companies must avoid **confused positioning**, leaving buyers with a confused image of a company. Good positioning helps build brand loyalty. In the case of hotels, it may not be enough to simply satisfy guests. Satisfied customers do not repurchase unless they are also attitudinally brand loyal.[43]

Underpositioning Failing ever to position the company at all.

Overpositioning Giving buyers a too-narrow picture of the company.

Confused positioning Leaving buyers with a confused image of a company.

Which Differences?

Not all brand differences are meaningful or worthwhile. Not every difference makes a good differentiator. Each difference has the potential to create company costs as

Casino resorts, such as the Marina Bay Sands in Singapore, need to gain the trust of their customers and establish an emotional bond with them. Marina Bay Sands.

well as customer benefits. Therefore, a hospitality company or a visitor destination must carefully select the ways in which it will distinguish itself from competitors. A difference is worth establishing to the extent that it satisfies the following criteria:

- *Important.* The difference delivers a highly valued benefit to target buyers. In the case of a visitor destination, personal safety has become a top benefit.
- *Distinctive.* Competitors do not offer the difference, or the company can offer it in a more distinctive way.
- *Superior.* The difference is superior to other ways that customers might obtain the same benefit.
- *Communicable.* The difference is communicable and visible to buyers.
- *Preemptive.* Competitors cannot easily copy the difference.
- *Affordable.* Buyers can afford to pay for the difference.
- *Profitable.* The company can introduce the difference profitability.

Some competitive advantages may quickly be ruled out because they are too slight, too costly to develop, or too inconsistent with the company's profile. Suppose that a company is designing its positioning strategy and has narrowed its list of possible competitive advantages to four. The company needs a framework for selecting the one that makes the most sense to develop.

Customers of casinos exhibit two critical reasons for maintaining a long-term relationship and recommending a particular casino to others. These are trust and emotional ties.[44] A positioning statement that emphasizes game pay-out will not succeed if customers don't believe this statement. Likewise, a positioning statement that emphasizes the latest technology may not succeed if customers feel the casino is cold and mechanical rather than a place to which they can relate.

Selecting an Overall Positioning Strategy

Value proposition The full mix of benefits on which a brand is differentiated and positioned.

The full positioning of a brand is called the brand's **value proposition**, the full mix of benefits on which a brand is differentiated and positioned. It is the answer to the customer question, "Why should I buy your brand?" Value Place is a low-priced hotel with a full kitchen and a low weekly rate. Sometimes low-priced hotels attract persons who do not have the credit or money to rent an apartment, drug dealers, and prostitutes. This can create an unsafe atmosphere. Value Place stresses safety as a point of differentiation in their value proposition. They stress the affordability, cleanliness, and safety of their properties. Fairmont, an upscale hotel chain, values providing exceptional service experiences that will create favorable memories for its guests. Firehouse subs uses "Piping hot and piled high for maximum deliciousness." Red Lobster uses "Sea Food Differently." Through these value propositions these companies strive to influence the perception prospective customers have of their brand.

Communicating and Delivering the Chosen Position

Having chosen positioning characteristics and a positioning statement, companies must communicate their positions to targeted customers. All of a company's marketing mix efforts must support its positioning strategy. If a company decides to build service superiority, for example, it must hire service-oriented employees, provide training programs, reward employees for providing good service, and develop sales and advertising messages to broadcast its service superiority.

Building and maintaining a consistent positioning strategy is not easy; many counterforces are at work. Advertising agencies hired by the company may not like a selected position and may overtly or covertly work against it. New management may not understand the positioning strategy. Budgets may be cut for critical support programs such as employee training or sales promotion. The development of an effective position requires a consistent, long-run program with continuous support by management, employees, and vendors.

Olive Garden opened a restaurant in Tuscany, Olive Garden Riserva di Fizzano, and developed the Culinary Institute of Tuscany. It added Tuscan dishes to its menu, sent its chefs to the Culinary Institute of Tuscany, and developed a Tuscan farmhouse design for its restaurants. It also included recipes and cooking tips on its Web site. The restaurant and Culinary Institute in Italy help communicate Olive Garden's position as an authentic Italian restaurant. Its advertisements enforced this by featuring Italian families dining at Olive Garden.[45]

A company's positioning decisions determine who its competitors will be. When selecting a positioning strategy, a company should review its competitive strengths and weaknesses and select a position that places it in a superior position against its competitors.

Positioning is enhanced and supported by creating memorable customer experiences. Hospitality companies provide many services throughout the day. Most of these become routine and are indistinguishable from competitors. The key to creating memorable and differentiating customer experiences is not simply to improve them but to layer an enjoyable/memorable experience on top.[46]

Positioning Measurement: Perceptual Mapping

In planning their differentiation and positioning strategies, marketers often prepare perceptual positioning maps that show consumer perceptions of their brand versus those of competing products on important dimensions. Figure 8–3 is a perceptual positioning map of hotels plotted on the attributes of price and perceived service. On this map we see there is a correlation between service and price; as price goes up, so does service.

Some hotels appear to offer a better value than others. For example, Italia offers a little higher level of service than the Palace but is less expensive. Two-by-two perceptual maps provide an easy-to-read picture, but one often has to study multiple maps plotting different attributes to obtain a good feel of the marketplace. Perceptual maps can also be developed using consumers' perceptions of a number of product attributes. Increased competition or an ineffective positioning strategy can make repositioning necessary. Perceptual maps provide data supporting the need for repositioning.

Figure 8–3
Positioning map of service level versus price.
Source: Lovelock, Christopher H; Wirtz, Jochen, Services Marketing: People, Technology, Strategy, 7th Ed., ©2011, p. 74. Reprinted and electronically reproduced by permission of Pearson Education, Inc., New York, NY.

CHAPTER REVIEW

I. **Markets.** A market is the set of all actual and potential buyers of a product. Most companies have moved away from mass marketing and toward target marketing. The three major steps in target marketing are: 1. market segmentation, dividing a market into distinct groups that might require separate products and/or marketing mixes; 2. market targeting, evaluating each segment's attractiveness and selecting one or more of the market segments; and 3. market positioning, developing competitive positioning for the product and an appropriate marketing mix.

II. **Market Segmentation.** Companies look for broad classes of buyers who differ in their product needs or buying responses. There is no single way to segment a market. A marketer has to try different segmentation variables, alone and in combination, hoping to find the best way to view the market structure.
   A. **Geographic segmentation** calls for dividing the market into different geographic units, such as nations, states, regions, counties, cities, or neighborhoods.
   B. **Demographic segmentation** consists of dividing the market into groups based on variables such as age, life-cycle stage, gender, income, occupation, education, religion, ethnicity, and generation. Demographic variables are the most popular bases for segmenting customer groups.
      1. **Age and life-cycle stage.** Consumer preferences change with age. Some companies offer different products or marketing strategies to penetrate various age and life-cycle segments. Other companies focus on the specific age of life-stage groups. Marketers must be careful to guard against stereotypes when using age and life-cycle segmentation most effective when combined with lifestyle and demographic information.
      2. **Gender.** Gender marketing is furnishings, leisure activities, reading habits, and retailers.
      3. **Income segmentation.** The lodging industry is particularly effective in using income segmentation, dividing a market into different income groups. However, income does not always predict which customers will buy a given product or service.
   C. **Psychographic segmentation** divides buyers into different groups based on social class, lifestyle, and personality characteristics.
      1. **Social class.** Social class has a strong effect on preferences for cars, clothes, home.
      2. **Lifestyle.** Marketers are increasingly segmenting the markets by consumer lifestyles.
      3. **Personality.** Marketers use personality variables to segment markets, for example "adventure seekers."
   D. **Behavioral segmentation** divides buyers into groups based on their knowledge, attitude, use, or response to a product. Many marketers believe that behavioral variables are the best starting point for building market segments.
      1. **Occasion segmentation.** Buyers can be grouped according to occasions when they make a purchase or use a product. Occasion segmentation helps firms build product use.
      2. **Benefits sought.** Knowing the benefits sought by customers is useful in two ways. First, managers can develop products with features that provide the benefits their customers are seeking. Second, managers communicate more effectively with their customers if they know what benefits customers seek.
      3. **User status.** Many markets can be segmented into nonusers, former users, potential users, first-time users, and regular users of a product. Potential users and regular users often require different marketing appeals.
      4. **Usage rate.** Markets can also be segmented into light, medium, and heavy product users. Heavy users are often a small percentage of the market but account for a high percentage of total consumption.
      5. **Loyalty status.** In the hospitality and travel industries, marketers attempt to build brand loyalty through relationship marketing.
   E. **Using multiple segmentation bases.** Marketers use multiple segmentation bases in an effort to identify smaller, better-defined target groups. Several business information services—such as Nielsen, Acxiom, and Experian—provide multivariable segmentation systems that merge geographic, demographic, lifestyle, and behavioral data to help companies segment their markets down to zip codes, neighborhoods, and even households.
   F. **Requirements for effective segmentation.** Market segments must have the following characteristics: measurability (the degree to which segments' size and purchasing power can be determined), accessibility (the degree to which segments can be served), sustainability (the degree to which segments are large enough to serve as markets), and actionability (the degree to which effective programs can be designed to attract and service the market).

III. **Market Targeting.**
   A. **Evaluating market segments**
      1. **Segment size and growth.** Companies analyze the segment size and growth and choose the segment that provides the best opportunity.
      2. **Segment structural attractiveness.** A company must examine major structural factors that affect long-run segment attractiveness.
      3. **Company objectives and resources.** The company must consider its own objectives and resources in relation to a market segment.
   B. **Selecting market segments.** Segmentation reveals market opportunities available to a firm. The company then selects the most attractive segment or segments to serve as targets for marketing strategies to achieve desired objectives.

1. **Undifferentiated marketing.** An undifferentiated marketing strategy ignores market segmentation differences and goes after the whole market with one market offer.
2. **Differentiated marketing.** The firm targets several market segments and designs separate offers for each. Differentiated marketing typically produces more total sales than undifferentiated marketing.
3. **Concentrated marketing.** Concentrated marketing strategy is especially appealing to companies with limited resources. Instead of going for a small share of a large market, the firm pursues a large share of one or more small markets.
4. **Micromarketing—Local marketing and SoLoMo.** Micromarketing is the practice of tailoring products and marketing programs to fit the tastes of specific individuals and locations. Local marketing and SoLoMo (social, local, mobile) marketing are forms of micromarketing.

C. **Choosing a market-coverage strategy.** Companies need to consider several factors in choosing a market-coverage strategy: company resources, the degree of product homogeneity, the degree of market homogeneity, and competitor's strategies.
1. **Socially responsible target marketing.** As marketers gain more information on customers, they must use this information responsibly.

IV. **Market Positioning.** A product's position is the way the product is defined by consumers on important attributes—the place the product occupies in consumers' minds relative to competing products.

A. **Positioning strategies.** Marketers can follow several positioning strategies. They can position their products based on price and product features. Product attribute positioning can be dangerous. The attribute has to create a benefit for the consumer. Products can also be positioned against another product class.

B. **Choosing and implementing a positioning strategy.** The positioning task consists of three steps: identifying a set of possible competitive advantages on which to build a position, selecting the right competitive advantages, and effectively communicating and delivering the chosen position to a carefully selected target market.

C. **Product differentiation**
1. **Physical attribute differentiation.** Unfortunately, many hotels, restaurants, and airlines lack physical differentiation. Motels in particular follow a standard architectural look that provides no differentiation. When this happens, price becomes the primary differentiating factor.
2. **Service differentiation.** Mature consumers place special value on friendly staff, guest name recognition by staff, assistance in making a product decision, opportunities to socialize, and no pressure to leave. These simple services can reap large rewards for members of the hospitality industry. Because so many companies overlook the importance of good service, those who truly emphasize service will achieve positive differentiation.
3. **Personnel differentiation.** Personnel differentiation requires that a company select its customer-contact people carefully and train them well. These personnel must be competent and must possess the required skills and knowledge. They need to be courteous, friendly, and respectful. They must serve customers with consistency and accuracy, and they must make an effort to understand their customers, communicate clearly with them, and respond quickly to customer requests and problems.
4. **Location differentiation.** Hospitality and travel firms should look for benefits created by their location, keeping in mind that this advantage is subject to chance. Factors such as a new highway bypass or criminal activity in a neighborhood can quickly turn an advantage into a problem.
5. **Image differentiation.** A company or visitor destination image should convey a singular or distinctive message that communicates the product's major benefits and positioning.

D. **Choosing the right competitive advantage**
1. **How many differences?** Many marketers think that companies should aggressively promote only one benefit to the target market (best quality, best service, lowest price, best value, best location...). Other marketers think that companies should position themselves on more than one differentiating factors. Companies need to avoid three major positioning errors: underpositioning, overpositioning, and confused positioning.
2. **Which differences?** Differences are worth establishing if they are important, distinctive, superior, communicable, preemptive, affordable, and/or profitable.

E. **Selecting an overall positioning strategy.** The full positioning of a brand is called the brand's value proposition.

F. **Communicating and delivering the chosen position.** Once having chosen positioning characteristics and a positioning statement, a company must communicate its position to targeted customers. All of a company's marketing mix efforts must support its positioning strategy.

G. **Positioning measurement: perceptual mapping.** In planning their differentiation and positioning strategies, marketers often prepare perceptual positioning maps that show consumer perceptions of their brand versus those of competing products on important dimensions.

IN-CLASS GROUP ACTIVITIES

*Exercises with an asterisk next to them are suitable for individual homework or online assignments. Students, always provide an explanation for your answer.

1. *Go to the Web site of a major brand of hospitality or travel company. Explain how it appeals to different segments through the Web site. Give specific examples.
2. In a small group, create an idea for a new restaurant or hotel business. Using the steps described in the chapter, develop a customer value-driven market strategy. Describe your strategy and conclude with a positioning statement for this business.
3. *Choose a hospitality business you are familiar with, for example, a hotel or restaurant. Explain some of the segments in its overall market (in this case, the hotel market or restaurant market), one of these markets that it targeted, and how it differentiated itself from its competitors to position itself in the market.
4. *Identify a restaurant or hotel market segment in your community that you feel would be a good market segment to target. Explain the marketing mix you would put together to go after this market segment.
5. *Some restaurateurs want to develop a restaurant with something for everyone. Why is this idea a dangerous policy?
6. What roles do product attributes and perceptions of attributes play in the positioning of a product? Can an attribute common to several competing brands contribute to a successful positioning strategy?
7. *Provide an example (other than one given in this chapter) of the use of SoLoMo marketing by a hospitality company.

EXPERIENTIAL EXERCISE

1. Find an advertisement from a hospitality or travel company that targets a specific segment, such as children, young adults, seniors, or upper-income customers. Then visit a location of that company. What does the company do at the location with its marketing mix to attract the segment that it targeted in the advertisement? This can include sales promotions, signage, product mix, location of the company, and pricing of products.

REFERENCES

1. Dan Peltier, "Interview: CitizenM Hotels Co-Founder on Making a Stay an Extension of Guests' Lifestyles," *Skift*, April 18, 2016, https://skift.com/2016/04/18/interview-citizenm-hotels-co-founder-on-making-a-stay-an-extension-of-guests-lifestyles/; "This is a Brand for Millennials," https://www.sayhellocreative.com/this-is-a-brand-for-millennials (accessed April 9, 2018); Liz Welch, "Entrepreneur Designs Upscale Hotels for Budget Travelers," *Inc.*, May 22, 2014, https://www.inc.com/magazine201406/liz-welch/citizenm-low-cost-high-end-hotels.html; Freek Vermeulen, "3 Steps to Break Out in a Tired Industry," *Harvard Business Review*, May 01, 2015 https://hbr.org/2015/05/3-steps-to-break-out-in-a-tired-industry; Michael Levie, "CitizenM Hotels Revolutionizes Guest Personalization," *Hospitality Technology*, February 18, 2009, https://hospitalitytech.com/citizenm-hotels-revolutionizes-guest-personalization; "citizenM Celebrates Yet Another Year of Affordable Luxury," December 15, 2017, https://www.citizenm.com/news/citizenm-celebrates-yet-another-year-of-affordable.
2. "Forecast of Retail Sales in the Foodservice Industry in the United States in 2014, by Venue Segment," *Statista*, http://www.statista.com/statistics/288612/retail-sales-us-foodservice-industry-by-venue-category/ (accessed July 22, 2015).
3. Elisabeth A. Sullivan, "Customer Spotting," *Marketing News* (March 15, 2008): 10.
4. https://order.dominos.com/en/pages/content/content.jsp?page=apps&so=hpnf&panelnumber=3&panelname=apps (accessed September 2014).
5. See Joan Voight, "Marriott Chain Adds Some Local Flavor," *Adweek* (January 7, 2013): 9; "Renaissance Hotels Launches New Navigator Program to Help Guests Discover 'Hidden Gems' of Various Cities around the World," January 8, 2013, www.adweek.com/prit/146321; http://renaissance-hotels.marriott.com/r-navigator (accessed September 2014).
6. Viking Cruises Web site, http://www.vikingcruises.com/terms-conditions/index.html (accessed July 28, 2015).
7. Paula Froelich, "Advertising's Untapped Market: Single Women," *Newsweek*, February 26, 2014, http://www.newsweek.com/2014/02/28/advertisings-untapped-market-single-women-245588.html (accessed July 25, 2015); Jamie Dunham, "Marketing Travel to Women: Eight New Trends You Need to Know," *The Lipstick Economy*, July 16, 2013, https://jamiedunham.wordpress.com/2013/07/16/marketing-travel-to-women-eight-new-trends-you-need-to-know/ (accessed July 25, 2015).
8. "Young Family Travelers," http://www.youngfamilytravelers.com/europe/novotel/novotel.htm (accessed October 31, 2004); "Family Adventure Traveler,"

http://www.colorado.com/family/default.asp; "Family Friendly" (accessed October 31, 2004); *Restaurant Hospitality* (June 1998): 48; Katie Smith, "Kiddin' Around," *Restaurant Hospitality* (April 2001): 52–64.

9. Peter Coy, "Why Price Is Rarely Right," *Bloomberg Business Week* (February 1 and 8, 2010): 77–78.

10. Richard Baker, "Retail Trends—Luxury Marketing: The End of a Mega-Trend," *Retail* (June/July 2009): 8–12, http://www.seadream.com/voyages/ (accessed July 24, 2015).

11. Dennis Ducharme, Fractional Ownership Puts Second Home within Reach for a New Generation, *Lodging Magazine*, June 21, 2018, www.lodgingmagazine.com/fractional-ownership-puts-second-home-within-reach-for-a-new-generation/; Milo Vanderbilt, Private Residence Clubs Make Luxury Vacation Homes Carefree and Affordable: Luxury Living International Predicts Growth for Fractional Ownership and Residence Clubs, *Luxury Living International*, October 7, 2015, www.luxurylivingmag.com/private-residence-clubs-make-luxury-affordable/; Les Christie, CNNMoney.com, June 23, 2006, www.money.cnn.com/2006/06/23/real_estate/fractionals_are_coming/.

12. Chris Reynolds, "Me, Myself and I," *American Demographics* (November 2003): 1; Gary M. Stern, "Solo Diners," *Restaurants USA*, 10, no. 3 (1990): 15–16; www.unmarriedamerica.org (accessed August 23, 2008).

13. See Kunur Patel, "Zipcar: An America's Hottest Brands Case Study," *Advertising Age* (November 16, 2009): 16; Paul Keegan, "Zipcar: The Best New Idea in Business," *Fortune* (August 27, 2009), www.fortune.com; Elizabeth Olson, "Car Sharing Reinvents the Company Wheels," *The New York Times* (May 7, 2009): F2; Stephanie Clifford, "How Fast Can This Thing Go, Anyway?" *Inc* (March 2008), www.inc.com; www.zipcar.com (accessed October 2010).

14. Information from www.rssc.com, http://nationofwhynot.com (accessed November 2010).

15. Andrew McMains, "Ad of the Day: Panera Gets into Lifestyle Branding with Manifesto about Healthy Living," *Adweek*, June 15, 2015, www.adweek.com/print/165330; Lisa Brown, "Panera Debuts New Ad Campaign: Food as It Should Be," *St. Louis Post-Dispatch*, June 16, 2015, www.stltoday.com/business/ local/panera-debuts-new-ad-campaign-food-as-it-should-be/ article_28c506b9-1a71-508d-9166-b1da12850076.html; and www. panerabread.com / en-us/our-beliefs / food-as-it-should-be-nopt.html (accessed September 2016).

16. Janet Hanner, "W London-A Hotel That Dares to Be Different," *Caterer & Hotelkeeper* (March 4–10, 2011): 26–28; Nancy Keates, "The Home Front: His Hotel, His Hangout," *The Wall Street Journal* (June 3, 2011): D6; Christina Binkley, "Putting the Hot Back in Hotel," *The Wall Street Journal* (August 18, 2011), http://online.wsj.com/article/SB10001424053111903596904576514293384502896.html; "W Hotels Unveils Innovative Design Concept of the Soon-to-Open W Paris-Opera by Acclaimed Rockwell Group Europe," Starwood Press Release, December 14, 2020 II, http://development.Starwoodhotels.comlnews/7/336-w_hotels_unveils_innovative_design_concept_of_the_soon-to-open_w_paris-opera_by_acclaimed_rockwell_group_europe; information and press releases from www.starwoodhotels.com/whotels/about/index.html (accessed September 2013).

17. www.smarttravel, www.rssc.com, www.royalcaribbean.com (accessed November 2007).

18. Quotes and other information from "Strong Comparable Sales Growth in the U.S. Drives Q1 Revenues for Dunkin' Brands," *Forbes,* April 28, 2015, www.forbes.com/sites/greatspeculations/ 2015/04/28/strong-comparable-sales-growth-in-the-u-s-drivesql-revenues-for-dunkin-brands/; Christine Champagne and Teressa Iezzi, "Dunkin' Donuts and Starbucks: A Tale of Two Coffee Marketing Giants," *Fast Company,* August 21, 2014, https://www.fastcompany.com/3034572/dunkin-donuts-and-starbucks-a-tale-of-two-coffee-marketing-giants; Janet Adamy, "Battle Brewing: Dunkin' Donuts Tries to Go Upscale, but Not Too Far," *The Wall Street Journal,* April 8, 2006, p. Al; "Dunkin' Donuts' Goes the Whole Nine Yards: Brand Keys Ranks Dunkin' Donuts Number One in Coffee Customer Loyalty for Ninth Straight Year," Dunkin' Donuts Newsroom, February 18, 2015, http://news.dunkindonuts.com; Khushbu Shah, "Starbucks or Dunkin Donuts? Where America's Coffee Loyalty Lies," *Eater,* January 15, 2015, www.eater.com/2015/1/15/7551497/starbucks-dunkin-donuts-peets-coffee-spending-percent; and www.dunkindonuts.com and www.dunkinbrands.com (accessed September 2016).

19. Robert C. Lewis, "Restaurant Advertising: Appeals and Consumers' Intensions," *Journal of Advertising Research*, 21, no. 5 (1981): 69–75.

20. From Starwood Hotel and Resorts, www.starwood.com/promotion/promo_landing.html?category=pets (accessed October 24, 2004); Elaine Sciolino, "Versailles Hotel Treats Dog Royally," *Denver Post* (December 4, 2003): 31A.

21. Victor J. Cook, Jr., William Mindak, and Arch Woodside, "Profiling the Heavy Traveler Segment," *Journal of Travel Research*, 25, no. 4 (1987).

22. Jiang Weizhong, Chekitan S. Dev, and Vithala R. Rao, "Brand Extension and Customer Loyalty," *Cornell Hotel and Restaurant Administration Quarterly*, 43, no. 4 (2002): 15.

23. A. Weissenberg, A. Katz, and A. Narula, "A Restoration in Hotel Loyalty—Developing a Blueprint for Reinventing Loyalty Programs," 2013, www.deloitte.com/view/en_US/us/Industries/travel-hospitality-leisure/72ce4f52478ab310VgnVCM1000003256f70aRCRD.htm (accessed July 23, 2014).

24. P. Mayock, "Personalization Equals Loyalty for Millennials," *Hotel News Now*, 2014, www.hotelnewsnow.com/article/13067/Personalization-equals-loyalty-for-millennials (accessed October 10, 2014).

25. John T Bowen and Shiang-Lih Chen McCain, "Transitioning Loyalty Programs," *International Journal of Contemporary Hospitality Management*, 27, no. 3 (2015): 415–430.

26. For this and other information on Experian's Mosaic USA system, see www.experian.com/marketing-services/consumer-segmentation.html and http://classic.demographicsnow.com/Templates/static/mosaicPDF/K40%20Bohemian%20Groove.PDF (accessed September 2014).

27. Type H 27: Birkenstocks and Beemers, http://library.demographicsnow.com/custom/img/mosaicPDF/H27%20Birkenstocks%20and%20Beemers.pdf (accessed July 27, 2015).

28. "Landry's reaches deal to sell Joe's Crab Shack," (2006) (accessed September 3, 2018) https://www.chron.com/business/article/Landry-s-reaches-deal-to-sell-Joe-s-Crab-Shack-1905117.php; Ron Ruggless (2017), "Fertitta wins Ignite bankruptcy auction; Judge set to rule on deal for Joe's Crab Shack, Brick House parent" (accessed September 3, 2018) https://www.nrn.com/mergers-acquisitions/fertitta-wins-ignite-bankruptcy-auction.

29. Eric Jackson, "Forget Kids, Investors Can Go for Chuck E. Cheese," *Breakout Performance*, Thursday, March 4, 2010, http://breakoutperformance.blogspot.com/2010/03/forget-kids-investors-can-go-for-chuck.html (accessed November 22, 2011).

30. Based on information found in Samantha Murphy, "SoLoMo Revolution Picks Up Where Hyperlocal Search Left Off," *Mashable*, January 12, 2012, http://mashable.com/2012/01/12/solomo-hyperlocal-search/; "Localeze/15miles Fifth Annual comScore Local Search Usage Study Reveals SoLoMo Revolution Has Taken Over: Business Wire," February 29, 2012; Joe Ruiz, "What Is So-Mole and Why Is It Important to Marketers?" *Business2Community*, February 1, 2013, www.business2community.com/marketing/what-is-somolo-and-why-is-it-important-to-marketers-039528; www.shopkick.com (accessed April 2014). For examples of successful retailer and brand SoLoMo efforts; see Jennifer Unger-felt, "What Airlines and Hotels Can Learn from Starbucks, Coca–Cola and Sephora's Approach to SoLoMo," *Joyalty360*, May 18, 2013; http://loyalty360.org/loyalty-today/article/what-airlines-and-hotels-can-learn-from-starbucks-coca-cola-and-sephoras-ap.

31. Ashtyn Douglas, "Go SoLoMo: Connecting with Your Local Customers," business.com, January 6, 2014, http://www.business.com/online-marketing/solo-mo-important-marketing-technique-local-businesses/ (accessed July 27, 2015).

32. Bill Carroll, "SoLoMo: Still Going Strong," *eCornell Blog*, April 9, 2013 (accessed July 27, 2015).

33. "Renaissance Hotels Launches New Navigator Program to Help Guests Discover 'Hidden Gems' of Various Cities around the World," January 8, 2013, www.adweek.com/ print/146,321; and www.renaissance-hotels.marriott.com/navigators (accessed September 2018).

34. See "McDonald's Introduces New Automatic Offerings of Fruit in Every Happy Meal," *PRNewswire*, January 20, 2012; "Judge Dismisses Happy Meal Lawsuit," *Advertising Age*, April 4, 2012, http://adage.corn/print/233946; Allison Aubrey, "McDonald's Says Bye-Bye to Sugary Sodas in Happy Meals," *NPR*, September 26, 2013, www.npr.org/blogs/thesalt/2013/09/26/226564560/mcdonalds-says-bye-bye-to-sugary-sodas-in-happy-meals.

35. http://www.marinabaysands.com/ (accessed September 11, 2011).

36. Airbnb, https://www.airbnb.com/about/about-us (accessed July 27, 2015).

37. Dean Houghton, "Close to the Consumer," *The Furrow* (September/October 2003): 12, John Deer Agricultural Marketing Center, 1145 Thompson Avenue, Lenexa, KS 66,219–2302.

38. Hilton offers global program for Chinese travelers, Fact Sheet, Hilton Worldwide, undated, http://hiltonglobalmediacenter.com/assets/HILT/docs/factsheets/HuanyingFactSheetEnglish.pdf (accessed July 27, 2015).

39. George Moschis, Carolyn Folkman Curasi, and Danny Bellinger, "Restaurant Selection Preferences of Mature Consumers," *Cornell Hotel and Restaurant Administration Quarterly*, 44, no. 4 (2003): 59–60.

40. "Taco Johns—the Fresh Taste of West-Mex," www.TacoJohn.com.

41. Chris Walsh, "New Partners to Preserve Old Charm of Telluride Ski," *Rocky Mountain News* (February 19, 2004): 7B.

42. Christopher Hosford, "A Transformative Experience," *Sales & Marketing Management*, 158 (June 2006): 32–36; Mike Beirne and Javier Benito, "Starwood Uses Personnel to Personalize Marketing," *Brandweek* (April 24, 2006): 9.

43. Back Ki-Joon and Sara C. Parks, "A Brand Loyalty Model Involving Cognitive, Affective and Cognitive Brand Loyalty and Customer Satisfaction," *Journal of Hospitality and Tourism Research*, 27, no. 4 (2003): 431.

44. Sui Jun Jian and Seyhmus Baloglu, "The Role of Emotional Commitment in Relationship Marketing: An Empirical Investigation of a Loyalty Model for Casinos," *Journal of Hospitality and Tourism Research*, 27, no. 4 (2003): 483.

45. Nancy Brumback, "Room at the Table," *Restaurant Business* (March 15, 2001): 71–82.

46. James H. Gilmore and B. Joseph Pine, II, "Differentiating Hospitality Operations vis Experiences," *Cornell Hotel and Restaurant Administration Quarterly*, 43, no. 3 (2002): 88.

Designing Customer Value-Driven Strategy and Mix

III

9 Designing and Managing Products and Brands: Building Customer Value
10 Internal Marketing
11 Pricing: Understanding and Capturing Customer Value
12 Distribution Channels: Delivering Customer Value
13 Engaging Customers and Communicating Customer Value
14 Public Relations and Sales Promotion
15 Professional Sales
16 Direct, Online, Social Media, and Mobile

Designing and Managing Products and Brands: Building Customer Value

Objectives
After reading this chapter, you should be able to:

1. Define the term *product* and explain critical elements to keep in mind when designing a product.
2. Define the term *brand* and explain strategies and decisions companies make in building and managing their brands.
3. Explain the new-product development process and product development through acquisition.
4. Describe the product life cycle and how it can be applied to the hospitality industry.
5. Identify the challenges of international product and services marketers.

When you hear someone mention Las Vegas, what comes to mind? Sin City? Wholesome entertainment for the entire family? An indulgent luxury vacation? Or perhaps a value-oriented reward for hard-working Americans? If you answered "all of the above," you wouldn't necessarily be wrong. The truth: All of these have been characteristics associated with Las Vegas over the years. In recent times, the Las Vegas Convention and Visitors Authority (LVCVA) fielded several national ad campaigns. Tourism is Vegas's biggest industry, and the LVCVA is charged with maintaining the city's brand image and keeping visitors coming to one of the world's most famous cities.

Although the positioning of the Vegas brand has changed from time to time, the town will probably never entirely lose the "Sin City" label. That title was born when Las Vegas was young—an anything-goes gambling town full of smoke-filled casinos, bawdy all-girl revues, all-you-can-eat buffets, Elvis impersonators, and no-wait weddings on the Vegas Strip.

But as the 1990s rolled around, many Las Vegas officials felt that the town needed to broaden its target audience. So they set out to appeal to—of all things—families. Some of the biggest casinos on the Las Vegas Strip built roller coasters and other thrill rides, world-class water parks, and family-friendly shows like Treasure Island's live-action swashbuckler spectacle, visible to everyone passing by on the street. Although this strategy seemed effective for a brief time, marketers came to realize that the family image just didn't sync well with casino gambling—the high-profit product that built Las Vegas.

As the LVCVA started to consider its options, the terrorist attacks of September 11, 2001, gave Las Vegas tourism one of its worst blows ever. Declining tourism led to 15,000 lost jobs. The LVCVA decided that it was time to unabashedly proclaim that Las Vegas was a destination for adults. That didn't just mean a return to the classic vices. The LVCVA engineered an image of Vegas as a luxury destination oozing with excess and indulgence. The theme parks were replaced by five-star resorts, high-rise condos, expansive shopping malls filled with the world's top luxury brands, and restaurants bearing the names of world-renowned chefs. A new breed of expensive stage shows for adult audiences replaced family-friendly entertainment. This change of strategy worked. Even as Las Vegas struggled through economic recovery in the post-9/11 world, visitors returned in record numbers. The LVCVA found that to the nearly 40 million who flocked to the city each year, Vegas is an emotional connection—a total brand experience.

And just what is the "Las Vegas experience"? Research showed that when people come to Las Vegas, they're a little naughtier—a little less inhibited. They stay out longer, eat more, do some gambling, and spend more on shopping and dining—an adult freedom.[1]

Based on these customer insights, the LVCVA coined the now-familiar brand slogan—"Only Vegas: What happens here, stays here." The catchphrase captured the essence of the Las Vegas experience—that it's okay to be a little naughty in Vegas. That simple phrase became the centerpiece of what is now deemed one of the most successful tourism campaigns in history. The campaign transformed Las Vegas's image from the down-and-dirty "Sin City" to the enticing and luxurious "Only Vegas."

The $75 million ad campaign showed the naughty nature of people once they arrive in Las Vegas. In one ad, a woman spontaneously married a visibly younger man in a Las Vegas wedding chapel. Then, ignoring his ardent pleas, she kissed him goodbye and pulled herself away, insisting that she had to get back to her business convention. In another ad, an outgoing young woman is shown introducing herself to various men, each time giving a different name. In a third ad, a sexy woman hops into a limo, flirts with the driver, and emerges from the car at the airport for her trip home as a conservative business woman. At the end of each ad was the simple reminder, "What happens here, stays here."

The LVCVA continued investing heavily in the bold and provocative campaign and in a variation on the theme, "Your Vegas is showing." All the while, Las Vegas experienced its biggest growth boom in history. Hotel occupancy rates hovered at an incredible 90 percent, visitors came in ever-increasing numbers, and there was seemingly no end to the construction of lavish new luxury properties. To top it off, Las Vegas was dubbed the number two hottest brand by respected brand consultancy Landor Associates, right behind Google. It seemed that the LVCVA had found the magic formula and that Vegas had found its true identity. With everything going so well, what could possibly go wrong?

Then in 2008, Las Vegas suffered two more punches. First, the worst recession since the Great Depression had consumers scaling back on unnecessary expenses. Second, in the wake of government bailouts and a collapsing financial industry, company CEOs and executives everywhere came under scrutiny for lavish expenses. Suddenly, Las Vegas's carefully nurtured, naughty, indulgent image made even prudent, serious company conferences held there look bad. It didn't help matters when President Obama delivered a statement that Las Vegas's mayor, Oscar Goodman, perceived as the straw that broke the camel's back. Obama scolded Wall Street executives by saying, "You can't get corporate jets; you can't go take a trip to Las Vegas or go down to the Super Bowl on the taxpayer's dime." As a result of the new economic realities, both leisure travel and the convention industry—two staples in Las Vegas's success—took a big hit.

As a result, 2008 and 2009 were some of the worst years ever for Las Vegas. In 2009, the total number of visitors dropped to 36.4 million, 7 percent less than the 2007 peak of 39.1 million. This translated into a 24 percent decrease in convention attendance, a 22 percent drop in room occupancy, and a 10 percent decline in gambling revenues. The Las Vegas hospitality industry responded by chopping prices. Rooms on the Las Vegas Strip could be had as cheaply as $25 a night. Gourmet meals were touted for half price. The town was practically begging for visitors.

After years of successfully pedaling Vegas naughtiness as the primary selling point, the LVCVA realized it had to make a shift. So in the middle of the economic carnage, with so much to offer and great deals to be had, it focused on the value and affordability of a Vegas vacation. A new ad campaign, "Vegas Bound," urged hard-working Americans to take a well-deserved break in Las Vegas to recharge their batteries before returning home to brave the tough economy. A series of Vegas Bound ads and online mini-documentaries showed average Americans in high-end nightclubs, spas, and restaurants. One grinning 81-year-old woman was even shown giving a thumbs-up after an indoor skydiving session. The campaign didn't eliminate glamour and luxury. Rather, it repackaged these traits in an "affordable" and "well-deserved" wrapper.

But after so many years of hearing about Las Vegas as a guilt-free adult playground, no matter what the ad campaign said, consumers had a hard time seeing Vegas as prudent. Research showed that even in a painful recession, consumers still saw Vegas for what it was: a place they could go to for simple pleasures not available at home. It took the LVCVA only five months to pull the plug on "Vegas Bound" and resurrect "What happens here, stays here." R&R Partners, the ad agency handling the Las Vegas marketing campaigns, made an important discovery through its research that, especially during hard economic times, people wanted to know that the same Vegas they've known and loved is still there.

Just as the needle started to budge, MGM Resorts International opened the most ambitious project Las Vegas had ever seen. In fact, its $8.5 billion CityCenter was said to be the largest privately funded construction project in U.S. history. A pedestrian-friendly resort, CityCenter, was designed as a small city in and of itself with four luxury hotels, two residential condo towers, and a 500,000-square-foot high-end shopping and dining center.

Adding 6,000 rooms and 12,000 jobs to the Las Vegas Strip has met with mixed reactions. Some speculate that this game-changing property will put an exclamation point on Las Vegas's image and provide additional oomph in a time of crisis.[2] Between 2010 and 2014, giant boutique and luxury lifestyle hotels have been sprouting up in Las Vegas. In 2010, the Cosmopolitan of Las Vegas, with 2,995 rooms, opened its doors to public. In 2013, Caesars Entertainment opened 181-room Nobu Hotel and co-branded it with Caesars Palace. In 2014, SLS Las Vegas, another high-end hotel, was added to Las Vegas hotel inventory, with 1,600 rooms, nightclubs, restaurants, and luxury shopping. The LINQ Hotel & Casino, designed for adventure seeking millennials, opened its doors with 2,253 rooms, suites, and poolside cabana guest rooms. The resort also offered attractions such as High Roller, a 550-foot observation wheel, and outdoor retail, dining and entertainment district.

Although there is rarely a magic bullet in a situation like the one Las Vegas faced, the LVCVA's return to its core brand message seemed to work. From 2010 to 2013, the visitor volume climbed from 37.3 million to 39.7 million. As 2017 unfolded, the city attracted 42.2 million visitors, a 4 percent growth.

Las Vegas has certainly had its share of ups and downs. The recovery is shaping up and times may be brightening now. Las Vegas has a long history of reinvigorating itself and bringing in new consumers. But the city faces new challenges. In the recession, the average consumer coming to Las Vegas put aside $650 to spend on gambling. In 2013, it was closer to $480. The crowd returned but gambled less. In 2017, among those who gamble, the average gambling budget was $540, still relatively low. Las Vegas also aims to attract more international visitors and set an ambitious goal of making international travelers 30 percent of the Las Vegas total visitors. In 2017, 16 percent of the 42.2 million visitors were international visitors, or about 7 million.[3]

As the Las Vegas example shows, in their quest to create customer relationships, marketers must build and manage products and brands that connect with customers. This chapter begins with a deceptively simple question: What is a product?

▪▪▪ What Is a Product?

A room at the Four Seasons in Toronto, a Hawaiian vacation, McDonald's French fries, a vacation package in Bali, a catered luncheon, a bus tour of historic sites, and a convention in a modern convention center with group rates in a nearby hotel are all products. Consider the variety of products in a typical casino hotel.

We define the term *product* as follows: *A product is anything that can be offered to a market for attention, acquisition, use, or consumption that might satisfy a want or need. It includes physical objects, services, places, organizations, and ideas.*

This definition refers to the planned component of the product that the firm offers. Besides the planned component, the product also includes an unplanned component. This is particularly true in hospitality and travel products, which are often heterogeneous. For example, a consumer entered a restaurant in Dallas and was greeted by the hostess, who presented him with a menu. When he opened his menu, he saw a dead roach stuck to the inside on the menu. After receiving this unexpected bonus, the consumer decided to leave the restaurant. The restaurant certainly did not plan on having a dead roach in the menu. The product the customer receives is not always as management plans. Managers of service organizations need to work hard to eliminate unexpected negative surprises and make sure guests get what they expect.

Today, as products and services become more commoditized, many companies are moving to a new level in creating value for their customers. To differentiate their offers, they are creating and managing customer *experiences* with their brands and companies. Many hospitality companies have developed brands—Moxy and Edition by Marriott International; W, Aloft and Element by Starwood Hotels & Resorts Worldwide; Indigo by InterContinental Hotels Group; and Andaz by Hyatt Hotels Corporation—to deliver a personalized and lifestyle experience: an eco-friendly, wellness, authentic, and/or local experience.

Experiences have always been an important part of marketing for some companies. Disney has long produced dreams and memories through its theme parks. It wants theme park cast members to deliver a thousand "small wows" to every customer.

The Hotel Le Royal is an MGallery Collection property of Accor-Hotels, and situated right in the heart of Lyon, between the Saône and the Rhône rivers. Its value proposition is traditional elegance in a convenient location, with proximity to attractions to experience and feel the city. Courtesy of Seyhmus Baloglu.

■■■ Product Levels

Hospitality managers need to think about the product on four levels: the core product, the facilitating product, the supporting product, and the augmented product (Figure 9–1). When developing products, marketers first must identify the core benefit that consumers seek from the product. They must then design the actual product and find ways to augment it to create customer value and a satisfying brand experience.

Core Products

Core product Answers the question of what the buyer is really buying. Every product is a package of problem-solving benefits and services.

The most basic level is **core product**, which answers the following question: *What is the buyer really buying?*

A four-day holiday in Dublin, Ireland, isn't a plane ride, hotel room, taxis, and meals. Depending on the visitor, it might be cultural enrichment, a return to one's roots, safe adventure, or even romance.

As all good steakhouses know, "Don't sell the steak, sell the sizzle." Marketers must uncover the core benefit to the consumer of every product and sell these benefits rather than merely selling features. A highway motel sells a good night's sleep, whereas a casino resort sells entertainment.

Facilitating Products

Facilitating products Those services or goods that must be present for the guest to use the core product.

Facilitating products are services or goods that must be present for the guest to use the core product. A first-class corporate hotel must have check-in and checkout services, a business center, a restaurant, and valet service, for instance. In an economy

Figure 9–1
Product levels.
Source: Adapted from C. Gonroos, "Developing the Service Offering—A Source of Competitive Advantage," in *Add Value to Your Service*, ed. C. Surprenant (Chicago, IL: American Marketing Association 1987), p. 83.

Supporting products Extra products offered to add value to the core product and to help differentiate it from the competition.

hotel, facilitating services might be no more than check-in and checkout service. Product design requires an understanding of the target markets and the facilitating services that they require.

A state park might not come to mind for customer service, but Chadron State Park in western Nebraska offers security for campers and cabin guests through a security station at the entrance. Late arrivals are welcomed by the security officer and given a key (cabins) as well as a map and instructions on how to find their location. Chadron State management knows that guests travel many miles to reach the park, and often arrive late at night.

Supporting Products

Core products require facilitating products but do not require supporting products. **Supporting products** are extra products offered to add value to the core product and help differentiate it from the competition. In a corporate hotel, an iPad in the room or a full-service health spa is a supporting product that exists to help draw and retain customers. The distinction between facilitating and supporting products is not always clear. Facilitating products for one market segment may be supporting products for another. For example, although families may not require restaurants and valet service when staying at a hotel, business travelers depend on them. Hyatt was among the first chains to offer a broad line of bathroom amenities, including shampoo, conditioners, and several choices of soap. When hotels first introduced these amenities, they were supporting the core product. Today, amenities have become facilitating products.

Hilton Worldwide announced the launch of Canopy by Hilton, a new lifestyle brand built on extensive market research, and opened world's first one in Reykjavik, Iceland, in 2016. Capitalizing on growing consumer interest in locally focused travel, each Canopy property uniquely reflects its neighborhood and local culture through its design, food and beverage, and art. Designed for today's leisure and business travelers, the hotel emphasizes open lobbies and comfortable spaces. "We saw an opportunity to not only enter the lifestyle space by developing a new brand, but also to redefine this category by creating a more accessible lifestyle brand," said Christopher J. Nassetta, president and CEO of Hilton Worldwide. "We identified the need to take the emphasis off of capital-intensive design and deliver exactly what the target consumer desires: an energizing, comfortable stay with more included value."

The more included value contains free Wi-Fi, a complimentary breakfast delivered to the room or to go, artisanal breakfast option, a local welcome gift, and evening tastings of local beer, wine, or spirits. Canopy aims to provide excellent service with its employees or "enthusiasts" in a "positively yours" service culture. Canopy properties will also offer guests the option of mobile straight-to-room arrival.[4]

In Aloft Hotels, a robot, nicknamed "Botlr" is being used to deliver items such as smartphone chargers, newspapers, or snacks from the front desk to guestrooms on request. The goal is to differentiate from competitors and create a value proposition. A futuristic Japanese hotel, named "Henn-na Hotel"—meaning "Evolve Hotel," will be run almost entirely by robots to perform duties such as manning the front desk, acting as porter, and cleaning.[5]

Hospitality firms should choose supporting products that are not easily matched by the competition. They should also be able to deliver supporting services in a professional manner. For example, some midscale hotels offer room service because they see it as a competitive advantage to attracting the business traveler. However, unprofessional delivery of supporting products can do more harm than good. Many mid-priced hotels offering room service lack a designated area in the kitchen for room-service carts, a room-service coordinator to answer the phone and write up the tickets, and designated room-service waiters. Necessary equipment and personnel are assembled at the time of the order, and as one might imagine, the results are sometimes disastrous. The person answering the phone lacks the proper training to ask the right questions (e.g., how the steak is to be cooked, the type of salad dressing the customer would like, and the type of potatoes desired). After taking the order, the next step is to find someone to set up the cart and take the order to the room. Likely candidates are the bell person, bus person, or a service person from the dining room. Personnel in the first two categories are not properly trained but may jump at the opportunity to gain a tip. Because they are not trained, the bell person and bus person may forget such essential items as salt and pepper, sugar, forks, and napkins when setting up the cart. To damage the hotel's image further, the guest puts the tray in the hallway after finishing the meal where it will sit until housekeeping picks it up the next morning.

Jogging is a popular means of exercise. Hotels are now offering jogging maps as well as bottles of water in the lobby for joggers. The Swiss Hotel in Boston provides serve-yourself coffee for early-morning flight crews. Some hotels place cold bottles of water as well as a note thanking the guest for staying at the hotel in the guest's car as the valet returns it to them after they have checked out of the hotel. These are examples of low-cost supporting products that add value.[6]

Increasing number of hotel brands provide amenity program for health- and wellness-conscious guests. Kimpton hotels have offered a brand-wide bicycle-share program for guests interested in experiencing outdoors while burning calories. The company made in-room yoga mats a nationwide standard in every guestroom and complimentary "Roll Out" service, which provides flavored water and fresh fruit in rooms. To meet the health and wellness needs of female guests, Omni Hotels & Resorts provide its select loyalty program members with a Fit Kit that includes complimentary weights and a yoga or stretch mat. JW Marriott Hotels & Resorts incorporated healthy living and sleeping into its turndown service with amenities such as an aromatherapy oil and bedtime snack bar developed by a known nutritionist.[7]

In summary, supporting products offer a competitive advantage, only if they are properly planned and implemented. They must meet or exceed customer expectations to have a positive effect.

Augmented Product

Augmented products
Additional consumer services and benefits built around the core and actual products.

The **augmented product** includes accessibility, atmosphere, customer interaction with the service organization, customer participation, and customers' interaction with each other. These elements combine with the core facilitating and supporting products to provide the augmented product.

From a managerial standpoint, the core product provides a focus for the business; it is the reason for being. Facilitating products are those that are essential for providing the core product to the target market. Supporting products can help position a product. According to Christian Gronroos, a services marketing expert, the core, facilitating, and supporting products determine what customers receive but not how they receive it.[8] The delivery of the service affects the customer's perception of the service, illustrated by the room-service example earlier. The augmented service offering combines what is offered with how it is delivered.

The augmented product is an important concept because hospitality and travel services require customer coproduction of the service. For most hospitality products, the customer comes to the service-delivery system and has to interact with the service-delivery system. For example, guests have to check in at the front desk, get to the room, and understand how to use the television and telephone systems. They also have to interact with other customers and employees. Because guests come to the service, atmosphere is an important part of the product. The augmented product captures the key elements that must be managed when the customer comes to the service factory (e.g., the hotel, restaurant, country club, conference center, amusement park). We now take a look at some of the elements of the augmented product.

Accessibility

If a product is not accessible, it has no value. Two barriers to accessibility are hours of operation and lack of knowledge. A hotel health club or a swimming pool that opens at 7 A.M. does not help the businessperson who wants to work out at 6 A.M., eat breakfast, and get to an 8 A.M. business appointment. A restaurant that opens at 7 A.M. becomes an irritant to a guest who has to leave at 6 A.M. for the airport. International hotels housing guests suffering from jet lag may find that opening the restaurant earlier in the morning would provide both a valued service and additional revenue. If there is a line of guests waiting for the restaurant to open in the morning, it may indicate that the hours need to be adjusted to make the restaurant more accessible.

The Palms Casino Resort in Las Vegas recently announced a 24-hour checkout policy for all guests at no extra cost. Guests can choose their departure time when they book rooms directly on the hotel's Web site.

Atmosphere: The Physical Environment

Atmosphere is a critical element in services. It can be the customer's reason for choosing to do business with an establishment. Burgundy's restaurant in Houston lacked street appeal and went out of business. The restaurant was located in a strip shopping center with a glass panel exterior and wall, common in many strip centers. The owners carpeted the concrete floor, put in booths, installed a sign over the door, and opened the restaurant. Perhaps they felt that their food quality and service would attract customers. But few ever reached the restaurant. The restaurant's exterior lacked identity or character and was not inviting to potential customers. People who saw Burgundy's simply did not come into the restaurant. Conversely, BJ's Restaurant and Brewhouse has used atmosphere effectively. It builds all of its restaurants, rather than move into existing locations, to give them a common look inside and out. This also ensures they operate efficiently. The exterior is modern and inviting; the interior is casual and promotes a relaxed and fun environment.

Atmosphere is appreciated through the senses. Sensory terms provide descriptions for the atmosphere of a particular set of surroundings.

- The main **visual** dimensions of atmosphere are color, brightness, size, and shape.
- The main **aural** dimensions of atmosphere are volume and pitch.
- The main **olfactory** dimensions of atmosphere are scent and freshness.
- The main **tactile** dimensions of atmosphere are softness, smoothness, and temperature.

When a strong atmosphere is created through the senses, it can set expectations for the fifth sense—taste. If loyal customers walk into a Starbucks, the atmospherics

---

Visual The dimension of atmosphere relating to color, brightness, size, and shape.

Aural The dimension of atmosphere relating to volume and pitch.

Olfactory The dimension of atmosphere relating to scent and freshness.

Tactile The dimension of atmosphere relating to softness, smoothness, and temperature.

Destination marketers have a special responsibility to carefully plan and help manage each of these phases. Tourism promotion organizations sometimes feel their responsibility is solely to bring "heads to beds," in other words, to increase the number of visitors. This simplistic thinking has resulted in a mix-match of attracting the wrong visitor to the community. It also ignores the organization's responsibility to use part of its funding for crime awareness and prevention programs, service-sector personnel training, signage, language instruction, beautification, and many other support activities to help ensure visitor satisfaction.

Customer Interaction with Other Customers

An area that is drawing the interest of hospitality researchers is the interaction of customers with one another. An airline flight on Friday afternoon from Dallas to Houston was sold out with a number of people on standby. Some on standby were construction workers returning home from their job sites. The airline's ground crew, in an effort to maximize revenue, put a construction worker in an empty first-class seat. The passenger paying a premium to sit in first class did not appreciate a worker in dirty construction clothes in the next seat. Hospitality organizations must manage the interaction of customers to ensure that some do not negatively affect the experience of others.

The issue of customer interaction is a serious problem for hotels and resorts. The independent nontour guest consistently objects to the presence of large group-inclusive tours (GITs). This problem is magnified if the GIT guests represent a different culture, speak a foreign language, or are from an age group years different from that of independent nontour guests.

The Shangri-La Hotel of Singapore dealt successfully with this problem by constructing three different hotel properties on the same grounds. The tower hotel serves GIT and lesser-revenue, independent nontour guests. The Bougainvillea section serves a more upscale guest, and a third executive property is for the exclusive use of very upscale guests. Interaction among the three groups is limited to the common outdoor swimming pool.

Ski resorts are facing a serious problem of guest interaction. Traditionally, skiers have been a fairly homogeneous group with common cultural norms, even though they arrive from widely separated geographic areas. German, French, Japanese, American, and Mexican skiers tended to have societal commonalities, despite differences in language.

The arrival of the snowboard changed this congenial mix of guests. Skiers began to complain that they must share the slopes with people dressed in counterculture clothing who often show blatant disregard for slope-side courtesy. The management of ski resorts was suddenly faced with a serious problem. Taos responded by refusing entry to snowboarders and positioned itself as "Skiing for Purists." Others turned part of the ski areas into terrain peaks with half pipes and other physical attractions popular with "riders."

Many hotels such as Embassy Suites provide free wine and cheese for guests during a set time period in the evening. These hotels commonly report that this act of hospitality has an added benefit of bringing guests together. Lasting friendships and business deals have resulted from the evening wine and cheese.

More and more hotels transform their lobbies into places to work, surf the Web, or meet friends for a drink. Aloft hotels by Starwood embraced this idea by creating the "social lobby" and XYZ Bar with a much younger vibe that appeals to millennials and draws them to socialize in the lobby. Moxy hotels by Marriott have adopted multi-zone lobbies that shift from quiet areas to social zones around the lobby bar. "Here's what we're hearing [from Millennials]: What I want is to be able to get out and see the city," says Indy Adenaw, VP of brand consulting at Marriott Hotels, and continues, "What I want is to be able to go downstairs and have a very lively and energetic bar experience. I want to meet people, I want to be communal. I want to be fiercely independent when I want to be, but also part of a larger community when it's active and when it's social."

Hotel Indigo by Intercontinental Hotel Group positions itself as a brand to deliver a local cultural experience. The director of brand management for Hotel Indigo brand says about their target market: "They want to sit in the lobby. They want to have local coffee, or they want to have local craft beer. They want to experience the neighborhood even if they don't get to leave the hotel."

Several hotels, such as Novotel by Accor, have taken the social lobby concept one step further with the use of LobbyFriend, an app that encourages hotel guests to meet and greet fellow guests and access a relevant and mobile stream of information about happenings within their hotel or city location. It also enables hotels to communicate with guests during their stay and connect hotel guests and hotel employees together.[18]

Customers as Employees

Customers often help hospitality organizations coproduce the product. Involving the guest as an employee can increase capacity, improve customer satisfaction, and reduce costs. Wait staff are not needed when guests help themselves.

The Las Vegas Sports Club used to have an attendant handing out keys and towels to members. The club installed a device that releases the locker key when the membership card is placed in a slot. Then someone observed that members could get their own towels if they were neatly stacked on shelves. The club no longer needed the space for the towel attendant in both the women's and men's locker rooms. It reconfigured the locker rooms and created a spa. The processes given to the customer resulted in considerable labor savings for the club and additional revenue for the spa. The members received a new amenity and gained control over their locker room experience.

Self-service technologies (SSTs) are a rapidly growing means for increasing customer coproduction in food-service experiences. For example, managers at Disney noticed guests at one of Walt Disney World's water parks standing in line at a snack bar just to get their refillable drink mug filled. This process cost the customer valuable time, added additional people to the queue, and required employees to take the drink order and refill mugs. The solution was an SST that saved time for the guest and labor. Management developed a drink-dispensing system that was activated by a bar code on the mug. The customer holds the mug in front of a scanner, which scans the bar code on the mug and activates the drink machine long enough for him or her to fill the mug. To prevent misuse of the system, Disney changes bar codes each day of the week. Recently, Rapid Fill refillable mugs have become available at Walt Disney World resorts. The soda stations in the food courts are activated by a radio frequency identification (RFID) chip embedded into the beverage mug. The chip is pre-programmed with guest's length of stay at the resort for a single or multiple days.[19]

Chili's has installed tabletop computer screens in its restaurants so customers can order directly and pay by credit card. The restaurant found users of the service spend more per check, in part because they buy more desserts and coffee when the screen is present.[20] You can add an app like WaitAway to your cell phone and be contacted by text message when your table is ready at a restaurant—and monitor the length of the line in the process.[21]

■■■ Branding Strategy

Building Strong Brands

A **brand** is a name, term, sign, symbol, design, or a combination of these elements that is intended to identify the goods or services of a seller and differentiate them from competitors. Some analysts see brands as the major enduring asset of a

Chili's has installed tabletop iPad-like tablets in its restaurants that allow customers to place orders and pay their bill at the table. Courtesy of Seyhmus Baloglu.

Brand A name, term, sign, symbol, design, or a combination of these elements that is intended to identify the goods or services of a seller and differentiate them from competitors.

TABLE 9–1
Marketing Advantages of Strong Brands

Improved perceptions of product performance
Greater loyalty
Less vulnerability to competitive marketing actions
Less vulnerability to marketing crises
Larger margins
More inelastic consumer response to price increases
More elastic consumer response to price decreases
Greater cooperation and support from suppliers
Greater support from marketing intermediaries
Increased marketing communications effectiveness
Brand extension opportunities

company, outlasting the company's specific products and facilities. Consumers attach meanings to brands and develop brand relationships. As a result, brands have meaning well beyond a product's physical attributes. A former CEO of McDonald's declared, "If every asset we own, every building, and every piece of equipment were destroyed in a terrible natural disaster, we would be able to borrow all the money to replace it very quickly because of the value of our brand. ... The brand is more valuable than the totality of all these assets."[22]

Branding is the process of endowing products and services with the power of a brand. It's all about creating differences between products. This process must be carefully developed and managed. In this section, we examine the key strategies for building and managing brands (Table 9–1).

Branding The process of endowing products and services with the power of a brand. It's all about creating differences between products.

Brand Equity and Brand Value

Brands are more than just names and symbols. They are a key element in the company's relationships with consumers. Brands represent consumers' perceptions and feelings about a product and its performance—everything that the product means to consumers. In the final analysis, brands exist in the heads of consumers. As one well-respected marketer once said, "Products are created in the factory, but brands are created in the mind."[23]

Brand equity The added value endowed on products and services. It may be reflected in the way consumers think, feel, and act with respect to the brand, as well as in the prices, market share, and profitability the brand commands for the firm.

A powerful brand has high brand equity. **Brand equity** is the added value endowed on products and services. It may be reflected in the way consumers think, feel, and act with respect to the brand, as well as in the prices, market share, and profitability the brand commands for the firm. It's a measure of the brand's ability to capture consumer preference and loyalty. A brand has positive brand equity when consumers react more favorably to it than to a generic or unbranded version of the same product. It has negative brand equity if consumers react less favorably than to an unbranded version.

Brands vary in the amount of power and value they hold in the marketplace. Some brands—such as Hilton, Marriott, and McDonald's—become larger-than-life icons that maintain their power in the market for years, even generations. Other brands create fresh consumer excitement and loyalty, such as NYLO, Moxy, Aloft, Westin, Mama Shelter, Red Mango, YouTube, and Twitter. These brands win in the marketplace not simply because they deliver unique benefits or reliable service. Rather, they succeed because they forge deep connections with customers.

Ad agency Young & Rubicam's Brand Asset Valuator measures brand strength along four consumer perception dimensions: *differentiation* (what makes the brand stand out), *relevance* (how consumers feel it meets their needs), *knowledge* (how much consumers know about the brand), and *esteem* (how highly consumers regard and respect the brand). Brands with strong brand equity rate high on all four dimensions. The brand must be distinct, or consumers will have no reason to choose it over other brands. But the fact that a brand is highly differentiated doesn't necessarily mean that consumers will buy it. The brand must stand out in ways that are relevant to consumers' needs. But even a differentiated, relevant brand is far from a shoe-in. Before consumers respond to the brand, they must first know about and understand it. And that brand recognition must lead to a strong, positive consumer–brand connection.[24] Thus, positive brand equity derives from consumer feelings about and connections with a brand. Consumers sometimes bond very closely with specific brands.

Brand value The total financial value of a brand.

A brand with high brand equity is a very valuable asset. **Brand value** is the total financial value of a brand. Measuring such value is difficult. According to some estimates, the brand value of McDonald's is a whopping $126 billion, with Hilton at $6.3 billion, and Marriott at $5.5 billion.[25]

High brand equity provides a company with many competitive advantages. A powerful brand enjoys a high level of consumer brand awareness and loyalty. Because consumers are loyal to strong brands, the brand has more leverage in bargaining with the consumer and the members of the distribution channel. Because a brand name carries high credibility, the company can more easily launch line and brand extensions. A powerful brand offers the company some defense against fierce price competition.

Above all, however, a powerful brand forms the basis for building strong and profitable customer relationships. The fundamental asset underlying brand equity is customer equity—the value of customer relationships that the brand creates. A powerful brand is important, but what it really represents is a profitable set of loyal customers. The proper focus of marketing is building customer equity, with brand management serving as a major marketing tool. Companies need to think of themselves not as portfolios of products but as portfolios of customers.

Brand Positioning

Marketers need to position their brands clearly in target customers' minds. They can position brands at any of three levels.[26] At the lowest level, they can position the brand on *product attributes*. For example, a hamburger restaurant can state that it uses only Angus beef. In general, however, attributes are the least desirable level for brand positioning. Competitors can easily copy attributes. More importantly, customers are not interested in attributes; they are interested in what the attributes will do for them.

A brand can be better positioned by associating its name with a desirable *benefit*. In the hospitality and travel industry, these benefits often relate to customer service or experience. Fleming's Prime Steakhouse and Wine Bar targets an upscale market that enjoys great wine, food, and service and has the resources to dine at a top restaurant. Fleming's positions the restaurant as a place where you can experience the celebration of exceptional food and wine.

The strongest brands go beyond attribute or benefit positioning. They are positioned on strong *beliefs and values*. Even a seemingly mundane brand such as Amtrak can be positioned this way. Recent Amtrak ads suggest that an Amtrak train ride does more than just get you from point A to point B. The moment you come on board Amtrak the journey begins. With more ways to relax on your journey, including plenty of legroom, spectacular views, and a unique dining experience, your state of mind will transform just like the land you're passing through.

Successful brands engage customers on a deep, emotional level. According to Stengel, "Marketing inspires life, and life inspires marketing."[27] Fleming's knows that its core customer enjoys wine. In order for a guest to try all one-hundred wines it has on its wine list, known as the Fleming's 100, a term it has trademarked, Fleming's provided a tasting of 25 wines each starting Friday at 5:30 P.M. for five consecutive weeks. It charged a nominal $25 for the tasting and sold small plates of food for those who wanted a snack.

Brand promise The marketer's vision of what the brand must be and do for consumers.

When positioning a brand, the marketer should establish a mission for the brand and a vision of what the brand must be and do. The **brand promise** is the marketer's vision of what the brand must be and do for consumers. The brand promise must be simple and honest. Motel 6, for example, offers clean rooms, low prices, and good service but does not promise expensive furnishings or large bathrooms. In contrast, The Ritz-Carlton offers luxurious rooms and a truly memorable experience but does not promise low prices.

Virgin America's brand promise is to enter categories where customers' needs are not well met, do different things, and do things differently, all in a way that better meets those needs. After flying for only a few years, Virgin America became an award-winning airline that passengers adore. It is not unusual for the company to receive e-mails from customers saying they actually wished their flights lasted longer!

Virgin America set to reinvent the entire travel experience, starting with an easy-to-use and friendly Web site and check-in. In flight, passengers revel in Wi-Fi, spacious leather seats, mood lighting, and in-seat food and beverage ordering through touch-screen panels. Some passengers remark that Virgin America is like "flying in an iPod or nightclub." The brand is seeking to be positioned as "an established player featuring discount pricing and a hip, stylish customer experience for travelers." Without a national TV ad campaign, Virgin America has relied on PR, word of mouth, social media, and exemplary customer service to create that customer experience and build the brand. To get customers more involved with the brand, Virgin America launched a digital marketing campaign offering the opportunity to upload a photo to Instagram from the flight. By tweeting the company's Twitter account, travelers can also upload their photo onto Virgin America's Times Square billboard or share it via their own social media accounts.[28]

Brand Name Selection

A good name can add greatly to a product's success. However, finding the best brand name is a difficult task. It begins with a careful review of the product and its benefits, the target market, and proposed marketing strategies. After that, naming a brand becomes part science, part art, and a measure of instinct.

Desirable qualities for a brand name include the following: (1) It should suggest something about the product's benefits and qualities: Luxury Collection, Sleep Inn, and Comfort Suites. (2) It should be easy to pronounce, recognize, and remember: Motel 6, Four Seasons, and JetBlue. (3) The brand name should be distinctive: Aloft, Moxy, and Element. (4) It should be extendable: Marriott began as a lodging company but chose a name that would allow expansion into other categories such as vacation ownership. (5) The name should translate easily into foreign languages. (6) It should be capable of registration and legal protection. A brand name cannot be registered if it infringes on existing brand names.

Many hotel corporations often market many different brands in a given product category. *Multibranding* offers a way to establish different features that appeal to different customer segments and capture a larger market share. If a hospitality company decides to brand its multiple concepts, it must choose which brand names to use. Hotel chains take various approaches to naming their brands.[29]

Individual Brand Names

Hospitality companies may choose to brand different products by different names. Starwood and Choice Hotels International use individual branding without including the family or corporate name. A major advantage of separate family brand names is that if a product fails or appears to be of low quality, the company has not tied its reputation to it.[30]

Corporate Umbrella (Family) or Sub-Branding

Hospitality companies may use their corporate brand as an umbrella brand across their entire range of products. Corporate-image associations of innovativeness, expertise, and trustworthiness have been shown to directly influence consumer evaluations. Marriott International used to include its corporate family name on majority of its brands. A sub-brand strategy, falling somewhere between, combines two or more of the corporate brand, family brand, or individual product brand names. For example, Hilton and Wyndham have used both individual and family

Co-branding: Four Seasons Hotel, Las Vegas, is located on floors 35 to 39 of the Mandalay Bay. Courtesy of Seyhmus Baloglu.

In response to guest demand for healthy travel options, "Stay Well" rooms at MGM Grand Hotel and Casino, in addition to private registration and lounge, include over 20 health and wellness features that allow business and leisure guests to maintain their healthy lifestyle practices. Courtesy of MGM Resorts International.

branding. Marriott International now uses both umbrella branding (e.g., Courtyard by Marriott, AC Hotels by Marriott) and individual branding (e.g., Moxy, Edition, Renaissance Hotels). Recently, Marriott created Moxy Hotels aimed at price-conscious and millennial consumers.

Leveraging Brands

Companies can leverage an existing brand by employing co-branding and ingredient branding.

Co-branding, or *dual branding*, can take advantage of the complementary strengths of two brands. For example, the Tim Hortons coffee chain is establishing co-branded Tim Hortons-Cold Stone Creamery shops. Tim Hortons is strong in the morning and midday periods, with coffee and baked goods, soups, and sandwiches. By contrast, Cold Stone Creamery's ice cream snacks are strongest in the afternoon and evening, which are Tim Hortons's nonpeak periods. The co-branded locations offer customers a reason to visit morning, noon, and night.[31] Taco Bell and Doritos teamed up to create the Doritos Locos Taco. Taco Bell sold more than 100 million of the tacos in just the first 10 weeks and quickly added Cool Ranch and Fiery versions.[32] Caesars Palace, the megaresort with 3,950 rooms, co-branded with the world's first Nobu Hotel, a luxury boutique hotel branded around celebrated Chef Nobu Matsuhisa. Co-branding enhances the credibility of the hotel's brand by borrowing credibility from other brands.[33]

Another form of co-branding is *same-company* or *retail co-branding* in which two retail establishments use the same location to optimize space and profits, such as jointly owned Pizza Hut, KFC, and Taco Bell restaurants. In 2012, Choice Hotels International unveiled a new dual-brand combination hotel prototype for its Sleep Inn and MainStay Suites brands. The new combo unit features a shared front desk, lobby and community room, fitness centers, and laundry facilities.[34] More recently, Hilton Worldwide opened a dual-branded property, the Hampton Inn and Homewood Suites in Washington, D.C. while Marriott International opened the dual-branded Aloft and Element hotel development in Dallas.[35] The main advantage of co-branding is that a product can be convincingly positioned by virtue of the multiple brands. Co-branding can generate greater sales from the existing market and open opportunities for new consumers and channels. It can also reduce the cost of product introduction because it combines two well-known images and speeds adoption. The dual-brand concept creates larger communal areas appealing to multiple target markets, business and leisure travelers, such as fitness center, and swimming pool.

Ingredient branding is a special case of co-branding. Ingredient brands can provide differentiation and important signals of quality. Many hotels use well-known brands for their in-room amenities such as care products, healthy meal options, and coffee. An interesting take on ingredient branding is self-branded ingredients that companies advertise and even trademark.[36] Westin Hotels advertises its own "Heavenly Bed"—a critically important ingredient to a guest's good night's sleep. The brand has been so successful that Westin now sells the bed, pillows, sheets, and blankets via an online catalog, along with other "Heavenly" gifts, bath products, and even pet items. The success of the bed has also created a halo for the Westin brand as a whole. Heavenly Bed enthusiasts are more likely to rate other aspects of their room or stay as more positive.[37] If it can be done well, using self-branded ingredients makes sense because firms have more control over them.

Hotels often have brands within a brand. Delos Living—a wellness design company—has observed a consumer demand for maintaining their health-conscious and wellness-oriented lifestyle while on the road, and designed a health and wellness hotel room concept—the "Stay Well" rooms. The company partnered with MGM Resorts International to convert 42 rooms of the MGM Grand in Las Vegas to Stay Well rooms. After receiving positive feedback, MGM Grand expanded the concept to 171 Stay Well suites, encompassing the entire fourteenth floor of the hotel's main tower. Among the numerous health and wellness features in the rooms are showers with vitamin C-infused water, an air-purification system, room lighting designed to combat jet lag and regulate levels of melatonin, aromatherapy, healthy menu options, and bedside lighting designed to enhance sleep.[38]

Brand Portfolios

A brand can only be stretched so far, and all the segments the firm would like to target may not view the same brand equally or favorably. Marketers often need multiple brands in order to pursue these multiple segments. Some other reasons for introducing multiple brands in a category include:[39]

1. attracting consumers seeking variety who may otherwise have switched to another brand;
2. increasing internal competition within the firm;
3. yielding economies of scale in advertising, sales, merchandising, and physical distribution.

The brand portfolio is the set of all brands and brand-particular category or market segment.

Recently, to target millennials and health- and well-being-sensitive customers, hotel chains have diversified their portfolio with lifestyle or boutique brands such as Moxy and Edition by Marriott International; W, Aloft, and Element by Starwood Hotels & Resorts Worldwide; Indigo by InterContinental Hotels Group; and Andaz by Hyatt Hotels Corporation. For example, Element by Westin Hotels and Resorts, an extended stay hotel concept, positions itself as an eco-friendly hotel offering a balanced experience where guests can "eat right, sleep well, exercise and relax."[40]

InterContinental Hotels Group has gone beyond providing in-room health and wellness amenities and created a single brand, the Even Hotels, targeting health- and wellness-conscious travelers. Even properties features elements based on four pillars:

- Eat well. Menus are focused on fresh, organic ingredients; food is clearly labeled; and free flavored filtered water is always available.
- Rest easy. Guestrooms feature natural eucalyptus fiber, high thread count linens, natural bath products, antibacterial wipes, and color LED mood lighting.
- Keep active. Exercise equipment such as yoga mats are provided in guestrooms.
- Accomplish more. Flexible space is provided for guests to work.[41]

Marriott International acquired nine distinct lifestyle brands that were developed by Starwood. Each brand, differentiated along emotional or experiential lines, conveyed different experiences and positions to establish an emotional connection with consumers. Consumer research suggested these positions for some of the brands:[42]

- **Sheraton** With the tagline "You don't stay here, you belong," Sheraton—the largest brand—is about warm, comforting, and casual. Its core value centers on "connections," an image aided by the hotel's alliance with Yahoo!, which cofounded the Yahoo! Link@Sheraton lobby kiosks and cyber cafes.
- **Four Points by Sheraton** For the self-sufficient traveler, Four Points strives to be honest, uncomplicated, and comfortable. The brand is all about providing high level of comfort and little indulgences like free high-speed internet access and bottled water. Its ads feature apple pies and talk about providing guests with "the comforts of home."
- **W** With a brand personality defined as flirty, for the insider, and an escape, W offers guests unique experiences around the warmth of cool. W's "Whatever/

- **Westin** Westin's emphasis on "personal, instinctive, and renewal" has led to a new sensory welcome, featuring a white tea scent, signature music and lighting, and refreshing towels. Each room features Westin's own "Heavenly Beds," sold exclusively in the retail market through Nordstrom, further enhancing the brand's upscale image.

The hallmark of an optimal brand portfolio is the ability of each brand in it to maximize equity in combination with all the other brands in it. Marketers generally need to trade off market coverage with costs and profitability. If they can increase profits by dropping brands, a portfolio is too big; if they can increase profits by adding brands, it's not big enough. The basic principle in designing a brand portfolio is to maximize market coverage so no potential customers are being ignored, but minimize brand overlap so brands are not competing for customer approval. Each brand should be clearly differentiated and appealing to a sizable-enough marketing segment to justify its marketing and production costs.[43]

Marketers carefully monitor brand portfolios over time to identify weak brands and kill unprofitable ones.[44] Brand lines with poorly differentiated brands are likely to be characterized by much cannibalization and require pruning.[45]

Marketing HIGHLIGHT 9.1 Extending your brand to China: What name do you use?

You are delegated with extending your brand to China. Your brand is well known and has a positive image. However, will you benefit from the brand's strong image in China? Do you use your foreign language brand name in China or do you adapt it to Mandarin or create a new name in Mandarin? Below are some considerations to help answer these questions, and some examples of what others have done.

Some names do not translate in Mandarin. Haagen-Dazs is an example of this category. The name does not have any meaning but because of the association with Denmark, it suggests high quality and a premium price can be charged. The name Haagen-Dazs was successfully used in China. In fact although it is an American company many Chinese view it as a Danish company. The name Hilton does not translate; however, Hilton decided to use a phonetic translation, Xi er dun; it hopes its strong worldwide brand name will carry over to China. Hyatt, realizing its name had no meaning in China, decided to use the name Yue, which translates into imperial. It used the name Kai Yue for Hyatt Regency, Juri Yue for Grand Hyatt, and Bo Yue for Park Hyatt.

Some brand names translate well into Mandarin. For example, Coca-Cola translates to Ke Kou Ke Le, which means tasty fun. Marriott Hotels is Wan hao, which translate to 10,000 wealthy elites. These brands and others have the benefit of being able to use their own brand name, which have a translated name that has a positive image.

Today for products appealing to a broader market, another important question is how the name will be searched online. Research shows that for many consumer products, the Chinese name is used to search online, not the international name. Also, the acronym can be a more frequently used search term than the full name. This should benefit a company like KFC, which changed its name from Kentucky Fried Chicken to KFC in 1991. In this age of digital marketing, it is important to know how your name will be used online, including how customers will try to find you online.

Chinese local brands have learned from observing how the brand names of multinational firms were accepted in China. For examples, a local company Paris Baguette and Croissants de France knows France is known for quality baked goods and uses a name that associates it with France. These shops are local but use foreign verbal elements to portray an association with a foreign culture. Such associations confer the brand some credibility and allow it to charge a premium. Chinese companies have also modified the names of multinational companies. Examples of this include Pizza Huh, KFG, and McDnoald.

Sources: Philip Kotler, Kevin Keller, Swee Ang, Siew Leong, and Chin Tan, *Marketing Management: An Asian Perspective*, 2013, Pearson, Singapore; Carly Chalmers, "12 Amazing Translations of Chinese Brand Names," *Today Translations*, September 27, 2013, http://www.todaytranslations.com/blog/12-amazing-translations-of-chinese-brand-names/ (accessed August 20, 2015); Michael Winesnov, "Picking Brand Names in China Is a Business Itself," *New York Times*, November 12, 2011, http://www.nytimes.com/2011/11/12/world/asia/picking-brand-names-in-china-is-a-business-itself.html?_r=3&partner=rss&emc=rss&pagewanted=all (accessed August 210, 2015); Clarissa Ward, "China's Logo Ripoffs: KFG, Pizza Huh and McDnoalds," ABC News, July 22, 2011, http://abcnews.go.com/Business/counterfeit-logos-hit-groupon-apple-pizza-hut-kfc/story?id=14131984 (accessed August 20, 2015); "Understanding Chinese Brand Names Online," *Lab Brand*, http://www.labbrand.com/brand-source/understanding-chinese-brand-names-online (accessed August 20, 2015).

Managing Brands

Companies must manage their brands carefully. First, the brand's positioning must be continuously communicated to consumers. Major brand marketers often spend huge amounts on advertising to create brand awareness and build preference and loyalty.

Brand identity is about positioning a brand in the minds of consumer. Brand image is about perceptions of the brand and differentiation by consumers, both features and feelings. Brand integrity is fulfilling the promise and delivering the experience claimed, connecting brand identity and brand image. It establishes the credibility and trust that consumers will establish after their actual brand experience. Companies should deliver experiences that they promise. Losing credibility will result in losing the community (online and offline) of potential buyers.[46]

Advertising campaigns can help create name recognition, brand knowledge, and perhaps even some brand preference. However, the fact is that brands are not maintained by advertising but by customers' *brand experiences.* Today, customers come to know a brand through a wide range of contacts and touch points. These include not only advertising but also personal experience with the brand, word of mouth, social media sites, and company Web pages. The company must put as much care into managing these touch points as it does into producing its ads. "Managing each customer's experience is perhaps the most important ingredient in building [brand] loyalty," states one branding expert. "Every memorable interaction ... must be completed with excellence and ... must reinforce your brand essence." A former Disney top executive agrees: "A brand is a living entity, and it is enriched or undermined cumulatively over time, the product of a thousand small gestures."[47] The brand's positioning will not take hold fully unless everyone in the company lives the brand. Therefore, the company needs to train its people to be customer centered. Even better, the company should carry on internal brand building to help employees understand and be enthusiastic about the brand promise. Many companies go even further by training and encouraging their distributors and dealers to serve their customers well.

Finally, companies need to periodically audit their brands' strengths and weaknesses.[48] They should ask: Does our brand excel at delivering benefits that customers truly value? Is the brand properly positioned? Do all of our customer touch points support the brand's positioning? Do the brand's managers understand what the brand means to customers? Does the brand receive proper, sustained support? The brand audit may turn up brands that need more support, brands that need to be dropped, or brands that must be rebranded or repositioned because of changing customer preferences or new competitors.

▪▪▪ The New-Product Development

A company can obtain new products in two ways. One is through acquisition—by buying a whole company or a license to use someone else's product. Large companies such as McDonald's sometimes buy a small restaurant chain such as Chipotle rather than develop their own new concepts. They are able to watch the fledgling chain grow. They sit back and observe its customer base, volume of sales per unit, and how easy or difficult it is to open new stores. When they are convinced that the new chain looks like a winner and makes a good strategic fit with their organization, the large company simply buys the chain. This is what Brinker International did when it purchased Romano's Macaroni Grill and PepsiCo purchased California Pizza Kitchen. This method of product development reduces the risk considerably for large companies that have the assets to purchase and then develop the chain. This acquisition strategy has a new class of restaurant entrepreneurs, those who try to develop a chain with the specific purpose of selling it to a large chain. Another technique is to purchase distressed chains. The mismanagement of a chain and resulting poor performance can drive the market value of the chain down. These chains become attractive targets for companies that believe they can turn them around.

The other is through the company's own new-product development efforts. To create successful new products, a company must understand its consumers,

Figure 9-2
Major stages in new-product development.

markets, and competitors and develop products that deliver superior value to customers. It must carry out strong new-product planning and set up a systematic, customer-driven *new-product development process* for finding and growing new products. Figure 9–2 shows the eight major steps in this process.

In 2004, Panda Restaurants developed a new retail line in partnership with Overall Farms of Texas, a supplier of frozen foods to the food-service industry. Panda placed two frozen entrées, beef with broccoli and mandarin chicken, into a test market within Costco and Sam's Clubs. "Consumers are ready to try our new frozen products because they feel a familiarity with the entrees and our company," said David Landsberg, vice president of business planning.[49]

Perhaps so, but other restaurant chains such as El Chico have also tried this form of product expansion and experienced severe problems. If consumers view the retail product the same as the restaurant one, they may question why they need to visit the restaurant. In some cases, consumers believe that the restaurant serves frozen rather than freshly prepared products. Two years after launching its fast-food line, Panda announced that it was discontinuing the line.[50]

Thus, companies face problems. They must develop new products but the risk of failure is high. The solution lies in strong new-product planning and in setting up a systematic new-product development process for finding and nurturing new products.

Idea Generation

New-product development starts with idea generation—the systematic search for new-product ideas. A company typically generates hundreds of ideas, even thousands, to find a few good ones. Major sources of new-product ideas include internal sources and external sources such as customers, competitors, and distributors and suppliers.

Awareness of External Environment

All members of the hospitality industry are highly dependent on the external environment. Recession, inflation, economic growth, terrorists, an aging population, and other external factors all directly affect this industry. Ideas for new products should come from a familiarity with what is happening in the external world. As an example, hotel security is of foremost importance, particularly to single women and other segments. A study of 930 hotel guests revealed a high acceptance of certain security measures. Guests younger than 40 said they would pay more for added security, including a first-aid kit in the room.[51]

Internal Sources

Using internal sources, the company can find new ideas through formal R&D. However, in one survey, 750 global CEOs reported that only 14 percent of their innovation ideas came from traditional R&D. Instead, 41 percent came from employees, and 36 percent came from customers.[52] Thus, beyond its internal R&D process, companies can pick the brains of its employees—from executives to scientists, engineers, and manufacturing staff to salespeople. Many companies have developed successful "intrapreneurial" programs that encourage employees to envision and develop new-product ideas. In 2012, Chick-Fil-A set up a large innovation center called "Hatch," where its staff and partners explored new ideas in restaurant designs, to train team members and improve the customer experience. In 2014, Chick-fil-A opened its Test Kitchen, an innovation center devoted to menu improvements. In 2018, Chick-fil-A opened a 6,000-square-foot Technology Innovation Center at Georgia Tech to develop solution for digital technology, machine learning, and data analytics.[53] Increasingly, restaurant chains are creating formal research and development facilities at their corporate headquarters staffed by a chef or team of chefs. For example, T.G.I. Friday's and Whataburger have these centers with kitchens replicating those found in their restaurants. The vice president of brand development for Whataburger states, "When it comes to menu development, having your own facility offers convenience, accessibility, and confidentiality." Quick-service chains such as Whataburger add around five items annually, whereas casual dining restaurants add 15 to 60 items. Usually new items are introduced as special promotions, with about 25 percent making it to the permanent menu.[54]

Within the hotel industry, new-product decisions are made at both the corporate and the property levels. New-product decision makers at the corporate level include mid-level to top management. In some cases, people not employed directly by the company but closely affiliated with it, such as bankers, lawyers, and consultants, become involved in this process.

Decision makers at the property level often include the owner if a chain does not own the hotel. In some cases, someone, such as a president, represents the owner. Others involved in the process are the general manager, department managers, and directors of various areas. Often a corporate vice president from the chain may participate in the process. A danger with this source is that managers and employees may say, "Yes the idea is good" when in fact they believe it is bad.

External Idea Sources

Companies can also obtain good new-product ideas from any number of external sources. For example, distributors and suppliers can contribute ideas. Distributors are close to the market and can pass along information about consumer problems and new-product possibilities. Suppliers can tell the company about new concepts, techniques, and materials that can be used to develop new products. Competitors are another important source. Companies watch competitors' ads to get clues about their new products. Other idea sources include trade magazines, shows, and seminars, government agencies, advertising agencies, marketing research firms, university and commercial laboratories, and inventors.

Restaurant and hotel managers visit restaurants when they travel, looking for ideas they can bring back to their businesses. It is important from both a competitive standpoint and a product development standpoint to visit the competition.

Perhaps the most important source of new-product ideas is *customers* themselves. The company can analyze customer questions and complaints to find new products that better solve consumer problems. Or it can invite customers to share suggestions and ideas. For example, Starbucks sponsors My Starbucks Idea, a Web site that invites customers to share, discuss, and vote on new product and service ideas.[55]

Crowdsourcing

Crowdsourcing An open-innovation new-product idea program.

More broadly, many companies are now developing **crowdsourcing** or open-innovation new-product idea programs. Jeff Howe is credited with developing the term. He defines *crowdsourcing* as "the application of open source principles to fields outside of software."[56] Crowdsourcing throws the innovation doors wide open, inviting broad communities of people—customers, employees, independent scientists and researchers, and even the public at large—into the new-product innovation process. The idea, says one analyst, is that when it comes to helping to improve "your products, services, Web site, or marketing efforts ... two heads—or 2,000 or 20,000—are better than one."[57]

Hospitality companies embrace the trend of crowdsourcing or "co-creation" and consider it a viable way to engage customers and generate new product ideas and innovative designs in a social-media-driven world. They can use crowdsourcing in many different ways such as building hotel bar menus, voting on logos and

Marriott International has opened a 10,000-square-foot Innovation Lab, located beneath the company's headquarters, to promote innovation and collaboration. Architects, designers, employees, and customers are invited to explore new concepts and product testing. Upon entry to the Innovation Lab, guests will traverse a gallery filled with projected images and presentations on walls, setting the scene for Marriott's newest designs. Courtesy of Marriott International, Inc.

room key designs, recommending names for new hotel spaces and concepts, and selecting games and entertainment options for lobbies.[58]

In 2013, Marriott International opened a new 10,000-square-foot Innovation Lab located beneath the company's headquarters in Bethesda, Maryland. The Innovation Lab is a place where employees, customers, and hotel owners brainstorm, design, and refine their ideas for the hotel of the future. Marriott invites frequent guests to its Innovation Lab to provide input on ideas and initiatives and "co-create" their next brand innovation.

Social media has empowered guests to let hotels know about their likes and dislikes in real time. Marriott Hotels and Resorts also turned to digital crowdsourcing and launched a "Travel Brilliantly" campaign aimed at millennials. The company solicited ideas from travelers on everything from design to technology to food and beverage on its Web site (travel-brilliantly.marriott.com). Among the 700 submissions, a panel of judges awarded the grand prize to the idea of a vending machine with healthful options.

Chris Baer, senior director of insight, strategy, and innovation at Marriott International, says, "There is no creation anymore except co-creation. To build any idea in a vacuum is more of a risk than building it with the insight of your guests and your associates."[59]

InterContinental Hotels Group's (IHG) partnered with Chase to develop a Priority Club Rewards Select Visa. This was targeted at members of its IHG's loyalty program. It hired Communispace, a provider of private online communities, to gather 300 current Priority Club Visa cardholders willing to share their opinions on the proposed card benefits and current card features. Based on the comments of this group, benefits were expanded to provide points on products other than IHG hotels. 4Food, a restaurant in New York, is using crowdsourcing to develop menu items. The restaurant serves hamburgers with a hole in the middle that is filled with the customer's choice of 40 different vegetarian dishes, including humus, salsa, and vegetarian chili. Customers can develop their own combination of these ingredients to create unique burgers and give them a name. If 4Food can get others to order "its" hamburger, it will get 20 cents for each burger sold. 4Food is using crowdsourcing to develop menu items and promote its restaurant.[60]

REO Eats in Lansing, Michigan, used crowdsourcing to gain ideas for its concepts. So, what does this mean? It means REO wants customers' input on everything, including its logo, interior design, exterior design of the building, menu ideas and pricing, and promotional strategy. It also used crowdsourcing to find investors and employees.[61] Crowdsourcing can produce a flood of innovative ideas. In fact, opening the floodgates to anyone and everyone can overwhelm the company with ideas—some good and some bad. "Even a small crowdsourcing event can generate a few hundred ideas. If I told you next year you're going to get 20,000 ideas from your customers, how would you process that?"[62]

Truly innovative companies don't rely only on one source or another for new-product ideas. Instead, according to one expert, they create "extensive networks for capturing inspiration from every possible source, from employees at every walk of the company to customers to other innovators and myriad points beyond."[63]

■■■ Idea Screening

The purpose of idea generation is to create a large number of ideas. The purpose of screening is to spot good ideas and drop poor ones as quickly as possible. Product development costs rise greatly in later stages, so the company wants to proceed only with ideas that will turn into profitable products. Marriott's healthy vending machine mentioned earlier is an example. Most companies require their executives to write up new-product ideas on a standard form that can be reviewed by a new-product committee. The executives describe the product, the target market, and the competition. They make some rough estimates of market size, product price, development time and costs, manufacturing costs, and rate of return. They also answer the following questions: Is this idea good for our company? Does it mesh well with the company's objectives and strategies? Do we have the people, skills, equipment, and resources to make it succeed? Many companies have well-designed systems for rating and screening new-product ideas.

The idea or concept screening stage is the appropriate time to review carefully the question of product line compatibility. A common error in new-product development is to introduce products that are incompatible with the company. The following describes major compatibility issues. How will the product assist us to:

- Fulfill our mission?
- Meet corporate objectives?
- Meet property objectives?
- Protect and promote our core business?
- Protect and please our key customers?
- Better use existing resources?
- Support and enhance existing product lines?

Concept Development and Testing

Surviving ideas must now be developed into product concepts. It is important to distinguish between a product idea, a product concept, and a product image. A **product idea** envisions a possible product that company managers might offer to the market. A **product concept** is a detailed version of the idea stated in meaningful consumer terms. A **product image** is the way that consumers picture an actual or potential product.

Major restaurant chains cannot afford to place an untested menu in all their restaurants. Burger King, like others, uses test market restaurants in selected cities. The Piedmont area of North Carolina was used as a test market for American fries. Apparently, the product performed poorly so it disappeared from the menus. Hotels commonly introduce new-product ideas to selected floors and to selected properties. Guests are sometimes invited to an afternoon product screening.

Concept Development

In the late 1970s, Marriott recognized that the urban market for its current hotel products was becoming saturated. It needed a hotel concept that would work in secondary sites and suburban locations. Marriott decided to focus its assets on the company's core business, lodging, through the development of a new product.

This was a product idea. Customers, however, do not buy a product idea; they buy a product. The marketer's task is to develop this idea into alternative product concepts, determine how attractive each is to customers, and choose the best one.

The concept for the new product was called Courtyard by Marriott. Marriott selected persons from different areas of the company to manage the development of this new product. The company conducted extensive competitor and market analysis and, as a result of this research, developed the following conceptual framework for the project:[64]

1. It would be tightly focused for the transient market.
2. It would house fewer than 150 rooms.
3. It would project a residential image. (Through its research Marriott identified a major segment of hotel users who did not like hotels. These consumers preferred homelike settings.)
4. It would not have significant cannibalization of Marriott's other hotels.

Product idea Envisioning a possible product that company managers might offer to the market.

Product concept A detailed version of a product idea stated in meaningful consumer terms.

Product image The way that consumers picture an actual or potential product.

5. It would have a limited-menu restaurant.
6. Public and meeting space would be limited.
7. It would be a standardized product with five to eight in a region.
8. The name Marriott would be attached for recognition and a halo effect. ("Halo" or "umbrella effect" refers to the carryover of a corporate or brand name to other products. The name Disney has a halo effect for many products, from movies to a cruise ship.)

Concept Testing

Concept testing occurs within a group of target consumers. New-product concepts may be presented through word or picture descriptions. Marriott tested its concept for the Courtyard Motel using a statistical technique called *conjoint analysis*. This involved showing potential target guests different motel configurations and having them rank the configurations from the most to the least desirable. The rankings were statistically analyzed to determine the optimal motel configuration.[65]

In most cases, however, simpler consumer attitude surveys are used. Suppose that 10 percent of the consumers said they "definitely" would buy and another 5 percent said "probably." The company would project these figures to the population size of this target group to estimate sales volume. But the estimate would be uncertain because people do not always carry out their stated intentions.

Unfortunately, the Marriott example is far too rare within the hospitality industry. The corporate headquarters of major hotel, resort, and restaurant chains do engage in professional concept testing, but smaller chains and individual properties often pass over this critical stage. They often move directly from product idea to full implementation.

In some cases, intuition or luck proves to be correct, and the new product is a winner, thus placing the company well ahead of competition. However, the history of the hospitality industry has proved that in many cases the idea needed concept testing because the product proved to be a disastrous mistake. In the case of a tactical product decision, such as a hotel room amenity or a new room service beverage, there may be relatively little damage from an incorrect new-product decision. This is not true of new-product decisions involving heavy capital expenditures, such as a new ship for a cruise line or a new destination resort. These decisions involve millions of dollars and have sometimes proved so disastrous that hospitality companies have been forced into bankruptcy. The expenditure of a few thousand dollars and a few extra months for concept testing might prove invaluable in the long run.

Marketing Strategy

The next step is marketing strategy development: designing an initial marketing strategy for introducing the product into the market. The marketing strategy statement consists of three parts. The first part describes the target market, the planned product positioning, and the sales, market share, and profit goals for the first few years. The target markets for Courtyard by Marriott were business travelers who wanted moderately priced, high-quality rooms and pleasure travelers who wanted a safe, comfortable room.

The second part of the marketing strategy statement outlines the product's planned price, distribution, and marketing budget for the first year. Statistical software enabled Marriott to build sophisticated models. These models provided information on pricing and expected market share based on these prices. The segmentation information gave Marriott the information it needed for marketing the hotels.

The third part of the marketing strategy statement describes the planned long-run sales, profit goals, and marketing mix strategy.

Business Analysis

Once management decides on the product concept and marketing strategy, it can evaluate the business attractiveness of the proposal. Business analysis involves a review of the sales, costs, and profit projections to determine whether they satisfy the company's objectives. If they do, the product can move to the product development stage.

Many communities view arenas and conference centers as essential products to serve the needs of the local populace and to attract out-of-town visitors. Unfortunately, many have suffered from a lack of sound business analysis. Political and emotional pressures often prevail in the planning stage. "This town needs a baseball team and that means we must have a new multimillion-dollar arena." Sentiments such as these often prevail. In the movie *Field of Dreams*, it was "If you build it, they will come." Sadly this has proven to be untrue for many arenas and convention centers.

The Generals from Greensboro, North Carolina, play in the minor-league East Coast Hockey League. To keep the team from folding, thus further affecting the coliseum's revenue, the City of Greensboro took over the day-to-day operations of the Generals. The team's coach became a city employee. The coliseum's authority assumed responsibility for marketing ticket sales, resulting in a loss of about $300,000 from operating the team.[66] Sports arenas brand their product with the name of corporate sponsors, such as Coors Field in Denver. This does not guarantee a long life for the brand because sponsoring companies have declared bankruptcy, including some involved in great corporate scandals.

Visitor products supported by tax money such as coliseums, convention centers, museums, and zoos should be developed only after careful and unbiased business analysis, including a professional marketing plan.

Product Development

If the product concept passes the business test, it moves into product development and into a prototype. Up to now it existed only as a word description, a drawing, or mock-up. The company develops one or more physical versions of the product concept. Restaurants can develop prototypes of menu items and run them as specials; hotels build guest room prototypes. It hopes to find a prototype that meets the following criteria:

1. Consumers perceive it as having the key features described in the product— concept statement.
2. It performs safely under normal use.
3. It can be produced for the budgeted costs.

Developing a successful prototype can take days, weeks, months, or even years. Marriott built a Courtyard room prototype with portable walks. It developed three room types: a standard, a short, and a narrow configuration. The consumers liked the overall concept. They rejected the narrow version but not the short version, which Marriott estimated would result in substantial cost savings.

One problem with developing a prototype is that the prototype is often limited to the core product. Many of the intangible aspects of the product, such as the performance of the employees, cannot be included.

Test Marketing

If the product passes functional and consumer tests, the next step is market testing in which the product and marketing program are introduced into realistic market settings.

Market testing allows the marketer to gain experience in marketing the product, to find potential problems, and to learn where more information is needed before the company goes to the great expense of full introduction. Market testing evaluates the product and the entire marketing program in real market situations. The product and its positioning strategy, advertising, distribution, pricing, branding, packaging, and budget levels are evaluated during market testing. Market testing results can be used to make better sales and profit forecasts.

The amount of market testing needed varies with each new product. Market testing costs can be enormous, and market testing takes time, during which competitors may gain an advantage. When the costs of developing and introducing the product are low or when management is already confident that the new product will succeed, the company may do little or no market testing. Minor modifications of current products or copies of successful competitor products might not need testing. For example, to take advantage of digital and mobile trends, Starbucks quickly introduced a less-than perfect mobile payment app, then worked out the flaws during the six months after launch. The Starbucks app now accounts for 8 million transactions per week.[67]

The costs of market tests are high but are often small compared with the costs of making a major mistake. When the risks are high, or when management is not sure of the product or its marketing program, a company may do a lot of test marketing. For instance, KFC conducted more than three years of product and market testing before rolling out its major new Kentucky Grilled Chicken product. The fast-food chain built its legacy on serving crispy, seasoned fried chicken but hoped that the new product would lure back health-conscious consumers who dropped fried chicken from their diets. More recently, KFC has announced that it is developing "meat replacements" such as a vegetarian version of its fried chicken that's made from plants. The product will be developed first for its locations in the United Kingdom.[68]

Commercialization

Market testing gives management the information it needs to make a final decision about whether to launch a new product. If the company goes ahead with commercialization, it will face high costs. It may have to spend several million dollars for advertising and sales promotion alone in the first year. For example, McDonald's spent $100 million on an advertising blitz to introduce its McCafe coffee in the United States. The media spend included TV, print, radio, outdoor, the internet, events, public relations, and sampling.[69]

When?

The first decision is whether it is the right time to introduce the new product. In Marriott's case the test market hotel experienced occupancy of 90 percent.

Where?

The company must decide whether to launch the new product in a single location, a region, several regions, the national market, or the international market. Few companies have the confidence, capital, and capacity to launch new products into full national distribution. Instead, they develop a planned market rollout over time. Small companies in particular tend to select an attractive city and put on a blitz campaign to enter the market. They may enter other cities one at a time. Large companies may decide to introduce their product in one region and then move to the next. Marriott decided to introduce the Courtyard in regional markets.

To Whom?

Within the rollout markets, the company must target its promotion to the best prospect groups. Management should have determined profiles of prime prospects during earlier market testing. It must now fine-tune its market identification, looking for early adopters, heavy users, and opinion leaders.

How?

The company must develop an action plan for introducing the new product into the selected markets and spend the marketing budget on the marketing mix.

▰▰ Product Life-Cycle Strategies

After launching a new product, management wants the product to enjoy a long and lucrative life. Although the product is not expected to sell forever, managers want to earn enough profit to compensate for the effort and risk. To maximize profits, a

Figure 9–3
Sales and profits over the product's line from inception to demise.

Product development
Developing the product concept into a physical product to ensure that the product idea can be turned into a workable product.

Introduction The product life-cycle stage when a new product is first distributed and made available for purchase.

Growth The product life-cycle stage when a new product's sales start climbing quickly.

Maturity The stage in a product life cycle when sales growth slows or levels off.

Decline The period when sales fall off quickly and profits drop.

product's marketing strategy is normally reformulated several times. Strategy changes are often the result of changing market and environmental conditions as the product moves through the product life cycle (PLC).

The PLC (Figure 9–3) is marked by five distinct stages:

1. **Product development** begins when the company finds and develops a new-product idea. During product development, sales are zero and the company's investment costs add up.

2. **Introduction** is a period of slow sales growth as the product is being introduced into the market. Profits are nonexistent at this stage because of the heavy expenses of product introduction.

3. **Growth** is a period of rapid market acceptance and increasing profits.

4. **Maturity** is a period of slowdown in sales growth because the product has achieved acceptance by most of its potential buyers. Although sales are still high, profits level off or decline because of increased marketing outlays to defend the product against competition.

5. **Decline** is the period when sales fall off quickly and profits drop.

The PLC concept can describe a product class (fast-food restaurants), a product form (fast-food hamburgers), or a brand (Popeyes). The PLC applies differently in each case. Product classes have the longest life cycles. The sales of many product classes stay in the mature stage for a long time. Product forms, in contrast, tend to have the standard PLC shape. Product forms such as the drive-in restaurant and roadside tourist court pass through a regular history of introduction, rapid growth, maturity, and decline. A specific brand's life cycle can change quickly because of changing competitive attacks and responses.

The PLC concept is a useful framework for describing how products and markets work. But using the PLC concept for forecasting product performance or for developing marketing strategies presents some practical problems. For example, managers may have trouble identifying a product's current life-cycle stage, determining when it has moved into the next stage, and enumerating the factors that affect how it will move through the stages. In practice, it is very hard to forecast the sales level at each PLC stage, the length of each stage, and the shape of the PLC curve.

Most marketing texts feature the PLC, yet very few managers claim that they use it in the development of marketing strategy. There are two explanations for this. First, managers make strategic decisions based on the characteristics of each stage of the PLC, without using the PLC itself as a tool. The second reason is that accurate prediction of the shape of the PLC is impossible. Many products do not follow the typical curve.

The PLC is not a predictive tool to determine the length of a product's useful life. It is, instead, a means of conceptualizing the effect of the market, the environment, and competition and understanding how that product may react to various stimuli.[70] Recognizing that products have life cycles with identifiable stages can provide insights into how to manage the cycle to extend its life. Unmanaged products travel along the life cycle with little resistance. Environmental and competitive changes move a product through its life cycle, and companies must react to keep their products salable. McDonald's has been able to extend by modifying the product concept. The McDonald's of today is a different concept than the McDonald's of the 1960s. The menu and the store design are different. McDonald's has evolved from stands with no seating into fast-food restaurants with attractive indoor seating areas and playgrounds for children. The company also changed its location strategy. In addition to its traditional suburban locations, McDonald's developed international, urban, and institutional locations such as hospitals and colleges. Often, when a product begins to peak in sales, management assumes that it has started its decline. The downturn could be attributable to many factors: ineffective marketing support, competition, economic conditions, or lack of market development. If managers wearing "PLC blinders" do not investigate these reasons, they risk seeing the PLCs as the cause of the slowdown.[71]

Using the PLC concept to develop marketing strategy can be difficult. Strategy is both a cause and a result of the product's life cycle. The product's current PLC position suggests the best marketing strategies, and the resulting marketing strategies affect product performance in later life-cycle stages. Yet when used carefully, the PLC concept can help in developing good marketing strategies for different stages of the PLC.

We looked at the product development stage of the PLC earlier. We now examine strategies for each of the other life-cycle stages.

Introduction Stage

The introduction stage starts when the new product is first made available for purchase. Introduction takes time, and sales growth is apt to be slow. Some products may linger in the introduction stage for many years before they enter a stage of rapid growth; suite hotels followed this pattern. Many companies watch others go into the market as pioneers. When suite hotels were introduced, many players sat on the sidelines until the product proved itself in the marketplace. Being a pioneer involves risk, but those who sit on the sidelines may watch others build market share quickly if the product is hot. The pioneers are then in an excellent position to defend their market share against attacks by late arrivals. Two new taco restaurant concepts, Taco Tote and Taco Palenque, may be examples. Time will tell. In the introductory stage, profits are negative or low because of low sales and high expenses. Promotion spending is high to inform consumers of the new product and encourage them to try it.

In the introductory stage, there are only a few competitors who produce basic versions of the product because the market is not ready for product refinements. Companies focus on selling to buyers who are ready to buy, usually the higher-income groups. Prices tend to be on the high side.

Growth Stage

If the new product satisfies the market, it enters the growth stage and sales start climbing quickly. The early adopters continue to buy, and later buyers start following their lead, especially if they hear favorable word of mouth. Competitors enter the market, attracted by the opportunity for profit. They introduce new product features, which expand the market.

Prices remain the same or fall only slightly. Companies keep their promotion spending at the same or at a slightly higher level to meet competition and continue educating the market. Profits increase during this growth stage, as costs are spread over a large volume and more efficient systems are developed.

Companies use several strategies to sustain rapid market growth as long as possible:

1. Product quality is improved and new product features and models are introduced.
2. New market segments are entered.
3. Advertising is shifted from building product awareness to building product conviction and purchase.
4. Prices are lowered to attract more buyers.

In the growth stage, a company faces a trade-off between high market share and high current profit. By investing heavily in product improvement and promotion, it can capture and dominate a position. But it sacrifices maximum current profit in the hope of making it up in the next stage.

Maturity Stage

At some point a product's sales growth slows down, and the product enters the maturity stage. This stage normally lasts longer than the previous two stages, and it poses strong challenges to marketing management. Most producers are in the maturity stage of the life cycle, and therefore, most marketing management deals with mature products.

The slowdown in sales growth causes supply to exceed demand. This overcapacity leads to greater competition. Competitors begin lowering prices, and they increase their advertising and sales promotion. "Burger wars" and "pizza wars" are the result of these products being in the mature stage. Real sales growth is about the same as population growth. The only way to increase sales significantly is to steal customers from the competition. Price battles and heavy advertising are often the means to do this. Both result in a drop in profits. Weaker competitors start dropping out. The industry eventually contains only well-established competitors in the main market segments, with smaller competitors pursuing the niche markets.

Applebee's restaurant chain has experienced product maturity. Things were not good when the founder, T. J. Palmer, said, "It doesn't have anything that would make me come back." In 2007, Applebee's found itself with falling profits, a lagging stock, and restless investors. According to *The Wall Street Journal*, "Applebee's didn't change quickly enough while a raft of competitors copied it. Applebee's stayed too long with a formula that had worked for it in the past."[72]

While Applebee's failed to change, U.S. customers were more exposed to ethnic cuisine and cooking shows. They also expressed concern about overprocessed foods and disliked the decor of high school sports paraphernalia and dark wood. In response, Applebee's made several product changes such as a high-low price strategy of offering a $14.95 New York strip steak on the front of the menu and a $5.99 soup and salad on the back. These did not stop the sales slide. In November 2007, Applebee's was bought by IHOP. The combination of IHOP and Applebee's resulted in the formation of DineEquity.

DineEquity was able to increase same store sales in 2010 for the first time since 2005, albeit the increase was only about 0.3 percent. DineEquity created new promotions such as "Sizzling Entrees," "Great Tasting Items Under 550 Calories," "2 for $20" (a shared appetizer and two entrees), and an advertising promotion called "There's No Place Like the Neighborhood." DineEquity through menu development, operating efficiencies, and effective advertising was able to create positive momentum. The Applebee's case shows how hard it is to create momentum in a mature product. It took DineEquity three years to change the direction of Applebee's. DineEquity's battle is not over; each year in a mature product is a battle to keep the product relevant and gain or maintain market share.[73]

In addition to old decor and an old menu, some blamed the lack of destination items. These are specialty items that diners seek out and are willing to go out of their way to purchase.

Wendy's has been rebranded to rejuvenate its image as a higher-end fast-food chain, with a sleek new look and new menu items such as premium Dave's Hot 'N Juicy burger. Courtesy of Seyhmus Baloglu.

Market Modification

At this point, the aggressive product manager tries to increase consumption of the product. The manager looks for new users and market segments and ways to increase use among present customers. McDonald's added breakfast, salads, desserts, and chicken sandwiches in its efforts to attract new users and increase use. Product managers may also reposition the brand to appeal to a larger or faster-growing segment. When anti-drunk-driving campaigns reduced alcoholic beverage consumption, Bennigan's emphasized its food.

Product Modification

The product manager can also change product characteristics, product quality, features, or style to attract new users and stimulate more usage. A strategy of quality improvement aims at increasing the performance of the product—its durability, reliability, speed, or taste. This strategy is effective when quality can be improved, when buyers believe the claim of improved quality, and when enough buyers want higher quality.

Wendy's has remodeled its restaurants to give them a modern and fact-casual look. The exterior features a contemporary design with large windows while the interior showcases open, bright dining areas, with multiple seating options. The restaurant has new menu items and a new customer ordering process, digital menu boards, and a high-definition television. Wendy's hopes to rejuvenate its image as a higher-end fast-food chain with the new design and changes.[74]

Responding to declining same-store sales, McDonald's pilot tested and expanded a custom-built burger program, which lets customers skip the counter and head to touch-screen tablet kiosks where they can customize their bun, cheese, toppings, and sauces, and pay for the orders. Dine-in customers can choose from 22 different ingredients, including caramelized onions, grilled mushrooms, red onions, pepper jack cheese, apple-wood smoked bacon, and sliced jalapenos.[75]

Marketing Mix Modification

The product manager can also try to improve sales by changing one or more marketing mix elements. Prices can be cut to attract new users and competitors' customers. A better advertising campaign can be developed. The company can also offer new or improved services to buyers.

Instead of just making cosmetic changes, hospitality companies may choose to *rebrand* the whole concept, with new marketing strategies. In 2005, Caesars Entertainment purchased the Imperial Palace, a 33-year run-down property offering lowest rates on the Strip, and changed the name to the Quad after limited renovation in 2012. Two years later, Caesars Entertainment invested $223 million toward revamping the 2,256-room Quad Resort & Casino, rebranded it as the Linq Hotel & Casino, and connected it with its newly developed outdoor dining, nightlife, and entertainment district. The resort now provides a social and connected environment and takes advantage of restaurant and shops and the High Roller (550-foot-tall observation wheel). The Linq Hotel offers new amenities such as spa, pool deck, a lobby bar for social hub to attract younger crowd, and automated check-in to reduce wait times.[76]

Decline Stage

Sales of most product forms and brands eventually decline. The decline may be slow or rapid, as in the case of Minnie Pearl Chicken. Sales may plunge to zero, or they may drop to a low level and continue there for many years.

Sales decline for many reasons, such as technological advances, shifts in consumer tastes, and increased competition. Carrying a weak product can be very costly to the firm and not just in terms of reduced profit but also in terms of hidden costs such as wasted management and sales force time and tarnished brand image in the future.

Companies must pay close attention to their aging products. Regularly reviewing sales, market share, costs, and profit trends for each of its products will help identify products in the decline stage.

Management has to decide whether to maintain, harvest, or drop weak products. Management may decide to harvest the product, which means reducing various costs. Successful harvesting may increase a company's profits in the short run. Management may also decide to drop the product.

Destination and hospitality marketers must be aware of the PLC as it affects retailers. Hotels are often located near centers of shopping. In fact, the giant mall in Edmonton, Alberta, contains a hotel. Restaurants have found malls to be excellent locations, but the PLC is changing.

Shopping malls are in the decline stage in many parts of the United States.[77] Crime, teenagers hanging around, huge parking lots, confusing layouts, fear of terrorism, and expensive rents are among the reasons for this decline. Stores such as JC Penney, Sears, and the May Company served as anchors in malls but are now

TABLE 9-2
Summary of Product Life-Cycle Characteristics, Objectives, and Strategies

	Introduction	Growth	Maturity	Decline
Characteristics				
Sales	Low sales	Rapidly rising sales	Peak sales	Declining sales
Costs	High cost per customer	Average cost per customer	Low cost per customer	Low cost per customer
Profits	Negative	Rising profits	High profits	Declining profits
Customers	Innovators	Early adopters	Mainstream adopters	Lagging adopters
Competitors	Few	Growing number	Stable number beginning to decline	Declining number
Marketing objectives	Create product engagement and trial	Maximize market share	Maximize profit while defending market share	Reduce expenditure and milk the brand
Strategies				
Product	Offer a basic product	Offer product extensions, service, and warranty	Diversify brand and models	Phase out weak items
Price	Use cost-plus	Price to penetrate market	Price to match or beat competitors	Cut price
Distribution	Build selective distribution	Build intensive distribution	Build more intensive distribution	Go selective: phase out unprofitable outlets
Advertising	Build product awareness among early adopters and dealers	Build engagement and interest in the mass market	Stress brand differences and benefits	Reduce to level needed to retain hard-core loyals
Sales Promotion	Use heavy sales promotion to entice trial	Reduce to take advantage of heavy consumer demand	Increase to encourage brand switching	Reduce to minimal level

Source: Adapted from Philip Kotler and Kevin Lane Keller, *Marketing Management*, 14th ed. (Upper Saddle River, NJ: Prentice Hall, 2012), p. 317. © 2012. Printed and electronically reproduced by permission of Pearson Education, Inc., Upper Saddle River, NJ.

moving to free-standing locations. This decline will make malls less attractive locations for restaurants.

Shopping remains one of the primary activities of travelers, particularly pleasure travelers. Additionally, thousands, if not millions, of travelers throughout the world plan overnight trips primarily for shopping. This includes international travelers. The motor coach industry in many nations derives a heavy percentage of income from shopping tours.

Table 9–2 summarizes the key characteristics of each stage of the PLC. The table also lists the marketing objectives and strategies for each stage.

Product Deletion

As we have seen, the PLC illustrates that most products will become obsolete and have to be replaced. Thus, understanding the product deletion process is just as important as understanding product development. A successful restaurant, Strawberry Patch, in Houston served a chicken breast topped with sautéed mushrooms. This dish enjoyed success for more than 10 years. When sales started to drop and the decline continued, it appeared that the product was no longer in favor with the restaurant's customers. Customers were asked about the dish, and they responded that it was too greasy. When the sautéed mushrooms were poured over the chicken breast, the butter collected at the bottom of the plate. When the product was first introduced, butter sauces were in vogue, but preferences changed. The restaurant removed the sautéed mushrooms and garnished the chicken with fresh sliced mushrooms. If management of the Strawberry Patch had been wearing life-cycle blinders, it would have deleted the product.

The deletion analysis is a systematic review of a product's projected sales and estimated costs associated with those sales. If a product no longer appears to be profitable, the analysis looks at possible ways to make modifications and return it to profitability. If the analysis indicates that the product should be deleted, there are three choices: phase-out, run-out, or drop it immediately.[78]

Phase-out is the ideal method; it enables a product to be removed in an orderly fashion. For example, a menu item would be replaced on the next revision of the menu. A **run-out** would be used when sales for an item are low and costs exceed revenues, such as the case of a restaurant serving a crabmeat cocktail with sales of only one or two items per week. If the restaurant decides to delete the product, it may choose to deplete its existing stock of crabmeat rather than reorder. The last option is an immediate **drop**. This option is usually chosen when the product may cause harm or complaints; it is best to drop the item rather than continuing to create unhappy customers.

The issue of dropping a product is particularly complex in the case of the properties of a hotel or restaurant chain. Management is usually quite aware of individual properties that should be dropped from the chain affiliation due to deterioration of the property or the neighborhood in which the property is located. In many cases, it is impossible or impractical to close the property quickly or drop it from chain affiliation:

- Contracts may prohibit a quick close.
- The property may have sentimental attachments to the community and to management.
- Closure might have a negative effect on the community.
- A buyer may not be readily available.
- Special relationships may exist between the franchisee and the franchisor.

Despite difficulties in closing hotels or disassociating properties from a chain, eventually the inevitable must occur. As in the earlier example of menu items, it is best to make this difficult decision as quickly as possible.

Phase-out The ideal method of removing an unpopular or unprofitable product; it enables a product to be removed in an orderly fashion.

Run-out Removing a product after existing stock has been depleted; used when sales for an item are low and costs exceed revenues, such as the case of a restaurant serving a crabmeat cocktail with sales of only one or two items per week.

Drop The action taken toward a product that may cause harm or customer dissatisfaction.

▪▪▪ International Product and Service Marketing

International product and services marketers face special challenges. First, they must figure out what products and services to introduce and in which countries. Then, they must decide how much to standardize or adapt their products and services for world markets.

On the one hand, companies would like to standardize their offerings. Standardization helps a company develop a consistent worldwide image. It also lowers the product design and marketing costs of offering a large variety of products. On the other hand, markets and consumers around the world differ widely. Companies must usually respond to these differences by adapting their product offerings. For example, by carefully adapting its menu and operations to local tastes and eating styles, YUM! Brands—parent company of quintessential fast-food restaurants KFC, Pizza Hut, and Taco Bell—has become the largest restaurant company in mainland China. Consider KFC.[79]

A typical Kentucky Fried Chicken meal in the United States features original, extra crispy, and a Pepsi. What do you get at a KFC in China? Of course, you can get some good old Kentucky fried, but more popular items include chicken with Sichuan spicy sauce and rice, egg soup, or a "dragon twister"

Global product adaptation: By adapting to local tastes and eating styles, KFC has achieved finger-lickin' good success in China. Michael Kemp/Alamy Stock Photo.

(KFC's version of a traditional Beijing duck wrap), all washed down with some soybean milk. Also on the menu: egg tarts, fried dough sticks, wraps with local sauces, fish and shrimp burgers on fresh buns, and congee, a popular rice porridge that is KFC's number one seller at breakfast. The Chinese menu also offers a large selection—some 50 items compared with 29 in the United States—meant to appeal to the Chinese style of eating, in which groups of people share several dishes. And although KFC outlets in the United States are designed primarily for takeout and eating at home, outlets in China are about twice the size of their U.S. counterparts, providing more space for eat-in diners, who like to linger with friends and family. Through such adaptation, KFC and YUM!'s other brands in China have positioned themselves not as a foreign presence but as a part of the local community. As a result, YUM! Brands has achieved finger lickin' good success in China. Its 5,000 KFC restaurants in more than 1,100 cities in China earned more revenue than all 19,000 of its restaurants in the United States combined, including KFC, Pizza Hut, and Taco Bell.

Many hotel chains—Marriott, Starwood, and IHG—have also globalized. The trend toward international growth of hospitality companies will continue. Today, hospitality companies are no longer simply following their manufacturing counterparts. Instead, they are taking the lead in international expansion.

CHAPTER REVIEW

I. **Products**
   A. **What is a product?** A product is anything that can be offered to a market for attention, acquisition, use, or consumption that might satisfy a want or need. It includes physical objects, service, places, organizations, and ideas.
   B. **Product levels**
      1. **Core product.** It answers the question of what the buyer is really buying. Every product is a package of problem-solving services.
      2. **Facilitating products.** These are services or goods that must be present for the guest to use the core product.
      3. **Supporting products.** These are extra products offered to add value to the core product and to help differentiate it from the competition.
      4. **Augmented products.** These include accessibility (geographic location and hours of operation), atmosphere (visual, aural, olfactory, and tactile dimensions), customer interaction with the service organization (joining, consumption, and detachment), customer participation, and customers' interactions with one another.

II. **Branding Strategy.**
   A. **Building strong brands.** Brand is a name, term, sign, symbol, design, or a combination of these elements that is intended to identify the goods or services of a seller and differentiate them from those of competitors. Brands are powerful assets that must be carefully developed and managed.
   B. **Brand equity and brand value.** Brand equity is the added value endowed on products and services. It may be reflected in the way consumers think, feel, and act with respect to the brand, as well as in the prices, market share, and profitability the brand commands for the firm. Brand value is the total financial value of a brand.
   C. **Brand positioning.** Companies can position brands at any of three levels. At the lowest level, they can position the brand on product attributes. A brand can be better positioned by associating its name with a desirable benefit. The strongest brands go beyond attribute or benefit positioning. They are positioned on strong beliefs and values.
   D. **Brand name selection.** A good name can add greatly to a product's success. However, finding the best brand name is a difficult task. It begins with a careful review of the product and its benefits, the target market, and proposed marketing strategies.
   E. **Leveraging brands.** Companies can leverage an existing brand by employing co-branding and ingredient branding.
   F. **Brand portfolios.** The brand portfolio is the set of all brands and brand-particular category or market segment. Marketers often need multiple brands in order to pursue these multiple segments.
   G. **Managing brands.** Companies must manage their brands carefully. First, the brand's positioning must be continuously communicated to consumers. The company should carry on internal brand building to help employees understand and be enthusiastic about the brand promise. Finally, companies need to periodically audit their brands' strengths and weaknesses.

III. **New-Product Development**
   A. **The new-product development process**
      1. **Idea generation.** Ideas are gained from internal sources, customers, competitors, distributors, and suppliers.
      2. **Idea screening.** The purpose of screening is to spot good ideas and drop poor ones as soon as possible.
      3. **Concept development and testing.** Surviving ideas must now be developed into product concepts. These concepts are tested with target customers.

4. **Marketing strategy.** There are three parts to the marketing strategy statement. The first part describes the target market, the planned product positioning and the sales, market share, and profit goals for the first two years. The second part outlines the product's planned price, distribution, and marketing budget for the first year. The third part describes the planned long-run sales, profit, and the market mix strategy over time.
5. **Business analysis.** Business analysis involves a review of the sales, costs, and profit projections to determine whether they satisfy the company's objectives.
6. **Product development.** Product development turns the concept into a prototype of the product.
7. **Market testing.** Market testing is the stage in which the product and marketing program are introduced into more realistic market settings.
8. **Commercialization.** The product is brought into the marketplace.

IV. Product Life-Cycle Stages
   A. **Product development.** It begins when the company finds and develops a new-product idea.
   B. **Introduction.** It is a period of slow sales growth as the product is being introduced into the market. Profits are nonexistent at this stage.
   C. **Growth.** It is a period of rapid market acceptance and increasing profits.
   D. **Maturity.** It is a period of slowdown in sales growth because the product has achieved acceptance by most of its potential buyers.
   E. **Decline.** It is the period when sales fall off quickly and profits drop.
   F. **Product deletion.** The deletion analysis is a systematic review of a product's projected sales and estimated costs associated with those sales. If a product no longer appears to be profitable, the analysis looks at possible ways to make modifications and return it to profitability. If the analysis indicates that the product should be deleted, there are three choices: phase-out, run-out, or drop it immediately.

V. **International Product and Service Marketing.** International marketers must figure out what products and services to introduce and in which countries. Then, they must decide how much to standardize or adapt their products and services for world markets.

IN-CLASS GROUP EXERCISES

*Exercises with an asterisk next to them are suitable for individual homework or online assignments. Students, always provide an explanation for your answer.

1. *Given all the changes in the branding strategy for Las Vegas over the years, has the Vegas brand had a consistent meaning to consumers? Is this a benefit or a detriment to the city as it moves forward?
2. *Use a product from the hospitality or travel industry to explain the following terms (provide an example in your explanation): (a) facilitating product, (b) supporting product, and (c) augmented product.
3. *As a hotel or restaurant manager, how would you gain new-product ideas?
4. *If you were the director of new-product development for a national fast-food chain, what factors would you consider in choosing cities for test marketing a new sandwich? Would the place where you live be a good test market? Why or why not?
5. *Give examples of co-branding and ingredient branding practices in hotel and restaurant industry. What are the advantages and disadvantages of these practices?
6. *Explain why many people are willing to pay more for branded products than for unbranded products. What does this tell you about the value of branding?
7. *Apply the concept of the product life cycle to a hotel. How does a company keep its products from going into the decline stage?
8. Walt Disney created the Disney brand from humble beginnings based on his love of drawing and animation. The Walt Disney Company has since expanded successfully into a global entertainment and media brand. Using the internet, research the components that make up the Disney brand and discuss how the Walt Disney Company has used branding strategies.
9. Go to the internet site of a hospitality or travel company. Think about the company's target market and the brand image it should portray. Does the company's Web site reinforce this brand image? Why or why not? What suggestions do you have for enhancing the image that the site portrays?

EXPERIENTIAL EXERCISES

Do one of the following:

1. Visit a hospitality or travel company. Look around at the physical facilities and the atmosphere of the company. Things you should look at include the exterior appearance, cleanliness, employees, atmosphere, and signage. Does the physical atmosphere support the image of the company or communicate to prospective customers and existing customers? Explain your answer.
2. Visit two locations of the same brand, such as two restaurants or two hotels. Does each location portray

the same brand image? Explain your answer. If the images are inconsistent, how could this affect prospective customers?

3. Visit http://www.brandme.jobs/en/. Explain how you would apply branding principles to brand yourself for job applications.

REFERENCES

1. Damon Hodge, "Tourism Chief Aims to Continue Vegas' Hot Streak," *Travel Weekly* (February 12, 2007): 64.

2. Jeff Delong, "After a Down Year, Vegas Hoping for a Rebound," *USA Today* (May 21, 2010): 2A; Nancy Trejos, "Las Vegas Bets the Future on a Game-Changing New Hotel Complex," *Washington Post* (January 31, 2010): F01; Tamara Audi, "Vegas Plans a New Push to Attract More People," *The Wall Street Journal* (January 7, 2008): B2; John King, "Luck Running Low in Las Vegas—Will It Turn Around," CNN.com (May 22, 2009), www.cnn.com; Tamara Audi, "Vegas Tries Luck with Old Slogan," *The Wall Street Journal* (May 13, 2009): B5; Damon Hodge, "Tourism Chief Aims to Continue Vegas' Hot Streak," *Travel Weekly* (February 12, 2007): 64; Tamara Audi, "Las Vegas Touts Its Affordability," *The Wall Street Journal* (February 4, 2009): B5.

3. Adam Nagourney, "Crowd Returns to Las Vegas but Gamble Less," July 31, 2013, http://www.nytimes.com/2013/08/01/us/as-las-vegas-recovers-new-cause-for-concern.html?_r=0;AnnFriedman, "Latest Trend in Las Vegas Is Boutique Hotels," *Las Vegas Business Press* (November 24, 2014): 7; Alison Gregor, "As Las Vegas Evolves, Boutique Hotels Gain," *The New York Times* (April 17, 2013): B10; Steve Green, "New Nobu Hotel at Caesars Palace Could Help Define Las Vegas as a City for Boutique Hotels," July 6, 2012, http://www.vegasinc.com/business/real-estate/2012/jul/06/new-nobu-hotel-caesars-palace-could-help-define-la/; "The LINQ Hotel & Casino Now Open After Complete Renovation," July 8, 2015, http://www.multivu.com/players/English/7,570,151-the-linq-hotel-casino-reopening/; Laura Carrol, "Las Vegas Aims to Benefit from Surge in Foreign tourism," *Las Vegas Review Journal*, January 8, 2012, http://www.reviewjournal.com/business/tourism/las-vegas-Aims-Benefit-Surge-Foreign-Tourism; http://www.lvcva.com/stats-and-facts/visitor-statistics (accessed September 2018).

4. "Say Hello to Canopy by Hilton," October 15, 2014, http://news.hiltonworldwide.com/index.cfm/newsroom/detail/27,567; "Hilton Launches 'Canopy' Lifestyle Hotel Brand," *TravelAgent*, November 3, 2014: P11; "Hilton Lifts Lid on Its New Lifestyle Brand," boutiqedesign.com (accessed November 2014); "Hilton Opens World's First Canopy in Reykjavik, Iceland," July 5, 2016, *Hotel Management*, https://www.hotelmanagement.net/openings/hilton-opens-world-s-first-canopy-reykjavik; "Experience Canopy," https://canopy3.hilton.com/en/relax-to-revive/index.html (accessed on September 15, 2018).

5. Elliot Mest, "Robots Make Their Way into Hotels," June 17, 2015, http://www.hotelmanagement.net/technology/robots-make-their-way-into-hotels-31,575; Junvi Ola, "Hotels Engaging Social Media-Savvy Guests with Perks and Prizes," February 23, 2014, http://hospitality.cvent.com/blog/junvi-ola/hotels-engaging-social-media-savvy-guests-with-perks-and-prizes.

6. Joseph A. Michelli, *The New Gold Standard* (New York: McGraw-Hill, 2008).

7. See "Creating a Balance: Help Guests Stay Healthy," April 9, 2014, *Hotel Business*, http://www.hotelbusiness.com/Amenities/Creating-a-Balance-Help-Guests-Stay-Healthy-While-Traveling/47,108; "Brands Focus on Health and Wellness Design," http://www.hotelnewsnow.com/Article/12,455/Brands-focus-on-health-and-wellness-in-design (accessed October 15, 2013).

8. Christian Gronroos, *Service Management Marketing* (New York: Lexington Books, 1990), p. 69.

9. http://www.starwoodhotels.com/alofthotels/about/index.html (accessed September 17, 2011).

10. Andrea Sachs, "Aloft Hotels: A Hip Addition to the Inn Crowd," *Washington Post*, July 15, 2009, http://www.washingtonpost.com/wp-dyn/content/-article/2009/07/14/AR2009071403194.html (accessed September 24, 2011).

11. Martin Lindstrom, *Brand Sense* (New York: Free Press, 2005).

12. Bernard Booms and Mary J. Bitner, "Marketing Services by Managing the Environment," *Cornell Restaurant and Hotel Administration Quarterly* (May 1992): 35–39.

13. See Le Méridien LM 100, http://www.starwoodhotels.com/lemeridien/lm100/index.html (accessed September 25, 2011).

14. Britt Aboutaleb, "Le Labo's Scent for Le Meridien Smells of Libraries and the Little Prince," Elle (September 23, 2011), http://fashion.elle.com/life-and-love/ (accessed September 24, 2011).

15. Philip Kotler, "Atmospherics as a Marketing Tool," *Journal of Retailing*, 49, no. 4 (1973–1974): 48–64.

16. Gronroos, *Service Management and Marketing* (New York: Lexington Books, 1990).

17. Karthik Namasivayam and Timothy R. Hinkin, "The Customer's Role in the Service Encounter," *Cornell Hotel and Restaurant Administration Quarterly*, 44, no. 3 (2003): 34.

18. See Scott Mayerowitz, "Making the Hotel Lobby a Place to See and Be Seen," September 4, 2013, http://news.yahoo.com/making-hotel-lobby-place-see-seen-070232759.html; Alissa Ponchione,

19. T. O'Brien, "Disney Looks to Fill Needs of Guests with Refill Soft Drink Mugs," *Amusement Business*, 114, no. 34 (2002): 7; Herb Leibacher, "Disney Puts RFID Technology in Cups at Walt Disney World," January 1, 2015, https://www.worldofwalt.com/disney-puts-rfid-technology-in-cups-at-walt-disney-world.html; Melissa Roden, "How Do Walt Disney World's Refillable Resort Mugs Work?" December 6, 2017, https://disneyaddicts.com/disney-world-refillable-resort-mugs-work-6806/.

20. Sarah Nassauer, "Chili's to Install Tabletop Computer Screens," *The Wall Street Journal*, September 15, 2013, http://www.wsj.com/articles/SB10001424127887323342404579077453886739272.

21. Sarah Turcotte, "The Wait Is Over," *Fast Company*, September 2012.

22. See "McAtlas Shrugged," *Foreign Policy* (May–June 2001): 26–37; Philip Kotler and Kevin Lane Keller, *Marketing Management*, 15th ed. (Upper Saddle River: Pearson Publishing, 2016), p. 316.

23. See "For Sale: Hessian, A Brand Without a Product," *Fast Company*, February 12, 2013, www.fastcodesign.com/1,671,819/for-sale-hessian-a-brand-without-a-product.

24. For more on Young & Rubicam's Brand Asset Valuator, see "Brand Asset Valuator," Value Based Management.net, www.valuebasedmanagement.net/methods_brand_asset_valuator.html (accessed May 2010); www.brandassetconsulting.com (accessed May 2010); W. Ronald Lane, Karen Whitehill King, and Tom Reichert, *Kleppner's Advertising Procedure*, 18th ed. (Upper Saddle River, NJ: Pearson Prentice Hall, 2011), pp. 83–84.

25. "Leading Companies Worldwide in 2018, by Brand Value (in Billion U.S. Dollars)," https://www.statista.com/statistics/269444/brand-value-of-the-most-valuable-companies-worldwide/ (accessed September 2018); "The World's Most Valuable Brands of 2018," *Lodging*, February 23, 2018, http://lodgingmagazine.com/worlds-valuable-brands-2018/.

26. See Scott Davis, *Brand Asset Management*, 2nd ed. (San Francisco, CA: Jossey-Bass, 2002). For more on brand positioning, see Philip Kotler and Kevin Lane Keller, *Marketing Management*, Chapter 10.

27. See www.jimstengel.com (accessed June 2010).

28. Lara O' Reilly, "Virgin America Bids to Banish Command Culture," *Marketing Week*, September 20, 2012; Joan Voight, "Where's the Party? At 30,000 Feet Virgin America Marketing Chief: 'What Would Richard Do?'" *Adweek*, February 5, 2013; Michael Bush, "Virgin America," *Advertising Age*, November 16, 2009, p. 12.

29. John W. O'Neill and Anna S. Matilla, "Hotel Brand Strategy," *Cornell Hospitality Quarterly*, 51 (February 2010), 27–34.

30. Jing Lei, Niraj Dawar, and Jos Lemmink. "Negative Spillover in Brand Portfolios: Exploring the Antecedents of Asymmetric Effects." *Journal of Marketing*, 72 (May 2008): 111–123.

31. "Tim Hortons and Cold Stone: Co-Branding Strategies," *BusinessWeek* (July 10, 2009), www.businessweek.com/smallbiz/content/jul2009/sb20090710_574574.htm; Steve McKee, "The Pros and Cons of Co-Branding," *BusinessWeek* (July 10, 2009), www.businessweek.com/smallbiz/content/jul2009/sb20090710_255169.htm.

32. See Austin Carr, "The Hard Sell at Taco Bell," *Fast Company*, July/August 2013, pp. 36–38; www.tacobell.com/food/menuitem/Doritos-Locos-Tacos-Supreme (accessed September 2014).

33. Steve Green, "New Nobu Hotel at Caesars Palace Could Help Define Las Vegas as a City for Boutique Hotels," July 2012, *VegasInc*, http://www.vegasinc.com/business/real-estate/2012/jul/06/new-nobu-hotel-caesars-palace-could-help-define-la/.

34. http://www.smartbrief.com/05/17/12/choice-unveils-new-fb-program-dual-brand-hotel-concept#.VRrqVnF_1Y; Mark Chesnut, "New Food, New Look at Choice Hotels Properties," June 7, 2012, http://www.orbitz.com/blog/2012/06/new-food-new-look-at-choice-hotels-properties/.

35. "Hilton Worldwide Opened Dual-Branded Property in Washington D.C.," Hotel Management (September 2, 2016), https://www.hotelmanagement.net/openings/hilton-opens-hampton-homewood-dual-brand-washington-d-c; "Dual-Branded Aloft and Element Open in Dallas," *Hotel Management* (February 15, 2017), https://www.hotelmanagement.net/openings/dual-branded-aloft-and-element-open-dallas.,

36. Philip Kotler and Waldermar Pfoertsch, *Ingredient Branding: Making the Invisible Visible* (Heidelberg, Germany: Springer-Verlag, 2011); Kalpesch Kaushik Desai and Kevin Lane Keller, "The Effects of Brand Expansions and Ingredient Branding Strategies on Host Brand Extendibility," *Journal of Marketing*, 66 (January 2002): 73–93.

37. Martin Bishop, "Finding Your Nemo: How to Survive the Dangerous Waters of Ingredient Branding," *Chief Executive*, March 15, 2010.

38. See http://www.mgmgrand.com/hotel/stay-well.aspx for MGM Stay Well suites features; "MGM Grand Hotel & Casino to Expand Stay Well Program to 171 Guestrooms," http://newsroom.mgmgrand.com/ (accessed September 17, 2013).

39. David A. Aaker, *Brand Portfolio Strategy: Creating Relevance, Differentiation, Energy, Leverage, and Clarity* (New York: Free Press, 2004).

40. Maria-Pia Intini, "Boutique Evolved: 5 Key Trends," November 14, 2011, http://www.hotelnewsnow.com/Article/6945/Boutique-evolved-5-key-trends.

41. Alicia Hoisington, "Brands Focus on Health and Wellness in Design," October 15, 2013, http://www.hotelnewsnow.com/Article/12,455/Brands-focus-on-health-and-wellness-in-design; http://www.evenhotels.com/hotels/us/en/reservation.

42. Christopher Hosford, "A Transformative Experience," *Sales and Marketing Management*, 158 (June 2006): 32–36; Mike Beirne and Javier Benito, "Starwood Uses Personnel to Personalize Marketing," *Brandweek* (April 24, 2006): 9; Deanna Ting and Greg Oates, "Every One of Marriott's 30 Hotel Brands, Explained," *Skift*, September 21, 2016, https://skift.com/2016/09/21/every-one-of-marriotts-30-hotel-brands-explained/.

43. Jack Trout, *Differentiate or Die: Survival in Our Era of Killer Competition* (New York: Wiley, 2000); Kamalini Ramdas and Mohanbir Sawhney, "A Cross-Functional Approach to Evaluating Multiple Line Extensions for Assembled Products," *Management Science*, 47 (January 2001): 22–36.

44. Nirmalya Kumar, "Kill a Brand, Keep a Customer," *Harvard Business Review* (December 2003): 87–95.

45. For a methodological approach for assessing the extent and nature of cannibalization, see Charlotte H. Mason and George R. Milne, "An Approach for Identifying Cannibalization Within Product Line Extensions and Multibrand Strategies," *Journal of Business Research*, 31 (October–November 1994): 163–170.

46. Phillip Kotler, Hermawan Kartajaya, and Iwan Setiawan. *Marketing 3.0* (New Jersey: John Wiley & Sons, Inc., 2010).

47. Stephen Cole, "Value of the Brand," *CA Magazine* (May 2005): 39–40. Also see "The Power of Customer Service," *Fortune*, December 3, 2012, www.timeinc-newsgroupcustompub.com/sections/121203_Disney.pdf; and "Community Engagement," https://aboutdisneyparks.com/citizenship/community (accessed September 2018).

48. See Kevin Lane Keller, *Strategic Brand Management* (Upper Saddle River, NJ: Prentice Hall, 2008), Chapter 10.

49. "Panda Restaurants Goes into Retail," *American City Business Journal* (February 2004).

50. Howard Riell, "High Expectations," *Kahiki*, July 12, 2006, http://kahiki.blogspot.com/2006/09/frozen-food-age-article.html (accessed September 19, 2011).

51. Julie Feickert, Rohit Verma, Gerhart Plaschka, and Cheikitan Dev, "Safeguarding Your Customers," *Cornell Hotel and Restaurant Administration Quarterly* (August 2006): 224.

52. John Peppers and Martha Rogers, "The Buzz on Customer-Driven Innovation," *Sales and Marketing Management* (June 2007): 13.

53. Urvaksh Karkaria, "Chick-fil-A puts 6,000-Square-Foot Innovation Center in Midtown," *Atlanta Business Chronicle*, March 8, 2017, https://www.bizjournals.com/atlanta/news/2017/03/08/chick-fil-a-puts-6-000-square-foot-innovation.html; Casey Miles, "Chick-fil-A Opens New Innovation Center," January 27, 2018, http://nique.net/news/2018/01/26/chick-fil-a-opens-new-innovation-center/.

54. Kate Leahy, "Discovery Zone," *Restaurants and Institutions* (July 15, 2007): 49.

55. http://mystarbucksidea.force.com/apex/idealist?lsi=1 (accessed December 16, 2015).

56. Joseph Mackenzie, "Can Hotels Use Crowdsourcing," February 5, 2009, http://www.hotelmarketingstrategies.com/can-hotels-use-crowdsourcing/ (accessed September 19, 2011).

57. Elisabeth A. Sullivan, "A Group Effort: More Companies Are Turning to the Wisdom of the Crowd to Find Ways to Innovate," *Marketing News* (February 28, 2010): 22–29.

58. Kristin Boyd, "Crowdsourcing Is Changing Hotel Design and Marketing," *Lodging*, May 5, 2014, http://lodgingmagazine.com/crowdsourcing-is-changing-hotel-design-and-marketing/.

59. Nancy Trejos, "Guests Help Design the Hotel of the Future," *USA Today*, November 15, 2013, http://www.usatoday.com/story/travel/hotels/2013/11/14/hotel-guests-millennials-design-marriott-holiday-inn/3,538,573/; "Designs on the Future—Big Ideas Become Reality at Marriott Hotels' New 'Underground' Innovation Lab," May 30, 2013, http://news.marriott.com/2013/05/designs-on-the-future-big-ideas-become-reality-at-marriott-hotels-new-underground-innovation-lab.html; Kristin Boyd, "Crowdsourcing Is Changing Hotel Design and Marketing," *Lodging*, May 5, 2014, http://lodgingmagazine.com/crowdsourcing-is-changing-hotel-design-and-marketing/.

60. Lauren McKay, "300 Current Priority Club Visa Cardholders Willing to Share Their Opinions on What Card Benefits and Services Are Important," December 8, 2010, http://www.emarketer.com/blog/index.php/case-study-using-online-community-crowd-source-customer-loyalty-strategies/ (accessed September 17, 2011); Amanda Kludt, "4Food, the Bonkers Techie Resto Coming Soon to Midtown," May 26, 2010, http://ny.eater.com/archives/2010/05/meet_4food_the_most_bonkers_restaurant_to_ever_hit_midtown.php (accessed September 17, 2010).

61. "The REO Eats Project," http://www.reoeatsproject.com/about-the-project/ (accessed September 17, 2010).

62. Guido Jouret, "Inside Cisco's Search for the Next Big Idea," *Harvard Business Review* (September 2009): 43–45.

63. Kevin O'Donnell, "Where Do the Best Ideas Come From? The Un-Likeliest Sources," *Advertising Age* (July 14, 2008): 15.

64. The Marriott example and this list were drawn from Christopher W. L. Hart, "Product Development: How Marriott Created Courtyard," *Cornell Hotel and Restaurant Administration Quarterly*, 27, no. 3 (1986): 68–69;

Jerry Wind, Paul E. Green, Douglas Shifflet, and Marsha Scarborough, "Courtyard by Marriott: Designing a Hotel Facility with Consumer Based Marketing," *Interfaces*, 19, no. 1 (1989): 25–47.

65. J. L. Heskett and R. Hallowell, "Courtyard by Marriott," *Harvard Case* 9–693-036 (Boston, MA: Harvard Business School Publishing, 1993).

66. Michael Lowrey, "Poor Attendance Plagues N. C. Arenas," *Carolina Journal*, 11, no. 3 (March 2004): 15.

67. Austin Carr, "Starbucks Leap of Faith," *Fast Company*, June 2013, pp 46–48; and "Starbucks' Mobile Transactions Top 8 Million Weekly," PYMNTS.COM, April 24, 2015, www.pymnts.com/news/2015/starbucks-mobile-transactions-top-8-million-weekly/.

68. Maria Malagna, "KFC is Right—People Are Gobbling up 'Meat Replacements'" *MarketWatch* June 17, 2018, https://www.marketwatch.com/story/kfc-is-right-people-are-gobbling-up-meat-replacements-2018-06-07.

69. See Emily Bryson York, "McD's Serves Up $100M McCafe Ad Blitz," *Cram's Chicago Business* (May 4, 2009), www.chicagobusiness.com; John Letzing, "Bing's Share Rises Again," *The Wall Street Journal* (June 18, 2009), http://online.wsj.com; Rita Chang, "With $100M Saturation Campaign, Droid Will Be Impossible to Avoid," *Advertising Age* (November 9, 2009): 3.

70. Theodore Levitt, *The Marketing Imaginization* (New York: Free Press, 1986), p. 173.

71. Christopher W. Hart, Greg Casserly, and Mark J. Lawless, "The Product Life Cycle: How Useful?" *Cornell Hotel and Restaurant Administration Quarterly*, 25, no. 3 (November 1984): 54–63.

72. Janet Adamy, "A Shift in Dining Scene Nicks a Once-Hot Chain," *The Wall Street Journal* (June 29, 2007): A1 and A3.

73. *Momentum!*, DineEquity Annual Report 2010.

74. Candice Choi, "Wendy's Outlines Airier, Modern Restaurant Look," *USA Today*, March 1, 2012, http://usatoday30.usatoday.com/money/companies/earnings/story/2012-03-01/wendys/53,315,420/1; Hank Hayes, "New-Look Wendy's Restaurant Opens on West Stone Drive," October 9, 2013, http://www.timesnews.net/article/9,068,456/new-look-wendys-restaurant-opens-on-west-stone-drive#ixzz3Ua3brTKg.

75. Bruce Horovitz, "McDonald's Expands Custom Sandwich Option," December 7, 2014, http://www.usatoday.com/story/money/business/2014/12/07/mcdonalds-fast-food-restaurants-create-your-taste-millennials/19,943,987/; Alexandria Fisher, "McDonald's Expands 'Build-Your-Own-Burger,'" September 11, 2014, http://www.nbcchicago.com/blogs/inc-well/McDonalds-Expands-Build-Your-Own-Burger-Test-274,815,801.html.

76. Richard N. Velotte, "Caesars to Spend $223 Million on Revamping Quad, Rebranding It as Linq Hotel," *Las Vegas Review-Journal*, July 1, 2014, http://www.reviewjournal.com/business/casinos-gaming/caesars-spend-223-million-revamping-quad-rebranding-it-linq-hotel; Leo Jakobson, "Outdoors Is In," *Successful Meetings*, January 15, 2015, pp. 56, 58.

77. Kortney Stringer, "Abandoning the Mall," *The Wall Street Journal* (March 24, 2001): B1.

78. William Pride and O. C. Ferrell, *Marketing* (Boston, MA: Houghton-Mifflin Publishing, 1995), pp. 312–313.

79. Based on information found in Celia Hatton, "KFC's Finger Lickin' Success in China," *CBS News*, March 6, 2011, www.cbsnews.com/2100-3445_162-20,039,783.html; Maggie Starvish, "KFC's Explosive Growth in China," *HBS Working Knowledge*, June 17, 2011, http://hbswk.hbs.edu/cgi-bin/print/6704.html; David E. Bell and Mary L. Shelman, "KFC's Radical Approach to China," *Harvard Business Review*, November 2011, pp. 137–142; www.yum.com/brands/china.asp (accessed October 2013); Harrison Jacobs, "KFC Is by Far the Most Popular Fast Food Chain in China and It's Nothing Like the US brand—Here's What It's Like," Business Insider, April 15, 2018, https://www.businessinsider.com/most-popular-fast-food-chain-in-china-kfc-photos-2018-4.

Zabotnova Inna/Shutterstock.

Objectives

After reading this chapter, you should be able to:

1. Explain why internal marketing is an important part of a marketing program.
2. Describe the steps in the internal marketing process.

10

Internal Marketing

Other exclusive resorts pamper their guests, but Four Seasons has perfected the art of high-touch, carefully crafted service. Whether it's at the elegantly "re-imagined" Four Seasons London, the regally attentive Four Seasons Hotel Riyadh in Saudi Arabia, the tropical island paradise at the Four Seasons Resort Mauritius, or the luxurious Sub-Saharan "camp" at the Four Seasons Safari Lodge Serengeti, guests paying $1,000 or more a night expect to have their minds read. For these guests, Four Seasons doesn't disappoint. Its mission is to perfect the travel experience through the highest standards of hospitality.

As a result, Four Seasons has a cult-like customer clientele, making it one of the most-decorated hotel chains in the world. As one Four Seasons Maui guest recently told a manager, "If there's a heaven, I hope it's run by Four Seasons."

But what makes Four Seasons so special? It's really no secret. Just ask anyone who works there. From the CEO to the doorman, they'll tell you it's the quality of the Four Seasons staff. Its people are responsible for the success of the organization, states Four Seasons founder Isadore Sharp. Just as it does for customers, Four Seasons respects and pampers its employees. It knows that happy, satisfied employees make for happy, satisfied customers.

The Four Seasons customer service legacy is deeply rooted in the company's culture, which in turn is grounded in the Golden Rule. In all of its dealings with both guests and staff, the luxury resort chain seeks to treat others as it wishes to be treated. If you expect your employees to treat your customers well, you must treat them well.

Most important, once it has the right people in place, Four Seasons treats them as it would its most important guests. Compared with the competition, Four Seasons's salaries are in the 75th to 90th percentile, with generous

A bell person at a Ritz-Carlton hotel delivered baggage to a guest about an hour after he had checked in due to an error. After he had delivered the luggage, he told his supervisor. The supervisor apologized to the guest and noted in the hotel's computer that this guest had experienced a problem and should receive exceptional service during the rest of his stay.[26] This seems like a rational way to handle the problem, but it is really an extraordinary event. In a hotel with a conventional organizational structure, if employees make a mistake, they hope their supervisor never finds out about it; they may even try to cover it up. They know that if their supervisor does find out about a mistake, they may be reprimanded. The Ritz-Carlton has a service culture; it has turned the organizational structure upside down. The bell person was concerned about the guest and knew his supervisor would take action that would enable the hotel to recover from his mistake. The supervisor was not afraid to communicate the department's mistake to other departments. When you turn the organization upside down, everyone works to serve the guest. When you have a conventional organizational structure, everyone works to please the boss. What is ironic is that when everyone works for the boss, the company loses. When everyone works for the customer, the financial performance is greater.

Nonroutine Transactions

An advantage of a strong culture is that it prepares employees to handle nonroutine transactions. A nonroutine transaction is a guest transaction that is unique and usually experienced for the first time by employees. The number of possible nonroutine transactions is so great that they cannot be covered in a training manual or in training programs. One benefit of a service culture is that it provides employees with the right attitude, knowledge, communication skills, and authority to deal with nonroutine transactions. The ability to handle nonroutine transactions separates excellent hospitality companies from mediocre ones.

An example of a nonroutine transaction is a guest who requested a late checkout so he could hold a business meeting in his room. Unfortunately, the hotel was fully booked, and the room was needed for guests arriving that afternoon. The policy manual would have said to tell the guest that he could not be accommodated in this situation. A service culture creates a desire to service the guest. The manager made provisions for him to use a vacant conference room free of charge. The guest offered to pay, but the hotel refused. The room would have never been rented at the last minute, so there was no lost revenue. The future business the hotel received from the guest who was a business consultant and the positive word of mouth was many times the amount the hotel would have received from the guest if it charged him for the room.[27] Empowered and innovative employees can handle nonroutine transactions.

A team of researchers studied the effect of employee empowerment on customers' perception of service quality. They found, "Ultimately, empowered and satisfied employees significantly influence how customers perceive the service quality of a restaurant. Therefore, restaurants must establish excellent HRM practices to empower and satisfy their employees, who in turn will deliver what the customer wants—a high quality of service."[28]

Management must be willing to give employees the authority to make decisions that will solve guests' problems. Management should exhibit confidence in its ability to hire and train employees by trusting the employees' ability to make decisions. Simon Cooper, former president of Delta Hotels and Resorts, believes that having staff do nothing but control other staff reflects poorly on the organization. He states that the job of an assistant housekeeper is to go around and check that the maids are doing their job. Having that position is an admission that we can't hire the right people. Cooper says that Delta has only a few assistant housekeepers, who are now in training positions. When their housekeepers finish a room, they know that the next person in it will be a guest. Cooper states that the degree of trust makes them far better workers.[29] When we trust employees, they solve guest problems more effectively and create fewer causes for the guest to complain.

Hospitality companies that rely on rigid policies and procedures rather than motivated, well-trained, and empowered employees have little hope of achieving maximum guest satisfaction.

The issue of nonroutine transactions will become increasingly important in the future. Hospitality firms are now using technology to serve routine customer transactions. This use of technology will become even more pervasive. Computerized check-in, video checkout, and robotics will be adapted to the hospitality industry, so employees will find themselves dealing more frequently with nonroutine tasks. Self-confident guests will take advantage of technology designed to enhance and hasten guest service. The uncertain guest or guests with problems will wish to deal with an employee. As the workplace becomes more automated, employees will take a greater role in answering questions and solving guests' problems. They must also be prepared to handle nonroutine transactions.

As Parasuraman says, "Customer service earned through several satisfactorily performed routine transactions can be badly damaged by just one botched attempt at processing a nonroutine transaction. No amount of written procedures, guidelines, or specifications can prevent the occurrence of such botched attempts; only true organizational dedication to customer satisfaction can."[30] A strong service culture enables employees to make decisions required to handle nonroutine transactions.

Development of a Marketing Approach to Human Resources Management

Creating Jobs That Attract Good People

Managers must use the principles of marketing to attract and retain employees. They must research and develop an understanding of their employees' needs, just as they examine the needs of customers. Not all employees are the same. Some employees seek money to supplement their incomes; others are looking for work that will be their sole source of income. Marketers can use marketing research techniques to segment the employee market, choosing the best segments for the firm and developing a marketing mix to attract those segments. For employees, the marketing mix is the job, pay, benefits, location, transportation, parking, hours, and intangible rewards, such as prestige and perceived advancement opportunities. Just as customers look for different attributes when they purchase a product, employees look for different benefits. Some may be attracted by flexible working hours, others are attracted by good health insurance benefits, and still others may be attracted by childcare facilities. Flexible working hours for office or housekeeping positions, cafeteria-style benefit programs in which employees design their own benefit package, and childcare can all be used to attract a certain type of employee. Advertising should be developed with prospective employees in mind, building a positive image of the firm for present and future employees and customers. Employees choose employers and leave them the same way that guests select certain hotels and then decide to switch. It is expensive to lose both guests and employees.[31] Using a marketing approach to develop positions and company benefits helps attract and maintain good employees. A reduction in turnover can result in hundreds of thousands of dollars in savings.[32]

Within the United Kingdom, turnover for the hospitality industry is estimated at 30 percent and higher in London. Recruitment and training is estimated at £1500 per employee making the total cost about £886 million.[33]

The Hiring Process

The service product, at least in part, is the attitude the employee displays as he or she delivers the service experience. It is unlikely that the service provider can teach the service attitude that all its customer-contact employees need. Service organizations need to hire for attitude and train for skills.[34] "Service characteristics like intangibility and customer contact require service employees to display more initiative, to cope more effectively with stress, to be more interpersonally flexible and sensitive, and to be more cooperative than their colleagues who work in manufacturing."[35] This idea means that service firms place more emphasis on personality, energy, and attitude than on education, training, and experience in their recruitment, selection, and training strategies. Finding employees who are good at creating a service experience is a vital goal and major hiring criterion of service organizations.

Several service marketing experts have stated there are lessons hospitality organizations can learn from theater. Dramaturgy (the craft of theatrical production) includes selecting people for a customer service role similar to casting people for roles in a theatrical production. The costumes help put some into character, just as uniforms do in a hospitality organization. The actors, stagehands, and theater attendants need to work together, just as the hostess, cooks, servers, and bus help do in a restaurant. Good actors know how to get into character and leave any personal problems at home so they can produce a great performance for the audience. Finally, they know the audience and work to please the audience. Dramaturgy also involves the setting for the theatrical production, something we have discussed in previous chapters.[36] The study of theater can provide useful insights for service marketers.

Swissair carefully screens its applicants, selects candidates for personal interviews, and puts them through a five- to six-hour selection process. The airline then puts successful applicants on probation for a three-month period. It invests a great deal in each candidate because it realizes it is better to spend money choosing the right employee than trying to repair mistakes caused by poor employees. Swissair understands the importance of hiring the right employees.[37]

Southwest Airlines strongly believes inherent attitudes cannot be changed in people. To test for behaviors such as a sense of humor, ability to work with others, and friendliness, Southwest's interview process includes group interviews where applicants tell jokes and role-play a variety of situations to demonstrate teamwork and the capacity to act spontaneously. Southwest can afford to be very selective because it receives an extremely large number of job applications with little active advertising, thanks to its reputation for being a unique and excellent place to work.

Southwest places special emphasis on preparing its people to perform and on teamwork. It considers employee training to be a continuous process rather than a single event. Throughout their careers, employees are cross-trained on multiple jobs to enrich every employee's work experience and to prepare them to perform flexibly in different positions as needed. In addition, employees are specifically assigned to work with a senior employee who serves as a mentor to provide a clear demonstration of Southwest's service quality and to be available to answer questions.[38] Colleen Barrett, president emeritus of Southwest Airlines, states that Southwest's real business is customer service; their product just happens to be air transportation.[39]

Cast members A term used for employees. It implies that employees are part of a team that is performing for their guests.

Disney World allows its best employees, its star "**cast members**," to pick future employees. Disney gives cast members who will be used in the selection process three weeks of training. They are then turned loose in a 45-minute interview session to select potential new employees. James Poisant, a former manager at Disney World, explains that employees choose employees who mirror their own values. "In 45 minutes the cast members pick up on who is fooling and who's genuine."[40]

Careful selection can also have a positive effect on the employees who are hired because they feel special. Adam Hassan, a Ritz-Carlton boiler operator, explains, "When people take so much time to select you, you really want to prove they made the right choice. So if I see anything unusual I take care of it."[41]

Danny Meyer, New York restaurateur and author of *Setting the Table*, sums up the essence of hiring in the hospitality industry by stating that he looks for people who have good technical skills, but more importantly they must also have good emotional skills. The emotional skills include optimistic warmth, a curiosity to learn new things coupled with the intelligence that enables one to learn, a work ethic that includes attention to detail, empathy, and self-awareness, and integrity.[42]

Selection methods that identify customer-oriented candidates must be used as part of the hiring process. Employee's attitude, appearance, and willingness to

The craft of theater productions provides principles that apply to the hospitality industry.
Lee Foster/Alamy Stock Photo.

handle the guest's requests help form a first impression of a hotel or a restaurant. Hiring and training, traditionally the responsibility of human resources management, are key areas in any internal marketing program. A marketing-like approach to human resources management starts with hiring the right employees.

Teamwork

If a company hires the right people, they will be team players. In companies that practice internal marketing, if one employee makes an error, other employees try to correct it before the guest notices. In these organizations, guests do not have to understand the hotel's organization and business to ensure that their needs are met. The front desk handles most requests, relaying the guest's desire to the appropriate department. In restaurants that have used internal marketing to create a service culture, staff members cover for each other. Employees who see that a guest needs something will serve the guest, even though it may not be their table.

Organizations that lack teamwork create an uncomfortable environment for the guest. For example, a guest called the front desk of a five-star resort and asked for extra towels. The front-desk clerk answering the telephone acted puzzled. Surely a guest would know to call housekeeping for towels. The operator stated that this was the front desk, not housekeeping, told the guest to call housekeeping, and hung up. Many restaurant guests have asked for a drink while they are sitting at their tables looking over the dinner menu. The response to some of these guests is that they have mistaken the food-service person for a cocktail-service person. The food serviceperson then tells the customers to redirect their requests to cocktail service and departs, leaving the guests' needs unfilled. In both of these incidents, the first employee contacted should have taken care of the customer's request and passed it along to the appropriate person. This is referred to as *ownership of the problem*. Customers should not have to learn the hotel or restaurant's organizational chart. They should not have to redirect their request for service to another employee. Hiring procedures need to identify those employees who are team players.

Older employees were one group that surprised some managers by their willingness to support other employees. Some managers believed the elderly might not be willing to cooperate with much younger workers or to accept direction from a youthful supervisor. KFC and McDonald's were among the first hospitality firms to prove the invalidity of these assumptions. A survey of National Restaurant Association members demonstrated that older workers were regarded to have better relations with guests and fellow employees than the "average employees."[43]

Coworker Support

The support or denial of support from coworkers may be the difference between a service-directed employee or an unhappy one whose negative feelings are transmitted to guests.

A study concerning the importance of coworkers concluded that, "It is important to train frontline employees concerning the critical role of co-worker support. Since such individuals have intense face-to-face or voice-to-voice interactions with customers, they are likely to be faced with various problems they may not be able to handle. Therefore, they need the support of co-workers. The availability of co-worker support appears to be essential, because co-worker support alleviates turnover intentions."[44]

"Fun in the workplace has both beneficial and potentially negative effects (if not carefully carried out) on employees in the hospitality industry." The authors of this statement recommended productive fun events such as productivity contests and social events. Fun may be an antidote to turnover challenge. Most individuals want more from work than financial compensation.[45]

The Importance of Initial Training

A guest overheard a conversation between a guest and the dining-room hostess of a hotel. The guest asked for a recommendation concerning a good place to eat in the area. Managers would hope that the hostess first would suggest the hotel's restaurant and then mention other restaurants in the area. Instead, the hostess said she had just moved to the area and had not yet found a good place to eat. Too often, employees know nothing about the hotel they work for or its products and other items of interest to guests. If employees are not enthusiastic about the company they work for and the products they sell, it will be difficult to create enthusiastic customers.

At the other extreme, a guest checked into the Quality Suites Tech Center South in Denver, Colorado, on a Saturday night and asked the front-desk clerk if he knew where the closest Catholic Church was for Mass the next morning. The clerk replied that he was not of that faith and did not know but would find out. Five minutes after the guest was in his room, the phone rang. It was from the front-desk clerk who said he had found three Catholic churches and Mass times and had personally called a Catholic friend to see which of the three he would recommend. At the same time, the desk clerk asked if the guest had eaten yet and when the answer was no, he proceeded to tell him of the great Mexican food in the hotel's restaurant and then offered to make a reservation. The guest enjoyed the Mexican food. If we hire the right employees and provide good training, we will be well on the way to having enthusiastic employees create repeat guests.

When we spend a great deal of time and effort selecting employees, we want to keep them. Consultant Jeanne d'Orleans provides some suggestions on how to make employees feel welcome during their first week.

Day One

- Ask employees to arrive at a time when someone has time to greet them.
- Make the team aware they are coming so *everyone* can welcome them.
- Use bulletin boards or even marquees to say "Welcome Robert!"
- Give them a basic tour and introduce them to as many people as possible.

Within Week One

- Make sure employees participate in an organized orientation.
- Provide them with a partner/mentor during those first tenuous days.
- Have a skills training program for them.
- Tailor training to the level of expertise they bring.[46]

To be effective, employees must receive information regularly about their company. The company's history, current businesses, and its mission statement and vision are important for employees to know. They must be encouraged to feel proud of their new employer. Desire to contribute to the company's success must be instilled in them. At Disney all new employees take a course called "Traditions," in which they learn about the company, its founder, and its values and beliefs. Employees then receive specific training for their particular assignments. Disney trains its ticket takers for four days because the company wants them to be more than ticket takers; it wants them to be cast members. The term *cast members* implies they are members of a team. Like other Disney cast members, they are putting on a performance. While they work in the ticket booths, guests will ask many questions. They must know the answers to these questions or be able to find them quickly. Disney understands the importance of these moments of truth. It provides its staff with extensive training before the first moment of truth is faced.[47] Disney has become so well known for its training and human resources management that it now conducts courses for other companies.

Opryland Hotel has developed a training program that begins with an orientation for new employees, designed to instill pride in the history, culture, and stature of the hotel. The purpose of the orientation process is to create an inspiring atmosphere and build a solid work commitment that helps reduce turnover. According to Marc Clark, former director of training at Opryland, "The new employee orientation program and all employee policies are built on a foundation of a sincere service attitude. If employees, particularly managers, are not serving guests directly, then they should be serving those who are."[48]

At citizenM hotels, front-line employees are called ambassadors. The ambassadors are there to help guests with anything they ask for. The ambassador training takes 6 to 10 weeks and begins with a casting on the hotel site. The hotels look for people who are genuine, who might even become friends with the client. At New York location, the company has hired many of ambassadors from drama school. The senior management team has come in from Holland to do culture training. They have send ambassadors to restaurants and retail stores and do group sessions afterward to discuss their service experience. Then, they have visited other hotel lobbies, hung around, and talked about that experience. They have also done workshops on creativity and trust. Finally, they have paid for their trips to Amsterdam for 10 days to do the training in citizenM hotels there.[49]

Continuous Training

Isadore Sharp, founder of Four Seasons Hotels and Resorts, told his managers, "Our competitive edge is service, service delivered by frontline employees we expect you to develop." "Your role then will be a leader, not a boss. Your job will be to bring out the best in all individuals and weld them into a winning team."[50]

Cross-training Training employees to do two or more jobs within the organization.

Two principal characteristics have been identified in companies that lead their industries in customer service: They emphasize **cross-training**, and they insist that everybody share certain training experiences. Most hotel training programs for college graduates rotate new employees through all departments in the hotel. This gives the trainees an insight into the importance of each department and how they work together to provide customer service. James Coney Island, a fast-food restaurant chain, cross-trains its employees so that they understand all the positions in the restaurant. Embassy Suites Hotels goes a step further, providing employees an opportunity to increase their wages based on the number of positions they have mastered.

Companies must make sure that their employees are familiar with all the products they sell. For example, all restaurant employees should be prepared to tell guests about the restaurant's Sunday brunch. A restaurant service person in a hotel should be able to give directions to the hotel's health club. Often, employees do not have knowledge of products in their own areas because they have never been given the opportunity to sample them. When a service person does not know how an item tastes, it promotes the perception that the employee or management does not care about the customer.

Truthful Training

It should not be necessary to place this warning in a textbook but feedback from embarrassed and angry employees indicates that in some cases individuals in responsible management positions purposely lie to employees. An actual example occurred to a daughter of one of the authors. The daughter acquired a part-time waitress position at an upscale restaurant. She was told that the pork roast featured that day would be served pink since it was from Durok hogs and their flesh was pink when fully cooked.

The new waitress took an order of roast pork to a customer who immediately summoned her back and complained that his roast pork was not sufficiently cooked. The waitress then told him what she had been trained to say about Durok hogs. At this, the customer became very angry and said, "Young lady, I am a farmer of Durok hogs and what you said is a bold face lie. The meat in this breed should be white when cooked properly, not pink. My meat is not cooked, and I refuse to eat it." The waitress returned the order to the chef and told him he was a liar, that she was embarrassed, and furthermore she would no longer work for a restaurant where the chef was a liar.

A front-desk clerk in a large casino resort said she felt uneasy when guests asked her about the show in the casino's showroom. The hotel had stressed the importance of promoting it favorably but did not give the front-desk employees an opportunity to see the show. As a result, the front-desk clerk would tell the guest that it was a great show. Sometimes, the guest would start asking specific questions about the show. When this happened, her answers usually reflected her lack of firsthand knowledge about the show and made her feel foolish. It would have been wise for the hotel to provide an opportunity for front-desk employees to see the show. They could have enthusiastically promoted the show with firsthand knowledge instead of cringing when someone asked about it. They may even have promoted the show on their own rather than waiting for a guest to ask about it.

In well-managed restaurants, employees know the menu. They are trained to direct guests to the menu selections that will best suit their taste and instructed in how to sell the choices on the menu. Every restaurant should have tastings where employees sample the products they are selling. Product training is a continuous learning process; it should be part of every company's employee training.

The Olive Garden brand promise is "the idealized Italian family meal"—characterized by "fresh, simple, delicious Italian food," "complemented by a great glass of wine," served by "people who treat you like family," "in a comfortable home-like setting." To live up to that brand promise, the Olive Garden has sent more than 1,100 restaurant general managers and team members on cultural immersion trips to Italy, launched the Culinary Institute of Tuscany in Italy to inspire new dishes and teach general managers and team members authentic Italian cooking techniques, conducts wine training workshops for team members and in-restaurant wine sampling for guests, and is remodeling restaurants to give them a Tuscan farmhouse look. Communications include in-store, employee, and mass media messages that all reinforce the brand promise and ad slogan, "When You're Here, You're Family."[51]

Product training sometimes must extend into the visual arts. The Grand Hyatt of Hong Kong is a magnificent hotel with caring and well-trained personnel. The Grand Hyatt is truly an art museum within a hotel. The decor features sculpture, paintings, and other fine works of visual art. If exquisite art is part of the product, it should be part of the training. Guests will be impressed, and employees will gain pride in the hotel.

This results in the circular effect of creating satisfied and proud employees who in turn create satisfied guests. The results of a study of this circular effect clearly demonstrated that "as employees' job satisfaction, job involvement, and job security improve, their customer focus also improves."[52]

Insurance executives checking out of the Sheraton Boca Raton locked their keys in their car. The car was blocking traffic, and the executives had a plane to catch. The bellman telephoned the car's make and serial number to a nearby locksmith, and the hotel staff rolled the car out of traffic. Fifteen minutes after the bellman's call, the locksmith arrived with replacement keys.[53] The employees were successful in handling the problem because they were prepared for such an incident. They knew that a car blocking the entrance could cause problems, so they stored a car jack attached to a dolly nearby. The bell staff contacted nearby locksmiths. They also understood the importance of keeping guests informed to relieve anxiety. Throughout this event, they kept the insurance executives apprised of what was going on. Leaving the Sheraton Boca Raton could have been a disaster; instead, it provided an exciting incident that enabled the staff to show their professionalism and to further convince the guests that they had indeed chosen the right hotel.

The Hyatt Sanctuary Cove in Australia has adjusted its training programs. Training is now conducted by each department instead of by a trainer from the human resources department. Departments decide what their training needs are and develop programs to fill those needs. The hotel also allows any employee to attend any training session and posts all training sessions on the employee bulletin board so every employee can review the hotel's training program for the coming month. During a visit to the Hyatt, an accounting department employee was observed training a food-service waiter on the hotel's computerized food and beverage accounting system. It became obvious from their conversation that each was learning about the other's department and how the departments could better support each other.

The development of a good training program can start organizations on an upward spiral. A research study found that service quality is related inversely to staff turnover. Properly trained employees can deliver quality service, which helps the image of the firm, attracting more guests and employees to the organization.

Employee turnover rates of 100 percent or more are common in the hospitality industry. For example, limited-service restaurants have a turnover rate of 123 percent, whereas full-service restaurants have a turnover rate of 88 percent for hourly employees.[54] Firms with high turnover often ask why they should spend money training employees if they are just going to leave. This can turn into a self-fulfilling prophecy for firms that have this attitude. The employees are not properly trained and thus are not capable of delivering quality service. Not being able to deliver good service, they will feel uncomfortable in their jobs and quit. Unfortunately, this reinforces employers' beliefs that they should not spend money training their employees, but not investing in employee training programs leads to a cycle of high employee turnover and guest dissatisfaction.

Hospitality companies with a strong commitment to employee training are well advised to make this philosophy well known to all employees in action and in word. The Centennial Hotel Management Company of Canada has a written statement of a human resources philosophy that includes orientation and training. This statement is an excellent internal marketing tool:

Orientation
- The purpose of Centennial Hotel orientation is to assure the new employee that he or she has made the right decision and to build a strong sense of belonging to the company, the team, and the industry.

- Orientation assures the employees that the company provides the support they require to be successful. It is also a time to share the values of Centennial Hotel and to introduce the facilities of the hotel.

Training
- Centennial Hotel is committed to providing consistent basic training throughout the company, as well as continuous upgrading. Training is for everyone and must be planned, systematic, and comprehensive. The success of training must be measurable.[55]

Part-Time Seasonal Help

One of the worst mistakes any hospitality firm can make is to hire part-time help and then fail to make them part of the team or properly train them.

Customers expect the same level of service from these people as from full-time employees. If large numbers of part-time and seasonal employees are used, it may be necessary to place one or more individuals in charge of making certain that they are given clear instructions concerning what is expected of them. When possible, consider using a working buddy system where full-time employees are asked to watch out and assist part-time ones. Good seasonal employees must be encouraged to remain for the full term of their contract (whether written or handshake). Consider an incentive program that both rewards them for excellent performance and gives them a bonus for remaining the full season. Nonmonetary motivations such as the promise of a positive letter of recommendation, planned parties, picnics, theater events, and other social gatherings with full-time and part-time/seasonable employees are generally winners.

Managing Emotional Employees

Just as we try to understand the needs of our customers, we need to understand the needs of our employees. One of these needs is the ability to manage their emotions. According to Zeithaml and Bitner, two services marketing experts, friendliness, courtesy, empathy, and responsiveness directed toward customers all require huge amounts of emotional labor from frontline employees who shoulder this

Emotional labor The necessary involvement of the service provider's emotions in the delivery of the service.

responsibility.[56] The term **emotional labor** was first used by Hochschild and has been defined as the necessary involvement of the service provider's emotions in the delivery of the service.[57] The display of emotions can strongly influence the customer's perception of service quality. To manage emotional labor, managers must hire employees who can cope with the stress caused by dealing with customers. Then emotional labor must be managed on a day-to-day basis. Some common techniques used to manage emotional labor include monitoring overtime and avoiding double shifts, encouraging work breaks, and support from fellow workers and managers. Managers are sometimes the cause of emotional stress, for example, by yelling at an employee before a shift and then sending the employee out to work with customers.

One of the biggest causes of emotional stress is long hours. Employees often find it hard to manage their emotions after working 10 hours straight. At this point, the employees are tired and often care little about the customer. We have all been in that position or observed service providers who were rude or uncaring after working a long shift. The cause of such behavior is that the employee is emotionally drained. The story is told of a waitress who was having a particularly hard day when a customer complained about the food. The customer shouted that his baked potato was bad. The waitress picked up the potato, slapped it a couple of times, yelling, "Bad potato, bad potato," put the potato back on the customer's plate, and walked away. Although this is a humorous story, the customer was not amused. When employees are overworked emotionally, service suffers.

Implementation of a Reward and Recognition System

To sustain a service culture, human resource policies must create a system that rewards and recognizes employees and managers that provide good customer service. Professors Sturman and Way state, "If you want to improve employee performance in the hospitality industry, ensure that the employees accurately perceive the practices, procedures, and behaviors that are rewarded, supported, and expected of them by your company."[58] Employees must receive feedback on how they are doing to perform effectively. Communication must be designed to give them feedback on their performance. An internal marketing program includes service standards and methods of measuring how well the organization is meeting these standards. The results of any service measurement should be communicated to employees. Major hotel companies survey their guests to determine their satisfaction level with individual attributes of the hotel. One researcher found that simply communicating information collected from customers changed employee attitudes and performance.[59] Customer service measurements have a positive effect on employee attitudes if results are communicated and recognition is given to those who serve the customer. If you want customer-oriented employees, seek out ways to observe them serving the customer and reward and recognize them for making the effort.[60]

Reward systems in the hospitality and travel industry used to be based only on meeting financial objectives such as achieving a certain labor cost or food cost or increasing revenue. Now well-managed companies are giving rewards based on customer satisfaction. If companies want to have customer-oriented employees, they must reward them for servicing the customer. Reward systems and bonuses based on customer satisfaction scores are one method of rewarding employees.

Unless an individual has taken a vow of poverty and wishes to live a communal spiritual life or is very wealthy, the rest of society is very concerned about monetary income. The subject of employee compensation is one that requires serious and continuous planning and sometimes modification. Professionals in the field should be retained or hired to work with members of management, particularly those in the Human Resources Department to ensure that all compensation programs provide incentives to excel. There is a subject that is not widely understood but has been proven in the hospitality industry and others to offer ongoing opportunities to provide earned financial rewards above the traditional financial programs. The purpose is to increase loyalty and longevity for employees and managers. This is an Employee Stock Ownership Plan (ESOP) and Phantom Stock.

One of the hospitality companies that successfully uses an ESOP program for managers and staff is the Waffle House. Many employees of the Waffle House have found that by retirement time their ESOP has grown to a position to provide financial assistance in retirement. Managers in many companies have an opportunity to participate in stock options or other programs but employees such as counter and grill staff may not have such opportunities. Conversations with counter employees at the Waffle House who have been in their ESOP for many years reveal that it has resulted in making a positive difference in their retirement funds.

An ESOP is generally used by privately held companies in which their stock is not traded on the stock market. The basic concept is to encourage managers and employees to dedicate effort to make certain that the company is successful so that their employment is secure and their stock value grows.

Phantom Stock is also a stock-based incentive program used by companies (public) whose stock is traded on an exchange. In this case, management may wish to offer employees an opportunity to participate in the value of the company's stock without providing actual equity ownership. This involves establishing a separate stock program (a phantom program) that tracks the company's stock price in the marketplace and rewards participating employees who own shares in the phantom stock with the price tied to the price of the actual stock. A record is maintained of the number of phantom shares an employee has earned and the current price.

Companies commonly establish conditions for participation in stock ownership programs including:

Number of years' employed

Ranking of the position held by the employee

Special stock incentives such as winning employee of the year

Professional council should be sought and used in the development of either an ESOP or a Phantom Stock program.

Nondiscrimination—Gender Gap

It is surprising in this era but apparently there still exist cases of wage discrimination. A recent study of "Gender Gap Wages" concluded, "It is clear that women still experience considerable wage discrimination in the U.S. hospitality sector." The researcher concluded, "The hospitality industry could expect to see higher turnover among women as several studies have shown that fair compensation is an important element contributing to career commitment among current students and graduates of hospitality programs."[61]

Dissemination of Marketing Information to Employees

Often, the most effective way of communicating with customers is through customer-contact employees. They can suggest additional products, such as the hotel's health club or business center, and they can upsell when it is to the guest's benefit. Employees often have opportunities to solve guest problems before they become irritants. To do this, employees need information. Unfortunately, many companies leave customer-contact employees out of the communication cycle. The director of marketing may tell managers and supervisors about upcoming events, ad campaigns, and new promotions, but some managers may feel employees do not need to know this information.

Beth Lorenzini, a restaurant trade magazine editor, states, "Promotions designed to generate excitement and sales can do just the opposite if employees aren't involved in planning and execution." Monica Kass, a former sales and marketing coordinator for Lawry's the Prime Rib, Chicago, says that employees and marketing people who develop promotions must communicate. Lawry's increased its Thanksgiving Day sales by 48 percent through employee involvement. Lawry's invited all the "wait staff" to a Thanksgiving dinner a week before Thanksgiving. This was the same meal it was serving to guests on Thanksgiving Day. The dinner not only was a festive affair to get everybody into the Thanksgiving holiday mood, but it also served as a training tool. Employees knew exactly what was going to be served on Thanksgiving Day, including wines. The management of Lawry's also asked the staff for their input as to how to make the promotion run smoothly. On Thanksgiving Day, each wait person was given a corsage or a boutonniere. Like the employees at Lawry's, all staff should be informed about promotions. They should hear about promotions and new products from management, not from advertisements meant for external customers.[62]

The actions of management are one way that an organization communicates with its employees. Management at all levels must understand that employees are watching them for cues about expected behavior. If the general manager picks a piece of paper off the floor, other employees will start doing the same. A manager who talks about the importance of employees working together as a team can reinforce the desire for teamwork through personal actions. Taking an interest in employees' work, lending a hand, knowing employees by name, and eating in the employee cafeteria are actions that will give credibility to the manager's words.

Hospitality organizations should use publications as part of their internal communication. Most multiunit companies have an employee newsletter, and larger hotels usually have their own in-house newsletters. Besides mass communication, personal communication is important to spread the word effectively about new products and promotional campaigns. Leonard Berry suggests having two annual reports, one for stockholders and one for employees. Many firms are now implementing his suggestion.[63]

Hire Quality People Who Want to Succeed

Many employees are self-selected. They know about the Lewis Hotels and want to work there. Why?

Each employee receives a thorough orientation in which the topic of personal and hotel success is foremost and accompanied by clear guidelines as to what is expected.

Employees participate in analyzing costs and for all areas of their work such as the cost of silverware and glasses. Expense and profit information is shared with employees; thus, they feel part of the management of the operation and continuously learn.

A Quality Management Team

Lewis Hotels calls this its SWAT Team. "Best investment in this hotel," Andria said of this team. In addition to assuming responsibility for critical areas such as food and beverage operations, the team is prepared to open new properties as Lewis Hotels expands.

Marketing HIGHLIGHT 10.2 — Internal marketing in action: Lewis Hotels

Burt and Andria Lewis of Boulder, Colorado, purchased second-rate failing hotels and turned them into award-winning properties with good rates and exceptionally high occupancy with strong guest and employee loyalty. The Golden Hotel in Golden, Colorado, was bought out of receivership. The Lewises were able to turn the hotel around and within two and a half years the property's occupancy was so high that even friends of the owners had difficulty acquiring a room. This hotel received awards from Choice hotels, including the Platinum Award, Best in Brand, and a nomination for Inn of the Year.

Although Burt has been in the hotel business for over 40 years, Andria joined the company eight years ago with no hotel experience. How was this accomplished by this husband/wife team from two very different backgrounds?

They used sound management practices and picked hotels in quality locations with limited potential for the development of new hotels. For example, they chose a city center hotel such as the Golden Hotel, where the availability and cost of a similar location would serve as a barrier to entry for other hotels. They also maintained their hotels.

One of the characteristics of their management was internal marketing. They created a quality product with amenities that created value for their guests. But they also wanted their employees to be able to say, "I am proud to work for this hotel." They also followed these internal marketing principles.

Food and Beverage Director Connie Laslow is representative of the quality of the SWAT Team. Connie speaks five languages and has extensive experience working for a variety of hospitality companies, including upscale restaurants and hotels. Connie is so customer focused that she can often recall what customers ordered a year later. Connie says, "You are only as successful as your staff" and works closely with them while allowing them to be creative. "You can put your fingerprints on many exciting things in the Lewis Hotels," says Connie.

Employee Empowerment

They empower employees and encourage staff to think creatively and not be bound to standardized rules. The Lewises believe that this is probably not possible for a company like McDonald's, but it is highly possible and desirable for Lewis Hotels and has much to do with providing a quality guest experience.

Managers Create a Service Culture and Show They Care About Guest Satisfaction

If a guest is dissatisfied and has left the hotel, Andria personally calls the person. Guests are often stunned that the owner has contacted them to resolve a problem. This has led to repeat business by otherwise angry guests who would select another hotel.

Burt and Andria Lewis realize that physical facilities, guest amenities, and a sound business plan are important. But they also realize customer-oriented employees are responsible for their guests returning. They use their physical environment and the warmth created by their employees to cause both guests and employees to say "wow" on a continual basis. This is accomplished by striving to exceed guest expectations at all times.

Snowshoe Mountain in Snowshoe, West Virginia, embarked on a marketing program to better brand the ski resort with a promise of an "authentic, rustic and engaging wilderness experience." In launching a branding initiative to define their goals and articulate what they wanted the Snowshoe Mountain brand to represent to visitors, the resort's marketers started inside. They incorporated the new brand promise in a 40-page brand book that contained the history of the resort and a list of seven attitude words that characterized how employees should interact with guests. On-mountain messaging and signs also reminded employees to deliver on the brand promise. All new hires received a brand presentation from the director of marketing to help them better understand the brand and become effective advocates.[64]

Ongoing communication between management and employees is essential—not just group meetings but regular individual meetings between the employee and management. Every customer-contact employee communicates with hundreds of customers. Managers should meet with these employees to gain customer need insights and determine how the company can make it easier for the employee to serve the customer.

DAILY BRIEFINGS. Many managers and consultants believe that daily briefings should be held at the beginning of each work day. As the name implies, these briefings must be short in duration. Ten or fifteen minutes are generally sufficient to inform staff about:

- Special guests
- New menu items
- Possible disruption of power during the day
- Special hospitality events such as a kitchen tour complete with appetizers
- Anything else that could affect the staff and guests in a positive or negative way

It has often been said that such briefings need to occur even on the busiest days since that is when problems usually occur.

EMPLOYEES WHO DO NOT UNDERSTAND YOUR LANGUAGE. The worldwide hospitality industry hires thousands of employees who are not familiar with the language spoken by management. If employees do not fully understand what management tells them, problems will occur and customer service will be negatively affected. Companies who hire large numbers of foreign employees must have a program to effectively communicate with them, including translation services and on-the-job training in the spoken language.

Research in this area showed that organizational practices do indeed influence manager's communication satisfaction with subordinates and specifically with those who have limited English skills.[65]

Front-desk clerks are the communication center of the hotel, yet they frequently do not know the names of entertainers or the type of entertainment featured in the hotel's lounges. They may also be unaware of special marketing promotions. Hotels can use technology and training to provide employees with product knowledge. Technology can be used to develop a database. Information can be readily accessible to employees, who should then be trained in the hotel's products and services. Finally, employees can be encouraged to try the company's products. They can eat in the restaurants, stay overnight in the hotel, and receive special previews of lounge entertainment. It is much more convincing if the front-desk employee can give a potential guest firsthand information rather than reading a description.

Employees should receive information on new products and product changes, marketing campaigns, and changes in the service delivery process. All action steps in the marketing plan should include internal marketing. For example, when a company introduces a new mass media campaign, the implementation plan should include actions to inform employees about the campaign. The first time that most employees see company advertisements is in the media in which the advertisement is placed. Before the advertisements appear in the media, the company should share the ad with its employees. Managers should also explain the objective of the campaign and the implications.

One of the authors once worked in a restaurant whose owner decided to install a computer system without discussing it with the staff. The system was first used during a busy lunch period, and the restaurant had given the staff almost no prior training. The system did not perform well, and the staff grew determined to get rid of it. They found that the system was sensitive to grease spots on the check. If a service person got butter on a check, the guest would be charged for all sorts of extra items. Some staff would deliberately put grease spots on their checks to develop false charges for the customer. When the customer complained about the bill, the server would explain to the guest the problems they were having with the new system. Customers quickly sided with the service personnel, and within three months the owner was forced to eliminate the new system. If management had consulted the employees before installation, the employees might have supported the computer. Management could have shown the employees how the system would help them better serve the guest by adding their tickets automatically and keeping them current. This would have created employee support. Instead, without the proper information and training, employees were determined from the beginning to get rid of the computer.

EMPLOYEE INVOLVEMENT IN UNIFORM SELECTION. Employees should be involved in the selection of the uniforms they wear every day. Selecting uniforms is often left to designers and managers, with little input from the service worker. Uniforms are important because employee dress contributes greatly to the guest's encounter with customer-contact employees. Uniforms also become part of the atmospherics of a hospitality operation or travel operation; they have the ability to create aesthetic, stylish, and colorful impressions of the property.[66] They distinguish employees from the general public, making employees accessible and easily identified. In cases where uniforms are lacking, guests may become frustrated because they have difficulty identifying employees when they need help. Uniforms have the ability to create attitudes about an employee's job. Employees dressing in formal wear state that they feel and behave differently once they put on their uniform. This anecdotal evidence has been supported by research. Clothing has been found to be a contributing factor in role-playing, acting as a vivid cue that can encourage employees to engage in the behaviors associated with the role of the employee.[67] Putting on the costume can mean putting on a role and shedding other roles. Employees' dress can direct employees' behavior to be more consistent with the goals and standards of behavior established

Managers should involve employees in the choice of uniforms. Andrey_Popov/Shutterstock.

by the organization. A study of resort employees found a significant relationship between employees' perceptions of their uniforms and their overall job attitude. The higher the employees' perception of the uniform, the more positive was their rating of their overall attitude toward their job.[68] Another study conducted in two different cultural settings, Hong Kong and Austria, found that employee uniform material, appropriateness, style, and functionality influence their overall job satisfaction.[69]

Uniforms should be functional and accepted by the employees. Management often looks for uniforms that represent the property, acting as a marketing tool—enhancing the image of the organization. It is paramount to allow employees to be involved in uniform choices regarding both function and projected image. For example, food servers at a pirate-themed restaurant complained about the loose-fitting sleeves on their shirts and blouses. The uniforms looked great until the servers began working. The sleeves dragged across plates when they were being cleared or when trays were being unloaded at the dishwasher. In a few hours the sleeves were stained with food. The employees stated that the problem embarrassed them when they approached a guest, and they became less outgoing in their dealings with guests. Other problems with functionality include uniforms that are designed without pockets and uniforms that are uncomfortable. The selection of uniforms can have an impact on both the employees' attitude and their ability to serve the customers well. Managers need to consider the employees and involve them in uniform decisions.

Isadore Sharp claims that customer service provided by employees of Four Seasons could be a point of distinction for the brand. Some managers replied that all good hotels gave good service. They said, "Look at their ads they all promoted smiling employees and great service." Sharp replied, "Your right they all do. By *their* standards. But we are going to do it differently. Do it so it is something we are known for." Creating an internal marketing program that produces distinctive service takes years to establish. Once one has created a competitive advantage based on employee service it creates a sustainable advantage. The competition may be aware of the advantage, but it will take them years to match the service levels—if they can.

CHAPTER REVIEW

I. Internal Marketing. Employee satisfaction and customer satisfaction are correlated. Marketers must develop techniques and procedures to ensure that employees are able and willing to deliver quality service. Internal marketing involves marketing to the firm's internal customers, its employees.

   A. Post face-to-face guest relations. It is important for members of the hospitality and tourism industry to review all public reviews and social media comments, favorable and unfavorable, by former guests.

II. The Internal Marketing Process. Internal marketing ensures that employees at all levels of the organization experience the business and understand its various activities and campaigns in an environment that supports customer consciousness. The process involves the following steps:

   A. Establishment of a service culture. Management must develop a **service culture**: a culture that supports customer service through policies, procedures, reward systems, and actions. Make the employees aware of the company story so that they share company values and culture. Empower employees so that they can decide what to do and how to do it to please customers. When a company has a service culture, the organizational chart is turned upside down. The customers are now at the top of the organization. Everyone is working to serve the customer.

   B. Development of a marketing approach to human resources management. Managers must use the principles of marketing to attract and retain employees. They must research and develop an understanding of their employees' needs, just as they examine the needs of customers. Service organizations need to hire for attitude and train for skills. This idea means that service firms place more emphasis on personality, energy, and attitude than on education, training, and experience in their recruitment, selection, and training strategies. Finding employees who are good at creating a service experience is a vital goal and major hiring criterion of service organizations. If a company hires the right people, they will be team players. In companies that practice internal marketing, if one employee makes an error, other employees try to correct it before the guest notices. Initial training is important. Knowledgeable and enthusiastic employees create enthusiastic customers. Companies that lead their industries in customer service emphasize cross-training and insist that everyone share certain training experiences. Part-time help must also be property trained. Make sure employees maintain a positive attitude. Managing emotional labor helps maintain a good attitude. Reward and recognize customer service and satisfaction. Provide equal pay and compensation.

C. **Dissemination of marketing information to employees.** Often, the most effective way of communicating with customers is through customer-contact employees. Employees should hear about promotions and new products from management, not from advertisements meant for external customers. Management at all levels must understand that employees are watching them for cues about expected behavior.

IN-CLASS GROUP EXERCISES

*Exercises with an asterisk next to them are suitable for individual homework or online assignments. Students, always provide an explanation for your answer.

1. *What is a service culture? Why is it a requirement for an internal marketing program?
2. *Discuss the possible ways that marketing techniques can be used by human resources managers.
3. *What are the benefits of explaining advertising campaigns to employees before they appear in the media?
4. *The handling of nonroutine transactions separates excellent hospitality companies from mediocre ones. What is a nonroutine transaction? Why is the proper handling of them so important?
5. Go to the site of an OTA such as Expedia, Travelocity, Priceline, or a social media site such as Yelp or Urban Spoon. For those outside of the United States, you may use your local OTAs and social media sites. Find 10 reviews where employee actions resulted in either a positive review or a negative review. Make a log of these employee actions.

EXPERIENTIAL EXERCISE

Do one of the following:

1. Visit a hospitality or travel company. Ask some questions about its products. For example, at a restaurant you may ask about the hours it is open and about menu items. You may state you are looking for a good steak restaurant and ask about its steaks. At a hotel you may ask about its rooms or restaurants. The idea is to have enough dialogue with its employees to be able to judge the customer orientation of the employees. Write your findings supporting how the employees demonstrated they had a customer orientation and ideas you have on how they could have been more customer oriented.

REFERENCES

1. Sources: Based on information from Jeffrey M. O'Brien, "A Perfect Season," *Fortune*, January 22, pp. 62–66; "The 100 Best Companies to Work For," *Fortune*, February 4, 2013, p. 85; Micah Solomon, "Four Seasons Hotels: Building Hospitality and Customer Service Culture," *Forbes*, September 1, 2013, www.forbes.com/sites/micahsolomon/201four-seasons-hotels-building-a-hospitality-service-cluture-without-starting-from-scratch/; http://jobs.fourseasons.com and www.fourseasons.com/about_four_seasons (accessed September 2018).
2. Danny Meyer, *Setting the Table* (New York: HarperCollins, 2006), p. 11.
3. Joseph W. Benoy, "Internal Marketing Builds Service Quality," *Journal of Health Care Marketing*, 16, no. 1 (1996): 54–64.
4. Julia Chang, "From the Inside Out," *Sales and Marketing Management* (August 2005): 14.
5. Richard Normann, *Service Management: Strategy and Leadership in Service Businesses* (New York: Wiley, 1984), p. 33.
6. Ibid., p. 9.
7. "Creating 'moments of trust': The key to building successful brand relationships in the Kinship Economy,"

IHG Intercontinental Group, January 21, 2014, https://www.ihgplc.com/-/media/949BED83794C-4C439156C28406C897F1.ashx.

8. Hyounae Min, Yumi Lin, and Vincent P. Magnini, "The Impact of Empathy, Professionalism and Speed, Factors Affecting Customer Satisfaction," *Cornell Hospitality Quarterly*, 58 (May 2015).

9. Bill Heatly, "Operators Who Make Staff Satisfaction a Top Priority Will Get Results on Bottom Line," *Nation's Restaurant News* (May 17, 2004): 24.

10. John P. Walsh, "Employee Training Leads to Better Service, More Profits," *Hotel and Motel Management* (January 12, 2004): 14.

11. William R. George and Christian Gronroos, "Developing Customer-Conscious Employees at Every Level: Internal Marketing," in *The Handbook of Marketing for the Service Industries*, ed. Carole A. Congram (New York: American Management Association, 1991), pp. 85–100.

12. Christian Gronroos, *Strategic Management and Marketing in the Service Sector* (Cambridge, MA: Marketing Science Institute, 1983), as cited in C. Gronroos, *Service Management and Marketing* (Lexington, MA: Lexington Books, 1990), p. 223.

13. Ibid., p. 85.

14. *The Australian* (October 10, 1990).

15. S. M. Davis, *Managing Corporate Culture* (Cambridge, MA: Ballinger, 1985).

16. John Bowen and Robert C. Ford, "Managing Service Organizations: 'Does Having a 'Thing' Make a Difference?'" *Journal of Management*, 28, no. 3 (2002): 447–469.

17. Terrence E. Deal and Allan A. Kennedy, *Corporate Cultures* (Reading, MA: Addison-Wesley, 1982), pp. 15–16.

18. http://www.kimptonhotels.com/hr/cul_moments.aspx (accessed September 21, 2011).

19. Brinker International, https://www.brinkerjobs.com/ (accessed October 2018); Branson, R., *The Virgin way: Everything I know about leadership* (New York: Portfolio/Penguin, 2014); Danny Meyer, *Setting the Table: The Transforming Power of the Hospitality Business* (New York: HarperCollins Publishing, 2008); Michael J. Tews, John W. Michel & Kathryn Stafford. "Does Fun Pay? The Impact of Workplace Fun on Employee Turnover and Performance," *Cornell Hospitality Quarterly* (November 2013), pp. 14–21.

20. Coleen Reinhart, "Organizational Culture in the Hospitality Industry," *Small Business Chronicle*, Houston Chronicle, http://smallbusiness.chron.com/organizational-culture-hospitality-industry-12969.html (accessed July 27, 2015).

21. Flora F. T. Chiang, Thomas A. Birtch, and Zhenyao Cai, "Front Line Service Employees Job Satisfaction in the Hospitality Industry," *Cornell Hospitality Quarterly*, 55, no. 4 (November 2014).

22. A. Parasuraman, "Customer-Oriented Corporate Cultures Are Crucial to Services Marketing Success," *Journal of Services Marketing*, 1, no. 1 (Summer 1987): 39–46.

23. Ibid.

24. Viceroy Hotel Group Web Site, http://www.viceroyhotelgroup.com/en/about_us (accessed July 27, 2015).

25. Ibid., p. 107; Nathan Tyler, *Service Excellence*, Tap. 2 (videotape) (Boston, MA: Harvard Business School Management Productions, 1987).

26. James L. Heskett, W. Earl Sasser, and Leonard A. Schlesinger, *Saving Customers with Service Recovery* (videotape) (Boston, MA: Harvard Business School Management Productions, 1994).

27. Karl Albrecht and Ron Zemke, *Service America!: Doing Business in the New Economy* (Homewood, IL: Dow Jones-Irwin, 1985), pp. 127–128.

28. Gabriel Gazzoil, Murat Hancer, and Yumi Park, "The Role and Effect of Job Satisfaction and Empowerment on Customers' Perception of Service Quality: A Study in the Restaurant Industry," *Journal of Hospitality and Tourism Research*, 34, no. 1 (February 2010): 70.

29. Carla B. Furlong, *Marketing for Keeps* (New York: Wiley, 1993), pp. 79–80.

30. A. Parasuraman, "Customer-Oriented Corporate Cultures," pp. 33–40.

31. Leonard L. Berry, "The Employee as Customer," *Journal of Retail Banking*, 3, no. 1 (1981): 33–40.

32. John J. Hogan, "Turnover and What to Do About It," Cornell Hotel and Restaurant Administration Quarterly, 33, no. 1 (February 1992), p. 41.

33. Caroline Cooper and Lacy Whittington, *Hotel Success Handbook: How to Achieve Great Customer Service*, Part 2, August 27, 2012, www.hotelsuccesshandbook.com.

34. Bowen, John, and Robert C. Ford. "Managing Service Organizations: Does Having a 'Thing' Make a Difference?." *Journal of management* 28, no. 3 (2002): 447–469.

35. B. Schneider and D. Bowen, *Winning the Service Game* (Boston, MA: HBS Press, 1995).

36. C. R. Bell and K. Anderson, "Selecting Super Service People," *HR Magazine*, 37, no. 2 (1992): 52–54; Stephen J. Grove, and Raymond P. Fisk, "The Dramaturgy of Services Exchanges: An Analytical Framework for Services Marketing" in *Emerging Perspectives on Services Marketing*, G. Lynn Shostack, Leonard L. Berry, and Gregory D. Upah, ed. (Chicago, IL: American Marketing Association, 1983), pp. 45–49.

37. Miliand Lele, *The Customer Is Key* (New York: Wiley, 1987), p. 252.

38. Andrew J. Czaplewski, Jeffery M. Ferguson, and John F. Milliman, "Southwest Airlines: How Internal Marketing Pilots Success," *Marketing Management* (September/October 2001): 14–17.

39. Steve Fisher, "Flying Off into the Sunset," *Costco Connection*, 22, no. 9 (2007): 17.
40. Tschohl, *Achieving Excellence Through Customer Service* (Englewood Cliffs, Prentice Hall, 1991), p. 113.
41. Joseph A. Michelli, *The New Gold Standard* (New York: McGraw-Hill, 2008), p. 77.
42. Danny Meyer, *Setting the Table* (New York: Harper Collins, 2006), p. 143.
43. Ibid., p. 58.
44. Osman M. Karatepe, "The Effects of Co-Worker and Perceived Organizational Support on Hotel Employee Outcomes," *Journal of Hospitality and Tourism Research*, 36, no. 4 (November 2012): 511.
45. Timothy R. Hinkin and J. Bruce Tracey, "What Makes it So Great," *Cornell Hospitality Quarterly*, 51, no. 2 (May 2015): 158–170.
46. Jeanne d'Orleans, "It's Basic Customer Service," *Hotel & Motel Management*, December 6, 2007, www.hotel-motel.com (accessed June 8, 2008).
47. N. W. Pope, "Mickey Mouse Marketing," *American Banker* (July 25, 1979), as included in W. Earl Sasser, Jr., Christopher W. L. Hart, and James L. Heskett, *The Service Management Course: Cases and Reading* (New York: Free Press, 1991), pp. 649–654.
48. Marc Clark, "Training for Tradition," *Cornell Hotel and Restaurant Administration Quarterly*, 31, no. 4 (1991): 51.
49. Liz Welch, "Entrepreneur Designs Upscale Hotels for Budget Travelers," *INC. Magazine* (June 2014), https://www.inc.com/magazine201406/liz-welch/citizenm-low-cost-high-end-hotels.html; citizenM news, https://www.citizenm.com/news/citizenm-celebrates-yet-another-year-of-affordable-luxury# (accessed March 18, 2018).
50. Isadore Sharp, *Four Seasons: The Story of a Business Philosophy* (Canada: Toronto, Penguin), p. 110.
51. Drew Madsen, "Olive Garden: Creating Value Through an Integrated Brand Experience," presentation at Marketing Science Institute Conference, *Brand Orchestration*, Orlando, Florida, December 4, 2003.
52. John R. Dienhart and Mary B. Gregoire, "Job Satisfaction, Job Involvement, Job Security and Customer Focus of Quick Service Restaurant Employees," *Hospitality Research Journal*, 16, no. 2 (1993): 41.
53. Christopher W. L. Hart, James L. Heskett, and W. Earl Sasser, Jr., *Service Breakthroughs* (New York: Free Press, 1990), p. 109.
54. Bruce Grindy, "The Restaurant Industry: An Economic Powerhouse," *Restaurants USA* (June/July 2000): 40–45.
55. Michael K. Haywood, "Effective Training: Toward a Strategic Approach," *Cornell Hotel and Restaurant Administration Quarterly*, 33, no. 6 (1992): 46.
56. Valarie A. Zeithaml and Mary Jo Bitner, *Services Marketing* (New York: McGraw-Hill, 1996).
57. A. R. Hochschild, *The Managed Heart* (Berkeley, CA: University of California Press, 1983); definition from Gunther Berghofer, "Emotional Labor," Working Paper (Bond University, Robina, Queensland, Australia, 1993).
58. Michael C. Sturman and Sean A. Way, "Questioning Conventional Wisdom: Is a Happy Employee a Good Employee, or Do Attitudes Matter More?" The Center for Hospitality Research, Cornell University, March 2008.
59. Albrecht, Karl and Ron Zemke. *Service America!* (Homewood, IL: Dow Jones-Irwin, 1985).
60. Chip R. Bell and Ron Zemke, *Managing Knock Your Socks Off Service* (New York: American Management Association, 1992), p. 169.
61. Susan S. Fleming, "Déjà Vu? An Updated Analysis of the Gender Wage Gap in the U.S. Hospitality Sector," *Cornell Hospitality Quarterly*, 56, no. 2 (May 2015).
62. Beth Lorenzini, "Promotion Success Depends on Employee's Enthusiasm," *Restaurants and Institutions* (February 12, 1992): 591.
63. Berry, Leonard L. "The employee as customer." *Journal of retail banking* 3, no. 1 (1981): 33–40.
64. Paula Andruss, "Employee Ambassadors," *Marketing News* (December 15, 2008): 26–27.
65. Mary Dawson, Juan Madera, Jack Neal, and Jue Chen, "The Influence of Hotel Communication Practices on Manager's Satisfaction with Limited English-Speaking Employees," *Journal of Hospitality and Tourism Research*, 38, no. 4 (November 2014): 558.
66. M. R. Solomon, "Dress for Effect," *Psychology Today*, 20, no. 4 (1986): 20–28.
67. A. Rafaeli and M. G. Pratt, "Tailored Meanings: On the Meaning and Impact of Organizational Dress," *Academy of Management Review*, 18, no. 1 (1993): 32–55.
68. Kathy Nelson and John Bowen, "The Effect of Employee Uniforms on Employee Satisfaction," *Cornell Hotel and Restaurant Administration Quarterly*, 41, no. 2 (2000): 86–95.
69. Guenther E. March and Mike Peters, "The Impact of Employee Uniforms on Job Satisfaction in the Hospitality Industry." *Journal of Hotel and Business Management* (February 9, 2017), p. 157. Retrieved from https://www.omicsonline.org/open-access/the-impact-of-employee-uniforms-on-job-satisfaction-in-the-hospitalityindustry-2169-0286-1000157.php?aid=86481.

11

Pricing: Understanding and Capturing Customer Value

Objectives
After reading this chapter, you should be able to:

1. Explain internal and external factors affecting pricing decisions.
2. Describe the differences among general pricing approaches.
3. Explain product pricing strategies for new products and existing products.
4. Describe revenue management and explain tools used by revenue managers.
5. Explain considerations in psychological pricing.
6. Discuss the key issues related to price changes.

Successful pricing at Wild Dunes® Resort requires coordinated planning and strategy. Located on the Isle of Palms near Charleston, South Carolina, Wild Dunes offers a mix of lodging, golf, tennis, dining, and family activities. This product mix combined with seasonal and special-occasion demand means that multiple factors must be considered in pricing decisions. Responsibility for planning and coordination of pricing is under the direction of the Director of Sales and Marketing.

Lodging at Wild Dunes involves three distinct properties. The first is the Boardwalk Inn, a 93-room hotel, with a private pool, billiards room, and the resort's fine dining restaurant option, the Sea Island Grill. The property is owned and operated by the resort.

The Village at Wild Dunes is the resort's newest offering, with 166 identically furnished rooms and suites and a family-style restaurant, fitness center, and day spa. Studios to three-bedroom suites and four-bedroom penthouses that were newly constructed were all sold to private owners who placed their units into the property rental program, and share in the revenues.

Additional lodging is available in nearby private homes, which Wild Dunes also manages for absentee owners. Property owners are free to use other booking and property management firms. The revenue management team must price these units to compete with them and also provide a good return to Wild Dunes and the property owners.

Wild Dunes also has other product lines—strategic business units (SBUs). These include two 18-hole golf courses, 17 tennis courts ranked in the top 10 by *Tennis Magazine*, and several tennis programs, including professional clinics and exhibitions. Island Adventures® offers recreational programs for preteen kids, teenagers, and adults. Each requires different pricing, such as the Pirate Adventure Pass and the VIP Club Pass for kids. Weekly entertainment events such as the Low Country Luau and the Blue Crabbing Expedition require price planning. Wellness programs such as group yoga, water aerobics, and spa services must also be price managed.

One of the major activities at any destination resort is dining, and Wild Dunes offers a variety in four restaurants, ranging from the Dunes Deli and Pizzeria to luxury dining at the Sea Island Grill. Dinner Delivered is another food and beverage (F&B) product that has become very popular with guests who rent condos or homes. Complete dinners are delivered to the guests' homes. Prices range from $145 to $220, but these also require careful price planning, particularly in times of increased competition and rising food costs.

Package pricing is a critical marketing responsibility. Golf is a major attraction for guests, and packages must be developed for commercial groups such as a group of salespeople, and for individuals with varying abilities and interest in golf. Packages typically include accommodations, golf, and breakfast. Specialty packages also include additional items such as a 50-minute massage in the Ladies Golf Package. Packages must be priced to be competitive with other destination resorts, but success also depends on creativity in packaging. For instance, would guests prefer breakfast on the links or a lunch following golf? "Dudes on the Dunes" is a creative package designed for men that includes poker in a guest room with snacks and beer. The "Romance Package" was designed for those celebrating an anniversary or perhaps just reconnecting.

Packages offer excellent opportunities for cross-merchandising and upselling, both of which are important factors in revenue management. Participation by employees in building packages is important since these people "know the guests" better than management.

Wild Dunes employs three full-time revenue management professionals and a director of revenue optimization with responsibility for budgeting, forecasting, and helping correctly positioning Wild Dunes and its product line.

Lodging revenue is the most important part of the product line and also the most variable. Golf and tennis lessons remain relatively stable, but the price of rooms is dependent on many variables. Therefore, the revenue optimization team, including the reservations manager, meets every Wednesday.

During the meeting, the team carefully examines room inventory at all price segments and also looks at the prices of two competitive sets: one in the Charleston area and another among a group of luxury destination resorts. According to the season and anticipated demand, Wild Dunes may decide to be the price leader and at other times to follow competitors.

Like most destination resorts, Wild Dunes faces prime, shoulder, and trough periods. Eight weeks during summer is prime and demand has been increasing 15 percent for this peak period. Rooms during this period were $295 per night but the same room sold for $495 earlier during Memorial Day in May.

The revenue optimization team is instructed to let the quality of the products drive price whenever they can. Sunday is traditionally a low-demand day. Package deals are often used to fill Sunday rooms.

The reservations sales team is also focused on increasing ancillary spending for products such as bike rentals, the spa, and excursions. This means cross-selling and creative packaging and promotions. Hotel guests are reminded of daily activities and items through a guest newsletter, the on-resort television channel, and the resort's magazine and vacation planner, which is the comprehensive resource for events and activities.

Wild Dunes has found that guests crave the ability to plan their vacation their way. The Wild Dunes Web site allows guests to plan their experience through their online concierge. The concierge is a Web page that shows a calendar with all possible activities. Guests can select their itinerary and submit it through the Web site, where it will be received by the reservations call center. A pre-arrival concierge staff member from Wild Dunes responds to the inquiry and confirms the requests if available. Users of the online concierge indicate whether they prefer a response by telephone or e-mail. Guest satisfaction with this has been high and ancillary spending has increased.

Upselling has improved as guests are encouraged to custom design their own packages. This allows guests to create their ideal experience. When guests build their own package, they commonly upgrade much like buyers of a car who add more accessories or a kid in an ice cream store who orders a double scoop with "the works" on top.

Menu prices for each F&B outlet are also regularly examined against a competitive set.

The head of revenue management states his position is complex. He states he is fortunate to have three areas that absolutely must work together report to him: reservations, group sales, and catering and marketing. All of these department heads participate in the development of the marketing plan. All new associates in these areas are required to spend one and a half days in orientation and two weeks in training. During this time, concepts such as teamwork, cross-selling, upselling, and revenue optimization are stressed.

He feels those responsible for revenue management must understand the needs of the hotel's departments and how pricing and occupancy will affect these departments. In order to do this, the person managing revenue must take an active role in the executive team.

Factors to Consider When Setting Prices

Price is the only marketing mix element that produces revenue. All others represent cost. Some experts rate pricing and price competition as the number-one problem facing marketing executives. Pricing is the least understood of the marketing variables, yet pricing is controllable in an unregulated market. Pricing changes are often a quick fix made without proper analysis. The most common mistakes include pricing that is too cost oriented, prices that are not revised to reflect market changes, pricing that does not take the rest of the marketing mix into account, and prices that are not varied enough for different product items and market segments. A pricing mistake can lead to a business failure, even when all other elements of the business are sound. Every manager should understand the basics of pricing.

Simply defined, **price** is the amount of money charged for a good or service. More broadly, price is the sum of the values consumers exchange for the benefits of having or using the product or service.

Marketers and managers must have an understanding of price. Charging too much chases away potential customers. Charging too little can leave a company without enough revenue to maintain the operation properly. Equipment wears out, carpets get stained, and painted surfaces need to be repainted. A firm that does not produce enough revenue to maintain the operation eventually goes out of business. In this chapter, we examine factors that hospitality marketers must consider when setting prices, general approaches, pricing strategies for new products, product mix pricing, initiating and responding to price changes, and adjusting prices to meet buyer and situational factors.

Internal and external company factors affect a company's pricing decisions. Figure 11–1 illustrates these. Internal factors include the company's marketing objectives, marketing mix strategy, costs, and organizational considerations. External factors include the nature of the market, demand competition, and other environmental elements.

Price The amount of money charged for a product or service, or the sum of the values that consumers exchange for the benefits of having or using the product or service.

Figure 11–1
Factors affecting price decisions.

Internal factors:
Marketing objectives
Marketing-mix strategy
Costs
Organization for pricing

→ **Pricing decisions** ←

External factors:
Nature of the market and demand
Competition
Other environmental factors (economy, resellers, government)

Internal Factors Affecting Pricing Decisions
Marketing Objectives

Before establishing price, a company must select a product strategy. If the company has selected a target market and positioned itself carefully, its marketing mix strategy, including price, will be more precise. For example, Four Seasons positions its hotels as luxury hotels and charges a room rate that is higher than most. Motel 6 and Formula One have positioned themselves as limited-service motels, providing rooms for budget-minded travelers. This market position requires charging a low price. Thus, the strategic decisions on market positioning have a major influence on price.

Survival A technique used when a company's or business unit's sales slump, creating a loss that threatens its existence. Because the capacity of a hotel or restaurant is fixed, survival often involves cutting prices to increase demand and cash flow. This can disrupt the market until the firm goes out of business or the economy improves.

SURVIVAL Companies troubled by too much capacity, heavy compensation, or changing consumer preferences set survival as their objective. In the short run, **survival** is more important than profit. Hotels often use this strategy when the economy slumps. A manufacturing firm can reduce production to match demand. During a recession, a 300-room hotel still has 300 rooms to sell each night, although the demand has dropped to 140 a night. The hotel tries to ride out the slump in the best way possible by cutting rates and trying to create the best cash flow possible under the conditions. This strategy directly affects immediate competitors and sometimes the entire industry. Competitors in the hospitality industry are highly cognizant of price changes and usually respond if they feel threatened. This results in soft markets: Not only does occupancy fall, room rates and profits also fall.

Observers of the hospitality industry have sometimes suggested that competition using a survival pricing strategy should be monitored carefully but not necessarily emulated. If the hotel is one of two in a market such as a small town, the effect of price discounting could be considerable. In contrast, if the hotel is in Orlando, Florida, it is one of many and represents a fraction of the total room supply. In this case, competitors with a strong marketing program may want to use their marketing skills to gain customers rather than cut their price. Also, for a hotel with good marketing it can make sense to allow a competitor to lower prices and skim off the budget-conscious customers, leaving more profitable business for them, particularly if the hotel using a survival strategy has a small market share.

CURRENT PROFIT MAXIMIZATION Many companies want to set a price that will maximize current profits. They estimate what demand and costs will be at different prices and choose the price that will produce the maximum current profit, cash flow, or return on investment (ROI), seeking current financial outcomes rather than long-run performance. For example, a company may purchase a distressed hotel at a low price. The objective becomes to turn the hotel around, show an operating profit, and then sell. If the hotel owners can achieve a successful turnaround, they may receive a good capital gain.

Some entrepreneurs develop a restaurant concept with the objective of selling the concept to a major chain. They realize that the concept's viability must be proved through a small chain that produces a high net profit. If they can do this, they may attract the attention of a major corporation. The pricing objective in this case is current profit maximization. The success of Steve Ells with Chipotle Mexican Grill and its sale to McDonald's is a prime example.

A study of a Restaurant in Arizona demonstrated that gross revenue could be increased 5 percent by carefully analyzing revenue factors and making appropriate changes. This study showed it is important to establish a measure of baseline revenue performance known as RevPASH, which is the revenue per available seat hour. The increase in revenue came from an improved table mix and improved service delivery. "Seat occupancy and RevPASH increased, dining duration and variation in that duration increased, and revenue and profitability increased."[1]

MARKET-SHARE LEADERSHIP Some companies want to obtain a dominant market-share position. They believe that a company with the largest market share will eventually enjoy low costs and high long-run profit. Thus, prices are set as low as possible. Marriott strives to be the market-share leader in its class. When it opens a new hotel,

Marriott builds market share as quickly as possible. For example, Marriott opened its resort on Australia's Gold Coast with rates well below market. Low opening rates created demand. A great hotel with good service created repeat customers and strong positive word of mouth. Six months after opening, the hotel moved its rates up to market rates. Such a strategy uses price and other elements of the marketing mix to create the awareness of better value than the competition.

PRODUCT-QUALITY LEADERSHIP The Ritz-Carlton chain has a construction or acquisition cost per room that can exceed $1,000,000. Besides a high capital investment per room, luxury chains have a high cost of labor per room. Their hotels require well-qualified staff and a high employee-to-guest ratio to provide luxury service. They must charge a high price for their luxury hotel rooms' product.

Groen, a manufacturer of food-service equipment, is known for its high-quality steam-jacketed kettles. Kitchen designers specify Groen equipment because of its known quality, enabling the company to demand a high price for its equipment. To maintain its quality, Groen must have a well-engineered product composed of high-quality materials. It also must have the budget to ensure that it maintains its position as a quality leader.

Quality leaders such as Ritz-Carlton and Groen charge more for their products, but they also have to reinvest in their operations continuously to maintain positions as quality leaders.

OTHER OBJECTIVES A company also might use price to attain other, more specific objectives. A restaurant may set low prices to prevent competition from entering the market or set prices at the same level as its competition to stabilize the market. Fast-food restaurants may reduce prices temporarily to create excitement for a new product or draw more customers into a restaurant. Thus, pricing may play an important role in helping accomplish the company's objective at many levels.

Marketing Mix Strategy

Price is only one of many marketing mix tools that a company uses to achieve its marketing objectives. Price must be coordinated with product design, distribution, and promotion decisions to form a consistent and effective marketing program. Decisions made for other marketing mix variables may affect pricing decisions. For example, resorts that plan to distribute most of their rooms through wholesalers must build enough margin into their room price to allow them to offer a deep discount to the wholesaler. Owners usually refurbish their hotels every five to seven years to keep them in good condition. Prices must cover the costs of future renovations.

A firm's promotional mix also influences price. A restaurant catering to conventioneers receives less repeat business than a neighborhood restaurant and must advertise in city guides targeted to conventioneers. Managers of restaurants who do not consider promotional costs when setting prices experience revenue/cost problems.

Companies often make pricing decisions first. Other marketing mix decisions are based on the price a company chooses to charge. For example, Marriott saw an opportunity in the economy market and developed Fairfield Inns, using price to position the motel chain in the market. Fairfield Inns' target price defined the product's market, competition, design, and product features. Companies should consider all marketing mix decisions together when developing a marketing program.

Costs

Costs set the floor for the price a company can charge for its product. A company wants to charge a price that covers its costs for producing, distributing, and promoting the product. Beyond covering these costs, the price has to be high enough to deliver a fair rate of return to investors. Therefore, a company's costs can be an important element in its pricing strategy. Many companies such as Southwest Airlines, Motel 6, or McDonald's work to become the low-cost producers in their industries. McDonald's has developed systems for producing fast food efficiently. A new hamburger franchise would have a hard time competing with McDonald's *on cost*. Effective low-cost producers achieve cost savings through efficiency rather than cutting quality. Companies with lower costs can set lower prices that result in greater market share. Lower costs do not always mean lower prices. Some companies with low costs keep their prices the same as competitors, providing a higher ROI.

Fixed costs Costs that do not vary with production or sales level.

Costs take two forms, fixed and variable. **Fixed costs** (also known as *overhead*) are costs that do not vary with production or sales level. Thus, whatever its output, a company must pay bills each month for rent, interest, and executive salaries. Fixed costs are not directly related to production level. **Variable costs** vary directly with the level of production. For example, a banquet produced by the Hyatt in San Francisco has many variable costs; each meal may include a salad, rolls and butter, the main course, a beverage, and a dessert. In addition to the food items, the hotel provides linen for each guest. These are called variable costs because their total varies with the number of units produced. **Total costs** are the sum of the fixed and variable costs for any given level of production. In the long run, management must charge a price that will at least cover total costs at a given level of sales.

Variable costs Costs that vary directly with the level of production.

Total costs Costs that are the sum of the fixed and variable costs for any given level of production.

Managers sometimes forget that customers are not concerned with a business' operating costs; they seek value. The company must watch its costs carefully. If it costs the company more than competitors to produce and sell its product, the company must either charge a higher price or make less profit.

Many hospitality companies are developing sophisticated models and software to better understand costs and their relations to price. Embassy Suites recognizes this relationship and believes the most valuable guest is not necessarily the one who pays the highest price for a suite. A contribution model developed by Embassy Suites now examines costs to acquire and service guests, such as room labor costs, advertising, special promotions, and associated costs.

Cost Subsidization

Revenue management Forecasting demand to optimize profit. Demand is managed by adjusting price. Fences are often built to keep all customers from taking advantage of lower prices. For example, typical fences include making a reservation at least two weeks in advance or staying over a Saturday night.

Destination ski resorts such as Steamboat Springs, Colorado, and Sun Valley, Idaho, depend upon air transportation to bring guests from distant markets. In many cases, these ski resorts are served by only one commuter airline during the nonski season. This is insufficient for the ski season when the resorts depend upon daily flights by major carriers.

Major carriers are unwilling to assume the entire financial risk of serving resort locations for only a few months each year. Therefore, the resorts and the nearby towns that profit from ski visitors are asked to help ensure that flights will be profitable by guaranteeing an agreed-to revenue base for the airlines. Steamboat Springs Local Marketing District (LMD) guaranteed $4.8 million to airlines for one ski season.[2]

Organizational Considerations

Royal Caribbean Cruises has developed a revenue management department with the responsibility for price, including coordinating with other departments that influence price. Solarysys/Alamy Stock Photo.

Management must decide who within the organization should set prices. Companies handle pricing in a variety of ways. In small companies, top management, rather than the marketing or sales department, often sets the prices. In large hospitality companies, pricing is typically handled by a revenue management department under guidelines established by corporate management. A hotel develops a marketing plan that contains monthly average rates and occupancies for the coming year. Regional or corporate management approves the plan.

Many corporations within the hospitality industry now have a **revenue management** department with responsibility for pricing and coordinating with other departments that influence price. Airlines, cruise lines, auto rental companies, and many hotel chains have developed revenue management departments.

The potential rewards are enormous from professional revenue management in a large hospitality company. According to Brian Rice, Director of Revenue Planning and Analysis for Royal Caribbean Cruise Line, "If the average yield at Royal Caribbean goes up by $1 a day, it is worth $5.5 million and 100 percent of it goes to the bottom line." Brian conservatively estimated the monetary benefits of "baby-sitting" the revenue on a day-to-day basis at Royal Caribbean at over $20 million per day.[3]

External Factors Affecting Pricing Decisions

External factors that affect pricing decisions include the nature of the market and demand, competition, and other environmental elements.

Market and Demand

Although costs set the lower limits of prices, the market and demand set the upper limit. Both consumer and channel buyers such as tour wholesalers balance the product's price against the benefits it provides. Thus, before setting prices, a marketer must understand the relationship between price and demand for a product.

Rudy's was one of the finest restaurants in Houston. It prospered during Houston's boom, but when Houston moved into recession due to low oil prices, the demand for fine dining fell and Rudy's suffered. Its lunches were just breaking even. Management considered a price increase as a way to push revenue above the break-even (BE) point. On the surface this may have seemed like a good idea: Just charge each customer $5 more, and the revenue would move above BE. This tactic assumed that the market was price inelastic.

Sales dropped at Rudy's because business expense accounts were being cut. An increase in price would have further reduced the size of the market that could afford the restaurant's prices. Another restaurant in Houston, La Colombe d'Or, adapted its pricing tactics to fit the recession. The restaurant booked many business luncheons. The host of a business luncheon generally does not force guests to order the cheapest item on the menu and may even encourage them to order wine, which is a high-margin menu item. As a result, La Colombe d'Or not only sold meals at regular prices but also enjoyed higher margin sales from business lunches.

Cross-Selling and Upselling

Cross-selling The company's other products that are sold to the guest.

Upselling Training sales and reservation employees to offer continuously a higher-priced product that will better meet the customers' needs, rather than settling for the lowest price.

The owner of La Colombe d'Or used **cross-selling**, one of the basics of effective revenue management. Cross-selling opportunities abound in the hospitality industry. A hotel can cross-sell F&B, exercise room services, and executive support services, and it can even sell retail products ranging from hand-dipped chocolates to terry-cloth bathrobes. A ski resort can cross-sell ski lessons and dinner sleigh rides.

Upselling, also part of effective revenue management, involves training sales and reservations employees to continuously offer a higher-priced product, rather than settling for the lowest price. One proponent of upselling believes that any hotel can increase its catering revenue by 15 percent through upselling.[4] Las Vegas resorts train front-desk personnel and incentivize them to upsell guests into suites and premium rooms.

Hundreds of upselling opportunities exist. They must be recognized and programs developed and implemented to ensure their success. The common practice of offering after-dinner coffee can be turned into an upselling opportunity by offering high-image upgraded presentations of coffee and tea rather than the standard pot of coffee. Price changes are easy to make and are often seen as a quick fix to a complex problem. Although it is easy to increase or decrease prices, it is hard to change a perception that your price is incorrect.

In this section, we look at how the price–demand relationship varies for different types of markets and how buyer perceptions of price affect pricing decisions. We also discuss methods for measuring the price–demand relationship.

Consumer Perceptions of Price and Value

In the end, it is the consumer who decides whether a product's price is right. When setting prices, management must consider how consumers perceive price and the ways that these perceptions affect consumers' buying decisions. Like other marketing decisions, pricing decisions must be buyer oriented.

"We can't see the value of our product," explains Carlos Talosa, senior vice president of operations at Embassy Suites. "We can only set price. The market value is set by our customers and our ability to sell to it." According to Talosa, "Even in recessionary times, consumers aren't necessarily buying the cheapest options, but they are demanding value for their dollars and rightly so. If you aren't value-selling, then you are giving away precious assets."[5]

Pricing requires more than technical expertise. It requires creative judgments and awareness of buyers' motivations. Effective pricing opens doors. It requires a creative awareness of the target market, why they buy, and how they make their buying decisions. Recognition that buyers differ in these dimensions is as important for pricing as it is for effective promotion, distribution, or product policy.

Marketers must try to look at consumers' reasons for choosing a product and set price according to consumers' perceptions of its value. Because consumers vary in the values that they assign to products, marketers often vary their pricing strategies for different segments. They offer different sets of product features at different prices. For example, a quarter-pound hamburger might cost $6 at McDonald's, $12 at a sit-down service restaurant, and $20 in an exclusive city club.

Buyer-oriented pricing means that the marketer cannot design a marketing program and then set the price. Good pricing begins with analyzing consumer needs and price perceptions. Managers must consider other marketing mix variables before setting price. Most hotel and restaurant concepts are designed by identifying a need in the marketplace. The product concept usually contains a price range that the market is willing to pay. Limited-service hotels identified a market segment that did not value many amenities found in a full-service motel. These guests did not use cocktail lounges, hotel restaurants, and banquet and meeting facilities. By eliminating these features, owners of limited-service hotels saved money in both construction and operating costs. They passed these savings along to the customer as lower prices, offering a sleeping room at a lower price than that of midscale hotels.

Consumers tend to look at the final price and then decide whether they received a good value. For example, two people dining in a restaurant receive their bill and see that it is $80. The diners then decide whether they were satisfied during the postpurchase evaluation. Rather than going over each item on the menu individually and judging its value, they judge the entire dining experience against the cost of that experience. If a restaurant offers good value on food but poor value on wine—charging $14 a glass for house wine, for instance—a couple who consume six glasses of wine may feel the check total is too high when $56 for wine is added to the bill.

Melvyn Greene, a hotel marketing consultant, once interviewed guests immediately after they had paid their bills and were leaving the hotel. Only about a fifth could remember the room rate they had just paid. They could, however, state whether they had received good value. Most of the guests had stayed for more than one day, used the internet, and dined in the hotel's F&B outlets. The room rate was only one part of the charges on their total bill. They tended to accept the charges and sign their charge card.[6] The guests based their perception of value on the total dollar amount of the bill, the products they had received, and their satisfaction with those products.

Different market segments evaluate products differently. Managers must provide their target markets with product attributes that the target market will value and eliminate those features that do not create value. Then they have to price the product so it will be perceived to be good value by the desired target market. For some markets, this means modest accommodations at a low price; for other markets, this means excellent service at a high price. Perceived value is a function of brand image, product attributes, and price.

Analyzing the Price–Demand Relationship

Each price a company can charge leads to a different level of demand. The demand curve illustrates the relationship between price charged and the resulting demand. It shows the number of units the market will buy in a given period at different prices that might be charged. In the normal case, demand and price are inversely related; that is, the higher the price, the lower the demand (Figure 11–2). Thus, the company would sell less if it raised its price from P_1 to P_2. Consumers with limited budgets usually buy less of something if the price is too high.

Most demand curves slope downward in either a straight or a curved line. But for prestige goods, the demand curve sometimes slopes upward. For example, a

Figure 11-2
Two hypothetical demand schedules.

A. Most goods

B. Prestige goods

luxury hotel may find that by raising its price from P_1 to P_2, it sells more rooms rather than fewer: Consumers do not perceive it as a luxury hotel at the lower price. However, if the hotel charges too high a price, (P_3), the level of demand will be lower than at P_2.

Most company managers understand the basics of a demand curve, but few are able to measure their demand curves. The type of market determines the type of demand curve. In a monopoly, the demand curve shows the total market demand resulting from different prices. But if the company faces competition, its demand at different prices will depend on whether competitors' prices remain constant or change with the company's own prices.

Estimating demand curves requires forecasting demand at different prices. For example, a study by the Economic Intelligence Unit (EIU) estimated the demand curve for holiday travel in Europe. Its findings suggested that a 20 percent reduction in the price of visiting a holiday destination increases demand by 35 percent, whereas a 5 percent decrease results in a 15 percent increase in demand.[7] The EIU study used vacation destinations in the Mediterranean and assumed that other variables were constant.

Researchers can develop models that assume other variables remain constant. For managers, it's not that simple. In normal business situations, other factors affect demand along with price. These factors include competition, the economy, advertising, and sales effort. If a resort cuts its price and then advertises, it would be hard to tell what portion of the increased demand came from the price decrease and what portion came from the advertising. Price cannot be isolated from other factors.

Economists show the impact of nonprice factors on demand through shifts in the demand curve rather than movement along it. Suppose that the initial demand curve is D_1 (Figure 11-3), the seller is charging P and selling Q_1 units. Now suppose that the economy suddenly improves or the seller doubles the advertising budget. Higher demand is reflected through an upward shift of the demand curve from D_1 to D_2. Without changing the price, P, the demand has increased.

Price Elasticity of Demand

Marketers also need to understand the concept of price elasticity, how responsive demand will be to a change in price. Consider the two demand curves in Figure 11-4. In Figure 11-4A, a price increase from P_1 to P_2 leads to a small drop in demand from Q_1 to Q_2. In Figure 11-4B, however, the same price increase leads to a large drop in demand from Q_1 to Q_2. If demand hardly varies with a small change in price, we say that the demand is inelastic. If demand changes greatly, we say the demand is elastic.

$$\frac{\% \text{ Change in Quality Demanded}}{\text{Price Elasticity of Demand}} = \% \text{ Change in Price}$$

Suppose that demand falls by 10 percent when a seller raises its price by 2 percent. Price elasticity of demand is therefore −5 (the minus sign confirms the

Figure 11-3
Effects of promotion and other nonprice variables on demand through shifts of the demand curve.

Figure 11–4
Inelastic and elastic demand.

A. Inelastic demand

B. Elastic demand

inverse relation between price and demand) and demand is elastic. If demand falls by 2 percent with a 2 percent increase in price, elasticity is 1. In this case the seller's total revenue stays the same: The seller sells fewer items but at a higher price that preserves the same total revenue. If demand falls by 1 percent when the price is increased by 2 percent, elasticity is 0.5 and demand is inelastic. The less elastic the demand, the more it pays for the seller to raise price.

What determines the price elasticity of demand? Buyers are less price-sensitive when the product is unique or when it is high in quality, prestige, or exclusiveness. Businesses are less price-sensitive when travel is needed to serve a client or potential client. Consumers are less price-sensitive when substitute products are hard to find. The only full-service hotel in an area where there is a high demand for four-star hotels will be able to charge and get good revenue for its rooms until competition arrives.

If demand is elastic rather than inelastic, sellers generally consider lowering their prices. A lower price may produce more total revenue. This practice makes sense when the extra costs of producing and selling more products do not exceed the extra revenue.

Factors Affecting Price Sensitivity[8]

We now look at some factors that affect price sensitivity. These include the unique value effect, the substitute awareness effect, the business expenditure effect, the end-benefit effect, the total expenditure effect, the shared cost effect, and the price quality effect.

UNIQUE VALUE EFFECT In Houston, the Pappas family has converted failed locations into successful restaurants, taking what had been dead restaurants and turning them into businesses with a one-hour wait on weeknights. The Pappas family did not have to use coupons or other price discounts to sell its food. It created a perception of value by giving large portions of food at a moderate price, which appealed to the upper lower class and the middle class.

Creating the perception that your offering is different from those of your competitors avoids price competition. In this way, the firm lets the customer know it's providing more benefits and offering a value that is superior to that of competitors, one that will attract either a higher price or more customers at the same price.

The guests may not always be able to describe what they mean by "value" but they certainly recognize it when they see or experience it. Price is a reflection of value and occasionally guests are highly offended by paying five-star prices for a three-star product. The internet offers photos of properties and even menu offerings but staged photos may not accurately reflect reality.

SUBSTITUTE AWARENESS EFFECT The existence of alternatives of which buyers are unaware cannot affect their purchase behavior. Hotel restaurants often charge more for meals based on the substitute awareness effect. The guest who arrives in the evening, being unfamiliar with the city, usually has breakfast in the hotel. The guest knows that a better value probably exists elsewhere but is unfamiliar with other restaurants in the city. Although the breakfast in the hotel may cost twice as much as a meal in a nearby restaurant, the search costs, the time it would take to find the restaurant, and the travel time to it are greater than the dollar savings of the meal.

Restaurants that target the convention market or out-of-town guests use the substitute awareness effect to their advantage. These restaurants have large advertisements in the city's entertainment magazines that are distributed in the hotels. They are often not the choice of the local resident, who perceives them as overpriced, but they do attract hotel guests who are unaware of alternatives.

When consumers discover products offering a better value, they switch to those products. Many hotel restaurants are empty in the evening. They are perceived as overpriced by the local market. Hotel guests have time during the day to find alternatives. These hotels often view F&B as a required amenity rather than an opportunity to compete for local business. A better philosophy is to use F&B as a means to attract customers. This requires unique offerings and concepts that provide realized value for the guest.

BUSINESS EXPENDITURE EFFECT When someone else pays the bill, the customer is less price-sensitive. This person will prefer to stay in an upscale hotel, and enjoy a good breakfast. When setting rates, management needs to know what the market is willing to pay. If a hotel can attract people traveling for business who have a generous travel allowance and are willing to pay high room rates, the hotel is leaving money on the table by offering discounts.

Airlines have been known to offer a second business-class ticket at a discount when one is purchased at full price. Hotels have been known to offer bonus frequent-flyer miles. Both of these promotions are taking advantage of the business expenditure effect. The airline knows that the employer or client will pick up the full-fare ticket, and the business traveler will be able to take a companion along at a discount. The hotel knows that because the traveler's company will pay for the hotel room, cutting prices by a few dollars might not bring in extra business travelers, but giving the business traveler bonus frequent-flyer miles that they can use for vacation trips will be effective. The business expenditure effect has numerous applications in the hospitality and travel industry.

END-BENEFIT EFFECT Customers are more price-sensitive when the price of the product accounts for a large share of the total cost of the end benefit. For example, a Japanese couple paying $3,000 in airfare to travel to Australia will pay $350 a night for a luxury ocean-front hotel. The $350 is a small cost of the end benefit (their vacation). Many families driving to the Gold Coast from Sydney (a 500-mile trip) are looking for less expensive accommodations. These families are often on a limited budget and prefer a less expensive motel a few blocks from the ocean.

When the Japanese couple goes to Dreamworld (a theme entertainment park), they pay the full per-person entrance fee without hesitation. The admission fee is a small portion of the price of their vacation. However, the local family of four looking for weekend entertainment may view the charges as high. In this case, the entry fee amounts to a large portion of their entertainment expenses for the month. To attract the local customer, Dreamworld offers yearly passes for just twice the single admission charge. Dreamworld knows that if it were to raise its prices by 20 percent, it would lose more local customers than international travelers. Thus, it is important for Dreamworld to know its customer mix. If 75 percent of Dreamworld's customers are local residents, Dreamworld must be cautious about its price increases. It is common for tourist attractions to provide special rates for local residents.

International visitors to the Gold Coast are less price-sensitive than local visitors.
Zstockphotos/123RF.

Upscale hotels can use the end-benefit effect as a tool to convince potential customers to pay an additional amount for hotel rooms. A company holding a two-day sales meeting may spend $750 in airfare, pay $500 in salary per day, and spend $100 in speaker fees per participant. A smart hotel salesperson may convince the meeting planner to upgrade by pointing out that the hotel costs are a small portion of the total costs. The sales presentation might be structured like this:

> And the difference between our luxury accommodations and the hotel accommodations you're considering is only $75 per night or $150 per participant, which is a small portion of your total cost per participant. Don't you think it's worth $150 to instill pride in your employees and show them that you care enough about them to put them in one of the best hotels in the city? Surely, the attitude difference this will create in the participants will play a significant role in the total success of the conference. Let's get the contracts drawn up for your sales meeting right now while we still have the space.

When working with price, the end-benefit price is an important concept to consider. The end-benefit price identifies price-sensitive markets and provides opportunities to overcome pricing objections when the product being sold is a small cost of the end benefit. To take full advantage of this effect, remember that many purchases have nonmonetary costs. For example, a mother planning the wedding of her daughter wants everything to be perfect to avoid embarrassing moments. High emotional involvement often makes the buyer less price-sensitive.

TOTAL EXPENDITURE EFFECT The more someone spends his or her own money on a product or service, the more sensitive that person is to the product's price. For example, limited-service chains such as Hampton Inns, Red Roof Inns, and La Quinta have made a successful effort to appeal to salespersons. The travel expenses of a salesperson can be significant, especially for those who average two to three days a week away from home. A salesperson who saves just $20 a night can realize annual savings of more than $2,000. This savings adds to the profit of salespeople on straight commission. Companies that pay the expenses of their salespeople can save $2,000 times the number of salespeople that they employ. Thus, a company with 12 salespeople can save $24,000.

The total expenditure effect is useful in selling lower-price products or products that offer cost savings to volume users. The hotel concepts mentioned earlier provide salespeople with the benefits that they seek in a hotel: clean, comfortable rooms; security; free telephone calls; and a coffee shop nearby.

The total expenditure effect is a dominant decision-making force for thousands of travelers who are provided with a set figure per trip. Many truckers are given a predetermined amount of cash, such as $500 for a trip. Expenditures over that level are not reimbursed. Not all motels desire the business of truckers, but those who do are highly cognizant of the fixed expenditures of their guests. They realize that ample parking for a 16- or 18-wheeler, a clean room with two beds, and a reasonable price will attract business.

Hotels that cater to upscale travelers frequently feature one king-size bed in a room because few people on unlimited or high-expense accounts wish to share a room. Quite the opposite is true of truckers or pipeline construction teams with fixed-expenditure travel budgets. A $70 room shared by two extends a fixed budget.

PRICE QUALITY EFFECT Consumers tend to equate price with quality, especially when they lack any prior experience with the product. For example, a friend may recommend that you stay at the Grand Hotel on your trip to Houston. If you call to make reservations and the reservationist offers you a $69 weekend rate, you may perceive this rate as too low for the class of hotel that you want and select another. The Grand Hotel may have met all your needs, but because of the low price, you assumed it would not.

A high price can also bring prestige to a product because it limits availability. Restaurants where the average check is more than $100 per person for dinner would lose many of their present customers if they lowered their prices. In cases where price is perceived to relate to quality or where price creates prestige, a positive association between price and demand may exist with some market segments. For example, the Gosforth Park Hotel, an upscale hotel in Newcastle, England, found that occupancy increased as its rates increased.[9]

HIDDEN FEES The hospitality industry is known for charging hidden fees or fees that a guest has to pay to use the product that are not included in the basic price. Resorts often add a resort fee that can be $30 or more. This fee usually covers items such as internet connection and the health club whether or not the guest uses these services. Many airlines charge baggage fee that can be from $25 to $100 per bag. Budget airlines will charge extra for an aisle or window seat. Some cruise lines add a $20–30 per day gratuity charge to the final bill on the cruise. In addition to alcoholic drinks some also charge for carbonated soft drinks. This charge is about $5 a day for children and $7 a day for adults. These charges allow the hotel, airline, or cruise to post a lower base rate, attracting price-sensitive customers and then collecting these hidden fees from the guest. These fees are unlikely to ever disappear from the hospitality industry. However, to avoid angry guests and embarrassment, it is important to keep such fees transparent to the guest before reaching the point of paying for the bill. If guests inquire at any time about extra fees, they should be given clear and direct answers.[10]

Competitors' Prices and Offers

Competitors' prices and their possible reactions to a company's own pricing moves are other external factors affecting pricing decisions. A meeting planner scheduling a meeting in Chicago will check the price and value of competitive hotels.

Once a company is aware of its competitors' prices and offers, it can use this information as a starting point for deciding its own pricing. For example, if a customer perceives that the Sheraton in Singapore is similar to the Hilton, the Sheraton must set its prices close to those of the Hilton or lose that customer. This is called a competitive set. The Star Report is a popular tool provided by STR. It compares a hotel with a set of competitors (usually 4), which they select. The Star Report compares price, occupancy, and RevPAR of your hotel with an aggregate of the competitive set.

Price-Rate Compression

During periods of weak demand, very few competitors escape the effect of a weak market. Those with a strong and loyal customer base are best suited to "ride out" such a market. In many cases, competitors are inclined to lower prices as a response rather than seek other strategies. Under these conditions, "price compression" may occur.

Price (rate) compression occurs when the difference between room rates for three- to four- and five-star properties is not significant. This occurs when higher-priced hotels lower rates to maintain occupancy and become direct competitors to lower-rated hotels. This creates margin problems for economy sector hotels, which may have less ability to lower rates.

Other External Elements

When setting prices, the company must also consider other factors in the external environment. Economic factors such as inflation, boom, or recession and interest rates affect pricing decisions. For example, when gasoline prices went from $2.40 a gallon to $3.80 a gallon, many families were paying $50 to $100 more a month for gasoline. This money reduced their discretionary budget, reducing the money they had to spend on restaurants. Many restaurants had to reduce their prices to maintain customer counts. Most cannot offer the same product at a lower price and survive. The restaurants create new menus with lower-cost items that can be sold at a lower price.

General Pricing Approaches

The price the company charges is somewhere between one that is too low to produce a profit and one that is too high to produce sufficient demand. Product costs set a floor for the price; consumer perceptions of the product's value set the ceiling. The company must consider competitors' prices and other external and internal factors to find the best price between these two extremes.

Companies set prices by selecting a general pricing approach that includes one or more of these sets of factors. We look at the following approaches: the cost-based approach (**cost-plus pricing**, BE analysis, and target profit pricing), the value-based approach (perceived-value pricing), and the competition-based approach (going rate).

Cost-plus pricing Adding a standard markup to the cost of the product.

Cost-Based Pricing

The simplest pricing method is cost-plus pricing, adding a standard markup to the cost of the product. F&B managers often use the cost-plus method to decide wine prices. For example, a bottle of wine that costs $14 may sell for $42, or three times the cost.

Cost as a percentage of selling price is another commonly used pricing technique in the restaurant industry. Some restaurant managers target a certain food cost and then price their menu items accordingly. For example, a manager wanting a 40 percent food cost prices the items 2.5 times greater than their cost. The multiplicand is found by dividing the desired food cost percentage by 100. A manager desiring a 30 percent food cost would multiply the cost by 3.33. Managers using this type of pricing should realize that a restaurant is not 100 percent efficient. To make up for spoilage, shrinkage, and mistakes, managers usually have to price three or four percentage points below their desired food cost. Thus, a manager wanting a 40 percent food cost would need to price the menu at 36 to 37 percent. The adjustment figure varies depending on the volume and efficiency of the operation. In high-volume, limited-menu operations, it is lower.

For managers using this technique, it is advisable to use prime cost, the cost of labor and food, when determining menu prices. There is often a trade-off between labor and food costs; thus, prime cost is a truer reflection of the cost of producing a menu item. For example, if a restaurant makes its own desserts, the cost of the ingredients is usually cheaper than that of buying a similar product from a bakery; however, there are no labor costs for the preparation of the purchased product. It is better to look at both labor and food costs to determine prices.

Does using standard markups to set prices make logical sense? Generally, no. Any pricing method that ignores current demand and competition is not likely to lead to the best price. Some items with high costs such as steaks may have a lower markup, whereas signature desserts or appetizers have a high markup. Most managers who use cost as a percentage of selling price to determine menu prices use this technique to develop a target price. They adjust individual prices for menu items based on factors such as what the market will bear, psychological pricing, and other techniques discussed in this chapter.

Wine was typically sold in restaurants at about three times cost. A growing trend is to reduce the markup as the price increases. For example, at three times markup, the sales price for bottles of wine costing $8, $25, and $75 would be $24, $75, and $225. A more rational approach is to sell less expensive bottles for three to four times markup and gradually reduce the cost multiplier on higher-priced bottles to 1.5 times cost. Using this model, the price of bottles that cost $8, $25, and $75 could be $28, $65, and $150. This type of pricing also attracts guests who enjoy finer wines and also tend to enjoy fine dining, increasing the overall check average.[11] In the case of exceptional wines, some establishments prefer to reserve them for a special gourmet dinner involving many courses and several wines. The price per person for such a dinner can easily exceed $200 per guest. The Steamboat Inn, situated 38 miles north of Roseburg, Oregon, on the Umpqua River, has built a strong reputation with such diners.

Markup pricing remains popular for many reasons. First, sellers are more certain about costs than about demand. Tying the price to cost simplifies pricing, and managers do not have to adjust as demand changes. Second, because many F&B operations tend to use this method, prices are similar, and price competition is minimized.

Break-Even Analysis and Target Profit Pricing

Another cost-oriented pricing approach is BE pricing, in which the firm tries to determine the price at which it will break even. Some firms use a variation of BE pricing called *target profit pricing*, which targets a certain ROI.

Target profit pricing uses the concept of a BE chart (Figure 11–5). For example, a buffet restaurant may want to make a profit of $200,000. Its BE chart shows the total cost and total revenue at different levels of sales. Suppose that fixed costs are $300,000, and variable costs are $10 per meal. Variable costs are added to fixed costs to find total costs, which rise with volume. Total revenue starts at zero and rises with each unit sold. The slope of the total revenue reflects the price. If the restaurant sells 50,000 meals at a price of $20, for example, the company's revenue is $1 million.

At the $20 price, the company must sell at least 30,000 meals to break even; that is, at this sales level, total revenues will equal total costs of $600,000. If the company wants a target profit of $200,000, it must sell at least 50,000 meals, or 137 meals a day. This level of sales will provide $1 million of revenue to cover costs of $800,000, plus $200,000 in target profits. In contrast, if the company charges a higher price, say $25 per meal, it will need to sell only 33,334 meals, or 92 a day, to meet its target profit. The higher the price, the lower the company's BE point. The selling price less the variable cost represents the gross profit or contribution that the sale makes toward offsetting fixed costs. Here is the formula for the BE point:

BE = Fixed Costs/Contribution (Selling Price–Variable Cost)

In the previous example,

BE = $300,000/$10 ($20 Selling Price – $10 Variable Cost) = 30,000 meals

Hotels use this concept of contribution margin to set rates when demand drops. Hotels set low rates, rationalizing that at least they are covering their variable costs.

Figure 11–5
Break-even chart for determining target price.

This can be effective if it creates additional demand. However, some hotels try to steal business during good times by cutting rates. This is a difficult strategy to manage, as recuperating from any substantial cut in prices in an inelastic market is not easy. A hotel that is 60 percent occupied with a room rate of $120 and a fixed cost of $40 per room and that cut its rates to $95 would have to increase its occupancy rate to 87 percent to BE on rooms profit. The fixed cost includes the cost of laundry, amentias, utilities, and cleaning of the room.[12]

Much depends on the relationship between price and demand. For example, suppose a company calculates that given its current fixed and variable costs, it must charge a price of $30 for the product to earn its desired target profit. But marketing research shows that few customers will pay more than $25 for the product. In this case, the company must trim its costs to lower the BE point so it can charge the lower price that consumers expect.

Value-Based Pricing

Value-based pricing Uses the buyer's perceptions of value, not the seller's cost, as the key to pricing.

An increasing number of companies are basing their prices on the products' perceived value. **Value-based pricing** uses the buyers' perceptions of value, not the seller's cost, as the key to pricing. Value-based pricing means that the marketer cannot design a product and marketing program and then set the price. Price is considered along with other marketing mix variables before the marketing program is set. The company uses the nonprice variables in the marketing mix to build perceived value in the buyers' minds, setting price to match the perceived value.

Any company using perceived-value pricing must learn the value in the buyers' minds for different competitive offers. Sometimes researchers ask consumers how much they would pay for each benefit added to the offer. One method of identifying how much customers are willing to pay involves using a technique called *trade-off analysis*. Researchers ask buyers how much they would pay for a hotel room with and without certain amenities. This information provides an idea of which features add more value than the cost. If the seller charges more than the buyers' perceived value, its sales will suffer.

More and more marketers have adopted value-pricing strategies. They strive to offer just the right combination of quality and good service at a fair price. This can result in redesigning existing brands to provide more quality or offer the same amount of quality for a lower price. Some companies even succeed by offering less value but at very low prices. For example, Spirit Airlines gives customers "Bare Fare" pricing, by which they get less but do not pay for what they do not get. Buying a ticket on a Spirit flight gets you one thing and one thing only—a seat on a plane to your destination. If you want more, you pay for it. Spirit charges extra for everything. You get only what you pay for—and not one peanut more. Understanding the value a segment places on a product can help marketers allocate their supply among the different segments. A study of meeting planners provided evidence that meeting planners perceived a greater value in paying $200 for a room than $175. Apparently, planners, like many guests, associate quality with higher price.[13]

The price of a hotel room may vary according to the type of customer. The hotel may have a rate for individual business guests, a group rate for groups of 10 or more, and a convention rate for associations that want to hold large functions at the hotel. If a hotel has the objective of maintaining 60 percent occupancy at an average rate of $180, it needs to determine its mix of customers and the average rate per segment. For example, it might develop the following mix to achieve a $180 rate:

	Percentage of Business	Average Rate ($)
Business	30	200
Corporate group	40	180
Association	30	160

To achieve its target rate of $180, the hotel would have to sell above the average rate in peak times to compensate for discounted prices during off-peak times. It is important to develop target rates and keep on track toward meeting these goals. If the hotel offers a group 100 rooms for three nights at a rate of $150, it will need to make up $4,500 [(100 rooms × 3 nights × $90 target rate) − (300 × $75 actual rate)] in revenue. It must sell to other groups above the $90 target rate, sell more business rooms at the $100 rate, or increase the targeted occupancy rate and sell additional rooms. A successful guest price mix depends on careful study of the behavior profiles of major guest segments. For most hospitality companies, this begins with a separation of guests into leisure and business segments. Subsegmentation of each category may occur, providing greater information about these major guest categories. Undoubtedly, the most important distinguishing profile characteristics of these two major segments are their relative degree of price elasticity. In general, business travelers exhibit inelastic price behavior and leisure travelers an elastic price response.

Competition-Based Pricing

Going-rate pricing Setting price based largely on following competitors' prices rather than on company costs or demand.

A strategy of **going-rate pricing** is the establishment of price based largely on those of competitors, with less attention paid to costs or demand. The firm might charge the same, more, or less than its major competitors. Some firms may charge a bit more or less, but they hold the amount of difference constant. For example, a limited-service hotel chain may charge $25 more than Motel 6 in markets where they compete. This form of pricing is quite popular.

▰▰▰ Pricing Strategies

New-Product Pricing Strategies

Pricing strategies usually change as a product passes through its life cycle. The introductory stage is especially challenging. Several options exist for pricing new products: prestige pricing, market-skimming pricing, and market-penetration pricing.

Prestige Pricing

Hotels or restaurants seeking to position themselves as luxurious and elegant enter the market with a high price to support this position. Nightclubs may charge a cover charge to attract a certain type of clientele and create an image of exclusiveness. In each of these cases, lowering the price would reposition the business, resulting in a failure to attract the target market.

Market-Skimming Pricing

Price skimming is setting a high price when the market is price-insensitive. Price skimming can make sense when lowering the price will create less revenue. For example, the owner of the only motel in a small town in South Dakota during pheasant hunting season can set high prices if there is more demand than rooms. Price skimming can be an effective short-term policy. However, one danger is that competition will notice the high prices that consumers are willing to pay and enter the market, creating more supply and eventually reducing prices. The hospitality industry is particularly affected by this because market entry by competitors is relatively easy.

The Hotel Vier Jahreszeiten Kempinski, built in 1858, is situated on Maximilianstrasse, regarded as Munich's most desirable street. Kempinski operates luxury hotels. It has a prestigious name and is often the price leader in the markets it serves. Manfred Bail/imageBROKER/Shutterstock.

Market-Penetration Pricing

Rather than setting a high initial price to skim off small but profitable market segments, other companies set a low initial price to penetrate the market quickly and deeply, attracting many buyers and winning a large market share. Theodore Zinck's, a cocktail lounge, opened in a new market with prices about 20 percent lower than the competition. Management had negotiated a low lease, giving Zinck's a competitive advantage. Competitors could not match Zinck's lower prices because of the higher overhead. The policy allowed Zinck's to attract many customers quickly.

Several conditions favor setting a low price: (1) The market must be highly price-sensitive so that a low price produces more market growth, (2) there should be economics that reduce costs as sales volume increases, and (3) the low price must help keep out competition.

Existing-Product Pricing Strategies

The strategies just described are used primarily when introducing a new product. However, they can also be useful with existing products. The following strategies are ones that can be used with existing products.

Product-Bundle Pricing

Product-bundle pricing
Combining several products and offering the bundle at a reduced price.

Sellers who use product-bundle pricing combine several of their products and offer the bundle at a reduced price. For example, hotels sell specially priced weekend packages that include room, meals, and entertainment or offer commercial rates that include breakfast and a newspaper. Product bundling can promote the sales of products that consumers might not otherwise buy, but the combined price must be low enough to convince them to buy the bundle. The items added to the core service must hold more value to the customer than they cost to provide.

Product-bundle pricing is a strategy that has been well developed by cruise lines, tour wholesalers, and casinos. Cruise lines typically offer fly-cruise or fly-drive cruise packages in which the services of an auto rental company, airline, cruise line, and hotel are combined at a price well under the cost of purchasing each separately. The internet has increased the use of product bundling by allowing companies to sell related products over their sites, such as airlines selling hotel rooms, rental cars, and vacation packages on their Web sites. Online travel agencies (OTAs) (Orbitz.com and Expedia.com), tour operators (Carlsontravel.com), destinations (Lasvegas.com), travel-related search engines (Kayak.com), travel agency consortia (Vacation.com), and global distribution systems (GDSs) (Amadeus and Sabre) all sell packages. With the internet as the distribution system, product bundles are expected to continue to grow in popularity.[14]

Price bundling has two major benefits to hospitality and travel organizations. First, customers have different maximum prices or reservation prices they will pay for a product. Thus, by packaging products, we can transfer the surplus reservation price on one component to another component of the package. For example, customer "A" may be willing to pay $280 for two nights in a hotel room near Disneyland and $350 for two three-day passes to Disneyland. Customer "B" is willing to pay $325 for two nights in a hotel room and $300 for two three-day passes.

Fast casual restaurants often bundle a burger, fries, and a soft drink at a lower "combo" price. (A customer enjoys a combo meal at a lower price in a fast-casual restaurant.) *Source:* Seyhmus Baloglu—author; model clearance—his son.

If a hotel that wants to get $160 for a night for its rooms is able to get discounted three-day passes to Disneyland and offer a package that includes a room for two for two nights and two three-day passes for $620, both customers will take advantage of the package. Even though the room price of $20 a night is above what the one customer wanted to pay, when the room and tickets are packaged together, the components are below the reservation price. In this case, the three-day pass was $50 below customer A's reservation price for the pass and the hotel price was $20 a night above what customer A wanted to pay. When they were packed together, the passes and the room were $10 less than customer A's reservation price for the package. Customers have different reservation prices; by bundling we can transfer surpluses from one component to another to expand the market.

A second benefit of price bundling is that the price of the core product can be hidden to avoid price wars or the perception of having a low-quality product. For example, a Las Vegas hotel that normally has an average rate above $120 may sell rooms to airlines for $55 to help fill the hotel. The airline bundles the hotel with a round-trip air ticket. The airline's package includes two nights in the hotel and airfare from Los Angeles for $299. This creates a much better perception for the hotel than if it ran an advertisement pushing $55 room rates. The $55 rates give a message to some that the hotel is desperate for business, to others who do not know the hotel it will give a perception of a hotel of the $55 quality level, and guests who had paid $129 for a room may ask for a refund. By selling the rooms to an airline and creating a bundled product, the hotel avoided the image problems that can come with low rates. Hotels can also create their own bundles. For example, the Royal Palms Hotel and Spa in Phoenix offered a "Royal Romance Package." The package included champagne, chocolate-covered strawberries, a rose-petal turndown, dinner for two, and a room for $456. The rack rate was $439 for a room for the same date. Rather than cut rates to try to attract guests, the exclusive resort bundled a number of products that have value to a couple wanting to get away.[15]

Dynamic packaging
A package vacation on a single Web site in which buyers can put together airline flights, lodging, car rental, entertainment, and tours in their own customer-designed packages.

Dynamic packaging is a relatively new term that refers to an old practice. Today it refers primarily to a package vacation on a single Web site in which buyers can put together airline flights, lodging, car rental, entertainment, and tours in their own customer-designed packages.

Price-Adjustment Strategies

Companies usually adjust their basic prices to account for various customer differences and changing situations. We look at the following adjustment strategies: discount pricing and allowances and discriminatory pricing.

VOLUME DISCOUNTS Most hotels have special rates to attract customers who are likely to purchase a large quantity of hotel rooms, either for a single period or throughout the year. Hotels usually offer special prices or provide free goods for association and corporate meeting planners. As an example, suppose that a convention held by an industry association is attended by people who pay their own room charges. The association may prefer to receive a free room night for every 20-room nights booked, rather than a lower room rate. It can use the free nights for its staff and invited speakers, reducing the association's total costs. Hotels offer corporate rates to companies that will guarantee their use of the hotel for an agreed-upon number of room nights per year.

DISCOUNTS BASED ON TIME OF PURCHASE Seasonal discounts allow the hotel to keep demand steady during the year. Hotels, motels, and airlines offer seasonal discounts during selling periods that are traditionally slower. Airlines often offer off-peak prices, based on the time of day or the day of the week that the passenger flies. International flights adjust the price according to seasonal demand. Restaurants offer early-bird specials to attract customers before their normal rush. Unfortunately, the various discount rates offered by a company sometimes clash to negate the desired positive effects. For example, restaurants that offer seniors 10 percent discounts have more difficulty offering early-bird specials. Seniors often feel no reason to accept the early-bird special because they will qualify for a discount at peak hours.

Discriminatory pricing
Refers to segmentation of the market and pricing differences based on price elasticity characteristics of the segments.

DISCRIMINATORY PRICING The term *discriminatory pricing* often invokes mental images of discrimination on the basis of ethnicity, religion, gender, or age. **Discriminatory pricing**, from the vocabulary of economics, refers to segmentation of the market and pricing differences based on price elasticity characteristics of these segments. Price discrimination as used in this chapter is legal and viewed by many as highly beneficial to the consumer.

Companies often adjust basic prices to allow for differences in customers, products, and locations. In discriminatory pricing, the company sells a product or service at two or more prices, although the difference in price is not based on differences in cost.

Suppose, for example, that a steak dinner has a menu price of $40, and the demand is 100 dinners at this price. If the restaurant lowers the price to $28, demand increases to 200 dinners. If the variable costs for preparing and serving the dinner are $16, the gross profit in each case will be $2,400. Price discrimination, a microeconomic concept, theoretically tries to capture the maximum amount someone would pay from each customer. From a practical standpoint, we might have several different prices to try to capture additional customers above the BE point.

In the case illustrated, we would charge $40 to customers willing to pay $40. Those who are willing to pay only $28 would be charged $28. How do we do this? We can't ask the customer, "Would you like to pay $40 or would you like to pay $28?" Obviously, everyone would say $28. Instead, we give different prices to different segments, offering the highest price to those segments that are less price-sensitive. For example, our standard price is $40 for the dinner. We offer an early-bird special of $28 to diners arriving before 6 P.M. A person who works until 5 P.M. probably is unwilling to rush home and rush to the restaurant to take advantage of the discount. This customer prefers to relax at home after work and arrive at the restaurant at 7 P.M. However, retired persons who may be more price-sensitive, but less time-sensitive, would be attracted by this special. The restaurant could also choose to send a coupon in a direct-mail package to prospective customers. The price-sensitive customers keep the coupon and use it the next time they go out to eat. Other people who receive the coupon throw it away. These customers do not want to be bothered with filing the coupon and then looking for it when they want to dine out. To these customers, the $12 savings is not worth the hassle of using the coupon. Price discrimination discriminates in favor of the price-sensitive customer.

The supersaver fares on airlines usually require an advance purchase and minimum stay. These criteria are both designed to eliminate business travelers, whereas the advance purchase eliminates business trips made on short notice. Airlines know that business travelers are less price-sensitive; that is, they exhibit inelastic price behavior. Airlines offer low fares with the leisure traveler in mind. The leisure traveler uses discretionary income to pay for travel and as a result is more price-sensitive than the business traveler. A reduction in price often results in additional demand from the leisure segment.

A flight between Detroit and Los Angeles provides an example of airline pricing. The flight had economy fares that ranged from $629 to $129, with 11 different fare categories. The least expensive fare was a special fare for seniors. Like the airlines, many hotels discriminate between the leisure and business segments. Business hotels in central business districts often suffer low occupancy on weekends. Many of these hotels have developed lower-priced weekend packages to entice the leisure traveler.

Low variable costs combined with fluctuations in demand make price discrimination a useful tool for smoothing demand and bringing additional revenue and profits to most businesses. This form of pricing uses lower prices to attract additional customers, without lowering the price for everyone.

Major sectors of the hospitality industry, such as airlines, hotels, cruise lines, and railroads, are faced with enormous fixed costs. Companies in these sectors are faced with the need to fill seats or beds. Marriott and other hotel chains employ a pricing system based on discriminatory pricing to fill rooms and maximize revenue opportunities using fencing to keep price-inelastic customers from using rates designed for price-elastic segments.

Fencing at Marriott is accomplished by establishing restrictions that allow customers to self-select price discriminatory rates that are best for them. Such fences include advance reservations and nonrefundable advance purchases. These policies permit price-sensitive customers to enjoy lower rates and inelastic segments to pay full fare without restrictions.

To price-discriminate successfully, the following criteria must be met:[16]

1. Different groups of consumers must have different responses to price; that is, they must value the service differently.

2. The different segments must be identifiable and a mechanism must exist to price them differently.

3. There should be no opportunity for persons in one segment who have paid a lower price to sell their purchases to other segments.

4. The segment should be large enough to make the exercise worthwhile.

5. The cost of running the price discrimination strategy should not exceed the incremental revenues obtained. This is partly a function of criterion 4.
6. The customers should not become confused by the use of different prices.

Revenue Management

One application of discriminatory pricing is revenue management. Revenue management involves upselling, cross-selling, and analysis of profit margins and sales volume for each product line. Revenue management systems are used to maximize a hospitality company's yield or contribution margin. In the case of hotels, this is done by the rates that a hotel will charge and the number of rooms available for each rate based on projected occupancies for a given period. These systems help hotels achieve the maximum contribution margin based on the demand for hotel rooms. The concept behind revenue management is to manage revenue and inventory effectively by pricing differences based on the elasticity of demand for selected customer segments.

Hotel companies are placing a great deal of emphasis on revenue management because the extra revenue it generates is pure profit that drops to the bottom line. However, at a meeting of revenue managers, half of the respondents indicated that their senior management did not understand revenue management.[17] If you are going into the hospitality industry, an understanding of revenue management is essential.

Marketing HIGHLIGHT 11.1 — Segmented pricing: The right product to the right customer at the right time for the right price

In most hospitality, travel and entertainment products capacity is fixed, but demand varies. In these situations, a common price may result in many people not being able to access the product during prime times and empty seats during off-peak periods. In some products such as airline transportation and events, all seats may not be the same.

Theaters, like the one in the Bellagio Hotel, Las Vegas, where the Cirque du Soleil show "O" is performed, often apply revenue management by charging more for seats with better views and during times when demand is higher. Kumar Sriskandan/Alamy Stock Photo.

Live performances, including sporting events, theater, and concerts, will charge more for seats with great views and less for seats father away from the event. Some airlines charge more for aisle and window seats. Customers wanting better seats with the capacity to pay for these seats will have the opportunity to purchase the seats they want. Those who want to see the event or want to get to a certain destination but want to spend less can purchase less expensive seats. Susan Greco gives an example of an opera company, which went from a single price for all seats to pricing based on the location of the seat, increasing the price for better seats and lowering the price for seats in the back. Seat prices on the weekends were increased and those during the week were reduced. The variety of prices allowed the customers to choose what they would pay and the opera company increased its overall revenue by 9 percent. Some customers who previously could not afford to attend now had the opportunity to attend by selecting tickets further from the stage on weekday nights.

The opera company had introduced a simple form of revenue management. Airlines, hotels, and restaurants call it revenue management and practice it religiously. This allows companies to attract customers by having the right product at the right price for the right customer.

Segmented pricing and yield management aren't really new ideas. For instance, Marriott Corporation used seat-of-the-pants yield-management approaches long before it installed its current sophisticated system. Back when J. W. "Bill" Marriott was a young man working at the family's first hotel, the Twin Bridges in Washington, DC, he sold rooms from a drive-up window. As Bill tells it, the hotel charged a flat rate for a single occupant, with an extra charge for each additional person staying in the room. When room availability got tight on some nights, Bill would lean out the drive-up window and assess the cars waiting in line. If some of the cars were filled with passengers, Bill would turn away vehicles with just a single passenger to sell his last rooms to those farther back in line who would be paying for multiple occupants. He might have accomplished the same result by charging a higher rate at peak times, regardless of the number of room occupants.

It is important to understand the demand cycles of your product and the motivation of your customers. For example, many resorts in Las Vegas will show their prices by day of the month. This provides transparency and lets the traveler who has flexibility in his or her travel dates to choose a date when there is less demand and prices are lower. For example, a retired couple driving to Las Vegas from the Los Angeles area will benefit by choosing lower-rated dates without reducing the benefits they receive from the trip. Shifting demand by charging higher prices when rooms are needed for convention delegates creates the ability to provide rooms for those who want to be in Las Vegas during the higher demand dates and are willing to pay the price for these dates. The transparency of the prices is important so that guests understand when a number of conventions are in town and the delegates to the convention will need rooms, the room rates will be higher.

Greco provides an example of a Cafe in Boston, which always had a wait over the lunch period but was empty by 3 P.M. until closing. The owner offered a 20 percent discount in the morning and after 2 P.M. By shifting some demand away from the lunch hour, he still remained full at lunch but was able to increase the off-peak business. He was able to increase overall revenue and even with the 20 percent discount he was still able to make a profit on the increased revenue.

These examples show that understanding your customers, what they value, and the demand for your product can create pricing that will allow you to create value for your customers and increase your revenue and profits.[18]

Revenue management involves the development and use of different rate classes based on the projected demand for the service. These rates are used to maximize yield. This is the formula for yield:

$$\frac{\text{room} - \text{nights sold}}{\text{room} - \text{nights available}} \times \frac{\text{actual average room rate}}{\text{room rate potential}} = \text{yield}$$

A hotel with sufficient history can project occupancy based on current booking patterns. If low occupancy is projected, the hotel keeps lower rate classes open to increase occupancy. The lower rates typically use price discrimination techniques that favor the leisure traveler. For example, a hotel may offer advance supersaver rates. The idea is to create extra demand with low rates, attracting guests that the hotel would not otherwise have. If the projected occupancy is high, the lower rates will be closed, and only the higher rate classes will be accepted. Today, several computerized systems are available that automatically project occupancy levels for a given date and suggest pricing levels for each day. It is common for a revenue-management system to increase revenues by at least 5 percent. Reservations for Hyatt's Regency Club concierge floors climbed 20 percent after Hyatt implemented revenue management. One Hilton hotel increased its average transient rate by $7.50 with no reduction in occupancy the first month after installing a revenue-management system.[19]

Three important concepts in revenue management are RevPAR, GopPAR, and RevPASH. RevPAR is revenue per available room. It takes into consideration both occupancy and average rate, by determining the average rate per available room. A 100-room hotel that sold 60 rooms at an average rate of $200 would have a RevPAR of $120 (60/100 × $200). GopPAR is the gross operating profit (Gop) per available room. Gop is equal to total revenue minus total departmental and operating expenses. GopPAR does not indicate the mix of a hotel property but it does provide a clear indication of a hotel's profit potential. GopPAR can reflect management's efficiency.[20]

RevPASH is the revenue per available seat hour. It is tracked hourly because we do not sell a seat for a day, like we do hotel rooms. For example, it identifies peak periods and periods of less demand. It supplies data to track the effectiveness of the promotions to fill the low-demand periods. For many restaurants, increasing RevPASH can be as easy as getting the right table configurations. Seating a deuce at a four-top results in zero revenue for two seats. Thus, having two-tops that combined to seat a party of four is a nonprice method of increasing revenue. The County Inn and Suites uses RevPAR measurements to compare renovated hotels in the chain to those it views as stabilized. An analysis of renovated rooms revealed a 5.7 percent favorable RevPAR, which equated to an additional $140,000 in annual revenue for an average 80-room hotel.[21]

This chain also uses a RevPAR index as a measurement to gauge nonperforming hotels. Terminated hotels had a RevPAR score that was far below others in the chain.

Another use of RevPAR by this chain is to compare its RevPAR improvement against that of competitive hotels. As an example, if RevPAR increased 10 percent for this chain but 13 percent for competitors, then the conclusion was that it was not performing as well as competitors. RevPASH can also provide data to help us with revenue management.[22]

Revenue management systems must be based on sound marketing. They should be developed with the long-term value of the customer in mind. One early yield-management system cut off reservations from travel agents when projected occupancy for a given date was high. This was done to eliminate travel agency commissions when the hotel could sell the rooms. This system saved money in the short term by saving travel agency commissions. However, in the long term, the hotel could lose a significant portion of its travel agency business. Think of the person who wants to stay at the Regal Hotel in Orlando and fly to Orlando on Delta. The travel agent informs the client that the airline is confirmed, but no rooms are available at the Regal, so a reservation was made at the Gator Hotel. The client calls the Regal only to find that rooms are available. The client now thinks the travel agent is pushing the Gator Hotel and gets upset with the travel agent. The travel agent becomes upset with the Regal and refuses to book future business with them. The Regal gains short-run extra revenue but loses the travel agent's business in the long term. Revenue management programs should focus on long-term profitability, not just the maximization of one day's revenue.

With some revenue management systems, customers staying a longer period can be charged more than those staying only a few nights. Normally, one might expect a concession for longer stays. Sometimes the longer stay may take the guest into a period of high occupancy. These systems average the occupancy over the guest's stay. For example, based on the occupancy levels in the following table, a guest checking in on May 8 and checking out on May 10 would be quoted a $65 rate as the lowest available rate. A guest checking in on May 8 and checking out on May 12 would be quoted $85 as the lowest available rate because the hotel can sell more rooms for May 10 and 11 at a minimum of $105 a night. Under this system, the staff must be well trained to explain rate differences to the guest.

	Projected Occupancy (%)
May 8	60
May 9	60
May 10	85
May 11	90

Revenue management systems can be useful in managing the number of rooms available for transient demand. Most hotels have a base of transient demand composed of individual guests who pay a high rate. Some of these transient guests are businesspersons who may stay in the hotel several times during the year. Groups make their reservations well in advance of the transients. When group business displaces transient business, the average rate drops, and some displaced transient guests may never return, deciding to stay at an alternative hotel. Revenue management systems help eliminate the problem of displaced transient guests by projecting the number of transient rooms that will be used on any given date.

If used properly, revenue management systems can provide extra revenue. A good revenue management system benefits both the hospitality company and the guest. It opens low-rated rooms for the leisure traveler during times of low occupancy and saves rooms during periods of peak demand for the business traveler willing to pay full rates. The company gains because revenue management focuses on maximizing revenue, not cutting costs.

A revenue management system requires the availability of good data. This has forced many hospitality companies to go back to the basics and develop sound information-retrieval systems for internal data, such as booking patterns, and to develop and use better forecasting methods. The end result is that without even using revenue management, the company is in a far better position to make intelligent management decisions.

An effective revenue management system depends on several variables.[23] These are the ability to segment markets, perishable inventory, ability to sell product in advance, fluctuating demand, low-marginal sales costs, high-marginal production costs (can easily add another room), booking pattern data, information on demand pattern by market segment, an overbooking policy, knowledge of effect of price changes, a good information system for internal and external data, and ability to fence customer segments.

Use of revenue management within the hospitality industry is expanding to new sectors. Many golf courses have started to track contribution margins, costs, and revenue per day and started using differential pricing (late-day specials and seniors' discounts), special events (local tournaments on off nights), and customer play time. The Dalmahoy Golf and Country Club Resort near Edinburgh, Scotland, implemented a revenue-management program for its golf course operation. This tied the costs of an annual membership to the time and day that the purchaser used the golf course.[24]

Hotel guests commonly realize that different prices are charged for similar rooms for a specific night. To offset customer perceptions of this being unfair, one study showed that if customers were given information about how the system works, the feelings of unfair prices were reduced. Specifically, when customers were told that rates vary according to day of the week, length of stay, and how far in advance the reservation was made, perceptions of fairness improved.[25]

Dynamic Pricing

Dynamic pricing Continually adjusting prices to meet the characteristics and needs of individual customers and situations.

A popular tool used by revenue managers is **dynamic pricing**. Dynamic pricing continually adjusts prices to meet the characteristics and needs of individual customers and situations. When demand increases or capacity is reduced due to previous sales, prices increase and the reverse is also true.

Airlines, cruise lines, and hotels use dynamic pricing. According to changes in demand, costs, or competitor pricing, they adjust what they charge for their products on a daily, hourly, or even continuous basis. Dynamic pricing is different from price discrimination. Dynamic pricing does not put up fences to restrict certain customers from taking advantage of lower prices. It raises or lowers prices based on demand for the hotel on a particular day, a particular flight, or cruise. It will raise the price of the lowest fare or rate available to leisure customers based on demand. Airlines change their rates several times if the demand for a flight keeps increasing and is predicted to be sold out. Prices will be lowered if the flight is predicted to leave with empty seats. Although dynamic pricing is different than price discrimination, often a revenue manager will use both techniques; they are not mutually exclusive.

In the extreme, some companies customize their offers and prices based on the specific characteristics and behaviors of individual customers. These days, online offers and prices might well be based on what specific customers search for and buy, how much they pay for other purchases, and whether they might be willing and able to spend more. For example, a consumer who recently went online to purchase a first-class ticket to Paris might get a higher quote on a hotel room. By comparison, a friend with a more modest online search and purchase history might receive an offer of 10 percent off on the same hotel room.[26]

Uber is an international app-based car dispatch service that lets customers summon cars from their app or by SMS. Uber uses a form of dynamic pricing called *surge pricing*. Under normal circumstances, Uber customers pay reasonable fares. However, using Uber in periods of surging demand can result in shocking price escalations, for example, on a stormy Saturday night in New York City. Uber knew that people would not want to walk in stormy weather, and demand would be high. Fares were eight times its average fare. On Uber's Web site, there is an explanation of surge pricing. They want to be able to provide service their customers can rely on whenever they need a driver.[27] Thus, the increase in prices is to encourage more drivers to be available. However, despite this explanation on their Web site and the fact that Uber's app warned customers of heightened fares before processing their requests, many customers were still outraged. They commented, e-mailed, and tweeted their displeasure with messages charging the company with price gouging. One customer shared an Instagram photo of a taxi receipt for $415. However, despite the protests, Uber experienced no subsequent drop in demand in New York. Uber's policy is working. Its higher fares offered to drivers attracted more drivers and increased capacity. The high fares reduced capacity, with some potential riders deciding to stay home. The end result was capacity and demand approached equilibrium. Thus, dynamic pricing can help sellers optimize sales and profits.[28]

BAR Pricing

Best available rate (BAR) pricing is a relatively new pricing technique used for guests who stay several nights. Instead of charging a single rate for a multiple-night stay, such as $100 per night, BAR pricing charges different rates for each night. Thus, some nights might be priced below $100 and others above the rate. These daily rates are determined through revenue management.

BAR pricing originated with the internet intermediaries Hotels.com, Expedia, Priceline, and Orbitz. The practice then spread to hotel companies. To assure customers that they are receiving the BARs for any date, price guarantees are often given. These vary in terms between firms offering them.[29] BAR is sometimes referred to as nonblended pricing.

Rate Parity

Hotel Rate Parity is a controversial strategy that has been challenged in court and survived. However, pressure against this strategy remains.

Rate Parity is essentially a strategy in which hotel chains agree to allow their product (rooms) to be shown and sold by OTAs provided the prices they offer are the same and are not lower than the hotel's BAR. The OTAs refer to these hotels as merchant model suppliers. Consumers are unlikely to find a rate lower than the BAR rate set by the hotel.

The OTAs ask for assurances of rate parity since they are assured that the hotel will not offer lower rates than what the OTAs can offer and make a profit. Rate Parity applies only to "public rates"—those available to the general public. It does not apply to affinity rates for special segments such as ministerial or military rates.

The hotel industry knows that many travelers search for a hotel room online first. With this price knowledge in hand, they then call the 800 number for one of the hotel chains for which they have price information. The hotel will quote a BAR as well as others. At this point, the hotel has an advantage over the OTAs since the hotel can offer a special *topper* (add-on offering) such as a meal or drink package.

In a particularly hot market, hotels do not need OTAs and could tell them they will not honor rate parities nor will they not pay commissions. However, when demand becomes weak, most hotels need the OTAs. "In down markets, many properties can't even break even without the steady flow of traffic from Expedia, Orbitz, and Travelocity and their subsidiaries."[30]

Nonuse of Revenue Management

Some members of the hospitality industry have chosen not to use a revenue management system. However, researchers on this subject concluded, "Waiting is part of life and particularly part of an experience with a restaurant. Having long waits for tables in a restaurant does not necessarily mean there is a problem. Demand in restaurants like Cheesecake Factory, Houston's, and Outback Steakhouse far exceeds supply on most days."[31]

Instead of using price discrimination and fencing, Outback Steakhouse sets a menu price but offers a streamline takeaway service to assist those who don't wish to wait for table service (uncaptured demand).

For popular restaurants like the Cheesecake Factory, demand far exceeds capacity on some days. *Source:* author—Seyhmus Baloglu.

Overbooking

Revenue management continues to provide great service to the hospitality industry. Nevertheless, occasionally there are problems with overbooking, which can create guest/passenger dissatisfaction. When overbooking occurs, the supplier has an ethical and legal responsibility to compensate the buyer and/or find alternative flights, hotels, and so on.

Airlines offer to pay passengers to give up their seats and accept an alternative flight. Guests of hotels are not interested in accepting a hotel room the next day or even hours later. The management of the hotel must, therefore, "walk" the guest, meaning the guest will be forced to accept a room in a different hotel. In fact, very few, if any, guests are expected to walk to a different hotel despite the name. Transportation is generally provided. In addition to providing an equal room elsewhere, some hotels follow the airline practice of providing extra compensation. This extra compensation may be in the form of vouchers or cash, as both seem to have about equal positive responses with the guest.[32]

Psychological Pricing

Psychological pricing considers the psychology of prices, not simply the economics. Earlier in this chapter, we discussed the relationship between price and quality. Prestige can be created by selling products and services at a high price.

Another aspect of psychological pricing is reference prices; these are prices that buyers carry in their minds and refer to when they look at a given product. A buyer's reference price might be formed by noting current prices, remembering past prices, or assessing the buying situation. Popular products often have reference prices. For a given type of restaurant, most consumers have a preconceived idea about the price or price range of certain items, such as a cup of coffee, a strip steak, or a hamburger. For example, a pizza chain may advertise its medium pizza for a price it knows is $2 less than the competition to establish a reference price for pizza eaters. But its price for beverages and extra items will be the same as that of the competition. The reference item creates the perception of value; consequently, little would be gained by cutting the price of the other items.

Price Endings

A study of hotel price-ending strategies demonstrated that "just under pricing strategies are utilized intentionally to signal value while round price endings of 0 and 5 are utilized to signal quality."[33] While dollar pricing is most commonly used by hotels, in the case of lower-rated hotels, odd ending prices are more common.

Customers tend to simplify price information by ignoring end figures. For instance, there is greater perceived distance between $0.69 and $0.71 than there is between $0.67 and $0.69. Consumers also tend to round figures. One restaurant study found that consumers round prices ranging from $0.86 to $1.39 to a dollar, from $1.40 to $1.79 to a dollar and a half, and from $1.80 to $2.49 to two dollars. If this is the case, there may be little change in demand caused by a price increase of $0.30 from $1.45 to $1.75, but there may be a significant decrease in demand if we raise the price by $0.40 to $1.85.[34]

The length of the field is another consideration. The jump from $0.99 to $1.00 or the jump from $9.99 to $10.00 can be perceived as a significant increase, although it is only $0.01. Taco Bell's value prices were all under $1, and therefore only two digits. Some psychologists argue that each digit has symbolic and visual qualities that should be considered in pricing. For example, because the number 8 is round, it creates a soothing effect, whereas 7 is angular, creating a jarring effect.

Perhaps the most interesting finding in this study was from a hotel management company of upscale, full-service hotels that added $0.95 to all of its managed properties. They reported no customer complaints but instead said that the practice added significant amounts to their EBITDA.

Promotional Pricing

When companies use promotional pricing, they temporarily price their products below list price and sometimes even below cost. Promotional pricing takes several forms. Fast-food restaurants price a few products as loss leaders to attract customers to the store in the hope that they will buy other items at normal markups. Donut shops may offer coffee for 75 cents, knowing a customer will usually buy at least one donut. Jack-in-the-Box offers special prices on its tacos because it often sells a soft drink with the order. During slow periods, hotels may offer special promotional rates to increase business. Rather than just lower prices, well-managed hotels create special events: a Valentine's weekend special, including a room, champagne upon arrival, a dinner for two, and a breakfast in the room, or a theater package, including a room, tickets to a play, dinner for two, and breakfast for two. These promotions give the guest a reason to come; the bundle of products adds value for the customer. The promotion creates a positive image, whereas straight price discounting can create a negative image.

The gaming industry is particularly aware of the importance of product bundling and promotional pricing. A casino executive stated, "We are in the adult entertainment business; our main product offering is gambling and there are many components that support it, such as hotels, entertainment facilities, and restaurants." Casino managers view hotel rooms as a means to entice and enable customers to gamble. Casinos must ensure that rooms are readily available for the most profitable gaming customers.[35] Hotel pricing reflects the fact that the company's main product offering is gaming, and a hotel room is only a supporting product for gaming.

Opaque pricing is a form of promotional pricing and used by some OTAs such as Priceline and Hotwire. Opaque offers do not identify the name of the supplier but usually give a general location and a rating such as a four-star hotel in the central business district offered at a very attractive price. Once the booking has been completed, the name and exact location of the property will be revealed to the buyer. Often exceptional price deals may be obtained in this manner.

Opaque pricing Selling products at a discounted price while hiding certain characteristics of the product from the consumer until after purchase.

Value Pricing—Low Price Approach

The term *value pricing* is confusing. It could be argued that anytime a product/service is purchased, at any price, the buyer must have perceived value in that product. Value pricing has become synonymous with the term *everyday low prices (EDLP)*. It has been used as a marketing strategy by some members of the hospitality industry, such as Taco Bell and Southwest Airlines.

"Value pricing can be extremely risky. Properly conceived and executed, it can earn positive results." It can also be disastrous.[36] In its simplest form, value pricing means offering a price below competitors permanently, which differs from promotional pricing, in which price may be temporarily lowered during a special promotion.

Value pricing is risky if a company does not have the ability to cut costs significantly. It is usually most appropriate for companies able to increase long-run market share through low prices (Taco Bell) or niche players with a lower-cost operating basis who use price to differentiate their product (Southwest Airlines). A study of value pricing in retail stores showed that "retailers can be profitable charging low prices but only when they have low costs."[37]

Prior to initiating a strategy of value pricing, managers must ask themselves these questions:

- What will happen if this starts a price war?
- Can our company significantly lower costs or increase productivity to compensate for lower prices?
- What is the price elasticity of our products?
- Can we gain significant market share or ensure a strong market niche position with this strategy?
- Can we reverse this strategy if it doesn't work, or will we create price levels that can't be sustained and can't easily be raised?

International Pricing

Many hospitality and tourism companies operate in multiple countries and decide what prices to charge in different countries. In some cases, a company can set a uniform worldwide price. For example, Boeing sells its jetliners at about the same price everywhere, whether the buyer is in the United States, Europe, or a third-world country. However, most companies adjust their prices to reflect local market conditions and cost considerations.

The price that a company should charge in a specific country depends on many factors, including economic conditions, competitive situations, laws and regulations, and the nature of the wholesaling and retailing system. Consumer perceptions and preferences also may vary from country to country, calling for different prices. A McDonald's Big Mac selling for a modest $4.20 in the United States might cost $7.8 in Norway or $5.65 in Brazil.

Marketing HIGHLIGHT 11.2 — Ryanair uses value pricing to attract customers and gains revenue from extra sales

Profits for discount European air carrier Ryanair have been sky-high, thanks to its revolutionary business model. The secret? Founder Michael O'Leary thinks like a retailer, charging passengers for almost everything—except their seat. A quarter of Ryanair's seats are free, and O'Leary wants to double that within five years, with the ultimate goal of making all seats free. Passengers currently pay only taxes and fees of about $10 to $24, with an average one-way fare of roughly $52. Everything else is extra: checked luggage ($9.50 per bag), snacks ($5.50 for a hot dog, $4.50 for chicken soup, $3.50 for water), and bus or train transportation into town from the secondary airports Ryanair uses ($24). Flight attendants sell a variety of merchandise, including digital cameras ($137.50) and iPocket MP3 players ($165). Onboard gambling and cell phone service are projected new revenue sources. Other strategies cut costs or generate outside revenue. Seats don't recline, window shades and seat-back pockets have been removed, and there is no entertainment. Seat-back trays carry ads, and the exteriors of the planes are giant revenue-producing billboards for Vodafone Group, Jaguar, Hertz, and others. More than 99 percent of tickets are sold online. The Web site also offers travel insurance, hotels, ski packages, and car rentals. Only Boeing 737–800 jets are flown to reduce maintenance costs, and flight crews buy their own uniforms. O'Leary has even discussed the possibility of pay toilets and 10 rows of standing room with handrails like a New York City subway car (to squeeze 30 more passengers aboard), though both suggestions drew much public concern and skepticism. Although his ideas may seem unconventional, the formula works for Ryanair's customers; the airline flies 58 million people to more than 150 airports each year. All the extras add up to 20 percent of revenue. Ryanair enjoys net margins of 25 percent, more than three times Southwest's 7 percent. Some industry pundits even refer to Ryanair as "Walmart with wings"!

Price Changes

Initiating Price Changes

After developing their price structures and strategies, companies may face occasions when they want to cut or raise prices.

Initiating Price Cuts

Several situations may lead a company to cut prices. One is excess capacity. Unable to increase business through promotional efforts, product improvement, or other measures, a hotel may resort to price cutting. As the airline, hotel, rental car, and restaurant industries have learned, cutting prices in an industry loaded with excess capacity generally leads to price wars as competitors try to regain market share.

Companies may also cut prices in a drive to dominate the market or increase market share through lower costs. Either the company starts with lower costs than its competitors or it cuts prices in the hope of gaining market share through larger volume. Price cutting to increase revenue must be carefully planned. Studies conducted across hotel sectors and in the United States and Asia have shown that in most mature markets, price cutting increases occupancy but the RevPAR decreases. Thus, the increased occupancy does not overcome the decrease in average rate. For an established hotel, the best tactic is to maintain prices slightly above the competitive rate.[38] Exceptions include hotels, such as casino hotels where high non-room expenditures, such as casino gaming or F&B, would offset the decrease in room revenue.

Initiating Price Increases Inevitably

Many companies must eventually raise prices. They do this knowing that price increases may be resented by customers, dealers, and their own sales force. However, a successful price increase can greatly increase profits. For example, if the company's profit margin is 3 percent of sales, a 1 percent price increase improves profits by 33 percent if sales volume is unaffected.

A major factor in price increases is cost inflation. Increased costs squeeze profit margins and lead companies to regular rounds of price increases. Companies often raise their prices by more than the cost increase in anticipation of further inflation. Companies do not want to make long-run price agreements with customers. They fear that cost inflation will reduce profit margins. For example, hotels prefer not to quote a firm price for conventions booked three years in advance. Another factor leading to price increases is excess demand. When a company cannot supply all its customers' needs, it raises its prices, rations products to customers, or it does both. When a city hosts a major convention, hotels may charge rates that are twice the average room rate. They know that demand for hotel rooms will be great, and they can take advantage of this demand.

Raising prices in the hospitality industry can be dangerous even when caused by inflation. It must be remembered that with the exception of some travel such as business or to attend funerals, the demand for travel generally faces an elastic demand curve. A couple may plan to celebrate their wedding anniversary with friends and relatives at a restaurant or resort, but if prices dramatically increase they may switch to a gathering at home or even a nearby park shelter. The travel industry has learned that much business travel can be postponed or conducted through electronic means, including the use of software such as GoToMeeting and Skype, which allow two-way audio-video using personal computers.

Cross substitutability of demand is a reality that always faces members of the hospitality industry, for example, the use of electronic communication rather than an airline trip.

In passing price increases on to customers, the company should avoid the image of price gouger. It is best to increase prices when customers perceive the price increase to be justified. Restaurants had an easier time implementing increased menu prices after the price of beef jumped because their customers noticed this price increase in the supermarket. If food prices are going down while the other costs of operating a restaurant are going up, it is difficult to gain customer acceptance of the need for a price increase. Restaurant managers should try to time price increases so they will be perceived as justified by customers, such as when increases in the price of food receive media attention, after an increase in the minimum wage, or when inflation is in the news. Price increases should be supported with a company communication program informing customers and employees why prices are being increased.

Buyer Reaction to Price Changes

Whether the price is raised or lowered, the action affects buyers, competitors, distributors, and suppliers. Price changes may also interest the government. Customers do not always put a straightforward interpretation on price changes. They may perceive a price cut in several ways. For example, what would you think when you see a restaurant advertising a buy-one-meal-get-one-free special? If you know the restaurant and have a positive feeling, you might be attracted. Someone who doesn't know the restaurant may feel it is having trouble attracting customers or something is wrong with the food or service. Or you might wonder if portion size has been reduced or inferior-quality food was being served. Remember, buyers often associate price with quality when evaluating hospitality products they have not experienced directly.

Similarly, a price increase that would normally lower sales may have a positive meaning for buyers. A nightclub that increases its cover charge from $5 to $10 might be perceived as the "in place" to go.

Competitor Reactions to Price Changes

A firm considering a price change has to worry about competitors' reactions. Competitors are most likely to react when the number of firms involved is small, when the product is uniform, and when buyers are well informed.

One problem with trying to use price as a competitive advantage is that competitors can neutralize the price advantage by lowering their prices. In a competitive market where supply exceeds demand, this often sets off price wars in which the industry as a whole loses. In the United States, Burger King and McDonald's are locked in a battle for market share. When one of these fast-food giants cuts its price, the other usually follows.

Competitors may choose to retaliate in different markets. For example, when Southwest Airlines cut prices on its Houston-to-San Antonio flights, its competitors reacted by cutting prices on their Houston-to-Dallas flights. The Houston-to-Dallas flights were Southwest's bread and butter. By hitting here, the competition hurt Southwest more than they could have by matching prices on the Houston-to-San Antonio route. Competitors may also react to a price cut with nonprice tactics such as additional baggage allowance. Before cutting prices, it is essential to consider competitive reactions. As we mentioned at the beginning of this chapter, price is a very flexible element of the marketing mix. It can easily be matched by the competition. A firm that lowers its price and has it matched by competition loses both its competitive advantage and profit.

Responding to Price Changes

Here, we reverse the question and ask how a firm should respond to a price change by a competitor. The firm needs to consider several issues. Why did the competitor change the price? Was it to gain more market share, to use excess capacity, to meet changing cost conditions, or to lead an industry-wide program change? Does the competitor plan to make the price change temporary or permanent? What will happen to the company's market share and profits if it does not respond? Are other companies going to respond? What are the competitors' and other firms' responses likely to be to each possible reaction?

In addition to these issues, the company must make a broader analysis. It must consider its own product's stage in the life cycle, its importance in the company's product mix, the intentions and resources of the competitor, and possible consumer reactions to price changes.

When Marriott's Fairfield Inns was just getting started, it offered a special discounted rate that was 40 percent less than its average daily rate. Its competitors decided not to match the rate because Fairfield had only 30 hotels at the time. Joan Ganje-Fischer, vice president of Super 8, said that if a major chain such as Super 8, Econo Inns, or Days Inn matched the discount, it would catch the attention of the other organizations. A price war would be the likely result of such a cut by a major chain. But because Fairfield Inns consisted of only 30 units, major competitors were unwilling to reduce rates across their 100-plus motel chains. Fairfield Inns used size to its advantage, recognizing that the larger chains would be unwilling to give up revenue from hundreds of hotels and thousands of rooms to match the price of a 30-unit chain.[39]

These examples show how companies can avoid competitive reactions to price changes by planning those changes carefully.

CHAPTER REVIEW

I. Factors to Consider When Setting Prices Simply defined, price is the amount of money charged for a good or service. More broadly, price is the sum of the values consumers exchange for the benefits of having or using the product or service.

A. Internal factors affecting pricing decisions

1. **Marketing objectives.** Survival is a technique used when a company's or business unit's sales slump, creating a loss that threatens its existence. Because the capacity of a hotel or restaurant is fixed, survival often involves cutting prices to increase demand and cash flow. This can disrupt the market until the firm goes out of business or the economy improves. Companies with an objective to maximize current profit may choose the price that will produce the maximum profit, cash flow, or ROI, seeking financial outcomes rather than long-run performance. Companies with a market-share leadership objective believe that a company with the largest market share will eventually enjoy low costs and high long-run profit; they set low opening rates and strive to be the market-share leader. Rates are moved up to market rates later on. Companies with a product-quality leadership objective charge a high price for their high-cost products to capture the luxury market. Other objectives include stabilizing the market, creating excitement for new product, and drawing more attention.

2. **Marketing mix strategy.** Price must be coordinated with product design, distribution, and promotion decision to form a consistent and effective marketing program.

3. **Costs.** A company wants to charge a price that covers its costs for producing, distributing, and promoting the product and that delivers a fair rate of return to investors. Costs are fixed and variable. Fixed costs do not vary with production or sales level. Variable costs vary directly with the level of production.

4. **Cost subsidization** is when other organizations have helped pay part of the cost.

5. **Organization considerations.** Management must decide who within the organization should set prices. In small companies, this will be top management; in large companies, pricing is typically handled by a corporate department or by a regional or unit manager under guidelines established by corporate management.

B. External factors affecting pricing decisions

1. **Market and demand** set the upper limit of prices.

2. **Cross-selling and upselling.** Cross-selling involves selling the company's other products to the guest. In upselling sales and reservation, employees are trained to offer continuously a higher-priced product that will better meet the customer's needs, rather than settling for the lowest price.

3. **Consumer perception of price and value.** It is the consumer who decides whether a product's price is right. The price must be buyer oriented. The price decision requires a creative awareness of the target market and recognition of the buyers' differences.

4. **Analyzing the price–demand relationship.** Demand and price are inversely related; the higher the price, the lower the demand. Most demand curves slope downward in either a straight or a curved line. The prestige goods demand curve sometimes slopes upward.

5. **Price elasticity of demand.** If demand hardly varies with a small change in price, the demand is inelastic; if demand changes greatly, the demand is elastic. Buyers are less price-sensitive when the product is unique or when it is high in quality, prestige, or exclusiveness. Consumers are also less price-sensitive when substitute products are hard to find. If demand is elastic, sellers generally consider lowering their prices to produce more total revenue.

6. **Factors affecting price sensitivity** are the unique value effect, the substitute awareness effect, the business expenditure effect, the end-benefit effect, the total expenditure effect, the shared cost effect, the price quality effect, and hidden fees.

7. **Competitors' price and offers.** When a company is aware of its competitors' price and offers, it

can use this information as a starting point for deciding its own pricing. Price-rate compression occurs when higher-priced hotels lower these rates to maintain occupancy and become direct competitors to lower-rated hotels. Other environmental factors include inflation, boom or recession, interest rates, government purchasing, and birth of new technology.

II. **General Pricing Approaches**
   A. **Cost-based pricing.** Cost-plus pricing: a standard markup is added to the cost of the product.
   B. **Break-even analysis and target profit pricing.** Price is set to break even on the costs of making and marketing a product, or to make a desired profit.
   C. **Value-based pricing.** Companies base their prices on the product's perceived value. Perceived-value pricing uses the buyers' perceptions of value, not the seller's cost, as the key to pricing.
   D. **Competition-based pricing.** Competition-based price is based on the establishment of price largely against those of competitors, with less attention paid to costs or demand.

III. **Pricing Strategies**
   A. **New product pricing strategies.** Pricing strategies usually change as a product passes through its life cycle. The introductory stage is especially challenging.
      1. **Prestige pricing.** Hotels or restaurants seeking to position themselves as luxurious and elegant enter the market with a high price that supports this position.
      2. **Market-skimming pricing.** Price skimming is setting a high price when the market is price-insensitive.
      3. **Marketing-penetration pricing.** Companies set a low initial price to penetrate the market quickly and deeply, attracting many buyers and winning a large market share.
   B. **Existing-product pricing strategies**
      1. **Product-bundle pricing.** Sellers using product-bundle pricing combine several of their products and offer the bundle at a reduced price.
      2. **Price-adjustment strategies.** Companies usually adjust their basic prices to account for various customer differences and changing situations. Strategies include volume discounts, seasonal discounts, and discriminatory pricing.

IV. **Revenue Management.** Revenue management involves upselling, cross-selling, and analysis of profit margins and sales volume for each product line. Revenue management systems are used to maximize a hospitality company's yield or contribution margin.
   A. **Dynamic pricing.** Dynamic pricing continually adjusts prices to meet the characteristics and needs of the marketplace.
   B. **BAR pricing.** Hotels charge different rates for each night for multiple-night stay.
   C. **Rate parity.** Rate Parity is essentially a strategy in which hotel chains agree to allow their product (rooms) to be shown and sold by OTAs provided the prices they offer are the same and are not lower than the hotel's BAR.
   D. **Nonuse of revenue management.** Some restaurants manage waiting time or offer takeaway service instead of raising prices during high demand periods.
   E. **Overbooking.** Selling airline seats or hotel rooms in excess of actual supply. When overbooking occurs, the supplier has an ethical and legal responsibility to compensate the buyer and/or find alternative flights, hotels, and so on.

V. **Psychological Pricing** includes aspects such as prestige, reference prices, round figures, and ignoring end figures. Prestige can be created by selling products and services at a high price. Reference prices are prices that buyers carry in their minds and refer to when they look at a given product.
   A. **Price endings.** Some psychologists argue that each digit has symbolic and visual qualities that should be considered in pricing.
   B. **Promotional pricing.** Hotels temporarily price their products below list price, and sometimes even below cost, for special occasions, such as introduction or festivities. Promotional pricing gives guests a reason to come and promotes a positive image for the hotel.
   C. **Value pricing.** Value pricing means offering a price below competitors permanently, which differs from promotional pricing, in which price may be temporarily lowered during a special promotion.
   D. **International pricing.** Many hospitality and tourism companies operate in multiple countries and decide what prices to charge in different countries. In some cases, a company can set a uniform worldwide price. However, most companies adjust their prices to reflect local market conditions and cost considerations.

VI. **Price Changes**
   A. **Initiating price changes**
      1. **Initiating price cuts.** Unable to increase business through promotional efforts, product improvement, or other measures, a hotel may resort to price cutting. Cutting prices in an industry loaded with excess capacity generally leads to price wars as competitors try to regain market share. Companies may also cut prices in a drive to dominate the market or increase market share through lower costs. Either the company starts with lower costs than its competitors or it cuts prices in the hope of gaining market share through larger volume. Price cutting to increase revenue must be carefully planned. Studies have shown that in most mature markets, price cutting increases occupancy but the RevPAR decreases.

2. **Initiating price increases inevitably.** Reasons for a company to increase price are cost inflation or excess demand.
3. **Buyer reactions to price changes.** Customers do not always put a straightforward interpretation on price changes. They may perceive a price cut in several ways. Remember, buyers often associate price with quality when evaluating hospitality products they have not experienced directly.
4. **Competitor reactions to price changes.** Competitors are most likely to react when the number of firms involved is small, when the product is uniform, and when buyers are well informed.

B. **Responding to price changes.** Issues to consider are reason, market share, excess capacity, meeting changing cost conditions, leading an industry-wide program change, temporary versus permanent.

IN-CLASS GROUP EXERCISES

*Exercises with an asterisk next to them are suitable for individual homework or online assignments. Students, always provide an explanation for your answer.

1. *One way of increasing revenue is through upselling. Give examples from the hospitality or travel industries of when upselling can result in a more satisfied guest.
2. *You have just been hired as the dining room manager at a local hotel. The manager asks you to evaluate the menu prices to see if they need to be adjusted. How would you go about this task?
3. *A number of factors affecting price sensitivity are discussed in this chapter. Provide some examples of the application of these factors in the hospitality or travel businesses.
4. *Give several examples of an effective use of price discrimination. State how these examples meet the criteria of price discrimination and creation of sales when they are needed.
5. *Can a hotel or restaurant increase or maintain customer satisfaction after implementing its first revenue management program? Explain your answer.
6. Airlines and hotels give bonus frequent-flyer miles, gifts, and free companion tickets to attract the business traveler. These promotions are often provided in lieu of a price cut. The traveler benefits personally, although his or her company does not get the benefit of lower rates. Is this ethical?
7. *You are going on a three-day business trip for your company to Pittsburgh, Pennsylvania. You have up to $300 a day to spend on lodging and food. If you do not spend the money you save money for your company; you do not get to keep the unspent money. You will check in next October 18 and check out on October 21. Choose the hotel where you would stay; what Web site would you use to pick the hotel? What did your search process involve? How many Web sites did you use to make your selection? What criteria did you make in choosing the hotel? (Note: Look up the hotel rates, but please do not make an actual reservation.)

EXPERIENTIAL EXERCISE

Do the following:
1. Conduct a price comparison of several hotels or restaurants in the same class. What price differences did you find? Do you feel the companies that had the higher prices could justify those higher prices by offering additional features or a higher-quality product?

REFERENCES

1. Sheryl E. Kimes, "Restaurant Revenue Management at Chevys Arrowhead," *Cornell Hotel and Restaurant Administration Quarterly*, 45, no. 1 (2004): 52–56.
2. Tom Ross, "Steamboat Airline Program Still Pursuing Service for Cities like Phoenix, Charlotte, Detroit," *Steamboat Today*, Friday, July 18, 2014.
3. Ibid., p. 6.
4. Howard Feiertag, "Up Your Property's Profits by Upselling Catering," *Hotel and Motel Management*, 206, no. 14 (1991): 20.
5. "Embassy's Suite Deal," *Scorecard: The Revenue Management Quarterly* (Second Quarter, 1993), 3.
6. Melvyn Greene, *Marketing Hotels and Restaurants into the 90s* (New York: Van Nostrand Reinhold, 1987).
7. Anthony Edwards, "Changes in Real Air Fares and Their Impact on Travel," *EIU Travel and Tourism Analyst*, 2 (1990): 76–85.
8. This section draws on Thomas T. Nagle, *The Strategy and Tactics of Pricing* (Upper Saddle River, NJ: Prentice Hall, 1987).

9. Melvyn Greene, *Marketing Hotels and Restaurants into the 90s*, p. 47.
10. Sarah Schlicter, "Hidden Hotel Fees," *Independent Traveler*, May 6, 2015; Erica Silverstein, Senior Editor, and Carolyn Spencer, "The 10 Hidden Costs of Cruising and How to Fight Back."
11. Juliet Chung, "Cracking the Code of Restaurant Wine Pricing," *The Wall Street Journal*, 1–4, online.wsj.com (accessed August 15, 2008).
12. *The Horwath Accountant*, 47, no. 7 (1967): 8.
13. Leo M. Renaghan and Michael Z. Kay, "What Meeting Planners Want: The Conjoint Analysis Approach," *Cornell Hotel and Restaurant Administration Quarterly*, 28, no. 1 (1987): 73.
14. Sarah Tanford, Seyhmus Baloglu, and Mehmet Erdem, "Travel Packaging on the Internet: The Impact of Pricing Information and Perceived Value on Consumer Choice," *Journal of Travel Research*, 51, no.1 (2012): 68–80; William J. Carroll, Robert J. Kwortnik, and Norman L. Rose, "Cornell Hospitality Report: Travel Packaging: An Internet Frontier," *The Center for Hospitality Research*, 7, no. 17 (2007): 7.
15. Royal Palms Resort and Spa Web site, http://www.royalpalmshotel.com (accessed January 23, 2009).
16. John E. G. Bateson, *Managing Services Marketing* (Fort Worth, TX: Dryden Press, 1992), p. 339.
17. "Survey Findings on Hotel Revenue Management," Hotelmarketing.com, September 16, 2008 (accessed September 25, 2008).
18. "Hospitality Revenue Management: Segmenting for Success," (January 27, 2016), https://www.hotelnewsresource.com/article87595.html; Susan Greco, "Are Your Prices Right?" *INC.* (January 1997): 88–89. Copyright 1997 by Goldhirsh Group, Inc., 38 Commercial Wharf, Boston, MA 02110; Robert G. Cross, *Revenue Management: Hard Core Tactics for Market Domination* (New York: Broadway Books, 1998); William J. Quain, Michael Sansbury, and Dennis Quinn, "Revenue Enhancement, Part 3: Picking Low-Hanging Fruit—A Simple Approach to Yield Management," *Cornell Hotel and Restaurant Administration Quarterly* (April 1999): 76–83. Also see Plumrao Desiraju and Steven M. Shugan, "Strategic Service Pricing and Yield Management," *Journal of Marketing* (January 1999): 44–56.
19. Eric B. Orkin, "Boosting Your Bottom Line with Yield Management," *Cornell Hotel and Restaurant Administration Quarterly*, 28, no. 4 (1988): 52–56.
20. Elie Younen and Russel Kett, GopPAR, A Derivative of RevPAR, March 2003, HVS International.
21. *Hotline: The Magazine of Carlson Hotels*, GBC, 2011, Vision in Action, pp. 38 and 41.
22. Gary M. Thompson and Heeju (Louise) Sohn, "Cornell Hospitality Report: Accurately Estimating Time-Based Restaurant Revenues Using Revenue per Available Seat-Hour," *The Center for Hospitality Research*, 8, no. 9 (2008).
23. Timothy Webb and Zvi Schwartz, "Revenue management analysis with competitive sets: Vulnerability and a challenge to strategic co-opetition among hotels," Tourism Economics, 23, no. 6 (2017): 1207; Zvi Schwartz and Eli Cohen, "Hotel Revenue Management Forecasting: Evidence of Expert-Judgment Bias," *Cornell Hotel and Restaurant Administration Quarterly*, 45, no. 1 (2004): 49.
24. Sheryl E. Kimes, "Applying Yield Management to the Golf-course Industry," *Cornell Hotel and Restaurant Administration Quarterly*, 41, no. 1 (2000): 127; William H. Kaven and Myrtle Allardyce, "Dalmahoy's Strategy for Success," *Cornell Hotel and Restaurant Administration Quarterly*, 35, no. 6 (1994): 87–88.
25. Sunmee Choi and Anna S. Mattila, "Impact of Information on Customer Fairness Perceptions of Hotel Revenue Management," *Cornell Hotel and Restaurant Administration Quarterly*, 46, no. 4 (2005): 444–445.
26. See Justin D. Martin, "Dynamic Pricing: Internet Retailers Are Treating Us Like Foreign Tourists in Egypt," *Christian Science Monitor*, January 7, 2011; and Mike Southon, "Time to Ensure the Price Is Right," *Financial Times*, January 21, 2012, p. 30.
27. "What Is Surge Pricing," Uber Web site, https://help.uber.com/h/6c8065cf-5535-4a8b-9940-d292ffdce119 (accessed August 3, 2015).
28. Jessi Hempel, "Why the Surge-Pricing Fiasco Is Great for Uber," Fortune.com, December 30, 2013, http://fortune.com/2013/12/30/why-the-surge-pricing-fiasco-is-great-for-uber/ (accessed August 3, 2015); Victor Fiorillo, "Will Everyone Please Shut Up About Uber Surge Pricing?" December 18, 2013. *Philadelphia Magazine*, http://www.phillymag.com/news/2013/12/18/uber-surge-pricing/#rhT8X23vORd-jS8Jd.99 (accessed August 15, 2015); Alison Griswald, "Everybody Hates Surge Pricing, So Why Does the D.C. Taxicab Commission Want to Introduce It?" *Slate*, http://www.slate.com/articles/business/moneybox/2014/04/uber_style_surge_pricing_does_the_system_make_sense_for_d_c_cabs.html (accessed August 3, 2015).
29. Kristin V. Rohlfs and Sheryl E. Kimes, "Customers' Perceptions of Best Available Hotel Rates," *Cornell Hotel and Restaurant Administration Quarterly*, 46, no. 2 (2007): 151.
30. Hotel Revenue Tools, Rate Parity, Definition and Strategies, Hotel Revenue Tools.com, 1–702-703–May 6, 4511, 2015; Sean O'Neill, Marriott, Expedia, Priceline and Other Brands Escape Hotel Rate Parity Suit, *TNooz*, February 19, 2014.
31. Alex M. Susskind, Dennis Reynolds, and Eriko Tsuchiya, "An Evaluation of Guests' Preferred Incentives to Shift Time-Variable Demand in Restaurants," *Cornell Hotel and Restaurant Administration Quarterly*, 45, no. 1 (2004): 82.

32. Buffie Noone and Chung Hun Lee, "Hotel Overbooking: The Effect of Over-Compensation on Customers' Reactions to Denied Service," *Journal of Hospitality and Tourism Research*, 35, no. 3 (August 2011): 334.

33. Michael Collins and H.G. Paisa, "Pricing Strategies to Maximize Revenues in the Lodging Industry," *Hospitality Management*, 25 (2006): 91–107.

34. JoAnn Carmin and Gregory X. Norkus, "Pricing Strategies for Menus: Magic or Myth," *Cornell Hotel and Restaurant Administration Quarterly*, 31, no. 3 (1990): 50.

35. "High Stakes at Harrah's," *Scorecard: The Revenue Management Quarterly* (First Quarter, 1993), 3.

36. David K. Hayes and Lynn M. Huffman, "Value Pricing: How Long Can You Go?" *Cornell Hotel and Restaurant Administration Quarterly* (February 1995): 51–56.

37. Stephean J. Hoch, Xavier Dreze, and Mary E. Park, "EDLP, Hi-Low, and Margin Arithmetic," *Journal of Marketing*, 58 (1994): 27.

38. Linda Canina and Cathy Enz, "Pricing for Revenue Enhancement in Asian Pacific Region Hotels: A Study of Relative Pricing Strategies," *Cornell Hospitality Report*, 8, no. 3 (February 2008).

39. "Fairchild Cuts Rates to Gain Stronger Presence," *Hotel and Motel Management* (June 19, 1989): 11.

12

Objectives

After reading this chapter, you should be able to:

1. Explain how and why companies partner with other companies to sell products.
2. Describe hospitality distribution channels.
3. Explain channel behavior and organization.
4. Describe key aspects of channel management for hospitality companies.

Distribution Channels Delivering Customer Value

Booking Holdings occupies the leadership position in online travel and related services.[1] It has a massive presence in more than 220 countries and territories, where it serves its customers via six well-recognized brands: Booking.com, Priceline, Agoda, KAYAK, Rentalcars.com, and OpenTable. Their mission is powerful: "*to help people experience the world.*"[1] The company started in 1998 as priceline.com, and through a number of smart growth strategies it was able to reach a successful market position in several verticals, such as airfare, hotel bookings, meta-search, car rental, and restaurant bookings. By doing so, Booking Holdings has consolidated its position across the entire travel experience, being able to carry a customer through air travel, hotel, restaurant, and ancillary services. This, in turn, creates sustainable competitive advantages that propel the company confidently into the future.

The company's omnipresence is supported by more than 28 million of places to stay[1] and gross travel bookings of $24.3 billion in the third quarter of 2018 alone[2] and its market capitalization was $77.115 billion at the beginning of 2019.[3] With such a strong presence in virtually every electronic market, Booking Holdings is reaching its customers via a variety of distribution strategies, from the classic merchant and agency models to "opaque strategies" (where a brand name is not revealed to the customer until the purchase), to metasearch (where customers can search for products on a variety of retail channels), to restaurant and car rental reservations. Thus, it is able to carry a customer through the entire sequence of travel, providing a seamless experience and reducing some of the uncertainty that comes from traveling to unfamiliar places. Moreover, it understands the main differences among customers from different cultures in their booking patterns.[4] For example, it has a strong presence in the

Maridav/123RF.

Asia-Pacific region with its Agoda brand. In addition to streamlining the travel experience for customers, Booking Holdings also provides superior value for hotels. For example, a study of over 72 million reservations revealed that booking.com is the best performing channel for hotels in United States and Canada.[5]

The company has seen tremendous potential for growth in emerging markets, and has invested substantially to establish a strong position in such markets. For example, it has invested substantially in several established and technology start-ups in China, trying to reach customers across a variety of demographic segments and offer a seamless travel experience.[4] Also, the company signed an agreement with Saudi Arabia to use their technology to assist the increasing number of pilgrims with making their accommodation reservations more convenient and secure.[2] Moreover, the company has seen the value of integrating popular platforms that allow customers to increase value while traveling, especially overseas. Specifically, Chinese customers using the Ctrip app could book restaurants reservations using OpenTable.[6] Booking Holdings is positioned for more growth in the future. It is able to see opportunities in the domestic as well as international markets, as the company understands very well the dynamics of travel and its relationship to the global economy.[7]

Partnering to Add Value

Supply Chains and the Value Delivery Network

In today's competitive and overspecialized market space, it is impossible to conceive that a single company can create a product from scratch and sell it to customers without the contribution of other companies. Therefore, a realistic view of company's ability to produce and sell products to the market includes other partnering companies, which contribute to the overall creation and selling of products. Throughout this process, the company gathers resources, raw materials, information, etc. and processes them into its products. The most logical representation of this process is chronological, which reflects the sequential and linear progression of resources from raw material to the final product that customers can purchase. This progression represents the **supply chain**, and is applicable to hospitality and travel. For example, a restaurant purchases raw ingredients, produces menu items, and sells them to customers. The company is viewed as located in the middle of the chain. The companies that provide the raw materials and other valuable resources that assist in the creation of a new product are considered upstream partners. In contrast, the companies that facilitate the sale of the product created by the company to the market are considered downstream partners. For the most part, distribution refers to the downstream side (marketing or distribution channels) that are oriented toward the customer.

Upstream partners represent companies that provide the resources needed to produce a product. Such companies include suppliers, consultants, financial institutions, resources, raw materials, components, services (e.g., business intelligence, information, finance). Downstream partners represent companies that provide the resources needed to sell a product by forming a connection between the business organization and the customers. Such companies include wholesalers, technology companies, and retailers, and the resources include inventory management, display, merchandising, etc.

A company can form supply chains with multiple companies, and those companies can be part of the supply chains of multiple competing companies. Therefore, designing the most appropriate and valuable supply chains is a very important and difficult strategic task for a company. For this reason, the supply chain partners contribute essentially to the success or failure of any company.

The term "supply chain" has limitations, as it views a business as only a make-and-sell company. A better approach is to consider the value delivery network that is created by the company, suppliers, distributors (intermediaries), and customers,

Supply chain Upstream and downstream partners. Upstream from the company is a set of firms that supply raw materials, components, parts, information, finances, and expertise needed to create a product. Downstream marketing channel partners, such as wholesalers and retailers, form a vital connection between the firm and its customers.

who partner to improve the performance of the entire network. For example, a restaurant such as Red Lobster does more than just selling menu items. It manages a network of producers, suppliers, and transportation partners that works together to ensure that the products are delivered on time and according to the required quality and safety standards. Throughout the hospitality industry, there are multiple examples of companies that manage relationships with partners on different continents. For example, seafood may come from farms in Central America, technology equipment may come from Asia, while a company's customer service call center may be located in Eastern Europe. Managing such relationships to add value to the entire delivery network is a critical and complex task.

The focus of this chapter is on distribution channels, or the downstream side of the value delivery network. However, distribution is only a part of the entire value network. In order to create and maintain value, companies work with both suppliers and distribution channel partners. Companies are increasingly influencing their upstream activities in addition to the downstream activities. Thus, companies expand their roles beyond managing distribution channels—they are becoming managers of the full value network.

Nature and Importance of Distribution Systems

Given its retail function (facilitating the sale of products to the ultimate customers), distribution provides a steady flow of customers. Well-managed distribution systems can make a difference between very successful companies and those struggling to survive. The hospitality industry provides many examples of companies making great use of the distribution channels available to them. For example, hotel companies such as Ritz Carlton receive substantial portions of business from travel agencies, as the company aggressively developed this channel. Airlines sell hotel rooms and car rental products on their Web sites, knowing that customers looking for a flight may also need to book a hotel reservation or rent a car. As the market becomes increasingly competitive, it is imperative for companies to develop and manage increasingly complex distribution channels.

There are several factors that increased the importance of distribution. For example, new brands that specialize on targeting specific types of customers have emerged, increasing the competition. Specifically, CitizenM hotels focuses on younger customers, and provides a vibrant lobby area and rooms filled with seamless technologies that allow customers to stream content or control the room using mobile tablets. In addition, the hotel market is becoming increasingly fragmented, as new boutique properties are emerging on the market. The global character of the industry is increasingly important, as customers from all over the world have unprecedented opportunities to travel internationally. Moreover, the intangibility and perishability of hospitality products make distribution challenging. Specifically, new Web sites have emerged that allow customers to book hotel rooms at the last minute, allowing hotels to sell last-minute inventory that otherwise could not have been sold. Moreover, the design of the distribution network can allow a company to reach very specific segments of customers, therefore fulfilling critical strategic goals. For example, Hilton's utilization of Hilton Honors mobile app created opportunities for the higher-tiered members of their rewards program to use the app to easily clear upgrades and access their rooms using their mobile phones, therefore increasing the value of the overall stay.

Nature of Distribution Channels

A distribution channel is a set of independent organizations involved in the process of making a product or service available to the customer or business user. A company starts the development of a distribution system by selecting channel members. Upon selection of channel members, the company shifts focus to managing the channel. The distribution networks in the hospitality industry are based on contractual agreements and alliances between independent organizations. In hospitality and travel, distribution systems are utilized to move the customer to the product: hotel, restaurant, airplane, cruise ship, or rental car.

Broker A wholesaler who does not take title to goods and whose function is to bring buyers and sellers together and assist in negotiations.

Agent A wholesaler who represents buyers or sellers on a more permanent basis, performs only a few functions, and does not take title to goods.

We can begin to examine distribution by looking at traditional distribution systems. Such systems lay the foundation for the development of hospitality distribution systems. The products used by hospitality and travel companies come through distribution channels; therefore, it is critical to understand their structure.

There are a variety of jobs that hospitality graduates can take within the complex distribution system. For example, in food service, two important jobs are broker and agent. A food **broker** works as an **agent** for a manufacturer, with the goal of creating demand for a specific product of the manufacturer. For example, when Alpha Industries developed a new organic cherry pie for the food service industry, brokers representing Alpha Industries would introduce the organic cherry pie to food service managers. These are just two examples of jobs in distribution that illustrate the diversity of the types of the labor market related to distribution.

Why Are Marketing Intermediaries Used?

Why would a company sell its products through intermediaries? Although selling through intermediaries decreases the ability of a company to control its pricing, it is difficult to imagine that a company can reach all its potential customers by itself. For example, the company selling silverware for a restaurant would have to have sales offices in all major markets, and employ salespeople to sell its products to potential buyers in those markets. This approach is unfeasible, as the company incurs substantial costs related to large sales force. Instead, the silverware company can work with an intermediary. The intermediary is specialized in making personal sales calls, displaying, and promoting products from a variety of restaurant vendors. The intermediary is in a better position than a single silverware company to promote and sell its products to restaurants. Therefore, this arrangement adds value for both the silverware company and the intermediary, as this form of intermediated distribution becomes more efficient than direct selling. Specifically, the silverware company can reduce its sales effort and therefore can focus on making better silverware, while the intermediary focuses on finding customers for the silverware company.

This arrangement is also beneficial for potential buyers. If a restaurant manager wants to buy different items (e.g., silverware, cases of beer glasses, napkins), he/she needs to make only one call to the intermediary. While each of the products listed may be manufactured by a different manufacturer, they are sold to the restaurant through one intermediary. To the restaurant, this means access to small quantities of products, as they become part of a larger order. This has beneficial effects on the restaurant, as this practice may reduce inventory requirements, number of deliveries, and the number of processed invoices. Therefore, restaurants may realize important benefits. Without the intermediary, the restaurant manager would have to contact individual manufacturers. In turn, the manufacturers would receive calls from individual restaurants, increasing the workload and cost. Figure 12–1 illustrates the workload and cost.

Figure 12–1
How a distributor reduces the number of channel transactions.

A. Number of contacts without a distributor
M x C = 3 x 3 = 9

B. Number of contacts with a distributor
M x C = 3 + 3 = 6

M = Manufacturer   C = Customer   D = Distributor

Distribution Channel Functions

A distribution channel facilitates the movement of products from producers to customers. This way, it closes the existing gaps in time, place, and ownership between the products and the customers. There are multiple functions performed by the members of distribution channels:

1. **Information**: Gathering and distributing marketing research and intelligence about the marketing environment
2. **Promotion**: Developing and spreading persuasive communication about an offer
3. **Contact**: Finding and communicating with potential customers
4. **Matching**: Shaping and fitting an offer to the customers' needs (developing/manufacturing, assembling, packaging)
5. **Negotiation**: Agreeing on price and other terms of the offer in order for ownership to be transferred
6. **Physical distribution**: Transporting and storing the products
7. **Financing**: Securing the funding that covers the cost of channel work
8. **Risk taking**: Assuming financial risks related to the inability of selling the inventory at full margin

While seemingly different, the functions optimize the distribution work of a company. Such functions can be interchanged among intermediaries. If a company shifts functions to an intermediary, it can lower its costs and prices, but it now has to pay the intermediaries for the shifted function. In order to optimize distribution, companies should assign functions to intermediaries that can perform those functions most efficiently.

For example, specialized trips (e.g., honeymoon, wellness tours) are becoming increasingly attractive.[14] Yet, such trips are complex, involving a variety of subdecisions for customers. For example, the customer has to decide which destination, which activities to book at the destination, and they may have questions about specific components of the overall experience. Therefore, it is likely that these types of services would be booked using a travel agency, as the agency could offer knowledge and expertise about the specifics of the trip. In contrast, most routine hotel stays could be booked using online travel agencies, as the customers do not have to make complex decisions about the specifics of the trip, and most information necessary to book the room is available online.

Number of Channel Levels

Channel level A level of middleman that performs some work in bringing the product and its ownership closer to the final buyer.

Direct distribution channel A distribution channel that has no intermediary levels.

Retailer Business whose sales come primarily from retailing.

Wholesaler Firms engaged primarily in wholesaling activity.

Distribution channels are characterized by the number of **channel levels**. The role of each level is to bring the product closer to the final customer. By default, every channel will have a producer and a final customer. The number of intermediaries used between the producer and the final customer determines the length of the channel. Figure 12–2 illustrates different types of distribution channels.

Channel 1 is called a **direct distribution channel**. The producer distributes directly to the customer. For example, a hotel sells rooms to customers who walk into the hotel without a reservation. Channel 2 contains one level. This level is generally a **retailer** in most markets. For example, a hotel has a direct contract with an online travel agency, and the online travel agency sells rooms to customers.

Channel 3 contains two levels. It includes a **wholesaler** and a retailer. For example, a hotel has agreements with a global distribution system (wholesaler) and an online travel agency (retailer) to sell rooms to customers. Channel 4 contains three levels. In addition to the wholesaler and retailer, it also includes a jobber. The jobber typically buys products from wholesalers and resells to smaller retailers that are not served by wholesalers.

Figure 12–2
Business-to-consumer and business-to-business marketing channels.

A. Customer Marketing Channels

- Channel 1: Manufacturer → Consumer
- Channel 2: Manufacturer → Retailer → Consumer
- Channel 3: Manufacturer → Wholesaler → Retailer → Consumer
- Channel 4: Manufacturer → Wholesaler → Jobber → Retailer → Consumer

B. Industrial Marketing Channels

- Channel 1: Business → Business customer
- Channel 2: Business → Business distributor → Business customer
- Channel 3: Business → Business representatives or sales branch → Business customer
- Channel 4: Business → Business representatives or sales branch → Business distributor → Business customer

Generally, the complexity of the cost to operate intermediated distribution channels increases with the number of levels added to the channel. The companies involved in any type of distribution channels are connected by several types of flows. Such flows include the following:

- Information
- Physical flow of products
- Promotion
- Ownership
- Payment

These flows, along with the nature of the product being distributed, increase the complexity of all distribution channels.

Given the complexity of hospitality and travel products, companies have a variety of choices of distribution channels. The following section describes the variety of participants to the distribution system: global distribution systems, tour wholesalers, travel agents, tourist agencies, etc.

Hospitality Distribution Channels

A large percentage of reservations comes from direct distribution without intermediaries using information technologies such as Web sites and mobile apps. In this situation, hotels, airlines, and car rental agencies sell their products directly to their customers using Web sites and mobile apps, without the help of any wholesalers or retailers. Such products are sold using the companies' main Web sites, such as hilton.com, united.com, or avis.com. The generic name given to these types of Web sites is "brand.com," because the companies use their brand name as their domain name for their Web sites. These Web sites represent the main portals of brands to sell their products to the final customers. They have a critical role in distribution as they sell their brand's products, and not the products of competitors.

In addition to the brand.com Web sites and apps, hotels and similar companies sell products directly to customers using central reservation offices. However, the cost of using a central reservation office is higher per reservation than the cost of using a Web site.

However, selling directly through brand.com Web sites or central reservation offices assumes that the customers will be motivated to find the Web site or call the company and book from there. In reality, it is difficult to expect that customers will do this, as in many cases, customers like to compare rates from different travel agencies, and make an informed choice about their purchase by looking at competing offers. Therefore, online travel agencies fulfill an important role in the market by providing retail environments where customers can compare rates. In addition, given the multitude of online travel agencies and brand.com Web sites, a new type of intermediary emerged: meta-search engines. Such companies allow customers to optimize their search and find a favorable deal regardless of the retail environment where the deal was originally located (e.g., on a brand.com Web site or an online travel agency Web site).

Managing such complexity becomes an important task in distribution, as it is directly related to the revenues that a company can make. For this reason, revenue managers are in charge of managing the various distribution channels utilized by a company, by changing the types of rates available through the multitude of channels that the company uses.

Direct Channels

Direct channels are distribution channels where reservations or purchases are made directly between the producer (e.g., hotel, airline, car rental company) and the final customer. Because there are no intermediaries involved, the transaction costs are low. The low costs reflect only the cost of maintaining the brand.com Web site and the central reservation office that handles customers' calls. Companies prefer this distribution channel because (1) it is low-cost, and (2) helps build a direct relationship between the company and the customer.

In order to stimulate customers' motivations to book/purchase directly, hotels and similar companies design useful and attractive Web sites and apps. They contain intuitive reservation engines, which are placed prominently on the Web site's homepage, along with persuasive information about current promotions and a portal for login for customers who are members of the rewards program.

A similar approach is followed by restaurants. Given the development in integrating restaurant point of sale systems with Web sites and mobile apps, a restaurant's Web site or app becomes a powerful tool for customers to make reservations and purchase products.

Companies generally promote their brand.com Web sites and apps as the main portals for retail and customer service. Brand.com Web sites and apps have critical retail goals, such as direct booking, allowing customers to access their already made reservations, and creating a profile for repeat purchasing. They also serve an important role in acquiring customers, with the goal of motivating them to become members of the rewards program.

Table 12–1 shows comparison of distribution costs across commonly used distribution in a typical upper-upscale chain-affiliated hotel.

Table 12–1
Comparison of Channel Costs

Channel	Rate ($)	Commission (%)	Total Cost ($)	Net Rate ($)
brand.com	200	5	10	190
Customer relations office or phone	200	5	10	190
Online travel agencies and others	200	14	28	172

Online travel agency (OTA)
A travel agency that conducts business through the internet with no physical locations or stores.

Online Travel Agencies

Online travel agencies (OTAs) conduct business over the internet without the need of having physical location and stores. They are popular among customers because they are able to provide a convenient market space where customers can make a buying decision by comparing the rates provided by multiple competitors. Given their well-designed Web sites, extensive promotional activities resulting in brand awareness, and reputation for allowing customers to find the best deal, online travel agencies attract large numbers of customers. Therefore, while costly for producers, distribution using online travel agencies is necessary. This is because it is very difficult for producers to sell all of their inventory through direct channels.

Distribution Models

There are multiple types of arrangements between producers and online travel agencies. Such arrangements are called models. Depending on their strategies, online travel agencies are using a combination of such models. One of the most common distribution models is the merchant model. According to the merchant model, an online travel agency (called a merchant) pays an agreed-upon rate to the producer, and then marks up the price according to its own pricing strategies. Major OTAs such as Expedia have used extensively the merchant model.[15] Another popular model is the agency model, where the hotel pays the OTA upon consumer's stay. Companies such as Booking Holdings, the parent company of booking.com, have traditionally relied on agency models. However, major companies may use combinations of such models, depending on the OTA brands that they manage.[15] Another distribution model is the auction model. According to this model, customers are bidding for desired products, and if their bid is accepted, they are allowed to purchase the product at the rate that they bid. Another distribution model is the referral model (pay per click). According to this model, customers are referred to an online travel agency Web site through other Web sites or Web services (e.g., search engines), for which the online travel agency pays referral fee.

One concern for producers using the models illustrated earlier is brand dilution. Brand dilution is a phenomenon by which the equity of a brand is diminished when customers ignore the brand qualities and focus primarily on the price of product when purchasing. Hoteliers have had concerns about customers comparing hotel rooms primarily on price on OTA Web sites, while disregarding the brand. As a result, different distribution models have emerged, such as the opaque model. In the opaque model, the online travel agency does not reveal the brand name of the hotel (or airline, car rental agency) to the customer first. Instead, a generic name, such as "3 star hotel" at the location sought by the customer will be provided. The brand name of the hotel would be revealed to the customer once the booking is made. This model takes the brand out of the customer's decision-making process.

Depending on the strategies of the hotel, some hotels would sell their last-minute unsold inventory using opaque online travel agencies. While this practice helps to bring additional revenues, it may have the drawback of diminishing the perceived value of a room for customers. One potential concern is the price, since customers can book the hotel room, but not spend additional money on ancillary services such as food and beverage once they arrive on the property.

One important aspect of distribution using online travel agencies is the information about the customers. When customers make reservations using OTAs, the information is collected by the online travel agency and is eventually transferred to the hotel.

In order to gain more control over the acquisition of customers and reduce distribution costs, hotels and other hospitality and travel producers have tried to stimulate customers to book directly. For example, reward points are given to customers booking directly through brand.com Web sites or apps, but not to customers booking through online travel agencies. In addition, customers who purchase products directly through apps are given additional benefits, such as the opportunity to use mobile device to access a guest room.[16] These strategies are designed to stimulate customers to book directly, therefore reducing the distribution costs of producers. In response to such strategies, online travel agencies created their own strategies that capitalize on the benefits of rewards programs. For example, hotels.com offers 1 night free after 10 nights purchased,[17] while Expedia offers reward points that can be used toward future purchases.

While it is important to understand the role of online travel agencies, certain producers have tried to focus on direct distribution. Such strategies have worked for large companies, who have well established brands. For example, Southwest Airlines is focusing its distribution strategy on their direct channels (e.g., the southwest.com Web site), but supports it by using third-party channels (e.g., Sabre, Apollo).[18] However, this approach is rare in the hotel industry, given the higher fragmentation in terms of brand and ownership. For example, smaller hotels, who do not have a nationwide recognized brand may have no choice but to distribute using OTAs, as their brand.com Web site is generally not sufficient to attract enough customers to sell the entire inventory every night.

The distribution models discussed so far are in use in a variety of OTAs. Their use depends on the strategic choices of the agency and the motivations of the customers it tries to attract. As OTAs tend to specialize by using specific models (e.g., Priceline uses the auction model, Hotwire uses the opaque model), new hybrid models have appeared.

There are two important developments: (1) the establishment of meta-search as a critical component of customers' decision making, and (2) the role of consumer-generated reviews in the decision making. Meta-search engines are technologies that allow customers to search for a hospitality or travel product over a large number of retail sites. This is different than searching on a OTA Web site, as the meta-search will return the results that appear on brand.com Web sites and all available retail places, while the OTA Web site will return results that appeared in their inventory. As a result, customer searches using meta-search engines broadens the scope of search and provides more opportunities for customers. Meta-search engines such as Kayak and SkyScanner allow customers to find the best airfare typically between airports, while hotel meta-search engines, such as Trivago, typically offer results to customer searches for hotels.[8] The second aspect is the increasing role of consumer-generated reviews. Historically, reviews were provided on separate Web sites rather than on the Web sites where purchasing took place. The landscape is changing now, because reviews are provided on the same Web site where customers are making their bookings, thus facilitating booking after reading reviews.

While the OTAs have demonstrated their usefulness to the distribution process, the strategies that they adopt combine the benefits of multiple models. For example, while Expedia predominantly uses the merchant model, it also incorporates a rich review section, which helps customers to make their purchasing decisions. As OTAs specialize and increase the value that they bring to the distribution process, they also become expensive. Consequently, to reduce the cost of distribution, the hotels and similar companies are trying to find ways to stimulate customers to purchase directly.[19]

Brick-and-mortar travel agents that specialize in unique travel experiences such as adventure tourism in Antarctica compete against OTAs by providing specialized services. Martin Schneiter/123RF.

Global Distribution Systems

Global distribution systems (GDSs) are computerized systems that serve as product catalogs for travel agencies and other intermediaries. They fulfill the wholesale function as they intermediate large volumes of transactions. They have been an integral part of the distribution arrangements for many hotels, airlines, and car rental agencies, as they developed interfaces that facilitated the sale of hospitality and travel products to retailers. GDSs have been developed by airlines in cooperation with information technology companies in order to speed up transaction process and reduce errors.[20] Generally, GDSs link a producer's central reservation system (CRS) or individual property management system with intermediaries, such as retailers. While there are a few major GDSs (Sabre, Amadeus, and Travelport, which includes Apollo, Galileo, and Worldspan), recently, a number of smaller GDSs have emerged. For example, SHR based in Houston provides services to numerous independent hotels.[21] While their legacy role is to develop links with retailers, the GDS roles have evolved over time. For example, given the rich transaction data that they have access to, some GDSs are moving closer to retailers. For example, Sabre Hospitality Solutions offers a platform provided as Software as a Service (Saas) to over 32,000 hotel properties.[22]

Travel Agents

While their function has been clearer in the past (reaching geographically diverse markets), their role has been diminished in recent years due to the proliferation of OTAs. Specifically, customers can make by themselves most of the reservations once made by travel agencies. However, travel agents still reflect the interests of specific groups of customers, and they are responsible for hotel, airline, and cruise line revenues. For example, hotels generally pay 10 percent commission to travel agents, while cruise lines pay typically 15 percent commission.

Hotels have generally not abandoned travel agents from their distribution strategies. Hotels send information packages to travel agents, and could invite the agents to visit the properties, in order to have a better idea about the services that could be promoted. Also, hotels direct promotional campaigns toward travel agents using trade publications such as Travel Weekly, Travel Trade, and Travel Agent. The use of promotional campaigns targeting travel agents is discussed in Chapter 14.

A specialized type of travel agents is the corporate travel agents. This is one of the most important segments of intermediaries. For these agents, U.S. corporations are major customers. Given the extensive travel budgets of U.S. corporations, their strategies are focusing on providing flexible services to their employees while reducing the overall cost of travel for the corporation. Some U.S. corporations created their own travel agencies, which manage travel exclusively for a particular corporation. Many corporations have exclusive travel arrangements with a specific agent, requiring all employees to make travel arrangements only through that specific agent. In turn, the agent assumes responsibility to find the best travel deals for the employees. While corporate travel agents specializing in specific type of travel for specific U.S. corporations (e.g., oil and gas, healthcare) and their main product sold remains travel, they provide additional services. For example, American Express Global Business Travel offers benefits such as broad representation in over 140 countries, offering help when travel is interrupted or in emergency, and providing reporting tools.[23]

Marketing HIGHLIGHT 12.1 Changing market dynamics

The market dynamics of the past 15 years have made distribution for specialized agents like brick-and-mortar (traditional) travel agencies difficult. The difficulty lies in the consolidation of the online market space for hospitality and travel products, and the shifting customers' tastes toward convenient purchasing options on the internet. The online market space is dominated by large online travel agencies (OTAs), such as Expedia, Hotels, Orbitz, as well as a variety of meta-search engines, such as Kayak, Google Flights, Trivago, or Google Hotel Ads.[8] In addition, hybrid Web sites such as TripAdvisor that offer customers an opportunity to make reservations while becoming informed via online reviews make it increasingly difficult for traditional travel agencies to survive. At the same time, airlines, hotels, and an increasing number of restaurants have concentrated their efforts on designing Web sites and mobile applications (apps) that attempt to attract customers to purchase directly from the companies providing such services.[9]

Yet, given today's technological advances, especially the market's orientation to mobile devices, the role of intermediaries is likely to increase in the future. Experts predict that travel intermediaries will exceed $2,200 billion, with compound annual growth rates (CAGR) in excess of 5.5 percent.[10] Such growth is expected in attractive sectors of the travel market, such as business travel. Specifically, the global business travel market is expected to reach $1,657 billion by 2023, with a CAGR of 4.1 percent for the period 2017–2023.[11] The same research report predicts that the group travelers will be the fastest growing market segment by 2023, exhibiting CAGR of 4.8 percent.[11]

Disintermediation

Such new dynamics are part of a complex phenomenon named disintermediation–reintermediation. Disintermediation represents the removal of a type of intermediaries from a distribution channel. Disintermediation occurs when a type of intermediary no longer adds value and a new type of intermediary emerges and offers better value. Traditional travel agencies have been the most representative intermediaries for hotel, airline, and car rental products. While they fulfilled multiple roles within distribution channels, their most important role was serving as retailers—that is, creating a market space where customers can find and purchase products. Traditional travel agencies have tried to adapt to the internet era. However, within the course of only a few years, OTAs have created highly valuable, convenient, comprehensive, and secure market spaces for hospitality and travel products.[12] In other words, OTAs served the retail function more effectively than traditional travel agencies. In such conditions, traditional travel agencies were no longer included within distribution channels. In other words, the distribution channels became disintermediated.

Reintermediation

Removing intermediaries from distribution channels leaves the channels incomplete, as customers cannot find and purchase products using those channels. Therefore, their important retail roles must be fulfilled by other intermediaries, which can serve the retail function better. The new types of intermediaries—the OTAs—were better positioned to serve the retail function, and as a result they were incorporated into the new distribution channels. This process is called reintermediation. The resulting distribution channels were predominantly online-retailer based, offering a variety of benefits that were nonexistent before. For example, customers could compare rates across different hotels and find the best deal only using a few mouse clicks. Moreover, customers could complete entire travel planning processes by themselves, without the specialized help of travel agents, therefore increasing the value retained.

Facing the difficulty of being removed from distribution channels, traditional travel agencies had to find ways to survive in the new market conditions. It was difficult for them to compete against OTAs, so they had to reposition in the crowded and highly fragmented hospitality and travel market. One way in which such travel agencies adapted was to specialize on particular travel activities. This was facilitated by the niches left, at that time, unfulfilled by the major online travel agencies. For example, while OTAs were very good at allowing customers to book routine trips, customers found it relatively difficult to book specialized trips (e.g., adventure tourism, specialized tours). Many traditional travel agencies filled those niches and began offering specialized products to customers who could not book these products by themselves using OTAs. This phenomenon allowed traditional travel agencies to capitalize on their unique skills—the ability to find and bundle customized travel products. By adding this type of value, many traditional travel agencies managed to survive and thrive.

Reintermediation is a process that should be viewed as continuous. For example, if the OTA industry is facing consolidation, it is likely that we will see a diminished number of retail Web sites where travel products can be purchased. In addition, large companies such as Google have already penetrated the travel market, offering a variety of options to customers.[13] Such dynamics are increasingly important for hotels, as such companies may have a large influence on the overall distribution environment for hotel, airline, and car rental products.

Travel Wholesalers and Tour Operators

Travel wholesalers facilitate the reservation of blocks of rooms and airline seats for specific groups, generally targeting leisure travelers. Such packages are sold to customers using travel agents or tour operators. Tour operators create packages and sell them to travel agents or directly to customers. Such packages are developed by direct negotiation with the hotels or airlines, which will provide discounts for booking multiple rooms or seats at the same time. Additional services, such as transportation, activities, logistics are also included into the package. When the package is complete, it is sold to the final customer through a travel agency, which receives a commission when the purchase is made. The value of a package like this resides in the price of the overall package, which must be lower than the sum of the individual components that individual customers can put together on their own. For this reason, the profit margin is small, so that generally 85 percent of the inventory has to be sold in order to break even.

Given the low margins, organization such as the U.S. Tour Operators Association requires members to post $100,000 indemnity bond for its customers' payments protection program. This measure helps customers receive refunds in the event of financial failure of member organizations.

Colonial Williamsburg and other historical sites often rely on bus tours as a source of guests. Ritu Jethani/123RF.

Given the high fragmentation of the international resort market, tour wholesalers are becoming valuable members of distribution. Wholesalers typically offer catalogs of resorts or destinations that are not known to travel agents. When customers inquire about a specific resort or a destination, they are presented with a catalog of resorts or destinations from a specific region. The tour wholesalers have control over the information that is presented to travel agencies, therefore influencing customers' decisions. This is important, especially in international markets, where the markets are highly fragmented, and there is a lack of information about specific properties.

The Caribbean resort industry is dependent on tour wholesalers, as they are responsible for a substantial portion of business. As these wholesalers influence the purchasing decisions, they have substantial impact on pricing and demand. For example, the wholesalers receive substantial discounts, regardless of seasonality. In turn, this situation influences the ability of hotel managers to control rates. This has implications for cash flow, as the wholesalers collect payments from customers three to six months in advance of travel, while the hotels are paid by wholesalers typically 60 days after customers' travel is completed.

While most producers use the brand.com Web sites to sell their own products, they sometimes fulfill tour operator functions. For example, United Airlines offers United vacations, a section of their Web site where the company offers specialized vacation packages based on the type of travel or destination choices of customers.[24] Similar strategies are employed by OTAs, which create packages aimed at simplifying the customers' products finding and bundling efforts. In addition, most brand.com Web sites offer travel products that are complementary to the main product sold by the company through the Web site. For example, Southwest Airlines offers the hotel and car rental bookings, even though it does not produce the services.

Specialists: Tour Brokers, Motivational Houses, and Junket Reps

Tour brokers sell motor coach tours, which are attractive in a variety of markets. In the United States, such tours include tours through New England to view the fall foliage, college and sporting events tours, entertainment events such as Mardi Gras tours, and regularly scheduled tours of Washington, D.C. Such tours are important source of revenues for the hotels and attractions that are located along the route of the tour. For example, Vacations By Rail offers a variety of train vacations in a variety of locations such as North America, Europe, or Australia. Customers can have access to expert advice, news, and book a variety of types of tours such as luxury tours, escorted tours, fall foliage tours, or combine train travel with cruises.[25]

Motivational houses Provide incentive travel offered to employees or distributors as a reward for their efforts.

Junket reps Serve the casino industry as intermediaries for premium players.

Motivational houses provide incentive travel offered to employees or distributors as rewards for their efforts. Travel is used as an incentive for companies' employees when they achieve specific performance goals. Such incentives include trips to resort areas or luxury properties, usually located in attractive destinations, such as New York, San Francisco, or Boston.

Junket reps are intermediaries in the casino industry for premium players. Such reps develop list of players who like to visit specific gaming destinations such as Las Vegas or Atlantic City and they work with only a few selected casinos. The reps are compensated typically by a commission on the amount of casino revenues produced by one of the rep's players, and may receive additional compensation such as air transportation, hotel, food and beverage, and entertainment.

Hotel Representatives

In certain situations, it is more efficient for a hotel (or other hospitality or travel producer) to hire a hotel representative, who is familiar with the market, to sell its products, then to rely on its own sales team. This is typical in situations where the producer is trying to penetrate the new market, with whom it is not familiar. For example, if a hotel in Philadelphia would like to penetrate the corporate market in Vancouver, Canada, it might be more effective to hire a hotel representative from Vancouver, who is familiar with the market. Such representatives receive a direct commission, a salary, or a combination of the two. It is important to select a hotel representative that is able to learn the specifics of the products to be sold, in addition to comprehensive knowledge of the market.

National, State, and Local Tourist Agencies

National, state, and local tourism agencies have the goal of promoting the destinations they represent. Outstanding promotion of the destination will result in bookings for the local businesses, and an increase in the overall economic impact of travel to the destination.

One of the most important promotional tools is to have representation in the main feeder markets—the markets where the customers who visit a destination generally come from. It is common for certain destinations to have physical offices overseas, which are staffed with salespeople who are knowledgeable about the destination and its offerings, and can provide printed and narrative material about the destination.

The promotional tools have traditionally relied on print advertising. For example, customers who contemplate traveling to a specific city or state can call or visit the destination's Web site and request a printed travel guidebook or brochure. The agencies will typically send that guidebook or brochure for free to the potential traveler. In addition, many states and cities have tourist information centers, with staff that is familiar with the local attractions and hospitality producers such as hotels and restaurants. Their goal is to persuade travelers to visit attractions in the area, and therefore increase the economic impact.[26]

While many destinations still provide free printouts that serve in the promotion of their attractions, a lot of the promotional material has been transferred to the internet. As a result, the main tool for promotion is the destination's Web site. While the designs and layouts of the destination Web site vary from destination to destination, certain elements remain the same, such as the focus on specific attractions, recommending activities at the destination, and finding hospitality service providers such as hotels, restaurants, entertainment venues, maps and driving directions.

Consortia and Reservation Systems

A consortium is a group of organizations that work together to provide mutual benefits to members. Such consortia include Global Hotel Alliance and Leading Hotels of the World.[27] They are expanding their legacy services (reservations) and provide a CRS for hotels. Given the fragmentation of the market, consortia provide opportunities for smaller producers to benefit from joining their budgets and increase their marketing power. Thus, hotel owners can still maintain preferred forms of ownership, such as independent hotels, but benefit from the marketing power of a larger organization.

Producers in certain geographical areas can also join efforts as consortia. For example, producers in the Bath region of the United Kingdom have formed the Association of Bath and District Leisure Enterprises (ABLE). By pooling together resources, the members of this association are able to create and distribute marketing material.[28] In addition, it is sometimes necessary for travel agents to form consortia in order to negotiate better rates with producers (e.g., better hotel rates). In addition, through the use of vertical marketing systems, consortia can negotiate better prices from their suppliers. By combining the marketing power of a number of relatively small members, consortia allowed their members to compete against bigger, more recognized competitors.

Restaurant Distribution Channels

Food Trucks

Food trucks have been popular for several years in the United States, as illustrated by the number of used food trucks. This distribution concept has increased in popularity during the past few years, especially due to the incorporation of social media features into most food truck business models. For example, truck operators can let customers know where they are located using Foursquare, which can be interfaced with other social media platforms such as Facebook and Twitter.

As a distribution platform, food trucks can be very flexible, as they can adapt to the specific consumption needs of the markets they serve. They can deliver products to specific locations, or they can claim specific locations and then let their customers know where they are located. Food trucks have been recently associated with other food distribution events, such as farmers' markets and music festivals. One interesting aspect of food trucks is that their services can complement greater travel/tourism initiatives. For example, it is increasingly common to organize catering services provided by food trucks for events and conventions, where customers can choose to pick up food items from various food trucks in a manner similar to that of a buffet-style restaurant. They combine the benefits of delivering through a window (offering convenience to customers) and that of producing small, customized products, that can increase the satisfaction of specific customers' segments that they serve. Moreover, food trucks have allowed for the development of interesting niches. For example, the popular Oh My Gogi food truck in Houston offers Korean-Mexican fusion food items and is enjoying a high popularity.

The future of food trucks is exciting, given the emergence of various services that address the desire of customers to consume restaurant-quality food items delivered at their current locations. The competition for this type of experience intensifies, as new and adapted delivery services find themselves increasingly popular for customers. For example, food delivery platforms (such as Grubhub and Favordelivery), ready-to-cook meals delivered to customers' residences (such as Blue Apron), delivery options offered by grocery stores (such as H-E-B in Texas), and the strong competition from established companies to deliver food (e.g., sandwich companies such as Jimmy Johns offer delivery options) are likely to reshape the delivery industry and created new creative niches for food trucks.

Food trucks have been recently associated with other food distribution events, such as farmers' markets, music festivals, and other gatherings. 123RF.

Food Delivery Platforms

A recently developed modality for distribution of food service is through food delivery platforms. Such platforms are technology-based services, that allow customers to place orders at different restaurants in the geographical area, and have products purchased from those restaurants delivered directly to the residences. Customers have access to the products of a variety of restaurants who participate in a specific geographical area. The merchandising of such products in the online space is designed by the food delivery company, which facilitates purchasing by allowing customers to compare different products from different restaurants. In a way, such platforms act like travel agencies, only for restaurant products. Typically, they charge a delivery fee. Platforms such as DoorDash, Grubhub, Yelp Eat 24, and FavorDelivery provide opportunities for customers to purchase restaurant food and have it delivered conveniently to their home. For example, DoorDash allows customers to order conveniently and then track their order until it arrives.[29] Such platforms typically have mobile app extensions, which facilitate purchasing due to the convenience of using mobile devices.

Concierges

Throughout the hospitality industry, there are certain types of employees in customer-facing roles, who develop extensive knowledge of various hospitality products available at the destination. Such employees can be concierges, bell staff, or front-desk employees, and can serve as important influencers for customers. Such roles are facilitated by their perceived credibility and expertise. They can be influential, as they combine the knowledge of producers in an area, with the specific knowledge of hotel customers who are staying on the property.

Typically, restaurants are cultivating relationships with hotel concierges, generally through inviting them to meals, allowing them to find reservations even during busy times. Sometimes, it is difficult to accommodate requests from concierges, as typically the guests making the request would be standing beside the concierge when making the call.

Channel Behavior and the Organization

The concept of distribution channels goes beyond simple groups of companies that act together to facilitate various flows. They represent complex behavioral systems, where people and companies interact to accomplish various goals. Such interactions range from formal interactions among loosely organized companies, to formal interactions guided by specifically designed organizational structures. Channel systems are also dynamic. Given the changing market conditions, customers' behaviors, and company strategies, new channels evolve to address such changes. We will examine channel behavior, and we will look at how members of a channel organize to facilitate the specific work within the channel.

A distribution system consists of dissimilar companies that have grouped together for their common good. Each channel member is dependent on the others, playing a specific role within the channel by specializing in performing certain functions.

The channel success is attributable to all members of a channel, which motivates members to work together. In order to realize the synergies necessary to accomplish channel goals, the members must understand their roles, coordinate their goals and activities, and cooperate to accomplish the overall channel goals. Only by cooperating they can operate efficiently and serve the target market effectively.

Channel Behavior

General members are driven by their own strategies. Such strategies reflect their own short-term goals, and behaviors that involve interactions predominantly with companies operating in their close proximity within the channel. Thus, cooperating to achieve better channel goals may mean giving up on individual company goals. Therefore, the channel members must balance their own short-term goals and strategies with the broad strategies of the overall channel. This could lead to disagreements in the role and goals of companies within the channel, which generate **channel conflict**.

Depending on the position of the company within the channel, conflict can arise at horizontal and vertical levels.

Horizontal Conflict

Horizontal conflict is conflict between companies at the same level of the channel. Companies situated at the same horizontal level have the same distance to the ultimate customer. For example, the franchisees of Burgers Place may complain that other Burgers Place franchisees might be cheating on ingredients and offering poor service, therefore influencing the overall Burgers Place image.

Vertical Conflict

Vertical conflict is conflict between companies situated at different vertical levels within the same channel. This is very common. In recent years, various companies

---

Channel conflict Disagreement among marketing channel members on goals and roles—who should do what and for what rewards.

Horizontal conflict Conflict between firms at the same level.

Vertical conflict Conflict between different levels of the same channel.

Vertical marketing systems (VMSs) Distribution channel structures in which producers, wholesalers, and retailers act as a unified system: Either one channel member owns the others, or has contracts with them, or has so much power that they all cooperate.

Corporate VMS A vertical marketing system that combines successive stages of production and distribution under single ownership. Channel leadership is established through common ownership.

Administered VMS A vertical marketing system coordinates successive stages of production and distribution, not through common ownership or contractual ties, but through the size and power of one of the parties.

Figure 12–3
Comparison of conventional marketing channel with vertical marketing system.

Conventional marketing channel
Manufacturer → Wholesaler → Retailer → Consumer

Vertical marketing system
Manufacturer / Wholesaler / Retailer → Consumer

had conflicts with their suppliers, stemming from disagreements in the types and quality of supplies provided and the timing of supply delivery.

Not all conflict is bad for the channel, if managed correctly. Some minor conflict is actually good for the members of the channel, as they keep the focus on understanding the roles and goals and acting to accomplish them in synergy with the other members of the channel. However, severe or extended conflict can harm the relationships among various members of the channel, and drive the overall channel's focus away from efficiency. Specifically, the members of the channel would dedicate substantial time and resources to manage and eventually solve the conflict, therefore diverting their focus away from the normal goals of the channel. Therefore, it is in everybody's best interest to keep channel conflict to a manageable level.

Channel Organization

Conventional Marketing System

A conventional marketing system consists of one or more independent producers, wholesalers, and retailers. Each is a separate business seeking to maximize its own profits, even at the expense of profits for the system as a whole.

Vertical Marketing Systems

The channels work perfectly when the synergies among the members are realized. For this to happen, each channel member's role must be specified, while managing any potential conflict. However, such roles and conflict cannot be properly managed in a vacuum. They are managed optimally if the channel includes a company, agency, or mechanism that provides leadership, and has power to assign the roles and manage conflict.

Historically, the conventional distribution channels have lacked such leadership and power, often resulting in high levels of conflict. Such conflict influenced the overall channel performance. To address these challenges, over the years, new channel developments have emerged in the form of **vertical marketing systems (VMSs)**, which are designed to provide channel leadership. Figure 12–3 contrasts the two types of channel arrangements.

Typical conventional distribution channels consist of one or more independent producers, wholesalers, and retailers. Each of these companies works as a separate business, with the goal of maximizing its own profits, regardless of the strategies of the other members of the channel. No channel member has substantial control over the other members, and there are no formal ways in which the channel roles are assigned or conflict is managed. In contrast, VMS includes producers, wholesalers, and retailers acting as a unified system. One channel member owns the others, has contracts with them, or has so much power that the other members must all cooperate. The producer, the wholesaler, or the retailer can dominate the VMS.

If we examine the three major types of VMSs, we can find that each type uses a different means for setting up leadership and power in the channel. Specifically, in a **corporate VMS**, common ownership at different levels in the channel represents the mechanism for coordination and conflict management. In contrast, in an administered VMS, the most dominant general members assume the leadership roles. Finally, in a contractual VMS, leadership and power are regulated by contractual agreements among the members of the channel.

Corporate VMS involves successive stages of production under a single ownership. Craft breweries often open their own pubs serving their own beers. For example, the St. Arnold brewery in Houston operates its Beer Garden & Restaurant, where the locally produced beers and food dishes are offered.[30]

An **administered VMS** coordinates successive stages of production and distribution through the leverage obtained by the size and power of the participants. For example, it is common to see administered

VMSs in many national airline markets. Specifically, the larger airline in a nation (also known as flag carrier) grows to a substantial size, which allows it to exercise additional amount of power over reservation systems, tour operators, and travel agencies within a specific nation.

A **contractual VMS** consists of independent companies located at different levels of production and distribution within channels who establish contracts in order to achieve strategic goals. For example, contracts with hotel representatives allow hotels to establish specific roles for themselves and their partners within distribution channels. Moreover, such contracts allow hotels to obtain benefits that they could not obtain by distributing alone. An important form of contractual VMS is franchising.

Contractual VMS A vertical marketing system in which independent firms at different levels of production and distribution join together through contracts to obtain more economies or sales impact than they could achieve alone.

FRANCHISING. Franchising is a method of conducting business where a franchisee is granted the right to engage in offering, selling, or distributing goods or services under a marketing format that is designed by a franchisor. This agreement allows the franchisee to take advantage of established trademarks, advertising, loyalty programs, and other notable marketing benefits already developed by a franchisor and currently successful.

Franchises have been very popular forms of distribution for hotels and restaurants. Franchised brands include Holiday Inn Express, Hilton Garden Inn, Fairfield Inn by Marriott, McDonald's, KFC, and many others. The development of franchising permitted the substantial growth of the hospitality industry by diversifying the types of operators. Specifically, the industry moved from individual operators to multiunit chains, therefore providing value to a variety of stakeholders.

Franchise A contractual vertical marketing system in which a channel member called a franchisor links several stages in the production distribution process.

The franchisee gains several advantages, typically from using established marketing methods and artifacts of an established, high equity brand. In order to obtain these benefits, the franchisee usually pays an initial fee, a royalty, and a marketing fee to the franchisor. For hotels, for example, there is a reservation fee and a fee for the loyalty program. The royalty and other revenue-based fees are based on the gross revenue. However, a contentious area in franchising is the marketing fee. Such fee is administered by the franchisor, but uses the fees paid by franchisees. If the manner in which such fees are utilized by the franchisor is not communicated well to the franchisees, conflict may arise. One way to avoid conflict is to encourage the franchisees to form a Franchisee Association and take advantage of the power of such a multi-company organization.

The size of the initial fee and royalty are correlated with the brand equity of the franchise. For example, recognizable brands such as Hilton and McDonald's are responsible for driving consumption around the world, as global customers are aware of such brands. Therefore, the higher the brand equity of the franchise, the higher the value that it can bring to a franchisee.

There are several advantages for the franchisees, which are in line with the factors that made the franchise brand successful over time:

- Recognition of the brand
- Low chance of business failure
- National advertising, predesigned advertising, and marketing plans
- Fast business growth, associated with the brand
- Help with site selection
- Architectural plans and other established design protocols
- Operational systems, software, and norms to maintain such systems
- National contracts with suppliers
- Product development and new product innovations
- Consulting
- Help with financing

However, there might be disadvantages of purchasing a franchise:

- Fees and royalties are required
- Limitations of the products sold and recipes used

- The franchisee is often required to be open for a minimum number of hours and offer certain products
- A poorly operated company can affect the repetition of the entire chain
- The franchisor's performance affects the profitability of the franchisees
- Some franchisees may not benefit from national advertising as much as other franchisees, which often causes conflict

Franchising is attractive for certain companies, especially given the opportunities for distribution. However, franchising is not effective for all companies. A franchisor must be able to offer a solid business concept, viable operational systems, good management support, and scalable technology. Especially for new businesses, it is challenging to provide a good franchisee package.

Franchising can be used as a strategic tool. For example, small restaurant chains franchise in order to help retain managers. It is difficult for smaller chains to compete against larger chains in terms of the compensation/benefits packages offered to their managers. This strategy allows chains to keep valuable managers who may otherwise leave the company. There are several advantages for the franchisors:

- Receive a percentage of gross sales
- Expand the brand
- Receive support for national advertising campaigns
- Are able to negotiate support for large-scale national contracts with suppliers

The disadvantages for the franchisors are the following:

- Limit the ability to expand distribution through other methods. For example, a company's ability to set up alliances may be restricted if such alliances violate the territorial agreements of the franchisees
- Franchisees must be continuously monitored to ensure product and production consistency.
- There are limitations when requiring franchisees to change operations. For example, Pizza Hut had a difficult time getting franchisees to add delivery when Domino's was developing heavily its delivery market.
- Franchisees want and need to have an active role in decision making

Marketing HIGHLIGHT 12.2 Restaurant franchising

These days, it's nearly impossible to stroll down a city block or drive on a suburban street without seeing a Wendy's, a McDonald's, a Pizza Hut, or a Starbucks. One of the best-known and most successful franchisors, McDonald's, has more than 37,000 stores in more than a hundred countries. Subway is one of the fastest-growing franchises, with more than 49,000 shops in over a hundred countries.

How does a franchising system work? The individual franchises are a tightly knit group of enterprises whose systematic operations are planned, directed, and controlled by the operation's innovator, called a franchisor. The franchisee is required to pay for the right to be part of the system. Yet this initial fee is only a small part of the total amount that franchisees invest when they sign a franchising contract. Start-up costs include rental and lease of equipment and fixtures and sometimes a regular license fee. McDonald's franchisees invest as much as $1 to $2 million in initial start-up costs. Subway's success is partly due to its low start-up cost of $100,000 to $300,000, which is lower than most other franchises. However, Subway franchisees pay an 8 percent royalty on gross sales, one of the highest in the food franchise industry, plus a 4.5 percent advertising fee.

The franchisor provides its franchisees with marketing and operations system for doing business. McDonald's requires franchises to attend its "Hamburger University" in Oak Brook, Illinois, for three weeks to learn how to manage the business; franchisees must also adhere to certain procedures in buying materials.

Through franchising, Subway has grown to become the largest restaurant chain. Courtesy of John Bowen.

In the best cases, franchising is mutually beneficial to both franchisor and franchisee. Franchisors can cover new territory in little more than the time it takes the franchisee to sign a contract. They can achieve enormous purchasing power. Franchisors also benefit from the franchisees' familiarity with local communities and conditions and from the motivation and hard work of employees who are entrepreneurs rather than "hired hands." Similarly, franchisees benefit from buying into a proven business with a well-known and accepted brand name. And they receive ongoing support in areas ranging from marketing and advertising to site selection, staffing, and financing.

As a result of the franchise explosion in recent years, some fast-food franchisors are facing worrisome market saturation. One indication is the number of franchisee complaints filed with the Federal Trade Commission against parent companies. The most common complaint is that franchisors "encroach" on existing franchisees' territory by bringing in another store. For example, McDonald's franchisees in California and other states complained when the company decided to open new company-owned stores in their areas. Franchisees may object to parent company marketing programs that may adversely affect their operations. Franchisees often strongly resist value promotions in which the company reduced prices on menu items in an effort to revive stagnant sales. Many franchisees believe that the value promotion cheapens the image of the chain and unnecessarily reduces their profit margins. Another complaint is higher-than-advertised failure rates. Subway, in particular, has been criticized for misleading its franchisees by telling them that it has only a 2 percent failure rate when the reality is much different. In addition, some franchisees feel that they've been misled by exaggerated claims of support, only to feel abandoned after the contract is signed and money has been invested.

International expansion is delivering both franchisor growth and franchisee earnings. Fast-food franchises have become very popular throughout the world. Domino's has entered Japan with master franchisee Ernest Higa, who built 180 stores in Japan and later sold them to Bain Capital for $67 million. Part of Higa's success can be attributed to adapting Domino's product to the Japanese market, where food presentation is everything. Higa carefully charted the placement of pizza toppings and made cut-mark perforations in the boxes for perfectly uniform slices.

It appears franchise fever will not cool down soon. Experts estimate franchises capture 50 percent of all U.S. retail sales. Of the top 13 franchisees in worldwide sales, 10 are related to the travel and hospitality industry. These franchises include McDonald's, KFC, Burger King, Subway, Domino's, Pizza Hut, Marriott Hotels, Wendy's, Taco Bell, and Hilton.[i]

[i] Richard Soloman, 2012, "Ernest Higa on leveraging US/Japanese biculturalism," Beacon Reports, http://beaconreports.net/en/higa-on-leveraging-usjapanese-biculturalism/ (accessed January 23, 2019); Franchise Times Top 200 Franchises, 2018, http://www.franchisetimes.com/Top200 (accessed January 21, 2019); Karin Shedd, 2018, "The Most Franchised Company in the World Isn't McDonald's or Starbucks," (accessed January 22, 2019); https://www.cnbc.com/2018/08/14/subway-franchises-mcdonalds-starbucks-fast-food.html; www.subway.com (accessed December 5, 2004); "The Top 200," *Franchise Times* (October 2003); Norman D. Axelrad and Robert E. Weigand, "Franchising—A Marriage of System Members," in *Marketing Managers Handbook* (3rd ed.), ed. Sidney Levy, George Frerichs, and Howard Gordon (Chicago, IL: Dartnell, 2004), pp. 919–934; Andrew E. Sewer, "McDonald's Conquers the World," *Fortune* (October 17, 1994): 103–116; Roberta Maynard, "The Decision to Franchise," *Nation's Business* (January 1997): 49–53; Cliff Edwards, "Campaign '55 Flop Shows Power of Franchisees," *Marketing News* (July 7, 1997): 9; Richard Behar, "Why Subway Is the Biggest Problem in Franchising," *Fortune* (March 16, 1998): 126–134; Patrick J. Kaufman and Sevgin Eroglu, "Standardization and Adaptation in Business Format Franchising," *Journal of Business Venturing* (January 1999): 69–85.

Alliances Alliances are developed to allow two organizations to benefit from each other's strengths.

ALLIANCES. Alliances represent another form of contractual agreement. Alliances are developed so that two or more companies can benefit from each other's strengths. Specifically, alliances allow companies to access resources that they do not have, while providing allies with new opportunities to develop in areas that are only accessible through the alliance. For example, United Airlines and Lufthansa (a major German carrier) are part of the Star Alliance. United Airlines can have access to passengers from the European Union market the travel to/from the United States and Europe through United Airlines major hubs (such as Houston, New York-Newark, and Chicago) and Lufthansa's major hubs such as Munich and Frankfurt in Germany. The alliance also allows travelers to book flights provided by Lufthansa on United Airlines Web site, and vice versa. Such alliances offer benefits to all partners, and such benefits could not be obtained in the absence of alliances. The alliance includes 28 airlines, including Air Canada, South African Airways, Turkish Airlines, Eva Air, and ANA, providing benefits to companies and travelers from all continents.[31]

A common form of alliance is the one between a hotel and a restaurant. Hotels ally with restaurants, offering benefits for both companies. For example, restaurants benefit from location and the flow of customers from the hotel. The hotel typically benefits from the brand value of the restaurant, and by offering guests a convenient option for food service. Such alliances are common, especially with established brands. For example, Trader Vic's has locations in several Hilton hotels. Las Vegas resorts are famous for bringing famous chefs to open restaurants at the resorts. Such a trend has expanded beyond Las Vegas, and now one can find famous upscale restaurants affiliated with hotels and most major cities.[32]

Horizontal Marketing Systems

Horizontal marketing system (HMS) Two or more companies at one level join to follow new marketing opportunities. Companies can combine their capital, production capabilities, or marketing resources to accomplish more than what one company can accomplish working alone.

A **horizontal marketing system (HMS)** is a system where two or more companies located at one level join to follow a new marketing opportunity. This way, companies can combine resources such as capital, production, innovation capabilities, and marketing resources to accomplish goals beyond what an individual company can accomplish alone. The development in information technology, especially data analytics, allows companies to develop better insight into their market segments and business intelligence, making it easier for them to find new partners for such systems.

Multichannel Marketing Systems

Alliances Alliances are developed to allow two organizations to benefit from each other's strengths.

The legacy distribution strategies of many companies involved using a single channel to sell products to a single market or market segment. The evolution of customer segmentation techniques and statistical analyses (e.g., cluster analysis, latent class analysis) allow companies to gain better insight into the specifics of new segments.[33] At the same time, technology development of such application program interfaces (API) allows for the development of technology platforms that facilitate better integration and data exchange among companies.[34] Overall, such developments created opportunities for companies to distribute their products using **multichannel marketing distribution**. Multichannel marketing occurs when a single company sets up two or more distribution channels to reach one or more customer segments. For example, Hilton Hotels Worldwide distributes its products through their own Web sites, mobile apps, and also through a variety of OTAs, review Web sites, meta-search engines, and social media Web sites.

Multichannel marketing distribution Multichannel distribution, as when a single firm sets up two or more marketing channels to reach one or more customer segments.

While this strategy is beneficial in that a company can increase its market reach, serve more segments of customers, or consolidate specific niches of customers, it increases the risk of distribution. Specifically, existent channels can find it unfair for new emerging channels to coexist, creating conflict or even legal challenges. Therefore, the company must think strategically about how the multiple channels can work together to support the main strategies of the company without alienating general members or cannibalizing sales.

■■■ Channel Management

Selecting Channel Members

Selecting channel members is a complex process and involves several factors, such as customer needs, the company's ability to attract channel members, the economic feasibility of the selected channel members, and the amount of control about to be given up in order to gain a general member. For example, hotels have to decide how many OTAs are allowed to sell their inventories online. With each new type of OTA, the hotel has to decide if the value provided by distributing through that OTA is high enough to justify the costs.

Customer Needs

It is important to envision the strategy by determining the types of services that are appropriate for various target market segments. For example, it is difficult for independent hotels to sell their inventory in the absence of using OTAs. However, using OTAs such as hotels.com, smaller independent hotels may gain international exposure, even when that exposure comes at a price.

Similarly, resorts in Caribbean destinations may consider aligning with wholesalers. Wholesalers are in charge of putting together packages that include airfare, rooms, ground transportation, and activities, and then distribute these packages through OTAs or specialized travel agencies. Customers looking for such packages find integrated packages through the OTA, thus eliminating the need to compose a package by themselves. This is less risky given the lack of knowledge that customers may have at the time of the booking about a specific product that can be found at the destination. Therefore, to effectively design the channel, a company must make an effort to understand the specific needs of its target market, and then balance the needs of those customers against the feasibility and the costs of meeting them.

Attracting Channel Members

Companies have different natural abilities to attract qualified channel members. For example, resourceful, well-known hotels that pay their commissions promptly and accurately honor the reservations of travel agents find it easy to find appropriate channel members. It is very important to do careful research by investigating the resources of the channel member to be used. This is important because these new channel members will eventually be responsible for creating and maintaining a company's image in front of the audience of customers that it serves.

Evaluating Major Channel Alternatives

ECONOMIC FEASIBILITY OF THE CHANNEL MEMBER. While each channel produces a certain level of sales, it also incurs a certain amount of cost. The sales must offset the cost and must support the channel member. Such costs can be grouped into two categories: direct costs and opportunity costs. For example, if a transportation provider is bringing customers to a casino, the casino may incentivize the transportation provider and even provide certain incentives to the customers that it brings. Such costs are lower than the amount of sales produced by those customers in the casino, therefore justifying the utilization of this particular channel member. Opportunity costs are created when products are discounted only to find out that such products can be sold at a higher price. For example, hotels can find differences in price between different channels, and act to diminish those differences (diminished opportunity costs).

Companies should always evaluate the performance of the other channel members (intermediaries). As market conditions evolve, the value of various channel members may change. The performance of the channel member may increase or decrease due to a multitude of factors. Such factors include the growth rate of the general member, growth rate of the market, the emergence of new competitors for the channel member, and new models of distribution. In such cases, the company needs to work with the channel member to accomplish the desired performance, or eliminate the general member from the channel if distributing through this channel is not profitable.

CONTROL CRITERIA. Control is very important in channel choice. For example, using the sales representatives offers less control to the hotel than building their own sales force. Such sales representatives may prefer to sell rooms in other hotels because it requires less effort. In contrast, building a sales force from scratch requires a lot of effort, such as recruiting, training, and designing the appropriate technology platforms. However, in the end it may be worth it because the sales force would be specifically trained and highly efficient in selling the hotel's products. While the technology has made great progress in allowing hotel decision makers to have an accurate idea about the efficiency of various components of the sales force, it is often very difficult to evaluate such efforts.

Control is also important in franchising and choosing multiple channel members. As companies use franchising, some portion of control is given up in exchange for a broader distribution arrangement. The franchisor may find it difficult to convince the franchisees to add specific new products or to participate in certain promotions. Quality control may be a problem, as establishing a protocol for control over franchisees' practices may be difficult due to logistical challenges.

In multichannel distribution arrangements, one particular challenge is represented by the rights of existing channel members. It is possible that existing channel members may limit their activities with new channel members, when the interests of various channel members are different. With each channel member that is added, the company may lose some of its flexibility while committing long term. For example, a hotel may use the sales representatives located in a foreign market. Such arrangements may be established through a five-year contract. During those five years, the hotel may develop alliances with other partners, such as OTAs, airlines, or tour operators that operate in that particular market. Thus, the services of the sales representative may not be needed. Yet, the hotel is unable to terminate the relationship until the contract has ended. Therefore, companies have to understand and anticipate the possible trade-offs that may occur when choosing channel members. This requires a good analysis of the market and viable business intelligence tools.[35] Today's technology also allows for such decisions to be made based on better information.

Determining Responsibilities of Channel Members

The channel members have to agree on the terms and responsibilities for each member. For example, the agreements between the hotel and OTAs must specify the type of rates to be commissionable, the amount of commission to be paid, and the amount of days by which the commission must be paid. In food service, the agreement between franchisors and franchisees must include the terms for promotional support, training, and systems development. Franchisees must specify how they will maintain the company standards for physical facilities and how they will participate in national promotions. It is critical to clearly and explicitly specify the terms in writing to avoid any potential misunderstandings and conflict.

It is critical to continuously motivate channel members. The company must market to its channel members. For example, periods of slow demand may be associated with positive incentives provided to the channel members, such as increased commissions. Also, companies can keep the channel members always informed about the new products being developed. Establishing a platform of healthy cooperation and communication among the channel members is a great foundation for support offered to channel members, which may increase their performance and stimulate good relationships in the channel.

Selecting Business Location

The Iconic Willard Hotel in Washington, D.C. has a great location near the White House and Monuments. Courtesy of John Bowen.

Location represents one of the most critical aspects of distribution for hospitality companies. It is especially important to have the right location for companies that provide services where customers go to the service delivery place. The well-known phrase "location, location, location" emphasizes this aspect. However, there is no single best strategy for finding the perfect location. For example, an ideal location for a Hampton Inn may be different than ideal location for a Four Seasons hotel. A similar logic is applied for food service. For example, restaurants choose their location based on the opportunities of a certain geographical area to provide customers. Location depends on the specifics of the company, the resources that it has, and the way the customers from its target market can access it easily. Most importantly, location depends on the company's marketing strategy, as each company has a set of criteria to evaluate a location. Generally, choosing the location involves four steps, which are discussed next.

Understanding the Marketing Strategy

First, it is important to clearly understand the target market and its alignment with the marketing strategy of the company. For example, La Quinta cater mostly to traveling salespeople and customers arriving primarily by car. Therefore, their locations include places along freeways or outside of cities. In contrast, many boutique hotels are appealing to customers who prefer to stay in vibrant downtown locations of cities, with access to a variety of other hospitality and entertainment services. Therefore, their location will be different.

Regional Analysis

The second step is the regional analysis, which consists of the selection of geographical market areas.[36] For example, expanding restaurants will have to find regions that could accommodate the desired number of new restaurants to be opened. Also, business hotels expanding into Eastern Europe may target cities such as Budapest, Sofia, or Bucharest. Such business hotels cover a substantial portion of the market of Eastern Europe, and offer services to business travelers who travel predominantly in that region.

One important characteristic of the region to be selected is the ability to provide sufficient and stable demand. In addition, the potential for growth is evaluated. Factors such as the overall economic drivers of the region are considered, as certain industries may drive the economic development in periods of strong economic boom, but may not provide sufficient demand during periods of economic slowdown. Other factors, such as weather, existing infrastructure, proximity to major commercial routes, the information technology infrastructure may be considered, as well as non-economic factors, such as population growth.

Choosing the Area Within the Region

The third step is the selection of an area within the selected region. For example, sites for restaurants need to be chosen within a specific metropolitan area. Typical criteria involved in the step include demographic and psychographic characteristics of the population in this area. Also, business intelligence could provide great insight into the competitive environment into the area. The result typically is a choice of five areas within the region that seem promising.

Choosing the Individual Site

The final step involves choosing individual sites. A critical consideration in site analysis is the existence of compatible businesses. Such businesses can generate demand. For example, a hotel is situated near major business office campuses, airports, shopping malls, residential areas may facilitate demand for a new location. While such businesses generally can increase demand, it is very critical for a company choosing a site to evaluate the specifics of the individuals in the market of those particular sites. For example, companies must obtain accurate profiles of their customers, in order to understand the degree of match between the potential market in the existing area and the products that the company is offering at that new site.

It is also important for a company to look at competitors that may exist in an individual site. If the market is served well by a number of competing companies, the new site may be rejected. This is because the new market can become oversaturated, which may hurt the demand for the products for all the competitors. However, sometimes companies choose to enter saturated markets only to have a presence in a particular city. Also, restaurants can be found in clustered location, offering a variety of choices to potential customers.

Another potential consideration is accessibility. The extent to which the site is accessible to traffic is critical. Factors to be considered include the location of the site relative to major highways, traffic going in both directions, the existence of a median, the speed of traffic, visibility of the site, etc. For example, restaurants located at intersections with a stoplight have the benefit of being exposed to waiting drivers. In addition, the overall attractiveness of the area is important. How attractive is the area? Are there any other attractions around? Is there an appropriate infrastructure allowing customers to access the area easily?

For companies to develop a profile of preferred sites for example, Carl's Jr. restaurants, a fast food hamburger restaurant, developed this profile:[37]

- Free-standing location in a shopping center
- Free-standing corner location (with a signal light at the intersection)
- Inside lot with 125-foot minimum frontage
- Enclosed shopping mall
- Population of 12,000 or more in a one-mile radius (growth areas preferred)
- Easy access of traffic to location
- Heavy vehicular/pedestrian traffic
- An area where home values and family income levels are average or above
- Close to offices and other demand generators
- A parcel size of 30,000 to 50,000 square feet
- No less than two or three miles from other existing company locations

Typically, companies utilize checklists and statistical analyses when determining the choice for a site. Checklists include specific items, such as those listed above. The development of easy-to-use and powerful statistical software during the past few years have allowed the utilization of such tools for site selection. For example, regression analyses could be conducted, in which the independent variable is typically sales, while the dependent variables include a variety of factors that describe the area such as the population size, household income of the market, competitors, and other attributes of the location.

It is also possible to use real estate development that is responsible for locations, or negotiating contracts for leases or purchases of desired properties. For example, commercial real estate agencies can be helpful to hospitality companies that choose new sites in specific markets. Such companies should be expected to participate in multiple phases of this process, from planning to the acquisition of properties.

CHAPTER REVIEW

I. Partnering to Add Value

A. Supply chains and the value delivery network. To produce and sell products requires the collaboration of partnering companies. A supply chain includes the sequential progression of resources from raw material to final product. Companies that provide the raw materials and other resources to assist in the creation of a product are called upstream partners. Companies that facilitate the sale are considered downstream partners. The term "supply chain" has limitations, as it views a business as only a make-and-sell company. A better approach is to consider the value delivery network that is created by the company, suppliers, distributors (intermediaries), and customers, who partner to improve the performance of the entire network.

B. Nature and importance of distribution systems. Distribution provides a steady flow of customers. Well-managed distribution systems can make a difference between very successful companies and those struggling to survive.

C. Nature of distribution channels. A distribution channel is a set of independent organizations involved in the process of making a product or service available to the consumer or business user.

1. **Why are marketing intermediaries used?** The use of intermediaries depends on their greater efficiency in marketing the goods available to target markets. Through their contacts, experience, specialization, and scale of operation, intermediaries normally offer more than a firm can on its own.
2. **Distribution channel functions** include information, promotion, contact, matching negotiation, physical distribution, financing, and risk taking.
3. **Number of channel levels.** The number of channel levels can vary from direct marketing, through which the manufacturer sells directly to the consumer, to complex distribution systems involving four or more channel members.

II. Hospitality Distribution Channels

A. Direct channels are where reservations or purchases are made directly between the producer and the final customer.

B. **Online travel agency.** A travel agency that conducts business through the internet with no physical locations or stores.
   1. **Distribution models.** Depending on their strategies, online travel agencies are using a combination of such models. One of the most common distribution models is the merchant model. According to the merchant model, an online travel agency (called a merchant) pays an agreed-upon rate to the producer, and then marks up the price according to its own pricing strategies. Other popular models include the agency model, the auction model, the referral model, and the opaque model.
   2. **Global distribution systems** are computerized systems that serve as product catalogs for travel agencies and other intermediaries. They fulfill the wholesale function as they intermediate large volumes of transactions.
   3. **Travel agents.** The role has diminished due to the proliferation of OTAs. Specialized type includes corporate travel agents.
   4. **Travel wholesalers and tour operators.** Travel wholesalers facilitate the reservation of blocks of rooms and airline seats for specific groups, generally target leisure travelers. Such packages are sold to customers using travel agents or tour operators. Tour operators create packages and sell them to travel agents or directly to customers. Such packages are developed by direct negotiation with the hotels or airlines, which will provide discounts for booking multiple rooms or seats at the same time. Additional services, such as transportation, activities, and logistics are also included into the package. When the package is complete, it is sold to the final customer through a travel agency, which receives a commission when the purchase is made.
   5. **Specialists: Tour brokers, motivational houses, and junket reps.** Tour brokers sell motor coach tours, which are attractive in a variety of markets. Motivational houses provide incentive travel offered to employees or distributors as rewards for their efforts. Junket reps are intermediaries in the casino industry for premium players.
   6. **Hotel representatives.** In certain situations, it is more efficient for a hotel (or other hospitality or travel producer) to hire a hotel representative, who is familiar with the market, to sell its products, then to rely on its own sales team. This is typical in situations where the producer is trying to penetrate the new market, with whom it is not familiar.
   7. **National, state, and local tourist agencies** have the goal of promoting the destinations that they represent. The main tool for promotion is the destination Web site.
   8. **Consortia and reservation systems.** A consortium is a group of organizations that work together to provide mutual benefits to members. They are expanding their legacy services (reservations) and provide a central reservation system (CRS) for hotels. Given the fragmentation of the market, consortia provide opportunities for smaller producers to benefit from joining their budgets and increase their marketing power. In addition, through the use of vertical marketing systems, consortia can negotiate better prices from their suppliers.
C. **Restaurant distribution systems**
   1. **Food trucks.** As a distribution platform, food trucks can be very flexible, as they can adapt to the specific consumption needs of the markets they serve. They can deliver products to specific locations, or they can claim specific locations and then let their customers know where they are located.
   2. **Food delivery platforms.** Such platforms are technology-based services, that allow customers to place orders at different restaurants in the geographical area, and have products purchased from those restaurants delivered directly to the residences.
   3. **Concierges** can be influential, as they combine the knowledge of producers in an area, with the specific knowledge of hotel customers who are staying on the property.

III. **Channel Behavior and the Organization**
Distribution channels involve complex behavioral systems, where people and companies interact to accomplish various goals. Such interactions range from formal interactions among loosely organized companies, to formal interactions guided by specifically designed organizational structures. Channel systems are also dynamic; new channels evolve to address changing market conditions, customer behavior, and company strategies.
   A. **Channel behavior.** The channel members must balance their own short-term goals and strategies with the broad strategies of the overall channel.
      1. **Horizontal conflict.** Conflict between firms at the same level.
      2. **Vertical conflict.** Conflict between different levels of the same channel.
   B. **Channel organization.**
      1. **Conventional marketing system.** A conventional marketing system consists of one or more independent producers, wholesalers, and retailers. Each is a separate business seeking to maximize its own profits, even at the expense of profits for the system as a whole.
      2. **Vertical marketing system.** A vertical marketing system consists of producers, wholesalers, and retailers acting as a unified system. VMSs were developed to control channel behavior and manage channel conflict and its economies through size, bargaining power, and elimination of duplicated services. The three major types of VMSs are corporate, administered, and contractual. A corporate VMS combines successive stages of production and distribution under single ownership. An

administered VMS coordinates successive stages of production and distribution, not through common ownership or contractual ties, but through the size and power of the parties. A contractual VMS consists of independent firms at different levels of production and distribution who join through contracts to obtain economies or sales impact. An important form of contractual VMS is franchising. Franchising is a method of doing business by which a franchisee is granted the right to engage in offering, selling, or distributing goods or services under a marketing format that is designed by the franchisor. The franchisor permits the franchisee to use its trademark, name, and advertising. Alliances are developed to allow two organizations to benefit from each other's strengths.
   3. **Horizontal marketing systems.** Two or more companies at one level join to follow new marketing opportunities. Companies can combine their capital, production capabilities, or marketing resources to accomplish more than what one company can accomplish working alone.
   4. **Multichannel marketing systems.** A single firm sets up two or more marketing channels to reach one or more customer segments.
IV. Channel Management
   A. **Selecting channel members** involves several factors:
      1. **Customer needs.** The company must make an effort to understand the specific needs of its target market, and then balance the needs of those customers against the feasibility and the costs of meeting them.
      2. **Attracting channel members.** Companies have different natural abilities to attract qualified channel members
      3. **Evaluating major channel alternatives.** While each channel produces a certain level of sales, it also incurs a certain amount of cost. The sales must offset the cost and must support the channel member. Such costs can be grouped in two categories: direct costs and opportunity costs. As market conditions evolve, the value of various channel members may change. Companies must understand the trade-offs of effort/control that may occur when choosing channel members.
   B. **Determining responsibilities of channel members.** The company and its intermediaries must agree on the terms and responsibilities of each channel member. According to the services and clientele at hand, the responsibilities are formulated after careful consideration.
   C. **Selecting business location.** There are four steps in choosing a location:
      1. **Understanding the marketing strategy.** Know the target market of the company.
      2. **Regional analysis.** Select the geographic market areas
      3. **Choosing the area within the region.** Demographic and psychographic characteristics and competition are factors to consider.
      4. **Choosing the individual site.** Compatible business, competitors, accessibility, drainage, sewage, utilities, and size are factors to consider.

■■■ IN-CLASS GROUP EXERCISES

*Exercises with an asterisk next to them are suitable for individual homework or online assignments. Students, always provide an explanation for your answer.

1. Discuss how you think technology will change distribution channels in the hospitality and travel industries over the next five years.
2. Explain how international travel changed distribution channels in the hospitality and travel industries.
3. *What are the major differences between a distribution channel for a business making tangible products and a firm producing hospitality and travel products?
4. *Can a business have too many channel members? Explain your answer.
5. *Explain the difference between a tour wholesaler and a travel agent.
6. *Why is franchising such a fast-growing form of retail organization?
7. According to the International Franchising Association, between 30 and 50 percent of all new franchise applicants are people who formerly worked in large corporations and who lost their jobs as a result of corporate downsizing. How do you think these midlevel, midcareer corporate executives will adapt to life as franchise owners? How will their previous corporate experience help them? How will it hurt them?

■■■ EXPERIENTIAL EXERCISES

Do one of the following:

1. Visit a restaurant that offers take-out service. What has it done to facilitate take-out service? For example, does it have a special order and pickup area; does it have paper menus to take home; does it accept phone, fax, or internet orders; and does it have special packaging for take-out? Report on what you find and any suggestion that you might have.
2. Investigate franchises available in the hospitality or travel business. Select a franchise you feel would be a good business investment based on what the franchise offers and the fees the franchisor charges. Support your findings in a two- to three-page report.

REFERENCES

1. Booking Holdings. *Factsheet*. January 10, 2019, https://www.bookingholdings.com/about/factsheet/#page-head-full.
2. Nicholas Rossolillo, "Booking Holdings and Saudi Arabia Strike a Travel Deal," Nasdaq.com (2018).
3. Yahoo Finance Inc. *Booking Holdings Inc.*, January 10, 2019, https://finance.yahoo.com/quote/BKNG?p=BKNG&.tsrc=fin-srch.
4. S. Y. Xie, "After a Comeback and a Name Change, Priceline Bets Big on China," *Wall Street Journal* (2018).
5. K. May, "Booking.com Leads the Way as Top Hotel Channel," *PhocusWire* (2018).
6. M. Cowen, Ctrip and Priceline Dine Out Together (2018).
7. S. Gharib, "Booking Holding CEO Is Upbeat About 2019: People Are Traveling a Lot," *Fortune* (2019).
8. M. Starkov, It's the End of the Hotel Metasearch Model as We Know It (2018).
9. R. Law et al., "Distribution Channel in Hospitality and Tourism," *International Journal of Contemporary Hospitality Management*, 27, no. 3 (2015): 431–452.
10. N. Popova, *Disrupt or be Disrupted*. HospitalityNet.org (2018).
11. Allied Market Research Business Travel Market to Reach $1,657 Bn, Globally, by 2023 at 4.1% CAGR, Says Allied Market Research. HospitalityNet.org (2018).
12. C. Morosan and M. Jeong, "Users' Perceptions of Two Types of Hotel Reservation Web Sites," *International Journal of Hospitality Management*, 27, no. 2 (2008): 284–292.
13. D. Schaal, Google's New Hotel Search Is a Greater Threat to Booking Rivals (2018).
14. L. Olmsted, "Why You Need a Travel Agent, Part 1," *Forbes* (2012).
15. D. Schaal, Booking Holdings Makes Major People Toward Prepaid Hotel Bookings (2018).
16. Hilton Hotels Worldwide Inc. Let Yourself in with Hilton Digital Key (2018).
17. Hotels.com (2018).
18. Southwest Airlines Corporate Travel (2018).
19. C. Estis Green and M. O. Lomano, *Distribution Channel Analysis: A Guide for Hotels* (HSMAI Foundation, 2012).
20. S. Andrew, <2018 about GDS .pdf>. Skift.com (2017).
21. SHR. *Distribution Platforms* (2016), http://shr.global/windsurfer/ (accessed August 4, 2016).
22. Sabre Hospitality Solutions (2018).
23. A. Express, The Benefits of Using a Corporate Travel Agency (2018).
24. Airlines, U. *United Vacations* (2018).
25. V. B. Rail, *Vacations by Rail* (2018).
26. C. Morosan, "The Influence of DMO Advertising on Specific Destination Visitation Behaviors," *Journal of Hospitality Marketing & Management*, 24, no. 1 (2015): 47–75.
27. Global Hotel Alliance (2018).
28. The Association of Bath Leisure Enterprises [A.B.L.E.]. Bath and Beyond (2018).
29. DoorDash (2018).
30. Saint Arnold Our Beer Garden & Restaurant Is Now Open (2018).
31. Star Alliance (2018).
32. Z. Quezada, "Celebrity Chefs Make Las Vegas Restaurants Shine," *Tripsavvy* (2018).
33. S. Okazaki et al., "A Latent Class Analysis of Spanish Travelers' Mobile Internet Usage in Travel Planning and Execution," *Cornell Hospitality Quarterly*, 56, no. 2 (2014): 191–201.
34. J. Schaap, "How Technological Accountability Can Boost Guest Service," HospitalityNet.org (2018).
35. W. Höpken and M. Fuchs, "Introduction: Special Issue on Business Intelligence and Big Data in the Travel and Tourism Domain," *Information Technology & Tourism*, 16, no. 1 (2016): 1–4.
36. A. Gosh, *Retail Management* (Fort Worth, TX: Dryden Press, 1990).
37. D. E. Lindberg, *The Restaurant from Concept to Operation* (New York, NY: Willey, 1985).

have become part of our passion and our brand." Who knows what the cows can accomplish in yet another 5 or 10 years. Whatever the future brings, the Chick-fil-A message will still be loud and clear: Eat more chicken![1]

Building good customer relationships calls for more than just developing a good product, pricing it attractively, and making it available to target customers. Companies must also communicate their value propositions to customers, and what they communicate should not be left to chance. All of their communications must be planned and blended into carefully integrated marketing communication programs. Just as good communication is important in building and maintaining any kind of relationship, it is a crucial element in a company's efforts to build profitable customer relationships.

The Promotion Mix

Promotional mix (marketing communications mix) The specific blend of promotion tools that the company uses to persuasively communicate customer value and build customer relationships.

Personal selling Personal presentation by the firm's sales force for the purpose of engaging customers, making sales, and building customer relationships.

Direct marketing and digital marketing Engaging directly with carefully targeted individual consumers and customer communities to both obtain an immediate response and build lasting customer relationships.

A company's total **promotion mix**—also called its marketing communications mix—consists of the specific blend of advertising, public relations, **personal selling**, sales promotion, and **direct-marketing and digital-marketing** tools that the company uses to communicate customer value and build customer relationships persuasively. Definitions of the five major promotion tools follow:[2]

Advertising: Any paid form of nonpersonal presentation and promotion of ideas, goods, or services by an identified sponsor

Sales promotion: Short-term incentives to encourage the purchase or sale of a product or service

Personal selling: Personal presentation by the firm's sales force for the purpose of making sales and building customer relationships

Public relations: Building good relations with the company's various publics by obtaining favorable publicity, building up a good corporate image, and handling or heading off unfavorable rumors, stories, and events

Direct and digital marketing: Engaging directly with carefully targeted individual consumers and customer communities to both obtain an immediate response and build lasting customer relationships

Each category involves specific promotional tools used to communicate with consumers. For example, *advertising* includes broadcast, print, internet, outdoor, and other forms. *Sales promotion* includes discounts, coupons, displays, and demonstrations. *Personal selling* includes sales presentations, trade shows, and incentive programs. *Public relations* includes press releases, sponsorships, special events, and Web pages. And *direct and digital marketing* includes direct mail, catalogs, online and social media, and mobile marketing.

At the same time, marketing communication goes beyond these specific promotion tools. The salesperson's manner and dress, the place's decor, and the company's stationery—all communicate something to the buyers. Every brand contact delivers an impression that can strengthen or weaken a customer's view of the company. The whole marketing mix must be integrated to deliver a consistent message and strategic positioning.

Integrated Marketing Communications

In past decades, marketers perfected the art of mass marketing: selling highly standardized products to masses of customers. In the process, they developed effective mass-media communication techniques to support these strategies. Large companies now routinely invest millions or even billions of dollars in television, magazine, or other mass-media advertising, reaching tens of millions of customers with a single ad. Today, however, marketing managers face some new marketing communications realities. Perhaps no other area of marketing is changing so profoundly as marketing communications, creating both exciting and challenging times for marketing communicators.

The New Marketing Communications Model

Several major factors are changing the face of today's marketing communications. First, consumers are changing. In this digital, wireless age consumers are better informed and more communications empowered. Rather than relying on marketer-supplied information, they can use the internet, social media, and other technologies to find information on their own. They can connect easily with other consumers to exchange brand-related information or even create their own brand messages and experiences.

Second, marketing strategies are changing. As mass markets have fragmented, marketers are shifting away from mass marketing. More and more, they are developing focused marketing programs designed to engage customers and build customer relationships in more narrowly defined micromarkets.

Finally, sweeping advances in digital technology are causing remarkable changes in the ways companies and customers communicate with each other. The digital age has spawned a host of new information and communication tools—from satellite and cable television systems to smartphones and tablets to the many faces of the internet (brand Web sites, e-mail, blogs, social media and online communities, the mobile Web, and so much more). Just as mass marketing once gave rise to a new generation of mass-media communications, the new digital and social media have given birth to a more targeted, social, and engaging marketing communications model.

Although network television, magazines, newspapers, and other traditional mass media remain very important, their dominance is declining. In their place, advertisers are now adding a broad selection of more-specialized and highly targeted media to engage smaller customer communities with more personalized, interactive content. The new media range from specialty cable television channels and made-for-the-web videos to online ads, e-mail and texting, blogs, mobile catalogs and coupons, and a burgeoning list of social media. Such new media have taken marketing by storm.

Some advertising industry experts even predict that the old mass-media communications model will eventually become obsolete. Mass-media costs are rising, audiences are shrinking, ad clutter is increasing, and viewers are gaining control of message exposure through technologies such as video streaming or digital video recorders (DVRs) that let them skip disruptive television commercials. As a result, the skeptics suggest that marketers are shifting ever-larger portions of their marketing budgets away from old-media mainstays and moving them to online, social, mobile, and other new-age media.

In recent years, although TV remains a potent advertising medium that captures a third or more of total advertising spending, its growth has slowed or declined. Ad spending in magazines, newspapers, and radio has also lost ground. Meanwhile, spending in digital media has surged. Growing at a rate of 15 percent a year, total digital ad spending is expected to pass TV spending this year. Digital media has captured an estimated 45 percent of all ad spending compared with TV's 33 percent. By far the fastest-growing digital category is mobile, and now accounts for an estimated 75 percent of all digital ad spending.

More and more, large advertisers are moving toward a "digital-first" approach to building their brands. For example, Unilever, one of the world's largest advertisers, now spends as much as one-quarter of its $8 billion global marketing budget on digital media. In countries such as the United States and China, digital media account for closer to 50 percent of its marketing budget.[3] Some marketers now rely almost entirely on digital and social media.

Thus, the explosion of online, mobile, and social media marketing presents tremendous opportunities but also big challenges. It gives marketers rich new tools for

Figure 13–1
Integrated marketing communications.

Carefully blended mix of promotion tools

- Advertising
- Personal selling
- Public relations
- Direct and digital marketing
- Sales promotion

Consistent, clear, and compelling company and brand messages

understanding and engaging customers. At the same time, it complicates and fragments overall marketing communications. The challenge is to bring it all together in an organized way. To that end, most companies practice the concept of integrated marketing communications (IMC). Under this concept, as illustrated in Figure 13–1, the company carefully integrates its many communication channels to deliver a clear, consistent, and compelling message about the organization and its brands.

IMC calls for recognizing all touch points where the customer may encounter content about the company and its brands. Each contact with the brand will deliver a message—whether good, bad, or indifferent. The company's goal should be to deliver a consistent and positive message at each contact. IMC ties together all of the company's messages and images. Its television and print ads have the same brand message as its e-mail and personal selling communications. And its PR materials are consistent with Web site, online, social media, and mobile marketing content.

A great example of a well-integrated marketing communications effort is Coca-Cola's "Mirage" campaign. Built around two Super Bowl ads, the campaign integrated the clout of traditional big-budget TV advertising with the interactive power of social media to create real-time customer engagement with the Coke brand.[4]

Coca-Cola's "Mirage" tells the story of three bands of desert vagabonds—Cowboys, Showgirls, and Mad Max-inspired "Badlanders"—as they trek through the blazing-hot desert pursuing the same elusive mirage—a frosty bottle of Coca-Cola. The Mirage campaign began two weeks before the Super Bowl with a 30-second teaser ad on American Idol and posted on YouTube and other online destinations inviting fans to visit CokeChase.com to get to know the story and teams. Then, during the big game, a 60-second Mirage ad set up the exciting chase, with a cliff-hanging close that urged viewers to visit CokeChase.com, where they could help decide the outcome by casting votes for their favorite team and throwing obstacles in front of rival teams. During the rest of the game, Coca-Cola listening teams monitored related activity on major social media, and put fans in the middle of the action by posting real-time chase updates on Facebook, YouTube, and Twitter and chase photos on Tumblr and Instagram. After the end of the game, a second Mirage ad announced the chase team with the most viewer votes—the Showgirls, in their glam pink and silver outfits, won the Coke. But the real winner was Coca-Cola. The Mirage campaign exceeded all expectations. In addition to the usual huge Super Bowl audience numbers, during the game, the campaign captured an eye-popping 8.2 million online and social media interactions and 910,000 votes, far exceeding the brand's internal goals of 1.6 million interactions and 400,000 votes. Contributing to these interactions was 4.5 million views of the ad on YouTube. Instead of fast-forwarding this ad, people are going to YouTube to watch it!

In the past, no one person or department was responsible for thinking through the communication roles of the various promotion tools and coordinating the promotion mix. To help implement IMC, some companies have appointed a marketing communications director who has overall responsibility for the company's communications efforts. This helps produce better communications consistency and greater sales impact. It places the responsibility in someone's hands—where none existed before—to unify the company's image as it is shaped by thousands of company activities.

In the new marketing communications world, rather than using old approaches that interrupt customers and force-feed them mass messages, new media formats let marketers reach smaller communities of consumers in more engaging ways. For example, think about television viewing these days. Consumers can now watch their favorite programs on just about anything with a screen—on televisions and also on laptops, smartphones, or tablets. And they can choose to watch programs whenever and wherever they wish, often without commercials. Increasingly, some programs, ads, and videos are being produced only for online viewing.

Despite the shift toward digital media, however, traditional mass media still capture a sizable share of the promotion budgets of most major marketing firms, a fact that probably won't change quickly. Thus, rather than the old-media model collapsing completely, most marketers foresee a shifting mix of both traditional mass media and online, mobile, and social media that engage more-targeted consumer communities in a more personalized way. In the end, regardless of the communications channel, the key is to integrate all of these media in a way that best engages customers, communicates the brand message, and enhances the customer's brand experiences.

As the marketing communications environment shifts, so will the role of marketing communicators. Rather than just creating and placing "TV ads" or "print ads" or "Snapchat branded story ads," many marketers now view themselves more broadly as **content marketing** managers. As such, they create, inspire, and share brand messages and conversations with and among customers across a fluid mix of paid, owned, earned, and shared communication channels. These channels include media that are both traditional and new as well as controlled and not controlled. It's not just advertising anymore. It's about understanding the customer journey, how and when they acquire information. Starting a conversation with them along this journey that leads to engagement, purchase, and advocacy (see Marketing Highlight 13.1).[5]

Content marketing Creating, inspiring, and sharing brand messages and conversations with and among consumers across a fluid mix of paid, owned, earned and shared channels.

Marketing HIGHLIGHT 13.1 — Thanks, just don't call it advertising: It's content marketing

In the good old days, life seemed so simple for advertisers. When a brand needed an advertising campaign, everybody knew what that meant. The brand team and ad agency came up with a creative strategy, developed a media plan, produced and placed a set of TV commercials and magazine or newspaper ads, and maybe issued a press release to stir up some news. But in these digital times, the old practice of placing "advertisements" in well-defined "media" within the tidy framework of a carefully managed "advertising campaign" just doesn't work anymore.

Instead, the lines are rapidly blurring between traditional advertising and new digital content. To be relevant, today's brand messages must be social, mobile, interactively engaging, and multi-platformed. Says one industry insider: "Today's media landscape keeps getting more diverse—it's broadcast, cable, and streaming; it's online, tablet, and smartphone; it's video, rich media, social media, branded content, banners, apps, in-app advertising, and interactive technology products."

The new digital landscape has called into question the very definition of advertising. "What Is Advertising Anyway?" asks one provocative headline. Call it whatever you want, admonishes another, but "Just Don't Call It Advertising." Instead, according to many marketers these days, it's "content marketing," creating and distributing a broad mix of compelling content that engages customers, builds relationships with and among them, and moves them to act and advocate the brand to others. To feed today's digital and social media machinery, and to sustain "always-on" consumer conversations, brands need a constant supply of fresh content across a breadth of traditional and digital platforms.

Many advertisers and marketers now view themselves more broadly as content marketing managers who create, inspire, share, and curate marketing content—both their own content and that created by consumers and others. Rather than using traditional media breakdowns, they subscribe to a new framework that builds on how and by whom marketing content is created, controlled, and distributed. The new classification identifies four major types of media: paid, owned, earned, and shared (POES):

Paid media—Promotional channels paid for by the marketer, including traditional media (such as TV, radio, print, or outdoor) and online and digital media (paid search ads, Web and social media display ads, mobile ads, or e-mail marketing).
Owned media—Promotional channels owned and controlled by the company, including company Web sites, corporate blogs, owned social media pages, proprietary brand communities, sales forces, and events.
Earned media—PR media channels, such as television, newspapers, blogs, online video sites, and other media not directly paid for or controlled by the marketer but that include the content because of viewer, reader, or user interest.
Shared media—Media shared by consumers with other consumers, such as social media, blogs, mobile media, and viral channels as well as traditional word-of-mouth.

In the past, advertisers have focused on traditional paid (broadcast, print) or earned (public relations) media. Now, however, content marketers have rapidly added the new digital generation of owned (Web sites, blogs, brand communities) and shared (online social, mobile, e-mail) media. Whereas a successful paid ad used to be an end in itself, marketers are now developing integrated marketing content that leverages the combined power of all the POES channels. Thus, many TV ads often aren't just TV ads any more. They're "video content" you might see anywhere—on a TV screen and also on a tablet or phone. Other video content looks a lot like TV advertising but was never intended for TV, such as made-for-online videos posted on Web sites or social media. Similarly, printed brand messages and pictures no longer appear only in carefully crafted magazine ads or catalogs. Instead, such content, created by a variety of sources, pops up in anything from formal ads and online brand pages to mobile and social media and independent blogs.

The new "content marketing" campaigns look a lot different from the old "advertising" campaigns. For example, consider Tecate—Heineken-Mexico's leading beer brand. In Mexico, Tecate stands for all things male, including soccer, Mexico's favorite sport. But Tecate faced a tough creative challenge during the recent Soccer World Cup. It wanted to tap into the fan fever surrounding the tournament but couldn't directly mention either the World Cup or the Mexican national team, both sponsored by competitor Corona. So instead of just running big-budget TV ads filled with the usual clichés, Tecate launched a novel, content-rich "Soccer Gentleman" campaign, that went well beyond traditional media:

Tecate's "Soccer Gentleman" campaign recognized that during the World Cup a real Tecate man must balance the two true loves of his life: women and soccer. So, the campaign set out to help men successfully juggle their love lives and watching soccer nonstop by being "perfect gentlemen." The campaign was built around a beautifully penned, 185-page love letter that took 90 minutes to read (which just happens to be the length of a soccer match).

In an opening TV spot aired a minute before a big match, a man touchingly presents the lengthy letter to his beloved and implores her to read it right away. Enchanted by his romantic gesture, she settles in to read his heartfelt words, so enrapt that she fails to notice as he races off to watch the World Cup match with his friends without interruption. During the match, five more TV spots, a campaign Web site, and 47 Facebook posts follow the reading of the letter in real time, with updates such as "She is now halfway through your 90-minute letter." A final post-game ad shows the man racing home just in time to greet his love as she emerges from her rapture and falls into his arms. Men could then download the entire letter for the next match and customize it by changing the woman's name; 16,000 people did so and lived the experience of reading the actual letter.

In another part of the campaign, a Tecate man refuses his new girlfriend's invitation to come inside after a first date, proclaiming his deep affection for her and his honorable intentions to be a perfect gentleman by defying the "macho culture" and the temptations of a one-night stand. As she swoons, he races off to catch the next game. "Watching World Cup soccer and being loved for it?" concludes Tecate. "Life doesn't get much better than that."

Skillfully integrated across POES channels, the "Soccer Gentleman" content campaign produced striking results. Tecate sales increased 11 percent during the World Cup period. During the four-month campaign, the brand saw a 228 percent increase in YouTube followers, added 1.2 million Facebook fans, and generated a flurry of media coverage and social media buzz. The campaign's ads and videos garnered 17 million YouTube views and accounted for two of YouTube's 10 most-watched ads during the World Cup. "Soccer Gentleman" was named by ad industry publication Advertising Age as the year's best integrated marketing communications campaign. "Soccer Gentleman" has "become a cultural phenomenon in Mexico," says a Tecate marketer. "The phrase is part of the popular culture; with memes, videos, and T-shirts. You hear it in restaurants and taxis. During the World Cup, without being able to say anything, we took everything!"

So, we can't just call it "advertising" anymore. Today's shifting and sometimes chaotic marketing communications environment calls for more than just creating and placing ads in well-defined and controlled media spaces. Rather, today's marketing communicators must be marketing content strategists, creators, connectors, and catalysts who manage brand conversations with and among customers and help those conversations catch fire across a fluid mix of channels. That's a tall order, but with today's new thinking, anything is POES-ible![6]

The Need for Integrated Marketing Communications

The shift toward a richer mix of media and content approaches poses a problem for marketers. Consumers today are bombarded by brand messages from a broad range of sources. But all too often, companies fail to integrate their various communication channels. Mass-media ads say one thing, whereas company's internet site, e-mails, social media pages, or videos posted on YouTube say something altogether different.

One problem is that marketing content often comes from different parts of the company. Advertising messages are prepared by the advertising department or an ad agency. Other company departments or agencies prepare public relations messages, sales promotion events, and online or social media content. However, consumers don't distinguish between content sources the way marketers do. In the consumer's mind, brand-related content from different sources—whether it's a Super Bowl ad, in-store display, mobile app, or friend's social media post—all merge into a single message about the brand or company. Conflicting content from these different sources can result in confused company images, brand positions, and customer relationships.

Thus, the explosion of online, mobile, and social media marketing presents tremendous opportunities but also big challenges. It gives marketers rich new tools for understanding and engaging customers. At the same time, it complicates and fragments overall marketing communications. The challenge is to bring it all together in an organized way. To that end, most companies practice the concept of **integrated marketing communications** (IMC). Under this concept, as illustrated in Figure 13–1, the company carefully integrates its many communication channels to deliver a clear, consistent, and compelling message about the organization and its brands.

Integrated marketing communications (IMC) Carefully integrating and coordinating the company's many communications channels to deliver a clear, consistent, and compelling message about the organization and its products.

Often, different media play unique roles in engaging, informing, and persuading consumers. For example, a recent study showed that more than two-thirds of advertisers and their agencies are planning video ad campaigns that stretch across multiple viewing platforms, such as traditional TV and digital, mobile, and social media. Such video convergence, as it's called, combines TV's core strength—vast reach—with digital's better targeting, interaction, and engagement.[7] These varied media and roles must be carefully coordinated under the overall integrated marketing communications plan.

Developing Effective Marketing Communication

A View of the Communication Process

IMC involves identifying the target audience and shaping a well-coordinated promotional program to obtain the desired audience response. Too often, marketing communications focus on immediate awareness, image, or preference goals in the target market. But this approach to communication is too shortsighted. Today, marketers are moving toward viewing communications as managing ongoing customer engagement and relationships with the company and its brands.

Because customers differ, communications programs need to be developed for specific segments, niches, and even individuals. And, given the new interactive communications technologies, companies must ask not only "How can we reach our customers?" but also "How can we let our customers engage us?"

Thus, the communications process should start with an audit of all the potential touch points that target customers may have with the company and its brands. For example, looking for a good restaurant may include talking to local residents, the hotel's concierge, and visit various online sites for reviews. The marketer needs to assess what influence each communication experience will have at different stages of the buying process. This understanding helps marketers allocate their communication dollars more efficiently and effectively.

Figure 13–2
Elements in the communications process.

There is a lot going on in this figure! For example, apply this model to McDonald's. To create great advertising—such as its long-running "i'm lovin' it" campaign—McDonald's must thoroughly understand its customers and how communication works.

[Diagram: Sender → Encoding → Message (Media) → Decoding → Receiver; Feedback ← Response; Noise affects Message/Media. Sender's field of experience and Receiver's field of experience overlap.]

To communicate effectively, marketers need to understand how communication works. Communication involves the nine elements shown in Figure 13–2. Two of these elements are the major parties in a communication—the *sender* and the *receiver*. Another two are the major communication tools—the *message* and the *media*. Four more are major communication functions—*encoding*, *decoding*, *response*, and *feedback*. The last element is *noise* in the system. Definitions of these elements follow and are applied to a McDonald's "i'm lovin' it" television commercial.

- *Sender:* The *party sending the message to another party*—here, McDonald's.
- *Encoding:* The process of *putting thought into symbolic form*—for example, McDonald's ad agency assembles words, sounds, and illustrations into a TV advertisement that will convey the intended message.
- *Message:* The *set of symbols* that the sender transmits—the actual McDonald's ad.
- *Media:* The *communication channels* through which the message moves from the sender to the receiver—in this case, television and the specific television programs that McDonald's selects.
- *Decoding:* The process by which the receiver *assigns meaning to the symbols* encoded by the sender—a consumer watches the McDonald's commercial and interprets the words and images it contains.
- *Receiver:* The *party receiving the message* sent by another party—the customer who watches the McDonald's ad.
- *Response:* The *reactions of the receiver* after being exposed to the message—any of hundreds of possible responses, such as the consumer likes McDonald's better, is more likely to eat at McDonald's next time, hums the "i'm lovin' it" jingle, or does nothing.
- *Feedback:* The part of the *receiver's response communicated back to the sender*—McDonald's research shows that consumers are either struck by and remember the ad or they write or call McDonald's, praising or criticizing the ad or its products.
- *Noise:* The *unplanned static or distortion* during the communication process, which results in the receiver getting a different message than the one the sender sent—the consumer is distracted while watching the commercial and misses its key points.

For a message to be effective, the sender's encoding process must mesh with the receiver's decoding process. The best messages consist of words and other symbols that are familiar to the receiver. The more the sender's field of experience overlaps with that of the receiver, the more effective the message is likely to be. Marketing communicators may not always share their customer's field of experience. For example, an advertising copywriter from one socioeconomic level might create ads for customers from another level—say, wealthy business owners. However, to communicate effectively, the marketing communicator must understand the customer's field of experience and what experiences will create value for the customer.

This model points out several key factors in good communication. Senders need to know what audiences they wish to reach and what responses they want. They must be good at encoding messages that take into account how the target audience decodes them. They must send messages through media that reach target audiences, and they must develop feedback channels so that they can assess an audience's response to the message.

Steps in Developing Effective Communications

We now examine the steps in developing an effective integrated communications and promotion program. Marketers must do the following: identify the target audience, determine the communication objectives, design the message, select the communication channels, select the message source, and collect feedback.

Identifying the Target Audience

A marketing communicator starts with a clear target audience in mind. The audience may be potential buyers or current users, those who make the buying decision, or those who influence it. The audience may be individuals, groups, special publics, or the general public. The target audience heavily affects the communicator's decision on what will be said, how it will be said, when it will be said, where it will be said, and who will say it. To create effective communication, a marketer must understand the target audience by creating a message that will be meaningful to them in a media they will understand. Managers need to understand their target markets before they can communicate with them.

Determining the Communication Objective

Once a target audience has been defined, the marketing communicator must decide what response is sought. Of course, in most cases, the final response is purchase. But purchase is the result of a long process of consumer decision making. The marketing communicator needs to know where the target audience stands in relation to the product and to what state it needs to be moved.

The Indian tribes of South Dakota wished to significantly increase tourist visitation to their reservations. These were their objectives:

- To provide guests for B&B operations
- To increase the market for Indian products
- To participate in other tourism-related incomes
- To correct misconceptions about the American Indian; it was deemed important to show that the Lakota, Dakota, and Nakota people are living cultures

This combination of economic and cultural education objectives led to the development of the Alliance of Tribal Tourism Advocates (ATTA) as a communication vehicle. Instead of depending on the South Dakota Department of Tourism or other organizations, Indians would promote themselves. "If you want to visit an Indian, the best person to talk with is a Native American," said Ronald L. Neiss, acting director of ATTA and a member of the Rosebud Sioux Tribal Council.[8]

Figure 13–3
Buyer readiness stage.

The target audience may be in any of six buyer readiness states: awareness, knowledge, liking, preference, conviction, or purchase, which are shown in Figure 13–3.

Awareness

First, the communicator must be able to gauge the target audience's awareness of the product or organization. The audience may be totally unaware of it, know only its name, or know one or a few things about it. If most of the target audience is unaware, the communicator tries to build awareness, perhaps by building simple name recognition. This process can begin with simple messages repeating the name. Even then, building awareness takes time. Suppose that an independent restaurant named the Hungry Hunter opens in a northern suburb of Houston. There are 50,000 people within a three-mile radius of the restaurant. Initially, the restaurant has little name recognition. The Hungry Hunter may set an objective of making 40 percent of the people living within three miles of the restaurant aware of its name.

Knowledge

The target audience might be aware of the company or product but know little else. The Hungry Hunter specializes in wild game, but the market may not be aware of this. The restaurant may decide to select product knowledge as its first communication objective.

The chain of Ruth's Chris Steak House restaurants uses a simple slogan and advertises on a quarter page in airline in-flight magazines. The message is directed at frequent flyers who deserve a "sizzling reward." The advertisement features a color photo of a very thick steak, a list of restaurant addresses, and a message that Ruth Chris focuses on serving excellent steaks. This simple message quickly gives the reader knowledge of restaurant location, size of the steak, and seriousness of the restaurant as a steakhouse.

Liking

If target audience members know the product, how do they feel about it? We can develop a range of preference, such as a Likert scale covering degrees of liking, for example, "dislike very much," "dislike somewhat," "indifferent," "like somewhat," and "like very much." If the market is unfavorable toward the Hungry Hunter, the communicator must learn why and then develop a communication campaign to create favorable feelings. If unfavorable feelings are based on real problems, such as slow service, communication alone cannot do the job. The Hungry Hunter has to fix its problems and then communicate its renewed quality.

Preference

A target audience might like the product but not prefer it to others. In this case, the communicator must try to build consumer preference. The communicator promotes the product's quality, value, performance, and other features. The communicator can check on the campaign's success by measuring audience preferences after the campaign. If the Hungry Hunter finds that many area residents like the name and concept but choose other restaurants, it will have to identify those areas where its offerings are better than competing restaurants. It must then promote its advantages to build preference among possible customers.

Conviction

A target audience might prefer the product but not develop a conviction about buying the product. Marketers have a responsibility to turn favorable attitudes into conviction because conviction is closely linked with purchase. Communication from the Hungry Hunter will work toward making its target market believe, it offers the best steaks at a fair value in its market area.

Purchase

Finally, some members of the target audience might have conviction but not quite get around to making the purchase. They may wait for more information or plan to act later. The communicator must lead these consumers to take the final step. Actions might include offering the product at a low price, offering a premium, or letting consumers try it on a limited basis. The Hungry Hunter may provide a "Tuesday Night Special," offering prime rib or its seafood of the day for $29.95 instead of the usual price of $34.95.

Designing the Message

Having defined the desired audience response, the communicator turns to developing an effective message. Ideally, the message should get attention, hold interest, arouse desire, and obtain action (a framework known as the AIDA model). In practice, few messages take the consumer all the way from awareness to purchase, but the AIDA framework does suggest the desirable qualities of a good message.

When putting the message together, the marketing communicator must solve three problems: what to say (message content), how to say it logically (message structure), and how to say it symbolically (message format).

Message Content

The communicator has to figure out an appeal or theme that will produce a desired response. The three types of appeals are rational, emotional, and moral.

Rational appeals relate to audience self-interest. They show that the product will produce desired benefits. Occasionally, rational appeals are overlooked.

Emotional appeals attempt to provoke emotions that motivate purchase. These include fear, guilt, and shame appeals that entice people to do things that they should (brush their teeth, buy new tires) or stop doing things they shouldn't (smoke, drink too much, or overeat).

Emotional appeals are widely used by resorts and hotels to stimulate cross-purchases:

- Commercials on in-room television, posters, and desktop tents promote the health center and the need to reduce stress and work off "pounds gained from eating in the hotel."

- The "Think of the Spouse and Kids at Home" theme is widely used to promote a myriad of products available in the hotel, from hand-dipped chocolates to stuffed animals. This appeal is also used to convince business guests to purchase a vacation for the family at one of the chain's resort properties.

Moral appeals are directed to the audience's sense of what is right and proper. They are often used to urge people to support such social causes as a cleaner environment, better race relations, equal rights, and aid to the needy.

Go RVing created a series of lifestyle ads promoting RVing. This one shows a father and daughter spending time together. Courtesy of Go RVing.

Message Structure

The communicator must also decide how to handle three message structure issues. The first is whether to draw a conclusion or leave it to the audience. Early research showed that drawing a conclusion was usually the most effective. More recent research, however, suggests that in many cases the advertiser is better off asking questions and letting buyers come to their own conclusions.

The second message structure issue is whether to present a one- or two-sided argument. Usually, a one-sided argument is more effective in sales presentations except when audiences are highly educated and negatively disposed.

The third message structure issue is whether to present the strongest arguments first or last. Presenting them first creates strong attention but may lead to an anticlimactic ending.[9]

"World's Largest Outdoor Swimming Pool" is the first message presented by the San Alfonso del Mar Resort in Chile. The accommodation and food actually take a second seat to the beauty and immensity of the 1-km-long salt water swimming pool, 115 feet deep and holding 66 million gallons of water.

Message Format

The communicator also needs a strong format for the message. In a print ad, the communicator has to decide on the headline, copy, illustration, and color. To attract attention, advertisers can use novelty and contrast, eye-catching pictures and headlines, distinctive formats, message size, position, color, shape, and movement. If the message is to be carried over the radio, the communicator has to choose words, sounds, and voices.

If the message is to be carried on television or in person, all these elements, plus body language, must be planned. Presenters plan their facial expressions, gestures, dress, posture, and hairstyle. If the message is carried on the product or its package, the communicator has to watch texture, scent, color, size, and shape. For example, color plays a major communication role in food preferences. When consumers sampled four cups of coffee that had been placed next to brown, blue, red, and yellow containers (all the coffee was identical, but the consumers did not know this), 75 percent felt that the coffee next to the brown container tasted too strong, nearly 85 percent judged the coffee next to the red container to be the richest, nearly everyone felt that the coffee next to the blue container was mild, and the coffee next to the yellow container was perceived as weak.

Selecting Communication Channels

The communicator must now select channels of communication. The two broad types of communication channels are personal and nonpersonal.

Personal Communication Channels

In personal communication channels, two or more people communicate directly with each other. They might communicate face to face, on the phone, via mail or e-mail, or even through an internet "chat." Personal communication channels are effective because they allow for personal addressing and feedback.

Some personal communication channels are controlled directly by the company. For example, company salespeople contact business buyers. But other personal communications about the product may reach buyers through channels not directly controlled by the company. These channels might include independent experts—consumer advocates, bloggers, and others—making statements to buyers. Or they might be neighbors, friends, family members, and associates talking to target buyers in person or via social media. This last channel, word-of-mouth influence, has considerable effect in many product areas.

Personal influence carries great weight for products that are expensive, risky, or highly visible. Hospitality products are often viewed as being risky because they cannot be tried out beforehand. Therefore, personal sources of information are often sought before someone purchases a travel package, selects a restaurant, or stays at a hotel.

Online recommendations have become a powerful influence on consumers. One survey found that recommendations from friends and family are far and away from the most powerful influence on consumers worldwide. More than 50 percent

Marketing HIGHLIGHT 13.2 Thank you—A great personal communication

Two of the most powerful words in any language are *thank you*. A sales manager for a limited service hotel in Indianapolis, Indiana, decided to initiate a special thank-you program for guests.

The manager's objectives were to increase corporate business and let guests know that the inn appreciated their patronage and wanted them to return. She felt that a handwritten note would be appreciated in this high-tech world of e-mail, internet, and voice-mail communications.

Names and addresses were obtained from business cards left by guests in a fish bowl qualifying them for a monthly drawing. After the drawing was held, any one of the three desk clerks would write thank-you notes during slow times on the desk. Each desk clerk is provided with personalized business cards that are included with the handwritten note.

The manager has spoken with many guests who were amazed that the inns took time to write a personal note to them. One client mentioned that he really liked having the business card sent from a front-desk associate rather than a general manager or salesperson. Because the desk associates are usually the ones to make reservations, guests like having the name of someone to ask for when they call back for future reservations.

The thank-you notes help build a relationship between the guests and the hotel. They let the guests know that the staff appreciates their business and cares about them as individuals. The manager's support of the program lets the employees know that creating positive guest relations is important to the hotel.

---

of consumers said friends and family are the number one influence on their awareness and purchase. Another study found that 90 percent of the customers trust recommendations from people they know and 70 percent trust consumer opinions posted online, whereas trust in advertisements runs from a high of 62 percent to a low of 24 percent, depending on the medium.[10]

The power of online ratings means that it is important to provide great service, to help eliminate negative reviews. It also means that one must monitor and respond to both negative and positive reviews. For negative reviews, it is best to take the conversation off-line. This can be done by apologizing online and asking the reviewer that had a problem to contact the manager directly by e-mail.

Companies can take steps to put personal communication channels to work for them. They can create *opinion leaders* for their brands—people whose opinions are sought by others—by supplying influencers with the product on attractive terms or by educating them so that they can inform others. **Buzz marketing** involves cultivating opinion leaders and getting them to spread information about a product or service to others in their communities.

Social marketing firm BzzAgent takes a different approach to creating buzz. It creates customers for a client brand, and then turns them into influential brand advocates.[11]

BzzAgent has assembled a volunteer army of natural-born buzzers, millions of actual shoppers around the world who are highly active in social media and who love to talk about and recommend products. Once a client signs on, BzzAgent searches its database and selects "agents" that fit the profiles of the product's target customers. Selected volunteers receive product samples, creating a personal brand experience. BzzAgent then urges the agents to share their honest opinions of the product through face-to-face conversations and via tweets, Facebook posts, online photo and video sharing, blogs, and other social sharing venues. If the product is good, the positive word of mouth spreads quickly. If the product is not so good, that's worth learning quickly as well. BzzAgent advocates have successfully buzzed the brands of hundreds of top marketing companies, including Disney and Dunkin' Donuts. BzzAgent's appeal is its authenticity. The agents aren't scripted. Instead, the company tells its advocates, "Be natural—after all, sharing the products we love is something we all do already."[12]

Buzz marketing Cultivating opinion leaders and getting them to spread information about a product to others in their community.

Nonpersonal Communication Channels

Nonpersonal communication channels are media that carry messages without personal contact or feedback. They include media, atmospheres, and events. Major **media** consist of print media (newspapers, magazines, direct mail), broadcast media (radio and television), display media (billboards, signs, posters), and online media (e-mail, Web sites, and online social and sharing networks). **Atmospheres** are designed environments that create or reinforce the buyer's leanings toward purchasing a product. The lobby of a five-star hotel contains a floral display, original works of art, and luxurious furnishings to reinforce the buyer's perception that the hotel is a five-star hotel. **Events** are occurrences staged to communicate messages to target audiences. PR departments arrange press conferences, grand openings, public tours, and other events to communicate with specific audiences.

The Scanticon Princeton (a conference center) used its lobby as a gallery for original artworks by members of the Princeton Artists Alliance. This resulted in excellent publicity, including a full-page story with pictures and the address of Scanticon Princeton in the Sunday edition of a major Philadelphia newspaper.

Nonpersonal communication affects buyers directly. In addition, using mass media often affects buyers indirectly by causing more personal communication. Mass communications affect attitudes and behavior through a two-step flow of communication. In this process, communications first flow from television, magazines, and other mass media to opinion leaders and then from these opinion leaders to others. Thus, opinion leaders step between mass media and their audiences and carry messages to people who are less exposed to media.

Media Nonpersonal communication channels, including print media (newspapers, magazines, direct mail), broadcast media (radio, television), and display media (billboards, signs, posters).

Atmosphere Designed environments that create or reinforce a buyer's leanings toward consumption of a product.

Events Occurrences staged to communicate messages to target audiences, such as news conferences or grand openings.

Selecting the Message Source

The message's impact on the audience is also affected by how the audience views the sender. Messages delivered by highly credible sources are persuasive. What factors make a source credible? The three factors most often found are expertise, trustworthiness, and likability. Expertise is the degree to which the communicator appears to have the authority needed to back the claim. Trustworthiness is related to how objective and honest the source appears to be. Friends, for example, are trusted more than salespeople. Likability is how attractive the source is to the audience. People like sources who are open, humorous, and natural. Not surprisingly, the most highly credible source is a person who scores high on all three factors: expertise, trustworthiness, and likability.

Memphis used prominent people to promote that city as a convention and meeting site. A video was produced in which convention planners, tour wholesalers, and association officials endorsed the city as an ideal convention location. Messages delivered by attractive sources achieve higher attention and recall. Advertisers often use celebrities as spokespeople, such as Michael Jordan for McDonald's. Celebrities are likely to be effective when they personify a key product attribute. But what is equally important is that the spokesperson must have credibility.

The use of living personalities to serve as spokespeople for a company or product carries inherent problems:

- Celebrities are often difficult to work with and may refuse to participate in important media events or to pose under certain conditions.

- Living personalities are still living out their lives and can do things that will publicly harm and/or embarrass the brand they represent. For example, Jared Fogel was a spokesperson for Subway

The message source in this ad, a young girl having a great time at the beach, will appeal to parents or grandparents with young children. Courtesy of Pettus Advertising, Inc. Courtesy of The Corpus Christi Convention & Visitors Bureau.

The Hilton Hotels and Resorts' logo is used in their advertising campaigns to increase awareness of the brand. Courtesy of John Bowen.

restaurants touting how he lost weight eating Subway's healthy sandwiches. While he was doing the Subway commercials he was accused and later convicted of child pornography and having sex with a minor.[13] One expert notes, "Ninety-nine percent of celebrities do a strong job for their brand partners."[14] It's important to pick the right celebrity for the brand.

- Symbols, animated animals, and other characters that the brand controls can be a safer way to promote a brand than using living personalities. Qantas Airlines has been successful using a kangaroo and a koala bear as symbols. For decades, McDonald's has effectively used the imaginary Ronald McDonald. Cartoon characters and animals are dependable and unlikely to create negative publicity.

Collecting Feedback

After sending the message, the communicator must research its effect on the target audience. This involves asking the target audience whether they remember the message, how many times they saw it, what points they recall, how they felt about the message, and their past and present attitudes toward the product and company. The communicator would also like to measure behavior resulting from the message: How many people bought a product, talked to others about it, or visited the store.

After not using television advertising for seven years, Sheraton Hotels and Resorts started an aggressive mass-media campaign that included television, radio, and print media. The objective of the ad was to tell travelers about Sheraton's upgraded services and amenities. Sheraton's iconic "S" was featured in its advertisements to reestablish the identity of the icon. A test found that the Sheraton "S" has an unaided recall of 93 percent. It is called unaided recall if there is no prompting with elements of the ads or commercials being examined. With prompting, the results are called aided recall.[15] After the campaign, Web bookings also increased by 20 percent.[16]

Figure 13–4 shows an example of feedback measurement. Looking at hotel brand A, we find that 80 percent of the total market was aware of it, 20 percent of those

Figure 13–4
Feedback measurement for two brands.

who were aware had tried it, but only 20 percent of those who tried it were satisfied. These results suggest that although the communication program created awareness, the product failed to give consumers the satisfaction expected. The company should, therefore, try to improve the product while continuing the successful communication program. With hotel brand B, the situation was different: Only 40 percent of the total market was aware of it. Only 10 percent of those had tried it, and 80 percent of those who tried it were satisfied. In this case, the communication program needed to be stronger to take advantage of the brand's power to create satisfaction.

Setting the Total Promotion Budget and Mix

We have looked at the steps in planning and sending communications to a target audience. But how does the company determine its total promotion budget and the division among the major promotional tools to create the promotion mix? By what process does it blend the tools to create IMC? We now look at these questions.

Setting the Total Promotional Budget

One of the hardest marketing decisions facing companies is how much to spend on promotions. John Wanamaker, the department store magnate, once said, "I know that half of my advertising is wasted, but I don't know which half. I spent $2 million for advertising, and I don't know if that is half enough or twice too much."

How do companies determine their promotion budget? Four common methods are used to set the total budget for advertising: (1) the affordable method, (2) the percentage of sales method, (3) the competitive parity method, and (4) the objective and task method.[17]

Affordable Method

Many companies use the affordable method: They set a promotion budget at what they think the company can afford. One executive explained this method as follows: "Why, it's simple. First, I go upstairs to the controller and ask how much they can afford to give this year. He says a million and a half. Later, the boss comes to me and asks how much should we spend and I say 'Oh, about a million and a half.'"[18]

Unfortunately, this method of setting budgets completely ignores the effect of promotion on sales volume. It leads to an uncertain annual promotion budget, which makes long-range marketing planning difficult. Although the affordable method can result in overspending on advertising, it more often results in underspending.

Percentage of Sales Method

Many companies use the percentage of sales method, setting their promotion budget at a certain percentage of current or forecasted sales, or they budget a percentage of the sales price. Some firms use this method because it is easy. For example, some restaurateurs know that the mean expenditure for promotion for restaurants is 4 percent; therefore, they set their promotion budget at 4 percent.

A number of advantages are claimed for the percentage of sales method. First, using this method means that promotion spending is likely to vary with what the company can "afford." It also helps management think about the relationship between promotion spending, selling price, and profit per unit. Finally, it supposedly creates competitive stability because competing firms tend to spend about the same percentage of their sales on promotion.

However, despite these claimed advantages, the percentage of sales method has little justification. It wrongly views sales as the cause of promotion rather than as the result. The budget is based on availability of funds rather than on opportunities. It may prevent increased spending, which is sometimes needed to turn around falling sales. Because the budget varies with year-to-year sales, long-range planning is difficult. Finally, the method does not provide a basis for choosing a specific percentage, except past actions or what competitors are doing.

Competitive Parity Method

Other companies use the competitive parity method, setting their promotion budgets to match competitors' outlays. They watch competitors' advertising or get industry promotion spending estimates from publications or trade associations and then set their budgets based on the industry average. For example, the advertising expenditure for the average hotel is 1 percent of sales, and the marketing budget is 5 percent. However, for limited-service hotels, the advertising expenditure is 2 percent of sales and the marketing budget.[19]

Two arguments are used to support this method. First, competitors' budgets represent the collective wisdom of the industry. Second, spending what competitors spend helps prevent promotion wars. Unfortunately, neither argument is valid. There are no grounds for believing that competition has a better idea of what a company should be spending on promotion. Companies differ greatly, and each has its own special promotion needs. Furthermore, no evidence indicates that budgets based on competitive parity prevent promotion wars.

Objective and Task Method

The most logical budget setting method is the objective and task method. Using this, marketers develop their promotion budgets by (1) defining specific objectives, (2) determining tasks that must be performed to achieve these objectives, and (3) estimating the costs of performing them. The sum of these costs is the proposed promotional budget.

The objective and task method forces management to spell out its assumptions about the relationship between dollars spent and promotional results. It is also the most difficult method to use because it can be hard to determine which tasks will achieve specific objectives. Management must consider such questions even though they are difficult to answer. With the objective and task method, the company sets its promotion budget based on what it wants to accomplish.

Shaping the Overall Promotion Mix

The concept of IMC suggests that the company must blend the promotion tools carefully into a coordinated *promotion mix*. But how does it determine what mix of promotion tools to use? Companies within the same industry differ greatly in the design of their promotion mixes. We now look at factors that influence the marketer's choice of promotion tools.

The Nature of Each Promotion Tool

Each promotion tool has unique characteristics and costs. Marketers must understand these characteristics in shaping the promotion mix. Often one promotional tool must be used to promote another. Thus, when McDonald's decides to run a million-dollar sweepstakes in its fast-food outlets (a sales promotion), it has to run ads to inform the public. Many factors influence the marketer's choice of promotion tools. Each promotional tool, advertising, personal selling, sales promotion, PR, and direct marketing has unique characteristics and costs. Marketers must understand these characteristics to select their tools correctly.

ADVERTISING. Because of the many forms and uses of advertising, generalizing about its unique qualities as a part of the promotion mix is difficult. Yet, several qualities can be noted. Advertising's public nature suggests that the advertised product is standard and legitimate. Because many people see ads for the product, buyers know that purchasing the product will be publicly understood and accepted. Advertising also allows the seller to repeat a message many times. Large-scale advertising by a seller says something positive about the seller's size, popularity, and success. Advertising can be used to build a long-term image for a product (e.g., Four Seasons or McDonald's ads) and also stimulate quick sales (as when Embassy Suites in Phoenix advertises a promotion for the Fourth of July holiday). Advertising can reach masses of geographically dispersed buyers at a low cost per exposure.

Advertising also has shortcomings. Although it reaches many people quickly, advertising is impersonal and cannot be as persuasive as a company salesperson. Advertising is able to carry on only a one-way communication with the audience, and the audience does not feel it has to pay attention or respond. In addition, advertising can be very costly. Although some forms, such as newspaper and radio advertising, can be done on small budgets, other forms, such as network TV advertising, require very large budgets.

For hotels, restaurants, and other hospitality companies that cater to traveling visitors in private vehicles, the use of advertising in billboards represents the largest expenditure item in their advertising budgets.

The Little America group of hotels has used a theme that all parents recognize with their tired and bored children: "Are we there yet?" In some cases, these hotels also advertise very inexpensive ice cream cones at the next exit, at Little America.

A critical challenge faced by hotel marketers is creating an immediate awareness of brand name to ensure that their properties are included in the traveler's evoked set of lodging choices. The evoked set of brand preferences and the relative impact of advertising and prior stay were investigated in a study of frequent travelers. It was found that chains whose names were well established in the traveler's evoked set most often won the traveler's business. There was little influence on chain name recall of prior stay without ad exposure or influence on ad exposure without prior stay. The combined effect of ad exposure and prior stay was an important influence on brand selection.[20]

PERSONAL SELLING. Personal selling is the most effective tool at certain stages of the buying process, particularly in building buyer preference, conviction, and purchase. Compared with advertising, personal selling has several unique qualities. It involves personal interaction between two or more people, allowing each to observe the other's needs and characteristics and make quick adjustments. Personal selling also lets all kinds of relationships spring up, ranging from a matter-of-fact selling relationship to a deep personal friendship. The effective salesperson keeps the customer's interests at heart to build a long-term relationship. Finally, with personal selling, the buyer usually feels a greater need to listen and respond, even if the response is a polite "no thank you."

These unique qualities come at a cost. A sales force requires a longer-term company commitment than advertising; advertising can be turned on and off, but sales force size is harder to vary. Personal selling is the company's most expensive promotion tool, costing industrial companies an average of $225 per sales call.[21] American firms spend up to three times as much on personal selling as they do on advertising.

Personal selling by members of the hospitality industry is used primarily for large key customers, travel intermediaries, and meeting planners and others with responsibility for group sales.

This restaurant manager is going over banquet menus with a prospective client. A well-managed personal selling program is effective for hotels and restaurants with banquet space. Jacob Lund/Alamy Stock Photo.

SALES PROMOTION. Sales promotion includes an assortment of tools, coupons, contests, cents-off deals, premiums, and others, and these tools have many unique qualities. They attract consumer attention and provide information that may lead the consumer to buy the product. Sales promotions offer strong incentives to purchase by providing inducements or contributions that give additional value to consumers, and they invite and reward quick response. Advertising says "buy our product." Sales promotion says "buy it now."

Companies use sales promotion tools to create a stronger and quicker response. Sales promotion can be used to dramatize product offers and to boost sagging sales. Its effects are usually short lived, however, and are not effective in building long-run brand preference.

PUBLIC RELATIONS. Public relations (PR) offers several advantages. One is believability. News stories, features, and events seem more real and believable to readers than do ads. PR can reach many prospects who avoid salespeople and advertisements. The message gets to the buyers as news rather than as a sales-directed communication. Like advertising, PR can dramatize a company or product.

A relatively new addition to the promotion mix is the infomercial, a hybrid between advertising and PR. Companies provide interesting stories on videotape for use on television during periods of light viewing, such as early morning. Infomercials provide enough information to keep the attention of viewers, combined with a "soft" approach to product or brand advertising.

Hospitality marketers tend to underuse PR or use it only as an afterthought. Yet, a well-thought-out PR campaign used with other promotion mix elements can be very effective and economical.

DIRECT AND DIGITAL MARKETING. Direct and digital marketing connections carefully targeted individual consumers to both obtain an immediate response and cultivate lasting customer relationships: the use of direct mail, the telephone, direct-response television, e-mail, online, mobile and social media, and other tools to communicate directly with specific consumers. Although there are many forms of direct marketing, they all share four distinctive characteristics. Direct marketing is *nonpublic*: The message is normally directed to a specific person. Rather than advertise reduced fares or room rates, airlines and hotels will send a direct marketing message to offering these promotions to their best customers. Direct marketing is *immediate* and *customized*: Messages can be prepared very quickly and can be tailored to appeal to specific consumers. Finally, direct marketing is *interactive*: It allows a dialogue between the marketing team and the consumer, and messages can be altered depending on the consumer's response. Thus, direct marketing is well suited to highly targeted marketing efforts and to building one-to-one customer relationships. Online, mobile, and social media marketing range from nonpublic text messages to Facebook sites and is one of the fastest growing areas of marketing.

Promotion Mix Strategies

Companies consider many factors when developing their promotion mix, including the following: type of product and market, push versus pull strategy, buyer readiness state, and product life-cycle stage.

TYPE OF PRODUCT AND MARKET. The importance of different promotion tools varies among consumers and commercial markets. When hospitality firms market to consumer markets, they spend more on advertising and sales promotion and often very little on personal selling. Hospitality firms targeting commercial organizations spend more on personal selling. In general, personal selling is used more heavily with expensive and risky goods and in markets with fewer and larger sellers. A meeting or convention is customized for the organization putting on the event. It takes a skilled salesperson to put together a package that will give clients what they want at an appropriate price that will provide good revenue for the company.

PUSH VERSUS PULL STRATEGY. The promotional mix is heavily affected by whether a company chooses a push or pull strategy. The two strategies are contrasted in Figure 13–5. A push strategy involves "pushing" the product through distribution channels to final consumers. The manufacturer directs its marketing activities (primarily personal selling and trade promotion) at channel members to induce them to order and carry the product and to promote it to final consumers. For example,

Figure 13-5
Push versus pull promotion strategy.

Push strategy

Producer → [Producer marketing activities (personal selling, trade promotion, other)] → Retailers and wholesalers → [Reseller marketing activities (personal selling, advertising, sales promotion, other)] → Consumers

Pull strategy

Producer ← Demand ← Retailers and wholesalers ← Demand ← Consumers

Producer marketing activities (consumer advertising, sales promotion, other)

Dollar Rent-A-Car offered travel agents a 15 percent commission instead of 10 percent to persuade them to order its brand for clients. Continental Plaza Hotels and Resorts developed a promotion that gave travel agents an extra $10 in addition to their normal commission for bookings. A push strategy provides an incentive for channel members to promote the product to their customers or push the product through the distribution channels.

Using a pull strategy, a company directs its marketing activities (primarily advertising and consumer promotion) toward final consumers to induce them to buy the product. For example, Sheraton placed an ad for its Hawaiian properties in the Phoenix, Arizona, paper. Interested readers were instructed to call their travel planner or Sheraton. If the strategy is effective, consumers will purchase the product from channel members, who will, in turn, order it from producers. Thus, under a pull strategy, consumer demand "pulls" the product through the channels.

BUYER READINESS STATE. Promotional tools vary in their effects at different stages of buyer readiness. Advertising, along with PR, plays a major role in the awareness and knowledge stages, more important than that played by cold calls from salespeople. Customer liking, preferences, and conviction are more affected by personal selling, which is closely followed by advertising. Finally, closing the sale is accomplished primarily with sales calls and sales promotion. Only personal selling, given its high costs, should focus on the later stages of the customer buying process.

PRODUCT LIFE-CYCLE STAGE. The effects of different promotion tools also vary with stages of the product life cycle. In the introduction stage, advertising and PR are good for producing high awareness, and sales promotion is useful in product's early trial. Personal selling must be used to get the trade to carry the product in the growth stage; advertising and PR continue to be powerful while promotion can be reduced because fewer incentives are needed. In the mature stage, sales promotion again becomes important relative to advertising. Buyers know the brands, and advertising is needed only to remind them of the product. In the decline stage, advertising is kept at a reminder level, PR is dropped, and salespeople give the product only a little attention. Sales promotion, however, may continue to be strong.[22]

INTEGRATING THE PROMOTION MIX. Having set the promotion budget and mix, the company must now take steps to see that each promotion mix element is smoothly integrated. Guided by the company's overall communications strategy, the various promotion elements should work together to carry the firm's unique brand messages and selling points. Integrating the promotion mix starts with customers. Whether it's advertising, personal selling, sales promotion, public relations, or digital and direct marketing, communications at each customer touch point must deliver consistent marketing content and positioning. An integrated promotion mix ensures that communications efforts occur when, where, and how *customers* need them.

To achieve an integrated promotion mix, all of the firm's functions must cooperate to jointly plan communications efforts. Many companies even include customers, suppliers, and other stakeholders at various stages of communications planning. Scattered or disjointed promotional activities across the company can result in diluted marketing communications impact and confused positioning. By contrast, an integrated promotion mix maximizes the combined effects of all of the firm's promotional efforts.

Advertising

Advertising Any paid form of nonpersonal presentation and promotion of ideas, goods, or services by an identified sponsor.

The remainder of this chapter examines advertising in more detail. Subsequent chapters deal with personal selling, sales promotion, and direct and digital marketing. We define **advertising** as any paid form of nonpersonal presentation and promotion of ideas, goods, or services by an identified sponsor.

The fast-food industry in the United States has reached the mature stage, and fast-food companies are fighting for market share. McDonald's, Yum Brands, Burger King, and Wendy's are stepping up their campaigns and trying to take market share from each other. Marketing wars such as the burger wars and pizza wars are fought with advertising dollars. Marketing wars break out in mature markets where growth of the market is slow. To increase their sales, companies must try to steal market share from their competitors.

Advertising is a good way to inform and persuade, whether the purpose is to sell Hilton Hotels around the world or to get residents of Kuala Lumpur, the capital of Malaysia, to stay at a nearby resort on the island of Langkawi. Organizations have different ways of managing their advertising. The owner or the general manager of an independent restaurant usually handles the restaurant's advertising. Most hotel chains give responsibility for local advertising to the individual hotels, whereas corporate management is responsible for national and international advertising. In some corporate offices, the director of marketing handles advertising. Other firms might have advertising departments to set the advertising budget, work with an outside advertising agency, and handle direct-mail advertising and other advertising not done by the agency. Large companies commonly use an outside advertising agency because it offers several advantages.

Major Decisions in Advertising

Marketing management must make five important decisions in developing an advertising program. These decisions are listed in Figure 13–6 and discussed next.

Figure 13–6
Major advertising decisions.

Objectives setting
Communication objectives
Sales objectives

Budget decisions
Affordable approach
Percentage of sales
Competitive parity
Objective and task

Message decisions
Message generation
Message evaluation and selection
Message execution

Media decision
Reach, frequency, impact
Major media types
Specific media vehicles
Media timing

Campaign evaluation
Communication impact
Sales impact

Setting the Objectives

The first step in developing an advertising program is to set advertising objectives, which should be based on information about the target market, positioning, and marketing mix. Marketing positioning and mix strategies define the role that advertising must perform in the total marketing program.

An advertising objective is a specific communication task to be accomplished with a specific target audience during a specific period of time. Advertising objectives can be classified by their aim: to *inform*, *persuade*, or *remind*. **Informative advertising** is used heavily when introducing a new product category and when the objective is to build primary demand. When an airline opens a new route, its management often runs full-page advertisements informing the market about the new service. Junior's Deli, in the Westwood section of Los Angeles, uses direct-mail campaigns to create new customers. New residents in the neighborhood receive a gift certificate for a Deli Survival Kit, which contains a chunk of beef salami, two types of cheese, a loaf of fresh rye bread, and a home-baked dessert. The kit is absolutely free, with no purchase required, but the certificate must be redeemed at the restaurant. More than a 1,000 new neighbors come in to claim their kits each year. Thus, the kit not only informs potential customers about the restaurant but also results in visits to the restaurant by customers who sample its products.[23]

Persuasive advertising becomes more important as competition increases and a company's objective becomes building selective demand. Some persuasive advertising has become comparison advertising, which compares one brand directly or indirectly with one or more other brands. For example, Dunkin' Donuts ran a TV and Web campaign comparing the chain's coffee to Starbucks's brews. "In a recent national blind taste test," proclaimed the ads, "more Americans preferred the taste of Dunkin' Donuts coffee over Starbucks. It's just more proof it's all about the coffee (not the couches or music)." "Try the coffee that won," the ads concluded.

Advertising is not a substitute for poor products. For an advertising campaign to create long-term sales, the product advertised must create satisfied customers. One mistake frequently made by the owners of new restaurants is advertising before the operation has gone through a shakedown period. Eager to get a return on their investment, the owners advertise before the restaurant's staff is properly trained and the restaurant's systems are tested under high-demand situations.

Because most people look forward to trying a new restaurant, advertising campaigns are usually effective, resulting in waits during peak periods. However, success can be short-lived when restaurateurs deliver poor-quality food, poor service, or poor value. Dissatisfied customers quickly spread negative word of mouth to potential customers, who are eager to find out about the new restaurant. Frequently, advertising a noncompetitive product quickens the product's death through negative word. The owner of a restaurant in Houston who went through this experience and ultimately went out of business blamed his loss on fickle customers. In his words, "The restaurant used to have waits every night of the week. Now, the restaurant is empty. I can't believe how fickle customers are." The customers weren't fickle; in fact, they knew exactly what they wanted: good food and good service. These were things the restaurant did not offer.

The president of a hospitality marketing, advertising, and PR firm believes that the implementation of an effective advertising campaign is one of the fastest ways to jeopardize the performance of a mediocre property. You must first be sure the property can live up to the promises your advertising makes. If your property or service is inconsistent with the claims made, the money you spend to generate additional business will probably do little more than increase the number of dissatisfied guests.[24]

Even highly satisfied customers need frequent reminders. Ski and scuba-diving resorts share a common problem. Satisfied guests often fail to return because they wish to experience new slopes and new dive areas. Years may pass before the guest is ready to return. Reminder advertising may shorten that period of time.

The goal of advertising is to help move consumers through the buying process. Some advertising is designed to move people to immediate action. For example, a direct mail promotional piece from a cruise line may feature specials that will expire in a few weeks. However, many ads focus on building or

Informative advertising
Advertising used to inform consumers about a new product or feature to build primary demand.

Table 13–1
Possible Advertising Objectives

Informative Advertising	
Communicating customer value	Suggesting new uses for a product
Building a brand and company image	Informing the market of a price change
Telling the market about a new product	Describing available services and support
Explaining how a product works	Correcting false impressions

Persuasive Advertising	
Building brand preference	Persuading customers to purchase now
Encouraging switching to a brand	Creating customer engagement
Changing customer perceptions of product value	Building brand community

Reminder Advertising	
Maintaining customer relationships	Reminding consumers where to buy the product
Reminding consumers that the product may be needed in the near future	Keeping the brand in a customer's mind during off-seasons

strengthening long-term customer relationships. For example, an airline may feature an ad showing how it is upgrading its airport lounges, giving its current customers another reason why they should continue to fly with the airline. Possible advertising objectives with examples for each objective are presented in Table 13–1.

Setting the Advertising Budget

After determining advertising objectives, a company can establish an advertising budget for each product. The role of advertising is to affect demand for a product. The company wants to spend the amount needed to achieve the sales goal. Four commonly used methods for setting the promotional budget were discussed earlier in this chapter. These methods—the affordable method, the percentage of sales method, the competitive parity method, and the objective and task method—are also often used when determining the advertising budget. The advertising budget also has some specific factors that should be considered when setting a budget:

- *Stage in the product life cycle.* New products typically need large advertising budgets to build awareness and gain consumer trial. Mature brands usually require lower budgets as a ratio to sales. For example, a casual neighborhood restaurant may want to budget heavily for advertising in its first year of operation and less per month after its first year. By the end of the first year, it should have established a clientele. After this point, it will need to maintain its existing customers and gain new customers (albeit at a lower rate than the first year). Its loyal customers should be spreading positive word of mouth by the end of the first year.

- *Competition and clutter.* In a market with many competitors and heavy advertising support, a brand must be advertised more frequently to be heard above the noise of the market.

- *Product differentiation.* A brand that closely resembles others in its product class (pizza, limited-service hotels, air travel) requires heavy advertising to set it apart. When a product differs greatly from those of competitors, advertising can be used to communicate differences to consumers.

No matter what method is used, setting the advertising budget is no easy task. How does a company know if it is spending the right amount? Larger companies have built sophisticated statistical models to determine the relationship between promotional spending and brand sales and to help determine the "optimal investment" across various media. Still, because so many factors affect advertising effectiveness, some controllable and others not, measuring the results of advertising spending remains an inexact science. In most cases, managers must rely on large doses of judgment along with more quantitative analysis when setting advertising budgets.

As a result of such thinking, advertising is one of the easiest budget items to cut when economic times get tough. Cuts in brand-building advertising appear to do little short-term harm to sales. In the long run, however, slashing ad spending may cause long-term damage to a brand's image and market share. In fact, companies that can maintain or even increase their advertising spending while competitors are decreasing theirs can gain competitive advantage.

Developing Advertising Strategy

Advertising strategy consists of two major elements: creating advertising messages and selecting advertising media. In the past, companies often viewed media planning as secondary to the message-creation process. The creative department first created good advertisements, and then the media department selected and purchased the best media for carrying those advertisements to desired target audiences. This often caused friction between creatives and media planners.

Today, however, soaring media costs, more-focused target marketing strategies, and the blizzard of new online, mobile, and social media have promoted the importance of the media-planning function. The decision about which media to use for an ad campaign—television, newspapers, magazines, video, a Web site, social media, mobile devices, or e-mail—is now sometimes more critical than the creative elements of the campaign. Also, brand content is now often co-created through interactions with and among consumers. As a result, more and more advertisers are orchestrating a closer harmony between their messages and the media that deliver them. As discussed in the previous chapter, the goal is to create and manage brand content across a full range of media, whether they are paid, owned, earned, or shared.

Creating the Advertising Message

Today, the average U.S. household receives about 190 TV channels and consumers have more than 7,200 magazines from which to choose.[25] Add in the countless radio stations and a continuous barrage of catalogs, direct mail, out-of-home media, e-mail, and online, mobile, and social media exposures, and consumers are being bombarded with ads and brand content at home, work, and all points in between. For example, Americans are exposed to a cumulative 5.3 trillion online ad impressions each year and a daily diet of 500 million tweets, 4 billion YouTube videos, 58 million photos shared on Instagram, 5 million article pins on Pinterest, and 4.75 billion pieces of shared content on Facebook.[26]

BREAKING THROUGH THE CLUTTER. If all this advertising clutter bothers some consumers, it also causes huge headaches for advertisers. Take the situation facing network television advertisers. They pay an average of $342,000 to make a single 30-second commercial. Then, each time they show it, they pay an average of $112,000 for 30 seconds of advertising time during a popular prime-time program. They pay even more if it's an especially popular program, such as *Sunday Night Football* ($803,000), *Empire* ($497,00), *The Big Bang Theory* ($348,000), or a mega-event such as the *Super Bowl* (averaging $5 million per 30 seconds!).[27] Then their ads are sandwiched in with a clutter of other commercials, announcements, and network promotions, totaling nearly 20 minutes of nonprogram material per prime-time hour, with commercial breaks coming every six minutes on average. Such clutter in television and other ad media has created an increasingly hostile advertising environment. According to one recent study, more than 70 percent of Americans think there are too many ads on TV, and 62 percent of national advertisers believe that TV ads have become less effective, citing clutter as the main culprit.[28]

It used to be that television viewers were pretty much a captive audience for advertisers. But today's digital wizardry has given viewers a rich new set of information and entertainment options—the internet, videostreaming, social and mobile media, tablets and smartphones, and others. Digital technology has also armed consumers with an arsenal of technologies for choosing what they watch or don't watch and when. Increasingly, thanks to the growth of DVR systems and digital streaming, consumers are choosing not to watch ads.

Thus, advertisers can no longer force-feed the same old cookie-cutter ad messages to captive consumers through traditional media. Just to gain and hold attention, today's advertising messages must be better planned, more imaginative, more entertaining, and more emotionally engaging. Simply interrupting or disrupting consumers no longer works. Instead, unless ads provide information that is interesting, useful, or entertaining, many consumers will simply skip them.

MERGING ADVERTISING AND ENTERTAINMENT. To break through the clutter, many marketers have subscribed to a new merging of advertising and entertainment, dubbed "Madison & Vine." You've probably heard of Madison Avenue, the New York City street that houses the headquarters of many of the nation's largest advertising agencies. You may also have heard of Hollywood & Vine, the intersection of Hollywood Avenue and Vine Street in Hollywood, California, long the symbolic heart of the U.S. entertainment industry. Now, Madison Avenue and Hollywood & Vine have come together to form a new intersection—Madison & Vine—that represents the merging of advertising and entertainment in an effort to create new avenues for reaching consumers with more engaging messages.

This merging of advertising and entertainment takes one of two forms: advertainment or branded entertainment. The aim of advertainment is to make ads themselves so entertaining, or so useful, that people want to watch them. There's no chance that you'd watch ads on purpose, would you? Think again. For example, the Super Bowl has become an annual advertisement showcase. Tens of millions of people tune in to the Super Bowl each year, as much to watch the entertaining ads as to see the game. And ads posted online before and after the big game draw tens of millions of views.

These days, it's not unusual to see an entertaining ad or other brand content on YouTube before you see it on TV. And you might well seek it out at a friend's suggestion rather than having it forced on you by the advertiser. Moreover, beyond making their regular ads more engaging, advertisers are also creating new content forms that look less like ads and more like short films or shows. A range of new brand messaging platforms, from Webisodes and blogs to online videos and apps, now blur the line between ads and entertainment.

For example, The Palm Restaurant created a series of Webisodes, which were promoted on its Web site, Facebook page, and were available through YouTube. These Webisodes were also promoted to the 100,000 members of the Palm's Loyalty program, 837 Club. The Webisodes featured "Chef Bruce," Bruce Bozzi, EVP of The Palms, and great grandson of the cofounder of the Palms, in a series of cooking demonstrations.[29] One of the most successful uses of Webisodes is McDonald's "Our Food, Your Questions," series. The series features Grant Imahara, who portrays an investigative reporter asking questions about McDonald's food and going to the food production facilities. The videos promote the quality of the production facility as well as the food ingredients that go into McDonald's products. The videos are promoted on the Web site and available on YouTube. Many of the videos have over a million views with some videos approaching 10 million views.

Dunkin' developed an integrated marketing program with the popular television show America's Got Talent. The elements of sponsorship included using Facebook, Snapchat, product placement on the show including Dunkin' cups which where prominently displayed on the judges table, a Dunkin's Lounge where interviews were held with the contestants and a Dunkin's save which allowed viewers to vote for their favorite contestant and keep them from being eliminated.[30]

So, Madison & Vine is now the meeting place for the advertising and entertainment industries. The goal is for brand messages and content to become a part of the entertainment rather than interrupting it. As advertising agency JWT puts it, "We believe advertising needs to stop interrupting what people are interested in and be what people are interested in. However, advertisers must be careful that the new intersection itself doesn't become too congested. With all the new ad formats and product placements, Madison & Vine threatens to create even more of the very clutter that it was designed to break through. At that point consumers might decide to take yet a different route."

MESSAGE STRATEGY. The first step in creating effective advertising messages is to plan a message strategy—the general message that will be communicated to consumers. The purpose of advertising is to get consumers to think about or react to the product or company in a certain way. People will react only if they believe they will benefit from doing so. Thus, developing an effective message strategy begins with identifying customer benefits that can be used as advertising appeals.

Ideally, the message strategy will follow directly from the company's broader positioning and customer value strategies. Message strategy statements tend to be plain, straightforward outlines of benefits and positioning points that the advertiser wants to stress. The advertiser must next develop a compelling creative concept—or "big idea"—that will bring the message strategy to life in a distinctive and memorable way. At this stage, simple message ideas become great ad campaigns. Usually, a copywriter and an art director will team up to generate many creative concepts, hoping that one of these concepts will turn out to be the big idea.

The creative concept may emerge as a visualization, a phrase, or a combination of the two. The creative concept will guide the choice of specific appeals to be used in an advertising campaign. Advertising appeals should have three characteristics. First, they should be meaningful, pointing out benefits that make the product more desirable or interesting to consumers. Second, appeals must be believable. Consumers must believe that the product or service will deliver the promised benefits. However, the most meaningful and believable benefits may not be the best ones to feature. Appeals should also be distinctive. They should tell how the product is better than competing brands.

MESSAGE EXECUTION. The impact of the message depends on what is said and how it is said: message execution. The advertiser has to put the message across in a way that wins the target market's attention and interest. Advertisers usually begin with a statement of the objective and approach of the desired ad.

The advertising agency's creative staff must find a style, tone, words, and format for executing the message. Any message can be presented in different execution styles, such as the following:

1. **Slice of life** shows one or more people using the product in a normal setting. Restaurants may show friends and family enjoying an evening together at their restaurant.

2. **Lifestyle** shows how a product fits with a lifestyle. For example, an airline advertising its business class featured a businessperson sitting in an upholstered chair in her living room, having a drink, and reading a book. The other side of the ad featured the same person in the same relaxed position with a drink and a book in one of the airline's business-class seats.

3. **Fantasy** creates a wonder world around the product or its use. For instance, Cunard's *Sea Goddess* featured a woman lying in a raft in the sea, with the luxury liner anchored in the background. A cocktail server in a tuxedo is walking through the ocean carrying a drink for the woman.

4. **Personality** symbol creates a character that represents the product. The character might be created by the company; for example, Jack in The Box

Restaurants uses the character Jack, a business person with a clown head, as their spokesperson.

5. **Technical expertise** shows the company's expertise with the product. Trivago claims to be able to find great hotel prices for its users.

The advertiser must choose a tone for the ad. Hyatt uses a positive tone, with ads that say something very positive about its own products. Hyatt ads avoid humor that might take attention away from the message or be misunderstood by its many international guests. By contrast, Taco Bell ads have used humor. To promote their new breakfast offering, they recruited and paid 20 people named Ronald McDonald. The Ronald McDonalds appeared in television ads and on YouTube. Taco Bell did include a disclaimer saying the Ronald McDonalds were not affiliated with McDonald's restaurants, but added "but man, they sure did love it."[31]

Finally, format elements make a difference in an ad's impact and cost. A small change in design can make a big difference in an ad's effect. The illustration is the first thing the reader notices. It must be strong enough to draw attention. Then the headline must effectively entice the right people to read the copy. The copy, the main block of text in the ad, must be simple but strong and convincing. These three elements must effectively work together. Even then, a truly outstanding ad is noted by less than 50 percent of the exposed audience. An even smaller percentage, about 30 percent, can recall the main point of the headline. Only 25 percent will remember the advertiser's name, and fewer than 10 percent read most of the body copy. Less-than-outstanding ads do not even achieve these results.

The Red Mountain resort shows what people come to a resort for in its ad: relaxation and rejuvenation. Courtesy of Red Mountain Resort.

CONSUMER-GENERATED MESSAGES. Taking advantage of today's interactive technologies, many companies are now tapping consumers for message ideas or actual ads. They are searching existing video sites, setting up their own sites, and sponsoring ad-creation contests and other promotions. Sometimes the results are outstanding; sometimes they are forgettable. If done well, however, user-generated content can incorporate the voice of the customer into brand messages and generate greater consumer brand involvement.

Many brands develop brand Web sites or hold contests that invite consumers to submit ad message ideas and videos. Not all consumer-generated advertising efforts, however, are successful. As many big companies have learned, ads made by amateurs can be well, pretty amateurish. Done well, however, consumer-generated advertising efforts can produce new creative ideas and fresh perspectives on the brand from consumers who actually experience it. Such campaigns can boost consumer involvement and get consumers talking and thinking about a brand and its value to them.[32]

Selecting Advertising Media

The major steps in media selection are (1) deciding on reach, frequency, and impact; (2) choosing among major media types; (3) selecting specific media vehicles; and (4) deciding on media timing.

DECIDING ON REACH, FREQUENCY, AND IMPACT. To select media, the advertiser must decide what reach and frequency are needed to achieve advertising objectives. Reach is a measure of the percentage of people in the target market who are exposed to the ad campaign during a given period of time. For example, the advertiser might try to reach 70 percent of the target market during the first year. Frequency is a measure of how many times the average person in the target market is exposed to the message. For example, the advertiser might want an average exposure frequency of three. The advertiser must also decide on desired media impact, the qualitative value of message exposure through a given medium. For products that must be demonstrated, television messages using sight and sound are more effective. The same message in one magazine (*Newsweek*) may be more believable than in another (*National Enquirer*).

Suppose that the advertiser's product has the potential to appeal to a market of 1 million consumers. The goal is to reach 700,000 consumers (70 percent of 1 million). Because the average consumer will receive three exposures, 2.1 million exposures (700,000 × 3) must be bought. If the advertiser wants exposures of 1.5 impact (assuming that 1.0 impact is the average), a rated number of exposures of 3.15 million (2.1 million × 1.5) must be bought. If 1,000 exposures with this impact cost $10, the advertising budget must be $31,500 (3,150 × 10). In general, the more reach, frequency, and impact that the advertiser seeks, the larger the advertising budget has to be.

Gross rating points (*GRPs*) show the gross coverage or duplicated coverage of an advertising campaign. GRPs are determined by multiplying reach times frequency. In the preceding example, an ad with a reach of 700,000 and frequency of three exposures would produce 210 GRPs if the market was 1 million. Each GRP is equal to 1 percent of the market.

Waste is the part of the medium's audience not in the firm's target market.[33] An entrepreneur owning a single restaurant in Worthington, Ohio (north of Columbus), will find that only about 20 percent of those reading the *Columbus Dispatch* will be in that entrepreneur's market area. Thus, he or she will probably advertise in other media. A travel agency may advertise in a newspaper targeted at seniors knowing that only 50 percent of the readers will spend more than $1,000 on travel annually. The travel agency factored this in when they purchased the media. Despite the waste, the medium still offered a good value. In choosing media, the circulation aimed at your target market is the important factor, not the total circulation.

CHOOSING AMONG MAJOR MEDIA TYPES. The media planner has to know the reach, frequency, and impact of each major media type. Table 13–2 summarizes the major advertising media. The major media types, in order of advertising volume, are newspapers, television, direct mail, radio, magazine, and outdoor. Each medium has advantages and limitations. For example, more than 75 percent of Holiday Inn Express guests arrive by car. Jennifer Ziegler, director of marketing for Holiday Inn Express, said, "Billboards serve as a reinforcement. They create top-of-mind awareness that make a difference when last-minute decisions about lodging are being made."[34]

Media planners consider many factors when making their media choices, including the media habits of target consumers. The nature of the product also affects media choices. Resorts are best shown in color magazines. Fast-food ads targeted at young children are best on television. Different types of messages may require different media. A message announcing a Mother's Day buffet would be conveyed effectively on radio or in newspapers. A message that contains technical data, such as an ad explaining the details of a travel package, might be disseminated most effectively in magazines or through direct mail. Cost is also a major factor in media choice. Television is very expensive; newspaper advertising costs much less. The media planner looks at both the total cost of using a particular medium and at the cost per 1,000 exposures, that is, the cost of reaching a 1,000 people.

Ideas about media impact and cost must be reexamined regularly. For many years, television and magazines dominated the media mixes of national advertisers while other media were neglected. Recently, costs and clutter (competition

Table 13–2
Profiles of Major Media Types

Medium	Advantages	Limitations
Newspapers	Flexibility; timeliness; good local market coverage; broad acceptance; high believability	Short lift; poor reproduction quality; small pass-along audience
Television	Combines sight, sound, and motion; appealing to the senses; high attention; high reach; appeals to the senses	High absolute cost; high clutter; fleeting exposure; less audience selectivity
Direct mail	High audience selectivity; flexibility; no ad competition within the same medium; personalization	Relatively high cost; junk mail image
Radio	Good local acceptance; high geographic and demographic selectivity; low cost	Audio only; lower attention ("the half-heard" medium) fragmented audiences, music stations being replaced by personal devices
Magazines	High geographic and demographic selectivity; credibility and prestige; high-quality reproduction; long life; good pass-along readership	Long ad purchase lead time; some waste circulation; no guarantee of position
Outdoor	Flexibility; high repeat exposure; low cost; low message competition	Little audience selectivity; creative limitations
Digital and social media	Audience selectivity; low cost; personalization; immediacy; interactive capabilities; user generated content can have high credibility	Potentially low impact; high audience control of content and exposure

from competing messages) have increased, and audiences have dropped. As a result, many marketers have adopted strategies targeted at narrower segments, and TV and magazine advertising revenues have leveled off or declined. Advertisers have increasingly turned to alternative media, including cable TV, outdoor advertising, specialty advertising, and internet advertising. Given these and other media characteristics, the media planner must decide how much of each type of media to buy.

SELECTING SPECIFIC MEDIA VEHICLES. The media planner must now choose the best specific media vehicles within each general media type. A comparison of the top television shows in the United States with younger (ages 18 to 34) and older audiences (age 35 to 54) showed that there were no shows that appeared on the top 10 list for both groups. Each group had a unique set. Thus, advertising must know the favorite media of its target market. Magazine vehicles include *Newsweek*, *Conde Nast Traveler*, *The New Yorker*, and *Town and Country*. If advertising is placed in magazines, the media planner must look up circulation figures and the costs of different ad sizes, color options, ad positions, and frequencies for various specific magazines. The planner then evaluates each magazine on such factors as credibility, status, reproduction quality, editorial focus, and advertising submission deadlines. The media planner decides which vehicles give the best reach, frequency, and impact for the money.

Media planners also compute the cost per thousand persons reached by a vehicle. If a full-page, four-color advertisement in the U.S. national edition of *Forbes* costs $163,000 and *Forbes*'s readership is 900,000 people, the cost of reaching a 1,000 persons is $181. The same advertisement in *Bloomberg Businessweek* may cost only $48,100 but reach only 155,000 persons, at a cost per 1,000 of about $310.[35] The media planner would favor magazines with the lower cost per 1,000 for reaching target consumers. In addition to the cost of the ad, the costs of producing ads for different media must also be considered. Although newspaper ads can cost very little to produce, flashy television ads may cost millions.

The media planner must thus balance media cost measures against several media impact factors. First, costs should be balanced against the media vehicle's audience quality. For a corporate hotel brand, business magazine would have high exposure to audience that use their product, whereas *People* magazine would have a low-exposure value. Second, the media planner should consider audience attention. Readers of *Vogue*, for example, typically pay more attention to ads than do readers of *Newsweek*. Third, the planner assesses the vehicle's editorial quality; *Time* and the *Wall Street Journal* are more believable and prestigious than the *National Enquirer*.

Media planners are increasingly developing more sophisticated measures of effectiveness and using them in mathematical models to arrive at the best media mix. Many advertising agencies use computer programs to select the initial media and then make further media schedule improvements based on subjective factors not considered by the media section model.[36]

DECIDING ON MEDIA TIMING. The advertiser must also decide how to schedule advertising over the course of a year. For a hotel or resort, effective advertising requires knowledge of the origin of its guests and how far in advance they make their reservations. If guests living in Connecticut make their reservations in November to go to a Caribbean resort in January, it will not be effective for a resort to advertise in December after consumers have already made their vacation plans. Mauritius launched a major campaign in the United Kingdom in October to create demand for the December holiday season.[37] Restaurants with a strong local demand may decide to vary their advertising to follow the seasonal pattern, to oppose the seasonal pattern, or to be the same all year. Most firms do some seasonal advertising.

Finally, the advertiser must choose the pattern of the ads. **Continuity** means scheduling ads evenly within a given period. **Pulsing** means scheduling ads unevenly over a given period. Thus, 52 ads could either be scheduled at one per week during the year or pulsed in several bursts. Those who favor pulsing feel that the audience will learn the message more completely and that money can be saved. However, some media planners believe that although pulsing achieves awareness, it sacrifices depth of advertising communications.

Evaluating Advertising Effectiveness and the Return on Advertising Investment

Measuring the communication effect reveals whether an ad is communicating well. Called **copy testing**, this process can be performed before or after an ad is printed or broadcast. There are three major methods of advertising pretesting. The first is **direct rating**, in which the advertiser exposes a consumer panel to alternative ads and asks them to rate the ads. Direct ratings show how well the ads attract attention and how they affect consumers. Although it is an imperfect measure of an ad's actual impact, a high rating indicates a potentially effective ad. In **portfolio tests**, consumers view or listen to a portfolio of advertisements, taking as much time as they need. The interviewer then asks the respondent to recall all the ads and their contents. The recall can be either aided or unaided by the interviewer. Recall level indicates the extent to which an ad stands out and how well its message is understood and remembered. **Laboratory tests** use equipment to measure consumers' physiological reactions to an ad: heartbeat, blood pressure, pupil dilation, and perspiration. The tests measure an ad's attention-getting power but reveal little about its impact on beliefs, attitudes, or intentions.

There are two popular methods of posttesting ads. Using **recall tests**, the advertiser asks people who have been exposed to magazines or television programs to recall everything they can about the brands and products that they saw. Recall scores indicate the ad's power to be noticed and retained. In **recognition tests**, the researcher asks readers of, for instance, a given issue of a magazine to point out what they have seen. Recognition scores can be used to assess the ad's impact in different market segments and to compare the company's ads with those of competitors.

Continuity Scheduling ads evenly within a given period.

Pulsing Scheduling ads unevenly over a given period.

Copy testing A process performed before or after an ad is printed or broadcast.

Direct rating The advertiser exposes a consumer panel to alternative ads and asks them to rate the ads.

Portfolio tests Consumers view or listen to a portfolio of advertisements, taking as much time as they need.

Laboratory test This test uses equipment to measure consumers' physiological reactions to an ad: heartbeat, blood pressure, pupil dilation, and perspiration.

Recall tests The advertiser asks people who have been exposed to magazines or television programs to recall everything they can about the advertisers and products that they saw.

Recognition tests The researcher asks readers of, for instance, a given issue of a magazine to point out what they have seen.

MEASURING THE SALES EFFECT. What quantity of sales is caused by an ad that increases brand awareness by 20 percent and brand preference by 10 percent? The sales effect of advertising is often harder to measure than the communication effect. Sales are affected by many factors besides advertising, such as product features, price, and availability. One way to measure sales effect is to compare past sales with past advertising expenditures. Another is through experiments.

MEASURING THE AWARENESS EFFECT. If the objective of the advertising is to inform, then conducting a pretest and a posttest of the target markets' awareness of the product or brand is often used as a method of measuring the effect of an advertising campaign. For example, in Figure 13–4, we saw that 60 percent of the market is not aware of the product of brand B. The objectives of brand B's advertising campaign are to increase awareness to 50 percent and increase trail from 30 to 50 percent of those who were aware of brand B. By replicating the research that produced the data for Figure 13–4, they could see if the campaign met its goals.

To spend a large advertising budget wisely, advertisers must define their advertising objectives, develop a sound budget, create a good message, make media decisions, and evaluate the results.

International Advertising Decisions

International advertisers face many complexities not encountered by domestic advertisers. The most basic issue concerns the degree to which global advertising should be adapted to the unique characteristics of various country markets. Some advertisers have attempted to support their global brands with highly standardized worldwide advertising, with campaigns that work as well in Bangkok as they do in Baltimore. For example, McDonald's unifies its creative elements and brand presentation under the familiar "'m lovin' it" theme in all its 100-plus markets worldwide. In recent years, the increased popularity of online marketing and social media sharing has boosted the need for advertising standardization for global brands. Most big marketing and advertising campaigns include a large online presence. Connected consumers can now zip easily across borders via the internet and social media, making it difficult for advertisers to roll out adapted campaigns in a controlled, orderly fashion. As a result, at the very least, most global consumer brands coordinate their digital sites internationally. For example, Coca-Cola Web and social media sites around the world, from Australia and Argentina to France, Romania, and Russia, are surprisingly uniform. All feature splashes of familiar Coke red, iconic Coke bottle shapes, and Coca-Cola's music and "Taste the Feeling" themes.

Standardization produces many benefits—lower advertising costs, greater global advertising coordination, and a more consistent worldwide image. But it also has drawbacks. Most importantly, it ignores the fact that country markets differ greatly in their cultures, demographics, and economic conditions. Thus, most international advertisers "think globally but act locally." They develop global advertising strategies that make their worldwide efforts more efficient and consistent. Then they adapt their advertising programs to make them more responsive to consumer needs and expectations within local markets.

Global advertisers face several special problems. For instance, advertising media costs and availability differ vastly from country to country. Countries also differ in the extent to which they regulate advertising practices. Many countries have extensive systems of laws restricting how much a company can spend on advertising, the media used, the nature of advertising claims, and other aspects of the advertising program. Such restrictions often require advertisers to adapt their campaigns from country to country. Thus, although advertisers may develop global strategies to guide their overall advertising efforts, specific advertising programs must usually be adapted to meet local cultures and customs, media characteristics, and regulations.

CHAPTER REVIEW

I. Promotion Mix
A company's total promotion mix consists of the specific blend of advertising, public relations, personal selling, sales promotion, and direct-marketing tools that the company uses to communicate customer value and build customer relationships persuasively.

II. Integrated Marketing Communications
The company carefully integrates its many communication channels to deliver a clear, consistent, and compelling message about the organization and its brands.
  A. The new marketing communications model. The digital age has spawned new information and communication tools. Customers are changing. Communication through mobile and social media are becoming more important. Marketers are shifting away from mass marketing to targeted communication. Content marketing involves creating inspiring and sharing brand messages and conversations with and among consumers across a fluid mix of paid, owned, earned, and shared channels.
  B. The need for integrated marketing communications. The explosion of online, mobile, and social media marketing presents opportunities and challenges. Most companies practice integrated marketing communications which involves the careful integration of all communication channels to deliver a clear, consistent, and compelling message about the organization and its brands. Some companies have appointed a marketing communications director who has overall responsibility for the company's communication's efforts to foster consistency and sales impact.

III. Developing Effective Marketing Communication
  A. A view of the communications process. Marketers are moving toward viewing communications as managing ongoing customer engagement and relationships with the company and its brands. Communications programs need to be developed for specific segments, niches, and even individuals. The communications process should start with an audit of all the potential touch points that target customers may have with the company and its brands. For a message to be effective, the sender's encoding process must mesh with the receiver's decoding process. The best messages consist of words and other symbols that are familiar to the receiver. The more the sender's field of experience overlaps with that of the receiver, the more effective the message is likely to be. Senders need to know what audiences they wish to reach and what responses they want. They must be good at encoding messages that take into account how the target audience decodes them. They must send messages through media that reach target audiences, and they must develop feedback channels so that they can assess an audience's response to the message.

IV. Steps in Developing Effective Communications
  A. Identifying the target audience. A marketing communicator starts with a clear target audience in mind.
  B. Determining the communication objective. The marketing communicator must decide what response is sought and needs to know where the target audience stands in relation to the product and to what state it needs to be moved. The six buyer readiness states are awareness, knowledge, liking, preference, conviction, and purchase.
  C. Designing the message. The message should get attention, hold interest, arouse desire, and obtain action (AIDA). When putting the message together, the marketing communicator must solve three problems: what to say (message content), how to say it logically (message structure), and how to say it symbolically (message format).
   1. **Message content.** The three types of appeals are rational, emotional, and moral.
   2. **Message structure** decisions involve whether to draw a conclusion or leave it to the audience, whether to present a one- or two-sided argument, and whether to present the strongest argument first or last.
   3. **Message format.** In a print ad, the communicator has to decide on the headline, copy, illustration, and color. To attract attention, advertisers can use novelty and contrast, eye-catching pictures and headlines, distinctive formats, message size, position, color, shape, and movement. If the message is to be carried over the radio, the communicator has to choose words, sounds, and voices. If the message is to be carried on television or in person, all these elements, plus body language, must be planned. Presenters plan their facial expressions, gestures, dress, posture, and hairstyle. If the message is carried on the product or its package, the communicator has to watch texture, scent, color, size, and shape.
  D. Selecting the communication channels
   1. **Personal communication channels.** Used for products that are expensive and complex. It can create opinion leaders to influence others to buy.
   2. **Nonpersonal communication channels.** Include media (print, broadcast, and display media), atmospheres, and events.
  E. Selecting the message source. The message's impact on the audience is also affected by how the audience views the sender. Messages delivered by highly credible sources are persuasive. The three factors most often found to make a source credible are expertise, trustworthiness, and likability.
  F. Collecting feedback. After sending the message, the communicator must research its effect on the target audience. This involves asking the target audience whether they remember the message, how many times they saw it, what points they recall,

how they felt about the message, and their past and present attitudes toward the product and company. The communicator would also like to measure behavior resulting from the message: How many people bought a product, talked to others about it, or visited the store.

V. Setting the Total Promotion Budget and Mix
A. Setting the total promotional budget
1. **Affordable method.** A budget is set based on what management thinks it can afford.
2. **Percentage of sales method.** Companies set promotion budget at a certain percentage of current or forecasted sales or a percentage of the sales price.
3. **Competitive parity method.** Companies set their promotion budgets to match competitors.
4. **Objective and task method.** Companies develop their promotion budget by defining specific objectives, determining the tasks that must be performed to achieve these objectives, and estimating the costs of performing them.

B. Shaping the overall promotion mix
1. **The nature of each promotion tool.** Advertising suggests that the advertised product is standard and legitimate; it is used to build a long-term image for a product and to stimulate quick sales. However, it is also considered impersonal one-way communication. Personal selling builds personal relationships, keeps the customers' interests at heart to build long-term relationships, and allows personal interactions with customers. It is also considered the most expensive promotion tool per contact. Sales promotion includes an assortment of tools: coupons, contests, cents-off deals, premiums, and others. It attracts consumer attention and provides information. It creates a stronger and quicker response. It dramatizes product offers and boosts sagging sales. It is also considered short-lived. Public relations has believability. It reaches prospective buyers and dramatizes a company or product. Direct and digital marketing are more targeted, immediate, and personalized. It includes direct mail, mobile, and social media.
2. **Promotion mix strategies.** Companies consider many factors when developing their promotion mix, including these: type of product and market, push versus pull strategy, buyer readiness state, and product life-cycle stage. To achieve an integrated promotion mix, all of the firm's functions must cooperate to jointly plan communications efforts.

VI. Advertising
This is any paid form of nonpersonal presentation and promotion of ideas, goods, or services by an identified sponsor.

A. Major decisions in advertising
1. **Setting objectives.** Objectives should be based on information about the target market, positioning, and market mix. Advertising objectives can be classified by their aim: to inform, persuade, or remind.
2. **Setting the advertising budget.** Factors to consider in setting a budget are the stage in the product life cycle, market share, competition and clutter, advertising frequency, and product differentiation.
3. **Developing the advertising strategy.** Advertising strategy consists of two major elements: creating advertising messages and selecting advertising media.
4. **Creating the advertising message.** Unless ads provide information that is interesting, useful, or entertaining, many consumers will simply skip them. Merging advertising and entertainment creates new avenues for reaching consumers with engaging message: advertainment and branded entertainment. The first step in creating effective advertising messages is to plan a message strategy—the general message that will be communicated to consumers. The purpose of advertising is to get consumers to think about or react to the product or company in a certain way. Ideally, the message strategy will follow directly from the company's broader positioning and customer value strategies. The advertiser must next develop a compelling creative concept—or "big idea"—that will bring the message strategy to life. Advertising appeals should be meaningful, believable, and distinctive. Taking advantage of today's interactive technologies, many companies are now tapping consumers for message ideas or actual ads.
5. **Selecting advertising media.** The major steps in media selection are (1) deciding on reach, frequency, and impact; (2) choosing among major media types; (3) selecting specific media vehicles; and (4) deciding on media timing.
6. **Evaluating advertising effectiveness and the return on advertising investment.** Measuring the communication effect is called copy testing. It can be done before or after an ad is printed or broadcast. There are three major methods of advertising pretesting: direct rating, portfolio testing, and laboratory testing. There are two major methods of post-testing ads: recall tests and recognition tests. Sales are affected by many factors besides advertising, such as product features, price, and availability. One way to measure sales effect is to compare past sales with past advertising expenditures. Another is through experiments.

B. International advertising decisions.
International advertisers face many complexities regarding how advertising should be adapted to the unique characteristics of various country markets.

IN-CLASS GROUP EXERCISES

*Exercises with an asterisk next to them are suitable for individual homework or online assignments. Students, always provide an explanation for your answer.

1. *Explain the concept of integrated marketing communications. Provide examples in your answer.
2. *Recently, a number of restaurants have shifted some of their promotional budget from advertising to public relations. What benefits does public relations offer that would make the restaurants spend more?
3. *The percentage of sales method is one of the most common ways of setting a promotional budget. What are some advantages and disadvantages of this method?
4. *Apply the five major tools in the marketing communication mix to a hospitality or travel company by showing how a company can use all these tools.
5. *According to advertising expert Stuart Henderson Britt, good advertising objectives spell out the intended audience, the advertising message, the desired effects, and the criteria for determining whether the effects were achieved (e.g., not just "increase awareness" but "increase awareness 20 percent"). Why should these components be part of the advertising objective? What are some effects that an advertiser wants a campaign to achieve?
6. Search YouTube for three hospitality or travel advertisements. For each ad identify the execution style, and the audience targeted. Do you feel it is an effective ad—why or why not?

EXPERIENTIAL EXERCISES

Do one of the following:

1. Provide an example of a communication from a hospitality or travel company that does a good job of communicating with a specific market segment. The example can be any form of communication (e.g., an advertisement, a sales promotion, or publicity).
2. Find an example of a promotion for a hospitality company that uses the push promotion strategy. Explain how the company is using the strategy.
3. Provide evidence that a hospitality company is using integrated marketing communications, by finding two communications by the firm that have the same message, look, and feel.

REFERENCES

1. Based on information from "The Cow Campaign: A Brief History," www.chick-fil-a.com/Cows/Campaign-History (accessed June 2014); "Company Fact Sheet," www.chick-fil-a.com/Company/Highlights-Fact-Sheets (accessed June 2014); Thomas Pardee, "Armed with a Beloved Product and a Strong Commitment to Customer Service, Fast Feeder Continues to Grow," *Advertising Age*, October 18, 2010, http://adage.com/prinV146491/; Brian Morrissey, "Chick-fil-A's Strategy: Give Your Fans Something to Do," *Adweek*, October 3, 2009, www.adweek.com/prinV106477; Information from various other pages and press releases at www.chick-fil-a.com and www.chick-fil-a.com/Pressroom/Press-Releases (accessed September 2014); Joe Mcgauley, "Chick-Fil-A Is about to Overtake Taco Bell, Wendy's, And Burger King," April 2, 2018 https://www.thrillist.com/news/nation/chick-fil-a-third-largest-fast-food-chain-us# (accessed September 10, 2018).
2. These definitions, except for sales promotion, are from *Marketing Definitions: A Glossary of Marketing Terms* (Chicago, IL: American Marketing Association, 1995). Other definitions can be found on www.-marketingpower.com/live/mg-dictionary.php
3. "Digital Ad Spending to Surpass TV Next Year," *e'Marketer*, March 8, 2016, www.emarketer.com/Article/Digital-Ad-Spending-Surpass-TV-Next-Year/1013671; Avi Dan, "Why P&G Is Quickly Shifting to a Digital-First Approach to Building Brands," *Forbes*, March 8, 2015, www.forbes.com/sites/avidan/2015/03/12/why-pg-is-quickly-shifting-to-a-digital-first-approach-to-building-brands/2/#552e75a03b68; Lara O'Reilly, "Almost a Quarter of Unilever's $8 Billion Ad Budget Is Now Spent on Digital," *Business Insider*, January 28, 2016, www.businessinsider.com/unilever-digital-advertsing-budget-up-to-24-2016-1.
4. See "Thrill of the Chase: Coca-Cola Invites Fans to Shape Story-line of Big Game Ad," *Coca Cola Journey*, January 25, 2013, www.Coca-colacompany.com/-stories/thrill-of-the-chase-coca-cola-invites-fans-to-shape-storyline-of-big-game-ad; Dale Buss, "Super Bowl Ad Watch: Crowdsourcing Peaks with Coke's 'Mirage' Campaign," *BrandChannel*, January 22, 2013, www.brandchannel.com/home/posV2013/01/22/SuperBowl-Coke-012213.aspx; Natalie Zmuda, "Watching the Super Bowl from Coca-Cola's War Room(s)," *Advertising Age*, February 4, 2013, http://adage.com/prinV239582/.
5. Lesley Bielby, "The 'A' Word—Does Advertising Still Exist?" *Advertising Age*, April 22, 2016, www.adage.com/print/303678.

6. "How PESO Makes Sense in Influencer Marketing," *PR Week*, June 8, 2015, www.prweek.com/article/1350303/peso-makes-sense-influencer-marketing; Randall Rothenberg, "What Is Advertising Anyway?" *Adweek*, September 16, 2013, p. 15; Paul Nolan, "The C Word: What Is Content Marketing," *Sales & Marketing Management*, January/February 2014; Peter Himler, "Paid, Earned & Owned: Revisited," *The Rack*, June 21, 2011, http://flatironcomm.com/2011/06/paid-earned-owned-revisited/; Laurel Wentz, "Integrated Campaign of the Year: 'Soccer Gentleman' for Tecate," *Advertising Age*, August 3, 2015, http://adage.com/article/print/299755; "Soccer Gentlemen," *Facebook Studio*, www.facebook-studio.com/gallery/submission/soccer-gentlemen-4 (accessed October 2016).

7. See "Advertisers Blend Digital and TV for Well-Rounded Campaigns," *eMarketer*, March 12, 2014, www.emarketer.com/Article/Ad-vertisers-Blend-Digital-TV-Well-Rounded-Campaigns/1010670.

8. Konnie Le May, "South Dakota Tribes Beating Tomtoms to Drum Up Increased Tourist Trade," *Star–Ledger* (May 8, 1994): Sec. 8, 6.

9. Michael Carey, Laurie Garnier & Robin Schwarz for Lyrics and Music.

10. For more on message content and structure, see Leon G. Schiffman and Leslie Lazar Kanuk, *Consumer Behavior*, 4th ed. (Upper Saddle River, NJ: Prentice Hall, 1991), Chapter 10.; Frank R. Kardes, "Spontaneous Inference Processes in Advertising: The Effects of Conclusion Omission and Involvement on Persuasion," *Journal of Consumer Research* (September 1988): 225–233.

11. Jonah Bloom, "The Truth Is: Consumers Trust Fellow Buyers Before Marketers," *Advertising Age*, February 13, 2006, p. 25; "Jack Morton Publishes New Realities 2012 Research," press release, January 26, 2012, www.jackmorton.com/news/article.aspx?itemiD=106.

12. www.bzzagent.com and http://about.bzzagent.com/ (accessed September 2014).

13. https://www.bzzagent.com/how-it-works (accessed May 2019).

14. Bill Chappell, "Jared Fogle Sentenced to 15 Years in Prison for Sex with Minors, Child Pornography," November 19, 2015, https://www.npr.org/sections/thetwo-way/2015/11/19/456622271/jared-fogle-to-learn-sentence-for-sex-with-minors-child-pornography (accessed September 10, 2018).

15. See T. L. Stanley, "Dancing with the Stars," *Brandweek*, March 8, 2010, pp. 10–12; and Chris Isidore, "Lance Armstrong: How He'll Make Money Now," *CNNMoney*, January 18, 2013, http://money.cnn.com/2013/01/16/news/companies/armstrong-endorsements/. Also see "Topic: Celebrity Endorsements," *Adweek*, www.adweek.com/topic/celebrity-endorsements (accessed October 2016).

16. *Marketing Glossary Dictionary*, American Marketing Association, http://www.marketingpower.com/-mgdictionary.php?Searched=1&SearchFor=recall%20test (accessed December 12, 2004).

17. "Sheraton Wakes Up," *Hotels* (January 2004): 20.

18. For a more comprehensive discussion on setting promotion budgets, see Michael L. Rothschild, *Advertising* (Lexington, MA: D.C. Heath, 1987), Chapter 20.

19. Quoted in Daniel Seligman, "How Much for Advertising?" *Fortune* (December 1956): 123.

20. The Hospitality Research Group of PKF Consulting, as cited in *Hotel and Motel Management* (May 15, 2000): 44.

21. Michael S. Morgan, "Traveler's Choice: The Effects of Advertising and Prior Stay," *Cornell Hotel and Restaurant Administration Quarterly*, 32, no. 4 (1991): 40–49.

22. "The Rise (and Fall) of Cost per Call," *Sales and Marketing Management* (April 1990): 26.

23. For more on advertising and the product life cycle, see John E. Swan and David R. Rink, "Fitting Market Strategy to Product Life Cycles," *Business Horizons* (January/February 1982): 60–67.

24. Leslie Ann Hogg, *50 More Promotions That Work for Restaurants* (New York: Walter Mathews Associates, 1989), p. 11.

25. "Number of Magazines in the United States from 2002 to 2014," *Statista*, www.statista.com/statistics/238589/number-of-magazines-in-the-united-states/ (accessed June 2016); Andrew Burger, "Nielsen: Despite Hundreds of Choices, Average Number of TV Channels Watched Is 17," *Telecompetitor*, May 9, 2014, www.telecompetitor.com/nielsen-average-number-of-tv-channels-watched-is-17/.

26. Peter C. Yesawich, "Execution and Measurement of Programs," *Cornell Hotel and Restaurant Administration Quarterly*, 29, no. 4 (1989): 89.

27. Kelsey Libert and Kristen Tynski, "Research: The Emotions That Make Marketing Campaigns Go Viral," *HBR Blog Network*, October 24, 2013, http://blogs.hbr.org/2013/10/research-the-emotions-that-make-marketing-campaigns-go-viral/; and data from YouTube, Facebook, Instagram, and Twitter (accessed October 2016).

28. "Results of 4A's 2011 Television Production Cost Survey," January 22, 2013, www.aaaa.org/news/bulletins/pages/tvprod_01222013.aspx; Sam Thielman, "The New Hour Is 43 Minutes Long," *Adweek*, June 24, 2013, p. 12; Jeanine Poggi, "TV Ad Prices," *Advertising Age*, October 20, 2013, http://adage.com/prinV244832; "Who Bought What in Super Bowl XLVIII," *Advertising Age*, February 3, 2014, http://adage.com/prinV244024.

29. "How Much Does Television Advertising Really Cost," *Houston Chronicle*, http://smallbusiness.chron.com/much-television-advertising-really-cost-58718.html (accessed October 2016); "AOL Says There Are More Ads on TV than Ever," *Wall Street Journal*, July 28, 2015, http://blogs.wsj.com/cmo/2015/07/28/aol-says-there-are-more-ads-on-tv-than-ever/; and "Cost for a 30-Second Commercial," Marketing Fact Pack 2016, *Advertising Age*, December 21, 2015, p. 18.

30. Amanda Baltazar, "The Palm Connects Through Webisodes," *Full Service Restaurant Magazine*, July 23, 2012, http://www.fsrmagazine.com/content/palm-connects-through-webisodes (accessed August 14, 2015).

31. Jon Lafayette, "Dunkin' Donuts Returns as Sponsor of NBC's 'America's Got Talent,'" May 23, 2017, https://www.broadcastingcable.com/news/dunkin-donuts-returns-sponsor-nbc-s-america-s-got-talent-166022 (accessed September 26, 2018).

32. David Griner, "Real Ronald McDonalds to Launch Its New Breakfast Errol Morris Finds 25 Subversive Spokesmen," Adweek.com, March 27, 2014, http://www.adweek.com/news/advertising-branding/ad-day-taco-bell-recruits-real-ronald-mcdonalds-launch-its-new-breakfast-156571 (accessed August 14, 2015).

33. For more on consumer-generated advertising, see Emma Hall, "Most Winning Creative Work Involves Consumer Participation," *Advertising Age,* January 6, 2010, http://adage.com/print?article_id=141329; Stuart Elliott, "Do-It-Yourself Super Ads," *New York Times*, February 8, 2010, www.nytimes.com; Michael Learmonth, "Brands Team Up for User-Generated-Ad Contests," *Advertising Age* (March 23, 2009): 8; Rich Thomaselli, "If Consumer Is Your Agency, It's Time for Review," *Advertising Age* (May 17, 2010): 2.

34. Joel R. Evans and Barry Berman, *Principles of Marketing* (Upper Saddle River, NJ: Prentice Hall, 1995), p. 432.

35. Jeff Higley, "Hoteliers Emphasize Importance of Billboard Marketing," *Hotel and Motel Management* (November 3, 2003): 76.

36. Forbes and Bloomberg Businessweek cost and circulation data found online at www.bloombergmedia.com/magazine/businessweek/rates/ and www.forbesmedia.com/forbes-magazine-rates/ (accessed October 2016).

36. See Roland T. Rust, *Advertising Media Models: A Practical Guide* (Lexington, MA: Lexington Books, 1986).

37. "Mauritius Launches 1 m ad Campaign," *Travel Trade Gazette* (October 29, 2004): 60.

14

Promoting Products: Public Relations and Sales Promotions

Objectives

After reading this chapter, you should be able to:

1. Define public relations and explain the different public relations activities.
2. Describe the public relations process.
3. Apply public relations activities in the hospitality industry.

With only two weeks left before the opening of the 2013 Calgary Stampede, the worst flood the city of Calgary, Alberta, Canada, had ever witnessed submerged much of the Stampede's park area.

Each July, Calgary hosts over 1 million visitors during the 10-day Stampede. This not-for-profit event is an integral part of Western Canada. The principal event—a world-class rodeo—is accompanied by musical events, exhibitions, and a myriad of food vendor booths with offerings ranging from hamburgers to scorpion pizza.

Visitor expenditures during the Stampede exceed $300 million for hotels, restaurants, and other local businesses. Additionally, the Stampede serves as a major unifying event.

The flood in Alberta had attracted the attention of worldwide media creating doubt about the future of the 2013 Stampede. Then an unexpected event occurred that initiated a dramatic marketing program.

The following was reprinted with the written permission of the Calgary Stampede:

Social Media Initiative—"Hell or High Water"

In the early afternoon of Saturday, June 22, an image appeared on Twitter featuring the Calgary Stampede name and the words "Hell or High Water." Very quickly the image was shared across social media. Developed by an unknown person, the popularity of the phrase was immediate and became a tagline to the optimism, power, and resiliency of the community to get the job done no matter what obstacles we faced. Unfortunately, at that point in time, Stampede Park was still in a state of emergency and as an organization we could not be so bold.

While we couldn't be certain there would be a Stampede, we could be certain of our support to our community and neighborhood. We adopted the phrase and the rallying spirit behind it and by the end of the day decided to design a t-shirt fitting within the already established Stampede brand. The shirt would be a tangible way to show individuals' support for Calgary and tell the world that this flood would not break the spirit of our community.

On Sunday, June 23, the t-shirt was posted for sale online at the Stampede Store, with proceeds donated to the Canadian Red Cross Alberta Floods Fund.

Target Audience

The Hell or High Water campaign was social in the truest sense of the word. It emerged from our social media community, was embraced by the Stampede, and promoted exclusively through our social and digital channels so our main target audience really was our social media community. While we thought the shirt would mainly resonate in Calgary, Alberta, and across Canada, we didn't expect how far the shirt would reach—truly showing the power of social media.

Execution

The shirt was promoted exclusively through social media and digital properties because of timing, costs, and to connect to the online purchase more quickly. We used Facebook, Twitter, Instagram, as well as our Web site to link directly to the online store. As demand for the shirts exceeded all expectations, we communicated daily updates through these channels and kept the interest in the shirts high which helped push sales. When our community asked if kids' sizing would be available, we went one step further and created a Heck or High Water version for the little ones that had adult-size attitude, with kid-friendly language!

From a logistics perspective, several partners and numerous volunteers assisted us in the packaging and distribution of shirts so that we could get them on people's backs in time for Stampede. To get some perspective on the scope of the project, the following were required to fulfill the overwhelming number of Hell/Heck or High Water shirts ordered:

  1 cargo plane
  2 warehouses
  2 shirt distributors
  3 volunteer sign up sites
  4 24-hour silk screeners
  5 data specialists
  5 distribution managers
  6 companies offering workers
  9 courier companies
  10 warehouse and customer service staff
  25 WestJet employees
  40 volunteers working 2 shifts per day, 7 days a week
  80 giant Canada Post containers
  100 rolls of packing tape
  35,000+ labels, bags, and boxes
  160,000+ black t-shirts

Results

Beyond individual sales, many corporations took the message to heart and jumped onboard as well. Canadian airline, WestJet, bought thousands of shirts for their staff around the country. Bennett Jones's law firm sent shirts to their associates in firms around the world. The Canadian Tourism Commission placed two orders as demand from tourism partners to support the cause continued to grow.

Calgary's media-savvy Mayor, Naheed Nenshi, sang the praises of the campaign and the spirit it defined whenever he had the chance. Both local and national media picked up on the groundswell of support, referencing the defiance of the campaign in their broadcasts. Sales of shirts spiked with more than 19,000 shirts being sold just one day. Shirts were shipped around the world to destinations including Australia, Switzerland, Denmark, Ireland, Japan, Norway, Sweden, New Zealand, Russia, and the United States. When sales were finally closed on July 14, just 21 days after they began, the Calgary Stampede presented a check to the Canadian Red Cross Alberta Floods Fund for $2.1 million. It was the largest single donation to the Fund, more than $1 million more than the next highest donation.

With the Hell or High Water campaign becoming such a success, an even bigger accomplishment was opening our gates for Stampede 101 on July 5. Expectations were modest, after all, more than 10,000 people were still displaced from their homes and much of the city was weeks or months away from returning to normal. Despite bad weather for much of the opening weekend, once again we welcomed more than 1.1 million people to Stampede Park.

Attendance figures were down slightly from 2012 and 2011, yet still spoke to the draw of the Stampede as a gathering place for the community. Comments on social channels were overwhelmingly positive with many people posting that they would be coming to Stampede Park to show off their shirts. Thousands of shirts were seen on-Park, tens of thousands more were sold on-Park, and Hell or High Water was a phrase that was heard in every corner of the Park.

Results from our 2013 guest experience survey showed that the flood had no real impact on guest experience on Park but did drive overall goodwill toward the event—46 percent cited their main reason for attending was to show their support of the community while 32 percent attended as support toward the efforts of rebuilding Stampede Park in time to open up the gates on July 5. Ninety-three percent of the guests indicated they would return, with 65 percent saying they definitely would return.

The local tourism industry was obviously affected by the floods as well. Calgary's hotel industry saw a slight drop in occupancy in June, but it rebounded in July with rates higher than 2012 when the Stampede celebrated its Centennial. The spirit of Hell or High Water would not be lost on the rest of the city as Tourism Calgary's marketing campaign soon after the flood assured everyone that Calgary was open for business.[1]

Public Relations

"Public relations, perhaps the most misunderstood part of marketing communications, can be the most effective tools."[2] Definitions for public relations differ widely. We think that this definition by Hilton best fits the hospitality industry: "The process by which we create a positive image and customer preference through third-party endorsement."[3]

Public relations (PR) is an important marketing tool that until recently was treated as a marketing stepchild. PR is moving into an explosive growth stage. Companies are realizing that mass marketing is no longer the answer to some of their communication needs. Advertising costs continue to rise while audience reach continues to decline. Advertising clutter reduces the impact of each ad. Sales promotion costs have also increased as channel intermediaries demand lower prices and better commissions and deals. Personal selling can cost over $500 a call. In this environment, PR holds the promise of a cost-effective promotional tool. The creative use of news events, publications, social events, community relations, and other PR techniques offers companies a way to distinguish themselves and their products from competitors.[4]

Public relations The process by which a positive image and customer preference are created through third-party endorsement.

The PR department of cruise lines, restaurant chains, airlines, and hotels is typically located at corporate headquarters. Often, its staff is so busy dealing with various publics—stockholders, employees, legislators, and community leaders—that PR support for product marketing objectives tends to be neglected. Many four- and five-star hotel chains have corrected this deficiency by hiring local PR managers.

In the past, it was common for the marketing function and PR function to be handled by two different departments within the firm. Today, these two functions are increasingly integrated. There are several reasons for this integration. First, companies are calling for more market-oriented PR. They want their PR departments to manage PR activities that contribute toward marketing the company and improving the bottom line. Second, companies are establishing marketing PR groups to support corporate/product promotion and image-making directly. Thus, marketing PR serves the marketing department.

Major Activities of PR Departments

PR departments perform five activities discussed next, not all of which feed into direct product support.

Press Relations

Press relations Placing newsworthy information into the news media to attract attention.

The aim of **press relations** is to place newsworthy information into the news media to attract attention to a person, product, or service. One reason for the growth of press relations in the hospitality industry is its credibility. Most types of publicity are viewed by the consumer as third-party information. A favorable write-up of a restaurant in the local newspaper by the food editor has more impact than an advertisement written by the restaurant's management.

Product Publicity

Product publicity Various efforts to publicize specific products.

Product publicity involves various efforts to publicize specific products. Special events such as food festivals, redesigned products such as a newly renovated hotel, and products that are popular because of current trends, such as nonfat desserts, are all potential candidates for publicity.

Tokyo's Narita International Airport transformed Terminal 3 walkways into a promotion for the 2020 Summer Olympic Games. The transformation also changed walking lanes into useful running tracks for travelers on a tight schedule to catch their flights. The running tracks look and feel like the shock absorbing tracks used in Olympic events. The architect chose not to install traditional moving sidewalks but instead decided to provide a change that would promote Olympics, promote good health, and assist in meeting tight schedules.[5]

New Products

New products are the lifeblood of any industry, including tourism/hospitality. Getting the word about new products is a major use of public relations. Public relations can be used to introduce a new menu item or a new restaurant. Hospitality products are perishable, so it is important that a new restaurant, airline route, cruise ship, or hotel does not have empty seats or rooms. The Royal Caribbean's Symphony of the Sea can accommodate over 6,600 guests. Thus, it needs to create demand for its cruises starting with the first one. As the world's largest cruise ship at the time it was launched it was able to get publicity in general news media as well as travel media. 816 New York created a campaign to promote the opening of Wild Rice Vegan Café in Watertown, Massachusetts. 816 New York did online research to identify food bloggers and media contacts. They searched social media to find foodie groups that would have interest in a vegan restaurant. Once they identified those individuals and organizations that could influence potential customers, they launched a campaign that included Promotional e-mail and social media outreach to maximize exposure. They also arranged interviews with the chef which resulted in coverage in print and broadcast media.[6] Successful public relations campaigns can help ensure the successful launch of new hospitality products.

Corporate Communication

Corporate communication This activity covers internal and external communications and promotes understanding of an organization.

Corporate communication covers internal and external communications and promotes understanding of the organization. One important marketing aspect of corporate communication is directed toward employees, such as company newsletters. Companies also need to manage their communication with stockholders to make sure they understand the company's goals and objectives.

Lobbying

Lobbying Dealing with legislators and government officials to promote or defeat legislation and regulation.

Lobbying involves dealing with legislators and government officials to promote or defeat legislation and regulation. Large companies employ their own lobbyists, whereas smaller companies lobby through their local trade associations.

Counseling

Counseling Involves advising management about public issues and company positions and image.

Counseling involves advising management about public issues and company positions and images.[7] Counseling is important when there may be sensitive issues associated with the business. For example, water is a scarce commodity in Las Vegas. Major resorts with water features, such as the Mirage, counsel their managers on the resort's water conservation efforts, such as recycling the hotel's wastewater to be used in the hotel's fountains.

Marketing HIGHLIGHT 14.1 Extreme Sports bring publicity and tourists

Today, a version of many outdoor sports known as Extreme Sports has built a following. These were formerly reserved for professional stunt people or highly advanced experts in a particular sport. Today, advocates exist within each sport such as frozen waterfall climbing or snowboarding and skiing on extremely dangerous terrain.

In some cases, a growth in tourism/hospitality has occurred as a result of these activities. Each of them offers opportunities for publicity and promotion. An example is the seaside town of Nazare, Portugal, and the beach of the Praia do Norte.

Garret McNamara, an American who is a champion in the sport of Jet Ski Surfing (a surfing sport in which a jet ski takes a surfer and board to a giant wave and then quickly gets out of the way), came to the attention of Dino Casimiro, a Portuguese surfer. Senor Casimiro knew of the town Nazare and the beach Praia do Norte and contacted Garret to visit and see for himself the size of the waves. Dino also convinced the town's development group to promote the waves as a visitor/surfer attraction.

Garret was intrigued and visited Nazare and quickly became hooked on the waves and the area. In 2011, McNamara broke the world's large wave record by surfing the biggest wave in the world at 78 feet. News of this event was carried by media throughout Europe. The French newspaper Le Parisien carried a headline, "Il Surfe la Plus Haute Vague du Monde" announcing McNamara's accomplishment. Garret was becoming a world celebrity and a near icon for Nazare.

Today, Nazare has attracted scores of surfers from all over the world to try their luck at surfing these giant waves. Several have surfed what are said to be 100-foot waves; however, none of these rides have been officially recognized. The town attracts thousands of visitors who were made aware of the town by the publicity it received from surfers riding the big waves. These visitors discover the beaches, great views from the cliffs above the beaches, seafood restaurants, and other attractions of the town while hoping to see a Jet Ski surfer riding a wave reaching 120 feet in height. In the meantime, Portugal and the town of Nazare benefit from observer and participant interest in this extreme sport at Praia do Norte. If you put Nazare into the search function in YouTube, you will be able to watch some of these surfers.[8]

Nazare, Portugal, waves which can reach heights of 100 feet plus have attracted Jet Ski surfers from around the world.
Rob Wilkinson/Alamy Stock Photo.

Publicity

Publicity is a direct function of PR. Publicity is the task of securing editorial and news space, as opposed to paid space, in print and broadcast media to promote a product or a service. Publicity is a popular PR tool used in the activities just described.

To be successful, the **press release** developed to gain the publicity must be of interest to the target audience of the media the company is targeting. For example, a food editor is interested in recipes and food history. A travel editor is interested in unique aspects of the destination, not just the hotel's features. A business editor is interested in the financial success of the operation. A press release should be written for a target audience and have value for the media's audience. We now look at some ways publicity can be used to enhance an organization's image.

Tourist destinations are particularly influenced by negative publicity. When disaster hits a region or city, tourists instantaneously learn of the problem and quickly find alternative destinations. Tourism recovery depends on the reintroduction of a tourism destination. The reintroduction must overcome the adverse publicity resulting from the natural disaster. It may take several

Press release Information released to the media about certain new products or services.

years to rebuild business to pre-disaster levels. The speed of recovery depends on these factors:[9]

1. The extent of damage caused by the disaster.
2. The efficiency with which tourism partners bring their facilities back online.
3. An effective marketing message that clearly states the destination is once again open (or still is) and ready for business.

Publicity builds corporate image in a way that is congruent with the organization's communication strategy. Olive Garden restaurants developed a charity program that tied in its sponsorship of a team entering the "Olive Garden Rafanelli V-10" in the American Le Mans races. The company worked with America's Second Harvest to help fill the food banks in its "Drive Against Hunger" program. The "Drive Against Hunger" was linked to race car "driving" by donating eight truckloads of food in the eight cities where the Le Mans races were held. By tying the two events together, Olive Garden was able to create synergy across the events in its PR efforts. This example illustrates the benefits of planning and integrating marketing communications.[10]

The Public Relations Process

Effective PR is the result of a process. This process must be integrated with the firm's marketing strategy. One common misconception about PR and publicity is that quantity is more important than quality. Some PR firms measure success by the number of articles placed in media. As in other marketing efforts, PR should be meaningful to the target market.

The PR process consists of the following steps: conducting research, establishing the marketing objectives, defining the target audience, choosing the PR messages and vehicles, implementing the PR plan, and evaluating the results.

Pamela Parseghian, a chef and food writer, provides a great example of the importance of using the PR process. She discusses a chef who proposed writing a column in a major newspaper. She states the chef had developed no previous relations with the newspaper and the newspaper had not even reviewed his restaurant. Thus, there was no chance that it was going to let a "stranger" write a column in its paper. She says that if you want to get a story in a publication, first research and read the publication. She states she has people calling her asking if *Nation's Restaurant News* publishes articles on restaurants! Obviously, these people have never seen the publication, but they are ready to send in an article. Once you know the media, you match their objectives and target market with your objectives. Then choose some news stories they will likely publish, such as recipes for new dishes, unique backgrounds, and themed dinners. She also states that making the story exclusive adds value. This process is the same whether it is print media or digital media. Once you get some articles placed, then you can decide whether writing regular columns makes sense based on the results the other articles created for your business.[11]

Conducting Research

Before a company can develop a PR program, it must understand the company's mission, objectives, strategies, and culture. It should know the vehicles that will be effective in delivering messages to the target audience. Much of the information needed by a PR manager is contained in a well-written marketing plan. Ideally, the PR manager should be involved in the formation of the marketing plan.

The firm's environmental scanning system is another important source of information for the PR manager. Analysis of this information should identify trends and give the firm insights into how to react to these trends. For example, many hotel and restaurant companies are now showing what they are doing to save and protect the natural environment.

Establishing Marketing Objectives

Once the PR manager has identified opportunities through product experiment and research, priorities can be established, and objectives set. Marketing PR can contribute to the following objectives:

- *Build awareness.* PR can place stories in the media to bring attention to a product, service, person, organization, or idea.

- *Build credibility.* PR can add credibility by communicating the message in an editorial context. Credibility can be enhanced through positive associations with respected institutions, companies, and individuals. Cabela's is a highly respected outdoor sporting goods company with several stores in many states. Hunting, fishing, and boating enthusiasts in these areas are very familiar with Cabela's and have faith in the products and services that Cabela's offers. Oak Tree Lodge in Clark, South Dakota, offers pheasant, duck, and goose hunting packages on 8,000 acres of hunting land at prices ranging from $750 to $1000 per day per hunter. These packages include upscale lodging and meals as well as the actual hunting experience. Oak Tree is a Cabela's certified hunting lodge. This designation gave the lodge great publicity, enhanced its image, and served as another channel of distribution. To receive this designation, the owner and staff of Oak Tree Lodge had to work closely with Cabela's and demonstrate that the lodge was indeed worthy of this designation and would maintain high standards.

    III Forks restaurant has received favorable reviews from Independent Retail Cattlemen's Association and Zagat. III Forks integrated these reviews into an advertisement which was used to provide evidence that its selection of top-quality meat helped earn the positive reviews.

- *Stimulate the sales force and channel intermediaries.* PR can help boost sales force and franchisee enthusiasm. Positive stories about a new menu item will make an impression on the customers, employees, and franchisees of a restaurant chain. The publicity Ritz-Carlton receives from winning the Baldridge Award provides its sales force with great ammunition when it makes a sales call.

- *Lower promotion costs.* PR costs less than direct mail and media advertising. The smaller the company's promotion budget, the stronger the case is for using PR to gain share of mind.

Specific Objectives Should Be Set for Every PR Campaign

The Wine Growers of California hired the PR firm of Daniel J. Edelman, Inc., to develop a publicity campaign to convince Americans that wine drinking is a pleasurable part of good living and to improve the image and market share of California wines. The following publicity objectives were established: (1) develop magazine stories about wine and place them in top magazines and in newspapers (food columns, feature sections); (2) develop stories about wine's many health values and direct them to the medical profession; and (3) develop specific publicity for the young adult market, college market, governmental bodies, and various ethnic communities. These objectives were refined into specific goals so that final results could be evaluated.

The Homestead of Hot Springs, Virginia, conducts special weekends that serve as a part of that hotel's promotion mix. These weekends bring members of the media to the resort and give them an event to write about in addition to the resort's amenities. The resort features events around long-weekend holidays such as Martin Luther King Jr. Day and President's Day. It has also created events for women. For example, "Just for Women" features a number of classes and seminars, including nutrition, financial advice, and organizing your life. It also includes luxurious spa treatments and a Friday night fashion show. Another feature has wine experts giving wine seminars and offering a special gourmet dinner on Saturday evening.[12]

The restaurant association in many cities sponsors a Taste of the Town, featuring food from the city's restaurants. Restaurants have a chance for exposure to many potential customers in one evening. The association usually charges an admission fee, which helps ensure that those attending are interested in restaurant fare rather than obtaining a free dinner. One of the largest of these events is the Taste of Chicago billed as "The Nation's Premier Food Festival." The Taste hosts upward of three million participants with many from out-of-town. The event features hundreds of menu items served from truck vendors and pop-up-booths along with concerts, musical acts from local artists, and rides such as a Ferris Wheel.[13]

Chicago hosts the Nation's Premier Food Festival.
Efrain Padro/Alamy Stock Photo.

Defining the Target Audience

A relevant message delivered to a target audience by the appropriate vehicle is crucial to the success of any PR campaign. Effective PR practitioners carefully identify the publics they wish to reach. They study these publics and find media that can be used to deliver their message. They identify issues that will be important to the public and form the message, so it will seem natural and logical to the target audience.

Choosing the PR Message and Vehicles

The PR practitioner is now ready to identify or develop interesting stories about the product or service. If the number of stories is insufficient, the PR practitioner should propose newsworthy events that the company can sponsor. Here the challenge is to create news rather than find it. PR ideas include hosting major academic conventions, inviting celebrity speakers, and developing news conferences. Each event is an opportunity to develop a multitude of stories directed at different audiences.

Publications

Print publications are being replaced by online publications. Media kits and images are commonly available online allowing instant access to stories and images. The online version is cheaper to produce, allows instant access, and can be updated quickly and inexpensively.

Natalie Norcross, CEO of A Design Partnership, states that only 28 percent of words in online media are likely to be read. To gain and retain attention the written component of online brochures should be condensed, and the visual content should be enhanced and appealing. Smart marketers who use printed publications and online publications will develop two different versions, one for print and one for online.

Events

Hospitality companies can draw attention to new products or other company activities by arranging special events, such as the Homestead Wine and Food Festival mentioned earlier. Events include news conferences, seminars, outings, exhibits, contests, and competitions, anniversaries, and sport and cultural sponsorships that will reach the target publics.

The Gaylord Palms Resort and Convention Center in Orlando created "Christmas at the Palms" to provide a demand for rooms in December. The festive event created a reason to stay at the Gaylord Palms, turning it into a destination. The result was articles in the media about the resort. The event gave the media a reason to discuss the resort. The outcome for the hotel was 135,000 visitors and increased room occupancy.[14]

A less elaborate event is Little Woodrow's Turtle Race. The weekly event features turtles with numbers on their backs starting from an elevated spot in the center of the race circle. The event creates excitement for the customers and helps create word of mouth. If you go on YouTube, you are likely to see several videos of the event, with some having thousands of hits.

New York's Vista Hotel decided to offer a Cajun dinner but needed a "hook" to make the event authentic and newsworthy. That hook was Paul Prudhomme, the colorful Cajun chef. The Vista arranged to host a publication party for Paul's Cajun cookbook at the hotel during the Cajun dinner. This type of creative thinking creates a great PR event from an otherwise interesting but not particularly newsworthy event.[15]

News

A major task of PR professionals is to find or create favorable news about the company, its products, and its people. News generation requires skill in developing a story concept, researching it, and writing a press release. But the PR person's skill must go beyond preparing news stories: getting the media to accept press releases and attend press conference calls for marketing and interpersonal skills. A good PR media director understands press needs for stories that are interesting and timely and for releases that are well written and attention getting. The media director needs to gain the favor of editors and reporters. As the press is cultivated, it is increasingly likely to provide better coverage to the company.

Social Media

Social media has proven to be a great way to reach thousands of customers and potential customers. Today, most PR campaigns use internet: Web sites, blogs, and social networks such as YouTube, Facebook, and Twitter are providing interesting new ways to reach more people. "The core strengths of public relations—the ability to tell a story and spark conversation—play well into the nature of such social media," says a PR expert.

Social media has increasingly become mainstream media, particularly for younger consumers of hospitality and tourism. The director of public relations for Choose Chicago stated that social media allows accessibility to international journalists through media such as WhatsApp and WeChat. She adds social media allows for a more personnel with media partners. Another benefit social media provides for public relations programs is that the influencers you are trying to reach use social media to quickly spread the message. Influencer marketing has become a popular way to promote hospitality products. Influencers have a following on social media typically through their blogs, Instagram, or YouTube channels. They develop a following of people who have similar interests and often aspire to have the experiences that the influencer is posting. The influencer is interested in what will be of interest to their followers and will want to create an authentic experience. The hospitality or tourist organization needs to make sure the influencer's following is large enough to be impactful and is part of their target market, so the followers will be interested in their products creating a win for the company and the influencer. The expectation is that the influencer will take professional pictures to post their social media site, thus promoting the hotel to their followers. For example, the public relations director for the Dallas CVB states during media familiarization trips the journalists are instantly sharing their experiences over social media with their audiences.[16]

Corporate Social Responsibility Activities

In our definition of marketing, we included marketing is the process by which companies create value for customers and society. Corporate social responsibility (CSR) has been found to be positively related to a customer's trust of the company and their loyalty toward the company. A recent study by Cone Communications found that Millennials were more affected by CSR, but the majority of all consumers are attracted to companies that have CSR initiatives.[17] Millennials not only prefer to purchase from companies that have an active CSR program, they also prefer to work for those companies. Many companies will support a cause and not only donate money to support the activities but also get their employees to volunteer their time. Companies realize that through public service activities they can create goodwill with the community and their employee. Some companies, including Choice Hotel, provide paid leave for public service activities.[18] Restaurant and hotel chains donate so much of each sale to a charitable cause for a given amount of time. For example, a fast-food restaurant may donate five cents from every sandwich purchased on a certain day to the Muscular Dystrophy Association. A common way for restaurants to give back to the community is to donate a percentage of sales to nonprofit on a given day. Any customers showing up with a flyer from the nonprofit will have a percentage of their purchase go toward the nonprofit. Part of a public relations campaign should include letting the publics know how the company is giving back to society and helping the local community.

Burger King has developed YouTube videos educating the public on issues relating to social justice and injecting itself into social media conversations. For example, women's and girl's products are often sold at a higher price than men or boy's products. This difference is referred to as the pink tax. In their video Burger King charged $1.69 for their chicken fries and the same product called chick fries was sold in a pink box to women for $3.09. The skit was done with real customers to show their reaction to the unjustified price difference, creating awareness that will hopefully lead to the end of this practice. This provides an example of how doing the right thing can benefit both society and the company.[19]

Implementing the Marketing PR Plan

Implementing publicity requires care. Consider the matter of placing information in the media. Exciting information is easy to place. However, most press releases are less than great and might not get the attention of busy editors. A chief asset of publicists is their personal relationship with media editors. PR practitioners are often former journalists who know many media editors and what they want. PR people look at media editors as a market to satisfy so they will continue to use the company's press releases.

Publicity requires extra care when it involves staging special events, such as testimonial dinners, news conferences, and national contests. PR practitioners need a good head for detail and for coming up with quick solutions when things go wrong. Most hotel corporations have a crisis plan included as part of their PR plan. In this plan, they state who can talk to the media and who should not. These plans usually state that staff should not speak to media but instead direct inquiries to the director of PR.

Evaluating PR Results

The contribution of PR is difficult to measure because it is used along with other promotion tools. If it is used before other tools come into action, its contribution is easier to evaluate.

Exposures

The easiest measure of PR effectiveness is the number of exposures created in the media. Publicists supply the client with a clipping book showing all the media that carried news about the product and a summary statement, such as the following:

Media coverage included 3,500 column inches of news and photographs in 350 publications with a combined circulation of 79.4 million; 2,500 minutes of air time on 290 radio stations and an estimated audience of 65 million; and 660 minutes of air time on 160 television stations with an estimated audience of 91 million. If this time and space had been purchased at advertising rates, it would have amounted to $1,047,000.[20]

This exposure measure is not very satisfying. There is no indication of how many people actually read, heard, or recalled the message and what they thought afterward. There is no information on the net audience reached because publications overlap in readership. Because publicity's goal is reach, not frequency, it would be useful to know the number of unduplicated exposures. It is also important that publicity reach target markets. A common weakness of publicity is that the persons exposed to it are not part of the company's target market.

Awareness/Comprehension/Attitude Change

A better measure is the change in product awareness/comprehension/attitude resulting from the campaign (after allowing for the effect of other promotional tools). For example, how many people recall hearing the news item? How many told others about it (a measure of word of mouth)? How many changed their minds after hearing it? The Potato Board learned, for example, that the number of people who agreed with the statement "Potatoes are rich in vitamins and minerals" went from 36 percent before the campaign to 67 percent after the campaign, a significant improvement.

Sales and Profit Contribution

Sales and profit impact is the most satisfactory measure, if obtainable. A well-planned PR campaign is usually part of an integrated promotional campaign. This makes it very difficult to isolate the impact of the PR campaign.

PR Opportunities for the Hospitality Industry

Promoting Individual Properties

PR is by far the most important promotional tool available to entrepreneurs and individual properties, such as a single restaurant, tourist attraction, bed and breakfast (B&B), tour operator, or hotel. Seldom can these enterprises afford costly advertising. Successful PR programs by individual operators have demonstrated winning strategies that can be emulated by others.

Employees should be trained to look for PR opportunities. For example, a bell person heard that a famous person would be a speaker at a dinner in the ballroom, and a room clerk found out that one of the hotel guests was 104 years old. This information was given to the hotel's PR firm through the manager, resulting in positive exposure for the employees' hotel.[21]

Promoting via Storytelling

Storytelling can be an effective way to connect with your target market. One of the reasons storytelling is so effective is that the human brain is story based. With information being stored and retrieved in the form of stories. Stories come with indices such as locations, decisions, attitudes, and actions that create awareness and an emotional connection.[22] The owner/operator of a fishing lodge in Costa Rica had been a circus trapeze artist before retiring to the jungles of Costa Rica. Each year, U.S. and Canadian TV and radio talk shows featured this entrepreneur and his fishing lodge. This owner/operator knew the media is always hungry for a good human-interest story. Many restaurants tell the story of their founder. These stories often discuss the founder's passion, their source of recipes, and how their dedication to authentic food and customer service created a popular restaurant. For example, Cyclone Anaya's Mexican Restaurant tells the story of Cyclone Anaya's wresting career and includes videos of his matches on their Web site. The story tells how he met his wife Carolina and after his wresting career was over, they decided to enter the restaurant business using Carolina's recipes. Fifty years later, his family still runs the restaurant and as the story goes, they welcome your family to join his family at their restaurant.[23]

Wall Drug Store is a major tourist stop and tourist attraction for the state of South Dakota. Located in a town of less than 1,000 residents, Wall Drug attracts 15,000 or more visitors daily during tourist season. Wall Drug's reputation was built on free ice water. Before the days of air-conditioned cars, Mr. and Mrs. Ted Hustead, the owners, saw tourists passing by on their way to the Black Hills. These folks looked thirsty and indeed they were. Ted hand-painted a few signs reading "Free Ice Water—Wall Drug" and placed them along the highway. Before Ted returned from planting these signs, tourists had already found their way to Wall Drug. They have never stopped coming. Today, many of the road signs have disappeared but the story of Wall Drug Store lives and continues to draw people to the store.

The Raffles Hotel in Singapore has a colorful and long history, but most visitors know it as the birthplace of the drink called the Singapore Sling. Today, the story of the Raffles Hotel being the creator of the Singapore is part of the Raffles Hotel public relations. The bar serves thousands of Singapore Slings each year in a souvenir glass which you can keep for an additional charge. The hotel's gift shop also sells Singapore Sling glasses, posters, placements and refrigerator magnets. These items serve a PR vehicle for the hotel when guests display them in their homes throughout the world. Hospitality enterprises everywhere have built a solid and long-lasting story around a drink, a dessert, a special entrée, fireplaces in the guest rooms, and even ducks. In the early 1900s, a general manager of the Peabody Hotel Memphis returned from a hunting trip and placed five ducks in the hotel's fountain. The story of the Peabody ducks has been memorialized by the ducks that still inhabit the Peabody Hotel. Every morning the flock of ducks waddles daily from the rooftop via the elevator to the fountain in the lobby and in the afternoon, they return with fanfare to their rooftop home. The morning and afternoon parade of ducks attracts scores of guests and tourists. When the Peabody opened their Orlando property, the Peabody ducks became one of the features of the property, creating publicity for the new hotel. Disney has developed YouTube testimonials of grandparents telling a story about their trip to Disney with their grandchildren. Disney has also created television advertisements showing grandparents enjoying a trip to Disney World with their grand kids. This is an example of integrated marketing communications; the same message used in public relations communications is also used in paid advertising.

Crisis Management

An important area of PR is crisis management. Not all publicity is good. Hotels are open 24 hours a day, major airline companies have thousands of flights a day, and fast-food companies serve millions of customers each day. There are times when things go wrong: sometimes it is management's fault and sometimes it is beyond management's control. Managers must realize that things do go wrong: people are poisoned by tainted or spoiled restaurant food, thieves rob guests, planes crash, and flooding occurs somewhere every spring. A crisis management program will reduce the negative effects of these events.

The first step in crisis management is to take all precautions to prevent negative events from occurring. As a communications consultant, Eric Bergman states that in crisis management we should concentrate more on the management and communication and less on the crisis.[24] Robert Irvine divides crises into two main categories—a sudden crisis and a smoldering crisis.[25] A sudden crisis is the one that comes without any warning. These can be natural disaster, such as earthquakes and floods, workplace or domestic violence, an outbreak of food poisoning, and fires. Smoldering crises can include sexual harassment by supervisors, safety violations that could result in fines or illegal actions, health code violations, and fire code violations.

Sudden crises need to be anticipated. Crisis management is a series of ongoing, interrelated assessment or audits of kinds of crises and forces that can pose a

Marketing HIGHLIGHT 14.2 Cheshire's Best Kept Stations, Cheshire, United Kingdom

In an era of jet travel and theme parks catering to millions, tourism and trains in a sleepy village in the heart of the English countryside surrounded by green fields and milk cows might seem to have little or no publicity value. John Hulme, a self-trained expert in publicity, would strongly disagree.

Although only 20 minutes away from Liverpool, home of the Beatles, and half an hour from the world famous Manchester United Football Club, Cheshire is a world apart. With its lush countryside, waterways, public gardens, and heritage, it has a lifestyle to aspire to and is a relaxing place where the visitor can discover and indulge in fine food and the better things in life. It is also the home of John Hulme, an UK entrepreneur, who following a brainstorming session at a business retreat repositioned his training-based company into a hospitality and tourism program and then successfully built up the brand based on PR. One part of his repositioning strategy was to move the business into a restored village railway station, theme his training center with railway memorabilia, and upgrade his catering to fine dining for the trainees, and suddenly he had a brand that could be sold by positive PR.

John differentiated his brand in his customer's minds so much that he was able to sell the business to a national competitor. This enabled him to retire and turn his attention to Cheshire and its railway stations.

Railway stations, for many visitors, provide first and last impressions when visiting Cheshire. In the United Kingdom, many railway lines have community rail partnerships to build cooperation between the rail operator and community served. They arrange events like music trains and establish groups at the stations to look after flower beds and keep the stations tidy.

To further promote the development of improved stations, John created a brand, "Cheshire's Best Kept Stations," that encouraged volunteers to improve the stations and culminated in a prestigious annual awards evening that recognized the work by the rail operators and the community. The guest list included local mayors, town hall officials, railway executives, and the local business community. With 16 annual awards presented each year, the result was 16 different storylines going into 16 newspapers, all supported by photos and comments from the invited guests. This became a PR bonanza.

In reviewing the success of the annual awards evening, John said, "Opportunities for awards ceremonies are endless. It is possible to transform a small private event into an overblown public affair resulting in a PR gravy train." For one awards evening, John invited Her Majesty's Representative for Cheshire, the Lord Lieutenant, as his guest speaker. A special postcard was produced in memory of the event. This allowed those in attendance to tell others about the evening, providing a chain-letter type of PR.

John also made certain that throughout the year endless positive stories were sent to newspapers and magazines. Four color spreads appear in glossy magazines. These remained in doctors' and dentists' waiting rooms for years.

John owned a 60-foot canal barge, the Bilbo Baggins, and entertained many people, including the editor of the local paper, onboard. During this social event, he persuaded the editor to run a weekly column, The Baggin Man, which talked about the picturesque Cheshire countryside with the story always starting from the railway station.

The local tourist office was coaxed into using his column in a 36-page full-color booklet promoting the local area. This was such a success that John wrote three different booklets, which resulted in a national circulation of 30,000 copies.

Ten years prior to the rash of publicity for Cheshire and the railway stations, the passenger trains serving the area had many spare seats and the line was always under the threat of reduced service. Through years of positive PR, today there are usually no spare seats and the UK government is under pressure to permit the train service to increase.

Tourism in Cheshire is not only increasing but is dramatically outperforming its targets.

John is convinced that for the hospitality and tourism industries PR/publicity including well-planned and managed events can provide excellent returns to the members and their community.

Cheshire has some great attractions for tourists; however, like any tourist destination, there must be good access. Through publicity Cheshire was able to increase the number of visitors and maintain its rail access, which was under the threat of being cut.
Travelbild/Alamy Stock Photo.

major problem to a company.[26] Companies and their management need to determine those crises that have a chance of occurring and develop plans in case they do occur. Hotels should have fire plans, and employees should know what to do in case of a fire. Hotels in areas where earthquakes are prevalent should have an earthquake plan. For example, Deborah Roker, PR director for Sonesta International Hotels, designed a crisis-communication program for each of the hotels in the 18-property chain. She conducts a half-day training session annually at each property, going over crisis management plans with department heads. Part of this training includes a session at which managers are asked challenging questions that may be asked by guests or the media.[27]

Smoldering crises can often be eliminated with good management. Smoldering crises give warning before they occur. It may be a lower grade on a health report, an informal claim that a supervisor is practicing sexual harassment, grease dripping from exhaust ducts, or strangers walking the property. Good sanitation practices reduce the risk of serving poisoned food. Strict policies regarding sexual harassment create a climate where sexual harassment is not tolerated. Regular cleaning of kitchen ducts and employee training can eliminate grease fires in the kitchen. Hotels that train all their employees to look out for suspicious actions and report them to security can reduce the risk of crimes against guests. A well-managed property is the best form of crisis management.

The internet is an area where major crises are being spawned. A damaging message about your organization (whether true or not) can be spread over the internet to millions of people. This has two important implications for management. First, the stakes of crisis management have been raised. It is very important to reduce the risk of a crisis occurring. Second, managers should monitor chat groups on the internet to find out what they are saying about their organization. For example, a hotel in Miami should monitor the various chat groups for tourists to Miami.

"In the online era, it becomes critical for the business of any size to have a social media crisis management plan—or even better, a crisis prevention plan in place for those times when things go wrong, and it is truly the matter of when vs if."[28] Today guests may post the crisis online, often with a picture online, before calling emergency responders. There have been cases where the corporate office knew about the crisis at a hotel before the hotel's general manager.

When a crisis does occur, having a crisis management plan will help an organization retain its reputation. The first step is to have emergency plans in place for events that might occur such as fire, weather emergencies, loss of water, loss of electricity, robbery, and terrorists or shooters. Second, train your staff in the procedures for these plans. Have a contact list so the appropriate staff can be notified when a crisis occurs. To have effective crisis management, the company should appoint a spokesperson. Other employees should be instructed to refer media to this person. This ensures that the company is giving a consistent story based on facts. Second, this person should gather the facts and speak only from fact. This person needs to make timely statements and keep the press updated. The spokesperson should never use the term *no comment* because it raises suspicion. Using the term, *I don't know at this time* is a better response.

The message about the event should be factual and transparent; this will reduce the impact of negative publicity. For example, a fire in a guest room resulting in no injuries could result in negative or positive publicity. If the hotel provides no information to the press, the headline might read, "Regal Hotel Fire Forces Evacuation of 360 Guests." If the hotel contacts the press, the hotel has a chance to tell its story. In this case, the hotel could state that there was a hotel fire. "The smoke alarm went off at 12:33 A.M. setting the hotel's fire plan into action. The fire department was called, and employees conducted an orderly evacuation of the hotel as a precautionary measure. No one was injured, and all guests were able to return to their rooms within 30 minutes. Ms. Roberta Dominquez, the general manager of the Regal, praised the quick action of the employees. She stated that as a result of the hotel's monthly fire drills, all employees knew exactly what to do." The headline from this story might read, "Well-Trained Employees Quickly Move Guests to Safety."

If the hotel has a PR agency, the agency should be contacted. In a major crisis, it is a good idea to seek the help of a PR firm. Every company should have a crisis management plan and instruct employees in crisis management as part of their initial training.

Sales Promotion

Sales promotion Consists of short-term incentives to encourage the purchase of sale of a product or service.

Sales promotion consists of short-term incentives to encourage the purchase or sales of a product or service. Sales promotion includes a variety of promotional tools designed to stimulate early or strong market response. It includes consumer promotion (samples, coupons, rebates, price-off, premiums, contests, and demonstrations), trade promotion-buying allowances (free goods, cooperative advertising, and push money), and sales force promotion (bonuses and contests). A well-planned sales promotion can result in publicity. The Omni San Antonio Hotel offered a Teacher's Appreciation Special in recognition of educators' contributions to the community. This sales promotion created goodwill among the teachers and the community and generated publicity for the hotel. It also generated room sales during a soft period. Applebee's gives a free meal to students who earn an A. This rewards students with good grades and provides the school with a no-cost way of recognizing students who have done well. In addition to the PR benefits, it brings the child's parents and siblings to Applebee's when the free meal is redeemed. Thus, Applebee's generates profitable sales from the promotion. Lenny's sends you a digital coupon Friday morning to get a sub free when you buy one sub and two fountain drinks on Friday, Saturday, or Sunday. This coupon drives business to Lennys over the weekend, while the purchase of two soft drinks (a high margin item) ensures that Lennys will not lose money on the promotion. While a coupon for Burger King on the back of a grocery store coupon offers a 2-for-1 Whopper promotion for the Burger King that recently opened in front of the grocery store. Burger King saw this as a good way to get people living in the area to become familiar with their new store. Sales promotion includes a wide variety of promotion tools designed to stimulate earlier or stronger market response.

Sales promotion tools are used by most organizations. Estimates of annual sales promotion spending run as high as $100 billion. Spending has increased rapidly in recent years. Several factors have contributed to the rapid growth of sales promotion, particularly in consumer markets. First, inside the company, product managers face greater pressures to increase current sales, and they view promotion as an effective short-run sales tool. Second, externally, the company faces more competition, and competing brands are less differentiated. Increasingly, competitors are using sales promotion to help differentiate their offers. Third, advertising efficiency has declined because of rising costs, media clutter, and legal restraints. Finally, consumers have become more deal oriented. In the current economy, consumers are demanding lower prices and better deals. Sales promotions can help attract today's more thrift-oriented consumers.

The growing use of sales promotion has resulted in promotion clutter, which is similar to advertising clutter. With so many products being sold on deal these days, a given promotion runs the risk of being lost in a sea of other promotions, weakening its ability to trigger an immediate purchase. Manufacturers are now searching for ways to rise above the clutter, such as offering larger coupon values, creating more dramatic point-of-purchase displays, or delivering promotions through new digital media—such as the internet or mobile phones. According to one study, 90 percent of the top 100 retailers use digital promotions—such as mobile coupons. Digital promotions can help drive both in-store and online sales.[29] In developing a sales promotion program, a company must first set sales promotion objectives and then select the best tools for accomplishing these objectives.

Setting Sales Promotion Objectives

Sales promotion objectives vary widely. Consumer promotions can increase short-term sales or they can be used to help build long-term market share. The objective may be to entice consumers to try a new product, lure consumers away from competitors, or hold and reward loyal customers. Sales force objectives include building stronger customer relations and obtaining new accounts.

Sales promotions should build consumer franchise; that is, they should promote the product's positioning and include a sales message. Ideally, the objective is to build long-run consumer demand rather than to prompt temporary brand switching. If properly designed, every sales promotion tool has consumer franchise-building potential.

When the economy tightens and sales lag, it's tempting to offer deep promotional discounts to spur consumer spending. In general, however, rather than creating only short-term sales or temporary brand switching, sales promotions should help to reinforce the product's position and build long-term customer relationships. If properly designed, every sales promotion tool has the potential to build both short-term excitement and long-term consumer engagement and relationships. Marketers should avoid "quick fix," price-only promotions in favor of promotions that are designed to build brand equity. Examples include the various frequency marketing programs and loyalty cards. Most hotels and airlines offer frequent-guest/buyer/flier programs that give rewards to regular customers to keep them coming back. Many restaurants are now starting to follow suit offering their own loyalty programs. Such promotional programs can build loyalty through added value rather than discounted prices.

Major Sales Promotion Tools

Many tools can be used to accomplish sales promotion objectives. The promotion planner should consider the type of market, the sales promotion objectives, the competition, and the costs and effectiveness of each tool. The main consumer promotion tools include samples, packages, coupons, premiums, patronage rewards, point-of-purchase displays, contests, sweepstakes, and games.

Sample Offers of a trial amount of a product.

SAMPLES. **Samples** are offers of a trial amount of a product. For example, for the past 37 years, Ben & Jerry's has set aside one day each year as Free Cone Day, on which it invites customers to stop by its scoop shops to sample any of a variety of the brand's classic ice cream flavors for free. Around the country, the unique sampling promotion is a huge success, with lines stretching out the doors and around the block at most shops. Officially, Ben & Jerry's uses Free Cone Day to thank its customers for being "so uniquely awesome." But the sampling program also generates tons of buzz and draws new customers into its shops, something that Ben & Jerry's hopes will turn into a habit.

Sampling by the staff who are employed by a hospitality firm such as a hotel, restaurant, or ski resort can be a very useful educational and promotional device. Thorough knowledge of the product is particularly beneficial to upselling. It is difficult for anyone to recommend a premium-priced Bordeaux or California merlot if he or she has no idea how the wine tastes. The sales and reservation staff of a hotel or resort can more convincingly sell a prospect on the idea of upgrading to a poolside cabana or suite if they have a personal knowledge of the product.

How does the staff obtain personal knowledge of the product or service of a company? Several successful approaches have been used to accomplish staff product knowledge:

1. Provide continuous training programs and invite suppliers such as vintners, cheese producers, and gourmet coffee distributors to provide samples and assist with product training.

2. Offer sales and performance incentives that include prizes on the property, such as a five-course meal, a month's use of the health club, or a weekend in the deluxe suite.

3. Create an employee's day in which the staff has full use of the facility. Country clubs often provide a special day in which employees and sometimes their families are treated to exclusive use of the pool, the golf course, the restaurant, and even the ballroom for an evening dance.

4. Share product information with employees through newsletters or product brochures. Often, product information brochures remain only in the offices of

the purchasing department, the food and beverage manager, or some other executive office.

5. Talk continuously about the company's products and services in a positive and upbeat manner. People have a tendency to forget the many positive attributes of the facilities and the services that surround us daily.

Preston L. Smith, the president and CEO of S-K-I Limited, regularly sends memos to company managers urging them to hit the slopes. Smith personally manages to ski over 60 times each season. "Everyone skis here. It's a way of sharing the customer's experience. It's also a way to achieve personal growth because skiing is exhilarating and exciting."[30]

PACKAGES. Packages can involve either bundling a number of a company's products or packaging a resort's products with attractions from the area. Ideally, the package creates a great experience for the guest and produces business for the hospitality or travel business. During a slow period in Las Vegas, two resorts of the same reputation took two different approaches to generating sales. One resort gave a discount on rooms and increased its projected occupancy. The other resort produced a package that included a room, dining, and show tickets. Like its neighbor, the price of the components of the package was greatly reduced, but the overall price was similar to what the resort would receive for the room during a busy period. The package sold well, and the resort also increased occupancy over what was projected. The difference between the two resorts was that the one selling the package achieved greater gaming revenue. The higher price of the package attracted a wealthier clientele, who also realized what they were saving by purchasing the package and were willing to spend these savings on the casino floor.

The Ritz-Carlton in Tyson's Corner developed a Fine Art of Cuisine weekend.[31] The weekend features gourmet meals matched with the appropriate wines. The hotel developed packages around the meals, tasting, and demonstrations. Guests received a room, tickets to the Grand Wine Tasting, and the Chef's brunch. Packages can also be developed around local events. The Best Western Palm Beach, Florida, created a three-night package that included a room for three nights, tickets to two baseball games (several teams and spring training near the hotel), and a continental breakfast.[32] Packages such as these bring in business during a slow period and create a memorable experience for the guest.

Coupons Certificates that offer buyers savings when they purchase specified products.

COUPONS. Coupons are certificates that offer buyers savings when they purchase specified products. In the United States, coupon redemption peaked at 3.5 billion in 2011, with 2.75 being redeemed in 2014.[33] Digital coupons could help the growth continue as 100 million digital coupons were redeemed in 2015. Forty percent of smartphone users will redeem at least one coupon using their phone.[34] Overall, mobile and online coupon redemption exceeds traditional newspaper coupon redemption. Coupons can be mailed, available through the internet, included with other products, or placed in ads. Coupons are most popular in the restaurant industry; however, hotel, rental car companies, tourist attractions, and cruise lines also use coupons.

Some restaurants have suffered from overcouponing. In the "pizza wars," the major chains fight for marketing share by distributing coupons at least once a week. Some pizza restaurants post signs saying they will honor competitors' coupons to neutralize the impact of competitor advertising. The price of a pizza dropped to the discounted coupon price for many customers. These customers feel they are getting a poor value if they purchased a pizza without a coupon. Overcouponing should be avoided because it can lower the price the customer is willing to pay.

Besides stimulating sales of a mature product, coupons are also used to promote the trial of a new product. For example, when a fast-food chain develops a new product, it often introduces the product in print advertisements featuring a coupon. The coupon provides an incentive and reduces the risk for customers trying the new product.

Cellfire (cellfire.com) distributes digital coupons to the cell phones of consumers nationwide who sign up for its free service.[35] Cellfire's list of clients includes Domino's Pizza, TGI Friday, and Hardee's restaurants. Cellfire sends an ever-changing assortment of digital coupons to users' cell phones. To use the coupons, users simply call up the stored coupon list, navigate to the coupon they want, press the "Use Now" button, and show the digital coupon to the store cashier. Domino's even permits consumers holding the mobile coupons to simply click on a link to have their cell phones dial the nearest Domino's store to place an order.

Coupons distributed through Cellfire offer distinct advantages to both consumers and marketers. Consumers don't have to find and clip paper coupons or print out Web coupons and bring them along when they shop. They always have their cell phone coupons with them. For marketers, mobile coupons allow more careful targeting and eliminate the costs of printing and distributing paper coupons.

Many professional marketing consultants and observers of marketing and sales practices feel that too much promotion creates a commodity out of a differentiated product. It is argued that companies spend millions of dollars and years of effort to develop a distinct image and a high level of product differentiation in the minds of consumers, only to have it destroyed by promotions.

In the hospitality industry where demand varies greatly by time period, coupons should have blackout periods during those times when a person using a coupon may displace a regular guest. For example, restaurants are typically busy on Fridays and Saturdays, so a new restaurant that is using coupons to attract customers should make the coupons good Sunday through Thursday. Coupons can serve an important part of a communications program, but their use should be part of an integrated communications plan.

Premiums Goods offered either free or at low cost as an incentive buy a product.

The Hard Rock Café is known for its logo shops selling T-shirts and other items, which promote Hard Rock Cafes around the world.
Source: Seyhmus Baloglu—author.

PREMIUMS. **Premiums** are goods offered either free or at low cost as an incentive to buy a product. For example, fast-food restaurants often offer a free promotional glass instead of their normal paper cup. A self-liquidating premium is a premium sold to consumers who request it. For example, McDonald's in Australia offered Batman figures for 95 cents with the purchase of a burger.

Many restaurants, such as the Hard Rock Café, have discovered that promotional items such as caps, T-shirts, and sweatshirts can be sold at a good profit, thus creating another profit center for the company. Others offer a premium-priced drink or dessert that is served with a special glass or plate. Guests actually pay for the glass or plate in the price of the product, take the "gift" home with them, and are reminded of a pleasant restaurant experience. Pat O'Brien's in the French Quarter of New Orleans serves a Hurricane cocktail in a commemorative glass. These glasses can be seen in homes throughout the world. The name recognition developed through its Hurricane glasses has helped make Pat O'Brien's a major tourist attraction in the French Quarter.

Marco Polo cruises gave a free flight to Europe for passengers from Sydney taking one of its Mediterranean cruises. The booking had to be made in the previous year and was restricted to Sydney, an area where the cruise line was trying to build additional business.[36]

Patronage rewards Cash or other awards for regular use of a company's products or services.

PATRONAGE REWARDS. **Patronage rewards** are cash or other rewards for regular use of a company's products or services. For example, most airlines offer frequent-flyer plans that award points for miles traveled. Most of the hotel chains have a frequent-stay program and many restaurants have frequent-dining programs. These programs reward loyal customers, gather guest information, and hopefully create a positive change in the consumer behavior of the member.

Often a dilemma for hotels, consumers feel that hotel frequent guest programs are worth less than those of airlines. Even so, a hotel company without a loyalty program may risk losing guests. Nevertheless, the majority of hotel guest program points are never redeemed. Starwood Hotels developed a program without blackout dates on free stays, instant online redemption, and the right to convert hotel points into airline miles. This proved so popular that Starwood signed 5 million new users or 50,000 each week.[37] Loyalty programs will be discussed in Chapter 16.

Hotels or restaurants can also create events to show their appreciation of loyal customers. For example, a casino invited 25,000 of its best customers to come to "Free Hug Friday." Five thousand players showed up to get a mug of Hershey's chocolate kisses and a hug from the company's executives. The players thought it was great, and the casino attracted 5,000 of its best players in one night.[38]

Another type of patronage rewards are specials for repeat customers. The Elephant Walk restaurants in Massachusetts are constantly looking for fine wines. Often their finds are wines that have limited availability. From their search for fine wines, they feature six wines each month. These are usually wines that do not have enough availability to put on their regular wine list. Customers are e-mailed information about the wines and can reserve a bottle for lunch or dinner. The restaurants sell these wines at normal retail levels, but half of what a restaurant would normally charge. This promotion creates goodwill with frequent customers and gives them another reason to dine at the restaurants. The unique promotion has also generated publicity for the restaurants.[39]

Point-of-purchase (POP) promotions Include displays and demonstrations that take place at the time of sale.

POINT-OF-PURCHASE (POP) PROMOTIONS. **Point-of-purchase (POP) promotions** include displays and demonstrations that take place at the point of purchase or sale. For example, a representative of Richmond Estate Wines might offer a taste of the estate's wines in the Robina Tavern package store.

The value of POP has long been recognized by the retailing industry and is making rapid inroads in restaurants, hotels, auto rental companies, and other hospitality industry firms. Hospitality firms have discovered that POP may be used (1) to disseminate information about the company's products or services and (2) to sell additional products and services, thus adding to gross revenue.

Hotels use display racks in the lobby to promote other hotels in the chain and additional services, from valet parking to sleigh rides. Restaurants such as Perkins, the Village Inn, and Denny's use the space near the cash register to create eye-catching displays of bakery items and desserts to be taken home by the guests.

Contests, sweepstakes, and games Give consumers a chance to win something, such as cash or a trip.

CONTESTS, SWEEPSTAKES, AND GAMES. **Contests, sweepstakes, and games** give consumers a chance to win something, such as cash or a trip. Viking River Cruises offers a chance to win a free trip on Viking by completing information online. This helps Viking to build a prospect list. A contest calls for consumers to submit an entry—a jingle, guess, or suggestion—to be judged by a panel. A sweepstakes calls for consumers to submit their names for a drawing. A game presents consumers with something every time they buy such as bingo numbers. A sales contest urges dealers or the sales force to increase their efforts, with prizes going to the top performers.

Dunkin' Donuts launched an integrated campaign to remind people of its roots as a doughnut maker and not just a coffee brand. From TV to internet to in-store displays, "you can't walk in the door without thinking about donuts," says Dunkin's vice president of consumer engagement. At the heart of the "donut domination" campaign was a "Create Dunkin's Next Donut" contest that urged people to visit the contest Web site and design their own doughnuts. "Put

Dickens on the Strand Parade. Galveston's Dickens on the Strand draws thousands of tourists to this seaside town in the winter. Mary Beth Bassett.

on your apron and get creative," the campaign urged. At the site, entrants selected from a list of approved ingredients to create the new doughnut, give it a name, and write a 100-word essay about why they think their doughnut creation was the best. Twelve semifinalists were selected, who cooked their creations at a bake-off in the company's test kitchen at Dunkin' Donuts University in Braintree, Massachusetts. The grand winner received $12,000 and the winning doughnut—Toffee for Your Coffee—was added to the company's everyday value menu. In all, contestants submitted nearly 130,000 creations online. "We were absolutely amazed at the number of entries in our contest," said Dunkin' marketing executive.[40]

Tom Feltenstein, a restaurant marketing consultant, suggests a program where loyal customers are sent two $20 gift certificates. They can use one toward the purchase of their meal and the other $20 certificate they give to an employee who provides them with the best service. Thus, the employee tries to earn as much money as possible by providing exceptional service.[41]

EEVENTS. Finally, marketers can promote their brands through event marketing (or event sponsorships). They can create their own brand-marketing events or serve as sole or participating sponsors of events created by others. The events might include anything from mobile brand tours to festivals, reunions, marathons, concerts, or other sponsored gatherings. Event marketing is huge, and it may be the fastest-growing area of promotion. Effective event marketing links events and sponsorships to a brand's value proposition. And with the social sharing power of today's digital media, even local events can have far-reaching impact. Tourism destinations use events to give people an additional reason to visit their destination. For example, the Galveston Historical Foundation puts on the Dickens on the Strand festival, tying in Galveston's Victorian style architecture with the sights and sounds of Charles Dickens' work to create a holiday festival attracting thousands of visitors.[42] Restaurants and hotels create wine tastings and craft beer tastings to attract customers.

Finding Creative Ideas

The internet makes it possible to see what sales promotion activities other companies are doing. If they are outside your market area, it is a good chance you can adapt the ideas to fit your needs. For example, at the Hilton Gaithersburg, Maryland, new Washington, D.C., the chef prepares Maryland crab cake sliders presented on soft mini rolls to accentuate a perfect combination of spices and sauces. Accompanying this scrumptious local dish is a collection of to-go crab flavors, including Crab chips, Old Bay crab cake classic mix, Gordon's Chesapeake Classics Maryland-style red crab soup, and spicy Chesapeake peanuts.

The Ritz-Carlton at Powerscourt in Ireland put together a package that included its regular offerings. However, by packaging the items, it created value for the guest and produced additional revenue. The package included:[43]

- Two nights' accommodation in a deluxe room
- Daily breakfast in the restaurant
- Dinner for two in Gordon Ramsay at Powerscourt for one night (excluding beverages)
- A one-hour aromatherapy massage

Friday's in the United Kingdom offered a twist on restaurant birthday clubs. Instead of telling persons celebrating their birthday what they will get, they can sign up for their gift when they join the birthday club. They can choose from free cocktails, champagne, or desserts for their party. Many people celebrate their birthday by dining out; thus, a well-designed birthday club can provide a reason for the birthday celebration to be held at your restaurant.[44]

Another reason to celebrate is with a dining experience on Father's Day. Mother's Day is the busiest day of the year for restaurants in the United States. So why not encourage families to eat out on Father's Day as well? That is exactly what Outback did. For anyone bringing their husband or father to Outback on Father's Day, Outback gave a $10 certificate valid on their next visit. This type of certificate is called a bounce-back certificate because it encourages diners to return. However, Outback went one step further by collecting information about who came on Father's Day. Dads activated the certificate online at http://outback.com/. The certificate was valid for five weeks and had to be used with a purchase of $25 or more. Thus, Outback was encouraging a quick return visit, and the minimum purchase of $25 ensured that Outback would at least break even on the bounce-back visit.[45]

Chick-fil-A is a master of promotions. One of its promotions is giving away 52 Chick-fil-A meal coupons to the first 100 people when it opens a new restaurant. Dan Cathy, president of Chick-fil-A, states that he could not believe it when fans showed up 18 hours in advance of the opening the first time it started the promotion.[46] The store opening creates local publicity. Newspapers, radio stations, and television stations cover the unique event and interview people who sleep in the parking lot so they can claim their free meals. The cost of the meals is more than offset by the publicity.

Consulting companies also give ideas online as a way to attract potential clients. One firm lists 10 promotional tactics for restaurants. One of these is partnering with a business or social organization to expose the restaurant to potential customers. They state that if you select the right group as partner, you can leverage resources to promote your restaurant, and you can also target your core audience. Partnering with a business or charitable organization works on many levels and can help stretch your marketing budget while delivering higher returns on investment than can be achieved with traditional advertising.[47] There is no end to the types of promotions one can do. But managers must remember to fit the promotion to the operation.

Developing the Sales Promotion Program

Beyond selecting the types of promotions to use, marketers must make several other decisions in designing the full sales promotion program. First, they must determine the size of the incentive. A certain minimum incentive is necessary if the promotion is to succeed; a larger incentive will produce more sales response. The marketer also must set conditions for participation. Incentives might be offered to everyone or only to select groups.

Marketers must determine how to promote and distribute the promotion program itself. For example, a $2-off coupon could be given out in an advertisement, at the restaurant, via the internet, or in a mobile download. Each distribution method involves a different level of reach and cost. Increasingly, marketers are blending several media into a total campaign concept. The length of the promotion is also important. If the sales promotion period is too short, many prospects (who may not be buying during that time) will miss it. If the promotion runs too long, the deal will lose some of its "act now" force.

Finally, the marketer has to decide on the sales promotion budget. It can be developed in two ways. The marketer can choose the promotions and estimate total cost. However, the more common way is to use a percentage of the total budget for sales promotion. One study found three major problems in the way that companies budget for sales promotion. First, they do not consider cost effectiveness. Second, instead of spending to achieve objectives, they simply extend the previous year's spending, take a percentage of expected sales, or use the "affordable approach." Finally, advertising and sales promotion budgets are too often prepared separately.[48]

Partnerships can stretch a budget. The Palm, a national upscale steakhouse, developed a promotion with a Chicago car dealer to promote its Chicago restaurant.[49] The car dealer offered a $50 gift certificate for the Palm to all who test drove its luxury model car. The cost of the certificate was split equally between the partners. Partnerships can also be used to acquire prizes in sweepstakes. Companies often discount or provide merchandise in exchange for advertising exposure.

PRETESTING AND IMPLEMENTING THE PLAN. Whenever possible, sales promotion tools should be pretested to determine if they are appropriate. Consumer sales promotions can be pretested quickly and inexpensively, yet few promotions are ever tested ahead of time. Seventy percent of companies do not test sales promotions before initiating them. To test sales promotions, researchers can ask consumers to rate or rank different promotions. Promotions can also be tried on a limited basis in selected geographic test areas.

Companies should prepare implementation plans for each promotion, covering lead time and sell-off time. Lead time is the time necessary to prepare the program. Sell-off time begins with the launch and ends when the promotion ends.

EVALUATING THE RESULTS. Many companies fail to evaluate their sales promotion programs. Various evaluation methods are available; the most common is sales comparisons before, during, and after a promotion. Suppose that a company has a 6 percent market share before the promotion, which jumps to 10 percent during the promotion, falls to 5 percent immediately after, and rises to 7 percent later. The promotion appears to have attracted new customers and more purchases from current customers. After the promotion, sales fell as consumers used inventories or moved purchases forward. For example, a person planning on traveling to see relatives in New York in June may move the trip forward to April to take advantage of an airline promotion that expires on April 30. The long-run rise to 7 percent means that the airline gained some new users, but if the brand's share returned to the pre-promotion level, the promotion changed only the timing of demand rather than total demand.

Surveys can provide information on how many consumers recall the promotion, what they thought of it, how many accepted it, and how it affected their buying patterns.

Clearly, sales promotion plays an important role in the total promotion mix. To use it well, the marketers must define objectives; select the best tools; design the sales promotion program; and pretest, implement, and evaluate the results.

Local Area Marketing (Neighborhood Marketing)

Local area marketing or neighborhood marketing is defined as a low-cost, hands-on effort to take advantage of all opportunities within the immediate trading area to promote and market a business.[50] Although all areas of the promotional mix are used, PR is the heart of any local area marketing program. Local area marketing is used by both small and large companies. Independently owned businesses, such as restaurants or travel agencies, have an advantage over large companies because the owners become permanent fixtures of the community, whereas large companies tend to replace store managers every two or three years. Research has shown that 75 percent of a restaurant's customers come from within a 10-minute drive. With fast-food restaurants, the radius shrinks to three to five minutes' drive time.[51]

Examples of PR activities included in local area marketing are providing tours of your facility. Primary schools look for places to take their students on field trips. A restaurant or hotel can be an exciting venue. A short tour, followed by tasting and providing the students with a coupon (so that they can show their parents where they went), can be a good way to create business and goodwill. (As a result of worldwide terrorism, many companies in all industries have stopped allowing tours.) Many suburban and rural areas have weekly papers, providing a weekly or monthly article on travel, food, or wine. If articles are well written, the paper will appreciate the free articles, and the writer will gain exposure and credibility in the local market. Being a speaker at meetings of local social and service clubs is another way to gain exposure. During the holiday season, a business can become a depository for charities collecting toys for disadvantaged children. But don't accept this task passively. For example, if the local firefighters ask you to collect toys for their campaign, suggest that the campaign be started with a kickoff drive, including fire engines, sirens, and firefighters in uniform in your parking lot on a Saturday. If they agree, call the local news station for television coverage.[52]

Organizations such as the school band, girl scouts, and the local little league team are always looking for fundraisers. Many restaurants will give a portion of their proceeds to these groups if they refer business. For example, at Sweet Tomatoes restaurant, the organization must hand out flyers redeemable at the restaurant on a specific night designated for that organization, resulting in a 15 percent donation to the organization. Sweet Tomatoes offers an alternative program. That organization sells script that can be used at face value at the restaurant. The group receives the script at a 10 percent discount and sells it at face value. Merchants, including restaurants, receive many requests to assist local groups with fundraising by donating merchandise or meals. Some restaurants have a policy of donating only products such as coffee mugs or T-shirts with the restaurant's logo/name.

Cause-related promotions are another local area marketing tactic. These promotions bring business to the hotel or restaurant and help the community. Rock Bottom Restaurant and Brewery frequently creates promotions that are cause related. For example, one of the beers the brew pub creates is Firechief Ale. The company developed a fiery line of appetizers and teamed them with its Firechief Ale to create a promotion that helps local firehouses. Through its CraftWorks Foundation, it develops and supports local charity partnerships.[53]

El Torito restaurants, based in California, had a television campaign that was based almost exclusively in Los Angeles because the chain could not afford to advertise in multiple markets. As a result, restaurants outside Los Angeles gained little benefit from the ads. Joe Herrera, the restaurant's manager, decided to scrap the television ads and build a local area marketing campaign. Its ad dollars went into local papers and community marketing. Now El Torito has a presence in all its markets, and Herrera stated the managers were happy to have the marketing help.[54]

A good local area marketing campaign creates goodwill in the community and exposure for the restaurant, which translates into increased business and customer loyalty. Successful local marketers should not give products or money away freely. They evaluate every opportunity and make sure the effort will be worthwhile. By being creative, managers can ensure that their local marketing efforts will be noticed.

CHAPTER REVIEW

I. Public Relations

The process by which a positive image and customer preference are created through third-party endorsement. Social media has become an important tool for public relations.

A. Major activities of PR departments

1. **Press relations.** The aim of press relations is to place newsworthy information into the news media to attract attention to a person, product, or service.
2. **Product publicity.** Product publicity involves efforts to publicize specific products.
3. **New products.** Getting the word out about new products is a major use of public relations.
4. **Corporate communication.** This activity covers internal and external communications and promotes understanding of the organization.
5. **Lobbying.** Lobbying involves dealing with legislators and government officials to promote or defeat legislation and regulation.
6. **Counseling.** Counseling involves advising management about public issues and company positions and image.

B. **Publicity.** Publicity is a direct function of PR. Publicity is the task of securing editorial and news space, as opposed to paid space, in print and broadcast media to promote a product or a service. Publicity is a popular PR tool. Three other popular uses of publicity are new product launches, special events, and crisis management.

II. **The Public Relations Process**
   A. **Conducting research** to understand the firm's mission, culture, and target of the communication.
   B. **Establishing marketing objectives.** Marketing PR can contribute to the following objectives: build awareness, build credibility, stimulate the sales force and channel intermediaries, and lower promotion costs.
      1. Specific objectives should be set for each PR campaign.
   C. **Defining the target audience.** Effective PR practitioners carefully identify the publics they wish to reach.
   D. **Choosing the PR message and vehicles.** The PR practitioner is now ready to identify or develop interesting stories about the product or service.
      1. **Publications.** The written component of online brochures should be condensed, and the visual content should be enhanced and appealing. Smart marketers who use printed publications and online publications will develop two different versions, one for print and one for online.
      2. **Events.** Companies can draw attention to new products or other company activities by arranging special events.
      3. **News.** PR professionals cultivate the press to increase better coverage to the company.
      4. **Social media** has proven to be a great way to reach thousands of customers and potential customers. Today, most PR campaigns use internet: Web sites, blogs, and social networks such as YouTube, Facebook, and Twitter are providing interesting new ways to reach more people.
      5. **Corporate social responsibility activities** has been found to be positively related to a customer's trust of the company and their loyalty toward the company.
   E. **Implementing the marketing PR plan.** PR practitioners need a good head for detail and for coming up with quick solutions when things go wrong.
   F. **Evaluating PR results**
      1. **Exposures.** The easiest measure. Publicists supply the client with a clipping book showing all the media that carried news about the product and a summary statement.
      2. **Awareness/comprehension/attitude change.** A better measure is the change in product awareness/comprehension/attitude resulting from the campaign (after allowing for the effect of other promotional tools).
      3. **Sales-and-profit contribution.** Sales and profit impact is the most satisfactory measure, if obtainable.

III. **PR Opportunities for the Hospitality Industry**
   A. **Promoting individual properties.** Public relations is by far the most important promotional tool available to entrepreneurs and individual properties, such as a single restaurant, tourist attraction, bed and breakfast (B&B), tour operator, or hotel. Seldom can these enterprises afford costly advertising or other promotional programs.
   B. **Promoting via storytelling.** PR around the owner/operator or history of the location.
   C. **Crisis management.** Take all precautions to prevent negative events from occurring. When a crisis does occur, having a crisis management plan will help an organization retain its reputation. The first step is to have emergency plans in place for events that might occur such as fire, weather emergencies, loss of water, loss of electricity, robbery, and terrorists or shooters. Second, train your staff in the procedures for these plans. Have a contact list so the appropriate staff can be notified when a crisis occurs. To have effective crisis management, the company should appoint a spokesperson. Other employees should be instructed to refer media to this person. This ensures that the company is giving a consistent story based on facts. Second, this person should gather the facts and speak only from fact. This person needs to make timely statements and keep the press updated.
   D. **Sales promotion** consists of short-term incentives to encourage the purchase or sales of a product or service.
      1. **Setting sales promotion objectives.** Sales promotion objectives vary widely and can include increasing short-term sales, increasing long-term sales, getting consumers to try a new product, luring customers away from competitors, or creating loyal customers.
      2. **Major sales promotion tools.** Many tools can be used to accomplish sales promotion objectives. The promotion planner should consider the type of market, the sales promotion objectives, the competition, and the costs and effectiveness of each tool. Common sales promotion tools include samples; packages; coupons; premiums; patronage rewards; point-of-purchase (POP) promotions; contests, sweepstakes, and games; and events.
      3. **Finding creative ideas.** The internet makes it possible to see what sales promotion activities other companies are doing. If they are outside your market area, it is a good chance you can adapt the ideas to fit your needs.
      4. **Developing the sales promotion program.** The following steps are involved in developing a sales promotion program:
         a. Decide on the size of the incentive
         b. Set the conditions for participation
         c. Decide how to promote and distribute the promotion program
         d. Set promotion dates
         e. Decide on the sales promotion budget

The marketer should pretest to determine if sales promotion tools are appropriate and the incentive size is efficient and effective. The company should evaluate the results against the objectives of the program.

E. **Local area marketing (neighborhood marketing).** A good local store marketing campaign is an effective way for both a chain and an individually owned restaurant or hotel to gain goodwill and exposure in the community.

IN-CLASS GROUP EXERCISES

*Exercises with an asterisk next to them are suitable for individual homework or online assignments. Students, always provide an explanation for your answer.

1. *What is meant by the term *public?* Can a company have more than one public?
2. Give examples of how a hospitality organization might be able to gain publicity.
3. *Compare and contrast publicity with advertising. What are the benefits and drawbacks of each?
4. *How can being socially responsible enhance a company's position in the community?
5. *Design a sales promotion campaign using online, social media, and mobile marketing for a restaurant or hotel in your area.
6. *Find two Web sites of hospitality or travel organizations that offer PR support. This could be corporate announcements, a "press room section," or a gallery of photos that one can download for publicity purposes. Report on the sites you found and the support they offered for persons wanting to write a story about the organization.

EXPERIENTIAL EXERCISE

Do one of the following:

1. Find a good example of publicity in a print medium that has been linked to a social medium such as Facebook. Explain how the print and electronic media complement each other.

REFERENCES

1. Reprinted with permission of The Calgary Stampede, Calgary, Alberta, Canada. Original—Social Media Initiative. Hell or High Water, Division 4.0, Inspiring Collaboration, Calgary Stampede.
2. Jessica Miller, "Marketing Communications," *Cornell Hotel and Restaurant Administration Quarterly*, 34, no. 5 (1993): 49.
3. Ibid.
4. Philip Kotler, "Public Relations Versus Marketing: Dividing the Conceptual Domain and Operational Turf" (paper presented at the *Public Relations Colloquium 1989*, San Diego, CA, January 24, 1989).
5. Shandrow Kim Lachance, "Tokyo Airport Terminal 3 Walkways Transformed into Racetrack Lanes," Fortune.com, April 13, 2015.
6. See "Wild Rice Vegan Café," https://816nyc.com/portfolio/wild-rice-vegan-cafe/#.W57gX0VKiu4 (accessed September 16, 2018).
7. Adapted from Scott M. Cutlip, Allen H. Center, and Glen M. Brown, *Effective Public Relations*, 6th ed. (Upper Saddle River, NJ: Prentice-Hall, 1985), pp. 7–17.
8. Eric Benson and Gotz Goppert, "A Good Break," *United Hemispheres*, January 2015, pp. 62–67, 98, 103; Damien Fletcher, "Surf's up to 100ft: Daredevil Breaks World Record for Largest Wave Ever Ridden," *Mirror*, January 30, 2013, http://www.mirror.co.uk/news/world-news/garrett-mcnamara-rides-100ft-wave-1563121 (accessed August 10, 2015); Chris Chase, "Watch: Surfer Nails Massive 100-Foot Wave," *USA Today.com*, October 29, 2013, http://www.usatoday.com/story/sports/2013/10/29/surf-big-wave-portugal/3296883/ (accessed August 10, 2015).
9. Joe Durocher, "Recovery Marketing: What to Do After a Natural Disaster," *Cornell Hotel and Restaurant Administration Quarterly*, 35, no. 2 (1994): 66.
10. "Olive Garden's Drive Against Hunger Raises More Than $1M," *Nation's Restaurant News* (June 25, 2001): 30.
11. Pamela Parseghian, "Chefs Looking for New Recipe to Drum Up Publicity Should Serve Up Side of Smarts," *Nation's Restaurant News* (September 6, 2004): 42.
12. The Homestead Resort Web site, http://www.-thehomestead.com/welcome/calendar.asp (accessed December 18, 2004); Karen Weiner Escalera, "How to Get News Out of Nothing," *Lodging* (March 1992): 25–26.
13. http://www.choosechicago.com/event/tasteofChicago 18479.
14. Christine Blank, "Driving Revenue," *Hotel and Motel Management* (October 4, 2004): 3.

15. Arthur M. Merims, "Marketing's Stepchild: Product Publicity," *Harvard Business Review* (November/December 1972): 111–112; see also Katharine D. Paine, "There Is a Method for Measuring PR," *Marketing News* (November 7, 1987): 5.
16. Angharad Miller—Swayy, August 30, 2018, "The Impact of Influencer Marketing on the Booking Journey," https://www.phocuswire.com/influencer-marketing-booking-journey (accessed November 14, 2018); "Tourism PR Professionals Say How Social Media Changed Their Jobs," http://skift.com/2014/10/23, p. 3.
17. See A. J. S. Stanaland, M. O. Lwin, & P. E. Murphy (2011), "Consumer Perceptions of the Antecedents and Consequences of Corporate Social Responsibility," *Journal of Business Ethics* (2011), 102: 47–55; "2015 Cone Communications Millennial CSR Study." (accessed September 18, 2018) http://www.conecomm.com/research-blog/2015-cone-communications-millennial-csr-study.
18. Choice Hotels Web site, http://careers.choicehotels.com/benefits/paid-leave.html (accessed August 20, 2015).
19. See https://www.youtube.com/watch?v=7rtHmSfYDbs (accessed September 25, 2018).
20. Arthur M. Merims, "Marketing's Stepchild: Product Publicity," *Harvard Business Review* (November–December 1972): 111–112. For more on evaluating public relations effectiveness, see Katharine D. Paine, "There Is a Method for Measuring PR," *Marketing News* (November 6, 1987): 5; Eric Stoltz and Jack Torobin, "Public Relations by the Numbers," *American Demographics* (January 1991): 42–46.
21. Tom McCarthy, "Add Publicity in the Mix," *Lodging Hospitality* (October 1999): 17.
22. See: A. G. Woodside, "Brand-Consumer Storytelling Theory and Research: Introduction to a Psychology & Marketing (special issue). *Psychology & Marketing* (2010), 27: 531–540. doi:10.1002/mar.20342; A. Lundqvist, V. Liljander, J. Gummerus, and A. van Riel, "The Impact of Storytelling on the Consumer Brand Experience: The Case of a Firm-Originated Story," *Journal of Brand Management* (February/March, 2013), 20: 283–297; R. C. Schank (1999), *Dynamic Memory Revisited* (Cambridge, U.K.: Cambridge University Press, 1999).
23. See https://cycloneanaya.com/ (accessed September 25, 2018).
24. Eric Bergman, "Crisis? What Crisis?" *Communications World*, 11, no. 4 (1994): 19–23.
25. Robert Irvine, "What's a Crisis Anyway?" *Communications World*, 14, no. 7 (1997): 36–41.
26. Ian Mitroff, "Crisis Management and Environmentalism: A Natural Fit," *California Management Review*, 36, no. 2 (1994): 101–114.
27. Julie Miller, "Crisis to Calm," *Hotel and Motel Management* (August 11, 1997): 261.
28. Ekaterina Walter, "10 Tips for Reputation and Crisis Management in the Digital World," *Forbes*, www.forbes.com/sites/ekaterinawalter/2013/11/12/10.
29. Jonathan Treiber, "Why Digital Promotions Are More Important Than Ever," *Retailing Today*, June 14, 2015, www.Retailingtoday.Com/Article/Why-Digital-Promotions-Are-More-Important-Ever; "Survey: The Vast Majority (87%) Of Retail Marketers Plan To Invest More In Mobile Marketing In 2016," *Pr Newswire*, March 3, 2016, www.Pmewswire.Com/News-Releases/Survey-The-Vast-Ma-Jority-87-Of-Retail-Marketers-Plan-To-Invest-More-In-Mobile-Market-Ing-In-2016-300230162.Html.
30. David H. Freeman, "An Unusual Way to Run a Ski Business," *Forbes* (December 7, 1992): 28.
31. Jennifer Coleman, "The Fine Art of Fine Dining," *Travel Agent* (September 18, 2000): 96.
32. David Cogswell and Sara Perez Webber, "Spring Flings," *Travel Agent* (February 21, 2000): 108.
33. Statista, "Total Number of Redeemed Consumer Packaged Goods (CPG) Coupons in the United States from 2007 to 2014," 2015, www.statista.com/statistics/247546/total-number-of-redeemed-consumer-packaged-goods-coupons-in-the-us/ (accessed August 10, 2015).
34. Trueship, "One-Click Savings: A Quick Look at 2015 Mobile Coupon Statistics," March 24, 2015, http://www.trueship.com/blog/2015/03/24/one-click-savings-a-quick-look-at-2015-mobile-coupon-statistics/#.VckNAVy-XA4 (accessed August 10, 2015).
35. Cellfire, www.google.com/cellfirecoupons.2015, Cellfire, Inc.
36. "Free-Flying Offer to Join Marco Polo Cruises," Travel-trade (October 20, 2004).
37. Ibid.
38. Tricia Campbell, "Cozying Up to Customers," *Sales & Marketing Management* (December 1999): 15.
39. Mary Ewing-Mulligan and Ed McCarthy, "Wine Lists Used Creatively Are Vintage Opportunity to Attract New Customers," *Nation's Restaurant News* (July 23, 2001): 43–46.
40. Based on information found in "Dunkin' Donuts Returns to Its Roots—Doughnuts—in $10 Million Campaign," Promo (March 18, 2009), http://-promomagazine.com/contests/dunkindonutscampaign/; "Time to Judge the Donuts," *PR Newswire*, May 18, 2009; Steve Adams, "Dunkin Donuts Contest Finalists Cook Their Unique Creations in Bake-Off," *Patriot Ledger*, May 29, 2009, http://www.patriotledger.com/businessx1594716181/doughnut-design-101; www.dunkindonuts.com/donut/ (accessed August 2010).
41. Tom Feltenstein, "Slay the Neighborhood Goliath," *Restaurant Hospitality* (October 1999): 38.
42. See http://www.galvestonhistory.org/events/dickens-on-the-strand/dickens-on-the-strand-3 (accessed September 28, 2018).
43. http://www.hilton.com/en/hi/promotions (accessed October 4, 2008).
44. https://www.tgigreattimes.co.uk/ (accessed October 5, 2008).

45. https://outback.com; http://www.thefashionable-house-wife.com/?p=3907 (accessed October 5, 2008).
46. https://www.reuters.com/article/pressRelease/idUS80974_06-Aug-2008+MW20080806 (accessed October 5, 2008).
47. https://www.quantifiedmarketing.com/learning_-center/restaurant-promotions.php (accessed October 5, 2008).
48. Roger A. Strang, "Sales Promotion-Fast Growth, Faulty Management," *Harvard Business Review* (July/August 1976): 98.
49. Steve Weiss, "Promotions Trend: Get Yourself a Partner," *Restaurants and Institutions*, 103, no. 26 (1993): 78–93.
50. National Restaurant Association, *Promoting the Neighborhood Restaurant: A Local Store Marketing Manual* (Chicago, IL: National Restaurant Association, 1988).
51. Tom Feltenstein, "Wily Underdogs with Fewer Resources Still Have Bite in Competitive Foodservice Industry," *Nation's Restaurant News* (May 7, 2001): 40.
52. Tom Felterstein, *Restaurant Profits Through Advertising and Promotion* (New York: Van Nostrand Reinhold, 1983).
53. CraftWorks Foundation Web site, http://www.craftworksfoundation.org/signature-programs/ (accessed August 11, 2015); Theresa Howard, "Charitable Promos Can Be Profitable Market Strategy," *Nation's Restaurant News* (June 9, 1997): 18.
54. Scott Hume, "Taking It to the Streets," *Restaurants and Institutions* (October 15, 1999): 101–108.

15

Objectives

After reading this chapter, you should be able to:

1. Explain the nature of personal selling and the objectives of the sales force.
2. Describe sales force structure and organization.
3. Identify the key issues in recruiting and training salespeople.
4. Explain the steps in the selling process.
5. Discuss supervising salespeople, including motivating and evaluating performance.
6. Discuss trends in social selling.

Professional Sales

The city of Grapevine, Texas, became an important tourism destination without the benefit of beaches or mountains or a Grand Canyon. Sales planning and team sales work brought this about. What Grapevine had was available land for development and access to seven major highways, the Dallas-Fort Worth (DFW) airport, and a team of salespeople consisting of a mayor, city council, and the city manager's office "Go Team" who sold Grapevine to prospective hospitality companies.

Situated just north of the DFW metroplex and the DFW airport, Grapevine decided that tourism and hospitality were the industries it wanted. While many Texas communities continued to seek manufacturing industries, Grapevine decided that tourism, hospitality, and shopping would create thousands of jobs and would attract out-of-area visitors as well as day shoppers and restaurant patrons from the DFW metroplex. It was felt that these were complementary to the historic nature of the community and would assist in preserving the culture of a small town.

The mayor, city council, and the city manager's office believed in the value of tourism and the hospitality industry. Tommy Hardy, assistant city manager, was charged to promote the destination and tourism economic development of Grapevine. Tommy decided that to be successful, he would need to fully understand tourism and the hospitality industry. This meant knowing the major players in the hospitality industry and understanding their language, such as ADR and RevPAR. It also meant that Grapevine would need to develop a marketing plan with desired target hospitality companies to become members of the Grapevine community and then pursue them with professional marketing/sales strategies.

Tommy and staff members attended hospitality industry conventions as well as the huge ICSC (International Council of Shopping Centers) show in Las Vegas. This permitted them to build a database, determine new trends, and establish contacts with executives who might bring a new hospitality company to Grapevine.

The city of Grapevine worked closely with developers, architects, and the financial community. Tommy Hardy and staff made sales calls on targeted companies. They conducted tours, hosted receptions for prospects to meet members of the community, and, most important, provided continuous follow-up to "close the sale." Tommy said that he and staff were never afraid to go to the private sector for assistance in planning and marketing. "We always took big steps," he said, and "the private community supported us. Our responsibility is to bring prospect companies together with brokers and developers. Once that has been accomplished, we walk out of the room."

The mayor of Grapevine was born and raised in the community and has great civic pride in Grapevine. Unlike some desk-bound mayors, he worked aggressively with Tommy and staff to bring desired hospitality and retailing companies to the community. He also has a reputation as a great "closer" and personally clinched many deals.

Developing and building a visitor infrastructure is critical, but all this must be supported by advertising and promotion. Sales and bed taxes generated by the complex support the Grapevine Convention and Visitors Bureau, which organizes visitor events such as GrapeFest, one of the top 100 festivals in the United States, provides promotional materials, conducts familiarization tours, and helps coordinate and promote activities with other organizations. Events have proven very popular with the local community and with day visitors from the metroplex, adding to tourism revenue.

Results

An area in northeast Grapevine was targeted for commercial tourism/hospitality development. One of the earliest companies was the Gaylord Texan mega-resort, which opened 1,511 hotel rooms and a 400,000-square-foot convention center. Nine additional hotels were located in the development area, including Great Wolf Lodge, a 402 all-suite hotel with a 50,000-square-foot indoor water park, and a conference center. Great Wolf then decided to add 203 more rooms and more meeting space. A typical Great Wolf water park is shown in the chapter opening picture.

Despite the growth in Grapevine hotel rooms, performance comparisons with other metroplex areas are excellent, as seen in the following table. Restaurant sales also increased during this time period by $3 to $5 million per year.

Attraction	Annual Visitors
Grapevine Mills Mall	13 million
Bass Pro Shops Outdoor World	2 million
Lake Grapevine	1.5 million
Festivals/events/historic district	1.15 million
Hotel guests	532,000
Grapevine Winery visitors	235,000
Heritage/information centers	150,000
Grapevine Vintage Railroad	80,000

Source: Based on Grapevine Convention and Visitors Bureau.

Tourism development planners know the importance of retail shopping, and a huge retail shopping area was developed, including Grapevine Mills Mall, an indoor mall of over 2 million square feet that annually attracts 15 million shoppers from a five-state region. The spectacular Bass Pro Shops Outdoor World with 200,000 square feet of space was built in proximity and by itself attracts 2 million visitors per year. Success attracts others, including the Glass Cactus, a 26,000-square-foot entertainment center, and Lone Star Crossing, a 120,000-square-foot shopping center.

Tourism development also occurred outside the destination corridor within the historic downtown Grapevine area and other areas of Grapevine. The Grapevine Vintage Railroad connects Grapevine with the renovated Fort Worth Stockyards. A complex of upscale restaurants known as the Epicenter was developed on South Main Street in Grapevine. This complex complemented other downtown retailers, restaurants, and art galleries.

Tourism in Grapevine means 13 million visitors annually. Thousands of individuals are directly employed in the industry, providing a healthy economy. Tourism has allowed downtown Grapevine to flourish as contrasted to the dying centers of many Texas towns. It has also encouraged historical preservation and cultural growth in the arts. Grapevine also saw over a 22 percent increase in its RevPAR, over twice the rate of its competitors.

None of this would have been possible without the teamwork between the private sector and the public. Nor would it have been possible without sales planning and strategy by a dedicated team of the mayor, city council, and city staff who wanted to see Grapevine grow in a desired and beneficial manner. The sales techniques presented in this chapter are utilized organizations both inside and outside of the sales office. The City of Grapevine Texas needed to sell their vision to the private sector; without an effective sales strategy and plan they would have not been able to build a tourist destination. To be effective as a manager in the hospitality you need to know how to sell.

Management of Professional Sales

Success or failure within the hospitality industry ultimately rests on the ability to sell. A roadside motel at an intersection of major highways or a popular restaurant with waiting lines is sometimes viewed as being above the need "to sell." No member of the hospitality industry can accept this as a long-term viewpoint.

These and all others who face the guest can drive away or attract business. In the best cases, they can upsell in a way that creates additional value for the guest, such as suggesting desserts, special drinks, and even a gift certificate for a friend. Higher-margin suites can be sold instead of the lowest-priced room.

Successful owners and managers know that they must sell continuously. County commissioners, tax evaluation officials, planning boards, the press, bankers, and the local visitor center must all be sold on one's hospitality business. The city of Grapevine, Texas, in the opening vignette clearly demonstrates the need to sell and the research that follows.

Libraries could be filled with tales of lost sales or needlessly fractured guest relationships because of a curt response or an unsavory attitude on the part of support staff who mistakenly believe that sales is not their responsibility.

Everyone must sell, but a few individuals have the specific responsibility for ensuring that payrolls can be met, invoices can be paid, and a fair return on investment (ROI) can be achieved. These are the professional salespeople.

Nature of Hospitality Sales

Sales personnel serve as the company's personal link to customers. The sales representative *is* the company to many customers and in turn brings back much-needed customer intelligence. Personal selling is the most expensive contact and communication tool used by the company. If managed effectively it can produce great returns.

Hotels are known for having a sales staff. However, other areas of the industry use salespeople. Newly designed restaurants increasingly include areas that can be closed off for private parties, creating an opportunity for a salesperson to sell meeting space and banquets. Rental car companies maintain sales staff, and the suppliers to industry hire salespeople. As a result of the importance of personal selling in our industry and the opportunities in selling, many graduates of hospitality programs find themselves in careers with personal selling.

The Burroughs Home is a historical mansion that serves as a museum and event venue. Museums have realized they can be attractive sites for weddings, receptions and meeting. This provides opportunities for hospitality graduates to sell and manage events. Brian Jannsen/Alamy Stock Photo.

Communicating Sales representatives communicate information about the company's products and services.

Information gathering Sales representatives conduct market research and intelligence work and fill in a call report.

Allocating Sales representatives decide on which customers to allocate scarce products.

Canadian resorts like Lake Louise, home to the iconic Fairmont Chateau Lake Louise, attract international meetings to Canada. Jimmy Wen/Alamy Stock Photo.

Cost estimates for making a personal sales call vary depending on the industry and the company, but one conclusion remains constant. However, measured, the cost is high! Add to this the fact that sales orders are seldom written on the first call and often require five or more calls, particularly for larger orders. The cost of obtaining a new client thus becomes enormously high. Despite the high cost, personal selling is often the most effective tool available to a hospitality company. Sales representatives perform one or more of the following tasks for their companies:

- **Prospecting.** Sales representatives find and cultivate new customers.
- **Targeting.** Sales representatives decide how to allocate their scarce time among prospects and customers.
- **Communicating.** Sales representatives communicate information about the company's products and services.
- **Selling.** Sales representatives know the art of salesmanship: approaching, presenting, answering objections, and closing sales.
- **Servicing.** Sales representatives provide various services to the customers—consulting on their problems, rendering technical assistance, arranging financing, and expediting delivery.
- **Information gathering.** Sales representatives conduct market research and intelligence work and fill in call reports.
- **Allocating.** Sales representatives decide which customers to allocate scarce products during product shortages.
- **Maintaining strategic partnerships.** Senior salespeople, including the sales manager, provide valuable planning assistance to clients.

The sales representative's mix of tasks varies with the state of the economy. During product shortages, such as a temporary shortage of hotel rooms during a major convention, sales representatives find themselves with nothing to sell. Some companies jump to the conclusion that fewer sales representatives are then needed. But this thinking overlooks the salesperson's other roles: **allocating** the product, counseling unhappy customers, and selling the company's other products that are not in short supply. It also ignores the long-run nature of hospitality sales.

Many conventions and conferences are planned years in advance, and hospitality salespeople must often work with meeting and convention planners two to four years in advance of the actual event. Resorts in the United States have concentrated much of their selling efforts on meetings and conferences, which by now represent 35 percent or more of their customers.[1] This was not achieved by viewing professional sales as a short-run tactic. A senior analyst with Tourism Canada demonstrated that Canadian resort salespeople are effective in reaching foreign markets. Guests in Canadian resorts are 60 percent Canadian and 40 percent foreign. By comparison, U.S. resorts have a mix of 91 percent American and 9 percent foreign.[2]

As companies move toward a stronger market orientation, their sales forces need to become more market focused and customer oriented. The traditional view is that salespeople should worry about volume and sell, sell, sell, and the marketing department should worry about marketing strategy and profitability. The newer view is that salespeople should know how to produce customer satisfaction and company profit. They should know how to analyze sales data, measure market potential, gather market intelligence, develop marketing strategies and plans, and become proficient at the use of sales tactics.

This has become very clear as micromarketing, including database marketing, online distribution, social media, marketing dashboards, and competitive information are readily available within the hospitality industry; salespeople need to understand how to analyze and effectively use the information.

After viewing the importance of marketing information to sales, a hospitality industry writer with *Hotel and Motel Management* magazine concluded the following:[3]

- Closing sales has more to do with professionalism than anything else.
- Understanding the identity of real prospects increases sales productivity.
- Sales force members can save hours of time by having information about prospect group clients.
- It is critical to know what groups have a history of booking rooms in your type of hotel.

Competitive Analysis and Competitive Sets

Sales managers within the hospitality industry are often held accountable for the performance of their properties against members of a competitive set. The selection of a comparable competitive set is, therefore, critical to meaningful comparative sales analysis.

Small bed and breakfasts (B&Bs) usually have no difficulty defining their competitive set. However, restaurants may not find this task an easy one. As an example, should a family-owned-and-run catfish restaurant be grouped with seafood restaurants such as Red Lobster? Perhaps it should be grouped with family-owned restaurants, but does this make sense to place it with Italian and Greek restaurants?

In the case of hotels, three common approaches are used to determine which competitive set or cluster is most appropriate.

ADR: The basis for average daily rate (ADR) clusters is that properties which are similar tend to sell for similar prices in a competitive market.

Product type: Properties may be grouped as luxury, resort, or in other ways such as the AAA diamond rating system or Mobil-star system. Whatever factors are selected to form a competitive set, there are certain to be inequalities.[4]

Management company set: Professional management companies may have contracts with a variety of hotels operating under different flags. It is tempting to use these hotels as a competitive set, but this practice is subject to criticism.

Hotels operating under the direction of an independent management company may have few competitive characteristics. Therefore, comparisons between these properties can be highly misleading.

Sales managers who focus on the actions and results of competitors may be focusing on the wrong variables. A study of customer orientation versus competitor orientation by management showed that "a customer orientation has a greater effect on a hotel's performance than does a competitor orientation." "A customer orientation that concentrates on acquisition, satisfaction and retention of customers is superior to a competitor orientation focused on monitoring, managing and outflanking competitors."[5]

Sales Force Objectives

Hospitality companies typically establish objectives for the sales force. Sales objectives are essential for two reasons:

1. Objectives ensure that corporate goals are met. Goals may include revenue, market share, and improved corporate image.

2. Objectives assist sales force members to plan and execute their personal sales programs. Objectives also help ensure that a salesperson's time and company-support resources such as personal computers are used efficiently.

Sales force objectives must be custom designed annually for each company. Individual sales objectives are established to support corporate goals and marketing and sales objectives. Annual marketing and sales objectives are normally broken into quarterly and monthly objectives. Sales force members break them down further into personal objectives by day and week.

It is the responsibility of the sales manager to establish and assign objectives to individual salespeople. These are often developed after consultation with the salesperson. An experienced salesperson is in the best position to understand what is happening in the marketplace and to assist the sales manager in formulating realistic objectives.

Occasionally, annual objectives must be changed before year end. This is generally due to a dramatic occurrence, such as the outbreak of war or a natural disaster.

Although sales objectives are custom designed, there are general objectives commonly employed by members of the hospitality industry.

Sales Volume

Occupancy, passenger miles, and total covers are common measures of sales volume within the hospitality industry. They all mean the same thing: Bring in as many customers as possible. An emphasis on volume alone inevitably leads to price discounting, attracting undesirable market segments, and cost cutting.

Sales Volume by Selected Segments

Exclusive resorts, charter flight services, and upper-end cruises tend to operate with the philosophy that if one establishes volume objectives but restricts **prospecting** to highly selective segments, price and profits will take care of themselves. Although appropriate for a few niche players, this thinking cannot be applied to the majority of the hospitality industry. Nevertheless, the concept of establishing sales objectives by specific market segment is feasible and basic to effective sales. Sales strategies must be analyzed and reviewed continuously in view of quantitative sales results.

Sales Volume and Price/Margin Mix

Establish sales volume objectives by product lines to ensure a desired gross profit. This system is the basis for revenue management. Salespeople often criticize the system as restrictive and unrealistic. The fact is it works. British Airways, Hertz, Sheraton Hotels, and Royal Caribbean Cruises are representative of the firms that use this system. Whether a revenue management system is in place or not, establishing objectives by volume and by price/margin segments leads to improved revenue.

Upselling and Second-Chance Selling

Excellent profit opportunities exist for hospitality companies, particularly hotels and resorts, to upgrade price and profit margins by selling higher-priced products such as suites through upselling. A related concept is second-chance selling, in which the sales department contacts a client who has already booked an event such as a two-day meeting. Opportunities exist to sell additional services, such as airport limousine pickup and delivery or to upgrade rooms or food and beverage (F&B) from chicken to prime rib. Second-chance selling encourages cooperation and teamwork between departments, such as catering, F&B, and sales.

Market Share or Market Penetration

Airlines, cruise lines, major fast-food chains, and rental car companies are highly concerned with market share and market penetration. These concepts have considerably less meaning to many restaurants, hotels, resorts, and other members of the hospitality industry.

The management of most hotels is concerned primarily with measures such as occupancy, average room rate, yield, and customer mix. The corporate marketing department of a chain, however, is likely to be concerned about market share, particularly if it is a dominant chain in a market such as Hawaii. Hilton, Sheraton, Aston, Outrigger Hotels, Marriott, and others actively compete for market share in that market.

Evidence indicates that hotel management companies are increasingly held accountable for clearly defined performance standards. Among these is the level of market penetration. This is a clear departure from the past when contracts between owners and hotel management companies contained vague references to standards of performance.[6]

As a result, it is very possible that the sales department of hotels and resorts will increasingly be required to measure market potential and will be held accountable for a predetermined level of market penetration. Independent measures of market penetration such as the STAR report will undoubtedly assume increased importance in the measurement of hotel sales. The STAR report provides information on average rate, occupancy, and RevPAR for the competitive set of a hotel.

Product-Specific Objectives

Occasionally, a sales force is charged with the specific responsibility to improve sales volume for specific product lines. This objective may be associated with upselling and second-chance selling but may also be part of the regular sales duties of the sales force. A sales force may be asked to sell more suites, higher-margin coffee breaks, holiday packages, honeymoon packages, and other product lines.

Excellent opportunities for enhanced revenues exist within many hotels and resorts from nonroom sales. Recreation club memberships, including children's programs, are sometimes sold to local residents. A properly designed club membership can generate substantial income from membership fees, dues, and F&B revenues. The Boca Raton Resort initiated a Premier Club Membership program that produced membership sales in excess of $40 million the first three years. The club gave residents access to its beach, spa, golf course, tennis course, children's activities, and concierge services. Additionally, special events were planned for career club members.[7]

Sales Force Structure and Size

The diverse nature of the hospitality industry means that different sales force structures and sizes have evolved. The structure of a sales force within the airline industry is different from that of a hotel or cruise line. In general, most restaurants do not use a sales force but depend on other parts of the marketing mix, such as advertising and sales promotion.

The hotel/resort industry traditionally uses a functional, hierarchical structure. Within this structure, hotel departments are organized around particular functions, such as housekeeping or sales. Department managers, including the sales manager, report to a GM. In smaller hotels such as roadside motels, the GM usually serves as sales manager because the organization is not large enough to support functional departments. Within large hotels and resorts, the sales department may have directors of specialized sales such as a convention and meetings sales director or a corporate accounts sales director.

The structure of a hotel sales department depends on the culture of the organization, size of the property, nature of the market, and type of hotel. A casino hotel might contain the same number of rooms as a ski resort hotel yet have a somewhat different organizational structure. Some casino hotels have sales directors who are responsible for working with junket reps and premium players. A resort hotel might have a sales director responsible for working with travel agents and tour wholesalers, or with nationwide ski clubs. The sales force structures commonly used in the hospitality industry today are described next.

Territorial-Structured Sales Force

In the simplest sales organization, each sales representative is assigned an exclusive territory to represent the company's full line. This sales structure has a number of advantages. First, it results in a clear definition of the salesperson's responsibilities.

As the only salesperson working the territory, he or she bears the credit or blame for area sales to the extent that personal selling effort makes a difference. Second, territorial responsibility increases the sales representative's incentive to cultivate local business and personal ties. These ties contribute to the sales representative's selling effectiveness and personal life. Third, travel expenses are relatively small because each sales representative travels within a small geographic area.

A territorial sales organization is often supported by many levels of sales management. Each higher-level sales manager takes on increasing marketing and administration work. Sales managers are paid for their management skills rather than their selling skills. The new sales trainee, in looking ahead, can expect to become a sales representative, then a district manager, and then a regional manager, and, depending on his or her ability and motivation, may move to still higher levels of sales or general management.

Territory Size

Territories can be designed to attempt to provide either equal sales potential or equal workload. Each principle offers certain advantages. Territories of equal potential provide each sales representative with the same income opportunities and provide the company with a means to evaluate performance. Persistent differences in sales yield by territory are assumed to reflect differences in ability or effort of individual sales representatives. Customer density varies by territory, and territories with equal potential can vary widely in size. The potential for selling restaurant supplies in Chicago is larger than in several Rocky Mountain states. A sales representative assigned to Chicago can cover the same sales potential with much less effort than the sales representative who sells in the Rocky Mountain West. The sales representative assigned to the larger and sparser territory is going to end up with either fewer sales and less income for equal effort or equal sales through extraordinary effort. A common solution is to acknowledge that territories differ in attractiveness and assign the better or more senior sales representatives to the better territories.

Alternatively, territories might be designed to equalize the sales workload. Each sales representative could then cover his or her territory adequately. This principle results in some variation in territory sales potential. This does not concern a sales force on straight salary, but when sales representatives are compensated partly on commission, territories vary in their attractiveness.

Territory Shape

Territories are formed by combining smaller units, such as counties or states, until they add up to a territory of a given sales potential or workload. Territorial design must take into account the location of natural barriers, the adequacy of transportation, and so on. Many companies prefer a certain territory shape because the shape can influence the cost and ease of coverage and the sales representatives' job satisfaction.

The territorial structure is most commonly used by airlines, cruise lines, and rental car companies, and at the corporate level by hotel chains. It is not frequently used by individual hotel/resort properties that instead seem to organize their sales departments by function or type of customer.

Market-Segment-Structured Sales Force

Companies often specialize their sales forces along market segment lines. Separate sales forces can be set up by different industries for the convention/meeting segment, the incentive travel market, and other major segments. This is the most common type of structure within the hotel industry. For example, associations have different needs than corporations; thus, one salesperson may be assigned to the association market, while another is assigned to the corporate market.

Market-Channel-Structured Sales Force

The importance of marketing intermediaries, such as wholesalers, tour operators, travel agencies, and junket reps, to the hospitality industry has created sales force structures to serve different marketing channels.

Targeting Sales representatives decide how to allocate their scarce time among prospects and customers.

The cruise line industry has historically depended on travel agents for the bulk of its sales. A study by Claritas, the marketing support company, showed that 96 percent of cruise line passengers purchased tickets through a travel agency, including OTAs. This company developed thematic maps **targeting** the areas in which the best prospects for a cruise line were concentrated. The cruise line then used these maps in presentations by its sales force to travel agents.[8]

A segment of the cruise line industry, cargo freighters are ships that carry freight everywhere in the world and offer a few berths to travelers. They lack the glamour and service of cruise ships but appeal to travelers with time. Highly specialized travel agents sell this product. Information is also available at www.freightword.com or www.traveltips.com.

Some hotels such as those near historical sites receive substantial bookings through motor coach tour brokers. The location, size, and type of hospitality companies greatly affect the relative importance of travel intermediaries. This in turn affects whether a company designs its sales force structure by travel intermediary.[9]

Customer-Structured Sales Force

A customer-structured sales force recognizes that specific customers who are critical to the success of the organization exist. The sales force is usually organized to serve these accounts through a key or national account structure.

Key Accounts

Large accounts (called key accounts, major accounts, or national accounts) are often singled out for special attention and handling. If the account is a large company with divisions operating in many parts of the country, it is likely to be handled as a national account and assigned to a specific individual or sales team. If the company has several such accounts, it is likely to organize a national account management (NAM) division.

NAM is growing for a number of reasons. As buyer concentration increases through mergers and acquisitions, fewer buyers account for a larger share of a company's sales. Another factor is that many buyers are centralizing their purchases instead of leaving them to the local units. This gives buyers more bargaining power. Still another factor is that as products become more complex, more groups in the buyer's organization become involved in the purchase process, and the typical salesperson might not have the skill, authority, or coverage to be effective in selling to the large buyer. In organizing a national account program, a company faces a number of issues, including how to select national accounts; how to manage them; how to develop, manage, and evaluate a national account manager; how to organize a structure for national accounts; and where to locate NAM in the organization.

Combination-Structured Sales Force

Some hotels and resorts have a sales force structured by product, market segment, market channel, and customer. A large hotel might have a catering/banquet sales force (product), a convention/meeting sales force (market segment), a tour wholesale sales force (marketing intermediary), and a national accounts sales force (customer). Proponents of such a sales force believe it encourages the sales force to reach most available customers. They also contend it is impossible for a single salesperson to understand and effectively sell all of the hotel's products to all available customer segments through all marketing channels. Sales specialists can become familiar with major customers, understand trends that affect them, and plan appropriate sales strategies and tactics.

Opponents of this system feel that in many cases this sales force structure indicates the hotel is trying to be all things to all people in the absence of long-term goals and strategies. They contend that such a structure is difficult to manage and can be confusing to the sales force and the customer because the same customer may be classified in different areas and thus be handled by more than one salesperson.

Regardless of which structure is used by a hotel or resort, a particular market segment neglected by many North American hoteliers is local markets. Many local markets offer potential for F&B and function room sales. Although a resort such as the Greenbriar in a rural area of West Virginia might not have a large local market, it is scarcely the case for most hotels. The Japanese seem to be particularly adept at penetrating local markets; 40 to 50 percent of Japanese hotel sales are accounted for by parties and other events from local companies.[10] Sales managers must be aware of the local market and develop a sales force structure appropriate for penetrating this market.

Seven months after opening, the Dalmahoy Golf and Country Club Resort near Edinburgh, Scotland, recognized the need for a strong sales effort in the local market and for a combination-structured sales force. Dalmahoy was experiencing low occupancy and less-than-desirable membership growth. Many factors were involved, such as a poor economy and almost no awareness by Edinburgh area golfers. As a member of the U.K.-based Country Club Hotel Group, Dalmahoy had the assistance of this company's national sales force. The management of Dalmahoy knew that a strong property-level sales effort was also needed and employed two salespersons to serve the local market, plus a travel trade manager to work with intermediaries to attract overseas business.[11]

Sales Force Size

Once the company clarifies its sales force strategy and structure, it is ready to consider sales force size. After determining the type and number of desired customers, a workload approach can be used to establish sales force size. This method consists of the following steps:

1. Customers are grouped into size classes according to their annual sales volume.
2. The desirable call frequencies (number of sales calls on an account per year) are established for each class.
3. The number of accounts in each size class is multiplied by the corresponding call frequency to arrive at the total workload for the country in sales calls per year.
4. The average number of calls a sales representative can make per year is determined.
5. The number of sales representatives needed is determined by dividing the total annual calls required by the average calls made by a sales representative.

Suppose that the company estimates its national market consists of 1,000 "A" accounts and 2,000 "B" accounts. "A" accounts require nine calls a year, whereas "B" accounts require six calls a year. This means that the company needs a sales force that can make 21,000 sales calls a year. Suppose that the average sales representative can make 1,000 calls a year. The company would need 21 full-time sales representatives.

The size of a sales force is determined by changes in the market, competition, and corporate strategies and policies. The sales process also directly affects decisions concerning sales force size. The following describes several of the factors that influence the size of a hotel's sales force:

- *Corporate/chain sales support.* Several major hotel chains have employed a corporate sales force to reach the meeting/convention/conference market. The concept behind this sales force is that individual hotel properties may not be in a position to search out and track this important market and that a sales force representing the chain can recommend and sell all appropriate hotels within the chain, not simply a single property. In recent years, some chains have begun to question the value of this sales force and may drop this area of sales support. If this occurs, individual properties may find it necessary to employ one or more additional sales force members to ensure coverage of this important segment.

- *Use of overseas independent sales reps.* Sales reps have traditionally been used by hotels and resorts to serve foreign countries. With the growing importance of many foreign markets, several companies are rethinking the use of independent reps and may substitute salaried sales staff in these markets.

- *Team selling.* Team selling has proved to be an effective and powerful tactic to reach and retain key customers. Its opportunities and limitations are only beginning to be realized in the hospitality industry.

- *Corporate selling.* Members of the travel industry sometimes join sales/marketing efforts to reach selected market segments. For example, a program offering 750 luxury properties in 85 countries was offered through credit cards targeted at United Airlines elite loyalty club members. This program offered guest privileges such as a buffet breakfast and available upgrades. An attractive color brochure was sent to members. It was apparent based on the location and rates of the hotel/resort properties that above-average income travelers were selected. Opportunities for cooperative sales programs in the travel industry are limited only by creativity and willingness of two or more companies/organizations to work together for their mutual benefit.

- *Electronic and telephone sales.* Electronic sales are now firmly entrenched as an important sales tool for the hospitality industry. Even local restaurants use a Web site as an informational and sales tool. This tool is particularly effective in international sales where customers and providers such as B&Bs can quickly interface. The majority of hospitality firms do not depend solely on this tool but have instead found that electronic sales is most effective when used as part of a marketing/sales mix, including database marketing, telephone (800 numbers), personal sales, and a carefully selected blend of media.

- *Search engine marketing sales.* Search engine marketing (SEM) focuses on using the internet effectively to market your hotel, restaurant, or tourism product. The importance of SEM has steadily increased over time as more travelers make reservations online. Hotel companies are putting more resources into SEM to help counter the need to pay commissions to online travel agencies (OTAs) to book their rooms. Some of the tactics used in SEM include the purchase of ads online and search engine optimization (SEO). SEO is a technique where the message on the Web is designed to catch the attention of search engines, so when a customer types in "Hotels in Vancouver" a company's hotel in Vancouver will come up on the first page of the search. Good SEM can be used to generate individual bookings as well as booking and leads for groups.[12]

- *Proprietary Web sites.* Effective SEM requires careful planning, including the development of a Web site.

A few strategies to create effective sales results from proprietary Web sites include the following:

A. Conduct data mining of potential guest profiles through information collected from frequent guest program databases or from guests at check-in.

B. Complement and support Web sites through direct mail sent to past guests inviting them to return and to use the company's Web site.

C. Provide Best Rate Guarantees that prices available on the Web site will match any price offered by an OTA.

D. Advertise on Google by "pay by click" to entice Google or another search engine to encourage the company's Web site to appear higher on the search.

E. Acquire the services of a Web page consultant to optimize key words that help locate a Web page higher on the search.

F. Entice customers to use a company's call center or on-site toll-free telephone number by offering "freebies," such as parking, breakfast, movies, and WiFi.

G. Experts in the field recognize that the use of toll-free numbers and call centers is labor intensive, but they say that the cost is less than paying commissions to OTAs.

The size of a sales force may need to increase to support new marketing strategies. The sales manager then has the responsibility to "sell" top management because a budgetary increase will almost certainly be necessary. Similarly, a professional sales manager must be aware of changing trends and new technology. Rather than tenaciously support a larger-than-necessary sales force, the sales manager must be prepared to downsize and substitute technology when appropriate.

Organizing the Sales Department

As discussed previously, hospitality companies traditionally design departments along functional lines. It is common to find hotels with several marketing-related departments, such as a sales department, a guest relations department, and an advertising and public relations department, but not a "marketing" department. In recent years, some hotels have given the title "sales and marketing" to the previously named sales department but with limited training in marketing for the sales manager.

Today's sales managers may have two types of salespeople within their departments: an inside sales force and a field sales force. The term *inside sales* can be misleading because many field salespeople spend a great deal of their time inside the hotel calling clients and prospects, meeting with them, making arrangements with other departments, answering mail, and performing many other duties, such as completing sales reports.

Inside Sales Force

Inside salespeople handle a number of sales tasks. There are technical-support persons, who provide technical information and answers to customers' questions. There are sales assistants, who provide clerical backup for the field salespersons. They call ahead and confirm appointments, carry out credit checks, follow up on deliveries, and answer customers' questions when they cannot reach the outside sales rep. Some inside sales specialists do prospecting and qualifying. This can provide the sales force with background information on the prospective client. The local Chamber of Commerce, internet, local news sources are all good sources of information. In the past these specialists would go to competitive hotels and gain information on their group customers by viewing their reader boards that list the groups that are meeting in the hotel. Today there are online services that provide this information, eliminating the need to leave the sales office. This information prioritizes the salesperson's time and the time of the prospective clients as the salesperson understands their needs.

There are also telemarketers, who use the phone, internet, and social media to find new leads, qualify them, learn about their business, and sell to them. Telemarketers can contact up to 50 customers per day compared with the four or five that an outside salesperson can contact. The information available over the internet, online RFPs and the over use of telemarketing in the past, has made cold calls through telemarketing less effective than it was on previous years. Telemarketing is being replaced by making contacts through networking and online request for proposals (RFPs).

Convention and visitor bureaus, plus hotel brands, have created Web sites where planners can post an RFP. This allows the meeting planner to make one RFP and gain competitive bids from a number of hotels in a region. For the hotel salesperson it gives her information on organizations who want to have a meeting on their area. So, they have hot leads rather than having to make cold calls over the phone. In responding to these electronic requests, hotel sales people need to be responsive, ideally responding to the request within 24 hours. More complex proposals take more time, but at least respond within 24 hours that you do have the space, with the time you expect to be able to deliver a complete proposal. Also, if you are unable to provide a positive response, state the reason why. For example, we do not have the space you need on the dates requested; however, if you are able to move it to these dates we could accommodate you. Larger hotels will often assign a dedicated internal sales person to handle all of the electronic RFPs. Some hotels develop templates for RFP and fill in the blanks with customization, where needed. When using templates make sure that any references to a previous client are eliminated from the RFP, also it is a good idea to customize the RFP with a unique touch to the proposal that creates value for the client. This shows that you understand the client, the attendees, and how you can create a unique experience for them.[13]

Information Needed by the Sales Force

At the least, salespeople need a database of their customers/clients. This helps them prepare for sales calls and also to answer questions while talking with customers.

Basic Database Needs

- List of clients alphabetically and by key client listing
- Sales history of client
- Volume of sales by client
- Seasonality of sales by client
- Products/services purchased by client
- Profitability of client (many companies will not release this to the sales force)
- Buyer contact information
  - Name
  - Title
  - Address (mailing, courier, and post office)
  - E-mail
- Special needs of client
- Past problems of/with client

This is a partial list of the type of information that may be provided to sales force members. Through cloud-based systems this information can be available to affiliated hotels and updated with information gained from scraping the Web.

Reservations Department

The reservations department is a very important inside sales area for many hospitality companies because reservationists may speak with 80 percent of a company's customers. This department is sometimes not viewed as part of the sales team. It is sometimes a separate department, and unfortunately, the reservations and sales departments may have little communication. In worst-case scenarios, they may actually find themselves at odds. This is not the case at Hyatt Hotels, where reservations are under sales/marketing.

A study of reservations departments at a hotel company, airline, and cruise line revealed that much can be done to improve the effectiveness of this critical inside sales force.[14] The results of this study showed that reservations training is critical. The training program prescribed was remarkably similar to that for any sales position. Hyatt focuses on technical aspects, including how to sell. Hyatt's philosophy is that the skills necessary to be an effective salesperson can be taught.

Reservationist candidates at American Airlines are interviewed and hired for their sales ability. Days Inns has a program to hire the elderly and the physically challenged and through training turn them into reservation salespeople. Training your reservationists to be good company representatives and teaching them how to sell will pay big dividends in the long run.[15]

Field Sales Force

Today, sales managers face an increasingly complex marketplace, which has created the need to review the organizational design of the field sales force. We next discuss different types of field sales forces currently used by hospitality companies.

Commissioned Reps

Hotels and resorts commonly use commissioned sales representatives in distant markets where the market potential does not justify employing a salaried salesperson. A Los Angeles hotel may contract with commissioned sales reps in New York or Miami to reach companies and associations that are known to the local sales reps. Commissioned sales reps normally represent several different properties or chains but attempt not to represent competing clients. This is sometimes difficult in the case of chains, which have competing properties.

It is important to follow a few simple rules when working with commissioned sales reps.

1. **Select markets with care.** Distant markets should be selected to match corporate goals and marketing/sales objectives, not simply to have someone represent the company in a location.

2. **Visit the market personally.** Meet with prospective sales reps, examine their offices, check out references, note their personal appearance, ask for a list of current clients, ask for a credit report, and clear the rep through the police and the Better Business Bureau or the equivalent. In general, it is important to be as careful or even more careful in hiring a sales rep to cover distant markets as in hiring salaried sales force members. In some developing nations, a commissioned sales rep is considered to be a member of the client company's workforce and is dependent on that company for livelihood. Local courts often decide in favor of the rep and may award the rep large financial settlements in cases such as dismissal for failure to meet performance standards.

3. **Include the sales rep as part of the hotel's sales force.** It is important to visit the offices of distant sales reps occasionally. This requires an adequate budget for travel and may entail considerable effort to convince the GM that such an expenditure of time and money is worthwhile.

Salaried Sales Force

Most hospitality industry sales force members are paid a salary plus benefits. Additional compensation is sometimes available through commissions, bonuses, profit sharing, or other financial remuneration. In some nations, a sales force, by law, is paid an additional month's salary at Christmas or New Year's and may qualify for benefits unknown to North American companies, such as a month of paid vacation each year.

Team Sales

Team sales have become a necessity in many industries. The hospitality industry is no exception. The concept of a sales team is two or more persons working in concert toward a common sales objective. These persons are not necessarily from the same company. The purpose for a team sales approach is to accomplish objectives through the synergism of two or more people that would be impossible or unduly costly through individual sales efforts.

In addition to traditional objectives, such as to increase occupancy in a hotel, other nonquantifiable objectives are sometimes established for teams. These generally deal with enhancing image and goodwill. People from various disciplines and departments are sometimes brought together to improve morale, teach teamwork, and cross-educate.

Teams within the hospitality industry have traditionally been used for specific tasks, which include but are not limited to the following:

- Sales blitz
- Travel mission
- Charity promotions
- Community improvement programs

Although teams are used for many purposes, the primary purpose for team sales should be to improve sales competitive position. Teams are best used when the needs of the customer or prospect are complex and require the input of specialists. An example might be a large conference that requires the expertise and cooperation of an airline, a golf resort, and a ground transportation company.

Today, the concept of team sales is moving beyond occasional use, such as during a sales blitz, to the allied concepts of relationship marketing and strategic alliances.

Relationship Marketing and Strategic Alliances

The goal of personal selling traditionally was viewed as a specific contract with a customer. But in many cases the company is not seeking simply a one-time sale. It has targeted a major customer account that it would like to serve for a long period of time. The company would like to demonstrate that it has the capabilities to serve the account's needs in a superior way. The type of selling to establish a long-term collaborative relationship is more complex than a short-run, one-time sales approach. Obtaining long-run commitment involves many more agreements than simply closing the sale.[16]

More companies today are moving their emphasis from transaction marketing to relationship marketing. Today's customers are large and often global. They prefer suppliers who can sell and deliver a set of products and services to many locations, and who can work closely with customer teams to improve products and processes.

McDonald's offers a special example of the value of building trust with suppliers. Unlike some restaurant chains, McDonald's supply chain is 100 percent outsourced as opposed to vertically integrated suppliers. Agreements with suppliers are done on a handshake basis. *McDonald's noncontractual agreements with suppliers, both large and small, are built on trust.*

When McDonald's expands into overseas markets, most of the cost is absorbed by suppliers such as McCain Foods, J.R. Simplot, and ConAgra. As McDonald's expands, its suppliers also expand into the same markets. These companies make investments in the hundreds of millions of dollars once McDonald's says it is entering a market such as India. In the case of India, McCain Foods (Toronto, Canada) purchased 8,000 acres to grow french fry potatoes assuring McDonald's of sufficient supply.[17]

Companies recognize that sales teamwork increasingly is the key to winning and maintaining accounts. They recognize that asking their people for teamwork doesn't provide it. They need to revise their compensation system to give credit for work on shared accounts; they must set up better goals and measures for their sales forces; and they must emphasize the importance of teamwork in their training programs while honoring the importance of individual initiative.

Relationship marketing is based on the premise that important accounts need focused and continuous attention. Salespeople working with customers under relationship marketing must do more than call when they think customers might be ready to place orders. They should monitor key accounts, know their problems, be ready to serve them in a number of ways, and strive to become part of the client's team.

When a relationship management program is implemented properly, the organization begins to focus as much on managing its customers as on managing its products. At the same time, companies should realize that although there is a strong move toward relationship marketing, it is not effective in all situations. Hospitality companies must determine which customers will respond profitably to relationship marketing.

The Boca Raton Resort and Club provides an example of the benefits that can accrue from relationship marketing. The resort took the approach that they could no longer confine themselves to selling rooms, conference space, and banquets. They focused on how the resort could partner with the client to help them achieve the goals of the conference.[18] To provide a competitive advantage, companies are

Hotels, resorts, and meeting venues hosting meetings should work with their clients to ensure the organization's desired outcome of the meeting is met. Derek Meijer/Alamy Stock Photo.

using consultative selling as a way of helping their clients and differentiating their product.

Strategic alliances are a highly developed form of relationship marketing that are common between vendor and buyer or between noncompeting vendors and a common buyer. "Alliances are relationships between interdependent parties that agree to cooperate but still retain separate identities."[19] A strategic alliance may involve sharing a combination of any of the following: confidences, database, market knowledge, planning resources, risks, security, and technology.

Strategic alliances have become a necessity due to a variety of factors: globalization, complicated customer needs, large customers with multiple locations, the need for technology, highly interdependent vendor/buyer relationships, intensified competition, and low profitability within the hospitality industry.

Strategic alliances directly affect the nature of the professional sales function within hospitality companies. The need for professional sales is dramatically enhanced.

Large customers may require services, such as assistance with planning, extended financing, and equity participation. In turn, these needs affect the policies and procedures of suppliers. A buyer who demands that all invoices be sent and settled through electronic data interchange (EDI) may create a need for new investment in hardware and software on the part of the suppliers.

Salespeople must be able to understand increasingly sophisticated buyer needs and communicate them to management. In many cases, the real test of a salesperson's skills comes in the ability of that person to convince his or her own management of the need to change policies and procedures.

The remainder of this chapter discusses the process of sales management. The topics selected are basic to sales managers of virtually all hospitality companies. Although these concepts have application to the management of an inside sales force, a commission sales force, and team selling, they were developed primarily for the management of a traditional sales force composed of individual salaried salespeople. The majority of the remaining examples in this chapter refer to this traditional form of sales force.

Recruiting and Training a Professional Sales Force

Importance of Careful Selection

At the heart of a successful sales force operation is the selection of effective salespeople. The performance difference between an average and a top sales person can be considerable. One survey revealed that the top 27 percent of the sales force brought in over 52 percent of the sales. Beyond the differences in sales productivity are the great wastes entailed in hiring the wrong person. When a salesperson quits, the cost of finding and training a new salesperson plus the cost of lost sales can be substantial. Additionally, a sales force with many new people is generally less productive.[20]

Characteristics of a Good Sales Person

Selecting salespeople would be simple if we knew what traits to look for. Most customers say they want sales representatives to be honest, reliable, knowledgeable, and helpful.

Look for traits common to the most successful salespeople in the company. A study of superachievers found that super sales performers exhibit the following traits: risk taking, powerful sense of mission, problem-solving bent, care for the customer, and careful planning.[21] Effective salespeople have two basic qualities: empathy, the ability to feel as the customer does; and ego drive, a strong personal need to make the sale.[22]

Establishing a Profile of Desired Characteristics Matching the Corporate Culture

The management of each hospitality company has a responsibility to determine a desired sales force profile. The GM, vice president marketing/sales, and others may help determine the preferred characteristics for a sales force.

The person who should first exemplify these is the sales manager. Management selects this person and then empowers him or her with the primary responsibility for recruiting, training, motivating, and controlling the sales force.

The rhetoric of most hospitality companies regarding a desired sales force is much the same, but actually putting words into action varies. This is due to the fact that managers sometimes overlook the importance of their unique corporate culture and simply adopt a generic profile description. All hotels are not alike, nor are all cruise lines, nor are the members of any hospitality company.

The corporate culture within some organizations is formal and authoritarian. In others, such as Southwest Airlines, fun is encouraged. Substantial differences exist among hospitality firms. Both the employer and the salesperson need to fully recognize that success cannot be realized if the two parties are incompatible. A salesperson might be very successful with InterContinental or Four Seasons Hotels but unable to adapt to the culture of Ramada or Novotel Hotels.

In service encounters, customers perform roles and employees perform roles. Satisfaction of both parties is likely when the customer and service provider engage in behaviors that are consistent with each other's role expectations. Ritz-Carlton realizes that its customers expect to be treated professionally and with a degree of formality. It communicates to its employees that they are ladies and gentlemen to prepare them for the role of providing professional service to their customers, who are also ladies and gentlemen.[23]

Matching Career Acquisitions with Corporate Objectives

The aspirations of a salesperson must first be clearly understood by that person and clearly communicated to the potential employer. The hospitality industry does not generally offer sales positions that allow a person to become wealthy from commissions or bonuses. Salespeople seeking great wealth are advised to seek careers in commercial real estate or securities. Despite this, the hospitality industry does offer many advantages to a salesperson:

- The industry is fun. Unlike selling funeral plots or cancer insurance, the product is by nature fun and even exciting.

- Clients are generally personable and willing to listen, unlike industries in which the client has little time to talk and exhibits an aggressive knock-you-over attitude.

- Fellow salespeople and other colleagues are generally people oriented, gregarious, and enjoyable.

- Opportunities for travel exist, particularly in sales of airlines, cruise lines, travel agencies, and travel wholesalers.

- Opportunities for movement within the hospitality industry exist. Considerable career movement occurs within the industry. Salespeople move among the various industry members, such as from a hotel or resort to a cruise line or rental car firm.

- Management opportunities exist. Career growth to positions of sales manager is quite feasible. Career growth to vice presidency of sales or marketing is also possible.

It should be recognized that career promotion to GM within hotels and resorts from sales historically has not often occurred but is beginning to happen. These positions generally call for individuals with broader experience and training, including F&B, front desk, and other operational areas.

Sales Force Training

Sales training is vital to success, yet unfortunately it remains a weak link within the hospitality industry. This is particularly problematic for recent graduates with little or no workplace experience. Fortunately, the situation is improving, and several hospitality companies now have training programs.

Sales training is not a one-time process but instead a career-long endeavor. Continuous training is part of the written philosophy of Singapore Airlines. This company believes that all employees must be trained and retrained continuously.

Types of Training Required

Members of a sales force require three types of training:

1. **Product/service training.** Technology creates continuous change within the hospitality industry. Reservation systems, equipment such as airplanes or cruise ships, and entire operational systems change. Service delivery systems, menus, branch locations, and other changes require regular and frequent training.

2. **Policies, procedures, and planning training.** As organizations increase in size and complexity, the need for formalized systems and procedures increases. Training is essential to ensure that all policies and procedures are understood.

    Effective salespeople continuously wink at some policies and procedures. This is generally done in an effort to satisfy customer needs and close the sale quickly. Unfortunately, a chronic failure to do things the "company way" leads to problems.

    Hospitality salespeople receive much criticism for their lack of attention to detail in the barrage of paperwork they must complete. Failure to complete paperwork correctly, on time, and in detail leads to costly errors, customer dissatisfaction, and ill will among other departments.

3. **Sales techniques training.** An age-old debate centers on the wisdom of attempting to teach techniques of selling. One camp firmly believes that salespeople are determined by genetics, personality, and motivation. The other side generally not only agrees that only a small percentage of individuals make effective salespeople but also contends their effectiveness can be enhanced by learning sales basics such as the following:

    - Prospecting
    - Obtaining the initial sales call (setting the appointment)
    - Conducting the sales dialog
      - Becoming acquainted
      - Asking questions and probing for prospects' needs
      - Listening to what the prospect says and doesn't say
      - Presenting benefits of product/service features to match prospects' needs
      - Overcoming objections
      - Further probing if necessary, to determine needs
      - Closing the sale
    - Follow-up
      - To continue sales dialog if prospect did not buy
      - To say thank-you for the order
      - To assure client that this was the correct thing to do
      - To look for opportunities to upsell or cross-sell
      - To ask for leads and testimonials
      - To ask for another appointment or ask for another sale when client is again ready to purchase

Although sales training is most effective when customized, general factors that contribute to the success or failure of a salesperson should be considered when developing a sales training program.

Six factors have been determined to contribute to sales failure. Each is relevant to salespeople within the hospitality industry.[24]

1. Poor listening skills[25]
2. Failure to concentrate on top priorities
3. Lack of sufficient effort
4. Inability to determine customer needs
5. Lack of planning for sales presentations
6. Inadequate product/service knowledge

Accor's Sofitel Hotel, Moorea, Society Islands, French Polynesia makes a great spot for incentive trips. Accor has created a loyalty program for meeting planners—Le Club **Accor Hotels for Meeting Planners.** ITPhoto/Alamy Stock Photo.

Sales training is a responsibility of the sales manager. It has been suggested that hotel sales management should spend 50 percent of their time selling; 30 percent supervising and training staff; and the remaining 20 percent with paperwork, meetings, and reviewing marketing plans.[26]

Members of upper management often assist in training by presenting an overview of the company and its history, culture, and norms. This sends a clear message to the sales force and helps establish an effective learning attitude.

Sales managers often invite people from other departments, such as the chef or reservations manager, to attend selected sales meetings for the purpose of discussing product improvements. It is also important for salespeople to experience the company's service. Salespeople for a cruise line cannot effectively sell the excitement of sailing if they have never left dry land.

The hospitality industry has historically offered free or low-cost "fam trips" (familiarization trips) to travel agents and wholesalers. This may be considered as training of sales intermediaries. Other benefits, such as free flight privileges and expense accounts to entertain guests in the company's lounge and restaurants, also enhance product knowledge. These perks are often viewed with suspicion by employees and managers from other departments. It is essential that they be used judiciously.

Training Materials and Outside Training Assistance

Formal training may sometimes be necessary in which technical details must be memorized. The use of interactive video for this kind of training has proved effective. Some fast-food chains use such systems to help train operational employees.

Today, many companies are adding digital e-learning to their sales training programs. Online training may range from simple text- and video-based product training and internet-based sales exercises that build sales skills to sophisticated simulations that recreate the dynamics of real-life sales calls. One of the most basic forms is virtual instructor-led training (VILT). Using this method, a small group of salespeople at remote locations log on to an online conferencing site, where a sales instructor leads training sessions using online video and interactive learning tools.

Training online instead of on-site can cut travel and other training costs, and it takes up less of a salesperson's selling time. It also makes on-demand training available to salespeople, letting them train as little or as much as needed, whenever and wherever needed. Although most e-learning is Web based, many companies now offer on-demand training from anywhere via almost any mobile digital device.

Many companies are now using imaginative and sophisticated e-learning techniques to make sales training more efficient—and sometimes even more fun. For example, some are creating a role-playing simulation video game to train its sales force.[27] Ultimately, all training is perfected on the job. Some managers continue to believe that effective training consists solely of learning from one's trials and errors while selling. What is overlooked is that this is costly. For many, this sink-or-swim system creates unnecessary turnover and morale problems.

As the new salesperson learns through experience, it is critical for the sales manager to monitor progress and offer encouragement and suggestions for improving areas of weakness. Effective sales managers are effective teachers. Individuals who do not enjoy teaching or coaching may find that their own management careers are limited.

All teachers dread a moment of truth. That is the time when grades must be given. Granting an "A" is pleasurable and easy but placing an "F" on someone's record requires soul searching. The same is true for a sales manager, who must eventually come to the conclusion that no amount of training will create a professional salesperson of an individual.

Once this decision has been reached after serious study and thought, the sales manager has no alternative other than to release the salesperson promptly. Those who rescind this decision in the face of emotion-laden pleas for a second chance only postpone the inevitable.

Managing the Sales Force

The research and study dedicated to this subject clearly indicate that successful sales management is not the result of following a formula.

Successful sales managers cannot be described by a narrow profile. Successful sales managers come in all sizes, shapes, colors, and backgrounds. Perhaps, if a universal truth exists, it is that long-run successful sales managers exhibit a strong affinity for their subordinates, are willing to learn, and are reasonably bright. Even these conclusions sometimes seem to be disputed by observing some sales managers who meet objectives and please upper management yet seem weak in virtually every skill and talent normally accorded to successful sales managers.

The fact is that market conditions often have an inordinate influence over a sales manager's failure or success. An economic climate in which guests are begging for hotel rooms versus three years of deep economic recession with a surplus of hotel rooms can produce very different results.

Hospitality sales management is neither a precise science nor a formula-based work procedure. Nevertheless, certain functions or processes have historically been associated with the management of a professional sales force.

Selecting Sales Strategies

Sales successes within the hospitality industry are not the result of a hit-and-run sales mentality. Success depends on the development of excellent long-run relationships with clients or accounts. The 80/20 rule prevails within the hospitality industry. A B&B, a highway motel, or a discount airline may find no relevance, but major hotels and major airlines know the phenomenon well. This concept says that a majority of a firm's business comes from a minority of its customers. These are commonly referred to as key, national, or major accounts. Certain corporate clients and travel intermediaries, such as OTAs, generally serve as key accounts. These companies provide large numbers of customers.

Based on the concept of key customers, six general sales strategies must be recognized by members of the hospitality industry:

1. **Prevent erosion of key accounts.** It does little good to attract new customers if key customers are lost. Companies operating on this kind of treadmill inevitably have higher than average sales force turnover and experience employee morale problems. Determine reasons why key customers leave and initiate corrective steps. Initiate and carefully manage programs that treat key customers as royalty. A single sales/service person may be assigned to work with only a handful of key accounts. Unless these accounts are provided highly personal service, the risk of loss to a competitor is great.

    The CEO of a large hotel chain reportedly once told franchisees that they should view their properties as buckets with holes in the bottom. From these holes escape large numbers of customers. The message was that franchises must place even greater efforts into sales to attract new customers. Some who attended this meeting reported that the message had a depressing effect on the audience, who viewed themselves on a treadmill that regularly increased in speed. This was undoubtedly not the desired effect of the analogy. Instead, the message should have been that each of us has holes in our respective buckets, but it is our responsibility to close or lessen the size of these holes, so we retain more of our customers.

Harrah's Casinos introduced a loyalty card program known as "Total Rewards." This allowed each Harrah's casino to track the gaming and purchasing activities of its customers. Data collected from this system were fed into an information system called "WINet," which linked all Harrah's properties, allowing the company to collect company-wide customer information.

This changed the corporate culture of Harrah's from an individual property focus to a chain-wide collaborative customer focus. The WINet system analyzes information such as gender, age, place of residence, and types of casino games played. Key customers and potential key customers are then identified, and promotional strategies are custom designed for them.

Harrah's discovered that 30 percent of its customers generated 80 percent of company revenues. Use of this information resulted in a $100 million increase in revenue from key customers in the first two years.[28]

2. **Grow key accounts.** As Harrah's clearly demonstrated, key accounts usually offer more sales potential than is currently realized. Key accounts may split their businesses between several provider companies. A hotel property or a hotel chain seldom obtains all or even a majority of a company's business. Increasing evidence indicates that companies are willing to reduce the number of hotel providers, and to give more of their business to a few hotels, if these companies meet their requirements for service and price.

    Sometimes the sales force of a hotel becomes enamored with what appears to be a sales opportunity gold mine. Unfortunately, when this happens, traditional customers and traditional marketing channels that have consistently produced for the hotel are momentarily forgotten. This is the old and familiar phenomenon of "the grass is always greener on the other side of the fence."

    The sales departments of many U.S. hotels thought they had discovered a "sure-fire" client that would fill their hotel rooms. Organizers of soccer's World Cup convinced hotels to reserve large quantities of rooms for thousands of anticipated fans. Some luxury hotels blocked off up to 1,000 room nights only to find that demand did not materialize, thus requiring them to release 50 to 80 percent of the reserved rooms.

    Hyatt International Sales Vice President Craig Parsons later described previous demand predictions as ludicrous. He claimed that by the time they were notified the World Cup was reducing the block, there was not enough time to sell them to summer tourists. Most of the summer tourists had already booked their rooms or chose an alternate destination because they could not find a room at a price they wanted to pay.[29]

    In addition to negating probable sales, hotels blocking rooms may have infuriated good customers who were unable to book reservations and probably selected another hotel. It is possible that some of the guests may be difficult to recapture, particularly if they liked the competitor's hotel.

3. **Grow selected marginal accounts.** Selected marginal accounts can become key accounts if given sufficient time and a consistent level of service. They are currently marginal accounts for a variety of reasons, such as the following:

    - Experimenting or sampling your product or service. If they like it, they might provide substantially more business.

    - Have received poor service in the past and therefore use your services only when necessary.

    - Account manager changes have resulted in splitting the business between various hospitality firms.

    - Comfortable with your service but competitors have acquired the bulk of their business through better follow-up.

4. **Eliminate selected marginal accounts.** Unfortunately, some accounts result in net losses for a hospitality company. These negative-yield customers should be identified and eliminated whenever possible. It may be difficult to eliminate these customers due to an inability to identify them when the order of reservation is placed. A professional sales force has the responsibility to remove these customers from its list of prospects or active accounts, and refrain from future sales calls or sales promotions directed to them.

5. **Retain selected marginal accounts but provide lower-cost sales support.** Many accounts represent infrequent purchases or low-yield business. These accounts cannot bear the cost of personalized sales calls or expensive promotions. A common method of dealing with these accounts is to assign them to an inside sales force. These salespeople don't make field calls but instead interact with customers via telephone, telemarketing, catalogs, direct mail, and fax machines.

6. **Obtain new business from selected prospects.** The process of obtaining new accounts is costly and time-consuming. Experienced salespeople know that it often requires five or more sales calls to obtain the business of a prospect. The cost of making a single sales call may be several hundred dollars when all costs are considered, such as travel expenses, salary, and benefits to the salesperson. The high cost of obtaining a new customer dictates that this person must have the potential to contribute significantly to profits. It is inefficient and nonproductive to pursue sales prospects who have little or no likelihood of ever providing significant returns to the company.

Sales Force Tactics: Principles of Personal Selling

We turn now to the purpose of a sales force: to sell. Personal selling is an ancient art. Effective salesperson have more than instinct. They are trained in tactics to achieve sales success. Selling today is a profession that involves mastering and applying a set of principles.

Today's companies spend hundreds of millions of dollars each year to train their salespeople in the art of selling. All the sales training approaches try to convert a salesperson from being a passive order taker to an active order getter.

In training salespeople to acquire signed orders (contracts), there are two basic approaches: a sales-oriented approach and a customer-oriented approach. The first trains the salesperson in high-pressure selling techniques, such as those often used in selling automobiles. The techniques include exaggerating the product's merits, criticizing competitive products, using a slick presentation, selling yourself, and offering some price concession to get the order on the spot. This form of selling assumes that customers are not likely to buy except under pressure, that they are influenced by a slick presentation and ingratiating manners, and that they will not be sorry after signing the order, or if they are, it doesn't matter.

The other approach trains salespeople in customer problem solving. The salesperson learns how to listen and question in order to identify customer needs and come up with good product solutions. Presentation skills are made secondary to customer-need analysis skills. The approach assumes that customers have latent needs that constitute company opportunities, that they appreciate constructive suggestions, and that they will be loyal to sales representatives who have their long-term interests at heart. The problem solver is a much more congruent concept for the salesperson under the marketing concept than the hard seller or order taker.

We examine briefly eight major aspects of personal selling.

Prospecting and Qualifying

The first step in the selling process is to identify prospects. Although the company will try to supply leads, sales representatives need skill in developing their own. Leads can be developed in the following ways:

- Through call-ins

- Having a booth at appropriate travel or trade shows

- Participating in international travel missions
- Asking current customers for the names of prospects
- Cultivating other referral sources, such as suppliers, dealers, noncompeting sales representatives, bankers, and trade association executives
- Through leads generated by the chain
- Joining organizations to which prospects belong
- Engaging in speaking and writing activities that will draw attention
- Examining data sources (newspapers, directories) in search of names
- Using the telephone and mail to find leads
- Dropping in unannounced on various offices (cold canvassing)
- Conducting a sales blitz

It is important not to overlook leads from internal sources. For example, working with the accounts payable department, a salesperson can find suppliers that may be sources of business. The reservations department should be trained to make inquiries of guests representing companies to find out if more business exists from those companies. Front-desk staff should talk with guests representing new companies and pass sales leads to the sales department. Prospecting internally and externally should be done daily. Once prospects have been identified, they need to be qualified.[30]

Sales representatives need skill in screening out poor leads. Prospects can be qualified by examining their financial ability, volume of business, special requirements, location, and likelihood of continuous business. The salesperson might phone or write to prospects before deciding whether to visit them.

Preapproach

Preapproach The step in which the salesperson or company identifies qualified potential applicants.

The salesperson needs to learn as much as possible about the prospect company (what it needs, who is involved in the purchase decision) and its buyers (their personal characteristics and buying styles). The salesperson should set call objectives, which might be to qualify the prospect or gather information, or to make an immediate sale. Another task is to decide on the best approach, which might be a personal visit, a phone call, or a letter. Do not depend solely on e-mail as many e-mail messages are ignored. The best timing should be thought out because many prospects are busy at certain times.

Approach

Approach The step in which the salesperson meets the customer for the first time.

The salesperson should know how to greet the buyer to get the relationship off to a good start. This involves the salesperson's appearance, the opening lines, and the follow-up remarks. The opening line should be positive, for example, "Mr. Smith, I am Alice Jones from the ABC Hotel Company. My company and I appreciate your willingness to see me. I will do my best to make this visit profitable and worthwhile for you and your company." This might be followed by key questions and active listening to understand the buyer and his or her needs.

Presentation and Demonstration

Presentation The sales step in which the sales persons tell the "value story" to the buyer showing how the company's offer solves the customer's problems.

The salesperson now tells the product "story" to the buyer, following the AIDA formula of gaining *a*ttention, holding *i*nterest, arousing *d*esire, and obtaining *a*ction. During the **presentation**, the salesperson emphasizes customer benefits throughout, bringing in product features as evidence of these benefits. A benefit is any advantage, such as lower cost, less work, or more profit for the buyer. A feature is a product characteristic, such as weight or size. A common selling mistake is to dwell on product features (a product orientation) instead of customer benefits (a market orientation).

A need-satisfaction approach to selling starts with a search for the customer's real needs by encouraging the customer to do most of the talking. This approach calls for good listening and problem-solving skills. The salesperson takes on the role of a knowledgeable business consultant, hoping to help the customer save money or make more money.

Negotiation

Much of business-to-business selling involves negotiating skills. The two parties need to reach agreement on the price and other terms of sale. Salespersons need to win the order without making deep concessions that will hurt profitability.

Although price is the most frequently negotiated issue, other issues include quality of goods and services offered, purchase volume, and responsibility for financing, risk taking, and promotion. The number of negotiation issues is virtually unlimited.

Unfortunately, far too many hotel salespeople rely almost exclusively on price as their negotiating tool. Even worse, they often begin negotiating from an already discounted price rather than from rack rates. Negotiations should always begin with rack rates, and price concessions should be given only when absolutely essential. Numerous bargaining tools exist, such as upgrades, complimentary tickets for the ski lift or golf courses, first-class coffee breaks instead of coffee and soft drinks, airport pickup, and use of hotel services such as the fitness center. A hotel sales force might package these amenities into bundles of services and give them names such as the President's Package, the Connoisseur's Package, and the Executive Package.

Sales force members should be taught to negotiate using services or bundled services as the primary negotiating tool rather than price. Table 15–1 shows the possible difference in service package negotiations versus price negotiation. It is easy to see that the hotel benefits by offering a package of services rather than a price discount at all levels other than a 10 percent discount. Sales force members must understand the economic value of these kinds of trade-offs before they enter into the negotiation process.

Salespeople who find themselves in bargaining situations need certain traits and skills to be effective. The most important traits are preparation and planning skills, knowledge of subject matter being negotiated, ability to think clearly and rapidly under pressure and uncertainty, ability to express thoughts verbally, listening skills, judgment and general intelligence, integrity, ability to persuade others, and patience. These will help the salesperson to know when and how to negotiate.[31]

WHEN TO NEGOTIATE. Consider the following circumstances in which negotiation in the hospitality industry is an appropriate procedure for concluding a sale:[32]

1. When many factors bear not only on price but also on quality and service.
2. When business risks cannot be accurately predetermined.

Table 15–1

Hotel Negotiation Cost Comparison: Offering a Service Package Versus Price
The booking below is for 50 guests for three nights for a total of 150 room nights.
Rack rate of $300/night × 150 room nights equals $45,000.

	50 Guests at 3 Nights Each	
	Cost/Guest	Total Cost
Special Service Package		
Welcome Reception	$50	$2,500
Use of Boardroom by the organization	$500 per day	$1,500
		$4,000

Price Cut (%)	Revenue Lost ($)
10	$ 4,500
20	$ 9,000
30	$13,500

Table 15–2

Examples of Hotel Customer's Negotiation Strengths and Weaknesses

Strengths	Weaknesses
1. Provide many guests.	1. Provide few guests.
2. Come in low or shoulder seasons.	2. Come in prime season.
3. Stay low-occupancy nights.	3. Stay high-occupancy nights.
4. Bring quality guests.	4. Bring undesirable guests.
5. Provide cross-purchase potential.	5. Provide little or no cross-sale potential.
6. Purchase upscale rooms.	6. Purchase lowest priced rooms.

Negotiation is appropriate wherever a zone of agreement exists.[33] A zone of agreement exists when there are simultaneously overlapping acceptable outcomes for the parties.

FORMULATING A BARGAINING STRATEGY. Bargaining involves preparing a strategic plan before bargaining begins and making good tactical decisions during the bargaining sessions. A bargaining strategy can be defined as a commitment to an overall approach that has a good chance of achieving the negotiator's objectives. For example, some negotiators pursue a hard strategy with opponents, whereas others maintain that a soft strategy yields more favorable results.

The sales force of a hotel or resort is in a position to use negotiating skills nearly every day of their professional lives. Their negotiation process can be enhanced by understanding the negotiating strengths and weaknesses of the client, as shown in Table 15–2.

BARGAINING TACTICS DURING NEGOTIATIONS. Negotiators use a variety of tactics when bargaining. Bargaining tactics can be defined as maneuvers to be made at specific points in the bargaining process. Threats, bluffs, last-chance offers, hard initial offers, and other tactics occur in bargaining.

Experts in negotiation have offered advice that is consistent with their strategy of principles negotiation. Their first piece of tactical advice concerns what should be done if the other party is more powerful. By identifying your alternatives if a settlement is not reached, it sets a standard against which any offer can be measured. It protects you from being pressured into accepting unfavorable terms from a more powerful opponent.[34]

Another tactic comes into play when the opposing party insists on arguing his or her position instead of his or her interests and attacks your proposals or person. Although the tendency is to push back hard when pushed, the better tactic is to deflect the attack from the person and direct it against the problem. Look at the interests that motivated the opposing party's position and invent options that can satisfy both parties' interests. Invite the opposing party's criticism and advice ("If you were in my position, what would you do?").

Another set of bargaining tactics involves opposition tactics that are intended to deceive, distort, or otherwise influence the bargaining. What tactic should be used when the other side uses a threat, or a take-it-or-leave-it tactic, or seats the other party on the side of the table with the sun in his or her eyes? A negotiation should recognize the tactic, raise the issue explicitly, and question the tactic's legitimacy and desirability—in other words, negotiate over it. Negotiating the use of the tactic follows the same principled negotiation procedure: Question the tactic, ask why the tactic is being used, or suggest alternative courses of action to pursue. If this fails, resort to your best alternative to a negotiated agreement and terminate the negotiation until the other side ceases to employ these tactics. Meeting these tactics by defending principles is more productive than counterattacking with tricky tactics.

Overcoming Objections

Customers almost always pose objections during the presentation or when asked for the order. Their resistance can be psychological or logical. Psychological resistance includes resistance to interference, preference for established hotel or airline, apathy, reluctance to giving up something, unpleasant associations about the other person, predetermined ideas, dislike of making decisions, and neurotic attitude toward money. Logical resistance might consist of objections to the price or certain product or company characteristics. To handle these objections, the salesperson maintains a position approach, asks the buyer to clarify the objection, denies the validity of the objection, or turns the objection into a reason for buying. The salesperson needs training in the broader skills of negotiation, of which **handling objections** is a part.

Handling objections The sales step in which the salesperson seeks out, clarifies, and overcomes any customer objections to buying.

Closing

Closing The sales step in which a salesperson asks the customer for an order.

Now the salesperson attempts to close the sale. Some salespeople do not get to this stage or do not do it well. They lack confidence or feel uncomfortable about asking for the order or do not recognize the right psychological moment to close the sale. Salespersons need to know how to recognize closing signals from the buyer, including physical actions, statements or comments, and questions. Salespersons can use one of several closing techniques. They can ask for the order, recapitulate the points of agreement, offer to help the secretary write up the order, ask whether the buyers want A or B, get the buyer to make minor choices, or indicate what the buyer will lose if the order is not placed now. The salesperson might offer the buyer specific inducements.

Follow-Up/Maintenance

Follow-up The sales step in which the salesperson follows up after the sale to ensure customer satisfaction and repeat business.

This last step is necessary if the salesperson wants to ensure customer satisfaction and repeat business. Immediately after closing, the salesperson should complete any necessary details on delivery time, purchase terms, and other matters. "Follow-up or foul-up" is a slogan of most successful salespeople. The salesperson should develop an account maintenance plan to make sure that the customer is not forgotten or lost.

Motivating a Professional Sales Force

Some sales representatives put forth their best effort without any special coaching from management. To them, selling is the most fascinating job in the world. They are ambitious and self-starters. But the majority of sales representatives require encouragement and special incentives to work at their best level. This is especially true of field selling, for the following reasons:

- *Nature of the job.* The selling job is one of frequent frustration. Sales representatives usually work alone, their hours are irregular, and they are often away from home. They confront aggressive, competing sales representatives; they have an inferior status relative to the buyer; they often do not have the authority to do what is necessary to win an account; and they lose large orders that they have worked hard to obtain.

- *Human nature.* Most people operate below capacity in the absence of special incentives, such as financial gain or social recognition.

- *Personal problems.* Sales representatives are occasionally preoccupied with personal problems, such as sickness in the family, marital discord, or debt.

Here is a basic model of motivating sales representatives:[35]

motivation → effort → performance → rewards → satisfaction

The model implies the following:

1. Sales managers must be able to convince salespeople that they can sell more by working harder or by being trained to work smarter.
2. Sales managers must be able to convince salespeople that the rewards for better performance are worth the extra effort.

Sales Force Compensation

To attract and retain sales representatives, the company has to develop an attractive compensation package. Sales representatives would like income regularity, extra reward for an above-average performance, and fair payment for experience and longevity. Management would like to achieve control, economy, and simplicity. Management objectives, such as economy, conflict with sales representatives' objectives, such as financial security.

The level of compensation must bear some relation to the going market price for the type of sales job and required abilities. If the market price for salespeople is well defined, the individual firm has little choice but to pay the going rate. The market price for salespeople, however, is seldom well defined. Data on the average take-home pay of competitors' sales representatives can be misleading because of significant variations in the average seniority and ability levels of the competitors' sales forces.

The company must next determine the components of compensation: a fixed amount, a variable amount, expenses, and fringe benefits. The fixed amount, which might be salary, is intended to satisfy the sales representatives' need for income stability. The variable amount, which might be commissions, bonuses, or profit sharing, is intended to stimulate and reward greater effort. Expense allowances enable the sales representatives to meet the expenses involved in travel, lodging, dining, and entertainment; fringe benefits such as paid vacation, sickness or accident benefits, pensions, and life insurance are intended to provide security and job satisfaction. Fixed and variable compensations give rise to three basic types of sales force compensation plans: straight salary, straight commissions, and combination salary and commission.

Many companies in the hospitality industry suffer from high sales force turnover. A variety of reasons have been given to explain this situation, such as burnout. A survey of college graduates preparing to enter the hospitality industry ranked salary as number 10 among variables relating to what they wanted in a job.[36] A different study of young managers who left hospitality careers demonstrated that money was indeed important. Pay-related issues were the second most common reason for leaving, following long hours and inconvenient scheduling as the primary reason. One respondent wrote, "I had poor pay, high stress, low praise and recognition, and worked 75 to 80 hours a week, all for the chance to be a GM in 10 or 15 years with the same job characteristics."[37]

The importance of monetary rewards to a hospitality sales force must not be minimized. These people are expected to maintain a large fashionable wardrobe, to work long hours, experience stress, and often give up family experiences for the sake of their career. Under these circumstances, monetary reward becomes very important.

Supplementary Motivators

Companies use additional motivators to stimulate sales force effort. Periodic sales meetings provide a social occasion, a break from routine, a chance to meet and talk with "company brass," and a chance to air feelings and to identify with a larger group. Sales meetings are an important communication and motivational tool.[38] They can also be used for training in subjects such as how to make effective presentations.[39] Thus, the sales meeting can and should assume increased importance to the sales force.

Companies also sponsor sales contests to spur the sales force to a special selling effort above what would normally be expected. The contest should present a reasonable opportunity for salespeople to win. If only a few salespersons can win or almost everyone can win, it will fail to spur additional effort. The sales contest period should not be announced in advance or else some salespersons will defer some sales to the beginning of the period; also, some may pad their sales during the period with customer promises to buy that do not materialize after the contest period ends.

Sales managers of hotels and resorts sometimes offer vacations at sister properties for winners of a sales contest. When the winners visit a sister property, they are introduced to the sales department and often learn new techniques. In turn, this information is transmitted to others when the winners return and give a report in the next sales meeting.

Evaluation and Control of a Professional Sales Force

Sales Quotas

Many companies set sales quotas prescribing what their sales representatives should sell during the year. Compensation is often tied to the degree of quota fulfillment. Sales quotas are developed from the annual marketing plan. The company first prepares a sales forecast. This forecast becomes the basis for planning production, workforce size, and financial requirements. Then management establishes sales quotas for its regions and territories, which typically add up to more than the sales forecast. Sales quotas are often set higher than the sales forecast in order to stretch sales managers and salespeople to perform at their best level.

The sales manager assigns the area's quota to each of the area's salespeople. There are three schools of thought on quota setting. The high-quota school sets quotas that are higher than what most sales representatives will achieve but are attainable. Its adherents believe that high quotas spur extra effort. The modest-quota school sets quotas that a majority of the sales force can achieve. Its adherents feel that the sales force will accept the quotas as fair, attain them, and gain confidence. The variable-quota school thinks that individual differences among sales representatives warrant high quotas for some and modest quotas for others.

Developing Norms for Salespeople

New sales representatives should be given more than a territory, a compensation package, and training. They need supervision.

Companies vary in how closely they direct their sales representatives. Those who are paid mostly on commission generally receive less supervision. Those who are salaried and must cover definite accounts are likely to receive substantial supervision.

The number of calls that an average salesperson makes during a day has been decreasing. The downward trend is due to the increased use of technology. It is also due to difficulties in reaching prospects because of traffic congestion, busy prospect schedules, and other complexities of contemporary business.

Companies often decide how many calls to make a year on particular-sized accounts. Most companies classify customers into A, B, and C accounts, reflecting the sales volume, profit potential, and growth potential of the account. A accounts might receive nine calls a year; B, six calls; and C, three calls. The call norms depend on expected account profitability.

Regardless of how a sales force is structured, individual salespeople must classify their customer base. A salesperson responsible for channel intermediaries, such as tour operators and travel agents, quickly learns that not all are capable of producing the same sales volume/profit. This is equally true for a salesperson who has responsibility for the conference/meeting segment and for those responsible for national accounts.

Omni International Hotels emphasizes account planning with its sales force. A former Omni president, Jon Canas, told a Harvard professor in a taped interview that not all prospects may be contacted in a particular year because they do not qualify as the best target customers. However, it is important to know the second- and third-tier prospects so that they can be contacted if a slowdown occurs within the top targeted groups.[40]

Companies often specify how much time their sales force should spend prospecting for new accounts. Companies set up prospecting standards for a number of reasons. If left alone, many sales representatives spend most of their time with current customers. Current customers are better-known quantities. Sales representatives can depend on them for some business, whereas a prospect might never deliver any business. Unless sales representatives are rewarded for opening new accounts, they might avoid new account development.

Using Sales Time Efficiently

Sales representatives need to know how to use their time efficiently. One tool is the annual call schedule, showing which customers and prospects to call on in which months and which activities to carry out.

Actual face-to-face selling time can amount to as little as 25 percent of total working time.[41] Companies are constantly seeking ways to improve sales force productivity. Their methods take the form of training sales representatives in the use of "phone power," simplifying record-keeping forms, and using the computer to develop call and routing plans and to supply customer and competitive information.

Managing Trade Shows

Trade shows are commonly used as a means of generating sales leads, keeping in touch with commercial customers, and writing business. Members of the hospitality industry participate in many trade shows, ranging from local/regional ones to international travel missions sponsored by visitor destinations, travel associations, and government departments or ministries of tourism.

Unfortunately, the cost/return effectiveness of trade shows is often placed in peril or disregarded through lack of effective planning and control. The conclusions of a study of hospitality trade show exhibitors were that "it is likely that the true marketing potential of trade shows is not being realized. Commitments to more effective planning would enhance the productivity of trade shows for most companies."[42]

Six steps were suggested to improve trade show effectiveness:

1. Construct a mailing list of prospects.
2. Identify potential leads and communicate with them before the show.
3. Promote the show with incentives that reflect the company's theme, products, and services.
4. Send letters to prospective buyers, inviting them to make a personal contact at the show or at an alternative location.
5. Keep good records of visitor contacts made during the show.
6. Follow up with qualified prospects after the show.

Sales force control and training are also needed to ensure success. The following are items a sales manager should implement before a trade show:

1. Review trade show objectives with the sales force before the show.
2. Designate a trade show captain responsible for managing sales activities.
3. Designate times when certain salespersons are expected to work the booth.
4. Prohibit smoking, drinking, eating, and bunching together in the trade booth.
5. Show sales force members how to deal with complaining/difficult visitors, greet customers/prospects (particularly key ones), develop prospects, identify nonprospects, and process and use leads, business cards, competitive data, and customer/prospect information acquired at the show.

Other Control Techniques

Management obtains information about its sales representatives in several ways. One important source is sales reports. Additional information comes through personal observation, customers' letters and complaints, customer surveys, and conversations with other sales representatives.

Sales reports are divided between activity plans and write-ups of activity results. The best example of the former is the salesperson's work plan, which sales representatives submit a week or month in advance.

The plan describes intended calls and routing. This report leads the sales force to plan and schedule their activities, informs management of their whereabouts, and provides a basis for comparing their plans and accomplishments. Sales representatives can be evaluated on their ability to "plan their work and work their plan."

Many hospitality companies require their sales representatives to develop an annual territory marketing plan in which they outline their program for developing new accounts and increasing business from existing accounts. This type of report casts sales representatives into the role of marketing managers and profit centers. Sales representatives write up their completed activities on call reports. Call reports inform sales management of the salesperson's activities, indicate the status of specific customer accounts, and provide useful information for subsequent calls. Sales representatives also submit expense reports, new business reports, lost business reports, and reports on local business and economic conditions.

These reports provide raw data from which sales managers can extract key indicators of sales performance. The key indicators are (1) average number of sales calls per salesperson per day, (2) average sales call time per contact, (3) average revenue per sales call, (4) average cost per sales call, (5) entertainment cost per sales call, (6) percentage of orders per 100 sales calls, (7) number of new customers per period, (8) number of lost customers per period, and (9) sales force cost as a percentage of total sales. These indicators answer several useful questions. Are sales representatives making too few calls per day? Are they spending too much time per call? Are they spending too much on entertainment? Are they closing enough orders per 100 calls? Are they producing enough new customers and holding on to the old customers?

Formal Evaluation of Performance

The sales force's reports along with other observations supply the raw materials for evaluating members of the sales force. Formal evaluation procedures lead to at least three benefits. First, management has to communicate its standards for judging sales performance. Second, management needs to gather comprehensive information about each salesperson. Third, sales representatives know that they will have to sit down one morning with the sales managers and explain their performance or failure to achieve certain goals.

SALESPERSON-TO-SALESPERSON COMPARISONS. One type of evaluation is to compare and rank the sales performance of a company's sales representatives. Such comparisons, however, can be misleading. Relative sales performance is meaningful only if there are no variations in territory market potential, workload, competition, company promotional effort, and so on. Furthermore, current sales are not the only success indicator. Management should also be interested in how much each sales representative contributes to current net profits.

CUSTOMER SATISFACTION EVALUATION. A salesperson might be very effective in producing sales but not rate high with customers. An increasing number of companies are measuring customer satisfaction not only with their product and customer-support service but also with their salespeople. Company salespeople who score high on satisfying their customers can be given special recognition, awards, or bonuses.

QUALITATIVE EVALUATION OF SALES REPRESENTATIVES. Evaluations can also assess the salesperson's knowledge of the company, products, customers, competitors, territory, and responsibilities. The sales manager should also review any problem in motivation or compliance. The sales manager should check that the sales representatives know and observe company policies. Each company must develop its own evaluation procedure. Whatever procedure is chosen, it must be fair to the salesperson and the company. If members of a sales force feel they are being judged against incorrect norms, they will quickly become dissatisfied.

Hospitality sales is a profession and must be treated as such. It is very much to the advantage of any hospitality company to develop a professional, loyal, and contented sales force. Measurement of a salesperson's value and contribution must not be left to the last minute or to inappropriate standards and measures. No aspect of sales management is more important than developing and using the correct appraisal system for members of a professional sales force.

Regardless of what evaluation system is used, it must be tied to performance. Sales performance and company performance are inherently married. Professor Bill Quain has said, "I believe it is getting harder and harder to find employees who have the drive to sell, the drive to create profits, and the drive to satisfy customers by filling more of their needs with ever improving products and services."[43]

Peer-to-Peer Sales

The rise of shared use or peer-to-peer sales within the travel/hospitality industry is in part due to the difficulty finding good salespeople as described by Professor Quain. The concept of allowing others to temporarily use one's auto, home, apartment, boat, or RV for a fee is not a new concept but technology such as iPhones and social media has certainly facilitated the process.

Other facilitating factors include (1) the high cost of buying and maintaining assets such as an automobile or second home, (2) increasing urbanization in which residents have few good choices for storing equipment, (3) high cost of alternative choices such as hotels or taxis, and (4) desire for increased socialization such as that available in a private home rental through a company such as Home Way, VRBO, or Airbnb or ground transportation available through Uber or Lyft.

Statistics concerning the size of this expanding industry are estimated to be in the billions of dollars. One thing is certain: Most entrepreneurs in this industry are young, technologically capable, and also familiar with social media. This industry will undergo change as governments pass legislation that directly affect the sales process as well as safety, security, and tax reporting issues. While there is little current concern that this industry will soon replace traditional hotels, train and bus service and asset ownership, it is obvious that peer-to-peer companies have discovered a profitable market niche.

Networking

One of the most effective sales tools anywhere in the world is networking. This is especially true for small hospitality members such as B&Bs, inns, fishing lodges, farm/ranch lodging, and many more. However, it remains important to all members of this industry.

The basis for networking is simple. Continuously contact members of the community. Tell these people what your enterprise offers and enthusiastically welcome them to visit and see for themselves.

Networking may at times (particularly for new hospitality members) require "cold calls" in which the owner/manager salesperson drops in without an appointment. In the case of a lodging owner, these calls are generally made on companies/organizations that might have clients or guests who need lodging. Sometimes assumptions are made that a particular business is not worth visiting but such assumptions are often wrong. One of the authors accompanied the owner of a new B&B during a day of cold calls. The owner said it was not worthwhile to call on government entities such as the Forest Service since they had low per diem rates available to them.

Nevertheless, a call was made. Upon talking with the Forest Service people in the office, it was discovered that they have several overnight visitors during the year such as consultants, reporters, outdoor enthusiasts, and others who were not limited to low rates. Additionally, it was discovered that the Forest Service had raised their per diem rates and that regional meetings were held at that site during times of the year that were low-occupancy periods for the B&B.

Later, a competitor B&B and a small motel were seen and once again the owner accompanying the author did not wish to visit them. Once again, they went anyway, and the competitors were welcoming and said they were delighted to know about the quality of the new B&B since they occasionally were overbooked and needed a reliable place to send their guests. Never accept assumptions.

Good contacts for networking can be made through membership in a service club, church, school activities, community theater, and other organizations. One can never predict the positive results of networking. Sales, of course, is the objective but other results occur, such as publicity through interviews on radio or TV or offers to speak at community gatherings. The social media site LinkedIn is a great networking site, because the people you are connected with will be updated when they move to a new position, allowing you to connect even after the person has changed jobs.

Remember that the most important product you will ever sell is yourself. Never rely on a resume or an e-mail to sell that important a product. Networking will serve you well throughout your life.

Social Selling: Online, Mobile, and Social Media Tools

Social Selling: Online, Mobile, and Social Media Tools

Social selling The use of online, mobile, and social media to engage customers, build stronger customer relationships, and augment sales performance.

The fastest-growing sales trend is the explosion in **social selling**—the use of online, mobile, and social media to engage customers, build stronger customer relationships, and augment sales performance. Digital sales force technologies are creating exciting new avenues for connecting with and engaging customers in the digital and social media age. Salespeople are using Web sites, online social media, mobile apps, video and conferencing technologies, and other tools that allow direct customer contact. One sales expert says, "There may be less face-to-face selling. But on the seller's side, there needs to be someone in charge of that (customer) interaction. That will remain the role of the salesperson." [17] Thus, online and social media technologies won't likely make salespeople obsolete. Used properly, however, they will make salespeople more productive and effective.

The new digital technologies are providing salespeople with powerful tools for identifying and learning about prospects, engaging customers, creating customer value, closing sales, and nurturing customer relationships. Social selling technologies can produce big organizational benefits for sales forces. They help conserve salespeople's valuable time, save travel dollars, and give salespeople new vehicles for selling and **servicing** accounts.

Servicing Sales representatives provide various services to the customers: consulting on their problems, rendering technical assistance, arranging financing, and expediting delivery.

Social selling hasn't really changed the fundamentals of selling. Sales forces have always taken the primary responsibility for reaching out to and engaging customers and managing customer relationships. Now, more of that is being done digitally. However, online and social media are dramatically changing the customer buying process. As a result, they are also changing the selling process. In today's digital world, many customers no longer rely as much as they once did on information and assistance provided by salespeople. Instead, they carry out more of the buying process on their own—especially the early stages. Increasingly, they use online and social media resources to analyze their own problems, research solutions, get advice from colleagues, and rank buying options before ever speaking to a salesperson.[44]

Thus, today's customers have much more control over the sales process than they had in the days when brochures, pricing, and product advice were available only from a sales rep. Customers can now browse hotel Web sites, and social media to qualify hotels. They can connect with other business users of the hotel on social media such as LinkedIn, Google+, Twitter, or Facebook to find out about the experiences other companies have had with the hotel. As a result, when customers contact the hotel they often know almost as much about the hotel's products as the salespeople do.

In response to this new digital buying environment, sellers are reorienting their selling processes around the new customer buying process. Hotels are providing cites for meeting planners, planning small events to book the event directly online. The hotel's site shows the dates and meeting rooms available, menus, audiovisual and sleeping rooms. The planner can book their event online and receive an instant confirmation of the event and the price of the event. This saves the meeting planner time and allows the hotel's sales staff to concentrate on larger events.

CHAPTER REVIEW

I. Professional Sales. Successful owners and managers know that they must sell continuously.
  A. Nature of hospitality sales. Sales personnel serve as the company's personal link to customers. Personal selling is the most expensive contact and communication tool used by the company. Sales reps perform the following tasks: prospecting, targeting, communicating, selling, servicing, information gathering, allocating, and maintaining strategic partnerships. The sales representative's mix of tasks varies with the state of the economy. As companies move toward a stronger market orientation, their sales forces need to become more market focused and customer oriented. Salespeople should know how to produce customer satisfaction and company profit. They should know how to analyze sales data, measure market potential, gather market intelligence, develop marketing strategies and plans, and become proficient at the use of sales tactics.
   1. **Competitive analysis and competitive sets.** Sales managers within the hospitality industry are often held accountable for the performance of their properties against members of a competitive set. For hotels, common approaches are measuring Average Daily Rate, Product Type, and Management Company Set.
  B. Sales force objectives ensure that corporate goals are met and assist sales force members to plan and execute their personal sales programs. Objectives must be custom designed annually for each company. Individual objectives must support corporate goals and marketing and sales objectives. The sales manager assigns individual objectives.
   1. **Sales volume.** Occupancy, passenger miles, and total covers are common measures of sales volume. An emphasis on volume alone leads to price discounting, attracting undesirable market segments, and cost cutting. Establishing objectives by volume and by price/margin segments leads to improved revenue.
   2. **Upselling and second-chance selling.** Profit opportunities exist by selling higher-priced products and additional services.
   3. **Market share or market penetration.** It is possible that the sales department of hotels and resorts will increasingly be required to measure market potential and will be held accountable for a predetermined level of market penetration. Independent measures of market penetration such as the STAR report will undoubtedly assume increased importance in the measurement of hotel sales.
   4. **Product-specific objectives.** Occasionally the sales force is charged with improving sales volume for a specific product.

II. Sales Force Structure and Organization
  A. Sales force structure and size
   1. **Territorial-structured sales force.** Each sales representative is assigned an exclusive territory in which to represent the company's full line. Territories are designed to provide either equal sales potential or equal workload. Territories are formed by combining smaller units until they add up to a territory of a given sales potential or workload.
   2. **Market-segment structured sales force.** Company structures its sales force based on market segments.
   3. **Market-channel structured sales force.** The importance of marketing intermediaries, such as wholesalers, tour operators, travel agencies, and junket reps, to the hospitality industry has created sales force structures to serve different marketing channels.
   4. **Customer-structured sales force.** Specific customers who are critical to the success of the organization exist. The sales force is usually organized to serve these accounts through a key or national account structure.
   5. **Combination-structured sales force.** A large hotel might have a catering/banquet sales force (product), a convention/meeting sales force (market segment), a tour wholesale sales force (marketing intermediary), and a national account sales force (customer).
   6. **Sales force size.** Customers are grouped into size classes according to their annual sales volume. The desirable call frequencies (number of sales calls on an account per year) are established for each class. The number of accounts in each size class is multiplied by the corresponding call frequency to arrive at the total workload for the country in sales calls per year. The average number of calls a sales representative can make per year is determined. The number of sales representatives needed is determined by dividing the total annual calls required by the average annual calls made by a sales representative.
  B. Organizing the sales department
   1. **Inside sales force.** The inside sales force includes technical support persons, sales assistants, and telemarketers.
   2. **Field sales force.** The field sales force includes commissioned reps, salaried reps, and sales team.
   3. **Team sales.** Two or more persons working in concert toward a common sales objective such as a sales blitz, relationship marketing, and/or the creation of strategic alliances. These persons are not necessarily from the same company. The purpose for a team sales approach is to accomplish objectives through the synergism of two or more people that would be impossible or unduly costly through individual sales efforts. Strategic alliances are a highly developed form of relationship marketing that are common between vendor and buyer or between noncompeting vendors and a common buyer.

A strategic alliance may involve sharing a combination of confidences, database, market knowledge, planning resources, risks, security, and technology. Strategic alliances have become a necessity due to globalization, complicated customer needs, large customers with multiple locations, the need for technology, highly interdependent vendor/buyer relationships, intensified competition, and low profitability within the hospitality industry.

III. **Recruiting and Training a Professional Sales Force.**
   A. **Importance of careful selection.** Effective salespeople have two basic qualities: empathy, the ability to feel as the customer does; and ego drive, a strong personal need to make the sale.
   B. **Establishing a profile of desired characteristics matching the corporate culture.**
   C. **Matching career acquisitions with corporate objectives.**
   D. **Sales force training.** There are three types of training: product/service training; policies, procedures, and planning training; and sales techniques training.

IV. **Selling**
   A. **Selecting sales strategies.** The 80/20 rule prevails within the hospitality industry. This concept says that a majority of a firm's business comes from a minority of its customers. These are commonly referred to as key, national, or major accounts. The following are six general sales strategies:
     1. Prevent erosion of key accounts
     2. Grow key accounts
     3. Grow selected marginal accounts
     4. Eliminate selected marginal accounts
     5. Retain selected marginal accounts, but provide lower-cost sales support
     6. Obtain new business from selected prospects
   B. **Sales force tactics: Principles of personal selling.** In training salespeople to acquire signed orders (contracts), there are two basic approaches: a sales-oriented approach and a customer-oriented approach. The first trains the salesperson in high-pressure selling techniques, such as those often used in selling automobiles. The techniques include exaggerating the product's merits, criticizing competitive products, using a slick presentation, selling yourself, and offering some price concession to get the order on the spot. This form of selling assumes that customers are not likely to buy except under pressure, that they are influenced by a slick presentation and ingratiating manners, and that they will not be sorry after signing the order, or if they are, it doesn't matter. The other approach trains salespeople in customer problem solving. The salesperson learns how to listen and question in order to identify customer needs and come up with good product solutions. Presentation skills are made secondary to customer-need analysis skills. The approach assumes that customers have latent needs that constitute company opportunities, that they appreciate constructive suggestions, and that they will be loyal to sales representatives who have their long-term interests at heart. The problem solver is a much more congruent concept for the salesperson under the marketing concept than the hard seller or order taker. There are eight major aspects of personal selling. These are prospecting and qualifying, preapproach, approach, presentation and demonstration, negotiation, overcoming objections, closing, and follow-up/maintenance.

V. **Supervising a Professional Sales Force.**
   A. **Motivating a professional sales force.** Sales reps require encouragement and incentives to work at their best levels because of the nature of the job, human nature, and personal problems. Motivation → effort → performance → rewards → satisfaction.
     1. **Sales force compensation.** The company must determine the components of compensation: a fixed amount, a variable amount, expenses, and fringe benefits. The fixed amount, which might be salary, is intended to satisfy the sales representatives' need for income stability. The variable amount, which might be commissions, bonuses, or profit sharing, is intended to stimulate and reward greater effort. Expense allowances enable the sales representatives to meet the expenses involved in travel, lodging, dining, and entertainment; fringe benefits such as paid vacation, sickness or accident benefits, pensions, and life insurance are intended to provide security and job satisfaction. Fixed and variable compensations give rise to three basic types of sales force compensation plans: straight salary, straight commissions, and combination salary and commission.
     2. **Supplementary motivators.** Sales meetings are an important communication and motivational tool. Sales contests spur the sales force to special efforts.

VI. **Evaluation and Control of a Professional Sales Force.**
   A. **Sales quotas.** Adherents of the high-quota school believe high quotas spur extra effort while adherents of modest-quota schools believe attaining achievable goals helps build rep confidence.
   B. **Developing norms for salespeople.** Companies often specify how much time their sales force should spend prospecting for new accounts.
   C. **Using sales time efficiently.** The annual call schedule shows which customers and prospects to call on when. Companies are constantly seeking to improve sales force productivity.
   D. **Managing trade shows.** Detailed planning can increase the effectiveness of attending trade shows to generate leads and keep in touch with customers.
   E. **Other control techniques** include reports, personal observation, customer comments, and other reps. The key indicators of sales performance are (1) average number of sales calls per salesperson per day, (2) average sales call time per contact, (3) average revenue per sales call,

(4) average cost per sales call, (5) entertainment cost per sales call, (6) percentage of orders per 100 sales calls, (7) number of new customers per period, (8) number of lost customers per period, and (9) sales force cost as a percentage of total sales.

F. **Formal evaluation of performance** includes salesperson-to-salesperson comparisons, customer satisfaction evaluation, and qualitative evaluation.

VII. **Social Selling**
  A. **Online, mobile, and social media tools.** The use of online, mobile, and social media to engage customers, build stronger customer relationships, and augment sales performance.
  B. **Peer-to-peer sales** have been facilitated by mobile technology and social media.
  C. **Networking** can be accomplished via face-to-face meetings and online via social networking.

IN-CLASS GROUP EXERCISES

*Exercises with an asterisk next to them are suitable for individual homework or online assignments. Students, always provide an explanation for your answer.

1. *What are the most common methods of structuring a sales force?
2. *Discuss the importance of establishing sales objectives and the various kinds of sales force objectives common to the hospitality industry.
3. *Why do all managers have to have selling skills.
4. Discuss the process of negotiation and how sales force members can use it effectively.
5. Good salespeople are familiar with their competitors' products as well as their own. What would you do if your company expected you to sell a product that you thought was inferior to the competitor's. Why?
6. *It has been said there are two parts to every sale: the part performed by the salesperson and the part performed for the salesperson by his or her organization. What should the company provide for the salesperson to help increase total sales? How does the sales manager's job differ from the sales rep's job?
7. *Name and explain the steps of the selling process.
8. Find a hotel Web site that has a section for meeting planners. Does this site appear to be taking the place of a salesperson or offering assistance to the sales department? Include the names of the sites you have visited in your response.

EXPERIENTIAL EXERCISE

Do the following:

1. Conduct an interview with a salesperson for a hospitality or tourism organization. Ask the salesperson about the job. Find out what a typical day is like, and what they like and dislike about the job. Ask how they feel technology will affect the sales department in the future. You may of course ask other questions that are of interest to you. Write up your finding in a report.

REFERENCES

1. Donna J. Owens, "To Offset Their Seasonality, Canada's Resorts Should Stretch Their Seasons by Appealing to Multiple Market Segments," *Cornell Hotel and Restaurant Administration Quarterly,* 35, no. 5 (1994): 29.
2. Ibid., p. 30.
3. Howard Feiertag, "Database Marketing Proves Helpful in Group Sales," *Hotel and Motel Management* (March 8, 1993): 14.
4. Jin-Young Kim and Linda Canina, "Competitive Sets for Lodging Properties," *Cornell Hospitality Quarterly,* 52, no. 1 (February 2011): 20–32.
5. Chekitan Dev, Kevin Zheng Zhou, Jim Brown, and Sanjeev Agarwal; "Customer Orientation or Competitor Orientation," *Cornell Hospitality Quarterly,* 50, no. 1 (February 2009): 25.
6. Peter Rainsford, "Selecting and Monitoring Hotel Management Companies," *Cornell Hotel and Restaurant Administration Quarterly,* 35, no. 3 (1994): 34.
7. Boca Raton Resort, http://www.bocaresort.com/PremierClub/PremierClubFeatures.aspx (accessed December 20, 2004); Michael P. Sim and Burritt M. Chase, "Enhancing Resort Profitability with Membership Programs," *Cornell Hotel and Restaurant Administration Quarterly,* 34, no. 8 (1993): 59–62.
8. "Cruise Lines, Boosting Bookings with Segmentation, Case Studies and Clients," www.claritas.com (August 2004).
9. Christopher Schulz, "Hotel and Travel Agents: The New Partnership," *Cornell Hotel and Restaurant Administration Quarterly,* 35, no. 2 (1994): 45.
10. Taketosh Yamazaki, "Tokyo Hotel Construction Push Roger On," *Tokyo Business Today,* 59, no. 3 (1991): 50–51.
11. William A. Kaven and Myrtle Allardyce, "Dalmahoy's Strategy for Success," *Cornell Hotel and Restaurant Administration Quarterly,* 35, no. 6 (1994): 86–89.

12. Alexandra Paraskevar, Ioannis Katsogridakis, Rob Law, and Dimitros Buhalis, "Search Engine Marketing: Transforming Search Engines into Hotel Distribution Channels," *Cornell Hospitality Quarterly*, 52, no. 2 (May 2011): 200.

13. See: Jaimie Seaton, December 6, 2017, "Electronic Requests for Proposals Have Created a Mess for Many Events," https://skift.com/2017/12/06/electronic-requests-for-proposals-have-created-a-mess-for-many/ (accessed on November 12, 2018); Betsy Bondurant, March 9, 2017, "How to Elevate the e-RFP Process: 10 Best Practices," https://www.meetingsnet.com/strategic-meetings-management/how-elevate-e-rfp-process-10-best-practices (accessed on November 12, 2018); Ann Ransom; "Hotel RFP Management Software: 5 Ways to Win More Bids," https://www.amadeus-hospitality.com/insight/win-more-rfp-bids/ (accessed on November 12, 2018).

14. Barbara Jean Ross, "Training: Key to Effective Reservations," *Cornell Hotel and Restaurant Administration Quarterly*, 31, no. 3 (1990): 71–79.

15. Ibid., p. 79.

16. See Neil Rackham, *SPIN Selling* (New York: McGraw-Hill, 1988); Frank V. Cespedes, Stephen X. Doyle, and Robert J. Freedman, "Teamwork for Today's Selling," *Harvard Business Review* (March/April 1989): 44–54, 58.

17. Shanna Asti, "2 Stealth Drivers of McDonald's Global Margins," *The Motley Food*, June 24, 2013.

18. Fred Conner, "Resorts Makeup Means Sweet Smell of Success for Long-Term Client," *Cornell Hotel and Restaurant Administration Quarterly*, 35, no. 3 (1994): 9.

19. S. Dev Chekitan and Saul Klein, "Strategic Alliances in the Hotel Industry," *Cornell Hotel and Restaurant Administration Quarterly*, 34, no. 1 (1993): 43.

20. George H. Lucas, Jr., A. Parasuraman, Robert A. Davis, and Ben M. Enis, "An Empirical Study of Salesforce Turnover," *Journal of Marketing* (July 1987): 34–59.

21. See Charles Garfield, *Peak Performers: The New Heroes of American Business* (New York: Avon Books, 1986; "What Makes a Supersalesperson?" *Sales and Marketing Management* (August 23, 1984): 86; "What Makes a Top Performer?" *Sales and Marketing Management* (May 1989); Timothy J. Trow, "The Secret of a Good Hire: Profiling," *Sales and Marketing Management* (May 1990): 44–55.

22. David Moyer and Herbert A. Greenberg, "What Makes a Good Salesman?" *Harvard Business Review* (July/August 1964): 119–125.

23. K. Douglas Hoffman and John E. G. Bateson, *Essentials of Services Marketing* (Fort Worth, TX: Dryden Press, 1997), pp. 92–93.

24. Thomas N. Ingram, Charles H. J. Sobuepher, and Don Hutson, "Why Salespeople Fail," *Industrial Marketing Management*, 21, no. 3 (1992): 225–230.

25. Judi Brownell, "Listening: The Toughest Management Skills," *Cornell Hotel and Restaurant Administration Quarterly*, 27, no. 4 (1987): 64–71.

26. Howard Feiertag, "Sales Directors Build Productivity and Profitability," *Hotel and Motel Management*, 207, no. 19 (1992): 14.

27. Based on information found in Sara Donnelly, "Staying in the Game," *Pharmaceutical Executive* (May 2008): 158–159; Bayer Health-care Pharmaceuticals, Inc., "Improving Sales Force Effectiveness: Bayer's Experiment with New Technology," 2008, www.icmrindia.org/casestudies/catalogue/Marketing/MKTG200.htm; Tanya Lewis, "Concentric," *Medical Marketing and Media*, July 2008, p. 59, www.hydra-frame.com/mobile/project_reprace.htm (accessed July 2012); Andrew Tolve, "Pharma Sales: How Simulation Can Help Reps Sell," *Eye for Pharma*, March 28, 2012, http://social.eyeforpharma.com/sales/pharma-sales-how-simulation-can-help-reps-sell; Krishna Depura, "Online Sales Training for Busy Sales Representatives," *MindTickle*, www.mindtickle.com/blog/online-sales-training-for-busy-sales-representative/#more-1474 (accessed June 2014).

28. Vincent P. Magnini, Earl D. Honeycutt, Jr., and Sharon K. Hodge, "Data Mining for Hotel Firms: Use and Limitations," *Cornell Hotel and Restaurant Administration Quarterly*, 44, no. 2 (2003): 97.

29. "U.S. Hoteliers Fail to Net Enough World Cup Trade," *Travel Trade Gazette, U.S. and Ireland* (June 1, 1994): 32.

30. Howard Feiertag, "Different People Should Perform Sales and Marketing Jobs," *Hotel and Motel Management* (February 4, 2002): 24.

31. For additional reading, see Howard Raiffa, *The Art and Science of Negotiation* (Cambridge, MA: Harvard University Press, 1982); Samuel B. Bacharach and Edward J. Lawler, *Bargaining Power, Tactics, and Outcome* (San Francisco, CA: Jossey-Bass, 1981); Herb Cohen, *You Can Negotiate Anything* (New York: Bantam Books, 1980); Gerald I. Nierenberg, *The Art of Negotiating* (New York: Pocket Books, 1984).

32. Lamar Lee and Donald W. Dobler, *Purchasing and Materials Management* (New York: McGraw-Hill, 1977), pp. 146–147.

33. This discussion of zone of agreement is fully developed in Raiffa, *Art and Science of Negotiation*.

34. Roger Fisher and William Ury, *Getting to Yes: Negotiating Agreement Without Giving In* (Boston, MA: Houghton Mifflin, 1981).

35. See Gilbert A. Churchill, Jr., Neil A. Ford, and Orville C. Walker, Jr., *Sales Force Management: Planning, Implementation, and Control* (Homewood, IL: Richard D. Irwin, 1985).

36. See Ken W. McCleary and Pamela A. Weaver, "The Job Offer: What Today's Graduates Want," *Cornell Hotel and Restaurant Administration* Quarterly, 28, no. 4 (1988): 28–31.

37. David V. Pavesic and Robert A. Brymer, "Job Satisfaction: What's Happening to Young Managers," *Cornell Hotel and Restaurant Administration Quarterly*, 30, no. 4 (1990): 90–96.

38. Richard Cavalier, *Sales Meetings That Work* (Homewood, IL: Dow Jones-Irwin, 1983).
39. See Joyce I. Nies and Richard F. Tas, "How to Add Visual Impact to Your Presentations," *Cornell Hotel and Restaurant Administration Quarterly*, 32, no. 1 (1991): 46–51.
40. Dunfey Hotels Corporation, "An Interview with Jon Canas, President," video case number 9-833-502 (Boston, MA: Harvard Business School, 1996).
41. "Are Salespeople Gaining More Selling Time?" *Sales and Marketing Management* (July 1986): 29.
42. Ali A. Poorani, "Trade-Show Management: Budgeting and Planning for a Successful Event," *Cornell Hotel and Restaurant Administration Quarterly*, 37, no. 4 (1996): 77–84.
43. Bill Quain, "No One Ever Made Money by Discouraging Their Customers from Spending It," *Cornell Hotel and Restaurant Administration Quarterly*, 4, no. 5/6 (2003): 172.
44. See Scott Gillum, "The Disappearing Sales Process,"- *Forbes*, January 7, 2013, www.forbes.com/sites/gyro/2013/01/07/the-disappearing- sales-process/; and Paul Nolan, "Mapping the Buyer's Journey," *Sales & Marketing Management*, March/April 2015, pp. 32–34.

16

Objectives

After reading this chapter, you should be able to:

1. Describe direct and digital marketing and discuss the benefits to customers and companies.
2. Explain how companies have responded to the internet and other powerful new technologies with digital and social media marketing strategies.
3. Describe how databases can be used to develop direct marketing campaigns.
4. Explain relationship marketing and loyalty programs.
5. List traditional forms of direct marketing used in the hospitality industry.
6. Explain the responsibilities of marketers to protect customer privacy and data security.

Stu/Alamy Stock Photo.

Direct, Online, Social Media, and Mobile Marketing

Hilton's Multi-Channel Digital Marketing Strategies—Integrating Legacy and Contemporary Media in Innovative Ways

One of the most innovative hotel companies is Hilton Worldwide Holdings Inc. Throughout its long history, Hilton has dedicated a lot of attention to innovating and taking advantage of all the technology opportunities that can be integrated into the best service models. Today, Hilton continues to innovate and seek innovative ideas. Their newly open Innovation Gallery is a clear example of the innovative directions that are paramount for Hilton's strategy. Such innovation is evident in their marketing approach. Throughout the years, Hilton has consolidated its position as a leading brand in the hotel landscape, with a marketing strategy that includes electronic media reinforcing this position. Most importantly, the discussion here shows how the various elements of an electronic marketing are integrated to provide a unified and seamless platform that supports the company. Here are some elements of the electronic marketing strategy and how they work together to sustain this leadership position.

Storefront Web Site

Like any highly respectable brand, the company uses its brand name as the domain name for the Web site: hilton.com. This makes it easier for customers to find the Web site in the crowded market of today. It also makes it easier for the customers driven to the Web site from other persuasive sponsored media, as the Web site represents the main portal of the company. The Web site is designed in accordance with the marketing strategies of the company. Simple, clean, and to-the-point design artifacts present information in a clear manner to the customers, facilitating purchasing through the prominently located search and booking engine. The main space of the homepage is dedicated to promoting special events or facilitating decisions around major calendar milestones, such as the winter holidays. The Web site also prominently features the buttons dedicated to the members of the Hilton Honors rewards program, with areas dedicated for "my reservations," signing in, and joining the program. Specifically promoted products are also featured on the homepage, along with reminders to join the Hilton Honors program and to acquire one of the Hilton Honors-related credit cards.

Link Between Storefront Web Site and Social Media

Promoting using social media is important for Hilton, and the Web site supports that strategy.

The bottom of the page includes the social media links, which customers can use to get redirected to Facebook, Twitter, Instagram, YouTube, Pinterest, and Google Plus. Importantly, the Web site features a link to @HiltonSuggests. Upon clicking on this link, the customer is redirected to a blog that features stories presented by contributing team member bloggers about specific destinations that might be of interest for any potential traveler. This section also features a link to Twitter, wherein you can tweet. Current tweets are presented in a scrolling manner at the bottom of the page. The fact that social media features are linked to the main storefront Web site of the company shows its orientation to capturing the attention of the younger travelers, who are active on social media. In addition, this section also helps connect strongly with the younger audience, as the stories provided by the contributors emphasize elements of travel that are attractive for younger travelers.

Mobile Marketing

Mobile marketing Marketing promotions, messages, and other content delivered to on-the-go customers through mobile phones, smartphones, tablets, and other mobile devices.

In addition to the main Web site, mobile technology artifacts are used extensively to support the strategies of Hilton. For example, the company has a well-developed app, which represents the foundation for booking, checking in, room access, clearing upgrades, and checking out for a variety of customers that are attracted to the mobile technology and want to stay connected with the company at all times. In addition, the mobile app integrated seamlessly its digital key feature, one of the most innovative and reliable mobile technology artifacts in the whole industry. The mobile app looks similar in design to the Web site, reinforcing the main aspects of the marketing strategy of Hilton: attention to detail, focus on loyalty, offering a broad range of products, and a very strong informational support for customer decisions. One of the best features of the app is the section dedicated to the loyal customers. The app shows the progression of any customer through the tiers of the loyalty program, therefore stimulating loyalty. Another innovative feature of the app is the contact section. This is the feature that allows for the integration between the use of a mobile device and the other touch points of the marketing strategy of Hilton. Communication between the customer and the company becomes seamless using a mobile device with the app, and does not constitute a bottleneck in service when customers switch from one device to another.

Social Media

Social media Independent and commercial online communities where people congregate, socialize, and exchange views and information.

Recognizing the benefits of social media, Hilton is present on all major social media. For example, the company has a comprehensive Facebook page with a variety of content areas for information and with areas dedicated to stimulating purchasing. In addition to the general information pertaining to the Hilton brand, the Facebook page features links to various specific properties from the Hilton family. This facilitates direct engagement between the customers and those specific properties, while making sure that the main values promoted by the general marketing strategy of Hilton are communicated consistently. A similar approach is provided by the Twitter, Instagram, and Pinterest: the core values are promoted by taking into account the specific of the medium, the type of communication, and the target audience on these platforms.

TV Media

In addition to traditional Web-based media, Hilton uses a TV campaign, featuring actress Anna Kendrick. The same strategy is followed on the TV space—the company aims at facilitating direct booking by emphasizing the benefits to the customers. For example, in the video ad titled "Acting," viewers are presented with the benefits of booking directly through the Hilton's channels rather than through online travel agencies (OTAs) and the price match guarantee strategy that the company is currently pursuing. Another video titled "Picking stuff" features actress Anna Kendrick explaining to a friend the benefits of booking directly to Hilton (such as choosing the room from a floor plan, using a digital key). Most importantly, the Hilton Honors app is clearly displayed in the video, as the benefits of booking directly are presented. This design method allows for the presentation of app features to a TV audience—one that may not have substantial exposure to the app itself. This is a good way to link traditional media channels to contemporary media channels in order to sustain the same integrated marketing communication strategy. In addition, the video titled "Poolside" presents some of the positioning attributes of some of the Hilton brands, emphasizing the diversity of the entire portfolio of brands.

Overall, the strategy of Hilton shows how multiple legacy and contemporary media can be joined together in creating marketing communications that take advantage of the specific of each medium while converging in the digital space. By integrating such messages, companies can reach multiple types of audiences according to their segmentation strategies, but not diminish the effectiveness of their messages, given that the message is consistent across media channels. Throughout this chapter, multiple aspects of digital marketing will be presented, with emphasis on the specific benefits that they bring to the company trying to emphasize one or multiple media.

Direct and Digital Marketing

Direct marketing Direct communications with carefully targeted individual consumers to obtain an immediate response and cultivate lasting customer relationships.

Direct and digital marketing involve the direct engagement of carefully targeted individual customer communities to obtain an immediate response and build lasting customer relationships. **Direct marketing** is used to tailor a message to the specific needs of narrowly defined market segments or individual customers. This way, companies can encourage customer engagement, development of brand communities, and ultimately realizing revenues.

For example, one of the most critical elements of direct marketing is the mobile app. All major hotel brands have a mobile app. For example, Hilton's *Hilton Honors* mobile app allows users to perform a variety of tasks using the app. Such tasks include reservations, managing a user profile, checking in/out, clearing upgrades, and receiving a digital key to access the guestroom. The app is also tied to the Hilton Honors rewards program, so that a member of the rewards program can use the app to take advantage of the membership to the program or accrue benefits.[1] In exchange, consumers share information with the hotel, allowing the hotel to use that information in designing and offering personalized products that are perfectly aligned with the needs and wants of the customer. This approach is similar throughout many hospitality verticals, including restaurants, clubs, events, and airlines. For example, in food service, Domino's Pizza mobile app allows customers to order through the app but also see a progression of their order from the moment the order is placed to delivery.[2] In addition, Domino's Pizza mobile app can be downloaded on the major mobile ecosystems (e.g., Apple, Android), and utilized via wearable technologies such as smartwatches, allowing customers more flexibility in the way they interact with the company.[3] These are just a few examples of direct marketing tools that could significantly influence the way customers interact with hospitality companies.

The New Direct-Marketing Model

Direct marketing is continuously transforming. The factors that influence such transformations are the development of new internet and networking protocols (e.g., 5G cellular networking standards),[4] new, powerful, customizable, and user-friendly computing devices (smartphones, tablets, wearable technologies),[5] social media tools and online communities,[6] and corresponding consumer behaviors.[7]

services, and become attached to brands. Most importantly, the internet and the digital tools created opportunities for companies to sell directly to customers. Such selling, while basic in the beginning, became more personalized over time, allowing customers to change the initial offerings of the firm and adapt such offerings through personalization in order to obtain the highest value.

Given these benefits, digital usage and impact of the digital environment is growing continuously. In addition, new trends have shaped the matter in which products are displayed, promoted, sold, and evaluated by the customers. For example, new developments in Web sites design, such as responsive design, facilitated a new wave of e-commerce, by allowing the appearance of a Web site to change based on the size of the device on which that Web site is accessed. This development took advantage of the variety of sizes of today's mobile devices, ranging from very small screens of smartwatches and other wearables, to the relatively high-resolution screens of certain tablets (iPad Pro) or smartphones (Samsung Galaxy). Moreover, such approaches in design allow customers to seamlessly blend multiple devices into a singular purchasing experience, therefore optimizing their purchasing.

Another important element in the development of digital marketing is the ability to synchronize content on the multiple devices that are typical to what the customer may have. Today's technologies allow customers to set up profiles with their favorite companies, and such profiles can be easily accessed through a multitude of devices. The content is synchronized so that the customer sees only the updated information regardless of the device. This facilitates purchasing and personalization, as the redundancies of using multiple devices to access the same content are eliminated. For example, the customer may start a search sequence for a hotel booking on the phone, and then abandon the session. A few days later, the customer can continue the search using the Web site, and eventually purchase using the Web site. This way, the entire sequence is optimized, with great benefits for the convenience offered to the customer, and ensuring multiple points of engagement between the customer and the company.

It is important to recognize that not all customers view the digital marketing tools the same way. Naturally, younger customers seem to be more attracted to using such technologies, and gravitate toward companies that utilize such technologies. This comes from their natural affinity toward novelty, and is in line with the use of technology in other parts of their lives.[13] In contrast, older customers may not be equally inclined to adopt and use newer technologies. In such contexts, companies have always found problematic design of strategies that include digital marketing tools in addition to the traditional tools, in order to prevent alienating any group of customers. In addition, it is difficult to generalize to all groups of customers. For example, not all older customers reject digital marketing tools, and not all young customers fully embrace it. There are multiple studies that have attempted to examine how various groups of customers utilize digital marketing tools, in order to ascertain how customers' personality, preferences, and the circumstances of their consumption influence the effectiveness of the digital marketing tools directed at them.[14] Yet, companies are always trying to encourage customers to use their digital marketing tools. For example, in most of their advertising, companies such as United Airlines or Hyatt hotels heavily promote their brand.com Web sites and apps.

Young tourists in London embrace digital technology.
Marco Govel/Westend61 GmbH/Alamy Stock Photo.

Given the popularity among consumers of digital media, and the effectiveness of such tools for companies, it is difficult to find companies that are not heavily using such tools. One of the most common tools is the brand.com Web site, where companies typically promote their brands, their values, their approach to service, and eventually sell their products and services. Even companies that traditionally did not have a heavy online presence have created online Web sites and other digital artifacts. For example, a variety of restaurants now developed comprehensive Web sites, and have become active users of social media in order to engage with their target markets. However, it is important to recognize that companies use their strategic insight into deciding which specific digital marketing tools to use, and the amount of emphasis of each of those tools within the overall digital marketing strategy. Such tools include online marketing, social media marketing, and mobile marketing.

Online Marketing

Online marketing refers to marketing via the internet using Web sites, online advertising and promotions, e-mail marketing, online video, and blogs. While social media and mobile marketing also use online environments, they have special characteristics and fast rates of growth. Therefore, we will discuss them as separate sections.

Online marketing Company efforts to market products and services and build customer relationships over the internet.

Web Sites and Branded Web Communities

One of the first steps in creating a marketing strategy online is to develop a Web site. While all companies have Web sites, such Web sites differ in size and scope. For example, some Web sites are primarily **marketing Web sites**, as they are designed to engage customers and move them closer to a purchase or other desired marketing outcomes (e.g., awareness, intention to return, word of mouth). The information on this Web site is persuasive in nature, and provides the information to support a customer's purchase. Information about products and services must be clearly explained, and the purchasing sequence should be intuitive. The information must be provided in a manner that is easy to be found by the customers; in other words, they should find it in the places where they are expected to be. In addition to the features that support purchasing, the Web site should also include information that is designed to engage the customers and make them return and interact with the site with the goal of creating an online community on the Web site. Such new approaches to Web site design includes information about the brand, videos, links to blogs, potential activities, and a variety of features that stimulate engagement among the customers.

Marketing Web site Web sites designed to engage consumers in an interaction that will move them closer to a purchase or other marketing outcome.

Buffalo Wild Wings has a rating of 4.7 out of five stars based on 1,133 reviews on Google search. Although the company has a large geographic footprint with over 1,100 locations throughout the United States, it also has a very strong online presence. Their Web site buffalowildwings.com is easy to navigate and allows customers to find the information that they are looking for very easily. For example, the left-hand side of the screen is occupied by the main informational areas, starting with food, promos, fan zone (rewards), and locations. The main space of the Web site is occupied by high-quality photos of promoted menu items. The upper part of the Web page is dedicated to online ordering, featuring buttons for online ordering locations and login for returning customers. Clicking on the left side titles opens submenus, which allows customers to navigate through specific menu items. Every time a menu or submenu is clicked, the main screen populates with larger square areas where specific products are being promoted. In turn, clicking on those squares provides suggestive photos of the menu items in addition to detailed descriptions of those menu items. The fan zone is an area that engages customers and promotes new initiatives of the company. For example, the company's commitment to new unique and revolutionary items is expressed through adding craft beers to the menu. One important feature is the online ordering area. When clicked, the system asks the customers about their location, and depending on their location it suggests potential stores where the order can be placed. The ordering interface is very easy to follow as the screen is divided in the same square areas where the products are being showcased in high-quality photos. One important feature is the customization. Each menu item has an option to be added to an order or to be customized. Each customization option provides the number of calories, which are added to the total number of calories of the item being ordered. Overall, the Web site of Buffalo Wild Wings shows the general orientation of restaurants to appeal to a larger audience—one that uses the Web site and the mobile devices as primary systems for information about the menus and ordering.[15]

While virtually all companies have Web sites, it remains challenging for companies to drive customers to visit their Web sites. This is important, as the Web site represents the integrated platform that supports all other promotional and retail activities. Therefore, companies make a great effort to promote the visitation of the Web site. For example, companies such as Hyatt and Delta Airlines heavily promote their Web site on print materials, direct marketing, TV advertising, in an effort to encourage potential customers to visit the Web site.

Another important feature of the Web site is its "stickiness."[16] Stickiness reflects the ability of a Web site to encourage customers to stay on the Web site instead of leaving the Web site. In order for a Web site to facilitate longer visitation sessions, it has to be well-designed and user-friendly. However, such features are only the foundation of good Web site design. In addition to such features, good Web sites must be aesthetically pleasing and playful, that is, allow customers to engage spontaneously with the Web site and derive satisfaction from such engagement. Another important feature of a good Web site is the manner in which the information is structured on the Web site. Many Web sites are designed in a similar way, to facilitate ease of navigation. For example, the logo of the brand is located in the upper left corner of the screen, while the upper right corner of the screen typically features login fields for customers who are members of the rewards program. The main part of the screen includes promotional information, and typically has a prominent area where the search and purchasing engine is located. This helps facilitate purchasing. Finally, to retain customers, a unified vision for design is sought between the Web site, mobile app, and all other marketing materials of the company. For example, the United Airlines Web site features a picture of a Boeing 737 on a blue background. The picture is similar among the Web site, tablet app, and smartphone app, therefore providing consistency in an aesthetically pleasant design.

Today's Web sites are designed not only to serve retail functions but also to encourage significant other marketing outcomes. One of such outcomes is brand awareness. This is important especially for large companies, where the main brand.com Web site may be slightly different by design than other brand.com Web sites or other affiliate Web sites. For example, Hilton.com represents the storefront Web site of the Hilton Worldwide Holdings Inc. company. While it heavily promotes products and facilitates the retail function, it is also designed to stimulate brand awareness, and help potential customers learn more about the brands. In addition, as the main portal of the firm in the digital space, the Web site also facilitates the access to the rewards program members to their accounts. This way, the Web site addresses the main customer relationship functions. However, when the customer wants to make a reservation to a specific Hilton property, the customer may be redirected to the storefront Web site of a particular property. For example, customers wishing to make a reservation for a room at a property located on the University of Houston's campus Hilton Hotel, would be redirected to that particular hotel's Web site.[17]

There are variations in design based on the purpose of the Web site. For example, brand.com Web sites primarily facilitate the sale of products by the company to customers. Specifically, Web sites such as Hilton.com or Marriott.com promote their products, as well as serve primary customer service functions. The Web sites are adapted to serve the purpose of the company or organization that it represents. For example, Web sites of Expedia.com or Priceline.com have retail as their main function. As their competitive advantage is the ability to provide customers with the optimal interface for comparing rates across different hotel properties, their search and reservation engine are prominently displayed on the Web site. Other companies have Web sites that are organized differently. For example, destination marketing organizations (DMOs) such as the convention and visitors bureaus' purposes are to promote entire destinations. Therefore, most of the DMO Web sites are designed around providing the right persuasive tools to promote the destination.

While today's Web sites are becoming increasingly comprehensive, designing Web sites is facilitated by the emergence of several environments where small companies can design their own Web sites. For example, Google Sites or Wix.com provides useful platforms for companies such as small independent restaurants, hotels, food trucks, travel agencies, and event planning firms to create, publish, and maintain their own Web sites. On such platforms, a restaurant, for example, can use a specific template that can be customized to the specifics of that particular restaurant. The restaurant designer doesn't have to be focused on the technical aspects of the Web site design (coding, hosting) and in return he or she can focus on the marketing aspects of the company.

Online Advertising

Given the large amount of time that customers spend online, companies are shifting efforts and advertising dollars to online advertising. The goal is to build brand sales, and eventually to consolidate traffic to their Web sites, mobile apps, and social media platforms. Therefore, online advertising has become a major promotional medium. The main forms of online advertising are display ads and search-related ads.

Online display ads may appear anywhere on an internet user's screen and may be related to the informational content that is being displayed. For example, a potential customer visiting Expedia.com may see an ad that advertises for American Airlines. There are two important components of display ads. One is the ability to persuade, by using rich media elements such as animation, sound, video, and interactivity. The second one is the ability to provide analytics to the company. Methodologies such as clickstream analysis allow marketers to determine the impact of an online ad in terms of its ability to generate sales or awareness.

Search-related advertising (or contextual advertising) remains one of the largest forms of advertising. When customers perform searches using popular search engines such as Google or Yahoo, advertising in the form of images, text, or links may appear on the top of the page or on the side of the page that displays the search results. For example, a person looking for restaurants in Austin Texas on Google may find a list of results, and also a series of ads that are aligned with the words that describe the search or the products being searched. Search-related advertising is a critical source of revenue for main search engines such as Google. While the search algorithms are always evolving, so are the methods to evaluate the effectiveness of such ads. Methodologies such as clickstream analysis allow marketers to determine the extent to which ads lead to purchasing.[18] In order to display ads on the side of search result pages, the company buys search terms from the search engine and pays when customers click on the ad.

Search-related advertising (or contextual advertising) Text-based ads and links that appear alongside search engine results on sites such as Google and Yahoo!

E-Mail Marketing

Despite the emergence and popularity of certain communication platforms online, such as text messages and social media postings, e-mail represents one of the main forms of online communication. This is because e-mail is associated with the work environment, and reflects a relatively formal way of communication. E-mail marketing is one of the oldest forms of electronic marketing, originating in 1978 with an e-mail campaign targeting 400 recipients.[19] In 2018, approximately 281 billion e-mails are sent daily.[19] Today, e-mail marketing can be adapted to increase the relevance of content to potential customers and can be adapted for mobile devices to reach the desired audience.[20]

E-mail can be a very effective direct marketing medium. It allows marketers to send highly personalized and very well targeted messages to customers. Such messages, when aligned properly with the persuasive strategies of a company, can be very powerful tools to stimulate purchasing or to obtain other brand-related outcomes. The developments in network technology allowed for the higher personalization of e-mail, which can include better graphics, high-resolution pictures, animations, and links to desired Web locations. However, while e-mail is popular, especially as a means to formally communicate inside companies, there are certain aspects of e-mail that negatively affect its utilization. For example, given the ease of such e-mail tools, and the access of marketers to potential customers' e-mail addresses, it is easy to get carried away and send unwanted e-mail marketing messages. When such an amount of unwanted e-mail eventually aggregates in an individual's inbox it takes the form of **spam**. Spam represents unsolicited, unwanted commercial e-mail messages that clutter e-mail inboxes. In addition, a variety of cyberattacks use e-mail as a medium. For example, phishing attacks have diversified in recent years, where e-mail recipients are tricked into clicking on links that eventually lead to attacks.[21] As a result of spam and phishing attacks, technology

Online marketing Company efforts to market products and services and build customer relationships over the internet.

Spam Unsolicited, unwanted commercial e-mail messages.

developers and many companies opted for using a variety of filters that limit the amount of unwanted e-mail that a person may receive. Such filters may decrease the effectiveness of e-mail marketing.

To address such challenges, companies use opt-in e-mail or permission-based e-mail. In such settings, e-mail is sent only to potential customers who agree to receive commercial e-mails from companies. For example, restaurants may ask customers to give permission to use customers' e-mail addresses in marketing communications. Given the integrated marketing communications using combinations of different online channels, it is common for Web sites that have retail functions to ask permission for using a customer's e-mail address for further marketing communications. This way, a consumer will receive only messages that are relevant to them, and will have a higher chance of being further pursued.

For the past 10 years, e-mail marketing was a direct reflection of a company's marketing strategy. For example, a hotel would capture a customer's e-mail address and then subsequently use that e-mail address for further communication. Hotels have relied primarily on their existing customers, sending e-mail messages to them after they had stayed at a property. Such e-mails promoted specific properties or services, often advertising for discounts.[22] However, the current systems have adapted to today's customer behaviors, who include Web behaviors that encompass their entire presence online (e.g., e-mail use, social media use, followers). Therefore, newer e-mail marketing systems take into account additional information about customers, such as their frequency of visitation, social media activity, and level of spending. Thus, e-mail marketing is seamlessly integrated with other customer relationship management (CRM) systems to form an integrated and more efficient platforms for communication with customers. For example, the technology company Clairvoyix has developed a cloud-deployed platform that can be utilized in direct marketing services and focuses on segmentation and personalization. In 2018, Clairvoyix has been named Top Hospitality Email Marketing and CRM by Hotel Tech Report.[23]

E-mail addresses of potential customers are very valuable tools in digital marketing. Therefore, companies such as Digital Alchemy have created software that allows for capturing e-mail addresses of guests making reservations on third-party platforms. Such systems are used to solicit information and feedback about potential stays. Given the instantaneous nature of such communications, managers can act quickly and prevent service failures or attenuate the effects of existing service failures. Given the fact that e-mail is ubiquitous, that is, almost everyone has an e-mail address set up on their smartphones or computers, e-mail marketing has likely bright future in the array of tools of the hospitality marketers. As long as the content is relevant to the recipient, and it provides value to the product or service being promoted, e-mail marketing can be a great tool that adds value to both customers and firms.

Online Videos

Online videos represent digital content posted on Web sites or social media platforms such as Facebook or YouTube. The typology of such videos is broad, as videos can be designed to emphasize certain attributes of products, promote the brand as a whole, or be used in public relations strategies. Other videos are designed for TV advertising but are converted to formats that can be easily displayed on Web sites.

As the number of people being engaged by video is increasing, the impact of online videos can be substantial. For example, online video consumption is estimated to increase by approximately 9 minutes per day annually until 2020.[24] One potential outcome of such videos is that a video would go viral. **Viral marketing** represents a digital version of word-of-mouth marketing that involves creating videos, ads, and other marketing content that is so infectious that customers will seek them out or pass them along to their friends. Because customers take the responsibility of sharing such videos, the distribution costs of viral videos are low. Also, the relevance of such videos for customers is high, as they typically receive them from friends or people whom they trust.

It's also important to recognize that not all videos posted online are presenting companies in a positive light. Companies must be aware of negative

Viral marketing The internet version of word-of-mouth marketing—Web sites, videos, e-mail messages, or other marketing events that are so infectious that customers will want to pass them along to friends.

videos. Also, companies sometimes use videos to defend product failures, or to address specific issues. Such videos can be very impactful, as they sometimes represent a company's sincere view of a past event. While viral marketing, where positive messages are "going viral," is desirable, it is very difficult to estimate the future viral impact of a video when it is published online. It is also difficult to estimate the effect of a video given the online video clutter. Given that the number of views of a video online can generate advertising revenue for the person or company posting that video, there are a lot of people posting videos online, especially on popular platforms such as YouTube. Therefore, the message to the company posts must be clear and targeted appropriately to the right audience in order to be effective.

Hemingways Resort is a luxury resort in Watamu, Kenya. It uses a video on its Web site to provide evidence that it is a luxury resort. Bill Gozansky/Alamy Stock Photo.

Blogs and Other Online Forums

Companies have found out that certain digital artifacts designed primarily for consumer-to-consumer communication can be effective in business-to-consumer communication. Such artifacts include blogs. Blogs (or Web logs) are online journals where people and companies post their thoughts, typically on narrowly defined topics. There are a variety of blogs published today, depending on the nature of information being discussed. As travel is one of the most exciting activities for people, there are a multitude of travel blogs. Such blogs discuss various aspects of travel, from finding a destination for a specific trip purpose to how to best utilize companies' reward programs. Many blogs are interconnected with other online content, as bloggers promote their work using social media. Yet, in all blogs, one thing is common—bloggers have a typically large and devoted following and a substantial influence on people's decisions.

Companies have designed blogs of their own, which promote brand-related information. For example, the Disney Parks Blog is designed for people to learn about the Disney company, including a behind-the-scenes area that includes posts about dance rehearsals new products, interviews with employees, and so on.[25]

Many companies understand well the influence of bloggers. They want to make sure that the bloggers have access to the most accurate information about products, in order to provide a clear and honest image of the products in the blogosphere. Therefore, it is common for hospitality companies to invite bloggers to stay in hotels or to eat in restaurants, in order for the bloggers to have the most accurate information. Honesty is very important, and companies are trying to provide enough information to bloggers so that they can write honestly about the company.

It is also common for leaders of organizations to have their own blog. For example, Sir Richard Branson, founder of the Virgin Group, has a comprehensive blog that addresses topics such as entrepreneurship, space travel, and company values.[26] Experts also believe that it is important to include blogs into the storefront Web sites. Blogs are updated regularly, which in turn may facilitate changing rankings in the search algorithms of the search engines. Although the use of blogs has become common among companies, it remains primarily a customer-driven online environment. Companies should monitor the blogs discussing their products and always be aware of the manner in which the products are discussed or presented.

Social Media Marketing

The fast and broad development of online tools have allowed for the emergence and consolidation of a variety of social media platforms. Such social media platforms attract customers, who congregate online, socialize, and exchange views and information. Platforms such as Facebook, Google+, Twitter, Instagram, YouTube, or professional-driven communities such as LinkedIn are important to the online interactions among potential consumers. As such platforms gather individuals who group together based on similarities in demographics, preferences, etc., such platforms became important for marketers. In addition, consumers of social media self-segment into narrow segments based on their sense of belonging to certain groups. Therefore, many companies have dedicated effort to understand the impact of social media and have an effective presence on social media.

Given the broad and deep informational content available on social media and the pace at which it is produced and consumed by individuals, it represents perhaps a feasible solution to the natural intangibility of hospitality products and services. Thus, it is not surprising to see the large amount of information available about hospitality and travel products online, and the amount of effort dedicated by companies to take advantage of this content. Most importantly, social media changed the manner in which marketing communications influence customers. For example, while most direct-marketing tools originate with the business and target the customer, social media allow consumers to create and disseminate information among themselves. Therefore, the focus of marketing shifts from one-to-many to many-to-many.

In addition, an important aspect of social media is the visibility of word-of-mouth communications. In the past, such communications did not cross the boundaries of the close and immediate social network of the consumer. Today, due to social media, communication spans beyond immediate networks and becomes public and very impactful. Such public information is impactful because it may influence the customers (what to buy, when to buy, from whom to buy) but also may influence the companies. Information is impactful for consumers because it is perceived to come from peers—therefore being devoid of any hidden marketing messages or goals. Also, information may come from people with expertise, whose opinions are important—therefore the information has value for the customers.[27] Companies monitor social media content closely and may adapt their products and service models based on the insight they gain from social media.

Using Social Media

Companies can use social media in two ways. First, they can use existent social media. Using existing media is the easiest, as such media accumulate a lot of content online and gather a large number of potential customers. It is difficult to find companies that do not have a presence today on YouTube, Facebook, Twitter, Pinterest, Instagram, etc. Using such standardized tools offers a seamless transition for potential customers from their personal communications they receive from friends, and the marketing communications that they engage with that come from companies. In doing so, companies need to adjust the matter of communication and design marketing messages that follow the rules of these major platforms.

One important use of social media is currently addressing customer service issues. Typically, customer service is addressed using a direct phone line (the typical 800-number), or online via the brand.com Web site or app. Typically, customers needing to interact with the company need to login to their accounts using the Web site, communicate to the company using the app, or call the 800 number. Yet, given the large number of customers using social media and the companies' willingness to respond faster to social media than through other means, social media use for customer service has become a very common tool in today's current customer service relationships. For example, United Airlines responds promptly to questions about service posted on Twitter, which adds benefits to customers who need a quick response from the company and may help other customers who have similar questions but have not had the chance to ask yet. Such responses are very valuable for customers especially during irregular operations (weather delays, rebookings), or when there is a large number of customers calling to traditional customer service channels.

Another important use of social media is having representatives of the company using social media and participating to the exchange of information about the customers. In many cases, representatives from hotel or airline companies are participants in online forums, where they are recognized for their expertise in the ability to provide answers to specific questions. This way, customers can find very precise answers to specific questions, thus being better equipped to make decisions, while the company is perceived as responsive and caring, with positive implications for the brand.

The second way in which social media can be used is to design online communities. This approach, while seemingly more difficult, has shifted the way certain brands are operating today. For example, Expedia designed an online community where customers provide feedback about the products that they have purchased. Given that the reviews are posted only by people who purchased products, having direct information about the quality of these products provides high value to the content. Because of the high credibility of such content, its ability to influence other potential customers' decisions is high as well. However, it is important to recognize that not all companies are capable of creating a large social media presence on the Web site.

In addition to the benefits of social media for targeting major groups of customers, social media can be very good at allowing narrower niches of customers to create a presence online. Despite the advancement in segmentation and targeting tools, it is still difficult to find such niches. Therefore, social media can provide access to these niches of consumers, diminishing the cost for companies, which is beneficial especially for new entrants into the market.

Social Media Marketing Advantages and Challenges

Using social media has both advantages and challenges. Some advantages include personalization and precise targeting, interactivity, real-time communication, timeliness, cost-effectiveness, engagement and social sharing capabilities, and possibility of creating brand communities.

First, social media allow for very precise targeting and personalization. Marketers can design specific marketing material that is aligned with the methods of communication and arguments that are important for specific demographic or psychographic groups that the company is targeting using social media. This increases the effectiveness of communication, as the messages have higher relevance to the potential customers.

Social media are also very interactive. They allow for immediate feedback to be exchanged between a company and potential customers. As discussed earlier, such approaches facilitate recovery from service failures and increase the satisfaction of customers when such failures occur. Moreover, based on the principles of cocreation of value, companies can listen and adapt immediately to the preferences of customers, therefore providing an opportunity for both customers and company to obtain a higher value.

Social media communications take place in real time. Therefore, companies can reach customers anytime, anywhere, and can design marketing communications that are relevant to the current events taking place. Companies may need to shift their vision from designing marketing material that anticipates events as they occur to designing marketing materials and adapting products based on current events that take place. Therefore, companies can respond better to trends, and consolidate their existing positions in the market.

Given the fact that communication takes place digitally, social media can be very cost effective. While creating and disseminating the content is not entirely free for companies, consumers' participation in social media is free. Therefore, companies can reduce their customer acquisition costs by relying on already formed consumer segments that congregate around their specific hobbies, interests, or affinities. Moreover, customers can further disseminate information provided to them using channels that span beyond the boundaries of a specific social medium. For example, a company can provide a nice ad that is funny and interesting, and their target customers who constantly visit the company's Facebook page may see that. If the customers like this content, they will be willing to share it with other friends on other platforms beyond Facebook. Such approaches diminish the marketing costs for the company.

Social media is an excellent tool for developing brand communities. Such communities emerge and consolidate as customers who are loyal congregate online and attract other loyal customers. They share experiences, ideas, and eventually provide enough informational content that puts the company in a good light, which in turn influences other potential customers. Once such communities have developed and consolidated, they become powerful advocates of brands.[28] They may convince other customers who are initially skeptical about the brand to become loyal, and may even defend the brand when service failures occur.

There are some challenges associated with social media. For example, many companies are still trying to find new ways to increase the effectiveness of guiding customers from awareness to purchase and further to post-purchase evaluation. Such approaches are difficult to measure, despite the advances of analytics and big data. Also, social networks are largely user controlled. It is difficult to permeate the fabric of the normal person-to-person communications. Other challenges include the continuous generation of content that is not necessarily relevant for the promotion of the company's products, or specific behaviors of customers who only acquire information about a brand, become aware of its products, but end up never purchasing the brand.

Managing User-Generated Social Media Content

User Generated Content (UGC) has its own unique role in the general marketing strategy of the firm. Positive comments help the company facilitate community development and encourage people to use the product. Negative comments allow the company to figure out ways to improve and detect specific attributes of the products that customers did not like. Companies should not discard UGC. UGC is generally credible for customers, as it comes from peers, therefore, being able to influence thousands of people. Such influences are found in switching brands, switching from one product to another, or changing specific attributes of a product.

It is also important to understand why people post messages. Studies show that customers post messages on social media out of altruism, that is, they like to help others.[29] Unfortunately, certain customers post messages in retaliation for poorly perceived products. Understanding the circumstances under which a customer posted a message is very important in responding to such comments. Both positive and negative comments should have response from the company. This is important because it gives the customers the impression that their opinions are considered by the company.

One common trend is for companies to respond to UGC. For example, hotels tend to respond to negative reviews by providing explanations why certain service failures occurred, and explaining the way in which pillars are less likely to occur in the future. While companies are involved in these types of responses, it is important for them to respond in the personalized manner. Customers seem to dislike standard responses that do not address the problem at hand.

In order to address the increasing amount of social media content, from both analytic and managerial points of view, companies have dedicated a lot of resources to hiring people with very good communication skills to work as social media representatives of the firm. The role is to monitor communications about the firm on social media and respond appropriately when needed. This is one of the fastest growing types of positions in the hospitality industry.

Listening to Customers on Social Media

Listening to customers' feedback on social media is critical for companies, as companies can gather valuable information. Such information pertains not only to their products and services but also to their competitors. Social media feedback often includes discussions that compare and contrast the product of the firm against the competitors' product. There are a lot of platforms available for people to comment: tripadvisor.com, hotelchatter.com, localyahoo.com, citysearch.com, yelp.com, expedia.com, opentable.com, flyertalk.com, etc. In line with the emergence and development of sites hosting social media content, the research trying to understand and summarize customers' feedback has increased as well. There are companies that provide services to hospitality organizations geared toward understanding accurately what customers are saying. Such analyses are called social media analysis, business analytics, or sentiment analysis.[30] In Chapter 5, we discussed the importance of establishing proper communication channels, so that feedback from customers is passed accurately to management.

The next natural step after listening to what consumers have to say is engaging in a conversation. The conversation has to be tailored to the ways of communication and specifics of the audience and product. For example, Marriott Hotels has a comprehensive Facebook page, which includes a variety of ways in which the company is engaging with its large audience.

One common approach for hospitality companies is to try to take the conversation off-line from social media. This will result in a de-escalation of a potential problem, and will prevent potential negative attitudes from being developed among customers. Many customers providing content expect the companies to respond promptly. In many cases, companies use live chats on their Facebook or Twitter pages in order to respond properly to customer concerns and complaints. This allows for a very personalized response, which can increase customer satisfaction about how a particular problem is handled. Therefore, there is a lot of opportunity to engage in conversations with customers using social media.

Other companies engage by embedding reviews from sites like TripAdvisor into their own brand.com Web pages. This facilitates customers' learning about the company from their peers' reviews, as well as offering employees an updated image of the company in the eyes of the customers.

International Social Media

One of the most important benefits of the internet is its international character. Social media has the same international character. Given the increased globalization of the hospitality business, understanding how various social media influence customers in different regions of the world is critical. In addition, multiple social media appeared in various regions of the world, and capitalized on the natural characteristics of people living in those areas. For example, some social media that are popular in the United States are not available in China. Instead, the Chinese customers have other platforms where they can post social media content, such as Wechat, Weibo, and YouTube. The popularity and manner in which people communicate using social media may depend from country to country. This is why it is important for companies of global scale to understand the specifics of communication in different countries, and the specific ways in which people in certain countries use social media.

Integrated Social Media Marketing

Having a social media presence can range from very simple postings on Facebook or providing updates on Twitter, to designing entire campaigns that take advantage of the interactions that take place in social media. Most companies have a dedicated strategy for social media, designing content specific for social media that takes advantage of its specific nature of interaction among its customers, but at the same time is integrated with other components of the overall marketing strategy. This way, the company can leverage the types of interactions among customers that are specific to social media with the effectiveness of other communication media, in an effort to (1) present a unified message to the customers and (2) to consolidate this image in the minds of the customers. Therefore, designing the right social media marketing strategy and incorporating it into the overall marketing strategy of the firm is critical.

Ultimately, the company wants not only to create an ideal image online, but also eventually drive customers to purchase the product. Certain companies, such as Starbucks, are engaging in social media and design content that encourage customers to go to the stores to

The popularity of social media changes across global regions. This smartphones show popular social media apps in China.
Chuck/Alamy Stock Photo.

purchase. Other companies, such as Marriott, provide redirect links and other tools to drive the customers to purchase online. For example, Marriott has a "Book now" button on its Facebook page, which redirects customers to the brand.com Web site for bookings. Generally, the industry offers multiple examples of how various companies use social media ingeniously, take advantage of the customers' willingness to share information online, and interact with the company.

Mobile Marketing

Mobile marketing features marketing messages, promotions, and other marketing content delivered to the customers through their mobile devices. This is important because, as customers have devices that are always on and connected to networks/internet, the company can engage with customers anywhere, anytime. Because of the personalized nature of the utilization of customers' own mobile devices, interactions with companies using such devices can lead to a high level of personalization, and over time to development of long-lasting relationships. The tremendous development in the hardware, software, service models, and customers behaviors regarding mobile devices produced important opportunities for companies to engage with customers. Such approaches determine the overall mobile marketing strategy of the company, which has an added layer of complexity given the mobile nature of communications.

The increased development in the capabilities of mobile devices has created opportunities for companies to engage with customers in real time. There are multiple examples of engagement platforms, which seem to take advantage of connectivity. For example, companies such as Alice App provide a pretty useful platform for engaging the customers while they are on hotel properties. The customer requesting extra towels in the room can check the status of the request in real time using their mobile phones, and therefore have a clear idea about when they will be delivered.[31] This approach allows customers to develop realistic expectations, and not be dissatisfied when employees take too long to deliver those towels.

One important use of mobile devices is engagement platforms in the pre-arrival stage of customers. The hospitality industry is unique in that there is a substantial amount of time between the booking and the actual consumption of a product. This is true for hotels, airlines, most events, and car rental companies. Traditionally, once the customer had made the reservation, there is little communication between the hotel and customer. At the most, the customer will receive an e-mail confirming the reservation. However, the new mobile engagement platforms are based on recognizing the need for delivering additional information to consumers, especially immediately prior to their arrival to the destination. Therefore, platforms such as Zingle[32] and Whistle[33] have developed mechanisms by which customers receive text messages on their mobile devices that simulate engagement. As customers arrive on the property, they already know what to expect, diminishing the intangibility of services, and eliminating the need to request additional information, therefore preventing service bottlenecks.

Another important feature of mobile devices is that they are always connected to the internet. The internet offers a variety of information, including social media reviews of various hospitality products. For example, a customer arriving at the hotel can have a variety of options to dine, and he or she can make the decision to dine in the restaurant on the go. This is because his or her phone can access a variety of reviews, process marketing communications, which facilitate decision making. This is facilitated by the development of reliable cellular data networks, which provide seamless connectivity to customers, and the development of service models offered by mobile carriers (e.g., T-Mobile's ONE plan offers data and texting abroad in more than 210 countries around the world).[34]

Given the popularity of mobile devices, a variety of tasks have moved to the mobile environment. For example, hotels are offering opportunities for customers to check in using their mobile devices, and using their phones as devices to unlock guestrooms and other restricted spaces.[35] For example, Hilton offers a digital key to their customers to facilitate ease of access to their rooms for their loyal customers. In addition, companies such as OpenKey have created platforms that allow hotels to offer similar services to their customers.[36] One other common application is to use the mobile app to perform certain tasks. This is especially common in the airline industry. For example, Southwest Airlines mobile app allows people to check in, check bags, book and manage reservations, and perform a variety of customer relationship tasks. By moving certain tasks from face-to-face interaction to mobile interaction where customers use their mobile devices, customers can complete the tasks using their own device, with which they are familiar, and at their own pace.

Companies use mobile devices to stimulate purchasing. A recent study[37] outlined the factors that lead to purchasing of ancillary services in the airline industry. It was found that the perceived usefulness, ease of mobile devices use, and trust in organization influence customers' adoption of mobile devices for purchasing ancillary services in air travel, such as internet access and meals.[37] In addition, companies stimulate purchasing by offering promotions exclusive on mobile devices. To stimulate purchasing, sometimes having customers using their smartphones is not sufficient. Companies need to design the proper infrastructure to take advantage of customers' use of their smartphones. One particular example of technology used to estimate this is beacon technology. Beacons are hardware devices installed in strategic places throughout the property (predominantly in hotels and casinos). Beacons can detect the presence of a customer's smartphone in the vicinity, and push marketing messages.[38] This way, the hotel or casino can take advantage of the information about location that the customer is disclosing through the smartphone, and can add value to the customer's stay by providing personalized services that the customer may want to purchase.

One interesting aspect of mobile technology is its playfulness. Smartphones and tablets are not only designed to facilitate tasks but also to entertain. Therefore, customers have expectations about the playfulness of such devices. Taking advantage of such expectations, companies have designed mobile applications or marketing campaigns targeting smartphones that allow for spontaneous interactions between customers and the app.

The advanced features of today's smartphones and tablets allow for the design of very interactive applications. For example, hotels.com app integrates a new Siri shortcut function. The function allows customers to use voice commands on the app, allowing them to retrieve important information by using voice recognition technology.[39]

In addition to stimulating purchasing, marketers have designed mobile artifacts that are stimulating customers to engage in longer-term relationships, beyond a specific task. For example, Starbucks has designed an app that allows customers to manage their accounts, while receiving analytics about their consumption. United Airlines mobile app has a feature that allows customers enrolled in the rewards program to know at any time their progression through the various tiers of the program. These types of features stimulate engagement and allow customers to continuously use such apps. Therefore, such apps are perfect vehicles for dissemination of marketing information, which can lead the customer to consume products of high value.

Finally, the mobile devices are equipped with opportunities to complete the purchasing loop. This is very important, as until recently, such devices were not used to complete purchasing, but only to facilitate various stages of customer behavior. For example, customers would imagine going on a trip, simulate a booking, read reviews about the destination or a hotel, but not book using the mobile device. Only recently, the Web-based and device-based payment systems have become secure and convenient to facilitate such tasks to be completed using the mobile devices. One of such examples is mobile payment. Starting with the iPhone 5 and Samsung S5, mobile devices have standard features such as Near Field Communications (NFC), which facilitate secure payment. As such, these devices can be used in the absence of other methods of payment, such as cash or credit cards, and eliminate the need for customers to carry the wallet with them while, for example, staying in the hotel. Such features of smartphones can also be used to unlock guestrooms, or facilitate access to other guest-only areas.

Overall, digital direct marketing including online, social media, and mobile marketing are becoming increasingly established in the fabric of today's marketing strategies of hospitality firms. While sometimes it is easy to envision a world of hospitality in which all things will be digital, a more pragmatic view will encourage us to accept the notion that marketing strategy should be based on both digital and traditional tools. This is necessary in order to create a unified marketing communication platform and a marketing mix that supports the strategies of the company.

▪▪▪ Customer Databases and Traditional Direct Marketing

Customer database An organized collection of comprehensive data about individual customers or prospects, including geographic, demographic, psychographic, and behavioral data.

Good customer databases are critical for effective direct marketing. A **customer database** is an organized collection of comprehensive data about individual customers or prospects, including geographic, demographic, psychographic, and behavioral data. A variety of marketing programs can be developed based on customer databases, with the long-term goal to build relationships. Given today's information overload, it is imperative for companies to have a good understanding of their customers, which can be achieved by analyzing data from customer databases.

Typical data stored in customer databases include demographics (e.g., age, income, names of family members, birthday), psychographics (e.g., activities, interests, opinions, beliefs), and buying behavior (e.g., buying preferences, and the recency, frequency, and monetary value—RFM—of past purchases). Given the increase in the use of interactive technologies, customers can disclose a variety of data that describes their purchasing behavior. For example, they can disclose their preferences for certain products, birthdays, hobbies, favorite foods, allergy information, etc.[11] The size and complexity of customer databases are increasing, offering increasing insight into the role of data in designing superior customer experiences. Specifically, the artificial-intelligence company Travelsify has collected data from hotel and restaurant reviews to create DNA-like descriptors for specific hotels and restaurants.[40] Such comprehensive data tools are especially valuable to hotels in designing market strategies.[41]

Database Uses

Once a company has built a database, it can use it in a variety of ways. For example, the company can try to identify their best customers, and use such information to generate sales leads. Also, the company can mine their database to learn about their customers' purchasing behavior, using this information in designing future products or designing appropriate communication. Overall, using the database can be a strong foundation for building strong relationships with customers.

Data warehouse A central repository of an organization's customer information.

One important aspect of database use is database integration. Today, data come from a variety of sources, and it is critical to integrate all of the sources in order to extract meaning from the data stored in the various databases. A **data warehouse** stores the data the company receives in the central repository of customer data. Having integrated databases is important for designing superior products. For example, using the benefits of competency databases, Hilton has developed its property management system OnQ by allowing the system to utilize data pertaining to all Hilton's brands. Moreover, OnQ facilitated the integration of CRS, CRM, and revenue management functions in a system that offers the right amount of information to the hotel employee when providing service to guests.[42] In addition, OnQ facilitated on-site training (as opposed to corporate-based) for operators, which increased the efficiency of operations.[42]

Once the data are stored in the database, companies can use specific database queries to find specific data within the database. For example, the hotel manager can obtain a report from the database and look for specific types of customers. Specifically, the manager can obtain data of all customers who have booked a reservation within three days of arrival, and build specific marketing communication targeting these customers. Similarly, a restaurant manager can obtain a report of customers who have ordered food online only for the past six months, and design a marketing campaign targeting these customers. For these specific managerial tools to exist, the development of relational databases was an important development.

Relational databases present data in the form of tables, typically with rows representing cases and columns representing variables. There are relationships among the various data in the table, and the database management offers the possibility of retrieving data that are related. Databases allow multiple users to access the same data simultaneously, hence the concern that not all users may see the same updated data. Therefore, the database management system—the software protocol that manages the data in the relational database—utilizes transactions to keep the data in a consistent form while multiple users are using the data.[43]

The examples presented earlier illustrate basic ways of utilizing databases for decision making. Specifically, they illustrated how managers use queries to obtain data stored in databases. While this is fundamental to database utilization, the database technology has evolved and now allows managers to employ automatic tools for database querying. For example, data mining is one such set of tools. Data mining represents a set of techniques and methodologies (e.g., cluster analysis, modeling, time series forecasting, factorial analysis) that allow for the discovery of unusual patterns within data with the purpose of adding value and discovering new knowledge.[44] Data mining originated from multiple areas of statistics and computer science, such as database management, artificial intelligence, machine learning, and statistical modeling and has evolved continuously over the past few years to keep up with the large volume of data available and to take advantage of decreasing cost of computing and storage.[45]

Recently, one important set of techniques related to data mining has produced encouraging results, allowing managers to have a good understanding of customer behaviors. Such set of techniques involve predictive analytics, which represent a set of tools that allow computers to examine data and predict how someone will make a decision in the future. Predictive analytics are based on predictive models, which include core variables that can be predicted—such as a customer's future purchasing behavior.[46] Predictive analytics have offered opportunities to companies that took advantage of big data, and streamlined processes in order to stay competitive.[47] Such insight is critical to companies' decision making and may have important implications for the value that customers receive during service encounters.[48] Typically, there are multiple data inputs to a predictive model, which provides an intelligence solution that is proprietary due to its value.[49] Most importantly, predictive models can be characterized by "uplift"—a term that describes the value provided to a firm in contrast to a setting where a predictive model was not deployed.[49] While an increasing amount of data is being collected from the various organizational systems and disclosed by customers, most predictive analytics strategies on companies are incipient.

Given the high fragmentation of the hospitality industry (e.g., large number of transactions, high frequency of purchasing among the general population), the concept of big data has applicability to the industry. One of the most fascinating technologies is artificial intelligence (AI), which, combined with predictive analytics and the information stored in databases, can allow managers to find patterns of consumption that would be difficult to observe by simple analysis. Experts recognize various types of AI, such as process automation (automation of physical and digital tasks), cognitive insight (detection and interpretation of valuable patterns from data), and cognitive engagement (engaging employees and customers using intelligent systems or machine learning).[50] There are a variety of benefits from using AI, centering around better decision making and better value offered to customers.[50] In hospitality, AI can be used to provide personalized services to customers, to better understand occupancy patterns and optimize revenues, management of reputation, and gather business intelligence data.[51]

Given the frequency, velocity, and the volume of data coming in from a variety of sources, it is important to recognize that such data must have high quality in order to be useful. If the quality of this data is low, the results obtained from it are unreliable. For example, one of the most common errors is duplication of records. For example, one customer can have two incomplete records, based on the manner in which data about the customer was collected at the time when his record was created in the database. Therefore, if a hotel designs a marketing campaign targeting this customer, he or she will receive duplicate messages. This could lead to frustration for the customer, as he or she might think that the hotel is not organized or that it does not really care about him or her.

Another important aspect directly related to the accuracy of data stored in the databases is the appropriate utilization of such databases. While most of the data comes from automatic sources, guaranteeing that the correct information is stored in the correct field, sometimes, errors occur, or the information is simply missing. Sometimes, such empty fields are completed manually, as new data become available. It is important for staff members writing data in the database or in customer profiles to understand exactly the types of data that are collected, and how to effectively use such information. In order to achieve this, employee training and establishing clear protocols for such position is critical.

Creating and maintaining a database are not simple or cheap. However, the past few years have brought tremendous developments in the hardware necessary to develop databases, as well as the software necessary to access and manage the data stored in them. For example, the development of cloud computing and the decreasing cost of storage has made the development of databases much more accessible to a variety of hospitality organizations. In addition, the development of software tools such as Oracle RDBMS, IBM DB2, or MySQL has created opportunities for a variety of companies to benefit from utilizing databases. In addition, the development of programming tools that are relatively easier to learn than their predecessors (e.g., Python) allows managers to obtain data from databases more easily and more effectively than ever before. However, to develop such databases, the company has invested in a variety of directions, such as in hardware, software, analytical programs, communication links, training, and security. Most importantly, companies must have strategic views regarding the development of databases, which guarantee effective and efficient utilization of such tools.

Personalization, Disclosure of Information, and Value for the Customers

Disclosing information to a company has been an important topic for managerial practice, not only in hospitality.[52] Customers are likely to disclose personal information in exchange for personalization.[53] However, they only disclose such personal information when they perceive the high value from disclosure.[54] Therefore, a good way in which a company may provide value to the customers is by offering personalized products. In the process of personalizing a product, a company relies on data from the database, which includes data disclosed by customers. Such personal data include general customer preferences and evaluations of certain products that the company offers. By receiving feedback, the company is in a better position to know which products or components of products are valued by the customers. In the past, such exchange of data was typically being conducted face-to-face, as customers would tell service staff about their preferences for certain products, and staff would make note of such preferences. Today, such exchanges are much easier and more accurate due to the use of information technology, especially mobile devices. Such exchanges occur automatically, as most companies have interactive tools, and customers have interactive hardware that can provide such data. For example, mobile apps are designed to exchange preference data, as well as location and other important data about the user's device and his or her consumption patterns. If companies develop methods to incorporate such data into new products and services, the value would be high for the customers.

One important aspect of utilization of databases is the value that it provides customers. The value that customers receive as a result of the strategies of the company must be in line with the utilization of databases. For this, companies may use databases in two ways: tactically and strategically. A tactical use of a database means that the database is used for immediate, finite purposes. For example, a company can use information about customers who purchased recently and create a marketing campaign targeting those customers. Such a campaign may help the company attract some of the customers to come back and purchase again. However, companies can obtain much more from the databases if they use them strategically.

That is, they can use the databases to learn more about their customers, and over time design products that fit better with the value that such customers expect from the company.

Major companies, such as Hilton or Marriott, regularly use databases to understand customer preferences and utilize such preferences for further service. For example, if a guest likes to drink Diet Coke and requests such drinks every time he or she is on the property, this data may be stored in the database and used in the future. For example, upon check-in, this guest will find Diet Coke products offered complementarily by the hotel. When companies utilize such tools strategically, they may obtain competitive advantages, based on the knowledge that they have of their customers. Now it is up to the company to develop feasible service models that take into account this knowledge, and provide valuable products to customers.

Relationship Marketing and Loyalty Programs

The goal of relationship marketing is to build long-term relationships with customers by delivering value on a consistent basis, resulting in a company that customers can trust. In order to accomplish that, companies must achieve synergies among various departments, which should work together to serve the customers. The relationships built with the customers involve many levels, such as economic, social, technical, and legal, and result in high customer loyalty. Marketing tools that support such programs include offers of financial benefits, social benefits, and structural ties.

Financial benefits are some of the most tangible benefits that companies can offer their customers. Most companies have programs that reward their customers for multiple purchasing by offering some form of financial benefits. For example, hotels can offer extra nights, or upgrades, while airlines can offer miles or points that can be used for future purchases or upgrades. In addition, many major companies have partnered with major credit cards to offer program benefits to cardholders. For example, Chase offers credit cards that allow customers to accrue miles that can be used for purchasing within the United Airlines MileagePlus program based on their amount of purchasing using that card.[55] The programs are structured in tiers, and the benefits are increasing as customers become members of such programs and go up through the tiers. For example, the program is structured in five tiers, beginning with member, premier silver, premier gold, premier platinum, and premium 1K. The benefits increase with the level of tier membership. For example, a premier silver member has a complimentary checked baggage allowance for United economy tickets of one bag, while a premier 1K member has an allowance of three bags. Also, the premier silver member has a complimentary premier upgrade confirmation as early as the day of the departure, while a 1K Premier member receives confirmation as early as 96 hours prior to departure.[56] The program allows members to exchange benefits with other airlines partners from the Star Alliance. To qualify for premier silver, a customer has to accumulate 25,000 premier qualifying miles or 30 premier qualifying segments (and $3,000). The requirement increases for premier gold to 50,000 premier qualifying miles or 60 premier qualifying segments (and $6,000). In order to qualify for the premier 1K®, a customer must earn 100,000 premier qualifying miles or hundred 20 premier qualifying segments (and $12,000).[57]

Social benefits are commonly added to the financial benefits offered by companies. Companies typically develop strategies to increase the social bonds with their customers by learning individual customers' needs and then personalizing such offers based on their needs. One may say that companies view their customers as clients. Clients have names, personalized needs, and are dedicated special attention by the company. For example, guests are recognized by service staff, and they are addressed by their names. Over time, service staff learn special guest preferences, and offer personalized services without customers requesting them. This creates a long-lasting bond between the company and the customer, which stimulate further engagement by the customer and cultivating this relationship by both sides. If this service philosophy is followed by all employees with whom the loyal customer has contact throughout the experience, the customer leaves the property

Like its competitors, Hyatt offers a loyalty program called World of Hyatt, providing members the opportunity to earn points when they stay at Hyatt Hotels such as the Beijing Grand Hyatt pictured above.
TongRoImageStock/TongRo Images/Alamy Stock Photo.

knowing that he or she is valuable to the company.

Structural ties require changes in the business operations. Such structural ties involve offering adjustments to products to loyal customers that are not necessarily offered to everybody else. For example, Hyatt offers late checkout to customers in higher tiers of the rewards program, platinum members can request late checkout at 2 P.M., while diamond members can check out at 4 P.M. Marriott offers the same benefits, such that silver, gold, and platinum tiers offer priority late checkout. This is a benefit that is not offered to everybody else. Specifically, this benefit is critical for business travelers, who use the hotel room as a flexible workspace. Therefore, not rushing such customers to check out and allowing them to stay a little longer and complete more of their productive work in the morning can result in very high satisfaction. When such structural changes in services are successfully deployed by the company, they can bring important benefits. However, they can be costly. They require rescheduling of staff, thereby reversing certain operations processes. As a result, they are difficult to implement by the competition, which can enhance a company's sustainable competitive advantages.

When building relationships, it is feasible to think that every customer will be engaged in a direct relationship with the company. Companies develop customer relationships selectively. Also, companies select customers based on the extent to which they can meet the customers' needs better than anyone else. Once customers are identified, the company plans and implements a program to develop a relationship with this target market. Table 16–1 illustrates how customers can be divided into categories based on their profitability, which is directly influenced by the frequency and amount of purchasing.

Benefits of Customer Relationship Management

Customer relationship management (CRM) relies on benefits for a company that result from building continuous patronage by loyal customers, reduced customer marketing (acquisition) costs, decreased price sensitivity of loyal customers, and partnership activities of loyal customers. Loyal customers purchase more than non-loyal customers do from companies that they are loyal to. They may also purchase a wider variety of items from these companies. Because loyal customers are familiar with the company and have a strong motivation to repurchase, the company does not need to spend marketing dollars to attract such customers to repurchase. This reduces the overall marketing cost of the company.[58]

Loyal customers also engage in positive word of mouth, which is extremely important in today's environment dominated by social media. For example, they are

Table 16–1
Types of Customers

	Low Frequency	High Frequency
High Profitability	Try to get these customers to come more often.	These are your best customers, reward them.
Low Profitability	These customers follow promotions. Make sure your promotions make money.	Some of these guests have the potential to become more profitable.

likely to defend their loyalty to companies, and they often do so publicly on online forums and other social media. This type of behavior is very impactful, as it creates an informational background that puts the companies in a good light, therefore stimulating other potential customers to become loyal. In addition, loyal customers often provide accurate descriptions of the benefits that they receive from companies. For example, online forums allow for photo uploading, where loyal customers discuss the benefits that they receive and illustrate such benefits in a manner that reduces the tangibility of products.

Loyal customers also are less likely to switch due to pricing, and are likely to purchase more than similar non-loyal customers.[59] They often act as partners of the company instead of as customers, and try to help the company fix problems and provide services rather than complain about such problems. They sometimes defend the company, even publicly, when the company makes an error, therefore reinforcing the notion that being loyal to a particular company is beneficial. Given all these benefits, it is attractive for companies to develop good rewards programs and to cultivate relationships with their loyal customers. Over time, even small increases in the number of loyal customers can have big impacts on the profits of companies.[59] Therefore, building a solid loyalty program is a strategic imperative for companies.[60]

Loyalty Programs

Loyalty programs have been developed in order to attract and maintain a company's best customers. Most basic fundamental loyalty programs were based only on financial rewards, which could be easily replicated by the competitors. Given the proven benefits of such programs, over time they evolved into the strategic programs that we see today. They evolved by offering tier-based systems, where customers can qualify to advance to the superior tier by spending more and receiving more benefits in return. Given the strategic place of such programs and overall strategy of today's companies, companies always adjust their loyalty programs. For example, recently, several airlines have changed the way they offer points to customers who are members of their loyalty programs by switching from miles traveled to dollars spent. Airlines such as United Airlines use combinations of dollars spent, miles traveled, and segments flown to qualify members of their rewards program from one tier to another.[57] For example, one of the benefits offered to especially lower-tier members (premier silver and premier gold tiers) is to provide upgrades to Business/First class travel.

Most companies identify their highest elite customers and extend invitations to join unique rewards programs designed for the super elites. This is the case of United Airlines Global Services. This program is offered by invitation only and the qualification criteria are not published. The program membership is reviewed annually and provides unique benefits to its members. Such benefits include highest upgrade priority, companion saver awards, Global First lounge access, and dedicated phone lines and e-mail addresses for customer service. Inquiries sent to the dedicated phone lines and e-mail addresses are addressed within hours. One of the most unique benefits is the use of high-end vehicles such as Mercedes-Benz to transfer between flights—such services are available at the main United Airlines hubs such as Chicago, Houston, Los Angeles, and San Francisco. Because the travelers who qualify for this program spend extensive amounts of money on airfare and travel frequently, they also receive benefits in terms of priority handling during irregular operations (e.g., flights being canceled due to weather, mechanical problems).

Companies developing loyalty programs generally have the objective of changing behavior, including the frequency and the amount of purchasing, and disseminating positive word of mouth, especially online. Many basic programs start with punch cards, offering a free product after, for example, 10 purchases. Such programs may track behavior, but do not necessarily change it. More complex programs (e.g., offering a coupon that expires after some time) may change behaviors. Specifically, free drinks offered to loyal customers that do not normally purchase such products may not give away revenue, but may offer the customer a newer experience, which the customer may purchase in the future without the incentive.

Table 16–2
Gap Analysis of Loyalty Features

Feature	Performance (%)	Importance (%)	Gap
The hotel provides upgrades when available.	18.7	69.4	50.7
You can request a specific room.	4.9	44.7	39.8
If the hotel is likely to be sold out at a time you normally visit, someone from the hotel will call you to ask if you would like to make a reservation.	3.0	37.7	34.7
The hotel uses information from your prior stays to customize services for you.	24.3	57.7	33.4
The staff recognizes you when you arrive.	15.1	38.3	23.2
Employees communicate the attitude that your problems are important to them.	24.0	42.6	18.6

Source: John Bowen, University of Houston and Stowe Shoemaker, University of Nevada, Las Vegas.

An important advantage of loyalty programs is the data that the loyal customers provide to the company. Such data, typically captured automatically using the information systems available to companies, provide insight into the customers spending patterns, and also may be based on the interactions that the customer has with the service staff. Hotels and airlines always survey their loyal customers to find out if certain features of their product result in customer value. For example, Table 16–2 illustrates the differences in luxury hotel customers' perceptions of importance and performance on 18 possible benefits offered to them by hotels. The difference between performance and importance is marked as a gap.

Many of the current loyalty programs have been developed in the 1980s for baby boomers. However, since then, the market conditions have evolved. Most importantly, the customers have evolved as well. Therefore, we have seen numerous changes and adaptations to such programs. Such adaptations have occurred to make the programs attractive to a variety of younger customers, who may seek more immediate benefits than older customers. Importantly, the focus of customers has shifted from offering a specific bundle of benefits, to offering highly personalized service. Especially, the millennial customers want to feel special throughout the entire consumption journey and value personalized services.[59]

The future challenges for the designers of loyalty programs will gravitate toward designing programs that are appealing for baby boomers and Generation X customers, as well as being able to attract Millennials and post-Millennials. This is critical, as the heterogeneity within each of this broad customer segment is increasing, and customers are focusing on more personalized offers than ever before. Yet, many service models have been redesigned to accommodate all members of rewards programs. Companies have responded to the increased importance of rewards programs by deploying service models and technologies that place the loyal customer center stage within the service sequence. For example, entire property management systems such as OnQ have developed interfaces that allow service staff to spot when a request comes from a loyalty member program, and to respond effectively, given the value of the customer to the overall hotel rewards program. In addition, various software vendors have developed customizable interfaces that allow service

Service staff in this Hilton in Antwerp, Belgium, are able to OnQ to spot when a request comes from a loyalty member program. PHOTOVALLEY-kris coppieters/Alamy Stock Photo.

staff to find very easily information about a specific rewards program member when he or she comes for check-in, and tailor the response that they offer to such customers in order to increase the value.

Traditional Forms of Direct Marketing

The traditional forms of direct marketing used in the hospitality industry are direct-mail marketing, telephone marketing, and kiosk marketing.

Direct-Mail Marketing

Direct-mail marketing Direct marketing through single mailings that include letters, ads, samples, foldouts, and other "salespeople with wings" sent to prospects on mailing lists.

Direct-mail marketing involves sending an offer, announcement, reminder, or other item to a person located at a particular address. This form of marketing is based on databases or lists. The types of communications being sent include letters, catalogs, ads, brochures, samples, etc. Direct mail is one of the largest marketing media. For example, the Data & Marketing Association (formerly Direct Marketing Association) is a trade organization that provides insight to marketers about the challenges of marketing in a data-driven economy.[61] In addition, DMA offers advice to consumers, especially in terms of protecting their data during the commercial exchange.[62]

Direct mail facilitates one-to-one communication. It allows marketers to select markets very accurately, personalize offers, and measure their effectiveness with precision. Despite the increase in electronic delivery tools such as e-mail and text messages, direct-mail marketing is still an important marketing tool, as it facilitates delivery of messages to better prospects. However, some experts predict that direct marketing has an optimistic outlook in the next few years, especially given the clutter caused by electronic marketing.[63] Direct marketing has its own advantages, mostly related to the durability of the marketing material and exposure of such material to multiple people. For example, an e-mail targeting an individual and promoting a specific hotel package may be seen by the recipient alone. In turn, if the same message is sent through direct marketing, the recipient may not discard it immediately but may keep it for some time, exposing other members to the material or facilitating repeat viewing of this message, therefore increasing its effectiveness. However, given the strategic orientation in today's marketing programs of hospitality companies, direct marketing becomes more effective if used seamlessly with other forms of marketing such as promoting Web sites, or text/e-mail marketing. In all these forms of marketing, integrating the marketing message is key.

Telephone Marketing

Telephone marketing Using the telephone to sell directly to customers.

Telephone marketing involves using the telephone to sell directly to customers and business customers. While telephone marketing used to represent a major marketing tool, the development in mobile telephony, and the changing customer behaviors and use of their phones along with the development of new service models from the mobile carriers changed the way the telephone is used for marketing.

For example, the service models that charge customers for all calls, including unwanted calls, have created behaviors in consumers that reject many unwanted phone calls. Such attitudes, aggregated at the level of the entire U.S. population led to the development of the national "Do-Not-Call Registry," managed by the Federal Trade Commission. This legislation bans sales calls to the registered phone numbers. Consumers can register their phone numbers for free and the majority of unwanted calls generally stop within a month from registration.[64] The Federal Trade Commission initiated legal action against companies who still call Do-Not-Call registered numbers, collecting over a billion dollars in judgments.[64] Businesses that break the Do-Not-Call laws can be fined up to $41,848 per call, which is a strong incentive for companies not to engage in these programs.[64] Despite the efforts to manage the unwanted marketing calls, two forms of telemarketing are still in extensive use. Inbound consumer marketing and outbound business-to-business telemarketing are still strong.

The development of Do-Not-Call lists have created barriers for marketers to call prospects directly on the phone. Facing such barriers, companies have shifted their efforts to targeting customers who manifested their willingness to receive such calls. Such customers are placed on "opt-in" lists, and are continuously used in opt-in marketing communications. Many experts believe that opt-in techniques are positioned to respond to the current markets rather than the previous invasive techniques, as customers may accept to interact with companies if such companies ask for permission.[65]

Kiosk Marketing

Kiosk marketing has developed in response to customers attraction to digital tools. Many companies have developed kiosks, which represent machines that offer information or allow customers to perform service tasks (e.g., check-in/-out, printing boarding passes). Given that some tasks result in service bottlenecks, the development of kiosks has been found to be beneficial for many customers in many service settings.[66]

For example, StayNTouch has developed ZestStation, which is a self-service station for hotels. It offers a streamlined check-in, key retrieval, and checkout procedure that facilitates service delivery and removes the inherent check-in and checkout service bottlenecks.[67] In certain business models, the kiosks are the fundamental part of the service system. For example, hotels that have removed or diminished their legacy front-desk function started to utilize kiosks extensively. Given the development in touch screen technology, the number of technology vendors providing kiosks has increased recently. Specifically, technology company Agilysys has developed the rGuest® Express Kiosk, which expedite guests' self-services such as check-in and checkout. In addition to providing benefits such as reducing the service lines, this kiosk integrates with the PMS system.[68]

Kiosks are responsible for the development of many of today's self-service technologies. Such technologies allow customers to engage in services by interacting with the machine, instead of a service staff member. For routine tasks, this is beneficial, especially in situations when customers are familiar with the property or with a service routine (e.g., printing baggage tags for bags when checking in for air travel). Many companies have shifted from providing full staff service areas to service areas where kiosks are predominant, while only a few staff members are available to assist when customers cannot complete the task using the kiosks alone. The development of kiosks and other touch screen devices has advanced tremendously during the past few years, due to the development in touch screen technology and the design of very user-friendly intuitive interfaces. Such developments have created more confidence among the customers that using such tools is actually beneficial. Most importantly, kiosks paved the way for other service technologies, such as tablets placed in rooms, smart TVs, or interactive text systems, which allow companies to provide many personalized services to customers.[69]

Interactive TV

Hotels are replacing the front desk with self-check-in kiosks. Aleksey Popov/123RF.

Interactive TV (ITV) lets viewers interact with TV programming and advertising using remote controls. Such tools have increased in popularity in recent years, as customers like to interact with such media under specific conditions. For example, Teleste's Hospitality Solutions offers an integrated solution that provides guest internet access and interactive TV using a hotel's existing cable network.[70] ITV allows marketers to target audiences based on their specific interests, and using interactive tools that are very engaging. By taking advantage of such engagement, the content of the marketing communications can be effective, stimulating purchasing and long-lasting relationships. Another important development in the area of TV entertainment is the increasing popularity of streaming services such as Netflix, Hulu, Amazon Prime, and live TV services streamed online such as SlingTV,

Vue, DirecTV Now, and Hulu Live. Along with the development of such services, many technology vendors have designed hardware that integrates with smart TV sets or other systems available in hotel rooms. Such systems allow customers to use their own credentials and stream services for which they have already subscribed. This way, the hotel expense can be enhanced. Similarly, airlines such as United Airlines have introduced mobile apps that can be used for streaming in-flight services. For example, a customer can download the United Airlines app and use the app to watch movies when connected to the airplane's Wi-Fi network.

▪▪▪ Online Privacy and Security

E-commerce The general term for a buying and selling process that is supported by electronic means, primarily the internet.

Online privacy is likely the number one concern for **e-commerce**. This is because marketing techniques and technology have evolved to an extent where they permit marketers to collect and analyze detailed data describing the customers. For example, visits to Web sites can be tracked, as well as the manner in which customers visit specific areas of a Web site or an app.

Privacy is very important for electronic marketing. For example, an increasing amount of data can be collected from customers, in addition to the data that they voluntarily disseminate using their mobile devices. Such data should only be used by companies according to the norms of consent agreed upon by the customers, and only to add value to customers. New privacy regulations have been enacted. For example, the European Union enacted the General Data Protection Regulation (GDPR), which offers privacy protections for customers who are residents of the European Union and stipulates penalties for organizations failing to comply with the GDPR rules.[71] The hotel and travel industries are likely to be affected due to the global character of travel and the information disclosed by customers in the process of service delivery.

An important aspect of online marketing is customers' security concerns. In many situations, customers fear that the data exchanged with Web sites can be intercepted by individuals with bad intentions. The industry is also susceptible to such feelings of customers, as it involves a large number of relatively small transactions, frequently using multiple vendors. For example, a couple visiting a destination and staying in a hotel may not know what attractions they are going to visit until they actually arrive at the destination and stay in the hotel. In that case, they would book tickets (e.g., for museums), likely using their mobile devices connected to the internet via the networks provided by the hotel. Many such networks are unsecured, presenting customers with potential cyber security risks, if customers do not take measures to protect the security of their internet sessions and transactions. Certain ways to minimize such security risks include using virtual private networks (VPNs), adopting very restrictive behaviors online, and avoiding clicking on redirect links.

If customers have security and privacy concerns, so do the companies. This is important, because a lot of the technologies that assist in the day-to-day business are attractive to individuals with bad behavior. For example, company databases and point-of-sale systems are used in exchanging a variety of customer information and preferences, including payment information. Therefore, one important aspect in safeguarding security and privacy is to maintain high standards at the level of the company, train the staff members, and create a culture of trust.[72] For example, companies are advised to use norms such as those provided by the Payment Card Industry Data Security Standards (PCI-DSS) to increase the security of their systems.[73] Moreover, companies conduct information security audits and design plans for unfortunate events when the privacy and the security of such systems have been compromised. In addition to the tools that they currently employ to safeguard security and privacy, companies should use their resources to better educate customers and employees to prevent them from falling victim to attacks. If companies engage in such activities, there will be trust among customers, with potential long-term effects on their engagement and loyalty.

CHAPTER REVIEW

I. **Direct and Digital Marketing.** This marketing involves engaging directly with carefully targeted individual consumers and customer communities to both obtain an immediate response and build lasting customer relationships. Companies use direct marketing to tailor their offers and content to the needs and interests of narrowly defined segments or individual buyers. In this way, they build customer engagement, brand community, and sales.

   A. **The new direct-marketing model.** In the wake of online social and mobile media, direct marketing has undergone a dramatic transformation. Direct and digital marketing are more than just supplementary channels or advertising media; they constitute a complete model for doing business.

   B. **Benefits of direct and digital marketing to buyers and sellers.** For buyers, direct and digital marketing are convenient, easy, and private. They give buyers anywhere, anytime access to an almost unlimited assortment of goods and a wealth of product and buying information. For sellers, direct marketing often provides low-cost, efficient, speedy alternatives for reaching their markets as well as greater flexibility. Especially in today's digital environment, direct marketing provides opportunities for real-time marketing that links brands to important moments and trending events in customers' lives.

   C. **Forms of direct and digital marketing.** Traditional direct-marketing tools include face-to-face selling, direct-mail marketing, catalog marketing, telemarketing, direct-response TV marketing, and kiosk marketing. In recent years, however, a new set of digital and direct-marketing tools have emerged. These include Web sites, online ads, promotional e-mail, online videos, blogs, social media marketing, and mobile marketing.

II. **Digital and Social Media Marketing.** Digital marketing tools and platforms directly engage consumers anywhere at any time via their computers, smartphones, tablets, smart TVs, and other digital devices. The use of the internet and digital technology impacts both buyers and the marketers who serve them.

   A. **Marketing, the internet, and the digital age.** The digital age has fundamentally changed customers' notions of convenience, speed, price, product information, service, and brand interactions. As a result, it has given marketers a whole new way to create customer value, engage customers, and build customer relationships. Also, companies that have traditionally operated off-line have now created their own online sales, marketing, and brand community channels.

   B. **Online marketing.** Online marketing refers to marketing via the internet using company Web sites, online advertising and promotions, e-mail marketing, online video, and blogs.

      1. **Web sites and branded Web communities.** For most companies, the first step in conducting online marketing is to create a Web site. Some Web sites are designed to engage customers and move them closer to a direct purchase or other marketing outcome, while others' primary purpose is to present brand content that engages consumers and creates customer-brand community.

      2. **Online advertising.** Online advertising has become a major promotional medium. The main forms of online advertising are display ads and search-related ads. Together, they account for the largest portion of firms' digital marketing budgets.

      3. **E-mail marketing.** E-mail can be the ultimate direct-marketing medium. Marketers can send highly targeted, tightly personalized, relationship-building messages. Many companies also use configurable e-mail systems that let customers choose what they want to get to steer clear of frustration from spam e-mails.

      4. **Online videos.** Online videos engage consumers and are a form of inexpensive marketing. Videos can go viral and harbor a vast amount of attention.

      5. **Blogs and other online forums.** Blogs (or Web logs) are online journals where people and companies post their thoughts and other content, usually related to narrowly defined topics. They usually appeal to specific special-interest groups.

   C. **Social media marketing.** For travel products, it can be argued that social media entails a change from one-to-one recommendations from individuals to many-to-many conversations. In the past, these personal sources often came from talking with a friend, relative, or local resident. Social media has now expanded the conversation, in terms of both breadth and depth.

      1. **Using social media.** Marketers can engage in social media in two ways: They can use existing social media, or they can set up their own. Using existing social media seems the easiest. Thus, most brands, large and small, have set up shop on a host of social media sites.

      2. **Social media marketing advantages and challenges.** Social media are targeted and personal—they allow marketers to create and share tailored brand content with individual consumers and customer communities. Social media are interactive, making them ideal for starting and participating in customer conversations and listening to customer feedback. Social media are also immediate and timely. Social media can be very cost effective. Social media marketing also presents challenges. First, many companies are still experimenting with how to use them effectively, and results are hard to measure. Second, such social networks are largely user controlled.

3. **Managing user-generated social media content.** UGC is valuable, whether it is positive or negative. The positive comments create community and encourage others to use the product. The negative comments provide feedback on what customers do not like and how the company did not meet their expectations. These comments help the company improve the service-delivery system.
4. **Listening to customers on social media.** One of the goals of a company's social media plan should be to engage its customers and create a conversation.
5. **International social media.** Social media managers working internationally will need to find out which sites are most effective as they move around the world.
6. **Integrated social media marketing.** Companies that use social media successfully are integrating a broad range of diverse media to create brand-related social sharing, engagement, and customer community.

D. **Mobile marketing.** Mobile marketing features marketing messages, promotions, and other marketing content delivered to on-the-go consumers through their mobile devices. Marketers use mobile marketing to engage customers anywhere, anytime during the buying and relationship-building processes.

III. **Customer Databases and Traditional Direct Marketing.** Effective direct marketing begins with a good customer database. A customer database is an organized collection of comprehensive data about individual customers or prospects, including geographic, demographic, psychographic, and behavioral data. A good customer database can be a potent relationship-building tool.

A. **Database uses.** Companies use databases to locate good potential customers and to generate sales leads. They can mine their databases to learn about customers in detail and then fine-tune their market offerings and communications to the special preferences and behaviors of target segments or individuals. In all, a company's database can be an important tool for building stronger long-term customer relationships.

B. **Personalization, disclosure of information, and value for the customers.** Customers are likely to disclose personal information in exchange for personalization. However, they disclose such personal information only when they perceive the high value from disclosure. Therefore, a good way in which a company may provide value to the customers is by offering personalized products.

IV. **Relationship Marketing and Loyalty Programs.** Direct marketing allows companies to develop a strong relationship with their customers, which helps prevent them from switching to competitors. Relationship marketing has a long-term orientation. The goal is to deliver long-term value to customers, and the measure of success is long-term customer satisfaction. Relationship marketing requires that all the company's departments work together with marketing as a team to serve the customer. It involves building relationships at many levels: economic, social, technical, and legal, resulting in high customer loyalty.

A. **Benefits of customer relationship management.** The benefits of CRM come from building continued patronage of loyal customers, reduced marketing costs, decreased price sensitivity of loyal customers, and partnership activities of loyal customers.

B. **Loyalty programs.** Loyalty programs were developed as a way to attract and maintain a company's best customers. The biggest change for North American hotel loyalty programs is the shift in the importance of generational trends, with millennials trending and baby boomers fading.

V. **Traditional Forms of Direct Marketing.** The traditional forms of direct marketing used in the hospitality industry are direct-mail marketing, telephone marketing, kiosk marketing, and iTV.

A. **Direct-mail marketing.** Involves sending an offer, announcement, reminder, or other item to a person at a particular address. Using highly selective mailing lists, direct marketers send out millions of mail pieces each year.

B. **Telephone marketing.** Involves using the telephone to sell directly to consumers and business customers.

C. **Kiosk marketing.** As consumers become more and more comfortable with computer and digital technologies, many companies are placing information and ordering machines called kiosks (in contrast to vending machines, which dispense actual products) in stores, airports, and other locations.

D. **Interactive TV.** ITV lets viewers use their remote controls to interact with TV programming and advertising.

VI. **Online Privacy and Security.** Marketers have a responsibility to protect the privacy of customer information and make sure personal information such as credit card numbers is secure.

▆▆▆ IN-CLASS GROUP EXERCISES

*Exercises with an asterisk next to them are suitable for individual homework or online assignments. Students, always provide an explanation for your answer.

1. *Find an example of a good video for a hospitality or travel company on YouTube. Why do you feel it was effective?

2. *You are going to a large city you would like to visit. How would you use the internet to determine where you would stay while visiting the city? Assume you will have to purchase accommodations in the city.

3. *If you were the owner of a restaurant explain how you would use mobile marketing.

4. *Define data warehouse and explain why it is a popular data management tool.
5. *Discuss ways an internet site can collect and use information from its visitors. You may refer to the site of a hotel, restaurant, club, or a destination marketing organization when answering your question.
6. Find an example of a hospitality or travel company effectively using social media.

EXPERIENTIAL EXERCISE

Do the following:

1. Sign up for a loyalty program for hospitality or travel organization. What information did it request from you? Did the information seem useful? Is there information it should have asked for but did not? Did it ask you if it was all right if it sent you information? See if you receive any response from the company after signing up.

REFERENCES

1. H.H.W. Inc., Travel easier with the Hilton Honors App (2018).
2. Domino's Pizza, Domino's Android App (2018).
3. Jonathan Maze, Domino's Debuts Smartwatch App. *Nation's Restaurant News* (2018).
4. S. Segan, "What Is 5G?" *PC Magazine* (2018).
5. S. Axon, "The Best PCs, Gadgets, and Wearables of CES 2018," *Ars Technica* (2018).
6. B. Freeman, "Find Your Community: Inspiring Travel Networks," *Lonely Planet* (2018).
7. C. Morosan and J. T. Bowen, "Analytic Perspectives on Online Purchasing in Hotels: a Review of Literature and Research Directions," *International Journal of Contemporary Hospitality Management*, 30, no. 1 (2018): 557–580.
8. Expedia.com. *Expedia Reviews*, December 10, 2018, https://www.expedia.com/reviews/.
9. E. Currington, "10 Best Restaurant Review Sites to Get Listed on," *The Digital Restaurant* (2018).
10. Doordash.com. *DoorDash*, 2018, https://www.doordash.com/ (accessed December 10, 2018).
11. C. Morosan and A. DeFranco, "Disclosing Personal Information via Hotel Apps: A Privacy Calculus Perspective," *International Journal of Hospitality Management*, 47 (2015): 120–130.
12. C. Morosan and A. DeFranco, "Co-creating Value in Hotels Using Mobile Devices: A Conceptual Model with Empirical Validation," *International Journal of Hospitality Management*, 52 (2016): 131–142.
13. A. Smith and M. Anderson, *Social Media Use in 2018* (2018).
14. A. Bilgihan et al., "Consumer Perception of Knowledge-Sharing in Travel-Related Online Social Networks," *Tourism Management*, 52 (2016): 287–296.
15. B. W. Wings, *Buffalo Wild Wings*, 2018, https://www.buffalowildwings.com/en/fan-zone/ (accessed December 18, 2018).
16. Y. Chen and Z. Lin, "Fashionability vis-à-vis Rationality: Investigating Factors Driving Users' e-Tourism Website Stickiness," *Current Issues in Tourism*, 21, no. 1 (2018): 41–57.
17. H.H.W. Inc., *Hilton University of Houston*, 2018, https://www3.hilton.com/en/hotels/texas/hilton-university-of-houston-HOUUHHF/index.html (accessed December 10, 2018).
18. Hotel Business, "OTAs Leading Travel Suppliers on Bookings, Research Shows," *Hotel Business*, 2017.
19. T. Wozniak, "What We Can Learn from Email Marketing's 40-Year Evolution," *Forbes* (2018).
20. A. Gomez, "Five Ways to Improve Your Email Marketing Content," *Forbes* (2018).
21. M. Drolet, "Don't Bite That Phishing Bait: Bet on These Five Simple Safety Rules," *Forbes* (2018).
22. V. Singh, "Hotel CRM Reality Check," *HospitalityNet.org*, 2018.
23. Clairvoyix, "Clairvoyix Named Top Hospitality Email Marketing, CRM Company," *Hospitality Upgrade* (2018).
24. K. Tran, "Time Spent with Digital Video will Grow 25 percent by 2020," *Business Insider* (2018).
25. Disney Parks Blog. *Disney Parks Blog*, 2018, https://disneyparks.disney.go.com/blog/.
26. S. R. Branson, Follow Richard Branson's blog, 2018.
27. M. Atwood and C. Morosan, "An Investigation of the Persuasive Effects of Firm-Consumer Communication Dyads Using Facebook," *Worldwide Hospitality and Tourism Themes*, 2015. Special Edition on Social Media.
28. M. E. Zaglia, "Brand Communities Embedded in Social Networks," *Journal of Business Research*, 66, no. 2 (2013): 216–223.
29. W. W. K. Ma and A. Chan, "Knowledge Sharing and Social Media: Altruism, Perceived Online Attachment Motivation, and Perceived Online Relationship Commitment," *Computers in Human Behavior*, 39 (2014): 51–68.
30. M. Geetha, P. Singha, and S. Sumedha Sinha, "Relationship between Customer Sentiment and Online Customer Ratings for Hotels—An Empirical Analysis," *Tourism Management*, 61 (2017): 43–54.
31. Alice. *Alice*, May 1, 2018, https://info.aliceapp.com/.
32. Zingle. *Zingle*, May 1, 2018, https://www.zingle.me.

33. Whistle. *Whistle*, May 1, 2018, http://www.trywhistle.com/.
34. T-Mobile. *T-Mobile ONE*, 2018, https://www.t-mobile.com/cell-phone-plans?icid=WMM_TM_Q417UNAVME_GHBARMBPJEO11768 (accessed December 17, 2018).
35. Hilton Hotels Worldwide Inc. Let Yourself in with Hilton Digital Key (2018).
36. OpenKey. *The World Is Your Front Desk*, 2018, https://www.openkey.co/ (accessed December 17, 2018).
37. C. Morosan, "Toward an Integrated Model of Adoption of Mobile Phones for Purchasing Ancillary Services in Air Travel," *International Journal of Contemporary Hospitality Management*, 26, no. 2 (2014): 246–271.
38. R. Ravikumar, *The Promise of Beacon Technology for the Hospitality Industry*, 2017.
39. hotels.com. *Hey Siri: Show Me the Shortcut to Hands-Free Travel with hotels.com, 2018*, http://press.hotels.com/us/hey-siri-show-me-the-shortcut-to-handsfree-travel-with-hotels-com/.
40. Video: Travelsify Unveils Hotel Brand DNA to Close the Gap Between Brand Personality and Guest Experiences, 2018, Skift: Skift.
41. Travelsify. Travelsify Hotel DNATM and Restaurant DNATM AI analytics platform, 2018, https://www.travelsify.com/en/.
42. J. OnQ Inge—"A Windows Pioneer Still in Global Use," *Hospitality Upgrade* (2017).
43. Oracle. *The JavaTM Tutorials*, 2018, https://docs.oracle.com/javase/tutorial/jdbc/overview/database.html (accessed December 18, 2018).
44. K. Gibert et al., "Which Method to Use? An Assessment of Data Mining Methods in Environmental Data Science," *Environmental Modelling & Software*, 110 (2018): 3–27.
45. SAS. *Data mining: What It Is and Why It Matters*, 2018, https://www.sas.com/en_us/insights/analytics/data-mining.html (accessed December 18, 2018).
46. N. Sharma and M. Dadhich, "Predictive Business Analytics: The Way Ahead," *Journal of Commerce & Management Thought*, 5, no. 4 (2014): 652–658.
47. B. T. Hazen et al., "Data Quality for Data Science, Predictive Analytics, and Big Data in Supply Chain Management: An Introduction to the Problem and Suggestions for Research and Applications," *International Journal of Production Economics*, 154, no. 72–80 (2014).
48. M. M. Malik, S. Abdallah, and M. Ala'raj, "Data Mining and Predictive Analytics Applications for the Delivery of Healthcare Services: A Systematic Literature Review," *Annals of Operations Research*, 270 (2018): 287–312.
49. M. Goul, T. S. Raghu, and R. D. St. Louis, "APC Forum: Governing the Wild West of Predictive Analytics and Business Intelligence," *MIS Quarterly Executive*, 17, no. 2 (2018): 157–183.
50. T. Davenport and R. Ronanki, "Artificial Intelligence for the Real World," *Harvard Business Review*, 96, no. 1 (2018): 108–116.
51. S. Redmore, "6 Ways Artificial Intelligence Is Already Impacting Hospitality," *Hotel Management* (2018).
52. R. Lin and S. Utz, "Self-Disclosure on SNS: Do Disclosure Intimacy and Narrativity Influence Interpersonal Closeness and Social Attraction?" *Computers in Human Behavior*, 70 (2017): 426–436.
53. M. J. Metzger, "Effects of Site, Vendor, and Consumer Characteristics on Web Site Trust and Disclosure," *Communication Research*, 33, no. 3 (2006): 155–179.
54. C. Morosan, "Information Disclosure to Biometric e-Gates: The Roles of Perceived Security, Benefits, and Emotions," *Journal of Travel Research*, 57, no. 5 (2017): 644–657.
55. JPMorgan Chase and Co. *The UnitedSM Explorer Card*, 2018, https://www2.theexplorercard.com (accessed December 18, 2018).
56. U Airlines, *Premier Benefits and More*, 2018, https://www.united.com/web/en-US/content/mileageplus/premier/default.aspx?int_source=loy&int_medium=uacom&int_campaign=mphomepage&partner_name=premier_benefits_helplink&asset_type=mphome_link&launch_date=2017-04-24 (accessed December 18, 2018).
57. U Airlines, *Premier Status Qualification Requirements*, 2018, https://www.united.com/ual/en/us/fly/mileageplus/premier/qualify.html (accessed December 18, 2018).
58. R. Nethercott, "5 Reasons Why Repeat Customers Are Better Than New Customers," (n.d.).
59. J. T. Bowen, and S.-L. Chen McCain, "Transitioning Loyalty Programs," *International Journal of Contemporary Hospitality Management*, 27, no. 3 (2015): 415–430.
60. A. Aluri, B. S. Price, and N. H. McIntyre, "Using Machine Learning to Cocreate Value through Dynamic Customer Engagement in a Brand Loyalty Program," *Journal of Hospitality & Tourism Research* (2018). Article ID: 109634801775352.
61. Data Marketing & Analytics. *Drive Data Further*, 2018, https://thedma.org/ (accessed December 17, 2018).
62. Data Marketing & Analytics. *Consumer Help* (2018), https://thedma.org/resources/consumer-resources/ (accessed December 17, 2018).
63. R. Niblock, "13 Direct Marketing Experts Reveal Their Predictions for the Future of Direct Mail," *Pro Active*, 2017.
64. F.T. Commission, *National Do Not Call Registry*. Consumer Information 2018, https://www.consumer.ftc.gov/articles/0108-national-do-not-call-registry (accessed December 17, 2018).
65. V. Kumar, X. A. Zhang, and A. Luo, "Modeling Customer Opt-In and Opt-Out in a Permission-Based Marketing Context," *Journal of Marketing Research*, LI (2014): 403–419.

66. H. Oh, M. Jeong, and S. Baloglu, "Tourists' Adoption of Self-Service Technologies at Resort Hotels," *Journal of Business Research*, 66, no. 6 (2013): 692–699.
67. StayNTouch. *Zest StationTM*, 2018, http://www.stayntouch.com/zest-station/ (accessed December 18, 2018).
68. Agilysys. *rGuest® Express Kiosk*, 2018, https://www.agilysys.com/en/solutions/by-products/property-management/rguestexpress (accessed December 18, 2018).
69. Intelity. *Guest Engagement Under One Platform*, 2018, https://intelitycorp.com/main/ (accessed December 18, 2018).
70. "Teleste Hospitality Solution: High-Speed Internet and Versatile TV Services to Every Room over Your Existing TV Cable," *HospitalityNet.org*, 2018.
71. "Hospitality: Unprepared for GDPR," *Hospitality Technology*, 2017.
72. N. Doyle Oldfield, "HITEC Houston 2018: Building Trust with Guests Is the Key to Creating a Competitive Advantage," *Hospitality Upgrade*, 2018.
73. L. Wainstein, "Data Security in Hospitality: Risks and Best Practices," *HospitalityNet.org*, 2018.

Managing Hospitality and Tourism Marketing

IV

17 Destination Marketing
18 Next Year's Marketing Plan

17

Destination Marketing

Why would anyone go to New Zealand for vacation? This was a question begging for an answer before the tourism board launched a new global campaign in international markets in 1999. The bold, simple, and concise statement of the brand campaign headline—"100% Pure New Zealand"—was aligned with images of nature, people, wilderness, activities, and sweeping landscapes in their purity. The key feeding markets were the United States, Australia, England, and Japan. The slogan was simple and straightforward in any language, not needing any translation on a global scale.

This was the first global marketing campaign for New Zealand that had a single message across all of its tourism markets. Interestingly, it resulted largely from a tight budget the tourism bureau, Tourism New Zealand (TNZ), has faced and the decision-makers realized that running a separate campaign in each country would be expensive. The umbrella campaign turned out to be an opportunity to communicate a distinctive voice and visitor experience combining landscapes, people, and activities. As part of the campaign, New Zealand also launched a comprehensive, vivid, and interactive Web site as part of its integrated marketing communication to engage potential visitors pre-trip and to sustain relationship and promote storytelling post-trip.

The Lord of the Rings movie trilogy, filmed in New Zealand and released over 2001 to 2003, made a significant contribution to raising New Zealand's profile as an adventure and breathtaking tourist destination in key markets. The campaign has undoubtedly become very successful and helped New Zealand to generate a positive image and brand recognition as a travel destination. Becoming a focal point in many advertising, public relations (PR), online marketing, and special events sponsorships, the international campaign demonstrated the economic and marketing impact of a movie-induced destination branding campaign and helped TNZ take advantage of wide coverage and publicity in local and international media. TNZ also actively worked to leverage the brand by building PR activities around the events such as America's Cup and Rally of New Zealand. Currently, TNZ's international media program hosts around 150 international journalists in New Zealand each year from print, online, and broadcast organizations.

Objectives

After reading this chapter, you should be able to:

1. Explain the essential aspects of tourism and destination marketing.
2. Explain tourism development and different options for creating and investing in tourism attractions.
3. Segment and monitor the tourist market.
4. Discuss how to communicate with the tourist market.
5. Explain how central tourist agencies are organized and managed.

Specific marketing campaigns have been linked to the release of each film and to significant film events such as the Oscars and other award ceremonies. For example, following Oscar nominations and successes, newspaper advertisements, and a poster campaign promoted New Zealand as "Best Supporting Country in a Motion Picture."

Over the years, the tagline has been used as "100% pure relaxation," "100% pure welcome," "100% pure adrenalin," and "100% pure you"—all connected back to the core premise of "100% Pure New Zealand." Feeder market-specific campaigns have also taken place under the "100% Pure New Zealand" umbrella brand campaign such as "What's On" in Australia, "What Do You Say UK?" in the United Kingdom, and "The New Zealand Life Back Promise" in the United States. The campaign has recently been extended beyond tourism to doing business, making investments, having education, and working and living in New Zealand (visit http://www.newzealand.com/).

From 1999 to 2004, the number of visitors grew at an average of 7 percent a year. Between 1999 and 2008, visitor arrivals grew 50 percent, from 1.6 million to 2.4 million and foreign exchange earnings from $3.5 billion to almost $6 billion. The International Visitor Survey from 2004 found that 6 percent of visitors to New Zealand cite *The Lord of the Rings* as being one of the main reasons for visiting New Zealand. In 2004, 63,200 visitors participated in a *Lord of the Rings* activity while there, and since then, an average 47,000 visitors each year have visited a film location.

The latest adaption, "100% Middle-earth, 100% Pure New Zealand" campaign, promotes New Zealand as a visitor destination through its association with the upcoming film releases of *The Hobbit* Trilogy. Association with films such as *The Hobbit* movies offers New Zealand a wider opportunity to enhance its international profile. The goal is to show potential travelers that the fantasy of Middle-earth is in fact the reality of New Zealand. Again, TNZ's marketing strategy focuses on stunning landscapes and converting the international attention drawn from starring in *The Hobbit* trilogy into travel demand. The new campaign was named the best destination marketing campaign at the 2012 World Travel Awards.

Research by the New Zealand Institute of Economic Research has found that the marketing of New Zealand as Middle-earth has had a significant and quantifiable impact on growth in visitor arrivals from Western markets. International Visitor Arrivals data for year ending August 2014 show holiday arrivals into New Zealand are up 7.2 percent on last year. Holiday arrivals from the United States, a key target market for the Middle-earth campaign, are up 14.2 percent on the same period last year. The International Visitor Survey shows that 13 percent of all international visitors surveyed in July 2013 to June 2014 say *The Hobbit* was a factor in stimulating their interest in New Zealand as a destination.

The image building "100% Pure New Zealand" campaign has now been broadened, beyond tourism, to attract businesses, trade, talents, employees, and students to further diversify the island country economy. The brand is extended to combine all things associated with the place economy (tourism, business, trade, arts, and education) under one brand.

Film tourism, also called movie-induced or film-induced tourism, consists of visits to a destination or attraction because of the destination's feature on television (TV) or cinema screen. The New Zealand case clearly demonstrates the critical role of movies in developing and communicating a destination image and the power of public and media relations for Destination Marketing Organizations' (DMOs) efforts of marketing and branding tourist destinations.

If you sell the sizzle, you need to deliver the sausage, as well. Once New Zealand set the expectations with the campaign, they also needed to deliver the experience. Therefore, TNZ made sure that the campaign would match the promise and initiated new quality guidelines and high standards for accommodations, tour companies, and visitor information centers. The DMO also partnered with Air New Zealand (ANZ) to develop special "Middle-Earth" fares and travel packages. In 2017, the international visitor arrivals to New Zealand reached 3.7 million visitors and generated $10.1 billion in international tourism receipts.

DMOs can exploit movie-induced tourism opportunities and engage in four types of marketing activities to promote film tourism: (1) proactive efforts to encourage producers to film at the destination, (2) generation of ongoing publicity around the film and destination, (3) marketing activities promoting the film location after production, and (4) leveraging the film tourism by developing activities.[1]

Marketing Tourism Destinations

The Globalization of the Tourist Industry

Tourism A stay of one or more nights away from home for leisure or business, except such things as boarding, education, or semipermanent employment.

The word **tourism** has many definitions. We use the World Tourism Organization's (UNWTO) and United Nations Statistics Division's (UNSTAT) definition of tourism: "a trip to a main destination outside usual environment, for less than a year, for any main purpose (business, leisure, or other personal purpose) other than to be employed by a resident entity in the country or place visited."[2] This book uses the words *tourism* and *travel* interchangeably.

The world has become a global community, opening places unimaginable decades earlier: the wonders of Antarctica, the secrets of the Himalayas, the rain forests of the Amazon, the beauty of Tahiti, the Great Wall of China, the dramatic Victoria Falls, the origin of the Nile, and the wilds of the Scottish islands. Travel is a global business with an expanding market. Table 17–1 lists the international tourist arrivals and receipts at the top tourist destinations.

Paris, "the City of Lights," attracts more than 15 million international visitors. The largest number comes from Britain, followed by the United States, Germany, Italy, and China. NaughtyNut/Shutterstock.

Table 17–1
The World's Top Tourism Destinations (International Tourist Arrivals and Receipts 2017)

Rank	Country	Arrivals in Millions	Rank	Receipts in U.S.$ Billions
1	France	86.9	3	60.7
2	Spain	81.8	2	68.0
3	USA	76.9	1	210.7
4	China*	60.7	12	32.6
5	Italy	58.3	6	44.2
6	Mexico	39.3	15	21.3
7	United Kingdom	37.7	5	51.2
8	Turkey	37.6	14	22.5
9	Germany	37.5	8	39.8
10	Thailand	35.4	4	57.5

Source: From Tourism Highlights 2018. Copyright © 2018 The World Tourism Organization. Reprinted by permission.
*Excludes Hong Kong (27.8 million arrivals, U.S.$33.3 billion receipts) and Macao (17.2 million arrivals, U.S.$35.6 billion receipts).

Tourism industry has shown uninterrupted growth in terms of international arrivals over the past six decades, from 250 million in 1950 to 1.3 billion in 2017. The international arrivals grew 7.0% in 2017, the highest increase since the 2009 global economic crisis. International tourism receipts reached U.S.$1,340 billion worldwide in 2017, up from U.S.$1,220 billion in 2016.[3] Many new destinations have emerged to benefit from tourism development. International arrivals are expected to reach nearly 1.6 billion by the year 2020.

France continued to top the ranking of international tourist arrivals with almost 87 million tourists, and came fourth in terms of international tourism receipts with U.S.$61 billion. Compared to 2016 arrivals, the top 10 countries list did not change. Spain climbed from third to second place in arrivals and held on to second position in receipts to become the world's second largest destination by both international tourist arrivals and receipts. Mexico climbed two places to sixth position in arrivals. Also, Australia was ranked seventh with U.S.$42 billion in terms of receipts, but could not make the top 10 in arrivals in 2017.

When ranking top international tourist destinations, one should consider two key tourism indicators—international tourist arrivals and international tourism receipts. Although seven of the top destinations appear in both lists, their rankings show marked differences. These destinations attract different types of tourists with varying average length of stay and spending per trip. Today many industries of the world are dominated by relatively few competitors (oligopolies), who hold major market shares. It is often difficult or impossible for potential new competitors to enter those markets. Market entry in tourism is open, and new destinations can acquire the economic and social benefits of tourism.

Students reading this book today can enter the world tourism industry and plan strategies to help drive tourism growth for their nations, states, and cities. Successful destination planning and marketing can bring hundreds of millions and even billions of dollars in revenue to destinations. New supportive industries and jobs can be created and standards of living can be increased. At the same time, the interchange of cultures assists the quest for world peace. Destination marketing is a career worthy of college and university graduates.

Tourist destinations do not need spectacular attractions such as an Eiffel Tower, Grand Canyon, or Leaning Tower to participate in today's tourism. Regions such as Eastern Europe and countries such as China and India are rapidly developing. They are now generators of tourists, as well as destinations for tourists. Africa recorded the strongest growth with an 8.6 percent increase in arrivals, followed by Europe (8.4 percent) and Asia and the Pacific (6.4 percent). China has become the number one tourism source market in the world, spending U.S.$258 billion on international tourism in 2017. By 2020, China is expected to be the largest inbound and outbound market in the world. China has 3.8 million hotel rooms and in 15–20 years is expected to have 5–7 million more.

Tourism accounts for more than 50 percent of Bermuda's foreign exchange. Elijah Lovkoff/123RF.

The Tourism Destination

Destinations Places with some form of actual or perceived boundary, such as the physical boundary of an island, political boundaries, or even market-created boundaries.

Tourists travel to **destinations**, places with some form of actual or perceived boundary, such as the physical boundary of an island, political boundaries, or even market-created boundaries such as those of a travel wholesaler who defines a South Pacific tour solely as Australia and New Zealand. Central America consists of seven nations, but few, if any, national tourist offices or tour planners view it that way.

Infrastructure The system according to which a company, organization, or other body is organized at the most basic level.

A commonly packaged tour of Central America includes only two or three nations, such as Costa Rica, Guatemala, and Panama. Others are excluded for reasons of political instability or deficient **infrastructure**.

Although Australia and New Zealand are often packaged together for the North American visitor, Australia has worked hard for many years to make it a single destination rather than share the limited vacation time of visitors. In turn, destinations within Australia, such as the state of Western Australia, or cities such as Perth or Adelaide, believe that they must develop a distinct destinations reputation to avoid being left out or used only as overnight stopovers.

The desire to become a recognized destination presents a difficult marketing challenge. Within eastern North Carolina, the town of New Bern has several interesting visitor attractions and events. The remainder of the county offers considerably less, yet visitor promotion funds are collected from a countywide hotel bed tax. Political pressure forced tourism officials to promote Craven County as a destination rather than just the town of New Bern. The promotion of a relatively unfamiliar town poses sufficient problems, but the promotion of a county greatly intensifies the challenge.

Macrodestinations Destinations such as the United States that contain thousands of microdestinations, including regions, states, cities, towns, and visitor destinations within a town.

Macrodestinations such as the United States contain thousands of microdestinations, including regions, states, cities, towns, and even visitor destinations within a town. It is not unusual to find tourists who view their Hawaiian destination as the Hilton Hawaiian Village in Honolulu and may rarely, if ever, venture outside the perimeter. Thousands of visitors fly to Orlando and proceed directly to Disney World, where most or all of their vacation is spent. These tourists do not view Florida or Orlando as their destinations, but rather Disney World.

For some pleasure travelers, the real destination is the vehicle of travel, such as a cruise ship, river paddle ship, or a special railroad such as the Orient Express. These "moving destinations" offer a variety of events for passengers, and dining is particularly important. Games, gambling, theater, musicals, participatory murder mysteries, seminars, dances, and a host of other onboard events enhance the pleasure of moving destinations. As industrialized societies experience enlarged numbers of senior citizens, these relatively passive moving destinations are likely to receive increased demand.

Destination Marketing System

Destination marketing is more challenging than marketing other products because a destination is a bundle of highly diverse products, including geographic size, attractions, accommodation, food and beverage, and entertainment. The complexity is augmented by limited control by DMOs and the number of public and private stakeholders involved in delivering a unified brand and destination experience.

Unlike business marketing in which target markets determine product strategy, initial destination marketing efforts usually start with the attractions and resources at hand that determine potential segments to target (except for man-made destinations). Figure 17–1 shows vital linkages between supply and demand in tourism to understand the role of marketing. Destination marketing is systematically linking supply (destination features and benefits) with demand (needs and wants of travelers) and enhancing competitiveness of a destination in a sustainable manner.

Destinations have varying natural, historical, and cultural attractions. To enhance competitiveness, destinations develop and offer facilitating, supporting, and augmented products such as infrastructure, lodging, food and beverage, transportation, tours, entertainment, visitor services, and hospitality of local people to appeal to existing markets or new markets. Therefore, a good knowledge of the demand side—current and potential visitor characteristics and destination selection behavior—is also necessary for successful destination marketing. Destinations need to understand what type of travelers they seek to attract and what they desire from their travel. They can improve their overall marketing effort by developing specific product offerings for specific segments. For example, millennials want customized experience and cocreate their destination experience. They are more interested than older generations in traveling abroad. The United Nations estimates that

Figure 17–1
Destination marketing system.

External environment
- Economic (i.e., exchange rates), social, technological, legal, and political (i.e., visa regulations) environment
- Competitor destinations' strategies
- Emergence of new destinations

Supply: destination
- Competitiveness
- Infrastructure and superstructure
- Attractions and events
- Environment
- Sustainable development

Destination marketing organizations (DMOs)
- Strategy
- Communication mix
- Internal marketing
- Marketing research

Transportation and distribution channels
- Airlines, cruises, car rental operators, and railways
- Tour operators and travel agents

Demand: travelers
- Visitor segments and behavior
- Brand awareness, image, and personality
- Satisfaction and loyalty
- Visitor experience

Destination performance and Benchmarking metrics
- Destination and demand metrics
- DMO performance
- Channel performance
- Visitor arrivals, length of stay, visitor Expenditures, and market share
- Well-being of residents
- Sustainable growth

23 percent of all international tourists, or nearly 275 million travelers, are young people, and that this demographic generates more than $286 billion in annual tourism revenue.[4]

Typically, DMOs, such as ministries of tourism, national tourism organizations (NTOs), and convention and visitors bureaus (CVBs), are the formal marketing organizations dealing with long-term strategy development. Funding is often provided by sales tax or special room tax receipts. The Las Vegas Convention and Visitors Authority (LVCVA) is the official DMO of Las Vegas funded by county hotel room tax. The LVCVA's responsibilities involve marketing activities, branding, market research, strategic planning, and operating convention and event centers. The responsibility for marketing destinations and delivering a memorable experience on location are generally shared by many diverse public and private organizations including chamber of commerce, hotel/motel associations, environmental organizations, and many more.[5] LVCVA Board of Directors involves both public and private industry members.

The selling function, to a great extent, is carried out by distribution channel and transportation companies such as airlines, tour operators, and travel agents. Distribution channel members and transportation companies play unique roles because they also have bargaining powers and strong influence on destination marketing and competitiveness. Tour operators and travel agents are significant information sources influencing the images and decisions of travelers.[6] Working closely with DMOs or independently, they develop and distribute travel packages and promote a destination. For most European and Mediterranean destinations targeting sun and sea markets, most vacation packages are sold via tour operators that determine "price" for destinations. They decide on destinations to be included in their sales portfolio, determine price quotes for hotels in host destinations as well as prices visitors pay for all-inclusive packages. Transportation companies get involved in developing and selling vacation packages through their own travel companies or strategic alliances. For example, United Vacations owned by United Airlines has its own list of destinations and offers leisure vacation packages that combine airfare with negotiated hotel rates in domestic and international destinations, car rentals, and entertainment.[7]

The trends in external environment will influence all elements of marketing system and destination competitiveness. Dramatic fluctuations in exchange rates (e.g., the recent decline in Russian ruble), visa regulations, terrorism attacks (e.g., India, Egypt, Bali, and Middle Eastern countries), disease outbreaks and epidemics (e.g., Ebola in Africa, SARS [severe acute respiratory syndrome] in Hong Kong, bird flu in Asia), and some natural disasters (e.g., tsunami in Thailand) significantly affect destination marketing and competitiveness. An increase in fuel costs makes distant (closer) destinations less (more) price competitive. The practices by destination's competitive set such as new tourism development and brand positioning will also impact the destination's marketing strategy.

Destination benchmarking should include not only outcomes and performance metrics in terms of number of visitors, market share, and revenue generated but also other elements such as visitor satisfaction and loyalty, brand recognition and image, performances of DMOs, and sustainable growth metrics. There are three main types of benchmarking: internal, external, and generic. Internal benchmarking is to keep track of changes over time (quarterly or annually) and compare current performance of a destination with its previous performances (e.g., changes in visitor satisfaction, brand image, number of arrivals, and tourism receipts). External benchmarking consists of selecting a major competitor and comparing performances in a given period (e.g., comparison of Jamaica and Dominican Republic). Generic benchmarking uses international standards and best practices (e.g., carbon footprints, European "Blue Flag" ecolabeling for beaches and marinas) for comparison. This type of benchmarking would particularly be appropriate for destination DMO performance to learn from best practices in terms of public and media relations, creating events, building partnerships, branding, and organizational effectiveness.[8]

Destination Competitiveness

Destinations have varying but similar resources and attractions. New Zealand has beautiful scenery and nature. Singapore offers multicultural urban attractions. Jamaica has beautiful beaches. So does Thailand. Turkey and Greece are rich in history, culture, nature, and beaches. Bali offers cultural traditions, while Italy has culture, cuisine, art, and fashion. Some destinations are rich in natural resources but seriously disadvantaged in other areas. Some have numerous resources and attractions and the luxury of targeting a wider selection of market segments.[9]

Destination competitiveness requires an understanding of two important concepts: comparative and competitive advantages. *Comparative advantage* is possession of resources, natural and/or man-made, critical to tourism development. It may include natural resources (climate, location, natural beauties), historical and cultural resources, factors such as human resources, capital resources, infrastructure (roads, water supply, public services), and tourism superstructure (hotels and restaurants, theme parks, golf courses). But having attractions and resources is not enough. The success in competitive arena lies in turning comparative advantages into strengths relative to competition. *Competitive advantage* is to make use of these resources efficiently and effectively to enhance competitiveness of destination.[10]

Travel and Tourism Competitiveness Index

Numerous, but interrelated, factors determine a place competitiveness in the regional and global marketplace. One comprehensive framework and measure of travel and tourism (T&T) competitiveness on a global scale is the Travel and Tourism Competitiveness Index (TTCI) developed and published each year by World Economic Forum (WEF).

The TTCI "is to provide a comprehensive strategic tool for measuring the set of factors and policies that enable the sustainable development of the travel & tourism

Figure 17–2
Travel and tourism competitiveness index.
Source: From Travel and Tourism Competitiveness Report 2017. Copyright © 2017 by World Economic Forum. Reprinted by permission.

The Historic City of Toledo, Spain, a UNESCO World Heritage Site, holds a cultural and monumental heritage of several historic civilizations, which has also been a traditional sword-making and steel-working center since about 500 BC. Sean Pavone/123RF.

sector, which in turn, contributes to the development and competitiveness of a country." It is derived from the Executive Opinion Survey, "hard" data from external sources for each country, and input from global agencies such as UNWTO, the Organization for Economic Cooperation and Development (OECD), the World Travel and Tourism Council (WTTC), and Deloitte.

Each country or destination (a total of 136 economies) score is composed of 14 pillars (Figure 17–2). The pillars were grouped under four broad categories or subindex: (1) *Enabling Environment* (5 pillars); (2) T&T Policy and Enabling Conditions (4 pillars); (3) Infrastructure (3 pillars); and (4) Natural and Cultural Resources (2 pillars) (see Appendix A for pillar descriptions).

Table 17–2 shows the overall ranking of the 10 countries—regional and world rankings-based on four main subindexes: (1) enabling environment; (2) policy and enabling conditions; (3) infrastructure; and (4) natural and cultural resources. The scores range from 1 (lowest) to 7 (highest). Spain maintains its top ranking position in the past two years, along with France (second) and Germany (third). It is a strong leisure tourism destination with both cultural and natural resources, combined with sound tourism service infrastructure, air transport connectivity, and strong policy support. It also scores highly for business travelers with a significant number of international conferences. However, it has relatively low scores in Subindex A because of its business environment (Pillar 1) and Subindex B because of its price competitiveness (Pillar 8), the 75th and 98th in World rankings, respectively. Regional ranking (America, Europe, North Africa, sub-Saharan Africa, Middle-East, and Asia Pacific) is also important because investors and travelers are interested in particular regions. Even though Japan ranks fourth in world rankings, it has the top ranking position in terms of regional rankings among Asia Pacific countries.

Beyond their economic value, events help create an identity for a community. Urban newspapers and suburban weeklies often publish a list of events, festivals, and celebrations occurring within a day's driving distance. State and local tourism offices do the same, making sure that travel agents, restaurants, hotels, airports, and train and bus stations have event-based calendars for posting.

Events can help destinations reduce seasonality problem. The Shakespeare Festival in Stratford, Canada, began as a small regional event and became a North American event for the United States and Canada. Most musical and cultural festivals in Europe followed the same pattern, such as Salzburg, Edinburgh, and Spoleto. Europe's Festival of Arts provides a selection among 50 musical festivals from Norway to Spain, with several dozen dance competitions, major summer art exhibits, and theater from London's West End to Berlin's Festival Weeks. The entire European continent, including Eastern Europe, has exploded in summer-place competition for tourists. Major U.S. cities have summer programs of scheduled events, and some, such as Milwaukee, have well-established year-round events. Milwaukee's June–September lakefront festivals (Festa Italiana, German Fest, Afro Fest, Polish Fest, and others) attract tourists regionally and nationally.

Wine festivals and wine trails and tours have been popular in Europe for generations. These are now occurring in the wine areas of Australia, New Zealand, and the United States. The Napa Valley of California has over 270 vineyards, each offering a unique visitor experience for the 5 million wine tourists annually.[31] Areas not previously known for wine production such as Texas, Missouri, Virginia, and North Carolina have established festivals and wine trails.

A study by the Washington State Wine Commission showed that 2 million visitors a year visit the 135 wineries in that state, generating $19 million in visitor income. The Australian Winemakers Association estimated that by 2025, wine tourism revenue would reach $1.1 billion.[32]

SUSTAINABLE EVENT MARKETING Events that attract a desired market and harmoniously fit with a community's culture can provide beneficial results, particularly if the event regularly reoccurs over a period of years. Events that occur only once or that require substantial capital investment for a community may not offer sufficient economic returns. A common reply by event promoters is that the PR value of the event outweighs cost considerations. This claim must be carefully and objectively analyzed before acceptance. Events must also be examined for the possible effect and cultural/societal impact they may have on the host community. "Destinations must choose their events to fit the needs of the locality, since each event draws on its own type of crowd."[33]

Some events are now marketed as being "green" or "sustainable." Green events can not only save money but also help the event stand out from the crowd. For example, events use downloadable content to decrease the carbon footprint and attract more crowd using online resources in an increasingly digital age.

Professional event planners within tourism agencies commonly establish requirements concerning desirable events. Here are some examples:

- Event must attract a minimum number of visitors.
- Event must complement and enhance the cultural nature of the community.
- Event should be replicable in future years, ideally on an annual basis.
- Workers from the community should be employed if part-time paid employees are needed.
- Events must not create destruction of private or public properties.
- As much as possible, events should use the services of local companies, such as food caterers.
- Events should provide guests for local hotels if hotel bed tax monies are used in their promotions.
- Events should allow/encourage participation by local residents.

Sydney, Australia's Darling Harbour, is an example of a well-planned tourist center. Chaiwat Leelakajonkij/123RF.

SPORTS EVENTS Many communities view sports events as attractive ways to bring visitors to their destinations. These events are often enjoyed by both visitors and residents.

Sports travel in the United States is estimated at $27 billion each year, with 75 million American adults traveling to attend a sports event as spectator or participant.[34] Las Vegas hosts major sports events such as NASCAR (National Association for Stock Car Auto Racing), the Las Vegas Bowl, and the National Finals Rodeo. The attendees spend more on lodging and non-gaming activities than on gambling. Golf has become a viable new market segment for Las Vegas.

Two very popular sports events are biking and marathons. An example is Ride The Rockies in which 4,000 people apply to ride 409 miles across Colorado. Riders come from all 50 states and many foreign nations. Host cities along the route benefit through travel expenditures from the riders as well as contributions from the sponsors to nonprofit charities in the host cities.[35]

The Walt Disney World Marathon covers a 26.2-mile course and attracts over 17,000 runners. This single event fills Disney World with 110,000 visitors during a normally slow part of the year. The success of this marathon prompted Disney to add a Princess Half Marathon for women. All Disney marathons sell out far in advance, despite comparatively high entry fees. "We literally take over Walt Disney World," said a spokesperson for Disney. "We overwhelm the property with runners."[36]

Attractions

Attractions may be natural, such as Niagara Falls or the Scottish Highlands, or manufactured, such as the shopping areas of Buckingham Palace, Hong Kong, or the Vatican.

Many nations have recognized the value of these natural attractions and have created national or state parks to protect them. However, the sheer numbers of visitors wishing to experience attractions threaten the ability of those in charge to protect them.

The long-run success of tourism will depend on manufactured attractions to satisfy the desire for travel. Historic attractions such as the pyramids of Egypt and Mexico are also at risk with increased visitor numbers. New attractions are continuously needed. This requires tourism investment.

Tourism investment ranges from relatively low-cost market entry for festivals or events to multimillion-dollar infrastructure costs of stadiums, transit systems, airports, and convention centers. Regardless of the cost, urban renewal planners seek to build tourism into the heart of their city's revitalization. Boston's Quincy Market, New York's Lincoln Center, and San Francisco's Fisherman's Wharf are examples. The ability to concentrate attractions, facilities, and services in a convenient, accessible location is essential to create a strong destination pull.

Mayan ruin in Chichen Itza is one of the most visited attraction in Mexico and one of the New Seven Wonders of the World. Matyas Rehak/123RF.

In centrally planned economies, governments control, plan, and direct tourist development. Tourism is necessary to earn hard currencies for trade and development and serves national purposes. Tourist expansion is highly dependent on public investments, which have proved to be woefully inadequate without private investment and market mechanisms to respond to changing consumer needs and wants.

Many nations promote private investment through joint ventures, foreign ownership, and time sharing for individual investors. The Mexican Riviera (e.g., Puerto Vallarta, Cancun, and Ixtapa) is an example of public/private combinations of successful tourism investments, where state investment in infrastructure works with private investment in tourist amenities, from hotels, restaurants, and golf courses to shopping areas.

UNESCO WORLD HERITAGE SITES   Regardless of one's opinion about the United Nations, the designation of World Heritage Sites by the United Nations Educational, Scientific, and Cultural Organization (UNESCO) is important to world tourism and very important to selected sites. This program designates and thereby hopes to help conserve sites of outstanding cultural or natural importance to the common heritage of humanity. In 2015, a total of 1,031 such sites were listed: 802 cultural, 197 natural, and 32 mixed. Each site belongs to the country in which it is located, but it is considered to be of international interest to preserve and protect these sites.[37]

Tourism authorities view inclusion on this list as very important. In 2008, Dresden, Germany, wanted to build a 2,100-foot-long bridge called Waldschlösschen Bridge over a picturesque river. UNESCO threatened to take Dresden off the list if it built the bridge.

WATERFRONT ATTRACTIONS   Throughout much of the world, cities and towns have finally realized the tremendous value of their river, lake, and ocean waterfronts.[38] Many of these were used for warehouses, docks, power generation facilities, and heavy industry. These were ugly, dangerous, and often polluted areas. Now cities such as Los Angeles and Baltimore, United States; Buenos Aires, Argentina; and Hamburg, Germany, have discovered there is gold in redeveloping these areas for upscale housing, restaurants, hotels, shops, and even maritime commerce all within a relatively small area. HafenCity (Harbor City) of Hamburg is the largest urban development project in Europe. This area is not strictly a tourist attraction. "We want to join economic, social, cultural, and architectural forces in a way that translates into lasting urbanity," said Mr. Bruns-Berentelg, chief planner.

It should not be a surprise that people attract people. The concept of distinct tourist attractions is only a part of tourism planning. New York, London, Paris, and other cities are tourist attractions. The development of areas of cities such as waterfronts for multipurpose living is an extension of the natural attraction that cities have always held for travelers.

Dubai is a good example of a city that has developed a good infrastructure along with tourist attractions. The airport at Dubai is world class and offers excellent duty-free shopping. The highway system is well designed and maintained, making it easy to get from the airport to the resorts. The hotels realize the importance of

The Diyarbakir Fortress, Turkey, was inscribed on UNESCO's World Heritage List in 2015. After the Great Wall of China, the Walls of Diyarbakir are the world's longest and best-preserved medieval walls, which form a shape like turbot and measure 5.5 kilometers in length. Courtesy of Merthan Anik, and Culture and Tourism Department of Diyarbakir Municipality.

service and customer satisfaction. Once at the hotel, the guest can select from a variety of activities, including water sports, tennis, golf, or sightseeing tours. Resorts spend a great deal of effort training their employees, who come from all over the world. The employee base also means that guests from almost any country will be able to find an employee speaking their language. Dubai set out on a strategy of using tourism to broaden its economic base and developed a plan to implement that strategy.

Two of the resorts in Dubai are the Burj Al Arab and the Jumeirah Beach Hotel. The Burj Al Arab is not only the world's tallest all-suites hotel but also one of the most luxurious. All of its 202 units are two-story suites. Guests staying at the Burj Al Arab have a choice of airport transportation: a Rolls-Royce limousine or a helicopter. Each floor features a private reception, and there is a personal butler for each suite. The Jumeirah Beach Hotel has 600 rooms and 18 restaurants and features a reef a mile offshore for scuba divers. The hotel also features extensive meeting and conference facilities to attract international meetings.

CASINOS AS ATTRACTIONS States and municipalities typically look at jobs and tax revenues. Prior to the U.S. recession, commercial casinos employed 366,000 people and paid over $5 billion in direct gaming taxes. Many observers say this is not all good news. They say (1) casinos often take business from other entertainment such as theaters and sports bars, (2) new casinos need fewer employees due to video poker machines, (3) revenues taken from local residents often leave the area as profits for out-of-state corporations, (4) casinos may actually destroy some jobs, (5) casinos don't provide the kind of societal benefits as a biotech firm, a hospital, a university, or other enterprises, and (6) casinos foster societal problems such as pathological gambling.

Research has shown that casinos do not take business away from local restaurants and they do create jobs. However, just as many other businesses, a poorly planned casino can be a determent to the area, whereas a properly planned one can be beneficial to the region. To maximize its benefits, gaming should be incorporated into a strategic plan for the area. From a tourism perspective, gaming works best when it is part of several tourism attractions for the area, not the only tourism attraction for the area. Gaming destinations that include entertainment facilities featuring nationally known performers, golf courses, fine restaurants, hotel rooms, and meeting facilities can attract leisure tourists as well as meetings and conventions. In fact, gaming can be the source of funds to create tourist destinations.

The Greektown Casino project in Detroit shows how a casino can work with the community to create tourism. As part of the casino's effort to create a symbiotic relationship with area business, the casino owners put $200 million into refurbishing Trappers Alley, a historical area around the casino featuring restaurants and clubs, which encouraged businesses to invest their own funds to give their operations a facelift. Greektown also created an innovative loyalty program (players club) that allowed players to redeem their points in over 20 restaurants in the Trappers Alley area, generating revenue for local business owners. In this case, the casino served as the catalyst to revitalize a tourist area that had fallen on hard times.[39]

The Burj Al Arab in Dubai is one of the world's most luxurious hotels. Melinda Nagy/123RF.

INDIAN GAMING Gambling (legalized gambling, mostly casinos) on 227 American Indian reservations has been described as "The Native American Success Story." The gambling operations and the businesses that support them are said to support 600,000 jobs. According to Ernest Stevens, chairman of the National Indian Gaming Association (NIGA), this has had a tremendous impact on reservation economies. Indian casino revenues have been estimated at $22.6 billion.[40]

Not all observers of Indian casinos believe they are healthy for the broader community. Critics say they exist despite the fact that state and neighboring communities do not recognize legalized casinos. Because these locations are often remote rural communities, they attract neighbors who are often bored, lonely, and not wealthy, who become addicted to gambling, thus creating financial hardships for their families.[41]

STOPOVER TOURISM Many visitor destinations are in fact only stopover destinations for travelers on their way elsewhere. Singapore has more than twice the number of annual visitors than its resident population, but visitors stay less than three days. Twenty-one percent are in transit or stopover guests.

Singapore's visitors shop, dine, and stay in world-class hotels. Sightseeing and entertainment represent only 3 percent of their expenditures. Despite short stays, Singapore ranks second in Asia and eleventh in the world in terms of tourism receipts.[42]

Kansas, Nebraska, Arkansas, Missouri, and many other states recognize the value of stopover visitors to their economies. Cities at the edge of large metroplex areas such as Lewisville, Texas, north of Dallas, also serve as stopover destinations. Many visitors prefer to stop outside a metroplex at a convenient roadside motel rather than attempt to find lodging in the city center.

Destination Life Cycle: Rejuvenating a Destination

Like a hotel or a restaurant, tourist destinations become dated, tacky, and undesirable for contemporary travelers. A resort destination will experience a life cycle similar to the product life cycle and eventually go into decline, or the destruction stage. Tourism managers must manage their products and make sure that during the growth stage the foundation is built for an infrastructure that will support future tourism demands. In some cases, sustaining tourism in the mature stage may mean limiting the number of tourists to a number that the infrastructure can handle. Tourist development must balance the temptation to maximize tourist dollars with preservation of the natural tourist attractions and the quality of life for local residents. This is often a difficult task. Those tourist destinations that do not manage their product may have a short life.

Tourist destinations that build solid infrastructures can look for increased business by expanding from a seasonal product to a multiseasonal product or by expanding the geographic base of their product. For example, Aspen, Colorado, expanded from winter skiing to summer recreation, education, and culture. Quebec promotes summer and fall tourism and its winter carnival and skiing. West Virginia is popular in the summer and fall seasons, but it also aggressively promotes the spring and winter seasons.

The Waikiki area on the island of Oahu fell victim to its life cycle. As of mid-2007, $2 billion had been spent to renovate Waikiki, with another $1 billion committed.[43] A 93,000-square-foot retail and restaurant center was built in the heart of Waikiki Beach Walk. Zoning restrictions were removed and Outrigger Enterprises Group tore down five of its older hotels. Many other improvements were made, including the removal of T-shirt and souvenir shops on one street making it the upscale Rodeo Drive of Hawaii.

Even the beach was expanded by back-pumping 10,000 cubic yards of sand from offshore. To prevent Waikiki from becoming another noisy waterfront, banana boats, parasailing, speedboats, and jet skis were prohibited. Ed Fuller, president of Marriott International, said, "The city made a major commitment to bring Waikiki back as a great destination."

Singapore has been a model of urban tourism in Southeast Asia. Luciano Mortula/123RF.

Rejuvenating a destination requires the cooperation of various government entities and several sectors of private enterprise including heavy involvement by the hospitality industry.

▪▪▪ Segmenting and Monitoring the Tourist Market

The decision to spend one's disposable income on travel versus furniture, a boat, or other purchase alternatives involves important psychological determinants. Table 17–3 lists some of the major psychological determinants of demand for tourism. These determinants can be used as segmentation variables. Demographics and lifestyles are also important segmentation variables.

Segmenting visitors based on push and pull motivations has been a common practice for benefit segmentation. The push factors are considered to be sociopsychological motivations that predispose the individual to travel, while the pull

Table 17–3
Psychological Travel Motivations

Prestige. A level of prestige has always been attached to travelers, particularly long-distance travelers. Marco Polo gained historical fame through travel, as did the heroes of Greek and Roman mythology, such as Ulysses. Travel to Aspen, the Riviera, Switzerland, and many other destinations provides the traveler with a level of prestige, if only in the mind of the traveler.

Escape. The desire to escape momentarily from the day-to-day rhythm of one's life is a basic human need. Travel marketers have long recognized this need, as reflected by glamorous advertisements in which the word *escape* is often mentioned.

Sexual opportunity. This has both a positive and an ugly side. Travel has long been viewed as a means to meet attractive people. This has been part of the heritage of transatlantic ocean travel, the Orient Express, and riverboat travel. Unfortunately, the existence of sex tours to certain Asian nations and the preponderance of houses of prostitution in some destination areas provide examples of a darker side.

Education. Travel in and of itself has historically been viewed as broadening. Many deeper psychological reasons for travel are masked by the rationale that educational benefits outweigh the cost, risks, and stress.

Social interaction. The opportunity to meet and interact with people previously unknown is a powerful motivator. Destination resorts and cruise lines commonly appeal to this need.

Family bonding. Family reunions have become an important market segment for many in the travel industry. In an era of intense pressure on the family, such as two careers, there is a strong need to refocus priorities and bond as a family. Unfortunately, the types of vacations selected by families do not always lead to bonding. If adults participate all day in activities such as diving, skiing, or golf, young children may be relegated to organized kids' programs and experience little bonding with parents.

Relaxation. Observers of human and animal conduct sometimes state that the human being is either alone or among a limited number of species that continue to play into adulthood. Destination resorts and cruise ships best exemplify need fulfillment for play. It is small wonder that cruise line travel has become a "destination" in direct competition with land-bound places.

Self-discovery. For many, travel offers the opportunity to "find oneself." Witness the action of many people following a dramatic event in their lives, such as a divorce or the death of a family member. Throughout recorded history, people have sought self-discovery by "visiting the mountain," "finding solace in the desert," and "losing oneself." Many cultures, including so-called primitive ones, have encouraged or even forced their youth to travel alone to find self-discovery. Youth hotels throughout the world serve a group of travelers, many of whom are seeking self-discovery. Temporary employment opportunities at resorts are often filled by those taking time off to learn more about who they are and wish to be. The concept of "holistic vacations" has been developed for people seeking self-discovery.

Sources: Peter Hawes, "Holistic Vacations," *Hemisphere* (March 1995): 85–87; A. J. Crompton, "Motivations for Pleasure Vacations," *Annals of Tourism Research*, 6 (1974): 408–424; A. Mathieson and G. Wall, *Tourism: Economics, Physical and Social Impacts* (Harlow, Essex, UK: Longman, 1982).

factors are destination attributes that attract the individual to a specific destination. The push–pull model considers both destination-specific characteristics and tourists' individualistic characteristics. A recent study segmented China's long-haul outbound travel market based on their push and pull motivations into three groups: entertainment/adventure seekers, life-seeing experience/culture explorers, and relaxation/knowledge seekers.[44]

The growing percentage of retirees in many nations has vastly expanded the tourism business. An increasing percentage of two-career couples has resulted in a trend toward shorter, more frequent vacations. Longer vacations (10 or more nights) have been declining for years in the United States; shorter vacations (three nights, including weekends) have become increasingly popular. Hotels and airlines have accommodated these trends with low-cost weekend excursion packages. Business travel now includes mixed business and leisure. To capture the trend toward shorter vacations within driving distance of home, new local and regional tourist attractions have been growing, as have family-oriented resorts.

Foreign visitor travel has become an increasingly important segment of the North American travel industry. Since the decline of the U.S. and Canadian dollars, foreign tourism has grown. British Isles visitors seek out New York, Florida, and Playa del Carmen, while continental visitors have a strong fascination for the U.S. West, particularly California. Hawaii targets Japan because of its high gross national product and spending and because 50 percent of all Japanese visitors to the U.S. mainland spend part of their trip in Hawaii. The Japanese repeat market outspends visitors from the U.S. mainland by a 4:1 margin.

In 2017, 16 percent of the 42 million tourists of Las Vegas were international visitors, which is about 6.8 million.[45] The LVCVA aims to benefit from the surge in foreign tourism and has set a goal of making international travelers 30 percent of the Las Vegas total visitors. The average international traveler spends about $1,100 per stay and remains in the Las Vegas longer than four days each trip. Compare that with domestic tourists who spend $580 per visit on average and stay about three days.[46]

About 60 percent of the city's international visitors now come from just three countries: the United Kingdom, Mexico, and Canada. The LVCVA through its international offices uses different market strategies. In the United Kingdom, the office focuses on lifestyle elements of Las Vegas, including shows, nightlife, and dining. Key sporting events such as boxing are also popular in the U.K. market. Canadians are more interested in food and wine culture, celebrity chefs, and culinary events. The LVCVA sees the emerging markets of Brazil, Russia, India, and China as the regions with the most untapped potential.[47]

Accommodating changing lifestyles and needs is a dynamic challenge for the tourism industry in light of demographic trends and income shifts. Where baby boomers once opted for status destinations and elaborate accommodations, many now opt for all-inclusive resorts and package tours that promise comfort, consistency, and cost effectiveness. Tourism planners must consider how many tourists are desired, which segments to attract, and how to balance tourism with other industries. Choices will be constrained by the destinations' climate, natural topography, resources, history, culture, and facilities. Like other enterprises, tourist marketers must know the actual and potential customers and their needs and wants, determine which target markets to serve, and decide on appropriate products, services, and programs.

The millennial generation is more interested than older generations in traveling abroad. The United Nations estimates that 20 percent of all international tourists, or nearly 200 million travelers, are young people, and that this demographic generates more than $180 billion in annual tourism revenue.[48]

Cave hotels in Cappadocia, Turkey. Cave hotels offer an authentic local experience and would be a more popular destination for millennials. Psvrusso/123RF.

A nationwide survey of millennials provided some insights for tourist destinations. It revealed that millennials are highly influenced by friends and family in selecting places to visit, and they are also more likely to travel with friends or to places friends have visited. Millennials visit online travel agencies as well as visit Web sites of destinations. They have strong preference to learn new things and fun and entertaining experience. Millennials are attracted to authentic destinations. This trend has sprouted into new accommodation concepts including hostels, Airbnb, couch surfing, and home exchanges. Millennials also care about environmental issues and engage in sustainable practices. They will prefer destinations that engage in sustainable practices.[49]

To appeal to millennials, destinations can involve locals in marketing efforts because millennial travelers rely on social media and word-of-mouth recommendations, and trust travel reviews from peers as well as strangers. Destinations can facilitate relationship building. "Visit a Swede" is a good example of this relational marketing. The Web site is designed to connect tourists to Sweden with residents. The result is local residents become involved in the cocreation of the tourist's experience. The residents also become tourism ambassadors for their country and city. BeWelcome has also opened up channels of communication between visitors and locals.[50]

Charleston, South Carolina, has several times won the South Carolina Governor's Cup for Travel and Tourism, been named the "most mannerly" city in the United States 10 times, and has been named a top-10 travel destination by *Conde Nast* magazine readers 11 times. It has also won awards from *National Geographic*, *Brides*, and *Travel & Leisure* magazines.

Another South Carolina travel destination, Myrtle Beach, attracts many more tourists, but Charleston remains "the Award Winner Jewel in South Carolina's Destination Crown."[51]

How does Charleston prevail as a top destination? The answer is that it does its best to preserve and retain what has historically attracted people to Charleston: history, charming architecture, pleasant and mannerly people, helpfulness, gardens, quaintness, and excellent cuisine.

These winning attributes could quickly disappear if discount shopping areas replaced old homes or if a multimillion-dollar theme park was built in the heart of the city. Vigilance is essential to preserve and further the genuine differentiating factors of a destination. These can disappear in a short period of time to the detriment of residents and visitors.

Not every tourist is interested in a particular destination. A destination would waste its money trying to attract everyone who travels. Instead of a shotgun approach, destinations must take a rifle approach and sharply define target markets. Many visitors to Myrtle Beach would find Charleston stuffy and boring. Attempts to attract those individuals would result in mutual dissatisfaction.

Agritourism

Agritourism Agriculture-based tourism that includes farms, ranches, and wineries. It provides rural areas with a means to attract tourists.

In an era in which most people in industrialized nations are urban or suburban dwellers, **agritourism** (farm or ranch tourism)—a niche ecotourism—has become one of the fastest-growing segments of the travel industry. This is particularly true in many European nations, North America, and Australia/New Zealand. Agri-destinations offer edutainment, relaxation, outdoor adventures, and dining experiences. It takes many forms, from just visiting a farm to staying and even working at a farm for education and hands-on experience. One can stay in an accommodation on farm premises and enjoy meals of farm produce.[52] Top agritourism destinations include Taiwan "leisure farms," Tuscany (Italy), Mallorca (Spain), Brazil, Hawaii, California for organic farming, and Philippines.[53] In Hawaii, agritourism options range from visiting coffee plantations in the Big Island's Kona region to exploring the plantations on Maui to staying on organic farms on the island of Oahu.

A study by Colorado State University provides evidence of the importance of agritourism. "Summer and fall had the highest agritourism visitation rates," said Dawn Thilmany, professor in Colorado State's Department of Agriculture and Resource Economics, who led the study.

In a state known for its skiing, agricultural activities have shown the potential to provide a real boost to Colorado's tourism efforts outside of winter months. Thilmany said, "Increased visitations during these times help fill the underutilized capacity of lodging and service industries." More than 20 percent of those surveyed took more than three agritourism trips each year, offering great potential for farm and ranch enterprises considering agritourism activities, according to the report.

Tourists from outside Colorado reported spending an average of $860 per trip; in-state tourists reported spending an average of $368, according to the report. Both in-state and out-of-state tourists said they would spend more during their next trip to Colorado ($450 for state residents; $1,023 for out-of-state tourists). Among the more frequent agritourism travelers, about 56 percent were Colorado residents.[54]

"We found there is sufficient interest in agritourism in Colorado to warrant active joint planning by communities and the agritourism enterprises they support," Thilmany said, offering as an example the joint marketing plan of Grand Junction's wine country. "Many regions of Colorado already see significant amounts of visitors to farm- and ranch-based diversions. Through coordinated marketing efforts, these regions can continue to capitalize on agritourism activities."

Space Tourism

In April 2001, Dennis Tito became the first space tourist when he paid $20 million to fly on the *Soyuz* taxi mission to the International Space Station. In October 2008, Richard Garrett paid $30 million to fly on a *Soyuz* mission and become the sixth space tourist. As a result of the Russians willingness to allow space tourists on their missions, there is now a travel agency, Space Adventures, specializing in space tourism.[55]

A number of private companies have been formed to provide trips into space for tourists. The founder of Virgin Atlantic Airline, Sir Richard Branson, has formed Virgin Galactic, with test flights scheduled soon. Commercial space travel for upscale tourists is planned from Las Cruces Spaceport America in New Mexico. Additional sites will be in the United Kingdom, Australia, and Sweden.

Space travelers will have to undergo elite cosmonaut training. They will be in a vehicle named SS2, which will climb to 50,000 feet altitude under a mother ship Space Ship Two. After release, the SS2 will free fall for a few seconds, fire its rockets, and accelerate into a vertical trajectory climbing to an altitude of 360,800 feet. Those aboard the SS2 will enjoy a 1,000-mile horizon of the earth in zero gravity. The entire flight will last about two and a half hours.[56]

NASA (National Aeronautics and Space Administration) is preparing for moon tourism, including developing plans to prevent looting of the six areas where manned space missions landed on the moon between 1969 and 1972. Under its guidelines, people can walk only within 246 feet of the first site where Neil Armstrong first walked on the moon. NASA's concern over protecting the sites was prompted by Google's $30 million prize for the first privately funded team to land a robot on the moon. It appears that NASA feels that people will soon follow robots on the moon. It wants to make sure that tourists don't trample on the footprint of Armstrong's "one small step for man."[57]

Multiday Hiking and Religious Pilgrimages

Many potential tourists are tired of traditional tourism opportunities, such as a beach resort. A huge and growing market exists for multiday trekking (hiking). In some cases, hiking has a religious basis, such as in pilgrimages to significant religious sites such as the Camino de Santiago de Compostela in northern Spain. This trip may be accomplished by foot, horseback, or bicycle and may be as long as a month or just a few days. In 1990, the Cathedral in Santiago registered 4,918 hikers (pilgrims), but today over 100,000 people are recorded each year and that is probably an underestimate.

Christian sites are by no means the only ones that are visited. Millions of pilgrims visit Hindu, Buddhist, Islamic, and other religious sites. Although most visitors arrive by some form of modern transport, many prefer to walk.

In western Japan, a walking pilgrimage to 33 sacred sites and the 1,300-km pilgrimage to the 88 holy sites of Shikoku Island are experienced by hundreds of thousands of hiking pilgrims. Most devotees on these pilgrimages carry a staff bearing the words, "We too walk together." Many of those on the Camino de Santiago carry a staff bearing a seashell.

Perhaps the most publicized pilgrimages are those of the Islamic faith such as that of Hajj, a pilgrimage to Mecca in which millions of Muslims participate, including 12,000 Americans in 2010. The Shrine of Iman Reza in Iran attracts over 12 million visitors each year. Visitors to these shrines arrive via many forms of travel.

Trails are available for special-interest hikers with cultural, scientific, religious, or gastronomical interests such as wine tours. Some trails such as the Milford in New Zealand are so popular that visitor numbers are restricted.

A North Sea Trail is being developed in Europe, which crosses six countries and extends for 3,000 miles and was funded by the European Union with nearly $15 million. The European Union already had 11 long-distance paths from Lapland to Gibraltar and Cyprus.

The 2,175-mile-long Appalachian Trail on the East Coast of the United States from Maine to Georgia has long been popular. Extended hikes such as this are supported by tourism organizations throughout the world as they disperse visitors, lessen the negative aspects of tourism, and provide economic support to rural communities.

Hundreds of cultural routes with tourism potential exist throughout the world, such as The Silk Road that started at the Chinese imperial city of Xian and extended across the Taklimakan desert to the Mediterranean. Long and arduous treks such as this will be completed in entirety by very few tourists, but many are likely to hike portions of the trail.[58]

Medical Tourism

Medical tourism is one of the fastest-growing and most lucrative segments of tourism, as people travel internationally to gain access to less expensive medical care. In 2003 there were 350,000 medical tourists, by 2010 that number grew to 6 million, and by 2019 the number is expected to grow to more than 20 million.

The growth in medical tourism is driven by four main factors: low cost, long waiting lines in national health-care services, accessibility to procedures and treatments, and opportunity for a vacation and privacy. Cost is the main driver. For people with no or inadequate insurance, low-cost health care at an international destination may be the only viable solution for health care. In an effort to stay young, baby boomers are seeking cosmetic surgery and dental work. These elective procedures are often not covered by insurance, creating a booming business for these procedures in Mexico, Central America, Asia, and Eastern Europe. In countries with national health care, such as Australia, Canada, and England, people needing elective surgery are often put on a waiting list. To some of those on the waiting list, a low-cost procedure overseas is often preferred to putting up with the malady for months. International health care also provides access to experimental procedures or treatments that are prohibited by law in one's home country. This includes experimental cancer treatments and treatments using stem cells. The privacy of having cosmetic surgery done overseas, recovering on the beach, and coming home healed and looking 10 years younger is a great alternative to hiding out at home while the scars are healing.

In Asia, Thailand is the most popular destination for Western European health-care tourists for cosmetic surgeries. About 2.5 million foreign patients visited Thailand in 2012, representing approximately half of the market share of total foreign tourist arrival in the Asian region. India attracts large number of patients for cardiac surgeries. Brazil (cosmetic surgery) and Mexico (weight loss surgery) receive patients from the United States because of geographic proximity. Turkey witnesses a growth in orthopedic, laser eye, and cosmetic surgeries.[59]

Medical tourism is being blended with the opportunity for a vacation. Some insurance companies in North America are offering their customers, who qualify for health care, the option to have it done at an international location. As an incentive,

Medical tourism One of the fastest-growing and most lucrative tourism markets. Tourists spend a large amount on medical treatment, stay in top hotels, and often travel around the country after their surgery.

they will waive the deductible and co-pay, as well as provide airfare and lodging during and after treatment. They sell both the cost savings and the opportunity for a free vacation to their client. The insurance company still comes out over the cost of having the surgery done in the United States. The biggest concern for the patient is the quality of the health care. Countries that want to capture the medical tourism market need to develop standards and accrediting procedures to create a perception of quality and build trust among medical tourists.[60]

Genealogical Tourism

The interest in knowing more about one's ancestors has grown substantially in recent years.[61] Many people plan vacations to visit genealogical research sites.

The Allen County Public Library in Fort Wayne, Indiana, hosts 400,000 visitors annually. The Church of Jesus Christ of Latter-day Saints in Utah has become a "must visit" site for 700,000 annual visitors. This is the world's largest depository of family records.

Other nations that received large numbers of immigrants from Europe such as Australia, New Zealand, Argentina, and Canada have growing numbers of genealogical tourists. Scotland refocused on genealogy tourism after VisitScotland, Scotland's national tourism organization, estimated that ancestral tourism in Scotland is worth more than $600 million a year. The destination initiated a promotion campaign and developed budget "genealogy packages." Malcolm Roughead, VisitScotland's chief executive, said, "We need to do all we can to make sure every visitor will have the experience of a lifetime. In our advertising campaigns we will be inviting people from all over the globe to come home and walk in the footsteps of their ancestors."[62]

Travel to Gallipoli battlefield of the First World War has become a "rite of passage" for younger Australian generations. The tourist trade is booming on Turkey's Gallipoli peninsula as thousands of Australians make their way to the World War I battlefields for the Anzac Centenary. Many Australians have paid between $7,000 and $10,000 to make the pilgrimage.[63]

Identifying Target Markets

A destination can identify its natural target markets in two ways. One is to collect information about its current visitors. Where do they come from? Why do they come? What are their demographic characteristics? How satisfied are they? How many are repeat visitors? How much do they spend? By examining these and other questions, planners can determine which visitors should be targeted.

The second approach is to audit the destination's events and attractions and select segments that might logically have an interest in them. We cannot assume that current visitors reflect all the potentially interested groups. For example, if Kenya promoted only safaris, it would miss groups interested in native culture, flora, or bird species.

Tourist segments are attracted by different features. The local tourist board or council could benefit by asking questions keyed to segmentation variables. These variables, including attractions sought, market areas or locations, customer characteristics, and/or benefits sought, can help define the best target markets.

After a destination identifies its natural target markets, tourism planners should conduct research to determine where these tourists are found. Which countries contain a large number of citizens who have the means and motivation to enjoy the particular place? For example, Aruba attracts mainly sun-and-fun tourists. The United States, Canada, and certain European countries are good sources. Eastern Europeans have been ruled out because they lack the purchasing power, but this is changing. Australians are ruled out because they have their own nearby sun-and-fun destinations, even though they are frequent travelers. This analysis can uncover many or few natural target markets. If many are identified, the relative potential profit from each should be evaluated. The potential profit of a target tourist segment is the difference between the amount that the tourist segment is likely to spend and the cost of attracting and serving this segment. The promotional cost depends on the budget. The serving cost depends on the infrastructure requirements. Ultimately, potential tourist segments should be ranked and selected in order of their profitability.

If the analysis identifies too few natural tourist segments, investments may be needed in infrastructure and visitor events and attractions. The payoff from these investments may come years later, but this lag is often necessary if the destination is to become an active participant in an increasingly competitive marketplace.

The Irish Tourist Board observed that many young European tourists visited the Emerald Isle to enjoy its natural, unspoiled beauty as backpackers and campers, but they spent little money. A serious question for Ireland was whether its tourism scorecard should be based on the number of tourists attracted (the prevailing standard) or their spending level. A consensus emerged that Ireland should try to attract a relatively small market of high-income tourists who stay longer, spend more, and are culturally and environmentally compatible.

Toward this end, the Irish Tourist Board now touts not only Ireland's mountains, water, and ancient buildings but also its literary giants, such as Oscar Wilde, George Bernard Shaw, and James Joyce. The board wants to attract high-income, culture-seeking tourists to Dublin, where the sparkling Irish speech and wit can be experienced.

Whatever tourist segment a destination seeks, it needs to be very specific. A ski area attracts skiers. Natural reefs attract snorkelers and divers. Arts and crafts attract the art crowd, and gambling attracts gaming tourists. Yet even with such givens, potential visitors must be segmented by additional characteristics. Sun Valley, Aspen, Vail, and Alta appeal to upper-income and professional skiers, and Keystone, Winter Park, Copper Mountain, and Telluride attract the family market. Tahoe and Squaw Valley draw the skiing and gaming markets. Monte Carlo appeals to an international gaming segment, whereas Deauville, France, promotes a more regional gaming market near Paris.

Tourism marketers know that even though an area may attract an activity-specific segment, there is great potential in providing reasons for others to come. For instance, a ski family or group often contains individuals who do not wish to ski. Why then should they come? If the answer is "we offer only a single activity," the group may decide to go somewhere else that offers broader vacation opportunities.

Las Vegas discovered that shopping, dining, and entertainment could attract nongamblers and also serve as secondary activities for all but the most dedicated gamblers. The Forum shopping mall at Caesars in Las Vegas provides continuous entertainment and a great variety of restaurants, making the retail sales areas some of the most costly and desirable to rent in North America. Today, the top attraction in Las Vegas is shopping and entertainment, not gambling.

Classification of Visitor Segments

Several classifications have been used to describe different visitor destination segments. The most commonly used classifications are based on whether the tourist travels with a group or independently. The common terms are group-inclusive tour (GIT) and independent traveler (IT). National tourism offices, international airlines, and others involved in international travel frequently use these designations.

Here are some classifications describing tourists by their degree of institutionalization and their impact on the destinations:

- *Organized mass tourists.* This corresponds to the GIT. These people have little or no influence over their travel experience other than to purchase one package or another. They commonly travel in a group, view the destination through the windows of a tour bus, and remain in preselected hotels. Shopping in the local market often provides their only contact with the native population.

- *Individual mass tourists.* These people are similar to the previous category but have somewhat more control over their itinerary. For instance, they may rent a car to visit attractions.

- *Explorers.* These people fall in the IT classification. They plan their own itineraries and make their own reservations. They tend to be very sociable people who enjoy interacting with people at the destination.

- *Drifters.* These people, the backpacker group, seldom, if ever, are found in a traditional hotel. They may stay at youth hostels with friends or camp out. They tend to mix with lower socioeconomic native groups and are commonly found riding third-class rail or bus. Most tend to be young.

- *Visiting friends and relatives (VFR).* VFR, as the name suggests, are people who stay in the homes of friends or relatives. For this reason, they are often discounted as important tourists. This is incorrect. They may not spend money on lodging, but they do spend on dining, attending attractions/events, and shopping.

- *Business travelers.* This often encompasses any form of business, including conventions, trade shows, and job seeking.

- *Pleasure travel.* This too is a very wide and all-encompassing classification. It may be of limited use without further segmentation.

- *Bleisure (Business and pleasure travelers).* Many conventions and business travelers plan to incorporate a period of relaxation prior to or after their business.

- *Education and religious travel.* This broad category includes students, those on a pilgrimage, missionaries, and a host of others. It may be of limited use in tourism planning unless further segmented.

- *Pass-through tourists.* These are extremely important visitors to states such as Kansas and Nebraska and to cities in Texas that serve as convenient rest or overnight stopping areas.

Another well-known tourist classification system is *Plog's categorization*.[64] Destinations can be placed on the psychographic curve based on the types of people who visit there most. Tourists' personality characteristics determine their travel patterns and preferences. These designations are similar to the groups mentioned previously but range from psychocentric to allocentric. Plog observed that destinations are first discovered by **allocentrics** (backpackers or explorers). As the natives discover the economic benefits of tourism, services and infrastructure are developed. When this occurs, allocentrics are turned off and find another unspoiled destination. The nature of visitors now changes, with each new group somewhat less adventurous than the preceding group, perhaps older, and certainly more demanding of creative comforts and service. Finally, a destination becomes so familiar that the least adventurous group of **psychocentrics** finds it acceptable.

A study of travelers' behaviors and preferences demonstrated that Costa Rica's position is evolving from being a destination for near allocentric to one that attracts mid-centrics. The researchers concluded that Costa Rica had indeed built its infrastructure to the point that adventurers are put off and mid-centrics are attracted, just as Plog's model predicted.

Knowing this, other nations in Central America, Honduras, Belize, and Nicaragua are pursuing the adventures market. Therefore, preservation of the natural environment in those nations is essential, including the need to set aside particular areas for special protection.

The researchers also noted that parts of Asia, China, Cambodia, Thailand, and Vietnam are rushing into a phase of development that is poorly planned based on the Plog analysis.[65]

Monitoring the Tourist Markets

Tourist markets are dynamic, and a marketing information system is part of any well-run tourist organization. Destinations need to closely monitor the relative popularity of their various attractions by determining the number and type of tourists attracted to each. The popularity of the Metropolitan Museum of Art, Big Ben, or the Coliseum can suddenly or gradually change. Marketing information systems help identify and predict environmental trends that are responsible for these changes. Information should be collected on changes, emerging markets, and potential target markets.

The LVCVA conducts an annual tourist profile. Information for this profile is collected through ongoing customer surveys. Survey results indicate that the

Allocentrics Persons with a need for new experiences, such as backpackers and explorers.

Psychocentrics Persons who do not desire change when they travel. They like to visit nonthreatening places and stay in familiar surroundings.

majority of visitors spend less than four hours a day gambling. The visitors are coming for entertainment and the non-gaming amenities of the mega-resorts. This information helped to attract a number of new restaurants, such as Spago, Wolfgang Puck's, Cafe Coyote, and Planet Hollywood. Las Vegas has developed a reputation as a restaurant town. This further enhances its image as a diverse destination rather than just a gaming venue.

One job of a tourist organization is to increase the accessibility of a destination. The LVCVA uses information from its survey to identify emerging markets that can support direct airline flights. Armed with current travel patterns and projected travel patterns based on its surveys, the LVCVA makes presentations to airlines, trying to convince them to start new routes, which will be profitable for the airlines and provide another region of the country with direct air service to Las Vegas. The accessibility of Las Vegas by frequently scheduled and relatively inexpensive airfare is in part responsible for it being one of the top convention centers in the United States. This did not happen by accident; it happened as a result of efforts by the LVCVA.

The Steamboat Springs, Colorado, Chamber Resort Association, and other resorts' visitor bureaus also work with airlines to ensure air accessibility to their cities. However, because these areas have a small population base and experience varying snowfall levels, airlines are reluctant to include them in their schedule without a financial guarantee. This means the visitor bureau must assume an active role to ensure that funding is available for the airline guarantees should this be necessary.

Tourist organizations need information to stay competitive. Tourist products must change to meet the needs of the changing market. Emerging markets must be identified and served. New markets that can be served by the existing tourist product must be identified. Tourist organizations trying to accomplish these tasks without good information are at a disadvantage.

First-Time Versus Repeat Visitors

First-time and repeat visitors are important segments for a tourist destination and they should be monitored. Destination wants to have a healthy balance of first-time and repeat visitors. Eighty percent of Las Vegas visitors are repeat visitors, which could create problems in the long run.

For some destinations, visitor satisfaction would be more important than repeat visitation loyalty because their target markets would seek more variety and are less likely to visit the same destination repeatedly. A study found that less loyal tourists to international destinations are either "Natural Switchers" or "Experiential Switchers." Natural switchers are variety seekers or price-sensitive travelers, whereas experiential switchers are those who are dissatisfied with their visit. These groups should be targeted differently.[66]

Short-Haul Versus Long-Haul Tourists

Tourists who travel short distances tend to stay for short durations. They also show preferences for package tours. Long-haul tourists tend to engage in longer duration, multi-destination trips and seek to fulfill multiple purposes, such as city sightseeing, country hikes, attending several cultural events, and participating in events.

Communicating with the Tourist Market

Competition for Visitors Involves Image Making

Destination images are heavily influenced by pictorial creations used in movies or TV, by music, and, in some cases, by popular entertainers and celebrities.

State media investment to attract tourists has grown rapidly. States such as Texas and Alaska have more than quadrupled their tourism media budgets. Nations and states invade and advertise in each other's markets. For instance, Illinois targets New York, California, Texas, and Japan. It produces multilingual travel guides, DVDs, and radio segments.

Destinations have formed partnerships with travel, recreational, and communication businesses on joint marketing efforts. They advertise in national magazines and travel publications and work with business-travel promotions to link the growing business-leisure segment of the traveling public, and they target travel agencies. Many states have located welcome centers along major interstate highways that include unstaffed two-way video systems to answer questions from a central location or otherwise assist travelers. States also target their own residents with brochures, maps, and a calendar of events.

Finally, effective destination imaging requires congruence between advertising and the destination. Glossy photographs of sunsets, beaches, buildings, and events need to have some relationship to what tourists actually experience; otherwise, destinations run the risk of losing tourist goodwill and generating bad word of mouth.

Many tourist destinations have discovered that it is important to show residents interacting with tourists in their advertisements. Thousands of mountain slopes and beaches exist in the world and most look alike in photos. Very few tourists seek a completely secluded vacation site. People are social creatures by nature and consciously or unconsciously seek the company of fellow humans.

Branding Destinations

Destination branding Creating a differentiated destination image that influences travelers' decision to visit a destination and conveys the promise of a memorable experience that is uniquely associated with the destination.

Tourist destinations increasingly embrace branding techniques to develop unique positions, images, and personalities in a highly competitive environment. **Destination branding** is creating a differentiated destination image that influences travelers' decision to visit a destination and conveys the promise of a memorable experience that is uniquely associated with the destination.[67] Branding opportunities for destinations exist at geographical levels such as country, city, and town (umbrella and sub-brands), specific attractions such as museums and theme parks, events such as mega-events and festivals, and lifestyle travel packages.

Destination visits or vacations express lifestyle, personality, and status. A study found that visitors who see a closer fit between their personality and Las Vegas's brand personality as a tourist destination are more likely to come back and to engage in positive word-of-mouth communication for the destination.[68]

PR and publicity (movies, news stories, events, and celebrities) are vital to develop brand awareness and image. The branding strategy of Las Vegas historically focuses on special events and appearance in movies.

Visitor-based brand equity measures such as brand recognition, image, loyalty, and brand advocacy are critical benchmarking performance measures for destinations. The Tourism Commission on Nevada launched a rebranded Nevada marketing campaign for other forms of tourism in neighboring states (California, Arizona, and Utah) and international markets. The goal is to promote rural areas and lesser-known sights, including "Wild West" experiences.[69]

Destination Tourism Slogans

A destination slogan is part of brand identity articulated to position a product. It is a short phrase that communicates descriptive or persuasive information about a brand. Slogans are considered an essential element to build brand awareness and image at country, state, and city levels.[70] Some popular slogans are "What Happens in Vegas Stays in Vegas," "I Love NY," and "Virginia is for Lovers" and "100% Pure New Zealand." Las Vegas actually has several lesser-known slogans aimed at narrow audiences, including "Not business as usual," aimed at meeting planners; "Overtime guaranteed," to promote special events; and "A world of entertainment," for international audiences.

Destinations can change their slogans as part of their rebranding strategy. Recently, the Greek National Tourism Organization (GNTO) launched a new global tourism campaign under a new slogan "Greece, All Time Classic." Jamaica ditched its longtime slogan "Jamaica—Once you go you know" after 10 years. It has been replaced by "Jamaica—Get All Right" to elicit a message that Jamaica is a place that makes visitors "feel alright." Singapore Tourism Board rebranded tagline "Uniquely Singapore" to "YourSingapore."

Effectiveness of Advertising/Promotion

The success of yesterday's advertising/promotion as a model for today is increasingly being questioned. The results of research on the subject of effectiveness of state expenditures to promote tourism are certain to be controversial.

One study concluded that "states with lower levels of tourism activity can enjoy small benefits from increased spending while states with higher levels of tourism would benefit from decreased spending."[71] Another study concerning the effectiveness of advertising suggested that "there was no significant difference between the control group that was not exposed to anything and the group that saw the advertisement as far as attitude formation and interest in visiting a destination were concerned."[72]

The two studies referred to may be in the vanguard of demonstrating the need for new marketing strategies to effectively market visitor destinations. Society has changed. Traditional media such as TV, newspaper and magazine ads, and AM/FM radio may not be utilized by target markets, particularly younger ones. In today's digital age, savvy DMOs are tapping social and mobile networks, smartphones and tablets, GPS (global positioning system) apps, e-commerce, and booking engines to economically reach consumers 24/7, and globally. Their Web sites can now interactively deploy video, text, audio, booking systems, photos and real-time comments from customers.[73]

New Zealand formed a global partnership with Facebook to build story-driven content together and to market the destination across their platforms of Instagram and Facebook. TNZ's Director of Marketing, Andrew Fraser, said,

> It was increasingly important to be able to work effectively across all digital platforms and working directly with Facebook was a great opportunity to ensure the campaign used the most effective best practice techniques. Essentially what we did was go to Facebook and ask them to create a content idea that addressed some of the barriers faced by people who are actively considering coming to New Zealand. Our research showed that while this audience understands the epic landscapes, there are gaps in their knowledge regarding their perceptions of our infrastructure, ease of travelling around New Zealand and the variety of things to do and see.

This collaboration resulted in an engaging and natural story of two American tourists missing the train to Wellington from Britomart and embarking on a Kombi road trip where they meet the locals and see the country.[74]

DMOs are usually in charge of developing and measuring the effectiveness of promotion campaigns. One significant outlet is major T&T fairs in Berlin, Las Vegas, and Madrid, which bring destinations, intermediaries, and travel trade together.

Developing Packages of Attractions and Amenities

An effective way of communicating with potential travelers is by offering packages. Tourist organizations must develop a package of attractions and amenities. Travelers make comparisons about the relative advantages and disadvantages of competing destinations. Destinations must provide easy access to attractions by bus, boats, carriages, and planes. They need to distribute brochures, audiotapes, and videotapes to travel agents and individual prospects. City bus companies might prepare half-day, full-day, and evening tours to highlight the destination's major attractions. Concentrating attractions, services, and facilities in a small area creates excitement, adventure, and crowds.

Destinations constantly discover hidden assets that have vast tourist potential. Illinois, for example, has more public and semipublic golf courses per population than any other state except Florida. It now promotes golf tours. Japanese tours responded to a package of golf and Chicago shopping. Pennsylvania has reclaimed old coal mining areas with championship golf courses, expanding its recreational facilities to promote tourism.

Victoria, Canada, "The City of Gardens," is home to The Butchart Gardens, a 55-acre abandoned quarry that was transformed into a beautiful living garden of flowers. The Butchart Garden has become synonymous with Victoria's tourist industry, featuring special events, dining, and gift shopping. When combined with other activities such as golf, shopping, dining, and museums, many packages can be developed for different visitor segments.

The Koshare Indian Museum at La Junta, Colorado, is an example of a cultural tourist attraction. The museum houses one of the largest collections of North American art and artifacts in the world and a library on Native American history. Native American dances are preserved by teaching them to the young men of the community, who perform throughout the nation as the Koshare Indian Dancers.

A destination may promote one, a few, or many of its attractions. Chicago's marketing theme "Chicago's Got It" featured pictures of its famous architecture, lakefront, symphony, world's tallest building, financial exchanges, and Wrigley Field (home of the Chicago Cubs) to suggest that the city had everything: business, culture, entertainment, recreation, and sports. In contrast, San Francisco played off its well-developed image as seductive and mysterious: a photo of a foggy, softly lit Golden Gate Bridge with the copy, "In the Beginning, God Created Heaven and Earth. San Francisco Took a Little Longer."

Competition among destinations extends to restaurants, facilities, sports, cultural amenities, and entertainment. Which place has the most four-star hotels, best culinary fare, most museums and theaters, best wine and drink, best chefs, or best native, cultural, or ethnic flair? Campaigns are carried out in specialty publications. Testimonials and rankings are found in travel brochures, advertising, and travel guides.

Despite the best offers of a destination to portray a positive image through PR and advertising, image building is affected by reports of disturbing societal problems, including human rights abuse.

Charges of human rights abuse from Western governments directly affect tourism development and growth. The government of Myanmar viewed its people as "contributing labor" to the development of the tourism-related infrastructure. International human rights observers viewed this development as forced labor. The U.K.-based Tourism Concern reported that the Myanmar State Law Order Restoration Council (SLORC) is "implementing projects earmarked for tourism through the use of forced labor and the displacement of people."[75] Tourism Concern reported that chained prison gangs and conscripted families had been used to build roads and prepare tourism sites. According to the reports, army members went from house to house taking people for forced labor.

The SLORC denied these reports and stated that people were contributing their voluntary labor happily. Whatever the truth, reports of human rights abuse, crime, disease, and other societal problems have a negative effect on tourism and may persist long after the problem is corrected.

Making a destination tourist friendly is the task of a central tourist agency, which may be public, quasi-public, nonprofit, or private. These agencies are referred to as **national tourist organizations (NTOs)**. Outside the United States, this agency is often run by the central government, state, or province, together with local government officials. The European Travel Commission, a 24-nation group bent on luring U.S. visitors to Europe, coordinates promotional activity in the United States.

National tourist organizations (NTOs)
A national government or quasi-government agency that markets destination tourism.

Creating and Managing Visitor Experiences

Attractions alone do not attract visitors. Most places seek to deepen the travel experience by providing greater value and making the experience more significant and rewarding. A destination is an amalgam of diverse products and environments generating a total destination experience.

The experience "clues" are building blocks of a product experience based on sensory information that collectively shape the consumer experience. Anything perceived and sensed (sight, sound, touch, taste, and smell) in the environment is an experience "clue" and must be managed. Unmanaged or random, negative clues can ruin the whole experience by canceling out the positive ones.[76] Applying it to tourism context, a typical international destination experience starts at the

Boulder City, Nevada, offers zip line tours that cover just over a mile and a half of the canyon. Courtesy of Las Vegas News Bureau.

airport (or even before if a visitor begins to "experience" the destination by surfing its Web site), continues with taxicab or shuttle service, hotel check-in, dining, sightseeing tours, and shopping and entertainment experiences.

Tourist destinations can create a net positive total experience by arranging the hundreds of clues. For example, negative clues such as smell and pollution that diminish the experience should be eliminated. In some cities, the roads between airport and the city were rerouted because old one included slums and shanty neighborhoods along for many miles. In Singapore, the airport road is always adorned with seasonal flowers and offers a scenic ride for very long miles. Singapore's cab drivers are known for their professional training and service, which include English-language exams, safety programs, and location skills. Some places invest little in that area, even though airport cabs and public transit may be the first encounter points that visitors have with a destination and can be critical to tourist satisfaction.

Specific attractions can also create and manage visitor experiences. Havana Club Museum of Rum, a renovated eighteenth-century colonial house, in the historic district of Old Habana implements some of the experiential marketing principles including a mule-driven cane mill show and tasting in the courtyard, history and real-time experience of rum-making process appealing to senses. A bar for rum tasting, local food, local live music, and a memorabilia store for rum and cigar is offered to enhance the experience. Destinations should find a delicate balance between designing or managing experiences and keeping the authenticity of the experience.

Cocreation of Destination Experience and Social Media

Developments in new media have transformed the relationship that individuals have with their social network and tourist destinations. Visitors now interact with different elements of destinations and tourism suppliers and cocreate their own experiences. Designing experiences in tourism should pay attention to interactivity, interactions between tourists and physical elements of destination, interactions with social elements of destination (other tourists, locals, employees, and social networks), and interactions with social media. The social platforms have become an integral part before the trip (cocreating), during the trip (sharing experiences real-time), and after the trip in the form of storytelling and helping others cocreate their own experience.[77] A 2014 Chase Marriott Rewards survey reveals that nearly all millennial travelers post on social networks and share experiences with friends while traveling.

DMOs and tourism providers can create interactive platforms for travelers to facilitate the process. Thailand (DMO Web site) focuses on traveler-generated stories and offers a platform, "Real Experiences" for cocreation, which includes exciting travel stories, insider travel tips, and travel videos and photos that showcase the many exciting activities, festivals, and destinations in Thailand.[78]

Live-Like-a-Local Experience

Younger generations want an authentic and "live-like-a-local" destination experience. "Like-a-local" site is an organization that enables visitors to taste and experience the local culture and destination like a local. All kinds of interactive workshops such as gastronomy, art, painting, and dancing are offered by local experts. For example, visitors to Istanbul can arrange a five-hour gastronomic walking tour by a local guide beginning on the European side of Istanbul and ending on the Asian side. One can also arrange bicycle or walking tours in Barcelona, gastronomic tours in Paris, or historical city tours in Prague.[79]

The Withlocals connects visitors with locals through food and experiences in Asian countries. Visitors can contact local guides for customized tours, taste the local culture by dining with a family in their home, and participate in activities and workshops led by locals. For example, they can try Mui Thai boxing, drive a Tuk Tuk, or have a typical Thai dinner in a local's home.[80]

The Canadian Tourism Commission (CTC) recently launched the Explore Canada Like a Local (ECLAL) Web site and mobile device app to facilitate travel research for people traveling in or planning a trip to Canada and to connect locals and travelers.[81]

Couchsurfing is not just about furniture. It is an online cultural exchange community and alternative travel platform for travelers to stay with locals instead of at hotels. Today, Couchsurfing has over 3 million members in more than 200 countries and facilitates tens of thousands of face-to-face encounters across the world each week. Members around the globe locate travel accommodation while traveling by staying in the homes of other members and organizing gatherings with fellow members. Members also use the community to exchange information, advice, stories, and culture. Couchsurfing offers "live-like-local" experience because members can also join local groups that plan social activities like happy hours, camping trips, and other gatherings.[82]

Organizing and Managing Tourism Marketing

National Tourism Organizations

Countries and states usually have government or quasi-government agencies that market destination tourism. On the national level, these are referred to as NTOs. An NTO has two marketing tasks: (1) The NTO can formulate and develop the tourist product or products of the destination and (2) it can promote them in appropriate markets. It can base its approach to development and promotion on market research and thus achieve a close match between the products and the markets. In doing this, the tourist organization is acting on behalf of the whole destination and is complementary to the development and promotion activities of individual tourist providers. The U.S. Travel Association is the national, nonprofit organization whose mission is to increase travel to and within the United States. It has more than 1,300 member organizations representing all components of the travel industry such as destinations, travel service providers, and travel associations. The association engages in lobbying efforts to further promote T&T and leads national promotion aimed at international travelers such as Brand USA.[83] Brand USA produces the official U.S. T&T Web site, www.DiscoverAmerica.com.

The NTO is responsible for the following functions:

- *Flow of research data.* The NTO coordinates tourism research for the area. Information on origin of visitors, length of stay, type of accommodation used, and expenditures on different tourism products are collected and disseminated to members of the organization. This information helps the NTO evaluate trends and develop marketing strategies. It also provides valuable information to hospitality and travel businesses.

- *Representation in markets.* The NTO often has offices in major markets. These promote the country within the market. The promotion comes in the form of advertising with response mechanisms, such as advertisements in travel magazines featuring a toll-free number to call for additional information. Respondents receive a tour manual. The offices answer questions from prospective visitors and facilitate the development of distribution linkages. They also serve as important sources of information about trends in the market.

- *Organization of workshops and trade shows.* The NTO facilitates the interaction of tourism with members of the distribution channels, such as travel agents and wholesalers. In addition to developing workshops, the NTO purchases

Familiarization trip (Fam trip) A trip where travel agents or others who can send business to a tourist destination attraction, cruise, or hotel are invited to visit at a low cost or no cost.

space at major travel shows and invites travel industry members to participate in the booth, by either displaying material or having a physical presence. This saves the member the cost of purchasing an individual booth.

- *Familiarization trips (Fam trips).* The NTO develops **familiarization trips** for key members of the distribution channel and travel writers. A fam trip is a low-cost or no-cost trip sponsored by a travel destination including hotels, cruise lines, and resorts for travel agents or others who can send business to the travel destination.

- *Participation in joint marketing schemes.* Some NTOs provide cooperative advertising support to help members promote to selected markets. The British Tourist Authority, for example, helps support British Airways advertising in the United States. It is hoped these advertisements will develop additional tourists for Britain, thus helping the British hospitality and travel industry.

- *Support for new or small businesses.* NTOs may provide support for new products and small businesses that are important to the overall tourism of the area. For example, rural tourism, regional festivals, and bed and breakfast (B&B) accommodations are often promoted by NTOs.

- *Consumer assistance and protection.* NTOs assist the consumer by providing product information. For example, in some countries there are classification schemes for lodging accommodations. These are designed to educate travelers concerning types of available lodging. Sometimes NTOs influence the design of lodging brochures and menus appropriate for a particular market segment.

- *General education.* NTOs conduct conferences and courses to educate travel industry providers from their nation to understand the needs of foreign markets.

Like other organizations, NTOs must develop a mission statement, goals, and a strategy. The underlying objective of national strategy formulation is to translate current conditions in the region into desired situations. For example, a federal government with the goal of increasing the economic benefits of tourism to a specific subregion may select a strategy to increase visitation to that area. A country that is highly dependent on one specific geographic market for its demand may adopt a strategy of diversification. For example, Mexico, known for its sun and sea destinations, has developed historical sites to attract a different segment of tourists.

Destinations marketers who are able to influence site selection of groups such as associations can expect invaluable visitors' income for the community. To have a chance of being selected as a meeting site, a destination must be included in the initial decision process. Careful study and research are needed of those responsible for site selection. Research of targeted associations and understanding who the real decision-makers are within the providence of the site selection committee is needed.[84]

Regional Tourist Organizations: State Associations and Convention and Tourist Bureaus

Many state or provinces have their own tourist organizations. Queensland in Australia has created Tourism Queensland, statutory authority of the Queensland government. State tourist organizations (STOs) perform many of the same functions of an NTO, only on a regional level. They also work with the NTOs, to obtain funds and effectively employ resources in their area. Tourism Queensland, working with other tourism organizations, has developed a 10-year strategic plan for the state.[85] New York State's STO developed the *I Love New York* campaign. Like many STOs, New York divided the state into regions that have a common theme for tourists. For example, some of the names of the regions are New York City, the Catskills, Greater Niagara, and the Thousand-Islands-Seaway Region.[86] The owners and managers of hospitality organizations such as hotels, restaurants, or attractions that entice tourists should work with STOs to see how they can promote their businesses.

City, county, or area convention and visitors' bureaus (CVB) promote tourism on the local level. Because they promote a specific destination, they are often

Destination marketing organization (DMO)
A group that promotes a specific destination. Often a local CVB serves as the DMO.

referred as a **destination marketing organization (DMO)**. A major focus of DMOs is to bring meetings and conventions to the local convention facilities and hotels with meeting space. The convention facilities are often owned by the local government and sometimes built knowing they would not make money off the rental of the facility. The dollars the tourists bring to the city and the sales taxes and hotel occupancy taxes would cover the loss on the convention center. Sometimes the DMO and the convention center management are two separate organizations, which calls for close communication between the two organizations.

Hotels, restaurants with banquet space, and restaurants near convention hotels should work closely with their CVB to make sure they get their fair share of the convention business. The local hotel association and restaurant association usually have board positions on the CVB's board to make sure their interests are represented.[87]

CVBs often work with airlines serving their area and create travel missions to visit markets, domestic and international, that represent opportunities for all tourist industry members within a destination to work together. Large enterprises such as a ski resort or a large attraction such as the Biltmore house in Asheville, North Carolina, may provide a booth with representatives, whereas small members such as a B&B may be able to only provide brochures and support the sponsoring tourist promotion organizations.

CHAPTER REVIEW

I. Marketing Tourism Destinations

A. **The globalization of the tourist industry.** Travel is a global business with an expanding market. Many new destinations have emerged to benefit from tourism development.

B. **The tourism destination.** Destinations are places with some form of actual or perceived boundary. Macrodestinations such as the United States contain thousands of microdestinations, including regions, states, cities, towns, and visitor destinations within a town.

C. **Destination marketing system.** Destination marketing is systematically linking supply (destination features and benefits) with demand (needs and wants of travelers) and enhancing competitiveness of a destination in a sustainable manner. Typically, DMOs, such as ministries of tourism, national tourism organizations (NTOs), and convention and visitors bureaus (CVBs), are the formal marketing organizations dealing with long-term strategy development. Funding is often provided by sales tax or special room tax receipts. The responsibility for marketing destinations and delivering a memorable experience on location are generally shared by many diverse public and private organizations including chamber of commerce, hotel/motel associations, environmental organizations, and many more. The selling function, to a great extent, is carried out by distribution channel and transportation companies such as airlines, tour operators, and travel agents. Tour operators and travel agents are significant information sources influencing the images and decisions of travelers.

D. **Destination competitiveness.** Comparative advantage is possession of resources, natural and/or man-made, critical to tourism development. Competitive advantage is to make use of these resources efficiently and effectively to enhance competitiveness of destination.

   1. **Travel and tourism competitiveness index.** It aims to measure the factors and policies that make it attractive to develop the T&T sector in different countries. Each country or economy is ranked on a set of indexes. Price competitiveness has a particular importance for tourist destinations because lower costs increase the attractiveness of some countries for many travelers.

E. **Sustainable tourism** refers to tourism that minimizes the environmental impacts and sociocultural changes, sustains the longevity of a destination, and creates economic opportunity for local communities.

   1. **Economic effects of tourism.** They are direct employment in hospitality and tourism industries, support for other industries, multiplier effect, tax revenue, and exports of locally made products.

   2. **Social/cultural effects of tourism.** Tourism growth affects the social/cultural basis of destinations in both positive and negative ways.

   3. **Environmental effects of tourism.** Too often, tourism planners focus mostly on tourism development without paying attention to retaining and preserving the destination attributes. Ecotourism is one of the fastest-growing niche markets in the travel industry and generally viewed as representing sustainable tourism. In fact, this occurs only when the government and the private industry cooperate in planning and strict enforcement of regulations and laws.

II. **Tourism Development and Investments.** Destinations must make more than financial or hospitality investments to attract tourists. Places find that they must expand public services, specifically public safety, traffic and crowd control, emergency health, sanitation, and street cleaning. They must also promote tourism internally to their own citizens and business retailers, restaurants, financial institutions, public and private transit, lodging, police, and public servants. They must invest in recruiting, training, licensing, and monitoring tourist-related businesses and employees.
   A. **Tourism events and attractions.** To attract tourists, destinations must still respond to the travel basics of cost and convenience.
      1. **Events** that attract a desired market and harmoniously fit with a community's culture can provide beneficial results, particularly if the event regularly reoccurs over a period of years.
      2. **Attractions** may be natural, such as Niagara Falls or the Scottish Highlands or a beach. They can also be manufactured, such as the shopping areas of Buckingham Palace, Hong Kong, the Vatican, or a casino resort.
   B. **Destination life cycle: Rejuvenating a destination.** Destinations will experience a life cycle similar to the product life cycle and eventually go into decline or the destruction stage.

III. **Segmenting and Monitoring the Tourist Market.** Tourism planners must consider how many tourists are desired and which segments to attract. Travel motivations, nationality, generational markets such as millennials, and lifestyles are effective segmentation base used by destinations.
   A. **Agritourism.** Agriculture-based tourism that includes farms, ranches, and wineries. It provides rural areas with a means to attract tourists.
   B. **Space tourism.** As private companies provide vehicles to send tourists into space, this form of tourism will develop. In the near term, it will just be for the very rich.
   C. **Multiday hiking and religious pilgrimages.** Trails are available for special-interest hikers with cultural, scientific, religious, or gastronomical interests.
   D. **Medical tourism.** It is one of the fastest-growing and most lucrative tourism markets. Tourists spend a large amount on medical treatment, stay in top hotels, and often travel around the country after their surgery. The aging baby boomers and the growing cost of health care will ensure the growth of medical tourism in the future.
   E. **Genealogical tourism.** Many people plan vacations to visit genealogical research sites.
   F. **Identifying target markets.** A destination can identify its natural target markets in two ways. One is to collect information about its current visitors. The second is to audit the destination's events and attractions and select segments that might logically have an interest in them. After a destination identifies its natural target markets, tourism planners should conduct research to determine where these tourists are found. Once identified, the relative potential profit from each should be evaluated. The potential profit of a target tourist segment is the difference between the amount that the tourist segment is likely to spend and the cost of attracting and serving this segment. The promotional cost depends on the budget. The serving cost depends on the infrastructure requirements. Ultimately, potential tourist segments should be ranked and selected in order of their profitability. If the analysis identifies too few natural tourist segments, investments may be needed in infrastructure and visitor events and attractions.
   G. **Classification of visitor segments.** The most commonly used classifications are based on whether the tourist travels with a group or independently. The common terms are group-inclusive tour (GIT) and independent traveler (IT). Plog's categorization divides travelers into allocentrics (persons with a need for new experiences) and psychocentrics (persons who like to visit nonthreatening places and stay in familiar surroundings).
   H. **Monitoring the tourist markets.** Tourist markets are dynamic and marketing information systems help identify and predict environmental trends that are responsible for changes. Information should be collected on changes, emerging markets, and potential target markets.
      1. **First-time versus repeat visitors.** Destination wants to have a healthy balance of first-time and repeat visitors.
      2. **Short-haul versus long-haul tourists.** Tourists who travel short distances tend to stay for short durations. They also show preferences for package tours.

IV. **Communicating with the Tourist Market**
   A. **Competition for visitors requires image making.** Tourist destinations largely compete on images held by current and potential travelers.
   B. **Branding destinations.** Destination branding is creating a differentiated destination image that influences travelers' decision to visit a destination and conveys the promise of a memorable experience that is uniquely associated with the destination. Branding opportunities for destinations exist at geographical levels such as country, city, and town (umbrella and sub-brands); specific attractions such as museums and theme parks; events such as mega-events and festivals; and lifestyle travel packages.
      1. **Destination tourism slogans.** Slogans are considered an essential element to build brand awareness and image at country, state, and city levels.
   C. **Effectiveness of advertising/promotion.** In today's digital age, savvy DMOs are tapping social and mobile networks, smartphones and tablets, GPS apps, e-commerce, and booking engines to economically reach consumers 24/7, and globally. Their Web sites can now interactively deploy video, text, audio, booking systems, photos, and real-time comments from customers.

D. **Developing packages of attractions and amenities.** An effective way of communicating with potential travelers is by offering packages. Tourist organizations must develop a package of attractions and amenities.
E. **Creating and managing visitor experiences.** Attractions alone do not attract visitors. Most places seek to deepen the travel experience by providing greater value and making the experience more significant and rewarding.
  1. **Cocreation of destination experience and social media.** Designing experiences in tourism should pay attention to interactivity, interactions between tourists and physical elements of destination, interactions with social elements of destination (other tourists, locals, employees, and social networks), and interactions with social media.
  2. **Live-like-a-local experience.** Younger generations want an authentic and "live-like-a-local" destination experience.
V. **Organizing and Managing Tourism Marketing.** Making a destination tourist friendly is the task of a central tourist agency, which may be public, quasi-public, nonprofit, or private. These agencies are referred to as national tourist organizations (NTOs), STOs, CVBs, or destination management organizations.

DISCUSSION QUESTIONS

1. How does a tourism destination determine what to promote and to whom it should be promoted?
2. What benefits and costs does tourism bring to your area?
3. Choose one of the psychological determinants of demand listed in Table 17–3 and describe a tourism product that is based on the determinant you have chosen.
4. Choose what you believe to be a good tourism promotion for a city, region, state, or country and explain why you think it is a good promotion. In your critique, discuss the media used, target audience, and benefits the destination offers.
5. Choose a visitor experience in a destination. Discuss how you can make it a memorable experience for visitors.

EXPERIENTIAL EXERCISE

Do the following:

1. Choose an event (festival, concert, play, etc.) in your area that draws tourists. Look into how the event is promoted and the benefits it brings to the community. Is this event effectively promoted? If yes, why? If no, how could it be improved?

IN-CLASS GROUP ACTIVITIES

1. Find two different sites of tourism marketing organizations, national, state, or CVB. Evaluate how effective you feel these Web sites are in promoting the destination. Explain your answer.
2. Visit Destination Marketing Association International (DMAI) homepage, http://www.destinationmarketing.org. What are the benefits for a DMO for becoming a member of the association?

APPENDIX A: 2018 TRAVEL AND TOURISM COMPETITIVENESS INDEX

Subindex A: Enabling Environment

1. Business environment pillar takes into account property rights, legal framework for disputes, cost to start a business, taxation on incentives and labor, and tax rates.
2. Safety and security pillar takes into account the costliness of common crime and violence as well as terrorism, and the extent to which police services can be relied upon to provide protection from crime as well as the incidence of road traffic accidents in the country.
3. Health and hygiene pillar measures drinking water and sanitation quality as well as the availability of physicians and hospital beds.
4. Human resources and labor market pillar takes into account the education and training levels in each economy as well as the availability and hiring of qualified labor.
5. Information and Communication Technology (ICT) readiness pillar measures ICT penetration rates (internet, telephone lines, and broadband), which provide a sense of the society's online activity as well the internet use by businesses in carrying out transactions in the economy.

Subindex B: T&T Policy and Enabling Conditions

6. Prioritization of the T&T sector pillar measures the extent to which the government prioritizes the T&T industry, such as ensuring the country's attendance at international T&T fairs and commissioning high-quality "destination-marketing" campaigns and branding, providing comprehensive travel and tourism data and statistics, and spending on T&T services to visitors.
7. International openness pillar captures the extent to which the government facilitates travel and services through its visa policy, the openness of the bilateral air service agreements, and the number of regional trade agreements in force.
8. Price competitiveness pillar measures the extent to which goods and services in the country are more or less expensive than elsewhere (purchasing power parity) as well as airfare ticket taxes and airport charges (which can make flight tickets much more expensive), fuel price levels compared with those of other countries, taxation in the country (which can be passed through to travelers), and the relative cost of hotel accommodations.
9. Environmental sustainability pillar measures the stringency and enforcement of the government's environmental regulations in each country, carbon dioxide emissions and the percentage of endangered species in the country, and the extent to which governments prioritize the sustainable development of the T&T industry in their respective economies.

Subindex C: Infrastructure

10. Air transport infrastructure pillar measures ease of access to and from countries, as well as movement to destinations within countries based on the quantity of air transport, the number of departures, airport density, the number of operating airlines, and the quality of the air transport infrastructure both for domestic and international flights.
11. Ground and port infrastructure pillar takes into account the quality of roads, railroads, and ports, as well as the extent to which the national transport network as a whole offers efficient, accessible transportation to key business centers and tourist attractions.
12. Tourism service infrastructure pillar takes into account the accommodation infrastructure (the number of hotel rooms), quality of tourism infrastructure, and the presence of major car rental companies in the country, as well as a measure of its financial infrastructure for tourists (the availability of automatic teller machines (ATMs)).

Subindex D: Natural and Cultural Resources

13. Natural resources pillar consists of a number of environmental attractiveness measures such as the number of UNESCO natural World Heritage sites, the quality of the natural environment, the richness of the fauna in the country as measured by the total known species of animals, and the percentage of nationally protected areas.
14. Cultural resources pillar includes the number of UNESCO cultural World Heritage sites, sports stadium seat capacity, the number of international fairs and exhibitions in the country, and cultural and entertainment tourism digital demand (online search volume).

REFERENCES

1. Graham Busby and Callu Haines, "Doc Martin and Film Tourism: Creation of Destination Image," *Tourism*, 61, no. 2 (2013): 105–120; Simon Hudson and J. R. Brent Ritchie, "Promoting Destinations via Film Tourism: An Empirical Identification of Supporting Marketing Initiatives," *Journal of Travel Research*, 44 (2006): 387–396; http://www.tourismnewzealand.com/about-us/what-we-do/campaign-and-activity/ (accessed June 16, 2015); http://www.tourismnewzealand.com/sector-marketing/film-tourism/ (accessed September 28, 2014); Daniela Carl, Sara Kindon, and Karen Smith, "Tourists' Experiences of Film Locations: New Zealand as 'Middle-Earth,'" *Tourism Geographies*, 9, no. 1 (2007): 49–63; "Celebrating 10 Years of 100% Pure New Zealand," http://www.tourismnewzealand.com/media/1544/pure-as-celebrating-10-years-of-100-pure-new-zealand.pdf (accessed July 31, 2015).
2. "Understanding Tourism: Basic Glossary," http://media.unwto.org/en/content/understanding-tourism-basic-glossary (accessed August 5, 2015); "International Recommendations for Tourism Statistics 2008: 10," http://unstats.un.org/unsd/-publication/SeriesM/seriesm_83rev1e.pdf.
3. Tourism Highlights 2018, UNWTO (August 2018): 2.
4. World Tourism Organization, Global Report on the Power of Youth Travel 2016, http://cf.cdn.unw-to.org/sites/all/files/pdf/wyse_powerofyouthtravel.pdf; Amanda Machado, "How Millennials Are Changing Travel," *The Atlantic*, June 18, 2014, http://www.-theatlantic.com/international/print/2014/06/how-millennials-are-changing-international-travel/373007/.
5. Robert Govers and Frank Go, *Place Branding: Gocal, Virtual and Physical Identities, Constructed, Imagined and Experienced* (New York: Palgrave Macmillan, 2009).
6. Seyhmus Baloglu and Mehmet Mangaloglu, "Tourism Destinations Images of Turkey, Egypt, Greece, and Italy as Perceived by US-Based Tour Operators and Travel Agents," *Tourism Management*, 22, no. 1, 1–9; Metin Kozak and Seyhmus Baloglu, *Managing and Marketing Tourist Destinations: Strategies to Gain a Competitive Advantage* (New York, NY: Routledge, 2011), 57.
7. See vacations.united.com.

8. Metin Kozak and Seyhmus Baloglu, *Managing and Marketing Tourist Destinations: Strategies to Gain a Competitive Advantage* (New York, NY: Routledge, 2011), 111–129.

9. Geoffrey I. Crouch and J. R. Brent Ritchie, "Conceptual and Theoretical Perspectives," in *Competitiveness and Tourism*, Vol. 1. eds. Geoffrey I. Crouch and J. R. Brent Ritchie (Northampton, MA: An Elgar Research Collection, 2012), p. 75.

10. Geoffrey I. Crouch and J. R. Brent Ritchie, "Introduction," in *Competitiveness and Tourism*, Vol. 1. eds. Geoffrey I. Crouch and J. R. Brent Ritchie (Northampton, MA: An Elgar Research Collection, 2012), pp. xii–xx.

11. "U.S. Consumer Online Travel Spending Surpasses $100 Billion for First Time in 2012," February 20, 2013, http://www.comscore.com/Insights/Press-Releases/2013/2/U.S.-Consumer-Online-Travel-Spending-Surpasses-100-Billion-for-First-Time-in-2012.

12. Peter Forsyth and Larry Dwyer, "Tourism Price Competitiveness," in *Competitiveness and Tourism*, Vol. 2. eds. Geoffrey I. Crouch and J. R. Brent Ritchie (Northampton, MA: An Elgar Research Collection, 2012), p. 8.

13. See www.economist.com/content/big-mac-index (accessed November 2018).

14. Salah S. Hassan, "Determinants of Market Competitiveness in an Environmentally Sustainable Tourism Industry," *Journal of Travel Research*, 38, no. 3 (2000): 244.

15. Andrew W. Savitz, *Triple Bottom Line* (San Francisco, CA: Jossey-Bass, 2006).

16. Terry Jicinsky and Seyhmus Baloglu, "Las Vegas—A Diversified Destination," in Metin Kozak and Seyhmus Baloglu, *Managing and Marketing Tourist Destinations: Strategies to Gain a Competitive Advantage* (New York, NY: Routledge, 2011), p. 155.

17. Ethan Hawkes and Robert J. Kwortnik, "Connecting with the Culture: A Case Study in Sustainable Tourism," *Cornell Hotel and Restaurant Administration Quarterly*, 47, no. 4 (2006): 369–381.

18. Sergei Khrushchev, Tony L. Henthorne, and Michael S. Latour, "Cuba at the Crossroads," *Cornell Hospitality Quarterly* (November 2007): 402–414.

19. Ibid.

20. Hugo Martin, "Utah's Wave Is a Rock Star Without a Crowd," *The Denver Post* (January 6, 2008): 1T, 6T.

21. Rex S. Toh, Habibullah Kahn, and Karen Kim, "Singapore Tourist Industry: How Its Strengths Offset Economic, Social and Environmental Challenges," *Cornell Hotel and Restaurant Administration Quarterly*, 42, no. 1 (2001): 46.

22. David Bruce Weaver, "Eco-Tourism as Mass Tourism: Contradiction or Reality?" *Cornell Hotel and Restaurant Administration Quarterly*, 42, no. 2 (2001): 112.

23. "Game on—Mega-Event Infrastructure Opportunities," April 2011, https://www.pwc.com/en_GX/gx/capital-projects-infrastructure/pdf/Mega-Events_with_Abadie_Change.pdf.

24. "Tourism Ministry to Undertake $34 Million 'Clean Coasts Project,'" *Jamaica Observer*, June 27, 2014, http://www.jamaicaobserver.com/news/Tourism-ministry-to-undertake-34-million-Clean-Coasts-Project-_17024117.

25. Jeffrey Ball, "The Carbon Neutral Vacation," *Wall Street Journal* (July 28–29, 2007): P1, P4, P5.

26. Ma Aiping, Si Lina, and Zhang Hongfei, "The Evolution of Cultural Tourism: The Example of Qufu, the Birthplace of Confucius," in *Tourism in China: Destination, Cultures and Communities*, eds. Chris Ryan and Gu Huimin (New York: Routledge, 2009), pp. 187–196.

27. Donald Getz, "Event Tourism: Definition, Evolution, and Research," *Progress in Tourism Management*, 29 (2008): 403–428.

28. Lisa Wirthman, "What to Expect at the 2015 Consumer Electronics Show," November 19, 2014, http://www.forbes.com/sites/lasvegas/2014/11/19/what-to-expect-at-the-2015-consumer-electronics-show/.

29. James R. Hagerty, "Loaves and Fish: Piscine Gluttony in Pennsylvania," *Wall Street Journal* (June 16–17, 2007): A1, A2.

30. http://www.bard.org/about/history.html#.VE1BB-vl4pKU (accessed August 9, 2015); "Economic Impact of the Utah Shakespeare Festival," January 4, 2012, http://www.le.utah.gov/interim/2012/pdf/00003264.pdf.

31. Martin A. O'Neill and Adrian Palmer, "Wine Production and Tourism: Adding Service to a Perfect Partnership," *Cornell Hotel and Restaurant Administration Quarterly*, 45, no. 3 (2004): 271.

32. Ibid.

33. Juergen Gnoth and Syed Aziz Anwar, "New Zealand Bets on Event Tourism," *Cornell Hotel and Restaurant Administration Quarterly*, 41, no. 4 (2000): 80.

34. Eliza Ching-Yick Tse and Suk-Ching Ho, "Targeting Sports Teams," *Cornell Hotel & Restaurant Administrative Quarterly* (February 2006): 49–59.

35. Susan Wargin, "Update," www.9news.com (accessed July 10, 2011).

36. "An Earful of Cheer, Disney Does Marathons the Only Way It Knows How," *Hemispheres Magazine.com* (May 2011).

37. World Heritage Centre, World Heritage List, http://whc.unesco.org/en/list/ (accessed August 11, 2015).

38. Deborah Steinborn, "On the Waterfront," *Wall Street Journal* (June 11, 2007): R11.

39. http://www.greektowncasino.com/Gaming/ClubGreektown/ (accessed October 11, 2008); R. Ankeny, "Greektown Casino: We'll Bring Neighborhood Firms to Table," *Crain's Detroit Business*, 15, no. 33 (1999): 3–4 (retrieved June 13, 2004, from EBSCOhost online article search engine); T. Lam, "Home Court Advantage: Greektown Casino Owners Are Betting on Metro

Detroiters' Affection for the Neighborhood," *Detroit/Windsor Casino Guide* (November 10, 2000), as originally printed in the Detroit Free Press, http://www.freep.com/casinoguide/greektown/greek.htm (accessed June 14, 2004).

40. www.fortune.com/sections, Special Advertising Feature, "Indian Gaming, The Native American Success Story," 2007.
41. Mark Whitehouse, "Bad Odds," *Wall Street Journal* (June 11, 2007): R5.
42. Rex S. Toh, Habibullah Kahn, and Karen Lim, "Singapore's Tourism Industry: How Its Strength Offsets Economic, Social and Environmental Challenges," *Cornell Hotel and Restaurant Administrative Quarterly*, 42, no. 1 (2001): 42, 48.
43. Norman Skiareivitz, Copley News Service, "Going Places: Waikiki $2 Billion Makeover," *Steamboat Pilot & Today* (November 4, 2007): 1D, 2D.
44. Xiang (Robert) Li, Fang Meng, Muzaffer Uysal, and Brian Mihalik, "Understanding China's Long-Haul Outbound Travel Market: An Overlapped Segmentation Approach," *Journal of Business Research*, 66, no. 6 (2013): 786–793.
45. "Vegas FAQ—Frequently Asked Questions," https://www.lvcva.com/stats-and-facts/visitor-statistics/.
46. "2017 Crosstab Report: Visitors by Origin (So California v International)," https://www.lvcva.com/stats-and-facts/visitor-profiles/ (accessed November 25, 2018)
47. "2017 International Visitation by Country & World Region," https://www.lvcva.com/stats-and-facts/visitor-origin/; Laura Carroll, "Las Vegas Aims to Benefit from Surge in Foreign Tourism," *Las Vegas Review Journal*, January 8, 2012, http://www.reviewjournal.com/business/-tourism/las-vegas-aims-benefit-surge-foreign-tourism; Laura Carroll, "Seeking International Visitors: Tourism Agency Widens Reach," *Las Vegas Review Journal* (February 29, 2012): 1d, 4d.
48. Amanda Machado, "How Millennials Are Changing Travel," *The Atlantic*, June 18, 2014, http://www.-theatlantic.com/international/print/2014/06/how-millennials-are-changing-international-travel/373007/.
49. Teresa Lee, "Top Millennial Traveler Trends," *Hotels Interactive*, April 16, 2013, http://www.hotelinteractive.com/article.aspx?articleID=28911; "Meet the Millennials: Insights for Destinations," 2011, from www.pgavdestinations.com/images/insights/Meet_the_Millennials.pdf; "Destination Marketing for Millennials," http://www.adventuretravelnews.com/destination-marketing-for-millennials (accessed November 13, 2014).
50. "Destination Marketing for Millennials," http://www.adventuretravelnews.com/destination-market-ing-for-millennials (accessed November 13, 2014).
51. Tom Crosby, "Kiawah Island Joins Charleston as Major South Carolina Destination," *Go Magazine* (March/April 2004): 29.
52. Sharon Flanigan, Kirsty Blackstock, and Colin Hunter, "Agritourism from the Perspective of Providers and Visitors," *Tourism Management*, 40 (2014): 395.
53. "Top 8 Agritourism Destinations in the World," http://www.mnn.com/lifestyle/eco-tourism/pho-tos/top-8-agritourism-destinations-in-the-world/-cul-tivate-your-knowledge (accessed August 5, 2015).
54. "Colorado's Agritourism Market Climbing Says New CSU Report," College of Agricultural Sciences, *AG Family* (Fall 2007), Colorado State University, p. 4.
55. *Houston Chronicle*, http://www.chron.com/disp/sto-ry.mpl/front/6052360.html (accessed October 11, 2008).
56. See www.virgingalactic.com.
57. Dan Vergano, "NASA Prepares for Moon Tourism," *USA Today* (November 10, 2011): 1.
58. *Centennial Journal* (May 2007): 11C, 12C.
59. "Medical Tourism Market (India, Thailand, Singapore, Malaysia, Mexico, Brazil, Taiwan, Turkey, South Korea, Costa Rica, Poland, Dubai, and Philippines)—Global Industry Analysis, Size, Share, Growth, Trends, and Forecast, 2013–2019," http://www.transparencymarketresearch.com/medical-tourism.html (accessed August 10, 2015); "Medical Tourism in 2013, Facts and Statistics," *Medical Tourism Resource Guide*, http://www.medicaltourismresourceguide.com/medi-cal-tourism-in-2013 (accessed May 9, 2015).
60. Michael D. Horowitz and Jeffrey A. Rosenweig, "Medical Tourism—Health Care in the Global Economy," *Physician Executive*, 33, no. 6 (2007): 24–30; "Healthcare Cost," *Healthcare Financial Management*, 62, no. 9 (2008): 12.
61. Carla Almeida Santos and Grace Yan, "Genealogical Tourism: A Phenomenological Examination," *Journal of Travel Research*, 49, no. 1 (February 2011).
62. "Scotland Urged to Refocus on Genealogy Tourism," *The Scotsman*, November 25, 2012, http://www.scots-man.com/lifestyle/arts/news/scotland-urged-to-refo-cus-on-genealogy-tourism-1-2658576.
63. James Glenday, "Gallipoli 2015: Tourist Trade Booms Ahead of Anzac Centenary," April 20, 2015, http://www.abc.net.au/news/2015-04-20/-gallipoli-tour-ist-trade-booms-ahead-of-anzac-centenary/6404628.
64. Stanley C. Plog, "Why Destinations Rise and Fall in Popularity," *Cornell Hotel and Restaurant Quarterly*, 14, no. 4 (1974): 55–59.
65. Zhaoping Liu, Judy A. Siguaw, and Cathy A. Enz, "Using Tourist Travel Habits and Preferences to Assess Strategic Destination Positioning," *Cornell Hospitality Quarterly*, 49, no. 3 (August 2008): 258–280.
66. Seyhmus Baloglu, "An Investigation of a Loyalty Typology and the Multidestination Loyalty of International Travelers," *Tourism Analysis*, 6, no. 1 (2001): 41–52.
67. Robert Govers and Frank Go, *Place Branding: Glocal, Virtual and Physical Identities, Constructed, Imagined and Experienced* (New York: Palgrave Macmillan, 2009).

68. Ahmet Usakli and Seyhmus Baloglu, "Brand Personality of Tourist Destinations: An Application of Self-Congruity Theory," *Tourism Management* 32 (2011): 114–127.
69. Laura Caroll, "Polishing a Silver Lining," *Las Vegas Business Press* (July 1–14, 2013): 6–9; Laura Carroll, "Seeking International Visitors: Tourism Agency Widens Reach," *Las Vegas Review Journal* (February 29, 2012): 4d.
70. Xinran Y. Lehto, Gwangjin Lee, and Joseph Ismail, "Measuring Congruence of Affective Images of Destinations and Their Slogans," *International Journal of Tourism Research*, 16 (2014): 250.
71. John Deskins and Matthew Seevers, "Are State Expenditures to Promote Tourism Effective?" *Journal of Travel Research*, 50, no. 2 (March 2011): 167.
72. Marsha Coleman and Kenneth F. Backman, "Walking in Memphis: Testing One DMO's Marketing Strategy to Millennials," *Journal of Travel Research*, 49, no. 1 (February 2010).
73. Bill Baker, "The Changing Role of DMOs in the Digital Age," http://destinationbranding.com/dmofuture (accessed December 24, 2014).
74. http://www.tourismnewzealand.com/news/-tourism-s-global-facebook-campaign-world-class/ Retrieved on July 28, 2015; see www.facebook.com/purenewzealand.
75. J. S. Perry Hobson and Roberta Leung, "Hotel Development in Myanmar," *Cornell Hotel and Restaurant Administration Quarterly*, 38, no. 1 (1997): 60–71. See also F. Doherty, "Come Ye Back to Mandalay," *Tourism in Focus*, 15 (Spring 1995): 8.
76. Lewis P. Carbone, *Clued In: How to Keep Customers Coming Back Again and Again* (Upper Saddle River, NJ: Pearson Education, Inc., 2004).
77. Noel Scott, Eric Laws, and Phillip Boksberger, "The Marketing of Hospitality and Leisure Experiences," *Journal of Hospitality Marketing & Management*, 18, no. 2–3 (2014): 99–110; Lis P. Tussyadiah, "Toward a Theoretical Foundation for Experience Design in Tourism," *Journal of Travel Research*, 53, no. 5 (2014): 543–564; Barbara Neuhofer, Dimitrios Buhalis, and Adele Ladkin, "Conceptualizing Technology Enhanced Destination Experiences," *Journal of Destination Marketing & Management*, 1 (2012): 36–46.
78. See http://www.tourismthailand.org/Real-Experiences.
79. See http://www.likealocalguide.com.
80. See https://www.withlocals.com.
81. See http://matadornetwork.com/goods/how-to-explore-canada-like-a-local.
82. Jennie Germann Molz, "CouchSurfing and Network Hospitality: It's Not Just About the Furniture," *Hospitality & Society*, 1 no. 3 (2011): 215–224; Devan Rosen, Pascale Roy Lafontaine, and Blake Hendrickson, "CouchSurfing: Belonging and Trust in a Globally Cooperative Online Social Network," *New Media & Society*, 13, no. 6 (2011): 981–998.
83. See https://www.ustravel.org.
84. Chris Ryan, *Recreational Tourism: A Social Science Perspective* (New York: Routledge, 1991), pp. 5–34; A. J. Burkhart and S. Medlik, *Tourism: Past, Present, and Future* (London: Heinemann, 1981), p. 256; T. C. Victor Middleton, *Marketing in Travel and Tourism* (Oxford, UK: Butterworth-Heinemann, 1994); Ernie Heath and Geoffrey Wall, *Marketing Tourism Destination* (New York: Wiley, 1992), p. 65; R. C. Mills and A. M. Morrison, *The Tourism System: An Introductory Text* (Upper Saddle River, NJ: Prentice Hall, 1985), p. 248; S. Crystal, "What Is the Meeting Industry Worth?" *Meeting News*, 17, no. 7 (1993): 1, 11.
85. http://www.tq.com.au/ (accessed October 11, 2008).
86. http://www.iloveny.com/home.aspx (accessed October 11, 2008).
87. "Best Practices Convention Center Sales and Convention Center Operations," A report from the Joint Study Committee, Destination Marketing Association International, and International Association of Assembly Managers, August 25, 2007.

18

Objectives

After reading this chapter, you should be able to:

1. Explain the purpose of a marketing plan.
2. Prepare a marketing plan.
3. Describe how to sell the marketing plan and use it to prepare for the future.

Next Year's Marketing Plan

The rationale is that the experience of the truly discerning traveler is shaped by the "little things," beyond guaranteeing merely a clean, comfortable room and a desirable package of amenities. In-depth guest input will also be used to shape the criteria that go into defining the on-property guest experience. Through a proprietary customer satisfaction program currently under development, Preferred Hotels & Resorts will refine still further fine points of detail that create a truly memorable and complete "luxury experience."

For example, at the Rittenhouse Hotel in Philadelphia, frequent guests are greeted nightly with an expensive pearl on their pillow instead of the usual chocolate. At Halekulani in Honolulu, named the number-one hotel in the world by *Gourmet* magazine, guests are escorted to their rooms for swift, private check-in and receive a welcoming box of chocolates made by their in-house chocolatier soon afterward.

Although "comment cards" and guest preference sheets remain commonplace at many luxury hotels, no other worldwide lodging brand has built into its core mission the complete and total fulfillment of the guests' individual tastes, requirements, and predilections.

We have found that complete attention to detail—a total commitment to guest satisfaction that saves guest time, energy, and efforts; provides completely personalized and individual service; and creates the experience of "intellectual surprise" for its consumers—is what drives repeat business among the affluent.

To better understand its affluent consumer, Preferred Hotels & Resorts launched a market research effort that "drills down" to the deepest level of guest preference and expectation. Using a prospect identification and lifestyle data collection system, detailed and segmented data are gathered not only about the preferences of luxury travelers but also about unperceived "micromarkets" that make up the luxury travel segment.

At the individual property level, the expectation is that property managers will soon be able to learn not only what kind of room guests prefer when they travel on business but also what their favorite leisure activities are, what kind of wine they like to drink—even their favorite reading material. At the macrolevel, Preferred targets programs, promotions, and partnerships tailored to the micromarket segments that make up its customer base. Examples are West Coast lawyers who golf or company CEOs who travel with children. Data collected from drilling down into the guest experience enable Preferred to provide the ultimate in-guest service. Unique data can assist to discover distribution channels to market to the affluent.

Initial Applications of the Research: "Experiential" Associations and New Marketing Programs

Although affluent guests value individuality and attention to detail, Preferred has begun to identify certain distinct attributes or expectations that define the affluent as a group. More than anything else, affluents tend to flock together around common symbols, expectations, and experiences. In a word, they associate themselves into groups. Membership in the group, in turn, comes to define participation in the affluent experience.

Association is built into the concept of the affluent experience so that Preferred's creation of programs that target the affluent can be understood as a universal affinity program for the discerning consumer. It is the ultimate "affinity program for the affluent."

Preferred has taken the affinity concept a step further by identifying an interlinked series of value and quality associations that respond to the affluent client's desire for unique, memorable experiences and superior service, and by using that information to provide experiences that cater directly and uniquely to that desire.

Seabourn/Windstar

An example of the research in action is a partnership between Preferred and Seabourn/Windstar Cruises. The linkage is the desire of guests who stay at exclusive Preferred hotel properties to take expensive cruises on these two cruise lines, among the world's finest. The customer reward is the ability to translate stays at Preferred hotels into free nights on these cruises. This allows Preferred and Seabourn/Windstar to share guest histories and databases that reveal a guest's preferences and thus guarantees the ability to best service the guest with the expectation of creating return business.

Golf the Preferred Way

Another example of the application of the lifestyle marketing approach is "Preferred Golf," a partnership with Wide World of Golf, a worldwide marketer of upscale golf services. Preferred Golf provides Preferred guests with access to the world's finest golf courses by means of staying at a Preferred hotel or resort.

Engaging New Partners: Travel Agents and the Lifestyle Client Building Program

Lifestyle marketing programs that target the affluent have applications that extend far beyond merely "selling room nights."

For example, through programs such as Wide World of Golf and the cruise redemption program, Preferred properties and travel agents can work together to sell complete "experiential packages" for the affluent traveler. Travel agents enter Preferred's luxury marketing "loop" as partners and build relationships with discerning travelers. This goes well beyond the usual booking of air travel and hotels on the basis of price and availability. Client building is achieved through educational seminars, training programs, and special package promotions. Agents are encouraged to position themselves as key components of Preferred's affluent marketing channel.[1]

Success in the marketplace is not guaranteed by understanding marketing concepts and strategies. Successful marketing requires planning and careful execution. It is easy to become so involved in the day-to-day problems of running a marketing department that little or no time is devoted to planning. When this occurs, the marketing department is probably operating without purpose and is being reactive rather than proactive. Even experienced managers sometimes fail to see that this is occurring until it is too late. This may be one of the root causes for high turnover within hospitality, marketing, and sales departments.

Purpose of a Marketing Plan

A marketing plan serves several of the following purposes within any hospitality company:

- Provides a road map for all marketing activities of the firm for the next year.
- Ensures that marketing activities are in agreement with the corporate strategic plan.
- Forces marketing managers to review and think through objectively all steps in the marketing process.
- Assists in the budgeting process to match resources with marketing objectives.
- Creates a process to monitor actual against expected results.

The development of a marketing plan is a rigorous process and cannot be accomplished in a few hours. Instead, it is best to set aside one or more days to develop next year's plan. Many marketing managers find it best to leave the office along with their staff and all necessary data while writing the plan. Constant interruptions that occur in the office are detrimental to the planning process.

To be effective, a new marketing plan must be written each year. Marketing plans written for periods longer than a year are generally not effective. At the same time, the annual marketing plan must be written against a longer-term strategic plan that states what the company hopes to achieve, say, three to five years down the road.

Many managers believe that the process of writing a plan is invaluable because it forces those writing it to question, think, and strategize. A plan should be developed with the input and assistance of key members of the marketing department. The discussion and thought process required to produce a plan are stimulating and very helpful in team building. It is also an excellent training device for younger staff members who wish to be managers.

Marketing plans are not created in a vacuum. To develop successful strategies and action programs, marketers need up-to-date information about the environment, the competition, and the market segments to be served. Often, analysis of internal data is the starting point for assessing the current marketing situation, supplemented by marketing intelligence and research investigating the overall market, the competition, key issues, and threats and opportunities. As the plan is put into effect, marketers use a variety of research techniques to measure progress toward objectives and identify areas for improvement if results fall short of projections.

Finally, marketing research helps marketers learn more about their customers' requirements, expectations, perceptions, and satisfaction levels. This deeper understanding provides a foundation for building competitive advantage through well-informed segmenting, targeting, differentiating, and positioning decisions. Thus, the marketing plan should outline what marketing research will be conducted and how the findings will be applied.

The marketing plan shows how the company will establish and maintain profitable customer relationships. In the process, however, it also shapes a number of internal and external relationships. First, it affects how marketing personnel work with each other and with other departments to deliver value and satisfy customers. Second, it affects how the company works with suppliers, distributors, and strategic alliance partners to achieve the objectives listed in the plan. Third, it influences the company's dealings with other stakeholders, including government regulators, the media, and the community at large. All of these relationships are important to the organization's success, so they should be considered when a marketing plan is being developed.

Unlike a business plan, which offers a broad overview of the entire organization's mission, objectives, strategy, and resource allocation, a marketing plan has a more limited scope. It serves to describe how the organization's strategic objectives will be achieved through specific marketing strategies and tactics, with the customer as the starting point. It is also linked to the plans of other departments within the organization. Suppose a marketing plan calls for selling 200,000 units annually. The production department must gear up to make that many units, the finance department must arrange funding to cover the expenses, the human resources department must be ready to hire and train staff, and so on. Without the appropriate level of organizational support and resources, no marketing plan can succeed.

Although the exact length and layout varies from company to company, a marketing plan usually contains the sections described in this chapter. To guide implementation effectively, every part of the plan must be described in considerable detail. Sometimes a company posts its marketing plan on an internal Web site, which allows managers and employees in different locations to consult specific sections and collaborate on additions or changes. We now discuss the following sections of a marketing plan in detail.

I. Executive Summary
II. Corporate Connection
III. Environmental Analysis and Forecasting
IV. Segmentation and Targeting
V. Next Year's Objectives and Quotas
VI. Action Plans: Strategies and Tactics
VII. Resources Needed to Support Strategies and Meet Objectives
VIII. Marketing Control
IX. Presenting and Selling the Plan
X. Preparing for the Future

We examine the role played by each section of the marketing plan.

Preparing a Marketing Plan

Section I: Executive Summary

Executive summary A short summary of the marketing plan to quickly inform top executives.

The **executive summary** and a few charts or graphs from the body of the plan may be the only parts ever read by top management. Consequently, it is of great importance to write this section carefully, with top management in mind.

The following few tips may assist in writing the executive summary:

- Write it for top executives.
- Limit the number of pages to between two and four.
- Use short sentences and short paragraphs. Avoid using words that are unlikely to be understood.
- Organize the summary as follows: Describe next year's objectives in quantitative terms; briefly describe marketing strategies to meet goals and objectives, including a description of target markets; describe expected results by quarter; and identify the dollar costs necessary, as well as key resources needed.
- Read and reread the executive summary several times. Never write it once and then place it in the plan. Modify and change the summary until it flows well, is easily read, and conveys the central message of the marketing plan.

Section II: Corporate Connection

Relationship to Other Plans

A marketing plan is not a stand-alone tool. Instead, it must support other plans, such as the firm's strategic plan. Whenever possible, the marketing manager should participate in or provide input to the development of a strategic plan. If this is not practical, it remains imperative to understand the contents of the strategic plan prior to the development of next year's marketing plan.

A marketing plan supports the company's strategic plan in several ways. Next year's marketing strategies and tactics must support strategic decisions such as the following:

- Corporate goals with respect to profit, growth, and so on
- Desired market share
- Positioning of the company or of its product lines
- Vertical or horizontal integration
- Strategic alliances
- Product-line breadth and depth
- Customer-relationship management (CRM)

Marketing-Related Plans

In large corporations, marketing-related plans are sometimes developed by people who do not report to marketing. This is usually the result of (1) originally establishing these departments independent of marketing, (2) political maneuvering in which a nonmarketing executive desired control of these areas, and (3) the failure of top management to understand the need to unify marketing-related activities.

Marketing-related areas in which plans are sometimes written independently of marketing include the following:

- Sales
- Advertising and promotion
- Public relations and publicity
- Digital marketing
- Marketing research
- Pricing
- Customer service

The director of sales works with his/her sales managers on the marketing plan. Antonio Diaz/123RF.

If these plans are developed independently of a marketing plan with no consideration as to how they tie together, the result is often chaotic, counterproductive, and a source for continuous infighting among marketing-related areas.

When the organizational design of a company fails to place major marketing activities under the marketing umbrella, the task of writing and implementing a marketing plan is made more complex. Under these conditions, it behooves the marketing manager to invite the managers of other marketing-related areas to participate in the marketing plan development process. This action should then be reciprocated.

The activities of marketing and many other departments within a company are closely intertwined. Operations and finance are two areas that affect and in turn are affected by marketing.

If guest experiences are diminished because of problem areas in operations, marketing will be adversely affected. Similarly, if financial projections are unrealistic for certain months or for various product lines, marketing will be called to task.

It is unrealistic to expect perfect harmony between marketing and other departments. It is by no means unrealistic to suggest that relations can usually be greatly improved and that a critical place to begin is by interchanging data, suggestions, and other assistance when department plans are being developed.

Corporate Direction

A good marketing plan begins with the fact that the only purpose of marketing is to support the enterprise. It is good politics and good sense to begin next year's plan by recognizing and restating these corporate elements. Let top management know that the following helped guide the development of next year's plan:

- Mission statement
- Corporate philosophy
- Corporate goals

Hospitality companies are highly sensitive to changes in their social, political, and economic environments. A manufacturer of food or toiletries may not immediately feel the impact of these changes, but airlines, hotels, auto rental firms, and cruise lines witness an instant reaction.

Section III: Environmental Analysis and Forecasting

A marketing plan is not a political or economic treatise, and hospitality marketers are not expected to be experts in these fields. They are expected to be aware of major **environmental factors** likely to affect the industry and the company, to consider their possible impact on marketing, and to respond quickly and intelligently to new events and trends. In Chapter 4 we discussed the environment and how to monitor it. An environmental analysis is essential for the development of an effective marketing plan.

Environmental factors Social, political, and economic factors that affect a firm and its marketing program.

Positioning Statement

A marketing plan should provide a positioning statement of how the enterprise intends to differentiate—position itself—in the marketplace. This provides essential guidance to the rest of the plan.

Major airlines such as American Airlines have traditionally positioned themselves as hub-and-spoke carriers serving multimarket segments and as market share companies. Other airlines have positioned themselves as low-price niche carriers, serving point-to-point markets.

Small resort hotels usually position themselves as providers of vacation/holiday service for individuals, couples, and small groups. Larger resort hotels position themselves as serving this market but also serving the corporate seminar, meeting, and conference market.

A limousine service positions itself differently from a taxi cab business. A tour bus business positions itself differently from a sightseeing bus business.

All members of the marketing and sales departments and their service suppliers such as ad agencies, public relations firms, marketing research firms, and others must know the desired positioning of the enterprise. Otherwise, their efforts may result in a confusing array of strategies, tactics, and results that may not serve the company well.

Tourist/visitor destinations usually have a more difficult task selecting a single unifying positioning statement due to political pressures and end up trying to be all things to all people. It is little wonder that their advertising and sales tactics mimic others.

Major Environmental Factors

Hospitality organizations need to anticipate the influence of these broad environmental factors on their business.

SOCIAL Consider the possible impact of major social factors, such as crime and changing demographics. These factors vary in their intensity and their geographic incidence. Social factors relevant to Los Angeles, California, or Sydney, Australia, may have little relevance to Rapid City, South Dakota.

Social conditions sometimes change rapidly to the benefit of alert marketers. The hotel market within India had long been considered as uninteresting by many hotel chains. Today, India's social and economic structures have become conducive to mid-priced hotel development. The emergence of a potentially gigantic market has attracted many chains, including Holiday Inn Worldwide, Choice Hotels, Carlson Hotels Worldwide, Southern Pacific Hotels (Australia), and Oberoi Hotels and Resorts (India).

POLITICAL Legislation affecting taxation, pension benefits, and casino gambling are only a few examples of political decisions likely to affect marketing directly. International politics is increasingly important to corporate hospitality marketing plans. The opening of Vietnam to investors and tourists after years of being off limits provides risk as well as rewards for the hospitality industry.[2] The same will undoubtedly be true with Cuba.

ECONOMIC Changes in economic variables such as employment and interest rates should be recognized. The hospitality industry, especially the lodging and cruising sectors, is highly sensitive to business-cycle movements.

TERRORISM The horrific terrorist attacks on the Taj Mahal Palace Hotel and the Hotel Oberoi Trident in November 2008 killed 164 people and wounded at least 308.[3] These attacks suddenly brought terrorism to the worldwide hospitality industry. In December 2014, the Lindt Café in Sydney, Australia, was the target of terrorism. In January 2015, the headquarters of Charlie Hebdo and a Jewish Kosher supermarket/deli in Paris also suffered terrorism attacks.

Clearly, all segments of the hospitality industry are at risk as targets of terrorism. A security plan concerning terrorism should be an integral part of the planning process for any company/organization within the hospitality industry. Your employees and guests are at risk in the absence of such a plan. It is not the function of a marketing plan, but marketing/sales executives have a responsibility to urge upper management to take this subject seriously if they have not already done so.

Economic Drivers of Growth

Economic drivers of growth have the ability to rapidly affect change. Marketers must be aware of these drivers before, during, and after entry into a market. An example is the Aerotropolis, which has been seriously considered for some communities.

THE AEROTROPOLIS The term *aerotropolis* was developed by Professor John D. Kasarda of the University of North Carolina. An aerotropolis is a transportation and urban development concept built around an airport. An aerotropolis is designed to serve as a powerful economic development force. These centers are built to facilitate the rapid movement of freight and passengers, such as Schiphol Airport in the Netherlands. A huge market for flowers and plants, Bloemenveiling Aalsmeer of Amsterdam, exists in tiny Netherlands as the largest and most important market in Europe. This is due in heavy part to the existence of Schiphol Airport.

Many aerotropolis centers are being built in China, Korea, and other nations where they serve as centers for tourism, transportation, and international business. Hotels, restaurants, and entertainment centers are critical participants in a successful aerotropolis.[4]

Competitive Analysis

Competitive analysis An analysis of the primary strengths and weaknesses, objectives, strategies, and other information relative to competitors.

It is common practice for hospitality companies to conduct a **competitive analysis**. In some cases, this analysis deals primarily with the observable physical properties of a competitor. For example,

Our Hotel	Their Hotel
500 rooms	600 rooms
One ballroom	Two ballrooms
Executive center	No executive center

An analysis solely of physical differences usually misses major competitive advantages or disadvantages. It is doubtful that most guests know or care about the room count of competitive hotels. They do recognize differences in service level, cleanliness, staff knowledge, and the responsiveness of the sales department. A competitive analysis must extend beyond inventory comparisons. True competitive advantages are factors that are recognized by guests and influence their purchase decisions. A creative and alert marketing manager recognizes competitive variables that are truly of importance to the customers and are controllable. Such a manager develops strategies and tactics to improve areas of weakness and enhance already strong points.

Based strictly on a comparison of physical attributes, many hospitality firms should not exist. Bed and breakfast (B&B) establishments are usually old homes without a swimming pool and may have shared bathrooms, yet they fill a competitive niche. Hertz and Avis may compete head-to-head, offering clean, late-model cars, but Rent-a-Wreck auto rental company successfully offers automobiles that many people would be ashamed to be seen driving.

The single best way to conduct a competitive analysis is to involve members of the marketing sales department, such as the sales force. These people often have difficulty discussing environmental variables such as interest rates, but they can talk knowledgeably for hours about the competition and guest preferences.

Market Trends

Market trends External trends of many types that are likely to affect the marketing in which a corporation operates.

Market trends are a reflection of environmental competitive variables. Market trend information for the hospitality industry is often available from outside organizations free of charge. Common sources include chambers of commerce, visitors' bureaus, universities, government agencies, banks, trade associations, and commercial organizations such as firms of certified public accountants or consultants who carry public information for publicity purposes.

Useful market trend information for writing a hospitality marketing plan includes the following:

- *Visitor trends:* Origination areas, stopover sites, visitor demographics, spending habits, length of stay, and so on.

- *Competitive trends:* Numbers, location, type of products offered (e.g., all-suite hotels), occupancy levels, average rates, and so on.

- *Related industry trends:* Interdependence of the members of the hospitality industry with airline flights, convention center bookings, new airport construction, and new highways. It is important to study trends for supporting or related industries.

Caterers of in-flight meals were dramatically affected by the trend among U.S. airlines to eliminate or reduce onboard meal service. Companies such as Dobbs International Services, which provided full-course meals, had to find new markets and new products. Caterair International Corporation diversified into the repair of airplane audio headsets, and Sky Chefs explored the private-label business and food preparation for prisons, schools, and hospitals. Randall C. Boyd, senior vice president of marketing and customer service for Sky Chefs, said, "We are good sandwich makers, salad makers, and pasta makers. Whether a prisoner or a college student is eating our sandwich, we don't care."[5]

Select only those trends that are useful in developing the plan. It is of no value to fill a plan with pages of information that have little or no direct relevancy. Unfortunately, it is common to read marketing plans prepared by professionals that are filled with "boilerplate" (statistics, tables, and graphs that are interesting and colorful but have little relevance to the marketing needs of a particular company or organization). Thousands of dollars are spent on so-called marketing plans filled with boilerplate.

Market Potential

Market potential The total estimated dollars or unit value of a defined market for a defined product, including competitive products.

Estimates of **market potential** often seem to be ignored by those who write hospitality marketing plans. Marketing managers in hotels sometimes feel that the concept has no application to them. "We view all travelers as potential guests" is a frequently heard comment. Others reply that the concept is theoretical for the hospitality industry and applies primarily to consumer-packaged goods.

These opinions are incorrect! Although it is true that measurement of true market potential is impossible, estimates can and should be made. The hospitality industry is notorious for ignoring or misinterpreting market potential estimates, thus leading to overbuilding, overcapacity, price cutting, and frantic advertising and promotion in an attempt to fill rooms or fill seats.

Market potential should be viewed as the total available demand for a hospitality product within a particular geographic market at a given price. It is important not to mix different hospitality products into an estimate of market potential.

It is common to hear individuals speak of the market for hotel rooms in a region as a number of room nights or gross number of travelers. For purposes of writing a marketing plan, such figures are interesting but do not indicate market potential for your products. Most markets consist of a mix of hotel properties, ranging from luxury to budget, with specialty lodging such as all-suites, condominium hotels, and B&Bs.

Each type of property faces its own peculiar market potential, except for times when a special event fills every bed in town. Estimates of market potential normally begin by examining the market for all hotels but should then shift to specific markets for your hotel and directly competitive properties, often referred to as a competitive set. To be precise, market potential estimates should be shown as demand estimates at various price points; however, this is generally unnecessary for most marketing plans. The average marketing manager for a property such as a hotel finds it impossible to make good quantitative estimates of market potential in room nights or dollars. These people lack marketing research support, and most were not trained in quantitative analysis. Therefore, market potential estimates are often expressed in "guesstimates," such as "The market seems to be growing or declining by about 5 percent a year."

There has been an explosion of branded hotels in Shanghai and throughout China. Lakov Kalinin/123RF.

Warning! Even though precise estimates may be beyond the abilities of many hospitality marketing managers, it is essential to go through the thought process of examining market potential. Never assume that market potential is static or unimportant to marketing success. The use of revenue management has created greatly improved estimates of market potential.

By engaging in the process of estimating market potential, those who develop marketing plans become aware of potentially important market conditions and can then adjust marketing strategies appropriately. Remember, the process of developing a marketing plan is not a precise discipline such as engineering or chemistry. The exercise of writing a plan is usually as important to marketing success as the plan itself.

Estimated marketing potential led U.S. ski resort developers to Asia. The world's highest and snowiest mountains remained virtually untapped for snow resorts. Developers estimated that 3 percent of the Chinese population might be potential skiers. This meant 43.3 million people.

The managing director of the project estimated a market potential of 100 million people with sufficient disposable income. Professor Simon Hudson of the University of Calgary said that there are 70 million skiers and snowboarders worldwide and that if 3 percent of India's population took up skiing that would be a 36.6 million person market.[6]

Although these estimates of market potential are not very sophisticated, they represent the kind of potential that excites entrepreneurs and investors.

LODGING MARKET POTENTIAL INDEX (L-MPI©) A joint research project between the School of Hospitality Business, Michigan State University's Center for International Business Education and Research (MSU-CIBER), and Global Edge developed the Lodging Market Potential Index.

According to the developers of this index, it is useful as a first step in hotel development, investment, and acquisition decisions. They state that this market index identifies market areas that show long-term potential for hotel development and will enable hotel developers and investors to conduct a relative comparison of the 25 largest lodging markets.[7]

Marketing Research

The need for marketing intelligence is ongoing. Much of the information acquired by marketing research in a current calendar or fiscal year serves as the basis for developing next year's marketing plan. Marketing research needs vary considerably by type and size of the hospitality company. Companies such as Hertz or Hilton Hotels have corporate marketing research departments. An individual hotel property or car rental location may have a need for additional marketing information. In these cases, the individual property or location is generally responsible for acquiring these data.

Marketing research needs can usually be divided into macromarket and micromarket information. Macromarket information includes, but is not restricted to, the following:

- Industry trends
- Socioeconomic and political trends
- Competitive information
- Industry-wide customer data

Micromarket information includes, but is not restricted to, the following:

- Guest information
- Product/service information
- New-product analysis and testing
- Intermediary buyer data
- Pricing studies
- Key account information
- Advertising/promotion effectiveness

Marketing Highlight 18.1 — The Indigo Pearl Resort: Facebook strategy and planning the Indigo Pearl

The Indigo Pearl Resort is an independent, luxury design property located in Phuket, Thailand. Michael Nurbatlain joined the resort as a sales manager, but this role quickly expanded to include managing digital marketing, e-commerce, and social media.[8]

Indigo Pearl Resort had witnessed a clear shift in its market mix: growing from a heavy reliance on tour operators to direct bookings and online channels. Michael Nurbatlain and the team at Indigo Pearl led this growth by developing a presence in a variety of channels, with Facebook emerging as one of the biggest successes. In just one year, Michael grew the resort's Facebook fan page to more than 8,000 followers. This is the result of having a good digital marketing plan.

Facebook Contents: The Key to Growth

In order to utilize Facebook fans, they were asked to post pictures, and then vote on their favorites. But Facebook contacted them, saying the contest setup violated terms and conditions. This forced them to set up an independent voting scheme allowing their fans to vote, which worked even better in the end. The contest generated great interaction among existing fans, strengthening their online community. Additionally, the contest generated a couple of hundred new fans—which was considered a great success at that time.

Latest Facebook Contest: Ultimate Holiday Package

This year's idea was to set up a new system. Rather than just asking fans to submit pictures, Indigo Pearl Resort wanted to add another layer of involvement. Michael and Indigo Pearl Resort asked fans to design their dream three-day holiday package. What would they like to do in Phuket? The resort was not very strict with the guidelines, so that if someone wrote some poetry about the perfect holiday, for example, it was still accepted as an entry. Michael worked a bit with the local media to get mentioned on their Web sites and sent out some tweets to promote it. But no other public relations or press releases were used. Everything was done through Facebook.

Within a few days they had 10–15 entries and then it started to get a snowball effect. They asked fans to send in their pictures, screened them, and placed the photos in the album called Ultimate Family Package. Once the photo was approved, the contest participants could ask their friends and family to vote on the entry. The contest exceeded expectations with one entry getting 1,000 likes.

Lessons Learned

- You work hard to generate friends and followers. Remember they are important assets of your online community. Treat them with respect and courtesy. Respond to comments whether they are positive or negative. Thank those who post positive comments and thank those who post negative comments for bringing the issue to your attention. Remember that other members of the community will observe how you handle negative comments.
- For online contests have multiple prizes. People realize that winning a contest online is a low probability. Having multiple prizes increases the perception that winning is a possibility and will result in more participation.
- Photos are an essential component of Facebook. Pictures of your guests enjoying your property, tourists enjoying a destination, or guests enjoying a trip you planned will receive more likes than a long post. Pictures attract attention, and it is often easier to post a picture with a short note than a written post.
- Avoid using Facebook as an advertising medium. Post items that will be of interest to your community. A special promotion may be of interest, but promotions should be infrequent. They should account for less than 10 percent of your posts.
- There should be consistency between the brand values and brand personality communicated to online communities and the brand values and brand personality guests observe when they visit your property and/or interact with your employees.

Section IV: Segmentation and Targeting

Segmentation Analysis

The heart of any marketing plan is careful analysis of available market segments and the selection of appropriate target markets. Not all market segments are appropriate for a hospitality company. The selection of segments is the result of (1) understanding what the company is and what it wishes to be and (2) studying available segments and determining if they fit the capabilities and desires of the company to obtain and secure them.

A common mistake within the hospitality industry is the selection of inappropriate segments. Marketing managers commonly err by allowing or encouraging the acquisition of low-yield segments in an effort to maintain occupancy. At the opposite extreme, companies sometimes feel they are serving "low-class" customers and attempt to attract quite different segments. If this is done in the absence of genuine product/service changes, the chances for success are slim to nonexistent.

In the case of a hotel, "A marketing plan tells you who is using your hotel and where you can look to expand your business."[9] The Los Angeles Biltmore Hotel had been the center of Los Angeles society for many years, but the property began to deteriorate and was sold. The new owners faced the task of restoring life to the hotel. One of the first discoveries by the new owners was that the Biltmore's marketing plan was confused. Some people believed that the hotel catered only to groups and tours, whereas others felt the hotel did not want their business and marketed only to commercial and transient guests. The guest mix was found to be 28 percent commercial, 40 percent groups, and 32 percent leisure. The new management decided that a more appropriate mix was 40 percent commercial, 50 percent groups, and 10 percent leisure. With this directive in mind, the hotel was able to establish a new marketing plan that included repositioning the hotel, changing food and beverage operations, and changing prices.[10]

Analysis of Internal Data	Analysis of External Data
Guest registrations	Published industry information
Credit card receipts	Marketing research
Customer surveys	Guesstimates after talking with competitors, vendors, and others in the industry
Customer database	

When developing a marketing plan, marketers must look at both internal and external data sources for information concerning market segments.

Market-Segment-Profitability Analysis (MSPA)

Information that identifies each of a company's existing customer segments by revenue, cost, and profitability is extremely valuable, but information about guests by segment is often not gathered or not analyzed. "Hotel marketers usually focus on customer segments. On the other hand, accountants record and report the operational results by department, not market segments."[11]

Market segment profitability data are even less likely to be available for most restaurants and are virtually nonexistent for tourism marketers such as those with most convention and visitor bureaus.

Targeting

No area of the marketing plan surpasses the selection of target markets in importance. If inappropriate markets are selected, marketing resources will be wasted. A high level of expenditures for advertising or sales promotion cannot compensate for misdirected marketing efforts.

Like the previous example of the Los Angeles Biltmore Hotel, targeting begins by defining the mix of desired guests. Commonly used broad groupings for guests are listed in the following table:

Business	Versus	Pleasure
Individual guests		IT (individuals who make their own reservations)
Conventions		
Seminars/conferences		GIT (group-inclusive tours)

The selection of a customer/guest mix must support the positioning strategy of the company. The mix should also support revenue management. This is not always the case. It is altogether too common for marketing/sales to plan and operate without consulting or working with the revenue management department.

Target markets are selected from the list of available segments. These include segments currently served by the company and newly recognized markets. The selection of target markets is a primary responsibility of marketing management. This requires careful consideration of the variables already discussed in the development of the marketing plan. Far too many marketing managers in the hospitality industry simply select last year's target markets. Although it is normally true that the majority of target markets remain the same, new ones appear and the order of importance can change between years.

Many Asian and Australian hotel managers discovered that their key segments in terms of spending and room nights were no longer American or European guests. Guests from Asian nations surpassed in importance than those from Western nations.

Women travelers represent a solid and growing percentage of travelers. Observation of hotel advertisements shows that hotel marketers realize the importance of this segment.

A study of gender-based lodging preferences showed that "there were several significant differences between male and female business travelers in their hotel selection and use criteria."[12] For instance, women considered security, room service, and low price to be more important, whereas men were more concerned about the availability of suite rooms with separate bed and office spaces.

Marketing planners need to stay abreast of such preferences, relay them to other departments within the hotel, and use this information in the selection of market segments.

An interesting market is couples expecting their first baby. These are people who delayed having children until their mid-thirties and want a "last hurrah" together before the infant arrives. The Bodega Bay Lodge and Spa in California offers a one-night babymoon package. Guest preferences change from champagne and a heated spa to bottled water and a gentle massage.[13]

TOURISM TARGETS Marketing plans for tourism marketers use a similar format to the hospitality industry for writing a marketing plan, but the initial definition of targets may be quite broad. The following example for the Tourism 2020 Strategy, Tourism Australia, provides an example of initially broad targets.

Global Market Strategy—Australia[14] "To achieve the Tourism 2020 Strategy, Tourism Australia will focus the majority of its global marketing resources on markets which represent the greatest potential for tourism growth to the year 2020. Tourism Australia will also target those emerging markets that have the strongest growth potential, and will continue to support rest-of-world markets.

Key markets have been categorized by the potential of growth in visitor spend by 2020. Visitor spend, tracked by the International Visitor Survey, refers to the amount of Australian dollar (AUD) spent by travelers in Australia."

The following were taken from the Global Market Strategy—Australia.

Visitor spend by the following markets has the potential to be worth over $5 billion by 2020:

- Greater China (China and Hong Kong)
- North America (the United States and Canada)
- United Kingdom
- Australia

Visitor spend by the following markets has the potential to be worth over $2.5 billion by 2020:

- New Zealand
- South Korea

- Singapore
- Malaysia

Visitor spend by the following markets has the potential to be worth over $1 billion by 2020:

- Japan
- Indonesia
- India
- Germany

After identifying major macromarkets, tourism planners/marketers tend to look for broad sub-segments such as leisure versus business and then sub-segments within these such as active-passive leisure travelers with more sub-segments such as saltwater sports, mountain bike enthusiasts, or snow skiing under active leisure travelers.

Further sub-segmentation may use postal codes such as those for Los Angeles and San Francisco in the United States. Business travelers may be identified as professional professors, medical doctors, engineers, or managers of corporations.

What are the sources of information for such segmentation? National (federal) tourism planners review travel information cards required by most nations for individuals entering their nations. Beyond that, tourism planners may build a database of studies compiled by universities, private consulting/research firms, airlines, cruise ships, and others. These organizations may also commission researchers to find out more about specific markets/market segments.

Tourism ministries, bureaus, visitor centers, and others responsible for tourism/marketing planning and implementation provide employment for many university/college graduates in business, economics, hospitality, tourism, and other related fields.

Section V: Next Year's Objectives and Quotas

Objectives

The establishment of objectives provides direction for the rest of the marketing plan. The purpose of marketing strategies and tactics is to support objectives. The marketing budget must be sufficient to ensure adequate resources to achieve objectives and to meet **timetables** that describe the time period in which expected sales results will occur.

Occasionally, there is confusion as to what constitutes an objective. Statements such as "To be the best in our industry" or "To provide excellent guest service" are accepted as objectives. That is always an error because these types of statements are slogans or mottos. They are not objectives. The following are examples of objectives:

- Quantitative (expressed in monetary terms [dollars, pesos] or unit measurements such as room nights, passenger miles, number of cars to rent, or occupancy)
- Time specific (one year, six months)
- Profit/margin specific (e.g., an average margin of 22 percent)

The process of establishing objectives is not an easy task and should not be accomplished by simply adding a random percentage to last year's objectives.

Objectives should be established after carefully considering the areas already discussed.

- Corporate goals
- Corporate resources
- Environmental factors

Timetable Specific dates to accomplish strategies and tactics.

- Competition
- Market trends
- Market potential
- Available market segments and possible target markets

To ensure profitability and remain competitive in today's marketplace, it has become necessary to establish several sub-objectives. For instance, a hotel with 1,000 rooms undoubtedly will have two broad objectives: average occupancy and average room rate. By themselves, these objectives do not serve as sufficient guides for developing marketing strategies. A set of sub-objectives is needed, as shown in Table 18–1.

Other sub-objectives may also be established by the marketing department. Again, these should support corporate goals and next year's primary objectives. They should never stand alone as objectives, unrelated to the primary function of the marketing department.

Each marketing support area needs to be guided by a set of sub-objectives. This includes areas such as advertising, promotion, public relations, marketing research, and, of course, sales.

Establishing measurable quantitative objectives for these areas is not an easy task, but increasingly, top management is requiring that such be done. Advertising and promotion are areas in which measurement of results is particularly difficult. Management would like to know what the dollar return was for advertising or how much market share or occupancy increased as a result of advertising/promotion. With few exceptions, such as direct advertising, current measurement techniques do not permit accurate measurements of this type. Consequently, objectives for advertising, such as share of mind and awareness level, are commonly used. These are not suitable substitutes.

RATING SYSTEM OBJECTIVES Some hotels are obsessed with ratings. The management of these hotels may drive corporate behavior, including marketing/sales, to help the hotel achieve another star or diamond or other symbol rating.

Because internet distribution, companies, and user customers rely on ratings, it is quite possible that many additional hotels will set objectives to attain higher ratings.

Quotas

Quotas Quantitative and time-specific accomplishment measurements established for members of a sales force.

No word creates more fear within the sales/marketing department than **quotas**. Yet, without quotas, the probability of accomplishing objectives is slim at best. To be effective, quotas must be:

- based on next year's objectives;
- individualized;
- realistic and obtainable;
- broken down to small units, such as each salesperson's quota per week; and
- understandable and measurable (e.g., quota = $10,000 sales for product line x in week 5). An example of a quota that is not understandable or measurable is "to obtain 10 percent increase of market share early in the year."

Communicating the Plan

A sophisticated and brilliantly developed plan is of no use if it is not understood, believed, or used. "A marketing plan should not be just a call to action or a benchmark by which to judge the efficiency and effectiveness of decisions. The plan should also serve as a method for communicating marketing strategy to people whose duty it is to implement or authorize the company's marketing strategies."[15] Several groups may serve as an audience for a marketing plan.

Table 18–1
Examples of Objectives Common to the Hotel Industry

Objectives	Average Occupancy	Average Room Rate
Sub-objectives	Occupancy per period of time Seasonal: prime, shoulder, trough 　Monthly 　Weekly 　Daily 　Weekend 　Midweek	Average rate per period of time and by type of room
	Types of Sleeping Rooms	**By Time**
	Suites Poolside Regular room	Seasonal Monthly Weekly Daily Weekend
	Occupancy by type of sleeping room 　Suites 　　Pool side 　　Cabaña 　　Cottage 　Regular sleeping rooms Occupancy per type of function room 　Ballroom 　Seminar room 　Executive conference room	*Note:* Yield objectives are used by many members of the hospitality industry, such as hotels, rental cars, cruise lines, airlines, and passenger rail

Objectives	Annual Sales by	Annual Sales by: Units Dollars
	Time period 　Seasonal 　Monthly 　Weekly 　Daily 　Weekend Department 　Group sales 　Incentive sales Sales territory 　Eastern United States 　Western United States Salesperson 　Joe 　Sally 　June 　Fred	

TOP MANAGEMENT This group must be convinced that the plan will accomplish the stated goals and objectives. Top management demonstrates acceptance or denial by its level of monetary support.

Marketing managers should strive for more than budgeting support. If top management buys in and demonstrates visible support, morale within the marketing department will increase, and other departments will be willing to lend support. To the contrary, the company grapevine quickly knows if marketing is only weakly supported by top management. Support from others will be weak at best if there is a perception that management is not solidly behind marketing.

BOARD OF DIRECTORS OR GROUP OF INVESTORS Occasionally, a board of directors or an investor's group may ask to be apprised of next year's marketing plan. This group generally does not seek details but instead wants to know the answers to the following questions:

- Does the plan support corporate goals?
- What are the dollars and unit objectives?
- What are the major strategies to achieve these objectives?
- What is the cost?
- When can we expect to see results?
- Does the plan support revenue management objectives?

SUBORDINATES Members of the marketing and sales departments must understand and support the marketing plan. It is important to develop a group mentality that the marketing plan for next year is a realistic and important road map. Unfortunately, far too many people in hospitality companies believe that the development of a marketing plan is a waste of time because no one will ever pay it any heed.

VENDORS It is important to transmit some aspects of the marketing plan to selected vendors. This is particularly true as strategic alliances develop. Vendors such as advertising agencies, marketing research firms, computer software providers, public relations firms, and consultants need to know and understand the marketing plan. It may be advisable to include these people in the plan's development. Supply chain management is not generally a responsibility assigned to marketing, but there are strategic alliances between hospitality companies and suppliers that affect the pricing, customer service, and other marketing functions. It is in the best interests of marketing to cooperate closely with those responsible for supply chain management. Advances in this management tool could and probably will affect what marketing will do. Such changes may need to be recognized in the marketing plan.

Supply chain management has been successfully used by manufacturers and by large retail chains for many years. The result has been cost savings and increased efficiencies of operators. Now, the restaurant industry is employing supply chain management.

Joseph O'Reilly provided information in restaurant logistics concerning restaurant supply management. O'Reilly reported that "Darden Restaurants (Olive Garden, Capital Grille, Longhorn Steakhouse) has more than 2,000 restaurants. Darden's supply chain manages more than $3 billion in capital and food product expenditures annually." "Because of its sheer size, Darden initiated a major supply chain overhaul that it expects will save $45 million annually through lower prices and less wasted food."[16] Starbucks decided to use this tool to team with other hospitality companies and purchase basic items such as sugar and milk.

The Gamboa Rainforest Resort is part of Bern Hotels and Resorts. Bern operates hotels throughout Panama. It is important that each hotel has a marketing plan that fits with the corporate plan. Rob Crandall/Alamy Stock Photo.

The need for this management tool is the result of worldwide price increases in agricultural commodities. Commodity price increases are the result of increased worldwide demand for food. Unless worldwide production increases sufficiently to meet this demand, restaurants will need to continuously seek new approaches to acquiring foodstuffs in a cost-effective and efficient manner.

Some restaurants (individual and chain) have decided to buy directly from producers. However, farmers are often not prepared to harvest, package, and prepare their crops for direct use by restaurants. The future marketplace for agricultural products could look quite different from the existing market in which producers view their crops as commodities, not table-ready products.[17]

OTHER DEPARTMENTS Other departments, such as revenue management, housekeeping, front desk, customer service, and maintenance, will be affected by next year's plan. They have a right to know key elements of the plan.

It is common for marketing managers to be asked to outline the marketing plan briefly and answer questions in a monthly managers' meeting. If a forum such as this does not exist, marketing managers should initiate a review of next year's marketing plan with other department heads after obtaining clearance from the general manager or president.

Section VI: Action Plans: Strategies and Tactics

Marketing strategies are designed as the vehicle to achieve marketing objectives. In turn, marketing tactics are tools that support strategies. Far too often, strategies and tactics have little relationship to objectives. This is always an error and is commonly the result of the following:

- Desire to maintain status quo.

- Management that wants to go with last year's tactics and do not want to risk their positions through new strategies and tactics.

- Failure to engage in marketing planning or to view the processes as serious and meaningful to decision making.

- Undue heavy influence of outside vendors, such as advertising agencies, which do not wish to change direction or try new media such as digital marketing.

- Failure to understand the relationship between objectives, strategies, and tactics.

- Myopic thinking that things are going well and one does not fix something that is not broken. Unfortunately, in the fast-paced, competitive hospitality industry, by the time the product is demonstrably broken, it is beyond repair.

It is important for cooperation between businesses that serve tourists, so they can co-promote each other's business. This Segway tour depends on part on recommendations from hotel staff. Kzenon/123RF.

Marketing strategies and tactics use advertising and promotion, sales and distribution, and pricing and product. Each must be custom designed to meet the specific needs of a company. It is unwise to follow ratios or industry averages concerning expenditures for advertising, new product development, or other strategy areas.

Strategies and tactics must always be custom made to fit the needs and culture of a company and to allow it to meet or exceed objectives. A study of marketing strategies and tactics used by restaurants was conducted. It was found that many restaurants use weak strategies, including following the leader, rather than developing individualized, unique strategies and tactics. The authors concluded that restaurants may be able to do well for a number of years, but over time their lack of strategy led to lower profits and even failure.[18]

Sales Strategies

The sales force must develop and use sales strategies to support objectives. Examples of sales strategies are as follows:

- Prevent erosion of key accounts.
- Grow key accounts.
- Grow selected marginal accounts.
- Eliminate selected marginal accounts.
- Retain selected marginal accounts but provide lower-cost sales support.
- Obtain new business from selected prospects.

A description of sales strategies should start with these six general strategies and indicate how the sales department is going to implement each one. The general strategy is supported by specific sales tactics, such as the following:

OUTSIDE THE COMPANY (EXAMPLES)

- Sales blitz of all or targeted accounts and projects
- Telephone, direct mail, and personal sales calls to selected decision makers and decision influencers
- Trade booths at selected travel shows
- Sales calls and working with travel intermediaries: tour wholesalers, travel agencies, incentive bonuses, and international sales reps
- Luncheon for key customers, prospects, or decision influencers
- Travel missions and other tactics

INSIDE THE COMPANY (EXAMPLES)

- Training of sales staff
- Involvement and support of nonsales personnel
- Motivational and control programs
- Involvement and support of management

Distribution Strategies

The selection of appropriate channels of distribution is basic to the development of successful sales strategies. Hospitality companies must be ever alert to changing distribution channels and the need for change.

Internet reservation systems, online travel agencies (OTAs), and the reduced number of traditional travel agents are important changes in the distribution system. It is critical for a marketing plan to identify each of the major distribution channels that is expected to produce sales and to forecast by week, month, and quarter the expected volume of sales each will provide.

Distribution systems do not provide equal sales volumes and, just as important, they do not provide equal profit margins. Hospitality managers will increasingly be tempted to accept ever greater sales volumes from independent companies such as Expedia, Travelocity, Priceline.com, and Hotels.com. This will almost assuredly erode profit margins.

In the absence of establishing sales and profit goals and sales limits for some distribution channels, hospitality managers may one day awaken to see a particular channel or company dominating their sales volume. Undoubtedly, other channels exist and should be added to a marketing plan if they are important to a company. (See Chapter 12 for a discussion on distribution channels.) Marketing and sales managers should be willing to sample and use new channels.

Advertising and Promotion Strategies

Advertising and promotion strategies should be established by people within the company responsible for these strategies, such as the director of advertising, the sales manager, or the marketing manager. It is critical for this person to work with supporting groups, such as an advertising agency, sales promotion firm, specialty advertising agencies, and consultants directly involved in the establishment and performance of advertising and promotion strategies.

It is inadvisable to give outside firms the sole authority for deriving and implementing these strategies. History has shown that when this occurs, the supporting group, such as an advertising agency, may produce brilliant copy and illustrations placed in well-respected media, only to find that these fail to meet objectives. The reason is that outside groups may not view objectives the same way as the client. Many advertising agencies have won distinguished honors for ads that did little or nothing to increase sales or market share for the client. Outside professionals correctly view their client as the company or the company's management, not the end consumer. Unfortunately, this view leads to pleasing the managers who hired them rather than achieving corporate or marketing objectives. Theoretically, corporate and marketing objectives and those of the manager should be synchronized. In fact, often a wide gap exists between the two. In some cases, outside professionals disdain client corporate or marketing objectives and view these as a detriment or obstacle to the creative process. The ideal is for corporate managers responsible for advertising/promotion to work as a team with selected outside professionals to derive strategies and tactics that satisfy objectives in a timely and cost-effective manner.

When this is accomplished, the team will develop an advertising/promotion mix of vehicles that includes tactics selected to achieve objectives, not simply to provide commissions, make life easy for the professionals, or produce a bland program that probably won't be criticized by management but may accomplish little.

Those who create advertising/promotion strategies have the following responsibilities:

- Select a blend or mix of media that may include commissionable mass media, direct mail, trade shows, billboards, specialty advertising, and social media (Facebook and others).
- Digital and social marketing must be considered as alternative media.
- Select or approve the message. This includes graphics, color, size, copy, and other format decisions.
- Design a media schedule showing when each medium, including noncommissionable media, will be used.
- Design a schedule of events, such as public relations events and familiarization (FAM) trips for travel writers.
- Carefully transmit this information to management.
- Supervise the development and implementation of advertising/promotion programs, with particular care given to timetables and budget constraints.
- Assume responsibility for the outcome. Increasingly, top management is requiring those in charge of advertising/promotion to prove effectiveness and to stand behind results.

Unfortunately, despite decades of marketing teaching and thousands of articles on the subject, many managers in the hospitality industry continue to equate marketing with advertising. They fail to realize that advertising is simply one part of marketing. The authors of the restaurant strategy referred to earlier concluded,

"Many firms [restaurants] have attempted to hold market share by increasing advertising expenditures. Advertising alone will not ensure success."[19]

Another area of the advertising/promotion mix that needs consideration in a marketing plan is cooperative advertising/promotion. This requires teamwork and a place in the budget. For example, in the case of a resort, cooperative opportunities exist between the following entities:

- Resort and resort community (e.g., all resorts, restaurants, and attractions in Provincetown, Cape Cod, Massachusetts)
- Resort and tourism promotion groups (e.g., state tourism department or local Chamber of Commerce)
- Resort and suppliers (e.g., Citrus Board or Columbia Coffee)
- Resort and transportation companies (e.g., airlines, motor coach, cruise lines)
- Resort and sister hotels or resorts

An example of cooperative advertising/promotion opportunities is offered by hotels in Mexico. After an examination of the brochures of 10 hotel chains in Mexico, it was found that most made minimal or no reference to other Mexican hotels operated by the chain. Club Med made good use of this marketing tool. Club Med had not only a Mexican brochure for all its properties but also a special supplemental brochure for its properties near prestigious archaeological sites.[20]

Digital Marketing Strategies

In addition to paid use of social media sites, a plan should be developed for the non-paid use of social media. One way of gaining good online reviews is to train the employees to be proactive. When a guest says how much they enjoyed their stay at the hotel, the employee should ask the guest to post a review on a popular Web site for travelers such as TripAdvisor. Another tactic is to encourage guests to share photos of their stay. One resort in Florida created a contest to post pictures that addressed this question, "How do you unwind in paradise?" The entries were featured on the hotel's Web site. The promotion resulted in additional 400 Instagram followers, 3,600 unique Web site visits, and a 44 percent increase in bookings. A study by the Content Marketing Institute found 70 percent of consumers who post content online claim this makes them feel closer to the company, which is an additional benefit of encouraging this type of engagement.[21]

Other digital marketing strategies include a blog that allows the hotel to discuss activities at the hotel. Blogs are especially effective at resorts as they are a great way to make the guest aware of the amenities the resort offers. For travel organizations that create experiences, such as cooking classes, sailing lessons, tours, and other activities, blogs are a great way to highlight these events. In Chapter 16, we discussed a number of ways to use digital marketing, which can be incorporated into the marketing plan.

Reputation management should be part incorporated into the digital section of a marketing plan. This section should include who is responsible for monitoring user generated content on social media. Most larger companies have a dashboard provided through an online service that will provide a site where one call find the comments made by customers on brand.com, OTAs, Meta sites, and other online sources. A study by CMB of 2,000 leisure customers found that during the information search process, online reviews were both the most used source of information and the most influential information.[22] Another study found that only 12 percent of travelers would include hotels with a rating under 3 in their search, while 32 percent search for a rating of 4 or higher. Researchers at Cornell and Penn State also found that travelers rarely searched for a hotel with a rating below 3 and that the rating was more important than price.[23] Additionally, these researchers found that the number of reviews was also important. A higher number of reviews gave credibility to the rating. The marketing plan should not only include who is responsible for monitoring UGC, but also set goals for overall ratings and the number of ratings on each major site.

Pricing Strategies

Pricing remains a function of marketing. Marketing managers must maintain control of this area; they must interface with revenue management. Marketing and sales departments will continuously be in conflict with pricing if pricing strategies are not understood and considered in marketing and sales plans. Today pricing is more critical than ever before due largely to the role of OTAs.

For instance, sales has responsibility for working with intermediaries such as tour wholesalers and with key customers. Both these customers will ask for price discounts. Commitments for large blocks of rooms, airline seats, autos, or ship berths will inevitably create problems with revenue or yield-management departments. Marketing and sales plans cannot be effective if they are developed without sales forecasts and revenue projections by major market segments. If forecasts and revenue projections are made without the input of the revenue management department, conflict will occur.

Review again the objectives and sub-objectives presented in Table 18–1. These call for average room rate objectives for each product class by season of the year. Using the concepts and practices of revenue management, pricing objectives may be considerably enhanced to include weekly objectives and objectives by subsegments. Marriott Hotels uses a strategy known as rational pricing. This calls for *fencing*, placing restrictions on customer segments selected due to their perceived level of price elasticity. Fencing restrictions will immediately affect marketing and sales plans. Marketing managers are also advised to work with the reservations department during the planning process. Reservations often have considerable latitude to adjust prices and may account for a significant percentage of sales.

Pricing objectives and strategies affect every facet of marketing and sales. The selection of appropriate target markets and the emphasis to be given to each again depend on pricing.

Marketing and sales managers who view themselves at war with pricing managers are probably doomed to eventual failure. The top managers in most hospitality companies realize that a 10 percent upward adjustment in rates can produce favorable profit results in excess of cost cutting or traditional marketing and sales strategies to increase the number of guests.

Pricing strategies are of great importance to chain restaurants and need to be reviewed constantly. As an example, food-service quality is the predominant influence on guest ratings for family, steakhouse, and casual dining restaurants. Family price appeal enhances a guest's rating for a family restaurant chain but not necessarily for a steakhouse or casual dining.[24]

A marketer who has gained experience in a family restaurant chain might make erroneous pricing decisions when hired by a steakhouse or casual dining chain. Despite the fact that restaurant chains may seem alike, different pricing strategies may need to be developed for each.

Product Strategies

Marketing has an important role to play in the improvement of existing products and the development of new ones. In some hospitality firms, marketing is expected to be heavily involved in the process; in others, marketing assumes only an advisory role; and sadly, in others, marketing is excluded from the process.

Marketing professionals can exert considerable input and strategic direction when planning basic product changes as dramatic as those occurring within the resort industry. Marketing can also help greatly to enhance revenue from product changes as additions to the current product line. Hundreds or thousands of new product opportunities exist in most hospitality companies. The Alexis Park Resort in Las Vegas invented "Cocktail Cruises," which is essentially a motorized cart driven by an employee who offers poolside guests drinks so they can stay by the pool.[25] The Opryland Hotel in Nashville uses a similar concept to sell hotel logo souvenir merchandise. "Whenever there is more to be sold than your customers are buying, profit potential is not being realized. Revenue boosting opportunities abound for the creative operator who is willing to offer facilities, services, and events that will attract customers and to train customer-contact employees to stimulate add-on sales and sales upgrades."[26]

The process of making product line changes requires the input and advice of many individuals and departments. Marketing may identify a need, such as the "neighborhood bakery" concept, for use in fast-food chains, but this product concept directly affects production, finance, and human resources. When McDonald's, Burger King, and Wendy's experimented with fresh biscuits or croissants, they discovered that these products prepared from scratch or frozen dough required additional working space, equipment, and employee training.[27]

Section VII: Resources Needed to Support Strategies and Meet Objectives

Marketing plans must be written with available resources, or those likely to become available, in mind. A common error in writing a marketing plan is to develop strategies that are probably highly workable but for which there is insufficient support. Another error is to assume that top management will not provide additional support regardless of the brilliance of the plan. Marketing plans can and must be sold to top management. A balance between mythical over-the-top plans and total acquiescence to perceived inflexibility of management is needed in any solid marketing plan.

Personnel

Generally, the most costly and difficult resource needed to ensure success with marketing/sales strategies is personnel. The addition of personnel is sometimes viewed as unnecessary, impractical, or unwise, given current budgetary restrictions.

Obviously, sometimes the addition of salespeople, secretaries, analysts, and others is absolutely essential. Be prepared to justify this request, and remember that many people, particularly salespeople, are not instantly productive. Training and recruiting costs must be considered with this resource request, as well as the time required by members of management to interview and work with these people.

The influence of the corporate culture cannot be overlooked in this process. Imagine a company such as the Ritz-Carlton with the philosophy that it not only treats its customers as ladies and gentlemen but also treats its employees as ladies and gentlemen. Fulfillment of this pledge with appropriate new personnel is demanding and may be time consuming.[28]

A marketing plan may need to specify the type of person required for a position if it is not described elsewhere, such as in company policies and procedures. Some hospitality companies operate under the philosophy that "we are always hiring excellent people." Marketing managers must plan personnel needs ahead for seasonal cost differences, such as a month with heavy trade show expenses or several weeks when brochures will be mailed to key customers and prospects. Budgets should reflect careful planning of resource use, such as temporary help on a week-by-week basis. A carefully constructed budget is simply a reflection of a well-thought-out marketing plan.

Other Monetary Support

Monetary support not accounted for by salary, wages, and benefits must be considered carefully and included. This includes travel expenses; motivational costs, such as a trip to Las Vegas; and other monetary needs.

Research, Consulting, and Training

Hospitality companies often have need for outside professionals to assist with marketing research, such as focus groups; training, such as sales training; or consulting to provide objective outside appraisals, advice, and revenue management.

Miscellaneous Costs

This area should not be a source of slush funds. Many expenses, such as subscriptions to professional books and journals, may be included here.

Budgets

In larger organizations, corporate policies and procedures may direct marketing managers as to categories of expenses and items that may be included. Marketing managers of smaller companies may need to develop their own list and to use it each year as a guide to ensure that all essential resources are included.

Budgets should be established to reflect projected costs weekly, monthly, quarterly, and annually. This is not simply to make life easier for the finance/account area personnel next year.

Section VIII: Marketing Control

This discussion of marketing control presupposes that the sales plan is part of the marketing plan. This is not always the case; some hospitality organizations separate the two functions.

The essentials for writing a sales plan follow the same general procedure as those described for a marketing plan. A sales plan does not need all the aspects of a marketing plan, such as advertising or marketing research, because these may be furnished by support departments. A sales plan should pay particular attention to the sales force and its objectives and to strategies to ensure that sales quotas are met and possibly exceeded.

Sales Objectives

Sales objectives must be established for each sales area, division, region, salesperson, and time period. The broad sales objectives discussed previously serve as the basis for establishing individual objectives. The sum of all sales objectives or quotas for members of the sales force must equal or exceed annual objectives.

One method of establishing annual sales objectives for the company is to begin with sales planning among members of the sales force. Each member should be expected to develop a list of all sales accounts currently served by that person, plus prospects for the coming year. From this, an estimate of potential sales by account and prospect will provide a means of forecasting next year's sales.

Management, beginning with the sales manager and ending with the general manager or other member of top management, then has the responsibility for critically examining these forecasts. Management seldom accepts the forecasts of the sales force without amending them, usually upward. This is known as bottom-up, top-down planning.

Management amends sales force forecasts for the following reasons:

- Sales force members often wish to protect themselves and give lower sales estimates than are actually possible.

- The company has certain sales objectives that it expects based on the needs of the company.

- Management may have access to marketing research information not available to the sales force.

- Management may have a history of dealing with the sales force and realize that forecasts are generally too high or too low by x percent.

- Management may be willing to provide the marketing/sales department with additional resources that are unknown to members of the sales force.

Table 18–2 shows a typical hotel sales forecast for a salesperson. Sales managers have the responsibility to work closely with their salespeople to ensure that sales forecasts are accurate. They must then provide a composite sales forecast for their department and present it to management.

Sales Forecast and Quotas

Eventually, all members of the sales force must be presented with sales quotas. Annual sales quotas should then be broken down into monthly and quarterly sales. Many sales managers and experienced salespeople break monthly quotas into weekly figures.

Table 18–2
Example of a Sales Forecast for a Hotel Salesperson

Salesperson: Janet Chin	SALES CURRENT YEAR			SALES PROJECTED NEXT YEAR		
	Room Nights	*Revenue*	*Avg. Rate*	*Room Nights*	*Revenue*	*Avg. Rate*
Major commercial accounts (key accounts)						
1.						
2.						
3.						
4.						
Other commercial accounts						
1.						
2.						
3.						
4.						
Major intermediary accounts						
1.						
2.						
3.						
4.						
Other intermediary accounts						
1.						
2.						
3.						
4.						
Airline accounts						
1.						
2.						
3.						
4.						
Other accounts						
1.						
2.						
3.						
4.						
Prospects for next year						
1.						
2.						
3.						
4.						
Total accounts/prospects	Total current year			Totals projected next year		

Sales managers have the responsibility for working with their salespeople to ensure that quotas are met or surpassed. It is important to evaluate sales results continually and develop corrective tactics if it appears that actual sales will not meet forecasts or quotas. Sales managers and salespeople who wait several months before evaluating actual sales against forecasts usually find it is too late to take corrective action.

Expenditures Against Budget

It is also important for marketing/sales managers to monitor actual expenditures continually against budgeted figures. This, too, must be done on a regular basis. As described in the Red Robin case, this chain now establishes budgets each quarter.

Periodic Evaluation of All Marketing Objectives

The role of marketing and sales managers is sometimes compared to that of an adult babysitter. A frequent comment made by people in these positions is that they spend a great deal of time simply making sure that people under their direction perform tasks in a timely fashion. There is much truth in this comment because a critical role of marketing/sales managers is to ensure that all objectives are met or exceeded on time.

Managers responsible for functions such as advertising, promotions, and marketing research also have a responsibility to ensure that all tasks are performed on time. If a summer brochure is printed three weeks after the due date, chances are very good that the sales force may miss the opportunity to send or deliver this advertising medium to prospects and key accounts during the time that they make travel decisions. In turn, the sales force may fail to make summer sales quotas. All marketing/sales tasks are important. If this is not true, the task and the position should be eliminated.

MARKETING ACTIVITY TIMETABLE One method commonly used by marketing/sales managers to ensure that tasks are completed on time is the use of a marketing activity timetable. This simple device lists major activities, the dates they must be completed, the person responsible, and a space for checking whether the task has been accomplished.

Readjustments to Marketing Plan

Human beings are incapable of devising a perfect marketing plan. Market conditions change, disasters occur, and many other reasons create a need to refine marketing plans. Generally, refinements should be made in the area of tactics, budgets, and timing of events rather than in major objectives or strategies. Changes in tactics normally do not require top management approval and are viewed as the normal responsibility of marketing/sales managers.

■■■ Presenting the Plan and Preparing for the Future

Section IX: Presenting and Selling the Plan

Changes in major objectives such as annual sales volume and in major strategies always require approval by top management. Marketing/sales managers are advised to refrain from considering changes in major objectives and strategies unless absolutely necessary. Top management will almost certainly view the necessity for change as a reflection of poor management by marketing/sales managers unless the cause was a disaster, such as a major fire in a hotel.

Never assume that a marketing plan is so logical that it will sell itself. A marketing plan must be sold to many people, including the following:

- **Members of marketing/sales department.** Many people within the marketing/sales areas do not believe in planning. They view the process of developing, writing, defending, and using a written plan to be a waste of time. Comments are frequently heard such as, "If management would just let us do our job and quit all this planning, the company would do better." This common sentiment may exist due to poor experience with prior planning, fear of the process, or genuine ignorance about the benefits. Marketing/sales managers need the support of subordinates in the planning process. It is best to sell the benefits of the process rather than to force acquiescence.

- **Vendors/ad agencies and others.** Outside organizations, such as advertising and marketing research agencies, need to be involved in the planning process. They must be made aware that their participation in the marketing planning process is an expected part of their responsibilities as team members.
- **Top management.** Top management must approve the annual marketing plan. It is seldom sufficient to write a lengthy plan, send it through company mail or e-mail to top management, and expect an enthusiastic endorsement. Marketing/sales managers must sell the plan to members of management through meetings, such as friendly luncheons and formalized presentations. Key members of the staff may be expected to participate in formal presentations. These appearances should always be treated with the same careful planning and professionalism that would be expected if a sales presentation were made to a key prospect for $2 million worth of business. Use professional presentation materials when appropriate, such as PowerPoint presentations, overheads, and bound copies of the annual plan. Prepare selected charts, graphs, and tables that are easy to understand and quickly reinforce key points.

Section X: Preparing for the Future

The process of marketing planning is a continuum. The task is never ending. Marketing/sales managers must always be planning. In reality, the development of next year's marketing plan begins the day this year's plan is approved.

Data Collection and Analysis

Marketing plan development depends on the availability of reliable information. This task can always be improved. The process of data collection and analysis from internal and external sources continues each day. Marketing/sales managers must always be alert for methods to improve the process.

Marketing Planning as a Tool for Growth

A good marketing plan will assist your company and department to prosper and grow. What is not so obvious to many is that a good plan will also enable people to prosper and grow. This occurs in the following several ways:

- The participatory planning process allows people to understand the management process.
- People learn to become team players during the process.
- People learn to establish objectives and set timetables to ensure they are met.
- The process of establishing realistic strategies and tactics to meet objectives is learned.
- People who approach the planning process with a receptive mind and use the marketing plan usually find it enhances their professional career.

Many hospitality companies have developed a planning culture in which there is a respect for planning as a positive process. This is a reflection of a corporate culture and top management support. Changes in top management sometimes mean that support for marketing planning will decrease or in some instances planning will be discouraged. A strong corporate culture that emphasizes and encourages planning within all levels of the company will be rewarded. Sometimes management becomes discouraged by the process, particularly when market conditions worsen as a new competitor threatens market share. It is at times like this that a corporate culture of planning provides stability and assurance of purpose and direction.

An example of the need for planning in poor economic times, rather than resorting to reactive "just-do-something" tactics, is offered by the California Country Club (CCC) of Los Angeles. This club, like many others in southern California, had a waiting list of potential members, but suddenly the waiting list changed to members wanting to leave the club.

Instead of panicking and grasping for an immediate marketing cure-all, the management of CCC pursued a process of market planning, starting with an analysis of the market and competitors. The planning process allowed CCC to recognize marketing opportunities, such as pricing strategies, including the elimination of golf-only fees. The need for a customer-directed policy of "just say yes" was also discovered and implemented. These and other changes represented a complete turnover from previous policies and procedures, thus allowing the club to increase market share and revenue.[29]

A study of the process used by hotels to develop marketing plans has shown that "the most important features in the development of a marketing plan appear to be management participation and commitment at all levels, sufficient time for development, specific training in developing a marketing plan, and tying incentives to the achievements of goals and objectives."[30]

In good times or bad, consistency in marketing planning pays good dividends for any hospitality company and its employees.[31]

CHAPTER REVIEW

I. **The Purpose of a Marketing Plan.** It serves as a road map for all marketing activities of the firm for the next year, ensures that marketing activities are in agreement with the corporate strategic plan, forces marketing managers to review and think objectively through all steps in the marketing process, and assists in the budgeting process to match resources with marketing objectives.

II. **Preparing a Marketing Plan.**
   A. **Section I: Executive summary.** Write it for top executives. Limit the number of pages to between two and four. Use short sentences and paragraph. Organize the summary as follows: Describe next year's objectives in quantitative terms; briefly describe marketing strategies to meet goals and objectives; identify the dollar costs necessary as well as key resources needed.
   B. **Section II: Corporate connection**
      1. **Relationship to other plans.** The marketing plan must support the firm's strategic plan.
      2. **Marketing-related plans.** When the organizational design of a company fails to place major marketing activities under the marketing umbrella, the task of writing and implementing a marketing plan is made more complex. Under these conditions, it behooves the marketing manager to invite the managers of other marketing-related areas to participate in the marketing plan development process. This action should then be reciprocated.
      3. **Corporate direction.** Begin the plan by reassuring management that the plan was guided by the firm's mission statement, philosophy, and goals.
   C. **Section III: Environmental analysis and forecasting**
      1. **Positioning statement.** It should explain how the enterprise intends to differentiate itself in the marketplace.
      2. **Major environmental factors.** Hospitality organizations need to anticipate the influence of social, political, and economic factors on their business as well as terrorism activities.
      3. **Economic drivers of growth** can rapidly affect change.
      4. **Competitive analysis** positions the primary strengths, weaknesses, objectives, and strategies relative to competitors. It's best to involve the sales force.
      5. **Market trends** are a reflection of environmental competitive variables including visitor trends, competitive trends, and related industry trends.
      6. **Market potential.** Market potential should be viewed as the total available demand for a firm's product within a particular geographic market at a given price. It is important not to mix different products into an estimate of market potential. Estimates of market potential normally begin by examining the market for all hotels but should then shift to specific markets for your hotel and directly competitive properties, often referred to as a competitive set.
      7. **Marketing research** can be divided into macro-market and micromarket information.
   D. **Section IV: Segmentation and targeting**
      1. **Segmentation analysis.** The selection of segments is the result of (1) understanding what the company is and what it wishes to be and (2) studying available segments and determining if they fit the capabilities and desires of the company to obtain and secure them.
      2. **Market-segment-profitability analysis (MSPA).** Information that identifies each of a company's existing customer segments by revenue, cost, and profitability is extremely valuable.
      3. **Targeting.** The most important area of the marketing plan. Targeting begins by defining the guest mix which must support the positioning strategy and support revenue management.

E. **Section V: Next year's objectives and quotas**
1. **Objectives** provide the direction for the plan. They should be measurable and quantitative. Strategies and tactics support objectives. Budget ensures resources to achieve objectives and meet timetables. Each marketing support area needs to be guided by a set of sub-objectives.
2. **Quotas** are quantitative and time specific accomplishment measurements.
3. **Communicating the plan.** The plan should serve as a method for communicating marketing strategy to people whose duty it is to implement or authorize the company's marketing strategies.

F. **Section VI: Action plans: Strategies and tactics.** Marketing strategies are designed as the vehicle to achieve marketing objectives. In turn, marketing tactics are tools that support strategies.
1. **Sales strategies** include preventing erosion of key accounts, growing key accounts, growing select marginal accounts, eliminating selected marginal accounts, retaining selected marginal accounts but providing lower-cost sales support, and obtaining new business.
2. **Distribution strategies.** It is critical for a marketing plan to identify each of the major distribution channels that is expected to produce sales and to forecast by week, month, and quarter the expected volume of sales each will provide.
3. **Advertising and promotion strategies.** Advertising and promotion strategies should be established by people within the company responsible for these strategies, such as the director of advertising, the sales manager, or the marketing manager. It is critical for this person to work with supporting groups, such as an advertising agency, sales promotion firm, specialty advertising agencies, and consultants directly involved in the establishment and performance of advertising and promotion strategies.
4. **Digital marketing strategies.** In addition to paid use of social media sites, a plan should be developed for the non-paid use of social media. Other strategies include use of blogs, and reputation management.
   a. **Pricing strategies.** Marketing managers must maintain control of this area; they must interface with revenue management.
   b. **Product strategies.** Marketing professionals can exert considerable input and strategic direction when planning basic product changes.

G. **Section VII: Resources needed to support strategies and Meet Objectives.** Marketing plans must be written with available resources, or those likely to become available, in mind.
1. **Personnel.** The most costly resource. Training and recruiting costs must be considered with this resource request, as well as the time required by members of management to interview and work with these people.
2. **Other monetary support** includes travel expenses and motivational costs.
3. **Research, consulting, and training** such as focus groups; training, such as sales training; or consulting to provide objective outside appraisals, advice, and revenue management.
4. **Miscellaneous costs** such as subscriptions to professional books and journals.
5. **Budgets** should be established to reflect projected costs weekly, monthly, quarterly, and annually.

H. **Section VIII: Marketing control**
1. **Sales objectives** must be established for each sales area, division, region, salesperson, and time period.
2. **Sales forecasts and quotas.** Annual sales quotas should be broken down into monthly and quarterly sales.
3. **Expenditures against budget** must be done on a regular basis.
4. **Periodic evaluation of all marketing objectives.** A critical role of marketing/sales managers is to ensure that all objectives are met or exceeded on time. One method is the use of a marketing activity timetable.
5. **Readjustments to marketing plan.** Generally, refinements should be made in the area of tactics, budgets, and timing of events rather than in major objectives or strategies.

III. **Presenting the Plan and Preparing for the Future.**
A. **Presenting and selling the plan.** A marketing plan must be sold to: members of marketing/sales department, vendors/ad agencies and others, and top management.
B. **Preparing for the future.** The development of next year's plan begins the day this year's plan is approved.
1. **Data collection and analysis.** Be alert for methods to improve the process.
2. **Marketing planning as a tool for growth.** A good plan assists the company, your department, and people to prosper and grow.

IN-CLASS GROUP EXERCISES

*Exercises with an asterisk next to them are suitable for individual homework or online assignments. Students, always provide an explanation for your answer.

1. *What is the purpose of a marketing plan? What happens if you do not do an annual marketing plan?
2. *What is the relevancy of environmental factors to an annual marketing plan?
3. *What is the determination of market potential and why is it so important?
4. Should marketing objectives be described in quantitative terms? Why or why not?
5. *What is the relationship, if any, between marketing strategies and marketing objectives?

6. *Is marketing control really necessary in a marketing plan, or is it an optional managerial exercise?
7. *Choose a hospitality or tourism organization in your area. On the internet find information that would be useful to you if you were developing a marketing plan for the organization. Explain how you would use this information.

■■■ EXPERIENTIAL EXERCISE

Do the following:
1. Meet with a director of sales of a hotel, a general manager of a hotel, or the director of a tourism marketing organization and ask him or her to go over the organization's marketing plan with you. Have him or her explain the process he or she uses to develop a marketing plan.

■■■ REFERENCES

1. Condensed with permission from Peter Cass, "Luxury Lifestyle Marketing: New Frontier," *Hospitality Business Review*, 2, no. 3 (Fall 1999): 27–30.
2. Perry J. S. Hobson, Henry C. S. Vincent, and Kye-Sung Chon, "Vietnam's Tourism Industry: Can It Be Kept Afloat?" *Cornell Hotel and Restaurant Administration Quarterly*, 35, no. 5 (1994): 42–49.
3. 2008 Mumbai Attacks, Wikipedia, http://en.wikipedia.org/wicki/2008_Mumbai_attacks.
4. John D. Kasarda and Greg Lindsay, *Aerotropolis: The Way We'll Live Next*, 2011, ISBN 978–03741001193.
5. Richard Gibson, "Flight Caterers Widen Horizons Beyond Airlines," *Wall Street Journal* (January 16, 1995): B1, B8.
6. David O. Williams, "Ski Execs Target Asian Markets," *Rocky Mountain News* (January 4, 2008): 5.
7. Lodging Market Potential Index, August 13, 2012, Global Edge.msu.edu and A. J. Singh, Raymond S. Schmidgall, and Tunga Kiyak, The Lodging Market Potential Index (L-MPI©) Ranking of Major Lodging Markets in the United States, Vol 7, No. 1, 2013.
8. Josiah Mackenzie, Michael Nurbatlian's Photo Contest Gained 2000+ New Faces in Two Weeks for Indigo Pearl Resort, Hotel Marketing Strategies—Technology for Better Guest Experiences, July 17, 2011, www.hotelmarketingstrategies.com.
9. Carl K. Link, "Developing a Marketing Plan: Lessons from the Inn at Plum Creek," *Cornell Hotel and Restaurant Administration Quarterly*, 34, no. 5 (1993): 35.
10. L. K. Prevette and Joseph Giudice, "Anatomy of a Turnaround: The Los Angeles Biltmore," *Cornell Hotel and Restaurant Administration Quarterly*, 30, no. 3 (1989): 32.
11. Karady Islam and Woo Gon Kim, "Comparing Market Segment Profitability Analysis with Department Profitability Analysis and Hotel Marketing-Decision Tools," *Cornell Hotel & Restaurant Administration Quarterly*, 47, no. 2 (2006): 155–173.
12. Ron Leiber, "A New Parenting Ritual: The Last Hurrah," *Wall Street Journal* (July 7, 2004): D1.
13. Ibid.
14. From Global Market Strategy Tourism Australia, 2013–2015, Retrieved from www.tourism.australia.com/markets/market-strategy.aspx. Copyright ©2013 by Tourism Australia. Reprinted by permission.
15. Francis Buttle, "The Marketing Strategy Worksheet: A Practical Tool," *Cornell Hotel and Restaurant Administration Quarterly*, 33, no. 3 (1992): 57.
16. Joseph O'Reilly, Restaurant Logistics: Serving Up the Perfect Meal, www.inboundlogistics.com, August 2012.
17. Julie Jargon, "Eateries' New Way to Shop," *Wall Street Journal*, Corporate News (April 1, 2011): B5.
18. Joseph J. West and Michael D. Olsen, "Grand Strategy: Making Your Restaurant a Winner," *Cornell Hotel and Restaurant Administration Quarterly*, 31, no. 2 (1990): 77.
19. Ibid.
20. Hana Ayala, "Mexican Resorts: A Blueprint with an Expiration Date," *Cornell Hotel and Restaurant Administration Quarterly*, 34, no. 3 (1993): 40.
21. Max Starkov and Mariana Mechoso Safer (2015), "The Smart Hotelier's Action Plan to Digital Content Marketing," https://www.hsmai.org/details.cfm?id=http://cdn.hsyndicate.com/econnect/4069939.html (accessed December 19, 2018).
22. Judy Melanson, "The New Hotel Booking Path to Purchase: The Mobile, Social, and Online Journey August," CMB, 2014.
23. Samantha Worgull, "How Guests Choose Hotels During Online Booking," June 2015, http://www.hotelnewsnow.com/Articles/26532/How-guests-choose-hotels-during-online-booking (accessed December 4, 2018).
24. Michael S. Morgan, "Benefit Dimensions of a Midscale Restaurant Chain," *Cornell Hotel and Restaurant Administration Quarterly*, 34, no. 2 (1993): 44–45.
25. Carl K. Link, "Internal Merchandising: Creating Revenue Opportunities," *Cornell Hotel and Restaurant Administration Quarterly*, 30, no. 3 (1989): 56.

26. Ibid., p. 57.
27. Regina Robichald and Mahmood A. Khan, "Responding to Market Changes: The Fast Food Experience," *Cornell Hotel and Restaurant Administration Quarterly*, 29, no. 3 (1988): 47.
28. William E. Kent, "Putting Up the Ritz: Using Culture to Open a Hotel," *Cornell Hotel and Restaurant Administration Quarterly*, 31, no. 3 (1990): 16–24.
29. Jeffrey L. Pellissier, "Remarketing: One Club's Response to a Changing Market," *Cornell Hotel and Restaurant Administration Quarterly*, 34, no. 4 (1993): 53–58.
30. S. Dev Chekitan, "Marketing Practices at Hotel Chains," *Cornell Hotel and Restaurant Administration Quarterly*, 31, no. 3 (1990): 54–63.
31. For more on developing a marketing plan, see James C. Makens, *The Marketing Plan Workbook* (Upper Saddle River, NJ: Prentice-Hall, 1985); *Hotel Sales and Marketing Plan Workbook* (Winston-Salem, NC: Marion-Clarence, 1990).

APPENDIX A: The Five-Gap Model of Service Quality

A widely used model of service quality is known as the five-gap model (Figure A–1). This model defines service quality as meeting customer expectations. In the words of those who developed the model, "Knowing what customers expect is the first and possibly the most critical step in delivering service quality. Stated simply, providing service that customers perceive as excellent requires that a firm knows what customers expect." This model is closely linked to marketing because it is customer based. The model has five gaps.

Gap 1: Consumer Expectations Versus Management Perception

Hospitality executives may fail to understand what consumers expect in a service and which features are needed to deliver high-quality service. When management does not understand what its customers want, a gap 1 exists. For example, a manager may develop a system to ensure that all guests wait no longer than 15 minutes to check in. However, if guests start getting upset after 10 minutes, this system will cause dissatisfaction. Talking to guests before developing the check-in system would enable the manager to learn that the critical time is 10 minutes, not 15 minutes. Marriott Hotels observed that guests were not using the complimentary bath crystals provided as a bathroom amenity. They discontinued the bath crystals in favor of cable television, a more important benefit to most guests than bath crystals. Originally, management believed that bath crystals would be considered a benefit. However, after observing its guests, management found that guest satisfaction could be increased by offering a different service.

Many firms conduct initial studies to find out what their market wants, but later they become internally focused and oblivious to the fact that customers' needs have changed. If customer needs change but the product does not, the marketing mix becomes less attractive to the target market, resulting in gap 1 increase. Managers should walk around their operations, talk with customers, and encourage feedback. Management can also gain information on customers from marketing information systems.

Gap 2: Management Perception Versus Service Quality Specifications

Gap 2 occurs when managers know what their customers want but are unable or unwilling to develop systems that will deliver it. Several reasons have been given for gap 2: (1) inadequate commitment to service quality, (2) lack of perception of feasibility, (3) inadequate task standardization, and (4) absence of goal setting.

Some companies look for short-term profits and are unwilling to invest in people or equipment. This almost inevitably causes service quality problems. Hotel owners who are reluctant to provide enough operating capital can be a cause of gap 2 errors. For example, the hotel owner who budgets for just enough linen to get by may discover that the linen inventory quickly drops below critical levels as

Figure A–1
Conceptual model of service quality: The gap analysis model.
Source: A. Parasuraman, Valarie Zeithaml, and Leonard L. Berry, "A Conceptual Model of Service Quality and Its Implication for Future Research," *Journal of Marketing* (Fall 1985): 44. Reprinted with permission of the American Marketing Association.

linen is stolen and destroyed. A visitor experienced this in Ft. Lauderdale, Florida. The guest returned from a walk on the beach to a freshly cleaned room, started to get ready to take a shower, and noticed there were no towels in the room. The guest called housekeeping and explained that he had to take a shower to get ready for a business appointment and there were no towels in the room. Housekeeping apologized, saying they were short on towels. In about 15 minutes, a housekeeper arrived with towels, causing the guest to arrive late for the appointment. Incidents such as this detract from a positive guest experience, create unnecessary tasks, and decrease employee morale. In this case, hotel management knew that the linen inventory was low, but the owner either did not want to invest in linen or did not have the money to supply the hotel properly.

Sometimes managers feel that improving an existing problem is not feasible. For example, most business guests want to check out after breakfast. They are usually in a hurry to get started with the day's business. Many hotel managers understand this but accept a 10- to 20-minute wait as the best they can do because they are unwilling to hire extra employees to help during the rush period. Bill Marriott Jr. felt that the problem was important enough to develop a system to solve it and invented express checkouts. Guests receive their bills the evening before. If the bills are accurate, the guests simply drop them off with their keys at the front desk. Today, most hotel chains use some type of express checkout system. Some hotels make use of technology and allow the guest to check the accuracy of bills on their television screens and check out using in-room television equipment. The express checkout system was developed by a person who viewed reducing checkout queues as a challenge rather than a problem that was an inherent part of the system. Bill Marriott eliminated this gap 2 error. He demonstrated that capital is not the only cure for a gap 2 problem. Innovative thinking can also eliminate gap 2 problems. Sometimes we need to look for unconventional solutions to the problem. Translating customer needs into service specifications is critical to service quality.

Finally, goals must be accepted by employees. Management must show its support through measurement of results, communication, and rewarding employees for superior service.

Gap 3: Service Quality Specifications Versus Service Delivery

Gap 3 is referred to as the service-performance gap. Gap 3 occurs when management understands what needs to be delivered and appropriate specifications have been developed but employees are unable or unwilling to deliver the service. Gap 3 errors occur during moments of truth, when the employee and the customer interact. Employees are expected to act cheerfully and solve the guests' problems. When they do not, guests may perceive a problem with functional quality. Often gap 3 errors occur when management assumes that the employees are delivering excellent service and do not pay attention to detail. It is important for management to inspect service delivery to let employees know it appreciates the job they are doing.

Gap 3 errors can be minimized through internal marketing programs. Management of the human resources functions (hiring, training, monitoring working conditions, and developing reward systems) is important in reducing gap 3 errors. Gap 3 errors are also the result of customer-contact employees being overworked. This can occur when a business is understaffed or an employee is required to work a second shift for an employee who called in sick. Under these conditions, employees become tired and stressed. They lose their enthusiasm for the job and become less willing to solve customer problems. This lack of customer orientation leads to gap 3 errors.

Gap 4: Service Delivery Versus External Communications

Gap 4 is created when the firm promises more in its external communications than it can deliver. Earlier in this book we mentioned the advertising campaign put on by the government of Bermuda, inviting travelers to enjoy the attractions of the island during its uncrowded low season. Visitors were disappointed when they discovered that many attractions were closed during the off season. Marketers must make sure that operations can deliver what they promise.

During the last week of ski season, skiers were surprised to find that only half the runs on one side of the mountain had been groomed. This was particularly annoying and even dangerous because the half grooming occurred on intermediate runs where less-than-expert skiers might suddenly encounter bad conditions. The runs had been perfectly groomed all seasons until that final week. Late-season arrivals undoubtedly felt that they had been slighted.

The Regent of Fiji encountered a severe problem when a military takeover occurred and discouraged tourism. A consultant, Chuck Gee, dean of the School of Travel Industry Management at the University of Hawaii, was hired to advise the hotel during this crisis. Chuck's advice was "Do nothing different. Do not reduce your staff, your lighting, your food quality, or your service." When asked why, Chuck's answer was that the Regent had positioned itself as a luxury resort and must continue to offer that level of service even if only one guest appeared. He further explained that the Regent knew there were risks when it entered this market and must now be prepared to accept them and pay the price to continue as an upscale resort.

Lack of consistency can also cause gap 4 problems. Hotel policies were discussed during a marketing seminar. After the seminar a manager from La Quinta told of a problem with a guest when the cashier refused to cash a personal check. The check was over the limit that La Quinta had set for personal checks. However, the guest had cashed a check for the same amount during a previous stay at a La Quinta Inn. The first desk clerk had given the implicit message that it was all right to cash personal checks for that amount. The clerk may have known the guest, had enough cash, and felt the guest should receive a favor. This clerk did not realize that problems were being developed for the next La Quinta. Customers expect chains to have similar products and policies. Inconsistency results in gap 4 errors.

Gap 5: Expected Service Versus Perceived Service

Gap 5 is a function of the others. As any of the other gaps increase in size, gap 5 also increases. It represents the difference between expected quality and perceived quality. The expected quality is what the guest expects to receive from the company. The perceived service is what the guest perceives he or she received from the company. If the guest receives less than he or she expected, the guest is dissatisfied.

The five-gap service model provides insights into the delivery of quality service. By studying this model, we can develop an understanding of the potential problem areas related to service quality. This insight will help to close any gaps that may exist in our operations.

APPENDIX B

Forecasting Market Demand

Defining the Market

Market demand measurement calls for a clear understanding of the market involved. The term *market* has acquired many meanings over the years. In its original meaning, a market was a physical place where buyers and sellers gathered to exchange goods and services. Medieval towns had market squares where sellers brought their goods and buyers shopped for them. In today's cities, buying and selling occur in what are called shopping areas rather than markets.

To an economist, the term *market* describes all the buyers and sellers who transact over some good or service. Thus, the limited-service hotel market consists of all the consumers who use limited-service hotels and the companies who supply limited-service hotel rooms. The economist is interested in the structure, conduct, and performance of each market.

To a marketer, a market is the set of all actual and potential buyers of a product or service. A market is the set of buyers, and the industry is the set of sellers. The size of the market hinges on the number of buyers who might exist for a particular market offer. Potential buyers for something have three characteristics: interest, income, and access.

Consider the market for Carnival Cruises. To assess its market, Carnival must first estimate the number of customers who have a potential interest in going on a cruise. To do this, the company could conduct a random sampling of consumers and ask the following question: "Do you have an interest in taking a cruise?" If one person out of ten says *yes*, Carnival can assume that 10 percent of the total number of consumers is the potential market for cruises. The potential market is the set of consumers that professes some level of interest in a particular product or service.

Consumer interest alone is not enough to define the cruise market. Potential consumers must have enough income to afford the product. They must be able to answer *yes* to the following question: "Can you afford to purchase a cruise?" The higher the price, the fewer the number of people who can answer yes to this question. Thus, market size depends on both interest and income.

For some market offers, Carnival might have to restrict sales to certain groups. Carnival requires passengers to be 21 years old, unless they are married; then they can be 18 years old. A particular state might not allow the signing of a contractual agreement by anyone under the age of 21. This eliminates the ability to sell to married couples between 18 and 21. The remaining adults make up the qualified available market: the set of consumers that has interest, income, access, and qualifications for the product.

Carnival now has the choice of going after the whole qualified available market or concentrating on select segments. Carnival's served market is the part of the qualified available market that it decides to pursue. For example, Carnival may decide to concentrate its marketing efforts on the East Coast, the Chicago area, and the Southwest. These areas become its served market. Carnival and its competitors will end up selling a certain number of cruises in their served market. The penetrated market is the set of consumers that has bought cruises.

Figure B–1 brings these market concepts together with some hypothetical numbers. The bar on the left of the figure shows the ratio of the potential market—all those who are interested—to the total market. Here the potential market is

Figure B–1
Levels of market definition.

A. Total market: Total population 100%, Potential market 10%.

B. Potential market: Potential market 100%, Available market 40%, Qualified available market 20%, Served market 10%, Penetrated market 5%.

10 percent. The bar on the right shows several possible breakdowns of the potential market. The available market—those who have interest, income, and access—is 40 percent of the potential market. The qualified available market—those who can meet the legal requirements—is 50 percent of the total available market (or 20 percent of the potential market). Carnival concentrates its efforts on 50 percent of the qualified available market—the served market, which is 10 percent of the potential market. Finally, Carnival and its competitors already have penetrated 50 percent of the served market (or 5 percent of the potential market).

These market definitions are a useful tool for marketing planning. Carnival's management can take a number of actions if it is not satisfied with current sales. It can lobby to get the age for signing a legal contract lowered. It can expand its markets in North America or in other areas of the world. Carnival can lower its prices to expand the size of the potential market. It can try to attract more buyers from its served market through stronger promotion or distribution efforts to target current customers. Or it can try to expand the potential market by increasing advertising to convert uninterested consumers into interested consumers. This is what Carnival did when it created the "Fun Ships."

Market Areas for Restaurants

In the restaurant industry, it is common to describe market areas geographically and call them *trade areas*, which vary by type of restaurant and area description. For example, in rural areas it is common for people to make a 100-mile round trip to dine at a favorite restaurant. In contrast, 90 percent of the customers of a fast-food restaurant in a residential area of a major city live within 3 miles of the restaurant. People are not willing to spend a great deal of time getting a fast-food meal. But if they eat at a specialty restaurant such as a Hard Rock Café, they are willing to drive across town. Thus, Hard Rock Café's trade area may encompass a 15-mile radius. A McDonald's in the same town may define its trade area as a 3-mile radius.

John Melaniphy, a restaurant site location expert, describes the trade area of a restaurant as an area that provides 85 percent of the restaurant's business. Restaurants that serve out-of-town guests can examine customers' zip codes and find out where their guests are staying while they are visiting the city. He gives other factors that influence the trade area of a restaurant. Topography defines trade areas. Rivers, lakes, or mountains may set boundaries. Psychological barriers can also exist. For example, expressways, airports, and industrial parks may create barriers. Demographic differences in neighborhoods can also create psychological barriers. For example, residents of a lower-class neighborhood may feel more comfortable eating in their own neighborhood than eating in a restaurant in an upper-middle-class neighborhood, even though both restaurants are the same distance from their houses and have the same average check.

Competition has a big impact on the trade area. Sometimes competition from the same chain may define a trade area. For example, in a city that has eight McDonald's, an adjacent McDonald's may set the boundaries of the trade area for another.

Traffic flows and road patterns also help define trade areas. Accessibility is an important consideration: The better the access, the more extensive the trade area. People also become accustomed to traveling in certain directions and are more likely to travel 4 miles to a restaurant that they pass every day going to work than 4 miles in a direction that they travel infrequently. Thus, a knowledge of normal traveling routes to major employment and shopping areas is useful in determining a trade area. Freeways can also present a perceived barrier. Even though the freeway may provide turnaround loops without stoplights, the multilane roadway will result in some consumers choosing restaurants on their side of the freeway.

Measuring Current Market Demand

We now turn to some practical methods for estimating current market demand. Marketers want to estimate three different aspects of current market demand: total market demand, area market demand, and actual sales and market shares.

Estimating Total Market Demand

The total market demand for a product or service is the total volume that would be bought by a defined consumer group in a defined geographic area in a defined time period in a defined marketing environment under a defined level and mix of industry marketing effort.

Total market demand is not a fixed number but a function of the stated conditions. One of these conditions, for example, is the level and mix of industry marketing effort. Another is the state of the environment. Part A of Figure B–2 shows the relationship between total market demand and these conditions. The horizontal axis shows different possible levels of industry marketing expenditure in a given period. The vertical axis shows the resulting demand level. The curve represents the estimated level of market demand for varying levels of industry marketing expenditure. Some base sales (called the market minimum) would take place without any marketing expenditures. Greater marketing expenditures would yield higher levels of demand, first at an increasing rate and then at a decreasing rate. Marketing expenditures above a certain level would not cause much more demand, suggesting an upper limit to market demand called the *market potential*. The industry market forecast shows the level of market demand corresponding to the planned level of industry marketing expenditure in the given environment.

The distance between the market minimum and the market potential shows the overall sensitivity of demand to marketing efforts. We can think of two extreme types of markets: the expandable and the nonexpandable. An expandable market, such as the market for air travel, is one whose size is affected by the level of industry marketing expenditures. In terms of Figure B–2, in an expandable market, the distance between Q_1 and Q_2 would be fairly large. A nonexpandable market, such as the market for opera, is one whose size is not much affected by the level of marketing expenditures; the distance between Q_1 and Q_2 would be fairly small. Organizations selling in a nonexpandable market can take primary demand—total demand for all brands of a given product or service—as a given. They concentrate their marketing resources on building selective demand—demand for their brand of the product or service.

Figure B–2 Market demand.

A. Market demand as a function of industry marketing expenditure (assumes a marketing environment of prosperity)

Q_1: Market potential
Market forecast
Q_2: Market minimum
Planned expenditure
Market demand in the specified period
Industry marketing expenditure

B. Market demand as a function of industry marketing expenditures (under prosperity vs. recession)

Market potential (prosperity) — Prosperity
Market potential (recession) — Recession
Market demand in the specified period
Industry marketing expenditure

Given a different marketing environment, we must estimate a new demand curve. Figure B–2 shows the relationship of market demand to the environment. A given level of marketing expenditure will always result in more demand during prosperity than it would during a recession. Marketers should carefully define the situation for which they are estimating market demand.

Estimating Area Market Demand

Companies face the problem of selecting the best sales territories and allocating their marketing budget optimally among these territories. Therefore, they need to estimate the market potential of different cities, states, and even national markets. Two major methods are available: the market-buildup method and the market-factor index method. The market-buildup method calls for identifying all the potential buyers in each market and estimating their potential purchases. The market-factor index method is used in the fast-food industry. A common method for calculating area market potential is to identify market factors that correlate with market potential and combine them into a weighted index.

Many companies compute additional area demand measures. Marketers now can refine state-by-state and city-by-city measures down to census tracts or zip code centers. Census tracts are small areas about the size of a neighborhood, and zip code centers (designed by the U.S. Postal Service) are larger areas, often the size of small towns. Information on population size, family income, and other characteristics is available for each type of unit. The area demographic information is appended with lifestyle information, such as Experian's Mosaic USA (mentioned in Chapter 8) and PRIZM by Claritas. Marketers can use these data for estimating demand in neighborhoods or other smaller geographic units within large cities.

Estimating Actual Sales and Market Shares

In addition to estimating total and area demand, a company will want to know the actual industry sales in its market. Thus, it must identify its competitors and estimate their sales. The industry's trade association often collects and publishes total industry sales, although it does not list individual company sales separately. In this way, each company can evaluate its performance against the industry as a whole. Suppose that the company's sales are increasing at a rate of 5 percent a year and industry sales are increasing at 10 percent. This company is actually losing its relative standing in the industry.

Forecasting Future Demand

Forecasting is the art of estimating future demand by anticipating what buyers are likely to do under a given set of conditions. For example, an association wants to book 100 rooms for three nights in a 250-room hotel next year. They will pay $225 per room per night. The current rate structure of the hotel is as follows: rack rate $275, corporate rate $245, and average rate $235. Should the manager take the 300 room-nights at a low rate, or does the manager turn down this request for $67,500 worth of business? Without forecasting, it is difficult to answer this question. Forecasts help managers maximize their profits.

Most markets do not have a stable industry or company demand, so good forecasting becomes a key factor in company success. Poor forecasting can lead to overstaffing and excess inventories or understaffing and running out of products. The more unstable the demand, the more the company needs accurate forecasts and elaborate forecasting procedures.

Forecasting Methods

Many firms base their forecasts on past sales. They assume that the causes of past sales can be uncovered through statistical analysis and that analysts can use the causal relations to predict future sales. One popular method, time-series analysis, consists of breaking down the original sales into four components—trend, cycle, season, and erratic components—and then recombining these components to produce the sales forecast. *Trend* is the long-term underlying pattern of growth or decline in sales resulting from basic changes in population, capital formation, and technology. It is found by fitting a straight line through past sales.

Cycle captures the medium-term wave movement of sales resulting from changes in general, economic, and competitive activity. The cyclical component can be useful for medium-range forecasting. Cyclical swings, however, are difficult to predict because they do not occur at regular intervals.

Season refers to a consistent pattern of weekly, monthly, or quarterly sales movements within the year. In the hospitality industry, we usually think of seasonal changes on a yearly basis, but weekly and hourly sales changes are important. The seasonal component can be related to weather factors, holidays, and trade customs. The seasonal pattern provides a norm for forecasting short-range sales. Yield management depends on forecasting demand by day, by flight or cruise, and by hour of the day. Historical sales patterns are carefully analyzed, such as examining sales for Tuesdays of the second week of September or total passengers and the mix of passengers on flight 482 each Wednesday at 3:30 P.M. Forecasting in the airline industry is further complicated by the presence of interconnecting stops. Large hospitality companies, such as hotel chains, and car rental firms, such as Hertz, depend on sophisticated software to analyze huge volumes of data.

Finally, *erratic events* include strikes, snowstorms, earthquakes, riots, fires, and other disturbances. These components, by definition, are unpredictable and should be removed from past data to reveal the more normal behavior of sales. Most of these events cannot be accurately forecasted, but a few, such as snowstorms and strikes, lend themselves to short-run forecasting. Hotel managers in Washington, D.C., know that if a major snowstorm is predicted for the city, room demand will increase. Visitors will be unable to leave the city and will want to retain their rooms. Office workers may be unable to return home and will also want a room. Managers who have a knowledge of the past behavior of demand when erratic events occurred can factor this into their thinking in times of crisis management.

The first step in managing demand is understanding the factors that affect the demand of the firm's market segments. The payday of a major employer may drive area customer demand. For example, in north Dallas the Friday and Saturday nights after a payday at Texas Instruments are much busier than non-payday weekends. There also may be seasonal variations. The Boulders, a resort in Arizona, charges more than $500 a room in season, yet it closes in July and August because of a lack of demand for rooms at less than half this price. Holiday periods have a positive influence on demand at most resorts. Business travel drops off between mid-December and mid-January, during the summer period, and over weekends. Although there is fluctuation in demand, much of the fluctuation can be explained. Managers must understand the factors that drive demand and build it into their forecasts.

Suppose that a 250-room hotel had an occupancy of 76 percent, selling 69,350 room-nights during the year at an average rate of $80. During the last seven years, the number of room-nights sold and average rate have both increased by 5 percent. The hotel has undergone two expansions to keep up with the growth. This information suggests that the next year the hotel will sell 72,818 room-nights (69,350 × 1.05) at an average rate of $84 (1.05 × $80). The manager first has to determine whether the hotel has the capacity to handle the increase. If the hotel sold out to business travelers from Tuesday to Thursday during February through May and September through October, it is unrealistic to expect that the growth will continue at a 5-percent rate because it will be constrained by capacity. The only opportunity to increase occupancy is during the low-demand periods.

Let us assume that a recession is expected next year. As a result, the number of room-nights is expected to drop by 10 percent, and the average rate is expected to decrease by 15 percent as competitors cut their rates to attract customers. If the manager did not factor in the recession and projected based solely on past information, the occupancy and average room rate would be greatly overstated. Taking the recession into consideration, the forecast will call for a lower occupancy at a greatly reduced room rate.

When a forecast calls for a decrease in sales, it is important to document the reasons for the decrease. This is especially true of regional recessions. A regional economy with a heavy dependence on one industry can suffer a regional recession when that industry declines while the rest of the country enjoys prosperity. When the hotel management sends its forecast showing a decline in sales to the home office, it will be rejected unless it is well supported. In many cases when a director of sales has presented a marketing plan calling for a decrease in sales without supporting documents to defend the projected decrease, corporate management required the director of sales to increase the forecast. In this scenario, the hotel fails to meet the revised forecast, and the director of sales is fired for not meeting the sales goal. Managers must forecast accurately and provide information to support their forecasts.

Statistical Demand Analysis

Time-series analysis views past and future sales as a function of time rather than as a function of any real demand factors. But many factors affect the sales of any product. Statistical demand analysis is a set of statistical procedures used to discover the most important real factors affecting sales and their relative influence. The factors most commonly analyzed are prices, income, population, and promotion.

Statistical demand analysis consists of expressing sales (Q) as a dependent variable and trying to explain sales as a function of several independent demand variables $X_1, X_2, \ldots, X_n$. That is,

$$Q = f(X_1, X_2, \ldots, X_n)$$

Using a technique called multiple-regression analysis, various equation forms can be statistically fitted to the data in the search for the best predicting factors and equation. For example, a restaurant near Marquette University in Milwaukee, Wisconsin, found that its sales were explained by whether Marquette University was in session and the preceding week's sales:

$$Q = 12750 + 6250X_1 + 0.21X_2$$

where X_1 is a dummy variable indicating whether Marquette was in session, with 1 given when it was in session and 0 used when it was not in session, and X_2 is last week's sales. For example, if Marquette had just finished a term and management wanted to predict sales for next week when last week's sales were $24,000, forecast sales for next week would be as follows:

$$Q = 12750 + 6250X_1 + 0.21X_2$$
$$= 12750 + 6250(0) + 0.21\,(24000)$$
$$= 12750 + 0 + 5040$$
$$= \$17.790$$

The manager could also expect a decline in sales (because the preceding week's sales will be falling) as activity around the campus slows down. For example, if the restaurant achieved the forecasted sales of $17,790, the next week's projected sales would be $16,486. The decline is due to the drop in the previous week's sales from $24,000 to $17,790 and caused by less people on campus.

Two precautions apply to the use of regression in forecasting. First, the equation just stated will not be sensitive to extraordinary events. For example, on parents' weekend the restaurant may generate very high sales. The equation does not include parents' weekend as a variable; therefore, it is unable to project sales accurately for this event. The sales for the week after parents' weekend will be overstated because the figure for the previous week will be extraordinarily high. Second, it is dangerous to forecast outside the range of the different variables used to build the forecast. For example, if a hotel manager examines the relationship between advertising and room sales, the manager may find that room sales increase $5 for every dollar spent on advertising. If the hotel advertising expenditures had ranged from $75,000 to $150,000, we could not necessarily expect this relationship to hold up for advertising expenditures of $250,000 because this level of advertising has not been tested.

The precautions cited earlier illustrate two types of errors caused by the misuse of regression analysis. Statistical demand analysis can be very complex, and the marketer must take care in designing, conducting, and interrupting such analysis. Yet constantly improving computer technology has made statistical demand analysis an increasingly popular approach to forecasting.

Two other forecasting techniques used in the hospitality industry are moving average and exponential smoothing. A moving average is the average of a set number of previous periods (n); this average is used to predict sales for the next period. For example, if a restaurant had sales of $12,000, $12,500, $13,000, and $12,500 over the last four weeks, using a four-week moving average, the sales forecast for the next week would be $12,500.

$$\frac{\$12,000 + \$12,500 + \$13,000 + \$12,500}{4} = \$12,500$$

A limitation of moving averages is that the latest period used in the average has the same weight as the current period. Exponential smoothing is a simple but useful mathematical technique, which allows recent periods to be weighted.

The forecasting techniques presented in this appendix represent a few of the techniques that managers use. It is not within the scope of this book to provide a detailed explanation of all forecasting techniques. We simply want to illustrate that tools are available to assist managers with their forecasts.

Case Studies

Guide to the Cases

Chapter	Cases	Chapter	Cases
1	4, 15	10	11, 12, 16
2	4, 12	11	14, 15
3	2, 6	12	18, 22
4	1, 8	13	13, 16, 18
5	3, 7, 22	14	8, 10, 13
6	1, 3	15	11, 20
7	1, 11	16	10, 13
8	1, 10, 19	17	7, 22
9	5, 9, 16	18	10, 17, 21

Case

1. Zipcar: It's Not About Cars—It's About Urban Life
2. Cafeteria I.C.E.
3. Airbnb: Making Hospitality Authentic
4. Chick-Fil-A Is Dominating The U.S. Fast-Food Market
5. The Hunt Room: Change the Concept or Just the Decor?
6. In-N-Out Burger: Customers Value the Old-Fashioned Way
7. The Australian Tourist Commission
8. The Witchery by the Castle
9. Mayo Clinic
10. Elk Mountain Hotel
11. The Ritz-Carlton
12. Grand Targhee
13. The Bleeding Heart Restaurant: Unique Positioning of a Restaurant
14. Pricing Almost Destroys and Then Saves a Local Restaurant
15. Good Value at Spirit Airlines: Getting Less but Paying Much Less for It
16. Apollo Hotel
17. The Cameron Trading Post and Lodge
18. Tropicana Fishing Lodge
19. Boulder Creek
20. International Travel Agency
21. Superior Hotels
22. Uber

Case 1 Zipcar: It's Not About Cars—It's About Urban Life

Imagine a world in which no one owns a car. Cars would still exist, but rather than owning cars, people would just share them. Sounds crazy, right? But Scott Griffith, CEO of Zipcar, the world's largest car-share company, paints a picture of just such an imaginary world. And he has nearly 800,000 passionate customers, or Zipsters, as they are called—who will back him up.

Zipcar specializes in renting out cars by the hour or day. Although this may sound like a minor variation on the established rental car agency business, car-sharing, a concept pioneered by Zipcar, is an entirely different concept. As Griffith took the driver's seat of the young start-up company, he knew that if the company was going to achieve cruising speed, it needed to be far more than just another car service. Zipcar needed to be a well-positioned brand that appealed to a customer base with unfulfilled needs.

A Car Rental Company That Isn't About Cars

As Griffith considered what Zipcar had to offer, it was apparent that it couldn't be all things to all people. But the concept seemed particularly well suited to people who live or work in densely populated neighborhoods in cities such as New York, Boston, Atlanta, San Francisco, and London. For these customers, owning a car (or a second or a third car) is difficult, costly, and environmentally irresponsible. Interestingly, Zipcar doesn't see itself as a car-rental company. Instead, it's selling a lifestyle, the urban life.

Initially, the Zipcar brand was positioned exclusively round a value system. As an urban lifestyle brand, Zipcar focused on traits that city dwellers have in common. For starters, the lifestyle is rooted in environmental consciousness. At first, Zipcar focused on green-minded customers with promotional pitches such as "We • Earth" and "Imagine a world with a million fewer cars on the road." Zipcar's vibrant green logo reflects this save-the-Earth philosophy. And Zipcar really does deliver on its environmental promises. Studies show that every shared Zipcar takes up to 20 cars off the road and cuts carbon emissions by up to 50 percent per user. On average, Zipsters travel 44 percent fewer miles than when they owned a car, leaving an average of 219 gallons of crude oil in the ground. Multiply all this out by 11,000 cars in Zipcar's fleet, and that's a pretty substantial impact on the environment.

But it wasn't long Zipcar realized that if it was going to grow, it needed to move beyond just being green. So the brand has broadened its positioning to include other urban lifestyle benefits, benefits that Zipcar appeals to on its site in response to the question, "Who exactly is the car-sharing type?" Zipcar provides these most common reasons for car sharing; eliminate the hassle and expenses of owning a car, save money and the environment by using public transportation, and the ability to use a car when you really need it.

One of most important benefits Zipcar provides is convenience. Owning a car in a densely populated urban area can be a real hassle. Zipcar lets customers focus on driving, not on the complexities of car ownership. It gives them "Wheels when you want them," in four easy steps: "Join. Reserve. Unlock. Drive."

Fulfilling Consumer Needs

To join, you pay around $70 for an annual membership and receive your personal Zipcard, which unlocks any Zipcar vehicle located in urban areas around the world. Then, when you need a car, reserve one, minutes or months in advance, online, by phone, or using a smartphone app. You can choose the car you want, when and where you want it, and drive it for as little as $9.00 an hour, including gas, insurance, and free miles. When you're ready, walk to the car, hold your Zipcard to the windshield to unlock the doors, and you're good to go. When you're done, you drop the car off at the same parking spot, Zipcar worries about the maintenance and cleaning.

Zipcar not only eliminates the hassle of urban car ownership; it also saves money. By living with less, the average Zipster saves $600 a month on car payments, insurance, gas, maintenance, and other car ownership expenses. That's like getting a $10,000 a year raise after taxes. In an era when consumers have become more frugal, this is a big plus, especially for those looking to live more minimally.

Zipcar isn't for everyone, it doesn't try to be. Instead, it zeros in on a narrowly defined urban lifestyle positioning. For starters, Zipcar "pods" (a dozen or so vehicles located in a given neighborhood) are stocked from a portfolio of over 50 different models that trendy urbanites love. The vehicles are both hip and fuel efficient: Toyota Priuses, Honda CRVs, MINIs, Volvo S60s, BMW 328s, Toyota Tacomas, Toyota Siennas, Subaru Outbacks, and others. And Zipcar now has plug-in hybrids, fully electric vehicles, and full-size vans for big jobs. Each car has its own personality, a name and profile created by a Zipster. For example, Prius Ping "jogs in the morning; doesn't say much," whereas Civic Carlos "teaches yoga; loves to kayak." Such personal touches make it feel like you're borrowing the car from a friend, rather than being assigned whatever piece of metal happens to be available.

To further eliminate hassles and make Zipcar as convenient as possible, company promotional tactics are designed to appeal to city dwellers. The company's goal is for Zipsters to not have to walk more than seven minutes to get to one of its car pods, no easy task. Zipcar's management realizes that even with targeted Web and mobile promotions it is hard to target at a block level. Zipcar sends street teams to understand the urban blocks. They use local ads and transit advertising. They use an on-the-ground guerilla-type marketing approach.

With its eye sharply focused on maintaining the Zipcar image, the company is consistently developing new features that appeal to the tech-savvy urbanites. Recently, the company has shifted its focus a bit from being a Web-based business to be an overwhelmingly mobile concern. Soon, Zipcars will have in-car device holders for smartphones that will allow for easy plug-in and hands-free navigation. The interface between the cars and the users will allow playlists stored on the phone to be played through the car's audio system. Users will be provided with information specific to the vehicle they are in, a personalized deal recommendation service, and a real-time feedback loop where users can report on vehicle cleanliness, damage, and fuel levels.

Fostering Brand Community

Zipcar's orientation around the urban, environmentally conscious lifestyle fosters a tight-knit sense of customer community. Zipsters are as fanatically loyal as the hardcore fans of Harley-Davidson or Apple, brands that have been nurturing customer relationships for decades. Loyal Zipsters serve as neighborhood brand ambassadors; 30 percent of new members join up at the recommendation of existing customers. "When I meet another Zipcar member at a party or something, I feel like we have something in common," says one Brooklyn Zipster. "It's like we're both making intelligent choices about our lives." And just like Harley owners get together on weekends to ride, the internet is littered with announcements for Zipster parties at bars, restaurants, and comedy clubs, among other places.

As Zipcar has taken off, it has broadened the appeal of its brand to include a different type of urban dweller, businesses, and other organizations. Companies such as Google now encourage employees to be environmentally conscious by commuting via a company shuttle and then using Zipcars for both business and personal use during the day. Other companies are using Zipcar as an alternative to black sedans, long taxi rides, and congested parking lots. Government agencies are getting into the game as well. The city of Chicago recently partnered with Zipcar to provide a more efficient and sustainable transportation alternative for city agencies. And Washington, D.C., now saves more than $1 million a year using Zipcar. Fleet management has proven to be a good market for Zipcar. As word of mouth spreads on savings that Zipcar can bring, organizations wanting to get rid of their fleet of cars are signing up with Zipcar. How is Zipcar's strategy of positioning itself as an urban lifestyle brand working? By all accounts, the young car-sharing nicher has the pedal to the metal and its tires are smoking. In just the past five years, Zipcar's annual revenues have rocketed nearly fivefold, to more than $270 million. Zipcar has also reached the milestone of being profitable. And with 10 million people now within walking distance of a Zipcar, there's plenty of room to grow. As more cars are added, Zipcar's reach will only increase.

Zipcar's rapid growth has sounded alarms at the traditional car-rental giants. Enterprise, Hertz, Thrifty, and even U-Haul now have their own car-sharing operations. Avis also had one. But recently, Avis decided to shut down its own service and buy Zipcar for nearly $500 million. The Zipcar brand will now benefit from cost savings that the large-scale rental service enjoys. As for the others, Zipcar has a big head start in terms of size and experience, cozy relationships in targeted neighborhoods, and an urban hipster cred that corporate giants like Hertz will have trouble matching. To Zipsters, Hertz rents cars, but Zipcar is a part of their hectic urban lives.

Sources: Based on information from Mark Clothier, "Zipcar Soars After Profit Topped-Analysts' Estimates," Bloomberg.com, November 9, 2012, www.bloomberg.com/news/2012-11-09/zipcar-soars-after-profittopped-analysts-estimates.html; Darrell Etherington, "Zipcar CEO Details In-Car Assistant, Personalized Deals and Member Onboarding for Mobile App," *TechCrunch*, October 9, 2012, www.techcrunch.com/2012/10/09/zipcar-ceo-details-in-car-assistant-personalizeddeals-and-member-onboarding-for-mobile-app/; Jerry Hirsch, "Zipcar CEO Talks About Car Sharing as Lifestyle Choice," *Seattle Times*, May 13, 2012, www.seattletimes.nwsource.com/html/businesstechnology/2018197748_inpersonzipcarl4.html; Paul Keegan, "Zipcar; The Best New Idea in Business," *Fortune*, August 27, 2009, www.moneycnn.com/2009/08/26/news/companies/zipcar_car_rentals.fortune/; Stephanie Clifford, "How Fast Can This Thing Go, Anyway?" *Inc.*, March 1, 2008, www.inc.com/magazine/20080301/how-fast-can-this-thing-go-anyway.html; www.zipcar.com (accessed May 14, 2019).

QUESTIONS FOR DISCUSSION

Chapter 4

1. What environmental factors would make Zipcar an attractive acquisition for Avis?

Chapter 6

1. Describe the beliefs and values associated with Zipcar's brand image.
2. How did Zipcar match the values and beliefs with lifestyle?

Chapter 7

Zipcar was developed for a consumer segment, but found an application for organizational markets. Use the organizational buying decisions presented in Chapter 7 in the text as a reference for your answers to the next two questions.

1. What problem does Zipcar solve for an organization?
2. What need does it fulfill?
3. What type of organization could Zipcar best serve?

Chapter 8

1. Evaluate Zipcar based on benefit-based positioning.
2. Compare Zipcar's positioning based on benefits to Zipcar's positioning based on beliefs and values. Which is stronger?

Case 2 Cafeteria I.C.E.

The cafeteria for employees of I.C.E. (the national electric company of Costa Rica: Instituto Costarricense de Electricidad) was experiencing difficulties, and top management felt compelled to see what corrective actions could be taken. Responsibility for correcting the problems had been assigned to Antonio F. Caas Mora, assistant manager for telecommunications.

The problems were of two types. First, no one was satisfied with the time required for lunch. The time often extended beyond the allocated half hour, resulting in loss of productivity. The second, related problem was how to change the lunchtime eating habits of the employees. The majority of employees used the main serving line, where they purchased a heavy traditional Latin meal. This required a considerable amount of time and also made the employees sleepy after eating. As a result, afternoon productivity among office personnel declined.

Background on I.C.E. and the Cafeteria

I.C.E. was the largest electric utility and the only telephone company in the nation of Costa Rica. It was owned and operated by the government of Costa Rica.

Although I.C.E. had field office locations throughout Costa Rica, the central administrative offices were located in the city of San José in a modern 15-story building. A total of 4,486 persons were employed by I.C.E. and 1,453 of these worked in the central office building. This group used the cafeteria facilities.

The cafeteria had been in operation for five years. It was under the management of an employee cooperative. This cooperative was managed by an elected board of directors consisting of employees of I.C.E. The board of directors of the cooperative hired a full-time manager who had direct responsibility for the cafeteria operation.

Description of Employees

Employees who worked in the I.C.E. building and used the cafeteria were primarily white-collar personnel. A minority of blue-collar employees such as maintenance personnel used the cafeteria. Employees who worked in the I.C.E. building consisted primarily of administrators, staff specialists, engineers, clerical personnel, secretaries, and receptionists.

The Menu and Eating Habits

The cafeteria consisted of two serving lines; the main serving line was the most popular with the employees and was the one with the long waiting lines. This line served what was known as the *casado*, a typical Latin meal. The menu changed each day. A typical meal consisted of a meat dish such as a small steak, sausage, or liver. This was accompanied with rice, beans, and a vegetable such as corn or, more commonly, potatoes.

The meals served in the main serving line reflected the cultural habits of Costa Ricans with traditional food. The noontime meal historically had been eaten with the family and required two or three hours, including family conversation and sometimes a short nap. This custom was the basis for closing stores during midday. It was still the custom in many parts of Latin America for all types of businesses to close until 2 or 3 P.M. The traditional long lunch hour meant that employees would arrive for work early in the morning, take a long lunch break, return for work, and stay late in the evening until 6 or 6:30 P.M. The management of I.C.E. had decided to break with this tradition to allow as smooth a workday as possible without the interruption of a long lunch break. The I.C.E. system closely paralleled that found in the United States.

There was evidence of change in eating habits in San José. Several U.S.-style restaurants had entered the market and did a brisk business at lunch with hamburgers, pizza, and other quick foods. McDonald's, Hardee's, and Pizza Hut were popular noontime restaurants, especially with younger people. After witnessing the success of restaurants such as McDonald's, the board of directors of the cooperative decided to open a sandwich line in the cafeteria. This was separate from the main serving line. It consisted of a long counter. Plastic food trays were placed on the counter and filled with stacks of unwrapped cold sandwiches such as cheese or ham and cheese. Other trays contained slices of fruits such as papaya or watermelon and cake. Coffee, milk, and carbonated beverages were available from dispensers located on the counter.

Two cash registers were located at the end of the main serving line, and one at the end of the sandwich line. Information was not recorded concerning the number of employees who used each line or the average expenditure per person in the sandwich line. However, it was felt that the average lunch expenditure per employee would probably be about two-thirds of the per-person expenditure in the main serving line.

Working Hours and Office Rules

The office hours at I.C.E. extended from 7:30 A.M. to 3:30 P.M., with half an hour for lunch. Employees were expected to arrive on time. This meant that some employees had to rise as early as 5:30 A.M., and few could rise later than 6:30 A.M.

Coffee breaks were not officially permitted, and there were no vending machines in the building. The policy of no coffee breaks had been instituted because many employees spilled coffee or other liquids on reports. It was also felt that a coffee break was unnecessary because half an hour was given for lunch. Workers would occasionally bring a cake or cookies from home and share them with employees in their work area, even though this was officially frowned upon.

A system had been devised to prevent all employees from crowding into the cafeteria at one time. The doors of the cafeteria were locked until 11 A.M., at which time employees began to arrive on a set schedule by floors. The line closed promptly at 1:30 P.M.

Survey Results

Before attempting to make changes to correct the situation in the cafeteria, management felt it would be wise to conduct a survey among the employees. This was done through the use of a written questionnaire, which was given to all persons using the cafeteria on a selected day. The results of this questionnaire follow.

Opinions Concerning Selected Factors (%)

FACTOR	VERY GOOD	GOOD	AVERAGE	BAD	NO OPINION
Quality	0.63	16.46	44.78	23.42	14.71
Variety	4.59	35.28	28.96	18.67	12.50
Cleanliness	1.74	18.67	36.55	29.75	13.24
Courtesy	5.38	27.37	39.24	25.16	2.85
Convenience	8.07	30.70	34.65	23.26	3.32
Quality of cooking	8.39	35.28	33.70	18.83	3.80
Quantity	3.16	28.48	39.72	20.41	8.23

Opinions Concerning Type of Food Served (%)

FOOD	VERY GOOD	GOOD	AVERAGE	BAD	NO OPINION
Chicken w/rice	8.86	43.04	29.59	7.59	10.92
Shrimp w/rice	1.11	12.34	33.23	31.64	21.68
Meatballs	2.37	12.97	31.33	31.65	21.68
Sea bass	10.28	37.18	25.63	8.86	18.04
Breaded steak	4.11	22.47	34.02	18.04	21.36
Flank steak in sauce	3.64	24.68	30.85	15.82	25.06
Tongue in sauce	5.54	26.58	26.42	17.41	24.05
Chicken in sauce	3.32	23.10	29.43	16.30	27.85
Fried chicken	2.37	23.89	30.70	12.97	30.06
Pork chop	3.32	19.15	29.43	21.99	26.11
Spaghetti w/meat	1.90	13.77	29.11	33.07	22.15
Spaghetti w/tuna	2.37	10.92	26.42	34.18	26.11
Chickpeas w/tripe	3.64	17.56	28.80	28.01	21.99
Chop suey	1.90	14.40	24.05	38.76	20.89

QUESTIONS FOR DISCUSSION

Chapter 3

1. Can the use of marketing concepts/strategies be of use in solving the problem with Cafeteria I.C.E.?

2. What effect can an individual organization such as I.C.E. have on changing ingrained cultural habits such as those of noontime dining?

3. What would you suggest be done to increase patronage of the sandwich and fruit line?

Case 3 Airbnb: Making Hospitality Authentic

Like many services industries, hotel companies have done a tremendous job of ensuring the quality of the customer experience through standardization. People booking rooms through any of the major hotel chains can be pretty much assured of certain basics. They'll enter the 13-by-25-foot room into a short hallway with a bathroom and closet on one side or the other. In the bathroom, they'll find the basics along with a sterile display of soaps, hair care products, and other toiletries. The room features a bed or two flanked on both sides by nightstands with a reading light by each. An upholstered chair and ottoman sit at an angle in the far corner with a desk opposite. A dresser topped with a flat-screen TV sits across from the foot of the bed. Visitors might also discover a mini-fridge and a microwave oven.

The artwork and decor are fairly contemporary although impersonal and nondescript. Other details throughout the hotel property are equally predictable. And although luxury level across these features varies from chain to chain, the vibe is the same. Many travelers count on this standard experience, and it assures that their experience will be within a set of narrow, expected boundaries. Minimizing the risk of negative outcomes typically results in a satisfactory lodging experience for most guests most of the time.

But one lodging provider is targeting travelers who have a different set of needs and expectations. Airbnb is turning lodging services upside down by promising a hospitality experience that is the complete opposite of the one provided by major hotel chains. A major player in the new sharing economy, Airbnb is an online community marketplace that connects people who want to rent out space in their homes with those who are looking for accommodations. Like a true online marketplace, Airbnb doesn't own any lodging properties. It just brings buyers and sellers together and facilitates transactions between them. But Airbnb's promise of value is what really sets it apart from the hospitality world's status quo. The new-to-the-game lodging provider pitches an authentic experience, a true sense of what life is like in the place you visit.

Whereas the hotel industry has spent decades sculpting its standardized offering, in just eight years Airbnb has built a global network of more than 2 million listings and 60 million guests throughout 34,000 cities in 191 countries. It has also built a market value of more than $25 billion. Although these numbers may sound impressive on their own, in its brief existence Airbnb has managed to exceed the accomplishments of the largest hotel chain in the world, 100-year-old Hilton Worldwide with its 5,700 properties and a market value of $27 billion.

How did Airbnb pull of this amazing feat? According to Brian Chesky and Joe Gebbia, the start-up's founders, Airbnb simply recognized that the travel industry had lost touch with its customers by offering only one cookie-cutter option, ticky-tack rooms in antiseptic hotels and resorts. This standardized model seemed to dictate an unintended goal for the entire hotel industry, to ensure that nothing remotely interesting happens. Once Chesky and Gebbia recognized this, they set out a strategy to bring authenticity back into the hospitality industry.

Two Million Rooms—No Two Alike

It all started when the founders had a hair-brained thought on how to generate some extra income to help pay the rent on their modest San Francisco loft apartment. During a major convention that had every hotel room in the city booked, they rented out three air mattresses on the floor of their apartment for $40 a night each. In the process, they discovered that the people who booked that real estate got more than just a place to stay at a time when they needed it most, they got a unique networking opportunity. From that moment, Chesky and Gebbia moved quickly to develop and formalize the business concept.

Today, using Airbnb to either list a property or rent one to stay in is relatively simple. For hosts, Airbnb's official term for property owners who want to rent out space, it's a simple matter of registering and being vetted to ensure legitimacy. Listings can be pretty much anything from a couch, a single room, a suite of rooms, or an apartment to a moored yacht, a houseboat, an entire house, or even a castle (Airbnb currently claims more than 1,400 castle listings). Some hosts even rent out space in their yards for guests to pitch a tent. With more than 2 million listed properties for rent, each is as unique as its owner. Because listings are in private homes and apartments, they are typically located in residential neighborhoods rather than commerce centers where national and global hotel brands abound. Bookings can be offered by the day, the week, or the month, and hosts decide on price and the other details of their service and listings. Airbnb keeps only 3 percent of the booking fees and returns the rest to the host within 24 hours.

For guests, the process is about like buying or booking most anything online. Registered users search by city, room type, price range, amenities, host language, or various other options, including entering their own keywords. Most listings provide photos and details that give potential guests a reasonably accurate idea of what their stay will be like. Guests can contact potential hosts with questions before booking. On top of the fee for the property, guests typically lay down a security deposit and pay a 6 to 12 percent service fee to Airbnb. Bookings are made through Airbnb, so money changes hands only through a secure interface. When guests arrive at the chosen property, the host either greets them or arranges for entry.

As the founders were getting Airbnb off the ground, they constantly faced a big challenge. Many people, investors included, were skeptical. In fact, during Airbnb's first year, the founders were turned down by every venture capitalist they approached. "When we started this company, people thought we were crazy," said Chesky. "They said strangers would never stay with strangers, and horrible things are going to happen." They also had a hard time convincing guests; few people were willing to risk staying with someone they'd never met.

But Airbnb overcame these concerns through various means. First, it set up a standard rating system for both hosts and guests, allowing each side to assess the other and reviewing what others have said about prior experiences. A "superhost" status gives an assurance of extensive booking experience and high-quality service. A "business travel ready" badge notes that the host provides specific amenities like Wi-Fi, a desk, and basic toiletries. Airbnb also puts guest and host minds at ease with its verification process, tips for safe and satisfactory bookings, and a 24-hour Trust and Safety hotline. Hosts are further protected by an included insurance policy that protects their property from damages of up to $1 million. Airbnb admits that although these measures do not guarantee that nothing bad will ever happen, the likelihood of a negative outcome is no greater than it is for staying at a chain hotel.

Seeing the World as the Locals Do

From the beginning, Airbnb primarily served budget-minded customers with prices for listings lower than those of comparable hotel rooms. But more and more, Airbnb is seeing a shift toward customers, leisure and business travelers alike, who want more than just low price. This is hardly an accident. Airbnb deliberately positions itself as a provider of unique and authentic experiences through its branding, communications, and other aspects of its business. In doing so, Airbnb has taken the uncertainty of staying in a stranger's house and turned it into an asset. Whereas hotels can compete on price and convenience, they cannot compete when it comes to the relationship between guest and host. "Guests are looking for experiences where they connect with people and connect with culture," says Chesky. "You can't automate hospitality."

Such was the theme of the second-annual Airbnb Open, a motivational event held in Paris, the company's biggest market, and attended by 5,000 hosts from 110 different countries. In his keynote address, Chesky explained that the entire hospitality industry caters to tourists in a way that makes them feel like tourists. But with an Airbnb experience, guests start to feel like they are a part of the neighborhood and the city.

As part of his presentation, Chesky summed up the entire Airbnb philosophy by illustrating the experience his own parents had when they arrived in Paris just days before the event. Pictures of their first day in town, hosted by typical tourist guides, were projected on a big screen. There was a picture of them on a double-decker tour bus, another on a generic boat ride, and a third standing in line at the Louvre. Chesky narrated each image with comical cynicism. "Every year, 30 million people go to Paris. They look at everything and they see nothing. We don't need to go to monuments and landmarks to experience a culture. We can actually stay with people." Then Chesky showed images from his parents' second day in Paris, guided by some of Airbnb's top hosts, where they experienced the city from the perspective of locals. They had coffee at an authentic sidewalk cafe, took a walk in a garden, and drank and danced at a cozy Parisian borte. "Maybe we should not travel to Paris," suggested Chesky. "Maybe what we should do is live in Paris."

Executing on the Promise

This ideal, one supported by all Airbnb employees, was the driving force behind a recent and ambitious rebranding effort by the tech start-up. The company tossed out its original straight, forward text logo in favor of something far more abstract, a symbol that resembles a puffy capital letter "A" with the two sides crossing over. Airbnb calls it the "belo," "the universal symbol of belonging." The new logo communicates a sense of belonging through something that transcends language, culture, and geography. A new slogan accompanies the logo, "Belong Anywhere."

To ensure that the Airbnb guest experience is as authentic and unique as possible, the company focuses first and foremost on its community of hosts. In fact, Airbnb considers its hosts to be its primary customers. As a result, Airbnb has been able to nurture a huge global community of lodging providers who are true believers in the Airbnb vision. Treated as active participants in the business, hosts develop a sense of ownership and devotion. In this manner, Airbnb influences hosts to follow certain guidelines toward creating the best guest experience possible. This is by no means intended to create a standardized model. But by urging hosts to offer guest services such as airport pickup and walking tours, Airbnb strengthens the connections formed with guests. "What's special in your world isn't just the home you have," Chesky tells the crowd at the Airbnb Open. "It's your whole life."

Sources: Max Chafkin, "Airbnb Opens Up the World?" *Fast Company*, February 2016, pp. 76–95; Marshall Alstyne, Geoffrey Parker, and Sangeet Choudary, "Pipelines, Platforms, and the New Rules of Strategy," *Harvard Business Review*, April 2016, pp. 54–62; Dan Peltier, "Airbnb's CMO on Authentic Travel Experiences," *Skift*, July 14, 2015, https://skift.com/2015/07/14/skift-global-forum-2015-airbnbs-cmo-on-the-meaning-of-authentic-travel-experiences/; and additional information from www.investopedia.com/articles/personal-finance/032814/pros-and-cons-using-airbnb.asp?performancelayout=true and www.airbnb.com/about/about-us (accessed July 2016); https://www.hilton.com/en/corporate/ (accessed May 28, 2019).

QUESTIONS FOR DISCUSSION

Chapter 2

1. How do the four characteristics of services apply to Airbnb? How does Airbnb deal with each characteristic?
2. Apply the service profit chain concept to Airbnb.
3. How does Airbnb differentiate its offer, delivery, and image?
4. How much of a threat is competition to Airbnb?

Chapter 5

1. You are the marketing director of a major hotel chain. How would you set up a study to determine how much, if at all Airbnb will affect your business?

Case 4 Chick-fil-A Is Dominating the U.S. Fast-Food Market

Chick-fil-A is dominating the U.S. fast-food market. Whereas McDonald's, Subway, Burger King, and Taco Bell trudge along at the top of the heap, Chick-fil-A has quietly risen from a Southeast regional favorite to become the largest chicken chain and the eighth-largest quick-service food purveyor in the country. The chain sells significantly more food per restaurant than any of its competitors, twice that of Taco Bell or Wendy's and more than three times what the KFC Colonel fries up. And it does this without even opening its doors on Sundays. With annual revenues of more than $6 billion and annual average growth of 12.7 percent, the chicken champ from Atlanta shows no signs of slowing down.

How does Chick-fil-A do it? By focusing on customers. Since the first Chick-fil-A restaurant opened for business in the late 1960s, the chain's founders have held tenaciously to the philosophy that the most sustainable way to do business is to provide the best possible experience for customers.

Applying Some Pressure

Chick-fil-A founder S. Truett Cathy was no stranger to the restaurant business. Owning and operating restaurants in Georgia in the 1940s, 1950s, and 1960s, his experience led him to investigate a better (and faster) way to cook chicken. He discovered a pressure fryer that could cook a chicken breast in the same amount of time it took to cook a fast-food burger. Developing the chicken sandwich as a burger alternative, he registered the name "Chick-fil-A, Inc." and opened the first Chick-fil-A restaurant in 1967.

The company began expanding immediately, although at a substantially slower pace than the market leaders. Even today, Chick-fil-A adds only about 100 new stores each year. Although it now has more than 2,000 stores throughout the United States, that number is relatively small compared to KFC's 4,100, McDonald's 13,000, and Subway's 27,000. Chick-fil-A's controlled level of growth ties directly to its "customer first" mantra. As a family-owned operation, the company has never deviated from its core value to "focus on getting better before getting bigger." The slow-growth strategy has facilitated that ability to "get better."

As another way to perfect its business, the company has also stuck to a limited menu. The original breaded chicken sandwich remains at the core of Chick-fil-A's menu today, "a boneless breast of chicken seasoned to perfection, hand-breaded, pressure cooked in 100% refined peanut oil and served on a toasted, buttered bun with dill pickle chips." In fact, the company's trademarked slogan, "We didn't invent the chicken, just the chicken sandwich," has kept the company on track for decades. Although it has carefully and strategically added other items to the menu, it's the iconic chicken sandwich in all its varieties that primarily drives the brand's image and the company's revenues. This focus has helped the company give customers what they want year after year without being tempted to develop a new flavor of the month.

Getting It Right

Also central to Chick-fil-A's mission is to "have a positive influence on all who come in contact with Chick-fil-A. Although seemingly a tall order to fill, this sentiment permeates every aspect of its business. Not long ago, current Chick-fil-A's CEO Dan Cathy was deeply affected by a note that his wife taped to their refrigerator. In a recent visit to a local Chick-fil-A store, she had not only received the wrong order, she had been overcharged. She circled the amount on her receipt, wrote "I'll be back when you get it right" next to it, and posted it on the fridge for her husband to see.

That note prompted Dan Cathy to double-down on customer service. He initiated a program by which all Chick-fil-A employees were retrained to go the "second mile" in providing service to everyone. That "second mile" meant not only meeting basic standards of cleanliness and politeness but going above and beyond by delivering each order to the customer's table with unexpected touches such as a fresh-cut flower or ground pepper for salads.

The experience of a recent patron illustrates the level of service Chick-fil-A's customers have come to expect as well as the innovative spirit that makes such service possible:

> My daughter and I stopped at Chick-fil-A on our way home. The parking lot was full, the drive-thru was packed ... but the love we have for the chicken sandwiches and waffle potato fries! So we decided it was worth the wait. As we walked up the sidewalk, there were two staff members greeting every car in the drive-thru and taking orders on little tablets. A manager was making his rounds around the building outside smiling and waving at cars as they were leaving.
>
> When we came inside, the place was packed! We were greeted immediately by the cashiers. Seth happened to take our order.
>
> He had a big smile, wonderful manners, spoke clearly and had great energy as a teenager! He gave us a number and said he'd be right out with our drinks. We were able to sit at a table as the other guests were leaving and before we could even get settled our drinks were on the table! While Seth started to walk away, our food was delivered by another very friendly person. Both myself and my 15-year-old daughter commented on how fast it all happened. We were so shocked that we started commenting on the large groups arriving behind us, and began watching in amazement, not only inside but outside!
>
> Everyone behind the counter worked together, used manners, and smiled. The teamwork was amazing! Then Ron, a gray-headed friendly man, made his way from table to table, checking on guests, giving refills, and trading coloring books for small ice cream cones with sprinkles for little kids. He checked on us twice and filled our drinks once.

Recently, the company instituted the "parent's valet service," inviting parents juggling small children to go through the drive-through, place their order, park, and make their way inside the store. By the time the family gets inside, its meal is waiting on placemats at a table with high chairs in place. But beyond the tactics that are taught as a matter of standard policy, Chick-fil-A also trains employees to look for special ways to serve—such as retrieving dental appliances from dumpsters or delivering smartphones and wallets that customers have left behind.

Give Them Something to Do

Beyond high levels of in-store service, Chick-fil-A has focused on other brand-building elements that enhance the customer experience. The brand got a big boost when the Chick-fil-A cows made their promotional debut as three-dimensional characters on billboards with the now famous slogan, "EAT MORE CHIKIN." The beloved bovines and their self-preservation message have been a constant across all Chick-fil-A promotional materials for the past 20 years. They've also been the linchpin for another Chick-fil-A customer experience-enhancing strategy, engage customers by giving them something to do.

Displaying any of the cow-themed mugs, T-shirts, stuffed animals, refrigerator magnets, laptop cases, and dozens of other items the company sells on its Web site certainly qualifies as "something to do." But Chick-fil-A marketers go far beyond promotional items to engage customers. For starters, there's "Cow Appreciation Day," a day set aside every July when customers who go to any Chick-fil-A store dressed as a cow get a free meal. Last year, the 10th anniversary of this annual event, about a million cow-clad customers cashed in on the offer.

Another tradition for brand loyalists is to camp out prior to the opening of a new restaurant. Chick-fil-A encourages this ardent activity with its "First 100" promotion, an officially sanctioned event in which the company presents the first 100 people in line for each new restaurant opening vouchers for a full year's worth of Chick-fil-A meals. Dan Cathy himself has been known to camp out with customers, signing T-shirts, posing for pictures, and personally handing coupons to the winners. And whereas some customer-centric giveaways are regular events, others pop up randomly. Take the most recent "family challenge," which awards a free ice cream cone to any dine-in customers who relinquish their smartphones to a "cell phone coop" for the duration of their meals.

To keep customers engaged when they aren't in the stores, Chick-fil-A has become an expert in social and digital media. Its newest app, Chick-fil-A One, jumped to the number-one spot on iTunes only hours after being announced. Nine days later, more than a million customers had downloaded the app, giving them the ability to place and customize their orders, pay in advance, and skip the lines at the register. And in a recent survey by social media tracker Engagement Labs, Chick-fil-A was ranked number one and crowned the favorite American brand on all major social media platforms, including Facebook, Twitter, and Instagram.

Every year, as the accolades roll in, it is apparent that Chick-fil-A's customer-centric culture is more than just talk. Among the many competitors, Chick-fil-A was rated number one in customer service in the most recent Consumer Reports survey of fast-food chains. In the latest annual Customer Service Hall of Fame survey, Chick-fil-A ranked second out of 151 of the best-known companies across 15 industries, trailing only Amazon. A whopping 47 percent of customers rated the company's service as "excellent," and Chick-fil-A was the only fast-food chain to make the list for the second year in a row.

After decades of phenomenal growth and success, Chick-fil-A is celebrating by firing the Richards Group, its long-standing agency of record. Additionally, the beloved cows that are so widely recognized as symbols of the brand will ease into the background of promotional materials. "The cows are an integral part of the brand. They're our mascot, if you will," says Jon Bridges, chief marketing officer for Chick-fil-A. "But they aren't the brand. The brand is bigger than that." For now, Bridges only says that the cows won't disappear. But a new "Cow-plus" is in the works, and the brand's promotional messages will expand beyond the bovines to tell engaging stories about the food, people, and service that make the brand so special. It's a risky move. With Chick- fil-A growing faster than any other major fast-food chain, it begs the question as to whether such a drastic change in the brand's symbolism will sustain its current growth for years to come, or send some customers out to pasture.

Prior to this recent announcement, one estimate has Chick-fil-A on track to add between $6 billion and $9 billion in revenues within the next decade. In that same period, giant McDonald's may add as much as $10 billion in U.S. sales but as little as only $1 billion. Clearly, all this growth is not an accident. As one food industry analyst states, "It's about trying to maintain high levels of service, high quality, not deviating dramatically, and giving customers an idea of what to expect." As long as Chick-fil-A continues to make customers the number-one priority, we can expect to find more and more access to those scrumptious chicken sandwiches.

Sources: Jessica Wohl, "Chick-fil-A Drops The Richards Group After 22 Years," *Advertising Age*, July 21, 2016, www.adage.com/print/305057; Micah Solomon, "Chick-fil-A Becomes a Customer Experience Thought Leader by Asking Families to Ditch Cell Phones," *Forbes*, March 3, 2016, www.forbes.com/sites/micahsolomon/2016/03/03/chik-fil-a-rewards-families-for-ditching-cellphones-the-genius-customer-experience-move-of-2016/#4e1830e65858; Micah Solomon, "The Chick-fil-A Way of Customer Service and Employee Engagement," *Forbes*, June 14, 2016, www.forbes.com/sites/micahsolomon/2016/06/14/the-chick-fil-a-way-of-customer-service-and-employee-engagement/#8587848660eb; Hayley Peterson, "How

Chick-fil-A's Restaurants Sell Three Times as Much as KFC," *Time*, August 5, 2015, www.businessinsider.com/how-chick-fil-a-is-dominating-fast-food-2015-8; Michael B. Sauter, "2015's Customer Service Hall of Fame," *USA Today*, August 2, 2015, www.usatoday.com/story/money/business/2015/07/24/24-7-wall-st-customer-service-hall-fame/30,599,943/; "Chick-fil-A One Surges to No. 1 Slot in iTunes App Store," *QSR*, June 10, 2016, www.qsrmagazine.com/news/chick-fil-one-surges-no-1-slot-itunes-app-store; "Chick-fil-A Beats Amazon, Netflix in Social Media," *QSR*, January 12, 2016, www. qsrmagazine.com/news/chick-fil-beats-amazon-netflix-social-media; and www.chick-fil-a.com/Company/Highlights-Fact-Sheets and www.chick-fil-a.com/Story (accessed June 2016).

QUESTIONS FOR DISCUSSION

Chapter 1

1. Give examples of needs, wants, and demands of Chick-fil-A customers, differentiating these three concepts.
2. Describe Chick-fil-A in terms of the value it provides customers. How does Chick-fil-A engage customers?
3. Evaluate Chick-fil-A's performance relative to customer expectations.

Chapter 2

1. How does Chick-fil-A use the concept of inseparability to deliver exceptional service?
2. Another tradition for brand loyalists is to camp out prior to the opening of a new restaurant. Chick-fil-A encourages this ardent activity with its "First 100" promotion. How does a parking lot full of a hundred or more people the night before opening provide tangible evidence?

Case 5 The Hunt Room: Change the Concept or Just the Decor?

The Rolling Hills Country Club is an established club in a major eastern city. Jimmy Johnson, the general manager of the club, had just convened the regular weekly meeting of the executive committee. The first item on the agenda was the Hunt Room.

Hans Krueger, the food and beverage manager, claims that sales have been declining for the last five years. He states the overall concept of the room is excellent. There have been some minor upgrades (replacing the chairs and the carpet), but no major renovation has taken place since 1997. He feels it is time for a major renovation. He claims that the food, service, and pricing are fine, but the atmosphere has grown tired. He claims that the comment cards returned by the guests have been highly favorable. Mr. Krueger has submitted plans for a $750,000 renovation package. His package calls for an updating of the same concept.

Alice Whitaker, the catering manager, claims the concept is no longer viable. She states that patronage of the restaurant has dropped. She says the people who use the Hunt Room may still enjoy it, but a very small percentage of the members use the room. Jimmy Johnson is concerned that if the changes to the room are major, he may lose the room's current customers and not be able to replace them with members drawn to the new concept. He is tending to side with Hans, viewing minor changes to the concept as a safe alternative.

The club has three restaurants: the Venetian Room, the Hunt Room, and the Terrace Room. The Venetian Room is the main dining room. It is a light, open room that overlooks the golf course. Its menu is eclectic and includes a selection of European, American, and Asian cuisine. The average check in the Venetian room is $28 for lunch and $75 for dinner. The Hunt Room is the casual dining room. It has rich wood paneling, red leather chairs, and features paintings of hunting scenes on the walls. The Hunt Room's menu features beef, quail, and several seafood items. The average check is $60 for dinner. The Hunt Room was closed for lunch in 2007, due to declining lunch sales. The Terrace Room is an informal room with the same menu for lunch and dinner. The menu is similar to one that might be found in a family-oriented restaurant. It is on the ground floor and features a patio that is popular with members using the swimming pool, who want more than the snack bar offers. The average check is $12 for breakfast, $17 for lunch, and $25 for dinner. Dinner business is very slow, except for the summer. In fact, Johnson is thinking of closing this room for dinner.

Referring to the Hunt Room, Alice Whitaker claims the club's members no longer want a heavy beef menu. She has also observed what she feels is a trend: Members are seeking new dining experiences. They want excitement in the menus and would enjoy a room with a casual atmosphere. Additionally, she claims that the restaurant prices have gradually crept up, and the restaurant is no longer considered casual dining. Those guests who want a casual meal usually end up in the Terrace Room or in a local restaurant. Ms. Whitaker feels the local restaurants offer better value for the money.

Mr. Krueger responded by stating that the restaurant offers a much better value than it did when it opened. He claims that beef prices have risen by 100 percent since 2009, but he has absorbed some of these increases and menu prices have only increased by 65 percent. He further stated that he was not in competition with every restaurant in town—the club has prestige and members come here because it is their club. Krueger claims the club gives good value compared with the fine dining restaurants in town.

Jimmy Johnson did not want the discussion to escalate into an argument. He, therefore, tabled the discussion on the Hunt Room until more information could be obtained. He was also proceeding very carefully. He has only been at the club for two years. He has been able to maintain the status quo of the club but has not made any significant changes. The club's membership wait list has continued its downward trend. The club had an average wait of four years in 2015; today the wait is 18 months. Food and beverage sales have remained flat over the last three years, despite an average menu increase of 4 percent per annum. Jimmy feels he has "stabilized the club," but he has not been able to show increases in sales. He feels the turnaround has come, but he also knows some board members are growing impatient. Thus, he feels a mistake with the new concept for the Hunt Room could cost him his job. He also knows many of the older board members enjoy the Hunt Room.

Another problem with the club is that the membership is aging. Most of the young members are sons or daughters of members. The club does not seem to attract members under 40. This makes it hard for Johnson to make changes because many of the older members do not want change, and the younger members who came to the club with their parents have grown used to it. They seem to like the club the way it is, yet they do not use the food and beverage facilities. Most of the younger members use the golf course and drop their children off at the pool. For the most part, their food and beverage sales are limited to the snack bars at the golf course and swimming pool.

Johnson ponders his options: Do nothing, or try to keep things from declining. He knows preventing further declines is a significant accomplishment. However, he feels the board is looking for increases. If he makes a mistake with the Hunt Room, he will quickly lose his job. If he does nothing, he may be able to hang on for several more years but if he does not turn sales around, eventually he will lose his job.

■■■ QUESTIONS FOR DISCUSSION

Chapter 9

1. If you were the general manager, what process would you go through to determine a new concept for the Hunt Room?
2. What information would you seek? Where would you find this information?
3. What makes restaurant concepts grow out of favor? How often should a room be re-concepted?
4. Should club restaurants compete with local restaurants?
5. Brainstorm to come up with possible concepts for the Hunt Room. You should include decor and menu ideas.

■■■ Case 6 In-N-Out Burger: Customers Value the Old-Fashioned Way

In 1948, Harry and Esther Snyder opened the first In-N-Out Burger in Baldwin Park, California. It was a simple double drive-thru setup with the kitchen between two service lanes, a walk-up window, and outdoor seating. The menu consisted of burgers, shakes, soft drinks, and fries. This format was common for the time period. In fact, another burger joint that fits this same description opened up the very same year just 45 minutes away from the first In-N-Out Burger. It was called McDonald's. Today, McDonald's boasts over 34,000 stores worldwide that bring in more than $88 billion every year. In-N-Out has only 281 stores in five states, good for an estimated $625 million a year. Based on the outcomes, it would seem that McDonald's has emerged the clear victor.

But In-N-Out never wanted to be another McDonald's. And despite its smaller size—or perhaps because of it—In-N-Out's customers like the regional chain just the way it is. When it comes to customer satisfaction, In-N-Out beats McDonald's hands down. It regularly posts the highest customer satisfaction scores of any fast-food restaurant in its market areas. Compared to McDonald's customers, patrons of In-N-Out are really "Lovin' it." Just about anyone who has been to an In-N-Out believes it's the best burger they've ever had. It comes as no surprise, then, that the average per-store sales for In-N-Out eclipse those of McDonald's and are double the industry average.

Breaking All the Rules

According to Stacy Perman, author of a definitive book on In-N-Out, the company has achieved unequivocal success by "breaking all the rules." By rules, Ms. Perman refers to the standard business practices for the fast-food industry and even retail in general. In-N-Out has maintained a tenacious focus on customer well-being, but it has done so by doing the unthinkable: not changing. The company's original philosophy is still in place today and best illustrates the basis for the company's rule breaking: "Give customers the freshest, highest quality foods you can buy and provide them with friendly service in a sparkling clean environment." The big burger giants might take exception to the idea that they aren't providing the same customer focus. But let's take a closer look at what these things mean to In-N-Out.

For starters, at In-N-Out, quality food means fresh food. Burgers are made from 100 percent pure beef—no additives, fillers, or preservatives. In-N-Out owns and operates its own patty-making commissaries, ensuring that every burger is fresh and never frozen. Vegetables are sliced and diced by hand in every restaurant. Fries are even made from whole potatoes. And, yes, milkshakes are made from real ice cream. In an industry that has progressively become more and more enamored with processing technologies such as cryogenically freezing foods and preparing all ingredients in off-site warehouses, In-N-Out is indeed an anomaly. In fact, you won't even find a freezer, heating lamp, or microwave oven in an In-N-Out restaurant. From the beginning, the company slogan has been "Quality you can taste." And customers are convinced that they can do just that.

In-N-Out hasn't changed its formula for freshness. But in another deviation from the norm, it also hasn't changed its menu. Unlike McDonald's or Wendy's, which introduce seemingly unending streams of new menu items, In-N-Out stays true to Harry Snyder's original mantra: "Keep it real simple. Do one thing and do it the best you can." This charge from the founder focuses on what the chain has always done well: making really good hamburgers, really good fries, and really good shakes, that's it. While others have focused on menu expansion in constant search of the next hit item to drive traffic, In-N-Out has tenaciously stuck to the basics. In fact, it took 60 years for the company to add 7up and Dr Pepper to its menu.

Although the limited menu might seem restrictive, customers don't feel that way. In another demonstration of commitment to customers, In-N-Out employees will gladly make any of the menu items in a truly customized fashion. From the chain's earliest years, menu modifications became such a norm at In-N-Out that a "secret" menu emerged consisting of code words that aren't posted on regular menu boards. So customers in the know can order their burgers "animal style" (pickles, extra spread, grilled onions, and a mustard-fried patty). Although the "Double-Double" (double meat, double cheese) is on the menu, burgers can also be ordered in 3×3 or 4×4 configurations. Fries can also be ordered animal style (two slices of cheese, grilled onions, and spread), well done, or light. A Neapolitan shake is a mixture of chocolate, vanilla, and strawberry shakes. The list goes on and on. Knowledge of this secret menu is yet another thing that makes customers feel special.

It's not just In-N-Out's food that pleases customers. The chain also features well-trained employees who deliver unexpectedly friendly service. In-N-Out hires and retains outgoing, enthusiastic, and capable employees and treats them very well.

It pays new part-time above the competition and gives them regular raises. Part-timers also receive paid vacations. General managers make over $100,000 a year plus bonuses and receive a full-benefit package that rivals anything in the corporate world. Managers who meet goals are sent on lavish trips with their spouses, often to Europe in first-class seats. For gala events, managers wear tuxedos. Executives believe that the men and women who run In-N-Out stores stand shoulder-to-shoulder with any blue-chip manager, and want them to feel that way. Managers are promoted from within. In fact, 80 percent of In-N-Out managers started at the very bottom. As a result, In-N-Out has one of the lowest turnover rates in an industry infamous for high turnover.

Happy, motivated employees help create loyal, satisfied customers. In fact, words like *loyal* and *satisfied* don't do justice to how customers feel about In-N-Out Burger. The restaurant chain has developed an unparalleled cult following. When a new In-N-Out first opens, the line of cars often stretches out a mile or more, and people stand in line for hours to get a burger, fries, and a shake. Fans have been known to camp overnight to be the first in line. When In-N-Out made its debut in Texas, one woman cried. "Pinch me, it just doesn't feel real," whimpered customer Danielle Deinnocentes, overcome with emotion as the reality of her newfound proximity to the burger chain set in.

Slow Growth Nurtures Fans

Some observers point out that it's probably more than just the food and the service that created In-N-Out's diehard customer base. Because of In-N-Out's slow-growth expansion strategy, you won't find one of the famous red-and-white stores with crisscrossed palm trees on every corner. By 1976, In-N-Out had grown to only 18 southern California stores, whereas McDonald's and Burger King had opened thousands of stores worldwide. It took In-N-Out 40 years to open its first non-California store in Las Vegas. And even as the company expands into Arizona, Utah, and Texas, it sticks tenaciously to its policy of not opening more than about 10 stores per year.

The lack of access to an In-N-Out in most states has created legions of cravers coast to coast. Fans have created countless Facebook pages, filled with posts by consumers begging the family-owned corporation to bring In-N-Out to their states. But In-N-Out's policy is driven by its commitment to quality. It will open a new store only when it has trained management and company-owned distribution centers in place.

The scarcity of In-N-Out stores only adds to its allure. Customers regularly go out of their way and drive long distances to get their fix. Having to drive a little further contributes to the feeling that going to In-N-Out is an event. Out-of-state visitors in the know often put an In-N-Out stop high on their list of things to do. Jeff Rose, a financial planner from Carbondale, Illinois, always stops at In-N-Out first when he visits Las Vegas to see his mother. "You have to pass it when you drive to her house," he says in his defense. "It's not like the time I paid an extra $40 in cab fare to visit an In-N-Out on the way to the San Diego airport."

Consistent with the other elements of its simple-yet-focused strategy, In-N-Out doesn't spend much on advertising—it doesn't have to. In fact, although the company doesn't release financial figures, some estimates place total promotional spending at less than 1 percent of revenues. In-N-Out's small promotional budget is for local billboards and radio ads. But when it comes to really spreading the word, In-N-Out lets its customers do the heavy lifting. Customers truly are apostles for the brand. They proudly wear In-N-Out T-shirts and slap In-N-Out bumper stickers on their cars. Rabid regulars drag a constant stream of new devotees into restaurants, an act often referred to as "the conversion." They can't wait to pass along the secret menu codes and share the sublime pleasures of diving into a 4 × 4 animal style. "When you tell someone else what 'animal style' means," says an analyst, "you feel like you're passing on a secret handshake. People really get into the whole thing."

In-N-Out doesn't use paid endorsers, but word-of-mouth praise regularly flows from the mouths of A-list celebrities. When former *Tonight Show* host Conan O'Brien asked Tom Hanks what he recommended doing in Los Angeles, Hanks replied, "One of the true great things about Los Angeles is In-N-Out Burger." Paris Hilton famously claimed she was on her way to In-N-Out when she was pulled over for a DUI. And paparazzi have snapped shots of scores of celebrities getting built for two. These are located in a lavishly restored seventeenth-century building just a few steps from the Witchery in Edinburgh's historic Castlehill. If possible, these suites are even more theatrical and opulent than the original two.

The gothic library suite overlooks the historic Royal Mile and includes masses of antique books, paisley-covered walls, and a book-lined bathroom with an open fire.

The Armory is discreetly located, overlooking a small private courtyard. This huge and glamorous suite is hung with dramatic tapestries and features an oak-paneled bathroom. The Guardroom is exceptionally spacious overlooking the historic old-town rooftops and a romantic bedroom paneled with antique leather.

Fully booked restaurants and suites did not occur without reason. The Witchery developed a worldwide reputation for sensational food in the most indulgent setting. The very best of Scotland's produce, such as Angus beef, lamb, game, and seafood, are served. Scottish lobster and Loch Fyne oysters are regularly featured alongside Witchery classic dishes such as hot smoked salmon with leeks and hollandaise or Angus beef fillet with smoked garlic broth.

The Witchery also developed a reputation for its wines, gaining a prestigious *Wine Spectator* Award for Excellence and many other awards for its cellar.

Its comprehensive list of almost a thousand wines covers all of the great wine-producing areas, varieties, prices, and styles with a special selection of 17 available by the glass. A skilled and enthusiastic wine team, supported by a respected sommelier, constantly taste, source, and buy wines to add to the already extensive cellar. Their extensive knowledge is available to guests in the restaurant.

Along with a large selection of old-world classics from Burgundy and Bordeaux, there are extensive selections from New World producers such as Australia, Chile, and New Zealand and a comprehensive Spanish and Italian list. Champagne is a Witchery specialty with selections from Pommery to the deluxe cuvées of Krug, Roederer Christa, and Dom Perignon.

An extensive range of malt whiskey, Armagnacs, and liqueurs are also available. Mineral water is locally produced by Findlay's in East Lothian, Scotland.

Obviously, much of the success of the Witchery, Secret Garden, and the suites may be attributed to their historic location, the ambience, the quality of the products, and the excitement and theater built into each.

James knows that these factors need to be continuously supported to ensure success. He is well aware of the tendency of hospitality guests to seek new dining and lodging experiences. He also recognizes the importance of word of mouth to deliver new guests. He believes that the product must be supported by staff loyalty and excellence, community involvement, personal leadership, and an appropriate use of technology.

Staff Development

Following attendance at the Disney Institute in Florida, James instituted a new mind-set in the company, encouraging staff to constantly seek to exceed guests' already high expectations. Staff members are empowered to deal with any guest request and are personally responsible for delivering each guest's total satisfaction. James encourages his team to develop rewarding long-term careers within his company, so staff turnover is significantly below the industry norm, and many of his staff have been with him long term. A large proportion have returned to work with him again after gaining experience with other organizations at home and abroad.

Community and Industry Involvement

James believes the hospitality industry offers exciting careers, and he encourages young people to enter. James supports and funds a number of educational initiatives at primary, secondary, and higher education levels, including supporting students in local high schools with cooking competitions, training with restaurant chefs, and work experience within his restaurants. Recently, he was delighted to see a student reach the Scottish final of the *Future Chef of the Year*.

He endowed the *James Thomson Award for Outstanding Customer Service*, which annually recognizes and financially assists a student who has shown outstanding commitment to excellence in customer service during his or her studies at Edinburgh's Telford College. He continues to be a significant sponsor of an annual exchange trip between Edinburgh students and the François Rabelais College in Lyon, France, giving up to 20 students and lecturers hands-on experience in Michelin-starred restaurants in France's culinary capital.

A strong believer in rewarding and recognizing the very best led James to sponsor the Scottish tourism "Oscars," the Visit Scotland Thistle Awards, the Caterer.com Best Tourism Website Award, and the recent Caterer.com Web Awards. Frequently asked to lend his expertise to others in the industry, he has judged the Caterer Hospitality Week Innovations Awards over recent years as well as being a regular judge for the Thistle Awards.

As an industry leader, James frequently speaks publicly to promote tourism and hospitality issues, and his restaurants maintain a high media profile in Scotland worldwide. He has written a food column in *The Herald* newspaper and speaks at industry events. Making his restaurants and suites available to the media has promoted a positive quality image of Scottish hospitality in dozens of publications, including *Vogue, Hello, Elle, Cosmopolitan*, and the *New York Times*, as well as on television around the world.

James believes that he has an obligation to assist in the growth of tourism to Scotland and especially to Edinburgh. Aware that visitors to Edinburgh were looking for more information about the historic but neglected Old Town, James supported the creation of the Caddies and Witchery Tours, the city's first customer walking tours. Tours leave from outside the Witchery every evening and have become a memorable part of the visitor experience for thousands of visitors to Edinburgh.

James works closely with several public- and private-sector organizations, including the Scottish Enterprise Innovation Group, the Scottish Borders Tourist Board, and the National Museums of Scotland to improve the standards of Scotland's hospitality products. An enthusiast for Disney's approach to customer care, James has encouraged a range of tourism businesses to learn from the best, including leading study tours to the Disney Institute in Florida. He often speaks on the lessons that can be learned from Disney. In 2002, in conjunction with other partners, he launched Castlehill Christmas, a joint initiative to bring business to local tourism enterprises at what was a traditionally quiet time of the year with a dramatic architectural lighting display and a program of events focused on Castlehill. James is a key member of the finance committee, raising over £300,000 in sponsorship to bring the prestigious Meeting Planners International Conference to Edinburgh in 2004, an international event with huge benefits for the city and Scotland.

Supporting the wider community, especially in Edinburgh's historic Old Town, has a place too. James acts as a trustee of the Old Town Charitable Trust, a member of the Board of the Queen's Hall, and support of the advisory group of the local homelessness initiative, the Edinburgh Streetwork Project. He also supports an under-10 football team. The Witchery supports a local community football team and the National Judo Academy. The innovative Just for Starters program that James pioneered as a collaborative venture brought a number of people with difficult backgrounds into the industry by harnessing the resources of a number of public- and private-sector organizations, including the police and army, to support, educate, and mentor them in the transition from homelessness to employment.

As sole shareholder, James is able to commit a significant proportion of the company's profits back to the community through ongoing support of charities, including the Hospitality Industry Trust, Crusaid Shelter, the Army Benevolent Fund, St. Columbia's Hospice, Save the Children, and the Royal Lyceum Theatre. Regular donations of dining or accommodation vouchers from the restaurants are also given to organizations to use for their own fundraising purposes.

Technology

James's basic concept of giving the diner a magical dining experience where each of the elements of food, wine, service, location, and decor all combine to create a magical dining experience was innovative when he established the Witchery, and constant innovation has been a hallmark ever since. He was ahead of other restaurants, installing specialist EPOS systems to process diners' orders and bills discreetly. James established a state-of-the-art mini call center to allow all guest enquiries for his restaurants to be dealt with centrally by a highly skilled team using specially developed reservation software. For guests looking to book online, he was an early investor in Web sites that have given the restaurants and suites a 24-hour worldwide presence with an average of a thousand hits each day. His restaurants were among the first in the United Kingdom to offer real-time table reservations online using his reservations database. James believes that hospitality firms can use the latest technology to provide a truly old-fashioned level of service. He credits much of his success to community and employee support. For James, marketing is far more than advertising or brochure development. He has demonstrated the importance of personal involvement by owners/managers in the community and the industry and strong product differentiation.

QUESTIONS FOR DISCUSSION

Chapter 4

1. From the preceding discussion, analyze the strengths and weaknesses of the Witchery.

Chapter 14

1. Discuss the Witchery's public relations efforts. Offer any suggestions you have for how the Witchery could gain publicity outside of Scotland. You might google the Witchery, Edinburgh, Scotland to gain ideas on what they might be able to do.

Case 9 Mayo Clinic

Mayo Clinic is the first and largest integrated not-for-profit medical group practice in the world. William and Charles Mayo founded the clinic over 100 years ago as a small outpatient facility and pioneered the concept of a medical group practice, a model that is widely used today.

Mayo Clinic provides exceptional medical care and leads the United States in many specialties such as cancer, heart disease, respiratory disorders, and urology. It consistently ranks at the top of *U.S. News & World Report*'s Best Hospitals list and enjoys 85 percent brand recognition among U.S. adults. It has reached this level of success by taking a different approach from most clinics and hospitals and putting a relentless focus on the patient's experience. The clinic's two interrelated core values trace back to its founders and are at the heart of all the organization does: placing the patient's interests above all others and practicing teamwork.

Every aspect of the patient's experience is considered at Mayo Clinic's three campuses in Rochester (MN), Scottsdale (AZ), and Jacksonville (FL). The moment a patient walks into one of Mayo Clinic's facilities, he or she feels the difference. New patients are welcomed by professional greeters who walk them through the administrative processes. Returning patients are greeted by name and with a warm smile. The buildings have been designed so that, in the words of the architect of one, "patients feel a little better before they see their doctors." The 21-story Gonda Building in Rochester has spectacular wide-open spaces with the capability of adding 10 more floors. Fine art hangs on the walls, and doctors' offices are designed to feel cozy and comforting rather than sterile and impersonal.

The lobby of the Mayo Clinic hospital in Scottsdale has an indoor waterfall and a wall of windows overlooking mountains. In pediatric exam rooms, resuscitation equipment is hidden behind a large cheery picture. Hospital rooms feature microwave ovens and chairs that really do convert to beds because, as one staff member explained, "People don't come to the hospital alone." The newest emergency medical helicopter was customized to incorporate high-tech medical equipment and is one of the most advanced aircraft in the world.

The other significant difference in serving patients is Mayo Clinic's concept of teamwork. A patient can come to Mayo Clinic with or without a physician's referral. At that time, the patient's team is assembled, which can include the primary physician, surgeons, radiation oncologists, radiologists, nurses, residents, or other specialists with the appropriate skill, experience, and knowledge.

Teams of medical professionals work together to diagnose patients' medical problems, including debating test results for hours to determine the most accurate diagnosis and best treatments. Once a team consensus has been reached, the leader meets with the patient and discusses his or her options. Throughout the process, patients are encouraged to take part in the discussion. If surgery is necessary, the procedure is often scheduled to take place within 24 hours, a dramatic difference from the long wait patients experience at many hospitals. Mayo Clinic's doctors understand that those who seek their care want action as soon as possible.

Mayo's doctors are put on salary instead of being paid by the number of patients seen or tests ordered. As a result, patients receive more individualized attention and care, and physicians work together instead of against each other. As one pediatrician at Mayo explained, "We're very comfortable with calling colleagues for what I call 'curbside consulting.' I don't have to make a decision about splitting a fee or owing someone something. It's never a case of quid pro quo."

Mayo Clinic is a not-for-profit, so all its operating income is invested back into the clinic's research and education programs. Breakthrough research is quickly implemented into the quality care of the patients. Mayo Clinic offers educational programs through its five schools, and many of its physicians come up through these programs with Mayo's philosophies engrained in their heads, including Mayo's motto: "The best interest of the patient is the only interest to be considered."

Third parties have recognized Mayo Clinic for decades for its independent thinking, outstanding service and performance, and core focus on patient care and satisfaction.

QUESTIONS FOR DISCUSSION

Chapter 9

1. Explain why Mayo Clinic is so good at customer service. Why has it been so successful practicing medicine differently from other hospitals?

2. How has the Mayo Clinic used tangible elements of the service product to enhance its service delivery?

Sources: Avery Comarow, "America's Best Hospitals," *U.S. News & World Report* (July 15, 2009); Chen May Yee, "Mayo Clinic Reports 2007 Revenue Grew 10%," *Star Tribune* (March 17, 2008); Leonard L. Berry and Kent D. Seltman, *Management Lessons from Mayo Clinic* (New York: McGraw-Hill, 2008); Leonard L. Berry, "Leadership Lessons from Mayo Clinic," *Organizational Dynamics* 33 (August 2004): 228–242; Leonard L. Berry and Neeli Bendapudi, "Clueing in Customers," *Harvard Business Review* (February 2003): 100–106; John La Forgia, Kent Seltman, and Scott Swanson, "Mayo Clinic: Sustaining a Legacy Brand and Leveraging Its Equity in the 21st-century Market," Presentation at the Marketing Science Institute's Conference on Brand Orchestration, Orlando, FL, December 4–5, 2003; Paul Roberts, "The Agenda—Total Teamwork," *Fast Company* (March 31, 1999).

Case 10 Elk Mountain Hotel

History of Elk Mountain Hotel

When Peter Thieriot first saw Elk Mountain Hotel, it looked like the proverbial money pit, an endless hole into which renovation funds could be thrown. Peter's lawyers strongly advised him to walk away and forget any thought of buying and remodeling this 1905 hotel in Elk Mountain, Wyoming.

Yet its history, its tranquil location in a beautiful grove of cottonwoods, the Old West appearance of the town of Elk Mountain, and the natural charm of the hotel and its proximity to Peter's buffalo ranch served as a magnet, and Peter became owner and renovator of Elk Mountain Hotel.

The Garden Spot Pavilion had sat on the grounds of the hotel for decades and attracted big names such as Louis Armstrong, Tex Beneke, Tommy Dorsey, and Les Brown, all popular with crowds in the 1940s and 1950s. Old-timers said, "You didn't have to know how to dance at the Pavilion, the floor would do it for you." Sure enough, the floor moved to the rhythm of the band and the crowd.

Peter Thieriot Renovates Elk Mountain Hotel

Wyoming winters and time took the Pavilion, but Peter believes that he can bring it back with modern construction and a special spring floor so once again "you won't need to know dancing to dance real good."

"We stripped the hotel and then built it back again room by room," said Trey Webb, the front-desk clerk and head waiter. Nine layers of wallpaper were removed from the dining room, but a large enough chunk of each remained to frame them and place them in the dining room.

Trey exemplifies the spirit and drive of Wyoming people that helped draw Peter to Elk Mountain from San Francisco. Trey, a high school senior, is headed to the University of Wyoming on a rodeo scholarship to study biology and eventually become a doctor. An expert in "bull dogging and calf roping," Trey knows horses and he knows people. He and other high school kids from the area find part-time employment at the hotel. Their native "Western personalities" and desire to help others makes them popular with guests. They also display a genuine affection for the hotel and pride in its renaissance.

It's easy for employees and guests to love the place because the restoration built warmth and coziness into the 12 guest rooms, the parlor, and the dining room. Peter developed an attic on the third floor into a conference room to host meetings of 16 people around a table with ample wall space for flip-chart pages temporarily held with masking tape, so common to meetings of this size.

Prior to renovations, the hotel served as a watering hole for a sometimes rough bunch of characters from the Medicine Bow area. Ten years before Peter bought the hotel, two of the rowdies took their argument to the hotel's parking lot where they settled it the old-fashioned way with six-shooters. Fortunately, neither of those would-be Wyatt Earps could aim straight, and the sheriff arrived before lead could accidentally find its mark.

Rowdies have been replaced by less colorful, middle-aged professional couples. "A few of the old customers returned looking for a beer and some action after renovations but when they spotted the wine and cheese, the Lexus and Lincoln cars in the parking lot, and heard English spoken without cussin' every other word, they promptly left and never returned," said Peter.

"Half this country loves what we did to this hotel and the other half has a different opinion." That was confirmed by a ranch family in McFadden 30 miles east who placed themselves squarely in the "love" section. Their opinion was that the renovated hotel added much to the community.

There is no fear that guests accustomed to fine dining when traveling and dining out at home will have to settle for less at Elk Mountain Hotel. The menu was designed to "combine a touch of flair, a hint of the Old West, and a big pinch of professionalism." With buffalo and caribou on the menu, there is more than a hint of the Old West. With a good selection of California and imported wines, seafood-based appetizers, and desserts such as crème brulée, compliments, not complaints, are most often heard.

The unanimous opinion of guests is that the hotel was renovated with style. The area on which the hotel sits had once been a stagecoach station for the Overland Trail. Although that building is gone, the Victorian style of the original 1905 building has been enhanced. The original embossed tin ceilings were cleaned and repainted, and the exterior asbestos shingles that used to hide the natural beauty were removed to expose the original cedar lap siding. Peter knew the hotel could be restored to this level of quality.

Susan and Arthur Havers Purchase the Hotel

Arthur and Susan Prescott Havers purchased the hotel 10 years ago. Susan was a marketing consultant in San Francisco, but had a culinary background. She had owned and managed a restaurant and catering company in Belgium and earned a Grand Diplome from Le Cordon Bleu in Paris. Arthur was vice president of international development for e-commerce. It was their dream to open a business together, and although they had this dream for many years, they were not able to find the right project. While searching the internet, Arthur came across the Elk Mountain

Hotel. The historic hotel aroused their curiosity. Although the hotel was not for sale, they contacted Peter, who also had a residence in San Francisco, to see if he would be interested in selling it. They visited Elk Mountain to see the hotel and the region. They found the people to be friendly, with a sense of humor. In addition to the people they enjoyed the wide-open spaces. A year later, the Havers were owners of Elk Mountain Hotel.

Susan's culinary background enabled the restaurant to be turned into a "hidden gem" and customers who discovered it encouraged people driving across I-80 to take the four-mile drive off the Interstate highway to Elk Mountain Hotel. The Havers used their marketing and culinary skills to create special dinners that pair food with wine, beer, or whiskey. They also have created unique events such as a women's handgun training weekend, for $1,100 per person. The fee covers handgun training, meals and three nights lodging, and dinner and breakfast during the stay.

They will be the only guests in the hotel and should be prepared to stay up till 1 A.M. helping track down shadows and bumps in the night. Package price is $250 per couple inclusive of room and dinner but excludes taxes and gratuities. Employees of the hotel swear it has a friendly ghost, and perhaps the guests at the dinner will find it.

Friendly or not, ghosts don't pay bills. That requires live paying guests, and getting more of those, particularly in the low season, requires marketing. Positive word of mouth can't be beaten, but it takes marketing to get enough of those mouths talking.

Peter Thieriot had the vision to renovate the Elk Mountain Resort; the Havers used marketing skills and Susan's culinary skills to turn the hotel into a destination. However, a town of 200 people cannot create the demand necessary to support. Elk Mountain needs to be a destination for people in nearby towns and a place for organizations to hold events and retreats.

Updated September 2015; Sources accessed November 20, 2011; "Elk Mountain, Wyoming," *MuniNetGuide*, http://www.muninetguide.com/states/wyoming/elk-mountain/; Jackie Borchardt, "Elk Mountain Hotel Offers Serenity, Escape," trib.com (March 27, 2011), http://trib.com/business/article_46602367-c87f-5f72-857b-3867c8734ae2.html; "Historic Elk Mountain Hotel Finding an International Flavor," *Rawlins Daily Times*, undated, http://www.elk-mountainhotel.com/-attachments/RawlinsDaily.pdf; Elk Mountain Hotel Web site; www.elkmountainhotel.com (accessed September 3, 2015).

▪▪▪ QUESTIONS FOR DISCUSSION

Chapter 8 or Chapter 18

Examine a map of the state of Wyoming and its neighboring states.

1. What percentage of lodging business would you expect from Wyoming residents in the three seasonal periods: peak, summer; shoulder, late fall and early spring; trough, winter? Which Wyoming towns are target markets?
2. From what markets would the remaining occupancy come?
3. What market targets would you select in terms of demographics and lifestyle?

Chapter 14

1. Develop a publicity/public relations campaign appropriate for Elk Mountain Hotel. Include cost estimates. Remember that free publicity costs something, such as room and board for travel writers.
2. Develop a series of creative packages that might be used to increase occupancy in shoulder and trough periods.

Chapter 16

1. The Havers have linked their site to TripAdvisor, and have posted photos on Flickr. Arthur stated if it was not for the internet, they would have not survived. How does the internet help a small hotel like Elk Mountain Hotel?
2. After visiting the hotel's Web site what suggestions would you have for additional uses of the internet to market the hotel?

▪▪▪ Case 11 The Ritz-Carlton

Few brands attain such a high standard of customer service as the Ritz-Carlton. This luxury hotel chain began with the original Ritz-Carlton Boston, which revolutionized the way U.S. travelers experienced customer service in a hotel. It was the first of its kind to provide a private bath in each guest room, fresh flowers throughout the hotel, and an entire staff dressed in formal white tie, black tie, or morning-coat attire.

In 1983, hotelier Horst Schulze and a four-person development team acquired the rights to the Ritz-Carlton name and created the concept by which it is known today, with its company-wide concentration on both the personal and the functional side of service. The five-star hotel not only provides impeccable facilities but also takes customer service extremely seriously.

The Ritz-Carlton fulfills this promise by providing impeccable training for its employees and executing its Three Steps of Service and 12 Service Values. The Three Steps of Service state that employees must use a warm and sincere greeting always using the guest's name, anticipate and fulfill each guest's needs, and give a warm good-bye, again using the guest's name. Every manager carries a laminated card with the 12 Service Values. A Ritz-Carlton executive explained, "It's all about people. Nobody has an emotional experience with a thing. We're appealing to emotions." The Ritz-Carlton's 35,000 employees in 29 countries go out of their way to create unique and memorable experiences for their guests.

Not only is the company known for training its employees to provide impeccable customer service, but it also reinforces its mission and values with them on a daily basis. Each day, managers gather their employees for a 15-minute "line up" to check in, resolve any impending problems, and read and discuss what the Ritz-Carlton calls "wow stories." These true stories, read to every employee around the world, recognize an individual employee for his or her outstanding customer service and also highlight 1 of the 12 Service Values.

One family staying at the Ritz-Carlton, Bali, needed a particular type of egg and milk for their son who suffered from food allergies. Employees could not find the appropriate items in town, but the executive chef at the hotel remembered a store in Singapore that sold them. He contacted his mother-in-law, who purchased the items and personally flew them more than 1,000 miles to Bali for the family. This example showcased Service Value 6.

In another instance, a waiter overheard a man telling his wheelchair-bound wife that it was too bad he couldn't get her down to the beach. The waiter told the maintenance crew, and by the next day they had constructed a wooden walkway to the beach and pitched a tent at the far end where the couple had dinner.

Wow stories can also be as simple as an employee's remembering how a guest prefers coffee and then preparing it that way without asking for the rest of his or her stay. According to Cooper, the daily wow story is "the best way to communicate what we expect from our ladies and gentlemen around the world. Every story reinforces the actions we are looking for and demonstrates how each and every person in our organization contributes to our service values." Each employee is empowered to spend as much as $2,000 without management approval to help deliver a guest's anticipated need or desire, supporting the company's intention to build lifelong positive relationships with each customer.

Ritz-Carlton measures the success of its customer service efforts through Gallup phone interviews, which ask both functional and emotional questions. Functional questions include: "How was the meal?" or "Was your bedroom clean?" while emotional questions reveal the customer's sense of well-being. The hotel uses these findings as well as day-to-day experiences to continually enhance and improve the experience for its guests.

Today Ritz-Carlton is owned by Marriott and now has 97 hotels in 30 countries; the company plans to expand further throughout Europe, Africa, Asia, the Middle East, and the Americas. It has also earned two Malcolm Baldrige Quality Awards—the only company ever to win the prestigious award twice.

Sources: Robert Reiss, "How Ritz Carlton Stays at Top," *Forbes*, October 30, 2009; Carmine Gallo, "Employee Motivation the Ritz-Carlton Way," *BusinessWeek*, February 29, 2008; Carmine Gallo, "How Ritz-Carlton Maintains Its Mystique," *BusinessWeek*, February 13, 2007; Jennifer Robison, "How the Ritz-Carlton Manages the Mystique," *Gallup Management -Journal*, December 11, 2008; Kelly Kearsley, "Taking a Cue from Ritz-Carlton's Customer Service," *Wall Street Journal*, March 1, 2013; Micah Solomon, "How Four Seasons and Ritz-Carlton Empower Employees and Uphold Customer Service Standards," *Forbes*, October 28, 2013; Micah Solomon, "A Great Customer Experience (Ritz-Carlton Caliber) Requires More Than Just Empowered Employees," *Forbes*, September 18, 2013, http://www.ritzcarlton.com/en/about/factsheet (accessed May 13, 2019).

QUESTIONS FOR DISCUSSION

Chapter 7

1. What market segments in Chapter 7 do you feel would be the best match for a Ritz-Carlton hotel?

Chapter 10

1. Explain how Ritz-Carlton applies the internal marketing concepts mentioned in Chapter 10.

Chapter 15

1. You are a sales person for the Ritz-Carlton in Cleveland, Ohio. A pharmaceutical company has contacted you about having a product introduction and information session for a new drug. It expects 100 medical doctors to come to the event. They are considering your hotel and another hotel. The other hotel is an independent brand equivalent to a business hotel such as a Marriott, Hyatt, or Hilton. The bid at the other hotel is 10 percent less. Your manager has told you not to lower your price. How would you overcome the price objection and close the deal?

2. How does the Ritz-Carlton match up to competing hotels? What are the key differences?

3. Discuss the importance of the "wow stories" in maintaining top-quality customer service for a luxury hotel like the Ritz-Carlton.

Case 12 Grand Targhee

In the competitive world of ski resorts, the race for profitability is always an uphill battle. But Grand Targhee Resort is carving out an innovative path to success that counters conventional wisdom and rethinks strategies popular with larger resorts. Personalized service gave Targhee the lift it needed.

At first glance, Wyoming's Grand Targhee Ski & Summer Resort would seem to have less chance of survival than a ball of its signature talcum-powder snow on a hot summer's day. The crucial element for a successful destination ski resort, according to conventional wisdom, is land. The skiers and snowboarders demand a return on their hefty investment in a roundtrip airline ticket, accommodations, and skyrocketing lift fees in the form of an enormous and varied terrain crisscrossed by numerous high-speed lifts. Off the mountain, it's no longer enough to throw up a couple of pseudo-chalets housing a lodge, a rental shop, and a cafeteria. Today, visitors expect a base village crammed with spiffy shops, luxury hotels, and high-octane restaurants, a destination in itself.

Based on those parameters, Targhee wouldn't appear to have what it takes. Located on the western side of the Grand Tetons about 30 miles from Jackson Hole, Targhee grabs the edge on size, 3,000 acres compared to Jackson Hole's 2,500, but accesses it with just four fill-size lifts and a snow card, compared to Jackson Hole's eight lifts, a gondola, and a tram. Similarly, visitors who white-knuckle their way up the long and hairpin approach road to Targhee find a handful of low-slung lodges, shops, and restaurants grouped around a plaza that can be explored thoroughly in 15 minutes, whereas Jackson Hole's crowded base village recently slotted in a Four Seasons hotel, and the town of Jackson is an easy 12 miles away.

Land usage in the base area is traditionally the key to a destination ski area's -bottom line. "Real estate has become a huge part of the business plans for all the major ski operations," says Mary McKhann, editor of *The Snow Industry Letter*, a trade publication covering the ski and snowboard industry. That real estate generates hefty rents from shops and restaurants and sizable amounts of income from sales of high-priced single-family homes, townhouse condominiums, and interval ownership (the latest euphemism for time-shares). The sale residential real estate and the sale and/or lease commercial real estate is often is needed to justify the development of the resort. Many times the sales of lift tickets along is not enough to sustain a ski resort.

Targhee's pristine terrain is located in the Targhee National Forest and is subject to strict regulations regarding the usage of public land. It took six years to get permission to build a new lift on Peaked Mountain; further expansion of either the slope system or the base area is unlikely in the near future.

Yet 80 percent of the skiers who have tasted Targhee's powder come back for seconds. Although that figure might not seem notable compared to an average return rate of 77 percent for destination skiers at 79 major areas nationwide, many of those areas are within just an hour or two of a significant urban center. Targhee's nearest city is Idaho Falls, Idaho, 80 miles away.

What Is Targhee's Secret?

Because Targhee literally could not expand into new territory, it was forced to take another look at what it already had. In doing so, it found that it was sitting on a mother lode of resources just waiting to be discovered. The light went on for Larry Williamson seven summers ago. At the time, Targhee's horseback riding concession was run by an outside outfitter that strictly scheduled everything: One-hour rides left at 9:00 A.M., 10:30 A.M., and 1:00 P.M., and two-hour rides went out at 10:00 A.M. and 1:30 P.M. "We couldn't get them to accept the idea that if it's 9:30 and you've got guests waiting and two wranglers and fifteen horses sitting down there, why wait half an hour to go on a ride?" Williamson recalls.

Targhee took over the riding program, and Williamson quickly realized that guests didn't want riding lessons per se; they wanted to enjoy being on a horse. The program was changed to accommodate their wishes. The result: "We went from $24,000 to more than $45,000 in one three-month season with no change in marketing, except that when you come in, we'll put you on a horse as soon as possible." Today, the horse concession is pushing $100,000 in revenues.

The next task is to figure out how to satisfy the customer when the snow fell. As a former ski instructor, Williamson knew that the ski school experience could make or break a guest's visit. A University of Idaho survey found that virtually 100 percent of the people who had taken lessons at Targhee's ski school planned on returning, whereas less than half who had not taken lessons were willing to come back. "The obvious answer was that if you're in ski school, you develop a friendship and become part of Targhee," says Williamson.

But there was a less obvious and even more compelling aspect to the lessons. Many ski schools judge their success on how much the student improves. One problem with that method is that success is defined by the instructor's parameters, rather than the guests' preferences.

Williamson came up with a different winning formula. "It really wasn't about how much the guest improved," he concluded. "It was more about how much fun the guest had. People don't like to pay for classes on vacation unless it's something fun. Fun became my focus for the industry."

A key element in Williamson's idea about fun is Mark Hanson, the snow sports school director. Hanson had run the children's program at Targhee for five years before becoming overall director. He knew the secret of a superb program: "If little kids don't have fun, mom's not going to bring them back again. And if they do have fun, mom isn't going to be able to keep them from coming back."

In transferring the successful elements of the kids' program to the adult lessons, Hanson had to take into account the fact that about 80 percent of Targhee's adult clientele is either level II or III skiers, compared to 60 percent at most other resorts. Such advanced skiers are not nearly as inclined to take a lesson as beginners. "We teach, on a percentage basis, far fewer lessons than Vail, so it became a particular challenge to get those advanced skiers into lessons," Williamson says. "Their attraction to powder is part of the answer. Customized options are another. Finding out what people want to accomplish became a priority. Rather than worrying about what they do with their bodies, get them doing things that help develop confidence."

Hanson examined Targhee's liabilities and realized that they could help the company differentiate itself and even provide opportunities. Targhee welcomes about a tenth of those who throng the slopes at Steamboat Springs, a Colorado resort with comparable acreage. But rather than sulk about empty slopes, Hanson says, "The lack of exorbitant volume becomes an advantage. We can be more personal with folks. We can say, 'It's just you and me now, so let's go play and do what you want.'"

Thanks to the small volume, Targhee's snow sports school can afford to be more flexible. At Big Sky, Montana, four hours to the north, semiprivate intermediate lessons go out in the afternoon only; if the snow has turned to slush by 2 P.M., that's tough luck. With so few crowds at Targhee, lessons billed as "group" frequently have attendance that would be more accurately labeled "semiprivate."

But it's the private lessons that best demonstrate Hanson's determination to bend over backward to achieve customer satisfaction. "You can go on a private lesson any time or any day," says public relations director Susie Barnett Bushong. "If you decide you don't want to learn a technical skill, that you just want the instructor to show you secret powder stashes, that's fine. And if you aren't happy with your lessons, you can come back the next day and get a free one."

As the program changed from the standpoint of value and product, the pay strategy changed too. Instead of being paid merely for the cost of their labor, Targhee instructors have a hefty incentive to ensure customer satisfaction through repeat business. "Instructors make much more money from returning mountain tours or returning private lessons than from lessons just assigned to them," Williamson says.

Although an expected amenity, a ski school is often something of a loss leader. Although larger areas amortize the various expenses involved in building up and staffing a school through other revenues, Targhee is too small to afford that kind of luxury. Hence the push to sell private and semiprivate lessons. "Financially, they're a win for us because they generate more revenue, they're a win for the instructors because they can make more money, and they're a win for the guests because they're getting what they want," says Hanson.

Hanson spends a lot of time ensuring he's got the right staff. "They have to be pros at working with people," he says. Again, Targhee's size is an advantage. "We might hire 10 or 12 people every year, whereas some resorts hire 200 each season," he says. "That smaller need allows me to be choosy."

It also enables him to keep a close eye on his staff; no supervisor is in charge of more than 15 instructors. Hanson monitors requests for private and semiprivate lessons and checks responses to guest surveys. "I don't do any formal spying, but I spend a lot of time on the hill myself," he allows. "I can say, 'Hey, I noticed you were doing this. Why?'"

Hanson's attentions have paid off. Grand Targhee's ski school brings in only 4.5 percent of revenue, compared to a national average of 7.5 percent. But in terms of EBITDA (earnings before interest, taxes, depreciation, and amortization), the school contributes a whopping 30.1 percent, whereas the national average is a little more than half that amount.

Targhee also bucks the industry trend by fervently pursuing the local market. "All the research will tell you that the destination guest spends more money, but to be successful, we can't afford to concentrate on that one aspect of our market," says Hanson. To broaden its share of the regional market, Targhee has adopted an all-encompassing approach, sponsoring ski programs in elementary, middle, and high schools, partnering with ski clubs in nearby Idaho Falls and at the University of Idaho at the other end of the state, and organizing programs aimed at niche audiences as narrow as, say, women from southeastern Idaho. Not surprisingly, discounted lessons and instructional weekends are a big part of the perks of membership in those ski clubs. "We get a lot of the same people who come to every instructional they can, and they generate more business for us by telling their friends," says Hanson.*

Targhee's drive for customer satisfaction and repeat business pervades every aspect of its efforts, from the parking lot attendants to the ski patrol. Each department is graded on its performance, with guest satisfaction accounting for a large portion of the rating. Five years ago, the ski patrol had a 44 percent performance rating. Then patrol staff members started to have lunch with guests, give demonstrations with their avalanche dog, and make themselves more visible. Last year, their score hit 88 percent.

Similarly, the parking lot attendants had barely eked out a 40 percent rating. They decided that guests wanted to see them working efficiently, so they donned bright orange vests, worked out a series of hand signals, were friendlier, and boosted their rating up to the 90s. Says Williamson, "The whites of the teeth are the number-one factor."

Williamson knows that Targhee will never be able to compete directly with places like Vail or Jackson Hole. It will never have the same number of chair lifts or the swanky base village that can be subsidized by real estate sales and rentals. "We try to focus not on competing with other resorts but on those features that make Targhee unique," he says. By mining those already existing assets, Williamson's team has figured out a way to turn Targhee's famous effervescent powder into cold, hard cash.

*Courtesy of Catherine Fredman.

QUESTIONS FOR DISCUSSION

Chapter 2

1. How did the management of Grand Targhee create a service culture?
2. How does fun relate to establishing a service culture?
3. What product did Grand Targhee focus on to create interaction between the guests and employees? Why was this product successful?

Chapter 10

1. Find evidence from the case to show that Grand Targhee practiced good internal marketing concepts.

Case 13 The Bleeding Heart Restaurant: Unique Positioning of a Restaurant

The Bleeding Heart Restaurant and Bistro has been a favorite with Londoners (UK) for 30 years. The perennially popular restaurant and Bistro was started in 1983 by Robert and Robyn Wilson, two former journalists, as a tiny basement wine bar in a deserted and derelict cellar that had once been the warehouse of a Victorian clock manufacturer. Despite warnings from fellow members of London's wine trade that a bar so hidden could never succeed, the Bleeding Heart prospered from the start. Today, it serves over a thousand guests per day.

History

Bleeding Heart Yard

The long-established and extremely popular Bleeding Heart restaurant offers superb French food in historical surroundings. The restaurant takes its name from the yard where it is located, which, according to the history books, was named after an eleventh-century beauty, Lady Elizabeth Hatton, who was found murdered there.

The Legend

Lady Elizabeth Hatton was the toast of eleventh-century London society. The widowed daughter-in-law of the famous merchant Sir Christopher Hatton (one-time consort of Queen Elizabeth I), Lady Elizabeth was young, beautiful, and very wealthy. Her suitors were many and varied, and they included a leading London bishop and a prominent European ambassador. Invitations to her soirees in Hatton Garden were much sought after.

Her annual Winter Ball, on January 26, 1626, was one of the highlights of the London social season. Halfway through the evening's festivities, the doors to Lady Hatton's grand ballroom were flung open. In strode a swarthy gentleman, slightly hunched of shoulder, with a clawed right hand. He took her by the hand, danced her once around the room and out through the double doors into the garden. A buzz of gossip arose. Would Lady Elizabeth and the European ambassador (for it was he) kiss and make up, or would she return alone? Neither was to be. The next morning her body was found in the cobblestone courtyard—torn limb from limb, with her heart still pumping blood onto the cobblestones. And from henceforth, the yard was to be known as the Bleeding Heart Yard.

Charles Dickens and the Bleeding Heart

Charles Dickens knew Bleeding Heart well. In *Little Dorrit* he wrote of folks in the yard, saying, "The more practical of the Yard's inmates abided by the tradition of the murder." But he went on to document another Bleeding Heart story: "The gentler and more imaginative inhabitants, including the whole of the tender sex, were loyal to the legend of a young lady imprisoned in her own chamber by a cruel

*Reprinted by permission from Catherine Fredman.

father for remaining true to her own true lover—but it was objected to by the murderous party that this was the invention of a spinster and romantic, still lodging in the Yard."

Today, the Bleeding Heart has grown well beyond that tiny basement wine bar but has preserved and enhanced the architectural, cultural, and historic value of its unique location while serving a multisegment market.

The Tavern has guarded the entrance to the Bleeding Heart Yard since 1746 with a history of conviviality encapsulated in its then boast of "drunk for a penny and dead drunk for two pence." Today, the Tavern offers a traditional neighborhood bar with real ale and a light lunchtime menu for those pressed for time.

Downstairs the Tavern Dining Room with its jolly farmyard illustrations features an open rotisserie and grill and provides a warm and comforting setting in which to enjoy free-range organic British meat, game, and poultry along with an excellent-value wine list.

The Tavern is also open for breakfast, with freshly squeezed orange juice, home-baked croissants, and "The Full English" with tasty Suffolk Bacon.

Early Days

In the early days, the Bleeding Heart's proximity to the headquarters of many of the national dailies—*The Times*, *The Mirror*, and *The Guardian*—coupled with the media connections (and the media's partiality to a decent bottle of wine) meant that from its inception the wine bar attracted a number of leading journalists and, in their wake, the public relations industry.

The Barristers Chambers of Gray's Inn were also but a corkscrew's throw away, and the Bleeding Heart became a popular lunch spot for this learned group to discuss their briefs over a decent bottle of claret and a platter of charcuterie or cheese.

The increasingly upscale clientele began to demand a more sophisticated menu than the simple wine bar fare originally offered. In response, the bar expanded its horizons into an adjoining basement and its kitchens to include a white tablecloth restaurant with more sophisticated, although still classically French, cuisine.

From that 40-seat bar, the Bleeding Heart expanded, above and around the ancient cobblestoned courtyard to encompass a formal fine-dining restaurant seating 160 with a 30-seat terrace, a 60-seat bistro with its own 40-seat terrace, a 70-seat tavern and bar, and two private dining rooms: the Parlor and the Wine Cellar. Adjoining Bleeding Heart Yard in Ely Place is the stunning medieval function room, the Crypt, and its intimate Crypt Café. The twelfth-century crypt, which seats 120, was the venue for the celebration following the wedding of Henry VIII and Catherine of Aragon.

Marketing

On opening day, the Wilsons deployed two French waitresses to hand out "How to Find Us" maps at the local underground station (subway). There was no advertising because there was no budget. As a launch tool, the leaflets were not an instant success; on that first day the restaurant earned only £39.37. However, within a week, word started to spread and turnover tripled. The week-long distribution of those leaflets was Bleeding Heart's only external promotion ever did.

Word of mouth was relied on to reach the right sort of customer. It worked, building a loyal and homogeneous clientele who believe that they have, by finding the tucked-away little Yard and the bustling bistro beneath it, made a personal discovery. The restaurant was a "best kept secret," a secret that, fortunately, lots of people were in on. The Unique Selling Proposition (USP) was their unique location.

Shortly after opening, Bleeding Heart was described by a New York reviewer as "bleeding hard to find but worth it." A London cab driver commented to a lost diner that the reason it was called Bleeding Heart was that it was Bleeding Hard to find. Robert and Robyn used the mantra that you had to discover Bleeding Heart rather than read an advertisement about it. They also worked hard building a database of regular customers, mainly by running monthly prize drawings to garner business cards, which, in those pre-e-mail days, had postal addresses and telephone numbers. It was a labor-intensive task, but they built a customer base of some 5,000 with a shorter list of 500 of those with a special interest in wine.

To the short list they promoted their regular wine and food evenings and any wine-related events such as the New Beaujolais Breakfast. Magnum Night was launched offering a special half-price deal on Friday evenings (the quietest night) for magnums of champagne. The Seagram Company had discovered a large stock of magnums of Heidsieck champagne in Ireland, which they were keen to offload at a very attractive price.

Despite the fact there was no promotion, Magnum Night became a rapid and astonishingly successful draw card. The hours it was available were cut from 5:30 until 7:00 P.M. only to discover that queues were forming in the yard. On one occasion, a journalist from the BBC phoned offering to pay in advance by credit card lest he should miss the 7:00 P.M. cutoff.

However, there was a downside to this promotion. Regular evening diners (long-term bread-and-butter customers) couldn't get in the door past the queues of Johnny-come-lately champagne quaffers, and with much regret, especially from the champagne drinkers; the promotion was stopped after a year. In its place the Magnum Club was created based on the premise that wine tastes better in bigger bottles. Regular customers were invited to join. Initially members were offered a discount on champagne. Then the offer expanded to include invitations to wine tastings and wine making dinners. The Club is still going strong and membership is free but by invitation only, and it is much sought after.

Today, the Wilsons still do no advertising for Bleeding Heart Restaurant, Bistro, or Tavern, but they have begun carefully targeted promotions for special functions in special publications aimed at the corporate event market and the wedding sector. These are always tied to associated editorial features.

Talking to regular customers has become much easier with e-mail, but the Wilsons are hypercautious about invading their e-space. Mailings are used only for major events such as the summer opening of the outdoor terrace when regular customers are given a complimentary glass of rosé wine to celebrate the sunshine.

The Wilsons believe that keeping a low profile has worked in an increasingly crowded marketplace. In 2008, despite the economic slowdown in the financial sector, turnover was still increasing. During this difficult economic period, the *London Evening Standard* newspaper wrote a feature about restaurants feeling the pinch of the recession. Bleeding Heart was one of the few restaurants to be lauded as "fully booked."

The restaurant received a number of favorable comments from both local and international media. The media praised the food, service, and ambiance of the restaurant. This media was more effective than any advertising the restaurant could place, as potential guests viewed it as a credible source of information. Thus, the press coverage proved to be a major factor in driving business to the restaurant.

Awards

During its first six months, the tiny wine bar/bistro was voted one of London's Top Ten Wine Bars by *Time Out* magazine and has continued to win plaudits from national and international press ever since, including "London's most romantic restaurant" from *The Times*, "Best Venue in Europe" from the *Guardian*, and "Best Private Dining."

The *Zagat Guide* put it in the top three restaurants in London for a business lunch. *Hardens*, the most authoritative London restaurant guide, and *Square Meal*, the city of London's eating-out bible, both rate it number one for business. Since its inception, Bleeding Heart has always been known for its extensive and well-priced wine list. The Wilsons have been frequent winners of an annual Award of Excellence for "One of the Best Wine Lists in the World" from *Wine Spectator* magazine.

QUESTIONS FOR DISCUSSION

Chapter 13

1. Explain the elements of the promotional mix that the Bleeding Heart Restaurant used.
2. Why do you think the Bleeding Heart was so successful with such a small budget for promotion?

Chapter 14

1. If you were hired as a public relations firm for the Bleeding Heart, how would you plan its public relations campaign?

2. There are a number of favorable mentions in popular media about the restaurant. How do you think it was able to get these mentions in the media?

Chapter 16

1. The Bleeding Heart has not changed its promotional strategy since it opened. If you purchased the Bleeding Heart, would you use social media? If you would, explain how you will use it. If not, explain why not.

Case 14 Pricing Almost Destroys and Then Saves a Local Restaurant

"As I pulled into the gravel parking lot I knew immediately that the Mexicatessan was a warm, friendly Mexican restaurant. There was nothing new here, and I don't mean that in a negative way. Nothing looked new but it all looked comfortable, well-worn with the passage of time. Mexican motifs line the walls and ceiling right next to the window air conditioners."

The restaurant, located in a lower-middle-class neighborhood, attracts both locals and Houston's rich and famous. The restaurant's profitability started to drop. The owner, Mr. Herrera, worked long, hard hours producing a high-quality product that his customers enjoyed, but he received very little reward for his time and investment. He had a good product, a good location, and a strong following. The problem was pricing. The prices at the Mexicatessan were far below those of the competition. Herrera wanted to offer good value, and he felt that he had to keep his prices below the chains. He used price to gain a competitive advantage against the chain's expensive buildings and their large regional advertising budgets.

Instead of attracting and maintaining loyal customers, the Mexicatessan's low prices almost destroyed the business. The prices were not high enough to produce sufficient cash flow to keep the restaurant in good repair. Herrera was unable to receive financial reward for his efforts. After several years of struggling, the owner commissioned a research project to see how he could increase his cash flow. The research suggested that his prices were 50 percent less than those of the competition, even though his customers thought the food quality was better. Herrera decided to increase his prices, so they were only 10 percent less than the competition. He felt this price difference and his food quality would offset the competitive advantages of the chains. He set out to achieve his strategy through a series of planned price increases. Because achieving his target would mean price increases of 70 percent or more on some items, the first price increase was about 25 percent, with subsequent price increases gradually moving him to his desired pricing levels. Over a three-year period, the menu prices increased by 40 to 70 percent. This was a bold move.

After the price increases, the Mexicatessan's revenues increased at a higher percentage than the price increases, indicating there was little resistance to the price increases. Herrera's customers still thought they were getting good value. The price increases allowed him to put a new roof on the building, hire additional staff, decorate the restaurant's interior, and receive a good return on his investment. This case study demonstrates the importance of price. Operations that charge too little often do not have money to maintain the business, although they have many customers and appear prosperous.

Herrera was lucky. It is easier to move up the price of a product that is underpriced than it is to lower the price of an overpriced product. Companies that overcharge create a negative attitude among those who have tried their products. Even when prices are lowered, customer attitudes may remain unchanged. Pricing must be a carefully planned management process.

QUESTIONS FOR DISCUSSION

Chapter 11

1. Why was Mr. Herrera reluctant to raise his prices? How did these low prices almost destroy the business?

2. Using this case as an example, explain how the concepts of demand, price, and profits are interrelated.

Case 15 Good Value at Spirit Airlines: Getting Less but Paying Much Less for It

There is a flood of social media comments posted regularly by dissatisfied Spirit Airlines customers. This isn't the kind of feedback most companies want to hear. What's more, adding to such negative social media testimonials, Spirit Airlines also recently earned the dubious distinction of being Consumer Reports' lowest-rated airline for the customer experience, receiving one of the lowest-ever overall scores given by the organization.

So Spirit Airlines must be headed down the path to bankruptcy and ruin, right? To the contrary, Spirit is one of the nation's fastest-growing carriers. It fills almost every available seat on every flight. And it turns a healthy profit every quarter, a difficult feat in the up-and-down airline industry. How does Spirit Airlines do it? By mastering the art and science of extreme good-value pricing. Spirit's value proposition: "Less money. More go."

Spirit Airlines is an "ultra-low-cost carrier," resulting in prices much lower than those of competitors, up to 90 percent lower in some cases. But to cash in on such rock-bottom fares, customers must accept less in return. Buying a ticket on a Spirit flight gets you one thing and one thing only, a seat on a plane to your destination. If you want more, you pay for it. Under what it calls "Bare Fare" pricing, Spirit charges extra for everything. Everything. You get only what you pay for and not one peanut more.

For example, whereas most airlines provide free beverages, Spirit charges $3 for a bottle of water or can of soda. Want a pillow or a blanket? Glad to oblige, that'll be $7, please. Getting a seat assignment costs $15, and it will cost you $10 extra to have a check-in agent print out your boarding pass. A full-size carry-on bag runs another $55. Adding insult to injury, seats on Spirit flights are crammed much closer together (what Spirit calls "a little cozier seating"), and the seats don't recline. If you do want a little more breathing room—you guessed it—for a fee you can get an exit row or first-class sized front-row seat.

Frill Control

Spirit refers to its pricing practices as "Frill Control," claiming that it gives customers more control over what they pay for and what they don't. It points out that the so-called free sodas and extra legroom on other airlines aren't really free. Customers are forced to pay for them in the all-inclusive ticket price whether they want them or not. On Spirit, passengers have the option. Although this approach sounds refreshing, some customers view it as cheap nickel-and-diming or, worse, as unfair and deceitful. The social media are filled with tales of unwary customers who say they ended up paying more for extras than they saved on the initial ticket.

Spirit Airlines takes a hardline approach in responding to customer complaints. When customers request pricing exceptions, Spirit agents stand their ground. The extra charges are optional, not mandatory, the airline explains. The base ticket price includes everything passengers need to get to their destinations. "We've rejected, for example, charging for bathrooms," says Spirit's CEO. "We're never going to do that. That's not an optional thing."

Defense of Poor Service and Pricing

Rather than hiding from its poor customer service record, Spirit Airlines seems almost to wear it as a badge of honor. When one recent study showed that Spirit ranked dead last in complaints made to the U.S. Department of Transportation,

Spirit turned it into bragging rights. Over the five years of the study, the airline averaged only eight complaints per 100,000 customers. Spirit celebrated by offering $24 discounts. "That's right, over 99.99 percent of our customers did not file a complaint with the Department of Transportation," Spirit declared in a press release. "To the 0.01 per-cent, that's OK, we know we aren't the airline for everyone (though we'd love for you to save by flying with us again!)."

The company further defends its pricing by noting that, for customers who take the time to look, it provides plenty of upfront information about what its fares cover. In fact, Spirit's online site offers "Spirit 101: Your Simple Guide to the Way We Fly," a detailed guide on what you get for what you pay and how to make the Spirit Bare Fare system work to your advantage. Despite the angst of the vocal few who think they are being fleeced, most Spirit customers seem to know exactly what they are getting and are happy with that. When asked if she resented paying $3 for water on a Spirit flight, one passenger replied, "Not at all. They're trying to cover their costs." That attitude is shared by most Spirit customers, who seem more than happy to give up the extras to get the super-cheap fares.

To see what all the fuss was about, one airline analyst put Spirit Airlines to the test, eyes wide open. After paying only $63 for a one-way flight from Detroit to LaGuardia, roughly $300 less than the same fare offered by Delta, American, or United, he reported on his experience. "After we landed I turned to my friend and said, 'I don't get it, what ... are people complaining about?'" He concluded that most dissatisfaction stems from misconceptions, that if people are aware of Spirit's policies ahead of time, they can avoid unpleasant surprises and add-ons they don't want. If you want entertainment, he suggests, bring along your own on a mobile device. Plan ahead and buy snacks and beverages before boarding. Think ahead and add in the fees for carry-ons or checked bags to calculate the true fare. Or pack light and jam everything into a small carry-on bag or backpack you can take on for free. And prepare yourself mentally that you might "be able to determine the shampoo used by the person in the row ahead of you." For flights no longer than three hours, being a little squished isn't all that bad.

For those customers who complain that the extras add up to more than the savings, official numbers suggest otherwise. Spirit's total flight price (all fees included) is still the lowest in the industry, an average of 40 percent below competitors' prices. Even at those super-low prices, thanks to its industry-lowest cost per seat-mile, Spirit Airlines still reaps industry-leading profit margins. For example, Spirit's total revenue per passenger is less than half of what United Airlines needs per passenger just to break even. Over the past four years, despite renewed challenges from its large competitors, Spirit's annual revenues shot up more than 80 percent to nearly $2 billion; net income soared almost 200 percent.

Thus, Spirit Airlines is thriving with its less, for-much-less positioning approach. True, you don't get much when you fly Spirit. Then again, you don't pay for what you don't get. And you end up with more money in your pocket to spend at your destination. If paying for the extras bothers you, don't buy them. Or just fly another airline and pay the full up-front fare. But Spirit won't be giving away those extras for free anytime soon. "[We won't] add costs for things that most customers don't value as much as our low fares just to reduce the complaints of a few customers," says the CEO. "Doing that would raise prices for everyone, compromising our commitment to what our customers have continuously told us they truly value, the lowest possible price."

Sources: Based on information from Shawn Tully, "Behind the Sudden Departure of Spirit Airline's Wildly Unconventional CEO," *Fortune*, January 8, 2016, http://fortune.com/2016/01/08/spirit-airlines-ceo-ouster/; "If Spirit Airlines Is So Unpopular, Why Are Its Flights So Full?" *CBS News*, March 23, 2014, www.cbsnews.com/news/if-spirit-airlines-is-so-unpopular-why-are-its-flights-so-full/; Justin Bachman, "Spirit Airlines Sees All Those Passenger Complaints as Mere Misunderstandings," *Bloomberg Businessweek*, April 18, 2014, www.businessweek.com/articles/2014-04-18/spirit-airiines-passenger-complaints-part-of-its-business-model; Jared Blank, "3 Myths About Spirit Airlines," *Online Travel Review*, September 10, 2012, www.onlinetravelreview.com/2012/09/10/3-myths-about-spirit-airlines-or-my-flight-on-spirit-was-perfectly-fine-really/; Adam Levine-Weinberg, "Why Houston Is Spirit Airlines' Next Big Growth Market," *The Motley Fool*, November 20, 2014, www.fool.com/investing/general/2014/11/20/why-houston-is-spirit-airlines-next-big-growth-mar.aspx;

"Value Airline of the Year-Spirit Airlines," *ATW*, January 23, 2015, http://atwonline.com/airlines/value-airline-year-spirit-airlines; and http://marketing.spirit.com/how-to-fly-spirit-airlines/en/, http://ir.spirit.com/financials.cfm, and www.spirit.com (accessed September 2016).

QUESTIONS FOR DISCUSSION

Chapter 1

1. How does Spirit Airlines create value for travelers?
2. Referring to needs, wants, and demands, what wants is Spirit Airlines satisfying for its customers?
3. For class discussion in North America, see which students have flown Spirit Airlines and which ones would fly again and why? Then see who would not fly again and why?

Chapter 11

1. What pricing principles and approaches are used in Spirit Airline's pricing strategy?
2. How does Spirit Airlines meet the expectations of travelers given the airfares charged?

Case 16 Apollo Hotel

After just 10 months of operation, Ryan Sawyer was proud of what he had accomplished managing the Apollo Hotel, but he knew that much work remained.

The Apollo was owned by the Williams Cosmetic Company and was located in Kentucky. The hotel had originally been built to serve as housing for students who attended the Williams Cosmetology School and was converted to an 82-room hotel in September 2002 to serve the general public.

In addition to the hotel, the complex contained a manufacturing plant for personal care products and the corporate headquarters of the Williams Cosmetic Company.

The Williams Cosmetic Company discontinued the operation of a cosmetology school and decided to concentrate on the manufacture and sale of cosmetics. The hotel was opened to use the existing building.

When the hotel opened, there were very few guests, almost no staff, and a limited budget. The hotel had no brochure, Web site, or even a listing in the yellow pages. Although Ryan had no previous hospitality industry experience, he was told to build the business and turn it into a profitable operation.

Ryan held a bachelor's degree in economics/business management from Colorado State University. He had worked with a large regional bank and with JCPenney Company.

Marketing Strategy

Ryan decided that the hotel should be marketed to a wide spectrum of guests. Over the years, Mr. and Mrs. Williams had met many people through their church and community work. These contacts proved useful in promoting the hotel.

The Convention and Visitors Bureau also proved to be helpful and referred many guests. Ryan contacted the Little League and secured contracts for teams to stay in the hotel by offering free lodging to referees on a double occupancy per room basis.

To entice guests during the season, Ryan decided to offer three nights for the price of two if guests would make reservations two months prior to arrival and pay in advance. This proved to be moderately effective.

A large electric utility company was offered very good rates to encourage their crews to stay at the hotel. This resulted in many nights of occupancy.

U.S. military personnel were also encouraged to stay at the hotel through very good rates. Ryan believed that with only 82 rooms, the best opportunity to fill beds was to contact organizations rather than attempt to market to individual travelers.

The hotel seemed to be gaining a reputation as "value lodging" and had experienced 58 percent occupancy on average for the last four months.

Ryan observed that the company's cosmetic items were not used or sold in the hotel even though they were manufactured on the grounds. This was corrected by placing Williams's amenity products in the rooms and opening a gift shop in the hotel, which sold the company's personal care products as well as other traditional gift shop items.

Personnel

As a small, privately owned hotel not operating as a flag property, the management of Apollo could explore different operational strategies. As an example, front-desk employees were paid a commission on business that they brought to the hotel. This encouraged front-desk people to continuously be aware of sales opportunities when someone called or dropped in. It also encouraged them to "sell" the hotel to their friends and to organizations they knew such as churches, schools, and clubs. Ryan said that with commissions, front-desk employees averaged more income than their counterparts in other area hotels.

Ryan believed that his primary responsibility was to "keep the lights on" by marketing the hotel and that operational decisions should be left to those responsible for the operational areas. He held the belief that most people who desired personal growth and responsibility could learn the operational tasks and would find ways to do the job better without top-down micromanagement. He also believed that all employees should be cross-trained and willing temporarily to accept responsibilities outside the primary department. The maintenance man had once been asked to wear a suit and serve as bellboy during a heavy occupancy period. This seemed to work well.

All new employees were expected to learn how to clean rooms and make beds so they could help with that important area in crunch times. The number-one criterion for employment with Apollo was, "Are you willing to learn and willing to work?"

Employees were also expected to constantly improve their professionalism. When decisions were needed by management, department heads were expected to type up their proposal and present it in a professional manner. This forced the department heads to think through the proposal, take it seriously, and be prepared to defend it.

Openness to New Ideas

Ryan said he was open to new ideas from employees and others concerning ways to improve occupancy and operations at the hotel.

■■■ QUESTIONS FOR DISCUSSION

Chapter 9

1. What recommendations would you offer to Ryan to:
   a. Increase occupancy
   b. Improve REVPAR
   c. Improve operations

Chapter 10

1. What would you do to further increase the level of personal responsibility that Ryan developed among employees?

2. Do you believe that employees should be cross-trained to do many tasks in a hotel? Does this alienate applicants who might otherwise be good employees?

Chapter 13

1. Should Ryan hire an ad agency to help position and market the hotel? Explain your answer.

■■■ Case 17 The Cameron Trading Post and Lodge

Travelers who venture 52 miles north of Flagstaff, Arizona, on Highway 89 are surprised and delighted when they stop at the Cameron Trading Post along the Little Colorado River Canyon. In reality, Cameron Trading Post represents most of the commercial activity in the town of Cameron. A decommissioned swayback suspension bridge built in 1911 sits next to the property.

Cameron began as a trading post where Hopi and Navajo residents bartered wool, blankets, and livestock for flour, sugar, canned goods, and household products. A trip to the post would take days of travel by horse-drawn wagon. Customers were always treated as family and fed and housed at the trading post. The local people trusted traders at Cameron because they understood local dialects and customers and explained the confusing American legal and social system.

Today, the trading post is owned by the employees and Joe Atkinson, a direct descendent of the original owners. It serves as a stopping point for travelers headed to the Grand Canyon, Lake Powell, the Painted Desert, and Utah.

The Cameron Trading Post and Lodge represent an example of:

Quality

Customer service

Respect for Native American culture

Excellent merchandising

Fair treatment and training of employees

Employee empowerment

Continuous product innovation

Cameron Trading Post may also represent a warning for the entire hospitality industry concerning the delicate balance between natural resource use, particularly water, and commercial growth.

The strength behind Cameron Trading Post is Joe Atkinson, a product and heir of Western pioneers and their attitudes, not the Hollywood version.

Joe's family came to Arizona and New Mexico as Indian traders. One was killed by Paiutes, Navajos, or outlaws in the 1840s as he carried trading goods by horse and mule to his customers.

Joe was born to the business at the Three Hogans Trading Post in Arizona. His uncles, CD and Hubert Richardson, moved to Arizona from Cleburne, Texas, and established a trading post at Cameron in 1916. In 1964, it was leased to Chevron Oil Company and later to the Harvey Corporation, a hospitality company pioneer who had built a successful western hotel, restaurant, and gift shop chain in cooperation with the Santa Fe Railroad.

Joe gained control of the Cameron Trading Post as well as Indian jewelry stores in Gallup, Santa Fe, Albuquerque, and Phoenix.

Joe didn't have the advantage of a college education but became an acknowledged expert in Indian jewelry and art and also learned to fly his own twin-engine Cessna. Joe discovered cigars at age four and until recently he and a good cigar were inseparable. That was the second time he had to give up cigars. The first was when he started grade school and the principal would not permit a cigar-smoking first grader.

The Cameron Trading Post serves as a source of southwestern art, souvenirs, and curios. The store features quality handcrafted traditional patterns on weaving, baskets, pottery, jewelry, and carvings. A free gallery of American Southwest Indian art is situated in a historic building of sandstone and log on the property.

Visitors dine in an atmosphere of antique luxury. A huge stone fireplace and beautiful local art provide a southwestern setting for breakfast, lunch, and dinner. The menu features American and Mexican foods as well as a signature "Navajo taco."

The 66-room lodge follows the upscale Southwest theme with exquisite furnishings and impeccable maintenance. Prices are moderate, yet 100 percent occupancy occurs only 25 to 30 nights a year.

ROOM RATES

March–October	$119–$199 plus tax
November–February	$ 79–$169 plus tax

Additionally, the property contains RV sites with full hookup, electricity, sewage, and water.

RV RATES

Nightly	$35 plus tax
Monthly	$350 plus tax

Joe said that marketing by Cameron Trading Post is almost nonexistent other than information in the AAA guidebook and a few signs. The Southwest has experienced a prolonged drought and the property has been strictly limited to 24 million gallons per year, which it pulls from the Little Colorado River. With current use at 22.5 million gallons, Joe said the management was forced to consider customer tradeoffs. Lodge customers use more water than restaurant guests or stop-by shoppers, yet hotel guests provide cross-sales in the restaurant and in the gift shop.

Prior to 9/11, the property hosted 45 tour buses per day. Forty percent of these were European tourists; the remainder were U.S. and Canadian retirees. The management originally felt that these guests would appreciate a cafeteria line because the stop time was only 30 to 40 minutes. Instead, the guests, particularly the Europeans, wanted sit-down service.

Once this was known, the management and staff found a system to serve all guests hot meals of their choice in 25 minutes. Joe expressed pride in the willingness of his employees to provide such service.

In 2004, bus tours had reached 18 per day, and further gains were expected unless another terrorist attack or unforeseen problem occurred in the United States. The European travelers from Germany, Italy, and France were particularly excited by the Indian products and gallery and the fact that 90 percent or more of the employees are Native American, largely of the Hopi and Navajo cultures.

The Alumni Club of Stanford University also discovered Cameron. Members of this group annually stayed in the RV camp or the lodge and brought their own chef who prepared open-air meals in the garden.

Collector's Auction

Although Joe downplayed his company's marketing activity, he said that tremendous success had been achieved with a collector's auction of Southwest Indian Art, first held in 1985 with only 15 to 18 people in attendance. By 1999, over 300 people attended filling rooms, RV sites, and the restaurant and gift shop. Eventually this was discontinued as the availability of antique Indian art diminished. The front cover of the final auction catalog featured four-year-old Joe sitting in a wooden rocking chair with cigar in hand.

Joe admitted that other promotional events could be organized to help increase occupancy in off-seasons. Typical occupancy percentages follow:

Summer	85%
Winter	30%
Fall/Spring	60–70%

U.S. vacation patterns account for the summer peak, but the best months for cool weather in northern Arizona occur in the trough seasons.

Management Style

Joe personally takes charge of selecting room furnishings, gallery displays, and overseeing future expansion ideas such as the possible construction of Navajo-style Hogans along the rim of the canyon to serve as unique guest rooms.

Mike Davis, general manager, is charged with daily operations, including the critical task of merchandise buying. Mike came from a strong retail background and Joe said he largely takes a hands-off approach yet consults with Mike.

Very little turnover exists among employees, and many retire with a retirement package that is quite good for the area. Joe said the following of his employees:

- They are dedicated to Cameron.
- They offer great input for improving operations.
- They want to learn and improve.
- They are customer friendly and provide good service.
- They are not afraid to say, "that's a dumb idea."
- They are cross-trained to work in different areas and willingly do so.
- They look on themselves and management as an extended family.

Joe and his management group realize the many advantages of the Native American workforce, the history of Cameron, and emphasis on quality that has been established. However, they know that the task of balancing customers and product offerings with the natural resource base will grow even more pressing in the future.

At present, merchandise sales represent the largest source of income with food and beverage second, followed by lodging. Joe believes it is important to have a mix of the three product areas and to resist any temptation to overemphasize merchandise. His goal is to maintain the cultural and historical foundation of the Cameron Trading Post and Lodge and provide a secure employment base for the 110 full-time employees who would otherwise be forced to drive or move to Flagstaff or Phoenix to support their families, thus disrupting their centuries-old cultural and societal heritage.

Source: Updated May 2019; http://www.camerontradingpost.com/.

QUESTIONS FOR DISCUSSION

Chapter 18

1. Discuss the tradeoff issues that Joe and his management team face concerning marketing, growth, natural resources, and the posts' traditional employment base.
2. What would you recommend to the management of Cameron Trading Post and Lodge?
3. What other sensitive resource issues are hospitality companies likely to face in the next 5 to 10 years? In the United States? In other countries?
4. What is the proper role for marketing in resource management?
5. What should Cameron Trading Post and Lodge do about the relatively low occupancy during the nonpeak seasons?

Case 18 Tropicana Fishing Lodge

How does a fishing lodge fit into our operations as a major producer of bananas? This was the question that faced the Costa Rican division of an international banana company.

Location and Description of Tropicana

Tropicana was a fishing lodge located on the Caribbean coast of Costa Rica. It was situated on the banks of the River Pastura. It could be reached by light plane because there was a paved landing strip on the nearby properties of Del Monte. It could also be reached by means of a mountain highway from San José. This road was 98 percent paved and required approximately three to three-and-a-half hours of travel. Fog could be a problem on this road and could impede travel. A small dock had been built to accommodate loading and unloading the boats. A series of steps, including rather steep steel ones with a rope handhold, led to the grassy bank above.

Immediately behind the lodge was a banana plantation. A cement sidewalk separated the plantation from the lodge and homes. The grounds surrounding the lodge were well kept and quite attractive. The beauty was not dramatic or awe inspiring but was instead peaceful and relaxing. Jungle growth could be seen on the opposite bank of the river, and monkeys could be heard howling in the forest.

The lodge was built in the fashion of a jungle building—it was not constructed on the ground but on wooden stilts. This allowed ventilation and helped prevent rotting. It also helped discourage insects and small animals from entering. The lodge was small but would accommodate 22 guests. Guest rooms were contained in a separate cabin that formed an "L" to the main lodge. The rooms were clean and well maintained. Each room had a bathroom with a shower and other bathroom fixtures. Beds were of the single-bed or bunk-bed style. There was no air conditioning in the rooms, but the evening breeze was pleasant. A light blanket was sometimes necessary.

Recreational Facilities

Fishing for tarpon and snook was the primary entertainment offered by Tropicana. This occurred in the intercoastal canal, which runs from Limón to the Nicaraguan border. It was also done in lagoons and the mouths of rivers. The river in front of Tropicana offered little opportunity for fishing; it was necessary to go downstream 30 to 40 minutes by boat to reach fishing sites.

Three principal areas were noted for tarpon and snook. One was in a lagoon 40 minutes downstream and to the south of Tropicana. Another was downstream and north of Tropicana near the village of Parismina. This was 45 minutes to an hour away and near a competitor's lodge. The third was much farther north, in the area of Tortuguero. This was roughly one-and-a-half hours away.

The scenery in the intercoastal canal and along the jungle rivers was beautiful. One could see a variety of bird life, including many rare species. Monkeys could be heard and sometimes seen in the trees. Both Walt Disney and Jacques Cousteau had made movies featuring the region. Crocodiles were difficult to see. Deer, marguary, jaguar, and many small animals also lived there but were rarely seen. Botanists and other nature lovers could find hours of enjoyment in the variety of trees, flowers, orchids, and other plant life, including a perfume tree that filled the air with a beautiful aroma in the evening.

There was little or no opportunity to exploit commercial hunting in the area. The area was not known for ducks or geese, and the deer were quite small. In addition, much of the area was gradually being turned into national parks, and wildlife would be protected. Swimming or water skiing in the lagoons and intercoastal waterway would be dangerous due to submerged logs. There was also the possibility of sharks. The Caribbean coast represented miles of uninhabited dark sandy beach. It had palm trees and was attractive but was not developed. Moreover, it was very difficult to reach the beach from Tropicana. The surf at the mouth of the river was too strong to permit entry into the sea with the flat-bottom boats and motors. Thus, the boats could not be used for ocean fishing.

Any large-scale building projects such as a lodge, modern tennis courts, or a golf course would require land. This would almost certainly have to come from land that was profitably planted in bananas.

Fishing Season

Although Tropicana remained open all year, guests were advised that fishing was impossible from November 1 to January 15. This was the time of year when the heaviest rains occurred. The longest periods of dry weather were from the latter part of January through most of May and then again from August through October. The best time for snook fishing occurred in late August until November 1. A schedule of the best fishing months versus the traditional months of high occupancy at Tropicana follows. This schedule presented certain difficulties in promoting Tropicana as a year-round lodge. During the months of May through August, Tropicana had to compete with vacation areas in the United States. September and October represented excellent months for fishing but relatively weak ones for occupancy due to the fact that school was open in the United States. In addition, these were fall months in the United States, with nice weather conditions there. November and December were winter months in the United States and could be promoted as vacation months, but fishing was impossible during that time. Increased promotion would be necessary to reduce the dependency on three to five months of natural draw. November, December, and half of January would remain poor months due to weather and fishing conditions. Thus, Tropicana would face, at a maximum, nine favorable months.

MONTH	FISHING CONDITIONS	FIVE HIGHEST MONTHS OF OCCUPANCY AT TROPICANA (APPROXIMATELY 80 percent OF TOTAL OCCUPANCY)
January	Good	
February	Excellent	1
March	Fair	2
April	Fair	3
May	Excellent	
June	Excellent	
July	Good	
August	Good	
September	Excellent	4
October	Excellent	5
November	Poor	
December	Poor	

Value of Lodge

It was difficult to estimate the market value of the lodge, but Eric estimated that it would probably be valued somewhere between $450,000 and $750,000 (United States). A difficulty in appraising the lodge was that its success was tied directly to the banana company, which owned and operated the source of electrical power for the lodge. A buyer might find this factor of concern. However, a generator and an independent well would not be difficult to acquire.

Competitors

- *Azul Grande.* The fishing lodge of Azul Grande was the primary competitor and could accommodate 24 guests. This lodge was located in the fishing village of Parismina and could be reached only by private airplane or boat. It was not as attractive as Tropicana. It was surrounded by poor fishing shacks and older in appearance than Tropicana. However, it was clean and well maintained. A monkey in the front yard greeted all visitors. Clients for this lodge were almost exclusively from the United States. The owners advertised in select outdoor magazines. The owner also appeared on TV talk shows when he was in the United States. Bookings in the United States were handled through an exclusive agent in Chicago who worked on a commission basis.

- *Isla Del Sol.* This fishing lodge was located at the mouth of the San Juan River, which forms a border for Nicaragua and Costa Rica. The manager/owner was a Mr. Laurie from Detroit. This lodge was experiencing difficulty in breaking even and was open six months or less each year.

- *Casa Fantastica.* This fishing lodge was also located at the mouth of the San Juan River and open six months or less each year. There was no information concerning the success of this lodge, but it was apparent that the management was fairly aggressive, as witnessed by advertisements from the outdoor magazine *The Salt Water Sportsman*.

Rates

Rates for competitive fishing lodges on the Caribbean coast ranged from $2,500 to $4,000 per person per week. Tropicana and other lodges did not encourage guests to come for periods of less than five days. This was due to the cost of transportation. It also provided a guest with more opportunities to catch fish. Guests who stayed for shorter periods of time sometimes arrived when fishing was poor and returned to spread stories of poor fishing. All lodges provided competitive services, although Tropicana provided even more individualized attention to guests and was willing to spend more time and money to transport guests to good fishing sites.

Promotion for Tropicana was handled primarily through ads in the English-print newspapers in San José. Word-of-mouth advertising seemed to be the primary means by which people heard of the lodge. A review of the guest book indicated that the majority of guests had been from the United States; the second largest group were Costa Ricans.

QUESTIONS FOR DISCUSSION

Chapter 12

1. What distribution channels would you use for the Tropicana Fishing Lodge?
2. How are distribution and segmentation related?

Chapter 13

1. What promotional strategies/tactics would you suggest for Tropicana?

2. Discuss the differences in management and marketing between a commercial fishing or hunting lodge and a commercial hotel.
3. Could the marketing of diverse hunting/fishing lodges be conducted effectively by an independent group responsible for multiple properties?

Case 19 Boulder Creek

One of the most difficult marketing tasks in any industry is to reposition a declining product, attract new market segments, and achieve market success. Yet that is exactly what Andrea Lewis did with a former Econo Lodge in a nonhighway location in Boulder, Colorado.

"This was the hardest thing I had ever done," said Andrea. When my husband Burt and I purchased the property, Burt was busy with real estate in Chicago and left most of the responsibility to me.

Andrea knew nothing about hotels but found that her training and experience supervising 26 salespeople in 19 states as manager of corporate sales for Tiffany & Company was invaluable. Andrea had just been offered a promotion with Tiffany's when Burt called to say they were purchasing an ignored Econo Lodge in Boulder that had great potential. "I need you to quit your job, move to Boulder, and remake this hotel," said Burt. Andrea had recently experienced the death of two young friends and said to herself, "I love Boulder, and I love Colorado. This will be a challenge, but life is short, so let's do it."

Life at Tiffany's was a dream compared to the task that confronted Andrea. The property contained a 100-year-old home suffering from lack of maintenance, a motel complex that had been built in stages with little or no curbside appeal, a lack of landscaping, a rutted parking lot, and a lack of physical amenities such as a swimming pool and exercise room. Located in a student residential area, the property did not easily lend itself to drive-by stopovers.

Employee quality and attitudes matched the property. Several employees were drug dealers or addicts, and an attitude of ignoring the guest prevailed. The management and staff seemed more interested in naked pool parties than guest interaction. One unusual guest service offered at the front desk was a tattoo on the ankle with real tattoo machines. Maintenance and housekeeping were not prepared to provide anything more than a barely acceptable level of guest satisfaction.

"The staff we inherited could not embrace customer service and consistently attracted low-life guests," said Andrea. It was not surprising that the front office was protected by bulletproof glass.

Management practices had discouraged customers from their nearest neighbors, the University of Colorado and Naropa University, a Buddhist institution. The hotel's policy had been, "No we won't direct bill even the most upstanding and desirable commercial clients, including Colorado University."

Turnaround

Within three years, this property changed from despair to being the winner of the gold award and a nomination for Platinum as the only Quality Inn in the United States. Repeat business at Boulder Creek was high and in a period of low hotel occupancy for the industry, Boulder Creek achieved a 78 percent average occupancy compared to 50 percent for Boulder hotels. Simultaneously, the Boulder Creek enjoyed an average daily rate (ADR) that was high for its category.

How did this remarkable turnaround occur?

Flag Change

Burt and Andrea believed that dramatic change was not possible under the Econo Lodge name but felt there was an advantage in remaining within the family of Choice Hotels International. They realized that the brand Quality Inn and Suites had not been used in the Boulder market. Andrea developed a presentation for the management of Choice Hotels that demonstrated the dramatic changes she planned and was granted the right as the first and only Econo Lodge to change to a Quality Inn.

Physical Property

The city of Boulder has very strict building codes and building permits are difficult to acquire. Knowing this, Andrea hired a respected architect with knowledge of the city and the elected officials. Andrea and the architect decided that the century-old home should be preserved and enhanced as a historic building and given multiple uses as front desk, business center, management offices, breakfast room, and two guest rooms upstairs.

A fireplace of colored river rock serves as a focal point near the front desk. The work of Colorado western artists was selected to furnish the historic home and the guest rooms. Curbside appeal was greatly enhanced by improving visibility, particularly of the historic home as a focal point. Landscaping with native wildflowers and rocks serves as the area of support for an attractive sign announcing the brands Quality Inn and Suites and Boulder Creek.

The 40 guest rooms and 6 suites were remodeled with "casually upscale lodge furnishings." Each room has many of the features expected in an upscale hotel such as Hyatt or Westin. Andrea sought local artisans to make Western-style lamps, furniture, and bedspreads. A fitness center was built and furnished with new state-of-the-art equipment. An inside sauna and a hot tub were built near a refurbished indoor swimming pool and a coin-operated laundry for guest use only.

The breakfast bar offers an assortment far beyond the typical cold cereal and doughnuts of many hotels. Free daily breakfast at Boulder Creek is a deluxe hot breakfast buffet of eggs, sausage, waffles, cereal, bakery goods, fruit, yogurt, and three types of juice, tea, or coffee.

Samantha

Samantha, a soft-coated Wheaton Terrier, is Andrea's personal pet and friend of the staff and guests. When Boulder Creek opened, pets were not accepted. This proved to be a bit awkward as Samantha found the space immediately beneath the No Pets Allowed sign perfect for naps. Several guest rooms are now reserved for guests with pets. Other rooms remain pet free because some guests have allergies to pets.

New Staff

Because retraining staff and changing old attitudes proved much more difficult than changing the physical structure, the entire original staff was fired.

Andrea originally went to an organization called the Boulder Workplace, which placed her in touch with individuals 50 years and older seeking employment. A manager lacked hotel experience but held a degree in operations management and exhibited the correct people skills and positive attitude.

Andrea personally took charge of employee training using a philosophy that if you treat your employees as gold, they will in turn treat you as gold. Although Andrea held an MBA from Vassar, she credited her training at Tiffany's and earlier at Estee Lauder with instilling the concept of "Excellence."

A constant theme of Andrea's that is taught to all employees is "Customer Service Doesn't Get a Day Off." Many of the first hires had to be taught computer skills, but recent hires generally bring these skills to the job.

Marketing/Sales

Unlike some hotels where the guest is expected to step around ladders and paint cans, Andrea refused to open until the hotel was ready. "Sure we needed the cash flow, but it was critical that the guests enjoy a finished product." Many people wanted to come even during remodeling, but were told, "You can't come here now, wait until we are ready; we do not want to disappoint you." Guests waited and were pleased that they did. Andrea said there is something in all of us that says, "If I can't have something, that is exactly what I want."

Andrea personally visited target organizations in Boulder. She felt that selected organizations could provide guests who would recognize and appreciate quality lodging. Those seeking only a "cheap sleep" were not viewed as target guests.

The University of Colorado and Naropa University had visiting professors, parents, and many others who visit during the year. Successful corporations, particularly those in technology, could provide many business travelers.

Direct billing was welcomed and individuals from these target organizations who might influence visitor hotel selection were personally given tours of the property. A list of potential guests and gatekeepers was developed and used for extending invitations to launch parties, swim parties, cocktail parties, and other planned events.

Travel writers were invited and given red carpet treatment as well as an honest and interesting story about the development of Boulder Creek. This resulted in many articles written in newspapers and magazines. Many free nights were given to individuals who could influence future business.

Andrea also targeted supportive hospitality businesses in which there might be a possibility of quid pro quo ("You scratch my back; I'll scratch yours"). Packages that supported local businesses such as restaurants were developed. Andrea felt that these built support among "local partners" and also provided the hotel guests with something above and beyond what they expect.

Now after building the business and understanding what is required to market the property successfully, Andrea said she was ready to hire a salesperson to ensure the continuation and growth of business.

Going Green

A majority of Boulder Creek's guests have some affiliation with one of the local universities. These guests ask for services that are regarded as healthy and environmentally friendly. A policy of no smoking was expected, but a recent request had caused Andrea to think creatively. The hotel offered quality amenities in each room such as shampoo, soap, and lotion. Lately many guests had stated these were not environmentally friendly and that amenities should be offered in a liquid dispenser.

Andrea was considering how to comply with this request without resorting to the common institutional look of dispensers and without offending guests who preferred the traditional mini-bottle amenities.

maintained that most of these had been ill planned and probably had little likelihood of long-range success. Jan personally believed that a major shakeup in the time-share industry was coming and that many existing projects would fail.

The Superior Hotel policy was to begin working with the developers of a time-share resort at the beginning of the project. It was felt that developers have a short-run viewpoint, but a management company must think of the long run. The policy was to become involved in the entire planning process of the project, including blueprints and interior decorations. If a developer refused to cooperate, Superior would remove itself from future management. Management believed that a time-share project differed considerably from a conventional hotel or resort development.

1. A time-share project has hundreds or thousands of owners. A conventional hotel or resort has one or a few.

2. Time-share projects receive high-intensity use, with 95 percent occupancy being normal. Furniture, carpeting, and other furnishings can wear out in a third of the time. Therefore, rules of thumb developed for hotels would often not apply in time-share.

3. The guest assumes a proprietary interest in a time-share. Guests are extremely critical because they view the units as theirs and complain about things that a hotel guest would accept.

4. A great deal of hype goes into the sales of a time-share unit, and guests arrive with extreme expectations. Superior has to bring reality into the dreams that the sales department creates.

5. The long-term success of a time-share unit depends on attracting the same guests each year for as long as 20 years or more. If guests became dissatisfied and enough guests decided to drop their ownership, resales can be very difficult, and the entire project can be in jeopardy.

Several management practices had been developed by Superior to deal with these complexities.

Owner Feedback

Owner comment sheets were distributed to each owner/guest during each visit. Jan took pride in the fact that she read each one personally. These sheets covered a variety of areas, from general appearance of the unit to any evidence of insects and rodents. If the comments were particularly bad, a member of management, including Jan, would personally contact the owner and report on the steps that had been taken to correct the problem.

Feedback was also received in "owner coffees." These weekly meetings with owners included attendance by one or more members of management. These could include the resort owner, the head of housekeeping, the director of internal management, and others. A quarterly newsletter was published by Superior and sent to all owners. In addition to information of a general nature such as changes in airfares to the resort, the newsletter was personalized to the extent that it reminded all owners of their vacation week.

Recreation Management

Superior Hotels believed that even the most beautiful and best-maintained resort could eventually become boring. To ensure that guests would find something new each year, a recreation program was established with a full-time professional in charge. Programs were designed for all ages. These employed some of the successful concepts of Club Med.

Supervised programs for children allowed parents a freedom they could not enjoy at most resorts. Hot dog parties, beach parties, tennis competitions, seashell classes, and many other programs offered a variety of recreational and educational pursuits. Each recreational program was monitored as to attendance and guest satisfaction, and weak ones were eliminated. A dominant feature of all the programs was the opportunity for interaction among guests. Jan believed that a guest at the average resort could spend a week and never develop new friendships. Ideally, the recreation programs encouraged friendships to develop.

Housekeeping and Maintenance

The turnover of a majority of the guests one day and the mass arrival of an equal number the next provides special housekeeping and maintenance problems for time-share projects. A full-time maintenance crew was employed, and a large inventory of replacement furnishings was carried. If a TV set or electric range had a problem, it was replaced immediately rather than sending a repair technician. With only one vacation week, Jan felt that a guest did not want to share it with a repair person. Housekeeping was performed for the time-share resorts under contract with an independent housekeeping company. Housekeeping managers were responsible for examining each room personally and ensuring that corrections immediately followed discovery of a problem.

The Superior Hotel Image and Philosophy

"All Superior properties must be first class; there is no room in this corporation for mundane or second-class properties." This statement by Jan summed up the company's philosophy. The philosophy concerning quality had led management to change its policy concerning the new properties it would manage. The company recently initiated a policy of holding an equity position in all future properties. This decision was made for two reasons. First, an ownership position would allow Superior to have a stronger voice in the development and management of properties and would help ensure quality. Second, Superior Hotels had no interest in "bringing up" properties to a desired quality and performance level only to find that the managers had decided not to renew the management contract.

Corporate Objectives

The management and ownership of Superior Hotels desired for the company to be recognized as a strong national resort and commercial hotel management company within 10 years. It was felt that resort properties offered limited growth opportunities because others had developed the most desirable locations.

The best strategy for the next five years seemed to lie in the development of first-class commercial properties within Sunbelt cities of 100,000 to 200,000 people. It was felt that the development of three new properties per year in this market was realistic. Sunbelt cities were believed to offer the best potential for growth because of the scarcity of 150- to 200-room high-quality hotels. These second-tier cities remained important industrial and agricultural centers and did not usually offer truly first-class hotel accommodations. In many cases a respected medical complex had been developed in these cities, and it was felt that this factor alone would serve as a magnet for visitors.

▪▪▪ QUESTIONS FOR DISCUSSION

Chapter 18

1. What are the core competencies of Superior Hotels? Management of resorts? Management of time-share resorts? Management of ski resorts? Management of commercial hotels? Other?

2. Do you believe that Superior Hotels should be entering diverse markets such as ski resorts and commercial hotels?

3. Do you believe that Superior Hotels can effectively market and manage a wide diversity of properties?

4. What would you advise Jan Trible to do?

Case 22 Uber

It's rare. But every now and then a company comes along that completely disrupts the traditional ways of distributing a product or service. Amazon.com radically transformed online selling, and Apple's iTunes and iPod turned music distribution on its ear. Now comes Uber, the app-based ride service that is revolutionizing urban transportation. Uber is giving conventional taxicab and car services a real ride for their money. In just seven short years, Uber has revved up operations in over 700 cities in more than 60 countries, already booking more than $10 billion in rides annually through its massive network of more than four million drivers.

A Disruptive Product

Why are so many customers around the world bypassing good old taxicabs in favor of newcomer Uber? It's all about convenience and peace of mind. No more stepping out into busy city streets to wave down a passing cab. Instead, Uber's smartphone app lets passengers hail the nearest cab or limo from any location, then track the vehicle on a map as it approaches. The Uber app gives riders an accurate estimate in advance of the fare to their destinations (usually less than that charged by a regular cab) eliminating guesswork and uncertainty. After the ride, passengers simply exit and walk away. Uber automatically pays the driver (including tip) from the passenger's prepaid Uber account, eliminating the often-inconvenient and awkward moment of payment. And it's the same process anywhere in the world, from San Francisco, London, Paris, or Abu Dhabi to Ashville, North Carolina, or Athens, Georgia. Compare the Uber experience to the uncertain and often-unsettling experience of using a standard taxicab.

One business reporter describes waiting in line at a taxi stand while a driver tried to convince another would-be passenger—a total stranger—to share the cab, thereby increasing his fare. The cab itself was ancient and filthy, with ripped and worn seats. During the entire ride, the cabbie carried on a phone conversation in a foreign language via his headset, causing safety concerns while distractedly navigating busy city streets. The reporter's conclusion: "I stepped out of the taxi in front of my house and realized I just don't have to put up with this garbage anymore. Uber has changed my life, and as God is my witness, [wherever Uber is available] I will never take a taxi again."

Uber drivers range from professional drivers who've switched over from conventional cab and transportation companies to regular people looking for a little adventure and some extra income in their spare time. All Uber drivers go through an orientation that requires proficiency in a market area's dominant language, ensuring that they can communicate effectively with customers. Although it may vary by location, in general Uber vehicles can be no more than ten years old. A two-way rating system—by which riders rate drivers and drivers rate riders in return—helps keep both sides on their best behavior. Poorly rated drivers risk being rejected by future passengers; poorly rated passengers risk rejection by drivers, who can choose which fares they accept.

Uber's disruptive innovation has brought a breath of fresh air to an industry begging for change. Urban transportation channels have long been characterized by cartel-like relationships between cab companies and local governments, high fixed fares, poor service, and little accountability. As one economics professor points out, the taxicab industry "was ripe for entry [by start-ups] because everybody hates it."

Uber has also been criticized for its "surge pricing" practices—a dynamic pricing mechanism that kicks in to raise prices when demand exceeds supply, sometimes resulting in shockingly high fares and accusations of price gouging. Uber justifies surge pricing by pointing that it provides an incentive for more drivers to be available during periods when passengers need them most. According to Uber, if a passenger faces a higher-than-normal fare because of surge pricing, the alternative without Uber would more than likely be no taxi at all. Moreover, Uber informs passengers in advance what the fares will be. If they don't like the fare, they can find another cab, take public transportation, or walk.

Competitors and Startup Costs

Uber's huge success has attracted a garage full of competitors, such as Lyft, Gett, Carma, and Zimride. Uber has a huge first-to-market advantage. Its bookings are 10 times those of nearest competitor Lyft, and Uber is adding new customers at a faster rate. Moreover, even as competition stiffens, Uber has little to fear from like-minded competitors. In fact, the more competitors adopt the new model, the more the revolutionary channel will grow and thrive versus traditional channels, creating opportunities for all new car-hailing entrants. Instead, the new distribution model poses the biggest threat to traditional taxicab and car-for-hire companies, which are now losing both customers and drivers to Uber and its competitors.

Despite its explosive growth, Uber—like every other ride-hailing company—has yet to turn a profit. Like Facebook, Amazon, and so many other revolutionary companies in today's internet-driven economy, Uber's start-up model is to build a big user base first, then worry about making money later. Uber keeps 20 to 30 percent of each fare—the rest goes to the driver. But Uber plows back most of its take into expansion and promotional expenses. Investors seem confident. Uber has raised more than $10 billion in venture capital. It went public in 2019 with a valuation of $82.4 billion. Your Lyft did an initial public offering (IPO) earlier in the same year that placed its valuation at $24.3 billion.

Challenges

Like any innovator, upstart Uber faces some significant challenges. For example, Uber has been criticized for exercising too little control over driver quality and security. So far, the company has ridden beneath the radar of industry regulators by not directly employing drivers (all Uber drivers are independent contractors) and not owning any vehicles (all vehicles are driver-owned). There have been charges of sexual harassment within the company and by drivers for Uber. Waymo a subsidiary of Alphabet, the parent company of Google, filed a lawsuit against Uber. Uber had acquired Otto, a self-driving company. The suit alleged an employee of Waymo downloaded confidential files of Waymo before leaving to start Otto. These incidents helped lead to the Uber replacing its founding CEO with Dara Khosrowshahi, the former CEO of Expedia.

Defining Its Business Beyond Ride Sharing

Under the new CEO Uber's mission became "We ignite opportunity by setting the world in motion," replacing, "Make transportation as reliable as running water, everywhere, for everyone." This expanded Uber's mission beyond just delivering people to their destinations. Uber is now looking at expanding into healthcare, package delivery, and other areas. As the population ages, many older people need rides to and from medical treatments. Uber Eats, a restaurant delivery service, has been very successful. "Once you're delivering cars in five minutes, there are a lot of other things you can deliver in five minutes."

Sources: "The Fall of Travis Kalanick Was a Lot Weirder and Darker Than You Thought," https://www.bloomberg.com/news/features/2018-01-18/the-fall-of-travis-kalanick-was-a-lot-weirder-and-darker-than-you-thought (accessed May 16, 2019); Uber.com (accessed May 16, 2019); Eric Newcomer and Ellen Huet, "Battling Lyft for Market Share, Uber Again Turns to Discounting," *Skift*, January 22, 2016, http://skift.com/2016/01/22/battling-lyft-for-market-share-uber-again-turns-to-discounting/; Alan Murray, "Uber-nomics," *Fortune*, January 2015, p. 6; Jim Edwards, "Uber Has Changed My Life and as God Is My Witness I Will Never Take a Taxi Again," *Business Insider*, January 22, 2014, www.businessinsider.com/uber-has-changed-my-life-and-as-god-is-my-witness-i-will-never-take-a-taxi-again-where-available-2014-1#ixzz3TYF7ZY29; Brad Stone, "Invasion of the Taxi Snatchers: Uber Leads an Industry's Disruption," *Businessweek*, February 20, 2014, pp. 38–42; Tracey Lien, "Lyft Defies Predictions by Continuing to Grow as a Rival to Uber," *Los Angeles Times*, January 5, 2016, www.latimes.com/business/technology/la-fi-0105-lyft-growth-20,160,105-story.html; Jon Russell, "Uber Makes First Big Expansion in China as It Aims to Reach 100 Cities in 2016," *TechCrunch*, January 18, 2016, http://techcrunch.com/2016/01/18/uber-sichuan-expansion/.

QUESTIONS FOR DISCUSSION

Chapter 5

1. You are thinking about using Uber Eats as a delivery service for your restaurant. Currently you do not have a delivery service, and customers have to receive the ordered food from the restaurant only. The manager has asked you to do a research project to see if it would be feasible to use Uber Eats. What information would you gather as data to present to the manager?

Chapter 12

1. Compare the distribution systems with taxicabs with that of Uber. That is how the customers gain access to a taxicab, compared with gaining access to an Uber ride.

2. What advantages did Uber create in their creation of a distribution system for people who needed transportation compared with taxicab companies?

Chapter 17

1. Explain how Uber could enhance opportunities for tourists.

2. As a destination manager would you embrace Uber? If so, how would you communicate your position with taxi drivers who have served your community for many years?

GLOSSARY

Administered VMS. A vertical marketing system coordinates successive stages of production and distribution, not through common ownership or contractual ties, but through the size and power of one of the parties.

Advertising. Any paid form of nonpersonal presentation and promotion of ideas, goods, or services by an identified sponsor.

Agent. A wholesaler who represents buyers or sellers on a more permanent basis, performs only a few functions, and does not take title to goods.

Agritourism. Agriculture-based tourism that includes farms, ranches, and wineries. It provides rural areas with a means to attract tourists.

Alliances. Alliances are developed to allow two organizations to benefit from each other's strengths.

Allocating. Sales representatives decide on which customers to allocate scarce products.

Allocentrics. Persons with a need for new experiences, such as backpackers and explorers.

Ansoff product–market expansion grid. A matrix developed by cell, plotting new products and existing products with new products and existing products. The grid provides strategic insights into growth opportunities.

Approach. The step in which the salesperson meets the customer for the first time.

Aspirational group. A group to which a person wishes to belong.

Atmosphere. Designed environments that create or reinforce a buyer's leanings toward consumption of a product.

Attitude. A person's enduring favorable or unfavorable cognitive evaluations, emotional feelings, and action tendencies toward some object or idea.

Augmented products. Additional consumer services and benefits built around the core and actual products.

Aural. The dimension of atmosphere relating to volume and pitch.

Baby boomers. The 78 million people born between 1946 and 1964.

Backward integration. A growth strategy by which companies acquire businesses supplying them with products or services (e.g., a restaurant chain purchasing a bakery).

Behavioral segmentation. Dividing a market into groups based on consumers' knowledge, attitude, use, or response to a product.

Belief. A descriptive thought that a person holds about something.

Big data. The huge and complex data sets generated by today's sophisticated information generation, collection, storage, and analysis technologies.

Brand equity. The added value endowed on products and services. It may be reflected in the way consumers think, feel, and act with respect to the brand, as well as in the prices, market share, and profitability the brand commands for the firm.

Brand image. The set of beliefs consumers hold about a particular brand.

Brand promise. The marketer's vision of what the brand must be and do for consumers.

Brand value. The total financial value of a brand.

Brand. A name, term, sign, symbol, design, or a combination of these elements that is intended to identify the goods or services of a seller and differentiate them from competitors.

Branding. The process of endowing products and services with the power of a brand. It's all about creating differences between products.

Broker. A wholesaler who does not take title to goods and whose function is to bring buyers and sellers together and assist in negotiations.

B-to-B digital and social media marketing. Using digital and social media marketing approaches to engage business customers and manage customers relationship anywhere, anytime.

Buying center. All those individuals and groups who participate in the purchasing and decision-making process and who share common goals and the risks arising from the decisions.

Buzz marketing. Cultivating opinion leaders and getting them to spread information about a product to others in their community.

Cast members. A term used for employees. It implies that employees are part of a team that is performing for their guests.

Causal research. Marketing research to test hypotheses about cause-and-effect relationships.

Channel conflict. Disagreement among marketing channel members on goals and roles—who should do what and for what rewards.

Channel level. A level of middleman that performs some work in bringing the product and its ownership closer to the final buyer.

Closing. The sales step in which a salesperson asks the customer for an order.

Cognitive dissonance. Buyer discomfort caused by postpurchase conflict.

Communicating. Sales representatives communicate information about the company's products and services.

Competitive advantage. An advantage over competitors gained by offering consumers greater value either through lower prices or by providing more benefits that justify higher prices.

Competitive analysis. An analysis of the primary strengths and weaknesses, objectives, strategies, and other information relative to competitors.

Competitors' strategies. When competitors use segmentation, undifferentiated marketing can be suicidal. Conversely, when competitors use undifferentiated marketing, a firm can gain an advantage by using differentiated or concentrated marketing.

Concentric diversification strategy. A growth strategy whereby a company seeks new products that have technological or marketing synergies with existing product lines.

Confused positioning. Leaving buyers with a confused image of a company.

Conglomerate diversification strategy. A product growth strategy in which a company seeks new businesses that have no relationship to the company's current product line or markets.

Consumption phase. Takes place when the customer consumes the service.

Content marketing. Creating, inspiring, and sharing brand messages and conversations with and among consumers across a fluid mix of paid, owned, earned, and shared channels.

Contests, sweepstakes, and games. Give consumers a chance to win something, such as cash or a trip.

Continuity. Scheduling ads evenly within a given period.

Contractual VMS. A vertical marketing system in which independent firms at different levels of production and distribution join together through contracts to obtain more economies or sales impact than they could achieve alone.

Convention. A specialty market requiring extensive meeting facilities. It is usually the annual meeting of an association and includes general sessions, committee meetings, and special-interest sessions.

Copy testing. A process performed before or after an ad is printed or broadcast.

Core product. Answers the question of what the buyer is really buying. Every product is a package of problem-solving benefits and services.

Corporate communication. This activity covers internal and external communications and promotes understanding of an organization.

Corporate meeting. A meeting held by a corporation for its employees.

Corporate mission statement. A guide to provide all the publics of a company with a shared sense of purpose, direction, and opportunity, allowing all to work independently, yet collectively, toward the organization's goals.

Corporate values. A set of corporate priorities and institutional standards of behavior.

Corporate VMS. A vertical marketing system that combines successive stages of production and distribution under single ownership. Channel leadership is established through common ownership.

Cost-plus pricing. Adding a standard markup to the cost of the product.

Counseling. Involves advising management about public issues and company positions and image.

Coupons. Certificates that offer buyers savings when they purchase specified products.

Cross-cultural marketing. This is the practice of including ethnic themes and cross-cultural perspectives within the mainstream marketing of the organization.

Cross-selling. The company's other products that are sold to the guest.

Cross-training. Training employees to do two or more jobs within the organization.

Crowdsourcing. An open-innovation new-product idea program.

Culture. The set of basic values, perceptions, wants, and behaviors learned by a member of society from family and other important institutions.

Customer database. An organized collection of comprehensive data about individual customers or prospects, including geographic, demographic, psychographic, and behavioral data.

Customer equity. The discounted LTVs of all the company's current and potential customers.

Customer expectations. Expectations based on past buying experiences, the opinions of friends, and market information.

Customer insights. Fresh marketing information-based understanding of customers and the marketplace that become the basis for creating customer value, engagement, and relationships.

Customer lifetime value (LTV). The customer LTV is the stream of profits a customer will create over the life of his or her relationship to a business.

Customer relationship management (CRM). CRM involves managing detailed information about individual customers and carefully managing customer "touch points" in order to maximize customer loyalty.

Customer satisfaction. The extent to which a product's perceived performance matches a buyer's expectations.

Customer touch point. Any occasion on which a customer encounters the brand and product—from actual experience to personal or mass communications to casual observation.

Customer value. The difference between the benefits that the customer gains from owning and/or using a product and the costs of obtaining the product.

Customer-engagement marketing. Fosters direct and continuous customer involvement in shaping brand conversations, experiences, and community.

Customer-perceived value. The customer's evaluation of the difference between all the benefits and all the costs of a market offering relative to those of competing offers.

Data warehouse. A central repository of an organization's customer information.

Data warehouses. Collect data from a variety of sources and store it in an accessible location.

Decline. The period when sales fall off quickly and profits drop.

Degree of product homogeneity. Undifferentiated marketing is more suited for homogeneous products. Products that can vary in design, such as restaurants and hotels, are more suited to differentiation or concentration.

Demands. Human wants that are backed by buying power.

Demographic segmentation. Dividing the market into groups based on demographic variables such as age, gender, family size, family life cycle, income, occupation, education, religion, race, and nationality.

Demography. The study of human populations in terms of size, density, location, age, sex, race, occupation, and other statistics.

Derived demand. Organizational demand that ultimately comes from (derives from) the demand for consumer goods.

Descriptive research. Marketing research to better describe marketing problems, situations, or markets, such as the market potential for a product or the demographics and attitudes of consumers.

Destination branding. Creating a differentiated destination image that influences travelers' decision to visit a destination and conveys the promise of a memorable experience that is uniquely associated with the destination.

Destination marketing organization (DMO). A group that promotes a specific destination. Often a local CVB serves as the DMO.

Destinations. Places with some form of actual or perceived boundary, such as the physical boundary of an island, political boundaries, or even market-created boundaries.

Detachment phase. When the customer is through using the product and departs.

Digital and social media marketing. Using digital marketing tools such as Web sites, social media, mobile apps and ads, online videos, e-mail, and blogs that engage consumers anywhere, at any time, via their digital devices.

Direct distribution channel. A distribution channel that has no intermediary levels.

Direct marketing and digital marketing. Engaging directly with carefully targeted individual consumers and customer communities to both obtain an immediate response and build lasting customer relationships.

Direct marketing channel. A marketing channel that has no intermediary levels.

Direct marketing. Direct communications with carefully targeted individual consumers to obtain an immediate response and cultivate lasting customer relationships.

Direct rating. The advertiser exposes a consumer panel to alternative ads and asks them to rate the ads.

Direct-mail marketing. Direct marketing through single mailings that include letters, ads, samples, foldouts, and other "salespeople with wings" sent to prospects on mailing lists.

Discriminatory pricing. Refers to segmentation of the market and pricing differences based on price elasticity characteristics of the segments.

Disintermediation. The elimination of intermediaries.

Drop. The action taken toward a product that may cause harm or customer dissatisfaction.

Dynamic packaging. A package vacation on a single Web site in which buyers can put together airline flights, lodging, car rental, entertainment, and tours in their own customer-designed packages.

Dynamic pricing. Continually adjusting prices to meet the characteristics and needs of the marketplace.

Dynamic pricing. Continually adjusting prices to meet the characteristics and needs of individual customers and situations.

Echo boomers. See millennials. Born between 1977 and 1994, these children of the baby boomers now number 72 million, dwarfing the Gen Xers and almost equal in size to the baby-boomer segment. Also known as Generation Y.

E-commerce. The general term for a buying and selling process that is supported by electronic means, primarily the internet.

Economic environment. The economic environment consists of factors that affect consumer purchasing power and spending patterns. Markets require both power and people. Purchasing power depends on current income, price, saving, and credit; marketers must be aware of major economic trends in income and changing consumer spending patterns.

Emotional labor. The necessary involvement of the service provider's emotions in the delivery of the service.

Empowerment. When a firm empowers employees, it moves the authority and responsibility to make decisions to the line employees from the supervisor.

Environmental factors. Social, political, and economic factors that affect a firm and its marketing program.

Environmental management perspective. A management perspective in which a firm takes aggressive actions to affect the publics and forces in its marketing environment rather than simply watching and reacting to it.

e-procurement. Purchasing through electronic connections between buyers and sellers, usually done online.

Ethnographic research. Trained observers interact with and/or observe consumers in their natural habitat.

Events. Occurrences staged to communicate messages to target audiences, such as news conferences or grand openings.

Exchange. The act of obtaining a desired object from someone by offering something in return.

Executive summary. A short summary of the marketing plan to quickly inform top executives.

Experimental research. The gathering of primary data by selecting matched groups of subjects, giving them different treatments, controlling related factors, and checking for differences in group responses.

Exploratory research. Marketing research to gather preliminary information that will help to better define problems and suggest hypotheses.

Facilitating products. Those services or goods that must be present for the guest to use the core product.

Familiarization trip (Fam trip). A trip where travel agents or others who can send business to a tourist destination attraction, cruise, or hotel are invited to visit at a low cost or no cost.

Family life cycle. The stages through which families might pass as they mature.

Financial intermediaries. Banks, credit companies, insurance companies, and other businesses that help finance transactions or insure against the risks associated with the buying and selling of goods.

Fixed costs. Costs that do not vary with production or sales level.

Focus group interviewing. Personal interviewing that involves inviting small groups of people to gather for a few hours with a trained interviewer to talk about a product, service, or organization. The interviewer "focuses" the group discussion on important issues.

Follow-up. The sales step in which the salesperson follows up after the sale to ensure customer satisfaction and repeat business.

Forward integration. A growth strategy by which companies acquire businesses that are closer to the ultimate consumer, such as a hotel acquiring a chain of travel agents.

Franchise. A contractual vertical marketing system in which a channel member called a franchiser links several stages in the production distribution process.

Generation X. A generation of 45 million people born between 1965 and 1979; named Generation X because they lie in the shadow of the boomers and lack obvious distinguishing characteristics; other names include "baby busters," "shadow generation," or "yiffies"—young, individualistic, freedom-minded few.

Generation Y. See millennials.

Generation Z. People born after 2000 (although many analysts include people born after 1995) who make up the kids, tweens, and teens markets.

Geographic segmentation. Dividing a market into different geographic units such as nations, states, regions, counties, cities, or neighborhoods.

Going-rate pricing. Setting price based largely on following competitors' prices rather than on company costs or demand.

Group. Two or more people who interact to accomplish individual or mutual goals.

Growth. The product life-cycle stage when a new product's sales start climbing quickly.

Handling objections. The sales step in which the salesperson seeks out, clarifies, and overcomes any customer objections to buying.

Horizontal conflict. Conflict between firms at the same level.

Horizontal diversification strategy. A product growth strategy whereby a company looks for new products that could appeal to current customers, which are technologically unrelated to its current line.

Horizontal integration. A growth strategy by which companies acquire competitors.

Horizontal marketing system (HMS). Two or more companies at one level join to follow new marketing opportunities. Companies can combine their capital, production capabilities, or marketing resources to accomplish more than what one company can accomplish working alone.

Hospitality industry. Made up of those businesses that offer one or more of the following: accommodation, prepared food and beverage service, and/or entertainment.

Human need. A state of felt deprivation in a person.

Human want. The form that a human need takes when shaped by culture and individual personality.

Incentive travel. A reward that participants receive for achieving or exceeding a goal.

Income segmentation. Dividing a market into different income groups.

Information gathering. Sales representatives conduct market research and intelligence work and fill in a call report.

Informative advertising. Advertising used to inform consumers about a new product or feature to build primary demand.

Infrastructure. The system according to which a company, organization, or other body is organized at the most basic level.

Inseparability. A major characteristic of services; they are produced and consumed at the same time and cannot be separated from their providers.

Intangibility. A major characteristic of services; they cannot be seen, tasted, felt, heard, or smelled before they are bought.

Integrated marketing communications. Under this concept, the company carefully integrates its many communication channels to deliver a clear, consistent, and compelling message about the organization and its brands.

Internal data. Internal data consist of electronic databases and nonelectronic information and records of consumer and market information obtained from within the company.

Internal marketing. Involves marketing to the firm's internal customers, its employees.

Introduction. The product life-cycle stage when a new product is first distributed and made available for purchase.

Joining stage. The product life-cycle stage when the customer makes the initial inquiry contact.

Junket reps. Serve the casino industry as intermediaries for premium players.

Laboratory test. This test uses equipment to measure consumers' physiological reactions to an ad: heartbeat, blood pressure, pupil dilation, and perspiration.

Learning. Changes in a person's behavior arising from experience.

Lifestyle. A person's pattern of living as expressed in his or her activities, interests, and opinions.

Lobbying. Dealing with legislators and government officials to promote or defeat legislation and regulation.

Local marketing. Tailoring brands and promotions to the needs and wants of local customer groups—cities, neighborhoods, and specific restaurant/hotel/store locations.

Macrodestinations. Destinations such as the United States that contain thousands of microdestinations, including regions, states, cities, towns, and visitor destinations within a town.

Macroenvironment. The larger societal forces that affect the whole microenvironment: competitive, demographic, economic, natural, technological, political, and cultural forces.

Macroenvironmental forces. Demographic, economic, technological, political, legal, social, and cultural factors.

Market development strategy. Finding and developing new markets for your current products.

Market homogeneity. If buyers have the same tastes, buy a product in the same amounts, and react the same way to marketing efforts, undifferentiated marketing is appropriate.

Market positioning. Formulating competitive positioning for a product and a detailed marketing mix.

Market potential. The total estimated dollars or unit value of a defined market for a defined product, including competitive products.

Market segmentation. Dividing a market into direct groups of buyers who might require separate products or marketing mixes.

Market targeting. Evaluating each market segment's attractiveness and selecting one or more segments to enter.

Market trends. External trends of many types that are likely to affect the marketing in which a corporation operates.

Market. A set of actual and potential buyers of a product.

Marketing concept. The marketing management philosophy that holds that achieving organizational goals depends on determining the needs and wants of target markets and delivering desired satisfactions more effectively and efficiently than competitors.

Marketing environment. The actors and forces outside marketing that affect marketing management's ability to develop and maintain successful transactions with its target customers.

Marketing information system (MIS). A structure of people, equipment, and procedures to gather, sort, analyze, evaluate, and distribute needed, timely, and accurate information to marketing decision makers.

Marketing intelligence. Everyday information about developments in the marketing environment that helps managers prepare and adjust marketing plans.

Marketing intermediaries. Firms that help the company to promote, sell, and distribute its goods to final buyers; they include middlemen, physical distribution firms, marketing service agencies, and financial intermediaries.

Marketing management. The art and science of choosing target markets and building profitable relationships with them, while creating value for society.

Marketing manager. A person who is involved in marketing analysis, planning, implementation, and control activities.

Marketing mix. Elements include product, price, promotion, and distribution (place). Sometimes distribution is called place resulting in the mix called the four Ps.

Marketing opportunity. An area of need in which a company can perform profitably.

Marketing research. The systematic design, collection, analysis, and reporting of data relevant to a specific marketing situation facing an organization.

Marketing research. The systematic design, collection, analysis, and reporting of data and findings relevant to a specific marketing situation facing a company.

Marketing services agencies. Marketing research firms, advertising agencies, media firms, marketing consulting firms, and other service providers that help a company to target and promote its products to the right markets.

Marketing strategy. The marketing logic by which the company hopes to create this customer value and achieve these profitable relationships.

Marketing Web site. Web sites designed to engage consumers in an interaction that will move them closer to a purchase or other marketing outcome.

Marketing. Marketing is the process by which companies create value for customers and society, resulting in strong customer relationships that capture value from the customers in return, while creating value for society.

Maturity. The stage in a product life cycle when sales growth slows or levels off.

Media. Nonpersonal communication channels, including print media (newspapers, magazines, direct mail), broadcast media (radio, television), and display media (billboards, signs, posters).

Medical tourism. One of the fastest-growing and most lucrative tourism markets. Tourists spend a large amount on medical treatment, stay in top hotels, and often travel around the country after their surgery.

Membership groups. Groups that have a direct influence on a person's behavior and to which a person belongs.

Microenvironment. The forces close to a company that affect its ability to serve its customers: the company, market channel firms, customer markets, competitors, and the public.

Microenvironmental forces. Customers, competitors, distribution channels, and suppliers.

Micromarketing. The practice of tailoring products and marketing programs to suit the tastes of specific individuals and locations.

Millennials (also called Generation Y or the echo boomers). Born between 1980 and 2000, these children of the baby boomers number 83 million, dwarfing the Gen Xers and larger even than the baby-boomer segment.

Mobile marketing. Marketing promotions, messages, and other content delivered to on-the-go customers through mobile phones, smartphones, tablets, and other mobile devices.

Moment of truth. Occurs when an employee and a customer have contact.

Motivational houses. Provide incentive travel offered to employees or distributors as a reward for their efforts.

Motive. A need that is sufficiently pressing to direct a person to seek satisfaction of that need.

Multichannel marketing distribution. Multichannel distribution, as when a single firm sets up two or more marketing channels to reach one or more customer segments.

Multiplier effect. Tourist expenditures that are recycled through the local economy, being spent and spent again.

Mystery shoppers. Hospitality companies often hire disguised or mystery shoppers to pose as customers and report back on their experience.

National tourist organizations (NTOs). A national government or quasi-government agency that markets destination tourism.

Observational research. The gathering of primary data by observing relevant people, actions, and situations.

Olfactory. The dimension of atmosphere relating to scent and freshness.

Online advertising. Advertising that appears while consumers are surfing the Web, including display ads, search-related ads, and online classifieds.

Online focus groups. Gathering a small group of people online with a trained moderator to chat about a product, service, or organization and gain qualitative insights about consumer attitude and behavior.

Online marketing research. Collecting primary data online through internet and mobile surveys, online focus groups, Web-based experiments, tracking of consumers' online behavior, and online panels and brand communities.

Online marketing. Company efforts to market products and services and build customer relationships over the internet.

Online social networks. Online social communities—blogs, social networking, Web sites, or even virtual worlds—where people socialize or exchange information and opinions.

Online travel agency (OTA). A travel agency that conducts business through the internet with no physical locations or stores.

Opaque channel. An opaque channel is one where the customer knows the general location and class of the hotel but does not know the specific name of the hotel he or she is purchasing.

Opaque pricing. Selling products at a discounted price while hiding certain characteristics of the product from the consumer until after purchase.

Opinion leaders. People within a reference group who, because of special skills, knowledge, personality, or other characteristics, exert influence on others.

Order-routine specification. The stage of the industry buying process in which a buyer writes the final order with the chosen supplier(s), listing the technical specifications, quantity needed, expected time of delivery, return policies, warranties, and so on.

Organization image. The way a person or group views an organization.

Organizational buying process. The decision-making process by which formal organizations establish the need for purchased products and services and identify, evaluate, and choose among alternative brands and suppliers.

Organizational culture. The pattern of shared values and beliefs that gives members of an organization meaning and provides them with the rules for behavior in that organization.

Overpositioning. Giving buyers a too-narrow picture of the company.

Patronage rewards. Cash or other awards for regular use of a company's products or services.

Performance review. The stage of an industrial buying process in which a buyer rates its satisfaction with suppliers, deciding whether to continue, modify, or drop the relationship.

Perishability. A major characteristic of services; they cannot be stored for later use.

Personal selling. Personal presentation by the firm's sales force to make sales and building customer relationships.

Personality. A person's distinguishing psychological characteristics that lead to relatively consistent and lasting responses to his or her environment.

Phase-out. The ideal method of removing an unpopular or unprofitable product; it enables a product to be removed in an orderly fashion.

Physical evidence. Tangible clues such as promotional material, employees of the firm, and the physical environment of the firm. Physical evidence is used by a service firm to make its product more tangible to customers.

Point-of-purchase (POP) promotions. Include displays and demonstrations that take place at the time of sale.

Political environment. Laws, government agencies, and pressure groups that influence and limit the activities of various organizations and individuals in society.

Portfolio tests. Consumers view or listen to a portfolio of advertisements, taking as much time as they need.

Positioning. Arranging for a product to occupy a clear, distinctive, and desirable place relative to competing products in the minds of target consumers.

Preapproach. The step in which the salesperson or company identifies qualified potential applicants.

Premiums. Goods offered either free or at low cost as an incentive to buy a product.

Presentation. The sales step in which the sales persons tell the "value story" to the buyer showing how the company's offer solves the customer's problems.

Press relations. Placing newsworthy information into the news media to attract attention.

Press release. Information released to the media about certain new products or services.

Price. The amount of money charged for a product or service, or the sum of the values that consumers exchange for the benefits of having or using the product or service.

Primary data. Information collected for the specific purpose at hand.

Problem recognition. The stage of the industrial buying process in which someone in a company recognizes a problem or need that can be met by acquiring a good or a service.

Product concept. The idea that consumers will favor products that offer the most quality, performance, and features, and therefore the organization should devote its energy to making continuous product improvements.

Product concept. A detailed version of a product idea stated in meaningful consumer terms.

Product development. Developing the product concept into a physical product to ensure that the product idea can be turned into a workable product.

Product idea. Envisioning a possible product that company managers might offer to the market.

Product image. The way that consumers picture an actual or potential product.

Product position. The way a product is defined by consumers on important attributes—the place it occupies in consumers' minds relative to competing products.

Product publicity. Various efforts to publicize specific products.

Product specification. The stage of an industrial buying process in which the buying organization decides on and specifies the best technical product characteristics for a needed item.

Product-bundle pricing. Combining several products and offering the bundle at a reduced price.

Promotional mix. The specific blend of advertising, public relations, *personal selling*, sales promotion, and *direct-marketing* tools that the company uses to communicate customer value and build customer relationships persuasively.

Prospecting. The process of searching for new accounts.

Psychocentrics. Persons who do not desire change when they travel. They like to visit nonthreatening places and stay in familiar surroundings.

Psychographic segmentation. Dividing a market into different groups based on social class, lifestyle, or personality characteristics.

Public relations. The process by which a positive image and customer preference are created through third-party endorsement.

Public. Any group that has an actual or potential interest in or impact on an organization's ability to achieve its objectives.

Pulsing. Scheduling ads unevenly over a given period.

Purpose of a business. To create and maintain satisfied, profitable customers.

Quotas. Quantitative and time-specific accomplishment measurements established for members of a sales force.

Recall tests. The advertiser asks people who have been exposed to magazines or television programs to recall everything they can about the advertisers and products that they saw.

Recognition tests. The researcher asks readers of, for instance, a given issue of a magazine to point out what they have seen.

Reference groups. Groups that have a direct (face-to-face) or indirect influence on a person's attitude or behavior.

Relationship marketing. Involves creating, maintaining, and enhancing strong relationships with customers and other stakeholders.

Reminder advertising. Advertising used to keep consumers thinking about a product.

Retailer. Business whose sales come primarily from retailing.

Return on marketing investment (or marketing ROI). The net return from a marketing investment divided by the costs of the marketing investment. It measures the profits generated by investments in marketing activities.

Revenue management. A pricing method using price as a means of matching demand with capacity.

Role. The activities that a person is expected to perform according to the persons around him or her.

Run-out. Removing a product after existing stock has been depleted; used when sales for an item are low and costs exceed revenues, such as the case of a restaurant serving a crabmeat cocktail with sales of only one or two items per week.

Sales promotion. Consists of short-term incentives to encourage the purchase of sale of a product or service.

Sample. (1) A segment of a population selected for marketing research to represent the population as a whole; (2) offer of a trial amount of a product to consumers.

Search-related advertising (or contextual advertising). Text-based ads and links that appear alongside search engine results on sites such as Google and Yahoo!

Secondary data. Information that already exists somewhere, having been collected for another purpose.

Self-concept. Self-image, the complex mental pictures people have of themselves.

Selling concept. The idea that consumers will not buy enough of an organization's products unless the organization undertakes a large selling and promotion effort.

Selling. Sales representatives know the art of salesmanship: approaching, presenting, answering objections, and closing sales.

Service culture. A system of values and beliefs in an organization that reinforces the idea that providing the customer with quality service is the principal concern of the business.

Service profit chain. A model that shows the relationships between employee satisfaction, customer satisfaction, customer retention, value creation, and profitability.

Servicing. Sales representatives provide various services to the customers: consulting on their problems, rendering technical assistance, arranging financing, and expediting delivery.

Share of customer. The portion of the customer's purchasing that a company gets in its product categories.

SMERF. SMERF stands for social, military, educational, religious, and fraternal organizations. This group of specialty market has a common price-sensitive thread.

Social classes. Relatively permanent and order divisions in a society whose members share similar values, interests, and behaviors.

Social media. Independent and commercial online communities where people congregate, socialize, and exchange views and information.

Social selling. The use of online, mobile, and social media to engage customers, build stronger customer relationships, and augment sales performance.

Societal marketing concept. The idea that an organization should determine the needs, wants, and interests of target markets and deliver the desired satisfactions more effectively and efficiently than competitors in a way that maintains or improves the consumer's and society's well-being.

SoLoMo (social+local+mobile). Marketing that targets on-the-go consumers as they come and go in key local market areas.

Spam. Unsolicited, unwanted, commercial e-mail messages.

Specific product attributes. Price and product features can be used to position a product.

Stakeholders. Stakeholders include customers, employees, suppliers, and the communities where their business is located and other people or organizations that have an interest in the success of the business.

Strategic business units (SBUs). A single business or collection of related businesses that can be planned separately from the rest of the company.

Strategic planning. The process of developing and maintaining a strategic fit between the organization's goals and capabilities and its changing marketing opportunities.

Subculture. A group of people with shared value systems based on common life experiences and situations.

Supplier search. The stage of the industrial buying process in which a buyer tries to find the best vendor.

Supplier selection. The stage of the industrial buying process in which a buyer receives proposals and selects a supplier or suppliers.

Suppliers. Firms and individuals that provide the resources needed by a company and its competitors to produce goods and services.

Supply chain. Upstream and downstream partners. Upstream from the company is a set of firms that supply raw materials, components, parts, information, finances, and expertise needed to create a product. Downstream marketing channel partners, such as wholesalers and retailers, form a vital connection between the firm and its customers.

Supporting products. Extra products offered to add value to the core product and to help differentiate it from the competition.

Survey research. The gathering of primary data by asking people questions about their knowledge, attitudes, preferences, and buying behavior.

Survival. A technique used when a company's or business unit's sales slump, creating a loss that threatens its existence. Because the capacity of a hotel or restaurant is fixed, survival often involves cutting prices to increase demand and cash flow. This can disrupt the market until the firm goes out of business or the economy improves.

Sustainable tourism. Tourism that minimizes the environmental impacts and sociocultural changes, sustains the longevity of a destination, and creates economic opportunity for local communities.

SWOT analysis. Evaluates the company's overall strengths (S), weaknesses (W), opportunities (O), and threats (T).

Tactile. The dimension of atmosphere relating to softness, smoothness, and temperature.

Tangible evidence. Tangible clues such as promotional material, employees of the firm, and the physical environment of the firm. Physical evidence is used by a service firm to make its product more tangible to customers.

Targeting. Sales representatives decide how to allocate their scarce time among prospects and customers.

Telephone marketing. Using the telephone to sell directly to customers.

Timetable. Specific dates to accomplish strategies and tactics.

Total costs. Costs that are the sum of the fixed and variable costs for any given level of production.

Tourism. A stay of one or more nights away from home for leisure or business, except such things as boarding, education, or semipermanent employment.

Transaction. Consists of a trade of values between two parties; marketing's unit of measurement.

Travel industry. The travel industry includes travel agencies, providers of land transportation for tourists, tour operators, resort retailing, entertainment activities for tourists, and convention centers.

Underpositioning. Failing ever to position the company at all.

Upselling. Training sales and reservation employees to offer continuously a higher-priced product that will better meet the customers' needs, rather than settling for the lowest price.

Value chain. The series of internal departments that carry out value-creating activities to design, produce, market, deliver, and support a firm's products.

Value proposition. The full mix of benefits on which a brand is differentiated and positioned.

Value-based pricing. Uses the buyer's perceptions of value, not the seller's cost, as the key to pricing.

Variability. A major characteristic of services; their quality may vary greatly, depending on who provides them and when, where, and how they are provided.

Variable costs. Costs that vary directly with the level of production.

Venue management. Forecasting demand to optimize profit. Demand is managed by adjusting price. Fences are often built to keep all customers from taking advantage of lower prices. For example, typical fences include making a reservation at least two weeks in advance or staying over a Saturday night.

Vertical conflict. Conflict between different levels of the same channel.

Vertical marketing systems (VMSs). Distribution channel structures in which producers, wholesalers, and retailers act as a unified system: Either one channel member owns the others, or has contracts with them, or has so much power that they all cooperate.

Viral marketing. The internet version of word-of-mouth marketing—Web sites, videos, e-mail messages, or other marketing events that are so infectious that customers will want to pass them along to friends.

Visual. The dimension of atmosphere relating to color, brightness, size, and shape.

Wholesaler. Firms engaged primarily in wholesaling activity.

Zaltman Metaphor Elicitation Technique (ZMET). A qualitative technique to uncover both conscious and unconscious motives, thoughts, and feelings of consumers.

INDEX

A. C. Nielsen, 149
Accepted Practices Exchange (APEX), 192
Accessibility, 216, 241
AccorHotels, 66–67
Acquisition, product development by, 252
Action plans
   advertising/promotion strategies, 555–556
   digital marketing strategies, 556
   distribution strategies, 554–555
   pricing strategies, 557
   product strategies, 557–558
   sales strategies, 554
   strategies and tactics, 553–558
Actionability, 216
Actual sales, estimation of, 574
Acxiom (business information services), 216
Administered vertical marketing system (VMS), 346
ADR (average daily rate), 426
Advertising, 7
   advertising budget, 381–382
   campaign evaluation, 379
   defined, 360
   developing strategy, 382
   informative, 380
   major decisions in, 379–381
   media selection, 385–388
   persuasive, 380
   reminder, 380
   setting the objectives, 380–381
Advertising budget, 381–382
   competition and clutter, 381
   product differentiation, 381
   product life cycle, 381
Advertising effectiveness, evaluating, 388
   measuring the awareness effect, 389
   measuring the communication effect, 388
   measuring the sales effect, 389
Advertising investment, 388
   advertising effectiveness and, 388
   return on, 388
Advertising message, 382–385
   breaking through the clutter, 382–383
   consumer-generated messages, 385
   creating, 382–385
   merging advertising and entertainment, 383–384
   message execution, 384–385
   message strategy, 384
Advertising strategies, 555–556
   developing, 382
Affordable method, 374
African American consumers, 159–160
Age and life-cycle stage, 166–167, 208–209

Agent (distribution channel), 333
Agoda (website), 331
Agritourism, 516
Airbnb (case study), 586–588
Alexis Park Resort, The, 557
Alliance of Tribal Tourism Advocates (ATTA), 367
Alliances, 349–350
All-inclusive resorts, 502
Allocentrics, 521
Amadeus (GDS), 340
Amenities (tourism), 524
American Airlines, 541
American Association of Retired Persons (AARP), 15
American Express, 42, 195
American family, changes in, 102
American Hotel and Lodging Association (AH & LA), 109
American Idol (television program), 362
American Le Mans races, 400
American Society for Quality Control, 273
American Society of Association Executives (ASAE), 194
American Society of Travel Agents (ASTA), 109
America's Second Harvest, 400
Amount of Australian dollar (AUD), 548
Andrews, Christine, 274
Ang, Swee, 251
Ansoff product–market expansion grid, 65
Apollo Hotel (case study), 618–619
Approach (personal selling), 444
Approvers, 186
Area customer demand, 575
Arthur D. Little, 59
Asian American consumers, 160
Aspen Skiing Company, 513, 520
Aspirational groups, 162
Association meetings, 194–196
   corporate meeting, 194–195
   decision variable matrix, 198
   incentive travel, 195–196
   meeting purpose segmentation, 198
   restaurants as venue, 199
   small groups, 195
   SMERFs, 196–197
Association of Bath and District Leisure Enterprises (ABLE), 343
Atmosphere, 241–242, 372
   aural dimensions, 241
   olfactory dimensions, 241
   tactile dimensions, 241
   visual dimensions, 241
Attitudes, 171–172

Attractions, tourism, 510–513
  casinos as, 512
  developing packages, 524–525
  rejuvenating destination, 513
  waterfront attractions, 511–512
Audiovisual (AV) companies, 188, 193
Augmented product, 240–245
  accessibility, 241
  atmosphere, 241–242
  customers as employees, 245
  interaction with other customers, 244–245
  service delivery system, 242–244
Aural dimensions, 241
Australia, global market strategy, 548–549
Australian Tourist Commission (case study), 596–600
Automated systems, 126
Automatic response loop, 173
Awareness, 368, 401
Awareness/comprehension/attitude change, 405
Baby boomers, 98
Backward integration, 67
Bain Capital (investment company), 349
BAR pricing. *See* Best available rate (BAR) pricing
Bargaining strategy, 446
Bargaining tactics, 446
Barrett, Colleen, 281
Barriers to entry, exit and competition, 95–97
Bed and breakfasts (B&Bs), 222, 426
Behavioral segmentation, 213–215
  benefits sought, 213
  loyalty status, 215
  occasion segmentation, 213
  usage rate, 215
  user status, 215
Beliefs, 171–172
Bellon, Pierre, 66
Benefits, customers seeking (behavioral segmentation), 213
Bergman, Eric, 406
Berry, Leonard L., 289, 568, 605
Best available rate (BAR) pricing, 320
The Big Bang Theory (television program), 382
Big Data, 119
  three Vs, 119
"Big Mac" index, 502
Blanchard, Ken, 278
Bleeding Heart Restaurant: Unique Positioning of a Restaurant (case study), 612–614
Blogs, 469
Bloomberg's Business Week, 387
Board of Directors, 552
Bodega Bay Lodge and Spa, 548
Booking Holdings, 331–332
Borchardt, Jackie, 607
Boulder Creek (case study), 625–628
Bowen, John, 482
Boyd, Randall C., 544
Brand(s), 235
  brand equity and value, 246–247
  brand name selection, 248–249
  brand portfolios, 250–253
  brand positioning, 247–248
  brand promise, 247
  brand strategy, 245–252
  branding, 245
  building strong brands, 245
  co-branding, 249
  defined, 245
  leveraging brands, 249–250
  managing, 252
Brand equity, 246–247
  defined, 246
  marketing advantages of, 246
Brand image, 175
Brand name selection, 248–249
Brand portfolios, 250–251
Brand positioning, 247–248
Brand promise, 247
Brand strategy, 245–252
Branding, 245
Branson, Richard, 242
Break-even (BE) analysis, 310–311
Broadcasting, 226, 360, 372, 388, 399
Broker (distribution channel), 334
Brown Palace (hotel), 223
Budgets, 558
  expenditures against, 561
Buffalo Wild Wings, 3–5
Burger King, 221, 349, 558
Business, purpose of, 6
Business analysis, new product development, 257
Business conduct, 183
Business expenditure effect, 306
Business markets, 94. *See also* Group business markets
Business portfolio
  design of, 64–65
  strategic business units (SBU), 65
Business travelers, 521
Business-to-business marketing channels, 336
Business-to-consumer marketing channels, 336
Buyer, buying center, 185
Buyer behavior model, 158
Buyer decision process, 173–177
  evaluation of alternatives, 174–175
  information search, 174
  need recognition, 173
  organizational buying process, 184–185
  postpurchase behavior, 175–176
  price changes, 325
  purchase decision, 175
Buyer readiness, 368–369, 378
Buyer-oriented pricing, 303
Buygrid framework, 188
Buying center, 185
Buyphases, 188
Buzz marketing, 162–163, 371

Index

Cabela's, 401
Caesars Entertainment resorts, 116–118
   customer experience, 117–118
   customer insights, 117
   data, gathering, 117
Cafeteria I.C.E. (case study), 581–585
California Country Club (CCC), 562
Cameron Trading Post & Lodge (case study), 619–621
Canada Like a Local (ECLAL), 527
Canadian Tourism Commission (CTC), 527
Capacity management, 48–49
   cross-training employees, 48
   customers and, 48
   demand management, 49
   downtime, 49
   overbook, 50–51
   part-time employees, 48–49
   price to create/reduce demand, 49
   promotional events, 53
   queuing, 51–52
   rent/share facilities and equipment, 49
   reservations, 50
   revenue management, 51
   service delivery system, 49
   shift demand, 53
   Spirit Airlines, 616–618
Carbon-neutral vacations, 505
Career acquisitions, 438
Carlson Hotels Worldwide, 542
Casa Santo Domingo (hotel), 223
Case studies
   Airbnb, 586–588
   Apollo Hotel, 618–619
   Australian Tourist Commission, 596–600
   Bleeding Heart Restaurant: Unique Positioning of a Restaurant, 612–615
   Boulder Creek, 625–628
   Cafeteria I.C.E., 581–585
   Cameron Trading Post & Lodge, 619–622
   Cheshire's Best Kept Stations, 407
   Chick-fil-A, 589–592
   Cuba Tourism Development, 506
   Disney, 50
   Elk Mountain Hotel, 605–607
   Extending Your Brand to China, 251
   Extreme Sports, 399
   Grand Targhee, 609–612
   Hunt Room: Change the Concept or Just the Decor?, 592–593
   In-N-Out Burger: Customer Value the Old-Fashioned Way, 593–596
   International Travel Agency, 628–629
   Mayo Clinic, 604
   Pricing Almost Destroys and Then Saves a Local Restaurant, 615
   Ritz-Carlton, 607–608
   Superior Hotels, 629–631
   Tropicana Fishing Lodge, 622–625
   Uber, 632–633
   W Hotels, 212
   Witchery by the Castle, 601–604
   Zipcar: Itar: Itw Travel, InItIt about Urban Life, 578–581
Casinos as attractions, 512
Cast members, 281, 283
Caterair International Corporation, 543
Cathy, Dan, 415
Causal research, 130
Cause-related marketing, 109
Cause-related promotions, 417
Channel behavior, organization and, 345–350
   alliances, 349–350
   franchising, 347–348
   horizontal marketing systems (HMS), 350
   multichannel marketing distribution, 350
   vertical marketing system (VMS), 346–347
Channel conflict, 345
Channel levels (distribution), 335
Channel members
   attracting members, 351
   control criteria, 351–352
   customer needs, 350–351
   economic feasibility of, 351
   marketing objectives and, 401
   responsibilities of, 352
   selection of, 350–352
Chen May Yee, 605
Cheshire's Best Kept Stations (case study), 407
Chez Panisse (restaurant), 223
Chick-fil-A, 415, 589–592
Chipotle Mexican Grill (restaurant), 223, 299
Choice Hotels, 542
Christensen, Glenn L., 138
Chuck E. Cheese (restaurant), 219
Cirque du Soleil, 43
Citizen-action publics, 94
CitizenM (hotel), 204–206
Closed-end questions, 142, 144
Closing (sales), 447
Club Med, 556, 630
Cluster (area) sample, 141
Co-branding, 249
Coca-Cola's "Mirage," 362
Cocktail Cruises, 557
Co-creation, 25–26
Cognitive dissonance, 176
Columbus Dispatch, 386
Comarow, Avery, 605
Combination-structured sales force, 430–431
Comment cards, 536
Commercial sources of information, 174
Commercialization of new products, 259
Commissioned reps, 435
Communication channels, 370–372
   nonpersonal channels, 372
   personal channels, 370–371
   selection of, 370–372

Communications, 360. *See also* Integrated marketing communications (IMC)
   awareness, 368
   campaign evaluation, 380
   channel selection, 370–372
   conviction, 368
   customer-contact employees, 288–289
   customers and, 226, 358–388
   effectiveness in, 388
   feedback, collecting, 373–374
   knowledge, 368
   liking, 368
   marketing plan, 550
   measuring the results of, 388
   message content, 369
   message design, 369–370
   message format, 369–370
   message source, 372–373
   message structure, 369–370
   objective of, 367–368
   preference, 368
   purchase, 369
   target audience, 367
   total promotional budget, 374–375
   tourist markets and, 522–523
Communications technology, 220
Community cooperation (tourism), 504
Company, 89
Company objectives and goals, 64, 217
Company records, 120
Company resources, 217
Comparison advertising, 380
Compensation, sales force, 448
Competition-based pricing approach, 312
Competitive advantage, 222, 499
   choosing, 225–226
   customer insights and, 118–120
Competitive analysis, 543
Competitive information, 129
Competitive parity method, 375
Competitive trends, 543
Competitors, 90–91
   barriers to entry/exit, 95–97
   future competitors, 95–97
   idea generation, 253
   levels of, 91
   price changes, 325
   prices and offers, 308
   strategies of, 220
Concentrated marketing, 219
Concentric diversification strategy, 66
Concept development and testing, 256–257
Concept testing, 257
Concierges, 345
   restaurants business and, 345
Conferences, 198
Confused positioning, 225
Conglomerate diversification strategy, 66

Conjoint analysis, 257
Consistency, 38–39
   hiring/training procedures, 39
   monitoring customer satisfaction, 39
   standardization of process, 39
Consortia, 343
   defined, 343
   purpose of forming, 343
   vertical marketing systems (VMS) development and, 343
Consumer behavior
   cross-cultural marketing, 160
   cultural factors, 158–159
   model of, 157–158
   personal characteristics, 158–172
   personal factors, 166–168
   psychological factors, 169–172
   social factors, 161–166
Consumer evaluation process, 174, 176
Consumer expectations *vs.* management perception, 567–569
Consumer markets, 94
   major segmentation variables, 207
Consumer perceptions, price *vs.* value, 302–303
Consumer preference, 368
Consumer promotion tools, 378, 410–414
   advertising, 375–376
   contests, sweepstakes, and games, 413–414
   coupons, 411–412
   digital marketing, 377
   direct marketing, 377
   events, 414
   packages, 411
   patronage rewards, 413
   personal selling, 376
   point-of-purchase (POP) promotions, 413
   premiums, 412
   public relations, 377
   sales promotion, 376–377
   samples, 410–411
Consumer-generated marketing, 19–20
Consumer-generated messages, 385
Consumption phase, 243
Contact methods, 135–137
   distribution channel function and, 335
   strengths/weaknesses of, 135
Contests, sweepstakes, and games, 413–414
Contextual advertising, 467
Continuity, 388
Continuous training, 284
Contractual vertical marketing system (VMS), 347
Control criteria, channel members, 351–352
Convenience sample, 141
Convention(s), 192–193, 198
   bureaus, 193
Convention and visitors bureaus (CVB), 466
Convention bureaus, 193
Conventional distribution channels, 346
   vs. vertical, 346

Conviction, 368
Copy testing, 388
Core product, 238
Corporate/chain sales support, 431
Corporate communications, 398
Corporate connection, 540–541
   corporate direction, 541
   marketing-related plans, 540–541
   relationship to other plans, 540
Corporate culture, sales force and, 438
Corporate customer, 126–127
Corporate goals, 541
Corporate meetings, 194–195
   small groups, 195
Corporate mission, 62–64
Corporate objectives, 438
Corporate philosophy, 541
Corporate values, 63
Corporate vertical marketing system (VMS), 346
Cost-based pricing, 309–310
   popularity, reasons for, 313
Cost-plus pricing, 309
Costs, 12, 300–301
   subsidization, 301
   types of, 302
Couchsurfing (website), 527
Counseling, 398
Coupland, Douglas, 98
Coupons, 411–412
Courtyard (hotel), 215
Crab Shack (restaurant), 217
Creative ideas, 414–415
Credibility, 401
Crisis management, 406–408
CRM. *See* Customer relationship management (CRM)
Crompton, A. J., 514
Cross-cultural marketing, 160
Cross-selling, 302
Cross-training, 284
Crowdsourcing, idea generation, 254–255
Cuba Tourism Development: A Time Travel
   (case study), 506–507
Cultural environment, 107–109
   persistence of cultural values, 107–108
   socially responsible actions and ethics, 108–109
Cultural factors, 158–161
   African American consumers, 159
   Asian American consumers, 160
   cross-cultural marketing, 160–161
   Hispanic American consumers, 159
   social class, 161
   subculture, 159–160
Cultural values, 107–108
Culture, consumer behavior and, 158. *See also* Cultural
   factors
Current market demand, 573–574
Current profit maximization, 299
Customer(s), 94
   capturing value from, 20–23
   consumer-generated marketing, 19–20
   direct marketing benefits, 463
   as employees, 245
   employees and, 6
   global customer, 5
   growing share of, 21
   idea generation, 253
   interaction with other customers, 244–245
   lifetime value of, 21
   personalization and value for, 478–479
   relating deeply and interactively, 19
   right relationships with right, 22
   selection of, 14
   service delivery system, 48, 242–244
   types of, 480
Customer care, 40–41, 273, 282
Customer databases, 434
   database uses, 476–478
   and traditional direct marketing, 476–479
Customer demands, 11
Customer equity
   building, 21–22
   defined, 22
Customer expectations, 12
Customer experiences, 12
Customer insights, 118–120
Customer lifetime value (LTV), 21
Customer loyalty and retention, 7, 21
Customer needs, 10
   channel members and, 350
   marketplace and, 10–13
Customer orientation, 6–7
Customer relationship management (CRM), 17–18, 540
   benefits of, 480
   building relationships, 16–20
   consumer-generated marketing, 19–20
   engaging customers, 19
   marketing and loyalty programs, 479–483
   partner relationship management, 20
Customer satisfaction, 12–13, 17–18
   evaluation of, 451
   marketing and, 5
   monitoring for consistency, 39
Customer share, 21
Customer touch point, 17
Customer value, 12–13
Customer wants, 10–11
Customer-contact employees, 288
Customer value-driven marketing
   strategy, 70–71
   customers to serve, 14
   design of, 13–16
   market differentiation/positioning, 71–72
   market segmentation, 70
   market targeting, 70–71
   marketing concept, 15
   marketing management orientations, 14–16

selling concept, 14–15
societal marketing concept, 15–16
Customer-engagement marketing, 19
Customer-perceived value, 17
Customer-structured sales force, 430
Cycle, 575
Daniel J. Edelman, Inc., 401
Darden Restaurants, 552
Data collection and analysis, 562
Data warehouses, 123, 476
Database needs, 434
Deciders, 186
Decline stage, 260, 263
Decoding in communication, 366
Degree of product homogeneity, 220
Demand, 11, 302
   elastic, 304–305
   inelastic, 304
   price and, 49
   price and, relationship between, 303–304
   price elasticity of, 304–305
   psychological determinants of, 514
   shifting of, 53
Demand management, 49
   low demand, 49
   overbook, 50–51
   price to create/reduce demand, 49
   promotional events, 53
   queuing, 51–52
   reservations, 50
   revenue management, 51
   shifting demand, 53
   short-term demand, 48
Demographic environment, 97–102
   age structure changes, 98
   baby boomers, 98
   education and, 102
   Generation X, 98–99
   Generation Z, 100
   generational marketing, 100
   geographic shifts in population, 102
   increasing diversity, 101
   millennials, 99
Demographic segmentation, 208–210
Demography, 97
Departmental organization, 60
Derived demand, 184
Descriptive research, 130
Destination branding, 523
Destination competitiveness, 499–502
Destination Digital Marketing, 96
Destination marketing organization (DMO), 26, 96, 529
Destination marketing system, 497–499
Destinations, 496. *See also* Tourism; Tourism destination(s)
   branding, 523
   competitiveness, 499–502
   life cycle, 513

live-like-a-local experience, 526–527
   marketing system, 497–499
   rejuvenation of, 513
   tourism, 496–497
   tourism, world's top, 495
   tourism slogans, 523
Detachment phase, 243
Differentiated marketing, 219
Differentiation, 76
   managing service, 41
Digital age, 23–24, 463–465
Digital Alchemy, 468
Digital and social media marketing, 23
   business-to-business, 191–192
   and business buyers, 190
   marketing, internet, and digital age, 463–465
   online marketing, 465–469
   social media marketing, 469–474
Digital marketing strategies, 556
Digital technology, 361
Digital video recordings (DVR), 361, 383
Direct and digital marketing, 335, 360, 377, 461–462
   buyers and sellers benefits, 462
   and customer databases, 476–478
   defined, 360
   described, 461
   direct-mail marketing, 483
   forms, 463
   gap analysis of loyalty features, 482
   interactive TV, 484
   kiosk marketing, 484
   mobile marketing, 460
   new direct-marketing model, 461
   telephone marketing, 483–484
   traditional forms of, 483–485
Direct Marketing Association (DMA), 483
Direct rating, 388
Direct-mail marketing, 483
Discretionary income, 103
Discriminatory pricing, 314–316
   criteria for successful, 315–316
   defined, 314
Disintermediation, 92–93, 341
Disney, 165
Disney Cruise Lines, 208
Disney Parks Blog, 469
Disney World, 242, 406
Distribution, 7
Distribution channels, 331. *See also* Marketing intermediaries
   contact and, 335
   control criteria, 351–352
   evaluating channel alternatives, 351–352
   financing and, 335
   functions of, 335
   importance of, 333
   information and, 335
   matching and, 335

Distribution channels (*Continued*)
  nature of, 333–336
  negotiation and, 335
  number of channel levels, 335–336
  physical distribution and, 335
  promotion and, 335
  risk taking and, 335
  selecting business location and, 352–354
Distribution models, 338–339
Distribution strategies, 554
Distribution systems, nature and importance, 333
Diversification growth, 66
  concentric strategy, 66
  horizontal strategy, 66
Diversity, 101–102
Dobbs International Services, 543
Domino's (restaurant), 349
Dominquez, Roberta, 408
Downstream partners, 332
Downtime, 49
Drifters, 521
"Drive Against Hunger" program, 400
Drop, 265
Drucker, Peter, 8, 77
Dunkin' Donuts, 214, 380, 413
Dunkin' Donuts University, 414
Dynamic packaging, 314
Dynamic pricing, 319
Eakin, Emily, 138
E-commerce, 485
Economic environment, 23, 103–104
  global economy, 103–104
  income changes, 103
  pricing and, 308
  super rich, 103
Economic feasibility, channel members, 351
Economic Intelligence Unit (EIU), 304
Economic situation, 167
Economic variables, 542
The Economist (newspaper), 502
Ecotourism, 504. *See also* Sustainable tourism
Education and religious travel, 521
Edwards, Cliff, 134
Effective communications, development of, 367–374
  designing message, 369–370
  feedback collection, 373–374
  message source selection, 372–373
  objective, determining, 367–369
  selection of communication channels, 370–372
  target audience, 367
Elasticity, price, of demand, 304–305
Electronic sales, 432
Elk Mountain Hotel (case study), 605–607
Elliott, Sheryl Marie, 507
Ells, Steve, 299
E-mail, 453
E-mail marketing, 467–468
Embassy Suites, 300–301, 375

Emotional appeals, 369
Emotional employee, 286–287
Employees
  cross-training of, 284
  customer-contact employees, 288–292
  customers and, 6
  marketing information and, 288–292
  as part of product, 46–47, 274
  part-time employees, 48–49
  training of, 39
  uniform selection, 291–292
Empowerment, 277, 290
Encoding in communication, 366
End-benefit effect, 306–307
Entry/exit barriers, 95–97
Environmental analysis and forecasting, 541–546
  competitive analysis, 543
  major environmental factors, 542
  market potential, 544–545
  market trends, 543–544
  marketing research, 545–546
  positioning statement, 541
Environmental factors, 187, 541
  economic, 542
  political, 542
  social, 542
  terrorism, 542
Environmental management perspective, 109
Environmental scanning, 109–110
Environmental sustainability, 63–64
E-Procurement, 190–191
Equipment limitations, 49
Erratic events, 575
Ethics, 108–109
Ethnographic research, 132
Evaluation of alternatives, 174–175
Event(s)
  in communication, 372
  sports, 508–509
  tourism, 507–510
Event marketing, 509
Everyday low prices (EDLP), 322. *See also* Value pricing
Exchanges, 13
Executive summary, 539
Existing-product pricing strategies, 313–316
  BAR (best available rate) pricing, 320
  discriminatory rising, 314–316
  distribution channels, 333
  nonuse of revenue management, 320
  price-adjustment strategies, 314–316
  product-bundle pricing, 313–314
  revenue management, 316–319
  time of purchase, 314
  volume discounts, 314
Expected service *vs.* perceived service, 570
Expedia (online travel site), 340, 554
Experian (business information services), 216
Experian's Mosaic USA system, 216

Exploratory research, 130
Explorers, 520
Exposures, 404–405
External benchmarking, 499
External environment, idea generation and, 253
External environmental analysis, 74–75
External idea sources, idea generation, 254
External marketing, 47
Extreme Sports (case study), 399
Facebook, 546
Face-to-face guest relations, 274
Facilitating products, 238–239
Fairfield Inn, 300, 326
Familiarization trips (Fam trips), 440, 528
Family life-cycle, 166
Family members, 163–164
Fast-food industry, 379
Federal Trade Commission, 67, 107
Feedback and control, 77
Feedback in communication, 366
Feltenstein, Tom, 414
Fencing, 315, 557
Feng shui, 107–108
Field of Dreams, 258
Field sales force, 434–435
Financial intermediaries, 93
Financial publics, 94
Financing, distribution channel function and, 335
Five-gap model of service quality, 567–570
   consumer expectations *vs.* management perception, 567
   expected service *vs.* perceived service, 570
   management perception *vs.* service quality specifications, 567–569
   service delivery *vs.* external communications, 569–570
   service quality specifications *vs.* service delivery, 569
Fixed costs, 301
Focus, 76
Focus group, 136–137
Follow-up/maintenance (in personal selling), 447
Food and Drug Administration, 107
Forecasting market demand, 571–577
   actual sales and market shares, 574
   area market demand, 574
   current market demand, 573–574
   defining the market, 571–572
   forecasting methods, 575–576
   future demand, 575–577
   restaurants, market areas for, 572–573
   statistical demand analysis, 576–577
   total market demand, 573–574
Forecasting methods, 575–576
Forms of direct and digital marketing, 463
Forward integration, 67
Four Cs, 71
Four Points (hotel), 250
Four Ps of marketing, 7, 16, 69, 71, 158

Four Seasons, 210, 219, 272–273
Franchise, 347–348
   advantages/disadvantages of, 347–348
Franchising, 347–348
   advantages/disadvantages of, 347–348
   restaurant, 347–348
"Free Hug Friday," 413
Frequency programs, 477
"Fresh Fit for Kids" program, 221
Future demand, forecasting of, 575–577
Galileo (GDS), 340
Gaming, Indian, 512–513
Gap analysis of loyalty features, 482
Gatekeepers, 186
Gender marketing, 209–210
Genealogical tourism, 519–521
General need description, 188
General public, 94
Generation X, 98–99
Generation Y, 99
Generation Z, 100
Generic benchmarking, 499
Geographic segmentation, 207–208
Geographic shifts in population, 102
Global distribution systems (GDS), 339–340
Global economy, 103–104
Global Hotel Alliance, 343
Globalization, tourist industry, 495–496
Goal formulation, 75–76
   differentiation, 76
   focus, 76
   objectives and tradeoffs, 75
   overall cost leadership, 76
   performance measures, 75–76
Going-rate pricing. *See* Competition-based pricing approach
Golf Resort, 224
Goodman, Oscar, 236
Government agency enforcement, 107
Government intervention, 104
Government legislation and regulation, 106
Government markets, 94
Government publics, 94
Grand Hyatt Hotels, 285
Grand Targhee (case study), 609–611
Great Depression, 236
Greco, Susan, 316
Greek National Tourism Organization (GNTO), 523
Green Meeting, 197
Greene, Melvyn, 303
Groen Kettle, 300
Gronroos, Christian, 241, 273, 276
Gross rating points (GRP), 386
Group(s), 161–162
Group business markets, 192–193
   conventions, 192–193
Group interviews, 136–137
Growth stage, 261, 378

Growth strategies, 66
　Ansoff product-market expansion grid, 65
　conglomerate strategy, 66
　integrative growth, 67
　market development strategy, 65
　product development, 65
Guest comment cards, 125
Guest information management, 125–126
　automated systems, 126
　guest comment cards, 125
　guest history information, 123
　listening/speaking with guests, 125
　mystery shoppers, 126
　point-of-sale information, 126
　point-of-sale (POS) systems, 126
Handling objections, personal selling principle, 447
Hard Rock Café, 412
Harrison, Jeffrey S., 60
Havana Club Museum of Rum, 526
Hawes, Peter, 514
Hendler, Flavia, 138
Herrera, Joe, 417
High-performance business
　nature of, 59–61
　organization and, 60–61
　processes and, 60
　resources and, 60
　stakeholders and, 59
Hiking, multi-day, 517–518
Hilton (hotel), 349, 459–461
Hiring process, 280–282
Hispanic American consumers, 159
Hochschild, A. R., 287
Holiday Inn, 64, 542
Horizontal conflict, 345
Horizontal diversification strategy, 66
Horizontal integration, 67
Horizontal marketing systems (HMSs), 350
Hospitality, 7–8
Hospitality and travel consumers, unique aspects of, 176
Hospitality industry, 8
　location as PR opportunities, 405
　marketing in, 8–10
　promoting individual properties, 405
　promoting via storytelling, 405–406
Hospitality sales, 424–426
　competitive analysis and competitive sets, 426
Hospitality Sales and Marketing Association International (HSMAI), 148
Hotel and Catering International Management Association (HCIMA), 109
Hotel industry
　objectives (examples of), 551
　performance measures in, 75
Hotel representatives, 343
Hotels.com, 320, 339
Howe, Jeff, 254
Hudson, Simon, 545

Huggar, Mary, 96, 97
Hulme, John, 407
Human need, 10
Human resources management
　continuous training, 284
　emotional employees, 286–287
　hiring process, 280–282
　initial training, 283–284
　jobs that attract talent, 280
　marketing approach to, 280–288
　reward and recognition system, 287–288
Human want, 10–11
Hunt Room: Change the Concept or Just the Decor? (case study), 592–593
Hustead, Ted, 406
Hyatt, 99, 137, 210, 238, 251, 277
Idea generation, 253–255
　awareness of external environment, 253
　crowdsourcing, 254–255
　external idea sources, 254
　internal sources, 253–254
Idea screening, 255–259
Illy, Andrea, 242
Image, 187
Image differentiation, 224–225
Implementation, 77
In Search of Excellence (Peters and Waterman), 47
Incentive travel, 195–196
Income segmentation, 210
Independent Retail Cattlemen's Association, 401
In-depth interviews, 137
Indian gaming, 512–513
Indigo Pearl Resort, 546
Individual factors, 188
Individual (intercept) interviews, 136
Individual mass tourists, 520
Industrial economies, 103
Industry cooperation (tourism), 504
Industry trends, 543
Influencers, 186
Information. *See also* Guest information management
　disclosure of, 478–479
　distribution channel function and, 335
　primary data, 131
　secondary information, 131
Information needs, 120–121, 188
Information search, 174
　commercial sources, 174
　internet, 174
　personal sources, 174
　public sources, 174
　word-of-mouth sources, 174
Informative advertising, 380
Infrastructure, 497
Initial training, 283–284
Inseparability, 36, 38
Inside sales force, 433–434
Instant messaging (IM), 139

Intangibility, 36–37
Integrated marketing communications (IMC), 358, 360–365
  communication process, view of, 365–367
  need for, 365
  new communications model, 361–363
Integrated marketing mix, 71
  four Ps of, 7, 16, 69, 71, 158
Integrated social media marketing, 473–474
Integrative growth, 67
Interactive TV (iTV) in marketing, 484–485
Intercept interviews, 136
Intercontinental Hotels Group (IHG), 274
Interdepartmental teams, 74
Internal benchmarking, 499
Internal data, 121, 122–127
Internal environmental analysis, 73–74
Internal marketing, 47
Internal marketing process, 275–292. *See also* Human resources management
  marketing information to employees, 288–292
  nonroutine transactions, 279–280
  organizational structure, 278–279
  service culture, 276–278
  steps in, 276
  weak culture, 277–278
Internal publics, 94
Internal sources, idea generation, 253–254
International advertising decisions, 389
International marketing research, 149–150
International markets, 94
International pricing, 323
International product and service marketing, 265–266
International social media, 473
International travel, 5, 501
International Travel Agency (case study), 628–629
Internet, 108, 138. *See also* Online marketing
  crisis management and, 406–408
  marketing communications and, 358
  word-of-mouth sources, 174
Interpersonal factors, 187–188
Interstate Commerce Commission, 107
Introduction stage, 261
Investors, 552
Irvine, Robert, 406
Island Adventures, 296
iTV. *See* Interactive TV (iTV) in marketing
Jet Blue, 18, 43
Joining stage, 242
Jordan, Michael, 372
Journal of Consumer Psychology, 170
Judgment sample, 141
Judgmental sampling, 136
Junket reps, 342
JW Marriott San Antonio Hill Country Resort & Spa, 35
KAYAK (online travel website), 331, 340
Kelleher, Herb, 15
Keller, Kevin, 251

Kennedy, John F., 43
Kentucky Fried Chicken (KFC), 121, 251, 265, 349
Key accounts, 430, 441–442. *See also* Customer-structured sales force
KFC. *See* Kentucky Fried Chicken (KFC)
Kimpton Hotels, 195, 240, 277
Kiosk marketing, 484
Knowledge, 368
Krishna, Aradhna, 170
La Forgia, John, 605
Laboratory tests, 388
Las Vegas Convention and Visitors Authority (LVCVA), 235–237, 498
LaTour, Kathryn A., 138
Le Parisien (French newspaper), 399
Leadership in Energy and Environmental Design (LEED) Green Building Rating System, 198
Leading Hotels of the World, 225, 343
Learning, 171
Legislation, 106
Leong, Siew, 251
Leveraging brands, 249–250
Lewis Hotels, 289
Lidia's (restaurant), 223
Life-cycle stage, 166–167, 208–209. *See also* Age and life-cycle stage
Lifestyle, 168, 211
Lifestyle marketing, 537
Lifetime value (LTV), 21
Liking, 368
LINQ Hotel, 237
"Listening post" concepts, 125
Live-like-a-local experience, 526
Lobbying, 398
Local area marketing, 416–417
  cause-related promotions, 417
  defined, 416
  PR activities in, 416
Local marketing, 220
Local publics, 94
Location differentiation, 224
Long-haul *vs.* short-haul tourists, 522
Los Angeles Biltmore Hotel, 547
Lovelock, Christopher, 227
Low price approach, 322–323
Loyalty
  features, gap analysis of, 482
  programs, 479–483
Loyalty status, 215. *See also* Behavioral segmentation
Macrodestinations, 497
Macroenvironment, 74, 95–109
  cultural environment, 107–108
  demographic environment, 97–102
  economic environment, 103–104
  natural environment, 104–105
  political environment, 106–107
  technological environment, 105–106
MADD (Mothers Against Drunk Driving), 108